息烽县志

1991—2010

息烽县地方志编纂委员会办公室　编

方志出版社
Publishing House of Local Records

《息烽县志（1991—2010）》编辑部

审 稿

▲ 息烽县城夜景（2016年摄　何超）

▲ 息烽县城（2016年摄　颜阳）

▲ 息烽县城（1990年摄　骆凡邦）

▲ 息烽县城（2013年摄）

▲ 息烽县城局部（2014年摄）

▲ 息烽县城局部（2017年摄）

▲ 息烽县城十字街（1998年摄）

▲ 息烽县城十字街（2013年摄）

▲ 息烽县虎城大道（2005年摄）

▲ 息烽县虎城大道（2010年摄）

▲ 息烽县城三角花园（1998年摄）

▲ 息烽县城三角花园夜景（2007年摄）

▲ 息烽县城东门片区（2003年摄）

▲ 息烽县城东门片区（2010年摄）

永靖镇示范小城镇建设（2013年摄）

小寨坝镇（2012年摄）

小寨坝镇农民安置新村（2012年摄）

▲ 小寨坝镇红岩村（2010年摄）

▲ 养龙司镇堡子村（2010年摄）

▲ 西山镇柏香山村（2016年摄）

▲ 永靖镇梨安村（2016年摄）

重钙厂厂区（2005年摄）

2003年8月6日，贵阳中化开磷化肥有限公司举行挂牌仪式

开磷集团磷酸一二铵装置（2008年摄）

▲ 小寨坝磷煤化工工业园区（2010年摄）

◀ 开磷集团息烽20万吨硫磺制酸装置（2008年摄）

▶ 2008年12月17日，小寨坝磷化工基地10亿块新型磷石膏砖配套黄磷生产装置技术改造项目开工

开磷磷酸二铵专用铁路站台包装线（2007年摄）

贵州西洋肥业有限公司（2008年摄）

开磷集团息烽60万吨磷酸氢二铵和24万吨磷酸氢二铵项目（2010年摄）

永靖镇阳朗花卉苗圃（2009年摄）

小寨坝镇王家坪村优质布朗李（2003年摄）

永靖镇阳朗大棚蔬菜（2008年摄）

▶ 小寨坝镇红岩葡萄（2007年摄）

▶ 流长乡前奔梨（2009年摄）

▲ 息烽中康园区猕猴桃基地（2016年摄）

息烽特驱希望公司标准化肉鸡养殖（2014年摄）

流长乡肉牛养殖（2009年摄）

九庄镇肉鸡养殖场（2016年摄）

▲ 青山苗族乡绿化村肉兔养殖（2006年摄）

▲ 息烽乌江网箱养鱼（2008年摄）

◀ 息烽稻田生态养鱼（2008年摄）

▲ 息烽坡改梯工程（2007年摄）

▲ 贵遵高等级公路息烽站出入口
（2006年摄）

▲ 贯穿县境的210国道、川黔铁路和贵遵高等级公路
（2005年摄）

▲ 贵遵高等级公路息烽站出入口（2010年摄）

▲ 贵遵高等级公路小寨坝段（2008年摄）

▲ 连接息烽县与金沙县的息烽流长大塘渡乌江大桥（2014年摄）

▲ 210国道阳朗段（2010年摄）

▲ 川黔铁路小寨坝段（2008年摄）

▲ 息烽乡村公路（2001年摄）

▲ 息烽火车站（2010年摄）

▲ 息烽火车站站房（2006年摄）

▲ 息烽客运站（2013年摄）

▲ 养龙司镇客运站（2015年摄）

▲ 温泉镇客运站（2010年摄）

▲ 石硐乡客运站（2010年摄）

▲ 息烽出租车免费接送高考学子（2013年摄）

▲ 息烽县出租车经营权拍卖会（2003年摄）

▲ 息烽县第一中学教学楼（2008年摄）

▲ 息烽县第一中学新校区教学楼（2015年摄）

▲ 息烽县第二中学（2007年摄）

▲ 底寨中学（2015年摄）

▲ 黑神庙中学网络教室（2010年摄）

▲ 息烽实验幼儿园（2006年摄）

▲ 石硐中学学生在学校少年宫下象棋（2010年摄）

▲ 息烽县云环小学（2009年摄）

▲ 息烽鱼简河水利工程开工（2002年摄）

▲ 息烽鱼简河水库（2010年摄）

▲ 温泉镇上沟水库（2010年摄）

▲ 息烽县永靖镇何家沟水库（2010年摄）

▲ 息烽县下洪马水库（2010年摄）

▲永靖镇板厂水库（2010年摄）

▲息烽水厂（2009年摄）

▲ 息烽县城污水处理厂（2010年摄）

▲ 永靖自来水厂（2010年摄）

电　　力

▲ 2011年1月6日，息烽县供电局工人在小寨坝镇南望山脉抢修因凝冻受损的供电线路

▲ 工人维修电力设备（2006年摄）

▲ 工人抢修因凝冻受损的电力设备（2008年摄）

▲ 九庄镇35千伏变电站（2008年摄）

▲ 贵州电网公司贵阳500千伏息烽变电站（2008年摄）

▲ 西电东送息烽50千伏安变电站（2009年摄）

▲ 息烽乡村电力网（2016年摄）

▲ 息烽工业园盘脚营220千伏变电站（2010年摄）

▲ 2008年2月20日，成都军区某部官兵抢修主供九庄、石硐的35千伏电力线路

▲ 1986－2005年县人民医院住院病房（2002年摄）

▲ 县中医院（2003年摄）

▲ 县人民医院综合大楼（2005年摄）

▲ 县中医院综合楼（2005年摄）

▲ 县人民医院住院大楼（2015年摄）

▲ 县中医院门诊及住院大楼（2016年摄）

▲ 永靖镇计划生育保健中心（2007年摄）

▲ 永靖镇卫生院（2010年摄）

▲ 息烽县计划生育生殖保健中心（2013年摄）

◀ 石硐镇卫生院（2015年摄）

▶ 疾控工作人员监测鹿窝乡农村生活饮用水（2007年摄）

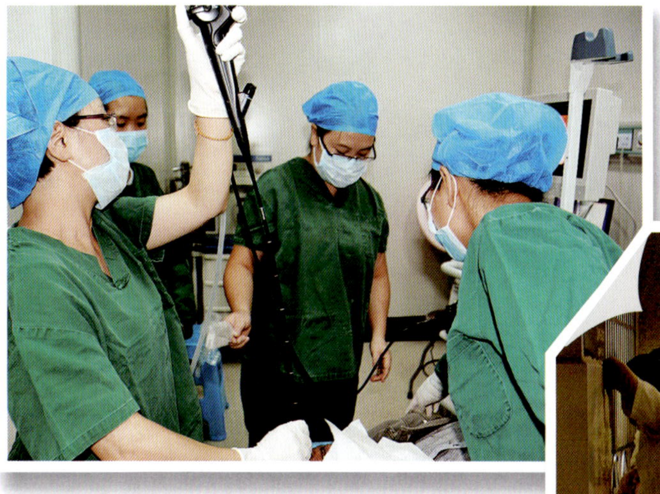

◀ 县人民医院医生用纤支镜做手术（2006年摄）

▶ 参合群众在医院排队报销“新农合”（2008年摄）

▲ 息烽县首届个体劳动者个体杯运动会（1990年摄）

▲ 息烽县体育场（2006年摄）

▲ 2003年，息烽县举办全民健身周展示大会

▲ 2011年9月，息烽县组织参加贵阳市第九届少数民族传统体育运动会武术比赛

▲ 2008年7月，息烽代表队参加贵州省首届农民运动会武术比赛项目。图为参赛队员合影

▲ 息烽县“三八”妇女节拔河大赛（2006年摄）

◀第三届少数民族运动会
（2009年摄）

▶小寨坝镇潮水龙舟比赛
（2010年摄）

▲息烽县千人体操拔河大赛（2010年摄）

◀ 息烽集中营革命历史纪念馆（2006年摄）

▶ 中国·堡子“半边天”文化陈列馆（2011年摄）

▲ 乌江峡（2008年摄）

▲ 杨虎城将军被囚禁处——玄天洞（2006年摄）

▲ 九庄镇烈士陵园（2010年摄）

▲ 西望山雨花瀑（2010年摄）

▲ 九庄镇龙滩洞（2010年摄）

▲ 西望山鹿溪（2014年摄）

◀息烽温泉疗养院二疗区（2002年摄）

▶息烽温泉泳池（2009年摄）

▲息烽温泉疗养院全景（2017年摄）

▲ 贵阳避暑季息烽县第三届红岩葡萄节开幕式（2009年摄）

▲ 贵阳避暑季息烽生态健康体验游系列活动暨青山苗族“四月八”活动开幕式（2009年摄）

▲ 息烽县举办“弘扬我们的价值观·家家户户贴春联”活动（2015年摄）

▲ 2007年8月，息烽集中营革命历史纪念馆在上海、上饶等地开展巡展

◀ 2006年，息烽县举办“名家写息烽、名家画息烽、名家摄息烽”活动

▲ 2005年8月19日，息烽集中营革命历史纪念馆第二期工程修复开馆

▲ 苗族芦笙舞

▲ 青苗服饰

▲ 苗族银饰

▲ 息烽县首届城建杯足球赛、首届房屋展示会开幕式文艺演出（2007年摄）

▲ 多彩贵州歌唱大赛息烽分赛区海选赛（2008年摄）

▲ 息烽龙灯（2009年摄）

▲ 息烽县老年大学学员展示民族舞蹈（2007年摄）

◀ 息烽县首届星火传承火炬传递活动（2009年摄）

▲ 多彩贵州舞蹈大赛西山分赛区海选赛（2007年摄）

▲ 苗族舞蹈《蒙待央》（2008年摄）

▲ 息烽女子威风锣鼓队锣鼓表演（2009年摄）

▲ 阳戏

▲ 息烽集中营红色情景剧《放飞自由》（2009年摄）

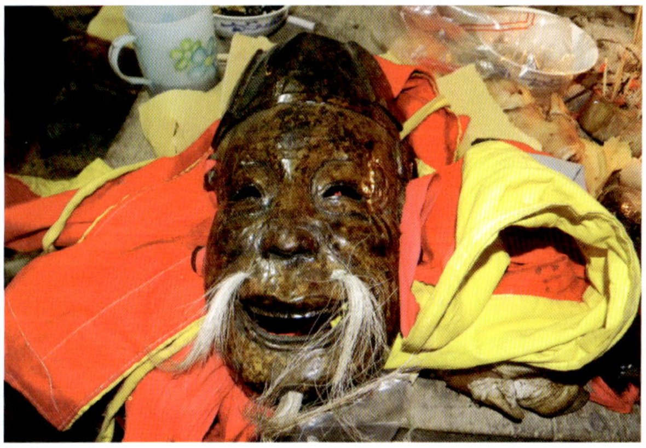

▲ 傩戏面具

▲ 息烽花灯

▲二姐山庄鲜果爆嫩兔（王项　摄）

▲“苗姑娘”小米鲊（王项　摄）

▲九酒八饭店吉祥玉子虾（王项　摄）

▲唐记潮水鱼火锅（王项　摄）

▲青山苗家灰豆腐（王项　摄）

▲西望山柴灰豆腐（王项　摄）

▲小寨坝啤酒鸭（王项　摄）

▲筑园酒楼排骨炖萝卜（王项　摄）

▲阳朗辣子鸡（王项　摄）

▲林之宝饭店菌香鸡（王项　摄）

▲ 西望山虫茶

▲ 红岩葡萄

▲ 贵州省名菜—息烽阳朗辣子鸡

▲“苗姑娘”油辣椒系列食品

▲乌江鱼

▲西望山禅贡米

▲2013年2月19日，息烽县举行第七届“龙腾息烽”新春游艺活动

▲节庆日舞龙活动（2009年摄）

▲小寨坝镇红岩葡萄节“彩虹跑”活动（2015年摄）

贵阳市商业银行息烽县支行
（2009年摄）

息烽县汽车站广场（2013年摄）

小寨坝镇廉租房（2010年摄）

▲九庄镇敬老院（2000年摄）

▲永靖镇廉租房（2008年摄）

▲温泉镇廉租房（2010年摄）

▲县城北门休闲广场（2010年摄）

▲被征地农民积极参加养老保险（2013年摄）

▲息烽县乡村移动、联通通讯基站（2013年摄）

▲息烽县ASDL（非对称数字用户线路）数据通信设备（2010年摄）

▲息烽县垃圾填埋场（2010年摄）

◀ 2002年6月，息烽县党员干部转移洪灾中被困群众

▶ 2007年9月28日，息烽县重兴燃气有限公司开业

▲ 凝冻期间，息烽机关干部职工“党员突击队”清除大林口路段路面冰雪（2008年摄）

2007年10月26日，息烽县首届房展会

2006年8月21日，息烽县首届农村劳动力非农技能比武大赛

2008年10月22日，息烽县中心敬老院落成

◀治安巡逻（2010年摄）

▶2009年12月10日，永靖镇硬寨村给群众发放温暖煤

▲息烽万人签名拒毒品（2008年摄）

▲合力超市（2009年摄）

▲“春风行动”招聘会（2010年摄）

▲凝冻期间，县消防官兵为群众送水（2008年摄）

▲“村村通”电话工程乐农家（2007年摄）

▲息烽县人民法院诉讼直通车进农村（2009年摄）

▲ 2017年11月6日，《息烽县志（1991—2010）》通过县级初审

▲ 2018年2月2日，《息烽县志（1991—2010）》通过市级复审

康示范县、开创更加美丽新息烽的伟大征程中，《息烽县志（1991—2010）》能赋予当代更加重要的意义。一是发挥史志的资政功能，为县委、县政府和全县广大领导干部的科学决策提供一个依据，为县域经济的发展提供借鉴，为今后的战略决策提供参考。同时，激励全县广大干部从历史出发，寻求初心，更好地为人民服务。二是为息烽的经济建设带来新的契机。史志工作为经济建设提供了一个平台，运用新的工作机制以及现代化的各种技术，将这些浓厚的历史积淀转换为经济建设的资源，将历史基因同当下经济建设相结合，走富有地方特色的路线，推动地方经济繁荣，为经济建设添砖加瓦。三是为我县的文化事业添上了浓墨重彩的一笔。通过《息烽县志（1991—2010）》的出版发行，唤起人们对历史、文物、遗迹的重视和保护，开启大家对历史的热忱，感召全县人民学史、懂史、用史，有力推动地方史志工作的开展，繁荣地方史志文化，也将史书、志书推向民间，提高全民文化素养和道德品质。

县志编撰过程中，数易其稿，增删无计，省、市地方志办公室给予最大的帮助，县委、县政府给予最大的支持，县地方志办公室以及全体编撰人员付出了最大的努力，全县上下、社会各界给予了最大的关注，才取得了今天的成果。在此谨致谢意！

中共息烽县委书记　卓　飞

息烽县人民政府县长　廖　勇

2019年11月15日

凡　例

一、本志编纂坚持以马克思列宁主义、毛泽东思想、邓小平理论、“三个代表”重要思想、科学发展观、习近平新时代中国特色社会主义思想为指导，坚持辩证唯物主义和历史唯物主义的立场、观点和方法，实事求是地记述1991—2010年息烽县政治、经济、文化、社会的发展变化。

二、本志是1993年版《息烽县志》的续志，上限为1991年，下限为2010年，个别地方为便于读者理清来龙去脉，适当追述和后延。部分图片超出时间限制。

三、全志除概述、“大事记”“人物”“附录”不设篇章外，主体部分设19篇87章365节。篇下设章、节、目、子目4个层次。概述统揽全志。“大事记”以编年体为主，辅以纪事本末体，横排门类，纵写史实，按时序记述大事、要事、新事。篇末有“人物”“附录”“编后记”。

四、本志采用语体文，记述体。总体以述为主，述议结合，寓理于事。语言文字、标点符号、数字数据、计量单位的使用和引文注释的书写等按国家有关标准执行。为符合时代发展，目录配以英文译文。

五、人物篇采用传、简介、名录形式，坚持“生不立传”原则。入传者主要是贡献突出和社会影响大的已故人物。有重大贡献的在世人物用“简介”或在有关篇章以事系人加以记述。副县级及其以上的干部、中高级职称的科技工作者和获市地级及其以上表彰的劳动模范分别以统计表和名录加以记载。入传人物和简介人物皆按其生年先后次序排列。

六、入志的文艺作品包含县内作者的文学、书法、美术、音乐、摄影等作品，坚持以质量为上，以曾经发表或获奖，能充分体现全县文艺创作的较高水平为选录标准。

七、本志数字资料主要是使用县统计局公布的法定统计数据，统计局缺少的则采用相关部门提供的数据。史实资料来源于历史文献、各单位档案和长篇资料、口述资料，所有资料一般不注明出处。

八、冠以“中华人民共和国”的法律法规一律使用全称；其他法律法规或其他可以使用简称的事物，第一次出现时使用全称，重复出现时使用简称。

九、全志具有科学计量和统计意义的数值一律使用阿拉伯数字。除表列数据外，文字记述使用整数，遇小数即用四舍五入法处理，涉及人数的个别数据因四舍五入会影响数据准确性的，则不改动。数据上5位至8位的以“万”为单位。反映比例、速度、结构的数据取原始数据计算，小数点后保留两位，不用无意义的“0”补位。

十、重量单位，不足1吨，用千克。涉及反映历史的内容，可用千克、斤、两。面积单位，根据语境，可用公顷，也可用亩。

十一、清代及其以前的纪年和夏历使用汉字，民国纪年、公元纪年、世纪年代和公历使用阿拉伯数字。公元纪年省写“公元”二字。

十二、地名一般使用现行标准地名。使用原地名之处，第一次出现时注以今名。

十三、正文主要用括注，括注不了的用页末注。专用名词简称在首次出现时加注，其后用简称。

十四、本志（除引文外）采用第三人称表述。人物直书其名，不加褒贬之词。职务名称置于姓名之前。

十五、前志补遗资料来自历史档案、有关书籍、报刊及社会调查等口碑资料，经考证后入志，一般不注明出处，尚属存疑的未补入本志。

目　　录

概　　述

大事记

第一篇　政区建置

第二篇　环境资源

第三篇　人口·民族·宗教

第四篇　政党·群团组织

第五篇 人大·政府·政协

第六篇 军 事

第七篇 政 法

第八篇 社会事务管理

第九篇 农业农村

第十篇　工　业

第十一篇　交通·邮政·通信

第十二篇　城乡建设

第十三篇　商　贸

第十四篇　财税·金融

第十五篇　综合经济管理

第十六篇　教育·科技

第十七篇　卫　生

第十八篇　文化·旅游·体育

第十九篇　社会生活

人　物

附　　录

Table of Contents

Part III Population, Ethnic Groups and Religion

Part IV The Political Parties and People's Organizations

Part V The People's Congress, Government and the CPPCC

Part VI Military

Part VII Procuratorial, Judicial and Public Security Affairs

Part VIII Social Affairs Management

Part IX Agriculture and Rural Affairs

Part X Industry

Part XI Transportation, Post and Communications

Part XII Urban-Rural Development

Part XIII Business and Trade

Part XIV Public Finance, Taxation and Finance

Part XV Comprehensive Economic Management

Part XVI Education, Science and Technology

Part XVII Health

Part XVIII Culture, Tourism and Sports

Part XIX Social Life

Characters

Appendix

概　述

一

息烽县位于贵州省中部、贵阳市北部，北纬26° 57′ ～27° 19′ ，东经106° 27′ ～106° 53′ 之间。东临开阳，南接修文，西北与遵义、金沙两县相望。县城所在地南距贵阳市中心66千米，北距历史名城遵义85千米。总面积1036.5平方千米，占贵阳市面积的12.91%。辖七镇三乡一社区，161个村，13个居委会。全县总人口268678人，其中非农业人口35221人，农业人口233457人；汉族人口253704人，少数民族人口14974人，少数民族人口占全县人口总数的5.57%。有苗族、布依族、土家族、彝族、侗族、仡佬族、白族、回族、满族、壮族、水族等24个少数民族，主要集中在1个民族乡和非民族乡的91个民族聚居村。

从底寨车田河出土的石斧、石锛，足以证明在新石器时期息烽就有了人类居住。夏时为梁州南徼。周为越国北境。春秋战国时期，先后属且兰、牂牁国境。秦始皇二十六年（前221）属新象郡且兰县。汉武帝元鼎六年（前111），置牂牁郡，县地在其境内。蜀汉建兴三年（225），昆明首领火济据有黔北、黔西北大部地区，县境在其管辖内。东晋简文帝咸安元年（371），置晋乐县，治所在今都拉营北，辖今贵阳及修文、开阳、息烽等。隋文帝时，县地属牂牁州。大业三年（607），改牂牁州为牂牁郡，治所在今安顺，县境隶牂牁郡。唐武德三年（620），设黔州都督府，羁縻51州，县境属蛮州，治所在今开阳。次年置矩州，治所在今贵阳，县境属之。宋乾德五年（967），罗甸国首领普贵“纳土内附”，命为贵阳刺史，统领今贵阳中、西、南部，县境属其辖地。开宝八年（975），县境由水东宋氏管辖。元至元十七年（1280），隶四川省顺元等处宣慰司。至元二十九年（1292），隶湖广行省顺元路军民安抚司。明洪武四年（1371），隶四川行省贵州宣慰司。永乐十一年（1414），属贵州布政司贵州宣慰司节制。万历年间（1573—1620），水西东侵，息烽归属贵州宣慰使司管辖，属水西安氏水外六目之地。明崇祯三年（1630），总督朱燮元平定水西，在今县境置诘戎守御千户所，旋改旋废。后经崇祯御批，取“平息烽火”之义，改设息烽、于襄两千户所。清顺治十五年（1658），撤所建卫，息烽、于襄两所属敷勇卫治理。康熙二十六年（1687）裁卫置修文县，息烽、于襄守御千户所入修文县，隶属贵阳府。同治十年（1871），缩建息烽城。民国3年（1914），开始建立息烽县。民国4年（1915），移贵筑县治于息烽城，改名息烽县。民国35年（1946），属贵州省督导室管辖。民国37年（1948），复归贵州省直辖区。1949年11月17日，息烽解放。11月23日，建立息烽县人民政府，隶属贵阳专区管辖。1952年11月15日，贵阳专区改称贵定专区，息烽县仍属其管辖。1956年5月10日，撤销贵定专区，划归安顺专区管辖。1958年10月4日，划归遵义专区管辖。1965年8月17日，复归安顺专区管辖。1996年1月1日，划归贵阳市管辖。

息烽属北亚热带和南温带季风气候区，气候温和，雨量充沛，冬无严寒，夏无酷暑，气候宜人。年平均气温14.5℃，年均降雨量1111毫米，大部分地区全年无霜期在270天以上。由于海拔高、纬度低、高差大，气候在空间分布上具有“一山有四季，十里不同天”的立体气候特点，适宜从亚热带到暖温带的多种农林作物生长。境内有南望山、西望山、天台山、团元山四大原生丛林，截至2010年，已查明的树木有104科263种，野草61科227种，药用植物110科227种，水生、陆生和两栖动物数百种。森林覆盖率达45.83%。

息烽地势南高北低，县境北濒贵州省储水量第一的乌江库区，境内的息烽河、瓮桶河、雨淋河多发源于东南，流向西北。境内河网密度达每平方千米17.8千米，流域面积大于20平方千米的河流有12条，多年平均流量5.85亿立方米，平水年常年保有储水量4.65亿立方米，水资源十分丰富。境内最长的河流息烽河发源于东北部的石硐镇南桥村，向东至南桥后折向北流，至大河口纳入头道河支流，在小寨坝镇瓮沙村和石桥村之间汇入乌江，全长50千米。

息烽是黔中交通要塞，自古有“川黔锁钥，黔中咽喉”之称。川黔铁路、210国道、兰海高速G75段、渝贵快速铁路南北纵贯县境东部的永靖、小寨坝、养龙司、西山4个乡镇，江都高速公路东西贯穿温泉、小寨坝、养龙司、流长、鹿窝、九庄6个乡镇，地处黔中南北交通大动脉交汇点上，是陇、川、渝三省市及省内遵义市南下出海的重要通道，也是贵阳市北上黔北及重庆、四川的“桥头堡”，兰海高速与都江高速在小寨坝镇十字交叉，成为贵州东西南北各市、州高速交通的连接点。息烽还是乌江水上航运的始发点，建设中的筑北码头连接水陆交通，通江达海。

息烽是筑北地质公园。息烽地处黔中山塬丘陵中部，南望山、西望山、团元山、乌江峡“三山一谷”构成县域地貌主骨架。境内峰峦起伏，沟壑纵横，主区域海拔1000～1200米，大部为低中山丘陵地，碳酸盐类岩分布广，喀斯特地貌发育充分，峰丛、洼地、溶丘、溶洞、暗河、漏斗、飞来峰等地质构造遍布，尤以多缤洞、龙滩洞、银子洞纵深最长、构造最奇、开发价值最大。北部边缘受乌江及支流侵蚀切割，沟谷纵横，危崖耸峙，形成姊妹峰、神女峰、导弹峰、鲤鱼峰和百里画廊等地质奇观。最高点为南望山南极顶，海拔1749.6米；最低点乌江出境处的大塘口，海拔609米。丹霞地貌特征明显，境内的西望山、团元山沉积了100多平方千米的侏罗纪石英岩，奇峰高耸，巨石林立，清泉流瀑，一步一景。团元山区发现的史前天地大冲撞形成的陨石坑、龙奔山发掘出的巨型食肉恐龙化石，均为贵州中部少有的地质奇观。境内矿产资源主要有煤、磷、铝、硫铁、褐铁、硅、水晶、重晶石、高岭土等，其中尤以煤、磷储藏最丰、品位最高。

息烽是红色热土。2004年，中宣部等十三部委公布第一批全国红色旅游经典景区，息烽集中营革命历史纪念馆和息烽乌江景区列入名录。息烽集中营革命历史纪念馆景区范围包括息烽集中营本部旧址、玄天洞杨虎城将军囚禁处旧址、快活岭张露萍等七烈士陵园；息烽乌江景区范围包括红军长征南渡乌江的大塘、梯子岩、江口三大渡口，乌江沿岸的红军长征南渡乌江纪念碑、流长没良坑红军烈士殉难处、鹿窝报恩寺红军烈士陵园、九庄红军烈士陵园，及红军长征过境息烽的7处战斗遗址。境内还有建国初期解放军平息匪患留下的草香沟、虎啸台等众多剿匪战斗遗址和温泉三宝山革命烈士陵园；有毛泽东题写编者按的中国男女同工同酬第一村、全国妇女教育基地、中国·堡子半边天文化陈列馆；有“大三线”建设时期核工业部国营二七六厂、贵州柴油机厂、贵州拖拉机电机厂、贵州拖拉机配件厂、贵州朝晖机械厂等企业留下的宝贵“三线”文化财富。红色文化底蕴厚重，红色旅游资源丰富多彩。

息烽是世界氡泉之都。息烽温泉在明、清时期的历史典籍中即有记载，开发建设于民国时期，名列世界三大氡泉、中国八大名泉，有“天下第一神汤”的美誉。20世纪90年代以来，县委、县政府邀请地质专家全面勘察温泉资源，发现永靖镇南山温泉、石硐镇胡家湾温泉、西山镇柏香山温泉和林丰温泉、小寨坝镇中心温泉、养龙司镇画眉湾温泉、鹿窝乡杨寨温泉、青山苗族乡青山温泉等8个温泉勘探点。其中新萝温泉、胡家湾温泉已钻探出水，且均含微量元素氡和锶、偏硅酸等对人体有益的矿物质。县旅游部门已编制息烽百里氡温泉城建设规划，投资4.5亿元开发建设南山温泉，林丰温泉、中心温泉已实施钻探取水工程。

息烽是贵州省级风景名胜区。息烽风景名胜区已列入贵州省人民政府1995年公布的第二批省级风景名胜区名录，以红色、温泉、森林、乡村四大旅游资源最具特色。南望山、西望山、团元山、天台山四大原生丛林构成长江上游息烽段的生态屏障，成为息烽森林旅游开发的重要依托，在建的南山驿站公园已列入省级示范性生态体育公园。县境东部的南望山巍峨雄奇，明朝时期即有半月道人在山中建玄天洞道观，是贵州道教文化发祥地，目前在阳朗建有贵州道教协会天龙道观。中部的西望山钟灵毓秀，清朝初年即有语嵩大师建凤池寺弘扬佛法，是贵州佛教禅宗发祥地，目前已建成国际定向越野、国际滑翔伞赛事基地。流传于民间的流长阳戏、息烽花灯、息烽龙灯、傩戏、苗族芦笙舞、苗族刺绣、苗族“四月八”活动、西望山虫茶制作技艺等已列入贵州省非物质文化遗产名录。还有源远流长的车田河石器、底寨黔商故里、流长东汉古墓、鹿窝明永乐五年盟誓碑等众多历史文化遗存。随着“旅游+”产业的持续开发和富美乡村、田园综合体建设持续推进，息烽已成为贵州中部、贵阳北部重要的休闲度假、文化体验、健康养生旅游度假区，进入2015年中国乡村旅游百强县行列。

1991—2010年，是息烽经济社会发展的黄金期。勤劳的息烽各族人民在历届县委、县政府的领导下，大力弘扬“自强不息，艰苦奋斗，赤胆忠诚，协力争先”的息烽精神，挑战贫困，奋起直追，先后经历了决战贫困、跻身强县、提速发展3个重大历史发展阶段，进入了经济全面发展、社会持续进步、文化全面提升和人的素质的整体提高的全面小康社会建设重要发展时期。

二

息烽是典型的喀斯特山地，大部分地区山高石多，土地破碎，工农业生产条件恶劣，经济社会发展基础脆弱。境内可开采的矿产资源主要为煤、磷和自然涌出的地热矿泉，分别归属贵州省林东矿务局南山煤矿、省地矿厅下属的国有企业息烽磷矿和省总工会下属的息烽温泉疗养院开采使用，对地方财政贡献不大。20世纪70年代乌江渡发电站建设期间，原属息烽县的养龙站、乌江片区划归遵义县管辖，不仅不能获得电厂财政税收，还要解决水库移民搬迁安置问题。加之地处西南内陆，不沿海、不沿边、不沿江，且1992年贵阳列入最后一批内陆开放城市时，息烽尚属安顺管辖，不具备对外开放条件和优势。工农业生产水平极低，第三产业总量小，县城面积不足0.5平方千米，只有三条破旧的瓦木、砖木房街道，“有县无城”。曾经辉煌的“大三线”企业，后来陆续搬离息烽，工业产值大幅下降，经济发展再次面临前所未有的压力，“一穷二白”的面貌一直得不到改善。1993年年底，全县10个乡镇中，贫困乡镇占3个，161个村有131个属贫困村，23.33万人口中，贫困人口达14.04万人，农民人均纯收入仅为628元，人均占有粮食310千克。1994年，国家实施“八七扶贫攻坚计划”，息烽被列入全国592个重点贫困县之一，启动“八七扶贫攻坚”历史征程。

新华社按照党中央、国务院安排，作为中央国家机关定点帮扶息烽。省委宣传部、省财政厅、省审计厅按照省委、省政府安排，作为省直机关定点帮扶息烽。新华社成立扶贫工作领导小组，下设扶贫办，在总社召开帮扶工作动员大会，先后派出16名扶贫工作队员，从1995年起分五批进驻息烽开展帮扶工作。省委宣传部、省财政厅、省审计厅先后组织65名队员，组成省委党建扶贫工作队，分五批进驻息烽扶贫。安顺地区也下派干部到息烽挂职，开展扶贫工作。1996年1月，息烽县行政区划调整，归属贵阳市管辖，成为贵阳市唯一的国定贫困县。市委、市政府对息烽的扶贫工作高度重视，组建市直扶贫工作队，先后从市直机关抽调58名队员到县、乡、村挂职帮扶，37家行政企事业单位、云岩区对息烽实施点对点帮扶。帮扶单位发扬动感情、动脑筋、动真格的“三动”精神，与息烽人一道打响了扶贫攻坚战，成功探索出了“息烽扶贫开发模式”，形成了“反贫困的职业技术教育”等一系列扶贫攻坚研究成果，走出一条靠发展治穷致富、靠发展抑制返贫、靠发展建设经济强县的路子，取得突出成效，得到国务院扶贫办和省委、省政府、市委、市政府的充分肯定。

息烽县委、县政府组织开展解放思想大讨论活动，进一步深化县情再认识，制定了“打基础、调结构、推科技、联市场、搞加工、抓转移、控人口”的总体工作思路。一是下大力改善农村基础设施，打开制约县域经济发展的瓶颈。8年时间共争取上级投资1.5亿元，发动群众投工投劳100多万个，完成坡改梯11.5万亩，新增灌溉面积2.78万亩，新修公路356.8千米，实施农村电网改造130多个村，基本实现村村通公路、通电话，组组通电、通广播电视信号。二是狠抓农业结构调整，坚持以市场为导向，以科技为动力，以农副产品加工为龙头，以实现土地产出增值为目标，8年内共投入扶贫开发资金5200余万元，兴办扶贫项目83个，形成了优质西瓜、秋淡蔬菜、辣椒、儿菜、晚熟果品、优质烤烟、“双低”油菜和稻田生态养鱼、网箱养鱼等具有一定规模的特色产业，建成一批绿色食品加工业。三是狠抓农村富余劳动力转移，拓展农村群众增收渠道。建起省内第一家农村富余劳动力就业培训基地，开展多形式、多层次的劳动力非农技能培训，采取干部带队、班组转移等多种形式，组织富余劳动力向东部沿海和省内发达城市有序输出，增加农民非农收入。四是发挥区位、交通、资源优势发展二、三产业，确立了旅游、医药、绿色食品、磷及磷化工、铝及铝加工五大优先发展的支柱产业，创造性地提出了“引得进，留得住，能发展”的招商引资工作“九字方针”，8年之间共从香港、台湾、广西、湖北、辽宁等地引进大小项目98个，引进资金9.8亿元，建成了贵州西洋肥业有限公司、贵州汉方药业有限公司、贵州太和制药有限公司、息烽铝厂等一批县内骨干企业，做大做强开磷集团息烽磷化工基地，工业经济显著提升，贫困人口就地转移就业率明显提高。到1996年，全县贫困村减少到71个，贫困人口减少到2.94万人，在全省贫困县中率先越过温饱线。2001年，全县国内生产总值提高到9.2亿元，农民人均纯收入达到1650元，全县经济增长幅度达19.7%，成为贵阳市经济增速最快的区县，产业结构实现从“一、二、三”向“二、一、三”再到“二、三、一”的两次跨越。建成2个小康镇、81个小康村，12万多人口基本过上小康生活。2002年，省委、省政府宣布息烽县脱贫。息烽人发扬战天斗地、艰苦奋斗的精神，用两年时间在全省率先越过温饱线，用6年时间率先摘掉贫困县的帽子，再用6年时间率先迈进全省建设经济强县行列，创造了令人瞩目的“息烽速度”。

三

1991—2010年，息烽县委、县政府围绕经济强县建设目标，创造性地组织实施“工业强县，农业稳县，科技兴县，旅游活县”四大战略，一、二、三产业齐头并进，经济社会发展驶入“快车道”。

产业发展持续提升，经济总量显著增长。1991年，息烽县国内生产总值1.62亿元，其中农业总产值1.06亿元；完成工业总产值0.63亿元。财政总收入0.17亿元，农民人均纯收入526元。到2010年，实现地方生产总值55.49亿元，其中农业总产值9.74亿元；完成工业总产值117.4亿元，占国内生产总值的2.12%；财政总收入5.5亿元；城市居民人均可支配收入14680元，农民人均纯收入5084元。三次产业结构实现从“一、二、三”到“二、一、三”再到“二、三、一”的两次跨越，经济结构更趋合理。

农业效益显著提高，农业产业化持续发展。“要想富得快，烤烟加油菜”，曾经一度是息烽农业经济的主要支撑。1996年，息烽县从安顺地区划归贵阳市管辖。按照市委、市政府“服务城市，富裕农村”的总体要求，息烽县从完善农村基础设施和调整农业产业结构两个方面入手，围绕贵阳城市菜篮子、米袋子、肉案子、果盘子，大力实施山、水、林、田、路综合治理，实施良种、良肥、良法“三良”工程，推进第二轮土地承包、林权制度和农村山塘水库产权制度改革，发展城郊型农业。20年间，全县持续推进实施“坡改梯”工程、土地综合治理工程、机耕道建设工程、水库、山塘建设和维修工程、天然林保护工程、长江防护林工程等，水资源配置更加合理，森林覆盖面积不断扩大。县、乡、村各级大力推进农业结构调整，实施农产品规模化、产业化发展。流长西瓜、南山秋淡菜、乌江网箱鱼、红岩葡萄、石硐晚熟果品、九庄辣椒、西山儿菜、养龙司次早熟蔬菜及中药材、生猪、肉鸡、肉牛、稻田生态鱼、高山灌草区黑山羊养殖等一批城郊型农业产业快速兴起并形成规模，农牧渔产品打入贵阳、遵义、广西、重庆等地城市市场。贵州汉方制药、贵州太和制药、味美食品、苗姑娘食品、玄天食品、天龙魔芋等一批农林产品深加工龙头企业相继建成投产。农产品市场网络不断完善，农业产业链不断延伸，农民人均纯收入持续增长。

工业经济快速发展，工业化进程全面提速。改革开放之初，20世纪六七十年代落户息烽的贵州朝晖机械厂、贵州拖拉机电机厂、贵州拖拉机配件厂、贵州汽油机厂等一批“三线”企业纷纷撤离息烽，息烽工业经济一度陷入困境。20世纪80年代末90年代初，贵州开阳磷矿矿务局谋求产业转型升级，实现以采矿为主业向采矿与化工齐头并进的发展方向转型，选址息烽县小寨坝镇，建设黄磷、重钙两个化工厂。息烽县紧紧抓住发展机遇，大力扶持开磷集团小寨坝磷化工基地做强做大，不断扩大生产规模，研发新产品，拓展新产业，延长产业链。1995年1月，开磷集团息烽重钙厂投产；同年，贵州太和制药有限公司成立。2002年，息烽铝厂投产。随着汉方制药、苗姑娘食品等一批新兴产业相继投产达产，标志着息烽工业经济走出了“三线”企业撤离后的“阴影”，实现了由传统的能源开采、国防工业、机械制造向磷及磷化工、铝及铝加工、生物制药、绿色食品四大支柱产业的转型。2001年，时任贵阳市市长孙国强率市直各部门负责人到息烽重钙厂调研，决定将重钙厂所在的小寨坝镇按县级城镇规划，以重钙厂为核心打造磷化工城。省、市、县三级加大企业“围墙外”基础设施建设，支持企业快速发展。1990—2010年，小寨坝磷化工基地实现了从化工厂到化工城到省级工业园区的两次跨越，企业规模不断扩大，经营业态不断延伸。县委、县政府把招商引资作为推进县域经济发展的重要抓手，先后设立招商办，组建招商局，出台招商、安商优惠政策，提供“保姆式”“一站式”服务，帮助企业完善“围墙外”基础设施，实施“三通一平”，陆续引进贵州西洋肥业有限责任公司、息烽铝厂、汉方制药厂、太和制药厂、银杏鹰药业、味美食品厂、苗姑娘食品厂、玄天食品厂、天龙魔芋加工厂等一批企业。工业总产值快速提升，农村富余劳动力有效转移，城乡居民增收致富渠道不断拓展。

旅游产业全面起步，第三产业综合发展。20年间，息烽县围绕“旅游活县”战略，全面开展旅游、文化资源调查，围绕“红色、温泉、森林、乡村”四大资源，推进旅游发展。1997年5月28日，息烽集中营革命历史纪念馆建成开放，标志着息烽红色旅游产业进入全新发展时期。20年间，纪念馆一期、二期工程相继实施，玄天洞杨虎城将军被囚禁处旧址、张露萍等七烈士陵园、九庄红军烈士陵园、流长没良坑红军烈士殉难处、鹿窝报恩寺红军烈士陵园、温泉三宝山革命烈士陵园相继建成开放。至2010年前，息烽集中营革命历史纪念馆先后列入全国爱国主义教育示范基地、全国廉政教育基地、全国国防教育基地、全省组工干部培训基地、全国首批100个红色旅游经典景区。中共十七大以后，国家实施公共文化服务体系建设，2008年，息烽集中营革命历史纪念馆列入全省第一批博物馆纪念馆免费开放试点，由中央财政每年补贴400万元免费开放专项经费，向社会免费开放，前来参观的省内外游客络绎不绝，红色旅游发展迈上了新的台阶。在此期间，县宣传、文化、旅游部门深入发掘息烽红色文化资源，通过新华社找到了1955年毛泽东为报道养龙司堡子妇女先进事迹的《在合作社内实行男女同工同酬》一文题写的编者按，并以此为依据向全国妇联申报妇女教育基地。2009年12月，时任全国妇联主席陈至立代表全国妇联授予堡子村“全国妇女教育基地”牌匾。2010年，县委、县政府组成专门班子，启动建设中国堡子半边天文化陈列馆；2011年8月12日，时任贵州省委常委、省委宣传部部长谌贻琴率省、市妇联、宣传部、文明办等多家单位和息烽县四大班子领导在堡子村举行隆重仪式，宣布陈列馆开馆。息烽红色旅游的文化内涵进一步丰富。

息烽是温泉富集地。息烽温泉开发于民国时期，拥有世界三大氡温泉之一的优质地热矿泉水资源，对皮肤病、风湿病、心脑血管病有显著疗效，深受游人推崇，成为全国总工会劳模职工疗休养中心。县委、县政府把温泉开发作为息烽旅游的主导产业和主打品牌，聘请国内一流地质勘探机构，对全县范围内的温泉资源进行勘探，确定了永靖镇南山、小寨坝镇中心、养龙司镇画眉湾、石硐镇胡家湾、西山镇柏香山、林丰、鹿窝镇罗家山等一批新的温泉开采点，于2009年实现南山温泉钻探出水，为温泉旅游开发打下了坚实基础。2005年10月，中共十六届五中全会作出建设社会主义新农村的决议，县、乡、村各级按照“生产发展、生活宽裕、乡风文明、村容整洁、管理民主”的总体要求，不断完善乡村基础设施，发展地方特色产业，挖掘地域特色文化，充分发挥农村生态、气候、空气质量等资源优势，加大政策、项目、资金扶持，发展乡村旅游，逐步形成了小寨坝镇红岩葡萄沟、养龙司幸福堡子两个乡村旅游示范点。引进贵阳商业银行，壮大农村信用合作联社，建立中国人寿保险息烽分公司，引进房地产企业，组建贵州广电网络息烽分公司，发展金融、保险、房地产、餐饮、文化娱乐、广告传媒、交通运输、批发零售等第三产业，实现了第三产业产值的快速增长。2010年，第三产业增加值12.84亿元，占国内生产总值的0.23%，实现对第一产业的超越。

城乡建设日新月异，城镇化步伐全速推进。1991—2010年，息烽县切实推进以县城扩容、示范小城镇试点和社会主义新农村示范点为重点的城乡建设。1996年1月划归贵阳市管辖后，县委、县政府在原西门田坝区域规划建设县城花园路新区，并统一楼层和房屋外立面设计，采取土地出让的方式引导和鼓励城乡居民投资征拨宅基地建房。1997年，县委、县政府向市争取到70万元建设资金，实施街区道路建设，建成息烽第一条人车分流的城市道路。同一时期，县建设局争取上级项目资金支持，在原东门田坝游泳池地块实施安居工程，解决干部职工住房难问题，建成东门河、河滨路、文化东路和县宣传文化中心（县文化馆），引进企业投资兴建光彩大楼、宏翔花园、明星公寓，息烽开始有了商品房。2001年，贵州中创房地产开发有限公司进入息烽，投资开发县城东门地块教师新村5号、6号楼。政府投资新建县青少年活动中心、县老年活动中心、息烽二中、县体育场、永靖镇政府、县质监局等公共建筑，扩建了息烽一中。引进企业投资兴建慧恒花园、水栖怡园、步行街楼盘，逐步完成了县城东门片区城市建设，实现了城市扩容。2002年，引进贵州广建房地产开发有限公司，按照城市发展规划，开发县城南片区。挖掉三座大山，建成了虎城大道南段和中段，规划建设了沿街商住楼，以及息烽大酒店、虎城大厦、龙港新城、县法院、县检察院、县消防大队等建筑，实现县城南移。2003年，贵州开磷集团购买原朝晖机械厂厂区，兴建开磷新城。2006年，重庆渝万集团息烽金穗房地产开发有限公司入驻息烽，对中街地块实施旧城改造，建成筑北大道商住区，并迁址新建了息烽县中医院。息烽县城面积逐渐扩大，“有县无城”的局面全面扭转。与此同时，为配合开磷集团磷化工基地扩容，小寨坝镇采取“产城互动”模式，规划建设南山小区安置失地农民，乡镇小城镇建设全面推进，九庄、温泉、养龙司、石硐、青山、流长等乡镇先后实施了城镇扩容，鹿窝镇配合乌江峡旅游开发建成了王家仓安置小区。2005年，中共中央十六届五中全会作出全面建设社会主义新农村的决定后，县委、县政府以流长乡水尾村为试点，启动新农村建设工作。各乡镇、村围绕富、学、乐、美“四在农家”的发展思路迅速推进，到2010年，全县已建成多个社会主义新农村示范点。城乡面貌大为改观，城镇化率迅速提升。

水电路信持续完善，基础设施进一步夯实。1991—2010年，息烽县农田水利、城镇自来水、农村人畜饮水基础设施全面推进，鱼简河水库、上沟水库等一批骨干水利工程相继建成投用，10个乡镇建起现代化的自来水厂，小桥河水库至小寨坝镇、鱼简河水库至小寨坝镇等一批重点引水管网开通，农村水利“三小工程”覆盖面广，水利水务改革全面推进。建成了永靖、立碑、流长、盘脚营等一批变电站，实施了农村电网改造工程，城乡供电有了充分保障。贵遵高等级公路南北纵贯县境，实现乡乡通油路、村村通硬化公路、户户通串户路。实施有线电话、互联网宽带、移动电话“村村通”工程，实现了有线、无线电话覆盖城乡，宽带网络进村入户。

教卫文体事业不断升级，民生保障水平持续提高。20年中，息烽县委、县政府持续推进实施“科教兴县”战略。以人为本，切实加大教育投入，通过实施基本普及九年制义务教育和基本扫除青壮年文盲“两基”工程，建成希望小学10所，新建、改扩建一批中、小学校和教学点，完善教学设施设备，改善乡村办学条件，引进高端人才，夯实教育发展基础，并向高标准扫盲、普及九年制义务教育、普及城乡中小学实验室目标延伸，夯实了全面提高人口素质的基础。加大投入，切实改善城乡医疗卫生条件，新建县医院、县中医医院、县妇幼保健站，全面改造提升乡镇卫生院，完善村级医疗服务点，实施城镇医疗保障和新型农村合作医疗制度，鼓励发展民营医院3所。深入开展计划生育“三结合”工作，深化城乡生殖服务，提高新生儿身体素质。加强公共文化服务体系建设，建成县宣传文化活动中心（县文化馆）、县图书馆、县体育场，建成10个乡镇综合文化站、161个村农家书屋和县、乡、村三级文化信息资源共享工程基层服务点，实现了乡、村两级农民体育健身工程全覆盖。实施息烽广播电视台台网分离，引进贵州广电网络息烽分公司，实施县城和乡镇集镇有线电视数字化改造提升和农村广播电视“村村通”“户户通”工程，全面解决了城乡群众收听、收看广播电视难的问题。深入挖掘息烽文物和非物质文化遗产，组织开展息烽红歌会、百龙千鼓闹新春、新春灯谜游艺、百村农民篮球赛等群众性文化体育活动，培育广场舞、舞龙、威风锣鼓、苗族芦笙舞等群众文体活动品牌。青山苗族芦笙舞《蒙待央》荣获全国第九届少数民族传统体育运动会表演项目金奖，永靖镇龙爪村农民舞龙队荣获全省农民运动会金奖。3项文化遗产列入省级非物质文化遗产名录、2项列入市级名录。县、乡、村各级扎实推进“平安息烽”建设，强化社会治安综合治理，先后荣获全省“无毒县”“平安建设先进县”称号。持续实施城乡最低生活保障制度，开展公共就业创业服务，加强劳动就业管理，切实保障农民工工资。2009年，贵阳市实施学有所教、劳有所得、病有所医、老有所养、住有所居、居有所安“六有”民生行动计划，教育、医疗、就业、养老及其他社会保障事业迈上了新台阶，群众幸福感、安全感显著提升。

改革开放不断深化，发展活力全面增强。县、乡各级按照中央、省、市安排部署，针对发展中的体制机制障碍，不断深化改革，扩大开放，激发内生动力，营造便利的投资贸易环境，高效的招商营商环境，开放的区域合作环境，优质的创新创业环境。组织实施政府机构改革、国有企业改革、林权制度改革、农村山塘水库产权制度改革等一系列改革。积极争取国家、省、市试点示范项目，创新行政审批、政务服务、土地利用、环保审查、人才引进、招商安商体制机制，健全市场化配置资源机制，切实增强发展活力，提高发展效益。

党的建设不断加强，精神文明建设持续推进。组织开展“三讲”“三个代表”重要思想学习教育活动，加强党的思想建设、组织建设和作风建设，深化干部人事制度改革，健全干部考核管理机制，推进党风廉政建设和反腐败斗争，党的建设全面加强。组织开展“整脏治乱”和文明县创建，推进生态文明县建设，实施覆盖城乡、全民共建的群众性精神文明创建活动，持续推进“三下乡”和精神文明“五进”活动。“自强不息，艰苦奋斗，赤胆忠诚，协力争先”的息烽精神全面弘扬。城乡生活环境极大改善，文明程度不断提高。

1991—2010年，息烽政治、经济、社会、文化、生态各项事业持续发展，人民物质文化生活水平持续提高，社会面貌发生了前所未有的深刻变化，为抢抓新机遇、迎接新挑战、实现新跨越奠定了坚实的政治基础、经济基础、文化基础和群众基础。

面向未来，息烽将站在全省建设经济强县的高起点，全面实施乡村振兴战略，以公园城镇、富美乡村建设为抓手，推动一、二、三产业融合，促进城乡一体化发展，努力打好新一轮脱贫攻坚战，建设更高水平的全面小康。

Overview

I

Xifeng County is located in the middle of Guizhou Province and the north of Guiyang City at 26° 57′ ~27° 19′ N and 106° 27′ ~106° 53′ E. It is adjacent to Kaiyang in the east and Xiuwen in the south, overlooking Zunyi County and Jinsha County in the northwest. The location of the county town is 66km away from Downtown Guiyang to the south and 85km away from the historical famous city Zunyi to the north. Covering an area of 1,036.5 square kilometers, accounting for 12.91% of the total area of Guiyang City, it has jurisdiction over seven towns, three townships, one community, 161 villages and 13 neighborhood committees. It has the total population of 268,678, including the non-agricultural population of 35,221 and the agricultural population of 233,457. Among the total population, the Han population is 253,704 and the ethnic population is 14,974 accounting for 5.57% of the total population of whole county. It has 24 ethnic groups including Miao, Buyei, Tujia, Yi, Dong, Gelao, Bai, Hui, Man, Zhuang and Shui, mainly concentrated in 91 ethnic villages of one ethnic township and non-ethnic townships.

Stone axes and stone adzes unearthed in Chetianhe, Dizhai Village prove that Xifeng was inhabited by human beings as early as in the Neolithic Age. It was the south boundary of Liangzhou Prefecture in the Xia Dynasty and the north border of Yue Kingdom in the Zhou Dynasty. It was under jurisdiction of the kingdoms of Julan and Zangke respectively in the Spring and Autumn Period and the Warring States Period. It was under jurisdiction of Julan County, Xinxiang Prefecture in the 26th year of the First Emperor of the Qin Dynasty (221BC) and Zangke Prefecture was established in the sixth year of Yuanding Period under the reign of Emperor Wu of the Han Dynasty (111BC) where the county was located. Huo Ji, a leader of Kunming occupied most regions of North Guizhou and Northwest Guizhou in the third year of Shuhan Jianxing Period (225) and the county was under the jurisdiction of the regions. In the first Xian' an Year of Jianwen Emperor of the Eastern Jin Dynasty (371), Jinle County was established with the seat of government located in the north of today' s Dulaying with jurisdiction over today' s Guiyang, Xiuwen County, Kaiyang County and Xifeng County. The county was under the jurisdiction of Zangke in the Emperor Wen Period of the Sui Dynasty. Zangke was changed into Zangke Prefecture in the third year of the reign of Emperor Yang of the Sui Dynasty (607) with the seat of government located in today' s Anshun and the county was under jurisdiction of Zangke Prefecture. In the third year of Wude Period of the Tang Dynasty (620), Qianzhou Governor' s Office was established with control over 51 prefectures, the county was under jurisdiction of Manzhou Prefecture and the seat of government was in today' s

Kaiyang County. Juzhou Prefecture was established in the following year with the seat of government located in today' s Guiyang and the county was under jurisdiction of the Prefecture.

In the fifth year of Qiande Period of the Song Dynasty (967), Pugui, leader of the Kingdom Luodian surrendered and was appointed as the governor of Guiyang with leadership over the middle, west and south of today' s Guiyang, and the county was subordinate to the regions. In the eighth year of Kaibao Period (975), the county was under jurisdiction of Song' s Family of Shuidong. It was subordinate to Pacification Office of Shunyuan, Sichuan Province in the 17th year of the Zhiyuan Reign Period of the Yuan Dynasty (1280), to Military Commission of Shunyuanlu, Huguang Province in the 29th year of the Zhiyuan Reign Period of the Yuan Dynasty (1292).

It was subordinate to Pacification Office of Guizhou, Sichuan Province in the fourth year of Hongwu Period of the Ming Dynasty (1371). It was under administration of Pacification Office of Guizhou, Guizhou Chief Secretary in the 11th year of Yongle Period (1414). During the reign of Emperor Wanli in the Ming Dynasty (1573–1620), Shuixi people invaded eastward and Xifeng was under the jurisdiction of Guizhou Pacification Office, belonging to the place of Shuiwai Liumu (6 regions to the south of Sancha River) of Shuixi An' s Family. In the third year of Emperor Chongzhen of the Ming Dynasty (1630), Zhu Xieyuan the Governor put down the rebellions in Shuixi and established Jierong Defending Qianhu Office (thousand households' administrative office of defense) in today' s Xifeng County, reformed and abolished subsequently. Later with the official reply of Emperor Chongzhen, two Qianhu Offices, Xifeng and Yuxiang were established. In the 15th year of Emperor Shunzhi of the Qing Dynasty (1658), office was canceled and Wei (guard town) was established, and Xifeng and Yuxiang were under administration of Fuyong Guard Town. Wei (guard town) was canceled and Xiuwen County was established in the 26th year of Kangxi Emperor (1687), and Xifeng and Yuxiang Defending Qianhu Offices were divided to Xiuwen County, under the jurisdiction of Guiyang Prefecture. It was reduced into Xifeng Town in the tenth year of Tongzhi Emperor (1871).

Xifeng County was established in the third year of the Republic of China Era (1914). Guizhu County Seat was moved to Xifeng Town and was renamed as Xifeng County in the fourth year of the Republic of China Era (1915). It was under the jurisdiction of Guizhou Province Supervision Office in the 35th year of the Republic of China Era (1946), and it was under direct administration of Guizhou Province once again in the 37th year of the Republic of China Era (1948). Xifeng was liberated on November 17, 1949 and the People' s Government of Xifeng County was established on November 23 of that year, under the jurisdiction of Guiyang Special District. Guiyang Special District was renamed as Guiding Special District on November 15, 1952 and Xifeng County was still under its jurisdiction. Guiding Special District was canceled on May 10, 1956 and it was put under the administration of Anshun Special District. It was put under the administration of Zunyi Special District on October 4, 1958 and put back to the administration of Anshun Special District on August 17, 1965. It was put under the administration of Guiyang City on January 1, 1996.

Xifeng is in an area of north subtropical and south temperate zone monsoon climate with mild temperature all year round and abundant rainfall. With the annual average temperature of 14.5° C and the annual average rainfall of 1,111mm, most regions have the annual frost–free period of more than 270 days. With high altitude, low latitude and big height difference, it has the three-dimensional climate of "one mountain with four seasons, ten miles with different weathers", suitable for growth of various crops and forests from subtropical zone to warm temperate zone. In the area there are four primary jungles respectively on the Nanwang Mountain, Xiwang Mountain, Tiantai Mountain and Tuanyuan Mountain. By 2010, it was proved to have 104 families of 263 species of trees, 61 families of 227 species of wild grass, 110 families of 227 species of medical plants and several hundred species of aquatic animals, terrestrial animals and amphibians, with the forest coverage of up to 45.83%.

Xifeng is high in the south and low in the north. It is adjacent to reservoir area of Wujiang River with the greatest capacity in Guizhou Province in the north. Xifeng River, Wengtong River and Yulin River in the area mostly originate in the southeast and flow northwestward. The river density in the area is 17.8km/square kilometer with 12 rivers with the single drainage area of more than 20 square kilometers. With the average long-term discharge of 585 million cubic meters and the average yearly storage capacity of 465 million cubic meters, it has abundant water resources. Xifeng River, the longest river in the area originates in Nanqiao Village, Shidong Town in the northeast, flows to the east and then to the north in Nanqiao, flows into the tributary of Toudao River at the big river mouth and flows into Wujiang River between Shiqiao Village and Wengsha Village, Xiaozhaiba Town, with the total length of 50km.

As the traffic fortress of Middle Guizhou, Xifeng has been known as "a strategic gateway of Sichuan and Guizhou and the throat of Middle Guizhou". Sichuan-Guizhou Railway, No. 210 National Highway, G75 Section of Lanzhou-Haikou Expressway and Chongqing-Guizhou High-speed Railway crosses four towns or townships including Yongjing, Xiaozhaiba, Yanglongsi and Xishan in the east of the county from south to north. Jiangkou-Duge Expressway crosses six towns or townships from east to west including Wenquan, Xiaozhaiba, Yanglongsi, Liuchang, Luwo and Jiuzhuang. Located at the juncture of the south-north traffic artery trunk of Middle Guizhou, it is an important way of Gansu Province, Sichuan Province and Chongqing City to the south as well as a "gateway" for Guiyang to connect North Guizhou, Chongqing and Sichuan in the north. The crossing of Lanzhou-Haikou Expressway and Duge-Jiangkou Expressway in Xiaozhaiba Town has been a connection point for each municipal and prefectural expressway of Guizhou to the east, west, south and north. Xifeng is also the starting point for marine traffic on the Wujiang River. Zhubei Dock (a dock in the north of Guiyang) under construction connects to both waterways and land ways.

Xifeng is a geopark in the north of Guiyang. Xifeng is located in the middle of the tableland and hills in Middle Guizhou, with Nanwang Mountain, Xiwang Mountain, Tuanyuan Mountain and Wujiang Gorge forming the main framework of the topography in the county. With rolling ridges and peaks, ravines distributed in length and breadth and the altitude of 1,000~1,200m in the major area, most areas in the county are low and medium-height hills with extensive distribution of carbonate rocks and full development of karst landform. Such geological structures are distributed everywhere as peak cluster, depression, karst hill, cave, underground river, funnel and klippe. In particular, Duobin Cave, Longtan Cave and Yinzi Cave are the deepest with the most peculiar structure and the greatest value of development. Eroded and cut by Wujiang River and its tributary, the north edge is distributed with ravines in length and breadth with towering cliffs, developing such geological wonders as Zimei Peak, Goddess Peak, Daodan Peak, Liyu Peak and Hundred-Mile Gallery. The highest point is at the south peak of Nanwang Mountain with the altitude of 1,749.6m and the lowest point is at Datangkou where Wujiang River flows out of the county, with the altitude of 609m.

With obvious characteristics of Danxia landform, more than 100 square kilometers of Jurassic quartzite is deposited on Xiwang Mountain and Tuanyuan mountain in the county. With towering peaks, rocks standing in great numbers and springs and waterfalls, it presents us diversified views. Craters formed from prehistorical collision of celestial bodies found in the area of Tuanyuan Mountain and the huge carnivorous dinosaur fossils unearthed in Longben Mountain are both geological wonders rarely seen in Middle Guizhou. Mineral resources in the county mainly include coal, phosphorus, aluminum, ferrous sulfide, limonite, silicon, crystal, barite and kaolin, of which coal and phosphorus boast the most abundant reserve and the highest grade.

Xifeng is a hot land for red culture. In 2004, 13 ministries and commissions including the Publicity Department of the CPC Central Committee announced the first batch of national classic scenic areas for red tourism, and Xifeng Concentration Camp Revolutionary History Memorial Hall and Xifeng Wujiang Scenic Area were among the list. The scope of Xifeng Concentration Camp Revolutionary History Memorial Hall covers the site of Xifeng Concentration Camp, the site of place where General Yang Hucheng was imprisoned in Xuantian Cave and the cemetery for seven martyrs including Zhang Luping in Kuaihuo Ridge. The scope of Xifeng Wujiang Scenic Area covers Datang Ferry, Tiziyan Ferry and Jiangkou Ferry where the Red Army crossed Wujiang River during the Long March, the monument for the Red Army crossing Wujiang River during the Long March on the bank of Wujiang River, Liuchang Moliang Pit where martyrs of the Red Army were killed, Baoensi Red Army Martyrs Cemetery of Luwo, Jiuzhuang Red Army Martyrs Cemetery and seven sites where the Red Army resisted the enemy when they passed through Xifeng.

In the county there are also a large number of battle sites for suppression of bandits such as Caoxianggou and Huxiao Stand where the Liberation Army pacified the bandits in the early period when the People's Republic of China was established as well as Wenquan Sanbaoshan Revolutionary Martyrs Cemetery. In the county there are the First Village of Equal Pay for Equal Work of Men and Women, National Women Education Base, China Baozi Half-the-Sky Culture Display Museum with the names inscribed by Mao Zedong and commented by the editor. There is also the precious "Three-Line" cultural wealth left from the big "Three-Line" Construction Period by such enterprises as State-owned 276 Factory of Nuclear Industry Department, Guizhou Diesel Engine Factory, Guizhou Tractor and Electric Engine Factory, Guizhou Tractor Accessories Factory and Guizhou Zhaohui Machine Works. With profound accumulation of red culture, it has abundant and diversified red tourism resources.

Xifeng is a worldwide well-known city of radon hot springs. Records about Xifeng hot springs are available in the historical books of the Ming and Qing Dynasties. Developed and constructed in the Republic of China Era, the hot springs of Xifeng are among the world top three radon hot springs and China's top eight hot springs, reputed as "No. 1 Hot Springs of the World". Since the 1990s, the CPC Committee of Xifeng County and the People's Government of Xifeng County has invited geological experts to have overall survey on the hot spring resources, finding eight hot spring survey points including Yongjing Nanshan Hot Spring, Shidong Hujiawan Hot

Spring, Xishan Baixiangshan Hot Spring and Linfeng Hot Spring, Xiaozhaiba Central Hot Spring, Yanglongsi Huameiwan Hot Spring, Luwo Yangzhai Hot Spring and Qingshan Miao Qingshan Hot Spring. Xinluo Hot Spring and Hujiawan Hot Spring have been drilled with water available containing such microelements beneficial to the human body as radon, strontium and metasilicic acid. The tourism department of the county has prepared the construction plan for the 100-Mile Hot Spring Town planning to invest RMB450 million Yuan in development and construction of Nanshan Hot Spring. Drilling work has been conducted for Linfeng Hot Spring and Central Hot Spring.

Xifeng is a provincial tourist destination of Guizhou. Xifeng Scenic Area has been listed among the second group of provincial scenic areas announced in 1995 by the People' s Government of Guizhou Province. It is mostly characterized with red tourism, hot spring tourism, forest tourism and countryside tourism. The primary jungles of Nanwang Mountain, Xiwang Mountain, Tuanyuan Mountain and Tiantai Mountain constitute an ecological barrier for Xifeng Section at the upper reach of the Yangtze River, becoming an important basis for development of forest tourism in Xifeng. Nanshan Posthouse Park under construction has been listed among the provincial demonstration ecological sports parks. The lofty Nanwang Mountain in the east of the county, where Banyue Taoist built Xuantiandong Taoist Temple as early as in the Ming Dynasty, is the birthplace of Taoism culture in Guizhou. Presently Guizhou Taoism Association Tianlong Taoist Temple has been built in Yanglang.

Xiwang Mountain in the middle endowed with supernatural talents, where Master Yusong built Fengchi Temple to carry forward Buddhism as early as in the early Qing Dynasty, is the birthplace of Zen Buddhism in Guizhou. Presently International Orienteering and International Paragliding Competition Base has been built. Popular in the folk, Liuchang Yang Opera, Xifeng Huadeng Opera, Xifeng Dragon Lantern Dance, Nuo Opera, Miao Lusheng Dance, Miao Embroidery, "Siyueba" Festival (April 8th Festival) of Miao People and Xiwangshan Insect Tea Art have been listed among the list of intangible cultural heritage of Guizhou Province. It has also a large number of cultural sites with a long history such as Chetianhe stoneware, Home of Guizhou Merchants in Dizhai Village, Tombs of the Eastern Han Dynasty in Liuchang and the Pledge Stele of the Fifth Year of Yongle Emperor of the Ming Dynasty in Luwo. With the continuous development of "tourism+" industry and the continuous promotion of countryside complex construction, Xifeng has become an important vacationing, cultural experience and health preservation tourism area in Middle Guizhou and North Guiyang, ranking among China' s top 100 counties for countryside tourism in 2015.

The period from 1991 to 2010 is a golden period for the economic and social development in Xifeng. Under the leadership of the CPC Committee of Xifeng County and the People' s Government of Xifeng County, Xifeng people have carried forward the Xifeng spirit of "striving to be stronger, working hard, being loyal and being united" to challenge poverty. Having successively experienced 3 major stages of the historical development periods with battling against poverty, ranking among counties of great strength and accelerating development, it has entered an important development era for the construction of a moderately prosperous society in all aspects with overall economic development, continuous social advancement, overall cultural improvement and general improvement of the people' s quality.

II

Xifeng is in typical karst mountainous area with most parts distributed with high mountains and rocks. With land distributed in a broken manner, it has poor conditions for industrial and agricultural production, hence the foundation for economic and social development is weak. In the county the mineable mineral resources are mainly coal, phosphorus, and geothermal and mineral water welling out naturally. Such resources are respectively mined and utilized by Nanshan Coal Mine of Guizhou Lindong Mining Bureau, Xifeng Phosphate Mine (a state-owned enterprise subordinate to Bureau of Geology and Mineral Exploration and Development Guizhou Province) and Xifeng Hot Spring Sanatorium subordinate to Guizhou Federation of Trade Unions, with limited contribution to the local finance. During the construction of Wujiangdu Hydropower Station in the 1970s, Yanglong Station and Wujiang Subdistrict originally under jurisdiction of Xifeng County were put under the jurisdiction of Zunyi County, so Xifeng County cannot get the financial tax revenue from the hydropower station and has to settle the problem of migrant resettlement for the reservoir. In addition, Xifeng is located in the southwest inland far away from any sea, border and river, and it was still under jurisdiction of Anshun when Guiyang was listed among the last group of inland opening cities in 1992, so it has no conditions and advantages for opening up.

The area of the county town is less than 0.5 square kilometer with extremely low industrial and agricultural production level and small volume of tertiary industry. With only three shabby streets of tile-wood and brick-wood houses, it is "a county without town". The big "Three-Line" enterprises once flourishing successively moved out of Xifeng later. With a sharp drop in industrial output value, the economic development of Xifeng faced unprecedented pressure once again and the backward state of poverty was never improved. At the end of 1993, three of ten towns and townships of the county were in poverty, 131 of the 161 villages were in poverty and 140,400 of the total population of 233,300 were in poverty. The per capita pure income of farmers was only RMB628 Yuan and the per capita cereal occupation was 310kg. In 1994, the national "Eight-Seven Poverty Alleviation Program" was implemented. Xifeng was listed as one of the 592 key poverty counties in China and started the history of "Eight-Seven Poverty Alleviation".

According to the arrangement of the CPC Central Committee and the State Council, Xinhua News Agency was appointed as a state organ supporting Xifeng, and the Publicity Department of the CPC Guizhou Provincial Committee, Department of Finance of Guizhou Province and Audit Office of Guizhou Province were appointed as provincial organs supporting Xifeng according to arrangement of the CPC Guizhou Provincial Committee and the People's Government of Guizhou Province. Xinhua News Agency established Poverty Alleviation Leading Team with a Poverty Alleviation Office set and held a poverty alleviation work mobilization conference in the Head Office. It successively designated 16 poverty alleviation team members who went to Xifeng for support in batches starting from 1995. The Publicity Department of the CPC Guizhou Provincial Committee, Department of Finance of Guizhou Province and Audit Office of Guizhou Province successively organized 65 members form a party construction poverty alleviation work team of the CPC Guizhou Provincial Committee who went to Xifeng for support in five batches. Anshun Region also delegated cadres to Xifeng for poverty alleviation work.

In January 1996, administrative division of Xifeng County was adjusted and it was put under the jurisdiction of Guiyang City, becoming the only state-designated poverty county in Guiyang City. The Guiyang Municipal Committee of the CPC and the Guiyang Municipal People' s Government attached great importance to the poverty alleviation work and organized a poverty alleviation work team directly under municipal administration. Totally 58 members were successively transferred from the municipal organs for support in the county, townships and villages. Thirty-seven administrative organs, enterprises and government-sponsored institutions and Yunyan District provided point-to-point support for Xifeng. With the spirit of being enthusiastic, hardworking and practical, the supporting units started the battle against poverty together with the people of Xifeng, successfully exploring "Xifeng Mode for poverty alleviation and development" with a series of research achievements gained including "anti-poverty vocational technical education" . They have developed the way of alleviating poverty, restraining returning to poverty and constructing a powerful county in economy by development with outstanding effect achieved, fully affirmed by the State Council Leading Group Office of Poverty Alleviation and Development, the CPC Guizhou Provincial Committee, the People' s Government of Guizhou Province, the Guiyang Municipal Committee of the CPC and the Guiyang Municipal People' s Government.

The CPC Committee of Xifeng County and the People' s Government of Xifeng County organized discussions on liberation of ideology to get further knowledge about the county situation, working out the general working thoughts of "laying foundation, regulating structure, promoting science and technology, linking market, carrying out processing, emphasizing shift and controlling population" .

Firstly, it is to vigorously improve the rural infrastructure to tackle the bottleneck restricting county-level economic development. In eight years, the county has got the investment of RMB150 million from the superordinate authority, mobilized the local people to input more than one million workers, completed the transformation slope into terraced fields with the area of about 7,666.67 hectares, increased the irrigation area of about 1,853.33 hectares, built the highways of 356.8km and conducted rural power grid reconstruction for more than 130 villages, basically realizing availability of highway and telephone for each village and availability of electricity and broadcasting &TV signals for each group.

Secondly, it is to emphasize the adjustment of agricultural structure. Oriented by market, driven by science and technology, led by agricultural and sideline product processing and targeted at realizing land yield value addition, the county invested more than RMB52 million Yuan in poverty alleviation and development in eight years with 83 poverty alleviation projects initiated. A number of green food processing industries have been established and some characteristic industries of certain scale have been developed such as high-quality watermelon, autumn vegetable, pepper, Ercai cabbage (*Brassica juncea*), late ripening fruit, high-quality flue-cured tobacco, "double-low" rape, ecological fish farming in paddy field and cage fish culturing.

Thirdly, is to attach great importance to transfer of surplus rural labor force to expand the channels for farmers to increase income. It established the first employment training base for surplus labor forces in Guizhou Province to carry out non-agricultural skill training of multiple forms and levels for rural labor forces. In multiple forms including leading by cadres and shift transfer, surplus labor forces were organized to output to the eastern coastal regions and developed cities in the province in an orderly manner, thus to increase the non-agricultural income of farmers.

And fourthly, it is to develop the secondary and tertiary industries based on the advantages in location, transport and resources. It has confirmed five pillar industries of prior development including tourism, medicine, green food, phosphorus and phosphorus chemical industry and aluminum and aluminum processing, creatively proposing the business invitation and capital introduction guidelines of "being able to introduce, retain and development". In the past eight years 98 projects of different size have been introduced from such places as Hong Kong, Taiwan, Guangxi, Hubei and Liaoning with the capital of RMB980 million Yuan introduced. A large number of backbone enterprises of the county have been established including Guizhou Western Fertilizer Co., Ltd., Guizhou Hanfang Pharmaceutical Co., Ltd., Guizhou Taihe Pharmaceutical Co., Ltd. and Xifeng Aluminum Factory. It has strengthened Xifeng Phosphorus Chemical Industry Base of Kailin Group with the industrial economy and nearby transfer employment rate of poor population significantly improved.

By 1996, the number of poverty villages of the county was decreased to 71 and the population in poverty decreased to 29,400, taking the lead to surmount the breadline among all the poverty counties in the province. In 2001, GDP of the whole county was increased to RMB920 million Yuan, per capita pure income of farmers reached RMB1,650 Yuan and the economic growth rate of the county reached 19.7%. It became the county of the highest economic growth rate in Guiyang City. The industrial structure realized leaps from "primary, secondary and tertiary" to "secondary, primary and tertiary" and to "secondary, tertiary and primary". Two moderately prosperous towns and 81 moderately prosperous villages were constructed with more than 120,000 people realizing comparatively well-off life. In 2002, the CPC Guizhou Provincial Committee and the People's Government of Guizhou Province declared that Xifeng County got rid of poverty. With the hard-working spirit, the people of Xifeng took the lead in Guizhou Province to surmount the breadline with two years, to get rid of poverty with six years and to rank among powerful counties in economy in Guizhou Province in another six years, creating the noticeable "Xifeng Speed".

III

From 1991 to 2010, centered on the construction goal of a powerful county in economy, the CPC Committee of Xifeng County and the People's Government of Xifeng County creatively organized and implemented four strategies, namely, "strengthening the county with industry, stabilizing the county with agriculture, prospering the county with science and technology and vitalizing the county with tourism". With simultaneous development of the primary, secondary and tertiary industries, the county has entered the "expressway" of economic and social development.

Industrial development was continuously improved and economic aggregate was significantly increased. In 1991, GDP of Xifeng County was RMB162 million Yuan including the total agricultural output value of RMB106 million Yuan, and the total industrial output value was RMB63 million Yuan. The total financial revenue was RMB17 million Yuan and the per capita pure income of farmers was RMB526.00 Yuan. By 2010, the local GDP reached RMB5.549 billion Yuan including the total agricultural output value of RMB974 million Yuan, and the total industrial output value was RMB11.74 billion Yuan, accounting for 2.12% of GDP. The total financial revenue was RMB550 million Yuan, per capita disposable income for urban citizens was RMB14,680.00 Yuan and per capita pure income of farmers was RMB5,084.00 Yuan. The industrial structure realized leaps from "primary, secondary and tertiary" to "secondary, primary and tertiary" and to "secondary, tertiary and primary", and the economic structure became more reasonable.

Agricultural benefits were significantly improved and agricultural industrialization was continuously developed. "To be rich, we develop flue-cured tobacco and rape." Flue-cured tobacco and rape were once major support for the agricultural economy of Xifeng. Xifeng County was put under jurisdiction of Guiyang City from Anshun Region in 1996. According to the general requirements of the Guiyang Municipal Committee of the CPC and the Guiyang Municipal People's Government for "serving urban areas, enriching rural areas", Xifeng County started with improving rural infrastructure and regulating agricultural industrial structure and focused on city vegetable basket, rice bag, meat table, and fruit tray to vigorously implement overall management of mountains, water, forest, farmland and road, carried out "high-quality seeds, fertilizer and method", promote the second round of reform on land contracting, forest right system and rural pond and reservoir property right system and develop outskirt agriculture.

In the past 20 years, the county has continuously promoted the implementation of the project of "transformation from slope to terraced field", overall land management project, tractor road construction project, reservoir and pond construction and repairing project, natural forest protection project and the Yangtze River protection forest project. Water resource allocation became more reasonable and the forest coverage area was continuously enlarged. The governments of county, township and village level vigorously promoted the regulation of agricultural structure and implemented large-scale and industrialized development of agricultural products. A large number of outskirt agricultural industry were rapidly developed and reached a considerable scale covering Liuchang watermelon, Nanshan autumn vegetable, Wujiang cage fish, Hongyan grapes, Shidong late ripening fruit, Jiuzhuang pepper, Xishan Ercai cabbage (*Brassica juncea*), Yanglongsi subprecocious vegetable, Chinese medicinal herbs, live pig, table poultry, beef cattle, ecological fish in paddy fields and black goat breeding in alpine bush and grass area. The agricultural, farming and fishery products of Xifeng County have entered the urban market in Guiyang, Zunyi, Guangxi and Chongqing. A number of leading agricultural and forestry product deep processing enterprises were successively established and put into production including Guizhou Hanfang Pharmaceutical, Guizhou Taihe Pharmaceutical, Weimei Food, Miaoguniang Food, Xuantian Food and Tianlong Konjak. The agricultural product market network was continuously improved, agricultural industrial chain continuously extended and the per capita pure income of farmers was continuously increased.

Industrial economy was rapidly developed and the process of industrialization was accelerated in all aspects. In the early period of reform and opening up, a number of "Three-Line" enterprises settled in Xifeng in the 1960s and 1970s including Guizhou Zhaohui Machine Works, Guizhou Tractor and Electric Engine Factory, Guizhou Tractor Accessories Factory and Guizhou Gasoline Engine Factory moved out of Xifeng successively, and the industrial economy of Xifeng was put in difficulty. At the end of the 1980s and the beginning of the 1990s, Guizhou Kaiyang Phosphorus Mining Bureau sought for industrial transformation and upgrading and realized transformation from mining industry to simultaneous development of mining and chemical industry by establishing two chemical plants of yellow phosphorus and heavy calcium in Xiaozhaiba Town, Xifeng County. Holding fast the development opportunity, Xifeng County provided great support for strengthening of Xifeng Phosphorus Chemical Industry Base of Kailin Group to continuously enlarge the production scale, research and develop new products, develop new industries and extend the industrial chain.

In January 1995, Kailin Group Xifeng Heavy Calcium Plant was put into production, and Guizhou Taihe Pharmaceutical Co., Ltd. was established in the same year. Xifeng Aluminum Factory was put into production in 2002. The successive operation of a number of emerging industries including Hanfang Pharmaceutical and Miaoguniang Food marked that the industrial economy of Xifeng got out of the "shadow" from moving of the "Three-Line" enterprises and realized the transformation from the traditional energy mining, national defense industry and mechanical manufacturing to four pillar industries including phosphorus and phosphorus chemical industry, aluminum and aluminum processing, biological pharmacy and green food. In 2001, Sun Guoqiang, then the mayor of Guiyang City, led the responsible persons of each department directly under administration of the city to go to Xifeng Heavy Calcium Plant for survey, making the decision to plan Xiaozhaiba Town as a county-level town where the heavy calcium plant is located and develop a phosphorus chemical industry town centered on the heavy calcium plant. The governments of provincial, municipal and county level strengthened infrastructure construction "out of enclosure wall" for enterprises to support their rapid development.

From 1990 to 2010, Xiaozhaiba Phosphorus Chemical Industry Base realized the leaps from a chemical plant to a chemical town and to a provincial industrial park, with the enterprise scale continuously improved and business forms continuously diversified. The CPC Committee of Xifeng County and the People's Government of Xifeng County took business invitation and capital introduction as an effective means of promoting county-level economic development, successively establishing Business Invitation Office and Business Invitation Bureau and issuing a series of preferential policies for business invitation and security to provide "one-station nanny" service, help enterprises to improve the infrastructure "out of the enclosure wall" and implement "three-accessibility and one-leveling". It has successively introduced a number of enterprises including Guizhou Western Fertilizer Co., Ltd., Xifeng Aluminum Factory, Hanfang Pharmaceutical Factory, Taihe Pharmaceutical Factory, Ginkgo Eagle Pharmaceutical, Weimei Food Factory, Miaoguniang Food Factory, Xuantian Food Factory and Tianlong Konjak Processing Factory. The total industrial output value was rapidly improved, surplus rural labor force was effectively transferred and the channels for urban and rural citizens to increase income were continuously expanded.

Tourism industry started in all aspects and the tertiary industry realized comprehensive development. In the past 20 years, Xifeng County conducted overall survey on tourism and cultural resources centered on the strategy of "vitalizing the county by tourism" and promoted tourism development centered on "red, hot spring, forest and countryside" resources. Xifeng Concentration Camp Revolutionary History Memorial Hall was built and opened on May 28, 1997, which marked that the red tourism industry of Xifeng entered a new era of development. In the past 20 years, Phase I and II of the Memorial Hall were successively constructed, and the site of place where General Yang Hucheng was imprisoned in Xuantian Cave, the cemetery for seven martyrs including Zhang Luping, Jiuzhuang Red Army Martyrs Cemetery, Liuchang Moliang Pit where martyrs of the Red Army were killed, Baoensi Red Army Martyrs Cemetery of Luwo and Wenquan Sanbaoshan Revolutionary Martyrs Cemetery were successively constructed and opened to public. By the time before 2010, Xifeng Concentration Camp Revolutionary History Memorial Hall had been appraised as a National Demonstration Base of Patriotic Education, National Base of Anti-corruption Education, National Defense Education Base, Provincial Cadre Training Base and one of the First Batch of National 100 Classic Red Tourism Attractions.

China started public culture service system construction after the 17th National Congress of the CPC. In 2008, Xifeng Concentration Camp Revolutionary History Memorial Hall was listed among the pilot sites for free opening, opened to the public free of charge based on the special fund of RMB4 million Yuan subsidized by the central finance. Countless visitors in and out of Guizhou Province were attracted and the development of red tourism took a further step. During that period, the publicity, culture and tourism departments of the county deeply dug the red cultural resources of Xifeng and found the editor' s comments on the article *Equal Pay for Equal Work for Men and Women within Cooperatives* reporting the advanced deeds of women in Baozi, Yanglongsi, written by Mao Zedong in 1955 through Xinhua News Agency. Based on that they applied for the Women Education Base with All-China Women's Federation. In December 2009, Chen Zhili, then the chairman of All-China Women's Federation, granted Baozi Village the tablet of "National Women Education Base" on behalf of All-China Women's Federation. In 2010, the CPC Committee of Xifeng County and the People' s Government of Xifeng County organized a special team to start the construction of China Baozi Half-the-Sky Culture Display Museum. On August 12, 2011, Chen Yiqin, a standing member of the CPC Guizhou Provincial Committee and director of the Publicity Department of the CPC Guizhou Provincial Committee then led officials of such units as the provincial and municipal women' s federations, publicity department and civilization office and the four leading groups of Xifeng to hold a grand ceremony in Baozi Village and declare the opening of the Display Museum. The cultural connotation of red tourism in Xifeng was further enriched.

Xifeng is a place with concentrated hot springs. The development of hot springs in Xifeng started in the Republic of China Era. It has the high-quality geothermal and mineral water resource as one of the world top three radon hot springs. With significant effect for skin diseases, rheumatism and cardiovascular diseases, it is highly favored by the people and Xifeng has become a rest center for model workers of All-China Federation of Trade Unions. The CPC Committee of Xifeng County and the People' s Government of Xifeng County took hot spring development as the leading industry and brand of tourism in Xifeng, inviting top-grade geological exploration institutions of China to explore the hot spring resources in the county. A number of new hot spring development points including Nanshan of Yongjing Town, Xiaozhaiba Town Center, Huameiwan of Yanglongsi Town, Hujiawan of Shidong Town, Baixiangshan of Xishan Town, Linfeng and Luojiashan of Luwo Town. Nanshan Hot Spring was drilled with water available in 2009, which laid a sound foundation for hot spring tourism development.

In October 2005, a resolution was made on the Fifth Plenary Session of the 16th Central Committee of the CPC to construct the socialist new countryside. According to the general requirements of "developed production, well-off life, civilized lifestyle, neat village look and democratic management" , the governments of county, township and village level continuously improved rural infrastructure to develop local characteristic industries, dig local characteristic culture, bring the advantage in rural areas in ecology, climate and air quality and enhance policy, project and capital support for development of countryside tourism, gradually forming two countryside tourism demonstration points respectively Hongyan Putaogou of Xiaozhaiba and Happy Baozi of Yanglongsi. It introduced Guiyang Commercial Bank, strengthened rural credit cooperatives, established China Life Insurance Xifeng Company, introduced real estate enterprises, organized Guizhou Broadcasting Network Xifeng Company, developed such tertiary industries as finance, insurance, real estate, F&B, culture & entertainment, advertisement media, transport, wholesale and retail and realized rapid growth of the output value of the tertiary industry. In 2010, the added value of the tertiary industry was RMB1.284 billion Yuan, accounting for 0.23% of GDP, successfully surmounting the primary industry.

Changes took place with each passing day in urban-rural construction and the pace of urbanization was promoted in full speed. From 1991 to 2010, Xifeng County practically promoted urban-rural construction focused on capacity expansion of the county town, demonstration town pilot and socialist new countryside demonstration point. After Xifeng County was put under jurisdiction of Guiyang City in January 1996, the CPC Committee of Xifeng County and the People' s Government of Xifeng County planned to construct Huayuan Road New Area of the County Town in the original Tianba Area of Ximen and unified the design of floors and external facade. Urban and rural residents were guided and encouraged to invest in land used for building a house in the way of land transfer.

In 1997, the CPC Committee of Xifeng County and the People' s Government of Xifeng County got the construction fund of RMB700,000 Yuan from the Guiyang Municipal People' s Government for road construction and built the first city road with pedestrians separated from vehicles in Xifeng. In the same time, the construction bureau of the county strove for project fund support from the superordinate authority to implement housing project at the plot of the original Dongmen Tianba Swimming Pool to settle the difficulty of cadres in housing. It built Dongmen River, Hoban Road, East Wenhua Road and Xifeng Publicity Culture Center (Xifeng Culture Center) and introduced enterprises to invest in building Guangcai Building, Hongxiang Garden Residential Quarter and Star Apartment. Xifeng started to have commercial housing. Guizhou Zhongchuang Real Estate Development Co., Ltd. entered Xifeng in 2001 to invest in the development of No. 5 and 6 buildings of Jiaoshi Xincun Residential Quarter at Dongmen Plot of the county town. The government invested in construction of such public buildings as Xifeng Youth Activity Center, Xifeng Activity Center for the Elderly, Xifeng No.2 Middle School, Xifeng Stadium, government of Yongjing Town and Xifeng Quality and Technology Supervision Bureau and expanded Xifeng No.1 Middle School. Enterprises were introduced to invest in building of Huiheng Garden Residential Quarter, Shuiqi Yiyuan Residential Quarter and the pedestrian street. City construction was gradually completed in the Dongmen Area of the county town and city capacity expansion was realized.

In 2002, it introduced Guizhou Guangjian Real Estate Development Co., Ltd. to develop the south area of the county town according to the city development plan. Three mountains were removed to build the south section and middle section of Hucheng Avenue. It planned and built street-front commercial and residential buildings as well as such buildings as Xifeng Hotel, Hucheng Building, Longgang New City, the People' s Court of Xifeng County, the Procuratorate of Xifeng County and Fire Brigade of Xifeng County, thus realized southward movement of the county town. In 2003, Guizhou Kailin Group bought the plant area of the original Zhaohui Machine Works to build Kailin New Town. Chongqing Yuwan Group Xifeng Jinsui Real Estate Development Co., Ltd. settled in Xifeng in 2006 and started old town reconstruction of Zhongjie Plot. It built Zhubei Avenue Commercial and Residential Quarter and rebuilt Xifeng TCM Hospital at a different site. The area of Xifeng County Town was gradually enlarged and the situation of "a county without town" was changed in all aspects. Meanwhile, in order to coordinate capacity expansion of Kailin Group Phosphorus Chemical Base, Xiaozhaiba Town adopted the mode of "industry-city interaction" to plan the construction of Nanshan Residential Quarter for resettlement of the farmers losing their land. Town construction was promoted in all aspects. Such towns and townships as Jiuzhuang, Wenquan, Yanglongsi, Shidong, Qingshan and Liuchang successively carried out town capacity expansion. Wangjiacang Resettlement Residential Quarter was built in Luwo in coordination with tourism development of Wujiang Gorge.

After the resolution was made on the Fifth Plenary Session of the 16th Central Committee of the CPC to construct the socialist new countryside in 2005, the CPC Committee of Xifeng County and the People' s Government of Xifeng County started the work of new countryside construction with Shuiwei Village of Liuchang Township as a pilot. The construction of each township and village was rapidly promoted centered on the thoughts of "getting rich, learning, entertainment and sharing beauty in rural areas" . By 2010, several demonstration points for socialist new countryside had been constructed in the whole county. Great changes took place in the urban and rural outlook and the urbanization rate was rapidly improved.

Water, electricity, road and telecommunications facilities were continuously improved and infrastructure was further strengthened. From 1991 to 2010, infrastructure of Xifeng County was promoted in all aspects covering irrigation and water conservancy, city water supply and drinking water for people and animals in rural areas. A number of major water conservancy projects were successively constructed and put into use including Yujian River Reservoir and Shanggou Reservoir. Modernized water supply plants were constructed in ten towns and townships. A number of key water diversion pipelines were opened including the pipeline from Xiaoqiao River Reservoir to Xiaozhaiba Town and from Yujian River Reservoir to Xiaozhaiba Town. "Three-small projects" of rural water conservancy realized extensive coverage and water conservancy reform was promoted in all aspects. A number of transformer substations were constructed covering Yongjing, Libei, Liuchang and Panjiaoying. In addition, it implemented rural power grid reconstruction project so that sufficient security was provided for urban and rural power supply. Guiyang-Zunyi Expressway crossed the county from south to north, each township was accessible to bituminous paved road, each village to hardened road and each household it accessible to cross-household road. "Accessibility of each village" to line telephone, internet and mobile phone was realized, line telephone and radio telephone covered urban and rural areas, and broad band network was accessible in villages and households.

The undertakings of education, health, culture and sports were continuously upgraded and the level of people' s livelihood security was continuously improved. In the past 20 years, the CPC Committee of Xifeng County and the People' s Government of Xifeng County continuously promoted the strategy of "prospering the county with science and education". Human oriented, it practically increased the input in education. By implementing the program of "basically popularizing nine–year compulsory education and basically eliminating illiterate youth", it built 10 hope primary schools, built and expanded a number of middle schools, primary schools and teaching points, perfected teaching facilities and equipment, improved rural schooling conditions, introduced high–end talents and strengthened the foundation for educational development. Besides, it extended to the goal of high–standard illiteracy elimination, popularization of nine–year compulsory education and popularization of laboratories in urban and rural middle and primary schools, strengthening the foundation for improving the population quality in all aspects. The county increased input to practically improve the urban and rural health conditions. It built Xifeng Hospital, Xifeng TCM Hospital and Xifeng Women and Children Health Station, reconstructed and upgraded the town health center in all aspects and improved the village–level medical service center. In addition, it implemented town medical security and new rural cooperative medical system and encouraged the development of three private hospitals. It conducted "three–combination" work of birth control in depth and deepened birth service in urban and rural areas to improve the physical quality of newborns.

The county strengthened the construction public culture service system. It built Xifeng Publicity Culture Activity Center (Xifeng Culture Center), Xifeng Library and Xifeng Stadium. In addition, it built 10 comprehensive town culture stations, 161 village–level farmers' studies and the county–, township– and village–level cultural information resource sharing project grassroots service centers, realizing full coverage of township– and village–level sports program for farmers. It implemented station–network separation of Xifeng Radio & TV Station, introduced Guizhou Broadcasting Network Xifeng Company, and carried out county and town cable TV digital upgrading and the project of "accessibility of each village and household" to radio and TV in rural areas to settle the difficulty of the urban and rural people in access to radio and TV. It deeply excavated the cultural relics and intangible cultural heritage of Xifeng, organized such mass culture and sports activities as Xifeng red songs performance, dragon dance and drum performance for the Spring Festival, lantern riddles parade for the Spring Festival and farmers basketball games, and fostered such activity brands as square dance, dragon dance, gong and drum performance and Miao Lusheng dance. Qingshan Miao Lusheng dance *Meng Dai Yang* won golden prize among performance programs on the Ninth National Minority Nationalities Traditional Sports Games, the farmers dragon dance team of Longzhao Village, Yongjing Town won golden prize on Guizhou Sports Games for Farmers. Two cultural heritages were listed among the provincial list of intangible cultural heritage and two listed among the municipal list. The county–, township– and village–level governments soundly promoted the construction of "safe Xifeng" and strengthened comprehensive social security management, successively entitled as "drug–free county" and "advanced county for safety construction" of Guizhou Province. It continuously implemented the urban and rural minimum life security system, carried out public employment and entrepreneurship service, enhanced labor employment management and practically secured pay to farmer workers. In 2009, the people' s livelihood program was implemented in Guiyang City covering teaching for students, pay to workers, medical care for those of disease, support for the elderly, housing for the people and life in peace. Education, medical care, employment, support for the elderly and other social security undertakings took further steps, and the sense of happiness and safety of the local people was significantly improved.

Reform and opening up was continuously deepened, development vitality was improved in all aspects. According to the arrangement of the central, provincial and municipal government, the governments of county and township level continuously deepened reform and expanded the scope of opening up based on the system barrier in development to stimulate the internal driving power and create a convenient investment and trade environment, high–efficiency business invitation and operation environment, opening regional cooperation environment and high–quality environment for innovation and entrepreneurship. A series of reforms were carried out on government agencies, state–owned enterprises, forest right system and rural pond and reservoir ownership system. Great efforts were made in striving for national, provincial and municipal pilot demonstration projects, innovating on administrative approval, government service, land utilization, environmental protection examination, talent introduction and business invitation system and perfecting the market–based resource allocation mechanism to practically improve the development vitality and benefits.

Party construction was continuously strengthened and spiritual civilization construction was continuously promoted. It organized "three–emphasis" (the intensive education in the need to stress study, political awareness and integrity) and the Theory of Three Represents learning and education activities to strengthen the ideological, organizational and work style construction of the party, deepen personnel system reform for cadres, improve cadre evaluation management mechanism and promote party conduct construction and fight against corruption. The party construction was strengthened in all aspects. It organized "rectification of the dirty and untidy look" and creation of a civilized county, promoted the construction of an ecological civilization county, carried out the mass spiritual civilization creation activities covering urban and rural areas with participation of all the people, and insisted the advancement of the program under which officials, doctors, scientists and college students went to the countryside to spread scientific and literacy knowledge and offer medical service to farmers as well as "five–entering" activities of spiritual civilization. The Xifeng spirit of "striving to be stronger, working hard, being loyal and being united" was carried forward in all aspects. The urban and rural living environment significantly bettered and the degree of civilization was continuously improved.

From 1991 to 2010, various undertakings of Xifeng was continuously developed covering politics, economy, society, culture and ecology, the material and cultural life of the people was continuously improved and unprecedented profound changes took place in the social outlook, laying a solid political, economic, cultural and mass foundation for holding fast new opportunities, embracing new challenges and realizing further development.

Facing the future, Xifeng will, on the high starting point of a powerful county for economic development in Guizhou Province, implement the countryside prospering strategy in all aspects. With constructing a park–like town and rich and beautiful countryside as important means, it will accelerate the integration of the primary, secondary and tertiary industry, promote urban–rural integrated development, make efforts in the new round of poverty alleviation work and construct a moderately prosperous society in all aspects with higher level.

大事记

1991年

1月 县政府印发《息烽县文化市场管理办法（试行）》。

2月1日 县政府成立政府系统纠正不正之风办公室，办公室设在监察局。

2月5日 县政府印发《关于贯彻国务院和省人民政府〈关于切实减轻农民负担的通知〉的通知》，明确由农业局成立“减轻农民负担监督管理领导小组”，负责减轻农民负担监督管理工作。

2月15日 省教育委员会、省人事厅批复县委党校试办成人中专专修班。当年招收学员30名。

3月17日 县委、县政府下发《关于1991年计划生育工作的安排意见》，提出全县人口出生率控制在17‰以内，自增率10‰，计划生育率95%以上，一胎率95%，多胎率2%。

3月20日 县计生协会、新场乡计生协会被国家计生委、全国计生协会评为先进单位。

3月28日 县公安局收审所发生被收审人员越墙逃跑事件。为此，有关领导及责任人作书面检查和接受批评教育；县公安局收容审查权被暂时取消，至次年1月恢复。

4月 县政府印发《关于做好劳动就业工作的通知》。

5月1日 县政府印发《息烽县个人建住房审批的暂行规定》和《息烽县永靖镇规划管理暂行办法》。

5月2日 县政府印发《息烽县商业一条街建设试行办法》。

5月4日 县政府印发《关于加强经济体制改革协调工作的通知》，明确县体改办改为县体改委，实行委员制，在县委、县政府领导下，统筹、组织、协调、督促和指导全县城乡经济体制改革工作。

5月16日 县境内部分地区遭受冰雹、暴雨袭击，永靖镇、石硐乡、九庄镇、西山乡等乡镇持续降冰雹40余分钟。

5月21日 县第十一届人大常委会第七次会议审议批准《息烽县人民政府关于在全县公民中开展法制宣传教育第二个五年规划报告》《息烽县人民政府关于社会治安综合治理五年规划报告》，并作出相应决议。

6月18日 县委、县政府命名表彰陈昌其、况力夫等9名首批县级专业技术拔尖人才。

6月 县委、县政府印发《关于进一步加强党的纪检机关和行政司法等监督部门建立联系制度的意见》。

7月 流长西瓜经省农科院、省农业厅有关专家鉴定，可溶性、固形物含量达11.6%，可食率

60.8%，超过当年全国西瓜良种鉴评规定指标。

7月　省山地资源研究所与县土地管理局共同开展的“息烽土地人口承载力研究”项目，被省级专家鉴定为国内先进项目。

8月17日　县城综合农贸市场建设工程启动，市场规划占地1424亩。1993年8月28日，综合农贸市场建成投入使用，有固定铺面128个，摊位395个，建设总投资320万元。

10月　县卫生系统“政治思想研究会”成立。同月，召开首次代表大会，选举产生理事会理事29名，常务理事10名，负责全县卫生系统的政治思想工作。

11月5日　县委、县政府下发《关于开展建镇并乡撤区工作安排意见》。至次年6月，建镇并乡撤区工作结束。全县撤销4个区25个乡镇，新组建永靖镇、小寨坝镇、九庄镇、温泉镇、养龙司乡、流长乡、鹿窝乡、石硐乡、西山乡和青山苗族乡10个乡镇。

11月　县综治委制定下发《息烽县维护社会治安秩序见义勇为奖励办法（试行）》。

11月　县中医院解放北路业务综合楼动工兴建，1995年9月竣工投入使用。

是年　县委、县政府印发《关于实现社会治安综合治理五年规划的决定》。

是年　县委、县政府推行“三公开一监督”制度，公开群众关心的招工、职工调动等热点问题的办理内容、政策、结果，接受群众监督。

是年　县政府出台《关于多渠道筹措基础教育经费的意见》。

是年　县委办公室、县政府办公室印发《息烽县党政机关信访工作暂行办法》。

是年　息烽重钙厂货运铁路专线动工，1995年竣工并投入使用。货运铁路专线长1.5千米，总投资1900万元，货站年吞吐量45万吨。

是年　县政府批转县畜牧局整顿恢复乡畜牧兽医站意见，明确乡畜牧兽医站经费实行民办公助，乡站人员报酬用防疫服务费支付。

1992年

2月24日　县第十一届人大常委会第十三次会议作出“撤销息烽县人民代表大会常务委员会永阳区、养龙区、九庄区、黑神庙区工作委员会”决定。

2月15日　永靖派出所更名为永靖镇派出所，黑神庙区派出所更名为小寨坝镇派出所，九庄区派出所更名为九庄镇派出所，养龙区派出所更名为养龙司乡派出所，永阳区派出所更名为西山乡派出所；新建温泉镇派出所、流长乡派出所、石硐乡派出所、鹿窝乡派出所、青山苗族乡派出所。

2月28日　县委印发《关于在全县认真开展社会治安综合治理宣传的决定》。

3月2日　县第十一届人大常委会第十四次会议补选黑卫平为县人民政府县长，陈福文为县人民法院院长。

4月　县政府出台《息烽县城镇集体职工养老保险费用社会统筹实施细则》，开始对集体企业、机关事业单位固定职工征收养老金。

5月15日至16日凌晨　县境内永靖镇、石硐乡、九庄镇、西山乡遭受冰雹、大风、暴雨袭击，降雨量70毫米，冰雹直径3厘米，持续降雹30余分钟。

5月 县政府出台《息烽县国营固定职工离退休费社会统筹实施细则》，开始对国有企业固定职工征收养老金。

5月 全县实行凭证生育制度。

6月27日 贵阳供电局息烽分局成立。

6月 县城市建设综合开发公司成立。

7月1日 县粮食局在全省范围内率先取消粮油供应证，实行放开经营，价格随行就市。

7月11日 息烽重钙厂年产10万吨重钙前期工程完工，年产硫酸5万吨、普钙15万吨生产线投产，副省长刘玉林等到厂祝贺。

8月6日 全县实行“蓝皮户口”（在本县范围内有效的城镇户口）制度。持“蓝皮户口”人员，除无粮油供应、副食品补贴及不得以非农业户口办理迁移手续外，其他方面与城镇居民享受同等待遇。

8月11日 县政府出台《息烽县农村社会养老保险办法》。

8月20日 县政府出台《息烽县优抚对象抚恤优待办法》。

8月21日 县政府下发《关于户政制度改革的通告》，凡自愿从农村到城镇（集镇）从事生产经营活动，离开农村后有稳定收入来源的县内外人员，均可申请办理城镇非农业户口。

9月12日 县举行首届“中小学教师师德演讲比赛”。

9月 小寨坝镇被省政府列为全省小城镇建设试点镇。

9月15日 全国“双拥”工作考察组到息烽考察拥军优属、拥政爱民工作。

9月20日 全国法院系统“两庭”建设会议代表到县人民法院考察。

9月21日 县第一所人口学校在永靖镇成立。首批招收18岁及以上未婚男女青年及新婚无孩夫妇学员共210名。

10月6日 县政府印发《关于执行〈贵州省水资源费征收管理〉的通知》，县水资源费征收工作正式启动。

11月10日 县十一届人民代表大会举行第四次会议，选举吴啸、姚继元、李以智、金春权、魏明禄、文昌碧为省第八届人民代表大会代表。

12月 经省级考核组抽查和测试，县社会治安综合治理工作全面达标。

是年 县委、县政府提出“一粮二烟三开发”经济建设思路。

是年 县畜牧局引进贵农黄、罗斯鸡、海赛克斯、衣沙明星和红布洛5个良种肉鸡种蛋进行孵化，当年向农户提供良种雏鸡1万余羽。

1993年

1—8月 县境内发生猪瘟传染病，发病率（占饲养量）27.3%，死亡率（占饲养量）16%。为控制疫情，全县开展生猪秋季防疫注射，并恢复1985年前的一年春秋两季防疫注射。次年，全县生猪死亡率降至6.7%。此后，生猪死亡率控制在国家规定的5%以内。

2月下旬至3月下旬 九庄镇和平村发生麻疹，先后发病30例。县卫生防疫部门对患者进行就地隔离治疗，保持室内通风换气和适当温度湿度，辅以药物防治，除死亡1例外，其余患者在发病8天后恢复正常。

3月5日 县水利电力开发公司成立。

3月 县农村信用合作联社成立，并召开第一次社员代表大会，审议通过联社章程，选举产生理事会、监事会。

3月 县医院“息烽红会血站”建成，生产的血浆和血液制品除满足本地区临床医疗用血外，外销省中心血站、卫生部成都生物制品研究所、解放军四川蜀阳制药厂、上海生物制品研究所等单位。

4月9日 县第十一届人大常委会举行第二十一次会议，会议决定将息烽温泉、乌江峡、西望山、多缤洞四景区和玄天洞、息烽集中营旧址、张露萍等七烈士墓三景点命名为县级风景名胜区。

4月23—27日 县政协四届全委会举行一次会议，选举县政协第四届委员会常务委员18名，选举蒋光国为县政协委员会主席，张其沾、黄及翔、文昌碧、余大维、陈继春为副主席。

4月24—28日 县第十二届人大举行一次会议，选举县第十二届人大常委会组成人员19名，选举路延科为县人大常委会主任，杨洪志、杨发礼、刘应龙、刘正菊为副主任；选举黑卫平为县人民政府县长，李贵菊、黄银忠、魏明禄为副县长；选举陈福文为县人民法院院长，童德权为县人民检察院检察长。

5月26—29日 县第八次党代会在县城召开。会议选举产生中共息烽县第八届委员会委员29名，候补委员4名；选举县纪委委员17名。会议期间举行八届县委一次全委会议，选举产生县委八届常委会组成人员7名：陈华祥为书记，黑卫平、李以智、刘兴明为副书记，刘权德、李贵菊、任国元为常委。

5月 县《乡（镇）土地利用规划》获国家土地管理局优秀成果三等奖。

6月10—12日 《息烽风景名胜区总体规划》通过专家论证。

6月21—23日 国家计生委计划生育工作检查组到息烽检查计划生育工作。

6月 县政府出台《关于鼓励乡镇企业引进人才的规定》《关于外商投资的暂行办法》《关于鼓励引进资金的暂行规定》《关于鼓励经济发展的建设用地优惠办法》《关于促进经济发展的税收优惠政策》5个文件。

6月28日 县委作出《关于鼓励机关人才走向经济建设主战场规定》，明确单位或个人可兴办或领办经济实体或从事经营活动。

7月29日 县第十二届人大常委会第三次会议作出《关于切实减轻农民负担的决议》。

7月 县政府出台《关于息烽县流动人口和个体从业人员计划生育管理办法》。

9月10日 县政府批准实施《贵州省息烽县风景名胜区总体规划》。

11月10日 永靖镇原贵州拖拉机电机厂10号宿舍楼发生特大恶性爆炸案，死亡4人，受伤2人。

11月 县开展首次第三产业普查登记工作，至次年9月结束。统计结果显示，1992年县内第三产业单位761个，从业人员12861人，分别比1991年增长2.28%和7.21%。

12月25日 县开始征收矿产资源补偿费、城市维护费、农村教育附加费。

12月 《息烽县志》出版发行。

是年 县医院开展丙型肝炎脑电图检查、成分输血、光量子血疗及细菌培养等项目获得成功。

1994年

1月1日 县进行财政管理体制改革，对各乡镇实行“划分财权，定收定支，定额上解，定额补助，自求平衡”。

2月20日 县委出台《关于农村小康建设规划意见》，提出小康建设以村为单元、户为基础，到2000年全县有80%以上的村达到小康目标。

2月 县政府印发《关于加强地产市场管理的决定》。

2月 县政府出台《关于高标扫除青壮年文盲的意见》。

2月 县政府办印发《关于县城交通市场秩序管理规定的通知》。

3月29日 息烽县关心下一代协会更名为息烽县关心下一代工作委员会。

4月1日 国务院扶贫领导小组下发国开发〔1994〕5号文件，息烽县列入全国592个贫困县之一。同日，县政府印发《息烽县土地出让金征收及其管理暂行办法》。

4月25日 县委、县政府召开洪马水库配套工程会审会议，审订工程总投资197.52万元，工程工期为两年，设计灌溉面积8693亩，解决1.85万人和2600头牲畜饮用水问题。

5月10日 县人民检察院设立反贪污贿赂工作局，撤销贪污贿赂检察科。

7月9日至8月12日 开磷集团息烽重钙厂硫酸车间发生二氧化硫尾气重大污染事故，小寨坝镇中心村、盘脚营村的9个村民组农作物受到污染，污染面积40.28公顷，减产稻谷4.55余万千克。

7月12日 省长陈士能、副省长姚继元率省直有关部门负责人到息烽，就息烽县实施国家“八七扶贫攻坚计划”，加快经济发展现场办公。

8月30日 县政府出台《关于拍卖非耕地使用权的暂行办法》，非耕地使用权拍卖期限为60年；坚持谁购买，谁开发，谁投资，谁受益原则。

8月 县档案馆修建工程动工，工程总投资35.54万元，建筑面积900余平方米，1995年5月竣工，1996年9月投入使用。

9月14日 县国家税务局和地方税务局分别成立。

9月16日 “中共贵州省委党校函授部息烽函授站”成立。是年招收经济管理、行政管理、现代文秘三个专业（大专班）学员135名。

10月27日 县第十二届人大常委会举行第十一次会议，审议通过《息烽县国家机关工作人员述职暂行办法》《息烽县人民代表大会常务委员会会议守则》《息烽县人民代表大会常务委员会关于〈贵州省乡镇人民代表大会主席团工作条例〉实施办法》。

11月6日 新华通讯社党组副书记、常务副社长夏赞忠到息烽对口联系扶贫工作。

12月5日 县委、县政府决定将小寨坝镇列为全县农村党的基层组织建设试点镇。

12月7日 省委办公厅、省政府办公厅下发《关于加强省级党政机关定点扶贫工作的通知》，确定省委宣传部、省财政厅等部门定点帮扶息烽县。

是年 县委、县政府作出《对以独生子女户　两女结扎户为重点的计划生育户实行优先优惠的规定》。

是年 县“坡改梯”工程获省政府一等奖。

是年 县畜牧局推行仔猪早期断奶补饲技术，使仔猪双月重由不补饲的10千克提高到15～20千克。

1995年

1月3日 县委、县政府印发《息烽县扶贫攻坚计划》。

1月20日 息烽重钙厂投产。该厂1988年10月动工修建，1994年12月竣工。设计年产高浓度过磷酸钙10万吨，配套生产硫酸10万吨、磷酸4万吨、磷矿粉16万吨、氟硅酸钠0.25万吨，总投资2.94亿元。

2月9日 县委召开息烽县人大工作会议。县委书记黑卫平作《提高认识　加强领导　推进人大工作上一个新台阶》的讲话，县人大常委会主任路延科作《坚持人民代表大会制度　为把我县人大工作提高到新的水平而奋斗》的讲话。

3月24日 新华社首批扶贫工作队入驻息烽。至2002年，新华社先后派出5批扶贫工作队到县开展扶贫工作，其间陆小华、宫喜祥、邵军、陈磊先后挂职任县委副书记；徐勇、胡晓光、王宇飞挂职任县政府副县长，王鹏远、王定一先后挂职任县长助理。

4月 县社会治安综合治理委员会下发《关于实行“依法治乡（镇）治村治厂”和“挂牌”管理的决定》，在全县推行“依法治乡（镇）治村治厂矿社区”和“挂牌”管理。当年挂牌43个单位、53个村14978户。

5月15日 国务院批准息烽县列为对外国人开放的29个县（市）之一。

5月 新华社捐资10万元修建青山希望小学。至2005年，相继有香港翁业坚先生、贵阳卷烟厂、贵州西牛王印务公司、贵州通海经济发展有限公司董事长陈林、宇宏经济开发有限公司、香港宝莲寺住持初慧大师及弟子能证法师、贵阳市地税局、中国银行总行、香港“庆委会”、共青团贵阳市委、贵州宠信畜牧发展有限公司、广明电器有限公司、香港人士吴仲敏等为息烽捐资290余万元，修建希望小学10所。

6月23日 全县10个乡镇遭暴雨袭击，至次日凌晨6时，平均降雨量165毫米，部分地区达200毫米。直接经济损失约1300万元。

6月30日 县城S-1240型3000门程控电话交换机开通（同时停用纵横制自动电话交换机），当年有用户2460户。至2010年，程控交换机容量扩大到5万门，用户3.5万户。

8月11日 新华社社长郭超人到息烽考察扶贫工作。

10月22日 贵阳供电局息烽分局划归贵阳市北供电局管辖，更名为贵阳市北供电局息烽分局。

10月26日 县人武部被国家综治委、中国人民解放军总参谋部、铁道部、公安部评为“全国铁路护路联防先进单位”。

10月28日 县城解放南路、交通路改造工程动工。该工程由省交通厅拨款150万元修建，设计为水泥路面，总长1.98千米。于1996年10月1日竣工。

10月 青山苗族乡被评为“全省民族团结先进集体”。

10月 贵遵高等级公路息烽段动工修建，至1997年5月20日，久长到息烽段通车，11月29日全线通车。道宽12米，县境内长28千米，途经4个乡镇24个行政村。

11月8日 县商会成立，与县工商联合署办公，实行一套班子，两块牌子。

同日 县光彩事业推动委员会成立。

11月28日 撤销县工商行政管理局、县物价局、县技术监督局，三局合并组建县工商行政管理局。

12月6日 息烽县被省政府评为“以工代赈”坡改梯先进县，并获三等奖。

12月16日 息烽县获省“八五”期间扶贫开发鼓励奖。

12月 息烽县获“全省铁路护路联防工作先进集体”称号，受到国家社会治安综合治理委员会、公安部、铁道部、中国人民解放军总参谋部联合表彰。

12月 县内第一家农村合作基金会在小寨坝镇成立。至次年11月，县农村合作基金会服务中心和全县10个乡镇农村合作基金会分别成立。1997年4月，县成立清理整顿农村合作基金会领导小组，11月撤销县农村合作基金会服务中心和永靖镇农村合作基金会。至1999年，其余9个乡镇农村合作基金会相继关闭清盘。2001年，农村合作基金会债权债务全部移交县清偿办公室。

是年 贵州太和制药有限公司在永靖镇成立。公司占地面积3.6万平方米，建筑面积8470平方米，总投资3.6亿元，设片剂、胶囊、颗粒3条生产线。

1996年

1月1日 根据国务院〔1995〕69号、贵州省政府〔1995〕56号文件精神，息烽县由安顺地区划归贵阳市管辖。

是日 县第三次工业普查登记开始。经普查，1995年年底，全县有乡及乡以上工业企业85个，从业人员3030人，其中工程技术人员171人。

1月15日 新华通讯社向息烽捐赠卡车、打字机、电话、卫星接收天线、书籍、衣服、被子等价值100余万元物资。

1月17日 县长锋耐火材料厂生产的磷酸盐高铝砖通过省冶金厅组织的专家评审会技术鉴定，各项指标达到部颁标准。

1月24日 县十二届人大第四次会议增选王忠碧、吴鹏、李贵菊、陈继春、聂明武、黑卫平、童金华、路延科、蔡汝达、魏忠润为贵阳市第九届人民代表大会代表。

1月26日 县科技局陈昌其主持选育的“息单七号”杂交玉米新品种，通过安顺地区品种审定委员会鉴定，列入贵阳市1996年度科技推广项目。陈昌其获1995年振华科技扶贫基金服务奖。

2月17日 温泉镇古家沟发生重大交通事故，死亡5人，轻重伤28人。

3月15日 县工商局、县消费者协会开展纪念“3·15”世界消费者权益日活动，当众销毁价值9.5万元的香烟等各类假冒伪劣商品。

3月29日 贵州省息烽县人民武装部收归军队建制交接仪式在县人武部会议室举行，贵州省军区、贵阳军分区首长出席。同日，贵州省息烽县人民武装部更名为中国人民解放军贵州省息烽县人民武装部。

3月 省政协委员郭建生捐款20万元资助青山苗族乡修建核桃坝小学。

4月8日 县首套电子汇兑系统在中国工商银行息烽支行开通。

同日 县腾龙化工公司正式投产，设计年产黄磷7200吨。

4月15日 中共息烽县委老干部工作局更名为中共息烽县委离退休干部工作局。

4月25日 县委、县政府召开帮村扶贫动员大会，县长李贵菊与贵阳市37家企事业单位签订帮村扶贫协议书。

4月 “息烽红会血站”划归县卫生局管理，更名为“息烽县单采血浆站”。

5月4日 养龙司乡新桥村残疾人兰吉发被评为“贵阳市十大杰出青年”。

5月5日 县第一次农业普查工作启动，至1997年10月，普查工作结束。

5月18日 县开通移动电话。至2010年，全县电信移动用户数达到1.2万户。

6月18日 中国儿童基金会委托林梁明教授一行10人对息烽县儿童健康、教育等进行为期10天的调查。

6月19日 全省“服务万村、创百争万”行动推进会暨青年开发扶贫工作研讨会在息烽召开。

6月 贵州汉方药业有限公司息烽药厂建设项目动工修建，项目规划占地1.6万平方米，建筑面积8240平方米，投资960万元。

7月30日 息烽县荣获贵州省1995年度发展乡镇企业“图强县”称号。

8月20日 县第十二届人大常委会举行第二十三次会议，作出《关于认真实施“三五”法制宣传教育规划的决议》。

8月28日 县政府发布《关于实行畜禽定点屠宰的通告》，规定凡永靖镇城关辖区内的单位、个人和屠工、屠商屠宰畜禽必须到县食品公司定点屠宰场屠宰。

9月3日 县委、县政府印发《关于发展农村集体经济中涉及农村土地承包责任制几个问题的规定》。

9月18日 县城公交车开始营运。运行路线由十字街至火车站至蚕桑坡，票价每客0.5元。

9月22日 县内首家私立中学“息烽永生私立中学”教学楼落成，主体工程建筑面积2080平方米，投资89万元。

9月28日 全县私营企业协会成立，并召开第一次全体会议，通过筹备工作报告和私人企业协会章程，选举产生协会第一届理事会。

9月 养（养龙站）温（温泉）公路路面硬化改造工程启动。工程全长16.2千米，总投资542万元，1997年5月28日竣工投入使用。

11月5日 市交警支队捐资12.25万元修建温泉镇大山村公路，公路全长9.8千米，于1997年12月25日竣工。

11月25日至12月2日 县公安局在全县范围开展“清理、整顿、收缴民间非法枪支专项行动”，查获非法制造火药枪窝点2个，销售点1个，收缴长短枪200余支。

11月27日 永靖镇联丰村通电，至此，全县实现村村通电。

12月19日 省委、省政府授予息烽县“率先解决温饱先进县”称号。

12月22日 县政府发布《关于在永靖镇城区禁止燃放烟花爆竹的通告》。

12月27日 县第十二届人大常委会举行第二十五次会议，审议通过《关于息烽县国民经济和社会发展“九五”计划及2010年远景目标纲要》，并作出决议。

是年 县委作出《关于促进乡镇企业持续 快速 健康发展的规定》。

是年 县委、县政府印发《关于实行社会治安综合治理领导责任制的若干规定》，明确各级各部门主要领导为社会治安综合治理第一责任人，分管领导为直接责任人，实行社会治安综合治理“一票否决权”制。

是年 息烽县被评为贵州省“粮食生产先进县”，并获三等奖。

是年 贵阳市政府投入资金155万元，为青山苗族乡修建人畜饮水工程41处，解决6859人和3783头牲畜饮水困难。

1997年

1月14日 息烽集中营旧址修复工程动工，工程总投资419.98万元，是年5月竣工并通过验收。

1月15日 息烽县提前4年完成造林10年规划，受省政府表彰和奖励。

1月20日 息烽县被省计生委评为“计生三结合”达标县，被市政府评为计划生育政策法规达标县，并获一等奖。

1月，养龙司乡新桥村残疾人兰吉发获“国际青少年消除贫困奖”提名奖。

3月24日 中宣部明确养龙司乡堡子村为创建文明村镇活动示范点。

3月27日 小寨坝综合饮水工程动工修建。工程以小桥河水库为水源，铺设管道19.93千米，设计日供水4300立方米，总投资382万元。于1998年7月25日竣工投入使用。

3月29日 南山煤矿井下发生瓦斯爆炸事故，18人死亡，7人受伤。

4月 息烽集中营旧址被市委、市政府命名为“贵阳市爱国主义教育基地”。

5月 息烽集中营旧址被省委、省政府命名为“贵州省爱国主义教育基地”。

同月 息烽集中营旧址正式对外开放。

6月24日 县邮电局可视电话会议开通。

6月29日 县文学艺术协会成立并举行首届代表大会。

7月18日 中共中央政治局常委、国务院总理李鹏率国家计委、经贸委、铁道部、交通部、农业部、财政部、人民银行、电力部、水利部等部门负责人到永靖镇河坎村上寨村民组视察扶贫工作。

7月 县档案局、档案馆合并，实行一个机构，两块牌子，两种职能体制，县档案局为县政府的档案行政管理部门，档案馆为集中管理档案的文化事业机构。

7月 全县2324户个体工商户、22户私营企业与县个体劳动者协会、私营企业协会签订“拒毒”责任书。

9月11日 县特殊教育学校成立并举行开学仪式。时有学生19人，其中盲生5人、聋哑生14人。学生一律免费入学。

9月25日 县铁锅厂被省政府授予“先进私营企业”称号。

24日 永靖镇河坎村上寨组就地改造扶贫示范工程竣工并通过验收。工程总投资200万元。建房屋24幢，建筑面积4732.8平方米，修建混凝土道路长306米，铺设自来水管网680米，维修公路6.7千米。

10月15日 县境内严禁生产、使用西南J211等图集空心板，建筑施工企业一律使用新的国家建筑标准93G436-1设计预应力混凝土空心板。

12月25日 县委组织部电教室制作的首部电教片《大山村的脊梁》在息烽举行首播式。

是年 县教育局制定第一轮中小学布局调整规划，将135所小学规划调整为128所。到2010年经过两次布局调整后，全县有小学60所，教学点22个，初级中学11所，完全中学1所，12年制学校1所。

1998年

1月13日 县文学艺术界联合会成立并举行首次代表大会。

1月 县委、县政府决定在县城建立“下岗职工小吃一条街”和“下岗职工百货一条街”，解决下岗职工再就业问题。

2月17日 息烽县被省政府授予“以工代赈坡改梯先进县”称号。

2月19日 《息烽县志》获贵州省优秀志书三等奖。

3月13日 “息烽英烈革命历史回顾展——烽火不息”在中国革命博物馆举行开展仪式。中共中央政治局委员、国务委员李铁映为开幕式剪彩。展览历时16天，共接待各界观展人士10余万人次。

3月16日 县公安局110报警服务台开通，实行24小时值班制。

3月22—26日 政协息烽县第五届委员会举行第一次会议，选举县政协第五届委员会常务委员19名，选举李以智为县政协委员会主席，张其沾、黄生谷、陈继春、余大维、汤太祥、米良才为副主席。

3月23—27日 县第十三届人大举行第一次会议，选举县第十三届人大常委会组成人员17名，选举刘兴明为县人大常委会主任，任国元、杨发礼、刘应龙、童德权、吴金奎、刘大英为副主任；选举陈长发为县政府县长，黄银忠、李光祥、魏燕飞、胡勇、刘正菊为副县长；选举关晓明为县人民法院院长，何志坚为县人民检察院检察长。

4月5日 联合国儿童基金会、国务院妇女儿童工作委员会访问团一行7人，对息烽《实施九十年代中国儿童发展规划纲要》《九十年代中国妇女发展规划纲要》试点工作进行6天考察，走访座谈3000余人。访问团对试点工作表示满意。

4月22—24日 县第九次党代会召开。会议选举产生中共息烽县第九届委员会委员31名，候补委员6名；选举县纪委委员16名。会议期间，举行九届县委一次全委会议，选举产生县委九届常委会组成人员12名：李忠为书记，陈长发、曾德书、吴德屏为副书记，宫喜祥、袁仁庆、韦奕松、黄银忠、刘权德、燕飞、魏发志、杨胜荣为常委。

4月 县人民法院推出“当日立案，排期开庭，一月审结，公正裁判”工作承诺制。

4月 西山乡卫生院郭庆书被卫生部医政司、妇幼司，健康报社，国家中医药管理局医政司，中国农村卫生协会5部门评为全国优秀乡村医生。

5月3日 县启动实施“国家贫困地区义务教育工程”，实施项目学校16所，投资989.24万元，配套改扩建校舍18615平方米，培训师资149人。

5月23日 息烽集中营旧址大型革命历史图片回顾展在贵阳市图书馆开展。

5月29日 县委、县政府举办“庆祝息烽集中营革命历史纪念馆开放一周年暨98息烽投资贸易洽谈会”，县政府与中外企业签订正式合同4份，资金1.33亿元，合作协议25份，资金3.99亿元。

5月 县政府出台招商引资优惠政策，规定出让土地使用权时间为：工业用地50年，开发性农业用地60年，商业娱乐用地40年，居住用地70年。投资者在出让期内有转让、出租、抵押、继承和赠予权利。

6月2日　省博物馆与县文体广播电视局对永靖镇后坝村鸦米寨龙背山东侧恐龙化石开展发掘抢救工作。出土恐龙化石160余块，化石体长6米，高3米，为1.4亿年前侏罗纪时期大型食肉恐龙。

6月6日　国家“幸福工程”组委会负责人方彬、陈会玲受王光美委托，到息烽考察“幸福工程”实施情况。

6月10日　国务院扶贫开发领导小组负责人刘成果、李延龄到息烽检查下洪马水库配套工程。

6月16日　县政府发布《息烽县市容环境秩序管理暂行规定（第一号令）》。

6月23日　县第二轮土地延包工作启动，历时3个月完成。全县有延包承包农户45994户201673人，承包耕地210051.9亩，非耕地12336.05亩。承包期50年。

6月26日　县开展禁毒宣传系列活动。组织4000余人进行游行宣传；召开公捕、公判大会；县领导发表禁毒电视讲话。

6月28日　温泉镇大山村党支部获“全国农村基层组织建设工作先进单位”称号。

6月29日　九庄镇新沙村下环山组扶贫安居工程动工。工程总投资86.79万元，建成砖混结构新房46幢，水、电、路“三通”及停车场、篮球场配套，当年11月20日竣工。12月25日，46户村民举行入住新居仪式。

6月　县政府印发《关于征收水土流失防治费的通知》《息烽县水土保持暂行规定》《关于实行水土保持方案许可制度的通知》《息烽县水土保持方案审批管理办法（试行）》《息烽县水土保持监督员水土保持管护员管理办法》。

7月7日　县委印发《关于开展依法治县工作的决定》。

7月16日　鹿窝乡程控电话开通。至此，全县实现乡乡通光缆和程控电话。

7月21日　流长乡引种巴西旱稻亩产275.5千克，通过省、市专家组验收。

7月24日　县首届西瓜节在流长乡举行，市领导罗大林、辛维光出席开幕式。

7月27日　息烽县被省委、省政府、省军区命名为“双拥模范县”。

7月　石硐乡洋荒煤矿发生瓦斯爆炸事故，死亡7人。

8月13日　越南民主共和国文化代表团在文化部部长孙家正陪同下参观息烽集中营革命历史纪念馆。

8月24日　成立“息烽县再就业服务中心”“息烽县职业介绍所”，统一指导全县国有企业下岗职工再就业工作。

8月27日　县委、县政府出台《关于进一步落实“两个确保”做好国有企业下岗职工再就业工作的实施意见》。

9月1日　息烽旱秋蔬菜基地建设项目通过市级验收。该项目于1996年实施，两年种植面积4897.5亩，亩产2568千克。

9月21日　县科技局实施的“黄磷炉渣粉在酸性田运用”科技项目通过市级验收。1996—1998年，全县使用黄磷炉渣改良冷、烂、锈田3.31万亩，净增产稻谷66.13万千克。

9月25日　县第十三届人大常委会第五次会议通过《关于开展依法治县工作的决定》。

10月1日　县邮电局分设为县邮政局和县电信局。

10月18日　息烽集中营“玄天洞——杨虎城将军被囚禁处”旧址修复后对外开放。修复工程总投资120万元。

10月26日 全县10个乡镇实现传真通信网络化。

10月27日 贵州汉方药业有限公司息烽药厂建设项目通过省级验收。

10月 县政府印发《关于深入开展依法治县工作的实施意见》。

11月10日 8集电视连续剧《小萝卜头》在息烽集中营旧址开机拍摄。

11月16日 贵州太和制药有限公司息烽制药厂奠基。项目规划占地3.27公顷，设计规模为胶囊、片剂、冲剂3条生产线，总投资1800万元。于2003年9月建成投产。

11月25—26日 全省以工代赈坡改梯现场会在息烽召开。省政府授予息烽县“1991—1997年坡改梯先进县”称号。

12月20日 县委举行九届四次全会，会议通过《关于认真做好农业和农村工作的意见》。

是年 息烽集中营革命历史纪念馆被国务院公布为“国家级文物保护单位”。

是年 息烽县荣获贵州省1997年度发展乡镇企业“图强县”称号。

1999年

2月3日 县委印发《中共息烽县委　息烽县人民政府关于对农村独生子女户　双女结扎户和其他计划生育户实行优先优惠的规定》。

2月8日 息烽县实施“国家贫困地区义务教育工程”项目成绩突出，受省政府表彰。

2月 县城旧城改造工程启动。

4月19日 8集电视连续剧《杨虎城的最后岁月》在息烽集中营旧址开机拍摄。

4月21日 联合国儿童基金会执行主席贝拉米女士率考察团到永靖镇河坎村上寨村民组、县特殊教育学校考察。

4月 县司法局“148”法律服务热线电话开通，向社会各界提供法律咨询。

5月26日 县十三届人大常委会举行第十二次会议，审议通过《关于人民群众旁听县人大常委会会议决定》。

5月 司法部授予永靖镇梨安村支部书记马发芬“全国模范人民调解员”称号。《贵州日报》《法制生活报》头版头条对马发芬的事迹进行报道。

5月 贵州旅游文史资料丛书息烽卷《筑北灵秀》由贵州人民出版社出版，7月13日在贵阳金筑大酒店举行首发式。

6月14日 湖北荆州铝箔实业公司投资兴建的息烽铝厂工程动工，总投资2.5亿元。

6月23日 省委副书记、省长钱运录，省委常委、市委书记庹文升率有关部门负责人到息烽考察永靖镇雨洒村坡改梯工程，到小坪坝组考察高标准农田建设。

6月 县农电网改造工程启动。至2003年10月，共完成工程项目270个。总投资5055.8万元。至此，县内实行城乡电费同网同价。

7月1日 全县各乡镇人民政府、县政府各工作部门实行政务公开，工作人员佩证上岗。

7月8日 县法律援助中心、中心法律事务所挂牌成立。

7月21日 县十三届人大常委会举行第十三次会议，审议通过《息烽县人大常委会对重大案件进行监审的决定》《息烽县人民代表大会选举及其常委会任命的国家机关工作人员述职评议办法》。

7月27日 息烽县被省委、省政府、省军区命名为“双拥模范县”。

同日 息烽县城首次使用洒水车清洁路面。

7月 实施工商行政管理体制改革，恢复县物价局、县技术监督局建制，县工商局上挂省、市局，实行省级垂直管理。

9月1日 县政府印发《息烽县国有资产管理 监督和营运体制改革方案》，明确县政府对国有资产管理的职能，组建县国有资产管理办公室、县国有资产经营有限公司。实现政府的社会经济管理职能与国有资产所有者职能分开，国有资产监督职能与国有资产经营职能分开。

9月 小寨坝镇前进村、大湾村试种优质蛋白玉米新品种“中单9409”通过市农办、市农业局验收。

是月 养龙司乡蚂蟥村利发煤矿发生瓦斯爆炸事故，死亡7人。

10月25日 由新华社《参考消息》报社捐赠20万元、邵云环烈士丈夫曹荣飞捐赠10万元修建的“息烽县云环小学”动工。该校规划占地7680平方米，建筑面积2250平方米。次年5月18日举行落成典礼。

11月17日 《息烽50年》出版发行。

12月17日 最高人民法院为九庄法庭记“集体一等功”。

是年 全县实现村村通公路，其中105个村通客车。

2000年

1月8日 县政府与辽宁西洋公司年产100万吨硫基复合肥投资项目协议签订会在贵阳金筑大酒店举行。

1月13日 息烽县实施的“国家贫困地区义务教育工程”通过省级验收。

2月17日 县委安排部署以“讲学习、讲政治、讲正气”为主要内容的党性党风教育活动。

2月18日 省卫生厅批复确认息烽县达到卫生部规定的“基本消灭麻风病县”标准，实现“基本消灭麻风病”总目标。

2月27日 息烽县被评为全省“国家贫困地区义务教育工程”特优县。

3月 县实施“孕产妇死亡率进一步下降，消除新生儿破伤风”项目。至2001年2月，孕产妇死亡率比1999年下降17.25%，新生儿破伤风发病率为零，通过卫生部检查验收。

4月16日 县委、县政府批准云环小学为县爱国主义教育基地。

4月27日 中共中央委员、国务院扶贫工作领导小组副组长胡福国考察永靖镇雨洒村漆树沟坡改梯工程。

4月 息烽县第二次进行煤矿“关井压产”，全县关闭年产3万吨以下煤矿20个。

6月24日 县境内普降大雨，局部降雨量达169.9毫米。全县受灾农户11302户，受灾人口46104人，死亡4人，受伤1人；农作物受灾面积37620亩，烤烟减产124吨；损坏、倒塌房屋1133间；死亡牲畜62头（只），造成经济损失1801万元。

8月3日 县“三五”普法依法治县工作通过贵阳市验收。

8月18日　县招商引资团参加2000年全国乡镇企业东西合作经贸洽谈会，签约项目11个。

8月　县政府批转《息烽县农村合作医疗实施方案（试行）》。

8月　卫生部副部长彭玉在市、县领导陪同下考察养龙司卫生院。

10月14日　教育部部长张保庆到息烽考察义务教育一期工程实施情况。

10月23日　县十三届人大常委会举行第二十四次会议，审议通过《息烽县城总体规划（修编）》。

10月29—30日　全县基本普及九年义务教育、基本扫除青壮年文盲工作通过省政府“两基”评估验收团验收。

10月　县村村通广播工程通过省级验收。

11月1日　县开始第五次全国人口普查登记工作。10日，普查登记工作结束。经普查统计，2000年11月1日零时，全县总人口221583人，其中男性117341人，占总人口的52.96%；女性104242人，占47.04%。

11月8日　中共中央宣传部常务副部长、中央文明办主任刘云山在省委有关领导陪同下考察县精神文明建设工作。

11月17日　县档案馆被省档案局评审委员会评定为省二级综合档案馆。

11月25日　县工商局、个体劳动者协会、私营企业协会发布公告，号召全县个体工商户、私营企业开展创建省级文明卫生县城活动。

11月　最高人民法院授予县人民法院“人民满意的好法院”称号。2001年、2002年县人民法院相继再次获此称号。

12月2日　深圳南华新龙首饰有限公司董事长付文斌、深圳兆亮珠宝有限公司董事长姚国亮捐资25万元修建的养龙司乡坪山小学举行落成典礼。

12月29日　县委召开九届九次全委扩大会议。审议通过《中共息烽县委关于制定息烽县国民经济和社会发展第十个五年计划的建议》，确定全县“十五”期间经济和社会发展的指导思想、总体思路、奋斗目标和政策措施。

是年　县委、县政府建立党员领导干部联系非公有制经济代表人士和少数民族代表人物制度。当年县、乡（镇）党员领导干部联系非公经济代表人士106人，少数民族代表人物122人。

是年　贵州汉方药业有限公司息烽药厂建设项目完成GMP规模建设。次年，一期工程建成投产，年产值1.5亿元。

2001年

1月5日　县委、县政府出台《进一步推进全县计划生育“村为主”及“村民自治”工作的实施意见》，提出到2001年5月，80%的村实现“村为主”；至9月，40%的村实现村民自治。至2002年9月，60%的村实现村民自治。至2003年，80%的村实现村民自治。

1月9日　开磷集团息烽重钙厂生产的“开磷”牌重过磷酸钙和工业黄磷获“贵州省名牌产品”称号。

2月15日　全县实现乡乡通移动电话。

2月23日　《息烽县城总体规划（修编）》通过省、市专家评审。

2月24日 省委常委、市委书记王晓东率市直8家单位到青山苗族乡调研。参与调研单位集资100万元扶持青山苗族乡“消灭茅草房”。至10月30日，青山苗族乡改造人居茅草房226户，成为贵阳市消灭茅草房第一乡。

3月28日 县委、县政府召开县农村税费改革动员大会，安排部署农村税费改革工作。

4月1日 县农村剩余劳动力技能培训在县人事劳动局开班，首期200余名学员接受上岗前技能培训。

5月11日 贵阳市商业银行息烽支行成立。

5月 永靖水厂动工修建，该工程总投资1239.92万元，设计日生产能力1.5万吨。2002年9月25日完工投入使用。

6月7日 县宣传文化中心奠基，次年11月9日建成并投入使用。中心占地6000平方米，建筑面积4186平方米，总投资650万元。

6月13日 县委、县政府在青山苗族乡举行“消除人居茅草房，建设农村新民居”工程开工仪式。至2004年，全县投入资金4200万元，投工17万个，改造农村人居茅草房2627户，全县实现消除人居茅草房。

6月14日 司法部部长张福森到息烽调研。

6月16日 鹿窝乡瓮舍村发生重大交通事故，死亡3人，重伤26人。

6月17日 省委组织部以全省共产党员名义出资55万元，用于修复息烽集中营革命历史纪念馆“忠斋”和“孝斋”。

6月 息烽集中营革命历史纪念馆被中宣部命名为全国爱国主义教育基地。

8月14日 《息烽县城总体规划（修编）》通过贵阳市政府批复实施。

8月17日 省扶贫开发办公室明确息烽县为马铃薯种薯扩繁基地。

8月24日 县生态渔业示范基地建设项目通过省、市验收。该项目投入资金286.15万元，面积2807亩；建鱼池1254口，修排洪渠1.5千米、主干渠2.6千米、支渠5千米；机耕道2.7千米；安装水泥桩柱1000根。生态带种植布朗李1万余株、葡萄苗5000株；投放鱼苗5.5万千克。平均亩产稻谷552千克，鱼107.5千克。

8月 县内首部乡镇志《小寨坝镇志》出版发行。

同月 小寨坝镇获全国创建文明小城镇示范点称号，受中宣部、中央文明办、建设部、国家环保总局、农业部联合表彰。

9月1日 县城自来水收费执行新标准：居民生活用水和机关、学校及事业单位用水1.2元/吨，工业用水1.25元/吨，商业用水1.8元/吨，建筑业、洗浴业用水2元/吨。

9月21日 老挝国家高级代表团到永靖镇雨洒村漆树沟坡改梯工程点、小寨坝镇贸易路和重钙厂生活区参观考察。

9月28日 养龙人民法庭被司法部评为“全国法院系统指导人民调解工作先进集体”。

12月19日 中共中央政治局委员、国务委员、中央军委副主席、国防部部长迟浩田到永靖镇龙爪村慰问退伍军人杨光义。

12月29日 团中央、公安部授予县消防大队“青年文明号”称号。

12月 县史志办获“全省第一届地方志编纂工作先进单位”称号，受省政府表彰。

是年 息烽县开始实施世界银行贷款卫生IX项目妇幼子项目，项目经费概算人民币283.49万元。至2007年10月，经卫生部、世行联合督导组检查，确认息烽县世界银行贷款卫生IX项目妇幼子项目各项指标超额完成。

是年 县政府引进贵阳苗姑娘食品公司投资1200万元兴建辣椒加工项目。

是年 县委、县政府印发《息烽县科技进步奖励办法实施细则》《息烽县科技发展“十五”计划及2015年长远计划》。

是年 县投资1750万元启动“乡乡通油路”工程。至2002年，投资5606万元，硬化路面109.5千米，实现乡乡通油路。

2002年

1月9日 县政府与贵州广建房地产开发有限公司在贵阳金筑大酒店签订《息烽县开发建设南大街协议书》，约定由广建公司出资建设县城南大街1696米道路，县政府以南大街道路两侧各25米范围内约9.2公顷土地整体出让给广建公司进行房地产开发建设。

1月10日 “贵阳市药品监督管理局息烽分局”挂牌成立。

3月11日 县政府印发《息烽县会计委派制度试行办法》。

4月8日 县公安局开通“DDN”专线，局机关内部电话与全国公安机关联通。

4月23日 全县农村税费改革工作正式启动。

5月27日 息烽县获“全国民政工作先进县”称号，受民政部表彰。

5月28日 全省农村非农技能培训现场交流会在息烽召开。

6月18日 县境内普降大雨、暴雨，降雨量115.2毫米，8个乡镇、103个村11463户农户不同程度受灾，直接经济损失2450余万元。

6月 省政府命名息烽县城为“省级卫生县城”。

9月9日 永靖镇老厂村、西山乡小鹿窝村、流长乡水尾村、营中村等8个村荣获第二批“贵阳市无公害农产品生产基地”称号。

9月 县永靖水厂建成投产。该厂总投资1080万元，于2001年动工兴建，日产水3万吨。

9月 县政府印发《关于对全县小型水利工程进行产权制度改革的实施意见》。

10月21日 西山乡底寨华氏四合院被列为县级文物保护单位。

10月29日 县城庆云山殡仪馆动工修建，占地25亩，总投资260万元。

10月30日 鱼简河水库举行开工典礼。该水库为集排洪、灌溉、供水为一体的中型水库，大坝高81米，坝长163米，总库容1050万立方米，兴利库容758万立方米，灌溉面积2.64万亩，总投资1.56亿元。

11月7日 县委党校教学综合楼（位于永靖镇玄天东路）动工修建。至2004年6月28日竣工并验收合格，是年9月投入使用。一期工程总投资440余万元，建筑面积3300平方米。

是年 全县乡镇卫生院划归县卫生局管理，人员经费由财政差额补助变为财政全额拨款。

是年 养龙人民法庭被最高人民法院、司法部授予“人民调解工作先进集体”称号。

是年 息烽县摘掉国定贫困县帽子。

2003年

1月5日 中国工程院院士、清华大学化学工程系博士生导师金涌，化工系生态工业研究中心主任胡山鹰，副教授薛东峰，博士周喆及副市长陈坚、宫喜祥等到开磷集团息烽重钙厂考察循环经济发展情况。

1月18日 息烽、黔西、修文、金沙、遵义五县政府联合发布《乌江库区水上交通安全管理联合公告》。

1月27日 国家计划生育委员会副主任潘贵玉一行到息烽考察计划生育工作，对息烽县计划生育工作取得的成绩予以肯定。

1月 山东信科环化有限公司投资1.1亿元在温泉镇兴建年产4万吨氯化钡、1.5万吨硫脲生产线。12月20日，一期工程建成投产。

1月 息烽县被省委、省政府、省军区命名为“双拥模范县”。

2月8日 县医院综合楼动工修建，占地3436平方米，建筑面积9057平方米，总投资1500万元。2005年9月29日建成并投入使用。

2月17—19日 县第十次党代会在县城召开。会议选举产生中共息烽县第十届委员会委员32名，候补委员6名；选举县纪委委员15名。会议期间，举行县委十届一次全委会议，选举产生杨彦峰、李志鹏、邓忠元、刘迪华、魏发志、陈康、刘大英（女）、汤太祥、陈德勇、王永平等县委常委会组成人员。

2月 《息烽县城控制性规划》通过省、市专家论证。

3月2—6日 县政协举行六届全委会一次会议，选举产生县政协六届常务委员会委员18名、选举吴德屏为县政协委员会主席，汤太祥、皮世凯、米良才、王忠碧、周鑫为副主席。

3月3—7日 县第十四届人民代表大会举行一次会议。选举县第十四届人大常委会委员19名，选举刘兴明为县人大常委会主任，任国元、胡勇、黄永辉、刘凤刚、李福燕、杜洪远为副主任；选举县人民政府县长，魏发志、刘正菊、赵永祥、魏永祥、蔡飞为副县长；选举张耀辉为县人民法院院长，莫智为县人民检察院检察长。

3月 县人民检察院荣获“全国检察机关首届预防职务犯罪工作”优秀检察院建议奖。

4月10日 中共中央政治局常委、国家副主席曾庆红到小寨坝镇黑神庙中学视察远程教育工作。

4月15日 全国人大常委会副委员长韩启德、副省长刘鸿庥一行到小寨坝卫生院考察指导防治“非典”工作。

4月18日 全县人口户籍管理实现微机化。

4月24日 县十四届人大常委会举行第一次会议，决定授予陈旭东、王宇飞息烽县荣誉县民称号。审议通过《息烽县人大常委会工作机构负责人就职宣誓誓词》《息烽县人民政府组成人员就职宣誓誓词》《息烽县人民法院法官就职宣誓誓词》《息烽县人民检察院检察官就职宣誓誓词》。

4月 县总工会困难职工援助中心成立。当年建立困难职工档案235个，为185名下岗职工推荐、安置工作。

6月20日 全省首家企业预防职务犯罪办公室在贵州开磷集团息烽重钙厂挂牌成立，省、市检察院及县四大班子领导出席挂牌仪式。

7月1日 县公安局“刑事案件信息库”建立。

8月4日 县委召开十届二次全委扩大会，通过县委《关于加大新阶段扶贫开发工作力度 全面推进小康社会建设的决定》。

8月5日 贵阳中化开磷有限公司出资3.6亿元兴建的大磷铵项目在小寨坝镇启动建设。

8月 县委、县政府出台《关于加快非公有经济发展的意见》。

8月 县人民检察院荣获最高检察院“第二届全国十佳公诉人暨全国优秀公诉人评选”特别奖。

9月10日 九庄镇堰坪小学教师陈永琪被教育部评为“全国优秀教师”。

同日 流长乡教育辅导站教师杨明仙被省教育厅、人事厅评为“贵州省优秀教师”。

9月15日 县政府发布《关于禁止燃放烟花爆竹的通告》，规定全县所有林区，县城东以川黔铁路为界，西以贵遵高等级公路为界，南以汉方制药厂接210国道路口为界，北以210国道公、铁路立交桥为界（殡仪馆内除外），为禁止燃放烟花爆竹区域。

9月 县委、县政府出台《关于稳定和引进人才的实施意见》。

10月20日 县委、县政府出台《关于加强机关效能建设 进一步改进机关作风的实施意见》。

10月26日 县委、县政府就全面推进农村卫生改革与发展，出台《关于进一步加强农村卫生工作的意见》。

11月10日 县委、县政府印发《关于进一步加强社会治安综合治理的意见》。

11月18日 县首次举行出租车经营权拍卖会，20辆出租车经营权分别以3.5万～4.3万元价格拍卖，总金额76.57万元。当月，县城出租车正式营运。

11月19日 县召开续修《息烽县志》动员暨业务培训会，省、市志办领导到会讲话，有关人员作修志专题发言。

11月21日 县城庆云山殡仪馆建成投入使用。

11月25日 香港佛教界文日一行12人到息烽走访慰问残疾人90户，每户发放大米15千克（1袋）、棉被1床（3.5千克）、食用油1瓶（2升）等。

12月17日 最高人民法院授予县人民法院“全国模范法院”称号。

12月22日 贵州银监局息烽县监管组成立。

12月23日 县委、县政府印发《关于加快生态畜牧业发展的意见》。

12月 县奶牛养殖协会（合作社）在永靖镇雨洒村成立。

是年 县政府制定《息烽县旅游市场治理整顿五年规划（2003—2007）》，委托省城乡规划院编制《息烽旅游发展总体规划》《息烽西望山风景区控制性详细规划》，启动《息烽乌江峡风景区控制性详细规划》。制定《息烽县“十五”环境保护规划》。

是年 县启动农家书屋建设工程。至2010年，全县161个村农家书屋全部建成，其中省级农家书屋5个（永靖镇红旗村、西山乡林丰村、温泉镇温泉村、石硐乡石硐村、养龙司乡江土村）。

是年 县城北门蚕桑坡田径运动场建成。运动场占地70256平方米，建400米标准跑道8条，四周阶梯看台可容纳观众5000余人。

是年 省政府批准：永靖镇红旗、永红、龙爪、南门、下阳朗等村的集体农用地、建设用地及原有农用、建设用地共计29.75公顷土地，作为永靖镇城镇建设用地，由县国土资源局代表县政府组织实施。

2004年

1月14日　息烽县获贵阳市2003年度人口与计划生育目标管理一等奖。

2月23日　贵州味美食品工业有限公司入驻息烽。

3月19日　县委召开实施创建"平安息烽"工程动员会，安排部署创建"平安息烽"工作。

4月7日　县委召开农村工作会议，传达省委、市委农村工作会议精神，讨论通过县委、县政府《关于促进农民增加收入的实施意见》。

4月25日　县委印发《关于人才强县战略的实施意见》。

5月　永靖镇禾丰村星火带头人王启发被共青团中央、农业部授予"2003年度全国农村青年创业致富带头人"称号。

5月　小寨坝镇养兔专业户林华锋、石硐乡前丰村龚星丹获贵阳市第五届"十大杰出青年农民"称号。

7月1日　息烽集中营革命历史纪念馆对中小学生免费开放。

7月16日　县委印发《关于进一步加强和改进未成年人思想道德建设的实施意见》。

7月23日　卫生部副部长朱庆生考察息烽县新型农村合作医疗试点工作。

8月12日　县委、县政府印发《关于加快农村专业技术协会发展的意见》。

8月20日　县委办公室、县政府办公室印发《关于息烽县人民政府机构改革的实施意见》。

9月3日　国务院安全生产督查组到息烽检查安全生产工作。督查组就贵州西洋肥业有限公司液氨贮罐无喷水装置和2名特殊工种人员无证上岗等问题，责令按规定落实整改。

9月15日　县政府印发《关于加强食品安全管理工作的通知》，明确建立食品安全责任追究制度，编制食品安全事故应急救援预案和食品安全事故处理程序。

10月1日　县第一次经济普查清查工作启动。至2005年12月30日普查工作结束，并发布普查公报。

10月8日　县农机厂、县酒厂等18家县属国有改革改制企业116名党员组织关系由县直属机关党委划转永靖镇党委管理。

10月　县教育局开展首届县级教育名师评选，汪政权、陈万立、张国生获县级"教育名师"称号。

11月5日　县第二次举行出租车经营权拍卖会，拍卖30辆出租车经营权。

11月26日　阳朗辣子鸡同业商会成立，时有会员22名。同日，举行首届会员代表大会，选举会长、副会长、秘书长各1名，聘请名誉会长1名。

同日　县现行文件阅览中心挂牌对外开放。

11月　县城实行生活垃圾袋装化管理，开始封闭住房楼道灰道。至2006年，县城住房楼道灰道封闭完毕。

12月5日　县城育才路40宗国有土地使用权在翠竹园二楼会议室成功拍卖，拍卖面积4498.4平方米，成交额495.9万元。

12月31日　县委印发《关于在领导干部任免表决中采用无记名投票方式的意见》。

12月 县施行住房公积金制度。

12月 县人民检察院控告申诉接待室被最高人民检察院授予全国检察机关“文明接待室”称号。

是年 县委实施干部任前廉政谈话制度。县委、县纪委领导对拟任职的乡科级领导干部进行任前廉政谈话并要求作书面承诺。当年对24名领导干部进行任前廉政谈话。

是年 息烽黔通快捷客货运输有限责任公司、息烽瑞达汽车运输有限责任公司成立，从此县内客运车辆实行公司化管理。

2005年

1月19日 县农村信用合作联社正式挂牌开业，成为按现代企业制度运行，具有独立法人地位的地方性金融机构。

1月21日 县委召开十届四次全委会议，会议对2004年工作进行总结，对做好2005年工作、提高党的执政能力、全力推进生态经济县建设作全面安排部署。讨论表决通过《中共息烽县委　息烽县人民政府关于进一步提高执政能力　全力推进生态经济县建设的意见》，确定建设生态经济县的总体思路，提出建设生态经济县分“三步走”的奋斗目标。

1月26日 县启动保持共产党员先进性教育活动。活动分县直机关、乡镇、村级党支部3个批次进行，共涉及基层党委、党总支各14个，党支部401个，党员8034名。

3月20日 最高人民法院、中央人民广播电台授予养龙人民法庭“2004中国十佳人民法庭”“全国优秀人民法庭”称号，并获“金天平奖”。

3月24日 贵州西洋肥业有限公司发生生产安全事故，死亡2人，中毒昏迷4人，直接经济损失25万元。

3月 息烽集中营革命历史纪念馆、息烽乌江峡景区被中宣部、国家发改委、国家旅游局等13个部委、局联合命名为“全国100个红色旅游经典景区和30条红色旅游精品线”。

4月9日 贵阳中化开磷化肥有限公司发生重大火灾事故，死亡5人，直接经济损失92万元。

是日 茅坡小学教师李光碧被国务院授予“全国先进工作者”称号，受到胡锦涛总书记、温家宝总理等接见。

4月30日 县举行县城南大街（息烽大道）开通仪式。

5月4日 鹿窝乡老窝村村主任黄世军被共青团中央、公安部、劳动和社会保障部授予“全国十大杰出进城务工青年”称号。

5月19日 县内首家从事液化气罐装、储、配经营燃料企业——重兴液化气储配有限公司挂牌营业。

5月 县政府创办《三农之窗》月刊向全县农民免费赠阅。该刊2007年改版，由县新闻中心承办。

5月 县医疗保险正式启动。

6月17日 贵州太和制药有限公司息烽制药厂提取车间发生药液喷出事故，死亡2人。

7月1日 石硐乡大兴田煤矿发生重大透水事故，死亡3人，直接经济损失62.8万元。

7月　县机关事业单位医疗保险启动。

7月　县张家沟引水工程开工建设。2008年8月全面完工。2009年5月全线贯通并通水试运行。

8月5日　县委召开十届五次全体（扩大）会议。

8月12日　鱼简河水库主体工程完工。

8月16日　息烽、遵义、重庆、广安四地红色旅游经典景区签订红色旅游区域无障碍通道协议，促进四地客源共享、信息互通、促销联合。

8月19日　息烽集中营革命历史纪念馆举行新馆开馆仪式。

同日　县政府与贵州千山旅游发展有限公司正式签约开发乌江峡景区，10月9日举行项目建设奠基仪式。

8月　息烽集中营革命历史纪念馆被国家旅游局命名为AAA级红色旅游景点。

9月8日　由复旦大学投资100万元在九庄镇修建的十二年一贯制学校——息烽乌江复旦学校正式动工。2008年9月建成并投入使用。

9月20日　息烽县被省民政厅命名为“贵州省村民自治模范县”。

10月24日　县委、县政府在温泉镇天台村三宝山举行王涌波等32烈士纪念碑揭幕仪式。

10月26日　县中医院综合楼竣工并投入使用。

11月28日　中国工商银行息烽县支行更名为中国工商银行股份有限公司息烽县支行，并挂牌营业。

11月　中国科协批复同意息烽县为“第三批创建全国科技示范县”。

11月　永靖镇计划生育办公室、计生服务站被国家人口计生委、中宣部表彰为“全国婚育新风进万家活动”先进集体。

12月9日　加拿大督查组到息烽检查“中国—加拿大法律援助与社区法律服务合作项目”资金使用情况。

12月30日　县委召开十届六次全体会议，审议通过县委、县政府《关于加快建设社会主义新农村实施意见》《息烽县“十一五”规划纲要》。

12月　扎南高等级公路息烽段动工建设，2007年12月31日竣工通车。息烽段总长38.53千米。

是年　县启动创建“无毒县”工作。

是年　青山苗族乡大林村山口洞移民新村动工修建，新村占地8180平方米，建房面积2835平方米，总投资186.3万元。于2007年2月建成，33户村民喜迁新居。

是年　全面消除县内2627户农村人居茅草房。

是年　县本级财政收入突破亿元大关，为11909万元。

是年　息烽县取消农业税，提前两年达到国务院五年内在全国取消农业税的要求。

是年　县内教师全部实行聘用制。

2006年

1月5日　县委、县政府印发《关于加快建设社会主义新农村的实施意见》，明确从当年起每年创建10个以上社会主义新农村村寨，用15年时间，全县161个村基本实现“生产发展、生活富裕、村容整洁、管理民主”目标。

1月15日 县公安局“110”“122”“119”三台合一指挥中心成功运行。

1月20日 县十四届人大常委会第二十二次会议作出息烽县与福泉市缔结为友好县市决定。

2月11日 中国歌剧舞剧院到息烽集中营革命历史纪念馆广场举行赴贵州首场“送文化下乡”演出。

2月17日 贵遵高等级公路息烽段81千米+500米处发生重大交通事故，死亡5人。

3月4日 世界卫生组织专家、国际狮子会、中国有关专家和中残联领导在省、市残联领导陪同下，对息烽县白内障患者进行手术后回访检查。

4月 贵阳市农村实用人才专业技术职称评审工作在息烽试点，首批210名农村实用人才分别获技师、助理技师及技术员职称。

5月24日 贵遵高等级公路小寨坝收费站立交桥拆除工程现场发生车辆高空坠落事故，死亡2人，受伤4人。

5月26日 县委、县政府召开“整脏治乱”专项行动、“创建平安畅通县”动员大会，安排部署相关工作。

6月7日 县中医院首例腹腔镜手术获得成功。

6月28日 县司法局与县电信局联合开通“96188”声讯法律服务台。

8月21日 永靖镇双龙井煤矿发生瓦斯爆炸事故，死亡4人，受伤1人，直接经济损失100余万元。

8月22日 贵州华信塑业有限公司落户温泉镇尹庵工业区，总投资850万元，设计年产彩印塑编包装袋5000万条。

9月9日 县青少年学生校外活动中心竣工，工程占地800平方米，总投资230万元。

9月25—28日 县第十一次党代会在县城召开。会议选举产生中共息烽县第十一届委员会委员39名，候补委员7名；选举县纪委委员21名。会议期间，举行县委第十一届一次全委会议，选举产生杨彦峰、罗德亚、陈德勇、王永平、黄永辉、张定超、李福燕、宋力等县委常委会组成人员。

9月28日 县中医院首例胰、十二指肠切除术获得成功，开创县级医院不能进行此类手术的先例。

10月24日 县启动有线电视“模改数”整体转换工程。

10月28日 县城北门休闲广场动工修建，占地4000平方米，总投资89万元。于次年1月16日建成投入使用。

11月3日 县老年活动中心建成并投入使用，占地7980平方米，总投资316万元。

11月15日 县十四届人大常委会举行第三十二次会议，会议同意县政府向中国农业发展银行息烽支行贷款1亿元，用于枧槽沟、两岔河、中坝、马家箐水库等农田耕地保护工程项目建设配套资金。

11月19—24日 县政协七届全委会举行一次会议，选举产生县政协第七届常委会委员19名，选举吴德屏为县政协第七届委员会主席，汤太祥、皮世凯、米良才、王忠碧、周鑫为副主席。

11月21—25日 县第十五届人大举行一次会议，选举产生县十五届人大常委会组成人员21名，选举刘大英为十五届人大常委会主任，胡勇、刘凤刚、胡亨超、刘其芬、魏永祥为副主任；选举县政府县长，黄永辉、李福燕、李红卫、杜洪远、佘龙、李华斌为副县长；选举李志强为县人民法院院长，钟雷为县人民检察院检察长。

12月5日　省委就息烽旅游资源开发事宜召开专题办公会议，确定将息烽乌江峡、温泉、西望山景区列入省重点建设项目，以获取政策、资金保证，促进息烽旅游资源开发。

12月28日　息烽黄南武阳朗辣子鸡店获贵阳十大名菜代表店辣子鸡系列金牌奖。

是年　县医院、县中医医院开展首例人工髋关节置换骨外科手术获得成功。

2007年

1月1日　县公安局实行网上“一站式”办理户口（贵阳市范围内市民在办理户口迁移时，不需再到原户籍地办理迁出手续，直接到迁入地派出所办理）。

1月25日　县委召开十一届四次全体（扩大）会议。审议通过《中共息烽县委关于构建“和谐息烽”的实施意见》，明确构建“和谐息烽”以科学发展观为统领，按照民主法治、公平正义、诚信友爱、充满活力、安定有序、人与自然和谐相处的发展思路，提出到2020年全面建成小康社会，全县物质文明、政治文明、精神文明和谐统一的奋斗目标。

1月　县第十五届人大常委会第一次会议作出设立100万元旅游发展专项资金的决定。

1月　县第二次农业普查工作全面展开，3月，普查工作结束。

2月1—3日　息烽县赴深圳参加“多彩贵州”图片展览，共展出红色旅游、自然风光、工业经济、城市建设、新农村建设等图片100余幅，展出息烽工业、医药、食品等特色产品20种，发放《息烽旅游指南》《招商指南》《烽火不息》等资料1万余份。

2月13日　县新闻中心、县广播电视台合并组建县新闻传媒中心。

4月10日　县委出台《关于进一步加强和改进人大工作的意见》。

4月16日　中化开磷化肥有限公司50万吨硫酸装置发生二氧化硫气体泄漏事故，造成小寨坝镇中、小学生和周边居民450余人中毒，县政府积极组织抢救，经过一周治疗，中毒者全部康复。

4月　县城污水处理厂及部分管网收集系统项目通过专家评审。

4—5月　九庄复旦学校发生甲肝疫情，81名学生被传染，省、市、县三级卫生组织采取应急措施处置，经医治，被传染学生全部康复。

5月15日　县委出台《关于深化文化体制改革　加快文化产业发展的实施意见》。

5月17日　县委、县政府决定命名潘世昌等15人为息烽县2007—2009年度专业技术带头人，陈华等30人为息烽县2007—2009年度中青年科技骨干。

6月27日　县残疾人综合服务中心办公楼投入使用。中心占地1079平方米，总投资83万元。

6月30日凌晨　县境内遭受强降雨袭击，降雨量达112.9毫米，全县7个乡镇不同程度受灾，直接经济损失800余万元。

8月14日　县委出台《关于开展乡（镇）党的代表大会常任制试点工作的实施意见》。

8月24日　县政府召开深入推进“整脏治乱”工作会，决定投入500万元改造县城人行道、公共厕所和绿化空地等。当月31日，县城文化西路、交通路人行道、排水、排污管道等改造工程动工。

9月10日　县城双拥广场动工修建，是年建成投入使用。

9月16日　中国红十字会和上海通用五菱汽车公司捐赠10万元援建“息烽县永靖镇博爱卫生院”。

10月1日　县新型农村社会养老保险全面启动。

11月8—21日　县政府组织有关单位及乡镇赴广州参加“贵阳——广州友好城市经贸合作交流会”，签订招商引资项目6个，协议总投资10.6亿元。

11月23日　息烽县被中国科学技术协会命名为第三批“全国科普示范县”。

11月　息烽县被商务部列入“东桑西移”示范县。是年12月27日，县政府出台《关于进一步加快蚕桑产业发展的实施意见》，明确从次年起，用3～5年时间，扶持发展10个蚕桑产业专业村和100户蚕桑专业大户。

12月20日　息烽县建立《烟花爆竹实施专用封签及防伪标识管理制度》，对烟花爆竹实施专用封签及防伪标识管理。

12月28日　县安委会印发《息烽县2008年烟花爆竹经营许可及安全管理工作方案》，明确自2008年1月1日起，烟花爆竹由禁止燃放改为限制燃放，允许县城永靖镇禁止燃放烟花爆竹的城镇区域在规定时间、地点、品种限制内燃放烟花爆竹。

12月29日　县委、县政府出台《关于全面加强人口和计划生育工作　统筹解决人口问题的实施意见》。

12月31日　贵遵高速公路扎佐至南白镇改扩建工程竣工通车。

是年　息烽县成为贵州省首批省级新一轮初保达标县。

是年　息烽县“创建全国科普示范县”工作通过省、市验收。

2008年

1月8日　县委召开第十一届四次全体（扩大）会议，审议通过《关于建设生态文明县的决定》，提出建设生态文明县坚持科学发展，统筹城乡，立足实际，分步实施，关注民生，促进和谐，创新机制，科学考评，党政推动，全民参与的原则，至2012年，生态产业快速发展，循环经济取得实效，服务业比重明显提高，“二、三、一”产业结构进一步优化，单位生产总值能耗比2005年降低25%以上，主要污染物排放总量减少10%以上，建成80个生态文明村寨的五年奋斗目标。

1月13日至2月15日　县遭受特大凝冻灾害，受灾22.6万人，损坏、倒塌房屋206栋9960间；农作物受灾面积7300公顷，绝收面积979.7公顷；因灾死亡大牲畜2409头。直接经济损失2亿元。

1月16日　县政府印发《息烽县集体林权制度改革实施方案》。

2月2日　天津市津南区红十字会向息烽捐赠10万元凝冻灾害救灾款。

2月18日　县污染源普查工作启动。于3月10日结束并汇总上报普查结果。

2月20日　县委、县政府召开“抗凝冻，保民生”总结表彰大会，授予县人武部、县供电分局等22个单位“突出贡献先进集体”称号，授予县消防大队、联通公司等69个单位“先进集体”称号，授予黄鲲、赵承瑞等338人“先进个人”称号。

2月22日　县委、县政府召开“抓重建、保民生”房开企业捐赠会，贵州弘晋、息烽伟业、重庆金穗等16家房开企业现场捐资133.6万元。

2月　县政府印发《息烽县招商引资奖励政策》。

3月6日　县启动“劳有所得”行动计划。

3月13日　县委、县政府出台《关于统筹城乡发展　推进城乡一体化的实施意见》。

3月19日　“息烽兴农兔业专业合作社”挂牌成立，时有社员105名，存栏种兔3000余只。

3月20日　贵阳富源盲人按摩院息烽分院在县残疾人活动中心开业。

4月28日　交通部在贵州实施的农村客运试点项目——九庄、温泉两个客运站投入运营，总投资160万元。

5月13日　县委、县政府号召全县各级各部门发扬“一方有难，八方支援”精神，开展向四川汶川地震灾区献爱心活动。

5月　县中心敬老院工程竣工。总投资200余万元，建筑占地面积784.43平方米，内设老人住房31间（62个床位）及活动室、餐厅、消毒间、厨房、休息室、卫生室等。

7月3日　县委、县政府命名息烽县档案馆为“息烽县爱国主义教育基地”。

7月18日　县生态文明建设民兵团成立大会在县城双拥广场举行。生态文明建设民兵团下设1个直属营和4个生态文明建设营，人员编制800余人，主要职责是参与发展生态经济、建设生态环境、完善农村基础设施；协助维护社会稳定、承担抢险救灾任务；进行全民国防教育、培养农村基层骨干等。

7月　县委、县政府决定向全县年满60周岁、累计任职5年以上的离任村干部发放定期定额补助。有720余名离任村干部列为补助对象，每人每年可获400～1700元补助。

7月　永靖镇安马村“脱毒马铃薯商品薯高产示范基地”重点建设项目通过省级验收，平均亩产脱毒马铃薯2512千克，超任务目标1012千克。

8月7日　县启动县委书记大接访活动。当日，全县共接待来访群众173批276人，现场解决问题24个，限时办理149个。

8月8日　省建设经济强县领导小组批准息烽县为省经济强县。

8月28日　县城污水处理厂工程开工奠基，工程投资2252.02万元。

9月1日　县为民服务全程代理中心正式成立，启动21项为民服务全程代理事项。

9月10日　县“金保二期”信息管理系统正式启用，全县社会保险实现“五统一”（统一基金征收、统一支付待遇、统一基金管理、统一政策制度、统一业务规程）。

9月14日　县政府印发《关于进一步加快服务业发展的意见》。

9月　县老年科技工作者协会成立，并召开第一次会员代表大会。

9月　县政务服务中心成立，为县政府办下属正科级事业单位。

10月1日　县新型农村社会养老保险全面启动。

10月24日　卫生部李熙、窦熙熙、张继泽等到息烽调研医患关系与医德医风建设工作。

11月26日　县十五届人大常委会举行第十八次会议，会议决定授予陈德伟息烽县“荣誉县民”称号。

11月　《息烽县工业发展规划（2008—2020年）》通过省、市专家论证。

同月　息烽县创建“无毒县”工作通过市禁毒委验收。

12月22日　西望山虫茶开发项目通过贵州大学、省科技厅、农业厅、林业厅等部门专家论证。

12月28日　息烽至金沙乌江大桥建设工程启动，总投资7860万元。

12月29日　县煤炭同业商会挂牌成立。即日举行首次会员大会，审议通过《息烽县煤炭同业商会章程》，选举执委会委员7名，会长1名、副会长2名，秘书长、副秘书长各1名。

12月 县城生活垃圾填埋处理工程动工，项目总投资4000万元。

是年 县国税局税收突破2亿元大关，累计入库各项税收2.01亿元。

是年 息烽县被列为国家石漠化综合治理试点县。

是年 县委下发《息烽县县级班子党员领导干部与统战对象联系制度》，每名县级党员领导干部分别联系2～3人，定期或不定期开展联系和慰问活动，听取统战对象对全县各项工作的意见和建议。

是年 县人民检察院控告申诉接待室被省人民检察院授予全省检察机关“文明接待室”称号。

2009年

1月1日 县工商局停止征收个体工商户管理费和集贸市场管理费。

1月19日 县委第十一届委员会举行第六次全体（扩大）会议，通过《关于抢抓机遇　进一步加快生态文明县建设的实施意见》。

1月 中国农业银行息烽县支行更名为中国农业银行股份有限公司息烽县支行。

1月 息烽县创建“无毒县”工作通过省禁毒委验收并授予“无毒县”称号。

2月20日 县政府印发《关于被征地农民社会保障的实施方案（试行）》。

3月17日 “息烽县青山长鑫种养殖农业专业合作社”登记成立。

3月 县委、县政府决定将村组干部生活补贴纳入财政预算。补贴标准每人每年360元，县、乡（镇）各负责50%。

5月11—13日 息烽县亚行贷款项目两岔河、枧槽沟、中坝3座水库供水工程可行性研究报告通过省级专家技术审查。

5月19日 省禁毒委员会授予息烽县“无毒县”称号，奖励人民币20万元。

5月27日 县政府与贵阳供电局签订息烽2009—2013年电网改造合作协议。贵阳供电局投资5亿元，与息烽县共同规划、共同建设息烽电网。

6月 县206.67公顷脱毒马铃薯二级良种扩繁和优质马铃薯生产基地两个项目通过省级验收。经现场测产，优质马铃薯最高亩产1927千克，二级良种最高单产2112千克。

6月 县政府印发《矿山环境保护与治理规划》。

7月7日 县委、县政府印发《关于进一步加快实施“旅游活县”战略的意见》。

7月21日 县政府印发《关于健全市场化配置资源机制　提高城乡统筹发展水平的意见》，明确以“市场化配置资源”为突破口，建立公开、公平、公正的市场环境。

7月 中国农业银行股份有限公司息烽县支行挂牌营业。

8月23日 息烽信科环化有限公司年产5000吨高纯度氯化钡生产线建成投产。

8月25日 县政府办印发《息烽县创建国家级创业型城市工作意见》。

8月 省综治委授予息烽县“平安建设先进县”称号。

9月4日 县政府办印发《息烽县农村土地承包经营权流转实施方案（试行）》，明确农村土地承包经营权流转按照土地所有权、承包权、经营权分离原则，在不改变土地集体所有性质和农业用途的前提下进行流转。

9月26日 息烽县与开磷集团签订“息烽县与开磷集团共谋贵阳市息烽循环经济磷煤精细化工工业园（2009—2015）发展合作协议”。

10月15日 全国妇联党组书记、副主席黄晴宜在省、市、县领导陪同下，考察养龙司乡农村妇女“双学双比”示范基地。

11月19日 “世界低碳与生态经济大会暨中国县镇绿色发展论坛”大会授予息烽县“中国绿色名县”称号。

11月20日 全国循环经济学会工作会议在息烽温泉召开。

11月 县委、县政府表彰2005—2008年度在平安建设和创建“无毒县”工作中成绩突出的70个先进集体和212名先进个人。

11月 息烽集中营革命历史纪念馆被国家国防教育办公室命名为“国家国防教育示范基地”。

12月17日 中华全国妇女联合会授予息烽县养龙司乡堡子村“全国妇女教育基地”称号。

12月 《息烽县石漠化综合治理试点实施方案（2008—2010年）》《息烽县2008年度石漠化综合治理试点工程初步设计》获省、市发改委审批。

是年 息烽县获“全省平安建设先进县”称号。

是年 县公安局打掉唐某某黑社会组织团伙，抓获犯罪嫌疑人17人，收缴涉案车辆2辆、自制手枪2支、制式子弹3发。

是年 县完成全国第三次文物普查，全县有不可移动文物88处。

是年 全县推广良种、良肥、良法工程，对坡度25度以下耕地，农民种植水稻、玉米、油菜、马铃薯等农作物，按20千克/亩的标准无偿补助磷酸二铵，所需磷酸二铵由开磷集团息烽磷化工基地负责生产并运送到全县161个村。

是年 县“两基”（基本普及九年制义务教育、基本消除青壮年文盲）工作通过“国检”。

2010年

1月 息烽县城电力管网入地工程启动。规划改造城镇道路建设1500平方米，总投资400余万元。

2月 息烽县获“贵州省绿化模范县”称号。

3月4日 县公安局看守所被公安部监所管理局授予2009年度一级看守所称号，明确为对外开放试点所之一。

3月22日 县委印发《关于推行党务公开的意见（试行）》。

3月25日 县政府印发《关于实行社会综合治税的意见》。

同日 县首家出租车客运公司——宏运出租车有限责任公司成立。时有出租车47辆，在岗驾驶员121人。

5月18日 县政府办印发《息烽县国家基本药物制度实施方案》。即日起，全县乡镇卫生院、村卫生室实行药品零差率销售。

同日 举行息烽大酒店建设项目奠基仪式。该项目投资7000万元，建筑面积1.7万平方米。

5月中旬 乌江库区息烽河段（磨河水至小溪口）网箱养鱼发生大规模异常死亡，死鱼260.8万千克。

5月26日 县委、县政府下发《关于息烽县人民政府机构改革的实施意见》。

5月 息烽集中营革命历史纪念馆被中纪委、监察部命名为全国廉政教育基地。

7月1日 在贵州省基层组织建设工作座谈会上，息烽县被评为“党的基层组织建设先进县”。

7月3日 县环境监测站挂牌成立。

7月8日 县内首个农产品商标——西山乡希望葡萄种植专业合作社“蜂布叮”商标注册成功。

7月31日 县城生活污水处理厂建设工程通过省级环保验收。该厂总投资2055万元，日处理生活污水7000吨。

7月 县林权流转交易服务中心成立。

7月 县石漠化综合治理工程获中央投资奖励200万元。

8月3日 全国政协副主席徐匡迪到小寨坝磷化工基地视察循环经济产业。

8月 青山苗族乡选送的芦笙舞《蒙待央》获省第九届少数民族传统体育运动会表演项目金牌。

10月 县工业园区建设开发办公室成立，内设综合协调部、建设开发部、招商引资部3个机构。

11月1日 县第六次全国人口普查工作启动。经普查登记，全县总人口257732人，其中男性134187人，占总人口的52.06%；女性123545人，占47.94%。

11月 息烽循环经济精细磷煤化工工业园成立。12月16日，工业园一期项目建设开工。

12月21日 中宣部、文化部、国家广电总局、新闻出版总署授予县旅游文化体育广播电视局综合执法大队“服务农民、服务基层”“基层文化市场管理和执法先进集体”称号。

12月17日 县西望山凤池寺修复工程启动。

12月 县社区矫正工作委员会成立。全县社区矫正工作全面启动。

是年 县政府引进广州石碣润丰国际蔬菜交易中心投资2亿元，在西山乡柏香山村建设“广州石碣润丰国际蔬菜交易中心”。

是年 县人民检察院控告申诉接待室被最高人民检察院授予全国检察机关“文明接待室”称号。

是年 县本级财政收入突破3亿元大关，为30769万元。

第一篇　政区建置

第一章　行政区划

息烽县位于贵州省中部，乌江南岸，北纬26° 57′ 42″ ~27° 19′ 45″ ，东经106° 27′ 29″ ~106° 53′ 43″ 。东与开阳县交界，南与修文县接壤，西北隔乌江与金沙县相望，北与遵义县毗邻。总面积1036.5平方千米。

1949年11月17日，息烽解放，23日建立息烽县人民政府，隶属贵阳专署。1952年11月，贵阳专署迁贵定，改称贵定专署，县属贵定专区管辖。1956年3月，贵定专署撤销，息烽划属安顺专区管辖。1958年10月，改属遵义专区管辖。1965年8月，划回安顺专区。1996年1月，划归贵阳市管辖。

中华人民共和国成立前，县内设永靖镇（镇公所驻县城）、文化乡（乡公所驻底寨）、镇南乡（乡公所驻阳朗坝）、邻文乡（乡公所驻石硐）、飞越乡（乡公所驻养龙司）、养龙乡（乡公所驻养龙站）、复兴乡（乡公所驻黑神庙）、九庄镇（镇公所驻九庄）、流长乡（乡公所驻流长）、西山乡（乡公所驻西山）10个乡镇，下辖84保809甲。

中华人民共和国成立后，县内设区，区辖乡镇，乡镇下设村。1951年2月，县内设4个区（永阳区、养龙区、九庄区、黑神庙区），同时将84个保改为84个村。1952年4月，增设底寨区。至此，原10乡镇全部废除。并将84个行政村合并为54个行政村，分属5个区管辖。1953年，将54个行政村改建为54个乡镇。1956年3月，调整区乡，撤销底寨区，54个乡镇调整为46个。1957年4月，46个乡镇合并为33个乡镇。1958年9月，33个乡镇调整改建为25个人民公社，实行政社合一，下设160个生产大队、1739个生产队。后实行一区一社，下辖管理区。1961年恢复区公所建制，下辖16个人民公社。1963年3月，将16个人民公社分建为32个，撤销管理区。1965年7月，全县32个公社合建为25个公社。1971年，乌江公社（即养龙站）划归遵义县，全县人民公社减为24个。1984年，撤销人民公社，恢复乡镇建制；增设九庄镇（乡级镇），青山乡改为青山苗族乡。至1990年，县辖4个区、1个区级镇、1个乡级镇、1个苗族乡、22个乡，乡镇下辖161个村、1642个村民组、5个街道居民委员会。

第一节　1991年行政区划

1991年，县辖4个区、1个区级镇、1个乡级镇、1个苗族乡、22个乡，乡镇下辖161个村、1642个村民组、4个街道居民委员会。

永阳区：区公所驻底寨，下辖：

梨安乡：辖梨安、安马、坪上、新萝4个村，35个村民组。

阳朗乡：辖阳朗、立碑、老街、猫洞、下洪马、上洪马、后坝、河丰8个村，35个村民组。

下阳朗乡：辖下阳朗、硬寨、联峰3个村，42个村民组、1个居民委员会。

三田乡：辖老厂、雨洒、马当田、管田、盘脚营、河坎6个村，79个村民组。

西山乡：辖小鹿窝、西山、新寨沟、联合、胜利5个村，55个村民组。

青山苗族乡：辖大林、青山、绿化、冗坝、马路岩5个村，62个村民组。

底寨乡：辖团元山、林丰、金星、田冲、猪场、文安、小堡、柏香山8个村，94个村民组。

养龙司区：区公所驻养龙司，下辖：

养龙司乡：辖幸福、灯塔、高坡、坝上、养龙司、堡子、坪山7个村，79个村民组。

茅坡乡：辖大山、茅坡、高洞、荆江、龙塘、蚂蟥6个村，61个村民组。

安江乡：辖高潮、大尖山、光荣、安江、江土、龙门、新桥、光华8个村，77个村民组。

温泉乡：辖温泉、兴隆、天台、赶子、三交、尹庵6个村，73个村民组，1个居民委员会。

九庄区：区公所驻九庄，下辖：

九庄镇：辖三合、同心、西门、新街4个村，28个村民组，1个居民委员会。

九庄乡：辖鸡场、桐梓、天鹅、腰寨、青堰、后陇、望城、大槽、鲁俐衙9个村，100个村民组。

竹花乡：辖竹花、杉林、清坪、和平、堰坪、新沙、柏茂、上坝、新田、团山、纸房、黄沙12个村，107个村民组。

新杨乡：辖新民、杨寨、瓮舍3个村，44个村民组。

鹿窝乡：辖鹿窝、田坝、老窝、三友、胡广、大石头、华溪、马吨8个村，70个村民组。

石硐乡：辖前锋、高峰、龙坪、光明、木杉、水头、石硐7个村，113个村民组。

猫场乡：辖新寨、南桥、泉湖、高青、新街、老街6个村，72个村民组。

何家硐乡：辖红星、玉龙、何家硐、中坝、大洪5个村，42个村民组。

黑神庙区：区公所驻黑神庙，下辖：

南极乡：辖南中、田兴、南桥3个村，42个村民组。

小寨坝乡：辖小寨坝、上寨、中心、高家坝、排杉、石桥、亲戚寨、茅草寨8个村，70个村民组。

流长乡：辖流长、大水井、茶园、大兴、前奔、龙泉、长涌、宋家寨、李安寨9个村，91个村民组。

新场乡：辖新中、水尾、四坪、营中4个村，65个村民组。

王家坪乡；辖王家坪、大湾、前进、瓮沙、甘溪、合箭、西安、红岩、大寨、潮水、关岭、龙塘坡12个村，88个村民组。

永靖镇：镇政府驻县城，下辖：

红旗、永红、南门、龙爪4个村，26个村民组，1个居民委员会。

第二节　建镇并乡撤区

1991年11月4日，县委、县政府、县政协、县纪委召开联席会议，学习贵州省委、省政府《关于建镇并乡撤区工作的指示》（以下简称“建并撤”），传达安顺地区“建并撤”工作会议精神；县成立“建并撤”领导小组和办公室，办公室下设规划建设、文书档案清理、财物清理、组织、宣传、后勤、选举7个小组。11月5日，“建并撤”工作正式开始，至1992年6月结束，共分3个阶段。

第一阶段为准备阶段（1991年11月5日至12月5日）：主要进行宣传，拟定行政区划变更方案、报批和新建乡镇政府驻地的选点和规划，以及原区乡镇财物和文书档案的清理登记、移交，乡镇干部的考核和第二阶段选举的准备工作。第二阶段为实施阶段（1991年12月6日至1992年2月29日）：省政府批复县建并撤行政区划变更的请示后，12月6日，县召开新建乡镇党的工作委员会组建大会，宣布撤销原4区1镇、24个乡镇，新建永靖镇、小寨坝镇、温泉镇、九庄镇、养龙司乡、流长乡、鹿窝乡、石硐乡、西山乡和青山苗族乡10个乡镇，下辖161个行政村、1575个村民组、8个街道居民委员会；同时成立各乡镇临时党的工作委员会。至1992年2月29日，先后选举产生和组建10乡镇党委、政府、人大主席团、纪检委、共青团、妇联。第三阶段为整章建制阶段（1992年3月1日至6月30日）：主要进行和完成政府有关部门延伸机构的建立和各种规章制度的制定工作。

永靖镇：驻地县城，由原永靖镇、阳朗乡、下阳朗乡、梨安乡、三田乡（盘脚营村并入小寨坝镇）5个乡镇合并组建，共辖24个村、214个村民组、3个居民委员会。

九庄镇：驻地九庄街，由原九庄镇（乡级镇）、九庄乡、竹花乡3个乡镇合并组建，下辖25个村、228个村民组、1个居民委员会。

小寨坝镇：驻地黑神庙街上，由原小寨坝乡、南极乡、王家坪乡的红岩、大寨、潮水、关岭、大湾、前进、长征、瓮沙8个村、三田乡的盘脚营村合并组建，下辖20个村、189个村民组、1个居民委员会。

温泉镇：驻地石头田，由原温泉乡和安江乡的光荣、安龙、高潮、安江、大尖山5个村合并组建，下辖11个村，132个村民组、2个居民委员会。

养龙司乡：驻地养龙司街上，由原养龙司乡、茅坡乡、安江乡的江土、光华、龙门、新桥4个村合并组建，下辖17个村、169个村民组、1个居民委员会。

流长乡：驻地流长街上，由原流长乡、新场乡和王家坪乡的甘溪、龙塘2个村合并组建，下辖15个村、135个村民组。

鹿窝乡：驻地鹿窝街上，由原鹿窝乡、新杨乡、王家坪乡的合箐、西安2个村合并组建，下辖13个村、124个村民组。

石硐乡：驻地石硐街上，由原石硐、何家硐、猫场3个乡合并组建，下辖18个村、205个村民组。

西山乡：驻地底寨柏香山，由原西山乡、底寨乡合并，下辖13个村、125个村民组。

青山苗族乡：驻地青山，下辖5个村、57个村民组。

第二章　乡镇概况

2010年，全县辖4个镇、5个乡、1个苗族乡。乡镇下辖161个村、1456个村民组、13个街道居民委员会。

第一节　永靖镇

永靖镇位于县境东南部，地理坐标北纬26° 58″ ～27° 09″ ，东经106° 39″ ～106° 47″ 。为县城所在地。是全县政治、经济、文化教育中心。东邻开阳县金钟镇，南接修文县久长镇，西与西山乡、青山苗族乡、石硐乡交界，北与小寨坝镇接壤。平均海拔1000～1200米，年平均气温14.7℃，最高温度25℃～30℃，最低温度2℃～3℃；年平均降雨量1200毫米，年平均日照1411小时，无霜期291天。镇域南北长约22千米，东西宽约7.6千米，总面积154.92平方千米；黔渝铁路、兰海高速（贵遵段）、210国道横贯南北；金阳公路东西连接，县道、乡村公路纵横交错。境内有3个火车站、1个高等级公路出入口、1个汽车站和1个客货综合停车场，全镇组组通公路。福—杭—贵—成通信光缆贯穿全境，数字化程控交换、移动电话网络覆盖全镇。有10千伏变电站1座、110千伏变电站2座。

2010年，镇政府驻县城育才路。辖24个村、180个村民组、6个居民委员会。

坪上村：辖坪上、菜子沟、牛角井、邓家林、宋家寨、石灰窑、下寨7个村民组。

新萝村：辖沙闸、沙田、老街、喜雅坝、四组、下丫口、上丫口、沟下坡8个村民组。

安马村：辖芦稿坪、旧屋基、鹞子岩、中寨、上寨、干田、洋土桩、老虎丫8个村民组。

梨安村：辖黑土坡、下坝、上寨、宋家寨、大院坝、马路湾、关冲、街上8个村民组。

老厂村：辖上寨、坪天坝、老厂、白岩厂、青山、田坝、上厂、张家沟、高茶树9个村民组。

河坎村：辖河坎、新寨、上寨、香子坪、堡山、坪上、大沟坎、坟坝8个村民组。

雨洒村：辖洒二、湾子、中心、牛硐、漆树沟、黄沙田、小坪坝、洒一、下坝、上坝10个村民组。

马当田村：辖大山沟、龙塘湾、水泥厂、马路边、马当田、大路边、长田坝、枫香树、鲁家寨、茶一、茶二、茶三、凤凰山、坪一、坪二、坪三、坪四17个村民组。

管田村：辖管田、螺蛳田、大寨、东边寨、猫山、安理寨、上东阳、下东阳8个村民组。

联丰村：辖板厂、金家厂、中寨、老安寨、老鹰岩、石关口、新田7个村民组。

龙爪村：辖东风、快活、洒岭沟、大型地4个村民组。

下阳朗村：辖北门、半边街、廖家沟、快活岭、毛栗冲、水井湾、西门塆、长岭岗8个村民组。

硬寨村：辖田坝、留旗湾、麻窝田、山脚、青关口、唐家湾、丁木树7个村民组。

上洪马村：辖麻窝寨、二坝田、水头上、上洪马4个村民组。

下洪马村：辖一、二、三、四、五、六、七、八、九、十组10个村民组。

猫洞村：辖猫洞、麦子溪、上坝河、三道拐、卢家湾、蔡家寨6个村民组。

立碑村：辖立碑、核桃湾、蒿枝湾、马场坝、毛狗冲5个村民组。

阳朗村：辖一、二、三、四、五、六组6个村民组。

老街村：辖一、二、三、四、五组5个村民组。

后坝村：辖后坝、朝房、鸦米寨、大田坎、坪上5个村民组。

河丰村：辖一、二、三、四、五、六、七组7个村民组。

南门村：辖一、二、三组3个村民组。

永红村：辖东一、东三、西一、西二、枧槽沟、柿花坪、沙石坡7个村民组。

红旗村：辖东二、田坝、拖电厂、北一、北二、北三、北四、北五、北六、蚕一、蚕二、蚕三、蚕四13个村民组。

居民委员会：有东门、南门、西门、北门、龙腾、新华6个社区居民委员会。

全镇总户数20749户，总人口54713人（其中非农业人口18146人），人口密度353人/平方千米。耕地面积23937亩（习惯亩），农业人口人均占有耕地0.65亩。农民人均年收入5084元。

辖区粮食作物以水稻、玉米、小麦、高粱为主，主要经济作物有油菜籽、烤烟、生姜、辣椒等，畜牧业以养殖猪、鸡为主，其次为肉兔和肉牛。粮食总产11259吨、油菜籽765吨、蔬菜23067吨；肉类总产2137吨、禽蛋464吨、水产品29吨、牛奶1390吨。全镇属亚热带常绿落叶混交林区，森林覆盖率39.21%，林木绿化率39.31%；建档挂牌保护的古、大、珍稀植物14株，被列为国家Ⅰ、Ⅱ级保护名录的有银杏、榉木、樟树、黄杨等。镇内河流主要有息烽河、永靖河、阳朗河、三田河。建有小（二）型水库5座、小（一）型水库1座、中型水库1座、山塘32口，总容量1514.26万立方米，可灌溉4万余亩稻田，解决全镇工业用水及人畜饮水。矿产资源主要有煤、硅石、石灰岩、硫铁矿、铝矾土、褐铁矿、硫铁矿和梨安温泉资源。

医疗机构有县人民医院、县中医院、县妇幼保健院、永靖卫生院，病床423张；27个村（居）卫生室和妇幼保健室。有协和、阳光、华西3家私立医院。学校有息烽一中、息烽二中、永靖中学、职业中学4所公办中学，特殊教育学校1所和永生私立中学1所，小学9所和5个教学点，1个公办幼儿园和15个民办幼儿园，1个敬老院。镇内有汉方、太和药业和味美、苗姑娘食品等工业园；三田、河坎、硬寨等地建材工业以生产砖、砂、水泥为主。

旅游资源有息烽集中营革命历史纪念馆、玄天洞杨虎城将军囚禁处纪念馆、张露萍七烈士陵园等红色旅游区和息烽县云环小学邵云环烈士纪念室等爱国主义教育基地；县城西南方有团元山景区，森林覆盖率80%以上，离县城约0.5千米，往南蔓延约4千米，起伏重叠，丘陵之间，绿树成荫，鸟语花香，风景别致，还有侏罗纪恐龙化石群。阳朗小镇以土特产品阳朗辣子鸡闻名，其中黄南武辣子鸡具有麻辣、酸辣、香辣等独特风味。集镇有永靖、阳朗、梨安3处，永靖星期三、星期日赶集，阳朗、梨安无场期。

第二节　温泉镇

温泉镇位于县境东北部，地理坐标北纬27° 19′ ~ 59′ ，东经106° 48′ ~ 55′ 。东与开阳县交界，南抵小寨坝镇，西与养龙司乡毗邻，北抵乌江与遵义县相望。东西宽8千米，南北长17千米，总面积85.03平方千米。海拔610 ~ 1260米，相对高差650米。年平均气温16℃，年降雨量1380毫米左右。

连接贵遵高速的养（龙司）温（泉）公路贯穿镇域，铁路交通有开阳支线经过镇内，镇内有火车站和专用货运站各1个，有7千米的276铁路专线和700米长的贵州息烽磷矿铁路专线。境内有客运汽车站1个，火车站1个。

2010年，镇政府驻石头田，距县城39千米。辖11个村，121个村民组、2个居委会。

温泉村：辖温泉、石头田、热水坪、新沟、窑上、赶子坡、方井、田坝8个村民组。

兴隆村：辖云峰、凤凰寨、胡子湾、高峰、干水井、田冲沟、干沟、小沟、坪上、族寨、三百块、沙埝、堰塘、龙尾、衙上、板桥、潘家坡、水淹凼、草香、旧寨湾20个村民组。

天台村：辖光石坡、茶园、鹿子山、新场坪、三宝山、湾子、后寨、关田坝、龙塘沟9个村民组。

尹庵村：辖大塘寨、马庄、瓦厂、中间、寨子、田坝、半坡、煤炭沟、大潮9个村民组。

三交村：辖大元、水井寨、高坎子、瓦厂、水井、太和寺、焦家坝、赵家林、垭角林、麻水、银坑、上寨、青㭎坪、沙塆14个村民组。

赶子村：辖高花、上寨、龙塘、花猫沟、塆子、坝上、枫香沟、田坝、柏香林、高山冲一、高山冲二、矿石槽、火石岭岗、下寨14个村民组。

安江村：辖阁上、后寨、长干子、袁家麻窝、大土、中寨、石头塆、龙洞、大沙坝、马渡10个村民组。

大尖山村：辖光腊湾、冯家寨、半坡、小麻窝、大尖山、坪上、田家塆、黄沙坡8个村民组。

安龙村：辖坝上、麻窝、坪子、田坝、大元、漆树坪、陶家湾、郑家寨、四坪、范塆10个村民组。

高潮村：辖唐家槽、山望陇、朗坡、大坡、下牛角坡、沙子田、烂田塆7个村民组。

光荣村：辖大田、上牛角坡、甲板沟、陈家沟、熊家湾、何家塆、林家湾、桐梓坡、柏杨坡、碾房、金坪、安清场12个村民组。

居民委员会：石头田居民委员会、西洋社区居民委员会。

全镇总户数7167户，总人口22155人（其中非农业人口4100人），人口密度260人/平方千米。耕地面积2.02万亩（其中田0.63万亩），农业人口人均占有耕地0.9亩。农民人均纯收入5941元。

辖区粮食作物以水稻、玉米为主，经济作物以油菜籽为主，其次是烤烟。畜牧业以养殖猪、鸡为主，有个别农户饲养梅花鹿。粮食总产10041吨、油菜籽1040吨、烤烟102吨、蔬菜12672吨；肉类总产1406吨、禽蛋82吨、水产品12吨。镇内林业用地58465亩，占土地总面积的42.1%。天台山林区，面积845亩，是县内植物种群数量较多，保护树种和珍稀树种也较多的地区。林区内有红豆杉古树群、银杏古树群、黄心夜合古树群、榉木古树群、枫香古树群、丝栗古树群。还分布有观赏价值较高的椤木石楠、常绿油麻藤、灯台树、枫香、珊瑚朴、乌柿等。乌江有近5千米的流段在镇域内，流经安江村、大尖山村、三交村，在大塘口与温泉河交汇。矿产资源有煤、铝土矿、硫铁矿、褐铁矿、磷矿、重晶石、高岭土、硅矿、石灰石9种。

学校有9年一贯制学校1所，初级中学1所，镇中心完小1所，村级小学4所，教学点1个，民办幼儿园3个；医疗机构有镇卫生院1所，病床20张，村级卫生室11个、妇幼保健室5个；2个企业医院，温泉疗养院有床位400张。

辖区大中型国有企业：贵州息烽磷矿、县磷肥厂、县磷矿粉厂、贵州省总工会温泉职工疗养院。民营企业：贵州西洋肥业有限公司、华信塑业有限公司、息烽合力化工有限责任公司、息烽龙泉磷肥厂。

旅游资源有温泉，泉水中氡含量较高，具有很高的医疗价值。是国内著名八大温泉之一。集市在石头田街，星期六赶集。土特产有小锅米粉、土豆鸡、咸味馅汤圆、拐枣酒。

第三节　九庄镇

九庄镇位于县境西北面，地理坐标北纬27° 09′ ~27° 13′ ，东经106° 27′ ~106° 36′ 。东与鹿窝乡交界，南与石硐乡接壤，西连修文县，北隔乌江与金沙县相望，总面积114.36平方千米。海拔610~1260米。一般气温-3℃~28℃，年平均气温15.5℃，全年无霜期270~300天，平均日照1410小时，年平均降雨量107.86毫米。

2010年，镇政府驻西门村新大街，距县城33千米。辖25个村，204个村民组，1个居委会。

鸡场村：辖大秧地、晏家沟、半边林、烂田塆、上坝、樱桃塆、梨树坡、鄢家槽、下坝、中坝、小寨沟、干田坝、大水沟、小寨14个村民组。

鲁俐衙村：辖白泥山、火麻塆、董家塝、旱禾、沙坝、仓上、鲁一、鲁二、鲁三、鲁四、占家槽、水淹坝、大坪13个村民组。

腰寨村：辖紫浸沟、八块田、大元、大土、坡成田、三口堰、上冲、山脚、中寨、大槽、白果树11个村民组。

桐梓村：辖毛一、前进、榨房、黄土坡、沙坝、杨家海、高坡、花底、中寨、毕甲山、大院、小寨坝、桐梓坡13个村民组。

桐枝驿村：辖大荒田、同一、同二、田家塆、上寨、下寨、中寨7个村民组。

三合村：辖巴麻窝、大垭口、贾角山、老白头、坪子、沙坡、瓦啄沟、堰塘、油房、中坝10个村民组。

大槽村：辖烟灯坡、大槽、烂田沟、关山、麻上、湾子、中坝、麻窝冲8个村民组。

新街村：辖和一、和二、和三、停车、环城、中北6个村民组。

西门村：辖羊叉、龙泉、东门、城墙、共和、中一、中二、场口8个村民组。

天鹅村：辖胜利、花坟、姜家坡、蜂子岩、高坡、甲堡、沙冲7个村民组。

清堰村：辖洋中、畜牧场、清堰、老油房、龙洞湾、魏家寨、田坝、上寨、彭家塆9个村民组。

望城村：辖朱家山、望城、龙塘、分水关、谭家湾、建设6个村民组。

后陇村：辖大塆、代家塆、老木冲、煤洞塆、桥边、毛坡、上寨、磨石沟8个村民组。

新田村：辖上寨、下寨、新春、中坝、下坝、大山脚、新田7个村民组。

竹花村：辖塆子、塝上、济沟、撒鸡堡、场口、街上、寨上、沙坝8个村民组。

杉林村：辖碾子沟、杉林、寨上、小农场、桥上5个村民组。

团山村：辖岩上、枣儿树、团山、碾房、高坡、煤洞坡、上寨、凉水井、中寨、下寨10个村民组。

纸房村：辖山堡、中坝、农中、磨刀石、中寨、燕山、龙井、大石板8个村民组。

清坪村：辖大寨、堰塘、小山、坪上、水明、兰家寨、宽丘、马家槽8个村民组。

和平村：辖漆树坪、大土、沙坡、塝上、湾子、下寨、贵子庆7个村民组。

堰坪村：辖坝子边、岩边、中寨、小庆、大堰、堰塘、鱼田、长冲8个村民组。

黄沙村：辖关家坝、田坎、上寨、塘子上、邱家院、垭口、武北门7个村民组。

新沙村：辖漆树湾、下环山、上寨、下寨、沙岗、下坝6个村民组。

柏茂村：辖岩脚、瓢儿箐、大坡、油洞、大槽、柏香湾6个村民组。

上坝村：辖大水井、田坝、下石坎、院子、大元5个村民组。

居民委员会：新街居民委员会。

全镇总户数9226户，人口31937人（其中非农业人口1489人），人口密度277人/平方千米。耕地面积33184亩（其中田10032亩、土23152亩），农业人口人均1.1亩。农民人均年纯收入5868元。

境内主产水稻、玉米、小麦、马铃薯、大豆、油菜、花生、辣椒、烤烟等。已建成团山10万羽肉鸡养殖小区，新田1000亩生姜种植基地，腰寨村300亩艳红桃基地示范园区，鸡场、桐梓、三合等16个村8000亩优质烟区，和平村200头肉牛养殖基地，杉林村山鸡养殖场等。粮食总产10903吨、油菜籽1326吨、烤烟764吨、蔬菜21218吨；肉类总产1633吨、禽蛋238吨、水产品70吨。森林面积66186亩，森林覆盖率38.5%。境内河流有九庄河、雨淋河以及客水乌江。建有小（二）型以上水库4座，总库容160.4万立方米，设计灌溉面积4020万亩；有山塘72口、水厂1座；共建有“三小”水池580口，总容积32122立方米。已探明地下矿藏有煤、硫铁矿、硅石、石灰石等，其中硫铁矿储量0.3亿吨，铁品位超过20%。

境内有小学13所、中学1所、公办幼儿园1所；镇卫生院1所，病床30张；卫生所25个。企业有砂石厂、砖厂、酒厂、汽车修理厂，粮油、木材加工厂等。

境内有4条县乡公路沟通各村公路支线；高低压电线形成电网，村村有动力线，户户有照明电；新建移动基站7座。

主要旅游景点有“多缤洞”“龙滩洞”“武北门”遗址、蜂岩寺、祖师观红军烈士陵园等。集市九庄街，星期六赶集。土特产有贡米、油炸麻花。

第四节　小寨坝镇

小寨坝镇位于县境东部，地理坐标北纬27° 07′ ~27° 18′，东经106° 37′ ~106° 48′，东与开阳县金中镇为邻，南与永靖镇、西山乡接壤，西与鹿窝乡、流长乡相连，北与养龙司乡、温泉镇以及遵义县乌江镇毗邻。东西长16.7千米，南北宽13.7千米，全镇总面积138.08平方千米。海拔760~1690米；年平均温度14.6℃，无霜期275天，平均降雨量1101.6毫米。黔渝铁路、兰海高速（贵遵段）、210国道横贯南北；县道、乡村公路纵横交错。有高等级公路进出口1个，火车站2个；建有移动和联通基站，通信网络覆盖全镇。

2010年，镇政府驻地黑神庙，离县城11千米。辖20个村、166个村民组、2个居委会。

小寨坝村：辖小寨坝、小寨沟、梅小山、上坝田、杉树坪、石碑、洗马坳、赖头山8个村民组。

亲戚寨村：辖龙井坪、四角寨、关田坝、亲二、亲三、长五间、芭蕉冲、猫坡、水沟、黄木沟、山垭11个村民组。

排杉村：辖交椅山、下甫、街一、街二、大屋基、大坡嘴、杨林、湾子、龙井沟、瓦厂10个村民组。

石桥村：辖石桥、荷包寨、荷包场、田湾、吴二寨、兰家箐、仲家坪、廖九寨、黄家沟、毛栗湾10个村民组。

高家坝村：辖高家坝、桶井坝、青枫林、洞口山、余家坪、康达、丰岩7个村民组。

上寨村：辖新村、林沟、上寨、核桃沟、后垄、干沟、五老湾7个村民小组。

茅草寨村：辖蒲小山、小沟子、大路坪、黄家坡、机房、半坡、堡子、杜家寨8个村民组。

中心村：辖堰塘沟、黄连沟、填方3个村民组。

红岩村：辖车头山、上红岩、下红岩、老杆山、山背后、红岗、上二屯、下二屯8个村民组。

大寨村：辖上寨、中寨、下寨、沙田、麒麟、长冲沟6个村民组。

潮水村：辖街一、街二、街三、街四、小桥、石盆、蔡家寨、何家坝、水流洞9个村民组。

关岭村：辖尹家坡、小岭岗、大沟、腊月坝、跑马路、单山坡6个村民组。

大湾村：辖龙井沟、跌马坎、上坝、桐子林4个村民组。

前进村：辖沙子溪、魏家寨、院墙、方家寨4个村民组。

王家坪村：辖仙佛寺、石灰窑、高家林、王家坪、赶场坪、大水井、雷打树、下坡土、坡头上9个村民组。

瓮沙村：辖上寨、河坎、中寨、湾子、魏家寨、下寨、沈家寨、牛耳坡8个村民组。

南中村：辖落脚坝、中坝、老房子、乌米沟、李家沟、潘家寨、水浸沟、狗脚塆一组、狗脚塆二组、白家山、上沟、下沟、石坟塆、涨水麻窝14个村民组。

田兴村：辖大坪一、大坪二、岩脚、曹田、石家沟、上沟、中沟、下沟一、下沟二、对门寨、杨家塆、坪上、张家塆、刘家塆、艾子坪、鸽子岩16个村民组。

南桥村：辖红中坪、牛耳坪、楠木桥、石笋沟、厂头、六八、新厂、桐梓湾8个村民组。

盘脚营村：辖新桥、干二、上街、下街、猫洞、三合土、潮水坝、大麻窝、石堡林、下大土10个村民组。

居民委员会：黑神庙居民委员会、磷兴园居民委员会。

全镇总户数12147户，总人口34665人（其中非农业人口5052人），人口密度251人/平方千米。耕地面积24720亩，农业人口人均0.5亩。农民人均年纯收入5265元。

辖区粮食作物以水稻、玉米、薯类为主，主要经济作物有烤烟、油菜籽等，畜牧业以养殖猪、鸡为主。粮食总产11163吨、油菜籽1180吨、烤烟138吨、蔬菜20653吨；肉类总产1557吨、禽蛋152吨、水产品40吨。境内林木属亚热带常绿落叶、阔叶混交林区。现有植被均属次生植物，森林面积7085公顷，森林覆盖率37.7%。有息烽河及其支流头道河、三田河3条雨淋型河流。建有小（二）型水库1座、小（一）型水库1座、山塘29口，总容量51万立方米。小寨坝引水工程建成后，解决全镇工业用水及人畜饮水。矿产资源主要有煤、硫铁矿、褐铁矿、硅矿等。

学校有初级中学1所、完小6所、教学点7个。医疗机构有镇卫生院，病床30张；7个村卫生室。镇卫生院能进行肝、胆、脾、胃、肾等中下腹部手术和泌尿外科手术。

辖区驻有贵州开磷（集团）磷煤化工基地（贵阳中化开磷化肥有限公司、开磷集团息烽磷业有限公司、息烽开磷合成氨公司、开磷磷石膏综合利用有限公司、开磷物业管理有限公司等）、林东矿务局南山煤矿等大中型国有企业，为西南地区最大的磷煤化工坑口加工基地。另有康裕来磷肥厂、黔豫纸厂、楠木桥煤厂等10余家非公有制企业。

土特产有红岩葡萄。集镇黑神庙，星期五赶集。

第五节 养龙司乡

养龙司乡位于县境东北部，地理坐标北纬27° 11′ 27″ ～27° 19′ 25″ ，东经106° 40′ 20″ ～106° 51′ 45″ ，东与温泉镇相连，南与小寨坝镇接壤，西与金沙县相望，北抵乌江，中被遵义县养龙站乡隔断。辖区东西长18千米，南北宽15千米，总面积96.26平方千米。海拔670～1240米，大部分区域处于780～920米之间。属亚热带湿润气候，年均气温15℃，年降水量1000～1040毫米，日照时数1411.9小时，无霜期250～290天。

2010年，乡政府驻养龙司新街，距县城30千米。辖17个村、162个村民组、1个居委会。

养龙司村：辖新街、场坝、场坡、水井坡、染房、院子、木莲坝、场口、后街、小水坪、赵家林、王岭沟、下坝、司栗坡、辽脚塆、大塆、十字路、上寨、下寨、油房共20个村民组。

幸福村：辖钟家院、中斗坡、吏目田、皮家湾、对门寨、新房子、纸槽沟、紫江田、下沟、半坡、大林、锡厂、小干溪、牛头山、王家寨15个村民组。

灯塔村：辖姜家塆、黄家塆、莲花寺、潘家寨、大岩、后寨、老街、院子、塆子、衙门、大石板11个村民组。

高坡村：辖院子、下油房、姜家湾、桃子坪、硐上、杨家山6个村民组。

堡子村：辖龙坑、堡子、高坎子、出行坡、懒家湾、院子6个村民组。

坪山村：辖麻林、紫江寨、郁家坡、上坪山、湾子、中坪山、下坪山7个村民组。

坝上村：辖茶园沟、柏果寨、田后坎、高坎子、青龙山、出口、上寨、下寨、大坪、中寨、兰垭、小水、毛栗岗、大桥14个村民组。

江土村：辖大上、大下、下一、下二、田坝、楠木坪、街上、三尖角、老院坝9个村民组。

光华村：辖旧寨、旧南、麻窝、沙坡、金土、关田、阿塘寨7个村民组。

新桥村：辖新寨、老岗寨、叶上、叶下、王上、王下、甘家寨7个村民组。

龙门村：辖云上、云下、龙上、龙下、水井湾、长门、长干7个村民组。

大山村：辖麻窝、梨树坪、大山、白岩沟、大土、马家沟共6个村民组。

蚂蟥村：辖周家堰、闵家湾、煤硐寺、陈家山、蚂一、蚂二、蚂三、油榨坪、水井湾9个村民组。

茅坡村：辖郑家林、苏家坪、街上、干水井、阳江、后坝、沙坡、芭蕉沟、冉家寨、上坪所、下坪所11个村民组。

龙塘村：辖马家井、马坡、黄私井、龙塘、下一、下二6个村民组。

高硐村：辖水沟、元山、陈家寨、下寨、团山、大沟、田坝、何家寨、对门、竹林、湾子11个村民组。

荆江村：辖湾子、水井坎、下坪坝、上坪坝、马排、龙井、陈家寨、石革闸、高塆、徐家寨10个村民组。

居民委员会：养龙司居民委员会。

全乡总户数6481户，24881人（其中非农业人口1506人）。人口密度244人/平方千米。耕地面积20017亩，农业人口人均0.97亩。农民年人均纯收入4858元。

主要农作物有水稻、玉米、小麦、蔬菜、油菜、烤烟等。畜牧业以养殖肉兔、肉牛为主，个别农户养殖野猪。粮食总产量8668吨、油菜籽1086吨、烤烟232吨、蔬菜28725吨；肉类总产量1585吨、禽蛋89吨、水产品290吨。森林覆盖率39.5%。有川黔铁路、贵遵高等级公路和210国道及温泉的旅游公路从境内穿过，县道方养公路、养紫公路、养温公路和33条村级公路（总长57.64千米）形成网络，全乡17个村170个村（居）民小组皆通公路，通车里程123千米。有火车站1个、水上运输码头3个。

全乡有3座小（二）型水库，蓄水量51.5万立方米；提灌工程38处，其中小（二）型8处、小（三）型30处，总灌溉面积6300亩。矿产资源主要有煤、铝矾土、硫铁矿。

乡内有中学1所、小学6所、教学点3个。医疗机构有卫生院1个，病床20张；17个村卫生室。有敬老院1个、民办幼儿园1个。

厂矿企业：息烽利发煤矿、息烽安黔煤矿、息烽农发磷肥厂、息烽温泉普钙厂、息烽龙泉磷肥厂硫酸分厂、息烽通州化肥厂、养龙司铸造厂。

旅游资源有乡西北以乌江河谷景点为主的观光旅游和乡东南以半边天农家乐为主的休闲旅游。集市养龙司新街，星期日赶集。

第六节 流长乡

流长乡位于县境西北部，地理坐标北纬27° 13′ ，东经106° 38′ 。东与养龙司乡、小寨坝镇以息烽河为界，南与小寨坝镇、鹿窝乡接壤，西以鹿窝河为界与鹿窝乡相隔，北隔乌江库区与金沙县相望。总面积105.8平方千米，海拔760～1304米。年平均气温15℃，降雨量1000～1300毫米，无霜期290天左右。

2010年，乡政府驻流长街上，距县城33千米。辖15个村、131个村民组。

流长村：辖街一上、街一下、街二上、街二下、梁家寨、田坝、马家寨、毛坡8个村民组。

大水井村：辖大水井、邓家寨、中坪、李家沟、翁仲、大巫山、大坪上、袁家寨8个村民组。

长涌村：辖路头坝、中寨、磨刀石、长冲沟、核桃坪、青㭎林、王化坪、黑硐、立新、田坝10个村民组。

李安寨村：辖路口、李安寨、水井湾、麻窝、浪坝槽、大湾、沟头、堰沟、马洪棚、卧龙溪10个村民组。

茶园村：辖青㭎坡、垮子、茶园寺、关口坡、三万塘、下茶园、对门寨、毛栗槽8个村民组。

宋家寨村：辖旧寨湾、马老山、宋家寨、客户寨、阳山沟、水槽上、大湾、梁家湾、蜂子岩9个村民组。

龙泉村：辖麻窝、大湾、田坝、对门坡、龙井、麻坪、下寨、三脚山、大槽、岩门10个村民组。

龙塘村：辖上龙塘、下龙塘、新寨、龙井沟、小甘溪5个村民组。

甘溪村：辖甘一、甘二、黄一、黄二、杜上、杜下、袁家陇、草坝8个村民组。

大兴村：辖汤家坝、坝子、新寨、大元、瓦房、下一、下二、磨河水、柒湾、徐家寨10个村民组。

前奔村：辖刘家寨、徐家寨、总寨、底下坝、林头、慢阳坡、大麻窝、中心、大林、上寨10个村民组。

四坪村：辖大一、大二、麻窝、大坪上、青㭎坡、陈家寨、竹林、古坟坝、李山坡、周四10个村民组。

营中村：辖上寨、下寨、对门寨、李家湾、堰坎5个村民组。

新中村：辖新场、大元、周家坝、黄泥坡、黄家沟、卢家寨、长干子、铁香寨、彭兜寨、南八、南九11个村民组。

水尾村：辖磨刀石、湾子、半坡、顺江、大寨、大水井、张家寨、火金山、田坝9个村民组。

全乡总户数6532户，21543人（其中非农业人口676人），人口密度203人/平方千米。耕地面积24125亩（其中田7258亩、土16867亩），农业人口人均耕地1.12亩。农民人均年纯收入5051元。

农作物以玉米、水稻、小麦、红薯为主，经济作物以油菜、西瓜、烤烟、花生为主。养殖业以猪、牛、鸡、鱼为主。粮食总产量7429吨、油菜籽1508吨、烤烟228吨、蔬菜11665吨；肉类总产1448吨、禽蛋36吨。森林覆盖率55.87%。建有小型水库3座、山塘24口。全乡三面环水，一面靠山，有89千米河段，水域面积1万余亩，网箱养鱼面积200多亩，水产品年产量2600吨。农副产品水路通过乌江出境，陆路通过息烽至流长公路直达县城。

境内有初级中学1所、完全小学5所、教学点1个、民办幼儿园4个；医疗机构有乡卫生院1个，病床15张；村卫生室15个。

旅游资源有红军长征南渡乌江战斗遗址和乌江七峡自然景观。集镇流长街，星期四赶集。

第七节　西山乡

西山乡位于县境中部，地理坐标北纬27°02′～27°06′，东经106°39′～106°43′。东邻永靖镇，南接青山苗族乡，西靠石硐乡、九庄镇、鹿窝乡，北与小寨坝镇毗邻，总面积74.19平方千米。海拔高度平均930米，最高海拔西望山为1590米，最低海拔小鹿窝为730米；年平均温度11℃～15℃，降雨量900～1100毫米，无霜期230～290天，日照1400小时。息烽至九庄，金竹坪至马路岩两条县道纵贯全境。

2010年，乡政府驻地柏香山村新寨组，距县城6千米。辖13个村，107个村民组。

林丰村：辖黄草坝、水岭沟、沙帽河、葫芦水、红岩林、大麻窝、包谷冲7个村民组。

文安村：辖旧一、旧二、中一、中二、大院、大坡、长冲、下坝、上寨、下寨10个村民组。

小堡村：辖山冲、高坎、中心、万兴、黄土坡、水头坝、桐梓坝、大土8个村民组。

猪场村：辖土地堂上组、土地堂中组、土地堂下组、龙堰、纸房沟、猪场、老房子、塆子、山背田9个村民组。

团元山村：辖石头田、东山、新房子、干堰、白坟、瓦房、龙塘沟、中心、滴水岩9个村民组。

田冲村：辖高山冲、马路槽、下坝、书房、下队、上队6个村民组。

新寨沟村：辖上寨、下寨、大土湾、关口、茶园沟5个村民组。

鹿窝村：辖木江山、中心、坪上、老鸦底、关口、蒿芝湾、宋井田、尾鲊、前寨、通树塆10个村民组。

金星村：辖龙井、棉花土、廖家湾、磨盘、中槽、煤幺冲、七堡寨、大槽、金竹坪、大水井、火金山、田坝、上寨、干田14个村民组。

西山村：辖凤池、苦草坪、谷米酒、张家沟、田丰、关田坝6个村民组。

联合村：辖半边山、付家寨、晚霞、杉树坪、烧炭塆5个村民组。

胜利村：辖杨家塆、黄泥田、沙土、柏杨寨、上寨、下寨、金钟、马粪寨8个村民组。

柏香山村：辖上街、下街、新寨、文阁、上大寨、下大寨、坡脚、磨老、青㭎寨、麒麟10个村民组。

全乡总户数6043户，人口19079人（其中非农业人口565人），人口密度238人/平方千米。耕地面积29800亩，农业人口人均0.83亩。农民年人均纯收入5000元。

粮食作物以水稻、玉米、薯类为主，主要经济作物有油菜籽、蔬菜等，畜牧业以养殖猪、鸡为主。粮食总产量6788吨、油菜籽728吨、蔬菜4.1万吨；肉类总产量1049吨、禽蛋73吨、水产品18吨。大面积林地系次生林，森林覆盖率45%。保护较为完好的森林有西望山、柏香山近4000余亩，有珍稀树种10余种100余株。境内有大小河流10余条，总长60.5千米，主要河流有底寨河、新寨沟河、胜利河3条。有2个小水库，蓄水17.6万立方米；120个小水窖、336个小水池，蓄水1500立方米。大型引水渠道有底寨河渠道、黄家大沟、大堰渠道、白岩堰渠道；另有灌溉渠道39条，总长96.3千米，灌溉面积4539亩。主要矿产资源是煤炭。

医疗机构有乡卫生院1所，病床5张；村级卫生室13个。学校有中学1所、小学2所、教学点1个。

2010年冬，在华府路两侧出售规划建房用地1600平方米，启动小集镇建设。

旅游资源有西山八庙人文景观和西山八景自然景观，土特产有西山贡米、虫茶、鸟笼。

第八节　石硐乡

石硐乡位于县境西南部，地理坐标北纬27° 01′ ~27° 05，东经106° 31′ ~106° 39′ 。东与青山苗族乡、永靖镇相邻，西南与修文县小庆乡接壤，北抵九庄镇。全乡总面积120.56平方千米。海拔1000~1450米，平均海拔1250米。多年平均气温14℃~14.5℃。年均降雨量1100~1200毫米，无霜期280天，最长290天。冬半年（10—3月）寒冷且凝冻较大，夏半年（4—9月）气候温凉。

2010年，乡政府驻石硐街上，距县城西南21千米。辖18个村、205个村民组。

光明村：辖高塝田、詹家塆、王家塆、康家塆、贵山、大坪、后山、湾子、龙洞沟、大荒土10个村民组。

木杉村：辖上街、中街、下街、上元坡、中元坡、下元坡、夏家塆、汪冲一、汪冲二、坡头上、枫香林、店子上、营山、大湾、高坎子15个村民组。

石硐村：辖大水塘上组、大水塘下组、狮子口上组、狮子口下组、桃子坪上组、袁家寨上组、袁家寨下组、水打凹、大路槽、龙家坡、桃子坪下组、沙坡、胡家田、鲊一、鲊二、鲊三、上雨鲊、大冲上组、大冲下组、安一、安二、高田坎、安多寨、马路岩、上沙槽、下沙槽、街一、街二、街四、街上三组、街下三组31个村民组。

水头村：辖下一、下二、下三、塔山、新杨、李家湾、小寨、黄泥堡、大坡、刘家塆、颜家塆、中坝12个村民组。

高峰村：一组、二组、三组、四组、沙坡、塆子、瓦厂、沟一、沟二9个村民组。

前丰村：辖旧衙坝一组、旧衙坝二组、上坝河、对门坡、上寨、下寨6个村民组。

龙坪村：辖上一、上二、中一、中二、下三、龙一、龙二、龙三、龙四、大苗寨、大麻窝11个村民组。

何家硐村：辖何家硐、关井、高坡、街上、坝子边、上寨、高山、罗家寨8个村民组。

玉龙村：辖小冲沟、大苗寨、马路丫口、白泥田、茨竹孔、敖五、敖六、严七、严八9个村民组。

红星村：辖半坡、红旗、田家埔、大岩方、红一、红二、高山、红子茨林8个村民组。

中坝村：辖汪冲、下坝、马家箐、梯子田、上坝、大冲、水井湾、营盘8个村民组。

大洪村：辖瓦房寨、下白岩、新寨、木弄、上排坡、下排坡、韦家寨、茨元门、林场、上白岩10个村民组。

高寨村：辖高寨、罗家坝、上街、中街、下街、大冲湾、毛栗林、山背后、山脚、筲箕塆、郑家冲11个村民组。

新寨村：辖李家山、水长冲二组、水长冲一组、周家湾、大块田、沟头、田坝、莫家湾、宋家寨、蔡家寨、汪家寨、姨妈寨一组、姨妈寨二组、王家寨、大洼子15个村民组。

难冲桥村：辖托幺寨、陈家湾、柏果树、桥边、胡家湾、新庄、大土、革家坝、小冲、陇共坡、麻窝、陇上、彭家寨、肖家湾、夏家湾、马路冲16个村民组。

泉湖村：辖革老冲、下坝二组、下坝一组、中坝一组、中坝二组、上坝、下坝三组、杨桂田、塆子、红房子10个村民组。

猫场村：辖松林、大树子、老街、杉棠树、王大山、小山边、李家坝、水流路、紫江山9个村民组。

高青村：辖胡家寨、张家寨、申家湾、吴家寨、猫洞、凉水井、郑家林7个村民组。

全乡总户数7914户26607人（其中非农业人口742人）。人口密度220人/平方千米。全乡耕地面积64367亩，其中田9735亩，旱地54632亩，农业人口人均2.49亩。农民人均年纯收入5086元。

石硐乡是典型的旱农作物乡。粮食作物以玉米、薯类、小麦为主，主要经济作物有烤烟、生姜、香葱、大蒜、黄花菜等，畜牧业以养殖猪、鸡为主，有蛋鸡、肉鸡、肉牛、肉兔养殖小区4个。粮食总产13655吨、油菜籽508吨、烤烟847吨、蔬菜10869吨；肉类总产1692吨、禽蛋89吨。森林覆盖率38%。有小（二）型水库7座、山塘18口；矿产资源有煤矿、硫铁矿、钾矿等，以煤储藏最丰。乡内有石硐至息烽、石硐至九庄镇、石硐至青山乡等县乡硬化公路，有石硐至修文县久长、大石、六桶等出境公路，到省城贵阳仅2小时车程。已建成35千伏变电站1个，建立移动、联通基站6个。企业有年产3万吨的马家箐、大兴田、石硐、小红寨4家煤矿，2家打砂厂和1家砖厂。有中学1所、小学6所、教学点4个。有乡卫生院1个，病床15张，18个村卫生室。

土特产：酒、核桃等。石硐酒有“小茅台”之称。集镇石硐街，星期五赶集。

第九节　鹿窝乡

鹿窝乡位于县境西北部，地理坐标北纬27° 10′，东经106° 35′，东与小寨坝镇、西山乡交界，南与九庄镇毗邻，西与金沙县隔河相望，北与流长乡接壤。总面积97.86平方千米。海拔762～1510米。境内属亚热带湿润季风气候，乡所在地年平均气温17.8℃，月均气温最高为7月26.1℃，最低为1月

4.6℃。无霜期280天以上。年日照1000～1100小时。年平均降水量950毫米。

鹿窝乡是典型的农业乡，无工业企业，无探明的矿产资源。森林植被丰富为其最大优势。

2010年，乡政府驻鹿窝街上，距县城59千米。辖13个村、126个村民组。

鹿龙村：辖老街、新街、李家窑、王家仓、场背后、孙家坡、邓阳寨、后山上、后山下、红土10个村民组。

老窝村：辖老窝寨、大屋基、毛家屯、水沟、马场坝、马安桥、沟头7个村民组。

马坉村：辖水浇莲、后河、余家湾、桐子林、马坉、纸厂沟、熊家庄、罗家火焰、小岭岗、周家塆、椅子山11个村民组。

胡广村：辖高寨、鱼陇、青树子、毛盖山、九峰山、黄土堡、龙崩塘、胡广寨8个村民组。

新民村：辖梯子岩、大土湾、黄马田上、黄马田下、明田、老树槽、云上坡、马洪棚、杉堂树、石关口、山林沟、新寨、岭岗、付家寨、沙坝、干田湾16个村民组。

三友村：辖桃子弯、黄家寨、何家寨、水头、湾田、高寨、垭口、晏家寨、麻窝田、高木桥10个村民组。

瓮舍村：辖梁子上、马鞍桥、瓦房、柿花树、麻窝、仓上、下河坝、桐梓堡、黄家湾、牟家坡10个村民组。

大石头村：辖填筑坪、下安、小箐口、大石头、新龙湾、阳雀坉、旧堰7个村民组。

西安村：辖河坝、毛栗坝、安二、安一、窑上、叶家沟、熊家庄7个村民组。

华溪村：辖大湾、高坡、龙洞沟、大堰田、潘家寨、平桥、仓上、大寨、彭家林9个村民组。

田坝村：辖麻窝、岩上、百家寨、四岭岗、大元、大坡、下寨、格塝8个村民组。

合箭村：辖小竹苗、磨盘山、箐林、箭杆林、回龙湾、黄泥井、毛家堰7个村民组。

杨寨村：辖上寨、湾子、下寨、石墙院、长连房子、马头山、杨柳湾、桶井、烧炭坡、下坡树、瓮桶河、山坪、新房子、杨柳井、小岩口、罗家山16个村民组。

全乡总户数4612户，16471人（其中非农业人口370人）。人口密度168人/平方千米。耕地面积17261亩（其中田7454亩、土9807亩），农业人口人均耕地1.05亩。农民人均年纯收入4584元。

农作物以水稻、玉米、小麦、大豆、红薯为主，经济作物以油菜、大葱、烤烟、西瓜、生姜、花生、草莓为主。养殖业以猪、牛、鸡为主。粮食总产6959吨、油菜籽822吨、烤烟63吨、蔬菜16018吨；肉类总产1082吨、禽蛋134吨、水产品390吨。森林覆盖率48.7%，有鹿窝河、瓮桶河、雨淋河3条河流。乡内建有县道4条、小型水库1座、山塘33口。

乡内有中学1所、乡中心小学1所、片区中心学校1所、村级小学4所、教学点5个。有乡卫生院1个，病床10张；村卫生室13个。集市鹿窝街，星期二赶集。

境内森林植被丰富。老窝寨地处乌江库区上游回水地段，河面宽阔，河水清澈，两岸植被茂密，奇山异石，峰峦叠嶂，景致迷人。著名景区有号称“小三峡”的乌江峡，峡内有“姊妹峰”等著名景点。

第十节　青山苗族乡

青山苗族乡位于县境西南部，地理坐标北纬270° 60′ ～270° 06′ ，东经106° 34′ ～106° 41′ 。

东与西山乡相邻，东南与永靖镇河丰村接壤，南与永靖镇坪上村相望，西南、西与石硐村为邻，西北与九庄乡相连，北与西山乡相接。总面积49.47平方千米。海拔1140～1347米；平均气温13.5℃，年平均降水量1122.9毫米，无霜期292天，年平均日照1182.1小时。县道青山公路、息九公路、金马公路、鹿马公路连接县城和周围乡镇，12条乡村公路进村，57个村民组有进组公路。全乡公路里程60千米。

2010年，乡政府驻青山村青山组，距县城19.5千米。辖5个村，57个村民组。

青山村：辖萝桂坝、青山、塘坎、大凹、河沟、下一、下二、尖山、中一、中二、烂箐、水淹槽12个村民小组。

大林村：辖下瓜种、上瓜种、杨柳冲、高田坎、黄家湾、土地垭、大林口、中果铺、林场、大土、马头山、打铁冲、革老冲、半坡、王依槽、大林、三口洞17个村民小组。

马路岩村：辖一组、二组、三组、四组4个村民小组。

绿化村：辖上河沟、下河沟、小桥河、沙沟、林场、后寨、大麻窝、沙塆、下塆、沙坡、中寨、五组、塆寨、岩脚寨14个村民小组。

冗坝村：辖煤洞、冗一、冗二、冗三、百花井、构一、构二、构三、马洞坡、后槽10个村民小组。

全乡总户数2115户，人口7250人（其中非农业人口254人）；少数民族2059人，占总人口的29.2%。

全乡耕地面积11969亩，其中田1545亩，土10424亩。人均耕地面积1.68亩。粮食作物以玉米、水稻、大豆、马铃薯为主，主要经济作物有油菜籽、烤烟、蔬菜等，畜牧业以肉猪、肉牛、肉羊、奶牛、肉鸡等为主。粮食总产4755吨、油菜籽98吨、烤烟125吨、蔬菜10943吨；肉类总产511吨、禽蛋36吨、牛奶620吨。农民年人均纯收入4493元。森林覆盖率50.31%，林木绿化率50.75%，境内植物种类繁多，有较为珍贵的兰花、红豆杉等，挂牌管理的古树、大树、珍稀树12棵。境内有息烽河与小桥河，建有小桥河水库，蓄水381万立方米，主要供西山、小寨坝两乡镇人畜饮水和工业用水；有山塘12口，蓄水380万立方米。地下矿藏有主要有煤、铀、硫铁矿、褐铁矿、汞矿5种。

乡内有初级中学1所、小学1所、幼儿园2所。医疗机构有乡卫生院1个，病床12张；村卫生室5个；敬老院1所。

集镇面积约1平方千米，房屋由1991年的几栋发展到2010年的108栋，其中住户81栋。

苗族擅长芦笙舞、板凳舞、苗族刺绣等。每年举办的文化节有苗族“二月十五跳厂节”“四月八”等，其中“四月八”为每年定期举办的苗族盛大活动。

旅游资源：青山湖、张氏祠堂（建于1877年，2007年重建后更名为张氏书苑）。

名优特色农产品：苗家腊猪肉、苗家腊狗肉、苗家糯米酒、苗家柴灰豆腐。

第二篇　环境资源

第一章　自然环境

县内地势起伏，沟谷纵横，东南西三面山脉绵延，地势较高，自南向北呈梯状下降。大部分地区海拔1000～1200米。境内岩溶地貌分布广泛，土壤类型复杂多样，气候温和，春暖秋爽，四季有春迟、夏短、秋早、冬长特点。境内河流属长江流域乌江水系，依县南高北低地势特点，呈羽状分布。降水趋势具有东南多、西北少的特征。

第一节　地质地貌

息烽县地处黔中山原丘陵中部，地势南高北低，一般海拔1000～1200米，大部分为低中丘陵地，碳酸岩分布广，喀斯特发育，峰丛、洼地、溶丘、溶洞、暗河、漏斗甚多，北部边缘受乌江及支流侵蚀切割，沟谷纵横。最高点南望山南极顶，海拔1749.6米；最低点乌江出境处大塘口，海拔609米。

一、地质

（一）地层

县境内地层分布为前震旦系、震旦系、寒武系、石炭系、二叠系、三叠系、侏罗系、第四系8个系，地台上层基底以上的地层最大总厚度5768米。分布岩石除侏罗系、第四系及三叠系二桥组为非碳酸盐岩外，其他各层均有碳酸盐岩分布。岩溶地区分布的主要有灰岩、泥灰岩、白云灰岩、白云岩、泥质白云岩；非岩溶地区分布的有紫色页岩、紫色沙页岩、页岩、沙页岩和砂岩。

前震旦系分布板溪群清水江组，面积0.47平方千米，占全县总面积的0.04%。分布在县境东北部温泉镇小河沟谷底，为砂岩、粉砂岩及黏土岩，系陆源海相碎屑岩沉积，沉积厚度5000米以上。

震旦系分布在县境东北部温泉镇小河沟、石头田一带，面积2.15平方千米，占全县总面积的0.2%，厚度609～688米。

寒武系主要分布在县境东部与遵义、开阳两县相邻边境一带，石硐乡东南部、何家硐西北部、养龙司乡茅坡东北部亦有分布，分布面积83.1平方千米，占全县总面积的8.1%。

石炭系县内有大塘组分布，为石灰岩夹泥质灰岩、白云岩，含硅质岩，厚10～30米。主要分布在温泉镇安江、小寨坝镇南极、永靖镇阳朗、梨安一带，养龙司乡茅坡东北部及石硐乡何家硐西北部亦有分布。面积约3.45平方千米，占全县总面积的0.33%。

二叠系分布在温泉镇安江、小寨坝镇南极、永靖镇阳朗、梨安、西山乡底寨、青山苗族乡、石硐乡何家硐、九庄镇等，沿乌江河谷的竹花、新场、新杨等地亦有分布，面积261.61平方千米，占全县总面积的25.23%，总厚度344～625米。

三叠系县内面积602.22平方千米，占总面积的58.09%，总厚度1218～1517米。是形成岩溶地貌的主要地层。

侏罗系主要分布在永靖镇的团元山，西山乡的西望山、小鹿窝一带，面积83.21平方千米，占总面积的8.03%，总厚度1002米。

第四系县内为松散堆积，连续性差，呈分散的小型斑块分布，面积约0.52平方千米，占总面积的0.05%，主要分布于山坡、沟谷、洼地及溶洞中。堆积类型有冲积、洪积、淤积、冰积、残积、坡积、化学堆积等。

（二）地质

县内地质构造主要为褶皱和断裂。褶皱主要为两组相互平行的北北东向复式褶皱。西部为流长至小箐复向斜，至西南向修文、清镇两县展延；东部为兴隆场至铁厂复背斜，也向修文、清镇两县展延。县内主要断裂构造是新华夏式构造体系的安靖至杨家寨断层，该断裂是县内流长至小箐复向斜与兴隆场至铁厂复向斜的分界线。南延至清镇卫城，中部纵贯息烽全境，在平面上呈波状弯曲，长约90千米，为压性枢纽断层。

二、地貌

（一）地貌类型

境内地貌属云贵高原梯状东斜坡的三级台阶，位于苗岭山脉北翼。以中低山为主，溶蚀地貌、剥蚀地貌、堆积地貌及构造地貌构成山地、丘陵和盆地组成的山原地貌。山地以中中山及低中山类型为主。主要分布在县境东部南望山、中部西望山一带，海拔1200米以上，相对高差200～300米，面积270.12平方千米，占全县土地总面积的26.06%。丘陵地貌形态有峰丛、溶洼、槽谷、沟谷、坡立谷及缓丘等。主要分布于县境南部和北部乌江沿岸，面积421.82平方千米，占全县总面积的40.68%。南部海拔1200～1350米，相对高差100～300米；乌江沿岸海拔800～1000米，相对高差100～200米。盆地分布在西山乡底寨、永靖镇阳朗、养龙司乡养龙司、九庄镇九庄等地区，地势平缓，相对高差小。海拔800～1100米，面积344.79平方千米，占全县土地总面积的33.26%。

（二）地貌分布

中中山沟谷区 分布在县境东部及东南部永靖镇的梨安、安马、坪上、新萝、上洪马、下洪马、联丰、河坎、雨洒、老厂10个村，石硐乡的泉湖、难冲桥；小寨坝镇的南中、田兴、南桥；温泉镇的兴隆，共16个村，面积167.41平方千米，占全县总面积的16.15%。平均海拔1300余米，相对高差200～300米。山大坡陡，溶丘、洼地、槽谷、坝子相互交替；草地、灌木林地、荒坡面积大，耕地少。

低中山丘陵区 分布在县境西南部石硐乡的猫场、高寨、高青、新寨、前锋、高峰、龙坪、光明、木杉、水头、石硐、红星、玉龙、何家硐、中坝、大洪；青山苗族乡的大林、青山、绿化、冗坝、马路岩，共21个村，面积146.54平方千米，占全县总面积的14.13%，海拔1200～1350米，相对高差50～200米。区内受河流切割不深，地势起伏不大，山间谷地、台地、洼地、丘堡面积大，山与山之间有较宽的槽坝。溶洞、漏斗、落水洞较多。

低中山盆坝区 分布在县境东南部永靖镇的红旗、永红、南门、龙爪、河丰、猫洞、老街、立碑、后坝、阳朗、硬寨、下阳朗、管田、马当田；西山乡的胜利、联合、鹿窝；小寨坝镇的盘脚营、小寨坝、上寨、中心、高家坝、排杉、石桥、亲戚寨、茅草寨、甘溪、瓮沙、王家坪、关岭、大湾、前进、大寨、潮水；养龙司乡的幸福、灯塔、高坡、坝上、养龙司、堡子、坪山；西山乡的团元山、林丰、金星、田冲、猪场、文安、小堡、柏香山；九庄镇的三合、同心、西门、新街、鸡场、桐梓、天鹅、腰寨、青堰、后陇、望城、大槽、鲁俐衙；温泉镇的温泉、尹庵、赶子、天台，共66个村。面积344.79平方千米，占全县总面积的33.26%。海拔800～1100米。区内除小寨坝镇王家坪片区因息烽河切割较深，形成耕地高、水位低地势特点外，其余地区地势平坦、坝子多、水源好、气候温和。

中中山峡谷区 分布在县境西部的整个西山山脉，包括鹿窝乡的鹿窝、田坝、老窝、三友、胡广、大石头、华溪、马纯、西安、合箐；西山乡的西山、新寨沟；小寨坝镇的红岩、龙塘，九庄镇的团山、纸房，共16个村，面积102.71平方千米，占全县总面积的9.91%，海拔1200～1500米，相对高差200～300米。以西山顶为主峰，山脉呈放射状向四周延伸，山与山之间峡谷深切，山上林木繁茂。是县内主要林区。

低中山丘陵河谷区 分布在县境北部乌江沿岸九庄镇的杉林、竹花、清坪、堰坪、和平、新沙、黄沙、新田、柏茂、上坝村、新民、杨寨、瓮舍，流长乡的流长、大水井、茶园、大兴、前奔、龙泉、长涌、宋家寨、李安寨、新中、水尾、四坪、营中，养龙司乡的大山、茅坡、高硐、荆江、龙塘、蚂蟥、江土、龙门、新桥、光华，温泉镇的大尖山、三交等村，面积275.28平方千米，占全县总面积的26.55%。海拔800～1000米，相对高差100～200米。区内多圆形山头和鱼背状山脊，谷地、洼地、山地、丘陵交错分布；岩溶地貌发育较全，漏斗、溶洞多，地表水易从溶洞流入乌江，沿江多峭壁峡谷，水低土高。是县内主要干旱地区。

（三）山脉·溶洞

县境山脉属苗岭山脉群北翼，东部及北部山岭大致呈北东走向，南部山岭呈东西走向，中部山群脉络不明显，走向基本与地质褶构线相一致。坡度一般20～50度，少数山坡大于50度。主要山脉有南望山，又名南山，距县城东5千米，总面积80平方千米，主峰南极顶，海拔1749.6米，为县内第一高峰。西望山，又名西山，距县城西15千米，总面积94平方千米，主峰团山岩，海拔1616.2米。其次，境东南有狼鸡岭，海拔1629米；龚家大岭，海拔1516米。南有盐井坡，海拔1545.7米；大金山，海拔1504米。西南有姨妈山，海拔1445.5米。西有漆山坡，海拔1444.1米。

由于境内碳酸盐类岩层经长期风化侵蚀，钙质释放与流失严重，形成溶洞较多，已探明43个，其中干洞16个，出水、潮湿洞27个；能容100～500人者28个，500～5000人者13个，5000人以上者2个。较著名的溶洞有玄天洞、玄天新洞、多缤洞、象鼻洞、箱子洞、九岭岗花洞等。

第二节 土 壤

县内土壤类型复杂多样，主要有黄壤、黄棕壤、石灰土、紫色土、潮土、水稻土，比例分别为20.59%、5.2%、55.7%、7.5%、0.01%、11%。耕地质量偏低，土壤普查统计，缺氮、磷、钾的耕地分别有562.9公顷、3319.1公顷、1216.2公顷，分别占耕地面积的1.7%、10.1%、3.7%；磷、钾均缺的耕地0.5公顷，占5.5%；缺有机质的耕地2.1公顷，占5.8%；共计缺素型耕地面积8789.7公顷，占26.8%。

黄壤分布在县境内各地，主要出现在海拔800～1400米地区。土层一般100厘米以上，pH值为4.5～6.5。黄棕壤出现在海拔1400米以上地区，主要分布于永靖镇、小寨坝镇、西山乡等，pH值为4～6.5。石灰土是县内主要岩成土，凡钙质基岩分布的乡镇均有，分布广，面积大，pH值为6.5～8。紫色土主要分布在鹿窝乡、西山乡、九庄镇、小寨坝镇、永靖镇、温泉镇等地海拔700～1500米地区，呈条状带分布，pH值为7.4～7.9。潮土由各种不同母质经河流或山洪冲击形成，主要分布在小寨坝镇王家坪、鹿窝乡等河流两岸，仅100余亩，pH值为4.7～7。水稻土主要分布在县内各乡镇条件较好的坝子、盆地、沿河两岸、沟谷、槽谷洼地、缓坡等地段上，海拔800～1400米地区较集中，pH值趋于中性。

县内第一次土壤普查于1958年实施，按习惯分类法，将耕地分为10土类，16个土组，22个土种，96个泥色。1983年，进行第二次土壤普查，按土壤发生学观点分类，共6个土类，14个亚类，46个土属，256个土种。

息烽县土壤分类统计表

表2-1-1

土壤名称	亚类（个）	土壤（个）	土种（个）			面积（亩）	占总面积比例（%）
			自然土	耕作土	小计		
黄壤	2	7	22	17	39	286704	20.56
黄棕壤	2	11	42	27	69	72981	5.24
石灰土	3	6	19	25	44	776717	55.72
紫色土	3	8	27	22	49	103998	7.46
潮土	1	1	—	2	2	100	0.01
水稻土	3	13	—	53	53	153526	11.01
合计	14	46	110	146	256	1394026	100

县内土壤pH值：酸性占40.67%、中性占40.61%、碱性占18.72%。

土壤质地比例：泥质面积占69.6%、黏质占26.07%、沙质占3.02%、砾质砾石占1.31%。

土壤容重：旱作土平均容重1.25克/立方厘米、水稻土平均容重1.16克/立方厘米。

第三节 气 候

一、机构

1991年，县气象站更名为县气象局，下设综合办公室、气象台、人工影响天气办公室、农村综合经济信息服务中心。1995年，建青山、九庄、青坪防雹站；2002年，建王家坪、流长防雹站；2007年，建养龙司、温泉防雹站。

2004年，完成10个乡镇自动气象观测站建设。2007年1月，县气象站由国家一般气象站升级为国家基本气象站，气象资料供国际交换。

二、气候特征

基本特征：1991—2010年，县内气温升高0.4℃，降水量偏少19.4毫米，日照减少310.3小时，主导风向与原来一致，风速减小0.7米/秒，蒸发减少59.9毫米，呈现温度升高、降水减少、阴霾天气增加的趋势，与全球气候变暖趋于一致。

四季特征：四季的划分以候平均温度为标准。候平均温度在10℃以上为春季，22℃以上为夏季，再降到22℃以下为秋季，继续下降到10℃以下为冬季。县内春季102天左右，夏季73天左右，秋季69天左右，冬季121天左右。进入春季后，北方冷空气逐渐减弱，南方暖湿气流逐渐增强，气温上升快；加上偏南大风，蒸发逐渐旺盛，所以初春相对干旱少雨。3月最高气温31.1℃，为历年气象资料记载中气温上升最快的月份。夏季太阳辐射强，空气热量大，温度上升迅速，气温高。

三、气候要素

日照：地势较高地区，遮蔽范围大，日照时数相对较少。中部、西北部海拔较低，地势相对平坦，日照较为充足。北部高差相对较大，主要农耕地在台地上，日照条件较好，全年可照时数4546.7小时。1991—2010年，日照时数共计20421小时，年平均日照时数928.2小时。其中，春季、夏季、秋季、冬季日照平均时数分别为261.2小时、382小时、253小时、124.9小时。全年日照时数以1992年8月最多，220.3小时；1996年11月最少，为3.4小时。

气温：全县历史最高气温36.5℃，最低气温-7.6℃。

1991—2010年，全县年平均气温14.9℃，最高为2002年7月17日35.7℃，最低为1996年2月20日-5.1℃；平均年积温5442.1℃，其中春季、夏季、秋季、冬季积温分别为502.9℃、1386.9℃、2128.6℃、1423.7℃。

息烽县2007—2010年乡镇月平均气温统计表

表2-1-2　　单位：℃

月份	小寨坝	青山	九庄	流长	养龙司	鹿窝	温泉	西山	石硐	永靖
1	4.17	2.45	3.3	3.45	4.35	5.22	4.25	4.4	3	3.85
2	8.02	6.7	7.3	7.35	8.47	8.5	8.25	8.37	7.05	7.97
3	11.67	10.3	11.17	11.4	12	12.45	11.95	12.25	10.72	11.92
4	14.65	13.02	13.97	13.97	14.72	15.37	15.05	15.2	13.5	14.62
5	19.85	17.85	19.1	19.2	19.52	20.1	19.97	20.12	18.32	19.57
6	21.57	19.7	20.95	20.97	21.85	22.05	21.9	22.07	20.12	21.45
7	24.57	22.22	23.67	23.85	24.7	24.82	24.87	24.82	22.92	24.25
8	24.45	22.05	23.37	23.77	24.35	24.37	24.6	24.47	22.5	23.92
9	21.17	20	20.07	20.22	21.2	21.47	21.65	21.35	19.6	21.05
10	15.85	14.05	15.2	15.22	15.9	16.45	16.25	16.32	14.57	15.67
11	10.72	9.18	10.25	10.4	10.72	11.82	11.2	11.02	11.82	10.7
12	6.57	4.97	5.97	5.92	6.55	7.97	6.9	7.07	5.65	6.5

息烽县1991—2010年各界限日平均温度统计表

表2-1-3

年份	0℃以下	0℃～9.9℃	10℃～19.9℃	20℃～29.9℃
1991	6天	108天	129天	122天
1992	0天	114天	137天	115天
1993	10天	103天	136天	116天
1994	3天	105天	134天	123天
1995	1天	127天	115天	122天
1996	9天	124天	110天	123天
1997	1天	117天	134天	113天
1998	4天	108天	116天	137天
1999	4天	108天	138天	115天
2000	10天	109天	128天	119天
2001	0天	94天	167天	104天
2002	3天	99天	147天	116天
2003	2天	106天	135天	122天
2004	6天	96天	149天	115天
2005	5天	115天	111天	134天
2006	1天	107天	135天	122天
2007	0天	93天	148天	124天
2008	26天	75天	136天	129天
2009	1天	109天	141天	114天
2010	1天	99天	157天	108天
平均	4.6天	105.7天	135.1天	119.6天

地温：1991—2010年观测结果分析，20年地表年平均温度17℃，地表下5厘米、10厘米、15厘米、20厘米年平均温度依次为16.4℃、16.4℃、16.6℃、16.7℃；月平均地表最高温度29.2℃（1992年8月），最低温度3.5℃（2008年1月）。

风向、风速：县内以西北风和东南风为主。1991—2010年，各月平均风速保持在1米/秒以上。夏半年平均风速1.4米/秒，冬半年平均风速1.1米/秒。月平均最大风速为2007年7月的2.7米/秒。各年极大风速及出现日期：2005年5月3日16.4米/秒，2006年4月3日16.7米/秒，2007年4月2日19.2米/秒，2008年4月18日16.9米/秒，2009年3月21日17.2米/秒，2010年2月28日16.5米/秒。

降水：县内年降水量一般950～1200毫米，最多年是温泉镇2007年的1498.4毫米，最少年是小寨坝镇2009年的788.5毫米。5—10月降水量相对较多，其他月份较少。多年平均降水量6月份最多，1月份最少。最多月份与最少月份相差10倍以上。雨量随地势升高而增多，从东南部向西北部减少。降水量随季节变化，也存在差别。春季雨量变化大，多雷雨天气；夏季降水充沛，是县内暴雨多发时段；秋季降水较夏季稍差，秋季有阵雨，偶有暴雨发生。

蒸发量：1991—2010年，全县蒸发量1104.1～1314毫米，平均值1195.9毫米。多年月平均蒸发量：1月32.4毫米，2月50.1毫米，3月82.2毫米，4月114.2毫米，5月136.7毫米，6月129.8毫米，7月177.2毫米，8月174.7毫米，9月132.7毫米，10月70.2毫米，11月50.7毫米，12月38.5毫米。其中，春夏两季蒸发量相对较大，7月蒸发为各月平均最大，秋冬两季蒸发量相对较小，1月蒸发量为各月平均最小。蒸发量与降水量基本保持平衡。

相对湿度：年平均相对湿度81.75%，历年变化范围在78%～86%之间。

霜期：1991—2010年，全县平均无霜期292天，平均初霜日12月15日，最早11月5日，最晚3月14日。最长无霜期354天，最短无霜期250天。

四、气候监测预报

1991—2004年，县内气候监测全是人工观测，项目仅有云、能、天、日照、蒸发、物候；以模拟天气预报为主，通过对物候观测，寻找相似性，制作天气预报，只能作一天趋势预报。随着数字预报模式的发展成熟，监测网络的完善，逐步减少物候观测，2007年以后停止物候观测。

2004年，县雷达雨量标校站投入使用。至2010年，县拥有七要素自动气象观测设备1套、TWR-01天气雷达设备1套、卫星接收系统1套、乡镇区域自动气象监测设备10套、山洪灾害防治单雨量站9套、自动土壤水分观测设备2套，气象监测实现10千米覆盖。随着短时临近预报系统的建立，全国雷达拼图、卫星云图及时联网更新，全省自动站资料的反馈，增强短时预报能力，提高气象防灾减灾水平。

2005年1月1日，县气象局启动地面气象自动观测与电脑编发报。建成气象手机短信平台，气象预测预报等服务信息发布渠道拓宽。2009年，各乡镇及部分单位和村安装气象预警电子显示屏，气象预测预报等服务信息覆盖面继续扩展，气象预报能力和时效进一步提升。气象预报服务信息有气象信息快报、气象信息专报、气象信息报告三大项。服务信息涵盖每日天气预报、一周气象服务信息、专题气象服务信息、重大天气服务信息、气象灾害预警信息等。

第四节　水　系

一、县内河流

境内河流属长江流域乌江水系，多发源于西望山和南望山。依县南高北低地势特点，呈羽状分布。总长187.25千米，河网密度17.4千米／100平方千米。流域面积大于20平方千米的河流有息烽河、瓮桶河、九庄河、雨淋河、猫场河、养龙司河、头道河、三田河、小鹿窝河、永靖河、小桥河、阳朗河、温泉河共13条。头道河、三田河、小鹿窝河、永靖河、小桥河、阳朗河是息烽河的支流。温泉河是界河——洋水河的支流。息烽河、瓮桶河、雨淋河、养龙司河直接流入乌江，九庄河、猫场河在下游变为伏流入乌江。

境内河流多属雨源型河流，主要靠大气降雨补水。大部分河流穿行于深沟峡谷之中，具有河床陡、落差大、流速快、河水暴涨暴落、冲蚀切割强烈、洪水汇流快、洪水流量占年径流比例大等特点。

（一）息烽河

境内第一大河，发源于修文县久长镇马场，南北流向。流经石硐、永靖、青山、西山、小寨坝、流长、养龙司7个乡镇，在养龙司乡荆江村小溪入乌江。全长60.1千米，总落差809米，平均比降12.2‰。流域总面积467.9平方千米（其中修文县境内4.7平方千米），占全县总面积的44.7‰。息烽河干流中上游处于县中部，水流较平缓，穿过阳朗、底寨、小鹿窝、潮水等山间盆地，便于引水灌溉。

头道河：发源于鹿窝乡西安村猫跳岩，由西南流向东北。经麻沙河、黄土田、头道河、瓮沙，在两河口入息烽河。流域面积40.5平方千米，河长12.3千米，落差195米，平均比降20.53‰。建有麻沙河、箭杆林、黄土田、头道河等引水工程。在瓮沙段河道上修建有排洪隧洞，将河道截弯取直，减少洪水对两岸农田的威胁。

三田河：发源于永靖镇河坎村上寨，东西流向。经河坎寨、螺蛳田、潮水坝后入息烽河。流域面积26.1平方千米，河长5.1千米，落差325米，平均比降63.73‰。已建有响水洞、象鼻洞等引水工程，平时余水引入底寨河渠道。

小鹿窝河：发源于西望山山脉，为西南至东北流向。上游为鹿溪、迷洗两支流。鹿溪源头在西山乡新寨沟村晚霞，经晚霞、新寨沟、关田坝、老鸦底，在前寨与迷洗支流汇合。迷洗支流源头在青山乡马路岩，流经马路岩、桶井坝、迷洗、黄泥田、蒿枝湾与鹿溪支流汇合，汇合后经石灰窑，在两岔河入息烽河。流域面积48.8平方千米，河长12.3千米，落差280米，平均比降22.76‰。

永靖河：主要源头是永靖镇红旗村的枧槽沟，东西流向。从县城穿过，经西山乡水岭沟、沙帽河，在葫芦水入息烽河。流域面积32.7平方千米，河长6.3千米，落差194米，平均比降30.79‰。

小桥河：发源于石硐乡新寨村水长冲，由西南流向东北。经青山乡下寨、小桥河、煤洞上，在西山乡车田河入息烽河。流域面积30.4平方千米，河长8.5千米，落差290米，平均比降34.12‰。

阳朗河：发源于南望山山脉，上游有下洪马、安马两条支流。下洪马支流源头在永靖镇联丰村金家厂，经老安寨、老安下坝、水头上、下洪马、洪马下坝，在三水寨与安马支流汇合。安马支流源头在永靖镇安马村鸡公岭，经安马、新萝、新萝下坝，在三水寨与下洪马支流汇合后经上坝河、老街、鸦米寨、后坝，在梅家桥入息烽河。流域面积53.1平方千米，河长17.75千米，落差496米，平均比降27.9‰。

（二）瓮桶河

发源于西望山山脉，由东北流向西南。鹿窝街以上有后河、水头两条支流。后河源头在鹿窝乡马垅村小箐口，经椅子山、后河，到鹿窝街与水头支流汇合。水头支流源头在鹿窝乡大石村兴隆湾，经龙洞沟、青龙嘴、水头到鹿窝街与后河支流汇合。汇合后经老窝寨、河尾巴、丁家岩，在江口入乌江。流域面积74.7平方千米，河长17.5千米，落差275米，平均比降15.7‰。

（三）雨淋河

发源于九庄镇纸房村凉水井，南北流向。经老虎冲、桐子堡、瓮舍田坝、雨淋河，在茂山入乌江。流域面积31.6平方千米，河长9.5千米，落差230米，平均比降24.2‰。乌江水库回水淹没河道4.5千米。

（四）九庄河

发源于西望山下九庄镇鸡场村打通湾，东西流向。经鸡场坝、九庄、竹花，在龙洞沟成伏流，在黄沙出露入乌江。河长22.4千米，落差245米，平均比降10.94‰。流域面积75.14平方千米。

（五）猫场河

发源于石硐乡新寨村锅圈岩，东西流向。经猫场、下坝，在龙旋窝成伏流入乌江。流域面积

21.79平方千米，出露河长5.1千米，落差90米，平均比降17.65‰。

（六）养龙司河

在养龙司以上有钟家山和茅草寨两条支流。钟家山支流源头在养龙司乡坪山村菜籽湾，由东南流向西北。经钟家山、养龙司，在斑竹林成伏流。茅草寨支流源头在小寨坝镇茅草寨村上坝田，南北流向，杜家寨、双涵洞，在袁家坝成伏流，在观音塘出露后，经小水、王家寨，在遵义县乌江镇盐仓坝入乌江。流域面积45.5平方千米，河长11.1千米，落差220米，平均比降19.82‰。

（七）温泉河

发源于温泉镇兴隆村干溪沟，南北流向。经温泉，在香岩入洋水河。流域面积21.3平方千米，河长7.2千米，落差225米，平均比降31.25‰。沿河建有小（二）型以下引水渠道。中游有息烽氡泉地热水，已被省总工会开发为中型疗养院。

二、县界河

（一）乌江

发源于贵州西部的乌蒙山区，由西北流向东南。在县境河段是息烽与金沙、遵义两县的界河。由县九庄镇柏茂村周家岩脚入境，经九庄、流长、养龙司、温泉四乡镇边境，在温泉镇三交村大塘口出境，长46.5千米。其中养龙司乡马排至盐仓坝8.5千米河段属遵义县。乌江水库建成后，水位升高135米。

（二）洋水河

发源于开阳县，南北流向。从温泉镇兴隆村入息烽境内，在香岩与温泉河汇合。经洪水营、岩灰洞在门前坝与开阳县石寸河汇流后，在大塘口入乌江。河长44.9千米，流域面积157.1平方千米。

第二章　自然资源

境内土地总面积10.37万公顷，动植物种类丰富，植被良好。水资源较为丰富，有地热资源可供利用。矿产主要有煤、磷、铝土、褐铁、重晶石、高岭土、水晶等。自然灾害主要有洪灾、旱灾、雹灾。

第一节　土地资源

1991年，全县土地总面积103753.6公顷，其中耕地36075.6公顷（稻田9033.13公顷、旱地27042.13公顷）、园地175.93公顷、林地37532公顷、牧草地9685.67公顷、城镇村及工矿用地2644.33公顷、交通用地907公顷、水域1796.67公顷、未利用地14936.73公顷（其中可开垦荒地279.87公顷）。

2009年6月，完成第二次土地调查。全县土地总面积103652.62公顷，其中农用地86997.06公顷，占土地总面积的83.93%；建设用地4444.59公顷，占土地总面积的4.29%；其他土地12210.97公顷，占土地总面积的11.78%。

农用地中，耕地面积33102.59公顷，占土地总面积的31.94%；园地662.56公顷，占土地总面积的0.64%；林地46938.73公顷，占土地总面积的45.28%；无牧草地；其他农用地6293.18公顷，占土地总面积的6.07%。

建设用地中，城乡建设用地面积3454.25公顷，占土地总面积的3.33%，其中城镇用地646.21公顷、农村居民点用地2616.13公顷、采矿用地40.48公顷、其他独立建设用地151.43公顷，分别占土地总面积的0.62%、2.52%、0.04%、0.15%；交通水利用地777.15公顷，占土地总面积的0.75%，其中交通用地665.6公顷、水利设施用地111.55公顷，分别占土地总面积的0.64%、0.11%；其他建设用地213.19公顷，占土地总面积的0.21%，其中风景名胜设施用地116.86公顷、特殊用地96.33公顷，占土地总面积的0.11%和0.1%。

其他土地中，水域面积1671.74公顷，占土地总面积的1.61%；自然保留地10539.23公顷，占土地总面积的10.17%。

第二节　矿产资源

县内已探明的矿产资源有4类14种，即能源类：煤、地热水；金属类：铝土矿、褐铁矿；非金属类：磷矿、硫铁矿、重晶石、高岭土、水晶、方解石、硅石、大理石、石灰岩矿；水汽类：地下水。矿藏特点：呈带状不均分布，东部种类多，西部种类少；多种矿产资源共生和伴生，赋存状态简单，易开采。永靖镇、小寨坝镇、温泉镇、养龙司乡、石硐乡、西山乡6个乡镇矿产资源较多。已开发利用煤、磷、硅、石灰岩、地热、硫铁矿、铝土矿、冶金用砂岩、页岩、重晶石等。

煤矿：县内煤矿以二叠纪龙潭组地层为主产层位。分布于温泉镇安青场，永靖镇南山、梨安，石硐乡，养龙司乡龙岗坡、西山乡周家田、青山苗族乡沙沟一带。煤矿呈层状产出，一般5～8层，可采1～3层，煤层厚度0.55～3.86米，发热量最高8000大卡，最低4500大卡。储量1.43亿吨。

磷矿：主要分布于县东北部的温泉和东南部的青沙河两处。温泉镇的乔巴山—松林坡矿段，矿体东西走向，倾角40～76度，矿体厚度0.55～9.35米，露头2000米，矿石含五氧化二磷30%～39%。青沙河矿段露头长500米，厚0.5～0.6米，矿石含五氧化二磷18.25%～29.45%。在磷矿岩层中尚伴生出铂、钯、镍、钒、钇、镉、锌等多种金属，其中钒部分富集成矿。储量2134万吨。

铝土矿：主要分布在赶子、天台、老厂、苦草坪、黑石头和水头寨6个矿段。各矿段含矿系2～20米，矿层厚1～11米，矿石含三氧化二铝29%～80%、二氧化硅0.89%～42%、三氧化二铁0.8%～16%。其中赶子的三氧化二铝含量较高。储量492万吨。

褐铁矿：主要分布于养龙司乡以西水头寨、茅坡，温泉镇天台、关田坝、后寨、银坑坪、安清，小寨坝镇的大坪，流长乡的流长、新场一带。含三氧化二铁50%以上。储量60万吨。

硫铁矿：主要分布于九庄镇的漆山坡、永靖镇的山岔沟、小寨坝镇的南桥、养龙司乡的茅坡、温泉镇的赶子等地，单一矿床以漆山坡、山岔沟储量为大。矿体平均品位13.72%～25.93%，平均厚度1.8～2.5米，总面积60.4平方千米。储量1.37亿吨。

重晶石：分布于温泉沟谷南面坡及窑上，厚1～2米，含硫酸钡95.6%，比重4.3。储量5万吨。

高岭土：出露于养龙司乡和温泉镇交界的上沟至“二七六”厂之间的山坡中，矿体厚1.5米，含二氧化硅40.74%、三氧化二铝35.41%、三氧化二铁1.28%。储量8万吨。

硅石：分布于永靖镇梨安、小寨坝镇楠木桥、大坪和西山乡小鹿窝一带。矿体厚5～40米，含二氧化硅95%～99%。储量1440万吨。

石灰岩矿：全县均有分布，储量丰富，多用作建筑材料和建材材料，部分用作矿物饲料。储量2.2亿立方米。

大理石：分布于养龙司乡茅坡、大山至油榨坪和关岩一带，长3000多米，宽60米，厚4米，有10余种花色。储量约72万立方米。

黏土矿：分布在梨安、猫场、石硐、九庄、流长、新场、茅坡、小寨坝、西山等地，含量未作测定。储量8000万立方米。

地下水：全县地下水枯水年1.01亿立方米，径流模数为3.84公升/秒/平方千米。赋存条件较为复杂，埋藏在50～300米之间，大部分不易开发利用。1996年开发利用率10.14%。明显的地下水富集区在团元山，底寨至盘脚营一带。

硅砂矿：主要产于永靖镇内的砂石坡、团元山、后冲等地，储量丰富。

第三节　动植物资源

一、植物资源

2008年，县林业绿化局委托贵州省林业学校牵头，调查县境内种子植物种类资源，查明境内主要有种子植物1126种，其中裸子植物22种、被子植物1104种。

（一）木本植物种质资源

县内木本植物种质资源共计622种，占种子植物的55.2%，其中裸子植物22种、被子植物600种。裸子植物和被子植物中，常绿乔木95种、落叶乔木164种；常绿灌木127种、落叶灌木149种；常绿藤本33种、落叶藤本39种；常绿藤状灌木5种、落叶藤状灌木10种。主要用材树种121种，其中裸子植物14种、被子植物107种。

天然植被以马尾松、柏木、白杨、桦木、丝栗、枫香、栎类、杉木等分布较广；人工植被主要有华山松、杨树、柳杉、杉木、刺槐、喜树、柏木等。灌木类植被分布较多的有火棘、马桑、荚蒾、黄金条、南天竹、杜鹃等。

（二）珍稀植物种质资源

县内珍稀植物共18种，其中：

国家Ⅰ级保护植物3种：红豆杉、珙桐、钟萼木。

国家Ⅱ级保护植物4种：闽楠、红豆树、榉木、香果树。

省级保护树种11种：三尖杉、铁坚油杉、深山含笑、紫楠、川桂、檫木、白辛树、刺楸、青檀、青钱柳、银鹊树。

（三）优良林分和优树资源

优良林分有铁坚油杉、光叶榉、丝栗栲；散生树木优良林分有蓝果树、香果树、银鹊树；优树群有黄心夜合、红豆树。

（四）古树名木资源

境内有古树763株，其中一级古树16株、二级古树84株。柏木古树最多，有314株，其次是枫香

67株、丝栗栲42株。

古猴樟：樟科樟属；地点：九庄镇桐梓村小学校旁，树龄在500年以上。

长穗桑：桑科桑属，生长于青山苗族乡青山村下寨村民组。树高25米，胸围543.2厘米，直径173厘米，冠幅直径15米，枝下高1.5米，树龄约300年。该树所在村寨为苗族村寨，当地村民视此树为“风水树”和“神树”，世代加以保护。

百日青：罗汉松科罗汉松。该树长于温泉镇天台村天台山国有林内。树高40米，胸围200厘米，平均冠幅11米，树龄约500年。

南酸枣树：漆树科南酸枣属。该树生长于流长乡甘溪村后土坎，树高32米，胸围764厘米，冠幅直径25米；是已知的贵州境内最大的南酸枣树，树龄约400余年。

古树群：底寨柏香山柏木古树群，天台山枫香古树群、银杏古树群。

（五）观赏植物

野生木本观赏植物280种，引种观赏植物110种。

（六）经济植物

果树植物106种，木本油脂植物97种，木本森林蔬菜植物51种，木本芳香植物86种，纤维植物69种，鞣料、染料植物60种，蜜源植物12种，饮料、饲料植物24种。

经济树种主要有油桐、乌桕、核桃、板栗、漆树、柑橘、桃、李、梨。草本植物以禾本科为主，其次为菊科、莎草科、豆科、蔷薇科。竹类有慈竹、荆竹、苦竹、斑竹、水竹、方竹、刺竹、川竹。

（七）药用植物

2003年，县农业局对境内药用植物进行全面调查后发现，境内有药用植物102科298属357种。其中木本65种、竹类4种、菌类4种、木质藤本25种、草本257种。野生中药材资源主要集中在西山、南山地区，主要有续断、沙参、盾叶薯蓣、穿山龙、天麻、喜树、金银花等。野生续断面积约3万亩，主要生长在南山山脉1300米以上高海拔地区。以永靖镇联丰、硬寨、老厂，小寨坝镇南极分布面积较大，温泉镇兴隆、石硐乡光明、青山苗族乡杨柳冲一带次之，年储量100吨干货。人工种植药材有黄檗、朝天罐、板蓝根、桔梗、太子参、皂角、杜仲、盐肤木、红花、续断、半夏、苦参、金花石蒜、瓜蒌。黄檗人工栽培主要在西山乡西山村、鹿窝村，面积15公顷，约30万株，树龄10年以上，胸径5～12厘米。杜仲主要分布在温泉镇大山村和养龙司乡，40万株，胸径6～8厘米者约8万株，胸径4～5厘米者约32万株，树龄10年以上。盐肤木种植主要在南山和西山一带，面积200公顷。

二、森林植被

境内植被主要类型有常绿阔叶林、常绿落叶阔叶混交林、落叶阔叶林、针叶林、针阔混交林、灌丛和灌草丛等。

常绿阔叶林以栲、青枫栎林为主，主要组成树种有栲树、小红栲、青枫、细叶青枫、木荷等，伴生树种多润楠、黄肉楠、山矾、黄心夜合，较高山地有水青枫、方竹等。因开发较早和长期人为活动干扰，此类原生森林植被仅残存于境内的天台山、西山和民族村寨的“风水林”。石灰岩常绿、落叶阔叶混交林以青枫栎、细叶青枫、乌枫栎、鹅耳枥、化香、朴树、青檀、椤木石楠、香叶树、黄连木、白栎为主，在破坏严重地段则以火棘、蔷薇、悬钩子、山胡椒和鼠李属等为常见。此森林以乌江边及民族村寨“风水林”为代表，其余多数遭到严重破坏。

境内有大面积的次生林，以马尾松、响叶杨、光皮桦、枫香、栎类以及人工马尾松、杉木、柳杉、竹林较常见。

三、野生动物

全县境内原有虎、豹、豺、狼等大型食肉动物，但久已绝迹。现存陆生动物主要有狐狸、野兔、穿山甲、野猪、野猫、貉、猴、刺猬、水獭、黄羊、獾子、丛林猫、林麝、斑羚等。多分布在西山、南山、天台、鹿窝等林区。

鸟类有斑鸠、鸢、雀鹰、百灵、黄莺、八哥、杜鹃、竹鸡、啄木鸟、喜鹊、乌鸦、山雀、锦鸡、金鸡、秧鸡、黄豆鸟、燕子、蜂鸟、麻雀、猫头鹰、老鹰、鹞等。

锦鸡、金鸡多分布于南极、西山、鹿窝等地丛林中；蜂鸟主要出现在乌江沿岸；竹鸡多栖于竹林、秧鸡多游于田坝。其余鸟类全县各地均有分布。

较为珍贵的动物有白鹳、穿山甲、丛林猫、林麝、斑羚、鸢、雀鹰、红腹锦鸡、杜鹃、啄木鸟等。

蛇类有乌蛇（乌梢蛇）、五步蛇、赤练蛇（野鸡项）、青竹标、黄颌蛇（构皮蛇）、兰蛇、脆蛇等10余种。以兰蛇、脆蛇较为珍贵，主要产于西山林区阴湿地带。

国家Ⅰ级保护动物：白鹳（老鹳）、林麝（獐子）。

国家Ⅱ级保护动物：水獭（獭猫）、大灵猫（狸子）、斑林猫、丛林猫（野猫）、斑羚（岩羊）、穿山甲、红腹锦鸡（金鸡）、啄木鸟、黑冠鹃隼（鹞子）、鸢（老鹰）、灰脸鵟鹰、白冠长尾雉、灰鹳、棕背田鸡、雕鸮、斑头鸺鹠（鬼瞪哥）等。

第四节　水资源

1998年3月，全县平水年水资源总量4.61亿立方米（不含乌江水库客水），其中地表水资源量3.37亿立方米、地下水资源量1.25亿立方米。2010年，全县地表水资源量3.84亿立方米、地下水资源量1.45亿立方米，水资源总量3.84亿立方米，全县人均年占有水资源量1492立方米。

息烽县2002—2010年水资源量统计表

表2-2-1

年份	降水量（毫米）	地表水资源量（亿立方米）	地下水资源量（亿立方米）	年人均水资源量（立方米/人·年）
2002	1169.7	7.26	1.84	2822
2003	805.6	4.72	1.43	1825
2004	1076.9	5.83	1.74	2240
2005	817.6	4.71	0.88	1913
2006	719.3	3.49	0.65	1415
2007	1109	5.17	1.89	2073
2008	1129.5	6.65	1.66	2657
2009	865	4.61	1.47	1840
2010	992.9	3.84	1.45	1492

由于地形地貌和降雨量的差异，全县水资源量的分布不均衡，东南部地区水资源量较西北部地区多。

除县境内水资源外，尚有乌江、洋水河两条界河，平水年拥有过境客水16.3亿立方米。全县水资源开发利用程度（用水量占年平均径流量之百分比）为14.93%，息烽河流域区为17.28%，九庄石硐区为14.27%，乌江沿岸区为8.3%。

水质：1996年调查，境内主要河流年接纳工业废水和生活污水113.5万吨，其中工业废水87.5万吨、医疗废水26万吨、城镇生活污水45万吨。工业废水中含有酚、氰、砷、氯、六价铬、铅和铀等有毒有害物质。另外，农药、化肥、煤渣、垃圾通过不同途径进入河道，造成地表水体污染。根据对全县地表水水质的感官性状，化学、毒理、细菌指标进行的测定，息烽河葫芦水以上干流，阳朗河、小桥河、三田河、小鹿窝河、头道河、九庄河、猫场河、瓮桶河、雨淋河、养龙司河等水域，水质良好，为Ⅱ类水域。温泉河为Ⅲ类水域。永靖河、息烽河葫芦水以下干流水域，水质较差，为Ⅲ类水域。息烽河干流红岩塘以下河段，水质差，为Ⅳ类水域。乌江水库水质较好，为Ⅱ类水域。洋水河水质差，为Ⅳ类水域。

县境内地下水大部分属重碳酸钙型水和重碳酸镁钙型水，局部地方为重碳酸硫酸钙型水。

地热水：息烽温泉地热矿泉水开发已有100多年历史。离县城40余千米的天台山脚，海拔约700米盆地中间有黑滩河及青水河相对贯穿而过，在两河接合处有4股清泉沿河畔露头，其中天然露头有3处。1959—1988年，多次取50件水样进行物理、化学、放射性、卫生等多种分析和水质对比检测。共检测72项指标，获得较全面的水质测试数据资料。其物理性质为无色、无味、无嗅、透明的地下水。色度2.5度，浊度3.6度，水温54℃～55℃。1990年7月人工取井一处，供罐装、瓶装矿泉水使用，日出产1500吨。

水质化学成分含有钾、钠、钙、镁、氯、重碳酸、硫酸根等10余种阴阳离子，含微元素近30种。其中锌、硒、钴、铜、铁、钼、镍、锡、碘、氟、铬、锰、钒等为人体必需的微元素；锶含量2.77毫克/升，偏硅酸含量58～61毫克/升，达到国内外饮用天然矿泉水标准。经检测，对人体有害的氟化物、铅、砷、汞、酚、阴离子合成洗涤剂等12项有毒指标均未超标。细苗总数测定无细菌生长，大肠菌小于3个/毫升，含放射成分属本底水平，未超过饮用标准。

此外，梨安凉水井一带有地热矿泉分布。

第三章　自然灾害与防治

1991—2010年，县境内发生较大水灾、旱灾、雹灾各6次，凝冻灾害1次。水灾造成房屋、设施损失较大，旱灾是造成粮食减产、农业减收的主要灾害。

第一节 自然灾害

一、水灾

1991年7月1—13日，县境内连续出现暴雨天气，13天降水量达428.8毫米，全县5个乡镇受灾，部分交通、通讯中断，死亡2人，受伤7人，房屋倒塌3306间，农作物受灾面积11065.53公顷，成灾面积5921.47公顷，直接经济损失220万元。水利设施经济损失共计40.73万元。其中16处山塘出现险情，13处垮塌；暴雨淹没和冲坏小（二）型提水工程8处、小（二）型水轮泵站3处、小（三）型提灌站工程12处、小（三）型水轮泵站2处，损毁渠道77.7千米，冲毁拦河坝14座、渡槽桥墩1个、倒虹管2处、排洪渡槽1处。

1995年6月23—24日，境内遭受特大暴雨袭击。铁路、主要公路和电力、通信、自来水全部中断。全县有5个乡镇、42个村、3个居委会、481个村民组受灾严重，涉及16210户、6.85万人。农作物受灾面积5273公顷，绝收面积2027公顷，不能恢复的农田367公顷，其中，阳朗坝淹没面积153.33公顷，老街村400余人被困在洪水中，死亡4人，受伤14人；淹死猪180头、耕牛17头、禽类数千只。直接经济损失3500万元。造成2口山塘缺口，冲垮渠道103处3452米，冲走250毫米管径水管6根24米、人畜饮水管1000多米，冲垮下洪马水库、底寨河渠道、小桥河水库三处小（一）型水利工程渠堤16段392米。雷击毁坏50千伏安变压器1台。

1996年7月1—4日，县境内连续降雨，县城累计降雨量176.7毫米，石硐、九庄、西山、青山等乡镇降水量达200毫米以上。全县10个乡镇161个村不同程度受灾，受灾村民5.4万余人，其中以永靖镇、石硐乡、九庄镇、西山乡等乡镇灾情较重，重灾区永靖镇阳朗坝一带平均积水3～4米，最深处10米；川黔公路（210国道）阳朗段被洪水淹没4昼夜，阻滞车辆4000余台、旅客10000余人。农作物受损面积23.18万亩。100余人临时搬迁。倒塌民房567间，损坏房屋900间，圈舍倒塌721间，校舍垮塌2970平方米；公路塌方38处，总长21.4千米，3条公路交通受阻，铁路停运。130家乡镇企业停产，10余家乡镇企业半停产。冲毁渠道378处，冲垮山塘2口，1口山塘大坝背坡滑坡，冲垮拦河坝13座，冲毁人畜饮水供水管6500米，影响8500人生活用水，受损水利工程影响灌溉面积767公顷。

2000年6月24日，全县普降大雨，局部降雨量169.9毫米，九庄、西山、永靖、小寨坝发生不同程度洪灾，因灾死亡4人，受伤1人。全县受灾农户11302户，受灾人口46104人，农作物受灾面积2508公顷，成灾面积1302公顷，绝收面积460.57公顷，其中毁损耕地面积114公顷，倒塌房屋515间，损坏房屋618间，损失粮食18吨，减产粮食6414吨，减产烤烟124吨，死亡猪39头，羊19只，毁坏电杆78棵，造成1条10千伏输电线路停电。公路路面毁坏87560平方米，塌方2691立方米，桥基足部毁坏2处，冲毁沟渠651处，计16830米，冲坏河床2500米，田土坎1500米，损坏通信光缆2处，导致1个乡通信中断，以上经济损失1801万元。

2002年6月18—20日，县内10个乡镇普降大到暴雨，3天内降雨量达215.5毫米。全县有139个村855个村民组受灾，受灾户13734户，人口55785人。紧急转移安置人口946人。农作物受灾面积1735公顷，当年减产粮食3726吨、减产烤烟25吨。倒塌房屋975间，损坏房屋953间，401户1046间房屋因灾成为危房，灾民家庭财产损失折款374万元，损失粮食349吨，农电、城建、水利、交通等基础设施受到严重损失，210国道阳朗段，息烽集中营革命历史纪念馆部分馆舍被淹。造成直接经济损失

2450万元，其中农业直接损失1235万元。

2007年7月30日，县内再次普降暴雨，造成县检察院、法院、消防大队及部分民房一楼被淹；阳朗片区有3586人不同程度受灾；广播电视设备多数受损，冲毁房屋5间，倒塌87间，损坏65间，被淹房屋多数成为危房；农作物受灾面积446.67公顷，绝收153.33公顷，冲毁耕地16.67公顷；毁坏水利灌溉设施17处，沟渠7800米；毁坏路面2500平方米、挡墙1650平方米，塌方6724平方米；210国道阳朗段多处被洪水淹没，交通中断。全县直接经济损失2450万元，其中农业直接经济损失1235万元。

二、干旱

1997年春夏，全县未降过大到暴雨。5月份降雨量122.6毫米，比正常年景偏少78.4毫米；6月份降雨量87.3毫米，比正常年景偏少112.7毫米。打田插秧面积4664.67公顷，占总田面积5196.2公顷的89.77%；已插秧的稻田受影响的460.87公顷，占插秧面积的9.88%；稻田脱水面积200公顷，占插秧面积的4.29%。7月26日至9月12日（除8月22日降雨22毫米）干旱81天，气温高、风力大、持续时间长，晚玉米受灾严重。全县实种玉米11624公顷，受灾7792公顷，成灾面积5609公顷，绝收面积1882公顷。

1998年6月1日，县境内连续40余天未下雨，九庄、鹿窝、流长、小寨坝等乡镇旱情严重，成灾面积5876.07公顷，占播种面积的75.1%。其中小寨坝镇最为严重，188个村民组2214.04公顷耕地受灾（833.33公顷减产，5806亩绝收）。

1999年3—5月，降雨量比多年平均减少78.8毫米，给打田插秧带来困难。又因上年下半年县境降雨量偏少，塘库蓄水量比正常年减少，至5月下旬，有5座水库和大部分山塘干涸。6月19日，小桥河水库水位降至死水位，只有基流淌出。

2001年，县内发生伏旱。自7月10日起，高温天气持续45天，造成稻田脱水，农作物干枯死亡，人畜饮水困难。全县受灾农民40606户164870人，成灾人口135438人；导致57705人、9265头大牲畜饮水困难。农作物受灾面积14045公顷、成灾面积10761公顷、绝收面积6269公顷。直接经济损失6454万元。

2006年1月1日至9月30日，境内总降雨量581.1毫米，属重旱年，尤其是6月份降雨比历年同期减少7成。全县农作物受旱面积5950公顷，其中轻旱2562公顷、重旱1858公顷、干枯1530公顷，因旱影响5.92万人、3.91万头牲畜饮水。

2010年，县遭受百年难遇大旱。从上年11月干旱出现苗头，持续到2010年9月29日。因灾造成11.7万人、6.43万头大牲畜饮水困难；农作物受灾面积9553公顷。其中成灾面积6967公顷、绝收面积450公顷。造成直接经济损失9191万元，其中农业经济损失4150万元、工矿企业损失5000万元、公益设施损失41万元。

三、雹灾

1991年5月16日，永靖镇、石硐乡、九庄镇、西山乡等乡镇持续降冰雹40分钟，冰雹大者直径4厘米，密度为20年来所罕见。冰雹过后，大风暴雨袭击上述乡镇，降雨量达79毫米，风力8～9级，百年大树被刮倒，327间房屋被毁坏。

1995年6月24日，县境内遭受冰雹、大风袭击，210国道息烽段交通中断，农作物和民房，猪、牛圈被打坏，树皮被打光，树枝被折断，照明电线被吹断。直接经济损失2300万元。

2000年4月13日下午5时，冰雹袭击小寨坝镇、流长乡、鹿窝乡等7个乡镇72个村，打坏房屋651

间，倒塌房屋265间，打死、打伤各1人，打死大牲畜12头，农作物大面积受损。造成直接经济损失1910万元。其中，小寨坝镇187个村民组4267户18538人受灾。农作物受灾面积1384.67公顷，倒塌房屋495间，毁损耕地15.1公顷、渠坎5349米。冰雹打毁油菜42公顷、小麦310公顷、蔬菜120公顷、地面卫星电视接收器6个，折断电杆18根，冲坏公路25千米。直接经济损失354万元。

2005年5月22日，石硐乡木杉村、光明村遭受暴风、冰雹袭击，小麦、油菜、马铃薯、烤烟被冰雹打成碎片。

2007年4月1日，境内8个乡镇46个村遭受冰雹袭击。农作物受损面积965公顷，其中绝收面积245公顷；打毁烟苗5188盘。养龙司乡的茅坡、龙塘、高硐、蚂蟥4个重灾村24公顷小麦、213.3公顷油菜绝收；小寨坝镇石桥村黄家、毛力湾组3.33公顷油菜、流长乡4.67公顷油菜绝收。因灾损毁房屋406间。紧急转移、安置人口950人。造成经济损失299万元。

2009年，石硐乡7个村遭受大风、冰雹袭击，冰雹持续半小时，小麦、油菜、马铃薯、杂粮、烤烟、蔬菜等农作物损失严重。

四、凝冻

2008年1月13日至2月15日，县境内出现罕见凝冻灾害，气温长时间维持在-3℃～-5℃。受灾22.6万人，因灾伤病286人，被困9698人，饮水困难13.12万人；农作物受灾7300公顷，绝收979.7公顷；倒塌民房206间，损坏民房9606间，死亡大牲畜2409头。直接经济损失2.3亿元，其中农业直接经济损失1.1亿元。春荒需口粮救济11139人、衣被救济2454人、伤病救济34人，需恢复住房3847户9970间，紧急转移1395人。森林受灾3.4万公顷，受灾活立林17万株、公路行道树1万余株、绿化灌木30万株、滇柏营养袋苗200万株，直接经济损失1200万元。全县18家规模以上企业因灾停产，直接经济损失9000多万元，产值损失5亿元，减少税收6810万元（其中地方财政收入3976万元）。29条供电线路（2条110千伏线路、8条35千伏线路、19条10千伏线路）出现故障，倒塌电杆962根，断线120处，毁损变压器22台。全县4个乡镇121个行政村停电，直接经济损失1100万元。乡村公路垮塌76处，直接经济损失66万元；全县公路路面、路基等直接经济损失188万元。客运班线车停运，受阻旅客6.5万人次。通信线路倒杆3178根324千米，140多个基站不同程度受损，直接经济损失600多万元。县城供水管道损坏333处5288米，冻坏水表5827块，1.6万人供水受到影响；乡镇水厂冻坏水表3110块、水龙头3290个、闸阀4170个、管网9800米，2.5万农村人口供水受到影响。直接经济损失120万元。

第二节　自然灾害防治

1995年以前，由每年一届的县防汛抗旱指挥部组织有关单位和灾区干部群众抗灾救灾。1996年，县防汛抗旱指挥部更名为县政府防汛抗旱指挥部，办公室设在水利局，负责全县防汛抗旱日常工作。农作物和森林病虫害防治工作分别由县农业局和县林业绿化局负责。旱灾、水灾发生时，县政府防汛抗旱指挥部办公室立即启动《息烽县防汛抗旱预案》和抗洪抢险预案。在县委、县政府领导和县政府防汛抗旱指挥部指挥下，组织全县人民抢险抗灾。解放军指战员、武警消防官兵、民兵预备役人员、救援应急队伍参加抗灾救灾，机关干部、企事业单位、社会团体到灾区参加义务劳动，民政部门干部职工到灾区查看灾情，下拨救灾款，组织社会为灾区捐款捐物，卫生防疫部门防治灾区疾病，帮助灾区恢复生产自救，重建家园。

一、抗水灾

由于洪水灾害具有区域性、突发性和破坏性等特点，县防汛抗旱指挥部决定：以各小（一）型以上水利工程、各乡镇为单位制定防洪抢险预案。县以武警消防支队、民兵预备役人员组成抢险应急队伍；各乡镇以基干民兵为主组成抢险应急分队。小（二）型以上水库实行行政首长和技术人员包库责任制。每年汛期（5月1日—10月31日），成员单位实行24小时值班制度。一旦出现洪水险情，指挥部统一调度抢险器材、物资和运输车辆，组织指挥抗洪救灾工作，保护人民生命财产安全，帮助灾民恢复生产，重建家园。

2002年6月，全县10个乡镇遭受不同程度洪涝灾害。2007年7月30日，县境内遭受强降雨袭击，7个乡镇不同程度受灾。灾情发生后，县委、县政府迅速启动防汛抗旱紧急预案。县委书记、县长率民政局、水利局、公安局、卫生局、农业局等县直单位负责人赶赴灾区，指导疏散被洪水围困的群众，抢救财物，县民政局为受灾群众提供饮食、饮水、住宿等后勤保障。县人武部、消防大队出动车辆、官兵，疏散转移群众600余人，抢救物资折款80万元。灾情发生当天，市长袁周率防汛办、水利局、农业局等相关部门负责人冒雨到永靖镇阳朗坝片区查看阳朗排洪大沟排洪情况，并到后坝村指挥抢险。县疾控中心组织人员对阳朗片区受灾单位和住户内外环境进行大面积消毒，防止灾后疫情发生。

二、抗旱灾

1999年5月18日至6月26日，县境内连续40天未降雨，禾苗枯死。县气象局实施人工降雨，24小时内，作业区的石硐、九庄、青山、流长、鹿窝、养龙司、温泉、永靖镇分别降雨74.5毫米、55毫米、48.6毫米、53.9毫米、47.7毫米、43.2毫米、39.5毫米、40毫米。

2002年，县政府制定《息烽县防旱抗旱预案》。县防办组建县抗旱服务队，购置抗旱机具、设备和专用车辆。具体抗旱措施：争取上级资金及相关物资，修理提水机具，疏通渠道，组织群众抗旱；停止水库农灌供水，城镇供水试行单双日供水制度，协调水源解决饮水困难。向缺水地区运送人畜饮水，打井找水，对无力取水的困难户实行专人包送；利用天气条件，开展人工增雨。

2010年，全县遭受罕见旱灾，县委、县政府及时成立“抗旱救灾指挥部”，组织、领导群众开展抗灾自救。下拨抗旱经费，用汽车拉水，解决人畜饮水问题。发动群众寻找水源，抗旱保苗。抗旱期间，新建抗旱应急水源，解决8.53万人饮水问题，组织汽车运水队送水，帮助1.75万人解决饮水困难。

三、抗凝冻

2008年1月13日至2月15日，县境内出现长时间凝冻灾害天气。灾害发生后，县委、县政府立即启动应急预案，明确提出“抗凝冻，保民生”指导思想和保路、保电、保水、保气、保物价、保安全、保吃饱穿暖的工作目标。县领导刘文新等先后多次深入受灾最严重的石硐、流长、鹿窝、九庄等乡镇察看灾情，指挥抢险救灾，率领消防官兵和有关部门为灾区干部群众送生活用水和物资。县直机关、各单位干部职工坚持每天清除县城街道冰雪；乡镇党员干部组成工作组，踏着冰雪，步行几十里深入村寨，为群众送去救灾物资。

到2月6日，全县乡村公路全部通畅，累计免费运送1000余名返乡民工和群众回家过春节。在确保县城照明的基础上，经奋力抢修，各乡镇部分恢复供电；至19日晚，全县161个行政村全面恢复供电。

第四章　环境保护

1996年，县开始环境质量监测，因技术力量和设备尚不能承担此项工作，均委托贵阳市环境监测中心站对县城环境进行质量监测。2010年4月，成立县环境监测站，主要开展大气、水、固体废弃物、噪声4个项目监测。

第一节　机　构

1980年9月，县成立环境保护局，隶属县计委。1982年，县环境保护局与建设局合并，成立县城乡建设环境保护局。1996年4月，县组建国土局，加挂环境保护局和地质矿产局牌子，环境保护局从城乡建设环境保护局分出，合并到国土局。1999年6月，县环保局单列为县政府环境保护的执法和监督管理部门，内设办公室、业务科和环保监理站（加挂监测站牌子）。2010年4月，成立县环境监测站，站内设监测室、实验室、质控室。

第二节　环境监测

一、大气污染及监测

1998年11月25日，贵阳市政府对环境空气质量进行功能区划，县内一类区包括温泉自然保护区（含天台山丛林）：以温泉为中心，面积4平方千米，周围外延500米为缓冲带。西望山自然保护区：面积4平方千米，周围外延500米缓冲带。三类区（小寨坝工业区）：西起息烽河，东到贵遵路，面积6平方千米，周围外延300米为缓冲带。其余为二类区。

1996—2010年县城大气环境质量监测数据统计表

表2-4-1

年份	监测点	监测项目			是否超标（倍）		
		二氧化硫	氮氧化物	悬浮微粒物	二氧化硫	氮氧化物	悬浮微粒物
1996	县环保局、重钙厂、县医院、县物资局、工务段	0.34	0.04	0.43	超2.25倍	优于国标1级	超1.45倍
1997	县环保局、县医院、工务段	0.21	0.03	0.4	超1.43	优于国标1级	超1.34
1998	县环保局、县医院、工务段	0.14	0.02	0.29	均未超过国标二级		
1999	县环保局、县医院、工务段	0.11	0.04	0.15	均未超过国标二级		
2000	县环保局、县医院、县交警队	0.04	0.01	0.24	均未超过国标二级		
2001	县环保局、县医院、县交警队	0.06	0.01	0.27	均未超过国标二级		

续表

年份	监测点	监测项目			是否超标（倍）		
		二氧化硫	氮氧化物	悬浮微粒物	二氧化硫	氮氧化物	悬浮微粒物
2002	县环保局、县交警队、县血站	0.04	0.01	0.24	均未超过国标二级		
2003	县环保局、县交警队、县血站	0.09	0.02	0.16	超0.49倍		超6.7%
2004	县环保局、县医院、县交警队	0.05	0.01	0.14	超6.7%		超13%
2005	县环保局、县医院、县交警队	0.04	0.01	0.07	均达国家二级标准		
2006	县环保局、县医院、县交警队	0.08	0.02	0.09	超66%		超20%
2007	县环保局、县医院、县交警队	0.02	0.01	0.06	均达国家二级标准		
2008	县环保局、县医院、县交警队	0.05	0.02	0.1	均达国家二级标准		
2009	县环保局、县医院、县交警队	0.02	0.03	0.08	均达空气质量二级标准		
2010	县环保局、县医院、县交警队	0.02	0.01	0.11	均达空气质量二级标准		

2000年，氮氧化物项改称二氧化氮；2004年，悬浮微粒物项改称可吸入颗粒。

2005年7月，连续3天对贵阳中化开磷化肥有限公司环境进行监测，共设高家坝村、重钙厂宿舍、大干沟3个监测点。监测项目为二氧化硫、氟化物、氮氧化物、可吸入颗粒物、五氧化二磷、一氧化碳、氨7个项目，取得数据252个。均达到国家环境空气质量二级标准（重钙厂宿舍执行二级标准，其余两个点执行三级标准）。

是年12月，连续3天对贵州西洋肥业有限公司环境进行监测，共设厂大门、尹庵村田坝组、赶子村龙塘组3个监测点。监测项目为二氧化硫、氟化物、二氧化氮、可吸入颗粒物、硫化氢、氨6个项目，取得数据216个。均达到国家环境空气质量二级标准。

二、水污染及监测

根据监测结果，息烽河、洋水河、黑滩河污染较为严重。息烽河污染主要由于生活污水未经处理直接排放、部分生产废水排入所致。黑滩河总磷超标原因是温泉疗养院洗浴水和附近居民生活用水排入所致。洋水河超标主要由于上游工业生产废水超标排放和生活污水直接排放所致。

息烽县1996—2010年水环境监测统计表

表2-4-2

河水监测			
时间	监测点	超标指标	水质
1997—2000年	息烽河政府招待所、纸厂、枧槽沟大桥	总磷、大肠杆菌超标	其余参数达地表水Ⅲ类水标准
2000年5月	乌江太阳大麻窝、大塘口		达到地表水Ⅱ类水标准
	洋水河大塘口、门前坝、洪水坝	TP、F-超标	达不到Ⅲ类水标准
	黑滩河	总磷超标	其余参数达地表水Ⅲ类水标准

续表

河水监测			
时间	监测点	超标指标	水质
2001—2005年	息烽河政府招待所、纸厂、枧槽沟大桥	总磷、大肠杆菌、氨氮、化学需氧量超标	水质达不到功能区要求
2003年4月	洋水河大塘口、门前坝、洪水坝	按地点排序分别超标3、4、5个指标	达不到Ⅲ类水标准
	黑滩河	总磷超标	其余参数达地表水Ⅲ类水标准
2006年4月	息烽河政府招待所、纸厂、枧槽沟大桥		全部达到相应标准
地表水监测			
2005年9月	地表水政府招待所、纸厂、枧槽沟大桥	招待所总磷超50%、大肠杆菌超0.1倍、纸厂氟化物超50%、枧槽沟大桥大肠杆菌超0.6倍	
2007年8月	地表水政府招待所、纸厂、枧槽沟大桥		所有项目均达到或优于Ⅱ类水质标准
2008年5月			
2009年9月			
2010年11月			
水源监测			
2006年6月	息烽水厂水源地	溶解氧5.9毫克/升，超标50%，五日生化需氧量5.0毫克/升，超标0.67倍	
2006年9月		溶解氧4.9毫克/升，超标率100%，硝酸盐19.25毫克/升，超标0.93倍	

1994年，县城乡建设环境保护局、水利局制定《息烽县地表水域环境保护功能区划分方案》，按方案要求，适时开展水环境监测。

三、固体废弃物污染及监测

1991—1996年，县内固体废弃物最低年4.5万吨，最高年13万吨。随着经济不断发展，固体废弃物产生量逐年增加。2002年161万吨，2004年138.2万吨（其中，磷石膏113.56万吨、冶炼废渣4.59万吨、粉煤灰1.82万吨、炉渣3.92万吨、煤矸石5.26万吨、其他废物9.04万吨），2006年超过200万吨，2010年500万吨。

四、噪声污染及监测

1996—2000年，县内城区域环境噪声总平均值54.47分贝。交通噪声总平均值70.32分贝，超标0.32分贝。2001—2005年，县内城区域环境噪声总平均值53.7分贝，交通噪声总平均值65.56分贝。2008—2010年监测统计，生活噪声66.4%、交通噪声22.6%、其他噪声11%左右（国家《城市区域环境噪声标准》：城区域环境噪声Ⅰ类55分贝，交通噪声Ⅳ类70分贝）。

第三节 环境治理

一、污水治理

（一）矿废水治理

20世纪90年代，县内大部分煤矿废水处于无序排放状态。1999年，县政府作出《息烽县2000年工业污染源达标排放工作安排意见》，限期治理煤矿废水。2000年，通过关井压产保留整改煤矿20个，经井下收集池收集，石灰中和处理后排入自然沟渠或者回用于矿区、农灌。2005年，县政府下发《关于下达环境污染限期治理项目的通知》，要求煤矿企业对废水限期治理，逐步实现一矿一污水站，通过“絮凝沉淀+曝气+锰砂过滤+消毒”等类似工艺进行废水处理，处理后的污水达标排放或者回用于矿区冲洗及农灌。2006年6月30日治理完毕，经监测，县内煤矿废水全部达标排放。

（二）磷化工废水治理

2000年，贵州西洋肥业有限公司投入460万元，对生产废水进行处理，污水经过石灰水中和、絮凝剂调理、戈尔膜过滤后循环使用。

2002年，贵阳中化开磷化肥有限公司投入2300万元，新建250立方米/小时污水处理站，采用三级石灰乳中和、三级絮凝沉淀加陶滤吸附过滤方式治理生产废水，2003年7月投入使用，实现生产废水稳定达标排放。

2006年，贵阳中化开磷化肥有限公司建成循环水站及循环水系统（50万吨/年硫黄制酸、60万吨/年硫黄制酸、20万吨/年磷酸装置）、200万吨磷矿浆输送和循环水系统、交椅山湿法堆存磷石膏和回水系统、全厂污水处理站技改工程。项目以新带老每年削减氨氮26吨、磷酸盐476吨、氟化物7470吨。次年，清理、排检厂区内废水地沟渗漏情况，对5#断面（干沟河渗漏水断面）收集回污水处理站和7#断面（山洞出水断面）的废水进行处理。

2007年，县政府印发《关于息烽河流域水污染物削减计划的通知》，要求加强污水治理工作。首先，环保部门加大沿河企业的监督管理力度，严格监管。其次，企业大力开展工程治理，中化开磷化肥有限公司大力发展循环经济，共投资近2亿元全面实施污水、中水回用工艺和工程，建成干沟河治理工程、潮水河调水工程、全厂水综合利用工程，对全厂跑、冒、滴、漏彻底收集，并安装废水在线监控系统，适时监控废水排放情况。第三，加大环保基础设施建设力度，解决沿岸城镇生活污染。2010年5月，贵阳市环境监测中心站对息烽河下游水质进行监测：pH7.8、化学需氧量18、氨氮1.5、总磷0.72、氟化物1.4，总磷下降60倍，水质从Ⅴ类改善到接近Ⅳ类水体。

（三）饮用水源保护及生活废水治理

1999年，县政府批复县环保局、水利局制定的《息烽县集中式饮用水源保护区划分方案》，将县城周围饮用水源划分为洪马水库、小桥河水库及枧槽沟三个集中式饮用水源保护区，采取相应措施保护区内水源。2004年5月，县环保局调查3个集中式饮用水源保护区污染源，制定《息烽县集中式饮用水源保护区内污染源整治实施方案》，整治饮用水源区污染源，设立“饮用水源保护区，禁止入内”警示牌等。2007年，在鹿窝乡王家仓新建日处理能力为300吨的生活污水处理厂1座，解决近百户居民的生活污水处理问题。2009年，建成日处理7000立方米的县城污水处理厂和5000立方米的小寨坝镇污水处理厂各1座。2010年，建小桥河水库饮用水源区围栏1600米。建垃圾处理场1个，处理县城生活垃圾。启动洪马水库集中式饮用水源保护区农村环境综合整治工程，搬迁村民19户68人，实施退耕还林43.85亩，总投资360万元。

二、固体废弃物治理

2008年，贵州开磷集团磷业有限责任公司投入28881万元，建成10亿块新型磷石膏砖生产项目，2009年投入生产，年可消耗磷石膏渣165万吨。此外，采取外售利用，引进废渣综合利用项目等措施，处理工业固体废弃物。2010年，县政府新建1个垃圾处理场，处理县城生活垃圾。同时，开展流域生态治理和农村污染防治，退耕还林，实施农村清洁能源工程建设，推广生态施肥和病虫草害生态控制技术，引导农民科学使用农膜、农药、化肥，开展“禁磷”“限塑”等群众性环保专项行动，减少污染。是年5月，经贵阳市环境监测中心站监测，息烽河下游水质指标为：pH7.8、化学需氧量18、氨氮1.5、总磷0.72、氟化物1.4，总磷下降60倍，水质从Ⅴ类改善到接近Ⅳ类水体。

息烽县1991—2010年工业固体废弃物产生与利用统计表

表2-4-3

年份	产生量（万吨）	综合利用量（万吨）	综合利用率（%）	贮存量（万吨）	处置量（万吨）	排放量（万吨）
1991	9.15	0.23	2.46	5.97	2.13	0.83
1992	13.32	0.03	0.2	6.76	4.66	1.87
1993	4.5	—	—	3	1.5	—
1994	7.3	—	—	—	7.3	—
1995	9.3	—	—	—	9.3	—
1996	10.99	0.1	—	10.89	—	—
1997	23.52	1.56	6.63	18.37	3.59	—
1998	61.3	37	60.36	24.3	—	—
1999	41.35	11.85	28.64	28.73	—	0.77
2000	41.1	11.2	27.3	29.17	—	0.73
2001	71.68	17.7	24.69	47.11	0.01	6.87
2002	161.04	14.99	9.31	57.41	89.72	—
2003	131.32	32.82	24.99	1.33	97.15	0.02
2004	138.2	38.67	27.98	1.08	98.84	—
2005	163.94	47.30	28.85	0.19	126.48	—
2006	226.32	54.29	23.81	27.82	145.92	—
2007	291.47	52.98	17.2	—	255.09	—
2008	338.55	61.8	17.3	—	295.5	—
2009	405.85	94.27	21.99	—	334.42	—
2010	502.72	142.96	28.4	—	360.36	—

第三篇　人口·民族·宗教

第一章　人　口

1991—2010年，全县人口自然增长率最高11.4‰，最低2.11‰，多数年份维持在3.82‰～7.72‰之间。

第一节　人口状况

一、人口数量

1991年年末，全县共有50708户220959人，人口自然增长率10.75‰。此后十余年间，除1994年人口自然增长率11.4‰外，其余年份皆维持在9‰～10.3‰之间。2005年，全县人口245934人，人口自然增长率2.11‰，为1991—2010年间人口增长最低的年份。2010年，全县有83097户257732人，人口自然增长率6.93‰。

息烽县1991—2010年人口统计表

表3-1-1

年份	总户数（户）	总人口（人）	自然增长率（‰）
1991	50708	220959	10.75
1992	51144	221825	9.91
1993	54192	224655	10.3
1994	55842	228454	11.4
1995	56464	231758	9.87
1996	58285	233332	9.62
1997	59782	235565	9.44
1998	60622	236593	5.89
1999	60382	239851	6.98
2000	62970	240563	7.72
2001	64549	241637	4.68

续表

年份	总户数（户）	总人口（人）	自然增长率（‰）
2002	60755	245509	4.15
2003	69602	246129	3.82
2004	69106	245535	4.16
2005	70122	245934	2.11
2006	71940	246571	4.07
2007	73222	249485	4.79
2008	73843	250186	4.9
2009	75505	250352	3.96
2010	83097	257732	6.93

二、人口密度

1991年，县辖国土面积1036.5平方千米，年末人口总数220959人，平均每平方千米213.18人。1992年6月，撤区并乡建镇后，各乡镇人口密度发生较大变化。其中，永靖镇原辖区面积8.62平方千米，撤区并乡建镇后，辖区面积增至154.92平方千米，人口密度由1990年的2119人/平方千米剧减为264.11人/平方千米，为人口密度变化最大的镇。

1992—2010年，永靖镇每平方千米增加4.69人，人口密度年平均值310.13人/平方千米，为全县各乡镇最高。其余依次为九庄镇277.47人/平方千米、温泉镇260.59人/平方千米、养龙司乡258.48人/平方千米、小寨坝镇251.05人/平方千米、西山乡238.78人/平方千米、石硐乡220.77人/平方千米、流长乡203.6人/平方千米、鹿窝乡168.32人/平方千米。青山苗族乡人口密度最低，19年内每平方千米年均增加0.92人，人口密度年均值为133.51人/平方千米。

第二节　人口构成

一、年龄构成

2000年和2010年，先后开展第五次、第六次全国人口普查。根据两个年度全县人口年龄构成统计，2010年，全县70～94岁人口占总人口的5.73%，较1991年的3.72%增加2.01%；95岁以上人口45人，较1991年的8人增加37人，县内人口呈现老龄化倾向。

息烽县2000年和2010年人口年龄构成统计表

表3-1-2

2000年			2010年		
年龄段	人数（人）	占比（%）	年龄段	人数（人）	占比（%）
0～4岁	16684	7.53	0～4岁	14115	6.63
5～9岁	21352	9.64	5～9岁	12787	6.01

续表

2000年			2010年		
年龄段	人数（人）	占比（%）	年龄段	人数（人）	占比（%）
10～14岁	23039	10.4	10～14岁	17016	7.99
15～19岁	16127	7.28	15～19岁	14755	6.93
20～24岁	16948	7.65	20～24岁	13376	6.28
25～29岁	22285	10.06	25～29岁	12974	6.09
30～34岁	22161	10	30～34岁	16834	7.91
35～39岁	15738	7.1	35～39岁	21606	10.15
40～44岁	11437	5.16	40～44岁	21137	9.93
45～49岁	14230	6.42	45～49岁	14987	7.04
50～54岁	11482	5.18	50～54岁	10646	5
55～59岁	8481	3.83	55～59岁	13115	6.16
60～64岁	7283	3.29	60～64岁	10075	4.73
65～69岁	6079	2.74	65～69岁	7243	3.4
70～74岁	4230	1.91	70～74岁	5536	2.6
75～79岁	2241	1.01	75～79岁	3869	1.82
80～84岁	1182	0.53	80～84岁	2014	0.95
85～89岁	512	0.23	85～89岁	616	0.29
90～94岁	84	0.04	90～94岁	151	0.07
95～99岁	7		95～99岁	40	
100岁以上	1		100岁以上	5	

二、性别比例

1991年，县内有男性113674人，占年末总人口的51.45%；女性107285人，男性比女性多6389人，性别比为105.96。1997年，男性126134人，占年末总人口的53.55%。女性109431人，男性比女性多16703人，性别比为115.26，为1991—2010年间最高值。2000年，男性125168人，占年末总人口的52.03%。女性115395人，性别比为108.47。2002年，男性127588人，占年末总人口的51.97%。女性117921人，男性比女性多9667人，性别比为108.2。2010年，男性134187人，占年末总人口的52.06%。女性123545人，男性比女性多10642人，性别比为108.61。

三、文化构成

2000年第五次全国人口普查和2010年第六次全国人口普查中，全县关于这两个年度的人口文化构成情况没有较详细的统计。

2000年，6岁及以上人口200699人，其中未上学者23629人，占6岁及以上人口的11.7%；接受扫盲教育的785人，占0.39%；接受小学教育的103808人，占51.72%；接受初中教育的56999人，占

28.4%；接受高中教育的7835人，占3.9%；接受中专教育的4701人，占2.34%；接受大学专科教育的2399人，占1.2%；大学本科学历539人，占0.27%；研究生及以上学历4人，不足0.01%。全县15岁及以上人口160508人，文盲或识字极少者22602人，其中男性5524人、女性17078人。

2010年，6岁及以上人口196440人，其中未上学者13921人，占6岁及以上人口的7.09%。接受小学教育的82752人，占42.13%；接受初中教育的74527人，占37.94%；接受高中教育的（含中专）15475人，占7.88%；接受大学专科教育的6760人，占3.44%；大学本科学历2954人，占1.5%；研究生及以上学历51人，占0.03%。全县15岁及以上人口168979人，文盲或识字极少者12186人，其中男性2889人、女性9297人。

四、职业构成

2000年，全县有在业人员127634人，按《职业分类与代码》规定分为6个大类：国家机关、党群组织、企业事业单位负责人1327人，占1.04%；专业技术人员4990人，占3.91%；办事人员和有关人员2093人，占1.64%；商业、服务业人员6328人，占5%；农林牧渔水利生产人员101355人，占79.41%；生产、运输设备操作人员及有关人员11487人，占9%。2002年，全县有政府机关国家公务员554人，其中县级政府机关国家公务员428人、乡（镇）级政府机关国家公务员126人；事业单位工作人员3648人、国有经济企业工作人员92人。2005年，全县有政府机关国家公务员567人，其中县级政府机关国家公务员439人、乡（镇）级政府机关国家公务员128人；事业单位工作人员3616人、国有经济企业工作人员、专业技术人员共146人。2008年，全县有政府机关国家公务员593人、参照公务员法管理的事业单位工作人员66人、事业单位工作人员3689人、国有经济企业经营管理人员、专业技术人员共61人。2010年，全县有政府机关国家公务员576人，其中县级政府机关国家公务员395人、乡（镇）级政府机关国家公务员181人。

五、民族构成

1990—1999年，县内有20个民族。2000年，县内有汉、蒙古、回、藏、哈尼、苗、彝、壮、布依、朝鲜、满、侗、白、土家、傣、毛南、畲、水、土、仫佬、纳西、黎22个民族。其中汉族209717人，占94.65%；少数民族11866人，占5.35%。是年，蒙古族新增35人，藏族新增8人，仫佬族新增4人，朝鲜族新增7人，畲族新增1人，哈尼族减少2人，纳西族减少11人。此外，尚有未识别民族10人。在已识别的少数民族中，苗族人口占比最高，为3.98%，布依族、彝族次之。

2010年，全县共有29个民族。其中汉族201104人，比2000年减少8613人，占94.46%；少数民族11793人，比2000年减少73人。在28个已识别的少数民族中，苗族所占比重最大，为常住人口总数的3.81%，布依族、彝族、土家族、仫佬、侗族次之，分别为0.81%、0.26%、0.16%、0.13%、0.1%，其他民族（含未识别民族）占0.27%。

六、城乡人口比例

1991年，境内非农业人口20555人，占总人口的9.3%；农业人口200040人，占总人口的90.7%。至2000年，由于境内朝晖机械厂、拖拉机电机厂、高强度螺栓厂等4家单位相继外迁，境内非农业人口在个别年份上有所减少。其中，1992年，境内非农业人口比1991年减少476人，非农业人口比例降至9.05%。1997年，境内非农业人口25164人，比上年同期增加657人，占总人口的10.68%，所占总人口比重比上年同期增加0.18个百分点。农业人口210401人，比上年同期增加1576人，占总人口的89.32%，所占总人口比重比上年同期降低0.18个百分点。到2010年末，境内非农业人口32848人，占总人口的12.75%。农业人口224884人，占总人口的87.25%。1991—2010年，非农业人口净增12293人，在总人口中占有比例增加3.45个百分点。农业人口净增24844人，在总人口中所占比例相应下降3.45个百分点。

息烽县1991—2010年城乡人口变动情况统计表

表3-1-3

年份	总人口	非农业人口		农业人口	
		人口数（人）	所占比重（%）	人口数（人）	所占比重（%）
1991	220959	20555	9.3	200040	90.7
1992	221825	20079	9.05	201746	90.95
1993	224655	20776	9.25	203879	90.75
1994	228454	23948	10.48	204506	89.52
1995	231758	24059	10.38	207699	89.62
1996	233332	24507	10.5	208825	89.5
1997	235565	25164	10.68	210401	89.32
1998	236593	25295	10.69	211298	89.31
1999	237851	25521	10.73	212330	89.27
2000	240563	26128	10.86	214435	89.14
2001	241637	26540	10.98	215097	89.02
2002	245509	26801	10.92	218708	89.08
2003	246129	30024	12.2	216105	87.8
2004	245535	29687	12.09	215848	87.91
2005	245934	30110	12.24	215824	87.76
2006	246571	30529	12.38	216042	87.62
2007	249485	30804	12.35	218681	87.65
2008	250186	31311	12.52	218875	87.48
2009	250352	32298	12.9	218054	87.1
2010	257732	32848	12.75	224884	87.25

第二章　计划生育

1991年，县计划生育委员会（简称县计生委）内设办公室，下辖计划生育宣传技术服务指导站、人口和计划生育协会、计划生育药具管理站。是年，人口和计划生育协会领导县、乡各级协会

30个。

1996年4月5日，县计生委更名为县计划生育局，内设办公室、统计科、宣传教育科。2004年8月25日，计划生育局更名为县人口和计划生育局。下设办公室、规划信息统计科、政策法规科。2009年4月，明确县计划生育协会为正科级群众团体。同年12月，省委组织部再次明确县计生协会为参照公务员管理的事业单位。2010年，县人口和计划生育局下辖县计划生育技术指导站、计划生育药具管理站、县人口和计划生育协会。是年，全县有人口和计划生育协会组织178个。

20年间，县委、县政府贯彻党和国家有关计划生育（简称计生）方针政策，相继推行计生工作“党政一把手负总责，亲自抓计划生育”，机关、企事业单位齐抓共管，实行目标管理，落实凭证生育制度，计生工作“一票否决”等措施。加强流动人口计生管理和加大计生工作投入，提高计生技术服务水平，全县人口增长速度得到有效控制，人口出生率和自然增长率分别从1991年的14.91‰、10.75‰降至2010年的12.02‰和6.93‰。

第一节　政策法规宣传

1991年，县委、县政府编印《加快全民性人口基础知识教育步伐　促进我县“八五”人口计划的顺利完成》的讲话材料，在全县进行宣传。发动群众结合本地实际开展算账对比活动，开展人口与计划生育基础知识教育。是年，共举办1583班，学员8.5万人，17.95万人次参加听课学习。1992—1996年，采取出墙报、黑板报，书写固定标语、电影宣传等多种形式，宣传中央、省、市、县有关计生法规及政策。同时，开班进行人口基础知识教育，其间，1992年、1993年两年，共办班3414个，参加学习人员19.75万人次。1998年7月，《贵州省计划生育条例》颁布实施，县人口与计划生育“三结合”（经济建设与计划生育相结合；扶贫奖励政策与计划生育相结合；小康建设与计生户建设幸福家庭相结合）工作领导小组下发《关于对〈贵州省计划生育条例〉的宣传实施意见》，利用赶场天向群众进行广泛宣传，发放宣传资料5000余份。

1999年，县委办公室下发《关于迅速掀起春耕大忙前集中宣传服务活动高潮的通知》，各乡镇共出动宣传车巡回宣传600余次，设专点进行计划生育宣传40余次，接受群众咨询4万余人次。县乡计生部门印发《致已婚育龄夫妇的公开信》1.5万余份、计生知识小折页4600份、计生对联3314副、新婚礼袋4000套、《流动人口管理办法》3000份、《村规民约》4000份，向广大群众宣传计生政策与法规。在宣传活动中，签订计生管理合同1.8万份。

2000年9月，县计生局、教育局、团县委、县妇联、息烽报社联合在《息烽报》开展纪念中共中央《关于控制我国人口增长问题　致全体共产党员　共青团员的公开信》（以下简称《公开信》）发表20周年征文活动。2003年，开展普及婚育新风，转变群众生育观念活动，县计生局组织乡镇分管计生工作的党政领导、计生干部深入学习《中华人民共和国人口与计划生育法》《贵州省人口与计划生育条例》（简称“一法一条例”）、《人口与计划生育宣传提纲》以及国家计生委主任张维庆在贯彻《中华人民共和国人口与计划生育法》座谈会上的讲话。全县共开展培训活动60次，受训人员5000余人次。县、乡两级利用赶场天、母亲节、计生协会活动日等，开展“一法一条例”宣传，确保计划生育政策法规家喻户晓。

2005年，县计生局开展“婚育新风进万家”“关爱女孩”活动，分别在“13亿人口日”“世界艾滋病日”“‘5·29’协会活动日”期间，组织开展大型宣传活动，全年共发放计划生育宣传材料60余万份。抓计生报刊的征订工作，做到村村有《中国人口报》《人口与家庭》《贵州人口墙报》《健康之友》《人生》等报纸杂志。2009年，启动人口文化精品建设工程，在永靖镇、小寨坝镇、养龙司乡打造“人口（生育）文化大院”精品宣传阵地；在永靖镇立碑村打造全省新农村、新农家、新农民“三新”建设宣传示范点，实施“生育关怀行动”；开展两期青春期性健康教育进校园活动，推进“婚育新风进万家”。2010年，采取多种形式学习宣传《流动人口计划生育条例》（以下简称《条例》）、《贵州省人口与计划生育条例（修正案）》，将人口计生宣传与全县“三创一办”宣传相结合，制作文明县、创新健康教育等宣传专栏；在息烽电视台开辟专栏，滚动播出1个月，同时，将《条例》内容印在日历上和编写进《息烽市民读本》，发给广大群众，提高《条例》知晓率。县、乡利用法制宣传日、世界卫生日、协会成立纪念日、“7·11”世界人口日等开展大型宣传咨询和文艺演出活动。

第二节　人口管理

1991年，全县出生人口3636人，出生率14.91‰。1993年7月，县政府出台《关于息烽县流动人口和个体从业人员计划生育管理办法》，要求由县计生部门牵头，公安、城建、工商等单位参与，组织联合行动，流动人口计划生育秩序。1997年，县计生部门增设流动人口管理科，对流出和流入人员的计生工作实行建档管理。1998年7月，开展流出人口计划生育普查，以村为单位进行登记造册。是年，全县有流动人口计划生育户968户，其中，办理计划生育流动人口证789个，办证率81.5%。

1999年，县计生部门统一拟定《村规民约》23条发到各村，供各村组织村、组干部、共产党员、共青团员和中心户长会议参考，讨论制定本村《村规民约》，在群众中公布后印发给计生对象，推进计划生育工作实现村级自我教育、自我管理、自我监督进程。是年，县计生部门印制计生合同2.5万份，合同明确计生管理部门和计生对象双方的权利义务和违约责任、计生政策、准生证发放制度及程序、独生子女病残儿鉴定程序、流动人口管理规定等。

2001年，县政府批转县人口与计划生育领导小组《关于对流动人口实行分乡镇管理的意见》，明确流动人口的计生工作实行流入地管理为主的原则。

2004年，全县推行“计划生育合格证”“一证先行”制度。

2006年，各乡镇落实房屋出租户对流入人口登记报告制度。至是年12月，全县流出人口54204人，其中18周岁以上育龄妇女18249人，已婚育龄妇女11832人，18周岁以上育龄妇女办理“流动人口生育证明”17786人，办证率97.5%；全县有流入人口6569人，流入人口验证率、妇检率100%。

2008年，县计生部门办理婚育证明2383人；慰问流动人口困难户139户，落实慰问资金及物资折价合计4.45万元；为125户计生户落实帮扶资金1.25万元。

2010年，全县计生工作围绕强化“两个服务”（流动人口计生管理服务和以计生技术服务为主的优质服务），落实“三项建设”（人口计生工作新机制建设、人口计生法治化建设、人口计生干部队伍建设），实现“五个转变”（从人治向法治转变、从重治标向标本兼治和综合治理人口问题转变、从管理主导型向优质服务型转变、从处罚多生向奖励少生与处罚多生并重转变、从人口计生部门自己抓向有关部门齐抓共管转变）开展工作。是年，全县出生人口3097人，人口出生率12.02‰。

息烽县1991—2010年人口出生率统计表

表3-2-1

年份	总人口	出生人口	出生率（‰）
1991	220959	3636	14.91
1992	221825	3457	15.58
1993	224655	3772	16.8
1994	228454	3859	16.89
1995	231758	4364	18.82
1996	233332	3802	16.29
1997	236565	3349	14.16
1998	236593	3729	15.46
1999	239851	3665	15.3
2000	240563	2932	12.18
2001	241637	2841	11.76
2002	245509	2835	11.54
2003	246129	2504	10.2
2004	245535	2531	10.31
2005	245934	2315	9.4
2006	246571	2104	8.53
2007	249485	2165	8.67
2008	250186	2313	9.24
2009	250352	2868	11.45
2010	257732	3097	12.02

第三节　计生服务

1991年，县、乡两级计生服务站配备有必要的器械、设备，有技术人员93人，基本做到人员、设备、场所“三落实”。

1995年，省委、省政府把息烽规划为全省首批实现计生“三为主”（宣传教育与经济限制，以宣传教育为主；避孕与人流引产，以避孕为主；经常工作与突击活动，以经常工作为主）县之一。1997年，息烽县被省政府命名为“计划生育‘三为主’达标县”。

1998年，启动创建市级计划生育优质服务县工作。县投入资金200余万元，建计生业务用房8380平方米。其中县站900平方米，10个乡镇平均每个服务站250平方米，166个村（居）委会计生服务室各30平方米；添置开展技术服务手术、检测以及试验用各种设备。是年，在妇检工作中充分利用B超、孕检试纸等技术手段进行一年四次的查环、查孕、查病工作。

2001年，在永靖镇、石硐乡开展省级中心服务站达标工作，在温泉镇、小寨坝镇、九庄镇、流长乡、青山苗族乡开展生殖保健优质服务示范乡（镇）创建工作。县成立以分管副县长为组长、各相关单位领导为成员的领导小组，将每年6月作为生殖保健优质服务月，为广大育龄妇女进行妇科病的普查普治，开展生殖保健知识宣传。是年，共完成药具发放4056例，妇检47320人次，发放准生证3778个。

2004—2006年，将查环、查孕与妇科病普查相结合，建立妇女生殖健康档案4万份，妇科病普查率94.3%，普治率97.53%。通过计生优质服务，全县三年内无重大技术责任事故，手术并发症发生率降至0.3‰以内，引产数占人流引产数的比例降至14.5%以内。2009年，县、乡计生服务站全面实行站长法人负责制，建立和落实站内激励机制。

2010年，开展创建国家级计生优质服务先进县工作，将工作指标分解下发各乡镇，为县、乡计生服务站购置21万余元的医疗器械。免费为27312人进行妇科病普查，对3867名计划怀孕、已孕妇女及18248名5岁以下儿童进行监测。完成出生缺陷干预2671人，新生儿疾病筛查160例。发放药具4706例，妇检85723人次。发放准生证3915个。全县计划生育率94.26%。

息烽县1991—2010年计划生育服务统计表

表3-2-2

年份	药具发放（例）	妇检（人次）	准生证发放（个）	计划生育率（%）
1991	—	—	3725	87.68
1992	—	—	4175	86.6
1993	—	—	3662	84.79
1994	—	—	3763	86.03
1995	—	—	3589	84.8
1996	—	51544	3709	91.05
1997	—	51416	3859	93.6
1998	—	65976	4027	94.64
1999	—	65976	3520	71.73
2000	—	63484	3809	91.6
2001	4056	47320	3778	90.22
2002	4097	57230	3848	91.49
2003	4517	54346	3995	89.61
2004	4154	56298	3864	91.76
2005	4260	62144	3720	95.44
2006	4273	59391	3645	96.96
2007	4543	64415	3809	97.27
2008	4188	75642	3807	95.22
2009	4068	82593	3991	93.17
2010	4706	85723	3915	94.26

第四节　计划生育协会

1991年，县、乡两级有计划生育协会30个。协会以老干部、老党员、老职工、老劳模、老教师“五老”为骨干，开办“计划生育活动室”“会员之家”“育龄妇女之家”等，组织会员学习党的计划生育政策和法律法规，落实计划生育任务，帮扶计生户、困难户，建立文明幸福家庭。1996年，县计生协会贷款18.9万元，各乡（镇）从统筹款中划出5万元，作为发展经济、帮助农民致富奔小康和建设文明幸福家庭的计生“三结合”发展基金。是年，帮扶农村独生子女户中的困难户281户发展种植、养殖业。1997年，县、乡计生部门共帮扶计生户558户。2005年6月，县计生局下发《关于转发息烽县计生协会〈关于抓好计生协会工作示范点实施意见〉的通知》，要求各乡镇抓好1～2个示范村（居）协会工作，促进后进协会工作转化。9月，贵阳市计划生育协会暨少生快富经验交流会在小寨坝镇红岩村召开。是年，全县共投入“三结合”帮扶资金约1000万元，共帮扶独生子女户、两女结扎户及一般计生户7500余户，帮助群众脱贫3000余户，为381户减免子女九年义务教育书杂费，免收411户外出务工办证费，为1172人提供农村合作医疗补助金。2006年，以“协会服务行动拓展年”活动为契机，开展“少生快富”试点工程、“生育关怀服务行动”“青春路上健康行”等活动，发挥协会五项职能作用。2007年，开展“生育关怀行动”“少生快富”以及新农村、新农家、新农民的“三新”活动。是年，全县投入资金850万元，共帮扶计生户17853户，帮扶面为91.05%。其中计生贫困户7747户19124人通过帮扶实现脱贫。2008年，开展支部加协会建设新农村，推进“政策法规进家”“婚育新风进家”“优质服务进家”“奖励扶助进家”“帮教致富进家”“生育关怀进家”等“六进家”服务活动。全年投入“生育关怀行动”资金99.8万元，落实求助项目25个，有1778户计生贫困户通过“生育关怀行动”在一年内实现脱贫。春节期间，慰问计生贫困户139户，送去慰问金2.68万元以及大米、菜油、猪肉、被子、棉衣等物。2009年，永靖镇立碑村被列为省、市“三新”示范点和全省“留守儿童乐园示范点建设村”。是年，为108名奖励扶助对象申报国家奖励扶助金7.14万元，为13户独生子女伤残或父（母）死亡、手术并发症家庭办理特别救助金1.8万元，为1820名农村独女户、两女结扎户父母申请“关爱女孩奖”8.96万元。2010年春节期间，发放慰问金3.6万元和价值2万余元的慰问物资。是年，小寨坝镇红岩村获国家级“基层群众自治示范村”称号，永靖镇立碑村获“支部加协会建设新农村省级示范村”称号。

第三章　民族·宗教

1991年，县民族事务委员会（简称县民委）为县管理民族事务的职能部门。1995年11月，县民委更名为县民族事务局，下设办公室。1996年2月，县民族事务局加挂“息烽县宗教事务局”牌子（简称民宗局），内设办公室、民族科、宗教科3科室。2002年3月，撤销原科室，单设综合业务科。2004年9月，县民族事务局与县宗教事务局合并，组建县民族宗教事务局。2005年11月，恢复民族事务局和宗教事务局称谓，撤销综合业务科，改设办公室、民族科、宗教科。

第一节　民　族

一、汉族

1991年，县境内汉族人口212072人，占全县总人口的94.94%，为县域内主体民族。汉族来源可追溯至明、清两代。明、清两代“调北征南”“改土归流”时，由四川、江苏、湖南、江西等地随军征战入境。抗日战争时期，难民流入大西南，部分进入县境。解放后，随军南下、西进到县接管政权以及经济建设中到县工作和兴建厂矿者，也使得汉族人口大幅度增加。1991—2000年，由于县境内中央及省属企事业单位相继外迁，汉民族有所减少。2000年，汉族总人口209177人。此后，随着经济发展，到县工作、生活的少数民族人口逐渐增加以及汉族的外迁，至2010年，汉族人口略有下降，为201104人。

二、苗族

1991年，县境内有苗族人口8262人。2000年，苗族人口8309人，占全县总人口的3.98%。2010年，苗族人口降至8114人，占全县总人口的3.81%。县内苗族主要分布于青山苗族乡青山村、冗坝村，永靖镇河坎村、雨洒村、安马村、河丰村、梨安村，九庄镇新沙村、柏茂村；石硐乡水头村、石硐村、木杉村，西山乡猪场村、金星村、新寨沟村等地。其他乡镇也有散居。

三、布依族

1991年，县境内有布依族人口1999人，占全县总人口的0.9%。2000年，布依族人口1846人，占全县总人口的0.83%。2010年，布依族人口1721人，占全县总人口的0.81%。主要分布于石硐乡大洪村，何家硐村高坡、坝子边，九庄镇和平村团坡寨、竹花村丫济沟，养龙司乡潘家寨、郁家坡，小寨坝镇亲戚寨村龙井坪等地。

四、彝族

1991年，县境内彝族人口472人，占全县人口的0.21%。2000年，彝族人口429人。2010年，彝族人口562人，占全县人口的0.25%。主要分布于永靖镇河坎村箱子坪、坪上村石灰窑，鹿窝乡新民村新雀、杨寨村梁子上，青山苗族乡大林村中合铺，石硐乡红星村田家铺、木杉村汪冲等地。其他各乡镇也有散居分布。

五、其他民族

1991—2010年，县境内有苗、布依、彝、回、满、壮、白、侗、水、黎、畲、羌、土、藏、佤、傣、瑶、蒙古、仫佬、朝鲜、仡佬、土家、哈尼、拉祜、毛南、纳西26个少数民族，2010年共有1701人，占全县总人口的0.66%。

第二节　民族工作

1991年，对少数民族继续贯彻执行计划生育优待政策，对夫妻双方都是少数民族的非农业人口或一方是少数民族的农业人口，允许生育第二胎；对农业人口中的少数民族夫妇，经批准可以生育第三胎；各大中专院校对少数民族考生，在同等条件下，降低分数线录取等。1992年，县民委组织开展少数民族困难帮扶活动，为18户少数民族建房2000余平方米，为少数民族购买耕牛10头。此后，县委、县政府每年争取上级有关项目经费和专款，协调中央、省、市帮扶单位、社会各界人士、企事业单位给予资金物资支持和建立帮扶点等，多渠道筹措资金，帮扶少数民族地区及少数民族困难户改善办学、生产、生活条件。至2001年，共投入资金846.6万元，为少数民族地区建学校2所，修建人畜饮水工程45处，解决约1万人和4000余头牲畜饮水问题。为300余户少数民族修建住房。其中，1997、1998两年，县委、县政府把永靖镇河坎村、九庄镇下环山村民组作为少数民族村寨扶贫点，拨款500余万元，为94户少数民族群众集中修建住房、圈舍，建提水站、水池，安装自来水等。2001年，市委书记王晓东率市直11家单位集资100万元，为青山苗族乡消灭人居茅草房226户。

2003年，县委、县政府拨款200余万元，在西山乡鹿窝村中心地段为该村木姜山村民组20户苗族同胞集中修建砖混结构楼房20栋、畜圈440平方米，动员苗族同胞从海拔1400米的木姜山集体搬迁到到新房居住，划出20亩地作为20户的蔬菜种植用地。

2007年1月，县委出台《关于进一步加强民族工作　加快少数民族和民族地区经济社会发展的实施意见》，提出加快少数民族和民族地区经济社会发展，集中力量改善0.6万少数民族贫困人口的基本生产生活条件；推进民族地区经济结构调整，把旅游业培育成为民族乡村新的经济增长点；发展民族地区教育事业。对农村少数民族考生报考息烽一中实行降低两个分数段录取政策。在“十一五”期间，落实“三个20万元”经费（民族工作经费、教育经费、基础设施建设经费）等。是年，争取项目资金91.3万元，为民族地区硬化串户路31.6千米，新修公路12千米，解决少数民族困难群众3200人的农村合作医疗保险困难，创办民族刺绣班1个，帮助55户少数民族困难户修建新房。2010年，争取上级民族资金380余万元，用于参加市的“四月八”活动、解决民族地区基础设施建设、补助少数民族生活困难的大学生在大学期间的相关费用。

第三节　宗教与宗教事务

一、教派

（一）佛教

1991年，全县有佛教僧尼3人。民间信教者多为老年妇女。此后，信教人员逐渐增多，至2002年，佛教信众增至895人。是年3月，县民宗局与小寨坝镇政府联系僧人释妙乐组织捐助善款修建普照寺。2003年5月，普照寺修建工程动工，2008年3月完工，占地面积1080平方米，建筑面积730平方米，总投资500余万元。2010年，全县僧众、佛教信众较之前略有增加。

（二）道教

20世纪90年代，玄天洞偶有道士活动。2009年，全县有道教教职人员76人，其中有牒符者39人，有法名者21人。2010年，道教教职人员减至65人，有牒符和法名者人数不变。

（三）基督教

1991年，全县有基督教信教人员170余人，主要分布于养龙司、流长、永靖镇、温泉等地，无固定活动场所，信教人员多在小寨坝镇茅草寨村小沟子村民组部分村民家中开展活动。1998年7月，经贵阳市宗教事务局批准，在小寨坝镇设立基督教教堂。12月，县政府批准在小寨坝镇中心村黄连沟建小寨坝基督教教堂。次年9月，县民宗局批准小沟子基督教临时活动点民主管理小组成立。2000年

11月，小寨坝基督教教堂建成，占地面积1200平方米，建筑面积589.4平方米。2002年，全县基督教信教人员增至562人，2010年降至160人。

二、宗教事务

1991年，由县委统战部牵头，组织民宗局及乡镇对全县宗教活动场所进行清理。1993年，对打着恢复龙王庙幌子，在流长小学内塑神建庙事件进行处理，恢复小学教学秩序。1994年，县委、县政府下发《关于认真执行宗教政策　做好宗教工作　坚决打击反动会道门和取缔封建迷信活动的意见》。1996年，组织全县村支书、主任和乡镇分管领导，开展宗教工作培训，学习宗教知识和宗教政策。是年，全县取缔邪教活动点9个，刑拘16人，拆除乱建庙宇28处，收缴迷信书刊49册、木鼓2个，48名住庙人员被遣回原籍。2002年，开展宗教活动情况普查登记工作，全县有信教人员1626人，其中基督教562人、佛教895人、道教168人、天主教1人。2003年，成立县宗教协调领导小组，建立县、乡（镇）宗教工作三级网络和两级负责制；建县级宗教网络1个，乡级宗教网络10个，村（居）委签订责任书169份。是年，拆除乱建寺庙2处。2004年，开展反邪教宣传活动，发放宣传资料1万份，制作展板29块，取缔非法传教信教场所19处，捣毁非法设置的佛像80尊。2007年，全县开展《宗教事务条例》宣传活动。是年，接受印度尼西亚、新加坡、厦门、昆明、遵义佛教组织捐款30.5万元，用于改善学校办学条件和农村基础设施建设。2009年，县委统战部、县公安局及乡镇成立调查小组，开展宗教活动摸底调查。据调查统计，全县有以家庭聚会方式开展宗教活动的场所6个，参加活动人员17人；以家庭聚会活动为主，私设基督教点6个，参加活动人员38人。2010年，香会活动期间，开展安全和宗教出版物审查，开展创建和谐寺观、教堂活动，加强宗教教职人员和宗教活动场所备案审查工作。是年，启动西望山凤池寺新寺建设工作。

第四篇　政党·群团组织

第一章　中共息烽县委员会

1991—2010年，中共息烽县委员会（简称县委）以建设有中国特色社会主义理论为指导，立足息烽实际，提出科教兴县、工业强县、环境立县、旅游活县发展战略，作出相应决策。一系列重大决策的实施，保持了息烽社会政治稳定，经济持续健康发展，提前两年完成“八七”扶贫攻坚计划，2002年摘掉国定贫困县帽子，2008年进入全省经济建设强县行列。2010年，全县地方生产总值55.49亿元，人均生产总值23218元；完成财政总收入5.5亿元，地方财政收入3.08亿元；城镇居民人均可支配收入14680元，农民人均纯收入5084元。

第一节　党员代表大会

1993年前，中共息烽县党员代表大会每3年召开一次，此后，每5年召开一次。会议主要听取审议上一届县委常委会工作报告、听取审议中共息烽县纪律检查委员会（简称县纪委）工作报告；选举县委委员和县纪委委员。1990—2010年，共举行会议5次。

一、党代表选举

根据《中国共产党章程》《中国共产党地方组织选举工作条例》规定，党代表名额根据党员数量确定，分配到各选举单位，由选举单位根据差额比例酝酿提出代表候选人，报县委组织部审查后，由选举单位召开党员大会投票选举。每次代表中，妇女、少数民族代表须占一定比例。对代表集中的县领导机关的部分代表，分派到各选举单位参加选举。第七次至第十一次会议代表名额分别为235名、200名、212名、218名、233名。

二、党代表会议

（一）第七次党代会

1990年7月24—28日在县城召开。出席会议代表235人。会议听取审议并通过县委书记陈华祥代表第六届县委作的《坚持基本路线　加强党的建设　努力推动我县政治　经济　社会的稳定发展》和县纪委书记黄友顺代表县纪委作的《从严治党　严肃执纪　进一步把党的建设推向前进》工作报告。选举产生县委七届委员会委员25名，候补委员3名；选举产生县纪委委员13名。

会议期间，举行七届县委一次全委会议，选举产生县委七届常务委员会（简称县委常委会）组成人员9名：陈华祥为书记，陈建忠、黄元法、邱志雄为副书记，罗新安、刘兴明、龙升明、李以智、罗筑云为常委。

（二）第八次党代会

1993年5月26—29日在县城召开。出席会议代表196人。会议听取审议并通过县委书记陈华祥代表第七届县委作的《换脑筋 抓机遇 鼓实劲 促发展》工作报告和县纪委书记刘权德代表县纪委作的工作报告。会议选举产生县委八届委员会委员29名，候补委员4名；选举县纪委委员17名。

会议期间，举行县委八届一次全委会议，选举产生县委八届常委会组成人员7名：陈华祥为书记，黑卫平、李以智、刘兴明为副书记，刘权德、李贵菊（女）、任国元为常委。

（三）第九次党代会

1998年4月22—24日在县城召开。出席会议代表211人，列席60人。会议听取审议并通过县委书记李忠代表第八届县委作的《解放思想 更新观念 抢抓机遇 奋力拼搏 把息烽各项事业全面推向二十一世纪》工作报告和县纪委书记刘权德代表县纪委作的工作报告。会议选举产生县委九届委员会委员31名，候补委员6名；选举县纪委委员16名。

会议期间，举行县委九届一次全委会议，选举产生县委九届常委会组成人员12名：李忠为书记，陈长发、曾德书、吴德屏为副书记，宫喜祥、袁仁庆、韦奕松、黄银忠、刘权德、燕飞、魏发志、杨胜荣为常委。

（四）第十次党代会

2003年2月17日在县城召开。出席代表218名。会议听取审议并通过县委书记杨彦峰代表第九届县委作的《开拓创新求发展 与时俱进奔小康》工作报告和县纪委书记邓忠元代表县纪委作的工作报告。会议选举产生县委十届委员会委员32名，候补委员6名；选举县纪委委员15名。

会议期间，举行县委十届一次全委会议，选举产生县委常委会组成人员：杨彦峰为书记，李志鹏、邓忠元、刘迪华为副书记，魏发志、陈康、刘大英（女）、汤太祥、陈德勇、王永平为常委。

（五）第十一次党代会

2006年9月25—28日在县城召开。出席代表233名。会议听取审议并通过县委书记杨彦峰代表第十届县委作的《增创新优势 谋求新发展 为实现强县目标而努力奋斗》工作报告和县纪委书记代表县纪委作的工作报告。会议选举产生县委十一届委员会委员39名，候补委员7名；选举县纪委委员21名。

会议期间，举行县委十一届一次全委会议，选举产生县委常委会组成人员：杨彦峰为书记，罗德亚为副书记，陈德勇、王永平、黄永辉、张定超、李福燕、宋力为常委。

息烽县委书记、副书记、常委名录

表4-1-1

届　次	姓　名	性别	民族	籍　贯	职　务	任职时间	备　注
第七届	陈华祥	男	汉族	贵州安顺	书记	1990年7月—1993年5月	
	黄元法	男	汉族	福建惠安	副书记	1990年7月—1993年5月	
	陈建忠	男	汉族	贵州贵阳	副书记	1990年7月—1992年2月	
	邱志雄	男	汉族	福建惠安	副书记	1990年7月—1991年10月	

续表

届 次	姓 名	性别	民族	籍 贯	职 务	任职时间	备 注
第七届	周延龄	男	汉族		副书记	1990年7月—1993年5月	
	罗新安	男	汉族	湖北武汉	常委	1990年7月—1991年7月	
					副书记	1991年7月—1992年10月	
	黑卫平	男	回族	贵州安顺	副书记	1992年2月—1993年5月	
	李以智	男	汉族	贵州遵义	常委	1990年7月—1992年1月	
					副书记	1992年1月—1993年5月	
	刘兴明	男	汉族	四川安岳	常委	1990年7月—1992年10月	
					副书记	1992年10月—1993年5月	
	罗筑云	男	汉族	贵州贵阳	常委	1990年7月—1992年1月	
	龙升明	男	侗族		常委	1990年7月—1993年5月	
	李贵菊	女	汉族	贵州息烽	常委	1992年10月—1993年5月	
第八届	陈华祥	男	汉族	贵州安顺	书记	1993年5月—1993年12月	
	黑卫平	男	回族	贵州安顺	书记	1993年12月—1997年9月	
	李 忠	男	汉族	山西稷山	书记	1997年9月—1998年4月	
	李以智	男	汉族	贵州遵义	副书记	1993年5月—1998年4月	
	刘兴明	男	汉族	四川安岳	副书记	1993年5月—1998年4月	
	李贵菊	女	汉族	贵州息烽	副书记	1993年5月—1998年4月	
	王海萍	女	汉族	山东龙口	副书记	1994年4月—1995年4月	挂职
	孙筑萍	女	汉族		副书记	1995年4月—1997年3月	挂职
	曾德书	男	汉族	贵州息烽	副书记	1995年8月—1998年4月	
	陆小华	男	汉族		副书记	1996年8月—1997年8月	挂职
	刘宝静	男	汉族	贵州贵阳	副书记	1997年3月—1998年3月	挂职
	宫喜祥	男	汉族	黑龙江北安	副书记	1997年10月—1998年10月	挂职
	刘权德	男	汉族	贵州清镇	常委	1993年5月—1998年4月	
	任国元	男	汉族	贵州息烽	常委	1993年5月—1998年4月	
	魏明禄	男	汉族	贵州息烽	常委	1993年12月—1998年4月	
	吴德屏	男	汉族	重庆	常委	1993年12月—1998年4月	
	燕 飞	男	汉族	—	常委	1993年3月—1998年4月	
	张巧楠	女	汉族	—	常委	1995年4月—1996年4月	挂职
	艾克勇	男	汉族	—	常委	1996年4月—1997年4月	挂职

续表

届 次	姓 名	性别	民族	籍 贯	职 务	任职时间	备 注
第九届	李 忠	男	汉族	山西稷山	书记	1998年4月—2000年7月	
	陈长发	男	汉族	浙江温州	副书记	1998年4月—2007年7月	
					书记	2000年7月—2003年2月	
	曾德书	男	汉族	贵州息烽	副书记	1998年4月—2000年9月	
	吴德屏	男	汉族	重庆	副书记	1998年4月—2003年2月	
	袁仁庆	男	汉族	贵州仁怀	副书记	1998年6月—2000年6月	挂职
	韦奕松	男	汉族	—	副书记	1998年6月—2000年6月	挂职
	曹晓明	男	汉族	—	副书记	1999年3月—2000年3月	挂职
	邵 军	男	汉族	—	副书记	1999年4月—2001年4月	挂职
	蒋志勇	男	汉族	—	副书记	2000年4月—2001年4月	挂职
	杨彦峰	男	布依族	贵州平塘	副书记	2000年7月—2003年2月	
	李志鹏	男	汉族	贵州清镇	副书记	2000年9月—2003年2月	
	陈德建	男	汉族	—	副书记	2001年4月—2002年4月	挂职
	陈 磊	男	汉族	—	副书记	2002年4月—2003年4月	挂职
	黄银忠	男	汉族	贵州息烽	常委	1998年4月—2003年1月	
	刘权德	男	汉族	贵州清镇	常委	1998年4月—2003年2月	
	燕 飞	男	汉族	—	常委	1998年4月—2003年2月	
	魏发志	男	汉族	贵州息烽	常委	1998年4月—2003年2月	
	杨胜荣	男	汉族	贵州息烽	常委	1998年4月—1999年7月	
	陈 康	男	汉族	贵州息烽	常委	2001年1月—2003年2月	
	邓忠元	男	汉族	贵州贵阳	常委	2001年2月—2003年2月	
					副书记	2003年2月—2006年9月	
	刘迪华	男	汉族	贵州贵阳	常委	2001年6月—2003年2月	
第十届	杨彦峰	男	布依族	贵州平塘	书记	2003年2月—2006年9月	
	丁旭东	男	汉族	湖北钟祥	副书记	2003年2月—2006年4月	
	黄秋斌	男	汉族	福建安溪	副书记	2006年5月—2006年9月	
	李志鹏	男	汉族	贵州清镇	副书记	2003年2月—2003年4月	
	刘迪华	男	汉族	贵州贵阳	副书记	2003年2月—2004年8月	
	罗德亚	男	布依族	贵州罗甸	副书记	2004年9月—2006年9月	
	刘大英	女	汉族	贵州息烽	常委	2003年2月—2004年3月	
					副书记	2004年3月—2006年9月	

续表

届　次	姓　名	性别	民族	籍　贯	职　务	任职时间	备　注
第十届	杨　宁	男	汉族	贵州遵义	副书记	2005年3月—2006年6月	挂职
	杨　樱	女	布依	贵州兴义	副书记	2005年10月—2007年10月	挂职
	向　阳	男	汉族	四川成都	副书记	2006年3月—2007年3月	挂职
	魏发志	男	汉族	贵州息烽	常委	2003年2月—2004年3月	
	陈　康	男	汉族	贵州息烽	常委	2003年2月—2006年9月	
	汤太祥	男	汉族	贵州息烽	常委	2003年2月—2006年9月	
	陈德勇	男	汉族	—	常委	2003年2月—2006年9月	
	王永平	男	汉族	贵州息烽	常委	2003年2月—2006年9月	
	黄永辉	男	汉族	贵州息烽	常委	2004年3月—2006年9月	
	张定超	男	汉族	贵州贵阳	常委	2004年3月—2006年9月	
第十一届	杨彦峰	男	布依族	贵州平塘	书记	2006年9月—2007年12月	
	刘文新	男	汉族	贵州修文	书记	2007年12月—2008年7月	
	黄秋斌	男	汉族	福建安溪	书记	2008年7月—	
	罗德亚	男	布依族	贵州罗甸	副书记	2006年9月—2007年12月	
	钟　阳	女	布依族	江西吉安	副书记	2009年5月—	
	陈德勇	男	汉族		常委	2006年9月—2008年6月	
	高开祥	男	汉族	贵州金沙	常委	2008年6月—2009年6月	
	张　昆	男	汉族		常委	2010年6月—	
	王永平	男	汉族	贵州息烽	常委	2006年9月—	
	黄永辉	男	汉族	贵州息烽	常委	2006年9月—	
	张定超	男	汉族	贵州贵阳	常委	2006年9月—	
	马　钊	男	汉族	贵州石阡	常委	2006年9月—	
	李福燕	女	汉族	山东历城	常委	2006年9月—	
	宋　力	男	汉族	贵州贵阳	常委	2006年9月—	
	佘　龙	男	汉族	湖南邵东	常委	2008年6月—2010年5月	
	方志立	男	汉族		常委	2010年5月—	
	向　阳	男	汉族	四川成都	副书记	2006年3月—2007年3月	挂职
	曹垒发	男	汉族	贵州石阡	常委	2008年4月—2010年4月	挂职
	梁小江	男	汉族	贵州绥阳	常委	2009年9月—2010年9月	挂职
	刘　彤	男	汉族	四川自贡	常委	2010年9月—	挂职
	李泽洋	男	汉族		常委	2010年9月—	挂职

三、县委工作部门

1991年，县委工作部门有县委办公室、组织部、宣传部、统战部、政法委、农村工作部、农村经济委员会、直属机关党委、老干部局、对台办（与县政府台湾事务办公室合署办公）、信访办、保密局（归口县委办公室）、机要局（归口县委办公室）。县委管理的事业单位：县委党校、党史研究室。此后，历经1995年、2001年、2004年、2009年四次机构改革，县委工作部门有撤、并、整合、重组及新建（详见本篇第三章《机构编制》）。2010年，县委工作部门有县委办公室（政策研究室，机要局、保密委员会办公室〈国家保密局〉）、组织部、宣传部（精神文明建设指导委员会办公室设在宣传部）、统战部（含对台工作）、政法委员会（社会治安综合治理委员会办公室与其合署办公，一个机构两块牌子；维护社会稳定领导小组办公室设在政法委员会）、机构编制委员会办公室、直属机关党委、离退休干部工作局（由组织部管理，不占机构限额）。县委管理的事业单位：县委党校。

四、区、乡（镇）党委

1991年，全县有永阳、养龙、九庄、黑神庙4个区委和永靖镇党委；有三田乡、梨安乡、下阳朗乡、阳朗乡、底寨乡、西山乡、青山苗族乡、养龙司乡、安江乡、茅坡乡、温泉乡、九庄镇、九庄乡、竹花乡、新杨乡、鹿窝乡、石硐乡、猫场乡、何家硐乡、小寨坝乡、南极乡、王家坪乡、流长乡、土城坝乡24个乡（镇）党委。是年11月，息烽县实施撤区并乡建镇，撤销原4区1镇和24个乡（镇）建制，组建4镇（永靖镇、小寨坝镇、温泉镇、九庄镇）6乡（西山乡、养龙司乡、流长乡、石硐乡、鹿窝乡、青山苗族乡），并分别建各乡（镇）党委。

第二节 县委全委会

县委全委会议由县委委员、候补委员出席，县委常委会主持。会议须有2/3以上县委委员出席方能举行。每年至少举行2次，根据工作需要，可增开或召开全体（扩大）会议。县纪委委员、非县委委员、候补委员的在职县级干部、县人民政府县长助理、曾经担任过副县级以上领导职务的离退休老同志、县人民法院、县人民检察院领导班子成员及县委各部办委局、县政府各部门、各人民团体领导班子成员列席。会议时间、议题，由常委会议确定。一般在会议召开5天前通知委员并送达会议材料。决定有关事项，由县委委员表决，以赞成票超过应到会委员的半数为通过。表决采取举手或无记名投票方式进行。决定多个事项时，逐项进行表决。会议内容：研究决定贯彻上级党组织的重大决策部署和县党代表会议决议、决定措施；对全县经济建设、社会发展、党的建设和其他涉及全局性问题作出决策；听取和审议县委常委会工作报告，对县委常委会及其成员的工作进行监督和评议等。

2000年12月30日，县委召开九届九次全会，传达贯彻党的十五届五中全会、省委八届六次全会、市委七届四次全会和中央、省经济工作会议精神，部署全县新世纪初的改革发展工作。会议审议通过《中共息烽县委关于制定息烽县国民经济和社会发展第十个五年计划的建议》。提出“十五”期间“转变观念，抢抓机遇，扩大开放，突出重点，调整结构，狠抓落实，实现跨越”的总体发展思路，到2005年，国内生产总值达到16.1亿元，在2000年基础上翻1.07番，全县基本实现小康，各项社会事业全面进步，迈入贵州经济强县行列的奋斗目标。要求全县上下要紧紧围绕奋斗目标，围绕经济建设这个中心，突出发展主题，贯穿结构调整主线，立足提高人民生活水平的根本出发点，高扬抢抓机遇、开拓创新、强县升位的时代主旋律，实施开放带动、科教兴县、可持续发展、全面创新、多元发展五大战略，为实现"十五"期间息烽经济超常规跨越式发展而努力奋斗。

2002年12月30日，县委召开九届十一次全会，学习贯彻党的十六大、市委七届八次全体（扩大）会议和省、市经济工作会议精神。审议通过县委、县政府《关于深入贯彻十六大精神 全面建设小康社会的实施意见》。提出到2020年，实现全面建设小康社会目标：至2004年，国民生产总值比2000年翻一番；到2008年，国民生产总值比2000年翻两番；到2014年，国民生产总值比2000年翻三番；到2020年，国民生产总值比2000年翻四番。

2005年12月30日，县委召开十届六次全会，讨论通过《息烽县"十一五"规划纲要》，提出以科学发展观统领全局，按"抓机遇、强产业、带农村、走前列"的发展思路和"科学定位，立足创新，整体推进，和谐发展，实现跨越"的总体要求，大力实施科教兴县、工业强县、环境立县三大战略，切实抓好城镇基础设施、农业综合生产能力、重点产业项目、人才队伍和发展环境五大建设，全力打造磷煤化工、制药、绿色食品深加工、建材和红色旅游五大产业，着力解决经济结构调整、经济增长方式转变、经济体制完善、经济社会协调发展、城乡二元结构和就业六大问题，正确处理改革、发展、稳定三大关系，到2010年，力争实现人均生产总值在2000年基础上翻2.7番，是2005年的2.2倍，经济总量在全市排位前移两位，进入贵州经济强县行列。

2008年1月8日，县委召开第十一届四次全体（扩大）会议，总结2007年经济社会发展工作，安排部署2008年经济社会发展工作；基层党委书记向县委全委会作党建工作专项述职报告。会议讨论通过《中共息烽县委关于建设生态文明县的决定》，提出建设生态文明县的五年奋斗目标：至2012年，生态产业快速发展，循环经济取得实效，服务业比重明显提高，二、三、一产业结构进一步优化；单位生产总值能耗比2005年降低25%以上，主要污染物排放总量减少10%以上；推进城乡环境生态化，建设80个生态文明村寨，全县生态环境质量进一步提升；生态文明观念在全社会牢固树立；民生显著改善，人民群众幸福感明显增强；文化特色逐步彰显；政府更加廉洁高效，生态文明发展基础进一步夯实，息烽更加适宜居住、适宜创业、适宜旅游。

第三节 县委常委会

县委常委会议须有半数以上常委出席方能举行，决定干部任免或提名的常委会议，须有2/3以上常委出席方能举行。县人大常委会、县政协党组书记列席会议。根据议题需要，吸收与会议议题直接有关的县其他班子领导和部门负责人列席（仅参加相关议题的汇报和讨论）。常委会会议由书记或书记委托的副书记主持。常委会会议一般每半月召开1次，需要时可临时召集。会议议题由书记或书记委托副书记确定。常委会讨论决定问题，根据讨论事项采取口头、举手、无记名投票或记名投票方式表决。2004年12月起，对干部任免事项采用无记名投票表决。决定事项编发会议纪要，不宜印发的会议纪要经会议主持人审阅后存档。

1991年4月22日，县委召开常委会议，传达《国务院关于调整粮油统销价格的决定》（以下简称《决定》）和安顺地区调整粮油统销价格紧急会议精神。会议认为：调整粮油统销价格是深化粮食流通体制改革的重要措施，做好这项工作，有利于社会稳定和发展，表示坚决拥护。要求各级党委、政府和干部、党团员要提高对调整粮油统销价格重大意义的认识，带头执行《决定》，做执行《决定》的表率、做宣传贯彻《决定》的标兵、做与破坏《决定》贯彻执行不良言行作斗争的模范。有关部门要及时做好调价前的准备工作。粮食部门从现在起做好粮油供应工作，改变服务态度，提高服务质量。物价、工商部门要切实加强市场管理，对搭车涨价、哄抬物价的要严肃处理。公安部门要做好调整粮油统销价格的保卫工作，为《决定》的贯彻执行创造良好的心理环境和社会环境。开好五大班子联席会，各区（镇）长、财政和粮管所长会，机关副局级（包括副主任科员）以上干部和全体党员参加的紧急动员会，各单位职工会，层层贯彻落实，及时反馈贯彻落实情况。

1995年6月7日，县委召开常委会议，就息烽县作为全省第一批率先脱贫县进行专题讨论。会议认为：1993年，息烽县农民人均纯收入在全省46个贫困县中排列第一，农业适用技术推广、粮食生产及乡镇企业发展速度等在全省县市中是比较好的，且位于省城贵阳与历史名城遵义之间，没有理由说不能在第一批脱贫，按省委、省政府的要求，同意作为全省第一批脱贫县，1996年率先脱贫。要求涉及有脱贫指标的单位、部门，要对照脱贫目标，结合县情，找出差距，算好账，提出问题和解决问题的办法、措施。报县扶贫办汇总，提交县委、县政府研究决定。

1996年5月17日上午，县委召开常委会议，讨论研究宣传思想、精神文明建设工作。指出现阶段党的宣传思想、精神文明建设工作，要以邓小平建设有中国特色社会主义理论和党的基本路线为指导，以创建卫生城镇为近期目标，以群众性精神文明建设活动为载体，采取多种形式，全方位开展精神文明建设系列活动。决定开展创建卫生城镇、文明村寨、文明单位，“做人民公仆”评比竞赛；评选“文明市场”和“文明个体工商户”；评选“优秀青年”“三八红旗手”“五好家庭”“三好学生”系列活动。要求各级各部门要加强对开展精神文明建设系列活动重要性的认识，切实加强领导，齐抓共管，形成合力，做到“两个文明”建设任务一起下，“两个文明”建设成果一起要。

1996年8月16日，县委召开常委会议，讨论研究大中专毕业生就业和中青年干部培养问题。会议决定：从1996年起，大中专毕业生原则上安排外出打工锻炼1～2年，同时有计划地组织部分在职30岁左右的青年干部外出打工锻炼，借地育才。议定：1996年本科以上毕业生由县安置到专业对口的县级事业单位工作，另外组织实践锻炼；警察院校毕业生安排到公安部门工作，政法院校毕业生，在单位编制范围内由县安置到对口单位工作，以缓解当前警力不足的现状；师范类、医药卫生类毕业生，选派一部分参加外出打工锻炼，一部分按生源流向，在编制范围内安置到鹿窝、石硐、青山等边远地区工作，解决师资不足和缺医少药问题；工程测量、地籍管理、果蔬等急需专业毕业生，直接安置到对口的事业单位工作。

2000年2月21日下午，县委召开常委会议，研究基层组织建设工作。议定：原则同意《息烽县2000年基层组织建设工作安排意见》和《关于2000年农村基层组织建设“六好”乡镇“五好”村创建活动的安排意见》，由县委组织部按照常委会意见修改后送县委主要领导审定，印发各乡镇、单位执行；同意召开全县组织工作会议暨农村基层组织建设工作会议，专门研究村级领导班子成员年轻化、发展党员问题等，要求组织部门要搞好调查摸底，提出解决方案；同意调整县农村基层组织建设领导小组成员。

2008年2月28日上午，县委召开常委会议，传达学习市委常委（扩大）会议和市“抓重建，保民生”工作领导小组会议精神，听取县发改局关于灾后重建项目编制和申报情况汇报。会议对全县“抓重建，保民生”工作进行安排部署，要求全县各级干部，特别是领导干部要牢记全心全意为人民服务宗旨，坚定不移地站在老百姓的立场想问题、办事情，一切从群众利益出发，把维护好最广大人民群众的根本利益作为“抓重建，保民生”工作的出发点和落脚点。发扬“情系人民、忠于职守，万众一心、共赴艰难，自强不息、敢于胜利”的贵阳抗凝冻精神和“自强不息、艰苦奋斗、赤胆忠诚、协力争先”的息烽精神，把每项工作抓紧抓实。对事关群众切身利益的各项设施的重建修复，要在规定时限内保质保量完成。各级各部门主要负责人要切实履行第一责任人职责，提前做好各种次生灾害和可能发生旱灾的预防工作；组织力量对企业设备设施进行安全生产大检查，确保不发生安全事故。县成立维稳安全工作指挥部，逐案逐厂制定应对措施，落实人员责任；以最硬的措施、最严格的纪律，坚决防止和严厉打击灾后重建工作中的各种腐败行为和违法行为。

第四节　重大决策

一、党组织建设

1990年2月24日，县委印发加强党组织建设意见，提出各级党组织要建立完善八项制度：定期议党建制度。县委每季度议一次，区、乡、镇党委每两个月议一次；党建工作联系点制度。县委、县纪委领导成员，县委工作部门和县直属机关党委要有自己的党建工作联系点，帮助、指导联系点围绕贯彻党的民主集中制、治理整顿、深化改革和党风建设、精神文明建设、思想政治工作以及“双带”“三带一联系”等进行调查研究，督促检查，协助解决存在问题；党建目标管理和考核制度。党建工作实行目标管理，年终检查考核，兑现奖惩；定期培训干部和党员制度。每年集中培训一次以上，时间不少于6天；定期研究“工青妇”工作制度。各级党组织每半年召开一次研究“工青妇”工作会议；干部教育管理制度。对干部在任期内进行一至二次评议考察，恢复干部“谈话”制度；坚持半年一次民主生活会制度；一年一次民主评议党员制度。

1993年2月，县委印发加强党的建设工作意见，提出加强党的思想理论建设，用邓小平建设有中国特色社会主义理论武装全体党员和群众，使广大党员从过去旧的观念中摆脱出来，树立适应社会主义市场经济发展的新思想、新观念。从因循守旧、安于常规的精神状态中摆脱出来，树立奋发进取、勇于开拓、敢为人先的精神面貌；加强各级领导班子建设，按照干部“四化”和德才兼备原则，打破论资排辈、求全责备等陈旧观念，通过县乡换届，把德才兼备的干部选拔、调配和充实进各级领导班子；加强党的基层组织建设，通过加强制度建设和党员的教育管理，落实党建工作目标责任制，发挥党组织的战斗堡垒作用和党员先锋模范带头作用。机关、企业、学校党建要根据自身特点，积极探索改革开放、市场经济新形势下党的建设工作的新方法、新举措；加强党风党纪教育，制定和完善监督约束机制；坚持民主集中制和完善共产党领导下的多党合作政治协商制度。

1995年1月，县委印发《关于加强党的建设的意见》，提出：坚持和健全民主集中制，完善各项工作制度。加强对党员干部、特别是党员领导干部进行民主集中制教育。建立完善党代表大会制度、各种会议制度、议事规则、决策程序和民主评议党员、评议干部制度。严肃党的纪律、加强党内监督。要围绕经济建设，加强基层党组织建设。农村党的基层组织建设，要围绕脱贫致富奔小康、“四个一”工程开展工作，实现农村基层组织“五个好”目标。企业党建要围绕生产经营、企业改革、转换经营机制、提高经济效益开展工作，科学合理规范企业党、政、工负责人交叉兼职，形成权责分明、管理科学，激励和约束机制相结合的内部管理体制。党政群机关基层党组织建设，从转变机关工作作风入手，抓好廉政建设和职工队伍建设，抓好党员教育管理。学校党组织建设，要围绕教育改革和发展，培养有理想、有道德、有文化、有纪律的社会主义事业建设者和接班人开展工作，重点解决好村级小学、民办小学和教学点没有党员或党支部的问题，凡有3名以上党员的学校都应建党支部。

二、计划生育

1991年10月20日，县委、县政府印发《关于进一步加强计划生育管理的规定》，提出：夫妻双方或一方是国家工作人员、企事业单位职工、城镇居民的只能生育一个孩子。其他几种情况可以生育第二个孩子：第一个孩子为非遗传性残疾的；夫妻双方为独生子女或少数民族的；夫妻结婚五年以上因患不孕症，已收养一个孩子，治愈后要求生育的；一方或双方是再婚的，一方生育过孩子，另一方未生育的；夫妻双方是农民，男方到独生子女家结婚落户成为女方家庭成员的；夫妻一方是少数民族，第一个孩子是女孩的。夫妻双方都是少数民族的农民，两个孩子中有一个为非遗传性残疾的，允许再生育一个孩子。提倡、鼓励晚婚晚育。机关事业单位干部职工晚婚的，婚假延长10天。女方晚育并系单位职工的，享受120天产假。在产假期间办理独生子女证的，产假延长到半年。领取独生子女证的夫妇，给予一次性奖金100元，从办证之日起，每月发给保健费4元，至小孩满14周岁止。从1991年起，用两年时间把计划生育工作逐步转向规范化轨道，从突击的孕后管理型向经常化的孕前服务型过渡，至1993年，实现基本无多胎县目标，1994年实现基本无计划外生育县目标。

1996年5月21日，县委、县政府印发《关于在农村全面开展计划生育“三结合”工作的决定》，提出在农村开展计划生育“三结合”，把广大群众特别是实行计划生育的育龄群众组织起来发展生产。对实行计划生育的农户给予政策优惠和经济扶持，使被帮扶的计划生育户真正得到实惠，真正感到实行计划生育光荣。指出：推行计划生育“三结合”，切忌一哄而起，急于求成，要防止形式主义。要组织县、乡计生协会，动员机关、单位、学校、干部职工、乡镇企业和公司对计划生育户实施帮扶。各级各部门结合自身业务，利用本部门掌握的项目、资金、技术向计划生育户倾斜，解决生产、生活和生育中的实际困难。要集中力量帮扶有发展实力的独生子女专业户、两女结扎户。政府部门帮助和扶持乡镇企业，支持集体经济和合作经济实体，吸收实行计划生育的家庭成员到企业务工。

1999年1月12日，县委、县政府印发《关于进一步加强计划生育工作的决定》，要求县级领导干部在联系乡镇、科局级单位包村工作中，把计划生育工作作为重点，予以督促指导。各单位每季度组织干部职工学习人口理论1次，积极参与计划生育“三结合”工作。宣传部门要配合抓好计划生育宣传。各级各部门干部职工属妇检对象的，要带头按规定参加妇检。加强计划生育干部队伍建设，配齐配好计划生育专职干部。继续坚持计划生育工作各级党政一把手亲自抓、负总责。是年2月3日，县委、县政府出台《关于对农村独生子女户　两女结扎户和其他计划生育户实行优先优惠的规定》，提出各级各部门对农村独生子女户、两女结扎户及其他计划生育户实行优先优惠政策，制定帮扶措施，落实帮扶责任人，对帮扶户实行挂牌管理和跟踪管理服务。在小学高年级和中学开设人口课，对学生进行国情国策和青春期卫生教育，对独生子女户、两女结扎户子女义务教育阶段上学免收学杂费。在扶贫济困工作中，对农村独生子女户、两女结扎户优先办理养老保险、发放救济款物、安排扶贫贷款。在提供化肥、农药，安排改水改厕，办理营业执照，审批宅基地，安排招工、劳务输出，征兵等方面，优先考虑安排。

2000年8月14日，县委、县政府印发《关于进一步加强人口与计划生育工作的决定》。指出：全县计划生育工作坚持“三个不变”，落实“三为主”，推行“三结合”，实现计划生育工作思想和工作方法两个转变。流动人口计划生育工作坚持流出地与流入地共同管理，以流入地为主的原则。围绕办证、租房、用工三个环节，做到部门间职责明确，齐抓共管；各级党委、政府把计划生育工作纳入国民经济和社会发展计划安排，坚持两手抓，两手都要硬，做到经济增长，人口下降，素质提高；以妇检为龙头，加强孕前管理，做好节育和生殖保健工作；落实法人代表责任制。国家机关、企事业单位、社会团体落实法人代表计划生育责任制，落实人员、经费、措施，兑现奖励和优惠政策；要面向基层、面向群众，宣传党的计划生育方针、政策、法律、法规和人口理论，营造良好的计划生育工作环境；运用利益导向机制，通过奖励、引导调节婚育行为。建立健全社会保障制度，逐步建立独生子女户、两女结扎户养老保险制度，对低保对象中的计划生育户优先给予保障补助等。至2005年，全县总人口控制在24.88万人以内（不含机械人口增长），人口出生率控制在15‰以内，人口自然增长率控制在7‰以内，计划生育率94%以上；至2010年，全县总人口控制在25.8万人以内（不含机械人口增长），人口出生率控制在13‰以内，人口自然增长率控制在5‰以内，计划生育率96%以上。

2001年1月5日，县委、县政府印发《关于进一步推进全县计划生育“村为主”及“村民自治”工作的实施意见》，提出：推进全县计划生育“村为主”及“村民自治”工作，遵循人口与经济社会协调发展、稳定现行政策、实行综合治理、推行行政管理和群众工作相结合和整体推进与分类指导相结合原则。抓好落实领导责任制。县计生主管部门、各乡镇党政一把手对“村为主”“村民自治”工作负总责；建立完善激励机制，严格奖惩制度，实行“一票否决”制；强化依法律、按政策规定办事，切实把生育、节育管理纳入规范有序的管理轨道；加强已婚育龄妇女计划生育工作。抓好婚前、孕前教育，提倡晚婚晚育、优生优育，引导群众转变生育观念；加强流动人口计划生育管理，有关部门要相互配合，齐抓共管；强化宣传教育，使党的计生政策深入人心，增强执行计划生育的自觉性；加强计生干部队伍建设，增加经费投入，实行双向考核等工作。至2001年5月，80%的村实现“村为主”，2001年9月前，40%的村实现村民自治，2002年9月前，60%的村实现村民自治，2003年底，80%的村实现村民自治。

2007年12月29日，县委、县政府出台《关于全面加强人口和计划生育工作　统筹解决人口问题实施意见》，提出：继续稳定低生育水平，到“十一五”期末，全县符合政策生育率达97%以上，人口出生率、自然增长率分别控制在10.58‰和5.4‰以内，全县总人口控制在27.05万人以内（不含机械增长和新增流动人口）。出生缺陷发生率逐年下降，出生人口素质不断提高。逐步建立覆盖城乡居民的养老保障制度和人口信息数据共享制度。提高人口和计划生育干部政治、经济待遇，对连续从事人口和计划生育工作满10年，年龄达到55周岁，已离开计生岗位的原村（居）计生专干，给予一次性生活补助2000元，县、乡计生干部岗位津贴从每月100元提高到200元。

三、扶贫攻坚

1995年1月3日，县委、县政府印发《息烽县扶贫攻坚计划》，提出：2000年，解决4万人、6万头牲畜的饮水困难；实现所有乡镇通公路、电话，90%的村通公路、有条件的村通电话；坡改梯3万亩；基本普及九年制义务教育，开展农民技术培训和职业技术教育，达到每户有1个掌握1～2项农业适用技术的劳动力；改善医疗条件，建立起县、乡、村三级防保网，基本控制地方病；人口自然增长率控制在11‰以内。做好七个方面工作：利用区位、资源、交通优势，开发有竞争力的名、特、稀、优产品和拳头产品；统一规划，连片发展有助于直接解决群众温饱、帮助群众脱贫致富的种植、养殖业，逐步形成一定规模的商品生产基地或区域性支柱产业；发展资源开发型和劳动密集型乡镇企业，外联市场，内联农户，带领群众脱贫致富；推广利用科技成果，推动企业技术改造，促进产品结构调整和技术水平提高；拍卖非耕地所有权，大面积种植经济林木，使之成为后续财源；培育劳动市场，引导、鼓励贫困户劳动力合理、有序向非农产业转移；大力发展非公有制经济。到20世纪末，实现全县国内生产总值达3.8亿元，工农业总产值达3.34亿元，财政收入达到3000万～4000万元，主要工农业产品有较大增长，产业结构明显改善，经济布局趋于合理，人民生活由温饱向小康迈进，人民群众科学文化素质和思想道德素质明显提高，社会秩序安定，社会风气更加健康向上，14万贫困人口全部脱贫，贫困户年人均纯收入达到500元以上，生活条件明显改善的目标。

2003年8月4日，县委作出《中共息烽县委关于加大新阶段扶贫开发工作力度　全面推进小康社会建设的决定》，明确新阶段扶贫开发工作以九庄、石硐、鹿窝、流长、养龙司5个贫困乡镇和84个贫困村8.04万贫困人口为重点。采取分类帮扶脱贫：对基本生产生活条件差、自我发展能力弱的2.34万贫困人口，实施开发式扶贫，帮助改善生产、生活等基础设施条件；对无生存条件的1954个贫困人口（包括在1类的2.34万人口中），用8年左右时间进行易地搬迁和配套解决土地、住房等生产生活问题，创造稳定脱贫的物质基础；对鳏寡孤独、因病因残丧失劳动力的0.44万特殊贫困人口，建立和实施特困群众救助制度，给予长期社会救助；帮助初步越过温饱线、人均纯收入在800～1200元之间的5.26万农村低收入人口改善基本生产生活条件，拓宽增收门路，早日脱贫致富。

四、乡镇企业发展

1996年，县委出台《关于促进乡镇企业持续　快速　健康发展的规定》，提出：发展乡镇企业实行党政一把手负责制，实行“四个放开”（登记、办证条件放开，经营范围和经营方式放开，从业人员和从业人数放开，生产经营地域放开）。支持党政机关干部、科技人员参与开发非耕地资源，领办和兴办乡镇企业。鼓励离退休人员到乡镇企业发挥作用。经县及县级以上乡镇企业局立项审批，在县内注册登记的乡镇企业享有税收减免优惠，鼓励以土地、资源、劳动力、闲置设备等参与投入办乡镇企业。1997年1月21日，县委、县政府制定《关于发展乡镇企业的优惠政策及服务措施》，对土地使用及管理、税收政策、奖励政策、人事劳动、用工政策、服务措施、部门承诺作出明确规定。1998年4月14日，县委、县政府出台《关于促进乡镇企业大发展大提高大突破的意见》，提出发展乡镇企业坚持一、二、三产业并举，农、林、牧、副、渔、工、商、建、运、服全面发展，取得四方面（工业、开发农业、第三产业、产权制度改革）突破。实施五项引资措施（以项目引资、以国家对中西部地区资金政策倾斜引资、以宽松环境引资、以主动出击宣传引资、以优质快捷服务引资）。至2002年，实现乡镇企业总产值、乡镇工业产值、乡镇企业营业收入增长速度保持在10%以上，乡镇企业上缴税金在县级收入中占40%以上比重。

五、农业和农村工作

1996年9月3日，县委、县政府对县内农村土地承包责任制中的有关问题作出规定：在土地承包期内全家农转非、死亡绝户及全家外迁出县的农户，其责任地、责任山、自留地，由村委会收回另行有偿发包或作发展村级集体经济用地。村民死亡后，子女尽了主要赡养义务，其承包的责任地、责任山、自留地可由其子女继续承包。国有企业职工原在农村的责任地、责任山、自留地，确因企业经营状况不好而无固定收入需要继续承包的可继续承包。

1998年12月20日，县委九届四次全会通过《关于认真做好农业和农村工作的意见》提出：到2010年农业总产值年均递增4.5%以上，粮食总产量年均递增2.5%以上；乡镇企业营业收入年均递增15%以上，总产值年均递增13%以上；工业总产值年均递增12%以上，工业增加值年均递增10%以上；农民人均纯收入年均递增10%以上；森林覆盖率38%以上；人口自然增长率控制在10.5‰以内。重点发展水果、蔬菜、畜牧、水产养殖、旅游等产业。

2004年8月12日，县委、县政府印发《关于加快农村专业技术协会发展的意见》，提出：加快农村专业技术协会发展，以民办、民管、民受益为原则，保留集体经济组织所有权、农户土地承包经营权和会员的财产所有权。坚持民办、自愿、民主原则，各乡（镇）选择1～2个有一定经济实力、信誉度高、运作规范、服务功能强的协会进行重点扶持，办成示范样板，总结推广经验。坚持“成熟一个，发展一个，建好一个”，逐步形成“发展一个协会，带出一群能人；创办一个实体，服务一方农户”的格局。到2005年底，符合登记条件的协会登记率100%。

六、再就业工程

1998年1月，县委、县政府决定在县城建立“下岗职工小吃一条街”和“下岗职工百货一条街”，拓宽就业门路，解决下岗职工再就业问题。1998年8月24日，印发《息烽县国有企业下岗职工基本生活保障和再就业五年规划》，提出：筹集资金确保国有企业下岗职工的基本生活和离退休人员养老金的发放；为下岗职工交纳养老金、失业金、医疗保险费，开展下岗职工转岗培训业务等。到2000年，基本建立能代替再就业服务工作的劳动力市场运作机制，取代再就业服务工作。1998年8月27日，县委、县政府出台《关于进一步落实“两个确保” 做好国有企业下岗职工再就业工作的实施意见》，提出：拓宽再就业渠道，加快再就业步伐；建立再就业服务组织，确保每年实现再就业人数大于当年新增下岗职工人数；确保国有企业离退休人员养老金的发放。

七、经济强县建设

1999年12月28日，县委、县政府印发《关于建设经济强县 促进经济发展的实施意见》，提出建设经济强县的战略思路：以国家产业政策为市场导向，以资源为依托，实施开放带动战略、科教兴县战略、可持续发展战略、非均衡推进战略；大力发展“六大支柱产业”（以旅游为重点的第三产业，以“一村一品”为重点的种植业，以“名、特、优”为重点的养殖业，以生物制药为重点的医药工业，以磷及磷化工为重点的化学工业，以铝及铝加工为重点的冶金工业）；做好向上争取资金，全方位招商引资，引导和扩大社会投资；盯住贵阳、遵义两大市场，发展以城郊型农业为主的农业产业化经营；放手发展非公有制经济，加快小城镇建设步伐，努力向贵州经济强县迈进；抓好产业结构调整和重点项目建设，用好用足国家经济政策，发展高新技术产业和非公有制经济，深化国有企业改革。

2010年1月26日，中共息烽县委第七次全体会议通过《关于巩固提升建设经济强县地位 纵深推进生态文明县建设的实施意见》，提出：以建设生态文明县为统领、“建强升位”为抓手，坚持以人为本、民生为重，抢抓“三创一办”机遇，突出加快基础设施建设，努力提高城镇化水平；加强生态建设和环境保护，大力推进产业生态化和特色优势产业发展；切实保障和改善民生，提高县域经济综合竞争力和人民群众幸福指数。2009—2010年，生产总值同比增长21.7%；全社会固定资产投资同比增长32.4%；社会消费品零售总额同比增长18.6%；城镇居民可支配收入同比增长14.6%，农民人均纯收入同比增长17.1%；招商引资到位资金同比增长25%；城镇化率年均增长率同比提高1.5%（力争2%）；城镇登记失业率控制在4%以内；单位生产总值能耗降低4%，主要污染物排放减少2%以上；高中阶段毛入学率每年提高5个百分点；符合政策生育率92.5%以上。至2010年，经济强县建设中期评估居于全省前20位。

八、实施“西部大开发”

2000年5月22日，县委、县政府印发《关于开展“西部大开发　息烽怎么干”大讨论的通知》，决定5月下旬至8月下旬，用3个月时间在全县党员、干部特别是各级领导干部中集中开展“西部大开发，息烽怎么干”大讨论。使广大党员、各级干部特别是领导干部在西部大开发中认识更深刻、思路更清晰、对策更得当、措施更有力。是年9月22日，县委、县政府出台《关于在西部大开发中强县升位　实现超常规发展的初步意见》，提出息烽在西部大开发中，重点抓好基础设施、城市、生态环境保护三大建设，突出发展旅游业、以生物制药为重点的制药业、以精细磷化工为重点的化学工业、以铝及铝加工为重点的冶金工业、以绿色食品为重点的绿色产业五大特色经济，实施开放带动、科教兴县、可持续发展、全面创新和多元化发展五大战略。实现一个跨越（从刚脱贫的农业县向省级经济强县跨越），两个转变（从依靠传统农业经济增长向主要依靠工业、旅游业、科技农业实现经济增长转变，从单纯依靠行政手段实现计划生育向村民自治实现计划生育转变），夯实三大基础（基础设施建设、城市建设、生态环境建设），四个指标（国民生产总值年均增长不低于18.56%，财政收入年均增长不低于19.36%，农民人均纯收入年均增长6%以上，计划生育率94%以上）的总体目标。

九、作风建设

2001年11月16日，县委、县政府印发《关于在县　乡（镇）党政机关深入开展作风教育整顿活动的实施意见》，提出：作风教育整顿活动分学习培训、对照检查、整改建制三个阶段进行。着力解决思想不够解放、开拓创新意识不强、工作思路不宽、大局意识不够、责任意识欠缺、群众观念淡薄；主观武断、高高在上的官僚主义和不求实效、只图虚名的形式主义以及学习不深入、脱离实际；群众观念淡薄、工作漂浮走过场和有章不依、抓而不实；职能不明、办事不公、执法不严；各种不良倾向和不正之风5个方面的问题。通过教育整顿活动，有效遏制铺张浪费、奢侈享乐、讲排场、比阔气和吃拿卡要等不良风气，提高反腐败能力，整治“四难”顽症，切实转变“冷、粗、硬、横”的作风，真正树立艰苦奋斗、甘于奉献、淡泊名利的思想和廉洁勤政的良好形象。

十、非公有制经济发展

2003年8月1日，县委、县政府印发《关于加快非公有制经济发展的意见》，提出全县非公有制经济发展分四步走战略，至2004年，非公有制经济增加值为8.19亿元，比2000年翻一番，年均增长26.5%；到2008年，非公有制经济增加值为19.3亿元，比2000年翻两番，年均增长25.2%；到2014年，非公有制经济增加值为65.29亿元，比2000年翻三番，年均增长24%；到2020年，非公有制经济增加值为110亿元，比2000年翻四番，年均增长19.32%，占国民生产总值的91.7%。围绕“调整结构提升一产，扶优扶强主攻二产，加快速度发展三产”的思路，确立全县非公有制经济发展产业。加快传统农业改造，调整农业生产布局。围绕服务城市、富裕农村，调整农产品结构，大力发展特色农业、精品农业；强力推进工业强县战略。以招商引资为动力，以重大项目为支撑，加速推进小寨坝新型工业区、尹庵磷化工业区、金星工业区、阳朗医药食品园区建设，大力发展磷化工业、现代药业、铝及铝加工业、绿色食品加工业；以发展旅游为龙头，以现代服务业为重点，加速发展第三产业。县非公有制经济管理和服务部门围绕重点产业的发展，抓紧制定全县非公有制经济发展规划，按“四步走”的战略目标，将各项经济指标层层分解落实，并纳入年终目标考核。

十一、社会治安综合治理

2003年11月10日，县委印发《关于进一步加强社会治安综合治理的意见》，提出积极开展“严打”斗争，着力解决突出治安问题：严厉打击严重刑事犯罪。重点打击有组织犯罪、带黑社会性质的团伙犯罪、流氓恶势力犯罪以及其他团伙犯罪，深挖黑恶势力的后台及其保护伞，坚决铲除其经济依托。建立破案责任制，挂牌督办，限期破案；开展打击经济犯罪专项斗争；坚持开展治安混乱地区和突出治安问题的排查和整治；坚持开展“扫黄打非”工作。维护社会稳定，消除不安定因素：加强隐蔽战线斗争，维护国家安全；做好县、乡（镇）中心学校的维护稳定工作；健全完善矛盾纠纷排查调处工作机制，妥善处理因人民内部矛盾引发的群体性事件；推进社会保障体系建设，做好下岗职工和失业人员再就业工作；继续开展平安工程创建活动。加强教育管理，预防和减少违法犯罪：建立健全流动人口管理和协调机制，维护和保障流动人口的合法权益；加强刑释解教人员的安置帮教工作；加大对吸毒人员管理教育力度，落实禁毒“七包”责任制；开展预防青少年违法犯罪工作，创建和办好流浪儿童救助保护中心，建立健全街道、村、政法部门、家庭“三位一体”管控体系。制定见义勇为奖励措施，落实社会治安综合治理领导责任制，实行社会治安综合治理“一票否决权”制。

十二、民族工作

2007年1月8日，县委印发《关于进一步加强民族工作　加快少数民族和民族地区经济社会发展的实施意见》，提出加快少数民族和民族地区经济社会发展，集中力量改善0.6万名少数民族贫困人口的基本生产生活条件；推进民族地区经济结构调整，把旅游业培育成为民族乡村新的经济增长点；发展民族地区教育事业，扩大“农村寄宿制学校建设工程”在民族地区的覆盖面。对农村少数民族考生报考息烽一中实行降低两个分数段录取政策；弘扬少数民族优秀文化，扶持民族地区卫生、体育事业，抓好少数民族传统体育项目进校园工作，办好四年一届的全县少数民族传统体育运动会；加大对民族乡财政转移支付力度，落实民族乡财政超收和节余部分留给民族乡继续使用的规定；“十一五”期间，落实“三个”20万元经费（民族工作经费、教育经费、基础设施建设经费）；加强民族地区人才队伍建设，大力培养、选拔少数民族干部。民族乡和民族工作部门选拔、竞争上岗配备领导干部，可划出相应名额和岗位，定向选拔少数民族干部。

十三、构建“和谐息烽”

2007年1月25日，十一届县委全会第四次会议通过《关于构建“和谐息烽”的实施意见》，提出：按照民主法治、公平正义、诚信友爱、充满活力、安定有序、人与自然和谐相处的总要求和“抓机遇、强产业、带农村、进前列”的发展思路，依托生态经济县建设，坚持科教兴县、工业强县、环境立县、旅游活县战略，着力发展社会事业，促进社会公平正义，建设和谐文化，增强基层民主，提高科学领导发展能力，推动社会建设与经济建设、政治建设、文化建设协调发展。到2020年，全县生产力布局科学合理，农村经济全面振兴，城镇乡村、经济社会发展更加协调，循环经济得到有效实施，基础设施完善，城乡社会和谐，生态环境优良，全县发展活力明显增强；基层民主法制更加完善，人民群众合法权益得到切实尊重和保障；服务型、责任型和效能型法治政府建设进一步加强，基本公共服务体系和社会管理职能更加完备；城乡统筹就业质量明显提高，劳动关系更加和谐，收入分配结构合理有序，人民生活安康，社会保障体系覆盖城乡居民；文化建设更加繁荣，群众思想道德、科学文化和健康素质全面提高，良好道德风尚、和谐人际关系进一步形成，学习型城镇基本形成；社会安定有序，广大人民群众幸福感、安全感和满意度大幅度上升。全面建成小康社会，全县物质文明、政治文明、精神文明和谐统一。

十四、文化体制改革

2007年5月15日，县委出台《关于深化文化体制改革　加快文化产业发展的实施意见》，指出：要牢牢把握社会主义先进文化的前进方向。坚持百花齐放、百家争鸣的方针，以改革创新为动力，以市场需求为导向，发展历史文化旅游业、文化艺术业、娱乐休闲业、广播电视业、体育业等文化产业项目，提高全县文化产业整体实力和竞争力。组建县新闻传媒中心，整合广播电视、报纸、刊物、网络等媒体，实现资源共享、优势互补，积极培育广告业。转变政府文化管理部门职能，实行政企、政事分开，管办分离，实施“农民文化家园”项目，扶持农户组建文化大院、文化室、图书室，允许个体兴办书社、个体放映队、业余表演团体等。把公益性文化设施建设纳入城乡建设总体规划，加大财政投入。乡镇组建集图书阅读、广播影视、宣传教育、文艺演出、科技推广、科普培训、体育健身和青少年校外活动等于一体的综合性文化站或文化服务中心。各文化单位可转换经营方式、拓宽业务范围，增加单位和个人收入。

十五、生态文明县建设

2008年1月8日，县委十一届五次会议作出《关于建设生态文明县的决定》，提出：建设生态文明县，坚持科学发展、统筹城乡、全面协调，立足实际、统筹规划、分步实施，以人为本、关注民生、促进和谐，创新机制、健全体系、科学考评，党政推动、全民参与、合力共建原则。发展循环经济、生态工业、旅游文化产业、现代农业。加强林业生态、节能减排、污染物防治、土地和水资源保护及“整脏治乱”各项工作。到2012年，实现八个目标：生态产业快速发展，循环经济取得实效，服务业比重明显提高，二、三、一产业结构进一步优化；单位生产总值能耗比2005年降低25%以上，主要污染物排放总量减少10%以上；推进城乡环境生态化，建设80个生态文明村寨，全县生态环境质量进一步提升，使“山更青、地更绿、水更碧、天更蓝”；生态文明观念在全社会牢固树立；民生显著改善，人民群众幸福感明显增强；红色文化特色逐步彰显；政府更加廉洁高效；生态文明发展基础进一步夯实，息烽更加适宜居住、适宜创业、适宜旅游。是年11月4日，县委、县政府印发《关于建设生态文明县目标绩效管理工作的意见（试行）》，就绩效目标内容及分类、绩效目标体系及分值安排、制定程序、签订时间，绩效目标管理、考核方式及奖惩等作出明确规定。

2009年1月19日，县委十一届六次全体（扩大）会议通过《关于抢抓机遇　进一步加快生态文明县建设的实施意见》，提出加快交通、农村、城镇和节能减排、生态环境等基础设施重大项目建设，推进“工业强县”战略、发展第三、第一产业，实施“学有所教”“劳有所得”“病有所医”“老有所养”“住有所居”“居有所安”的“六有”民生行动计划，继续深化各项改革，探索体制机制创新，营造良好投资环境，2009年、2010年，实现全社会固定资产投资增长30%以上，“十一五”规划任务全面完成。

十六、其他

1991年11月5日，县委、县政府出台《关于开展建镇并乡撤区工作安排意见》，成立领导小组负责组织协调建镇并乡撤区工作。至次年6月，建镇并乡撤区工作结束：撤销原4个区1个区级镇和24个乡镇，组建永靖镇、小寨坝镇、养龙司乡、温泉镇、流长乡、鹿窝乡、九庄镇、石硐乡、青山苗族乡、西山乡10个乡（镇）。

1993年6月28日，县委出台《关于鼓励机关人才走向经济建设主战场的规定》，提出：鼓励机关干部带薪留职兴办、领办、联办扶贫型、开发型、示范型、服务型乡（镇）企业或租赁亏损企业；机关和事业单位人员（教师和卫生技术人员除外），可脱离机关事业单位另谋职业；机关事业单位可兴办经济实体、从事生产经营；教育部门、学校可组织勤工俭学、兴办企业或经济实体，举办各种培训或提供其他有偿服务；卫生业务技术员可在本单位兴办的实体兼职，由单位组织开展医疗单位之间有偿协作服务和面向社会有偿服务。机关和单位办经济实体所得合法收入受法律保护。

2003年8月，县委、县政府提出“十五”期间教育发展目标：到2005年，小学入学率99.7%，辍学率降到0.3%；初中净入学率95%，辍学率降到3%以下；高中招生人数占初中毕业生人数的60%以上；县城幼儿学前三年入园率80%以上，农村学前一年入园（班）率90%以上。9月，将县特殊教育学校过渡为9年一贯制学校。

12月23日，县委、县政府出台《关于加快生态畜牧业发展的意见》，提出：在贵遵高等级公路沿线建成奶牛生态养殖区，在息九公路沿线建成肉牛、肉兔生态养殖区，在息流公路沿线建成生态型优质肉鸡养殖区，形成畜牧业发展三角经济带。到2005年，实现年出栏优质肉牛0.5万头，优质肉兔10万只，生态鸡50万羽，年存栏奶牛0.1万头，肉类总产量1.49万吨，奶类产量2500吨，人均占有量分别为55千克、10千克。畜牧产值占农业总产值的40%，力争达到45%。到2010年，实现年出栏优质肉牛2万头、优质肉兔50万只、优质肉禽300万羽，年存栏奶牛0.5万头以上，实现全县肉、奶分别达到2.2万吨、1.2万吨，人均占有量相应为82千克、40千克，实现畜禽产品市场商品率90%，畜牧业产值占农业总产值的50%，力争达到60%。

2004年4月25日，县委出台《关于人才强县战略的实施意见》。提出：抓住培养、吸引、用好人才三个关键环节。实施“高层次人才培养工程”，建设高素质党政人才队伍；以盘活现有专业技术人才为基础，以稳定、培养和引进急需的优秀人才为重点，培养造就专业技术人才队伍；实施高技能人才培养工程，发展壮大技能人才队伍；实施农村实用人才培养工程，整合培训资源，创新培训形式，把农业科技示范场、科技园区作为农村实用人才的实践基地；构建终身教育体系；创造人才汇集的吸引环境，以较大的竞争力引进人才。

2005年12月30日，县委十届四次全体会议通过《息烽县“十一五”规划纲要》，提出实施三大战略（科教兴县、工业强县、环境立县战略），抓好五大建设（城镇基础设施、农业综合生产能力、重点产业项目、人才队伍、发展环境建设），打造五大产业（磷煤化工、制药、绿色食品深加工、建材、红色旅游产业），正确处理三大关系（改革、发展、稳定的关系），实现五大目标（发展基础进一步夯实，生态环境明显改善，农村经济快速发展，优势产业全面形成，历史性跨越目标的战略构想）。

2006年1月20日，县委出台《关于创建“无毒县”的实施意见》，提出创建“无毒县”总体要求和目标任务。2006年，完成“五创”（创“无毒乡镇”“无毒村居”“无毒单位”“无毒学校”“无毒家庭”）任务；抓好三个落实（禁毒工作“一票否决”权落实、禁毒工作经费投入落实、禁毒工作措施落实）；实现辖区内无新增吸毒人员，无贩毒、无制毒、基本无非法种植毒品原植物、无复吸毒品人员。做到现有吸毒人员（不含正在劳教、服刑的吸毒人员）落实帮教措施、尿检率和外流吸毒人员跟踪调查3个100%；戒断巩固三年以上人数达到80%以上；下落不明4年以上吸毒人员不超过8%；本地人员外流涉毒违法犯罪不超过辖区常住人口的8/10万，实现全县登记在册吸毒人员大幅度下降。

2008年3月13日，县委、县政府出台《关于统筹城乡发展　推进城乡一体化的实施意见》，提出到2010年，初步建立城乡一体经济社会发展管理体制和运行机制，全县城镇化率达50%左右，城镇人口达10万左右，建成区面积达24平方千米以上，转移农村富余劳动力3万人以上，农民人均纯收入达到4180元，实现县改区目标。2015年，全县城镇化率达60%左右。至2020年，全县三城中心区域（永靖城区、小寨坝城区、西山城区）城镇化率达80%左右。其他乡镇区域：温泉镇、鹿窝乡、青山苗族乡、石硐乡建设以旅游服务业为主。九庄镇以农贸及特色农产品种植加工为主，流长乡大力发展渔牧业，养龙司乡以农贸及特色农产品种植加工为主。九庄、流长、养龙司三个乡镇作为县城卫星城镇，每个乡镇人口容纳约2万～3万人，建城区面积2～3平方千米。

第五节　重大活动

一、“三讲”教育活动

2000年2月，按中央和省、市委安排部署，息烽县在县级党政领导班子、领导干部中开展以讲学习、讲政治、讲正气（简称“三讲”）为主要内容的党性党风教育活动。参加“三讲”集中教育活动的有县委、县人大、县政协、县政府、县纪委、县人民法院、县人民检察院、县公安局8家单位及54名领导班干部。县委成立“三讲”教育领导小组，制定《“三讲”教育活动实施方案》。在省、市委巡视组指导下，整个活动按思想发动、学习教育，自我剖析、听取意见，交流思想、开展批评与自我批评，认真整改、巩固成果四个阶段进行。参加人员每人学完规定的38篇必读篇目，做读书笔记2万余字，并写出学习心得体会和学习小结。3月中旬起，活动转入第二阶段，各家单位开展自我剖析，广泛听取各方面建议意见，对有条件的立说立行，即知即改；对需要时间解决的问题，抓紧研究解决。4月19日，召开全县领导班子、领导干部“三讲”教育民主测评会，对8家单位和54名领导干部的剖析材料进行测评，测评结果为：领导班子剖析材料满意率最高100%，最低95.8%；领导干部个人剖析材料满意率最高100%，最低80.4%，全部达到市三讲办要求。至5月9日，全县“三讲”集中教育活动告一段落。10月中下旬，开展“三讲”教育“回头看”活动，8家单位分别召开专题民主生活会，查摆、分析工作中存在的问题，修订完善整改方案。班子成员间交换工作意见，相互提醒、批评，各自剖析存在的问题，提出改进方向和措施。

二、“三个代表”重要思想学习教育活动

2001年，县委按中央和省、市委安排部署，从2月起，在全县开展“三个代表”重要思想学习教育活动（简称“学教”活动）。“学教”活动分乡镇、部门和村三个层面进行。是年2—6月，开展乡镇“三个代表”重要思想学习教育活动，参学对象1215人；6—9月，开展部门“三个代表”重要思想学习教育活动，参学单位77个，参学对象1986人；11月中旬至次年1月底，开展村级“三个代表”思想学习教育活动，参学单位165个村（居）委员会，参学对象3.11万人。通过学习培训、对照检查、整改提高三个阶段的工作，全县干部受到深刻教育，思想认识、理论水平有新提高，服务意识、发展意识增强，思想作风和工作作风明显转变。活动期间，全县各级各部门共投入资金1160万元，进村入户为群众办好事、实事1560件，解决急难问题3800余个。次年3月，开展“学教”活动“回访复查”，巩固和扩大“学教”成果。

三、党政机关作风教育整顿活动

2001年11月16日起，息烽县开展为期62天的党政机关作风教育整顿活动。活动围绕全县改革、发展和稳定大局，以密切党同人民群众血肉联系为核心，以“八个坚持、八个反对”为主要任务，突出实践“三个代表”重要思想，着力解决五个方面问题：思想不够解放、开拓创新意识不强、工作思路不宽、大局意识不够、责任意识欠缺、群众观念淡薄；主观武断、高高在上的官僚主义和不求实效、只图虚名的形式主义；学习不深入、脱离实际、群众观念淡薄、工作漂浮走过场和有章不依、抓而不实；职能不明、办事不公、执法不严；各种不良倾向和不正之风等。通过学习培训、对照检查、整改建制三个阶段工作，基本实现干部思想素质有新进步，班子活力有新增强，工作效率有新提高，工作作风有新改进和中央提出的“八个坚持、八个反对”的目标。全县各级党政机关按照县的统一要求，研究制定推动机关作风建设经常化、制度化的保证措施和形成良好作风的长效机制。活动中，全县各级党政机关共协调资金1000万元，帮助基层和群众办好事实事，建立完善规章制度1356个，配套落实保障措施700余条。

四、保持共产党员先进性教育活动

2005年1月，开展保持共产党员先进性教育活动。活动分县党政、人大、政协、法院、检察院和人民团体机关；组织关系在县直属机关党委的事业单位和直管部门、乡镇机关及企事业单位、县派驻乡镇的基层单位、非公有制企业和县属各中小学；农村、社区居委会、承担先进性教育活动组织和指导工作的县有关部门等三批进行，每批时间6个月。参加教育活动共涉及基层党委14个、党总支14个、党支部401个，参学党员8034名。学教活动按学习动员、分析评议、整改提高、“回头看”四个阶段进行。先后开展“做合格党员”、支部“结对共进”和以“保持先进性、致富奔小康”为内容的主题实践活动；落实党员承诺制和无职党员设岗定责；实施“三大工程”（农村党支部“双带致富”、农村党员干部现代远程教育和“双千”工程），健全“三个组织”（村民自治、集体经济和群团组织），实行“四项制度”（县级领导联系党建工作责任制、党建工作例会制、组工干部联系农村基层党组织工作责任制、村级党员目标管理制）等，全县各级党组织和广大党员通过引资金、带项目、送技术、送文化、送物资、送培训、送岗位等形式，为群众办实事、解难事。全县各级党员领导干部和党员联系企业和贫困村30个，结帮扶对子4200对，实施项目348个，协调解决帮扶资金357.9万元、水泥846吨、化肥168.5吨，安装电话50门等，一批群众关心关注的农村基础设施建设、农业结构调整、合作医疗、农资价格上涨等热点难点问题得到解决。

第六节 县委办公室工作

一、文秘工作

1991年，围绕“两个提高”加强和改进文秘工作。1996年落实工作责任制。1999年起，加强文秘工作规范化管理，至2003年，相继制定《中共息烽县委办公室公文办理及管理办法（试行）》《中共息烽县委办公室公文处理暂行规定》《中共息烽县委办公室公文处理规定》，规范公文格式和处理程序，提高工作效率。2009年，牵头或指导完成《息烽县磷煤化工产业生态化研究》《应对危机 推动息烽工业经济平衡较快发展的思考》等20余个课题调研报告，撰写《招商引资 推动后发地区经济发展的加速器——息烽县招商引资工作10年启思录》。2010年，完成《息烽县“十二五”宏观环境分析》《地方政府在生态文明建设中的职责分析和路径选择（以息烽为例）》等课题调研，撰写《息烽县新型农村合作医疗良性运行探析》《息烽县城镇化建设的回顾与展望》《党务公开之“四字诀”》调研文章；与省委政研室联合完成《从国定贫困县到建设经济强县的跨越——息烽县经济社会发展情况汇报》《从走出滞后“迷局”到黔北工业重镇——息烽县小寨坝镇工业化和城镇化的做法和体会》调研。

二、信息工作

1995年前，县委办公室设综合科，负责信息工作。1996年4月设信息科。是年，举办骨干信息员培训。全年上报信息428条，采用122条，其中被评为好信息5条。1999年，信息工作实现与省委办公厅信息微机联网，列为省信息直报点。聘请信息员80余名。是年，信息工作获全市综合一等奖、信息单项一等奖及信息调研奖。2000年，开展县、乡两级信息员顶岗轮训。2001年，实现信息传输微机与市机要专线联网。是年，撰写新闻稿件300余篇（条），被省、市报刊采用30余篇（条）。2003年，首次选派信息员到市委办公厅顶岗培训。至此，县办政务信息员培训初步形成选派上挂培训、县级集中培训、基层网点培训的“三级培训”模式。建立重要紧急信息迟、漏、错报责任追究制。2008年，创办《息烽信息网络资讯》，当年出刊27期。2009年，开通“书记、县长—百姓交流台”，依托网络、邮政信件、电话、短信平台、视频约访5个载体，架起百姓与县委、县政府之间的沟通桥梁。至2010年，百姓交流台共收到有效信件1674件，意见建议253条，百姓交流台“倾听百姓意见、汇聚百姓良策、疏解百姓情绪、维护百姓利益”的作用得以显现。

三、督查工作

1996年4月前，督查工作由综合科代行。4月，县委办设督查科。1997年11月，改设县委督查室。是年，制定出台《息烽县督查工作制度》。围绕“10件实事”及县委中心工作开展督查调研。2001年，实行督查工作目标化，对县委重点工作进行细化分解，制定考核标准和评比办法，加大督查力度，增强督查实效。2004年，开展市级文明县创建、“卫生与秩序”综合整治、普法依法治县、勤政廉政建设、茅草房改造、农村合作医疗、“平安息烽”工程、小寨坝磷化工基地建设和拟办“10件实事”等10余个专题项目督促检查。对全县人才队伍建设、非公有制经济发展、推动生态立县战略、公路建设、西部开发战略存在问题、政务村务公开、基层组织建设、小额扶贫贷款、循环经济发展等26个专题开展督查调研。次年，息烽县被省委督查室列为督查工作联系县。单独或会同有关部门就息烽旅游发展、扎南高速公路建设、返乡创业资金、农民收入增长、生态经济示范村建设、农村合作医疗、就业与再就业开展专题督查调研。其中对扎南高速公路建设的建议引起省委领导的重视并作出批示。2010年，坚持每月对全县“十件实事”、每季度对“整脏治乱”工作进行督促检查，不定时对全县部分重点项目、县委领导批示、“生态文明县建设”“职业素养教育周”“三创一办”“创先争优”等活动落实情况开展跟踪督查，印发《督查通报》27期。

四、政研工作

1996年4月，县委办设政策研究室。1997年，开展农村经济工作研究，对全县非耕地资源开发利用、村级集体经济现状、小康村建设等开展调研，撰写调研报告及发展规划。2003年，与市委政研室开展联合调研5次，撰写调研报告6篇。向省、市委政策研究室报送《息烽调研》5期；向《今日贵阳》编辑部组稿10余篇及专页宣传息烽1期。次年，对循环经济、农村改革情况、西望山村民异地搬迁、小寨坝磷化工基地建设、小额信贷、返乡创业资金使用、新型农村合作医疗试点及农民合作经济组织的培育发展等进行调研。其中《西洋公司发展循环经济的情况》一文在“首届中国·贵阳生态经济城市建设高层论坛”上交流。2007年，县成立重点调研课题管理领导小组。是年，完成农业产业结构调整、远程教育、工业布局、新农村建设等重点调研课题26个。

五、保密工作

1991年，县国家保密局与县委保密委员会办公室合署办公，实行两块牌子、一套人马，归口县委办公室管理。是年，对县五大班子（县委、人大、政府、政协、纪委）27名领导干部及四区一镇、县直21个单位进行保密检查28次。组织、指导县人民法院、县人民检察院、县委组织部、县人事局等单位开展保密工作。1995年，分期对县委办、人大办、政府办、人民检察院、人民法院、人武部等18个重点涉密单位，县城区内打字、复印店及废品收购点，县辖区内造纸厂进行保密检查。审查县直86个单位经管国家秘密事项专兼职人员96人。次年，县国家保密局对外挂牌，编制、文件单列，党务和行政后勤工作由县委办公室统一管理，业务工作独立运行。1997年，制定《息烽县“三五”普法期间保密法规宣传教育规划》。是年5月28日，息烽集中营旧址对外开放，印发做好“5·28”活动期间保密工作通知，要求各有关单位及个人做好活动期间保密工作。对活动参展资料进行保密审查。开展《办公自动化设备和通信设备》《科学技术保密规定贯彻落实情况》《息烽粮油食品经营总公司保密工作》等专题调查。2004年，推广应用保密技术产品，为保密部门安装计算机物理隔离卡1套，开通宽带上国际互联网检查系统。2005年，保密部门配置计算机安全保密管理检查工具、TD-2电话保密检查装置和通信、办公自动化保密技术检查设备，为县政府会议室安装保密技术设备1台，开展县内有关单位国际互联网站使用情况调查统计和保密检查。2010年，开展通信和计算机信息系统以及重点部门、要害部位和重大事项保密工作，对重点涉密单位进行保密检查，编发《保密工作简报》24期，撰写调研文章2篇。

六、机要工作

1991年，县委机要局归口县委办公室管理。机要工作重点抓完善制度，加强管理，做好密码通讯、密码安全和信息化密码保障工作。2001年，开展办公室计算机党政机要系统专网通信接入工作。次年，县委机要局更名为县委办公室机要局，规格降为副科级，内设综合科。2003年，全县10个乡镇计算机电子邮件报送材料系统开通。编制出台《党政综合信息保密网使用和管理规定》。次年，成立县密码管理委员会，办公室设在机要局；2007年，恢复县委机要局，县密码管理委员会办公室更名为国家密码管理局，与县委机要局一套人马，两块牌子，主要负责全县密码使用和管理、信息化密码保障、密码安全保密的监督及检查、指导工作，行使政府管理职能。2008年，开展党委部门和10乡镇党政办计算机信息安全保密大检查。

第七节　组织工作

一、机构

1991年，县委组织部内设办公室、干部科、干部调查审理科、组织科，下设党员电化教育办公室（中心）。县委知识分子工作领导小组办公室设在县委组织部，归口县委组织部管理。1995年8月，县委组织员办公室设在县委组织部，接受县委组织部业务指导和日常管理。2002年3月机构改革，县委组织部设办公室、组织科、干部科、知识分子工作办公室（县委知识分子工作领导小组办公室）、干部监督科、组织员办公室（县委农村基层组织建设领导小组办公室）6个职能科室和党员电化教育中心。2004年9月，撤销党员电化教育办公室，设立息烽县农村党员干部现代远程教育办公室，为县委组织部下设副科级事业单位。2007年3月，增设公务员管理科。2009年9月，知识分子工作办公室（县委知识分子工作领导小组办公室）更名为人才科（息烽县人才工作协调小组办公室）。2010年9月，增设信息科为县委组织部内设机构。

二、党员队伍建设

（一）组织建设

1991年，全县有基层党组织414个，其中，基层党委27个、党总支9个、党支部378个。是年，开展后进党支部调查、整改，改选村支部42个，调整支部书记21人、支部委员28人。1992年，撤区并乡建镇后，原区（镇）、乡（镇）党委撤销，组建永靖镇、小寨坝镇、温泉镇、九庄镇、西山乡、石硐乡、流长乡、鹿窝乡、养龙司乡、青山苗族乡10个乡镇党委。1993年起，县、乡、村三级党建工作实行目标管理，建立“定期议党建”“党建工作联系点”“三会一课”等制度。是年，调整改选支部班子120个，调整支部书记40名、副支部书记14名、支委85名。培训支部书记428人次。1998年3月，成立公安局、教育局党委。2005年，全县基层党委14个、党总支14个、党支部401个。2010年，全县有基层党委16个、党总支13个、党支部352个。

（二）党员发展

1991年，全县有党员5013名，其中正式党员4790名、预备党员223名。次年，学习贯彻中组部《发展党员工作实施细则》和《关于加强在企业　农村生产第一线发展党员的工作意见》，按照“坚持标准，保证质量，改善结构，慎重发展”方针，注重在生产第一线发展党员。全年发展党员200名。1995年，县下发《关于进一步加强发展党员工作的意见》，明确把发展党员工作重点放在企业、农村、生产一线和党的力量比较薄弱的地方。是年，发展党员422名。1996—2003年，全县年发展党员227～389名。2004年，针对党员队伍年龄老化、文化程度偏低、发展不平衡等情况，县委组织部下发《息烽县2004—2006年发展党员工作指导意见》，提出到2006年，力争35岁以下农村党员占村级党员总数的20%，妇女党员占村级党员总数的18%，高中（中专）以上文化程度的党员占村级党员总数的18%，没有三年不发展党员的村。是年，全县有党员7641名，其中农村党员3910名，占51.2%。机关党员2654名，占34.7%，企业党员231名，占3%。2006年起，发展党员工作全面推行公示制和票决制。2010年，全县有党员8962名。

（三）党员教育管理

1991年，县委从县直机关抽调105名干部组成工作队，深入到区、乡、村围绕“一个中心，两个基本点”（以经济建设为中心，坚持四项基本原则，坚持改革开放）对党员开展社会主义思想教育。在机关举办党员“三基本”（马克思主义基本理论，党的基本路线和党的基本知识）学习班，101个党支部1050名党员参加教育学习。播放电教片85场次，参加观看的党员5692人次。是年，开展先进党组织、优秀共产党员和优秀党务工作者表彰活动，表彰39个先进党组织、50名优秀党员、16名优秀党务工作者。1992—1995年，通过集中轮流培训、组织播放电化教育片等形式，对党员进行教育学习。

1996年起，党员电化教育内容增加市场经济理论、法律和农业科技知识等，旨在提高广大党员综合素质。是年，全县196个电化教育播放点播放电教片284部（其中，党的基本知识电教片184部，经济管理和科技知识电教片20部，农科技术专集片73部，政策法规类电教片7部）325场次，观众3.04万余人次，其中，党员1.33万余人次、入党积极分子2940人次、群众1.4万余人次。

1998年起，抓党员电化教育制度建设，至1999年，相继建立、完善《电教设备使用管理规定》《播放负责制》和“五制四册一手册”等。播放电教片166部308集420场次，观众5.49万人次，其中党员2.53万人次。2002年，县委表彰先进基层党组织23个、优秀共产党员43名、优秀党务工作者7名、纪检监察先进集体2个、优秀纪检监察干部4名。

2003年起，息烽县实施农村党员干部现代远程教育工程。是年5月，县、乡（镇）分别成立农村党员干部现代远程教育工作领导小组，明确专人负责远程教育工作。6月，县委党校现代远程教育B级站正式开通。同月，10个乡镇远程教育卫星接收站建立，至10月，建成村级播放站点161个。2004年9月，成立息烽县农村党员干部现代远程教育管理办公室，是年，建成村级卫星接收站136个。此后，现代远程教育取代党员电化教育。

2005年，开展“村校共携手，远教进万家”活动，落实“四联一帮”（学校党支部班子联系村党支部班子、学校党员教师联系农村普通党员、学校普通教师联系农村科技示范户、学生联系家长；学校党支部帮助村党支部进一步探索教学组织与管理的有效途径），建教学示范基地62个。是年，省、市远程教育教学组织与管理工作现场会相继在息烽召开，息烽县作为全省三家远程教育单位之一参加在山东召开的全国远程教育工作座谈会并作经验交流发言。次年，结合党员先进性教育活动的开展，在农村广泛开展无职党员设岗定责活动和党员承诺制，以“党员活动日”为载体，规范和完善农村党支部在党员教育和管理上的组织形式，不断增强党员的宗旨意识和责任意识。

2007年，开展“远教领跑新农村，信息构建致富路”系列宣传活动。在青山苗族乡、石硐乡开展远程教育进组入户工作试点。在村民组、自然村寨建立播放分点912个，有线电视入户1.95万户（本年新增3000户），卫星电视入户3.45万余户（本年新增2100户）。

2010年，建成息烽党建网，设远程教育专栏，实施清华大学远程教育扶贫工程。在县委党校、永靖中学、云环小学等21所中小学实施“清华伟新远程教育扶贫中小学在线”项目，培训基层干部、中小学教师、农业技术人员、农村卫生人员和普通农民400余人。全县10个乡镇和170个村（社区）站点开展“远教助创办，构建新家园”“远教助创办，学用促争优”知识竞赛活动，开展集中学习1000余期（次），培训农村党员干部3万余人次。举办各类培训学习班311期，培训党员和农民群众5万余人次。参加远程教育学习农户达70%以上。其中，参与远教“绿卡通”计划学习6次，积分30分以上2100余户，享受优惠政策161户，得到相关扶持200余万元。

（四）农村基层组织建设

1991年，继续以农村经济建设为中心，开展党员“带头致富，带领群众致富”活动（简称“双带”活动）和整顿后进党支部工作。至1993年，调整改选支部班子120个，组织发动群众集资30.35万元，投劳7.5万个，修建人畜饮水工程31处，解决43个村民组6300余人的饮水困难，修通乡村公路49千米。拉通照明输电线26.7千米，为民办好事实事2300余件。涌现出小寨坝镇南中村，温泉镇三交村，西山乡猪场村、柏香山村，石硐乡红光村等“双带”活动先进典型。

1994年，贯彻落实《中共中央关于加强农村基层组织建设的通知》精神，在西山乡、小寨坝镇开展农村党的基层组织建设试点。试点期间，两个乡镇共调整村党支部书记8名、副支书1名、支委成员12名。发展党员27名，处置不合格党员6名。次年，农村党的基层组织建设工作在全县铺开，建立党建工作联系点，实行党建工作责任制，县、乡（镇）、村（居）层层签订目标责任书。至1997年，全县整改充实支部班子97个，调整支部书记89名，支委157名，培训村支部书记743人次。发展农民党员576名，其中35岁以下360名，占58.3%，较1994年增长7.2个百分点。初中以上文化程度448名，占75.6%，较1994年增长11.9个百分点，无党员村民组从133个减少到46个。依法选举充实村委班子121个，改选委员131名。村办经济实体126个，104个村有经济积累。全县涌现出农村先进党组织38个、优秀支部书记26名、优秀党员53名，分别受县委表彰，其中，先进党组织18个、优秀支部书记12名受省、市表彰。

1998年起，根据中央新一轮农村基层组织建设安排部署，息烽县开展以创建“六好”乡镇、“五好”村和农村基层组织建设先进县（简称“三创”活动）为载体的新一轮农村基层组织建设。下发《息烽县1998—2000年农村基层组织建设实施意见》，各乡镇制定建设规划。县委采取县级党员领导干部帮乡联点、部门包村。县直单位和乡镇抽调48名后备干部驻村帮扶，要求不脱贫不脱钩，实行目标管理，年终考核。至2000年年底检查验收，全县161个村达到“五好”村标准的92个，占57%，10个乡镇达到“六好”乡镇标准的6个，占60%。161个村基本实现村村有集体经济收入3000元以上，村村有办公用房和村务公开栏，实行村务公开；“四位一体”配置达70%，村村有5名以上后备干部，基本消除无党员村民组，农民人均纯收入1514元。

2004年，制定《息烽县“双带致富”贴息资金使用和管理办法》，县农村信用联社为村支书贷款600万元，扶持启动项目46个。县财政下拨贴息资金12.02万元兑付双带致富项目领办人。修订村级经济发展规划86个，投入“双带致富”资金2790余万元，启动实施“双带致富”项目197个。

2006年，县委出台《在社会主义新农村中加强基层组织建设的实施意见》《关于建立党委书记党建工作述职制度的实施意见》，要求基层党委书记按年度以会议或书面形式，就各项党建工作开展情况进行述职。是年，在10个乡镇的10个村开展农村党支部换届“公推直选”试点工作。

2008年，开展党的基层组织建设年活动，推行农村党支部书记“公推直选”。建立乡镇党代会常任制。是年起，进行党务公开试点，凡是群众关心的党内热点问题，只要不涉及党和国家秘密和不违反党组织原则的，都进行公开。2009年，从县直机关选派副科级干部到乡镇挂任专职党委副书记，负责抓基层党建工作。以“抓基层、打基础、重服务”为工作目标，开展“五抓五强”（抓素质，强队伍；抓阵地，强堡垒；抓保障，强效能；抓作风，强意识；抓产业，强发展）活动，扎实推进基层党建“1234”（“建强一支队伍、完善两个机制、落实三个保障、实现四个突破”）工程的实施。是年，中央组织部《全国基层组织建设工作情况通报》《贵州日报》头版头条以《让领头雁羽翼丰满飞得更高——息烽县农村基层党建抓“双基”纪实》为题对息烽县抓基层党建工作进行报道，中央学习实践办1021期简报刊发息烽县“四抓村党支部书记队伍建设”成功经验。次年，省委常委、市委书记李军在《决策参考》2010年第6期刊发的《基层党组织建设科学途径的创新探索—息烽县农村基层党组织建设“1234”工程调查》上作出批示：“这篇调研报告内容很好，请市委组织部转发，供各区市县在创先争优活动中借鉴。”8月，中央政策研究室主办的《学习与研究》第8期以《“1234”工程——农村基层党建科学发展的新样本》为题进行刊发。

2010年，开展“五个一”（亮明一个身份、当好一个标兵、践行一个承诺、强化一个意识、结好一个对子）、“四百”（进百家门、知百家事、解百家难、暖百家心）活动和党员志愿服务活动。全县建党员志愿服务队325个，党员结成帮扶对子8000余对，为群众办好事实事3000余件。是年1月起，提高村干部待遇，村主要干部工资由每月420元增加到550元。建立离任村干部补贴机制，720余名离任村干部列为补助对象，每人每年可获补助400～1700元。

三、干部队伍建设

（一）干部教育培训

1991年1月，编发《息烽县干部培训三年规划》。是年，29名干部获一年制党政中专专修班毕业文凭。至1993年，共举办干部轮训、培训班7期，培训干部324名。

1994年，编发《息烽县1994—1998年干部培训五年规划》。是年，举办学习《邓小平理论》第三卷小集中读书班、中青年干部、乡局级干部及文秘干部培训班共9期，培训干部524名；选派38人参加省、地委党校干部培训班学习、10名干部到沿海及经济发达地区挂职学习锻炼。1996—2000年，举办乡科级干部、中青年干部、文秘干部和村支书、主任培训班18期，培训干部882人次。358人获省委党校经济管理、法律、文秘专业函授专科毕业文凭。

2003年，县成立干部教育领导小组，制定《息烽县2003—2007年干部教育培训规划》，明确干部是否参加过各级党校和行政院校培训学习作为选拔任用重要条件之一。县委、县政府投入专项资金260余万元新建县委党校，改善干部教育培训条件。次年，县委出台文件，鼓励干部参加各级各类教育培训学习，规定：县级领导干部参加公共管理硕士（MPA）课程、工商管理硕士（MBA）课程进修培训，取得学历证书，其学习费用由县干教经费承担60%，单位承担30%，个人承担10%；推荐优秀干部到省内外院校参加学习培训，学习费用由县干教经费承担70%，单位承担30%；选派县级干部和乡科级干部到国外、港澳地区或经济发达地区考察培训，其考察培训经费由县干教经费承担60%，单位承担40%。

2005年，选派38名县级领导干部、55名科级干部、14名一般干部参加“西部地区管理人才创新培训工程研修班”“全省县市领导干部安全生产管理培训班”“省委党校2005年春季学员培训班”“乡镇、街道办事处领导干部培训班”等各类班次的培训学习。选派乡科级干部、中青年干部参加城市建设与管理、农业管理、会计业务、办公英语、普通话等培训，参加培训干部2181人次。是年，全县组织1256人干部职工参加全省《中华人民共和国公务员法》考试，全部合格。2006年，县委组织部下发《关于学习贯彻〈干部教育培训工作条例（试行）〉的意见》，要求全县各级党组织按《干部教育培训工作条例》要求，抓好干部教育培训工作。把《干部教育培训工作条例》列入各党委、党组中心学习组、干部职工政治业务学习内容，纳入年终目标考核。

2007年，制定《息烽县2007—2010年干部教育培训规划》，建立干部教育培训“月讲座”制度。是年，举办“月讲座”12期，请省、市有关专家进行纪检监察、财务、农技、统战知识等授课，培训乡科级领导干部2500余人次。至2009年，相继邀请清华大学、省委党校、市委党校教授，国家海洋局海洋发展战略研究所副所长，省人大常委会副主任，县委领导等专家和领导就“旅游产业与息烽经济发展”“领导干部健康知识”“贵州文化与区域发展”“深入贯彻落实科学发展观”“坚持科学发展建设和谐息烽”等主题进行授课。共举办月讲座30余期，培训副科级以上领导干部5900余人次。

2010年，邀请省内外知名专家学者到息烽为乡科级以上干部作旅游经济发展、生态文明城市建设、中共十七届四中全会精神、管理心理学等专题讲座。是年，与清华大学联手，采取“请进来”或“派出去”方式，进行干部培训，培训农村基层法律服务人员、乡科级和中青年干部512人次。

（二）干部选拔任用

1991—1994年，干部选拔任用基本沿用“推荐、考察、任命”程序。1995年起，贯彻落实中共中央《党政领导干部选拔任用工作暂行条例》，逐步推行干部任用改革。是年，下发《关于推荐选拔优秀年轻干部到党政机关、企事业单位培养锻炼的通知》，采取公开选拔形式，在全县党政群机关、企业、事业单位选拔干部。对82名报名干部按照公平竞争，择优录取原则，经过面试、答辩、考核，选拔32名干部分配到机关、乡镇以及企业任职。2001年起，推行干部竞争上岗和干部任前公示制。印发《息烽县党政机关推行干部竞争上岗的实施意见（试行）》，是年，县人民法院5名干部经过竞争上岗走上法院中层领导干部岗位。全县任前公示乡（局）级干部4批55人，股级干部1批3人。

2002年起，贯彻中共中央《党政领导干部选拔任用工作条例》，严格按照条例规定开展干部选拔任用工作。干部提拔任职必须经过民主推荐，实行干部考察工作预告制，考察对象公示制，增强干部选拔任用工作透明度，防止和避免选人用人上的失察。2009年，选拔6名村支书、主任到乡镇任副科级领导职务。是年9月，面向社会公开选聘基层团组织兼职副书记，来自非公企业、个体经营户和公安、教育等系统的5名同志成为兼职团委副书记人选。

2010年6月，面向全县公开选拔专职党建副书记7名、科级领导干部5名。是年，制定《息烽县乡镇党委书记公推直选实施方案》《息烽县西山乡 青山苗族乡乡长选拔配备方案》，分别通过电视、报刊、网络发布公告，向社会公布空缺职位、岗位要求、任职条件、选拔方式、选拔程序等。先后召开两次初步候选人公推直选公开推荐大会，按1∶2比例确定初步候选人，在媒体、涉及的乡和考察对象所在单位同时进行公示。完成3个乡（西山乡、青山苗族乡、流长乡）党委书记公推直选和西山乡、青山苗族乡乡长公开选拔。根据《贵阳市市县联合公开选拔领导干部工作实施方案》，完成县委政研室副主任、党校副校长（正科级）、县环保局副局长、县人民医院副院长和中医院副院长等5个职位的公开选拔任用。

（三）干部调配、交流及监督管理

1992年7月，息烽县撤区并乡建镇，县委组织部门加强与执纪、执法部门联系，汇集干部被审查处理情况，调整、充实、选配新建10个乡镇党政班子成员。是年，交流干部14人，提任科局级干部

17人。1995年，在县级机构改革中，共任免干部84名，调整乡镇班子6个。选派10名年轻干部到乡镇任职，9名科技人员到乡镇担任科技副乡镇长，2名干部到企业任职锻炼，推荐1名干部到经济发达地区挂职锻炼。对全县招聘干部进行考察考核，对表现较好的238名招聘干部续签合同，对工作不称职或违法违纪的15名招聘干部作解除聘用合同或缓签合同处理。1999年，对副科级以上领导干部执行"三项规定"情况实行申报制度。

2001年，学习贯彻《中共中央组织部关于加强组织部门干部监督工作若干意见》，县委制定《党政领导干部选拔任用工作纪实办法（试行）》。是年，试行干部任用公示制，推行干部监督联席会议制度，制定完善《经济责任审计制度》，建立干部选拔任用试用期制度和推行重大事件（项）干部跟踪考察机制等。对1名干部进行组织函训，4人进行组织谈话打招呼。

2005年起，实行《乡科级领导干部收入申报制度》。是年，对新提任的32名干部进行任前公示和任前谈话，签订廉政承诺书。对3名干部进行诫勉谈话、2名领导干部进行任期经济责任审计。次年起，实行科局级干部男年满53周岁、女年满51周岁不再担任领导职务，保留原职级待遇制度，当年对不再担任领导职务的52名科局级干部免职，保留原职级待遇。

2007年，开展贯彻执行《党政领导干部选拔任用工作条例》情况监督检查。是年，对新提任的31名乡科级干部实行任前公示和任前谈话，签订廉政承诺书；对9名试用期满正式任职干部实行任前谈话；对26名领导干部进行任期经济责任审计。

2010年，调整充实9个乡镇、32个县直部门领导班子，共调配干部212名。调整交流乡科级干部139名。

四、知识分子与人才工作

20世纪90年代，知识分子工作继续执行"政治上关心、生活上照顾"政策，为符合条件的知识分子、专业技术人员办理生活补贴、家属子女"农转非"和解决子女招工就业等。对知识分子、专业技术人才实行拔尖管理。其间，1991年，县委知识分子工作部门到知识分子比较集中的部门和单位开展调查研究，建立知识分子工作联系点，开展优秀知识分子、专业技术拔尖人才选拔工作。是年6月，县委、县政府决定表彰首批命名的狄光华、简富明、冯世忠、况力夫、陈昌其、许中和、李国良、戴传声、罗文敏9名县级"专业技术拔尖人才"，在全县营造尊重知识、尊重人才氛围。次年，为127名知识分子办理生活补贴，调查整理中级以上专业技术人员家属子女需"农转非"147户367人基本情况。12月，召开全县知识分子工作座谈会，县委、县政府通报表彰优秀知识分子47名。"专业技术拔尖人才"简富明当选省党代会代表。1994年，全县有在职知识分子3460人，其中大学本科566人，大专161人，中专及以下2733人；高级职称26人，中级职称461人，初级职称2007人。未评专业职称996人。1996年3月11日，县委组织部下发《关于选拔县级第二批专业技术拔尖人才的通知》，启动第二批县级"专业技术拔尖人才"选拔工作。

2001年起，开展乡土人才开发工作，将乡土人才纳入人才管理范围。

2003年，县成立人才工作协调领导小组、"息烽县稳定和引进人才工作领导小组"，制定《息烽县"十五"人才规划》。县委、县政府出台《息烽县关于稳定和引进人才的实施意见》，规定：对无住房的主要引进对象由用人单位提供一套80平方米以上住房，政府发给一次性安家费5000元；重点引进对象和取得博士学位的人员到县工作的，由县政府提供一套100～120平方米住房，发给一次性安家费1万元；主要引进对象和重点引进对象若愿意自主购房的，县政府补助2万元购房款等。

成立乡土人才开发工作领导小组，启动乡土人才开发工程，建立乡土人才档案，实行建档立卡管理。制定《息烽县“三百二千”人才工程方案》，把乡土人才开发纳入人才发展规划；推荐高级专业技术带头人和中青年科技骨干人选各5名，建立30名县级专业技术人才后备库。全县10乡镇配备科技副乡（镇）长，161个村都配齐科技副主任，形成以科技副县长为龙头，科技副乡（镇）长为骨干的科技网络。是年，开展知识分子（中专以上学历）、专业技术人员（初级以上专业技术职称）调查，掌握人才基本状况。次年4月，县委、县政府命名表彰2004—2006年度专业技术带头人和中青年科技骨干33名、教育名师3名。

2005年，建立《息烽县县级领导干部联系优秀人才工作制度》，27名县领导分别与县级专业技术带头人、中青年科技骨干、驻县非公企业负责人和省、市下派挂职干部等优秀人才共81人建立结对关系。次年，组织17名县级专业技术带头人到云南考察学习。引进急需专门人才7名，公开招聘事业单位人才98名。评定农村农技师23人，助理技师35人，技术员152人。

2007年，县委、县政府出台《中共息烽县委　息烽县人民政府关于人才强县战略的实施意见》《息烽县关于稳定和引进人才的实施意见》。2008年，县委、县政府印发《关于进一步加强人才队伍建设的实施意见》《息烽县引进高层次人才暂行办法》，开辟人才引进“绿色通道”，引进急需紧缺专业人才，至2009年，引进急需紧缺专业人才22名。

2009年，县成立人才开发专项规划编制工作领导小组，制订《息烽县“十一五”人才规划》。是年，培训党政人才3226人次、企业管理人才193人次、专业技术人才3685人次、技能人才244人次。评定农村实用人才助理技师9名，技术员56名。县委、县政府决定对潘世昌等15名息烽县2007—2009年度专业技术带头人、陈华等30名中青年科技骨干进行命名表彰。

2010年，全县人才总量4.34万人。其中，党政人才930人，企业经营管理人才3202人，专业技术人才2854人，技能人才7300人，农村实用人才25028人，社会工作人才4074人。是年，县委、县政府安排25.5万元资金作“人才资源开发专项经费”。评审农村实用人才职称资格46人，培训农村实用人才203人。从清华大学引进博士、硕士在读研究生6人，从中化开磷集团引进4人到县挂职。

第八节　宣传工作

1991年，县委宣传部内设宣传通讯科、理论教育科、办公室。县精神文明建设委员会办公室设在县委宣传部。1999年7月，创建息烽报社，隶属县委宣传部。2003年9月30日，《息烽报》停刊，息烽报社撤销。2004年4月，原息烽报社编辑部改为息烽县新闻中心，隶属县委宣传部。

一、理论宣传教育

1991—1995年，全县各级党组织组织广大党员、干部和群众学习宣传中共十三届六中、七中全会及十四大精神，学习《社会主义若干问题学习纲要》、邓小平建设有中国特色社会主义理论、社会主义市场经济理论知识、中共中央《关于加强党的建设几个重大问题的决定》等。开展社会主义思想教育和脱贫致富奔小康学习讨论。组织征订各类学习辅导材料和宣传资料7651余册（套），张贴宣传标语1871条，办宣传专栏148期，专题广播264次，先后3次组织机关单位干部职工参加安顺地区举行的理论学习统一考试。举办“建党70周年电影周”活动。

1996年1月，息烽县划归贵阳市后，理论宣传教育工作力度加大，县委印发广泛开展邓小平理论和中共十五大精神学习通知，要求县直机关干部职工每周至少安排半天时间、乡镇中心学习组每月一次学习邓小平理论和中共十五大精神，《中央关于加强农业和农村工作的决定》。县委宣传部征订、发放中共十五大学习辅导资料等3250余份，在《息烽报》开辟专栏刊载中共十五届三中全会精神知识问答，举办学习十五大精神读书班3期，参加学习干部340余名，培训学习十五大精神理论辅导员（理论骨干）140余人，组织开展“学习建设有中国特色社会主义理论百题知识竞赛”“贵阳市党员干部‘双学’和党纪党风知识竞赛”活动。开展“西部大开发，息烽怎么干”大讨论。

2001年，县委组建宣讲团，到10个乡镇开展“三个代表”重要思想、《公民道德建设实施纲要》和江泽民“七一”讲话宣讲教育活动，乡镇机关干部职工、党员和村干部1250余人听讲。邀请市委宣传部和市委讲师团专家和领导三次到县就“三个代表”重要思想和江泽民“七一”讲话作专题报告。次年起，要求副科级以上领导干部每年每人撰写两篇理论或调研文章，并列入工作目标考核。当年收到副科级以上领导干部撰写的理论、调研文章532篇。

2003年，县委出台《关于加强全县政治理论学习的意见》，对干部职工政治理论学习提出明确要求。是年，先后邀请市领导孙国强、秦家伦，市委宣讲团成员罗思源等到县作《学习贯彻十六大精神与贵阳市全面建设小康社会》和学习贯彻《“三个代表”重要思想学习纲要》专题报告。全县副股级以上领导干部、离退休老同志、乡（镇）机关理论辅导员1900余人听讲。组织全县各部门党员干部职工2400余人参加全省学习《“三个代表”重要思想学习纲要》知识竞赛和党员干部3000余人参加全市学习中共十六大精神理论考试。

2005年起，开展“学习型息烽”建设活动。是年，县委宣传部编辑出版县领导干部学习贯彻中共十六届三中、四中全会精神，树立和落实科学发展观理论调研文集《探索·创新·发展》一书。次年起，实行副科级以上领导干部月讲座学习制度，邀请有关专家、学者授课。

2007年10月，中共十七大召开期间，组织5000余名党员、干部职工收看中共十七大开幕式和闭幕式，学习《人民日报》社论。是年，邀请市委宣讲团成员为全县副科级以上干部宣讲中共十七大精神。县委宣讲团到各乡镇、县直部门宣讲中共十七大、市委八届四次全会和县委十一届五次全会精神，宣讲生态文明建设等20余场次。举办纪念改革开放三十周年座谈会和图片展活动。元旦、春节期间开展送政策理论下乡活动，发放理论宣传资料1万余份。开展“读书学习进万家”活动，举办读书学习进万家——林城家庭读书事迹巡回报告会，开展“书香人家”评选活动，县委命名表彰18个学习型领导班子、14个学习型机关、5个学习型企业、2个学习型社区、3个学习型村镇、427户学习型家庭。

2010年，邀请清华大学和省、市有关专家、学者、领导为县委中心学习组成员作依法治国、息烽县域经济发展、社会主义新农村建设和城市规划专题讲座。组织县级领导开展读书评书活动，为每位县委中心学习组成员购买西西弗书店购书卡。副科级以上领导干部撰写调研文章80余篇，其中《息烽县磷煤化工产业生态化研究》《息烽县新型农村合作医疗良性运行探析》《息烽县发展壮大村级集体经济小记》等文章在省、市刊物登载。

二、新闻宣传

1991—1995年，县内近200名业余通讯员为省、地、县新闻单位提供以报道县内抢险救灾、冬修水利、经济建设和讴歌时代精神、颂扬先进模范人物为主的新闻稿件和信息年均3000余条。县委宣传部采写自办《思想信息》《宣传工作简报》《学习通讯》等刊物，免费发送县直各机关单位和区、乡（镇）。

1996年后，县委宣传部门借助各类新闻媒体，以开辟专栏、办专版等形式，加大息烽对外宣传力度，至2004年，相继在《贵阳晚报》办“息烽专版”，介绍县内自然资源、环境和发展状况；配合《贵州日报》《瞭望》周刊、香港《大公报》《西部开发报》《贵州画报》等报刊，通过办专版形式介绍息烽投资环境、招商引资优惠政策和两个文明建设成果。年均在市级以上报刊发表稿件700余篇（条）。县委宣传部多次被《贵阳晚报》（后组建为《贵阳日报》）、《贵州日报》表彰为通联工作先进集体，多人被评为优秀通讯员或获优秀作品奖。

2004年起，利用网络媒体开展息烽宣传。是年，建息烽人民政府网站，在新华网、林城贵阳网设息烽网页（简称“一站两网页”）。当年，在新华网、“林城贵阳”两网站累计用稿500余篇（条）。制作《息烽集中营纪念馆开馆仪式纪念册暨首日封》《走进息烽》画册等。组建息烽千人合唱团。向省、市新闻媒体投稿近800篇（条）。编辑出版《息烽宣传》20期。

2007年，县委组织赴贵阳、上海、江西、深圳等地举办息烽集中营革命历史纪念馆陈列图文暨旅游风光图片展活动。编辑、拍摄、出版《杨虎城将军的最后岁月》《笔行山水间》《名家画息烽》《息烽漫步》《红军长征过息烽》《息烽外宣电视片》等文化图书和电视专题片。邀请《贵州日报》、贵州电视台等5家省、市主流媒体到县采访，对息烽党建工作、旅游开发、文化产业、磷化工业建设、远程教育、新农村建设等重大课题进行采访报道。

2009年，对县政府网站进行改版，建立网评员队伍，启动“依法治县网”“科技信息网”等二级网站建设。是年，全国百家电视台红色旅游巡礼在息烽集中营革命历史纪念馆启动，全国30多家媒体记者到息烽集中营、乌江峡、息烽温泉等景区采访，专题报道息烽红色旅游资源；中央驻黔媒体记者10余人到息烽采访“平安先进县”建设工作、小寨坝磷煤化工基地建设等；是年1月26日，中央电视台《焦点访谈》栏目，对息烽2008年凝冻期间“风雪中送产妇”的先进事迹进行回访，播出时间长达10余分钟；息烽电视台制作《抗凝冻·保民生》电视专题片；11月13日，中央电视台新闻频道报道息烽低保评审工作先进经验。

2010年，在县自办媒体上开设“‘三创一办’息烽在行动”“整脏治乱树新风”“科学发展看息烽”“又好又快、更好更快发展乡镇行”“创先争优、党务公开”“回顾‘十一五’、展望‘十二五’”、深入开展“四帮四促”活动等栏目或专题，宣传报道全县各项重点工作。是年，在县自办媒体刊登、播出新闻、专题稿件等3000余篇（条、幅），在市级以上媒体外宣用稿800余条。县相关部门制作《责任重于泰山——息烽县“十有县”创建工作纪实》《行阳光之举　兴磊落之风》《阳光低保：晒出公平——息烽县农低保工作纪实》等专题片。建“网上息烽集中营”“息烽科技网”等子网站，网站访问量从每日2000人次提升到每日6000人次。投入资金近50万元，在上级媒体开设专版或专栏，加大息烽对外宣传力度。协助中央电视台“探索与发现”栏目组、高清频道栏目组、《生活567》“5000元改厨改卫”行动栏目组拍摄“巾帼英雄”张露萍在息烽集中营的英勇故事、改厨改卫农户节目。协助湖南电视台、重庆电视台、中央台12家媒体到息烽采访抗干旱保民生、红色旅游开发、生态文明建设等重要课题。12月6日起，息烽电视新闻上传省、市“新闻荟萃”平台。

三、《息烽报》与《息烽宣传》

（一）《息烽报》

1998年7月，县委宣传部筹备创办县委机关报——《息烽报》。10月1日，《息烽报》创刊第一期出版，为四开四版。至是年底，试刊免费发行计12期。次年1月1日起，《息烽报》正式出版发行，为周报（每周五出版），四开四版。每期发行1200份（其中100份为免费赠阅），每份年定价30元。2000年1月，《息烽报》改为周二报，每周二、五出版。次年1月，《息烽报》恢复为周报。2003年9月30日，根据中办发《关于进一步治理党政部门报刊散滥和利用职权发行　减轻基层和农民负担的通知》和贵阳市委办公厅文件精神，《息烽报》停刊。1998年10月至2003年9月，《息烽报》共出版303期，每版除消息、通讯、领导讲话、图片外，在二、三、四版开辟"金钥匙""连心桥""大家谈""经济观点""息烽人""法之声""走遍息烽""西望诗坛""艺苑小花"等栏目。

（二）《息烽宣传》

2004年3月起，以原《息烽报》编辑部采编人员为主体，开始编印《息烽通讯》，免费发县直各机关、各乡镇和企事业单位，供学习交流之用。《息烽通讯》为16开本内宣刊物，每月底印发一期，每期20～40页不等，印数400份。《息烽通讯》以"工作报道、经验交流、决策参考、信息荟萃"为办刊宗旨。2005年2月，《息烽通讯》更名为《息烽宣传》。是年10月，《息烽宣传》由月刊改为周报（每周一发行），为四开四版。2007年3月，息烽新闻中心（含《贵阳日报》息烽县记者站）、《"三农"之窗》、县政府网及新华网息烽网页、林城贵阳网站息烽网页整合，组建息烽县新闻中心，由宣传部分出，隶属县委管理。2005年10月至2007年2月，《息烽宣传》共出版64期。

四、精神文明建设

（一）文明单位、乡村建设

1982年起，息烽县开展以富裕、文明、民主为主要特征的"文明村寨"建设。1991年6月，县委宣传部开展"党在我心中"系列活动，举办"建党70周年电影周"活动，组织干部职工观看《中国革命之歌》《四渡赤水》《百色起义》等影片。是年，县委、县政府命名表彰文明单位6个、文明村寨10个。1992年3月，县委、县政府再次修订《文明村寨建设竞赛先进区乡评比标准及奖励办法》。是年，九庄镇杉林村、县乡镇企业公司、息烽县分别受中共安顺地委、安顺地区行署，省委、省政府授予文明村、文明单位、精神文明建设工作先进单位称号，并通报表彰和授牌命名。

1996年起，在全县开展创建卫生城镇、文明村寨、文明单位及片区社会治安综合治理、群防群治活动；开展"做人民公仆""文明市场""文明个体工商户""优秀青年""优秀三八红旗手""五好家庭""三好学生"评选活动。至1998年，全县创建文明单位22个、文明村20个、文明村寨38个。养龙司乡堡子村被中宣部命名为全国文明村镇创建示范点。

1999年，开展创建"十星级文明户"（劳动致富星、遵纪守法星、履行义务星、计划生育星、科技应用星、文化知识星、尊老爱幼星、清洁卫生星、团结和睦星、移风易俗星）活动。是年，创建"十星级文明户"1000户。次年，在全县中小学开展"五不"（不说脏活、粗话，不随地吐痰，不乱扔杂物，不损坏公共设施，不违反交通规则）活动，在机关开展创建花园式单位、院落评选活动，在农村开展以村寨环境建设，整治村容村貌为中心的"五改"（改水、改沟、改厕、改圈、改房）、"五通"（通水、通电、通电话、通广播电视、通客车）活动。

2001年11月，县委宣传部、县文明办、息烽一中、二中等单位利用赶场天在县城新大街、校园举办“崇尚文明，反对邪教”大型图片展；开展纪念“一二·九”运动系列活动，组织1000余名青少年开展《公民道德实施纲要》万米跑和成人宣誓活动等。次年2月，在县城灯光球场举行“争做文明人，创建文明城”启动仪式和游演活动。县委宣传部、文明办组建《公民道德建设纲要》宣讲团分赴10个乡（镇）进行宣讲。

2003年3月，息烽县、永靖镇和永靖镇阳朗村获省精神文明委2002年度“卫生和秩序”“文明大道”创建工作“先进单位”称号。6月，开展“革陋习，树新风”集中整治活动，查处和纠正市民不文明行为110余起，清理过期横幅40余条，清运垃圾50余吨，清洗垃圾池和果皮箱165个。11月20日起，开展取缔县城非法营运二、三轮摩托车和其他机动车，投入“的士”20辆从事城市客运。2006年，小寨坝镇红岩村获贵阳市“十大文明生态村”称号；磷兴园社区、开磷新城社区获贵阳市2003—2005年度文明示范社区和文明社区称号；小寨坝镇获全省“文明单位”和“文明单位”创建工作“先进集体”称号。

2008年起，开展生态文明机关（单位）、企事业、学校、社区、村寨创建、评选、推荐活动。至2010年，命名表彰县级生态文明单位173个、村寨45个、学校20所、乡镇6个、社区2个、示范户160户、文明窗口36个、十星级文明户3380户、五好文明家庭1.3万户。推荐98个文明单位、19个文明村寨、10个文明窗口、110户五好文明家庭参加市级生态文明单位评选。

（二）文明县创建

2004年起，息烽县开展文明县创建工作。是年，县委、县政府召开创建文明县动员大会和誓师大会，印发《息烽县创建文明县工作方案》、制作曝光城市不文明行为电视专题片《城市的呼唤》和反映文明县建设成果专题片《文明之路》进行播放宣传。次年，组织交通、司法、妇联、团县委等20余家单位，上街开展“公民道德宣传咨询”活动，发放宣传资料、倡议书等1万余份。举办市民素质教育骨干培训班，建市民文明学校70余所，开展市民素质培训。

2010年，县委、县政府印发《息烽县创建文明县工作方案》《文明县创建暨“三创一办”近期宣传工作要点通知》《关于在全县组织“三创一办”知识测试的通知》和《关于做好“三创”知晓率　支持率　满意率测评工作的通知》等系列文件。组织乡镇、机关企事业单位干部职工，各中小学师生及村（居）干部3.2万人进行“三创一办”知识测试。举办“三创一办”暨创建文明窗口知识竞赛活动和文明礼仪培训。组织志愿者1万余人次对“三创一办”相关知识进行“六进”宣传讲解，印制、张贴、发放各类宣传资料及《市民文明手册》共43万份。在县政府网、《息烽宣传》和息烽电视台开设“三创一办”“打响创模攻坚战”“‘三创一办’息烽在行动”“‘三创’大家谈”征文，“亮亮不文明，看看该谁管”“小手牵大手，共做文明人”曝光台等专栏，适时报道创建先进典型，曝光不文明行为等。开展创建全国文明城市、城市公共文明指数、公众对城市环境保护满意率测评工作。全县17.83余万人参加调查测评，公众对创建全国文明城市满意率94.05%，对城市公共文明指数满意率96.75%，对城市环境保护满意率97.15%。

（三）整脏治乱

2004年，县成立“整脏治乱”领导小组，下设办公室在县建设局。2006年，制定《息烽县“整脏治乱”行动规划（2006—2010）》《2006年息烽县“整脏治乱”工作方案》，召开700余人参加的全县“整脏治乱”动员大会，层层分解任务，明确各单位具体职责。是年，夺得贵阳市“整脏治乱”第一面流动红旗。

2007年，印发《2007年息烽县“整脏治乱”专项行动工作方案》，完善考评办法，实行季评季查季通报；制作“整脏治乱”专项行动宣传标牌200余块、“整脏治乱”图片展板17块在城乡巡回展出；开展“讲文明，树新风，‘整脏治乱’美息烽”宣传咨询活动，印制宣传资料10万份发放全县中小学。成立县“四创”工作领导小组，开展“文明值勤岗”活动，县直70余个单位、部门参加每周三轮流值勤。2008年，落实“门前三包”责任制、楼群院落环境卫生整治和管理实施方案、农村环境卫生整治工作方案。是年，贵州省“整脏治乱”明察暗访排名中，息烽县第一、二、三季度排名分别为全省第一、十、十五名。

2009年起，开展“文明与秩序”专项整治活动。至2010年，完成道路维修改造20余处，对群众反映县城占道经营、垃圾清理不及时、噪声扰民等51起投诉进行及时处理。是年1月，在贵州省精神文明建设指导委员会2009年“整脏治乱”专项行动年度考核中，息烽县获贵阳市第一名并被通报表彰。

第九节　政法委工作

一、机构

1991年，县社会治安综合治理领导小组成立，下设办公室在县委政法委。5月，更名为县社会治安综合治理委员会（简称县综治委），下设办公室（简称县综治办）。1996年4月，县委政法委、县综治办合署办公。1997年3月，县委政法委机关与县综治办实行一个机构，两块牌子。同月，成立县禁毒工作委员会（简称县禁毒委），下设办公室（简称县禁毒办）与县综治办合署办公，实行两块牌子，一套人员。是年8月，县委政法委内设办公室。1998年8月，县铁路护路联防领导小组办公室（简称县护路办）由县人民武装部改设在县综治办。1999年5月，成立县维护社会稳定工作领导小组，下设办公室（简称县维稳办）在县委政法委。2001年11月，县国家安全领导小组办公室（简称国安办）由县委办公室改设在县委政法委，承担县国家安全领导小组日常业务工作。

2009年5月，县委政法委、县综治办、县维稳办（县委防范和处理邪教问题工作领导小组办公室）合署办公，设政工科、办公室（研究室）、执法监督科、综治科、维稳科（防范和处理邪教工作科）、铁路护路办、流动人口服务和管理办公室7个科室。

二、社会治安综合治理

1991年，开展社会治安综合治理达标工作，制定《息烽县社会治安综合治理达标实施方案》，各乡（镇）成立社会治安综合治理委员会及办公室，按编制配齐专职干部。县直党、政、群机关成立综合治理领导小组47个，负责本系统、本单位综合治理达标工作。次年，综合治理达标工作实行县委、县政府领导，县综治委成员单位包乡（镇）、联点、分类指导。明确各乡（镇）党政主要领导是综合治理工作责任人，实行目标管理，量化考核。是年，县综治委组织达标督促检查4次。全县建专兼职联防队412个1215人，群防群治队伍调解各种民事纠纷1000余起，调解成功率90%以上。全县128个村、1380个村民组和1360个自然村寨无民事积案。评定达标红旗乡镇2个，县直机关单位5个，中央、省属驻县企事业单位2个。12月，经省考核组抽查和测试，息烽县社会治安综合治理工作全面达标。1993年，继续实行社会治安综合治理承包责任制，县、乡、村、机关、学校、企事业单位层层签订治安承包责任状，落实综合治理达标巩固工作。是年，小寨坝镇、永靖镇、流长乡、养龙司乡被县委、县政府命名为社会治安综合治理“红旗单位”，温泉镇、九庄镇、石硐乡、青山苗族乡、鹿窝乡、西山乡为社会治安综合治理达标合格单位。

1995年起，开展“依法治乡（镇）、治村、治厂矿社区”和“挂牌”管理。县综治委印发《关于实行“依法治乡（镇）、治村、治厂”和“挂牌”管理决定》。全县新建治安联防队18个，建立综治委11个（县级1个、乡镇级10个）、综治办11个（县级1个、乡镇级10个），政法领导小组17个，治保、调解组织204个，治安联防队190个，护村、校、厂队542个，关心下一代协会10个。定期帮教“八种人员”“两劳人员”和有轻微违法人员，列帮率100%。对43个单位、53个村1.5万户实施挂牌管理。

1996年，开展创建“平安工程”试点工作。县委、县政府制定《息烽县社会治安综合治理第三个五年规划》和《息烽县1996—2010年推行“平安工程”实施方案》。是年，全县建治保委员会、调解委员会各249个，保安公司1个，护厂、校、村、村寨队1.1万余个，专兼职联防队255个，农村维护社会治安民兵队伍88支。全年调解民事纠纷2546件，调解成功2419件。次年，“平安工程”创建工作全面铺开。至1998年，全县建立村（居）委治安室42个，协助公安机关抓获犯罪嫌疑人426人，夜间巡逻截获被盗耕牛33头、马14匹。各级调解组织调解民间纠纷1265起，调解成功1216起，成功率96%。

2000年，县委、县政府将社会治安综合治理年终考核95分以上的鹿窝乡、流长乡、永靖镇、青山苗族乡、养龙司乡、西山乡、小寨坝镇、温泉镇命名为“实施社会治安综合治理平安工程模范乡（镇）”，将90分以上的九庄镇、石硐乡命名为“实施社会治安综合治理平安工程红旗乡（镇）”。是年，鹿窝乡推行联户守护责任制，以2～3户、5～7户、10～15户不等实行联户守护。全乡13个村中，未发生刑事案件的村11个，未发生治安案件的村6个。

2004年，县综治委在青山苗族乡绿化村创建“五进社区”示范点，设“社区（村居）”警务室、法律服务室、文化活动室，建立服务承诺制，将工作职责、任务、纪律、监督电话、工作人员照片、报警灯箱上墙公示。次年，在全县推行“治安门前三包责任制”，实行门前治安承包。以自然村寨或村民小组为基本单位，按20～30户为一组设立“治安中心户长”为警民联系点，全县设“治安中心户长”1601名，构建以“治安中心户长”制为依托的新型农村治安防控网络。

2006年，以派出所和责任区巡警、交警、刑警为骨干，以村（居、社区）治保会、义务巡逻队等群防群治力量为辅助，以创建平安村（居、社区、单位、企业）为载体，健全村（居、社区）治安防控网络。全县170个村（居）组建850人农村义务巡防队伍（每村〈居〉5人），实现社会治安综合治理横到边，纵到底，无死角的防控格局。流长乡营中村“千户联户”经验被推荐到市“创安”现场会交流。是年8月，省综治委授予息烽县“平安建设先进县”称号。12月，息烽县创建“平安息烽”工程经市级检查验收达标。

2009年起，推行“一主三横五纵”网格式群防工作。

2010年，县委、县政府印发《息烽县社会治安综合治理一票否决权制实施细则》《息烽县社会治安综合治理领导责任追究制实施细则》，对各乡（镇）、各单位主要领导和分管领导履行社会治安综合治理工作职责情况进行细化考评。

三、“严打”斗争

1991年起，县委政法委组织、指导、协调县公安、法院、检察院、司法局各家集中统一行动，开展“反盗窃”专项斗争，专项斗争统一行动分“打团伙，破大案”“追逃犯，打流窜”两个步骤，对特种行业和重点人口、暂住人口以及流动人口进行清理整顿三个阶段进行。至1994年，摧毁犯罪团伙111个，击毙犯罪逃跑分子2人，破获各类刑事案件207起，查获犯罪分子118人，追回耕牛、马、猪、羊、鸡等家畜家禽94头（只），查获摩托车、电视机、放像机、布匹、建材、高档酒1批。

1995年，开展以打击持枪抢劫、拦路抢劫、入室抢劫、车匪路霸和拐卖妇女儿童犯罪，流氓恶势力犯罪和黑社会性质的团伙犯罪为重点的春季、夏秋严打斗争，破获盗窃案件12起，治安案件39起；摧毁犯罪团伙9个52人，抓获违法人员70人；缴获赃物和赃款1.5万元。

1996年，县建立“严打”斗争领导小组及办公室，各乡（镇）及驻县中央、省属厂矿企业相继成立“严打”领导小组及办公室17个，抽出181人具体抓“严打”工作。是年，开展“破大案，追逃犯，抓现行，打团伙”专项斗争，共组织集中统一行动9次，发放宣传资料近2000份，张贴通告、规劝书、通缉令3000份，典型安全宣传小册子200册，“严打”宣传提纲近1万份，自印资料5000份，发送宣传录音磁带10盒，张贴大小标语2647条（幅），出动宣传车辆265台次，出墙报、黑板报167期，专栏39期，广播、电视宣传196次，破获刑事案件208起，抓获各类违法犯罪人员778人，召开严打公捕公判大会3次。

1997—2008年，相继组织开展“双打双反”（打团伙、打暴力犯罪，反盗窃、反抢劫）、“三打一防”、打击“两抢一盗”“破大案，追逃犯，打团伙”“打黑除恶”“冬季百日破案会战”等“严打”专项斗争和集中统一行动，侦破刑事案件2698件，抓获犯罪分子1024人，查破犯罪团伙30个，侦破“2·23”杨某某故意杀人案、“8·23”蔡某某被杀案和“9·22”周某某故意杀人案，召开公捕、公处、公判大会10次。

2009年，按照“有黑打黑，无黑除恶，无恶打霸，无霸打帮，无帮打痞”和“打早打小，不任其坐大成势”的工作要求，打掉唐某某黑社会组织团伙1个，抓获该团伙犯罪嫌疑人员17人，收缴涉案车辆2台、自制手枪2支、制式子弹3发。侦破“4·9”温泉镇王某某故意杀人案、“5·21”石硐乡汪某某故意杀人案、“6·27”永靖镇柿花坪轮奸杀人案和“9·10”永靖镇小意思夜市故意伤害致人死亡案。

2010年，以“打黑除恶”为重点，相继开展“严打‘两抢一盗’，保卫百姓平安”“社会治安重点地区排查整治”“夏季严打”“冬季百日破案”等严打专项行动12次，出动警力2554人次，警车581台次，破获刑事案件634起，抓获犯罪嫌疑人279人，打掉恶势力犯罪团伙2个，缴获毒品126.7克，解救被拐卖妇女儿童6名，为群众找回失踪和离家出走的少女、儿童各2名，女青年1名。

四、重点人口管理

1993年起，开展对管制、缓刑、假释、监外执行、剥夺政治权利、免予起诉、免予刑事处分和保外就医人员（简称“八种”人员）和劳改释放、解除劳动教养人员（简称“两劳”人员）及流动人口实行流进流出登记管理，对贵阳市以外到息烽临时居住人员实行办理暂住证制度，对房屋出租户进行建档管理，签订流动人口管理责任书，对“两劳”和“八种”人员进行建档立卡，回访监改帮教帮扶。是年，对“两劳”和“八种”人员473人建档立卡，开展回访监改帮教帮扶。2001年，全县建帮教小组461个，与977名帮教对象签订帮教责任书。2010年，安置刑释解教人员

112人就业。

五、维护社会稳定

（一）取缔、打击邪教组织

20世纪90年代初，县境内部分边远地区出现邪教组织，少数不法分子打着信教幌子进行非法活动，影响群众正常生产生活秩序。县委政法委协调组织有关国家机关，严厉打击不法分子和邪教组织的非法活动，向人民群众开展以“崇尚科学，关爱家庭，珍惜生命，反对邪教”为主题的反邪教警示教育活动，维护社会稳定。1994—2006年，取缔有害气功社团和非法宗教活动传教场所13处，解散非法教会4个，收缴音像制品、书籍344盒（本）；取缔邪教“门徒会”组织27个，拆除非法建庙宇25处，依法惩处相关人员41人，送劳教3人。

（二）排查调处纠纷、处置群体事件

1999年5月，县维护稳定工作领导小组成立。是年起，维护稳定工作贯彻“预防为主，调防结合”方针，坚持“分级负责，归口督办，一把手负总责”和领导干部“一岗双责”制。县委政法委不定期组织相关单位召开矛盾纠纷排查调处会，及时掌握矛盾纠纷信息，早预测、早发现、早调处，把矛盾纠纷解决在萌芽状态。依法打击别有用心、煽动群众闹事，造成社会危害结果的违法犯罪分子。2001年3月7日，永靖镇三田片区200余名村民非法聚集、围攻党政干部、强行封堵贵遵高等级公路1个多小时。政法机关对涉嫌策划堵塞交通的3名首要分子依法抓捕处理。是年4月20日，永靖镇联丰村石关口村民组发生胡家马槽果园价值4.3万元的经果林遭村民砍毁，并围攻永靖镇派出所事件，政法机关依法抓捕涉嫌围攻冲击派出所闹事的7名不法分子，平息事态发展，维护社会稳定。

六、禁毒工作

（一）禁毒宣传

1991—1996年，县内禁毒宣传为常规性开展。1997年县禁毒委员会成立后，加大禁毒宣传力度。是年，组织相关单位开展禁毒宣传咨询活动，在县城和乡镇集镇悬挂、张贴“维护社会稳定，人人有责”“吸毒可耻”“吸毒危害社会、家庭、个人身体，千万不可沾”等标语，发放禁毒宣传资料1.6万余份，书画6.8万册（份）。

1998年起，县禁毒宣传步入高潮期。至2008年，连续11年坚持开展“6·26”禁毒日宣传活动，相继组织开展“珍爱生命，远离毒品”，消除艾滋病万人签名，禁毒宣传游行，召开公捕、公判大会，举办禁毒文艺演出、演讲比赛、讲座和征文等大型禁毒宣传活动10余次。采取赶场天在县城、乡镇集镇摆摊设点，“致妈妈的一封公开信”，接待群众禁毒法律知识咨询，为中小学师生上禁毒知识课，播放禁毒电视教育片，在报刊开辟禁毒宣传专栏，领导发表禁毒电视讲话，举办禁毒培训，悬挂、张贴禁毒宣传标语，出禁毒墙报等多种形式开展禁毒宣传。累计召开公捕公判大会2次，举行万人签名活动3次、游行活动2次，接待群众禁毒法律咨询5000余人，为中小学师生上禁毒知识课62次，听课师生1万余人次，征集文章2000余篇，发放宣传资料6万余份（册）等。

2010年1月22日，县委政法委组织县公安、检察、法院和司法各家单位利用石硐乡赶集之机，在石硐乡召开禁毒严打整治专项行动“公捕、公处”大会，对陈某、云某某、徐某、卿某某等8名涉毒违法犯罪嫌疑人员进行“公捕”“公处”。6月2日，在县城三角花园开展纪念《中华人民共和国禁

毒法》颁布实施2周年暨“6·3”虎门销烟71周年宣传活动。是年，县公安局共出动宣传车12辆次、警力23人次，分别在全县7个社区、86个村、7家厂矿企业、10所学校巡回播放《中华人民共和国禁毒法》《娱乐场所管理条例》等录音。举办行业场所业主及从业人员禁毒知识培训会2次，参加培训87人。与行业场所业主签订娱乐场所禁毒承诺书19份。

（二）创建“无毒县”

息烽创建“无毒县”工作始于2005年。是年，县政府印发《息烽县创建“无毒县”实施方案》。2006年1月20日，县政府召开创建“无毒县”动员大会，出台《关于进一步加大禁毒“五大战役”工作力度的意见》《关于开展创建“无毒县”攻坚战的实施意见》《息烽县禁毒及创建“无毒县”工作领导责任追究暂行规定（试行）》《息烽县禁毒工作保证金制度》《息烽县禁毒帮教对象优惠扶持意见》等文件。将创建“无毒县”工作纳入各级各部门一级目标管理，实行禁毒工作“一票否决”权。是年，县禁毒专项经费预算从2004年的10万元增至100万元。永靖镇财政预算禁毒经费20万元，其余乡镇财政预算禁毒经费3万～5万元不等，为创建“无毒县”提供经费保障。2008年，为县禁毒办和县公安局禁毒大队各增加人员8名。各乡镇党委、政府配备禁毒工作专职人员，乡镇禁毒办人员增至3～5人。各部门明确1人专管禁毒工作。是年，全县建禁毒帮教小组308个，成员1352人。县禁毒委员会制发《息烽县集中整治涉毒娱乐场所　建立长效管理机制专项行动实施方案》《息烽县禁毒严打战役攻坚战实施方案》《息烽县创建“无毒县”堵源截流实施方案》等文件。县、乡镇、村居、村民组四级明确信息员500余名，县公安机关开展“飓风”“雷霆”“猎狐”、禁种铲毒、打击苯丙胺类毒品犯罪、打击零包贩毒等专项行动10余次。采取“一对一帮村”“多对一帮人”措施，全县副科级以上领导干部直接联系帮教吸毒人员308名，并实行干部帮教保证金制度（县处级2000元、正科级1500元、副科级1000元）。印发《息烽县禁毒帮教对象优惠实施意见》。为社区戒毒（康复）工作招聘专职人员24名，每个康复中心配备专（兼）职医生1名等。是年11月，息烽县创建“无毒县”工作通过市禁毒委员会验收。2009年1月，息烽县创建“无毒县”工作通过省禁毒委员会验收。5月19日，省禁毒委员会授予息烽县“无毒县”称号。是年，县委、县政府下发《关于进一步巩固“无毒县”的工作意见》，将禁毒工作纳入经济社会发展的总体部署，层层分解细化禁毒工作目标责任，落实禁毒工作领导责任制。开发公益性岗位24个，专职从事社区戒毒（康复）工作。此后，禁毒工作转入常态化。2010年，县公安、司法、卫生食品药品监督等部门对10个乡镇创建“无毒乡镇”“无毒村居”“无毒单位”“无毒学校”“无毒家庭”等工作进行督导检查。

七、铁路护路联防

（一）组织机构

1991年，县整顿铁路治安秩序领导小组办公室设在县人民武装部，组建铁路护路民兵连，编4个排、12个班、19个点段组、122人。1994年8月，县整顿铁路治安秩序领导小组更名为县铁路护路联防领导小组。1996年，县铁路护路民兵连精减人员，编1个连、4个排、10个班，共87人。次年调整为4个排、9个班，62人。1998年7月，撤销县铁路护路民兵连，组建县公安局铁路护路保安大队，设三个中队，共19人，铁路护路民兵改称护路治安员。是年8月，县铁路护路联防领导小组办公室（简称县护路办）改设在县综治办。1999年，铁路护路保安大队设四个中队20人，次年设五个中队，人员增至25人。

（二）主要工作与活动

1991年3月20日，护路民兵巡查至川黔铁路K362处，发现火车在运输途中被盗铝锭105块，报当地派出所与公安警察，抓获行盗人员3名。4月10日，护路民兵巡查到川黔铁路K345处，从行进中的火车头前救出1名坐在钢轨上喂奶的妇女及其怀中女婴。7月11日，县境内发生暴雨洪灾，川黔铁路K341处被山洪冲垮50余米，县人武部组织民兵抢修36小时，恢复通车。1994年7月28日，息烽县被评为“全省第五轮承包铁路护路联防工作先进单位”。1995年10月1日，川黔铁路K358处危岩大塌方，重约3吨的3块巨石坠入铁路道心，永靖镇下洪马村护路民兵汪银华、郭世伦发现后，立即分头将上海至重庆的一列特快旅客列车拦停在离塌方点100米处，避免了一场特大列车事故，2名民兵受到省护路办公室通报表彰并各奖励2700元。是年，息烽县被中央综治委、铁道部、公安部、中国人民解放军总参动员部评为“全国护路联防先进县”。1996年7月9日，县护路办被评为全省铁路护路联防先进单位。1997年5月25日，全省护路民兵与巡道工交叉联网巡查现场会在息烽铁路工务段召开，会上介绍息烽铁路护路联防工作经验。7月26日，县铁路护路联防工作受省通报表彰，再次荣获“全省第五轮承包铁路护路联防工作先进单位”称号，成为连续5年受省表彰的3个先进县之一。

1998年起，铁路护路实行重点路段重点守护，对铁路道口落实专人守护，一般路段列入乡镇社会治安综合治理行政管理内容，实行一票否决权。2005年，县综治办、护路办组织铁路沿线28个村665户机动车户主、978户人家与县护路办签订机动车辆、耕牛管理责任书，对妨碍铁路畅通重点对象进行再教育。2008—2009年，在全县范围内开展爱路护路宣传月活动2次。广播宣传60小时，播放光盘60小时，制作展板51块，发放《致沿线群众及中小学生一封公开信》2.6万封，出动宣传车4台次，到铁路沿线乡村巡回宣传16次，召开群众会议13场次。铁路沿线乡（镇）政府与各村，村与组，组与农户签订责任书，各村与978户大牲畜户主、665户机动车户主、26户精神病人及“五残”儿童监护人签订管理责任书。2010年，建立以统一研究策略、统一安排部署、统一发动宣传、统一检查督导（“四个统一”）领导工作机制，制定《息烽县铁路护路保安队伍管理暂行规定》《息烽县铁路护路保安队伍量化管理评分细则》。开展百日整治行动，两次对铁路沿线15户废旧金属收购站进行清理整治。

第十节　统战工作

一、机构

1991年，中共息烽县委统战部（简称县委统战部）内设办公室。县政府台湾事务办公室与中共息烽县委对台工作小组办公室合署办公，实行两块牌子、一套人员，设在县委统战部。1992年4月，“中共息烽县委对台工作小组办公室”更名为“中共息烽县委台湾工作办公室”。1996年，县委统战部增设对台办，撤销中共息烽县委台湾工作办公室、县政府台湾事务办公室。2002年，设综合科，撤销对台办。

二、非党干部培养、任用、联系工作

1991年，按照中央各级政协委员中非党人士比例不得少于60%的要求，有非党人士78人担任县政协委员。是年，选派3名党外干部分别到省社会主义学院和厦门台湾知识讲习班培训学习。1993年组织非公有制经济代表人士和非党干部共10人参加省委统战部、省社会主义学院举办的“金三角”

边贸经济考察研讨班学习。1995年，县委统战部在乡（镇）和部分县直机关建立非党知识分子联系点13个。开展非党知识分子调查统计工作，全县有非党知识分子1800人。是年，从教师队伍中选拔优秀人才12人到县机关任职。1997年，在6个乡（镇）和17个县直部门领导班子中各配备非党干部1名，安排进入后备干部培养101人，同年选派19名大中专毕业生到村挂职锻炼。1998年，任用非党副县级干部5名，选拔13名非党干部担任科级领导职务。推荐安排75名党外人士担任县政协委员。1999年6月，县委办公室印发《关于建立县级党员领导干部与非党干部　非党知识分子　非公有制经济人士和少数民族代表人士联系制度的通知》，28名县级党员领导干部联系非党干部135名、非党知识分子136名、非公经济代表人士92名和少数民族代表人物108人，定期了解非党干部、非党知识分子、非公经济代表人士的工作、生活和生产经营情况，及时帮助排忧解难。2000年，县委、县政府建立非公有制经济代表人士联系制度和少数民族代表人物联系制度，县、乡（镇）党员领导干部共联系非公经济代表人士106人，少数民族代表人物122人。是年，县委下发《关于加强和完善党外科级后备干部队伍建设的通知》，明确把党外后备干部队伍建设纳入“十五”计划进行安排。2008年，县委下发《息烽县县级班子党员领导干部与统战对象联系制度》，明确每名县级党员领导干部分别联系统战对象2～3人，定期或不定期开展联系和慰问活动，听取统战对象对全县各项工作的意见和建议。是年，开展无党派人士政治交接主题教育活动，组织无党派代表人士学习党的路线、方针、政策，交流思想，提高认识。2010年，选派11名党外人士到省社会主义学院和市、县委党校培训学习。

三、台务与侨务

1991年，县台湾工作办公室组织召开各种会议18场次，宣传党的对台方针政策。走访台侨属313户575人。1992年，开展中秋、春节慰问活动，走访、慰问台、侨属438户575人。分别送给礼品和年画。此后，县委统战部门坚持每年开展走访、慰问台侨属活动。

1995年，县委统战工作部门为台胞给县内台属汇款28起，邮寄往来信件475封提供必要帮助。接待台胞8起12人次，台胞台属来信来访17件17人。1998年，组织台、侨属50余人参加“庆回归，迎中秋”座谈会。次年，组织台、侨属100余人召开座谈会，学习中央关于台湾问题的“八项主张”，声讨台湾地区领导人李登辉的“两国论”。帮助办理台属证200余个。2001年4月，县台办、团县委、教育局、文明办、电视台组织开展“祖国宝岛在我心中”征文演讲比赛活动。次年8月，县委办公室下发《关于加强对涉台事务进行通报的通知》，就有关涉台问题作出具体规定，建立县、乡（镇）涉台事务通报备案制度。10月，全县开展台属、台胞普查工作，普查统计，全县有台属628户1926人，台胞257人，其中：军界53人、政界14人、商界35人，其他155人。引进台湾佛教慈善慈济事业基金会出资250万元，购买物资帮助息烽抗灾赈灾和灾后重建工作。

2004年，开展侨情普查登记工作，全县有华侨 4 户13人、海外华人13户47人、港澳同胞25户55人、归侨 3 户 5 人、侨眷14户46人、外籍华人眷属17户77人、港澳同胞眷属28户118人。是年，接待台侨胞属16起19人。

2005年 5 月，开展侨法宣传活动。县政府下发《关于在全县深入开展侨法宣传的通知》，全县悬挂宣传横幅标语15条，张贴宣传标语650余条，发放宣传资料 2 万余份、侨法手册100余本，办黑板报20期。12月 2 日，贵阳市外侨办在永靖镇北门社区召开全市侨务工作现场会，为北门社区举行“侨务工作进社区示范单位”授牌仪式。是年，推选省侨联代表大会代表 1 名。

2007—2009年，相继组织“中国台湾问题图片展”“乡情行动”和台胞台属向台湾灾区捐赠活

动，组织捐款1.73万元送县红十字会转交台湾灾区。引进台胞游昌华投资150万元参与息烽中医院建设。2010年，县委、县政府在中秋、春节期间组织慰问台、侨属200余户。统战工作部门协助办理台胞寻亲事务 1 件，接待台湾参访团两批92人；接待台胞王锡�等 7 人祭拜张露萍等七烈士墓。

1991—2010年，接待来信来访89件97人次；走访台、侨属688户次；中秋、春节等慰问425户；办理台属证277个，引进海外资金940万元、美金7万元办企业、建学校及进行赈灾和灾后重建等。

第十一节　党校工作

一、机构

1991年，中共息烽县委党校（简称县委党校）内设办公室、教务处、总务处。1997年5月，县编委明确县委党校相当于副县级事业单位，其内设机构升为副科级规格。是年，教务处、总务处更名为教务科、行政科。2009年12月增设科研办公室，行政科更名为总务科。

1991—2010年，县委党校除1993年6月至1994年1月设专职校长外，其余时间均由县委副书记兼任校长，配备正科级常务副校长主持日常工作。2007年，贵阳市机构编制委员会批复县委党校领导职数，明确县委党校设常务副校长（副县级）。

二、校舍建设与师资队伍

（一）校舍建设

1991年，县委党校校址位于县城环城路49号。占地面积约800平方米，校舍为砖木结构三层楼房，建筑面积926平方米。设教室2间，办公室、图书室、简易厨房及餐厅各1间等。有黑白电视机、收录机、洗衣机各1台，被褥30套、床100张、课桌110套、办公桌20张、铁皮炉23个，图书2000余册。1999年11月，购置彩色电视机2台，录放机、VCD、功放机各1台，课桌椅300套、文件柜11个、直拨电话机2台、小车1辆、教学电脑20台等。

2004年7月，县委党校迁到永靖镇南门村大型地玄天东路新教学综合楼办公。新教学综合楼校区占地1.52公顷（22.8亩）。建筑面积3300平方米，设教室12间，阶梯教室1间，教职工办公室14间，会议室2间，图书室、阅览室、多功能厅各1间，篮球场1个，档案室2间，活动室6间，车库2间，配电房、值班室各1间。教学设施：中央党校远程教育B级站、农村党员干部远程教育网各1个，小车1辆，扫描仪、刻录机、传真机、摄像机各1台，打印机2台，电话机4台，课桌椅192套，各办公室办公桌椅、电脑等设施齐备。

（二）教师队伍

1991年，县委党校有专职教员7人，其中大学本科学历4人，专科及以下3人；7人中具有高级职称2人。此后，专职教员有调进调出（含退休）。多数时间保持在7人左右。2010年，有专职教员9人，均为本科学历，其中高级讲师3人、讲师5人、助理讲师1人。

三、教学

（一）干部培训

县内各级干部到县委党校培训学习，其对象由县委组织部按干部培训规划，分期分批安排，县委党校负责授课。培训学习时间1周至3个月不等。培训学习内容主要有马克思列宁主义、毛泽东思想、邓小平理论、“三个代表”重要思想和党的路线、方针政策、法律法规、当代经济、领导科学、管理科学、写作知识、现代科学文化知识，WTO知识及党风廉政建设等。根据不同培训对象，设置相关业务知识培训。对农村党支部书记、村主任的培训，除安排政治理论和党的路线方针培训学习外，特别安排《人口与计划生育》《经济林种植与管理》《乡镇企业的创办及集体经济的管理》《农民人均纯收入的简易算法》和种植、养殖技术培训课程。教学方式：除党校教师按计划授课外，聘请有关领导、专家授课，辅以电教、经验交流、社会考察等。培训结束后，发给培训结业证书。1991—2010年，共举办干部培训70个班次，培训干部4588人次。其中乡（科）级、中青年干部培训27个班次，培训1288人次；村干部培训15个班次，培训1334人次；干部轮训6个班次，培训284人次；其他22个班次，培训1682人次。

（二）学历教育

脱产学历教育：1991年，县委党校开办一年制党政管理专业干部中专专修班。招生对象为具有初中文化程度的副区、局级以上干部和乡股级业务骨干。参加全省统一考试成绩合格者，由省教委发给录取通知书。学员学完规定课程，经考试、考查成绩合格，由省教委统一验印，县委党校发给中专毕业证书。学员毕业后从事与所学专业一致工作的，其使用和待遇与取得国民教育中等专业毕业生同等对待。是年9月，招收学员30名，次年7月，30名学员全部毕业。1998年2月，经省委组织部、省委党校招生办批准，县委组织部、县委党校联合行文，举办村级后备干部经济管理中专班。招生对象为35岁以下具有初中毕业以上文化程度、坚持四项基本原则、拥护改革开放、身体健康、立志改变农村面貌的男女青年。学制为脱产学习两年。学员学完规定课程，经考试、考核合格，颁发经省干教委验印的毕业证书，承认其中专学历。是年招录学员30名，于2000年7月毕业。2005年，为提高农村剩余劳动力基础文化知识和专业技术水平，拓宽就业渠道，实现农民增收致富，经县委批准，县委党校与贵州省机械工业学校联合举办两年制数控与模具专业中专班，学员在县委党校学习一年基础文化知识后，转入贵州省机械工业学校学习相关专业知识。学员学完规定课程，经考试考核合格，颁发贵州省机械工业学校中专毕业证书，并推荐就业。是年9月招收学员24名，于2007年7月毕业。

函授学历教育：1994年9月始，县委党校承办省委党校函授专科学历班，开设经济管理、行政管理及现代文秘3个专业，学制三年。是年招生135名。1995年，承办省委党校函授本科学历班，开设经济管理、法律两个专业，学制3年（从2000年起改为两年半）。是年招收学员62名。1998年9月，开办息烽县村级后备干部经济管理中专班，学制二年，是年招生30名，此后停止招生。1999年秋季始，举办贵阳市委党校业余专科班，学制两年半。开设行政管理、法律两个专业。是年招生39名。

2000年秋季始，承办中央党校函授学院本科班，开设法律、经济管理和公共管理3个专业，学制两年半。是年招生35名。2004年秋，承办中央党校经济管理函授专科班，学制3年。当年招生27人。是年，根据中共贵阳市委组织部《关于开展全市农村党员干部中专学历教育的通知》精神，县委党校运用现代远程教育网络，开展农村党员干部中专学历教育，招生对象为50岁以下村党支部书记、村委会主任及村级后备干部。以乡（镇）为单位设立教学班，各乡（镇）党委负责学员管理，县委党校负责教学工作，当年招收学员308名。此后，农村党员干部中专学历教育未再招生。2006年后，中央、市委党校停止招生。至2008年，县委党校（息烽函授站）承办中央、省、市委党校的各级经济管理、行政管理、现代文秘、法律等专业及农村党员干部中专班共49个班次，学员3164人，毕业

3092人，毕业率97.7%。2008年后，省委党校函授部停止招生。

四、科研成果

1996—2010年，县委党校教师完成市级课题研究9个。其中《农村一事一议筹资筹劳制度研究》《贵阳市林权制度改革跟踪研究——以息烽县集体林权制度改革为例》《息烽县磷、煤化工产业生态化研究》3个课题经贵阳市社科联验收合格，并颁发“社会科学研究项目验收证书”。《息烽县委党校教学科研工作服务息烽经济和社会发展的思考》《贵阳市农村扶贫开发模式研究》《被征地农民生活保障问题研究》《贵阳拓展农民增加收入的办法研究》《贵阳市新农村建设中党支部建设研究》《贵阳市失地农民老有所养问题研究》获中共贵阳市委颁发的“结项证书”或“荣誉证书”。在省、市级刊物上发表理论文章39篇。

第十二节　老干部工作

1991年，中共息烽县委老干部工作局（简称县委老干局）内设办公室，下设事业机构干休所。县关心下一代协会办公室挂靠老干局。是年，全县有离休干部92人，其中享受副地级待遇6人、县级待遇44人、一般离休干部42人。1996年，县级退休干部纳入县委老干局服务管理范围。4月，县委老干局更名为“中共息烽县委离退休干部工作局”（简称县委离退局）。2002年起，副县级（含享受待遇）以上干部退休后纳入离退局管理和服务对象。2010年，全县有离休干部38人，其中享受副地级待遇4人，享受县级待遇22人，一般干部12人。有享受副县级以上待遇退休干部53人，其中曾经担任副县级以上实职23人，享受副县级待遇30人。

一、落实老干部“两费”

20世纪90年代，部分县属企业因生产经营不景气，有的甚至停产倒闭，部分事业单位经济收入差，出现拖欠老干部离退休费、医药费（简称“两费”）现象。1997年8月，县属企业拖欠9名离休干部工资3023.1元，行政单位拖欠11名离休干部工资9281.5元。1999年6月，县供销社拖欠7名离休干部生活费1.68万元。县委老干局用单位业务经费购买粮、油等送到老干部家里，帮助解决生活困难。2001年，县委、县政府作出决定，对无力支付老干部离退休费单位的老干部离退休费由县计经局统一解决，医药费由县社保局解决。2002年，县委组织部行文明确：企事业单位离退休老干部的“两费”由县财政统一计发。从此，全县离退休老干部“两费”有了保障，同时解决了22名老干部工资偏低问题。2003年8月，县委行文强调，对离休干部“两费”问题，必须健全“三个机制”，确保老干部“两费”按月足额发放，不得克扣和拖欠。至2010年，有关老干部特需费、取暖费、护理费、生活补贴费、交通费、高龄补助费及遗孀生活困难补助等，按政策规定按时足额发放。

二、落实离休干部基本政治待遇

1991—2010年，县委离退局坚持每月15日老干部例会制度，组织老干部传达学习上级文件和时事资料，邀请县领导和有关单位领导到会通报县有关工作情况。组织老干部参加县党代会、人代会、政协会等重要会议和重大活动。组织老干部开展参观视察和文娱体育活动。在县人民医院、中医医院设置老干部病房，确保老干部生病能够得到及时医治和护理。定期为老干部进行健康体检，坚持到医院看望生病住院的老干部及每年春节对老干部进行慰问等。20年间，为老干部体检600余人次。接送老干部生病住院540余人次，前往看望740余人次。组织开展扑克、麻将、象棋、跳棋、门球、台球、钓瓶、夹弹子、击鼓、投篮球等文体活动。按政策规定落实老干部行政级别等。

三、发挥老干部余热

1991年以来，县委离退局通过组织老干部对县的新农村建设、农业产业结构调整、乡村旅游发展，重大工程项目建设、工业企业生产、教育工作等开展视察，听取老干部对有关工作的建议意见，发挥老干部奉献余热、奉献社会作用。1999年6月，组织老干部98人视察永靖镇南山坡改梯工程，老干部们提出对丢荒土地不耕种要进行造林绿化，要严格控制占用田土建房等建议意见。2001年，组织老干部56人视察息烽铝制品厂、富源磷矿、磷矿编织袋厂。老干部对几家厂矿从无到有，从小到大，效益可观的发展状况表示肯定，但对存在的环境污染问题表示担忧，建议企业要创造条件，解决好环境污染问题。2008年，县境内发生50年一遇的凝冻灾害，县委离退局组织老干部参与“抗凝冻，保民生”活动。是年，四川汶川发生“5・12”特大地震，组织老干部捐款捐物，支援灾区人民抗震救灾，有4名离退休干部每人捐款1000元以上，1名老干部一次缴纳“特殊党费”5000元。

第十三节　县直属机关党建工作

一、党员代表大会

1993年1月11—12日，召开第六次代表大会。应到代表120名，实到107名。会议听取审议第五届委员会工作报告和纪检工作报告；会议选举书记1名、副书记2名；纪委书记、副书记各1名。通过会议决议事项。

1998年4月12—13日，召开第七次代表大会。应到代表119名，实到109名。县委副书记曾德书到会作“加强机关党建工作　保证机关为实现息烽跨世纪宏伟目标”讲话。会议听取审议第六届委员会工作报告和纪检工作报告；选举第七届委员会委员6名，书记、副书记各1名；纪律检查委员会委员5名、书记1名。通过会议决议事项。

2006年12月4日，召开第八次代表大会。应到代表109名，实到97名。县委副书记罗德亚到会并讲话。会议听取审议第七届委员会工作报告；选举第八届委员会委员7名，书记、副书记各1名；纪律检查委员会委员3名。通过会议决议事项。

二、组织建设

1991年，县直机关有党总支8个，党支部105个，党员1135名，其中女党员230人，少数民族党员39人。是年，举办党员学习马克思主义基本理论、党的基本路线和基本知识（简称“三基本”）学习班，101个党支部，1050名党员参加“三基本”教育学习。1994年，直属机关党委印发《关于加强党的制度建设的意见》，要求各支部建立健全“四簿四册”（《支部组织生活记录簿》《党员“三带一联系”记录簿》《好人好事登记簿》《党员奖惩登记簿》和《党员花名册》《领导干部花名册》《入党积极分子花名册》《党费收缴花名册》）。1996年起，推行机关党支部标准化管理，印发机关、企业、学校党支部标准化管理考核内容，并加强督促检查。次年，17个行政事业单位党支部、2个学校党支部和11个企业党支部标准化管理考核达标。2002年，县直属机关党委配合县委组织部对原县农机厂、纸厂、乡企公司等33家县属国有企业党组织建设情况开展调查，撰写《县属国有改革改制企业党建工作存在的问题及建议》，为县委决策企业党建提供参考。是年，县委出台《关于进一步做好县属国有改革改制企业党建工作的意见》。2004年，县农机厂、酒厂等18家县属国有倒闭企业116名党员组织关系划转到永靖镇党委。是年，协调联系县政府办、建设局、林业绿化局、机关党委党支部和公安局党委分别与市规划局党总支，林业绿化局、住房公积金管理中心机关党支部和市政府办公厅、公安局党委开展“结对共建”活动，相互学习，取长补短，实现市县党建工作“双赢”。2005年，县直属机关党委印发《息烽县县直机关党支部规范化建设的若干意见》《中共息烽县直属机关委员会关于开展机关支部“结对共进”活动的实施意见》，对机关党支部抓党员教育管理、思想政治和发展党员工作提出明确要求。是年，县直73个机关支部结成“对子”36个。开展支部党员互帮互学，共同促进，共同提高活动。推行党务公开、实行机关党建工作目标管理责任制。至2008年，各机关党支部制定党务公开工作方案，将组织建设、制度建设、作风建设、经常性党务工作等事项按规定时限和范围进行公开。不少单位聘请老干部老党员作为党务公开监督员，接受党员群众和监督员监督。2010年，建立完善党风廉政建设责任制和党风廉政建设责任追究制。对任期届满的16个基层党组织换届选举候选人实行“公推直选”。是年，县直属机关有基层党委1个，党总支2个，党支部81个，党员1285名。

三、党员发展

1991年，县直属机关党委按照“坚持标准，保证质量，改善结构，慎重发展”方针，坚持“先培养、考查、培训，后发展”程序，做好发展党员工作。是年，培训入党积极分子46名，发展党员25名、预备党员转正28名。以后数年，培训入党积极分子和发展党员人数均有增加。1997年，培训入党积极分子63名，发展党员40名，按期考查审批预备党员转正32名。2000年起，贯彻落实《中国共产党党员发展细则》。是年，县直属机关党委修订完善党员发展计划，建立培养对象花名册，制定培养措施，做好发展前的培养、政审、谈话、审批工作。2004年起，实行发展党员公示制，严把党员入口关。1991—2010年，共计培训入党积极分子964名，发展党员511名，考查审批预备党员转正467名。

四、党费收缴

1991年，收党费1.26万元。以后数年，党费收缴逐年增加。1997年，收缴党费3.3万元。1998年，中央组织部下发文件，对党费收缴标准作出调整。县直属机关党委召开支部书记、组织委员会议，传达学习文件精神，要求各党组织组织党员学习，严格执行新的党费收缴标准，做好党费收缴工作。是年，收缴党费3.74万元。2008年，中央组织部再次调整党费收缴标准，直属机关党委转发县委组织部《关于认真做好党费收缴 使用和管理工作的通知》《关于认真做好部分党员交纳“特殊党费”用于支援抗震救灾工作的通知》。是年，实行党费收缴情况公示制度。收缴党费18.25万元。收缴“特殊党费”26.74万元，支援四川汶川“5·12”大地震受灾群众。2010年，收缴党费24.1万元。

第十四节 党史工作

一、机构

1991年，设中共息烽县委党史研究室，为正科级事业单位。1995年7月县级机构改革，党史研究室与县地方志编纂委员会办公室合并，组建息烽县史志办公室，内设综合科。2009年1月，县史志办公室列入参照公务员管理范围。2010年5月，县级机构改革，撤销史志办公室，组建档案局（档案馆、地方志编纂委员会办公室），为正科级参公管理事业单位，实行一套人员、三块牌子，地方志编纂委员会办公室下设史志编纂科。

二、主要工作

1991年6月，编纂出版《解放初期的息烽》。1996年，到鹿窝、流长、九庄、青山等乡镇走访当年红军过息烽相关情况，征集到红军在息烽的资料共计6万余字，以及红军在息烽留下的医药箱、“红毯子”、马灯、宣传标语等革命遗物。1997年，征集抗日战争时期国民党军统设在息烽阳朗的“息烽集中营”历史资料近10万字，图片80帧，实物1件。是年，县史志办向中共辽宁省委党史研究室发函查明黄显声是周恩来1936年8月介绍入党的中共党员。1998年3月，参与组织“息烽英烈革命历史回顾展”在北京展出活动。1999年，根据中央、省党史部门要求，开展查实钱壮飞牺牲地点专题调查，撰写《关于钱壮飞南渡乌江时牺牲在息烽县流长乡的调查报告》报中共中央党史研究室。2005年，开展中华人民共和国成立55周年系列纪念活动，制作图片展板32幅参加全市巡展。是年，县政府拨款20万元修建流长“没量坑”红军烈士殉难处遗址。2007年5月，启动《中国共产党息烽历史》一卷本编纂工作。2008年8月，《中国共产党息烽历史大事记》编纂出版。2010年5月，启动革命遗址普查工作，8月结束。普查统计，全县有各类遗址24处，其中革命遗址23处，其他遗址1处。

第二章　纪检监察

1991—2010年，县纪检监察机关坚持把开展党风廉政建设和反腐倡廉宣传教育贯穿工作始终，建立起宣传教育、制度建设、监督检查工作格局。采取集中培训学习、播放电教片、办墙报专栏、组织参观展览、举办廉政文艺演出、开展知识竞赛和警示教育等形式，加强党风党纪教育，提高广大党员干部防腐能力，防止各种腐败现象的滋生和蔓延。

第一节　机　构

1991年，中共息烽县纪律检查委员会（简称县纪委）设办公室、研究室（县委廉政建设领导小组办公室）、控告申诉室、纪律检查室、案件审理室。县监察局下设办公室、信访股、监察股、审理股。1993年7月，县纪委、县监察局合署办公。实行一个领导班子、一套工作机构、两个机关名称。下设办公室、监察综合室、纪检监察室、案件审理室、信访室（举报中心）、教育研究室、党风廉政建设室。1996年8月，增设县纠正部门和行业不正之风工作领导小组办公室（简称纠风办），与党风廉政建设室合署办公，一个机构，两块牌子。2002年3月，撤销教育研究室。2009年4月，增设宣教政研室。2010年，县纪委、监察局内设办公室、监察综合室、纪检监察室、党风廉政室（县委廉政工作领导小组办公室、县党风廉政建设责任制领导小组办公室）、纠风室（县政府纠正行业不正之风办公室）、信访室（监察局举报中心）、案件审理室、宣教政研室。

第二节 党风廉政建设

一、党风党纪教育

1991年，县纪委组织开展党员干部集中培训6次，培训党员干部1100余人次；组织全县机关单位播放电教片《普通一官》《中流砥柱》《锦旗下的鬼蜮》《惩治腐败案例》；组织全县近千名党员干部和职工参加全省党风党纪百题知识竞赛活动。次年，组织播放电教片《党的基本知识》《共产党人》《面对五光十色》等215场，参加观看的党员干部和职工1.12万人次。举办党风党纪教育培训23期，培训党员干部5000余人次。

1996年起，全县各乡镇、县直机关、企事业单位和驻县厂矿开展“电化教育月”活动，至1998年，播放《枪声响后的思索》《不醒的梦》等电教片204场，参加观看的党员干部和职工群众6220人次。组织党员干部参加“党纪政纪条规知识竞赛”，《党纪处分条例》《廉政准则》和《行政监察法》知识竞赛3次，参赛人数6000余人次。1999—2003年，组织广大党员干部集中培训学习《邓小平关于党风廉政建设和反腐败的论述》《党纪处分条例》《党内监督条例（试行）》，县纪委选派人员为县委党校乡局级干部、中青年干部、村干部、计生干部等培训班学员作《领导干部要清正廉洁》《计生干部如何遵纪守法》《清正廉洁是领导干部必备素质》《切实加强党风廉政建设 深入开展反腐败斗争》等专题讲座。邀请省纪委常委李云龙到息烽为县四大班子领导和全县党员干部作反腐倡廉专题报告。在县广播电视台、各乡镇和部分县直部门播放《中国共产党纪律处分条例》电视系列片，参加观看的各级领导和党员干部1.87万人次。结合“三个代表”重要思想学习教育活动，组织学习《为人民服务》《整顿党的作风》《保持艰苦奋斗的传统》等论著和中共中央《关于改进和加强党的作风建设的决定》，要求副科级以上领导干部撰写1.5万字以上读书心得体会。其间，县纪委、监察局与县委组织部、宣传部、党校及新闻部门等单位建立反腐倡廉宣传教育联席会议制度，明确各成员单位在反腐倡廉宣传教育工作中的职责和任务，整合资源，形成合力，加大党风党纪宣传教育力度。

2004年3月，县委印发《关于认真贯彻落实〈中国共产党党内监督条例（试行）〉和〈中国共产党纪律处分条例〉的通知》（简称“两个条例”），部署贯彻落实“两个条例”工作。是年起，实行干部任前廉政教育谈话制度，要求拟任干部在新岗位上贯彻落实党风廉政建设责任制，并作出书面承诺。

2005年，开展廉政文化“六进”（进机关、进社区、进农村、进校园、进企业、进家庭）活动和“争做廉洁从政表率”活动。是年，首次举行党风廉政文艺演出，参演节目44个。2006年，在县城东门小区建“廉政文化一条街”，将郑培民、牛玉儒等勤政廉政模范人物画像及有代表性的廉政格言制作成公益灯箱广告，安装于街道两旁路灯杆上，用以引领和教育广大党员干部和职工群众。是年，围绕“四大纪律”（政治纪律、组织纪律、经济工作纪律、群众工作纪律）、“八项要求”（要同党中央保持高度一致，不阳奉阴违、自行其是；要遵守民主集中制，不独断专行、软弱放任；要依法行使权力，不滥用职权、玩忽职守；要廉洁奉公，不接受任何影响公正执行公务的利益；要管好配偶、子女和身边工作人员，不允许他们利用本人的影响谋取私利；要公道正派用人，不任人唯亲、营私舞弊；要艰苦奋斗，不奢侈浪费、贪图享受；要务实为民，不弄虚作假、与民争利）和领导干部廉洁从政行为准则、廉洁从业各项规定，加强领导干部廉洁自律教育。组织开展廉政歌曲传唱和廉政文艺演出15场次，观看群众2万余人次。在全县纪检监察干部中开展“做党的忠诚卫士，当人民群众的贴心人”主题实践活动。

2008年，组织全县副科级以上领导干部120余人到省羊艾监狱接受警示教育。组织县、乡、村三级干部300余人旁听县人民法院审理国家机关工作人员受贿、贪污案，用身边的人和事对广大党员干部开展警示教育。

2010年5月，中央纪委、监察部命名息烽集中营革命历史纪念馆为第一批全国廉政教育基地后，县纪检监察机关收集图片和文字资料，制作廉政教育基地宣传资料，撰写廉政教育讲解词；行文要求各乡镇各部门组织各级党员领导干部到廉政教育基地缅怀革命先烈，重温入党誓词，接受廉政教育。是年，对新提拔和交流岗位的46名正、副科级领导干部进行任前廉政谈话，签订廉政承诺书。

二、廉政建设

1991年，县纪委在县农业银行、县酒厂、石硐乡和阳朗乡开展廉政建设试点，指导和帮助试点单位建立廉政建设责任制。1993年起，要求全县科局级以上领导干部把执行廉洁自律有关规定情况作为专题民主生活会的必查内容，接受与会人员的评议，有针对性地进行整改。至1995年，通过专题民主生活会反映出来的少数机关干部参与打麻将、领导干部利用公车学驾驶、党政机关车辆违规挂军警号牌等问题，在纪检监察机关的监督下等得到纠正。1997年，县纪委、监察局贯彻落实《中共中央　国务院关于厉行节约　制止奢侈浪费行为的规定》，作出县直机关和乡镇工作接待必须在县政府食堂、县招待所和乡镇政府食堂就餐，规定就餐标准和陪餐人数，推行工作接待审批、核算和监督制度。1998年，全县工作接待费用共计35.89万元，较1997年减少15.33万元。1999年，县委印发《贯彻落实党风廉政建设责任制意见》，县委、县人大、县政府、县政协、县直各单位及乡镇建立党风廉政建设责任制，制定考核办法，纳入年终目标管理。2000年，县委、县政府印发《息烽县党风廉政建设责任追究制度》，修订完善《息烽县党风廉政建设责任制》，10个乡镇和55个县直部门完善和制定相应制度。是年，对9名失、渎职干部进行责任追究。

2002年起，建立领导干部廉政建设打招呼制度，制定《息烽县乡科级领导干部廉政教育谈话实施办法》，修订完善党风廉政建设责任制，明确各级党组织一把手是抓党风廉政建设第一责任人。至2005年，县纪检监察部门对14名领导干部在党性党风方面的苗头性问题实施打招呼，对17名党员干部进行责任追究。其间，2004年开展党员领导干部“争做廉洁从政表率”活动，召开领导干部廉政谈话大会，县委主要领导代表县委对全县300多名副科级以上领导干部作集体廉政谈话。

2006年，县委印发《领导干部廉洁自律　落实党风廉政建设责任制和加强党内监督工作安排意见》《关于党风廉政建设和反腐败各项工作任务进行责任分解的通知》，县委、县政府主要领导与县直各部门、各乡镇党政主要负责人签订党风廉政建设目标责任书。是年，建立完善领导干部廉政审查、廉政承诺、个人重大事项报告、责任追究等8个廉政制度。2008年，制定《息烽县党政领导班子党风廉政建设责任制考核办法（试行）》。次年，贯彻落实“党委统一领导、党政齐抓共管、纪委组织协调、部门各负其责，依靠群众支持和参与”的领导体制和工作机制，将党风廉政建设同经济建设、社会发展一起安排、一起检查、一起考核。

2010年，党风廉政建设责任制延伸到基层站所和村居党支部。党风廉政建设和反腐败各项工作任务责任分解到单位，层层签订责任书，做到责任到人。是年，贯彻落实《关于领导干部报告个人有关事项的规定》，375名科级以上干部填报《领导干部个人有关情况报告表》。开展干部述职述廉工作，全县339名乡科级领导干部在单位干部职工会上进行述职述廉，并进行民主测评。

三、廉政监督检查

1991年，开展年度党风检查，全县抽查42个党组织，听取5个区（镇）党委情况汇报，实地查看4个乡党委、6个机关支部、10个农村支部工作材料和实绩。次年，县委下发《关于加强党风和廉政建设的意见》，抽调92人组成33个检查组，深入220个基层党组织检查执行党风和廉政建设情况。1993—1996年，采取单位自查，纪检监察部门抽查方式开展廉政监督检查。2000年，开展领导干部收受礼金、有价证券、支付凭证专项检查。全县358名乡科级领导干部填报《清理接受和赠送现金 有价证券 支付凭证登记表》和《领导干部配偶 子女个人经商办企业情况登记表》。是年，5名领导干部向县纪委上交收受的香烟和礼金1500元。

2004年起，党风廉政建设、反腐败工作与物质文明建设、政治文明建设、精神文明建设工作一起安排部署、一起检查落实、一起考核。2010年，按《党风廉政建设责任制》和《惩治和预防腐败实施纲要》要求，开展半年和年终两次监督检查，督促375名科级以上干部填报《领导干部个人有关情况报告表》。

第三节 行政监察

一、行政效能监察

2003年10月，县委、县政府印发《关于加强机关效能建设 进一步改进机关作风的实施意见》。2004年起，县纪检监察部门有计划、择重点对机关事业单位开展行政效能专项监察。是年，对县教育局、环保局、建设局开展行政效能监察，通过与单位干部职工座谈、走访服务对象，听取干部群众对被监察单位工作的意见建议，分析整理，提出行政效能监察意见12条。至2006年，相继对县农办、城乡规划建设局、财政局、林业绿化局开展机关效能监察，提出监察建议4条，查处违法建筑39起，督促指导有关单位建立完善资金管理等制度。2009年，组织干部职工收看市“整建办”专题片《老周三年的困惑》，要求广大党员干部职工引以为戒、举一反三。次年，对5家群众反应比较强烈的单位和部门进行明察暗访，对工作人员不按时到岗，或工作中态度不端正、服务意识不强、办事效率不高、上班时间玩电子游戏、网上聊天等进行公开曝光，对相关人员作出严肃处理。

二、治理中小学乱收费

1995年，县纪检监察部门组织县财政、工商、物价、教育等部门对中小学乱收费情况进行监督检查，抽查全县30所中小学的收费情况，查出违规收费15.83万元，纠正明令取消的收费项目10个，取消自立收费项目13个，提高标准收费项目2个，督促清退违规收费11.58万元。至2003年，相继检查全县中小学校搭车收费、超标准收费、自立项目收费及农村教育费附加收取情况，督促取消违规收费项目9项，清退乱收费197.37万元，提出监察建议9条，工作建议30条，对2所学校负责人给予纪律处分。

2004年起，对中小学执行“一费制”收费标准、贯彻落实“两免一补”政策（免收义务教育阶段贫困户、两女结扎户和独生子女户学生杂费，补助农村义务教育阶段寄宿制困难学生生活费）情况进行监督检查，至2010年，未发现挤占、截留、挪用等违纪问题。

三、减轻农民负担与企业负担监督

（一）减轻农民负担监督

1993年起，县纪检监察部门按中央有关文件精神，开展减轻农民负担监察工作。至1995年，取消涉农收费文件8个，取消农民负担收费项目23个，纠正涉农收费项目36个，涉及资金14.37余万元。1997年，发放农民负担监督手册4.62万册。1998年，会同有关部门开展农民负担情况调查统计。是年，全县农民人均负担20.17元，低于国家标准。要求财政部门在乡镇财政所建立“三提五统”专门账户，对收取的涉农资金实行专户管理。

1999年，在全县推行农民负担监督卡，让老百姓知道、明白收费情况。是年填发农民负担监督卡4.5万户，填发率97.93%；督促各乡镇对农民负担进行专项审计。2001年，县纪检监察部门组织相关部门对各乡镇和县直9个部门的涉农物资价格和涉农收费进行专项检查，查处1个部门10个基层站所违规收费1.04万元，杂交玉米销售中多收成本费2.45万元。

2002年，取消“五统筹”，取消面向农民征收的行政事业性费用、政府性基金和集资，取消屠宰税，调整农业税和农业特产税等，改革村提留征收和使用办法。2003年起，实行减轻农民负担工作“一票否决”制。对涉农税收、物资价格和收费标准实行公示制度。是年，督促清退农村中小学多收学生课本费9.52万元、补课费0.83万元和国土部门违规收取农民集资建房征地管理费0.94万元。至2009年，全县政策性减轻农民负担1366.62万元，督促发放政府补贴补偿资金1914.19万元。其间，2005年推行涉农收费部门签署《减轻农民负担承诺书》，公开作出不向农民乱收费承诺。

2010年，采取财政监督、审计监督、行业监管、群众监督、法纪监督方式，对农村危房改造、“三良”工程等资金情况开展监督检查，对涉农项目资金、扩大内需项目资金和扶贫救灾资金实行登记备案制。是年，全县18个涉农单位登记备案资金2.4亿元。

（二）减轻企业负担监督

1995年4月，县纪委、县监察局以永靖镇老鸦河水泥厂为调查点，检查行政事业单位对企业收费情况，通过调查统计，有14个单位在该厂收费共计9.38万元，其中违规收费3个单位，收费2.9万元。1997年，县纪检监察机关查处7个单位以收取风险金、会务费、联营费、治安管理费、消防应急保险费等名义向13家企业收费4.47万元，按规定进行督促清退和纠正。1998年，县纪委、监察局印发《关于治理向企业乱收费 乱罚款和各种摊派等问题的意见》，规范各执收执罚单位的收费和罚款行为。1999年，在全县各有关单位及企业推行“收费许可证”制度。是年，帮助95个收费单位更换和补办“收费许可证”；取消不合理收费项目10个，涉及金额21.07万元。

2002年，县政府印发《关于对危害投资环境行为的处理意见（试行）》，就向企业乱收费、乱罚款、乱摊派提出处理规定，规范行政行为。次年6月，成立“息烽县投资环境监督中心”，聘请涉企负担义务监督员4名。2004年，县纪检监察部门对全县涉及行政许可和行政审批的28家单位的有关收费进行清理，取消收费项目32项，下调收费标准2项。次年，建立减轻企业负担工作联系制度、督查督办制度和出台煤矿安全事故保证金监督管理工作方案等。2007年，减轻企业负担工作实行目标管理，县政府与减轻企业负担成员单位签订《企业治乱减负工作目标责任书》。

2010年，开展整顿规范行业协会和市场中介组织服务收费专项整治，废止不合理行政事业性收费文件3个，取消涉企行政事业性收费项目13个，涉及金额41.6万元。

四、项目资金监督

1998年，县纪检监察部门会同有关单位对1997年度扶贫资金的管理和使用情况进行专项检查，在要求14个涉及扶贫资金管理和使用单位自查的基础上，抽查11个单位，涉及资金1446.8万元，扶贫贷款1487万元。通过检查，收回违纪资金2.58万元，提出监察建议2条。2000年，专项检查永靖镇雨洒人畜饮水、玄天洞小流域综合治理和林业局天然林保护3个工程项目使用国债资金的情况，涉及资金321万元，纠正违规资金0.8万余元，提出监察建议9条。次年，监督检查3个单位国债资金使用情况，涉及资金498万元，提出监察建议12条。

2001年起，连续7年坚持开展扶贫资金管理和使用情况专项检查，共涉及资金1.57亿元，对发现存在收支手续不全、票证使用不规范等问题的单位实施打招呼，对票据使用、发放贷款和资金管理不规范、调整项目计划未按程序办理申报手续、审签手续不完备、监督力度不到位等问题，提出监察建议10条。

五、农资、医药供应市场监督

（一）农资供应市场监督

1996年，县纪检监察部门配合有关部门对10个乡镇集贸农资经营市场监督检查2次，查处非法经营化肥户8户，涉及资金1.44万元，督促有关部门撤销农资经营服务部2个，收回营业执照2个，取消植保服务点3个。至2010年，县纪委、监察局共督促、参与、配合相关部门开展农资经营市场监督检查4次，查处违规经营户45户，案件25件，取缔无证经营户18户；没收假劣不合格种子249.5千克、农药15千克、无证肥料14吨、假劣磷肥92吨。罚款8.47万元。

（二）药品供应市场监督

1994年，县纪检监察部门组织相关单位检查卫生用药单位16家、药品经营企业2个、个体药店30户，查出伪劣药品15种，取缔无证售药点及游医18个。1999年，会同县卫生局对县人民医院、中医医院及乡镇卫生院的药品购销进行专项检查，严肃处理个别卫生院有关人员在药品采购中吃回扣的问题。2000年，组织卫生、工商局等部门，检查113个医疗单位的药品，查处假药14批次，没收假冒伪劣药品30批次，价值0.28万元。

2001年起，督促县卫生局推行药品集中采购制度，将乡镇卫生院药品采购统一纳入市卫生局招投标采购范围，规范进药渠道。次年，集中采购药品87.3万元，让利患者39.2万元。

2003年，督促各医疗单位实行常用药品价格和服务收费公示制、医药分开核算制。2005年，围绕群众“看病难”“看病贵”“用药难”问题，开展把好“五个关”（把好“进药关”，严格执行药品集中招标采购政策；把好“价格关”，严格执行药品价格政策，对常用药品明码标价进行公示，住院病人实行就医清单制；把好“出口关”，严防划价、收费、调剂、复核、发药等环节出差错；把好“处方关”，严禁药房工作人员擅自为药品供应商提供用药数据；把好“服务关”，落实服务公约、上墙公布）活动。是年，在全县启动新型农村合作医疗网络信息平台管理，加强进村入户指导，有效遏制医药购销中的不正之风。2007年，在全县医疗单位推行以农村新型合作医疗为核心的“五个一”（一个醒目的药品价格和医疗服务收费公示栏；一本药品购进记录；一套完整的药品标价签；一张负责的就医处方；一份真实的就医清单）工程。

2009年起，对全县各医疗卫生单位实行廉价就医情况进行监督检查。督促两家县级医院参加省卫生厅等部门组织的网上采购。至2010年，全县卫生系统共招标和集中网上采购药品5788.78万元，招标和集中网上采购率88.9%以上。

六、其他监督

20世纪90年代初，县监察局开展干部职工违法违章违规建私房清理工作，清理干部职工违法违章违规建私房53人，面积4688.79平方米。作拆除处理115.4平方米，收回土地151.64平方米；没收房屋203.9平方米，变价没收房屋511.72平方米；其他处理3706.13平方米。2005年起，县纪检监察机关坚持“公开、平等、竞争、择优”原则，会同有关部门对全县招考国家公务员和事业单位人员、干部竞争上岗等人事工作进行全程监督。对各单位及干部评先选优的报审进行党风廉政建设和领导干部廉洁自律等情况进行监督。对县乡两级换届中拟提拔、交流、调整的276名干部进行廉洁自律、勤政廉政考察；配合有关部门开展整治违法排污企业，保障群众健康专项行动。查处环境违法案件13起，调处污染纠纷36件，参与评审项目56个。

配合有关部门推进司法体制改革，督促司法机关健全完善《违法审判责任追究制度》、公开审判制度、案件流程管理制度、人民陪审员制度、审判委员会制度，《检务公开制度》《人民警察办案工作责任制》、查办案件工作责任制等制度，实行立审分离、审执分离、审监分离，防止违法审判，维护司法公正，从源头上防止和纠正执法办案中的违法行为；深化财政制度改革，在全县推行财政国库集中收付，撤销使用性质重复的银行账户16个，推行“乡财县管乡用”，配合财政、审计等部门对行政事业单位预算外资金和行政事业性收费项目进行清理，清理出预算外资金651.93万元，组织收缴财政管理资金520.49万元。取消不合理收费项目14个，纠正收费标准25个。全面落实“收支两条线”；全程参与出租车拍卖，20万元以上建筑工程的招标投标，经营性土地出让的监督；参与农资经营市场监督和国债资金的使用和管理等。

七、评议行风

1997起，县纪检监察机关开展民主评议行风工作。是年，开展“纠行风，树新风”活动，印发《关于转变党政机关工作作风和加强工作纪律的意见》，对工作作风和工作纪律提出明确要求。检查金融系统、工商、公安等9个窗口服务行业，倡导金融部门率先实行“服务承诺制”。1998年，按省委办公厅《关于开展民主评议行风　切实加强行风建设的通知》精神，建立县行风评议领导小组，聘任行风评议代表10人，对县工商局、供电局进行行风评议。此后，采取选聘民主评议代表、走访群众、召开座谈会、发问卷调查等形式开展行风民主评议。至2009年，相继对卫生、教育、建设、农业、民政、林业6个系统，国税、电信、国土、文体广电、交通、物价、质监、旅游、环保局，乡镇政府、工行、自来水公司、电信公司、移动通信公司、食品药品监管部门等24个单位的行风进行民主评议，提出建议意见864条，整改意见38条。2010年，聘请评议代表87人，民主评议基层站所31个，发放行风调查问卷6298份，收集群众意见152条。

第四节　信访办理和案件查处

一、信访办理

1991年，接待群众来信来访105件，办结90件，办结率85.7%。1992—2009年，收接人民群众来信来访（含电话举报）2778件次，办结2769件次，办结率99.67%。2010年，接待群众来信来访117件，办结117件，办结率100%。

1991—2010年，县纪检监察机关通过办理群众来信来访，为查处违法违纪案件提供线索313条，为受误告、错告的143名党员干部澄清是非。

二、案件查处

1991年6月，县委、县政府印发《关于进一步加强党的纪检机关与行政司法等监督部门建立联席会议制度的意见》，就联席会议的内容、工作任务、联席会议领导小组职责和建立查办案件联席会议制度相关事宜作出明确规定。2001年，纪检监察机关内部实行领导干部案件负责制。2005年，实行常委分工包片负责制、室主任履行办案职能负责制、承办人履行案件基本事实和卷宗质量负责制，加大案件查办力度。

1991—2010年，县纪检监察机关共立案1013件，结案1003件，结案率99.01%。受党纪处分634人，其中开除党籍173人，留党察看137人，撤职6人，其他318人。受政纪处分366人，其中降级15人，撤职29人，开除留用14人，开除19人，其他289人。通过查处案件，挽回经济损失900余万元。

第三章　机构编制

1979年8月，县成立机构编制委员会（简称县编委），是县委、县政府议事协调机构，负责全县行政管理体制、机构编制领导工作。下设办公室（简称县编委办）。1991—1995年，县编委办挂靠县人事局。1996年起，挂靠县人事劳动局。2001年机构改革，县编办独立设置，列入县委机构序列，是县编委的常设办事机构，内设综合业务科和事业单位登记管理局。

第一节　机构设置

一、县级机构设置

（一）1991年县级机构设置

党的纪律检查机构：县纪律检查委员会（简称县纪委）。

县委直属机构：县委办公室、组织部、宣传部、统战部、政法委、农村工作部、农村经济委员会、直属机关党委、老干部局、对台办（与县政府台湾事务办公室合署办公）、信访办、保密局（归口县委办公室）、机要局（归口县委办公室）、县委党校、党史研究室。

法定设置机构：县人大常委会、政协息烽县委员会、县人民法院、县人民检察院。

政府直属机构：县政府办公室、计划委员会、经济委员会、经济体改委、经济协作办公室、科学技术委员会、财政局、劳动局、人事局、编委办公室（挂靠人事局）、建设局、外协办、人防战备办公室、司法局、民族事务委员会、公安局、民政局、监察局、审计局、统计局、物价局、工商行政管理局、税务局、技术监督局、土地管理局、交通局、轻工业局、商业局、粮食局、乡镇企业局、农业局、林业局、水利水电局、畜牧局、物资局、文化局、教育局、卫生局、计生委、体育运动委员会、广播电视局、扶贫开发办公室、农机局、移民办、档案局、县志办、县农业区划办。

群团组织：县总工会、团县委、县妇联、县工商联、县科协、县残联。

1993年7月，县纪委、县监察局合署办公，实行一套工作机构，两个机关名称。

1994年，县税务局分设为国家税务局和地方税务局。国家税务局隶属国家税务总局垂直管理，县地方税务局实行县政府和上一级地方税务局双重领导，以县政府为主的管理体制。

1995年，县党史研究室与县志办合并，改称县史志办公室。

（二）机构改革

1995—1997年县级党政机构改革

机构调整：撤销计划委员会、经济委员会独立建制，合并组建计划与经济贸易局；撤销商业局、轻工业局、物资局行政序列建制，合并组建为贸易公司，其行政职能并入县计划与经济贸易局；撤销县委农村工作部、县农村经济委员会和县扶贫开发办公室独立建制，合并组建农业办公室，加挂扶贫开发办公室和农业综合开发办公室牌子，列入政府序列，同时为县委农村工作领导小组办事机构；撤销农业局、畜牧局独立建制，合并组建农业局，下设农业技术开发服务中心和畜牧水产技术开发服务中心，为农业局领导下的副科级事业单位；撤销工商行政管理局、技术监督局、物价局独立建制，合并组建工商行政管理局，对外加挂技术监督局和物价局牌子；撤销人事局、劳动局独立建制，合并组建人事劳动局；撤销民族事务委员会和宗教科独立建制，合并组建民族宗教事务局；撤销文化局、广播电视局独立建制，合并组建文化广播电视局；撤销人防办独立建制，其行政职能分别由有关部门承担；土地管理局改为国土局，同时承担环保、地矿、土地测绘和移民工作，加挂环境保护局和地质矿产局牌子；档案局、农机局、体育委员会改为县政府直属科级事业单位，受县政府委托行使部分行政管理职能。粮食局与粮油贸易总公司为一个机构，两块牌子。

改革调整后，县委直属机构设置：县委办公室（同时承担政研、信访工作，挂信访办公室牌子。县委机要局和保密局对外挂牌，编制、文件单列，党务和行政后勤工作由县委办公室统一管理，业务工作独立运行）；县委组织部（同时承担干部教育、知识分子联系、审干和组织员工作业务）；县委宣传部（同时承担精神文明建设指导和对外宣传工作，与人武部共同承担国防教育工作）；县委统战部（加挂县委台湾工作办公室和政府台湾事务办公室牌子）；政法委员会（社会治安综合治理委员会与政法委员会合署办公）；离退休干部工作局（原老干部局改为离退休干部工作局，归口县委组织部管理，不占机构个数）；机构编制委员会办公室（编制、经费、文件等分别在有关部门单列户头，挂靠人事劳动局，不占机构个数）。县委管理的事业单位：县委党校。

改革调整后，县政府机构设置：县政府办公室（同时承担法制、体改、侨务、外事、旅游、信访工作。加挂信访办公室、经济体制改革委员会牌子）；计划与经济贸易局（同时承担经济协作，非公有经济和医药管理工作）；农业办公室（同时承担农业区划管理工作）；农业局（同时承担畜牧、水产、饲料和两烟工作）；教育局（同时承担成教、职教和教育督导工作）；工商行政管理局；审计局；监察局（与县纪委合署办公，不占机构限额）；地方税务局；财政局（同时承担国有资产管理工作，对外加挂国有资产管理局牌子）；公安局（同时承担国家安全工作）；民政局（同时承担军供支前工作）；人事劳动局（同时承担安全、科工工作）；卫生局（加挂爱国卫生运动委员会牌子，承担爱国卫生运动委员会日常工作）；计划生育局；民族宗教事务局（同时承担民族、宗教两项职能）；国土局（加挂环境保护局和地质矿产局牌子）；建设局（同时承担房改和人防建设工作，加挂人防战备办公室、住房制度改革领导小组办公室牌子）；司法局；交通局（同时承担战备支前运输工作）；文化广播电视局；林业局（同时承担绿化、森林防火工作）；水利电力局（同时承担防汛抗旱工作）；乡镇企业局（加挂煤炭工业局牌子）；统计局；科学技术局。政府管理的事业单位：史志办公室、旅游事业局。

1998年，县地方税务局上划省垂直管理。1999年，工商行政管理局、技术监督局、物价局三局分建。是年，工商行政管理局、技术监督局上划省垂直管理。

2001—2002年县级党政机构改革

机构调整：计划与经济贸易局更名为发展计划与经济贸易局；人事劳动局更名为人事劳动和社会保障局；水利电力局更名为水利局；林业局更名为林业绿化局；国土局更名为国土资源局；老龄委员会更名为老龄工作委员会，其办事机构设在民政局。县体育事业局与县文化广播电视局合并组建县文体广播电视局。组建维护社会稳定领导小组办公室（设在政法委员会）、招商引资局。县机构编制委员会办公室单独设置，列入县委工作部门。撤销农机局，其行政管理职能交由农业局承担。县委党史研究室和县志办合署办公，统称县史志办公室。

改革调整后，县委直属机构设置：县委办公室（政策研究室，机要局、保密委员会办公室〈国家保密局〉，信访办公室设在县委办公室）、组织部、宣传部（精神文明建设指导委员会办公室设在宣传部）、统战部（含对台工作）、政法委员会（社会治安综合治理委员会办公室与其合署办公，一个机构两块牌子；维护社会稳定领导小组办公室设在政法委员会）、机构编制委员会办公室、直属机关党委、离退休干部工作局（由组织部管理，不占机构限额）、县委党校。

改革调整后，县政府直属机构设置：县政府办公室（含外事、侨务、人防、经济体制改革调研、国防教育工作；法制办公室设在政府办公室）、发展计划与经济贸易局（含非国有经济管理和外协工作），教育局、科学技术局、民族宗教事务局、公安局（含国家安全工作）、监察局（与县纪律检查委员会机关合署办公，列入县政府工作部门序列，不计入县政府机构个数）、民政局（老龄工作委员会办公室设在民政局）、司法局、财政局（含国有资产管理工作）、人事劳动和社会保障局、国土资源局、建设局、交通局（含战备支前运输工作）、水利局（含小水电建设和防汛抗旱工作）、农业局（含农机、畜牧、水产、饲料工作）、林业绿化局、环境保护局、卫生局（含爱国卫生工作）、计划生育局、审计局、统计局、粮食局、乡镇企业局（挂煤炭工业局牌子）、文体广播电视局、物价局（物价所与其合署办公，不占机构限额）。政府议事协调机构的常设办事机构：农业办公室（加挂农业综合开发办公室、扶贫开发办公室牌子）、旅游事业局、招商引资局、移民开发办公室、档案局（与档案馆合一体制，一个机构，两块牌子）、供销合作社联合社、史志办公室。

2004年县政府机构改革

机构调整：发展计划与经济贸易局更名为发展和改革局；计划生育局更名为人口和计划生育局。在县发展计划与经济贸易局安全监察科的基础上组建县安全生产监督管理局，县安全生产委员会办公室设在县安全生产监督管理局。县政府法制办公室设在县政府办公室，加挂县政府行政复议办公室、县政府法律事务顾问室牌子，党务、行政后勤工作由县政府办公室统一管理。

改革调整后机构设置：县政府办公室、发展和改革局、教育局、科学技术局、民族宗教事务局、公安局、监察局（与县纪委合署办公，列入县政府工作部门序列，不计入县政府机构个数）、民政局、司法局、财政局、人事劳动和社会保障局、国土资源局、建设局、交通局、水利局、农业局、林业绿化局、环境保护局、卫生局、人口和计划生育局、审计局、统计局、粮食局、乡镇企业局（加挂煤炭管理局牌子）、文体广播电视局、物价局（与物价所合署办公，一个机构两块牌子，不计入政府机构个数）。政府议事协调机构的常设办事机构：农业办公室。受政府委托行使部分行政管理职能的直属事业单位：旅游事业局、招商引资局、移民开发办公室、档案局（与档案馆实行局馆合一体制）。其他机构：供销合作社联合社。

2004年，撤销县委、县政府联合信访办公室，组建县信访局，归口县政府办公室管理，业务上受县委办公室、县政府办公室领导，党务、行政后勤工作由县政府办公室统一管理。

2009年，县人口和计划生育协会更名为县计划生育协会（简称计生协会），列入群团序列。

2010年县级政府机构改革

机构调整：组建发展和改革局，撤销物价局、粮食局，其职责整合划入发展和改革局。建县工业和信息化局，原发展改革经贸局工业、煤炭、能源、科技（知识产权）、信息化等管理职能划入工业和信息化局。组建旅游文体广播电视局，挂新闻出版局（版权局）牌子，原旅游局、文体广播电视局职责整合划入旅游文体广播电视局。不再保留旅游局、文体广播电视局。组建卫生和食品药品监督管理局。原卫生局和由省以下垂直管理的食品药品监督管理局的职责，整合划入卫生和食品药品监督管理局。不再保留卫生局、食品药品监督管理局。组建交通运输局。原交通局职责和建设局指导和管理城市客运职责，整合划入交通运输局。不再保留交通局。原农业办公室（扶贫开发办公室、农业综合开发办公室）中农业办公室（扶贫开发办公室）的职责、乡镇企业局（煤炭管理局）农产品加工的行政管理职责划入农业局，挂扶贫开发办公室牌子。农业综合开发办公室职责由财政局承担。不再保留农业办公室（扶贫开发办公室、农业综合开发办公室）。组建安全生产监督管理局，原发展和改革局安全生产监督管理职责、乡镇企业局（煤炭管理局）煤炭安全生产监督管理职责划入安全生产监督管理局。不再保留乡镇企业局（煤炭管理局）。人事劳动和社会保障局更名为县人力资源和社会保障局。建设局更名为住房和城乡建设局。建设局除指导和管理城市客运以外的职责划入住房和城乡建设局。不再保留招商引资局，其职责划入政府办公室。组建水利水电工程移民局，为县政府直属事业单位，原移民开发办公室水利水电工程移民管理职责划入水利水电工程移民局，不再保留移民开发办公室。组建档案局（与档案馆、地方志编纂委员会办公室合署办公，撤销县史志办，相应职责划入档案局）。供销合作社联合社由县政府管理。

（三）2010年县级机构设置

党的纪律检查机构：县纪委（县监察局与其合署办公，实行一套工作机构，两个机关名称）。

县委直属机构：县委办公室（政策研究室、机要局、保密委员会办公室（国家保密局））、组织部、宣传部（精神文明建设指导委员会办公室设在宣传部）、统战部（含对台工作）、政法委员会（社会治安综合治理委员会办公室与其合署办公，一个机构两块牌子；维护社会稳定领导小组办公室设在政法委员会）、机构编制委员会办公室、直属机关党委、离退休干部工作局（由组织部管理，不占机构限额）、县委党校。

法定设置机构：县人大常委会、政协息烽县委员会、县人民法院、县人民检察院。

政府工作机构：县政府办公室、县发展和改革局（加挂县科技局、县煤炭管理局、县知识产权局牌子）、教育局、民族事务局（县宗教事务局）、公安局、监察局（与县纪律检查委员会机关合署办公，列入县政府工作部门序列，不计入县政府机构个数）、民政局、司法局、财政局、人力资源和社会保障局、国土资源局、环境保护局、住房和城乡建设局、交通运输局、农业局、水利局、旅游文体广播电视局（县新闻出版局、县版权局），卫生和食品药品监督管理局、人口和计划生育局、审计局、林业绿化局、统计局、安全生产监督管理局、工业和信息化局。县政府直属事业单位：水利水电工程移民局、档案局（加挂县档案馆、地方志编纂委员会办公室牌子）。其他机构：供销合作社联合社。

群团组织：总工会、团县委、妇联、工商联、科协、残联、文联、红十字会、计生协会。

二、乡镇机构设置

（一）1991年乡镇机构

1991年，全县设4区（永阳区、养龙区、九庄区、黑神庙区）1个区级镇（永靖镇）、1个乡级镇（九庄镇）、23个乡（三田乡、梨安乡、下阳朗乡、阳朗乡、底寨乡、西山乡、青山苗族乡、养龙司乡、安江乡、茅坡乡、温泉乡、九庄乡、竹花乡、新杨乡、鹿窝乡、石硐乡、猫场乡、何家硐乡、小寨坝乡、南极乡、王家坪乡、流长乡、土城坝乡）。是年11月，开展撤区并乡建镇工作，至次年初，全县新组建4个镇（永靖镇、小寨坝镇、温泉镇、九庄镇）6个乡（西山乡、养龙司乡、流长乡、石硐乡、鹿窝乡、青山苗族乡）。各乡镇机构设置：党委设党委办公室、武装部；人大主席团；纪律检查委员会；群团组织设共青团、妇联；政府设政府办公室、经济科技办公室、计划生育股、民政福利股、文教卫生股、社会治安综合治理办公室。

（二）机构改革

1995—1997年乡镇党政机构改革

本次乡镇党政机构改革，按乡（镇）地域面积、人口和社会经济发展状况，分三种类型设置内设机构：永靖镇设纪律检查委员会（监察室）、党政办公室、政法委员会、社会治安综合治理办公室、人民武装部、教科文卫办公室、民政办公室、计划生育办公室、街道管理办公室；小寨坝镇、九庄镇、温泉镇、流长乡、养龙司乡、石硐乡、西山乡、鹿窝乡分别设纪律检查委员会（监察室）、党政办公室、政法委员会、社会治安综合治理办公室、人民武装部、教科文卫办公室、民政办公室、计划生育办公室；青山苗族乡设纪律检查委员会（监察室）、党政办公室、政法委员会、社会治安综合治理办公室、人民武装部、教科文卫办公室、民政办公室、计划生育办公室。

2001—2002年乡镇党政机构改革

机构调整：各乡镇民政办公室更名为社会事务办公室，街道管理办公室更名为城镇管理办公室。新设立经济发展办公室。撤销教科文卫办公室，保留计划生育办公室。

党的机构设置：各乡镇设纪律检查委员会（监察室与其合署办公，实行一套工作机构，两个机关名称体制），党政办公室（承担文秘、档案、组织、宣传、统战、工会、人事劳动、信访、计划统计等工作）、政法委员会（社会治安综合治理委员会办公室与其合署办公，实行一个机构两块牌子）、人民武装部。

政府机构设置：永靖镇、小寨坝镇、九庄镇、温泉镇、养龙司乡、石硐乡、流长乡、青山苗族乡设社会事务办公室（承担民政、文教、卫生、科技、广播电视、民族、宗教、老龄、残联等工作）；计划生育办公室（承担计划生育与人口管理工作）；经济发展办公室（承担经济发展的协调服务和村镇建设等工作）；城镇管理办公室。西山乡、鹿窝乡设社会事务办公室、计划生育办公室、经济发展办公室。各乡镇农技、农推、畜牧、水产、农经等站合并为“农业服务中心”，文化广播电视站更名为“文化服务中心”；撤销村镇建设管理所。

2010年乡镇机构改革

本次乡镇机构改革，按照乡镇党政办事机构不超过5个，人口在5万人以上的不超过6个的原则规定：永靖镇、小寨坝镇设党政办公室、社会事务办公室、经济发展办公室、人口和计划生育办公室、社会治安综合治理办公室、安全生产监督管理办公室；九庄镇、温泉镇、养龙司乡、石硐乡、流长乡、鹿窝乡、西山乡、青山苗族乡设党政办公室（挂社会事务办公室牌子）、经济发展办公室（挂安全生产监督管理办公室牌子）、人口和计划生育办公室、社会治安综合治理办公室。

公安派出所、司法所、人民法庭、工商行政管理所、国土资源管理所、中小学校、卫生院为县政府部门设在乡镇的机构。党组织关系按规定实行属地管理。

乡镇党委、政府管理的事业机构：农业综合服务中心、人力资源和社会保障服务中心、科技宣教文化信息统计服务中心、村镇建设服务中心、人口和计划生育技术服务站、水利站、林业站、安全生产监督管理站、财政所。

第二节 人员编制

一、编制管理

1991年，县机构编制管理继续实行“一支笔”审批制度，凡涉及机构、机构职能调整，人员编制事项，统一由机构编制部门审核，按程序报同级或上级机构编制委员会或党委、政府审批，其他任何部门和单位无权决定机构编制事项。1993年7月起，县编办根据省机构编制委员会《关于在全省各级党政群机关和事业单位使用〈机构编制管理证〉的通知》精神，开展机关事业单位使用《机构编制管理证》核发工作。1998年，县机构编制委员会印发《关于各级党政机关 事业单位办理〈机构编制管理证〉的通知》，明确在全县各级机关和事业单位实行“一证”（机构编制管理证）“一册”（工资基金管理手册）管理。

2002年3月，县编办转发《贵州省机构编制委员会办公室〈关于严格机构编制管理有关事项的通知〉的通知》，对全县各级机关和事业单位建立和实施控编补员审批制度提出补充意见，规定从2002年3月起，对全县各级机关和事业单位实施控编补员审批制度，各级机关和事业单位要求补充人员，必须在县编办办理控编补员审批手续后，组织、人事劳动部门方能按干部管理权限办理调动、派遣、安置和录用手续。

2007年，息烽县在贵阳市各区（市、县）中独家创新使用“个人编制管理证”，与“单位机构编制管理证”（简称“双证”）一起年审管理制度，通过“双证”对全县各级机关和事业单位实有人员实施“实名制”管理，建立和实施“实名制”登记管理制度，控制人员编制总量，防止超编进人、行政编制与事业编制混用和“吃空饷”等现象的发生。是年，向全县发放“行政机关工作人员编制管理证”1205个、“事业单位工作人员编制管理证”3651个。2010年，县编办完成“机构编制管理证”年审换证工作；办理“行政机关工作人员编制管理证”年审换证1115个、“事业单位工作人员编制管理证”年审换证3820个。

二、编制核定

（一）县级编制核定

1991年，县级党政机关594人。1994年，《贵州省县级机构改革方案》核定息烽县为三类三档县，省机构编制委员会下达息烽县行政编制456名，其中县委机关定编81名，县政府机关定编306名，其他机关定编69名。1997年5月，按县人大、政协、法院和检察院机构改革“三定”批复意见，核定县人大常委会定编20名，县政协定编15名，县人民法院定编58名（含县人民法院派出的5个人民法庭的编制），县检察院定编41名。

2001—2002年县党政机构改革，市委、市政府批复《息烽县党政机构改革方案》，下达息烽县县级党政群机关（不含公、检、法、司机关）行政编制337名（县委机关95名，政府机关191名，其他机关46名，预留机动编制5名）。根据省、市有关文件精神，县机构编制委员会核定县党政机关单列（参公）编制62名；事业（参公）编制93名；核定机关后勤服务人员事业编制64名。

根据市机构编制委员会办公室《关于全市公安专项编制精简的通知》《关于全市、县（区、市）两级人民法院政法专项编制调整的通知》《关于全市、县（区、市）两级人民法院、检察院政法专项编制精简的通知》精神，核定县公、检、法、司机关总编制231名；公、检、法、司机关后勤服务人员事业编制23名。

2004年，县政府机构改革，核定县政府机关行政编制为191名；增加事业参公编制17名，其中县安全生产监督管理局12名、县政府法制办公室5名。

2010年，县政府机构改革，县政府工作部门核定行政编制432名；县政府直属事业机构核定事业编制26名，原县安监局、财政局、旅游局、物价局等共46名事业编制由县机构编制委员会办公室收回；核定机关工勤人员编制61名。

（二）乡（镇）编制核定

1992年1月，县机构编制委员会核定新建乡（镇）人员编制338名：按乡（镇）面积、人口等情况定编：永靖镇定编47名、小寨坝镇定编41名、温泉镇定编28名、九庄镇定编43名、西山乡定编27名、养龙司乡定编33名、流长乡定编33名、石硐乡定编36名、鹿窝乡定编26名、青山苗族乡定编24名。2月，对新建乡（镇）社会化服务体系机构人员编制进行核定：10个乡（镇）公安派出所定编80名，财政所定编69名，土地管理所定编28名，文化广播电视站定编59名，教育辅导站定编64名，计划生育技术指导（服务）站定编45名，农业技术经营管理综合服务站定编64名，林业站定编51名，水利站定编30名，卫生院定编109名，畜牧站定编28名，农机管理站定编15名。

1995—1997年，乡（镇）机构改革，省机构编制委员会办公室核定下达给息烽县10个乡（镇）行政编制329名，县编办预留10名作为机动编制，以319名核定下达各乡（镇）：永靖镇定编46名，小寨坝镇定编36名，九庄镇定编34名，温泉镇定编30名，流长乡定编30名，养龙司乡定编32名，石硐乡定编32名，西山乡定编30名，鹿窝乡定编28名，青山苗族乡定编21名。

2001—2002年机构改革，市委、市政府批复《息烽县党政机构改革方案》，下达给息烽县乡（镇）机关行政编制283名；核定乡（镇）机关后勤服务人员事业编制32名。

2010年，乡（镇）机构改革，核定10乡（镇）行政编制283名，机关工勤人员编制42名；核定事业编制719名。

第三节　事业单位登记管理

2000年12月起，根据国务院《事业单位登记管理暂行条例》《贵州省事业单位登记管理实施细则》要求，县编办开展事业单位法人登记管理工作。2001年起，开展事业单位年检工作。至2004年，累计完成196家事业单位法人初始登记。2007年7月起，开展网上登记。是年，完成196家事业单位网上登记数据整理上传，实现事业单位登记管理网络化。至2010年底，全县已登记事业单位201家，全部实现网络化管理。是年，年检事业单位200家（按规定不参加年检1家），参检率、合格率100%。

第四章　人民团体

县工、青、妇等群众团体组织，围绕县委和县政府各个时期的中心工作，宣传贯彻党的路线、方针政策和国家的法律法规，开展职工群众思想政治教育。组织干部职工开展扶贫济困、下岗职工再就业、青年志愿者、希望工程、“双学双比”　“拥军优属”等活动。开展科普宣传，弘扬科学精神，传播科学思想，普及科学知识，营造讲科学、爱科学、学科学、用科学的良好社会风尚，助推息烽经济社会发展。2007年，建成“全国科普示范县”。

第一节　工　会

一、代表大会

第七次代表大会：1993年5月18—19日召开，出席会议代表140名。会议听取审议武斌代表县总工会第六届工会委员会作的《真抓实干　求实创新　提高工会工作整体水平》工作报告、县总工会经费审查委员会工作报告；选举第七届工会委员会委员21人，常务委员7人，工会主席1人、副主席1人；经费审查委员会主任、副主任各1人。通过会议决议事项。1998年8月，召开七届五次全委会，补选第七届工会委员会委员3名；选举七届工会委员会主席、副主席各1人。

第八次代表大会：1998年9月召开，出席会议代表100人。会议听取审议黄兴华代表县总工会第七届委员会作的《高举邓小平理论伟大旗帜　团结动员全县各族职工　为实现富民兴息和跨世纪宏伟目标立新功》工作报告、县总工会经费审查委员会工作报告；选举第八届委员会委员25人、常务委员9人、工会主席1人、副主席2人；经费审查委员会委员3人，主任、副主任各1人。通过会议决议事项。

第九次代表大会：2003年10月30—31日召开，出席会议代表93人。会议听取审议杨朝国代表县总工会第八届委员会作的《实践“三个代表”重要思想　维护合法权益　团结动员全县职工为实现小康社会努力奋斗》工作报告、经费审查委员会工作报告；选举第九届工会委员会委员21名、常务委员9人、工会主席1人、副主席2人；经费审查委员会委员5名、主任、副主任各1人。通过会议决议事项。2006年9月21日，召开九届五次全委会，选举工会主席、副主席各1人。

第十次代表大会：2008年10月24—25日召开，出席会议代表115人，特邀代表30人。会议听取审议龙泽琴代表县总工会第九届委员会作的《发展和谐劳动关系　凝聚职工群众力量　为构建“和谐息烽”再铸辉煌》工作报告、县总工会经费审查委员会工作报告；选举第十届工会委员会委员21名，常务委员9人，工会主席、常务副主席各1人、副主席2人；经费审查委员会委员5名，主任、副主任各1人。通过会议决议事项。

二、基层组织建设

1991年，全县有基层工会组织140个。按照全国总工会“最大限度地把职工组织到工会中来”的指示精神，县总工会加大基层工会组织发展力度。次年11月，县总工会召开女职工代表大会，选举产生首届女职工委员会。至1995年，全县女职工在25人以上的基层工会组建女工委员会，不足25人的明确女工委员负责女工工作。1996年，县总工会与统战部、工商局、人事劳动局联合下发《关于在私营企业组建工会的意见》，与县乡镇企业局联合下发《关于在乡镇企业组建工会的通知》。是年6—8月，相继建立老鸦河水泥厂、阳朗水泥厂两个乡镇企业工会组织和金西磷矿粉厂、息烽铁锅厂两个私营企业工会组织。至1998年，基层工会组织发展到155个。1999年，县委组织部、县总工会联合下发《关于推进基层工会改革和建设的意见》，要求10个乡镇成立具有县总工会性质的工会委员会。是年，县计经贸、粮食、烟草、供销、卫生完善系统工会工作委员会，县委机关、县政府职能部门、私营企业及乡镇企业分别成立工会联合会。至2000年，全县有基层工会组织200个，会员7604人。

2001年8月，县委组织部行文为永靖镇、小寨坝镇、温泉镇、西山乡配备工会专职副主席，九庄镇、石硐乡、养龙司乡、流长乡、鹿窝乡、青山苗族乡由各乡镇党委行文配备兼职工会干部。是年，全县有基层工会组织353个，会员9689名。2003年，县总工会会同乡镇企业局下发《煤炭生产企业工会组织建设的实施方案》，组建全县煤炭生产企业工会组织。

2006年，继续探索“党建带工建，工建促党建，党工共建”的建会工作机制，“扩大工会覆盖面、增强工会组织凝聚力”，加大在非公有制企业和农民工中组建工会组织力度。永靖镇、九庄镇、小寨坝镇、温泉镇建立村、社区工会和行业工会委员会；在养龙司乡、西山乡、青山苗族乡、流长乡、石硐乡、鹿窝乡建立村（居）、行业工会委员会。至2008年，有村级工会组织192个。其中村（社区）工会委员会38个，行业工会66个，行业工会小组88个。会员1.41万人。2010年，全县有基层工会组织473个，会员2.89万人。

三、主要工作与活动

（一）职工学习教育

1991年，各级工会组织在广大职工中组织学习宣传中共十三届六中、七中全会精神。1992年后，组织职工学习中共十四大精神、邓小平建设有中国特色社会主义理论、社会主义市场经济理论知识、全总十二大、省总九大精神及学习贯彻《中华人民共和国劳动法》《中华人民共和国工会法》《中华人民共和国妇女权益保障法》《工会章程》。1997—2004年，学习中共十五大、十六大精神和“三个代表”重要思想，省委十届四次会议文件和县委《关于贯彻中共贵阳市委〈关于进一步全心全意依靠工人阶级和加强工会工作的决定〉的意见》，学习党风廉政建设决议和国有企业改革文件。开展“双文明”建功立业竞赛和以“热爱家乡、建设息烽、奉献岗位”，为企业扭亏增盈，提高工作效率，改善服务质量为主要内容的建功立业活动、“掌握安全生产知识，争做遵章守纪职工”为主题的安全知识学习和应用活动。2005—2009年，组织职工学习和贯彻中共十七大和中国工会十五大精神，引导职工正确认识和对待改革中的利益关系调整，落实职工民主管理制度，完善维权机制。开展“百万职工大练兵”“职工读书评书”和“创建学习型组织，争做知识型职工”活动。2010年11月23—30日，县总工会与县人力资源和社会保障局牵头，组织县教育局、卫生局和食品药品监督局、住房和城乡建设局、交通运输局等工会组织，开展8个项目的职工技能大赛，来自基层工会的150余名职工参加比赛，9名职工获一等奖，18名职工获二等奖，27名职工获三等奖。

（二）文体活动

1991年，县总工会、县体育运动委员会联合开展春节文娱活动，举办“五一”职工运动会，“五一”税务杯篮球赛、税法知识竞赛活动，庆“七一”《党在我心中》系列活动和国庆文娱晚会，活跃全县职工文娱生活。1992—2008年，每年节假日期间，县总工会坚持与有关单位联合举办篮球、乒乓球、卡拉OK、拔河、环城跑、中老年迪斯科、棋类、登山、广播体操、工会法规知识抢答、安全知识演讲等比赛活动和文艺晚会等文体活动，丰富职工体育文化生活，增进了解和友谊，促进社会和谐。

2009年起，举办息烽县“天翼迎春杯”职工羽毛球比赛、“建强杯”机关职工拔河赛和中华人民共和国成立60周年慰问职工演出等活动。2010年10月，举办以“攀高峰、推和谐、促三创”为主题的息烽县首届职工秋季登山比赛活动，有40支代表队288名运动员参赛。

（三）维权

1991年，县总工会开展企业民主参与和民主监督专题调研，推进企业民主管理。是年，督促县酒厂领导严格按政府文件精神处理该厂调资中存在的不合理现象，维护职工权益。1994年，在职工中开展提合理化建议活动。基层工会在召开职代会期间，提合理化建议238条，采纳76条，实施23条。次年，各级工会建立职工代表会议制度，重大问题提交职代会讨论决定。

1996年，黑神庙中学一女教师在孕期被单位解除劳动合同，县总工会与县人事劳动局联合开展调查，依法仲裁，维护女教师的合法权益。1997年，核工业二七六磷业有限公司在职工调资中，入股方31名职工利益受到侵害，县总工会牵头协调处理，对入股方职工工资进行补调。是年，全县33家企业与职工签订集体合同。39家企业建立劳动法律监督委员会、35家企业建立劳动争议调解委员会。

1999年，县委办、政府办相继下发《关于在国有企业实行“厂务公开，民主监督”制度的通知》《息烽县关于进一步推行厂务公开工作的意见》，县总工会下发《息烽县关于进一步推行厂务公开工作的意见》，向84个企事业单位发放厂务公开学习资料及厂（校、院）务公开工作量化考核标准，推进企业“厂务公开，民主监督”工作。至2002年，有102家国有、集体、股份制企业实行厂务公开并建立相关制度，医院、学校实行内部事务公开，新签订集体合同70份，续签集体合同24份。2004年起，县总工会开展为农民工追讨工资工作。是年，为农民工追回拖欠工资100余万元。至2008年，为农民工追回拖欠工资1000余万元。

2010年，县委、县政府下发《关于进一步开展“劳动关系和谐企业”创建活动的实施意见》，县总工会指导全县各企业工会组织开展劳动关系和谐企业创建活动。全县270家企事业单位实行厂（事）务公开，98个企业建立调解委员会。是年，开展企业劳动用工、职业病防治、企业工会组织建设情况检查，检查国营和非公企业25家。对未签订劳动合同、缴纳工资保证金和实行厂务公开的单位下发询问通知书2份，责令整改决定书4份。免费为困难职工、农民工提供法律援助18件次，涉案金额近50万元，为农民工索回工资和工伤赔款37.6万元。

（四）扶贫济困

1991年春节前，县委、县政府组织有关单位慰问县饮料厂、磷肥厂特困职工40人，发给生活补助金1700元。1995年起，县总工会开展“送温暖工程”活动，及时慰问困难职工。1997年，建立特困职工基金。是年，慰问特困职工140人，发放慰问金3万元。1998年起，实施再就业工程。在县城建立“下岗职工小吃一条街”和“下岗职工百货一条街”，拓宽下岗职工再就业渠道。7月，成立“息烽县国有企业下岗职工再就业咨询服务中心”。是年，为240名困难职工和203名下岗职工建档。培训下岗职工119人，安置下岗职工再就业161人。2003年，成立“息烽县总工会困难职工援助中心”。是年慰问特困职工30户、困难职工90户，发放慰问金3万元，为185名下岗职工推荐、安置工作。次年，举办计算机、美容美发、家政服务、法律法规、政策咨询等培训，培训下岗职工407人次，介绍下岗职工305人就业，安置下岗失业人员407人。通过小额担保贷款发放再就业起始资金，使45户125名下岗职工实现自谋职业。为下岗职工申办《再就业优惠证》826个。2007—2008年，举办“民营企业招聘周”活动两次，省内外56家企业提供空岗信息8000余个，697名求职者签订就业意向表；签订技能培训协议1031人。2010年，成立县帮扶工作领导小组，各乡镇建立困难职工帮扶站。是年，慰问困难职工和农民工600余名，发放慰问金21.5万元。开展再就业技能培训8期，培训下岗职工278人，就业56人。发放助学金7.6万元，帮助80名困难职工子女圆大学梦。

第二节 共青团

一、代表大会

十五次代表大会：1997年5月23—24日召开，应到代表100名，实到91名。会议听取审议共青团息烽县第十四届委员会工作报告。选举产生共青团息烽县第十五届委员会委员19人、常务委员7人，书记1人。通过会议决议事项。

十六次代表大会：2000年12月5—6日召开，应到代表105名，实到101名。会议听取审议共青团息烽县第十五届委员会工作报告。选举产生共青团息烽县第十六届委员会委员19人、常务委员7人，书记1人、副书记1人。通过会议决议事项。

十七次代表大会：2003年11月3—4日召开，应到代表105名，实到103名。会议听取并审议共青团息烽县第十六届委员会工作报告。选举产生共青团息烽县第十七届委员会委员19人、常务委员7人，书记1人、副书记1人。通过会议决议事项。

十八次代表大会：2006年12月13—14日召开，应到代表105名，实到93名。会议听取并审议共青团息烽县第十七届委员会工作报告。选举产生共青团息烽县第十八届委员会委员19人、常务委员7人，书记1人、副书记1人。通过会议决议事项。

十九次代表大会：2009年12月29—30日召开，应到代表115名，实到112名。会议听取审议共青团息烽县第十八届委员会工作报告，选举产生共青团息烽县第十九届委员会委员35人、常务委员7人，书记1人、副书记1人。通过会议决议事项。

二、基层组织建设

1991年，全县有基层区（镇）团委5个，乡（镇）团委24个，团总支10个，团支部198个。是年，发展新团员1588名，推优入党33名。1992年，撤区并乡建镇，建立基层团委11个，团总支13个，团支部263个，发展团员1765名，推优入党40名。此后10年间，基层团组织和团员有较快发展。至2002年，全县基层团委24个，团支部366个，团员10308人。2003年后，按照《关于进一步加强全县基层“党建带团建”工作的实施意见》精神，坚持抓好基层团组织建设和团员的发展工作。至

2010年，全县基层团委20个，团总支35个，团支部397个，团员2.58万人。

三、主要工作与活动

（一）青年志愿者活动

1994年起，团县委组织开展“息烽县青年志愿者活动”，组建青年志愿服务队伍48支，开展“双收双增”“青年安全岗”“五小成果”（小发明、小革新、小改造、小设计、小建议）、“技能比武”等活动，参加活动的青年志愿者3万余人次，增创产值17.71万元。1995年6—7月，县境内遭受特大暴雨和持续干旱，团县委行文组织青年开展“向灾区群众献爱心”活动，广大青年志愿者积极参与，为灾区群众投工投劳5200余个，捐资1.85万元。县直中小学及小寨坝镇中心学校募捐鸡蛋8600余个，现金600元，慰问56029部队官兵。至1999年，相继组建农业科技、医疗卫生、法律服务3支青年志愿者专业服务队。青年志愿者队伍发展至6400余人。2003年防治“非典”期间，组织团员青年缴纳防治“非典”特殊团费1.13万元。次年，团县委被贵州省委评为“西部计划工作先进集体”。2007年，组织志愿者1000余人次开展未成年人保护、消防安全、拒绝毒品宣传教育活动，发放宣传资料8000余份，解答和接受法律咨询100余人次。参与公众安全感调查活动，发放问卷1600余份。2010年3月，组织全县1000余名青年志愿者开展“贵阳市万名森林保护志愿者在行动”活动，青年志愿者进村入户开展森林防火和“三创一办”宣传，发放宣传资料2万余份。

（二）“希望工程”

1992年起，在县委领导下，团县委组织实施“希望工程”，制定《息烽县“希望工程”实施管理细则（试行）》，从管理内容、操作程序及要求、监督与奖惩等方面作出明确规定。各乡镇成立“希望工程”领导小组负责组织协调相关工作。1995年，团县委首次接受社会各界捐款2.43万元，帮助226名失学儿童解决入学问题。是年，养龙司乡教师李光碧被授予“全国第三届‘希望工程’园丁奖”。1996年，团县委开展“息烽县希望工程志愿者劝募行动”，接收捐款（含物资折价）5.3万元。1997年，息烽县列为全国首批基本消除适龄儿童因贫困失学问题试点县。是年，省青基会拨款21.71万元，资助贫困学生549人，援建希望小学6所。1999年元月，吴德屏、陈久琪分别被省青基会和团省委授予“希望工程贡献奖”。2002年9月，美国康德基金会捐款30万元，县政府匹配7.7万元，修建希望小学2所。是年，募集资金8.83万元，资助900余名贫困学生入学。2003年1月，网友“爱心工程”首批来自全国各地的80余名网友到鹿窝乡胡广小学开展捐资助学活动。是年，网上筹集捐款11.08万元，资助贫困学生694名。

2005年，全县各级团组织开展“对口帮扶，一助一”活动。是年，接受社会各界捐款近100万元，图书2000余册。救助学生1500人次，修建希望小学3所，修建爱心桥1座。2008年9月25日，大西南矿业股份有限公司董事局主席陈德伟捐赠198万元，在息烽设立“健康希望工程德伟爱心基金”，连续三年为息烽7500余名中小学住校生每人每天无偿提供鸡蛋1个。2010年，团县委通过希望工程、网友爱心工程、“习酒——我的大学”助学资金、“圆梦大学”行动助学金等，募集资金5.39万元，帮助66名中小学贫困生解决上学难问题，为8名大学生圆大学梦。

（三）未成年人保护

1994年，县成立未成年人保护工作领导小组。团县委在有关部门配合下，开展《中华人民共和国未成年人保护法》《中华人民共和国预防未成年人犯罪法》《贵州省未成年人保护条例》（简称“两法一条例”）宣传教育活动，参与清查使用童工企业和有害青少年身心健康的非法出版物、未成年人帮教、打击侵害未成年人合法权益不法分子等活动。1996年，配合县法院审理未成年人刑事案件10件11人。次年，组织开展“两法一条例”知识竞赛活动。1998年，团县委组织有关单位开展“两法一条例”、禁毒知识、体育法宣传咨询活动，发放宣传资料2000余册。2000年4月，团县委会同有关组织将受父母虐待的小女孩文娥救出并送医院治疗，向社会各界发出倡议，募集资金1.2万余元为其支付医疗费。是年6月，永靖中学学生陈刚双腿被火车碾断，团县委发起捐款倡议，募集资金4000余元。2010年，团县委通过“3·15”维权日、“六一”儿童节、“6·26”国际禁毒日、“未成年人保护法宣传周”等，开展以学校为重点的宣传教育活动。

第三节　妇女联合会

一、妇女代表大会

第七次代表大会：1993年5月11—12日召开。出席大会代表90名，特邀列席代表8名。会议听取审议县妇女联合会（简称县妇联）第六届委员会《坚持改革开放　发扬四自精神　开创妇女工作新局面》工作报告。选举产生县妇联第七届执委会委员21名，常务委员9名，其中主任1名。通过会议决议事项。

第八次代表大会：1998年9月21—22日召开。出席大会代表98名、列席代表10名、特邀代表9名。会议听取审议县妇联第七届委员会《加快妇女工作的发展　为实现富民兴息的目标而努力奋斗》工作报告，选举产生县妇联第八届执委会委员23名，常务委员9名。其中主任1名。通过会议决议事项。

第九次代表大会：2003年9月22—23日召开，出席大会代表102名，列席代表10名，特邀代表6名。会议听取审议县妇联第八届委员会《与时俱进　开拓创新　加快妇女工作发展　为强县升位目标而努力奋斗》工作报告，选举产生县妇联第九届执委会委员21名，常务委员9名，其中主任、副主任各1名。

第十次代表大会：2008年10月21—22日召开。出席大会代表137名，列席代表13名，特邀嘉宾63名。会议听取审议县妇联第九届委员会《创新方法　拓展载体　引领妇女为生态文明县建设再立新功》工作报告。选举产生县妇联第十届执委会委员25名，常务委员11名，其中主席、副主席各1名。

二、基层组织

1991年年初，全县有区（镇）妇联5个、乡镇妇联24个，村妇工委161个，专兼职妇联工作干部305人。1992年，撤区并乡建镇后，全县10个乡镇设妇联组织。2010年年底，全县有乡镇妇联10个，县直机关、企事业单位妇委会、村（居）妇代会共179个，专兼职妇联工作干部189人。

三、主要工作与活动

（一）学习宣传

1991年4月，县妇联会同有关单位下发《关于加强税法宣传活动的通知》。是年，全县出宣传周刊42期，撰写广播稿65篇，举办培训班30期，培训宣传骨干2663人次。次年3月，下发《关于在全县妇女中开展“二五”普法学习的通知》，要求各乡镇妇联组织宣传学习《社会主义法制建设若干问题的讲话》《中华人民共和国宪法讲话》《中华人民共和国妇女权益保障法》。乡镇妇联及村妇委会利用妇女之家、妇女活动中心、妇女禁赌协会等组织，多形式开展法律法规宣传学习。1995年

5月，组织2045人参加安顺地区举办的《中华人民共和国母婴保健法》知识竞赛，1人获一等奖，多人获二、三等奖。2002年“三八”妇女节、“六一”儿童节期间，开展男女平等、基本国策、“两纲”“两规”、《中华人民共和国妇女权益保障法》《中华人民共和国未成年人保护法》《中华人民共和国婚姻法》宣传活动，制作宣传展板60块，累计发放宣传资料5万余份、宣传读本2万余册，接受法律咨询1300余人次。2007年，开展送法下乡、送法进社区、送法进家庭活动。利用赶场天、“三八”妇女维权周、“法律宣传月”开展相关法规宣传，印发《中华人民共和国妇女权益保障法》1.1万份，开展法律义务咨询活动3场次，接受1200余人咨询。次年，开展“百万妇女学法律，平安和谐进万家”活动，全年开展法律宣传活动5次，举办培训班1期，发放宣传资料近3万份，组织干部职工学法40余次。

2010年，在“三八”维权宣传周、“5·26”综治宣传日期间，县妇联与县综治办、司法局等单位联合在县城十字街、三角花园开展法律法规宣传活动。组织宣传车、腰鼓队沿街宣传，印发法律宣传资料2000余份，现场接受咨询服务1000余人次。

（二）维权

2005年7月6日，遵义县一名9岁女孩被父母遗弃，县妇儿工委协调永靖派出所、县医院共同出资1100余元为小女孩治病，治愈后将女孩送回家乡。次年1月18日，小寨坝镇潮水村蔡家寨组村民余某某，因丈夫李某某怀疑其与他人有不正当男女关系，将其杀伤（经法医鉴定为重伤）。余某某到县妇联请求给予法律援助，县妇联与司法局联系，明确专人为余某某提供法律服务。经县法院审理，决判李某某犯故意伤害罪，判处有期徒刑4年。是年7月31日，永靖镇下阳朗村村民贾某某（残疾人）到县妇联反映，结婚后长期受丈夫虐待，经村干部多次调解无效，故起诉离婚，但苦于无钱交诉讼费。县妇联与县法院协调，为其减免离婚诉讼费。2009年，流长乡前奔村廖某某（18周岁、学生），因家庭贫困，利用暑假在一家私营米粉加工店打工赚取学费，工作中，右手食指、中指和无名指被机器轧断（经鉴定为伤残8级），事后米粉加工店老板拒绝给予赔偿。县妇联领导协调司法部门，为廖联系律师，依法向人民法院提起诉讼。经法院调解，达成赔偿2.2万元协议，维护了廖的合法权益。

1991—2010年，县妇联接待来信来访1953件次，其间，为8名受害妇女申请办理法律援助，协助解救被拐卖妇女、儿童56人。

（三）“双学双比”活动

1991年，县乡成立“双学双比”协调小组，下设办公室在县妇联，负责“双学双比”（学文化、学技术，比成绩、比贡献）活动日常工作。是年，县妇联举办养猪培训班2期。1994年，全县各级妇联加强对“双学双比”活动的领导，制定“双学双比”年度计划、并纳入年终工作目标考核。是年，建联系点27个，完成烤烟种植220亩，坡改梯4425亩、渠道防渗维修926千米。1997年，实施帮扶“结对子”工程，全县妇联组织结对子565对；建扶贫联系点120个，联系1155户4669人；帮助8000户贷款1400万元。12月，九庄镇和平村熊光英获贵州省“双学双比”竞赛活动协调领导小组授予“农民女状元”和双学双比“女能手”称号。是年起，开展“千万农家女，百项新技术”活动。至1999年，举办各类培训班1314期，培训妇女6.07万人次，掌握1～2项实用技术妇女3.1万名、3项以上实用技术妇女2.23万人；建科技示范户1947户；组织妇女劳务输出2004人；扫除妇女文盲2706人。2000年10月，在全省妇联系统开展的“树九县、促千村”活动中，永靖镇获“先进集体”称号，小寨坝镇王家坪村、永靖镇下阳朗村、西山乡猪场村、石硐乡南桥村、九庄镇大曹村妇代会获“先进村（居）妇代会”称号。

2002年起，实施“巾帼科技致富工程”，至2005年，举办各类科技培训班362期，培训妇女1.1万人次，以妇女为主体科技示范户8365户，4.5万名妇女掌握三项以上实用技术。油菜、玉米育苗移栽，新法养猪，西瓜、大棚蔬菜种植管理等技术被广大妇女所掌握。

2006年起，开展创建“巾帼示范点”活动。县妇联在小寨坝镇创建农业网络信息站和农业科技辅导站，为农村妇女获取新知识和对外交流提供方便。通过网络发布提供种子、果苗、蔬菜、萝卜等商品信息50余条。

2010年，县委下发《关于建立息烽县妇女小额担保贷款工作联席制度》，启动妇女小额担保贷款，全年为112名妇女发放贷款1052万元。是年，举办农村妇女适用技术、技能培训班30余期，培训农村妇女3000余人次。县妇联配合有关单位举办息烽县2010年“春风行动”招聘会暨“创业孵化园”揭牌仪式，提供以制造业、服务业为主的女性就业岗位1800余个，达成用工意向628人。

（四）“三八”绿色工程

1991年起，县妇联组织指导全县广大妇女参与以“林业发展，改善生态环境”为主要内容的“三八”绿色工程。县妇联率先在王家坪乡建立长防林示范点，带动全县建绿色工程示范点30个，造“三八”林950亩，义务植树419.2亩5.03万余株。王家坪乡瓮沙村上寨组组织50名妇女开展造林竞赛活动，每名妇女造林20亩。次年，全县建“三八”林示范点11个，面积3000余亩。妇女参与造林1579亩。

1994年，西山乡金星村农家妇女陈再荣购买荒山100亩，通过七年精心栽培，至2001年，出售果苗70余万株，获得经济收入20余万元。1995年，石硐乡难冲桥村妇女李正秀购买荒山600亩，逐年开发，建成果品基地250亩，用材林基地350亩，种树成活率95%以上。

1995年起，举办“绿色证书”培训学习，至2006年，办培训班181期，2332名妇女获“绿色证书”。全县建“三八”绿色基地72个，造“三八”绿色工程林1.8万亩。2008年2月，县妇联会同有关单位在县城十字街开展“森林保卫战”宣传活动，发放宣传资料近2万份、“森林保卫战”倡议书2000余份，号召全县妇女发扬不怕吃苦、连续作战、敢打敢拼精神，广泛开展植树造林、森林管护、森林维权等活动。

（五）堡子教育基地建设

2008年，启动堡子“妇女教育基地”建设。县委、县政府主要领导两次到堡子村开展妇联工作调研，就有关工作作出指示。县妇联在堡子村创建“全国巾帼示范村”，为堡子村申报“全国妇女教育基地”打基础。2009年，全国妇联党组书记、副主席、书记处第一书记黄晴宜率全国妇联调研组一行到堡子村视察农村妇女“双学双比”、蔬菜基地、乡村旅社、农家乐以及村委会建设情况。是年12月17日，全国妇联授予养龙司乡堡子村“全国妇女教育培训基地”称号。县委、县政府决定从2009年起，县财政每年预算50万元用于堡子村“全国妇女教育基地”建设。2010年，成立息烽县养龙司乡“‘半边天’文化发祥地——全国妇女教育培训基地”建设工作领导小组，规划“半边天”文化“六个一”建设工程（制作一部片子、出一本文集、举办一次论坛、建立一个网站、拟定一个规划、建立一个陈列馆）。同年6月，堡子村“半边天”文化陈列馆动工建设，占地5408.1平方米，计划投入331万元。

第四节　残疾人联合会

1990年12月，县残疾人联合会（简称县残联）成立，为副局（科）级机构，由县民政局代管。1995年11月，升格为正科级机构，与民政局合署办公。1998年4月，县残联机构独立，下设残疾人劳动就业服务所。2002年6月，撤销残疾人劳动就业服务所，设办公室、康复教育就业科。

一、代表大会

一次会议：1990年12月20日召开。出席会议代表61名（健全人代表23名、残疾人代表38名），特邀代表6名。县委、县人大、县政府、县政协、县纪委主要领导出席开幕式，各乡镇分管民政工作的副乡镇长列席。大会选举产生第一届主席团成员21名，主席1名，副主席4名；推举理事长1名；聘请名誉主席1名。

二次会议：1998年9月18日召开。出席会议代表70名（健全人代表34名，残疾人代表36名），特邀代表30名。县委、县人大、县政府、县政协、县直机关单位主要领导出席开幕式。会议总结一次会议以来县残联的工作。选举产生新一届残联主席团成员49人，主席1名，副主席2名；推举理事长1名；聘请名誉主席1名，副主席2名。

三次会议：2005年9月14日召开。出席会议代表80名（健全人代表38名，残疾人代表42名），特邀代表40名。县委、县人大、县政府、县政协分管和联系残联工作领导、县直机关单位主要领导出席开幕式。会议总结二次会议以来县残联工作。选举产生新一届主席团成员55人，主席1名，副主席3名；推举理事会理事2名；聘请名誉主席3名。

二、基层残联组织

1993年，全县各乡镇相继组建残联组织，设主席和专职理事长。是年起，县、乡政府先后成立残疾人工作协调委员会（简称残工委），此后，根据人员变动情况，适时进行调整充实。1996年6月，成立县精神病防治康复工作领导小组。8月，成立县残疾鉴定委员会，下设办公室和肢体残疾、视力残疾、听力残疾、言语残疾、智力残疾6个鉴定小组。

县残联下设盲人、聋哑人、肢体残疾人、智力残疾人、精神残疾人5个专门协会。全县各村（居）设残疾人协会。2010年，全县161个村、9个居委会均成立残疾人协会，选聘180名残疾人专职委员协助乡镇残联理事长、村（居）残协主席工作。

三、残疾人队伍

1991年，全县有残疾人9379人，占全县人口的4.2%。其中肢体残疾1685人、视力残疾565人、言语（聋、哑）残疾932人、智力残疾1032人、其他残疾人5165人。至1996年，全县残疾人基本保持在9400人左右。1997年，有残疾人1.16万人，占全县总人口的4.99%。其中肢体残疾1786人、视力残疾1681人、智力残疾2282人、精神残疾440人、听力、言语残疾3869人、多重残疾1506人。2010年，有残疾人14095人，占全县总人口的6.4%。其中视力残疾2262人、肢体残疾4652人、听力残疾4844人、言语残疾327人、智力残疾935人、精神残疾1075人、多重残疾2596人。

四、主要工作

（一）康复工作

1991年，施行小儿麻痹（简称儿麻）矫治手术39例，做白内障复明手术131例，聋哑训练2人，低视力配镜5人。此后，县残联或请专业技术员诊疗、或举办相关培训等，适时开展各类残疾人康复治疗、训练工作。1996年，县精神病防治康复工作领导小组成立。是年，对精神病患者实行建档立卡管理。2001年6月，息烽县被省残联列入精神病康复工作新增试点县，下拨经费1万元。次年，县残联向精神病患者无偿发放价值1万余元的精防康复药品。2003年10月16日，县残联举办“精防康复工作培训”，各乡镇分管残联工作领导，残联干部、精防医师、精神病患者家属、县精防康复工作领导小组成员参加。邀请市残联康复部领导授课。2005年6月，县政府办公室转发市政府有关部门《关于进一步加强全市残疾人康复工作　实现残疾人“人人享有康复服务”目标的意见》，要求各单位结合工作实际认真贯彻执行。10月，县残工委印发《开展城镇社区及农村基层康复服务的若干意见》。是年，培训精防医生26人。2010年，县残联举办康复管理干部培训班，培训县残联康复工作管理干部、乡镇残联理事长、残疾人工作者、乡镇卫生院精防医生等32人。为精神病患者1553人建档。

1991—2010年，县残联组织儿麻患者作矫正治疗康复手术64例，做白内障复明手术813例，送精神病患者到指定医院治疗142人次，为29名低视力患者配镜或助听器，组织指导聋哑、肢残、脑瘫、盲人、智障残疾人训练320人，为肢残患者安装大小腿假肢27例，发放残疾人辅助用品用具707件。

（二）培训就业

1991年，全县有21名残疾人从事个体商业经营，减免税金5000余元。1992—1995年，全县培训残疾人60人，安排就业213人。小寨坝镇盘脚营村盲人李发伦参加“盲人按摩培训班”学习后，开办息烽县首家盲人按摩诊所。1996年，“息烽县残疾人劳动就业工作领导小组”成立。是年，开展残疾人就业情况调查。全县106个单位有残疾职工100人，占职工总人数的0.78%。养龙司乡新桥村村民兰吉发（双下肢高位截肢），自学成才经营家电维修，劳动致富后，自筹资金举办两期“家电维修培训班”，培训残疾人26名，为4名失学儿童承担小学到高中的学费，被共青团省、市委评为“十佳青年”，树立为全省青年学习榜样。

1998年9月，县政府批转《息烽县分散按比例安排残疾人就业暂行办法》。次年，收取残疾人就业保障金9500元；开展实用技术培训220人。2001—2005年，安排按比例就业62人，个体就业90人；收取残疾人就业保障金12.6万元；开展实用技术培训669人。2010年，实施残疾人就业创业工程，投资培训经费4.8万元，举办蔬菜、果树栽培，农药识别，养殖，机械操作培训4期，培训370人；县残联争取扶持资金1万元，扶持残疾人曾士勇发展养殖业。安排残疾人就业20人，征收残疾人就业保障金50.4万元。

（三）帮扶与社会保障

1991年起，县残联开展为残疾人事业捐赠1元钱活动。至1993年，共收到社会各界人士捐资2.54万元。用于帮助残疾人发展生产和解决生活困难。1998年起，发放残疾人专项贷款，安排贫困残疾人家庭发展种植、养殖和加工业等。至2000年，发放残疾人专项贷款170.6万元，帮扶残疾人家庭688户发展生产。办理残疾人个体开业证书156个。2000年，下拨残疾人危房改造资金30.7万元，安排补助114户残疾人家庭建房和危房改造；发放助学补助款8.39万元，资助175名学生就读；残疾人家庭969户纳入低保，低保覆盖率100%；春节走访慰问残疾人家庭100户。2005年，为467人办理低保（农村392人、城镇75人），低保覆盖率100%，结队帮扶残疾人家庭110户，扶贫1020人次，解决温饱160人。2009年，利用“彩票公益金项目”和“扶残助学”资金，帮助140名贫困残疾学生及残疾人子女就学。2010年，下拨危房改造资金14.85万元。帮助残疾人30户建房。

第五节　工商业联合会

1988年，恢复成立县工商业联合会（简称县工商联）。1993年7月，恢复成立县工商经济开发公司，隶属县工商联直接管理。1995年11月8日，县商会成立，与县工商联合署办公，实行一套班子，两块牌子。2002年4月18日，县工商经济开发公司更名为县商汇经济开发中心，2010年，因未开展经营业务被县工商局注销。

一、会员代表大会及基层组织

（一）会员代表大会

第五次会员代表大会：1992年4月28—29日在县商业局会场召开。出席会议代表85名。安顺地委统战部副部长施建超、县委书记陈华祥出席会议并作重要讲话。各乡镇党委分管副书记和统战干事、县直部分单位负责人列席会议。会议传达学习《中共中央批转中央统战部〈关于工商联若干问题的请示〉》、中共中央《关于传达学习邓小平同志重要谈话的通知》及省发〔1991〕40号、县发〔1992〕4号文件；听取审议县工商联第四届执委会工作报告；选举县工商联第五届执委会委员23名，执委会主委1名、副主委3名。通过会议决议事项。

第六次会员代表大会：1997年4月29日在县商业局会场召开。出席会议代表100名。市委统战部副部长、市工商联党组书记王汪、县委书记李忠出席开幕式并作重要讲话，各乡镇党委分管副书记和统战干事、县直部分单位负责人列席会议。会议听取审议县工商联五届执委会工作报告。选举县工商联（商会）第六届执委会委员37名、常委会委员12名、会长1名、副会长9名、秘书长1名。通过会议决议事项。

第七次会员代表大会：2001年11月29日在县民政局接待中心会场召开。出席会议代表120名。县委书记陈长发，市委统战部副部长、市工商联党组书记谭亦先，副会长张大炼及部分县领导出席开幕式。各乡镇党委分管副书记和统战干事、县直部分单位代表列席会议。陈长发、谭亦先作重要讲话。会议听取审议第六届工商联（商会）执委会工作报告；选举县工商联（商会）第七届执委会委员43名、常委会委员18名、会长1名、副会长7名、秘书长1名。通过会议决议事项。

第八次会员代表大会：2006年7月27日在县翠竹园宾馆会场召开。出席会议代表160名。县委书记杨彦峰、市工商联秘书长薛常辉及县四大班子部分领导出席开幕式。县总工会、团县委、县妇联、县科协等单位负责人列席会议。杨彦峰、薛常辉分别作重要讲话。会议听取审议县工商联（商会）第七届执委会工作报告；选举县工商联（商会）第八届执委会委员47名、常委会委员29名、会长1名、副会长9名、秘书长1名。会议表彰2002—2006年工作突出的永靖镇、小寨坝镇、青山苗族乡、石硐乡4个基层商会，7名优秀企业会员、13名优秀会员。通过会议决议事项。

（二）基层组织

1991年，全县有会员347名。其中团体会员6名，公有制企业会员55名，民营企业会员4名，个人会员278名。有个体工商户2562户。此后，随着经济体制改革，计划经济逐步转入市场经济，公有制团体和企业会员逐步退出，会员发展重点转向非公有制企业和个体工商户。1994年，永靖镇、小寨坝镇、九庄镇、温泉镇、石硐乡、流长乡、养龙司乡工商联分会成立；青山苗族乡、西山乡、鹿窝乡成立工商联小组。2001年，有会员502名，其中公有制企业会员9名，私营及股份制企业会员20名，个人会员473名。2002年，乡（镇）工商联分会、工商联小组更名为乡（镇）商会。2004年11月

26日，息烽阳朗辣子鸡同业商会成立，同日，举行首次会员大会，审议通过《息烽县阳朗辣子鸡同业商会章程》，选举会长1名、副会长1名、秘书长1名，聘请名誉会长1名。2008年12月29日，县煤炭同业商会成立。同日，举行首次会员大会，审议通过《息烽县煤炭同业商会章程》，选举执委会委员7名、会长1名、副会长2名、秘书长1名、副秘书长1名。2010年，全县工商联有会员462名，其中非公有制企业会员65名、个人会员397名。

（三）工作辑要

1991年，县工商联就县城规划区建商业一条街和农贸市场一事，在广大会员和集体企业、个体工商户中广泛动员宣传，提出“人民城镇人民建，建好城镇为人民”口号，两次组织召开会员代表、个体工商户和有关单位负责人座谈会，听取各方面建议意见，为政府决策提供参考。是年7月，县内遭受特大水灾，各级工商联组织会员、个体工商户捐款4.8万元，捐衣物274件、食盐1吨、水泥15.5吨、砖1万块、化肥5吨、抽水泵2台，帮助灾区群众解决生产、生活困难。1992年后，县工商联通过召开执委会、非公有制人士座谈会、乡镇商会会长会议等，传达学习党的路线、方针政策，中央、省、市、县有关发展非公有制经济文件或会议精神。鼓励会员、个体工商户“放心、放胆、放手”发展非公有制经济，教育、引导会员、个体工商户文明、诚实经商，做“爱国、敬业、诚信、守法”公民。1999年，县工商联会同县委统战部等单位开展非公有制经济发展状况调查。提出解放思想，放手发展非公有制经济，为非公有制经济发展创造良好环境和条件；制定规划，建立专门机构抓非公有制经济发展；强化服务意识。增强为非公有制经济发展服务的自觉性和主动性；加强法制宣传和监督力度，为非公有制经济发展保驾护航和加强非公有制经济人士教育培训等10条建议意见。受到县委、县政府领导高度重视，批示通过县委《情况通报》转发全县。2003年，县工商联组织非公经济人士两次对县委、县政府即将出台的《关于加快非公有制经济发展的意见》进行讨论，提出修改建议意见。是年起，县工商联（商会）开展对已故原工商业者无工作配偶享受低保待遇调查申报工作。2008年，县工商联开展“遍访会员企业，携手共渡难关”活动，鼓励会员、企业坚定信心，化危机为机遇，同舟共济，共度金融危机难关。组织会员开展《百城连动儿童慈善一日捐》、“圆梦住有所居”、向灾区人民“伸援手献爱心”活动，累计接收捐款420.95万元。用于预防“非典”、茅草房改造和支援四川汶川“5·12”大地震灾区人民恢复生产，重建家园。3月，在县“两会”期间，工商联界别政协委员提出提案12件，其中《加强煤炭行业纳税监管　防止税收流失》《本土企业与外来企业应享受同等政策》《加快团元山陨石坑考察论证工作　促进息烽旅游快速发展》三个团体提案，得到政府有关部门高度重视和认真办理。是年，开展非公有制经济人士综合评价工作，纳入评价对象65人。2010年，贯彻落实县委、县政府《关于进一步加快非公有制经济发展的实施意见》。对36家服务企业、个体经营户172名从业人员进行礼仪培训。是年，组织非公企业及非公经济人士开展助学济困、抗旱救灾等活动，共捐款捐物折合人民币80余万元。

第六节　科学技术协会

一、代表大会及基层科协组织

（一）科协代表大会

2005年9月15—16日，县科学技术协会（简称县科协）第三次代表大会召开。会议听取审议县科协《团结和动员全县广大科技工作者　为息烽经济和社会发展做贡献》工作报告，审议通过《贵阳市息烽县科学技术协会章程》。选举产生县科协第三届委员会委员27名、常务委员15名，主席1名、副主席4名（其中兼职副主席3名）。

（二）基层科协组织

1991年，县科协下设农学、畜牧兽医、林学、水电、青少年、烤烟研究6个专业学术学（协）会；28个区、乡（镇）建有科协组织，有会员1779人。次年，撤区并乡建镇，区、乡（镇）科协组织解散。1996年5月，县委办批转县科协《关于恢复乡镇科普协会的报告》，8—9月，全县10个乡镇科普协会相继恢复成立。是年，县科协在永靖镇、温泉镇、养龙司乡筹建县第一批农村专业技术协会（简称农技协会），当年建成永靖镇果蔬、种植养殖，养龙司乡养猪、蔬菜，温泉镇农民致富研究5个农技协会。至1999年，农技协会发展到38个。由于部分农技协会成立比较仓促，引导和服务工作跟不上等原因，不久就名存实亡。2003年6月，全县农技协会12个，有会员714人。2004年，县委、县政府出台《加强农村科技协会发展的意见》。全县农技协会发展到19个、会员1477人。2005—2006年，相继成立贵阳中化开磷化肥有限公司、贵州太和制药有限公司、贵州汉方制药有限公司、贵州信科环化有限公司4个企业科协组织，有会员253人。2008年，成立老年科技协会（简称老科协）。2010年，全县有县直专业学（协）会6个、乡镇科普协会10个、企业科协4个、农科协会27个。

二、科协活动

（一）科普宣传

1991年起，县科协通过开展“科普日”系列活动、编印《科技信息》、办科技橱窗等进行科普宣传。是年，开展科普赶场16场次，接待群众咨询4560人次，向农民群众发送科普信息资料1600余份。至1994年，编印《科普信息》49期，办科普橱窗32期，出科普专栏142期。

1996年起，开展以消除碘缺乏病为重点的科普宣传，至1997年，每年利用赶场天进行历时一周的消除碘缺乏病宣传，受教育群众1.5万余人次。为中小学生举办碘缺乏病防治讲座1次，参加讲座400余人。

2003年5月，开展以“依靠科学，战胜非典”为主题的防治“非典”科普宣传周活动，展出防治非典型肺炎图片600余幅、挂图23幅、宣传画1000余张，发放“非典”防治资料2.2万余份、有奖答卷1000余份。

2004年6月，开展“科学普及——你我共参与”为主题的科普宣传系列活动。在县城新大街举行“全国科普日”活动启动仪式暨大型科普宣传活动，悬挂宣传口号布标5幅，展出科普展板23块44个版面，发放农村实用技术资料1万余份，送科技图书2500册，提供科技咨询1000余人次，为民义诊120余人次，播放科普录像10场次。

2006年起，开展以“树立科学发展观，共建和谐社会——健康、安全、文明、创新”为主题的系列科普宣传活动。至2009年，组织“健康生活进农村”活动30次，送科技、送卫生下乡、送科教进社区22次及“健康安全教育进校园”等活动，提供健康咨询9100余人次，作心理健康讲座、科普禁毒报告24场次，播放录像14场次，为群众义诊3600余人次，赠图书5000余册，展出展板10块18个版面，挂图600余张次，出专栏204期，发放计生药具4000余盒及宣传资料5万余份等。

2010年9月，县科协举行“息烽县2010年全国科普日启动暨科普进校园活动仪式”，组装科普大篷车在县境内巡回宣传，各乡镇利用赶场天开展科普日宣传活动，发放科普宣传资料1.5万份。

（二）青少年科技活动

1991年起，县科协、县教育主管部门以开展青少年科技活动月活动为载体，组织中、小学观看科教片、读科普书、听科普报告、做科学小实验，办科技墙报、开展科技竞赛、写科普小论文、参观科研单位（基地）等形式为中小学生普及科技知识，开启智力，提高学生的思维能力和创造能力，培养中小学生学科学、爱科学、勤动手动脑的良好习惯。至2010年掌握1项农业实用技术的农村初中毕业生2035人，占初中毕业生的77%；掌握2项农业实用技术的农村初中毕业生1019人，占初中毕业生的38.6%。其间，1996年，在县城举办有息烽一中、二中，私立高中学生参加的青少年科普报告会，接受教育学生2000余人；在永红小学、南门小学、向阳小学播放科教片和两次科普讲座，500余人参加。2001年4月，全县129所中小学在校生41730人参加青少年科教系列活动：参加文艺活动20023人次；科学故事会35283人次；参观科研单位（基地）的学生34次，听科普讲座46场14892人次，科技竞赛活动52次，看科普录像35场2416人次；读科普书26899人次；实用技术培训79期4077人次；办科技墙报83期；征集到科普小论文1255篇，小制作小发明7868件，计10173人次等。2008年4月，县组织开展“智力七巧板”竞赛活动和小论文、小制作评选活动。学校活动有科技讲座、文艺演出、出科技墙报、野外考察、科技竞赛、小论文、小制作、科普录像、实用技术培训、智力七巧板竞赛等。各乡镇推荐171名学生参与县“智力七巧板竞赛”，参赛小论文410篇、小发明小制作50件。

2010年4月，全县中小学学生25686人参加青少年科技活动月系列活动，占在校学生的91%。活动内容有科技讲座、科技文艺演出、办科学墙报、科学参观考察、科技竞赛、实用技术培训、科普影片、读科普书及期刊等；共撰写小论文4052篇；小发明小制作2579件。

（三）科技培训与推广

1991年，县科协举办农业实用技术培训61期，参训4480人次，推广“两杂”良种、旱地分带轮作等15个项目。推广地膜玉米100余亩，产量比常年增长10%～15%。次年，举办栽桑养蚕、“三杂”良种、旱地分带轮作等农业实用技术培训54期，参加培训人员6100余人次。1996年，举办食用菌栽培、水稻旱育浅植科普培训772期，受训9.86万人次，发放有关资料500余份；为408名群众颁发绿色证书。在流长乡刘培富家采用更新西瓜品种，使用种植新技术，种高产示范西瓜3亩，亩产量5445千克，产值3500元。2004年，开展水稻新品种推广示范、高产玉米种植、脱毒马铃薯基地培育、经果林种植与管理、肉牛肉免养殖、中药材引种种植、生态渔业发展等培训。是年，举办培训、讲座955期，参训人员6.02万人次。2010年，组织开展葡萄、艳红桃、莲藕种植和养鱼等实用技术培训500余期，参加培训4万余人次。

（四）科技扶贫与学术交流

1992年，县科协划拨科技扶贫基金4万元在流长乡发展蚕业生产，栽桑400.5亩，扦播桑苗10.5万株，为农民创收1.2万元；引进西瓜良种特大新红宝4千克，种植60亩，亩产量4000千克。次年，在全县推广栽桑养蚕科技扶贫项目，栽桑183亩，投放春、夏、秋种蚕90张，产鲜蚕3400千克。在流长乡推广优质西瓜种植，选种“特大新红宝”100余千克、“新澄”30千克，种植面积2100亩，产量610万千克，产值122万元，缴纳农特税10.32万元。2003年3月，举办首届“农村经济发展学术交流会”，收到论文79篇，其中9篇在会上作交流发言，为29人颁发荣誉证书。次年11月，举办第二届农村经济发展学术交流活动，县直学会、乡镇组织人员参加会议。收到学术论文14篇，其中7篇在会上交流。

（五）创建全国科普示范县

2005年11月，息烽县被中国科协确定为第三批“全国科普示范县”创建单位。是年，县委、县政府成立创建“全国科普示范县”工作领导小组，下设办公室（简称创建办）在县科协，负责创建日常工作。编制《息烽县创建全国科普示范县的实施方案》。各乡镇、县直有关责任单位相应成立创建工作领导小组。2006年2月10日，召开创建全国科普示范县动员大会，县、乡（镇）、村（居）层层签订创建工作目标责任书，将创建工作纳入年度目标考核内容。“创建”经费由每年3万元增加到8万元，次年，科普经费增加到12.5万元（人均0.5元）。县委、县政府督查室坚持不定期对创建工作进行督促检查，及时通报创建进展情况和存在问题，确保创建工作顺利推进。县创建办两次组织乡镇及县直相关部门的创建工作负责人外出考察观摩学习“创建”工作，同时对相关人员进行创建工作业务培训。2007年，县“创建全国科普示范县”工作通过省、市验收。

第七节　关心下一代工作委员会

一、机构

1991年，县关心下一代协会（简称县关协），内设学校工作组、宣传工作组、社会工作组和办公室，办公室设在县老干局。是年，有基层关协10个，关协小组41个，会员2131人。至1993年年底，全县共建基层关协28个，关协分会129个，关协小组121个，有会员1.03万人。1994年3月，县关协更名为“息烽县关心下一代工作委员会”（简称县关工委）。1998年，全县建关工委4个，关协分会135个，关协小组419个，会员1.52万人。1999年3月，撤销社会工作组，增设法制工作组、农村工作组、机关街道工作组。6月，理顺乡镇关协工作关系，乡镇关协及机关、街道、村民组关协小组更名为关工委或关工委工作小组。2005年，撤销农村工作组、机关街道工作组，设农村（社区）工作组。2009年起，各级关工组织均称关工委。2010年，全县有乡镇、部门一级关工委14个，村（居）、学校一级关工委196个。

二、主要工作与活动

（一）思想道德教育

1991年起，每年清明节前后，县关协组织青少年到张露萍等七烈士墓开展扫墓活动，对青少年进行革命传统教育。是年，在全县中小学开展学雷锋、学赖宁活动，在中小学学生中进行社会主义、爱国主义、集体主义和革命传统教育。

1995年，开展纪念抗日战争胜利和世界反法西斯战争胜利50周年活动，组织学生观看影片《大决战》，在县教育系统组织学生开展“听一场报告，讲一个故事，写一篇心得”活动224场，参加活动6.49万人次。邀请“五老”（老干部、老战士、老专家、老教师、老劳模）为青少年作德育教育报告338场，受教育3716人次。次年，县关工委在全县中小学教职工中开展纪念中国工农红军二万五千里长征胜利60周年活动，组织师生到烈士墓开展入团宣誓仪式，观看百部爱国主义影片。

1997—1999年，全县各级关工委组织举办革命传统教育、爱国主义教育报告会近50场次，接受教育近3万人次。印发《长征精神　光照千秋》《鲜血染得山河秀　精神永励后来人》《板桥献身

躯 史册留英名》等文章，介绍在息烽境内牺牲的革命先烈的生平事迹。举办“勿忘国耻，振兴中华”知识竞赛、“共和国迈进新世纪”征文活动。

2000年起，开展以“三无两有”（无辍学、无不孝子女、无犯罪，青年有技术、少年有文化）为主要内容的创建关心下一代工作先进村活动。永靖镇永红村创建“三无两有”经验被推选到全国关工委厦门会议上交流。永靖镇永红村、立碑村，小寨坝镇前进村、养龙司乡坝上村“创关心下一代工作先进村”工作受到市关工委表彰。

2006年起，贯彻落实中共中央、国务院《关于进一步加强和改进未成年人思想道德建设的若干意见》。是年4月，县关工委在10个乡镇巡回开展“珍惜生命、远离毒品万人签名暨青少年参观禁毒教育巡回展”活动，全县4万余名师生受到禁毒教育；7月起，在全县青少年中开展“弘扬长征精神，建设美好贵州”征文演讲、“社会主义荣辱观教育”活动。在农村开展创建“四无三有”（无辍学、无不孝子女、无犯罪、无吸毒，青年有技术、少年有文化、青少年有公德）先进村，在学校创建“四好”（组织建设好、“五老”发动好、活动开展好、教育效果好）关心下一代先进学校活动。2007—2009年，县关工委在全县青少年中组织开展“知荣辱、树新风、促和谐”歌咏比赛活动，以“学习十七大精神、举旗帜、颂改革、讲文明、迎奥运”和“抗震救灾”为主题的讲故事比赛活动。2010年，县关工委组建法制宣讲团，到永靖镇南门、云环、三田、永靖等7所小学和黑神庙中学开展法制宣传教育活动，接受法制教育师生5000余人，教育中、小学生从小事做起，争做文明礼貌、助人为乐、爱护环境、遵纪守法的文明小公民。组织中小学生开展“看看我的家，比比谁干净”“除陋习，树新风，争当文明少年”千人签名，参加义务监督、捡拾白色垃圾等活动。

（二）帮教

1991年春节前，县关协组织老同志到县公安局收容所、看守所、行政拘留所和省中八劳教所探望息烽籍失足青少年，送去毛巾、牙刷等生活用品，对失足青少年进行规劝、教育。是年，县社会治安综合治理办公室与中八劳教所签订为期两年的帮教协议。此后，县关协坚持每年组织帮教团赴劳教单位开展帮教活动，至2000年，有38名在中八劳教所劳教的息烽籍失足青年获得提前解教。

2001年4月，县关工委组织人员赴永靖镇雨洒村、温泉镇尹庵村、大山村开展“两劳”回归青年继续教育专题调研。同月，与省沙子哨监狱联合开展“走出高墙，接回家乡”社会帮教活动，组织在该监狱服刑的息烽籍失足人员参观息烽集中营旧址和家乡的变化，在县城灯光球场开展帮教文艺演出活动。次年，开展“两劳”回归青年走访活动，了解回归青年思想、就业、生产、生活状况，帮助解决生产、生活困难。与沙子哨监狱合作，把57名息烽籍服刑人员接到息烽，参观家乡建设，开展刑属见面、座谈、文艺演出等活动。2005年11月，县关工委与省沙子哨监狱在息烽宣传文化中心联合开展以“爱自己、爱亲人、爱家乡”为主题的大型社会帮教活动和文艺演出，县教育局组织800余名师生参加。活动中，省监狱管理局把息烽命名为“贵州省沙子哨监狱帮教基地”，并举行授牌、授旗仪式。2006年6月，县关工委与贵阳市三江劳教所在息烽宣传文化中心开展以“爱亲人、爱生命，远离毒品——参与禁毒你我他，利己利民利国家”为主题的禁毒帮教活动。2010年11月，县关工委、永靖镇关工委联合派员组成关爱团，赴省未成年人犯罪管教所对息烽籍20名失足少年进行帮教，送去衣物、书籍等物品。是年，各乡镇关工委走访辖区内刑释解教青年，帮助解决生产、生活困难。小寨坝镇4名刑释解教人员回家后，除1人因年高外，其余3人均通过关工委的帮助到重钙厂工作。鹿窝乡合箐村青年农民陈某因吸毒被送劳教，回家后，其住房因年久失修成危房，无法居住。乡关工委协调建房资金1万元，为其新建住房。养龙司乡养龙司村刑释人员龚前国在政府关心下，养殖山羊100余只，走上养殖致富之路。

（三）关爱与济困

1991年，县关协副秘书长白先发组织县经委关协老同志帮助协调安置4名职工子女就业。1996—1997年，县关工委协调、争取引进“宇宏公司”投入资金30余万元、香港宝莲禅寺义工简光先生投入20余万元，分别在石硐乡高峰村、永靖镇坪上村各建“希望小学”一所。县关工委农村工作组组织协调举办种植、养殖等培训班583期，培训近2000人次。1998年，县关工委老同志自发捐资，为3名重病青少年送去救助金1000元；为4名少数民族特困学生争取助学金2600元。1999年，县关工委会同有关单位、组织向社会各界发出倡议，募捐资金5000余元，帮助永靖镇坪上村下坎村民组张某某的小孩解决患股骨关节坏死的部分治疗费。次年4月，8岁女孩文娥被父母虐待，县关工委、县妇联、团县委联合发出倡议，呼吁社会各界人士“少抽一包烟、少喝一杯酒，救救可怜不幸的女孩”，向社会各界筹集捐款1.2万余元为其解决住院治疗费。2005—2006年，县关工委派员参与审理未成年人犯罪案36件，帮教犯罪未成年人26名。

2008年5月，县关工委开展留守儿童情况专题调查。调查统计，全县农村有留守儿童2333人，其中幼儿326人，小学1456人，中学414人，不在校适龄儿童137人。针对留守儿童现状，就重视和加强“留守儿童”关爱工作提出建议意见，供县委、县政府决策参考。次年，永靖镇立碑村关工委主任况武英多方奔走呼吁，为本村患病做手术的王某某同学筹集手术费2.07万元。县关工委、县残联领导为石硐乡聋哑学生文某捐资1150元，资助解决部分学费，为其圆大学梦。

2010年，县关工委派员参与县法院对王某等4人（在校学生）涉嫌故意伤害案的审理，组织被告人和被害人亲属座谈协商，求得被害人亲属对被告的谅解，法院对王某4人给予从轻处罚，重回课堂。是年，为300余名贫困学生发放助学金27.8万元，为农村少年儿童订阅《贵州民族报——少儿书画》周刊1178份。

第八节　文学艺术界联合会

1997年6月，县文学艺术协会成立，时有会员95人。次年1月，息烽县文学艺术界联合会（简称县文联）成立，下设文学、书法、美术、音乐和摄影5个专业协会。2008年，增设舞蹈、园艺2个专业协会。2009年，园艺专业协会撤销。

一、会员代表大会

第一届代表大会：1998年1月13日召开。会议选举产生文联委员24名，主席1名。

第二届代表大会：2003年12月18日召开，出席会议代表及特邀人员125人。会议审议通过文联《章程》，选举产生文联委员43名，主席1名。

第三届代表大会：2009年12月18日召开。选举主席1名。

二、文联活动

1998年1月，县文联参与贵阳市新春“五下乡”服务团大型迎春活动，与有关部门联合举办“息烽县第七届青少年歌手大赛”。2月，举办县内首部长篇小说《利剑斩毒魔》首发式。5月后，相继举办“息烽风光”展、“8·28”艺术作品巡回展和玄天洞杨虎城将军囚禁处旧址书画展活动。1999—2003年，县文联与有关部门配合开办声乐、器乐、舞蹈、书画等培训班，培训青少年2000余人次，其中50余名学员参加市级以上文艺竞赛并获奖；书协、摄协、美协等专业协会创作作品入选国内外作品选集或参展，息烽木烙画代表贵州参加昆明世博会；先后成立民族艺术团、学生合唱团、女子合唱团等文艺团队，音协排练、指挥的童声合唱《摘菜调》在“全国童声合唱节”大赛中获二等奖。协助县内外有关部门完成《走近息烽》《息烽风光VCD光碟邮票珍藏册》《军统魔窟》《杨虎城将军在息烽》等一批宣传品制作和《杨虎城将军的最后岁月》《小萝卜头》《小萝卜头的故事》等电视剧拍摄任务。

2004年年初，组织书协会员参加“三下乡”活动，义务为群众书写春联；组织16名少年儿童参加“贵州省少儿影视之星选拔赛”，其中5名入选参加省级赛。6月，组建“息烽县千人合唱团”，有成员1468人。是年，成功举办“西洋杯”交流音乐会，受到美国科本音乐学院教授、指挥家马可·威廉姆斯的高度评价。次年8月，千人合唱团排练的《十送红军》《息烽美景看不够》《保卫黄河》《七月的榴花》《红星歌》等歌曲，在息烽集中营革命历史纪念馆开馆仪式上演出获得成功。

2005—2009年，县文联与有关单位联合举办“迎新春文艺联谊会”“‘争创文明城市，共建美好家园’摄影展”“‘西洋杯’名家画息烽‘2006年油画风景精品展’”“鑫悦怀”书画作品展、“名家摄息烽”“名家写息烽”等活动。文学协会会员创作的《卖鸡蛋的妇人》《风雨过后是彩虹》《中国没有过不去的坎》等作品被有关报刊采用。

2010年，选送5名音协会员参加“贵阳市舞蹈编导创作暨群众文化活动组织工作培训”。邀请省内知名作家、文艺评论家徐成森、申元初、李寂荡、冉正万到息烽作文学创作专题培训讲座。配合“多彩贵州”小品大赛息烽分赛区海选，组织专业会员到机关、乡镇、企业和学校指导编排参赛小品，县建设局和九庄镇选送的小品《等人》《合作医疗好》代表息烽参加贵阳市“多彩贵州”小品大赛贵阳赛区海选赛。组织摄影协会会员拍摄20余幅反映息烽精神文明建设、新农村建设、文明县创建为主题的图片参加“贵阳市‘三创一办’成果摄影联展”。

第九节　红十字会

一、机构

2002年前，县红十字会挂靠在县卫生局，无人员编制，其工作由卫生局代管。2002年，县委办公室、县政府办公室联合下发《关于印发〈息烽县红十字会机关机构改革方案〉的通知》，明确县红十字会为副科级群众团体建制，配置参公管理人员 3 人，工勤人员 1 人。虽然已明确县红十字会机构独立建制，但人员配置未到位，县红十字会的工作仍由县卫生局代管。2006年 6 月，县组织人事部门为县红十字会配备专职人员 2 名，从此，县红十字会开始独立开展工作。

按惯例，县红十字会名誉会长由县委书记兼任，会长由分管副县长兼任。2006—2010年，县红十字会名誉会长先后由杨彦峰、刘文新担任，会长先后由刘正菊、李福燕担任。

基层组织：2006年，县红十字会在息烽二中开展教育系统建立红十字会基层组织试点，组建息烽二中红十字会，发展学生会员246人。是年，九庄、石硐、鹿窝、流长、小寨坝、温泉、西山等 7

个乡（镇）红十字会成立，发展农村会员1400余名。至2010年，全县有8所中学、10个乡镇、26个机关、厂矿、企事业单位建立红十字会组织，共有成人会员3624人，青年会员6284人。建社区红十字会工作站6个，招募志愿者9人。

二、主要工作与活动

（一）备灾救灾

2007年4月，县内部分地区遭受风雹袭击，尤以流长、养龙司两乡受灾面积大，灾情严重。灾害发生后，县红十字会向县内社会各界发出“一方有难，八方支援”，为灾区群众捐款捐物的倡议书，得到社会各界的积极响应，收到捐款3.29万元、衣物894件、化肥5吨。县红十字会及时将所收到的捐款、捐物及上级调拨的价值2万多元的大米、棉被、药品等慰问物资送到灾民家中，帮助灾民改善生活，渡过难关。

2008年1月12日—28日，息烽县遭遇百年罕见的凝冻灾害，造成县境内公路交通中断，水电设施严重损坏，房屋倒塌等。灾害发生后，县红十字会立即启动自然灾害与突发事件应急预案，及时为永靖、温泉、鹿窝等乡镇受害最严重的36户困难户送去棉被。组织人员深入灾区开展灾情调查。凝冻灾害期间，县红十字会接收省、市红十字会调拨的灾害救助大米20吨、衣物100箱、救助包150个（内装大米、食物等物品）等价值15万元的救灾物资和5万元重建资金；天津市津南区红十字会汇来善款15.3万元。慰问受灾群众800户2600余人，为2400多户灾民发放救灾物资和善款。是年5月12日，四川汶川发生8.0级特大地震，灾区人民生命财产遭受特大损失。次日，县红十字会向社会公布募捐电话，印发《向四川汶川地震灾区进行捐款的倡议书》2万余份，向全县各机关、企事业单位和社会各界发起募捐活动，并在县城十字街设立固定募捐款接收点等。至5月23日，共募集捐款66.02万元，衣物等物资折款2万余元。其间，在县人民医院接受治疗的流长乡村民黄永生看到汶川地震电视报道后，致电县红十字会表达捐款意愿，并向病友借款400元，凑足2000元交到县红十字会。居住贵阳的县烟草公司退休职工朱维凤委托息烽的亲人代其捐款1000元。县教育系统教职员工捐款近23万元。县看守所50名在押人员从电视上看到四川地震灾情后，向灾区人民捐款4000余元。

2010年6月、7月，县内遭受伏旱灾害，县红十字会启动《自然灾害应急方案》，实行24小时值班制度，双休日坚持上班，全力投入抗旱工作。及时将上海生物制品公司、天津市津南区红十字会为灾区捐献的25万元善款和部分物资通过各乡镇红十字会发放到灾民手中，帮助灾民恢复生产，渡过难关。

（二）红十字“博爱送万家”活动

2006年起，县红十字会开展“红十字博爱送万家活动”。是年春节期间，县红十字会联合县民政局、民宗局、疾控中心等单位，走访慰问困难群众3000余户和5户麻风病人，为他们送去衣物1万件和价值1万余元的棉被、大米等。国庆、中秋节期间，县红十字会组织人员到永靖镇南门、北门两社区，慰问困难户、低保户、鳏寡孤独和残疾群众，给他们送去月饼和大米等慰问品。此后数年，县红十字会坚持开展“红十字博爱送万家活动”，利用每年春节、国庆、中秋等节日走访慰问困难群众，至2010年，共计走访慰问困难群众4874户次，发放慰问金2.34万元，送去大米、食油、月饼、棉被等生活物资折款53.62万元。

（三）医疗救助

2006年，县红十字会组织医疗救护培训50余次，接受培训9000余人次。9月，开展“世界急救日”宣传活动，印发各种宣传资料5万余份和培训书籍1700册。是年，息烽县被中国红十字会总会列为红十字会参与新型农村合作医疗工作试点县。省市红十字会下拨贫困医疗补助专项基金3万元，印发农村新型合作医疗补助宣传资料10万份，发放到全县农村农户家中，为1000名农村红十字会员缴纳参合费1万元，向26户困难农户发放医疗救助金1.01万元。下拨“丽珠得乐胶囊”100箱（价值28万元），通过息烽县、乡（镇）红十字会配发给困难群众开展医疗救助。至2009年，县红十字会共为5050户困难农户缴纳参合费用5.05万元，向220户困难农户发放医疗救助金10.85万元。其间，2008年，永靖镇代立祥、小寨坝镇牛杰、温泉镇方婷庆三位青年学生身患白血病，县红十字会、团县委联合向息烽社会各界发起募捐救助活动，收到捐款1.7万元，县政府拨出专款6万元。县红十字会及时将社会捐款和政府拨款送到三位白血病患者手中，帮助患者治病。

（四）无偿献血

2006年以来，县红十字会加强《中华人民共和国献血法》和《贵州省献血条例》宣传，坚持自愿、尊重的原则，至2010年，相继组织全县干部职工、企事业单位人员和广大人民群众开展无偿献血活动15次，共计3422人次参加，累计献血83.34万毫升。

第五篇　人大·政府·政协

第一章　人民代表大会

1990—2010年，县人民代表大会（简称县人大）历经第十一至十五届，共举行会议25次。会议主要听取审议县政府、县人民法院、县人民检察院（简称“一府两院”）、县人大常务委员会（简称县人大常委会）工作报告；审查批准县年度国民经济、社会发展计划和财政预算报告；审查批准县中、长期国民经济和社会发展计划、规划，并作出相应决议。选举县人大常委会组成人员、“一府两院”领导和市人大代表。

县人大常委会履行宪法和法律赋予的监督、讨论决定重大事项和人事任免职权，在工作实践中，不断探索、总结和创新：安排人民群众旁听常委会会议，增加常委会工作透明度；常委会会议设“无主题”发言，更直接地听到人民群众对国家机关各方面工作的意见建议；审议“一府两院”工作报告实行“审议卡”制度和“票决制”，提高审议质量；开展述职评议、工作评议、听取审议意见办理和整改意见落实情况报告，拓宽监督工作渠道，增强监督实效；人事任免设法律知识考试、作拟供职报告和举行就职宣誓仪式程序，增强供职人员的法律意识、履职意识和为民服务意识。宣传人民代表大会制度工作成效显著，曾获省人大宣传人民代表大会制度好新闻一、二等奖各1次、全国人大宣传人民代表大会制度好新闻三等奖1次。

第一节　人大代表选举

根据《中华人民共和国全国人民代表大会和地方各级人民代表大会选举法》县级人大代表由选民直接选举规定，县每届人大代表换届选举，主要经过准备工作（成立选举工作机构、制定选举工作方案、培训选举骨干、划分选区等）、宣传发动和选民登记、提名推荐和酝酿协商代表候选人、投票选举、召开人民代表大会、换届选举工作总结等阶段。1993年前，县人大代表每届任期3年，此后任期为5年。1990—2010年，县人大代表历经第十一至十五届换届选举，共选举人大代表683名。届中，因代表工作变动、代表辞职、代表资格终止或其他原因，依法适时进行补选。

息烽县第11—15届人大代表选举统计表

表5-1-1

届次	选举时间	参选数（万人）	参选率（%）	选举代表（人）	结构			
					中共党员（人）	非中共党员（人）	妇女（人）	少数民族（人）
十一	1990年4月	13.3	95.8	171	103	68	44	24
十二	1993年3月	12.92	92	172	101	71	44	18
十三	1997年1月	14.8	94.8	169	105	64	44	14
十四	2002年9月	15.6	96	171	103	68	44	16
十五	2006年8月	16.17	95.4	171	108	63	48	15

第二节　历届人民代表大会

一、十一届人民代表大会

本届人民代表大会举行会议4次。一次会议于1990年4月24—28日在县城召开。出席会议代表166人，有关部门负责人61人及出席县政协三届一次会议的政协委员列席会议。会议听取审议“一府两院”、县人大常委会工作报告，审查批准县1990年国民经济和社会发展计划、财政预算草案报告。会议认为，过去三年，县政府贯彻“决不放松粮食生产，积极发展多种经营”方针，坚持“六个稳定不变”，深化农村改革，不断完善家庭承包责任制，调整农业产业结构。1989年，实现农业总产值6411万元，比1986年增长27.6%，年均递增8.5%，实现财政收入1602万元，比1986年增长1.27倍，年均递增31.4%，各项工作取得较好成绩。会议选举刘兴贵为县十一届人大常委会主任，刘厚生、杨晓年、魏恩高、路延科为副主任，常委会委员14名；选举陈建忠为县政府县长，罗筑云、李贵菊、蒋光国、黄银忠为副县长，戴敬嘉为县人民法院院长，廖宗华为县人民检察院检察长。会议通过各项决议。二次会议听取和审议“一府两院”、县人大常委会工作报告，审查批准当年国民经济和社会发展计划、全县及县本级财政预算草案报告。会议认为，1990年，息烽遭受百年不遇的特大旱灾，县政府深化对农业基础地位的认识，坚持以科技兴农为主导，团结全县各族人民与自然灾害做斗争，把灾害造成的损失降到最低。建议各级政府1991年要在中共十三届七中全会和省、安顺地委扩大会议精神的指引下，努力争取经济稳步发展，保持社会稳定。要强化农业基础地位，千方百计夺取农业丰收。深入开展“质量、品种、效益年”活动，增强企业活力，提高经济效益，保持经济适度增长。三次会议听取和审议“一府两院”、县人大常委会工作报告，审查批准当年国民经济和社会发展计划、全县及县本级财政预算草案报告。会议认为，1991年，县政府加快改革步伐，把发展农业作为头等大事来抓，以科技兴农为先导，多渠道增加对农业的投入，推广农业实用技术，大抓粮食生产，发展多种经营，促进农业增产，农民增收。全县农业总产值完成1.06亿元，粮食总产量实现5645.8万千克，为历史最高记录。农业综合开发在温泉、小寨坝、西山、石硐、流长等地起步，收到一定效益。完成财政收入1669万元，创历史最高纪录。农民人均纯收入526元，人民群众生产生活条件有较大改善。会议补选黑卫平为县政府县长，陈福文为县人民法院院长。

二、十二届人民代表大会

本届人民代表大会举行会议7次。一次会议于1993年4月24—28日在县城召开。出席会议代表170名，有关部门负责人58人及出席县政协四届一次会议的政协委员列席会议。会议听取审议“一府两院”、县人大常委会工作报告，审查批准县1993年国民经济和社会发展计划、财政预算草案报告。会议认为，县十一届人大一次会议以来，县政府坚持把农业和农村工作放在首位，组织人民群众克服困难，战胜各种自然灾害，开展生产自救。继续稳定和完善家庭联产承包责任制，增加农业投入，推广农业适用技术。大搞以坡改梯和兴修水利为主要内容的农田基本建设，注重农业综合开发，使全县农业连续三年遭受自然灾害的损失降到最低。1992年，工农业总产值1.67亿元，财政总收入1768.3万元；粮食总产量4101万千克，农民人均纯收入496.5元。各项社会事业稳步发展。建议：今后五年，县政府要按照建立社会主义市场经济体制的要求，进一步解放思想，深化认识，抓住有利时机，加快改革开放和经济建设步伐。强化农业基础地位，提高农业综合能力，切实解决好减轻农民负担问题。扩大对外开放，积极引进外资，兴办“三资”企业，大力发展乡镇企业、第三产业和个体私营经济。加强城镇建设，改善投资环境。会议选举路延科为县十二届人大常委会主任，杨洪志、杨发礼、刘应龙、刘正菊为副主任，常委会委员13名；选举黑卫平为县政府县长，李贵菊、黄银忠、魏明禄为副县长，陈福文为县人民法院院长，童德权为县人民检察院检察长。通过各项决议。二次会议听取和审议“一府两院”、县人大常委会工作报告，审查批准当年国民经济和社会发展计划、全县及县本级财政预算草案报告。会议认为，1993年，县政府坚持“一个中心、两个基本点”的基本路线，坚持“一粮、二烟、三开发”发展思路，经过全县上下齐心协力，国民生产总值达到1.88亿元，工农业总产值达到2.01亿元，创造粮食总产量、烟叶产量、财政收入三个历史最高纪录。采取多轮驱动、多轨运行发展乡镇企业，加强管理，狠抓技改，提高效益。建议各级政府要服从服务于深化改革、扩大开放、促进发展、保持稳定的大局，围绕建立社会主义市场经济体制，加大各项事业改革力度，组织实施财税、计划、金融等重点领域改革。四次会议选举王忠碧、吴鹏、李贵菊、陈继春、聂明武、黑卫平、童金华、路延科、蔡汝达、魏忠润为贵阳市第九届人民代表大会代表。五次会议听取和审议县国民经济和社会发展“九五”计划及2010年规划纲要草案报告，县人大常委会、人民法院、人民检察院工作报告。审查批准县1996年国民经济和社会发展计划及财政预算草案报告。会议认为，“八五”期间，县政府在县委领导下，认真贯彻中共十四届三中、四中、五中全会精神，完成县国民经济和社会发展第八个五年计划。国民经济持续增长，农业和农村经济稳步发展，乡镇企业发展驶入快车道。各项改革不断深入完善，扶贫攻坚取得初步成效，各项社会事业不断进步，民主法制与廉政建设不断加强。建议：鉴于市“九五”计划和2010年远景目标规划纲要尚待批准，县政府应根据市的纲要要求和落实项目以及本次会议的审议意见，对国民经济和社会发展“九五”计划及2010年规划纲要草案报告进行必要调整和补充后，报县人大常委会审查批准（会议授权）。会议补选马跃进、许成彪、陈康、罗开俊为县第十二届人大常委会委员。通过其他决议。六次会议听取和审议“一府两院”、县人大常委会工作报告，审查批准当年国民经济和社会发展计划、全县及县本级财政预算草案报告。会议认为，过去一年，县政府围绕“加大扶贫力度，基本解决温饱；加快经济发展，增强发展后劲”总体目标，实现国内生产总值4.35亿元，农民人均纯收入1200元，人均占有粮食335千克，基本解决7.26万贫困人口温饱问题，成为全省48个国定贫困县中率先解决温饱的6个县之一。会议对县政府的工作表示满意。七次会议选举李忠、罗大林、兰义彤、杨育军、杨黔灵、赵治华、刘孟杰、路延科、吴鹏、王忠碧、杨静、李贵菊、陈继春、骆凡邦为贵阳市第十届人民代表大会代表。

三、十三届人民代表大会

本届人民代表大会举行会议6次。一次会议于1998年3月23—28日在县城召开。出席大会代表169名，有关部门负责人81人、出席县政协五届一次会议的政协委员列席会议。会议听取审议“一府两院”、县人大常委会工作报告，审查批准1998年县国民经济和社会发展计划、财政预算草案报告。会议认为，五年来，县政府在县委领导下，坚持党的基本理论、基本路线和基本方针，不断深化改革，扩大开放，推进经济体制和经济增长方式两个根本性转变，国民经济持续、快速、健康发展，社会事业全面进步，人民生活水平不断提高，为县实现跨世纪发展创造了有利条件。会议建议：今后五年，县政府要进一步深化改革，实施开放带动战略、科教兴县战略和可持续发展战略，坚持精神文明和物质文明“两手抓、两手都要硬”的方针，进一步解放思想，更新观念，推进经济社会全面发展。会议选举刘兴明为县十三届人大常委会主任，任国元、杨发礼、刘应龙、童德权、吴金奎、刘大英为副主任，常委会委员10名；选举陈长发为县政府县长，黄银忠、李光祥、魏燕飞、胡勇、刘正菊为副县长，关晓明为县人民法院院长，何志坚为县人民检察院检察长。会议通过各项决议。四次会议听取审议县国民经济和社会发展“十五”计划纲要草案报告，县人大常委会、县人民法院、县人民检察院工作报告，审查批准县国民经济和社会发展“十五”计划纲要草案报告，2001年国民经济和社会发展计划、财政预算草案报告。会议认为，“九五”期间，县政府抓住国家实行积极财政政策和实施西部大开发机遇，以经济建设为中心，积极工作，国民经济持续增长。2000年国内生产总值7.49亿元，“九五”期间年均增长10.54%，实现翻两番的战略目标；实现工业总产值9.46亿元，“九五”期间年均增长30.19%。扶贫攻坚成效明显，农民人均纯收入1567元，城镇居民人均可支配收入4696元，人民生活水平不断提高。实施“科教兴县”战略，基本消除中小学危房，教育“两基”达标工作通过省级验收，初级卫生保健通过市级验收，基本实现创建省级卫生县城目标。会议补选杨彦峰为县政府县长，张耀辉为县人民法院院长，孔凡明为县十三届人大常委会委员。会议通过各项决议。六次会议选举陈仁贵、陈长发、张新建、罗大林、雷友达、常本荣、刘兴明、杨彦峰、王忠碧、魏永祥、陈顺琴、夏培玉、杨明芬、刘才文为贵阳市第十一届人民代表大会代表。

四、十四届人民代表大会

本届人民代表大会举行会议5次。一次会议于2003年3月3—7日在县城召开。出席会议代表169名，有关部门负责人76人及出席县政协六届一次会议的政协委员列席会议。会议听取和审议“一府两院”、县人大常委会工作报告，审查批准2003年国民经济和社会发展计划、财政预算草案报告。会议认为，5年来，县十四届人民政府按照“提高一产，主攻二产，加速发展三产”工作思路，加快产业结构调整步伐，三次产业结构从1997年的38.3∶36.5∶25.2调整到2002年的20.7∶57∶22.3，实现从“一、二、三”到“二、三、一”的历史性跨越。固定资产投资完成5.71亿元，比1997年翻两番，年均增长42.58%。国有企业改革改制面达到95%。建立财务核算监督体系，成立会计核算中心，启动乡镇财政“零户统管”。提前两年实现国家“八七扶贫攻坚计划”目标，全县1.94万贫困人口基本脱贫，城乡人民生活水平明显提高。各项社会事业发展步入新阶段，实现创建省级卫生城市和人人享有初级卫生保健目标；依法治县工作不断深入，民主法制建设进一步加强。会议选举刘兴明为县十四届人大常委会主任，任国元、胡勇、黄永辉、刘凤刚、李福燕、杜洪远为副主任，常委会委员10名；选举县政府县长，魏发志、刘正菊、赵永祥、魏永祥、蔡飞为副县长；选举张耀辉为县人民法院院长，莫智为县人民检察院检察长。会议通过各项决议。二次会议听取和审议“一府两院”、县人大常委会工作报告，审查批准当年国民经济和社会发展计划、全县及县本级财政预算草案报告。会议认为，2003年，县政府贯彻中共十六大和县委第十次党代会精神，围绕全面建设小康社会“四步走”战略目标和“调整结构提升一产，扶优扶强主攻二产，加快速度发展三产”的思路，解放思想，奋力拼搏，完成国内生产总值15.04亿元、社会固定资产投资7.57亿元、县属固定资产投资6亿元、地方财政收入7632万元。三次会议补选胡亨超为县十四届人大常委会副主任。五次会议听取审议“一府两院”、县人大常委会工作报告、《息烽县国民经济和社会发展第十一个五年规划纲要》，审查批准2005年国民经济和社会发展计划、财政预算草案报告和《息烽县国民经济和社会发展第十一个五年规划纲要》。会议认为，过去5年，息烽经济结构调整步伐加快，经济总体实力明显增强，全县生产总值从2000年的7.5亿元增加到2005年的23.7亿元，增长2.16倍。财政总收入从2000年的6330万元增加到2005年的2.39亿元，增长2.78倍，首次突破2亿元大关。地方财政收入从2000年的4073万元增加到2005年的1.27亿元，增长2.1倍。固定资产投资累计完成35.79亿元。2002年摘掉国定贫困县帽子。“十五”期间，引进一批在全国有较高知名度的企业入驻息烽，招商引资到位资金29.4亿元，是“九五”期间的10倍。会议选举刘其芬为县人大常委会副主任。

五、十五届人民代表大会

本届人民代表大会2006年11月至2010年3月，举行会议5次。一次会议于2006年11月21—25日在县城召开，出席大会代表171名，有关部门负责人96人、出席县政协七届一次会议的政协委员列席会议。会议听取和审议“一府两院”、县人大常委会工作报告。审查批准县2003—2006年国民经济和社会发展情况报告、财政工作报告。会议认为，过去4年，县政府全面贯彻落实“三个代表”重要思想和中共十六大精神，依靠全县各族人民，坚持以经济建设为中心，克服改革、发展中的困难，大力实施“工业强县、科教兴县、环境立县”三大战略，保持国民经济持续、快速、健康发展，圆满完成本届政府四年来提出的各项经济社会发展目标任务。2006年，完成地方生产总值27.99亿元、农业总产值3.09亿元、全社会固定资产投资15.65亿元、财政总收入3.7亿元、地方财政收入4.8亿元。会议对县政府的工作表示满意。会议强调，今后5年，县政府要坚持把发展作为执政兴县第一要务，以科学发展观统领工作全局，实施科教兴县、工业强县、环境立县、旅游活县战略，全面抓好经济、政治、文化与和谐社会建设。依法行政，建设廉洁高效、运转协调、行为规范的服务型政府，推进富民强县事业。会议选举刘大英为十五届人大常委会主任，胡勇、刘凤刚、胡亨超、刘其芬、魏永祥为副主任，常委会委员15名；选举县政府县长，黄永辉、李福燕、李红卫、杜洪远、佘龙、李华斌为副县长，李志强为县人民法院院长，钟雷为县人民检察院检察长。会议通过各项决议。四次会议听取和审议“一府两院”、县人大常委会工作报告，审查批准当年国民经济和社会发展计划、全县及县本级财政预算草案报告。会议认为，2008年，县政府积极组织县各族人民开展抗凝冻、保民生、生产自救和重建家园工作，经受住百年不遇的凝冻灾害和全球性金融危机考验。围绕建设生态文明县总体目标，解放思想，扎实工作，全县经济社会呈现结构优化、质量提高、民生改善的良好态势。全年完成地方生产总值40.87亿元、财政总收入4.45亿元、地方财政收入2.22亿元、全社会固定资产投资28.51亿元，实现城镇居民人均可支配收入11623元，农民人均纯收入3826元，迈入全省建设经济强县行列。会议选举张定超为县政府县长，刘勇为县十五届人大常委会副主任，张著权、冯劲锋、唐慧为县十五届人大常委会委员。五次会议听取和审议“一府两院”、县人大常委会工作报告，审查批准当年国民经济和社会发展计划、全县及县本级财政预算草案报告。会议认为，2009年，县政府深入学习实践科学发展观，以“保增长、保民生、保稳定”为落脚点，较好完成各项目标任务。全年完成地方生产总值47.84亿元、固定资产投资37.11亿元。农民人均纯收入4575元。森林覆盖率45.3%，荣获“中国绿色名县”称号。治安环境不断改善，群众安全感明显上升，荣获全省“平安建设先进县”和“无毒县”称号。会议选举吕仕龙、况武德为县十五届人大常委会委员。会议通过各项决议。

息烽县第十一届至第十五届人大常委会主任、副主任名录

表5-1-2

届次	姓名	性别	民族	籍贯	职务	任职时间
第十一届	刘兴贵	男	苗	贵州息烽	主　任	1990年4月—1993年4月
	刘厚生	男	汉	四川岳池	副主任	1990年4月—1993年4月
	杨晓年	女	苗	贵州黔南	副主任	1990年4月—1993年4月
	魏恩高	男	汉	贵州息烽	副主任	1990年4月—1993年4月
	路延科	男	汉	贵州息烽	副主任	1990年4月—1993年4月
第十二届	路延科	男	汉	贵州息烽	主　任	1993年4月—1998年3月
	杨洪志	男	汉	贵州息烽	副主任	1993年4月—1998年3月
	杨发礼	男	汉	贵州息烽	副主任	1993年4月—1998年3月
	刘应龙	男	汉	贵州息烽	副主任	1993年4月—1998年3月
	刘正菊	女	汉	贵州息烽	副主任	1993年4月—1998年3月
第十三届	刘兴明	男	汉	四川安岳	主　任	1998年3月—2003年3月
	任国元	男	汉	贵州息烽	副主任	1998年3月—2003年3月
	杨发礼	男	汉	贵州息烽	副主任	1998年3月—2003年3月
	刘应龙	男	汉	贵州息烽	副主任	1998年3月—2003年3月
	童德权	男	汉	贵州开阳	副主任	1998年3月—2003年3月
	吴金奎	男	汉	贵州息烽	副主任	1998年3月—2003年3月
	刘大英	女	汉	贵州息烽	副主任	1998年3月—2003年3月
第十四届	刘兴明	男	汉	四川安岳	主　任	2003年3月—2006年11月
	任国元	男	汉	贵州息烽	副主任	2003年3月—2006年11月
	胡　勇	男	汉	贵州息烽	副主任	2003年3月—2006年11月
	黄永辉	男	汉	贵州息烽	副主任	2003年3月—2006年11月
	刘凤刚	男	汉	贵州金沙	副主任	2003年3月—2006年11月

续表

届次	姓名	性别	民族	籍贯	职务	任职时间
	李福燕	女	汉	山东历城	副主任	2003年3月—2006年11月
	杜洪远	男	汉	贵州息烽	副主任	2003年3月—2006年11月
	胡亨超	男	汉	贵州息烽	副主任	2004年4月—2006年11月
	刘其芬	女	汉	贵州息烽	副主任	2006年3月—2006年11月
第十五届	刘大英	女	汉	贵州息烽	主　任	2006年11月—
	胡　勇	男	汉	贵州息烽	副主任	2006年11月—
	刘凤刚	男	汉	贵州金沙	副主任	2006年11月—
	胡亨超	男	汉	贵州息烽	副主任	2006年11月—
	刘其芬	女	汉	贵州息烽	副主任	2006年11月—
	魏永祥	男	汉	贵州息烽	副主任	2006年11月—
	刘　勇	男	汉	贵州乌当	副主任	2009年3月—

第三节　人大常委会

一、工作机构

1991年，县人大常委会机关设办公室、财政经济工作委员会、法制工作委员会、代表工作委员会、教科文卫工作委员会5个工作机构。在九庄区、永阳区、黑神庙区、养龙区分别设人大工作委员会，为县人大常委会派出机构。1992年2月，因撤区并乡建镇，各区人大工作委员会撤销。2002年，代表工作委员会更名为选举任免联络工作委员会。

二、常委会会议

县人大常委会会议每两个月举行一次，因特殊情况，经常委会主任会议决定，可临时召集。会议由常委会主任或其委托的副主任主持。会议须有常委会全体组成人员过半数出席方能举行。“一府两院”领导及其有关工作部门负责人、乡镇人大主席团主席或副主席、县人大常委会工作机构负责人列席会议。必要时，邀请县委、县政协领导，驻县省、市人大代表列席。会议议程（草案）由常委会主任会议提出，常委会讨论表决通过，主要内容有学习法律法规、传达学习有关会议及文件精神，听取审议“一府两院”工作报告、讨论决定有关重大事项及人事任免等。2000年9月起，常委会审议“一府两院”工作报告提出的需要报告单位研究办理的意见、建议，整理形成常委会审议意见，印发“一府两院”，要求报告单位认真研究办理落实，并在下一次常委会会议报告办理结果。2005年9月起，每次会议安排3~5名人民群众旁听；每次会议议程结束后，由会议主持人安排一定时间作“无主题发言”；审议“一府两院”工作报告实行“审议卡”制度，于会前10天将听取审议的工作报告及“审议卡”送达常委会组成人员，所提批评、建议和意见写入“审议卡”，会后交回，汇同会议审议发言一并整理，形成常委会审议意见，印发“一府两院”办理落实；审议“一府两院”工作报告、办理落实常委会审议意见报告、述职评议整改落实情况报告等实行“票决制”，票决获得“满意”“基本满意”票超过常委会组成人员过半数者通过，未获通过的责成在下一次会议重新报告。常委会表决决定问题，须获全体组成人员过半数赞成票通过。常委会表决决定问题以举手或无记名方式表决，2009年11月起，使用电子表决器表决。

1991—2010年，常委会共举行会议156次。

第四节　工作辑要

一、监督工作

（一）法律监督

1990年4月至1993年4月，县十一届人大常委会听取审议县政府贯彻实施《中华人民共和国传染病防治法》《中华人民共和国土地管理法》《中华人民共和国档案法》《中华人民共和国标准化法》《职业教育暂行条例》《计划生育试行条例》《国家预算管理条例》《中华人民共和国义务教育法》《中华人民共和国食品卫生法》《中华人民共和国计量法》，国务院《兽药管理条例》《未成年人保护条例》《农业技术推广条例》《价格管理条例》等23部法律法规情况报告，对个别单位“有法不依，执法不严，违法不究”问题，要求县政府及其职能部门把实施法律法规放在重要位置，加强领导，建立执法责任制，做到依法行政，依法管理各项事务。

1993年4月至2003年3月，县十二、十三届人大常委会听取审议“一府两院”贯彻实施《中华人民共和国矿产资源法》《中华人民共和国环境保护法》《中华人民共和国国家赔偿法》《中华人民共和国妇女权益保障法》《中华人民共和国教师法》《中华人民共和国消费者权益保护法》《中华人民共和国劳动法》《中华人民共和国农业法》《中华人民共和国义务教育法》《中华人民共和国森林法》《中华人民共和国药品管理法》《中华人民共和国农业技术推广法》《中华人民共和国婚姻法》《中华人民共和国村民委员会组织法》《中华人民共和国乡镇企业法》《中华人民共和国科学技术进步法》《中华人民共和国刑事诉讼法》，国务院《全民所有制工业企业转换经营机制条例》《公路管理条例》《贵州省计划生育条例》《贵州省广播电视管理条例》等37部法律法规情况报告；配合省、市人大常委会对《中华人民共和国职业教育法》《中华人民共和国测绘法》《中华人民共和国红十字会法》《中华人民共和国老年人权益保障法》《贵州省测绘管理条例》等9部法律法规贯彻实施情况进行检查。参与《减轻农民负担监督条例》《贵州省禁毒条例》《贵阳市公路管理办法》《贵阳市房屋拆迁管理条例》《贵州省气象管理条例》等11部地方性法规的调研修改和征求意见。

2003年3月至2006年11月，县十四届人大常委会听取审议“一府两院”贯彻实施《中华人民共和国建筑法》《中华人民共和国人口与计划生育法》《中华人民共和国煤炭法》《中华人民共和国水污染防治法》《中华人民共和国行政监察法》《中华人民共和国水土保持法》《中华人民共和国村民委员会组织法》《中华人民共和国招标投标法》《中华人民共和国安全生产法》《中华人民共和国农业技术推广法》《中华人民共和国职业教育法》，国务院《殡葬改革条例》《突发公共卫生事件应急条例》《法律援助条例》，贵州省《宗教事务管理条例》《城市房屋拆迁管理办法》《职业技术教育暂行条例》等29部法律法规情况报告，提出审议意见152条。配合全国、省、市人大对《中华人民共和国传染病防治法》《中华人民共和国科学技术普及法》《中华人民共和国工会法》《中华人民共和国法官法》《中华人民共和国检察官法》《科学技术投入资金管理条例》贯彻实施情况检查，完成《贵州省征兵工作条例修正案》《城市市容和卫生管理条例》《扶贫资金使用条例》《外来投资者权益保障条例》和贵阳市《养犬管理办法》《禁止选择性终止妊娠规定》等9部地方性法规的立法调研。

2007—2010年，县15届人大常委会听取审议县政府贯彻实施《中华人民共和国煤炭法》《中华人民共和国公路法》《中华人民共和国残疾人保障法》《中华人民共和国政府采购法》《中华人民共和国道路交通安全法》《中华人民共和国科学技术进步法》《中华人民共和国水污染防治法》《中华人民共和国治安管理处罚法》《中华人民共和国义务教育法》《中华人民共和国传染病防治法》《中华人民共和国行政复议法》《中华人民共和国劳动合同法》，国务院《互联网上网服务营业场所管理条例》等16部法律法规的情况报告。其间，2010年4月29日，县十五届人大常委会第三十二次会议听取审议县政府贯彻实施《中华人民共和国传染病防治法》情况报告，提出强化对传染病预防及传染病人的跟踪服务，随时掌握传染病人治疗情况、治疗效果、去向及从业情况等。加强对个体餐饮店和摊贩卫生管理的审议意见。县政府召集有关单位开会，对审议意见进行研究，抓好落实：制定《息烽县传染病人收治管理办法》，明确县人民医院为县境内传染病定点收治单位；是年，卫生药监局开展餐饮业许可审查189户，查出患五类传染病不能从事餐饮服务人员8名。检查夜市小吃摊点71户；全县农村建无害化厕所6500间，村级垃圾池74个等。8月，县十五届人大常委会第三十四次会议听取审议县政府贯彻实施《中华人民共和国劳动合同法》情况报告，提出指导和帮助职工签订劳动合同，加大劳动保障监察执法力度，依法查处不签订劳动合同、不参加社会保险等侵害劳动者权益的违法行为的审议意见。县人事劳动监察部门在3个月内开展各项专项检查6次，检查用人单位236户次，指导和帮助职工签订劳动合同2028份，督促企业法人与劳动者签订劳动合同326份。对不依法与劳动者签订劳动合同、不缴纳社会保险等侵害劳动者权益的6家用人单位下达责令整改决定书，对两家未整改的用人单位给予经济处罚。

（二）工作监督

1990—2010年，县人大常委会围绕县委的中心工作、全县改革开放和经济社会建设，人代会提出的目标任务和人民群众普遍关心的热点难点问题，通过听取审议工作报告，开展调查、视察，工作评议和述职评议等，对“一府两院”及国家机关工作人员实施工作监督。坚持按年度听取审议国民经济和社会发展计划、财政预算执行情况，财政决算、财政预算执行和其他财政收支审计报告，办理代表建议报告。

听取审议工作报告：1990年4月至1993年4月，县十一届人大常委会听取审议“一府两院”关于工业生产、实施长江防护林工程、社会治安综合治理、教育收费、水利设施建设、烤烟生产、乡镇企业发展、粮专资金使用、审计及监察工作、民事及刑事审判、打击刑事犯罪和贪污贿赂犯罪等方面的工作报告28个。

1993年4月至1998年3月，县十二届人大常委会听取审议县政府建立行政执法责任制、减轻农民负担、农田基本建设、文化教育市场管理、普法依法治理、城市建设、医疗卫生收费、企业生产经营、领导干部廉洁自律、乡镇企业发展等工作报告38个。

1998年3月至2003年3月，县十三届人大常委会听取审议县“一府两院”实施社会治安综合治理创建“平安工程”活动、创建省级卫生县城、农业技术推广、国有企业改革改制和配套改革、非公有经济发展、人口与计划生育、普法教育、实施“十五”计划纲要、农村费改税、举报控告申诉等工作报告29个。其中就人民群众反映殡葬改革部分项目收费过高的问题向县政府提出建议意见，县政府召开会议研究，调低相关收费标准，推进殡葬改革工作的开展。1998年9月，县人大常委会审议县政府执行国民经济和社会发展计划报告，针对报告基本情况不清楚、多处数据错误、未反映政府执行计划所做的工作等提出严厉批评，对该报告不予通过，责成在下一次常委会上重新报告。

2003年4月至2010年，十四、十五届人大常委会听取审议“一府两院”开展科技进步考核、招商引资、10件实事办理、教育“两基”复查和“普实”验收、新型农村合作医疗、创建“无毒县”、村村通广播电视、社会治安综合治理、“创建全国科普示范县”反渎职侵权、移民工作、社会主义新农村建设、农村贫困户特危住房及配套设施改造项目建设专项贷款使用、农村富余劳动力转移培训、农村低保、农村公路建设、生态文明总体规划、扩大内需增加投资、依法行政、“四五”普法依法治县、预防职务犯罪、反贪、民事审判、刑事审判、反贪污贿赂、监所检察、国民经济和社会发展“十一五”规划中期评估、农村危房改造、矿山安全生产管理、司法为民等工作报告102个。

述职评议：1993年起，县人大常委会开展对常委会任命的国家机关工作人员述职评议。至1997年，先后对县水利、农机管理、民政、司法、农业、建设、劳动、计划生育、教育、国土、交通、监察、乡企、文化广播电视、粮食、林业等16个局的局长及县法院副院长、县检察院副检察长各1名进行述职评议。通过评议表决，评定为优秀等次12名、称职等次6名。1999年7月，县十三届人大常委会制定出台《息烽县人民代表大会选举及其常委会任命的国家机关工作人员述职评议办法》，进一步完善和规范述职评议工作，首次把人民代表大会选举的国家机关工作人员纳入述职评议对象。至2007年，共述职评议国家机关工作人员29名，其中县政府县长1名、副县长4名、县政府组成人员19名；县人民法院院长1名、副院长2名，县人民检察院检察长、副检察长各1名。提出述职评议整改意见100余条。常委会适时分别安排听取被述职人员的整改落实情况报告。在对1名副县长的评议调查中，了解到其分管的某部门领导班子涣散，内部管理不力，有法不依、执法不严现象突出，干部群众意见大，职工对个别领导的工作写照为“干部交流，浪费汽油，星期一姗姗来迟，星期五鞋底擦油”。常委会对此提出评议意见，并向县委汇报。组织采取措施，调整该部门领导班子。根据《中华人民共和国各级人民代表大会常务委员会监督法》有关规定，2008年起，不再开展对国家机关工作人员的述职评议。

工作评议：县人大常委会开展工作评议始于1995年。是年，十二届人大常委会组织人大代表对县公安局永靖镇、小寨坝镇、九庄镇、石硐乡4个派出所的工作开展评议。在走访调查、召开座谈会听取各方面意见建议和查阅案卷等工作的基础上，针对存在问题，提出加强干警队伍建设，严肃法纪，强化服务意识，建立完善制度等评议整改意见。次年，对县人民法院永靖、永阳、九庄、黑神庙、养龙司5个基层人民法庭的工作进行评议。此后，工作评议工作一度间断。2008年起，县十五届人大常委会恢复开展工作评议工作。每年按计划、有重点选择1～2个单位作评议对象。至2010年，先后对人口和计划生育局、水利局、住建局3个单位进行工作评议。评议工作坚持“不评功摆好，重在找准问题，抓好整改落实”。2009年，对县人口和计划生育局进行工作评议，提出统筹做好人口和计划生育工作，落实部门齐抓共管机制，加大社会抚养费征收力度，提高妇检履约率等评议意见，促进人口和计划生育工作的开展。当年，人口和计划生育工作实现县委提出的在全市排位前移目标。

视察调查：1991—2010年，历届人大常委会坚持围绕全县中心工作、经济社会发展中的重大事项和人民群众关心的热点、难点问题，组织人大代表开展视察调查，提出工作建议意见，交“一府两院”研究办理。先后组织代表对县政府贯彻实施《中华人民共和国土地管理法》《中华人民共和国水法》《中华人民共和国行政诉讼法》《中华人民共和国国家赔偿法》《贵州省行政事业单位收费管理条例》《贵州省计划生育试行条例》《贵州省未成年人保护条例》、全县“区以下小学生辍学和教师垫付书本费情况”、水利设施建设工程、公路建设工程、社会治安综合治理、乡镇企业发展、减轻农民负担情况、环境治理、城市建设等法律法规的实施情况和专项工作进行视察。其间，1992年3月，县人大常委会组织驻会常委会委员考察西山乡西望山水土流失情况。认为县政府落实安顺地委、行署关于治理西望山水土流失意见不力、对要求补种910亩长防工程林任务未落实、修建谷坊（拦河坝）尚未作施工准备、严禁在陡坡地段开荒的问题未完全禁止等，向县政府提出要采取措施，敦促开垦单位严格按照林业、水利部门计划，迅速落实造林、种草、修建谷坊等补救措施，要求在三月内完成以上工作。要求县政府及其职能部门要加大对《中华人民共和国森林法》《中华人民共和国水土保持法》宣传力度，对不利水土保持的开垦要坚决纠正。有关单位要派专人前往西望山监测沙土流失情况，及时组织抢险，防止意外事故发生等意见建议。1998年，永靖镇上厂水库建成后发生渗漏，县人大常委会组织市、县人大代表对此开展视察，提出批评和意见，但有关职能部门未引起重视，导致发生坝堤垮塌事故。县人大常委会责成县政府对此进行专题调查，提出处理意见。通过跟踪监督，有关责任人因渎职被追究法律责任。2005年6月，县人大常委会组织部分驻县省、市及县人大代表对县看守所有无超期羁押情况进行视察，发现市人民检察院在办理部分刑事案件时，存在对当事人换押法律手续不完备，有假性超期羁押现象，为此提出严格执行有关纠、防超期羁押规定，保障犯罪嫌疑人、被告人合法权益的建议。对此，市人民检察院联合市人民法院、市公安局制定《关于贯彻落实〈贵州省关于羁押犯罪嫌疑人　被告人实行换押制度的暂行规定〉的补充规定》，避免假性超期羁押的发生。2008年，县人大常委会组织部分市、县人大代表对息烽磷矿排土场进行视察，对排土场存在的安全隐患，建议县环保局、县安监局等部门帮助息烽磷矿制定科学治理方案，确保企业生产安全。息烽磷矿立即作出整改，最大限度降低安全隐患。

二、讨论决定重大事项

（一）县人大讨论决定重大事项

县人大通过一年一次的代表会议，听取审议县“一府两院”、人大常委会工作报告，审查批准县国民经济和社会发展中、长期规划，年度计划、财政预算草案，作出决议方式决定全县重大事项。1991—2010年，作出决议决定100余项。

1991年3月30日，县十一届人大二次会议审议《县人民政府工作报告》（以下简称《报告》），认为1990年县政府在大灾之年，团结全县各族人民与自然灾害作顽强斗争，把灾害造成的损失降到最低，为全县经济发展、社会稳定、人民生活安宁作出应有的成绩和贡献。《报告》提出1991年的工作方针和任务，符合息烽实际，会议决定批准政府工作报告。指出：1991年是实施十年规划和“八五”计划的第一年，做好1991年的工作，对全县今后的发展意义重大，强调各级政府要在党的十三届七中全会和省、地委扩大会议精神指引下，强化农业的基础地位，增强企业活力，提高经济效益，全面完成会议确定的各项目标任务，为今后的发展创造条件。2003年3月3—7日，县十四届人大一次会议审议《政府工作报告》（以下简称《报告》），认为1998—2002年，县十三届人民政府按照县委“提高一产，主攻二产，加速发展三产”的工作思路和“抢抓机遇，奋力拼搏，加速发展，强县升位”的总体要求，顺利完成“九五”计划和开创“十五”计划的良好局面，取得2002年全县国内生产总值完成11.85亿元，比1997年翻一番，年均增长15.15%的好成绩。三次产业结构从1997年的38.3：36.5：25.2调整到2002年底的20.7：57：22.3，实现从“一、二、三”到“二、三、一”的历史性跨越。对政府所做的工作和取得的成绩予以肯定。对《报告》提出的今后五年高扬开拓创新、强县升位主旋律，实施工业强县、环境立县、科教兴县战略，按照提高一产、主攻二产、加速发展三产的工作思路，实现全面建设小康社会第一步战略目标表示认同。提出的2003年国内生产总值达到13.89亿元，增长18%（其中，第一产业增长5%，第二产业增长25%，第三产业增长13%），地方财政收入增长16%，招商引资到位资金增长25%，固定资产投资增长27%，社会商品零售总额增长13.2%，城镇居民人均可支配收入增长8%，农民人均纯收入增长5%，计划生育率达到90%的主要预期目标符合县的实际，会议决定对《政府工作报告》予以批准。指出：息烽经济和社会发展还存在整体实力不强，人均收入水平低，财政收入总量小，结构调整力度不大，农业基础设施薄弱，农产品商品率低，农民增收缓慢，就业和再就业压力大，部分地方社会治安不够稳定等问题。强调今后五年，县政府要坚持把发展作为第一要务，继续把“强县升位”作为主旋律，以调整产业结构为主线，以改革开放和科技进步为动力，以提高人民群众生活水平为根本出发点，以实现超常规跨越式发展为目标，坚持三个文明一起抓，正确处理改革与稳定的关系，努力完成大会提出的各项目标任务。

2009年3月3—7日，县十五届人大四次会议审议《政府工作报告》（以下简称《报告》），认为2008年，面对百年不遇的凝冻灾害和全球性金融危机，县人民政府在市委、市政府和县委的领导下，围绕建设生态文明县的总体目标，积极应对，攻坚克难，努力工作，完成地方生产总值40.87亿元，同比增长24.1%；财政总收入4.45亿元，增长34.9%；地方财政收入2.22亿元，增长22.19%；实现城镇居民人均可支配收入11623元，增长8.35%；农民人均纯收入3826元，增长20.05%；迈入全省建设经济强县行列，社会各项事业协调发展。对《政府工作报告》提出的2009年预期目标（生产总值增长15%；财政总收入增长14%，地方财政收入增长14%；全社会固定资产投资增长30%；社会消费品零售总额增长20%；城镇居民人均可支配收入增长10%；农民人均纯收入增长13%；招商引资到位资金增长20%；城镇登记失业率控制在4%以内；单位生产总值能耗降低5%，主要污染物排放减少2%以上，实现建设经济强县保位前移）表示认同，会议决定批准《政府工作报告》并作出决议。指出息烽经济总量小，财政收支矛盾突出；规模以上企业不多，受全球金融危机影响，部分企业产值下滑；旅游资源未得到充分开发，第三产业发展仍较滞后；招商引资项目不多，发展后劲不足；农业基础仍然薄弱，农业标准化、产业化水平不高；教育、医疗等公共服务设施有待改善，社会事业发展仍需进一步加强等。强调要切实转变经济发展方式，以建设生态文明县为统揽，以实现建设经济强县保位前移为目标，以改善民生、促进社会和谐为落脚点，全力抓好项目建设和招商引资工作，强力推进“科教兴县、工业强县、环境立县和旅游活县”战略，全面完成会议确定的各项目标任务。

（二）县人大常委会讨论决定重大事项

县人大常委会通过举行会议，就审查批准县国民经济和社会发展计划、财政预算调整，批准县财政决算、县政府建设项目贷款；审议城市规划，开展依法治县工作、法制宣传教育，决定“一府两院”主要领导代理人选和主要领导辞去职务、授予荣誉县民称号等作出决定决议。1991—2010年，历届县人大常委会作出重大决定决议110余项。

1991年11月23日，县十一届人大常委会第十一次会议审议县人民政府《关于调整变更1991年财政预算（草案）的报告》，认为1991年全县遭受历史上罕见的洪涝灾害，工农业生产受到影响，烤烟减产，烟税减收，加之政策性税收调减和政策性增支扩大，造成收入完不成，会议批准将预算收入1850万元调整为1650万元，预算支出1419万元调整为1749万元。并作出决议：要求县人民政府采取有力措施，加强税收征管，开展税收、财务和物价大检查，做到应收尽收，增加财政收入。加强管理，严肃财经纪律，控制社会集团购买力，减少非生产性开支，把收支逆差降到最低限度，力争实现财政收支平衡，略有节余；审议县人民政府《关于调整一九九一年工业产值及夏收作物生产计划的报告》，作出决议：同意夏粮播种面积由11万亩调为13.7万亩，产量由1000万千克调为1640万千克，油菜籽播种面积由8万亩调为6.8万亩，产量由680万千克调为700万千克；对1991年的工业产值计划不作调整变更，仍执行年初县十一届人大二次会议批准的5792.9万元。

1993年7月29日，县十二届人大常委会第三次会议审议县人民政府《关于切实做好减轻农民负担工作情况的报告》，认为自中央、国务院关于减轻农民负担系列文件下发后，县人民政府在减轻农民负担方面做了一定的工作，初步遏制了农民负担不断增长的势头，但离中央、国务院的要求还有很大差距，政府有关部门对减轻农民负担的问题还未引起高度重视，或行动迟缓，或按兵不动，农民负担过重的问题仍未得到解决，农民意见很大。会议作出决议：各级人民政府和各部门领导，要进一步提高认识，把减轻农民负担、保护农民的生产积极性当作一项紧迫的政治任务，摆在重要议事日程，切实加强领导，狠抓落实，坚决地、不折不扣地执行中央、国务院关于减轻农民负担的一系列指示和国务院颁布的《农民承担费用和劳务管理条例》（以下简称《条例》），对已经公布取消的项目，坚决执行，不留死角，不走过场，更不得以任何借口拖延不办或变相收费。对县、乡两级及部门出台的涉及农民负担的文件和项目，要认真清理，一律取消，并向社会公布。各级人民政府和职能部门，要深入宣传减轻农民负担的各项政策法规，让人民群众了解党中央、国务院是关心农民疾苦，反对增加农民负担的，要让每个农民知道《条例》的具体规定，依法保护自己的合法权益。各级监督管理部门要认真履行职责，真正把减轻农民负担的监督管理工作落到实处。县人大常委会对各级、各部门贯彻落实中央办公厅、国务院办公厅涉及农民负担项目审核处理意见的通知和《条例》的情况进行一次全面检查，对阳奉阴违、顶着不办的单位和个人要严加追究，责成有关部门严肃处理。对农民“三提五统”的收费，控制在上一年度农民人均纯收入的5%以内。县人民政府〔1993〕20文件，因不符合中共中央办公厅、国务院办公厅关于涉及农民负担项目审核意见的通知和《条例》的规定，应停止执行。县人民法院、县人民检察院应根据中央、国务院关于减轻农民负担指示精神，作出贯彻实施意见。

1995年4月27日，县十二届人大常委会第十四次会议审议县人大常委会八名委员提出的《关于对治理县城环境作出决议的议案》，认为县城环境虽经几次治理，但由于环境意识不强、责任不清晰、制度不健全，监管不到位等，县城脏、乱、差的问题未得到根本解决。会议作出决议：县人民政府及有关职能部门要从县城容貌关系到全县的形象，关系到息烽改革开放、经济发展和精神文明建设的高度提高认识，切实加强领导，把治理县城环境当作攻坚战来打，主要领导要亲自过问，分管领导要具体抓，职能部门要现场抓，通过几年的努力，把县城环境治理好；加强宣传教育，提高公民的环境意识，形成人人爱护环境、保护环境的良好社会风气；城建、工商、交通等有关职能部门要在县人民政府的统一领导下，各司其职，协调配合，排除一切干扰和阻力，保证县城环境治理工作的顺利进行；县人民政府要制定县城环境治理规划，落实措施，分阶段、分步骤地实施解决路面低洼、淤积泥水及垃圾乱倒、污水乱排、车辆乱停乱放、乱搭乱建、占道设摊经营等问题；各有关职能部门要按照各自职责，建立健全规章制度，使管理工作制度化、规范化。

1996年8月20日，县十二届人大常委会第二十三次会议审议县人民政府《关于我县实施法制宣传教育第三个五年计划安排意见的报告》认为，全县法制宣传教育工作经过十年努力，取得一定成效。指出普法工作是一项艰巨的、长期的工作，要持之以恒，常抓不懈，使学法、用法、守法成为全体公民的自觉行动。作出《息烽县实施法制宣传教育第三个五年计划决议》：法制宣传教育是全社会的共同任务，县、乡（镇）人民政府要加强领导，各部门、各系统要各司其职，密切配合，齐抓共管，积极主动地开展法制宣传教育。要重点抓好领导干部、司法人员、行政执法人员、企业经营管理人员、青少年和农村的普法工作。各级国家机关工作人员，特别是领导干部要带头学习法律知识，做学法、守法的模范，影响和带动广大干部群众学法、守法，形成全社会学法、用法、守法的良好风气。司法机关、行政执法机关的执法人员，要精通相关的法律、法规，努力提高自身素质和执法水平，做到有法必依、执法必严、违法必究。各乡镇、各部门、各系统以及农村、企业、机关、学校等，要逐步将社会和经济事务的管理纳入法制轨道，结合实际开展依法治理活动，加快依法治县进程。建立健全执法责任制和监督制约机制。县、乡（镇）人民政府要充实普法工作力量，保证法制宣传必需的经费，改善工作条件，提高法制宣传的效果和质量，要根据普法规划，制定切实可行的实施办法，使普法工作落到实处，做好组织协调、督促检查、分类指导工作。

1998年9月25日，县十三届人大常委会第五次会议作出《关于开展依法治县工作的决定》，指出：开展依法治县，是党领导全县各族人民治理息烽的基本方略，是发展社会主义市场经济的客观需要，是兴县富民、长治久安的重要保障。要按照“有法可依、有法必依、执法必严、违法必究”的社会主义法制的基本要求，围绕经济建设这个中心和改革、发展、稳定的工作大局，发展社会主义民主，健全社会主义法制。全县各族人民在县委的领导下，依照宪法、法律和法规的规定，通过各种途径和形式管理国家事务、经济文化事务和社会事务，推进经济持续、快速、健康发展和社会全面进步。县、乡（镇）人民政府要依照法律、法规和规章赋予的行政管理职权严格依法行政。推行行政执法责任制，做到主体明确、责权明晰、行为规范、奖惩分明，切实解决执法不严、越权执法、滥用职权的问题，努力实现“执法权限法定化、责任明晰化、程序公开化、行为规范化、检查经常化、监督机制完善化”。司法机关必须坚持以事实为根据，以法律为准绳的原则，依法独立行使审判权和检察权，坚决抵制来自各方面的非法干预，防止和克服司法活动中的地方保护主义和部门保护主义。要推行司法人员办案责任制和冤案、错案责任追究制度。要加强律师、公证、仲裁和法律援助工作。抓好执法队伍的思想、纪律和作风建设，坚决查处执法队伍中的腐败分子，清调、辞退不合格人员，努力造就一支政治坚定、业务精通、纪律严明、作风正派、公正廉洁、乐于奉献的高素质执法队伍。县人大常委会要对全县经济、社会发展以及人民群众关注的重大问题，加强对“一府两院”的法律监督和工作监督，有计划、有重点地开展执法检查，组织人大代表视察、评议“一府两院”工作。乡镇人大主席团要按期召开例会，适时听取和审议本级人民政府开展依法治理工作情况报告。要密切同人民群众的联系，组织代表开展视察和评议工作，为依法治县工作提出建议、批评和意见。县人民政府要加强对所属工作部门和乡镇人民政府的行政监督，健全、完善行政监督制度，提高监督实效。县人民法院要加强行政审判工作，维护和监督行政机关依法行使职权。县人民检察院要认真履行法律监督职责，确保公正司法。各级领导干部要带头学法，执法人员、企业经营管理人员要熟悉与本职工作相关的法律法规，提高依法决策、依法管理、依法履职水平，防止和纠正有法不依、执法不严、以言代法、以权压法的行为，维护社会主义法制的统一和权威。各级各部门和基层组织要广泛深入地开展学法和法制宣传教育工作，形成人人知法、懂法、守法、护法的良好风尚。基层政权组织和群众自治性组织，要深入贯彻落实《中华人民共和国村民委员会组织法（试行）》和《中华人民共和国居民委员会组织法》，要坚持和完善村（居）民会议制度或村（居）民代表会议制度，逐步形成民主决策、民主管理、民主监督的规章制度及其运行机制。以财务公开为重点，凡属村民普遍关心的热点问题、村里的重大问题向村（居）民公开，接受群众监督。全县各级国家机关必须在县委的领导下，把依法治理工作列入重要议事日程，动员全社会力量，协调一致，齐抓共管，认真做好依法治县的各项工作。

2005年4月25日，县十四届人大常委会第十六次会议审议县人民政府《关于请求县人大常委会审议项目贷款的报告》后决定：同意县人民政府向贵阳市商业银行息烽县支行贷款200万元，用于县气调保鲜库项目还贷。明确该项目贷款纳入2008年县财政还贷预算。至2010年，县人大常委会根据县人民政府的提请报告（议案），相继作出有关贷款决议15项。次年1月20日，县第十四届人大常委会第二十二次会议作出息烽县与福泉市缔结友好县市决议，会议认为息烽县与福泉市同处黔中腹地，自然条件、资源优势、经济状况、人文环境具有相似性和互补性，为充分发挥地缘优势、资源优势和互补优势，促进两地经济社会共同发展，同意息烽县与福泉市缔结为友好县市。

2010年4月29日，县十五届人大常委会第三十二次会议审议县人民政府提请审议《息烽生态文明县总体规划（2007—2020）》（简称《总体规划》）议案。会议认为，该规划符合《中华人民共和国城市规划法》、建设部《城市总体规划编制办法》等法律法规要求，能够与《贵州省城镇体系规划》《贵阳市城市总体规划》衔接，符合息烽县实际及发展趋势。规划的基础资料较为翔实，发展策略研究基本到位，城市定位定性、总体布局基本合理，功能分区明确，具有前瞻性和可操作性。会议同意《总体规划》由县人民政府按程序上报审批。强调县人民政府要高度重视总体规划修编工作，使空间布局适应息烽经济与产业发展。修改后的规划要及时向社会公布，确保社会公众对规划的知情权、参与权、监督权。要牢固树立“规划先行”的意识，维护规划的严肃性和权威性，扎实推进规划的落实，促进息烽经济社会全面协调可持续发展。

三、人事任免

（一）任免程序

20世纪90年代，县人大常委会任免国家机关工作人员，由提请机关提出书面报告，并附被提请任免干部简历和考察材料，提请机关或县委组织部门派员到会介绍相关情况，负责解答与会人员提问。县人大常委会组成人员经过审议，采用无记名投票方式表决，以获得常委会全体组成人员过半数赞成票始得通过。表决通过的行文通知提请机关，并对外公布，颁发由县人大常委会主任签署的任命书。每届人大换届后，常委会任命的县政府办公室主任、局长等组成人员提请县人大常委会重新任命。县人大常委会工作机构主任、副主任和县人民法院副院长、庭长、副庭长、审判委员会委员、审判员，人民检察院副检察长、检察委员会委员、检察员等，职务未作变动的，不再重新任命。在人民代表大会闭会期间，县人大常委会接受县人大常委会组成人员，县长、副县长，县人民法院院长、人民检察院检察长辞职的，报下一次人民代表大会备案。2003年4月起，“一府两院”提请任命的国家机关工作人员，任命表决前，须通过法律知识考试和作拟供职报告。未参加法律考试或考试不合格者，暂缓提请任命表决。2005年9月起，任命表决通过者，须手持《中华人民共和国宪法》面向国徽举行就职宣誓仪式。

（二）人事任免辑要

1990—2010年，县十一至十五届人大常委会任命国家机关工作人员466人次，免职136人次，接受辞职28人，任命人民陪审员19人次，决定代理职务6人；任免的县级人事67人次中，任命35人次，决定代理职务11人，决定接受辞去职务16人次，免去职务5人。

1991—2010年县级人事任免统计表

表5-1-3

姓　名	时间	会议次／届	人事类别	职务
周治权	1991年9月	9／十一	决定任命	县人民政府科技副县长
戴敬嘉	1991年9月	9／十一	决定接受	辞去县人民法院院长
陈福文	1991年9月	9／十一	决定代理	县人民法院院长
罗筑云	1992年1月	12／十一	决定接受	辞去县人民政府副县长
黑卫平	1992年2月	13／十一	决定任命	县人民政府副县长
			决定代理	县人民政府县长
倪　田	1992年2月	29／十一	决定免去	县人民政府副县长
周治权	1993年7月	2／十二	决定任命	县人民政府副县长
黑卫平	1994年1月	6／十二	决定接受	辞去县人民政府县长
李贵菊	1994年1月	6／十二	决定代理	县人民政府县长
李光祥	1994年2月	7／十二	决定任命	县人民政府副县长
周治权	1994年6月	9／十二	决定免去	县人民政府副县长
魏宗华	1994年8月	10／十二	决定任命	县人民政府副县长
张巧楠	1995年4月	14／十二	决定任命	县人民政府副县长
杨洪志	1995年2月	17／十二	决定接受	辞去县人大常委会副主任
艾克勇	1996年6月	22／十二	决定任命	县人民政府副县长
潘　剑	1996年6月	22／十二	决定任命	县人民政府副县长
魏燕飞	1996年12月	25／十二	决定任命	县人民政府副县长
陈福文	1997年12月	31／十二	决定接受	辞去县人民法院院长
关晓明	1997年12月	31／十二	任命	县人民法院副院长
			决定代理	县人民法院院长
何志坚	1997年12月	31／十二	任命	县人民检察院副检察长
			决定代理	县人民检察院检察长

续表

姓　名	时间	会议次/届	人事类别	职务
魏明禄	1998年3月	33/十二	决定接受	辞去县人民政府副县长
韦奕松	1998年6月	2/十三	决定任命	县人民政府副县长
吴仲萍	1998年6月	2/十三	决定任命	县人民政府副县长
胡晓光	1999年4月	11/十三	决定任命	县人民政府副县长
徐　勇	1999年4月	11/十三	决定任命	县人民政府副县长
陈长发	2000年7月	21/十三	决定接受	辞去县人民政府县长
杨彦峰	2000年7月	21/十三	决定任命	县人民政府副县长
			决定代理	县人民政府县长
丁旭东	2000年9月	23/十三	决定任命	县人民政府副县长
杨明晋	2000年9月	23/十三	决定接受	辞去县人民政府副县长
关晓明	2000年12月	26/十三	免去	县人民法院院长
张耀辉	2000年12月	26/十三	任命	县人民法院副院长
			代理	县人民法院院长
魏永祥	2001年1月	27/十三	决定任命	县人民政府副县长
何志坚	2001年1月	27/十三	决定接受	辞去县人民检察院检察长
莫　智	2001年1月	27/十三	代理	县人民检察院检察长
陈旭东	2001年4月	29/十三	决定任命	县人民政府副县长
王宇飞	2002年5月	40/十三	决定任命	县人民政府副县长
范祖燕	2003年11月	5/十四	决定任命	县人民政府副县长
黄永辉	2004年4月	9/十四	决定任命	县人民政府副县长
			决定接受	县人大常委会副主任
魏发志	2004年4月	9/十四	决定接受	辞去县人民政府副县长
范祖燕	2005年11月	21/十四	决定接受	辞去县人民政府副县长
任国元	2006年1月	21/十四	决定接受	县人大常委会副主任
丁旭东	2006年3月	24/十四	决定接受	辞去县人民政府县长
黄秋斌	2006年3月	24/十四	决定任命	县人民政府副县长
			决定代理	县人民政府县长
李福燕	2006年9月	30/十四	决定任命	县人民政府副县长
李华斌	2006年9月	30/十四	决定任命	县人民政府副县长
钟　雷	2006年9月	30/十四	任命	县人民检察院副检察长
			决定代理	县人民检察院检察长
曹垒发	2008年4月	12/十五	决定任命	县人民政府副县长

续表

姓　名	时间	会议次／届	人事类别	职务
刘凤刚	2008年6月	14／十五	决定任命	县人民政府副县长
			决定接受	辞去县人大常委会副主任
佘　龙	2008年6月	14／十五	决定免去	县人民政府副县长
黄秋斌	2009年1月	20／十五	决定接受	辞去县人民政府县长
张定超	2009年1月	20／十五	决定任命	县人民政府副县长
			决定代理	县人民政府县长
李红卫	2009年5月	24／十五	决定任命	县人民政府副县长
曾文平	2009年6月	25／十五	决定任命	县人民政府副县长
梁小江	2009年9月	27／十五	决定任命	县人民政府副县长
刘　彤	2010年9月	34／十五	决定任命	县人民政府副县长
李泽祥	2010年9月	34／十五	决定任命	县人民政府副县长
梁小江	2010年9月	34／十五	决定免职	县人民政府副县长

四、议案建议办理

20世纪90年代初，人大代表议案、建议办理，主要由常委会工作部门分类整理后，转“一府两院”办理，办理结果书面答复代表。常委会每年适时安排听取办理情况报告。1998年，县人大常委会《办理县人大代表建议　批评和意见的办理办法》出台后，对“一府两院”及其承办单位办理人大代表建议、批评和意见作出时限规定，制发“息烽县人大代表建议、批评和意见办理情况征询意见表”，代表对办理答复意见不满意的，承办单位与代表联系，听取代表意见，作出解释或重新办理。2003年起，常委会代表工作机构每年与县政府办公室联合召开人大代表建议交办会，对代表建议实行集中交办。2004年后，对涉及全县经济社会发展，人民群众关心关注、带有普遍性和办理难度大的代表建议，实行常委会主任会议督办制度。1991—2010年，共收到人大代表议案2件，建议、批评和意见2393件，办复率100%，代表满意率96%以上。

1995年3月，县十二届人大三次会议期间，代表提出治理县城脏、乱、差的建议，人大常委会组织代表对县城脏、乱、差进行视察，作出《关于治理县城环境的决议》。对此，县政府及时召集有关部门召开会议，安排部署县城环境治理工作，签订目标管理责任书。2006年3月，县十四届人大五次会议期间，代表提出《调查处理息烽磷矿与石头田村民组矿山地界纠纷》的建议，经常委会主任会议督办，承办单位通过召开协调会，邀请技术人员对矿山地界进行实地放样测量，确认企业采矿是否超越地籍界线，并埋桩定界，使一桩多年未解决的矿山地界纠纷得到较好解决。2009年，开展代表建议评比表彰活动，有10名优秀代表、10条代表好建议和10个办理代表建议先进单位受到表彰。

五、信访办理

20世纪90年代，县人大常委会信访工作，坚持“分级负责，归口办理”原则，及时转办、交办和跟踪督办。2003年10月，县人大常委会印发《息烽县人民代表大会常务委员会关于县人大常委会和县政府、县人民法院、县人民检察院领导干部下基层接待人民群众来信来访的决定》，要求县人大常委会和“一府两院”建立领导干部下基层接待人民群众来信来访制度，每季度分别下基层接待人民群众来信来访不得少于一次，实行挂牌接待。2005年9月，县人大常委会印发《息烽县人民代表大会常务委员会联合接待人民群众来访意见》《息烽县人民代表大会常务委员会转办交办信访事项办理意见》，明确县人大常委会、县政府组成人员，县人民法院、县人民检察院班子成员联合接待人民群众来访，每月15日为联合接待日。

1990年3月至2010年4月，共接待人民群众来信来访2949件，做到该解释的解释，该答复的答复，该协调的协调，该转办的转办，该责成有关部门办理的责成有关部门办理，件件有着落，事事有回音。

第五节　乡镇人民代表大会

1992年，建镇并乡撤区后，乡镇行政区域变更，新建乡镇进行人大换届选举，届次统一为第一届。1992—2002年，乡镇人大每届任期3年，此后每届任期5年，并与县级人大换届同步进行。至2010年，共进行6次换届选举。

息烽县1992—2006年乡镇人大换届选举情况统计表

表5-1-4　　单位：人

年份	届次	人大代表	乡镇人大主席团			乡镇政府	
			主席	副主席	成员	乡镇长	副乡镇长
1992	一	497	10	7	42	10	22
1993	二	538	10	7	36	10	28
1996	三	541	10	7	39	10	37
1999	四	543	10	18	47	10	37
2002	五	551	10	15	50	10	40
2006	六	551	10	10	50	10	29

第二章　人民政府

1991—2010年，县政府围绕县委的决策部署，执行县人大的决议决定，坚持以经济建设为中心，组织政府工作部门实施科教兴县、工业强县、环境立县、旅游活县战略。举全县之力，打好扶贫攻坚战。大力招商引资，狠抓产业结构调整，不断推进经济和社会事业向前发展。2002年，国内生产总值完成11.86亿元，产业结构从1997年的38.3∶36.5∶25.2调整到2002年的20.7∶57∶22.3，实现从“一、二、三”到“二、三、一”的历史性跨越。2004年地方财政收入突破亿元大关，为1.11亿元。2008年进入全省建设经济强县行列。2010年，全县国内生产总值55.49亿元，县地方财政收入突破3亿元。

第一节 县政府班子

县政府班子由县长、副县长组成。县长、副县长由县人民代表大会选举产生，并随县人民代表大会换届而换届。届中有政府班子成员人事变动时，县长由县人大常委会决定代理县长履行县长职务或召开县人民代表大会补选产生；副县长由县人大常委会任命产生。上级下派的科技、挂职副县长履行法律程序后到岗履职。1991—2010年，县政府班子经历5次换届。

县政府十一至十五届县长、副县长名录

表5-2-1

届次	姓　名	性别	学历	职务	任职时间	备注
第十一届	陈建忠	男	大学	县长	1990年4月—1992年2月	
	罗筑云	男	大专	副县长	1990年4月—1992年1月	
	李贵菊	女	大专	副县长	1990年4月—1993年4月	
	龚德昭	男	大学	副县长	1990年4月—1993年4月	
	蒋光国	男	大专	副县长	1990年4月—1993年4月	
	黄银忠	男	大专	副县长	1990年4月—1993年4月	
	倪　田	男	大专	副县长	1990年8月—1993年2月	挂职
	周治权	男	大专	副县长	1991年9月—1993年4月	科技副县长
	黑卫平	男	大学	副县长、代理县长	1992年2月—1993年4月	
第十二届	黑卫平	男	大学	县长	1993年4月—1994年1月	
	李贵菊	女	大专	副县长	1993年4月—1994年1月	
				副县长、代理县长	1994年1月—1994年3月	
				县长	1994年3月—1998年3月	
	黄银忠	男	大专	副县长	1993年4月—1998年3月	
	魏明禄	男	大专	副县长	1993年4月—1998年3月	
	杨明晋	男	大专	副县长	1993年4月—1998年3月	
	周治权	男	大专	副县长	1993年7月—1994年6月	
	李光祥	男	大专	副县长	1994年2月—1998年3月	
	魏宗华	男		副县长	1994年8月—	
	张巧楠	女	大专	副县长	1995年4月—1997年3月	挂职
	潘　剑	男	大学	副县长	1996年6月—1997年6月	挂职
	艾克勇	男	大专	副县长	1996年6月—1997年6月	挂职
	魏燕飞	男	大专	副县长	1996年12月—1998年3月	
	王定一	男	大学	副县长	1997月—	挂职

续表

届次	姓　名	性别	学历	职务	任职时间	备注
第十三届	陈长发	男	大专	县长	1998年3月—2000年7月	
	杨彦峰	男	大专	副县长、代理县长	2000年7月—2001年2月	
				县长	2001年2月—2003年3月	
	黄银忠	男	大专	副县长	1998年3月—2003年3月	
	杨明晋	男	大专	副县长	1998年3月—2000年9月	
	李光祥	男	大专	副县长	1998年3月—2003年3月	
	魏燕飞	男	大专	副县长	1998年3月—2003年3月	
	胡　勇	男	大专	副县长	1998年3月—2003年3月	
	刘正菊	女	大专	副县长	1998年3月—2003年3月	
	韦奕松	男		副县长	1998年6月—2001年5月	挂职
	吴仲泮	女		副县长	1998年6月—2001年5月	挂职
	胡晓光	男		副县长	1999年4月—	挂职
	徐　勇	男		副县长	1999年4月—	挂职
	丁旭东	男	研究生	副县长	2000年9月—2003年3月	
	魏永祥	男	大专	副县长	2001年1月—2003年3月	
	陈旭东	男		副县长	2001年4月—2003年3月	挂职
	糜　亚	男	大专	副县长	2002年1月—2003年1月	挂职
	王宇飞	男	大专	副县长	2002年5月—2003年3月	挂职
第十四届	丁旭东	男	研究生	县长	2003年3月—2006年5月	
	魏永祥	男	大专	副县长	2001年1月—2006年11月	
	魏发志	男	大学	副县长	2003年3月—2004年4月	
	赵永祥	男		副县长	2003年3月—2006年1月	
	蔡　飞	男	大专	副县长	2003年3月—2004年10月	
	刘正菊	女	大专	副县长	2003年3月—2006年11月	
	范祖燕	女	大学	副县长	2003年11月—2005年11月	
	黄秋斌	男	大学	副县长、代理县长	2006年5月—2006年11月	
	黄永辉	男	大学	副县长	2004年4月—2006年11月	
	李福燕	女	大学	副县长	2006年9月—2006年11月	
	李华斌	男	大学	副县长	2006年9月—2006年11月	
	李红卫	男	大专	副县长	2006年3月—2006年11月	

续表

届次	姓　名	性别	学历	职务	任职时间	备注
第十五届	黄秋斌	男	大学	县长	2006年11月—2009年1月	
	张定超	男	研究生	副县长、代理县长	2009年1月—2009年3月	
				县长	2009年3月—	
	黄永辉	男	大学	副县长	2006年11月—	
	李福燕	女	大学	副县长	2006年9月—	
	李华斌	男	大学	副县长	2006年9月—	
	李红卫	男	大专	副县长	2006年11月—2009年5月	
	杜洪远	男	大专	副县长	2006年11月—	
	佘　龙	男	研究生	副县长	2006年11月—2008年6月	
	刘凤刚	男	大学	副县长	2008年6月—	
	曹垒发	男		副县长	2008年4月—	挂职
	曾文平	男		副县长	2009年6月—2010年3月	
	梁小江	男		副县长	2009年9月—2010年9月	挂职
	刘　彤	女		副县长	2010年9月—	挂职
	李泽洋	男		副县长	2010年9月—	挂职

第二节　县政府工作机构

一、直属机构

1991年，县政府工作部门有政府办公室、农业区划办、移民办、县志办、人防战备办和外事办、计划委员会、经济委员会、农村经济委员会、科学技术委员会、民族事务委员会、体育运动委员会、计划生育委员会、民政局、人事局、劳动局、公安局、司法局、档案局、统计局、物资局、物价局、城乡建设环境保护局、土地管理局、监察局、财政局、税务局、工商行政管理局、标准计量管理局、审计局、轻工业局、交通局、粮食局、商业局、农业局、林业局、水利电力局、畜牧局、农业机械管理局、乡镇企业管理局、教育局、文化局、广播电视局、卫生局、气象局、烟草专卖局。

1994年税务局分设为国税局、地税局。

此后，县政府工作机构历经1995年、2001年、2004年、2010年四次机构改革，有撤、并、整合、重组及新建（详见本志第四篇第三章机构编制）。

2010年，县政府工作机构设置为：政府办公室、发展改革经贸局（科技局、煤炭管理局、知识产权局）、教育局、民族事务局（县宗教事务局）、公安局、监察局（与县纪律检查委员会机关合署办公，列入县政府工作部门序列，不计入县政府机构个数）、民政局、司法局、财政局、人力资源和社会保障局、国土资源局、环境保护局、住房和城乡建设局、交通运输局、农业局、水利局、旅游文体广播电视局（县新闻出版局、县版权局）、卫生和食品药品监督管理局、人口和计划生育局、审计局、林业绿化局、统计局、安全生产监督管理局。

直属事业单位：水利水电工程移民局、档案局（县档案馆、地方志编纂委员会办公室）。

办事机构：社会治安综合治理办公室、禁毒办公室、烤烟生产办公室、教育督导室。

其他机构：县供销合作社联合社。

二、派出机构

1991年11月前，县政府派出机构有：永阳、养龙、九庄、黑神庙4个区公所及永靖镇（区级镇）人民政府，是年12月，因撤区并乡建镇而撤销。

三、乡（镇）人民政府

1991年11月，息烽县实施撤区并乡建镇，撤销原4区1镇（永阳区、养龙区、九庄区、黑神庙区、永靖镇）、24个乡镇（三田乡、梨安乡、下阳朗乡、阳朗乡、底寨乡、西山乡、青山苗族乡、养龙司乡、安江乡、茅坡乡、温泉乡、九庄镇、九庄乡、竹花乡、新杨乡、鹿窝乡、石硐乡、猫场乡、何家硐乡、小寨坝乡、南极乡、王家坪乡、流长乡、土城坝乡）建制，组建4镇（永靖镇、小寨坝镇、温泉镇、九庄镇）6乡（西山乡、养龙司乡、流长乡、石硐乡、鹿窝乡、青山苗族乡）。1992年上半年，各新建乡（镇）相继进行人大换届选举，选举产生乡（镇）长10名、副乡（镇）长22名。2006年，各乡（镇）人大进行第六次换届选举，选举产生乡（镇）长10名、副乡（镇）长29名。至2010年，各乡镇政府历经6届。

第三节　县政府会议

一、政府全体（扩大）会议

县政府全体（扩大）会议每半年举行一次，必要时由县长或县长办公会决定临时召开。会议由政府全体组成人员出席，政府办公室副主任和负有行政职能的部门、公司及重点企业负责人列席。会议由县长或常务副县长召集和主持。主要内容是传达贯彻县人大及其常委会的决议、上级国家行政机关有关决定和命令，制定行政措施；通报全县经济和社会发展情况；讨论和决定县政府重要工作部署；讨论和通过需要全体会议决定的事项。1991—2010年，全体会议内容主要有：讨论《国民经济和社会发展五年计（规）划》《政府工作报告》《国民经济和社会发展计划执行情况及次年计划安排（草案）》，产业结构调整，招商引资，推进工业经济发展，抓好农业农村工作，落实旅游活县战略，构建稳定环境和转变工作作风等。

二、常务会议

常务会议一般一月召开一次，必要时可临时召开。由县长、副县长、政府办公室主任、督查室主任组成，必要时各乡镇长及县政府有关工作部门负责人列席。由县长或县长委托常务副县长主持。主要内容是传达上级党委、政府及县委的重要指示、决定和会议精神，研究贯彻执行措施；研究执行县人民代表大会及其常委会的有关决议；讨论和审定向上级党委、政府及县委的请示、报告和以政府名义发布的决定；讨论提请县人民代表大会及其常委会审议的议案和重要报告；讨论决定各乡镇政府、县政府各工作部门请示县政府的重要事项；通报经济和社会各方面重要工作情况；讨论决定政府工作中其他重要问题。1991年12月6日，县政府召开常务会议，研究烤烟生产有关事宜。议定：继续抓好烤烟专卖法宣传，组织一次较大规模的宣传活动，活动方案由烟草局拟定，所需经费由烟草局负责；1992年烤烟生产所需复合肥，县供销、农资部门务必于1992年1月组织到位。安顺地区烟草局划拨的180吨复合肥，原则上由县烟草局掌握安排；1991年的烤烟税，烟草系统务必于12月底前全部结清；县烤烟办整理1989年烤烟生产奖励相关资料，写出报告提交下次常务会议研究，1991年烤烟生产奖励兑现问题，由县烤烟办写出报告，按县发文件规定，研究后给区、乡明确；1992年烤烟生产任务按新建的四镇六乡分配，提前安排落实。

三、县长办公会议

县长办公会议一般两周召开一次，由县长、副县长、县政府办公室主任、督查室主任组成，必要时有关部门参加。由县长或县长委托副县长召集和主持。主要研究、通报政府工作中的重要情况和问题。

1991年8月31日，县政府召开县长办公会，研究和讨论开发西山有关事宜等，议定：开发西山分三步走，坚持以山养山原则。第一步建3000亩中药材基地，其次考虑水、电、路“三通”问题，第三步恢复名胜古迹，发展旅游业。实行承包开发。由县政府代表区、乡、村、组及部分农户与开发（承包）方签订协议，具体范围由林业、水电、城建、土管、文化、交通、农经委研究划定；开发用工由县劳动部门提出参照意见，在同等条件下，优先考虑西山乡剩余劳动力；由林业、水电、城建、土管、文化、交通等部门根据有关法律法规作好开发西山近期及远景的山、水、林、田、路及旅游综合规划，注意名胜古迹、古树名木和珍稀动、植物的保护；承包方须在10月1日进山动工。

1995年8月3日，县政府召开县长办公会，研究部署全县抗旱保苗、抗旱救灾工作。会议认为，自7月10日始，全县旱情持续20余天，平均气温高达30℃以上，严重影响全县农作物生长和群众生产生活。会议决定：迅速把当前农村工作的重点转移到抗旱保苗、抗旱救灾、抓好烤烟收购和作好“三秋”生产准备上来，集中精力，组织群众，全面搞好农村工作。成立3个抗旱工作组，分赴乡镇开展抗旱工作：向乡镇和群众传达全县旱情及近期天气预报情况，帮助群众树立长期抗旱夺丰收思想，立即行动起来，搞好抗旱保苗和抗旱救灾；现场解决抗旱工作中的实际问题；帮助乡镇搞好计划用水，协调解决用水纠纷等。

1998年8月19日，县政府县长办公会研究《息烽县农村合作医疗实施方案》。会议决定，该工作先选择小寨坝镇搞试点，总结经验后再行文全面组织实施。农村合作医疗组织必须实行建管结合，不能重建轻管。以村卫生室为重点，统筹各医疗单位的收费标准，认真解决群众看病难和看不起病等问题，确保实现国务院提出的2000年人人享有初级医疗卫生的保健目标。11月30日，县政府县长办公会研究县国有企业改革改制有关问题。会议决定，国有企业改革，要认真执行国务院1998年1月5日电报精神，制定贯彻实施意见由县政府另行行文。关于高负担（资产少人员多）企业的改制，原则同意改制领导小组的思路，有关部门要认真执行。关于中西药公司职工拖欠公款问题，列为清欠重点。会议研究县人民医院转让贵州盛康医药有限责任公司股权、县中西药公司和县印刷厂改革方案的批复。

1999年7月2日，县政府县长办公会研究东门小区规划，会议决定，小区规划的道路占地与小区规划布局要科学合理，必须有利于小区的开发和利用。规划要留出足够的空地和绿化带，并尽量与道路相连接。原规划的体育场用地应考虑用作商业用地。

2009年11月4日，县政府召开县长办公会，听取县甲型H1N1（一种RNA病毒，属于正黏液病毒科）流感疫情防控领导小组办公室汇报息烽县甲型H1N1流感防控工作情况，研究相关工作。议定：

各乡镇、各部门要高度重视甲型H1N1流感防控工作，坚持预防为主，构建和完善防控甲型H1N1流感的组织体系和工作机制；加大宣传力度，提高群众对甲型H1N1流感防控知识知晓率，发动群众自觉防控；进一步强化各项防控制度和措施的落实，确保防控工作有序、有力开展；抓好防控物资储备，防患于未然；医疗部门要积极治疗甲型H1N1流感确诊病例，力争不出现重症病例，确保不出现死亡病例；报县委常委会审定。

2009年12月30日，县政府召开县长办公会，安排元旦期间相关工作。议定：继续抓好“整脏治乱”、道路保洁工作，加大对车辆乱停乱放巡查力度，确保交通井然有序。各单位、各乡镇要通过悬挂彩旗、灯笼、空飘和布置花坛等方式，营造整洁、靓丽、有序的节日氛围；全力抓好安全生产工作。县安全监管、乡企、建设、交通、公安等相关部门加强对煤矿、危险化学品、道路交通、建筑工地等的监管，确保万无一失。县交通、公安部门继续加大上路巡查力度，坚决查处超速行驶、疲劳驾驶、酒后驾驶、超员超载等违章违法行为。县消防、安全监管等部门加强娱乐场所的消防安全检查，防止发生安全事故，切实维护社会稳定。抓好全县社会治安工作，防止发生影响恶劣的治安、刑事案件，扎实做好信访维稳工作，坚决打击违法上访行为；切实安排好困难群众的生产生活。特别是对五保户等弱势群体，县直相关部门和各乡镇要加大救灾救济力度，广泛开展形式多样的帮扶帮助和送温暖、送爱心活动；认真做好疾病防控，特别是要做好甲型H1N1流感等重大传染性疾病防控，切实保障人民群众身体健康；县直各部门、各乡镇要严格执行节日期间值班和领导带班制度，严禁擅离职守，确保信息畅通；要厉行节约，自觉执行中央、省、市、县有关廉洁自律规定。

四、政府专题会议

政府专题会议主要研究处理县政府日常工作中的具体业务问题，听取有关工作汇报或情况通报；安排近期某项工作；研究处理各乡镇政府、县政府各工作部门向县政府专题请示事项以及协调部门之间的重要问题。专题会议由县长或副县长主持，根据会议内容通知县政府有关工作部门以及中央、省、市驻县单位和部门负责人参加。1991—2010年，政府每年召开专题会议的次数不等，多数年份在50～70次，2009年超过100次，2010年达到181次。

第四节　施政辑要

一、农业和农村经济

1991—1997年，县第十一、十二届政府围绕“一粮二烟三开发”发展思路，发展农村经济，增加农民收入，解决人民群众温饱问题。深化农村改革，继续稳定和完善家庭联产承包责任制。实施以坡改梯和兴修水利为主要内容的农田基本建设。推广“两杂”良种和旱地分带轮作、两段育秧、配方施肥、综合病虫害防治农业适用技术，提高粮食产量。烤烟生产采取定点扶持、让利基层、集中连片、规模经营，推广营养块、袋育苗移栽及打顶抹芽等新技术，提高质量，增加烟农收入。出台发展农村庭院经济意见，鼓励支持农民发展种植、养殖和加工业，发展多种经营。实施农业综合开发，在温泉、西山、小寨坝、石硐等乡镇发展柑橘、葡萄、梨、桃等经果种植。其间，1996年全县粮食总产量68993吨，创历史最高水平。至1997年，累计完成坡改梯4.38万亩，治理沙土流失19.55平方千米。兴建小水池900口4.58立方米，治理金家厂、烂泥沟等一批病险水库，新增和恢复灌溉面积4.17万亩。2003年，十四届政府以农民增收为核心，优化农业产业结构，以味美、美满等农产品加工企业为龙头，捆绑项目、资金，扩大订单农业。推进种植、养殖业向特色化、规模化、市场化发展。推行“政府引导、企业带动、农户种植、协会经营”的模式和种植、养殖业小区化建设。2005年，全县实现全面免征农业税。2009年，十五届政府与贵州开磷有限责任公司合作，实施“政企联合、以工哺农”政策，在全县推广“三良”（良种+良肥+良法）工程。至2010年，种植水稻133.7万亩、玉米19.4万亩、油菜21.4万亩、马铃薯5.8万亩，农民人均纯收入5084元。

二、乡镇企业

1991年，县政府出台《关于加快乡镇企业发展步伐的有关规定》，提出建立县、区、乡三级乡镇企业管理机构，完善管理制度，推行以产量、产值、收入、税金、利润、安全6项指标为主要内容的经济责任制和岗位责任制。要求各有关部门为乡镇企业发展创造宽松外部环境，用足、用好、用活上级有关发展乡镇企业政策，严禁任何单位和个人向企业乱摊派、乱收费，平调财产。对乡镇企业实行经营范围、经营区域和生产经营方式放宽。在税收政策上给予优惠。对新办乡镇企业，从投产之时起，免征1年的产品税、增值税或营业税。对在西山、青山、梨安、新场、南极、茅坡、猫场、石硐、何家硐、王家坪等15个边远乡镇企业不发达乡新建的乡镇企业，按实际生产时间，免征两年的产品税、增值税或营业税，免征4年所得税。对引进乡镇企业技术和管理人才，征收二分之一个人调节税。鼓励各级党政干部、离退休职工和科技人员兴办、领办、协办乡镇企业。对国家分配到乡镇企业工作的大中专毕业生，享受国家正式干部待遇，符合条件的提前半年转正，上浮一级工资，户口留在县城。采取“农民集资、引进外资、乡村借垫、财政补贴、金融扶持”，鼓励使用扶贫贷款和建立乡镇企业发展基金等多渠道筹措资金发展乡镇企业。采取国家、集体、个体一起上，乡、村、组、联户、个体“五个轮子”一起转，多种形式发展乡镇企业。至1992年，全县建成乡镇企业2695个（个体2402个），从业人员9506人，实现总产值7736万元。

1993年3—6月，县政府相继出台《关于鼓励乡镇企业引进人才的规定》《关于鼓励引进资金的暂行规定》（关于外商投资的暂行办法），规定：引进管理人才承包1个企业或1个车间，年新增税后利润5万元以下的，每年提取利润的10%奖励本人；年新增利润5～20万元、20万元以上的，分别每年提取利润的15%、20%奖励本人。为县内乡镇企业牵线搭桥，从国外引进新项目、新技术、新产品成功的，连续5年按当年实现税后利润的5%～8%提取奖金；辞去公职到县乡镇企业工作的，经考核重新吸收为国家干部，工龄连续计算，办理入户手续；鼓励和支持县直机关、企事业单位人员到县乡镇企业工作，保留原住房；引进境外资金兴办生产性企业、公益性事业的，每5万元可申办1名“农转非”户口；通过申报经济建设项目引进国家无偿投资的，县乡两级财政按谁受益谁奖励办法，给予引资总额5‰～10‰的奖励；对外商投资企业用地实行有偿出让，享受出让价10%～25%的优惠或出让方以地价入股等。实施“多轮驱动，多轨运行”策略发展乡镇企业。1996年7月30日，息烽县获贵州省1995年度发展乡镇企业“图强县”称号。1997年，全县乡镇企业实现总产值6.41亿元。1998年，息烽县再次获贵州省发展乡镇企业“图强县”称号。

三、劳动就业

1991年4月29日，县政府印发关于做好劳动就业通知，提出支持集体企业发展多种经营，开辟生产门路和新产品，开辟就业岗位，安排本单位待业子女就业；发展服务型行业和劳动密集型企业，鼓励支持各单位组织各种形式的服务型企业，安置待业人员就业；提倡鼓励待业人员自谋职业；积极组织劳务输出，鼓励待业青年到沿海地区务工；实行安置就业目标责任制，各单位待业人员原则上自行消化，矛盾不上交；对外来劳动力实行“务工许可证”制度；实行优惠扶持政策，鼓励企业安置待业人员就业。5月3日，县政府印发《息烽县社会劳动力管理暂行规定》，对社会劳动力管理对象、办法及有关收费标准作出明确规定。1997年，十二届政府成立解困与再就业工程领导小组，当年，安置失业人员和下岗职工127人。1998年8月24日，县委办、县政府办印发《息烽县再就业服务组织实施意见》，成立“息烽县再就业服务中心”与“息烽县职业介绍所”，统一指导全县国有企业下岗职工的再就业工作。27日，县委、县政府出台《关于进一步落实“两个确保”做好国有企业下岗职工再就业工作的实施意见》。至2000年，安置下岗再就业人员342人。2008年2月25日，十五届政府印发《息烽县创建充分就业社区工作实施意见》，提出：创建充分就业社区，以促进社会和谐为核心，以实现劳动者充分就业为目标，全面落实促进就业政策，广开就业门路，拓宽就业渠道，建立促进就业再就业工作长效机制。社区有劳动能力和就业愿望的登记失业人员就业率达98%以上，无持续失业一年以上登记失业人员；对“零就业家庭”做到出现一户，帮扶一户，解决一户，稳定一户，社区内“零就业家庭”动态管理为零；辖区内有培训要求的失业人员和其他求职人员参加技能培训和创业培训，参训率100%。是年，创建充分就业社区2个。至2010年，创建充分就业社区9个。

四、财政体制改革

1992年6月10日，县政府出台《息烽县乡级财政包干体制管理办法》，规定县、乡两级财政实行“分级包干，分灶吃饭”“核定基数，收支包干，定额上解，超收分成”管理。1994年10月10日，出台《息烽县乡级财政体制管理办法》，规定乡级财政收支范围，核定上解、补助定额，取消超基数分成规定，执行分税制财政管理体制。2005年5月8日，县政府印发《息烽县乡镇财政体制管理实施意见》，提出乡镇财政体制管理实行划分收支范围、核定基数、实行激励机制、定额上解、超收分成、基数补助、自求平衡。根据乡镇不同情况采取不同管理形式：以收入基数加两税返还、所得税基数返还和转移支付补助减刚性支出、农村税费改革转移支付安排的支出、教育附加和城市维护建设税专项上解、公务费、医疗费后余额部分的一半作为定额上解。每年对超过收入基数部分实行县乡镇分成。其中：永靖镇、温泉镇、小寨坝镇按4∶6分成，西山乡、石硐乡按2∶8分成；青山苗族乡财政收入县级不参与分成，自求平衡；九庄镇实行定额补助基数10万元，逐年按10%递增补助；养龙司乡、流长乡、鹿窝乡实行财政体制补助，以第一年补助为基数，逐年按10%递增补助。

五、实施扶贫攻坚计划

1993年，全县有贫困人口14.04万人，占农业人口的70%，其中人均年纯收入200元以下的极贫人口7.4万人，201～300元的3.89万人，在301～400元的2.74万人。1994年“国家八七扶贫攻坚计划”将息烽县列入全国592个贫困县后，中央、省、市相继派出新华社、省委宣传部、省财政厅、省审计厅及37家省、部属、市属企事业单位到息烽开展定点帮扶和帮村扶贫，贵阳市云岩区与息烽开展结对帮扶。县成立以县委书记为组长、县长为副组长，有关职能部门负责人为成员的扶贫开发领导小组，明确8家驻县工矿企业、38个县直机关、事业单位，帮扶71个贫困村和13个经济不发达村。抽调机关干部组成扶贫工作队，深入村、组、农户帮助指导制订脱贫计划，采取县领导联系乡镇、单位包村，干部包户，不脱贫不脱钩办法开展扶贫攻坚。引进扶贫资金和项目，加大对贫困地区交通、通信、水利、卫生、教育等基础设施建设力度，改善贫困地区的生产条件和生活环境。发展种植、养殖、加工业，组织劳务输出增加农民收入。至1996年，全县农民人均纯收入1200元，人均占有粮食335千克，有7.26万贫困人口基本解决温饱，成为全省48个国定贫困县中率先解决温饱的6个县之一。1997年起，扶贫工作进入攻坚阶段，县、乡两级实行“一把手”负责制，层层签订目标责任书，实行目标管理。开展农业实用技术、农民绿色证书和农村劳动力非农技能培训，增强贫困地区和贫困户自身“造血”能力。1998年后，县十三届政府加大扶贫力度，拓宽扶贫渠道，转变和完善扶贫方式，对贫困村组和贫困户采取从资金扶持、寻找路子、科技投入、物质注入、劳务输出、农产品销售等方面给予帮扶；增加贫困地区基础设施建设投入，进一步改善生产条件和生活环境。至2000年，投入水利建设资金6500万元，兴建水库5座，治理病险水库11座，修建一批小水池和人饮工程；累计完成坡改梯8.35万亩、沼气池4900口、改厕10857座、改圈4000间。全县贫困人口除极少数特殊困难人口外，温饱问题基本解决。开展“135”帮扶和创建小康乡镇、小康村活动。提前两年实现国家“八七扶贫攻坚计划”目标。2002年，息烽县正式摘掉国定贫困县帽子。

六、调整产业结构

1998年起，县政府通过发展特色农业和订单农业，实施种植、养殖业基地建设，提升农业在县域经济建设中的基础地位，相继建成优质烤烟、双低油菜、优质西瓜、秋淡蔬菜基地和养龙司万亩无公害蔬菜等基地建设，全县有12个村被贵阳市命名为“无公害农产品生产基地”；建立仔猪繁殖基地、肉牛养殖基地、奶牛基地、网箱养鱼和生态养鱼基地；建立招商引资机构，落实招商引资“一站式”服务承诺制，按照“引得进，留得住，能发展”的招商引资工作指导方针，实施政策招商、服务招商、全民招商、项目招商、形象招商、网络招商、“外脑”招商、以商引商策略，实行招商引资“一把手工程”制度、引资项目跟踪落实责任制、政府与企业的双向承包制度、监督检查制度、招商引资奖励制度等五项举措，营建良好的招商引资“软环境”。2000年后，县委、县政府先后提出“提高一产，主攻二产，加速发展三产”和“唯有招商引资，唯有抓项目建设，唯有培植税源，唯有稳农富民，唯有推进工业强县”的发展思路，提出“抢抓机遇，奋力拼搏，加速发展，强县升位”“谋发展，抓重点，调结构，进强县”等要求。通过招商引资，抓工业项目的引进和建设，推进工业经济发展。至2002年，合同引进项目100余项，到位资金11.1亿元。全县国内生产总值完成11.86亿元，三次产业结构由1997年的38.3：36.5：25.2调整到2002年的20.7：57：22.3，实现从“一、二、三”到“二、三、一”的跨越。至2010年，三次产业结构调整到11.6：65.3：23.1，二、三产业比重进一步提升，“二、三、一”的产业格局进一步优化。

七、实施“工业强县”战略

2003年起，县十四届政府通过编制全县工业发展规划，修订完善相关招商引资政策及措施，优化投资环境。完善和规范项目库，增强招商引资针对性和成功率，引入更多工业企业入驻，提升工业增加值在地方生产总值中的主导地位。加大招商引资力度，相继组团参加贵阳·港澳经贸洽谈会、哈尔滨国际经济贸易洽谈会、黄果树瀑布节经贸洽谈会等全国性和区域性经贸洽谈活动。至2006年，引进世界500强企业中国化工进出口总公司及息烽信科环化、息烽合力化工、味美食品、苗姑娘食品等一批规模以上企业入驻息烽，招商引资到位资金25.4亿元，初步形成磷及磷化工、铝及铝加工、食品医药、建材四大支柱产业。以小寨坝磷化工基地建设为重点，争取协调技改、贴息资金支持帮助企业扩大生产规模和生产技术改造，提高企业的知名度和产品竞争力，西洋肥业、中化开磷等6家企业14个产品分别获国家免检产品，省、市名牌产品称号。2006年，全县工业总产值完成

17.47亿元，占地方生产总值27.99亿元的62.42%，工业总产值占地方生产总值的比重较2002年提高5.42个百分点。2010年，工业总产值占地方生产总值的65.3%。

八、生态文明县建设

2008年，县十五届政府围绕县委《关于建设生态文明县的决定》，开展生态文明县建设。建成生态文明新农村46个。至2010年，建成清洁能源工程示范村2个、生态文明新农村77个。采取关、停、并、转措施淘汰高能耗、高污染、低效益企业，关停淘汰制砖厂5家、造纸厂4家、铝厂1家。实施10亿块磷石膏砖、30万吨合成氨尾气综合利用、低温余热回收等循环经济项目，年创产值上亿元，重点工业固体废物综合利用率47%。投资8000余万元，建成县城污水处理厂、县城垃圾填埋场、小寨坝污水处理厂、鹿窝污水处理厂等环保基础设施。开展石漠化综合治理。2010年，全县森林覆盖率45.8%，获得"中国绿色名县"、全国集体林权制度改革"百强县"和全省"绿化模范县"称号。

九、依法行政与政务公开

（一）法制建设

1993年8月，县政府办公室内设法制办公室（简称法制办），负责政府机关法制建设工作，对县政府出台的规范性文件及政府行政行为的合法性进行审查把关。至2003年，法制办先后参与《关于切实做好实施中华人民共和国国家赔偿法准备工作的通知》《关于在全县行政机关开展行政法治"六化"建设工作方案的通知》《关于印发〈息烽县人民政府行政复议案件受理办理程序〉的通知》《息烽县人民政府关于印发〈息烽县行政执法监督管理实施意见〉的通知》《息烽县人民政府办公室关于办理县人民政府行政复议案件处理程序若干问题的通知》等13个文件起草及审核工作。参与行政应诉案2件，办理行政复议4件。

2004年，举办《中华人民共和国行政许可法》学习培训班，集中培训公务人员700余名。组织1491名公务人员参加全省"行政许可法"统一考试。推行行政执法责任制和行政执法考评制、行政处罚备案制，定期对行政执法情况进行检查。各行政许可单位的行政执法纳入年终目标考评。对县国土资源、环保、建设等部门重大行政处罚备案36件。受理申请行政复议案件16件，办理行政应诉案件2件，审查规范性文件5件、各类合同（协议）6份，清理行政许可事项315项。是年12月16日，法制办公室从县政府办公室分出，升格为县政府法制办公室，加挂县政府行政复议办公室、县政府法律事务顾问室牌子，内设综合科、行政执法监督科和行政复议应诉科。

2005年，县政府出台《贯彻落实国务院全面推进依法行政实施纲要的具体规划》《贯彻落实国务院〈全面推进依法行政实施纲要〉实施意见》，制定《息烽县行政执法评议考核制度》。次年，县法制办对31家涉及行政执法的单位落实行政执法责任制情况进行检查。审查行政强制执行案件6件，重大行政案件备案审查126件。受理申请行政复议案件15件，结案6件。2008年，向各行政执法部门印发《关于进一步加强市县政府依法行政的决定》学习读本1000册，组织全县行政执法人员1300余人考试。

2009—2010年，对43个行政执法单位执行《中华人民共和国行政许可法》情况检查2次，对个别单位存在程序违法、越权许可等问题，下达整改指令，要求限期整改。对8名行政执法人员在行使行政职务过程中的违法行为进行责任追究。受理行政复议申请22件、各级行政机关行政应诉案件42件。开展行政执法单位行政许可、非许可类行政审批事项清理，行政许可审批事项由清理前的305项减少为158项；非行政许可事项清理94项，减少为69项。服务项目由清理前45项增加至75项。开展

《中华人民共和国行政复议法》颁布实施十周年系列纪念活动，全县各乡镇、各部门利用赶场天向干部群众宣传《中华人民共和国行政复议法》，印发宣传资料5万余份，悬挂宣传标语50余幅。

（二）依法行政

1991年起，开展行业不正之风监督检查，制止行政不作为、乱作为、乱收费现象。至1993年，全县取消部门不合理收费项目14个，纠正收费标准25项，取消对农民不合理负担收费项目23个，纠正和修改18个，查处金额7万余元。1998年，印发《关于在全县行政机关开展行政法治“六化”建设工作方案》，要求各乡镇、机关单位开展形式多样的普法教育和培训学习，加强行政法治“六化”（权限法定化、责任明晰化、程序公开化、行为规范化、检查经常化、监督机制完善化）建设，行政执法部门按照“公正、公开、效益、合法”要求，建立完善执法责任制、行政执法立案、审批、文书档案等制度和行政确认、行政决定、行政许可、行政处罚、行政监察等行政执法程序，建立和完善行政执法公示制度，实行政务“五公开”（办事程序、办事时限、办事标准和质量、办事结果、办事责任公开）。是年10月，县政府印发《关于深入开展依法治县工作的实施意见》。要求加强行政管理、规范行政执法行为，严格依法行政。加强行政执法监督，建立健全监督机制，保障法律、法规、规章的正确实施。2000年，县政府对1992年以来以县政府名义发出的文件进行清理，决定废止《承包人奖励办法》《息烽县流动人口和个体从业人员计划生育管理办法》《关于促进经济发展的税收优惠政策》《关于调整开征城镇土地使用税和房产税有关规定》《关于鼓励经济发展的建设用地优惠办法》《息烽县城镇房屋拆迁及安置暂行规定》《息烽县扶贫贷款到村到户实施办法》7个政府文件。2002年4月，县政府印发《息烽县行政执法监督管理实施意见》。8月，县政府废止1954年以来以县政府（含县革命委员会、县人委会）名义下发的有关或者影响贸易的，主要内容与新的法律、法规、规章和政策措施不相适应的，被新的法律、法规、规章和政策措施所代替的，以及适用期已过或者调整对象已经消失、实际上已经失效的120个政策措施类文件。次年，审查重大行政处罚案件6件，督促部门纠正不合理行政处罚案件1件；接行政复议案件14件，办理行政应诉案件3件。2005年7月，县政府印发《关于贯彻落实国务院〈全面推进依法行政实施纲要〉的实施意见》。11月，县政府印发《息烽县行政执法评议考核制度》，落实行政执法责任制，规范行政执法行为。2007年4月13日，县政府办公室印发《关于加强行政复议和应诉工作的通知》，要求各行政机关提高依法行政水平，对人民法院依法受理的行政诉讼案件，行政机关要按法定时限提供答辩，自觉执行人民法院的生效判决和裁定，积极纠正违法和不当行政行为。2009年，开展行政审批事项清理，清除行政审批事项114项，保留80项；清除非许可类行政审批事项12项，保留35项；服务类项目由9项增加到12项。2010年，息烽县“五五”普法依法治理工作通过国家、省、市考核验收，获全国法治县创建活动“先进单位”称号。

（三）政务公开

1991年，县政府推行“三公开一监督”制度，对群众关心的招工、职工调动等热点问题实行公开办理内容、公开政策、公开结果，接受群众监督。1999年4月，县政府各工作部门、乡镇政府机关实行政务公开。印发《关于县人民政府各工作部门实行政务公开的通知》。是年7月1日起，各乡镇、县政府各工作部门实行政务公开，工作人员佩证上岗。在工程建设项目招投标、大中专毕业生就业、退伍军人安置、预算外资金管理、土地出让等方面，建立公开办理运行机制，推行行政执法责任制、行政执法公示制、服务承诺制，提高政府工作透明度。至2001年，全县71个县属国有企业和驻县企事业单位推行厂务公开，161个村全部实行村务公开。县乡各部门结合“三个代表”重要思想学习和机关作风整顿活动，开展“三优”“两满意”创建活动，落实办事公开、公布承诺、公布监督电话、聘请监督员进行行业行风评议等，针对群众反映的问题，及时整改、解决和答复。2009年3月，政府办印发《关于将息烽县行政审批和服务事项纳入县政务服务中心集中办理的实施意见（试行）》，要求驻县垂直管理部门、县政府各工作部门和单位，其行政许可事项、非许可类行政审批事项和涉及改善息烽投资环境、促进招商引资工作等服务事项全部进入行政事务大厅，实行“一站式”办理。是年10月起，推行网络新闻发言人制度，及时、主动、准确发布政务信息。2010年，完善村务、厂务、政务公开内容，对事关群众利益的重大决策部署，广泛征询社会各界意见和建议，推进政府决策民主化、科学化、规范化。

十、作风教育与效能建设

1991年3月，出台政府工作制度建设意见。次年8月，制定《息烽县人民政府若干工作制度》，对会议、工作联系、请示报告、出差、礼仪等工作行为予以规范。1998年10月，县政府印发《息烽县人民政府目标管理实施办法》，建立领导干部下基层调查研究制度，要求副县长以上领导干部实行“下基层登记卡”制度，年均下基层时间须达3个月；各乡镇、县直机关建立考核、考勤制度和帮助基层解决实际问题备查制度。至2003年，县政府相继出台、印发《息烽县人民政府工作规则》《关于改进政府会议会务工作的意见》《关于进一步加强会议纪律　改进会议作风的通知》《息烽县人民政府办公室公文办理制度》等文件。从职业道德、责任意识、敬业精神、提高服务质量和办事效率、严禁有令不行等方面作出规定，提出要求，着力解决不依法行政和对县委、县政府的决议、决定消极抵触或执行不力，搞不明利益第一，上有政策，下有对策等问题；严禁办事拖拉，着力解决违反服务承诺制度，政务不公开或政务公开流于形式，搞暗箱操作，办理事项不能限时办结，效率低下，推诿扯皮，对群众要求办的事项敷衍塞责等问题；严禁吃拿卡要，着力解决办事不讲规则讲关系，不给好处不办事，给了好处乱办事，巧立名目乱检查、乱收费、乱罚款、乱摊派等问题；严禁态度刁蛮，着力解决服务态度差、刁难群众、作风霸道等问题。2008年9月，成立“息烽县政务服务中心”，为人民群众办事提供“一站式”方便快捷服务。至2009年，全县建成8个县级代理窗口、10个乡（镇）级代理室、169个村（居）代理点。政务服务坚持能在窗口办理的事项立即办理，不能办理的明确时限督促办理。县、乡、村三级为民服务全程代理中心共收件1.23万件，办结1.15万件，办结率93.5%，满意率100%。2010年，政务服务中心建成“三网（项目申报大厅局域网、行政审批政务网、电子监察专网）一站（息烽县政务服务中心网站）六平台（业务支撑管理平台、网上行政审批平台、电子监察系统平台、视频监控系统平台、信息发布系统平台、信息查询系统平台）”。制定服务承诺制、一次性告知制、限时办结制、岗位责任制等制度。入驻部门和单位32个，共收件3.2万件，办结3.06万件，办结率95.75%，群众满意率100%。是年，县委、县政府命名表彰三八红旗手标兵、三八红旗手60名，“双学双比”活动先进工作者、“双学双比”活动女能手35名，先进工作者、先进劳动者30名，三八红旗集体、城乡妇女“岗位建功”先进集体25个。

第五节　实事工程

1988年起，每年年初，县政府广泛征求意见，遴选出一批关系人民群众切身利益的事项写进工作报告，作为当年为民办实事项目，经县人代会批准后实施，实施完成情况向人代会报告，接受监督。1998—2001年，每年拟办实事13～16件不等；2002年起，每年拟办实事均为10件。

1998年实事工程：解决全县最后1.5万贫困人口温饱问题。完成“息烽集中营”旧址的玄天洞部分修复工作。抓好息烽铝厂、息烽110千伏变电站建设。建成1000亩杂交玉米制种基地。解决1万人、5000头牲畜饮水困难问题。开工建设3所精神文明活动中心。完成西山至马路岩公路建设任务。完成8个村57千米的公路建设。完成老厂灌区建设任务。改造县城东风路至蚕桑坡公路，完成县城文化南路道路建设。新建三所希望小学。启动安居工程3000平方米。创建县级文明单位10个、文明村10个、市级文明单位5个、文明村5个。兴建黑神庙—流长—鹿窝光缆。完成1个村（组）异地搬迁任务。规划建设息烽公墓。

1999年实事工程：完成水土保持综合治理工程6平方千米，在玄天洞公路沿线实施农业科技组装配置。培育优质西瓜基地1万亩。示范种植巴西旱稻500亩，其中良种提纯200亩。建成石硐晚熟果品基地，是年栽培八月李2000亩、柰李3000亩、雪梨3000亩。实现村村通公路。分步实施，分阶段治理息烽河。分步实施，分阶段维修，治理底寨河主干渠。建成农村山庄1个（在玄天洞附近）。完成农村人畜饮水工程15处，解决6000人、5800头牲畜的饮水问题。完成微型“三小”水利工程（建小水池1200口3万立方米）。建成石硐、流长、西山、鹿窝4个卫生院业务用房。建成县特殊学校1所。建成息烽客货综合停车场1个。新增教学用房1.6万平方米、教师住房2400平方米。

2000年实事工程：建成温泉次早熟蔬菜基地23.73公顷。建成底寨河渠道修复改造工程15.3千米。建成云环小学暨邵云环烈士纪念室。实施2660公顷优质油菜籽基地，平均每亩单产121.8千克。完成汤木沟生态环境治理工程，其中退耕还林21.47公顷，荒山造林50.3公顷。建成饮水工程12处，解决3000余人、2000余头牲畜的饮水困难。建成西山乡、鹿窝乡精神文明活动中心。解决400户农村贫困户危房问题，使他们乔迁新居。建成30个小康村和1个小康镇。创建省级卫生县城。完成石硐至梨安公路路基工程97%，整体工程完成80%。启动县城东门小区建设，完成小区河滨路工程95%。完成“村村通电话”148个村，占全县“村村通电话”总数的91.9%。启动县城精神文明活动中心建设工程。

2001年实事工程：启动永靖镇上沟水库工程，建成贵州西洋肥业有限公司供水管道工程。开工建设县城日供水1.5万吨供水工程。完成九庄1000吨日供水工程建设。完成火麻湾、板厂两座小（二）型水库和鱼简河水库前期工程。建成老厂至二〇五、竹花至黄沙、石硐至梨安3条四级公路，启动关田坝至西山公路建设。完成硬化县乡公路35千米公路工程量的50%。建成185公顷生态渔业示范基地。完成息烽农副产品综合批发市场前期工程，建成1000吨气调保鲜冷藏库房。解决农村536户贫困户住房困难。建成13座移动通信基站。完成县宣传文化中心建设主体工程。动工修建息烽中学教学大楼并建成学生宿舍。完成县城南大街控制性详细规划。

2002年实事工程：建设县城南大街一期工程和十字绿化广场，建成县城北门桥综合商场和农资商场，建成县城东门小区一期工程。启动鱼简河水库一期工程，兴建“三小”工程5万立方米，治理3座病险水库，建成西山净水、日供水能力5000吨及养龙司净水、日供水能力1000吨的两个供水厂。建成息烽中学教学大楼、职教综合大楼和县实验幼儿园，完成息烽二中校园规划并年内启动建设。建成沼气池4000口，改圈4036间，改厕4000个。完成县乡公路改造硬化工程74.5千米，实现乡乡通油路。动工建设县城西门片区集贸市场、流长乡顺江码头。帮助426户特困户改造茅草房和危房，在小寨坝、永靖镇实施110户贫困户以工代赈异地扶贫安置。动工修建县城殡仪服务中心及宝山公墓。启动县城垃圾填埋场、生猪屠宰场建设项目。启动县医院和县中医院门诊大楼建设工程。

2003年实事工程：完成鱼简河水库一期工程，累计投资2500万元；投资682.02万元治理小桥河、烂田沟、猪嘴田3座病险水库，启动水落洞水库、阳朗排洪大沟、县城排洪一期工程，动工修建流长、温泉两个日产1000吨（净水）水厂。启动县城南大街道路二期建设工程，到年底完成总工程量的70%；完成县城“城中城”综合市场一期工程，投资1500万元，建筑面积1.32万平方米；建成消防大楼并投入使用，投资11.58万元，建筑面积1964平方米。完成小寨坝县级磷化工城一期改造工程（含南山大道）和磷化工基地一期工程。投入资金206.4万元，超额完成帮助农村特困户改造茅草房和危房518户。九庄镇土地开发整理项目工程，因财政部门尚未拨款而未实施。建成息烽县第二中学教学大楼并投入使用，完成24所中小学校实施远程教育工程设备安装。完成养龙司万亩蔬菜基地一期配套工程。投资1179万元，新建、改造及硬化县乡公路7条68.4千米。完成县人民医院综合大楼建设项目主体工程，开工建设县田径场。在农村建沼气池3000口，配套改厕3000座、改圈3000间，实际完成3420口及其配套的改厕、改圈工程。

2004年实事工程：投资315万元完成九庄河道治理，投资98.6万元治理病险水库1座；因受国有宏观土地调控政策影响，计划投资619万元和670万元改造的下阳朗河道、阳朗排洪大沟一期工程完成工程量的10%和54%；计划投资1588万元的水落洞水库二期工程完成设计工作。全面完成顺江商贸码头总体规划，投资90万元建成顺江水产品交易市场；硬化县、乡公路117千米；硬化贫困村村级公路25千米，完成路基及路肩墙230千米。兴建九庄镇、小寨坝镇、温泉镇3个汽车客运站，因建设资金筹措不到位而未开工。投资998万元完成县城“城中城”综合市场二期工程，投资60万元完成县城垃圾填埋场搬迁。完成县城南大街北段主干道建设，小寨坝镇磷化工基地南山大道二期工程。息烽集中营革命历史纪念馆二期建设工程完成500万元年度目标任务；完成县老干活动中心大楼建设前期工作及团元山森林公园勘测、规划，建成县田径场。分别投资427.13万元、172.35万元和231万元，建成永靖镇彭家垭口水厂、唐家湾水厂和石硐水厂。农村新建沼气池2000口及配套改厕2000座、改圈2000间，完成1411户茅草房改造，完成村通电视1200户。完成县人民医院综合大楼二期工程建设，建成县疾病控制中心综合楼，投资103.6万元动工修建县卫生局监督所业务楼。分别投资630万元和520万元，基本完成县一中、二中配套设施建设工程。

2005年实事工程：建成小水池1820口，人畜饮水工程37处，解决1万人、8000头牲畜饮水困难；治理病险水库1座；启动何家硐、鹿窝、青山3座日产500～2000吨净水水厂建设工程。创建10个经济生态示范村；完成市第二环城林带工程建设166.67公顷；新建农村生态沼气池1500口，配套改厕、改圈、改灶1500个；构筑农村维权网络，将“12315”延伸到农村。完成农村100户危房改造，硬化农村串户路80千米，建成县级“三农”科技专家服务中心办公楼；完成10个贫困村宣传文化室和党员活动室修建工程。完成小寨坝磷化工基地南山大道1万平方米拆迁安置房主体工程；新建3个水冲式公厕、5个垃圾转运台；完成团元山森林公园建设总体规划的审批；全面清理拖欠农民工工资。改造县乡公路68.4千米，硬化贫困村公路200千米。改造农村中小学危房7500平方米；建成九庄中学寄宿制学校；建成农村中小学小伙房、厕所各60个。启动8个乡镇卫生院改扩建工程；建立新型农村合作医疗信息平台；建成县人民医院传染病区并投入使用。建成6个乡镇计生服务站办公楼；实现符合条件的农村独生子女户、双女结扎户计划生育养老保险覆盖面达到100%的目标。建成县劳动力人才市场及5个乡镇司法所和九庄镇人民法庭办公楼。完成42个行政村电视“模改数”、200个自然村寨通电视、广播工程；开通边远村电话3000门；完成息烽集中营革命历史纪念馆广场扩建和新馆建设工程。

2006年实事工程：新建生态沼气池5654口，建成10个100户以上的生态养殖小区、新建机耕道20千米；利用阳光工程培训人员2000人次。治理病险水库2座；整修山塘12口；实施“万户小水池工程”1800口；人饮工程10处。新增就业岗位1456个；实现城乡统筹就业6220人（其中农村剩余劳动力转移4400人）；城乡统筹培训4300人（其中农村技能培训3600人），完成县劳动力人才市场信息网络建设并投入使用。实施易地扶贫搬迁200人；完成农村人居危房改造438户，建成串户水泥路200千米；完成阳朗片区土地整治项目1个，标准农田改造项目2个；在全县十个乡镇创建11个社会主义新农村示范村寨。完成息烽乌江复旦学校主楼建设和养龙司、流长、青山民族中学寄宿制学校建设1.5万平方米；建成县中小学生校外活动中心；在3个贫困乡镇实施“两免一补”政策。新建县城北门休闲绿化广场并投入使用；建成县城公厕3个；改造城镇道路4000平方米；新建小寨坝南山大道安置房4万平方米；修建县城至团元山森林公园大门公路1200米，园区步道2000米；新增县城绿地2万平方米。新建九庄镇、永靖镇、小寨坝镇3个司法所和黑神庙法庭；动工修建九庄镇、西山乡、青山苗族乡3个乡镇派出所；完成公安“三台合一”和3个报警监控站、60个监控网点建设。建成贫困村公路150千米；完成县乡公路硬化改造27.3千米，进村公路改造10千米；新建农村社会客运站3个，完工2个。完成42个行政村电视“模改数”200个自然村寨10625户通广播电视工程，超任务2400户；建成15个村级综合楼。继续推进农村合作医疗制度，覆盖全县农村现有农民；建成1个中心敬老院和1个社会主义新农村科技活动窗。

2007年实事工程：新建生态沼气池5300口，配套改厕、改圈、改灶5300套；新建机耕道20千米；新建规模以上养殖小区38个，无公害蔬菜基地22个；完成新型农民科技培训1200人。完成农村小水池505口，安全饮水工程和烟水配套工程53处，容积5万立方米，解决1.34万人饮水困难。完成农村危房改造530户，串户路260千米；土地整治项目1个，面积4600公顷：标准化农田建设项目3个，面积377.6公顷；创建社会主义新农村示范村10个并实施种植和养殖等示范；续建社会主义新农村示范点12个。新增就业岗位1760个；完成城镇失业人员就业1430人，下岗失业人员就业220人；实现农村富余劳动力非农技能培训8944人，有序就业转移7894人。落实“两免一补”政策，到位资金640.52万元，农民工子女入学就读问题全部解决。新增绿地面积2万平方米。完成团元山森林公园园区旅游步道、景观亭、景观绿化等基础设施；建成9个乡村旅游示范点并通过旅游行业认证，完成鹿窝乡安置小区污水处理工程，创建绿色社区1个，各项创建指标通过市级验收。完成县城道路改造6000平方米，修建垃圾中转站1座。建成“双拥广场”1个，其中广场4950平方米，周边道路3000平方米；完成小寨坝镇南山大道安置房3.84万平方米。完成213个自然村通电视、广播工程。建设38个“四室合一”村级综合楼。县乡公路完成盘脚营至红岩7.3千米；完成村公路185.5千米。新型农村合作医疗参合人数19.44万人，参合率92.68%，农村特困群众实行“应保尽保”，共发放保障金416万元。

2008年实事工程：投入资金6843.9万元，完成农村危房改造2271户，消除危房18.17万平方米，新建住房面积21.46万平方米。完成硬化村寨串户路421.9千米；完成“四改一气”2500套和后续服务网点25个；完成新建标准化奶牛养殖小区1个；建成无公害蔬菜基地10个，完成蔬菜种植353.33公顷，改造农家店32个。完成治理九庄镇盘龙山、石硐乡水沟病险水库2座；实施安全饮水工程59处，解决8000人的饮水安全。完成未成林林地补植补造826.67公顷；建成贵遵高速公路息烽段通道景观绿化工程40公顷。完成新增就业岗位1700个；培训非农技能农村劳动力4700个，转移就业4551人；创建充分就业社区2个。完成经济适用房建设5000平方米、廉租房建设5000平方米。完成北门桥至开磷新城道路改造；投入300万元，完成新增县城绿地2万平方米；延伸团元山森林公园步行道1000米；动工修建总投资5666万元的县城垃圾填埋场和县城、小寨坝污水处理厂；投资400万元，改造县城旱厕15个。做好进城务工人员子女接受义务教育工作，全年接收4347名进城务工人员子女就近入学；在全县范围内免除义务教育阶段学生（含民办学校学生）的书费和杂费，并对生活困难的住校生给予生活补助。新建温泉中学学生宿舍2000平方米，食堂400平方米。全面推行城乡医疗救助。筹集农村贫困医疗救助资金43.5万元，共救助农村贫困群众1.41万人次；资助城镇低保人员901人参加城镇居民基本医疗保险，资助金额7041.4元，资助因病造成家庭生活困难的城市居民4户，资助金额1.2万元；启动城镇居民基本医疗保险，实施城镇居民基本医疗保险2940人；19.56万人参加新型农村合作医疗。出台惠民医疗政策，普及到县级医疗机构和10个乡镇卫生院。建成小寨坝潮水片区办事处“博爱卫生站”，新建妇幼保健院综合业务用房。安装城市中心区110群众报警定位标志679个。完成续修村公路60千米，新建县乡公路15千米。新建和扩建村级综合楼27栋。

2009年实事工程：实施农村饮水安全工程，解决4400人安全饮水困难；治理病险水库2座。完成“四改一气”农村生态能源建设3292套；硬化串户路200千米，完成农村危房改造1484户。完成西山乡小鹿窝基本农田建设项目1个、永靖镇马当田片区农业综合开发土地治理项目1个；完成永靖镇硬寨村、青山苗族乡冗坝村2个清洁工程建设点，安装太阳能100台，改厕54户，建花池608.8平方米，庭院美化81户。安装频振杀虫灯12盏，建设公用生活垃圾收集箱5个，生活污水处理联户型93个，安装排污主管1498.4米，排污支管2869.5米，修建沉渣池37个，硬化路面5400平方米；新建供销社农家店15个。完成村公路硬化50.69千米，超额完成20.69千米；完成永温至温泉公路和息烽至九庄公路大修工程8.7千米A、B标段主体施工。按政策规定在春、秋两个学期为进城务工人员随迁子女5536人提供免费教科书；完成乌江复旦学校实验楼主楼建设2400平方米。加快县城景观建设，完成县城东门河道亮丽工程，并投入使用。完成新建廉租房5000平方米，并将人均住房面积不足15平方米的城镇低保户纳入保障范围。完成县计划生育宣传技术服务指导站主楼建设。完成4000户村通电视和67个自然村通广播工程；实现村村都有“农家书屋”。建立城乡临时救助制度，并对35户107人开展临时救助，发放救助资金6.35万元；完成10个乡镇劳动保障所和9个居委会（社区）劳动服务窗口平台建设；创建充分就业社区4个；新增就业岗位1695个，完成城乡统筹培训5883人，完成城乡统筹就业8036人。

2010年实事工程：完成息烽二中综合楼和永靖中学学生宿舍及食堂3200平方米建设。完成基本养老保险扩面1.12万人，城乡统筹就业8069人，新增就业岗位2097个，开发公益性岗位521个；创建新华、西门和东门3个充分就业社区；建成县政务服务办事大厅并投入使用。完成政府开办的社区卫生服务机构及乡镇卫生院、村卫生室，实行国家基本药物零差率销售，下发药品零差率销售补助金90万元；建成健康档案6万份；建成居民健康档案信息系统并进入试运行阶段，建立电子健康档案3万余份；完成县人民医院综合住院大楼和县中医院改扩建项目主体工程。启动2.9万平方米廉租房建设项目。其中：永靖镇廉租房、小寨坝廉租房进入主体施工阶段，采取购置方式完成5000平方米廉租房；为644户住房面积不足15平方米的城镇低保家庭发放租赁补贴。为困难群众无偿办理法律援助案件129件，提供义务法律咨询790人次，完善报警与监控管理系统，增加县城报警管理监控点39个。完成串户路339千米，基本农田建设项目7个；11个整村推进项目全部完工；完成农业综合开发土地治理项目1个；完成农村饮水安全工程5处，解决3019人、2170头牲畜饮水安全工程；何家沟病险水库治理工程全面完成；启动枧槽沟、廖九寨水库建设。完成县城文化路二标段（800米）建设，县城三角花园一标段500米电力管网入地工程；完成改造城镇道路建设1.31万平方米；完成10个农贸市场的改造建设并投入使用。完成村村通广播电视工程8420户，微机信息录入8420户；完成县图书馆新馆建设；建成文化信息资源共享工程县级支中心。完成续建村公路22.3千米；完成仡佬冲桥、中寨桥、底寨中桥3座危桥改造；马路岩至关田坝旅游公路工程建设完工通车；开工建设息烽县鹿窝旅游公路；启动息烽至开阳高速公路工程建设。完成国家退耕还林工程封山育林533.33公顷、退耕还林补植补造740公顷、人工造林466.67公顷、石漠化综合治理633公顷；县环境监测站建成并投入使用；开展集中式饮用水源综合治理。

第六节　信访工作

一、机构

1991年，县委、县政府设联合信访办，负责全县群众来信来访接待办理工作。1995年县级机构改革，撤销“县委、县政府联合信访办”，设县委办公室信访办。2001年，恢复成立“县委、县政府联合信访办”。2004年，成立“息烽县处理信访突出问题及群体性事件联席会议办公室”，下设土地征用问题、城镇房屋拆迁问题、国有企业改革改制问题、涉法涉诉问题、企业军转干部问题、维护社会稳定问题6个工作小组。是年9月，撤销“县委、县政府联合信访办”，成立县信访局，归口县政府办公室管理，业务受县委办公室、县政府办公室领导。内设综合科、信访接待科（对外称“中共息烽县委、息烽县人民政府来访接待室”）、督查科。下设“人民群众来信办理及信访预测研究办公室”。

二、工作辑要

1991年，县信访工作继续坚持县领导信访接待日制度，每周三为县领导信访接待日。县信访部门编制县领导信访接待时间安排表，信访接待当日，实行署名挂牌接访。是年，县联合信访办公室翻印《贵州省信访条例》400本发到区、乡、村，供学习宣传用，向全县区、乡（镇）、县直有关部门印发《息烽县党政机关信访工作暂行办法》。全年接待人民群众来信来访261件次。2001年，县委、县政府主要领导到石硐、小寨坝、九庄等乡（镇）开展挂牌接待人民群众来访活动，现场解决人民群众上访问题。县长杨彦峰在石硐乡专题调研群众上访工作，红光村群众反映因修路挖断自来水管，导致石硐上街群众无水吃，杨彦峰当即表态责成县水电局帮助解决水管问题，使群众尽快吃上自来水。2005年，开展学习宣传新修订《信访条例》活动，组织干部职工群众集中收看《信访条例》光碟和用宣传车到企业、村居滚动播放《信访条例》光碟，发放宣传资料1万余份。2008年8月，开展县委书记大接访活动。县委办公室、县政府办公室行文下发《息烽县开展县委书记大接访活动实施方案》，成立由县人大、县政协、县纪委领导牵头组成的督查组，全程督查大接访活动的开展及信访事项的处理情况。是年，县领导接访1147批1757人次，其中个人访1063批1423人次，集体访84批334人次。办结答复信访事项1075批，占接访总量的93.7%，群众满意或无异议的895批，占办结答复总量的83.3%。2009年，县信访局牵头，有关单位配合，采取进村入户、利用赶场天、广播电视滚动、发放资料和悬挂标语等宣传形式，向人民群众宣传信访法律法规，接待群众咨询信访问题。是年，开展宣传活动3次，发放宣传资料1万余份。

2010年5月，县信访局、县公安局在县城开展《信访条例》实施五周年宣传活动，发放《信访条例》《信访工作及相关法律法规宣传手册》《信访知识问答》《群众来信“绿色通道”平常邮件寄送须知》等资料3000余份，接待群众咨询1000余人次。是年，县领导接待人民群众来访113件240人次。阅批群众来信125件。

息烽县1991—2010年来信来访统计表

表5-2-2

年份	来信（件）	来访（人）	集体访人/批	立案（件）	结案（件）
1991	181	80	23/5	29	28
1992	133	51	25/5	49	49
1993	195	73	19/5	25	25
1994	126	129	325/6	25	25
1995	58	53	178/4	21	21
1996	125	285	149/19	40	40
1997	80	216	86/12	39	39
1998	59	233	187/17	55	55
1999	86	383	—	98	98
2000	70	249	334/23	85	85
2001	54	333	662/44	63	63
2002	23	250	760/38	58	58
2003	24	216	687/38	256	256
2004	34	423	376/49	142	142
2005	30	237	776/46	76	76
2006	81	243	962/48	80	80
2007	89	233	861/54	96	96
2008	184	1356	334/84	1270	1198
2009	273	140	632/31	287	281
2010	144	229	575/52	273	270

第七节　档案工作

一、机构

1991年，县设档案局、档案馆（归县档案局管理）。1995年11月，县档案局、档案馆合并，实行一个机构，两块牌子。1996年4月，县档案局（馆）内设办公室、业务科。2004年3月，成立县现行文件阅览中心，隶属县档案局（馆）管理。2010年12月，组建县档案局（息烽县档案馆、息烽县地方志编纂委员会办公室），为县政府直属事业单位。内设办公室、档案管理科、档案业务科、史志编纂科、信息资料科。

二、法制建设与业务培训

1991年起，县档案局（馆）采取与县直单位协作，通过会议、干部培训等开展档案法律法规宣传和业务培训指导。至1995年，为财政系统80余人、县委党校干部培训班学员89人授课，宣传、学习《中华人民共和国档案法》《档案法实施办法》《中华人民共和国保密法》和江泽民在视察上海市档案局工作时的重要讲话。进行财会、文秘档案业务知识培训、实际操作示范演练。

1996—1997年，开展新修订《中华人民共和国档案法》颁布实施、第十三届国际档案大会召开和《中华人民共和国档案法》颁布10周年纪念活动。在县城中心地段张贴宣传标语，出宣传专刊，向群众发送档案法规等宣传资料，接待群众咨询等。组织县直机关61个单位近100人参加贵阳市档案局举办的《中华人民共和国档案法》暨第十三届国际档案大会知识竞赛活动。

1998年，组织17个立案单位100余人参加国家档案局组织的“中宝杯”档案知识有奖问答活动。2001年起，配合“四五”普法、依法治县宣传，开展《中华人民共和国档案法》《档案法实施办法》《归档文件整理规则》《贵州省档案管理条例》《贵阳市档案管理规定》宣传。至2006年，对乡镇、县直机关、企事业单位专兼职档案工作人员66人进行归档文件价值鉴定、整理组织工作、分类、编号、编目、装盒等培训。对170名村（居）委会主任进行“三农”档案工作的规范管理培训。2010年，配合乡镇举办短期培训班3次，对村级档案员100余人进行“林改档案”和“污染源普查档案”业务培训。

三、业务监督与指导

1991年，根据省政府办公厅转发省档案局关于在撤区并乡建镇工作中加强档案工作意见精神，县档案局选派6人分两个小组到区、乡、镇监督、指导档案资料收集、整理、立卷、归档工作。至次年元月，全县4个区24个乡镇共整理档案4560卷，按时完成撤区、并乡、建镇前档案清理工作。1992年起，开展档案规范管理和达标升级督促检查，坚持执法检查与业务指导同步进行。是年，检查县直机关87个单位的档案室工作，达到规范管理要求的83个，占95.4%。1997年起，开展农村村级建档监督指导工作。在养龙司乡灯塔村进行村级建档试点。开展乡镇、农业科技档案工作现状调查，撰写《息烽县乡镇档案工作调查报告》《息烽县农业科技　乡镇企业档案工作情况调查报告》，提出村级建档工作意见。至1999年，建立以土地延包、村级换届选举、村务公开资料为主建档的村140个，未建档的21个。

2000年3月，召开全县档案工作会议，县政府分管领导与46个单位分别签订档案工作达标目标责任书，纳入年终工作目标考核。是年，经考评，达县直机关一级标准单位1个、二级标准单位31个。县档案馆经省、市考评达省二级档案馆标准。

2003年，县委、县政府将村级建档工作纳入年终目标考核。县档案局印发《关于搞好村级建档的函》，制定《息烽县村级档案归档范围》。对170名村（居）委会干部进行档案业务培训。是年，对10个乡镇进行档案执法检查。督查指导县税改办整理税改文书档案205卷、声像档案6盒，乡镇税改档案166盒9601件，退耕还林档案33盒。在小寨坝镇开展“小城镇建设档案规范管理试点”。2004年明确小寨坝镇为省、市、县农业农村档案工作联系点。2008年，贯彻落实国家档案局、农业部、民政部《关于加强社会主义新农村档案工作的意见》，在10个乡镇分别选定1～2个村为村级档案规范化管理示范点。全县161个村和9个社区全部建档。完成10个乡镇集体林权制度改革档案资料收集、立卷归档。次年，县档案事业发展综合评估工作通过市级验收。2010年，村级档案规范化管理全面推进。

四、档案征集、接收与开发利用

（一）档案征集与接收

1991年初，县档案馆馆藏档案76个全宗，16771卷；资料3230种，11999册。是年接收进馆档案524卷，资料32种318册。1992年，县档案局整理全县建镇并乡撤区前档案4667卷，资料32种405册入库。以后数年，县档案局加大档案征集接收工作力度，馆藏档案数量逐年增加，内容更加丰富，至2001年，县档案馆馆藏档案98个全宗，20318卷；档案资料8483卷（册）；照片36本，1731张。照片底片73张（套、盒）。2005年，县档案局印发《关于到期档案移交进馆通知》，强调按时做好档案清理移交工作。是年接收档案20个全宗，1011卷。现行文件阅览中心接收现行政策性、法规性、公益性、服务性文件313件，专题资料汇编17册。2010年，县档案馆馆藏档案100个全宗，29920卷（盒）。

（二）档案开发利用

1991年，县档案馆接待利用档案用户169人次，提供档案941卷，资料96卷册，为25名干部职工解决工龄等问题，解决土地、山林权属纠纷9起，为政法机关提供依据4起。1992年，接待利用档案用户189人次，为编写《息烽县志》提供档案1742卷（册）；为县、乡镇两级党政部门落实政策提供档案768卷，资料487卷（册），解决139起土地、山林权属纠纷；为政法机关提供4起依据。此后，由于第一轮修志工作结束，加之机构调整，企业改革等因素，查阅利用档案数量明显下降。1997年，接待利用档案用户68人次。2001年起，县档案馆开展电话代查业务，为机关企事业单位和个人利用档案信息资源提供方便。是年，接待查阅利用档案信息328人次，查阅档案1077卷。2004年起，息烽县二轮修志工作开始，此后数年，接待查阅档案和利用档案信息资源数量剧增。2008年，接待查阅档案信息1960余人次，利用档案1.13万余卷，为1991年以来最高。2009年，举办档案展览一期。接待查阅1010余人次，利用档案2020卷。2010年，接待档案查阅570余人次，利用档案3500余卷。

1991—2010年，县档案馆共接待查阅档案22698人次，利用档案99876卷（次），资料2769卷（册）。解决山林、土地、婚姻等民生纠纷3798次，工作查考6784次，为政法机关提供依据80余次。

第八节　地方志工作

一、机构

1991年，设县地方志编纂委员会办公室，为正科级事业单位。1995年7月，县级机构改革，县地方志编纂委员会办公室与中共息烽县委党史研究室合并，组建县史志办公室，内设综合科。2009年1月，县史志办公室列入参照公务员管理单位。2010年5月县级机构改革，撤销史志办公室，组建档案局（档案馆、地方志编纂委员会办公室），为正科级参公管理事业单位，实行一套人马，三块牌子，地方志编纂委员会办公室下设史志编纂科。

二、工作辑要

1991年，完成《息烽县志》总纂稿。1992年1月16—18日，完成《息烽县志》县级评审。11月2日，《息烽县志》通过省地方志办验收并同意出版。1993年12月，《息烽县志》出版发行。是年，出版发行《息烽县财政志》等14部专业志。1995年6月，《息烽县商业志》出版发行。次年11月，《息烽县烟草志》出版发行。1997年，《息烽县志》获贵州省地方志优秀成果三等奖。1999年5月，《息烽县教育志》出版发行。2001年8月，县内首部乡镇志《小寨坝镇志》出版发行。是年，县史志办被评为全省第一届地方志编纂工作先进单位，受到省政府表彰。2003年，启动《息烽县志（1991—2010）》编修工作。2007年起，《息烽县志（1991—2010）》编修工作纳入各单位年度目标考核，并签订目标责任书。是年，息烽县城旧城改造工作启动，县史志办开展县城旧城图片拍摄工作；《息烽县军事志》编纂出版。2009年，启动西山乡《鹿窝村志》编修工作，拟订编纂篇目，培训编纂人员，当年完成6个篇的初稿编纂。

第三章　人民政协

1991—2010年，中国人民政治协商会议息烽县委员会（简称县政协），遵照“长期共存、互相监督，肝胆相照、荣辱与共”方针，围绕全县政治、经济、文化等重大问题，认真履行“政治协商，民主监督，参政议政”职能，发挥政协位置超脱、联系广泛、人才荟萃优势，积极服务大局，反映社情民意，建言献策。20年间，提出议案1830件。履职中，探索总结出例会协商、专题协商、对口协商等多种协商方式，畅通协商渠道，丰富协商内容，增强协商的针对性和实效性。

第一节　政协全委会

县政协全体委员会议（简称全委会）每年至少召开一次。委员会由各党派、各民族、各界别代表和知名人士组成。委员中非中共党员所占比例不低于60%。委员实行任期制，1993年前，每届任期3年，此后，每届任期5年。届中根据人员变动或工作需要，进行个别补充和调整。全委会会议主要听取县政协常委会工作报告、提案工作报告和会议提案审查情况报告；列席同期召开的县人民代表大会，听取讨论县政府工作报告和其他报告；通过各项决议。部分会议安排传达省、市政协会议精神，听取县委领导、市政协领导讲话，补选、增选县政协副主席、秘书长、常务委员。每届一次会议安排换届选举事项，选举县政协委员会主席、副主席、秘书长和常委会委员。1990年4月至2010年，县政协全委会经历5届，举行会议22次，提出议案1830件。

一、第三届委员会全体会议

第三届委员会委员130名。其中：中共10名、无党派人士5名、共青团3名、总工会3名、妇女联合会3名、农林6名、工商业联合会5名、文化艺术界3名、科学技术界15名、教育界15名、社会科学界3名、医药卫生界9名、工商经济界8名、少数民族4名、体育界3名、台港澳侨7名、特别邀请人士28名。

一次会议于1990年4月23—28日在县城召开。出席会议委员130名。会议听取审议政协常委会工作报告、提案工作报告；听取讨论县政府工作报告和其他报告；选举黄永刚为县政协第三届委员会主席，刘守珍、蒙锡琚、吕莹琳、黄及翔为副主席，常务委员20名。通过各项决议。收到委员提案59件。

二次会议于1991年3月25—30日在县城召开。出席会议委员128名。县委书记陈华祥到会作重要讲话。会议听取审议政协常委会工作报告、提案工作报告；听取讨论县政府工作报告和其他报告；选举张其沾为县政协第三届委员会副主席兼秘书长，闫国畅、武国勋为常委会委员。通过各项决议。收到提案90件。

三次会议于1992年3月27—31日在县城召开。出席会议委员128名。陈华祥到会并讲话。会议听取审议政协常委会工作报告、提案工作报告；听取讨论县政府工作报告和其他报告；通过各项决议。收到委员提案86件。

二、第四届委员会全体会议

第四届委员会委员129名。其中：中共11名、无党派人士5名、共青团3名、总工会3名、妇女联合会3名、工商业联合会7名、科学技术协会3名、文化艺术界3名、科学技术界12名、社会科学界3名、经济界11名、农林界10名、教育界12名、体育界3名、医药卫生界7名、少数民族4名、台港澳侨7名、特别邀请人士22名。

一次会议于1993年4月23—27日在县城召开。出席会议委员112名。陈华祥到会作题为《回顾过去　展望未来　加强协商监督　努力参政议政　为振兴息烽经济而奋斗》的重要讲话。会议听取审议县政协常委会工作报告、提案工作报告；听取讨论县政府工作报告和其他报告；选举蒋光国为县政协第四届委员会主席，张其沾、黄及翔、文昌碧、余大维、陈继春为副主席，武国勋为秘书长，常务委员18名。通过各项决议。收到委员提案100件。

二次会议于1994年3月22—24日在县城召开。出席会议委员105名。县委书记黑卫平到会作重要讲话。会议传达贯彻省政协七届二次会议精神；听取审议政协常委会工作报告、提案工作报告；听取讨论县政府工作报告和其他报告；补选杨政敏为县政协秘书长，增选黄生谷为常务委员。通过各项决议。收到委员提案56件。

三次会议于1995年3月14—16日在县城召开。出席会议委员126名。县委书记黑卫平到会作重要讲话。会议听取审议政协常委会工作报告、提案工作报告；听取讨论县政府工作报告和其他报告。通过各项决议。收到委员提案33件。

四次会议于1996年3月19—21日在县城召开。出席会议委员112名。黑卫平、市政协副主席牛秉璋到会并讲话。会议传达省、市政协会议精神；听取审议政协常委会工作报告、提案工作报告；听取讨论县政府工作报告和其他报告；通过各项决议。收到委员提案42件。

五次会议于1997年3月17—19日在县城召开。出席会议委员105名。黑卫平、市政协副主席张道煌、市委统战部副部长董淑琴到会并讲话。会议听取审议政协常委会工作报告、提案工作报告；听取讨论县政府工作报告和其他报告；通过各项决议。收到委员提案50件。

三、第五届委员会全体会议

第五届委员会委员125名。其中：中共13名、无党派人士5名、总工会3名、共青团3名、妇女联合会3名、工商业联合会10名、科学技术协会3名、文化艺术界3名、科学技术界12名、社会科学界3名、经济界11人、农林界13名、教育界12名、体育界3名、医药卫生界7名、少数民族5名、特别邀请人士16名。

一次会议于1998年3月21—26日在县城召开。出席会议委员120名，县副县级以上领导干部和部分离退休干部列席会议。会议听取审议政协常委会工作报告、提案工作报告；听取讨论县政府工作报告和其他报告、县委书记李忠和市政协副主席张道煌讲话；选举李以智为县政协第五届委员会主席，张其沾、黄生谷、陈继春、余大维、汤太祥、米良才为副主席，黄生谷为秘书长（兼），常务委员19名。通过各项决议。收到委员提案原案133件，归纳合并为108件，审查立案71件，其余作其他处理。

二次会议于1999年1月31日—2月3日在县城召开。出席会议委员108名，县副县级以上领导干部列席会议，李忠作重要讲话，市政协副主席施建超到会祝贺。会议听取审议县政协常委会工作报告、提案工作报告；听取讨论县政府工作报告和其他报告；补选凌瑞梁为县政协第五届委员会秘书长。通过各项决议。收到委员提案原案103件，归纳合并为89件，审查立案55件，其余作其他处理。

三次会议于2000年2月20—24日在县城召开。出席会议委员124名，县副县级以上领导干部列席会议，李忠作重要讲话。市政协副主席毛彝铭到会祝贺。会议听取审议政协常委会工作报告、提案工作报告；听取讨论县政府工作报告和其他报告。通过各项决议。收到委员提案120件，归纳合并为107件，审查立案106件，其余作其他处理。

四次会议于2001年2月8—12日在县城召开。出席会议委员119名。县副县级以上领导干部列席会议，县委书记陈长发作重要讲话，市政协副主席孙立忠到会祝贺。会议听取审议政协常委会工作报告、提案工作报告、会议期间提案审查情况报告；听取讨论县政府工作报告和其他报告。通过各项决议。收到委员提案原案108件，归纳合并为98件，审查立案94件，其余作其他处理。

五次会议于2002年1月20—24日在县城召开。出席会议委员118名，县副县级以上干部列席会议。陈长发作重要讲话，市政协孙立忠、市委统战部副部长谭亦先到会祝贺。会议听取审议政协常委会工作报告、提案工作报告；听取讨论县政府工作报告和其他报告；选举皮世凯为县政协第五届委员会副主席。通过各项决议。收到委员提案原案120件，归纳合并为107件，审查立案106件，其余作其他处理。

四、第六届委员会全体会议

第六届委员会委员152名。其中：中共13名、无党派民主人士6名、共青团4名、总工会4名、妇女联合会3名、工商联17名、科学技术协会4名、文化艺术界3名、科学技术界13名、社会科学界3名、经济界18名、农业界16名、教育界13名、体育界3名、医药卫生界7名、少数民族宗教界7名、特别邀请人士18名。

一次会议于2003年3月1—6日在县城召开。出席会议委员149名，列席人员70名。会议听取审议政协常委会工作报告、提案工作报告；听取讨论县政府工作报告和其他报告；选举吴德屏为县政协第六届委员会主席，皮世凯、李光祥、米良才、王忠碧、谢荣忠为副主席，张正方为秘书长，常务委员18名。通过各项决议。收到委员提案原案124件，归纳合并为117件，立案105件，其余作其他处理。

二次会议于2004年2月7—11日在县城召开。出席会议委员152名，列席人员51名。会议听取审议政协常委会工作报告、提案工作报告；听取讨论县政府工作报告和其他报告；增选政协第六届委员会常务委员2名。通过各项决议。收到委员提案原案155件，归纳合并为127件，立案114件，其余作其他处理。

三次会议于2005年2月24—28日在县城召开。出席会议委员153名，列席人员51名。会议听取审议政协常委会工作报告、提案工作报告；听取讨论县政府工作报告和其他报告；增选县政协第六届委员会常务委员1名。通过各项决议。收到委员提案原案149件，归纳合并为128件，立案116件，其余作其他处理。

四次会议于2006年3月5—8日在县城召开。出席会议委员152名，列席人员62名。会议听取审议政协常委会工作报告、提案工作报告；听取讨论县政府工作报告和其他报告。通过各项决议。收到提案原案147件，审查合并为126件，立案116件，其余作其他处理。

五、第七届委员会全体会议

第七届委员会委员163名。其中：中共14名、无党派民主人士5名、共青团4名、总工会4名、妇女联合会3名、工商业联合会26名、科学技术协会4名、文化艺术界4名、科学技术界14名、社会科学界3名、经济界17名、农业界15名、教育界15名、体育界3名、医药卫生界7名、少数民族宗教界6名、特别邀请人士19名。

一次会议于2006年11月19—24日在县城召开。出席会议委员159名，列席人员56名。会议听取审议政协常委会工作报告、提案工作报告；听取讨论县政府工作报告和其他报告；选举吴德屏为县政协第七届委员会主席，汤太祥、皮世凯、米良才、王忠碧、周鑫为副主席，何海忠为秘书长，常委会委员19名。通过各项决议。收到委员提案原案160件，审查合并为132件，立案127件，其余作其他处理。

二次会议于2007年3月5—8日在县城召开。出席会议委员160名，列席人员60名。会议听取审议政协常委会工作报告、提案工作报告；听取讨论县政府工作报告和其他报告。通过各项决议。会议收到委员提案原案32件，归纳合并为29件，立案26件，其余作其他处理。

三次会议于2008年3月3—6日在县城召开。出席会议委员163名，列席人员59名。市政协副主席刘建军，市委统战部副部长、市对台办主任李静到会祝贺。会议听取审议政协常委会工作报告，政协第七届委员会第一、二次会议提案工作报告；补选县政协第七届委员会常务委员2名；通过各项决议。收到提案原案104件，审查合并为97件，立案92件，作建议意见处理5件。

四次会议于2009年3月2—5日在县城召开。出席会议委员163名，列席人员63名。市政协副主席刘建军，市委统战部副部长、市民族宗教事务委员会主任李华到会指导。会议听取审议政协常委会工作报告、提案工作报告；听取讨论县政府工作报告和其他报告。通过各项决议。收到委员提案原件104件，审查合并为97件，立案92件，作建议意见处理5件。

五次会议于2010年3月1—5日在县城召开。出席会议委员163名，列席人员53名。刘建军、李华到会指导。会议听取审议政协常委会工作报告、提案工作报告；听取讨论县政府工作报告和其他报告；补选县政协常委会委员3名。通过各项决议。收到委员提案原件105件，审查合并为95件，立案94件，作建议意见处理1件。

息烽县政协1990—2010年历届主席、副主席名录

表5-3-1

届 次	职 务	姓 名	性别	任职时间	备 注
第三届	主席	黄永刚	男	1990年4月—1993年4月	
	副主席	刘守珍	女	1990年4月—1993年4月	
		蒙锡琚	男	1990年4月—1993年4月	
		吕莹琳	女	1990年4月—1993年4月	
		黄及翔	男	1990年4月—1993年4月	
		张其沾	男	1991年3月—1993年4月	补选
第四届	主席	蒋光国	男	1993年4月—1998年2月	
	副主席	张其沾	男	1993年4月—1998年2月	
		黄及翔	男	1993年4月—1998年2月	
		文昌碧	女	1993年4月—1995年8月	
		余大维	男	1993年4月—1998年2月	
		陈继春	女	1993年4月—1998年2月	
第五届	主席	李以智	男	1998年2月—2003年3月	
	副主席	张其沾	男	1998年2月—2001年3月	
		黄生谷	男	1998年2月—2003年3月	
		陈继春	女	1998年2月—2001年6月	
		余大维	男	1998年2月—2000年8月	
		汤太祥	男	1998年2月—2003年3月	
		米良才	男	1998年2月—2003年3月	
第六届	主席	吴德屏	男	2003年3月—2006年11月	
	副主席	皮世凯	男	2003年3月—2006年11月	
		李光祥	男	2003年3月—2006年11月	
		米良才	男	2003年3月—2006年11月	
		王忠碧	女	2003年3月—2006年11月	苗族
		谢荣忠	男	2003年3月—2006年11月	
第七届	主席	吴德屏	男	2006年11月—	
	副主席	汤太祥	男	2006年11月—	
		皮世凯	男	2006年11月—	
		米良才	男	2006年11月—	
		王忠碧	女	2006年11月—	苗族
		周 鑫	男	2006年11月—	

第二节 政协常委会

一、工作机构

1991年，县政协常务委员会（简称县政协常委会）设办公室、学习宣传委员会、提案法制委员会、文史资料委员会、经济科技委员会、教卫文体委员会、社会联谊委员会，在九庄区、永阳区、黑神庙区、养龙区和永靖镇分别设政协息烽县委员会常委会政协工作联络组（一度改成工作委员会）。县政府智力支边办公室设在县政协。1992年撤区并乡建镇，全县新建10个乡（镇）分别设政协工作联络组。1996年6月，乡镇政协联络组撤销。1997年5月，撤销提案法制委员会、文史资料委员会、社科联谊委员会，组建提案法制社联委员会、经济科技委员会、教卫文体委员会。2003年9月，增设人口资源环境委员会。

二、常委会会议辑要

县政协常委会由主席、副主席、秘书长、常委会委员组成。常委会会议每季度召开一次，必要时可临时举行。会议主要议题：审议县政协及常委会会务和工作中的重大事项；协商讨论县委、县政府重大方针政策和社会生活中的重大事项，提出建议、意见；审议县政协全体会议文件和重要建议案、提案、视察报告、调查报告等。1991—2010年，县政协常委会举行会议127次。

（一）三届常委会会议辑要

1991年3月11—12日，举行第五次会议，协商讨论县政府工作报告；讨论县政协三届常委会工作报告和提案工作情况报告。6月28—30日，举行第八次会议，传达学习全国政协会议精神；听取县政府领导通报1991年上半年全县经济工作情况、社会治安综合治理情况；听取县政协赴乌当、云岩考察组参观考察两地乡镇企业、街道企业情况汇报、经科委赴省蚕科所考察学习栽桑养蚕情况汇报；听取县委对台办通报对台工作情况。9月17—19日，举行第九次会议，传达贯彻上级有关会议精神；听取县政府有关情况通报；协商讨论《息烽县国民经济和社会发展“八五”计划和十年规划》草案。11月27—29日，举行第十次会议，贯彻学习中央和省、地有关会议精神；讨论如何围绕经济中心开展政协工作；听取各专门委员会和区、镇工作委员会汇报1991年工作情况。1992年6月25—27日，举行第十三次会议，传达学习省发（1992）11号文件；听取县政府领导通报1992年前5个月经济工作情况及加快改革开放步伐的措施；协商讨论县房改实施方案（草案）。11月18—20日，举行第十五次会议，传达学习中共十四大精神；听取县政府1—10月经济工作情况通报；听取各专门委员会和各乡镇联络组工作情况汇报；协商决定1993年县政协换届方案。1993年2月25—26日，举行第十六次会议，传达学习政协七届一次会议精神；听取县委书记陈华祥通报安顺地区三干会精神和1993年全县工作安排。讨论通过政协三届常委会工作报告。视察全县基本农田建设情况。

（二）四届常委会会议辑要

1993年6月28—30日举行第二次会议，传达学习县第八次党代会精神和省政协安顺地区工委第十五次会议精神。听取县政府领导通报全县1993年上半年经济工作情况；讨论通过《中国人民政治协商会议息烽县委员会关于政治协商 民主监督的暂行规定》《政协息烽县第四届常务委员会工作规则》《政协息烽县第四届委员会专门委员会组织通则》《政协息烽县第四届委员会乡镇联络组工作暂行办法》；协商通过各专门委员会组成人员名单和人事任免事项。9月28—29日，举行第三次会议，传达学习上级有关反腐倡廉文件和会议精神；听取县委副书记、县长黑卫平关于统战和政协工作讲话、县纪委领导通报全县反腐倡廉工作情况、县政协有关调查和视察情况报告等。12月7—9日，举行第四次会议，传达学习江泽民、李瑞环在全国统战工作会议上的重要讲话，中共中央关于建立社会主义市场经济体制若干问题的决定，省第七次党代会精神；县领导通报县委、县政府1994年工作打算、1993年农村经济情况和今冬明春农村工作安排等。1994年6—12月，相继举行第七次至第九次会议，学习新修订的人民政协章程、《中共中央关于加强党的建设几个重大问题的决定》、全国政协主席李瑞环会见贵州省政协领导同志时的重要讲话、全省政协工作会议精神；听取讨论县政府领导通报县国营工业企业和乡镇企业情况、1994年国民经济和社会发展情况、县教育发展情况和政协委员提案办理情况、“八七”扶贫攻坚计划草案等。1995年6—12月，县政协相继举行第十二次至第十五次会议，传达学习中共中央关于制定国民经济和社会发展“九五”计划和2010年远景目标的建议和有关会议精神；听取讨论县政府关于全县农业综合开发情况通报、扶贫工作和乡镇企业情况通报和1—8月经济工作情况。听取县政法委通报1995年全县社会治安综合治理情况，县委书记黑卫平通报1995年财政收支情况和扶贫开发、经济发展思路；听取各专门委员会和乡镇联络组1995年工作情况汇报等。1996年3—10月，相继举行第十七次至第十九次会议，审议通过县政协《关于切实纠正烤烟收购中的不正之风　确保我县烤烟生产顺利发展》建议案；听取讨论县政府领导通报非公有制经济发展情况、县“严打办”通报“严打”斗争情况、《息烽县乡镇企业优惠政策及服务措施（征求意见稿）》；听取县政协经科委视察报告。1997年7—12月，相继举行第二十三次、第二十五次会议，听取讨论县禁毒委员会通报全县禁毒工作情况；听取县政协有关调查、视察报告；协商讨论县政府提交的息烽县发展非公有制经济等5个专题草案。

（三）五届常委会会议辑要

1998年5—9月，相继举行第二次至第六次会议，传达学习李瑞环主席在全国政协九届一次常委会上的讲话、中共中央《关于全党深入学习邓小平理论的通知》《江泽民总书记在第二期中央委员和候补委员学习邓小平理论和十五大精神研讨班结业式上的讲话》和省第八次党代会精神；听取、讨论县政府创建省级卫生县城工作通报、县政府《关于息烽县村级公路建设工作汇报》《关于息烽县水利建设和管理情况的汇报》；审议通过县政协《关于政治协商　民主监督　参政议政的规定》、常务委员会工作规则、专门委员会通则、《关于深入学习邓小平理论的意见》和治理底寨河渠道建议案、扩大巴西陆稻试种面积建议案；听取县政协教卫文体委员会《关于“国家贫困地区义务教育工程”在我县实施情况的视察报告》、经科委、支边办《关于冬瓜嫁接西瓜和巴西陆稻试种情况的报告》等。

1999年4—12月，相继举行第九次至第十三次会议，传达学习全国、省、市政协会议精神、《中共中央关于国有企业改革和发展若干重大问题的决定》和江泽民主席在庆祝中华人民共和国成立50周年大会上的讲话、县委九届七次全会精神等；听取并讨论县政府关于禁毒工作和巴西陆稻种植情况通报，息烽县近年油菜生产情况汇报、秋淡菜生产情况汇报、1999年1—8月份经济工作情况通报、村级民主制度建设情况通报、合作医疗试点情况通报和国有企业改革情况；协商讨论《县人民政府工作报告（征求意见稿）》、县建设局关于永靖镇东门小区规划说明；审议通过县政协《关于认真学习宣传贯彻落实中共十五届四中全会精神的决定》和人事任免事项；讨论通过县政协经科委《关于建立我县优质（双低）油菜生产基地的调查报告》、智力支边办《关于息烽县发展秋淡蔬菜的调查报告》等。

2000年4—12月，相继举行第十六次至第二十次会议，学习李瑞环主席在全国政协九届三次会议闭幕会上的讲话、全国政协九届三次会议决议、“三个代表”重要思想和江泽民总书记在全国统战工作会上的讲话；组织收看电教片《胡长清案件警示录》；听取讨论县政府关于底寨河渠道改造、“双低”油菜基地生产和巴西陆稻扩种的情况通报、2000年上半年国民经济和社会发展计划执行情况、息烽县城总体规划方案、生猪发展情况、“牛改”工作情况和扶贫项目及资金管理情况的通报和县政协各视察、调查组的视察、调查报告。会议决定：将修改后的《生猪发展调查报告》作为常委会建议案和其他两个调查、视察报告报送县政府参考。听取讨论县卫生局《关于息烽县初级卫生保健达标工作进展情况的通报》、县教育局《关于我县“两基”达标工作情况汇报》、县民宗局《关于我县民族地区经济社会发展的情况通报》；审议通过县政协政治协商、民主监督、参政议政的实施意见，民主监督评议工作实施意见和提案、建议案、意见、建议工作实施意见。

2001年3—12月，举行第二十二次至第二十六次会议，学习江泽民总书记在江苏、浙江、上海考察工作时的讲话、中共中央办公厅《关于在农村开展“三个代表”重要思想学习教育的意见》《息烽县“三个代表”重要思想学习教育活动方案》《全国政协九届四次会议主要精神及贯彻意见》《全国人大四次会议精神传达提纲》《中共贵州省委关于加强政协工作的决定》，全国地方政协工作经验座谈会议精神和李瑞环主席在全国地方政协工作经验座谈会结束时的讲话；听取讨论县政府关于《我县生态渔业基地建设情况》《关于我县烤烟生产前期工作情况通报》《农村贫困户建房和茅草房改造工作情况》《我县乡（镇）卫生院　村卫生室基本情况及工作开展情况》、县委精神文明办负责人通报《全县精神文明活动中心建设情况》；协商讨论县政府《工作报告》和计划、财政报告；协商决定有关人事任免事项。

2002年4月4日至12月，举行县政协五届三十二次至三十四次会议，学习全国政协九届五次会议精神和李瑞环主席在全国政协九届五次会议闭幕会上的讲话、江泽民总书记在中央党校省部级干部学习班毕业典礼上的讲话；协商讨论县政府《关于我县退耕还林工程实施情况的通报》《关于我县流动人口计划生育齐抓共管工作的情况报告》、全县沼气池生态项目建设情况和基层公安派出所建设情况、2002年政协委员提案办理情况、“渴望工程”建设、管理、使用情况、县城城市建设情况和县委关于党政机关贯彻落实《公民道德建设实施纲要》情况；协商决定有关人事任免事项。

（四）六届常委会会议辑要

2003年4—12月，举行县政协六届一次至四次常委会议，学习中共十六大、十六届三中全会和全国“两会”精神、“三个代表”重要思想；听取讨论县政府关于防治“非典型肺炎”、小寨坝磷化工基地一期工程和南山大道建设情况，关于集镇规划、建设、管理，全县农业产业结构调整、基础设施建设，加强公安工作、全县养殖业发展、司法工作，办理县六届政协一次会议委员提案，办理县政协建议案的情况通报；听取讨论县检察院2003年检察工作、县人民法院关于充分发挥审判职能为全县经济和社会发展提供司法保障、县纪委2003年党风廉政建设、纪检监察工作的情况通报；审议通过《中国人民政治协商会议息烽县委员会常务委员会工作规则（草案）》《息烽县政协各专门委员会通则（草案）》等。

2004年1—12月，举行县政协六届五次至九次会议，学习中共十六届四中全会精神、《政协章程》；协商讨论“一府两院”工作报告；听取县政府“双拥”工作、“五五”普法和依法治县工作、办理六届二次会议以来提案工作情况通报；听取县工商联民营企业的发展和对策的调研报告；协商决定县政协六届二次会议有关事项；审议通过县政协六届委员会优秀提案和提案承办先进单位优秀政协委员奖励办法、2004年工作要点等。

2005年2—12月，举行县政协六届十二次至十六次会议，学习《中共中央关于进一步加强中国共产党领导的多党合作和政治协商制度建设的意见》《中共贵州省委关于进一步加强中国共产党领导的多党合作和政治协商制度建设的实施意见》和全国政协主席贾庆林在政协十届全国委员会常务委员会第十次会议上的讲话；协商讨论县国民经济和社会发展“十一五”规划纲要、县政协2005年调研视察题目、县委统战部提出补选常委会委员建议名单；听取县政府通报2005年上半年经济运行及下半年经济工作安排、“四五”普法依法治县县级验收、创建“平安息烽”、办理《加强农村缺水地区水利工程规划、建设、管理的建议案》、县人民法院刑事审判工作、县人口与计生工作、国土资源开发利用和管理、环境保护、国民经济和社会发展“十一五”规划编制工作进展情况通报等。

2006年2—11月，举行县政协六届十七次至二十一次会议，学习《中共中央关于加强人民政协工作的意见》《中共贵州省委关于加强人民政协工作的实施意见》《中共中央关于学习〈江泽民文选〉的决定》及《中共贵阳市委关于加强人民政协工作的实施意见》；协商讨论县政府工作报告、县政协七届一次会议的有关事项、主席会议督办提案；听取县政府关于建设社会主义新农村、2006年上半年经济和社会发展、整脏治乱工作的情况通报和县政协关于县人口与计划生育村民自治、全县商品房市场情况、全县“无毒县”创建情况的调研通报；听取审议县政府办理县政协关于对全县“无毒县”创建工作、加强全县商品房建设管理、进一步加强和规范全县自来水的使用和管理建议案的办理情况报告。

（五）七届常委会会议辑要

2007年1—12月，举行一次至四次会议，学习中共十七大精神、省委办公厅、省政府办公厅转发的《贵州省政协办公厅关于加强和改进提案工作的意见》《中共贵阳市委关于加强人民政协工作的实施意见》、全国政协贾庆林主席的《运用科学理论指导和推动新世纪新阶段人民政协工作》和《中共贵州省委关于巩固和壮大新世纪新阶段统一战线的实施意见》等；听取县政府安全生产情况、办理县政协建议案、“抓重建，保民生”，建设生态文明县、县纪委2006年党风廉政建设情况、县人民武装部《关于息烽县人民武装工作情况通报》、县法院、县检察院、县公安局工作的情况通报；协商通过召开县政协七届二次会议有关事项和县政协2007年工作要点。

2008年2—12月，举行十次至十八次会议，学习中共十七届三中全会精神、胡锦涛在中央各部委、各省、市、自治区领导大会上的讲话、县委领导关于“抓重建，保民生”工作的重要讲话精神，学习《贵州日报》社论《论〈守土有责　守土尽责〉》；协商讨论“一府两院”工作报告；协商通过政协七届三次会议有关事项；审议通过县政协增补常务委员候选人建议名单（草案）；听取县政府关于“抓重建，保民生”，建设生态文明县、2008年上半年全县经济和社会发展、县政法委“无毒县”创建、县检察院监所检察等工作情况通报和县政协有关工作机构视察通报等。

2009年2—12月，举行二十一次至二十六次会议，学习中共十七届四中全会决定、公报和胡锦涛总书记在庆祝人民政协成立六十周年大会上的重要讲话；听取县政府“两基”迎国检、“五五”普法、依法治县、创建法治息烽、农村危房改造、打击“两抢一盗”、保卫百姓平安、2009年上半年全县经济社会运行工作情况通报，县政府有关工作部门关于2009年财政运行、计生工作、低保工作和甲型H1N1流感防控、办理县政协关于息烽旅游产业发展建议情况通报，县人民法院贯彻实施全国人大常委会《关于完善人民陪审员制度的决定》、县人民检察院控告申诉检察，县政协有关工作机构关于旅游资源开发及旅游产业发展、乡村旅游发展、农村土地流转及农村劳动力转移情况调研汇报等。

2010年3—12月，举行二十九次至三十三次会议，学习全国两会精神、息烽县创建“四优”“三好”“一满意”活动实施意见和余心声《论又好又快　更好更快发展》文章；听取县政府创建国家卫生城市、创建国家环境保护模范城市、创建全国文明城、西望山虫茶产业发展、抗旱救灾、县城旧城改造、县住建局关于阳朗片区新城规划及工程进展和县林业绿化局森林防火工作情况通报；协商通过县政协经科委关于民营煤矿企业生产及建设造成地质灾害解决办法的调研报告等。

第三节　主要工作与活动

一、政治协商

1991—2010年，县政协坚持对全县政治、经济、文化和社会生活的重要问题，在县委、县政府作出决策之前或在决策执行过程中的重要问题进行协商。主要通过政协全体会议、常委会议、主席会议、常委会专题会议、政协各专门委员会会议等形式进行讨论协商；县政协主席列席县委常委会议，副主席列席政府、人大有关会议等，就列席会议涉及的议题进行协商。县政协每年除全委会围绕党政中心工作开展政治协商外，还拟出议题进行调研，组织专题协商活动，为县委、县政府决策提供参考。其间，1991—1993年，县政协三届常委会就县委、政府委托及自拟的有关两个文明建设、加强党风和廉政建设、社会主义民主与法制建设、国民经济和社会发展十年规划、“八五”计划、改革开放中的重大决策、住房制度改革方案等进行协商讨论。至1997年，县政协四届常委会相继就“八七”扶贫攻坚计划、国民经济和社会发展“九五”计划及2010年远景目标纲要、“九五”期间社会主义精神文明建设规划及非公有制经济、国有企业、乡镇企业及教育事业发展、农业综合开发、反腐倡廉、社会治安综合治理、“严打”斗争、全县禁毒工作等进行协商。其中，1996年3月21日县政协四届常委会十五次会议提出的《关于切实纠正烤烟收购中的不正之风　确保全县烤烟生产顺利发展的建议案》，县委、县政府采纳后作出相应决定。

1998年起，县政协建立县委、县政府工作部门与县政协专门委员会对口协商制度，拓宽政治协商领域，使政治协商落到实处，更具针对性。2000年8月5日，县委转发县政协关于《政协息烽县委员会履行政治协商　民主监督　参政议政职能的实施意见》，明确政治协商的原则、主要内容、主要形式、方法及要求，使政治协商更加科学规范。

2005年9月26日，县政协六届常委会十五次会议，听取县国土资源开发利用和管理情况通报。会议认为：国土资源开发利用和管理工作取得一定成绩，但还存在几个问题：土地利用总体规划在用地布局上不尽合理，急需进行规划修编，调整用地布局；非农建设用地审批程序多、时间长，导致未批先用的情况时有发生；无证采矿，特别是无证采煤现象屡禁不止。建议县国土局针对以上问题，采取相应措施，确保“十一五”人口资源环境工作健康、有序发展。

2006年3月，县政协六届常委会十八次会议，听取县政府关于建设社会主义新农村的情况通报。会议认为，县委、县政府贯彻中央、省、市关于加快社会主义新农村建设的若干意见，决定用5～15

年时间，扎实开展社会主义新农村建设工作，是全面建设小康社会，构建社会主义和谐社会的客观要求，是抓好“三农”工作的有力举措。建议：建设社会主义新农村要科学规划，结合实际，因地制宜，分类指导，抓好试点，逐一推进；加大扶贫开发力度，建立长效机制，为社会主义新农村建设打下基础；加大宣传力度，转变观念，整合资源，找准载体，成熟一个发展一个。

2006年7月，县政协六届常委会十九次会议，听取全县“无毒县”创建情况的调研通报。会议指出，禁毒工作是关系国家和民族兴旺发达的大事，息烽各界群众对创建无毒县工作非常关注，各级各部门要高度重视，把创建工作纳入本部门工作的议事日程，要进一步加大宣传力度，动员全县人民共同参与创建，千方百计堵住毒品来源；建立长效机制，巩固创建成果警钟长鸣，常抓不懈；要建立好各类档案，做到底数清，情况明，进一步采取有力措施，把禁毒工作抓落实。议定将调研报告上升为建议案供县委、县政府决策时参考。

2007—2010年，县政协七届常委会举行会议31次。通过召开常委会议、主席会议、专题协商会议，对全县“三创一办”（创建国家卫生城市、创建国家环境保护模范城市、创建全国文明城市，办好2011年第9届全国少数民族传统体育运动会）、“十二五”规划制定、生态文明县建设、城镇规划建设与管理、旅游发展、交通建设、商品房维修基金管理、“清理并完善职工集资建房手续”“西望山景区开发”“阳朗新区规划建设”和“县城旧城改造”“息烽河治理”、农村劳动力转移培训、加强对灾后重建项目资金的监督管理、加大县城环境绿化力度、“两基”迎国检、农村危房改造、“五五”普法等工作进行讨论协商。

二、民主监督

1991年，县政协通过开展调查、视察和参与有关职能部门工作检查等，就工作中存在的问题提出意见和建议，履行民主监督职能。是年，县政协各专门委员会组织政协委员开展调查、视察11次，形成调查、视察报告10篇，就有关方面工作提出意见、建议52条，被有关部门采纳39条。县政协主席、副主席及各专委会主任、副主任参加县委、县政府及有关部门组织的活动和工作检查43次。次年，采取“专门委员会牵头，分管主席挂帅，吸收政协委员参加，职能部门配合”的方法，自拟题目，开展专题调查16次、专项视察10次，写出调查、视察报告各10篇，提出建议、意见108条。

1993年，县政协有关专门委员会对西山乡群力小学搬迁问题、九庄计划生育合同管理情况等8个项目开展专题调查，对县粮食专区项目区水利工程建设实施情况进行视察，写出调查报告6篇、视察报告1篇，提出建议、意见30条。至2002年，县政协先后就县农村经济结构调整、非公有制经济发展、扶贫开发、部分国有企业和乡镇企业发展情况、乌江流域息烽县境治理情况、贵遵高等级公路息烽段第一期工程建设情况、下洪马水库配套工程、养龙司生猪养殖发展情况、城市建设规划、交通、水利建设、生态养殖、教育、文化、卫生、计划生育、旅游、社会治安、精神文明建设、少数民族聚居区经济发展、扶贫项目资金的使用和管理、农村医疗卫生工作、计划生育工作中持证生育情况、果品生产及农业科技推广情况、合作基金会运行等工作开展调查、视察和考察活动79次，提出意见、建议486条。

2003年起，县政协以民主评议为载体，探索民主监督新途径，增强民主监督针对性和有效性。是年，在县工商行政管理局开展民主监督评议试点，制定民主监督评议试点实施方案，从组织动员、调查研究、监督评议、整改回访四个阶段对县工商行政管理局进行民主监督评议。评议工作以“正面评议，民主监督、献计献策，共谋发展”为目的，按“统一部署、量力而行、先易后难、实事求是、客观公正、务求实效”进行。通过民主监督评议，授予县工商行政管理局“民主监督评议满意单位”牌子。是年，派员参与县质监局、教育局、旅游局民主评议行风工作。2004年，对县交通局进行民主监督评议，采取听、看、查、访、议方式，发问卷调查表100份，广泛听取群众意见。召开各类座谈会9次，收集意见、建议74条，汇总梳理后提出改进意见、建议13条。

2010年，组织政协委员对县虫茶产业发展情况、人畜饮水情况、创建国家卫生城市、环境保护模范城市及饮用水源环境保护情况等16个方面开展调研视察，撰写调研视察报告8篇，梳理出存在困难或问题36个，提出意见、建议53条。

三、参政议政

1991—2010年，县政协编发《工作简讯》《社情民意》，在报刊刊登各类信息、文稿等及时反映社情民意。2005年年初，县政协广泛听取干部群众意见，编发《增强住房公积金透明度　让广大职工明白放心》一文，引起贵阳市住房公积金管理中心领导的重视。是年8月，该中心领导专程到息烽县政协听取意见，解答问题。两个月后，该中心将息烽县作为全市第一家发放“住房公积金缴存凭证”试点县，在开户银行安装查询设备，方便职工查询，解除职工疑虑。

四、提案办理

1990年4月至1992年3月，县政协三届委员会举行全体会议3次，收到委员提案249件，内容涉及农业、工业、乡镇企业、交通运输、教育科技、医疗卫生、城乡建设、人口与计生、环保等领域。经审查整理归类合并为174件，审查立案145件，作建议意见处理29件。对立案的145件送承办单位办理。办理过程中，县政协提案法制委员会组织委员走访承办单位，了解办理情况，共同协商，促进提案办理落实。其间，县政协有关专委会对提案的提出、立案及办理等进行积极探索总结，组织外出考察学习，借鉴外地成功经验和做法，不断改进工作方法，提高提案质量和办理实效，发挥政协“参政议政、民主监督”主渠道作用。

1993年4月至1997年3月，县政协四届委员会举行全体会议5次，收到委员提案261件，内容涉及工业、农业、城建、交通、邮电通讯、文教卫生、社会治安、勤政廉政建设、人民群众生产生活等方面。经审查整理归类合并为241件，立案127件，作建议意见处理114件。其间，1993年，县政协审查提案时，本着有利于息烽经济、社会发展，有利于党委、政府决策，有利于发挥政协职能的要求，筛选出重点提案，或提交主席会议审定，作视察调查课题，明确相关委员会牵头实施；或提请常委会审议后作建议案送县政府处理，加大重点提案的办理力度，增强办理效果。

1998年2月至2002年1月，县政协五届委员会举行全体会议5次，收到委员提案559件，内容涉及经济建设、精神文明建设、科技、文化、卫生、人事劳动和社会保障、民族宗教、民政、农业、水利、电力、交通、通讯等。经审查整理归类合并为475件，其中立案374件，作意见或建议处理101件。其间，1998年，县政协为避免由于会议期间审查提案时间紧，易发生疏漏现象，改会议期间审查为会后集中审查，提高提案审查质量。县委、县政府把提案办理工作列入年度目标管理，年终进行考核。开展提案办理信息反馈工作，要求承办单位将办理提案情况以书面形式答复提案人，征求提案人意见。1999年，县政协五届委员会通过主席会议、常委会议、委员活动，组织委员学习党和国家的方针政策，邀请党政部门通报全县政治经济和改革开放情况，组织委员调查、考察，为委员订阅报刊等，帮助委员“知情知政”，为委员提高提案质量打基础；制定调研、审查立案、督促催办、跟踪问效反馈四项制度，提升提案工作规范化、制度化管理水平。要求委员提出提案前，须深入实际调查研究，掌握第一手资料，使所提提案具有严肃性、科学性和可操作性。要求做到“五个不提”（未经核实的问题不提，非重要问题不提，政策、法律法规未弄清楚的不提，涉及司法诉讼、国家机密的问题不提，没有解决办法的不提）；严格按立案标准审查立案，对不符合立案标准的作意见建议处理。要求把好“五关”（格式关、文字关、内容和事实关、政策和法律关、保密关）；要求有关专委会在提案办理过程中，采取电话、信函和深入承办单位催办等方式，了解提案办理情况，协调解决办理中的问题；对已办复的提案进行跟踪问效。2000年8月，县委转发《政协息烽县委员会提案　建议案　意见建议工作实施意见》。同月，县政协在市提案工作回顾和研讨会上，作《加大提案办理力度　提高提案办理质量》专题发言，会后，《人民政协报》《贵州政协报》《息烽报》分别以《息烽县政协采取六条措施　加大提案办理力度》《采取新措施　切实做好委员提案办理工作》《雷厉风行　切实做好提案办理工作》为题对县政协提案工作进行报道。次年4月，县人大、县政府、县政协联合召开县人大代表建议、政协委员提案表彰暨交办会，表彰优秀提案人、提案办理先进单位和先进个人。

2003年3月至2006年3月，县政协第六届委员会举行全体会议4次，收到委员提案556件，内容涉及财税、金融、农业、林业、水利、广播电视、供电、通讯、国土、城建、教育、卫生等。经审查整理归类合并为495件，其中立案451件，作建议意见处理38件，超出范围转市政协交有关部门办理4件，不予立案2件。其间，2005年，县政协六届常委会修订出台《政协息烽县委员会提案工作条例》，对提案的选题、撰写、提交、办理、督办等方面作出明确规定。

2006年11月至2010年3月，县政协七届委员会举行全体会议5次，收到委员提案原案678件，内容涉及财政、金融、农业、林业、水利、交通、城建、旅游、文化、教育、医疗卫生等。其间，2009年，县政协在息烽电视台、《息烽宣传》及“息烽人民政府网”开辟征集提案线索专栏，建立“向市民征集提案线索”窗口平台，广泛征集提案线索。是年，《贵州政协报》刊登《“无毒县”：凝聚政协提案里的智慧与汗水》《息烽县政协积极为“旅游活县”出谋划策》，报道县政协提案工作。

优秀提案辑录：

县政协四届一次会议期间，政协委员提出《切实纠正烤烟收购中的不正之风　确保我县烤烟生产顺利发展》的提案，县政协常委会将该提案作建议案送县政府，县政府采取措施加强烤烟收购工作领导，修订完善相关规章制度，强化监督机制，使烤烟收购秩序明显好转，受到烟农好评。

县政协四届二次会议期间，政协委员提出《尽快维修底寨中学危房　消除不安全因素》提案，县政府召开县长办公会议研究，决定将底寨中学暂时搬迁至原螺栓厂子校上课，保证该校秋季按时开学。

县政协五届一次会议期间，政协委员提出《尽快修复底寨至养龙司坪山渠道》提案，县政府将其列入1999年拟办的实事之一，制定《底寨河道清淤方案》，组织县直机关单位职工、沿线受益农户参加底寨河渠道清淤义务劳动，为落实该提案奠定基础。

县政协五届三次会议期间，政协委员提出《建议加大对少数民族地区基础设施和经济发展的投入力度》提案，县政协提案法制社联委员会部分委员与县委统战部、县民宗局、扶贫办等单位人员组成调查组，调查10个乡镇少数民族聚居的5个村67个村民组经济发展、基础设施建设和文化教育情况，针对存在问题，提出建议10条，为县委、县政府做好民族工作，发展少数民族聚居地区经济提供决策参考。县民宗局投入资金5.62万元，解决少数民族地区修公路、人畜饮水、教学设备、贫困户建房等问题，新修教学点1个，解决41名少数民族学生就地入学问题。

县政协六届一次会议期间，政协委员提出《加强对个体饮食餐馆的卫生管理》提案。是年8月，县卫生局组织实施“食品放心工程”，督促饮食单位加大卫生设施硬件投入，要求无自行消毒条件的饮食单位使用消毒公司提供的消毒餐饮具；建立健全食品市场准入制度，规范食品卫生许可证发放管理工作；加强日常性卫生监督，每年监督检查不少于4次；培训食品从业人员，提高卫生知识和法律意识。

县政协六届四次会议期间，政协委员提出《改善县城人行道路面质量》提案，县建设局接到该提案后，筹集资金，修复县城文化北路、镇府路等路段共1.2万余平方米。

息烽县政协1998—2010年委员提案统计表

表5-3-2　　单位：件

年份	提案原案	归类整理	立案	其他处理
1998	133	108	71	37
1999	103	89	55	34
2000	120	107	106	1
2001	108	98	94	4
2002	120	107	106	1
2003	124	117	105	12
2004	155	127	114	13
2005	149	128	116	12
2006	307	258	243	15
2007	32	29	26	3
2008	104	97	92	5
2009	104	97	92	5
2010	105	95	94	1

五、文史征编

1991年，县政协文史工作主要开展各类史料征集。至1994年，征集各类史料100余万字。是年，编辑出版《息烽文史资料》5辑共65万字，其中第三辑中《军统在息烽》获安顺地区社科成果二等奖。与省、市政协文史委协作，编辑出版《息烽集中营》《杨虎城将军被囚息烽》两个专辑。

1998年7月，启动《贵州旅游文史系列丛书·息烽卷〈筑北灵秀〉》组稿、编辑工作。由主席领衔成立编委会，拟定篇目和编写方案。是年底出版发行。全书25万余字，图片54幅。从三大类（人文景观、旅游疗养、自然景观）、四大景区（息烽集中营旧址风景区、温泉风景区、西望山风景区、乌江峡风景区）、一大景群（息烽溶洞群）全面介绍息烽旅游资源。

1999年起，收集整理史料，相关工作交叉进行，适时编辑出版书籍。至2010年，相继编辑出版《息烽政协工作（1950—1997）》《军统魔窟·息烽集中营》《政协工作文件选编》《息烽政协工作（1998—2002）》《息烽政协委员手册》《中央红军过息烽》《国泉神汤·息烽温泉》《崛起黔中》等书籍，其中，《中央红军过息烽》《国泉神汤·息烽温泉》（简称“两本书”）出版发行后，受到社会各界好评，建议把“两本书”列为全县干部职工和中小学生必读书目。县委书记批示：“同意将《中央红军过息烽》《国泉神汤·息烽温泉》作为县农家书屋藏书，建议将《中央红军过息烽》作为推荐书目，向全县干部群众推荐。”县委宣传部行文向全县干部职工、中小学生推荐，要求各乡镇、各部门将“两本书”作为“读一本好书活动”中干部职工必读书目。中小学校将“两本书”作为课外辅导读物必读书目。为此，县政协开展“情系农家书屋”赠书活动，向全县161个村农家书屋、学生较多的中小学、县职校赠送“两本书”。

2010年，开展挖掘整理“全国妇女教育基地”养龙司乡堡子村半边天文化，收集整理资料10万余字，图片100余幅。是年，完成《妇女能顶半边天》一书初稿编写。

六、智力支边

1991年，县政协智力支边工作主要面向边远、贫困、少数民族地区开展适用技术推广和师资培训，组织政协委员开展科技扶贫和科技咨询，为发展农村经济服务。至1992年，邀请省教科所教育专家来县举办语文教学学术讲座；组织政协委员两次到流长乡、石硐乡开展义诊和医疗卫生保健咨询服务，到青山苗族乡各学校听课、进行现场指导，组织学生开展职业技术教育活动。

1993年起，智力支边工作以办科技示范点为重点，为人民群众传授先进种植技术，实施科技扶贫。至2002年，共办烤烟示范点8个、小麦示范点1个、油菜育苗移栽示范点4个、西瓜种植示范点1个、五倍子种植基地9个等。为九庄、石硐、青山、永靖4个乡镇引进优质花椒种苗20余万株。为养龙司乡引进紧凑型玉米种子100余千克。引进“中玉6号”玉米种，巴西陆稻、“K优4号”“K优5号”水稻种在养龙司、小寨坝等乡镇试种成功。引进小麦“96-195”“贵农12号”“96-166”，与“绵阳26号”包衣种和油菜“油研9号”进行试种试验。举办科技文化培训40期，培训人员5759人次。

2003年起，智力支边工作从输血型向造血型转变，重点在培训提高素质上做工作。至2006年，争取并组织实施智力支边项目117个，其中，培训、进修学习类项目108个，培训各类人员1.03万人次。争取农业专项资金32.5万元，引进捐赠资金47.5万元。联系、协调保送50名贫困初中生到省外职业学校免费学习。组织县政协委员到10个乡镇巡回义诊，为农村群众送医送药432人次。2007—2010年，组织实施智力支边项目89个，其中，培训项目60个，培训农业、医卫、教育人员1100余人次。为群众义诊500余人次。组织实施农村基础设施建设项目5个，投入资金213.92万元；协调组织各类捐赠活动20余次，捐赠物款204.22万元。

七、社会联谊

1991—2010年，县政协组织政协委员和各界人士开展走访“三胞两属”和接待台胞活动，广泛联络交友，促进祖国统一。利用春节、中秋等传统节日，举行“三胞两属”亲属代表会、座谈会等，宣传党的方针、政策，交流感情，增进互信。开展走访政协委员和各界人士活动，听取各方面建议、意见。

根据不同时期政协工作要求，与各级政协开展工作交流。接待省内外政协到息烽考察参观学习的团体或个人，组织政协委员、县政协机关干部外出考察学习，交流政协工作，取长补短，增进友谊。县政协相继参加川、黔、渝毗邻县市区政协工作协作会、贵州省乌江流域部分县市政协工作协作会和贵阳市区（市）、县政协工作研讨会。按每次会议要求组织材料，派员出席交流工作，学习其他成员单位工作经验。应邀参加贵阳市政协承办的十一个省会城市主席联谊会，列席省、市政协常委会和省政协委员约谈会等。2006年4月、2007年9月、2009年4月，县政协分别举办“川黔渝毗邻县政协工作协作会第二届第十四次年会”、贵州省乌江流域部分县市政协工作协作会和贵阳市区、市、县政协工作研讨会第二十八次会议。

20年间，县政协相继与近30个省内外区、市、县政协建立联系。县政协四届委员会接待省、市、区、县政协参观考察团（组）44个618人。组织政协机关干部职工、政协委员外出参观考察学习10余次。其间，2010年，组织政协委员到陕西、宁夏、福建等省区考察学习；到独山、平塘、惠水、兴仁、纳雍等县市就文史工作、提案办理、民营煤矿管理、旅游资源开发与佛教文化保护等进行考察学习。

第六篇　军　事

第一章　军事机构

县人民武装部（简称县人武部）是县委的军事工作部门和县政府的兵役机关，接受上级军事部门和地方党委、政府双重领导，并领导乡镇、厂矿基层武装部工作。基层武装部接受同级党委、政府和上级军事机关的双重领导，完成地方党委、政府和上级军事机关交给的其他任务。

第一节　人民武装部

一、县人民武装部

1991年，县人武部为副县级单位，隶属安顺军分区和县委、县政府双重领导。下设军事、政工、后勤三个科和办公室。1996年1月1日，息烽县由安顺地区划属贵阳市，县人武部由安顺军分区转属贵阳军分区。

1996年4月起，县人武部收归军队建制，改称中国人民解放军息烽县人民武装部，为军队正团级单位，属本地区军事领导指挥机关、县委的军事工作部门和县人民政府的兵役机关，接受上级军事机关和县委、县政府的双重领导。县委书记兼任人武部党委第一书记，人武部一名主官为县委常委，一名主官参加县人民政府常务会议。县人武部属二类人武部。

二、基层人民武装部

（一）区（镇）、乡（镇）武装部

1991年，全县有区（镇）武装部4个、乡（镇）武装部24个。1992年，撤区并乡建镇后，全县新建4镇6乡分别设武装部，有专职武装干部编制20人。其中永靖镇武装部3人、青山苗族乡1人，小寨坝镇、温泉镇、九庄镇、西山乡、石硐乡、鹿窝乡、流长乡、养龙司乡武装部各2人。2010年，全县10个乡镇武装部部长10人、干事10人。

（二）厂矿武装部

1991年初，全县有驻县厂矿武装部4个。是年2月、10月，相继建立息烽温泉疗养院武装部、息烽重钙厂武装部。此后，驻县厂矿武装部有撤、建、迁、合。2010年，全县有驻县厂矿武装部6个。

第二节　县人民武装组织

一、人民武装委员会

县人民武装委员会（简称县武委会），是县委领导下的人民武装力量的领导组织和领导机构，任务是贯彻执行上级武委会的指示，研究解决人民武装工作中的重大问题，协调各方力量，保证完成人民武装建设工作任务。县武委会主任由县委书记担任，副主任由县委副书记、县长担任，委员由县委常委、副县长、人武部部长、政委和宣传、人事、民政等有关部门负责人担任。县武委会每年召开会议1～2次，总结、研究和部署全县人民武装工作。1991—2010年，武委会成员进行过12次调整。

二、县国防动员委员会

1996年4月9日，县委、县政府、人武部联合行文，成立县国防动员委员会（简称县国动委），明确县武委会与县国动委为“一个机构，两块牌子”。规定县国动委为县政府领导下的国防动员组织机构，履行组织全县国防动员工作，协调经济与军事、政府与军队之间的关系职责，以增强国防实力和提高平时与战时的转换能力。县国动委设人民武装动员、人民防空、交通战备、经济动员4个办公室。1996年4月至2010年12月，县国动委召开全体委员会议28次。每年“八一”建军节，组织武委会、国动委成员过军事日，交流、研讨国防后备力量建设。

第二章　驻　军

1991—2010年，中国人民武装警察部队息烽县中队（简称县武警中队）、中国人民武装警察部队贵州省息烽县消防大队（简称县消防大队）、贵阳预备役工兵团二营、78088部队72分队、中国人民解放军56029部队、77146部队和贵州省武警部队一支队等部队，或参加县内抗洪抢险、救灾，或支援地方建设等，为息烽经济建设和社会稳定做出贡献。

第一节　县武警中队

1991—1995年，县武警中队隶属武警安顺地区支队。1996年1月1日起，隶属武警贵阳支队、县公安局双重领导。县武警中队为连级单位，负责看守在押犯人，维护安全稳定，支援地方两个文明建设等工作。

一、组织建设

1991年起，县武警中队按照《政治工作条例》，由中队指导员担任党支部书记，中队长担任副书记，副指导员担任团支部书记，排长或司务长担任团支部副书记。2004年7月，县武警中队党支部被贵州省武警总队党委表彰为“先进基层党组织”，指导员宋仁磊被表彰为“优秀党务工作者”。12月31日，县中队党支部被武警总队表彰为“党风廉政建设先进单位”。2005年5月，县中队团支部被贵州省武警总队团委表彰为“先进团支部”。至2010年，党支部发展党员80余人，团支部发展团员186人。

二、训练、执勤

县武警中队按照军队《队列条令》《纪律条令》《执勤条令》《军队基层建设纲要》教育管理部队，建立起正规的战备、训练、执勤、学习工作秩序，通过严格的教育、训练，提高官兵德、智、体素质。1991—2010年，看守在押犯人8309人次，参加全县“严打”，追捕人犯行动786次，出动官兵8767人次。2000年、2003年、2005年被评为贵州武警总队“基层建设先进中队”。

第二节　县消防大队

1975年，成立贵州省息烽县公安局消防股。次年，成立贵州省息烽县公安局消防中队。1982年2月，消防股改称消防科，消防中队改称中国人民武装警察贵州省息烽县消防中队。1991年，明确消防科为副营级单位，受武警安顺地区消防支队和县公安局双重领导。1996年1月16日，消防科、消防中队随行政区划变更，由安顺地区消防支队转隶贵阳市消防支队管理。1997年10月16日，县公安局消防科和县消防中队合并，组建中国人民武装警察部队贵州省息烽县消防大队（简称县消防大队），接受县公安局和贵阳市消防支队的双重领导。县消防大队主要负责消防安全知识宣传教育培训、进行防火检查、建立防火检查档案、扑救火灾、处理火灾事故等工作，保护人民的生命财产安全。

第三节　贵阳预备役工兵部队

1999年6月，省军区在息烽、修文、开阳3县组建贵阳陆军预备役工兵团，团部设在修文县；在息烽县永靖镇、小寨坝镇、养龙司乡、温泉镇组建预备役工兵团道路桥梁二营和团直属反地雷爆破连，二营营部设在县人武部民兵训练教学楼，由县人武部负责组建。8月2日，在修文县召开工兵团成立大会。9月15日，在县人武部举行道路桥梁二营各连、排干部任职和授预备役军衔仪式，县长、工兵团副团长陈长发宣布预备役工兵团二营正式成立。

第四节　其　他

1995年4月4日，中国人民解放军56029部队官兵驻县担负60.3千米光缆通信线路施工任务。部队指挥部驻县人武部民兵训练基地，一营驻养龙司，二营驻小寨坝，三营驻阳朗小学。该部队完成任务后，于6月8日离开息烽。

2002年10月，中国人民解放军78088部队72分队在县龙爪村建立通信站，负责军队通信光缆息烽段的维护。

2008年1月12日至2月27日，中国人民解放军77146部队和贵州省武警总队一支队官兵奉命于2月17日到县救援，负责抢修县境内因凝冻灾害损坏的供电供水线路及设备。经过15天昼夜奋战，县南山老厂村、大林口至九庄路段、青山苗族乡等重灾区恢复正常供水供电。3月3日，两支部队完成任务后返回贵阳。

第三章　兵　役

1991—1998年，县内实行义务兵役制，1998年《中华人民共和国兵役法》修订后，实行义务兵为主，与志愿兵相结合，民兵与预备役相结合的兵役制度。每年兵员征集时，在征兵领导小组的领导下，通过深入宣传和严格的体检、政审，确保征兵质量。至2010年，已有25年26次征兵无责任退兵，多次受到上级表彰。1991—2010年，全县输送的兵员中，有2人在服役期间荣立一等功，13人荣立二等功，25人荣立三等功，985人被评为“优秀士官”或“优秀士兵”。

第一节　兵役管理

一、兵役制度

1991—1998年，义务兵服现役为：陆军3年，空军和海军4年，期满可超期服役1～2年。服现役满5年，已成为专业技术骨干的义务兵，经本人申请，报经师以上机关批准，改为志愿兵，延长服役期8～12年，年龄不超过35岁。

1998年12月29日，《中华人民共和国兵役法》（以下简称《兵役法》）修订后，实行义务兵与志愿兵相结合、民兵与预备役相结合的兵役制度。服现役期限为2年，期满后根据军队需要和本人自愿，经团级以上单位批准，改为志愿兵，志愿兵称士官，延长服役期至少3年，不超过30年，年龄不超过55岁。

二、兵役登记

1991年起，县人武部按照《兵役法》和上级军事机关指示，组织全县各乡镇、厂矿武装部设立兵役登记站，对当年年满18周岁的公民进行兵役登记，填写《公民兵役登记表》。1996年起，为适龄公民填发“兵役证”。乡、镇、厂矿武装部组织开展适龄公民目测初检、病史调查，对其现实表现、文化程度、年龄、家庭情况等进行初审，合格者定为当年应征公民，上报县人武部，由县人武部从中挑选政治素质好、身体合格、文化程度较高的应征公民作当年的征集对象，并登记造册，通知到乡、镇、厂矿武装部及本人。对退出现役返乡的士兵、军官逐一登记造册，符合服预备役条件的，办理预备役登记手续。

三、专业技术人员登记

1993年5月18日，县成立地方与军队专业对口技术人员预备役登记领导小组，县长任组长，副县长、人武部部长、政委任副组长，组织县直机关，企、事业单位、10个乡镇、厂矿开展地方与军队专业对口技术人员预备役登记。全县登记3287人服预备役，其中18～28岁的2136人，29～35岁的1151人；以后逐年进行登记更换，年满35岁的退出预备役，符合预备役条件的登记服预备役。至2010年12月31日，登记服预备役的专业对口人员4218人，其中，中共党员687人、共青团员3521人。

四、国防潜力调查

1995年7月，县、乡镇、厂矿成立国防潜力调查工作领导小组，开展国防潜力调查工作，填写县国民经济及社会发展、兵员潜力、预备役军官、士兵、军地专业对口人员、医疗设备、邮电通信设备、交通运输、工程机械设备、人防战备工程、粮油储备、战备物资储备、战时民转企业、计算机配置等调查统计。至2010年，县人武部每年7—8月均开展国防潜力调查统计、核对工作，为战时兵员动员、物资供给动员打基础。

第二节 兵员征集

1990年起，兵员征集改春季征兵为冬季征兵。兵员征集时，成立以县长任组长，常务副县长、县人武部部长、政委任副组长，县有关单位领导为成员的县征兵领导小组，下设办公室（在县人武部）和宣传、纪检、体检、政审、优抚、后勤保障6个组，分别承担有关征兵事宜。

1993年起，在征兵中对体检的应征公民进行文化测试。1997年10月，在温泉镇进行征兵工作改革试点。次年5月，县武委会制定《息烽县征兵工作的若干规定》，进一步保证县境征兵质量。2001年9月，《征兵条例》修改后，《息烽县法制征兵试行办法》继续沿用。2002年6月，县制定《预征对象管理规定》，做到兵员质量、数量、流向“三个清楚”，以保证适龄青年报名率。2006年8月，县人武部出台《征兵工作检查评比标准》，对整个征兵工作实施量化管理，征兵经费、车辆物资保障等指标列入年度财政预算。

2010年，开展征兵工作与接兵方式改革。征兵走访调查与政审工作同步开展，女兵实行网上报名，由过去突击报名、体检、政审改为结合平时民兵工作确定预征对象，搞好初审、初检和病史调查，逐步实现征兵工作法律化、规范化、制度化。广泛宣传《中华人民共和国兵役法》《征兵工作条例》。此外，通过县广播电视台，县移动、联通公司将10万条征兵宣传信息发送给手机用户。

1991—2010年，县人武部召开各级征兵工作会议512次，进行广播电视宣传4567次，办征兵宣传专栏782期，发征兵宣传提纲1.8万余份，张贴大小标语2万余条，出动征兵宣传车452台次；全县入伍新兵在服役期间，2人荣立一等功，13人荣立二等功，252人荣立三等功，985人被评为“优秀士官”或“优秀士兵”；县人武部被省政府、省军区表彰为征兵“三化一廉（法制化、规范化、公开化，廉洁征兵）”建设“先进单位”和10次表彰为“征兵工作先进单位”；被安顺地区行署、军分区，贵阳市政府、军分区表彰为“征兵工作先进单位”；1998年被贵阳市政府、军分区表彰为“无责任退兵先进单位”。

第四章 民 兵

民兵是不脱离生产的群众武装人员，是中国人民解放军的助手和后备力量。民兵的任务是参加社会主义现代化建设，带头完成生产和各项任务，担负战备执勤，维护社会治安，随时准备参军参战，抵抗侵略，保卫祖国和人民的生命财产安全。

第一节　民兵队伍

一、民兵组织

1991年年初，全县民兵分为普通民兵和基干民兵。全县设民兵团一个，由人武部部长任团长，人武部政委任民兵团政委。乡、镇设民兵营；乡、镇人武部部长任民兵营营长，书记任教导员。村、办事处设民兵连，村、办事处支书任民兵连连长。排、班负责人临时任命。凡18～35岁符合服役条件的公民（除已服现役的），编入民兵组织，服预备役。28岁以下的退伍士兵、经过军训的人员和地方专业对口技术人员编为基干民兵，其余18～35岁符合服兵役条件的公民，编为普通民兵。县人武部对民兵营以上干部，每年组织学习训练不少于2次，连以上干部每年组织学习训练不少于1次，根据战时需要分营、连组织民兵学习、训练。民兵组织管理由分散、流动性大的松散管理走向集中、规范化管理，更加适应新时期战场和市场需要。

二、民兵应急分队

1991年10月，永靖镇组建民兵应急分队，通过培训，成为组织严密、军事过硬、结集迅速、勇敢顽强的民兵突击队。1998年6月，省军区到县人武部摄制《民兵应急分队建设专题片》，在省电视台“贵州新闻联播”和中央电视台7频道“军事新闻”栏目中播出。2000年8月1日，县委、县政府授予民兵应急分队“铁骑神鹰”荣誉称号。2010年4月，组建县民兵应急队伍骨干分队，隶属县人武部统一管理，主要任务是协助公安机关进行治安巡逻，维护社会稳定及参加抢险救灾等。

1991—2010年，县应急分队6次参加军事比武，2次获省军区军事全能比武第二名，3次获贵阳警备区军事全能比武第一名。参加县境内团元山、西望山、南山森林火灾扑灭行动16次，6次参加永靖镇阳朗坝、九庄鸡场坝抗洪抢险，协助县公安维护社会治安360余人次，为国家和人民群众挽回经济损失4860余万元。荣立集体三等功2次，1人荣立二等功，17人荣立三等功，268人次受嘉奖、表彰，14人加入中国共产党。中央、省、市电视台，报纸杂志36次报道民兵应急分队先进事迹。受省委、省政府、省军区、市委、市政府、贵阳警备区通报表彰。

第二节　民兵教育、训练

一、民兵教育

1991年，县人武部在基层民兵连开展“青年民兵之家”建设活动，连部设图书室、文化娱乐室，为民兵学习科学文化知识和开展文娱活动提供场所。1992年起，县人武部对全县民兵采取集中学习与自学的方式开展政治学习教育，每年用3～5天时间组织民兵学习《民兵政治教育读本》《民兵工作条例》《中华人民共和国兵役法》《中华人民共和国国防法》和农业科普知识。学习期间组织民兵到“息烽集中营”旧址、张露萍等七烈士陵园进行爱国主义和革命英雄主义教育，为全县民兵连、排、班和民兵连长以上干部征订《中国民兵》《中国国防报》《西南民兵》《两用人才报》《国防大视野》等学习刊物。1997年8月1日，养龙司乡基干民兵连“青年民兵之家”被成都军区表彰为“先进青年民兵之家”。至2010年，县人武部8次被成都军区通报表彰为“民兵刊授教育先进单位”。

二、民兵军事训练

1991年，县人武部对民兵的军事训练采取分类训练，根据不同的训练对象设置不同的训练科目，训练时间一周至一个月不等。训练的科目主要有队列、射击、战术、擒敌拳、警棍术、防空袭、防化防毒、远距离奔袭、抢险救灾、专业技能（维修、通信、医疗、车辆驾驶、计算机使用管理、后勤保障）等，每年按计划对民兵进行训练。1999年6月，县民兵应急分队科技兴训的一组照片参加成都军区科技兴训成果展示，受到军区领导好评。

第五章 国防教育

1991年7月，县成立全民国防教育领导小组，下设办公室在县人武部。1998年8月，县全民国防教育领导小组更名为县全民国防教育委员会，办公室改设在县委宣传部。2006年5月设专职主任，明确专兼职人员、联络员、教员120余名，形成党委领导、政府主管，驻地军事机关、宣传、教育、民政、文化、工青妇等有关部门密切配合的工作机制。县全民国防教育委员会在县委、县政府领导下，通过多种形式的宣传、报警演练以及采取将防空战备设施纳入城市建设规划等措施，加强人防战备工作，使全民人防战备意识大为提高。

第一节 宣传教育

1997年5月，息烽集中营革命历史纪念馆开馆后，至2010年，相继有中国人民解放军第二炮兵政治部、成都军区空军政治部、贵阳警备区、武警贵阳市支队、县人武部把息烽集中营革命历史纪念馆作为理想信念教育基地。其间，2009年11月，息烽集中营革命历史纪念馆被国家命名为“全民国防教育示范基地”。

在全民国防教育活动中，每年悬挂宣传标语200余条，发放国防教育宣传资料5万余份，展出宣传展板30余次，户外宣传专刊40余期，组装宣传车巡回宣传，在机关、学校、企业举办国防知识专题讲座。在每年“4·28”《中华人民共和国国防教育法》颁布纪念日、“9·20”全民国防教育日、11月全民国防教育月期间开展集中宣传活动。将国防教育纳入高中教学内容，全年不少于4课时，每年入学的高一、中职新生（约1200人）进行军事训练。通过新闻媒体及手机短信等形式宣传国防教育法律、法规和国防知识。1992年，县广播电视台开办“国防之声”栏目。1994年，县组队参加全国国防知识竞赛，2人获省优秀奖；1998年8月组队参加全国“科凌杯”国防知识竞赛，县国教办获组织奖，1人获全国三等奖，1人获全省三等奖，3人获纪念奖。2006年建立国防教育网，县政府门户网站建立国防教育网页。2009年4月，启动“全民国防教育万映计划”，每年免费放映国防教育影片44场。1992—2010年，先后19次组织机关干部职工、民兵、学生、社会各界人士参加中央、省、市（地区）举办的国防知识答题竞赛，参赛1800余人，获各级奖励64人次。

第二节　人民防空

1991年，县人防战备办公室（简称县人防办）设在县政府办公室。1995年，人防战备工作划归县建设局管理，县人防办改设县建设局。2001年，人防战备工作复归县政府办公室管理。2002年、2003年，先后成立县人防音响警报器鸣响演练指挥所和交通战备办公室。

2003年，县人防办发放宣传资料8000余份，编制《息烽县交通战备重点目标保障方案》，对县内交通战备重点目标进行安全检查。2004年，县政府制定《关于贯彻贵阳市人民防空工程建设管理办法的实施意见》和《息烽县房地产开发优惠政策》。加大人防执法力度，对警报器进行维修管理，新安装防空警报器1台，保障人防音响警报覆盖率达到90%以上。对辖区内交通战备重点目标进行安全检查；对交通战备正规化建设情况、交通战备资料、数据进行收集整理，分类建立档案；绘制县境内平、战时交通战备保障工作图初稿。2005年，组织开展“爱我中华，心系国防”电视大赛，以县内中小学校为基础，出黑板报80余期，悬挂标语10余条（幅），发送宣传资料5000余份。与县人武部组织召开县委、县人大、县政府、县政协领导及国防教育委员会成员参加的军事活动日和国防教育座谈会。及时消除交通战备目标隐患，并实行24小时值班制度。2006—2008年，在县城开展大规模人民防空教育4次，接受教育群众1万余人。试鸣人民防空音响警报器3次。向12所中学发放《永远的蓝天》《铸就和平之盾》等专题片和《中华人民共和国人民防空法》（以下简称《人民防空法》）、《贵州省人民防空条例》等宣传资料6000余份，对交通战备重点目标定期进行安全检查。在乡镇、社区、厂矿企业指定人民防空联络员，组建人民防空志愿者队伍。

2009年7月21日，县政府印发《关于规范人防工程审批和防空地下室易地建设费征收管理的通知》《关于完善社区群众人民防空组织的通知》，要求凡在县城镇规划区域内新建民用建筑按规定应修建人防工程的（即防空地下室），建设前必须按照规定权限办理相应人防审批手续。城市规划区域内新建的民用建筑，因条件限制不能同步配套建设防空地下室的，建筑单位应向县人防办提出易地建设申请，经县人防办批准，建设单位按应建防空地下室的建设面积和规定的易地建设费标准缴纳费用。是年，完成县城防空预案修编，乡镇、社区、厂矿、企业建立群众人民防空组织，并指定基层人民防空组织联络员。2010年，开展纪念《人民防空法》《中华人民共和国国防教育法》颁布实施宣传教育活动，组织防空袭警报演练；在县城设点宣传人民防空法、国防教育法和相关法律、法规，印发宣传资料3万余份，接受群众咨询700人次；利用广播、电视、报刊宣传人民防空知识，对中学学生8000余人和县委党校学员100余人进行人民防空知识教育。为九庄、温泉安装人民防空音响报警器各1台，对县内溶洞进行勘察、登记和建档。

第六章 拥政爱民

1991—2010年，县人武部组织干部、职工、民兵，开展植树造林、修建串寨公路、坡改梯和土壤改良、兴修小水窖、沟渠等工作；积极参加各种抢险救灾，均出色完成任务，多次受到上级表彰和记功。

第一节 支援地方建设

一、修建公路与植树造林

1991—2010年，县人武部组织干部、职工、民兵5.38万人次修整、修建乡村公路、串寨路126条273千米。在团元山、梨安、南山、西山等地植树造林6.68万亩。其中，1996年，武警县中队15名官兵平整县水厂至县粮食局仓库公路路面500米，帮助大型地村民修建通组公路400米。1997年1月，组织干部、职工、民兵120人到温泉镇修建通村公路8.7千米。2000年7月，贵阳军分区出资3万元，官兵24人与县人武部干部、职工、民兵138人劳动3个月，修通下洪马通村公路3千米。是年12月，组织干部、职工、民兵100余人修筑县工业园区1.4千米水泥路，经验收，被评为优质工程。2002—2003年，组织全县民兵协调县内退耕还林工作，在各乡镇退耕还林区植树造林2900亩，在南山、梨安、团元山等国有荒山植树造林3200余亩。2004—2009年，相继修建县砖厂经团元山到西山林丰村公路9.8千米，为西山乡金星村、田冲村修建饮水工程等。

二、参与农业基本建设

1991—2010年，县乡镇人武部组织民兵2.73万人次参与农业基本建设，修筑修整农用灌溉沟渠186条986千米；修建小型水库10个、小水窖348个、沟渠268条1687千米。完成坡改梯工程11.2万亩。其间，1999年，县人武部组织干部、职工、民兵162人次，参加底寨河、息烽河治理，清除220米河段淤泥120吨。2002年，组织民兵120人，修建阳朗至息烽排洪沟2.4千米，清理垃圾2680余吨，清除污泥6729吨。2005年12月，组织全县民兵1.26万人次，完成改造和改良土壤任务6.7万亩。2008年6月，组织民兵80人，清除东门河道垃圾3.8吨、污泥12.5吨。

第二节 帮村扶贫

1991年起，县人武部负责水、电、路三不通，人均年收入不到200元的鹿窝乡瓮舍村帮扶工作。干部、职工161人次，筹集资金13.8万元，修建水池2个，安装入户水管1.87千米，架通村供电线4.8千米，修建通村公路3.2千米，解决全村人畜饮水、照明、交通问题。另筹资3.2万元维修村办小学，解决学生上学难问题。请县农科技术员到瓮舍村开展科学种田、烤烟种植和养殖技术培训，指导村民发展种植业和养殖业。1998年该村脱贫，2010年迈进小康村行列。

1998年5月，县人武部帮扶石硐乡大洪村，部领导带头，组织干部职工捐款、捐物，解决特困村民和贫困学生的衣食、上学问题。部长到省水利厅引资10万元修建饮水、农田灌溉水利设施；政委协调县交通局出资修建通村公路；协调县农业局科技人员到村开办科技种植、养殖培训班；请有关土壤改良专业人员指导治理冷、酸性田。2002年8月，大洪村实现水、电、路三通。多数农户种植花椒、李树、梨树等经济作物和发展养殖业。至2004年9月，全村165户茅草屋全部改建为砖瓦结构平房，人均年收入从1998年的218.6元增长到1126.8元，全村无一失学儿童。2010年，大洪村跨入小康村行列。

1991—2010年，县人武部先后帮扶6个村，筹资68.3万元，维修村小学5所，修通村公路187千米，送化肥50余吨，使6个村脱贫。全县各乡镇武装部帮扶87个村，285个村民组372个扶贫点摆脱贫困。

第三节　引资捐资建校助学

1991—1995年，县人武部干部、职工先后6次为扶贫点贫困群众捐款3600元，捐衣物1876件。1996—1997年，县人武部干部、职工2次给扶贫点合箐小学捐款6005元，让12名儿童重返校园。为小学生捐赠铅笔2000支、钢笔186支、作业本2000个、篮球2个；为141户贫困户捐赠衣物165件。1998年，人武部出资4万元，协调资金3万元，为村办小学硬化操场、维修教室，购置课桌、板凳等。

2000年4月，县人武部通过省军区领导引资25万元，修建养龙司乡坪山小学。共修建教学楼3层，教室6间，建筑面积1693平方米，操场1000平方米。县教育局将坪山小学更名为“息烽县文亮希望小学”，并立碑记。之后，县人武部通过筹资、引资方式，筹措资金1万元为文亮希望小学购置教学用品和图书300册、篮球架1副。

2003—2004年，县人武部出资和协调资金6.2万元，为石硐乡大洪小学平整操场，重修教室，购买教学用具，为学生购置3800元的书籍和学习用品。2009年6月1日，购置书包、文体用具等到石硐乡前丰村小学进行慰问。2010年9月1日，县人武部干部职工为青山苗族乡冗坝村贫困学生王明亮捐款6000元。

此外，县人武部组织干部职工相继为长江中下游遭遇洪水的灾民和四川汶川地震灾民捐款2.6万元，衣物1169件。

第四节　抢险救灾

1991年7月11日，县部分乡镇遭暴雨袭击，公路、铁路、河道桥梁被洪水毁坏。县人武部组织当地民兵208人对川黔铁路341千米处被洪水冲垮的50余米路段进行抢修，在36小时后通车。组织县应急分队50名民兵对被洪水冲毁的九庄镇天鹅桥进行修复，经过48小时连续战斗，保障息九公路畅通。是年，九庄区委、区政府送县人武部“架通桥梁，为民造福”匾牌，县人武部被县委、县政府表彰为“抗洪抢险先进单位”。

1993—1999年，在县内发生的4次较大洪灾中，县人武部均组织干部、职工及民兵参与抗洪抢险，战斗在抗洪第一线，县人武部被省军区、贵阳军分区和息烽县委、县政府表彰为“抗洪抢险先进单位”各1次。为县民兵应急分队记集体三等功1次，为民兵李光祥等7人记三等功1次，对王玉岭等21人进行通令嘉奖1次。

2000年6月24日深夜，九庄镇遭暴雨袭击，鸡场村民兵连长组织民兵14人，从洪水中救出群众19

人。县人武部组织应急分队民兵142人投入抢险救灾。疏通沟渠850米，恢复农田1820亩，为灾民捐款6800元、衣被367件。2002年6月18—19日，全县遭暴雨袭击，永靖镇阳朗村受灾严重。县人武部组织民兵140余人投入抗洪抢险，协调贵阳军分区机关干部，白云区、清镇市、花溪区民兵应急分队出动210人、10艘皮划艇赶到现场援助。救出被困群众317人，抢救集中营纪念馆陈列物资200余件，搬运救灾物资80余吨。组织民兵1730人次参加灾后重建。

2008年1—3月，县遭受百年难遇的凝冻灾害。县人武部组织干部、职工、民兵应急分队1630人次深入到永靖镇、鹿窝乡、九庄镇、青山苗族乡等灾区展开“抗凝冻，保民生”行动，抗击灾害。先后清理积冰路面1.6万余米，修复水、电线路3780余米；为被困群众送盐1800千克、粮食22吨、水150吨、棉衣被1637件；组织干部、职工、民兵投入到受灾最严重的青山乡大林口一带、永靖镇南山老厂片区，九庄至鹿窝、流长公路沿线，铲除公路积冰，撒盐57.6千米，修复受损公路63.8千米等。

2008—2010年，乡镇、厂矿武装部抗洪抢险136次，县人武部8次受上级表彰，县民兵应急分队2次荣立集体3等功，1人荣立二等功，21人荣立三等功，92人受表彰、嘉奖，县人武部部长、政委被省军区表彰为“抗凝冻，保民生”先进个人。

1991—2010年，县人武部17次组织民兵1026人次扑灭火灾，使1.4万亩林木免遭烧毁。乡镇武装部286次组织民兵1.13万人次，保护森林3.2万余亩，挽回经济损失数千万元。

第五节　军民共建活动

1991—2010年，县人武部先后与息烽集中营革命历史纪念馆、息烽一中、县劳动人事局、县民政局、养龙司文亮希望小学开展军民共建文明单位活动，建成军民共建文明单位12个；与永靖镇老街村、下阳朗村，小寨坝镇关岭村、王家坪村，温泉镇天台村、温泉村，九庄镇大槽村、和平村，石硐乡水头村、高峰村、泉湖村、猫场村等开展军民共建文明村寨活动，共建文明村寨55个。其间，1991年9月，县人武部与县职业技术学校建立军民共建文明学校和文明单位关系，互帮互学，携手创建文明单位。1993年2月，县人武部抓鹿窝乡瓮舍村共建点。12月，瓮舍村被县委、县政府命名为“文明村寨”。1994年12月，瓮舍村被安顺地委、行署命名为“文明村寨”。1995年8月，瓮舍村被省委、省政府命名为“文明村寨”。

第七篇　政　法

第一章　公　安

1991—2010年，县公安机关坚持“打防结合”方针，在上级公安机关统一部署和相关部门配合下，通过集中开展“严打”和专项治理活动，重点打击杀人、抢劫等暴力犯罪和有组织、涉枪涉爆涉毒犯罪，打击黑恶势力和拐卖妇女儿童犯罪。适时开展打击车匪路霸，盗窃机动车、耕畜等违法行为专项斗争，加大对各类刑事犯罪行为打击力度，为维护全县政治稳定、社会安定，保护人民生命财产安全和经济建设顺利进行做出了贡献。20年间，立各类刑事案件10900件，破7408件，破案率67.9%。全县公安系统被评为市级以上先进集体19次、先进个人36人次，记集体三等功3次、个人三等功20人次。

第一节　机　构

一、内设机构

1991年，县公安局内设政保科、经文保科、治安科、预审科、政工科、秘书科、纪检组、刑事侦查队、看守所、行政拘留所、收容审查所、保安公司。1992年6月，增设法制科、户政科。12月，成立县保安综合贸易总公司，下设商业、汽车维修、废旧物资回收、保安4个分公司，保安公司并入保安分公司。

1996年1月，县公安局由安顺地区公安处划归贵阳市公安局管辖。10月，县公安局内设秘书科、政工科、政保科、经文保科、治安科、预审科、户政科、缉毒科、法制科、纪检监察室、拘留所（兼收容审查所）、看守所、戒毒所、刑侦队和交通警察大队。12月，撤销收容审查所。1997年8月，秘书科更名为办公室。1998年6月，成立公路巡逻民警大队（与交通警察大队一个机构，两块牌子）；行政拘留所内设临时戒毒所；撤销刑侦队、预审科，成立刑事侦查大队（内设综合科、技术科、一中队、二中队、三中队）；缉毒科更名为禁毒科。1998年，保安综合贸易总公司撤销。1999年1月，设立监察室。12月，设立警务督察队。2002年12月，县公安局内设机构调整为1室2科9个大队。即：办公室（指挥室）；政工科、法制科；国内安全与经济文化保卫大队、刑事犯罪与经济犯罪侦查大队、治安警察大队、监所管理大队、禁毒工作大队、交通警察大队、警务督察大队、公共信息网络安全监察大队、巡逻警察大队。2008年5月，办公室更名为指挥中心，加挂办公室牌子；刑事犯罪侦查与经济犯罪侦查大队更名为刑事侦查大队；交通警察大队更名为交通管理大队，加挂公路巡逻民警大队牌子；禁毒工作大队更名为禁毒大队，加挂县禁毒委员会办公室牌子；政工科与警务督察大队合并，设政工监督室，加挂纪检、监察室、督察大队；法制科更名为法制室，设警务保障室和特警大队；撤销监所管理大队，恢复看守所和拘留所（合署办公）。2010年2月，指挥中心设情报信息研究室。

二、派出机构

1991年，县公安局设永靖、永阳区、九庄区、黑神庙区、养龙司区和温泉6个派出所。是年7月，永阳区派出所设长岭岗中学片区治安室。1992年2月，撤区并乡建镇，新建石硐乡、鹿窝乡、流长乡、青山苗族乡、温泉镇5个乡镇派出所；永靖派出所更名为永靖镇派出所、永阳区派出所更名为西山乡派出所、九庄区派出所更名为九庄镇派出所、黑神庙区派出所更名为小寨坝镇派出所、养龙司区派出所更名为养龙司乡派出所；撤销温泉派出所。是年，撤销永阳区派出所长岭岗中学片区治安室。

三、双重管理机构

1991年，消防科、消防中队（现役）、县武警中队、县公安交通警察中队，永红、硬寨、金竹坪3个厂矿派出所及林业派出所为县公安局与有关部门或单位双重管理机构。1992年撤销永红、硬寨、金竹坪3个厂矿派出所。1994年11月，交通警察中队更名为交通警察大队，内设综合办公室，交通警察第一中队、第二中队。1997年10月16日，设中国人民武装警察部队息烽县消防大队，原县公安局消防科和消防中队并入消防大队，由武警贵阳市支队与县公安局双重管理。林业派出所由县公安局与县林业局双重管理。中国人民武装警察部队息烽县中队1991年1月至1995年12月隶属武警安顺支队，1996年1月行政区划变更后，转隶武警贵阳市支队与县公安局双重管理。

第二节　户政与出入境管理

一、常住人口管理

1991年，县公安局对常住人口实行登记管理，由各派出所对辖区内公民填写《常住人口登记表》，用以证明公民身份状况及家庭成员之间的相互关系，作为常住人口管理的基础材料。常住人口变动情况以定期统计为主，每年统计1次，统计主要内容为户数、性别人数、非农业人口数、出生、死亡、迁入、迁出等。由派出所将辖区人口情况报县公安局户政部门核实汇总后，报送上级公安户政部门和县统计局。1992年8月，县内实行“蓝皮户口”（指在本县范围内有效的城镇户口）。持“蓝皮户口”人员，除无粮油供应、副食品补贴及不得以非农业户口办理迁移外，其他与城镇居民享受同等待遇。1996年7月，启用新的《常住人口登记表》和“居民户口簿”。2000年，开展第五次全国人口普查，培训户籍民警44名、核对人员845人，利用广播、电视、报刊、黑板报、宣传栏、标语、公开信等形式向群众宣传，设咨询点11个，出宣传车16辆次，民警86人次，印发《关于解决和处理有关户口问题的通告》和《致全县人民的一封公开信》1.5万份。遵照“组不漏户，户不漏人，人不漏项”要求，对错登、漏登、应注销户口未注销、身份证差错等问题予以纠正。2003年4月，县内人口户籍实现微机管理。2008年，县公安局制发《息烽县公安局为民服务全程代理工作实施方案》，6月起，对息烽籍大中专院校毕业生、复员（退伍）军人、随军人员、新生婴儿、购买商品房或“二手房”居住入户、夫妻投靠等入户和户口注销，实行“一站式”代办。

二、流动人口管理

1991年，对境外到县内暂住人员实行登记管理，不定期进行清查、整顿。1996年，全县开展清理人口统一行动，共清理房屋出租户203户，暂住人口647人。查获违法嫌疑人47名。1998年起，对暂住人口、流动人口除进行登记管理外，协助流入地公安机关管理，即：外地公民到县内居住3日以上，持本人身份证或其他有效证件到暂住地派出所申报登记，离开时注销。暂住1个月以上、年满16周岁人员须申领“暂住证”；服刑、劳教人员因病、因事请假回家暂住，持监狱、劳教机关证明到辖区派出所申报暂住登记，离开时注销；暂住旅馆、饭店、宾馆、招待所、客货栈、浴室等人员，凭“居民身份证”或其他有效证件进行《旅客登记簿》登记，定期交辖区派出所查验。

2000年9月起，永靖镇、小寨坝镇、温泉镇派出所与当地计生办、站实行每周二合署办公制度，对流动人口进行管理。2001年起，对房屋租赁户实行每月考核，季度审查，年终总评管理。是年，登记流入暂住人口1094人，办暂住证909人，办证率83%。清理整顿全县范围内流动人口，清理出租房屋218间、复杂场所49个、特种行业18家。清查暂住人口646人，清查婚育情况220人，抓获赌博、卖淫嫖娼11人，其他5人。

2005年8月起，开展流动人口核查登记。2008年6月起，人口“暂住证”改为“居住证”。是年，全县设流动人口管理办公室11个、流动人口服务站22个。2009年9月，开展流动人口和出租屋普查登记。普查统计，全县有流动人口4068人，出租屋1026户。同时，开展建立流动人口和出租屋信息库工作，全年录入暂住人口信息3058人，租赁户796户。

2010年，在各乡镇设立流动人口服务和管理工作中心，配备协管员20人，实行“五个统一”（统一录用、统一培训、统一管理、统一考核、统一标识）管理。169个村（居）设流动人口服务和管理工作站。是年，全县有流动人口1.3万余人，租赁房屋7176户。

三、证件办理

（一）“居民身份证”办理

1987年起，开始办理“中华人民共和国居民身份证”。至1989年9月，全县13.02万人办理“居民身份证”，占16周岁以上应办证人数的91.16%。此后，“居民身份证”办理转入公安常规业务。2000年起，“居民身份证”号码由15位数升到18位数。公民申领、换领、补领“居民身份证”由辖区派出所管理，县公安局负责审核、签发。2004年6月起，换发第二代“居民身份证”，当年办理第二代“居民身份证”5763人。2005年6月1日起，婴儿出生即可办理“居民身份证”。2007年2月，县公安局下发《关于在春节前后集中开展为外出返乡群众办理第二代“居民身份证”的通知》，集中一段时间为外出返乡群众办理第二代“居民身份证”。至2010年，共办理第二代“居民身份证”6.49万张。

（二）“临时身份证”办理

县境内居民申领“临时身份证”，由本人向住所地公安派出所申请，县公安局统一制证和颁发。“临时身份证”有效期为1年或2年。1989年10月1日起，“临时身份证”有效期统一为3个月。1992年7月29日起，对收容审查、拘留、逮捕及送劳动教养人员持有的居民身份证或“临时身份证”予以收缴，居民身份证随案移交，“临时身份证”移交发证机关注销。2000年起，居民“临时身份证”停办。2006年起，恢复办理“临时身份证”。至2010年，共办理“临时身份证”11110人次。

（三）边境通行证办理

县境内居民到国家规定的边境地区时，需办理“中华人民共和国边境通行证”（简称“边境通行证”）。办理“边境通行证”由本人申请，填写相关表格，乡镇或单位签出同意前往意见，报辖区公安派出所审查同意后，到县治安警察大队（2002年前为治安科或户政管理科）办证。1992年7月13日，息烽县启用新版“边境通行证”。2006年1月起，停止办理“边境通行证”。

四、出入境管理

（一）入境管理

1991年，县公安机关对入境人员实行登记管理。2007年10月，县公安机关启动省公安厅出入境管理系统，对入住县内旅店的入境人员，由入住旅店登记后，电话与所在地派出所或县国内安全与经济文化保卫大队联系，民警上门登记，将其入住、离开情况在省公安厅出入境管理系统进行登录。

1991—2010年，共有入境人员349人，其中，外国人入境55人，港、澳、台地区人员入境294人。入境事由主要有探亲、旅游和商务活动。

（二）出境管理

1991年，县公安机关对县内公民出境（到外国或港、澳、台地区）实行申请审批管理。即出境人提出申请，报省公安厅审批。是年，县内公民申请出国人员11人，到港、澳、台地区5人。1992年7月，省公安厅下发《关于改进出入境外事管理工作的通知》，明确省内公民前往港、澳、台地区探亲、奔丧和出国探亲，自费留学、定居、访友审批权下放给各州、市公安机关。2006年6月20日起，简化出入境管理办证手续，除出境定居由县公安机关审定上报审批外，其他出境手续一律由市公安局出入境管理分局办理。

1991—2010年，县内共有出境人员745人，其中，出国206人，赴港、澳、台地区539人。

第三节 治安管理

一、枪支弹药及民用爆炸物品管理

（一）枪支弹药管理

1991年年初，县境内有私人佩带用于狩猎的各种枪支共548支。1992年，县公安局对公务用枪进行清理，全县有各类公务枪支221支。其中，公安系统112支、检察系统21支、法院系统28支，企事业公安、保卫部门39支、林业公安8支，县体育运动委员会管理使用体育运动用枪13支。

1993年9月，县公安局对县境内内部保卫单位枪支进行清理，收回枪支7支。是年，收回县公安退休人员配枪4支送安顺地区公安处集中保管。

1995年12月13日，县公安局印发《关于进一步加强警用枪支弹药管理的通知》，规定除科、所、队长配专用枪外，各科、所、队其他枪支作为公用枪支使用，由各科、所、队长掌握使用情况。1996年7—9月，县公安局开展公务用枪和民用枪支清理、核实、登记工作。清理统计，全县共有公务用枪261支，其中，公安系统143支、检察系统23支、法院系统36支、林业公安7支、内部保卫系统52支。民用枪支324支。10月，县公安局对国营276厂公安科发生枪支被盗和1名干警用枪打死其妻事件进行通报，决定将该科配发的公务用枪收回集中保管，并规定各单位公务用枪集中保管，对经常酗酒、纪律作风不好、政治素质不高人员，坚决不予佩用枪支。次年11月，县公安局在全县范围内开展收缴民用非法持有枪支专项行动，共收缴各种枪支194支（其中，长筒火药枪59支、短筒火药枪122支、高压气枪13支），军用枪子弹6发。查破非法制造火药枪窝点2个、销售点1个。

1997年1月起，取消民用枪支佩带，不再办理新的民用枪支“持枪证”。1998年，县公安局开展队伍集中教育整顿，收回不适合配枪民警枪支12支。

2001年4月起，县公安局在全县范围内开展“治爆缉枪”专项行动，至2007年，收缴火药枪172

支，查处涉爆案件2起、违反枪支管理规定案件1起，涉爆人员4人，治安拘留1人。其间，2006年，县公安局正式投入使用“枪支管理信息系统”，并与贵阳市公安局联网。

2008年3月31日起，县公安局在全县开展集中收缴非法枪支专项行动，至10月，收缴火药枪47支。是年，按市公安局统一部署，县公安局将历年收缴的144支火药枪上交市公安局治安支队统一销毁。

（二）民用爆炸物品管理

1991年，县内有炸药、雷管类民用爆炸物品储存仓库3个（息烽县物资局炸药库、息烽磷矿炸药库、南山煤矿炸药库）、爆竹生产厂（九龙爆竹厂）1个。1996年，开展清理民用爆炸物品专项行动，清理民用爆炸物品储存单位5个、使用单位31个，签订《民用爆炸物品安全管理责任书》33份。1999年，清理涉及民用爆炸物品单位95家，储存民用爆炸物品单位20家。查获私造炸药2起，收缴炸药251千克、雷管413发、导火绳1373米，查处隐患11起，发出《整改通知书》9份，督促整改11起。取缔非法生产爆竹点3个、非法销售烟花爆竹点5个，治安处罚9人。是年，县公安局收回乡镇派出所对爆破器材的审批权，为100余名爆破员换发“爆破作业证”。

2001年，成立县永兴物资有限责任总公司，负责全县炸药、雷管类民用爆炸物品销售。4月起，开展民用爆炸物品专项检查活动，至2004年1月，公安机关共出警994人次、警车143台次，检查村寨30个，涉爆单位49个，爆竹生产厂及销售点51个，炸药库（含临时储存点）14个，矿山、采石场64处，查处隐患7起，收缴炸药3箱6包40节，责令娱乐场所停业整改2家。2004年，破获息烽磷矿黄磷厂技改工程工地“5・2”炸药被盗案，抓获犯罪嫌疑人1人，缴获炸药24千克。2007年1月，培训涉爆单位爆破员、保管员、安全员、押运员250人。2010年起，县永兴物资有限责任总公司4个爆破站，对销售爆破器材实行购买、保管、运输、使用、清退“五统一”服务。是年，全县有爆破器材仓库8个（固定库房6个、临时库房2个），使用单位56家。办理民用爆破物品购买证、运输证各943次。审批使用民用爆炸器材700吨。

二、剧毒化学品、放射性物品管理

2002年3月15日，国务院颁布《危险化学品管理条例》（以下简称《条例》），县公安局按照《条例》规定，对需要购买剧毒物品单位，持县级主管业务部门证明，经县公安局批准，发给“剧毒物品购买证”，到指定单位按批准的品种、数量、用途购买；自带生产所需且数量不超过500克或500毫升，可以直接购买（有特殊限量和规定的除外）。2004年，息烽磷矿、贵州黔能息烽天吉磷化工有限责任公司、贵州西洋肥业有限责任公司、开磷集团息烽重钙厂、黄磷厂等5家企业列入县公安局管理使用剧毒化学品单位。2006年6月，乡镇派出所与生产、使用剧毒化学品单位签定《剧毒化学品治安责任书》《剧毒化学品销毁承诺书》14份。6月26日，市公安局、县政府在南极公路纵深400米处组织有关部门开展危险化学品事故紧急救援模拟演习。2008年，列入县公安局管理的剧毒化学品生产、经营、使用单位13家，69人。

三、烟花爆竹管理

1991年，县农资日杂公司负责县境内烟花爆竹总经销。县公安机关在九龙爆竹厂查获非法生产爆竹原料氯酸钾23箱（1150千克）、硫黄粉200千克、银粉两桶（40千克），作统一处理。1996年12月22日，县政府发布《关于在永靖镇城区禁止燃放烟花爆竹的通告》，规定从1997年1月1日零时起，永靖镇城区范围内禁止燃放烟花爆竹。2003年10月24日，县公安局、县供销合作社联社（简称县供销社）联合发出《关于规范息烽县烟花爆竹经营管理的通知》，规定在全县设4个烟花爆竹批发点，各零售点凭《烟花爆竹零售许可证》从批发点进货，九庄幅光鞭炮厂凭县公安局核发的“烟花爆竹零售许可证”销售本厂产品。2006年3月起，实施国务院《烟花爆竹管理条例》，烟花爆竹不再列入民用爆炸物品，县公安局负责办理《烟花爆竹道路运输许可证》和查处非法生产、购买、运输、销售烟花爆竹行业。2007年2月8日，县政府发布《关于春节期间限放烟花爆竹的通告》，规定允许燃放烟花爆竹时间为：农历正月除夕至正月十五（2007年2月17日0时至2007年3月4日24时）；限放区域：春节焰火晚会在县体育场进行，民间燃放区域为县城西门农产品直销市场场坝内和南大街人劳社保局旁边空地，其他场所一律禁止燃放。此后，在县境内烟花爆竹由禁放改为限放。次年，县公安机关查获小寨坝镇居民蔡某某驾小货车从贵阳运载各类烟花爆竹90余件回小寨坝，蔡某某被行政处罚。

四、公共娱乐场所管理

1991年12月，县公安局在有关部门配合下，开展专项治理和“扫黄”行动，在县城及城郊清理播放黄色录像放映点2个，收缴放映机、电视机各6台，黄色录像带200余盒、淫秽书刊4本，审查20人。1993年，县公安、文化、工商等部门联合印发《关于加强对电动转盘游乐机管理的暂行规定》，明确电动转盘、游乐机业主必须到文化、工商部门办理登记手续；坚决取缔利用电动转盘、游乐机进行赌博的场所。1999年5月，县公安机关配合有关部门，清理出租房屋118户、建筑工地45个、旅社23家，破获刑事案1件，抓获涉赌人员16人。7月1日，《中华人民共和国娱乐场所管理条例》实施。是年，清理娱乐场所41家，提出整改意见26条，限期改正。

2002年3月，县公安、综治、法院、司法、工商、文化等部门联合开展“禁娼禁赌”专项治理活动。全年统一组织“禁娼禁赌”行动3次，检查、清理公共娱乐场所144家次，查获赌案8件37人，没收赌资2888元，治安罚款1.04万元；查处卖淫嫖娼案9件30人，立刑事案4件，涉案20人；立治安案5件，治安拘留10人；清理网吧8家，责令停业整改2家。次年，查处治安案件12件，治安处罚67人，其中涉赌涉毒9件，拘留2人，罚款58人，没收赌资、毒资9906.5元，罚款6.08万元；卖淫嫖娼案2件6人，罚款3万元，并责令具结悔过；出租、出售淫秽光碟1件，治安处罚1人，罚款2500元，没收淫秽光碟11张和违法所得。2005年起，美容、美发业列入公共娱乐场所管理。2006年2月，县公安局印发《录像放映室管理规定》《台球室管理规定》《桑拿洗浴按摩业管理规定》《歌舞厅（夜总会）管理规定》《茶馆（室）管理规定》《大型商场管理规定》《音响出租管理规定》《酒吧管理规定》《游戏机室管理规定》等文件，并组织业主集中学习，要求业主将各项规定张贴在营业厅内，遵照执行。7月，县公安局组织县内旅社、歌舞厅、酒吧、茶室、网吧、废旧物品收购等132家经营业主培训学习《治安管理处罚法》《娱乐场所管理条例》，对县境内营业性娱乐场所进行全面登记。2010年，全县有公共娱乐场所179家（个），11月起，县公安局与贵州同望科技有限公司对县内娱乐服务场所及其从业人员进行信息采集。

五、特种行业管理

（一）旅馆业管理

1991年，全县有旅馆66家。1992年，公安机关检查旅馆112家次，查出登记不完整、漏登、不及时送辖区派出所审查等问题，责令限期整改。1997年，对旅馆业进行清理整顿，清理55家，补办“特种行业许可证”5家，停业整改1家。2004年，全县有旅馆44家，其中国有与集体所有各2家、个体40家。

2006年，有旅馆65家，其中国有2家、集体1家、个体62家。县公安局先后印发《旅客住宿须知》《旅客住宿登记制度》《旅客财物保管制度》《旅馆业违法犯罪情况报告制度》《门卫制度》

《值班巡逻制度》，强化规范旅馆管理。2008年9月起，全县旅馆业实行联网管理。2010年，有旅馆72家。县公安局组织旅馆业主及其电脑操作员进行电脑登录、录入、添加、删除、查询、对比等培训2次。参训270余人次；召开旅馆业治安管理推进会2次，参加220余人；66家旅馆安装VPN新系统，登记入住上网传输旅客信息7.86万人，上网联网传输率100%；发放旅馆业特种行业许可证18个。

（二）刻字业与印刷业（含打字、复印）管理

刻字业：1991年，县内有刻字业4家。1995年，对刻字业进行清理整顿，保留2家。至2005年，县内刻字业保持1～2家。2006年6月1日起，按上级有关部门规定，县境内新建立企业单位、院校、社会团体和民办企业机构刻制单位公章、财务章、合同章、税务专用章、法人名章印鉴，统一纳入贵阳市印章治安信息中心计算机网络管理，各用章单位或个人更换或刻制上述五种印章时，须到县公安局治安警察大队办理准刻手续，到经公安机关批准持有准刻网络印章的刻制企业按照全国统一标准，刻制带有编码的新型印章。是年，县公安局批准贵州国盾宝图防伪技术有限公司在治安警察大队设工作点，负责办理网络印章传输等工作。批准永靖镇严世武刻字店挂靠贵阳利达工艺美术厂承制网络印章。当年，共办理、刻制网络印章82枚。2010年，县内有刻字业2家。

印刷业（含打字、复印）：1991年，县内有集体所有制印刷厂1家。此后，随着个体印刷业的发展，电脑打字的普及，印刷业（含打字、复印）在县城快速发展。至2004年，县内有印刷厂5家（个体），打字、复印店13家（个体）。2006年，县公安局制发《印刷业管理规定》，严禁各印刷厂印刷涉黄、赌、毒、邪教、迷信等文件资料；严禁印刷反动、暴力、恐吓等影响社会稳定的文字材料；要求建立从业人员登记簿、工作日志；持证经营，配合公安机关开展印刷业安全管理工作等。2008年，县内有印刷厂3家，打字、复印店15家。2010年，全县有印刷厂3家，打字、复印店13家。

（三）旧货业管理

1997年3月，县公安局制定《清理整顿旧金属收购点　严厉打击盗窃生产性旧金属犯罪活动方案》，成立以县长为组长的“清理整顿工作协调领导小组”，对全县废旧金属收购业进行清理整顿，清理废旧金属收购站（点）5家，小红炉15家，查获永兴铸造厂非法收购铸铁管1800千克，取缔废旧金属收购站（点）3家。1998年，县境内有废旧金属收购站5家，2000年增至14家。2002年12月，根据公安部通知，取消“生产性废旧金属收购企业特种行业许可”设立及办理。

2006年2月，县公安局制发《废旧收购业管理规定》，要求县境内金属收购站（点）合法、文明经营；不收购来历不明、无任何手续的废旧物品；建立从业人员登记簿和收购台账；发现嫌疑人或涉嫌物品，立即报告公安机关。2010年，县境内有金属收购站（点）10家。

（四）美容、美发与金银首饰加工业管理

美容、美发业：1991年，县境内有美容、美发店2家。此后，随着经济发展，城乡人民群众生活水平提高，美容、美发业在县城或乡镇集镇较快发展，至2004年，县境内美容美发店增至21家。2009年起，美容、美发店不再列入特种行业管理。2010年，全县有美容、美发店（院）18家。

金银首饰加工业：1991—2003年，县内金银首饰加工店保持在4家以下。2004年增至5家。2005年，根据有关规定，公安机关不再为金银首饰加工业办理“特种行业许可证”，但仍列入特种行业管理范围，进行登记管理。是年，有金银首饰加工业4家。2008年增至6家，其中：铸造厂、金银首饰加工店各3家。2010年，县内有金银首饰加工业4家。

第四节 侦 查

一、刑事犯罪侦查

1991年，立各类刑事案578件，破案394件，破案率68.16%。此后数年，刑事立案呈下降趋势，至1998年，每年立刑事案件375～448件。

1999年起，县公安局利用“全国在逃人员信息系统网”和公安部“网上追逃”光盘开展“网上追逃”。2000年9月，县公安局在永靖镇召开公捕、公处大会，将涉嫌破坏电力设备、盗窃、伤害的11人逮捕，吸毒、诈骗的7人送劳动教养。

2003年7月，县公安局建立“刑事案件信息库”。

2004年，开展“侦破命案专项行动”，印发《息烽县公安局命案必破保障机制》，制定命案防范、快速处置、领导亲侦、整体联动、后勤保障、破案奖励、侦破责任、个案讲评、挂牌督办、责任倒查10项措施。成功侦破“2·23”“3·19”“6·3”“6·10”“6·11”5件命案。次年，在九庄镇召开“命案必破”和打击“两抢一盗”犯罪专项斗争公捕、公处大会，会后，抢劫、杀人犯罪嫌疑人黄某某在其父陪同下到公安机关自首。2006年起，县公安局逐步推行网上办案。2008年4月，省公安厅政治部授予县公安局“2005—2007年度全省公安机关侦破命案工作先进集体”称号，并颁发奖牌、奖金5000元。

2010年，县公安局制发《息烽县公安局打击扒盗等多发性违法犯罪行动方案》，开展专项斗争12次，立刑事案1513件（为历年最高），侦破刑事案634件（当年案498件、年前案27件、外辖区案109件），其中“两抢一盗”221件。县政法部门组成联合督导组，出动检查车辆235台，清查旅店39家、网吧10家、娱乐场所15家、出租房135户312人、废旧金属收购点3个，破获刑事案20件，抓获犯罪嫌疑人53人，暂扣违章摩托车38辆，缴获海洛因4.3克。

息烽县1991—2010年刑事立案破案统计表

表7-1-1　　单位：件

年份	立破案	合计	杀人	伤害	抢劫	强奸	绑架	放火	投毒	爆炸	盗窃	诈骗	涉毒	其他
1991	立案	578	9	23	28	26	—	2	—	2	410	15	1	62
	破案	394	8	22	19	26	—	2	—	2	245	15	1	54
1992	立案	424	—	—	—	—	—	—	—	—	—	—	—	—
	破案	301	—	—	—	—	—	—	—	—	—	—	—	—
1993	立案	374	4	15	35	10	—	3	—	2	224	2	3	76
	破案	297	4	15	26	10	—	2	—	2	163	2	3	70
1994	立案	448	8	14	16	15	—	2	6	—	311	8	4	64
	破案	368	5	13	12	15	—	2	6	—	247	7	4	57
1995	立案	372	11	21	29	14	—	3	8	2	213	6	29	36
	破案	313	9	20	25	14	—	3	8	2	164	6	29	33

续表

年份	立破案	合计	杀人	伤害	抢劫	强奸	绑架	放火	投毒	爆炸	盗窃	诈骗	涉毒	其他
1996	立案	306	—	—	—	—	—	—	—	—	—	—	—	—
	破案	249	—	—	—	—	—	—	—	—	—	—	—	—
1997	立案	375	8	33	11	18	—	2	—	5	185	3	31	79
	破案	272	8	32	9	17	—	1	—	5	92	2	31	75
1998	立案	375	7	32	17	17	—	7	—	2	196	4	49	44
	破案	295	7	30	12	17	—	5	—	2	130	2	49	41
1999	立案	266	3	30	29	18	—	3	1	9	123	3	16	31
	破案	179	2	26	18	18	—	2	—	4	63	2	16	28
2000	立案	558	1	33	19	2	1	3	—	8	416	10	13	52
	破案	247	4	22	10	3	1	1	—	2	123	4	13	64
2001	立案	639	5	41	29	16	—	2	—	1	462	30	18	35
	破案	318	4	36	11	13	—	1	—	1	135	33	15	69
2002	立案	628	8	33	24	5	—	4	—	2	477	9	15	51
	破案	456	7	24	38	7	—	2	—	2	290	13	15	58
2003	立案	591	4	33	31	11	1	1	—	1	432	13	13	51
	破案	366	7	26	18	32	1	1	—	1	217	9	15	39
2004	立案	506	4	38	16	18	—	3	—	—	344	10	10	63
	破案	421	5	38	9	14	—	1	—	1	207	2	12	132
2005	立案	409	5	37	32	10	—	1	—	—	269	6	12	37
	破案	281	5	39	21	10	—	—	—	—	147	5	13	41
2006	立案	362	1	45	14	11	1	2	—	—	204	7	15	62
	破案	335		39	16	14	—	1	—	—	134	4	15	112
2007	立案	477	5	53	12	6	—	—	—	—	290	9	12	90
	破案	489	5	56	11	8	—	—	—	—	243	16	12	138
2008	立案	576	2	38	20	15	—	1	—	—	410	33	8	49
	破案	546	3	50	14	11	—	20	—	—	295	90	8	55
2009	立案	1123	3	42	39	18	—	2	—	—	919	46	8	46
	破案	647	3	37	66	17	—	—	—	—	261	195	9	59
2010	立案	1513	1	47	49	13	—	1	—	—	1061	176	24	141
	破案	634	1	34	24	14	—	—	—	—	295	122	24	120

二、经济犯罪侦查

1991年，县公安局设经济文化保卫科（股），负责侦查经济犯罪案件。1997年前，经济犯罪侦查归属刑事案件统计。1998—2004年，立各类经济犯罪案33件，破23件，破案率69.7%。其中挪用资金案5件，破4件；职务侵占案12件，破8件；诈骗案10件，破8件；偷税案3件，破1件；使用、购买假币案2件，破2件；公司企业人员受贿1件。涉案金额880余万元，追回经济损失90余万元。2005—2010年，立经济犯罪案17件，破18件（含旧存1件），涉案金额近700万元，挽回经济损失278万元。其中，公司、企业人员受贿案4件、职务侵占案6件、挪用资金案4件，其他3件。

三、打击拐卖妇女儿童犯罪

1991年5月，开展“打击拐卖妇女儿童专项治理”统一行动，抓获拐卖妇女儿童犯罪嫌疑人6名。1998年4月，县公安局刑事侦查队选派民警4名，辗转河南、安徽、江苏等8个省，行程5000余千米，抓获拐卖妇女儿童犯罪嫌疑人1名，解救被拐卖妇女5名。

2000年4月，县公安局按照公安部在全国开展打击拐卖妇女儿童专项斗争统一行动安排部署，在全县范围内开展被拐卖妇女儿童调查。调查统计，全县有被拐卖妇女59名、被拐卖或失踪儿童22名。县公安局抽调16名民警组成5个解救（破案）组赴浙江、江苏、福建、河南、河北、山东、广东、山西、广西、内蒙古等省份解救被拐卖妇女、儿童。至2001年，解救被拐卖妇女43名、被拐卖儿童7名。破获拐卖妇女儿童案件15起，抓获拐卖妇女儿童犯罪嫌疑人及买主30名。协助外地公安机关抓获拐卖妇女儿童犯罪嫌疑人1名，解救被拐卖妇女2名。

2002年4月，县公安局在县城、乡镇集镇及农村村寨张贴《致全县儿童家长的一封公开信》，各乡镇派出所将《公开信》送到全县101所小学、12个教学点，5所幼儿园，公安局局长在县电视台发表电视讲话等，开展防止盗抢儿童宣传工作。

2005年后，县内拐卖妇女儿童犯罪逐渐减少，公安机关的工作重点逐步向解救被拐卖妇女儿童转移。至2010年，共解救被拐卖妇女22名、儿童1名，破获拐骗儿童案件1起。为群众找回离家出走少女、儿童25名。

四、打击车匪路霸

1991起，县公安机关采取蹲点守候等措施开展打击车匪路霸工作，至1995年，破获车匪路霸案件（盗、抢）21起，抓获作案人员20人（其中当场击毙1人），缴获轿车1辆、匕首1把、自制手枪3支、子弹7发、制枪工具1套，人民币500余元。

1996年5月，县公安机关在永靖、小寨坝、温泉、九庄、养龙司、西山、石硐、流长9乡（镇）开展打击盗抢机动车犯罪专项斗争，出动警力228人次，车辆22台次，设卡14处。暂扣125型摩托车44辆、三轮摩托车1辆，汽车、农用车4辆，抓获犯罪嫌疑人1名。

1998年3月起，县公安局开展“打击盗、抢、走私机动车”专项行动。至2006年，破获盗窃摩托车案件42起，抓获犯罪嫌疑人28人，缴获摩托车36辆，赃款和赃物折款10万余元。

2006年后，打击车匪路霸纳入其他专项行动和日常侦查工作。

五、案件简介

（一）张某军、张某春故意杀人案

1997年5月11日7时40分，县公安局刑事侦查队接到小寨坝镇派出所电话报称：该镇小寨坝村梅小山组的一堰塘里发现一具男性尸体。接报案后，刑事侦查队当即成立专案组前往现场，经对现场勘查和走访群众，查明死者黄某书的身份和大概死亡时间，并排查出两名作案嫌疑人。当晚，在小寨坝镇二屯岩将嫌疑人张某军甲抓获，次日凌晨在永靖镇将嫌疑人张某春抓获。

经审讯和侦查查明：张某军、张某春将一张挖煤得到的煤票交给黄某书兑换现金，黄当时未付钱。两名嫌疑人于1997年5月10日上午找到黄某书索要煤票，双方发生争执，经商议，三人一同到小寨坝镇猫猫坡郑某某家收钱，因郑不在，未得到钱。下午2时许，三人从郑家返回小寨坝。行至梅小山村民组罗树旗湾处的小路时，张某军趁黄某书不备，用包有石块的衣服猛击黄某书头部，张某春用拳头猛击黄的胸部，致黄当场死亡。二人将黄某书尸体藏在路旁水沟中，天黑后，将黄的尸体拖至梅小山组一水塘边，用皮带将石头捆在黄的尸体上沉入水塘内。

1997年11月15日，贵阳市中级人民法院以故意杀人罪判处张某军死刑，剥夺政治权利终身；以故意杀人罪判处张某春无期徒刑，剥夺政治权利终身。

（二）吉某发、陈某江、张某国、张某、吴某发破坏电力设备案、盗窃案、销售赃物案

2003年3月27日15时，县公安局永靖镇派出所接到群众电话报称：永靖镇老厂村青山组电线被盗400米，价值960元。永靖镇派出所随即派人对现场勘查并立案侦查。

2004年2月15日晚，吉某发、陈某江、张某国携带铁钳、蛇皮口袋等作案工具准备作案时，被永靖镇派出所巡逻人员抓获，经审讯和调查取证，查明2003年3月—2004年2月，吉某发、陈某江、张某国、张某、吴某发以非法占有为目的，在息烽县永靖镇、小寨坝镇多次破坏正在使用中的电力设备，危害公共安全。其中，吉某发参与作案31次，盗割电线774.5千克，价值1.25万元；陈某江参与作案32次，盗割电线782.75千克，价值1.16万元；张某国参与作案26次，盗割电线1190.25千克，价值1.35万元；张某参与作案7次，盗割电线307.25千克，价值4375元；吴某发参与作案2次，盗割电线110千克，价值1848元。吉某发、张某、吴某发以非法占有为目的，在永靖镇窃取公私财物1次，吴某发单独窃取公私财物1次，总价值6300余元。吴某发还多次在明知是犯罪所得赃物的情况下而予以收购并转卖给他人。

2004年6月29日，县人民法院以破坏电力设备罪判处吉某发有期徒刑10年，以盗窃罪判处其有期徒刑2年，并处罚金2000元，总合刑期12年，决定执行11年；以破坏电力设备罪判处陈某江有期徒刑10年；以破坏电力设备罪判处张某国有期徒刑9年；以破坏电力设备罪判处张某有期徒刑5年，以盗窃罪判处其有期徒刑2年，并处罚金2000元，总合刑期7年，决定执行有期徒刑6年，并处罚金2000元；以破坏电力设备罪判处吴某发有期徒刑3年，以盗窃罪判处其有期徒刑2年，并处罚金2000元，以销售赃物罪判处其有期徒刑1年，并处罚金1000元，总合刑期6年，决定执行有期徒刑5年，并处罚金3000元。

（三）董某均、董某斌、陈某故意杀人案

2004年3月20日11时35分，县公安局刑侦大队接到流长乡派出所电话报称：流长乡大兴村磨河水河边发现一具尸体，性别不详。接报后，刑侦大队立即组织侦技人员赶赴现场，经勘查发现，死者为男性，双手被绳子捆住，身上绑着一块石头，因头部受钝器多次打击，造成严重颅脑损伤而死亡，系他杀。抛尸时间大概在2日内。经进一步查明，死者名叫董某华，住流长乡大兴村新寨组。

当天17时许，办案人员在董某斌卧室内发现了第一现场，经勘查和使用警犬搜寻，在董某华堂弟董某均卧室床下发现一把带血的铁锤，董某均已去向不明。当即调集警力在董某均可能外逃的路线设卡堵截，并派人做董某均亲友思想工作，吩咐发现董某均后劝其投案自首。同月21日12时29

分，董某均、董某斌在其亲戚劝说下，到流长乡派出所投案自首。随后，办案民警将另一名作案嫌疑人陈某（女性）抓获。

经调查和对犯罪嫌疑人审讯查明：2004年3月19日19时许，陈某为摆脱董某华的骚扰，与董某均、董某斌商量后，决定将董某华杀死。同日23时许，由陈某持手电筒照亮，董某均、董某斌分别持斧头、铁锤进入董某华卧室，用斧头和铁锤猛击董某华头部、胸部，致董某华当场死亡。随后，三人将一块石头绑在董某华尸体腹部，用棉絮裹住尸体抛入流长乡大兴村磨河组的头沟河。

2004年9月1日，贵阳市中级人民法院以故意杀人罪判处董某均无期徒刑，剥夺政治权利终身；判处董某斌有期徒刑15年，剥夺政治权利5年；判处陈某有期徒刑10年，剥夺政治权利1年。

六、打击毒品犯罪和强制戒毒

（一）打击毒品犯罪

20世纪90年代初，县境内有少量吸毒、贩毒活动发生。1991—1996年，共破获涉毒案件31件。1997年3月，县公安机关组织350人（以公安干警为主）、汽车25辆参加贵阳市禁毒统一行动，破获毒品案件5起，端掉海洛因零售点3个、贩卖精神药品窝点6个，抓获贩毒人员9人，吸毒人员22人；缴获海洛因2.5克、罂粟壳粉55克、三唑仑等精神药品4087片、安定注射液212支、吸毒工具2套。6月起，县公安局开展“禁毒专项治理”集中统一行动，至7月底，共破获各类刑事案件79起，查破犯罪团伙3个10人，抓获各类犯罪嫌疑人50名；收缴海洛因82.8克、鸦片150克；缴获其他赃款、赃物折款共15.87万元。次年，开展春、秋两季严打会战，遏制毒品犯罪。开展“禁种、禁吸、禁贩”工作，破获涉毒案9件，抓获嫌疑人24人，缴获海洛因50.4克，铲除罂粟2041株。送强制戒毒75人，劳教6人，移送起诉涉毒违法犯罪25人。

1999—2004年，相继开展“90天扫毒”“百日剿毒会战”“春夏扫毒风暴”行动和“创无毒，保净土”等活动，破获涉毒案件52起，缴获海洛因408.8克，捕判54人，强制戒毒325人，劳教89人，行政拘留40人。

2005年2月，县公安局开展“冬季缉毒会战”行动。是年，破获特大运输毒品案件1起，抓获犯罪嫌疑人7人，缴获海洛因82.4克，强制戒毒3人。次年3月起，县公安局开展“雷霆”扫毒行动，至2007年，共破获毒品案件15起，抓获犯罪嫌疑人18人，缴获海洛因346.9克、K粉2.8克，强制戒毒7人，劳动教养5人。

2008年，县公安局开展打击外流贩毒专项行动。是年，破获贩毒案件7起，抓获贩毒嫌疑人7人，缴获海洛因3.4克、K粉0.4克。

2010年，破获贩毒案件23起，抓获毒品犯罪嫌疑人28人，缴获毒品126.7克，查处吸毒人员18人。

（二）强制戒毒

1990年11月，县戒毒所成立，有所长1名、副所长2名，配备医生3人，接收戒毒人员14人。其中年龄最大67岁，最小17岁，毒龄5~6年、1~2年不等。1997年起，息烽县贯彻“三个一律”（对贩毒者一律追究刑事责任；对吸毒者一律送强制戒毒；对复吸者一律送劳动教养戒毒）政策。是年，县公安局首次将抓获的12名吸毒人员送市公安局戒毒康复中心强制戒毒，经检查，收戒7人，退回5人。1998年6月，县公安局行政拘留所内设“临时戒毒所”，负责3~6个月吸毒成瘾人员的强制戒毒。至2000年，共收治强制戒毒人员237人（男185人、女52人）。此后，“临时戒毒所”撤销。

2003年起，县境内吸毒成瘾人员送开阳县公安局戒毒所戒毒。开阳县公安局戒毒所撤销后，送修文县公安局戒毒所戒毒。对经过强制戒毒后又复吸毒品人员，报请贵阳市劳动教养管理委员会批准后实行劳动教养（男性送三江或中八劳动教养管理所，女性送省女子劳动教养管理所）。是年，开展“吸毒人员基础信息调查”统计，全县共登记吸毒人员223人（男185人、女38人），其中劳教在所39人，劳改在场13人，社会面吸毒152人，下落不明4年以上11人，死亡8人。收集吸毒人员照片155份。

2004年11月，县禁毒委开展“吸毒人员基本情况普查”，经统计，全县登记在册吸毒人员340人（男265人、女75人）。其中劳教在所37人，正在服刑三年以上15人，下落不明的19人，死亡19人，现有吸毒人员250人。

2006年8月起，按国家禁毒委“8·28”电视电话会议精神，对吸毒人员信息数据实行上网录入管理。是年，上网录入97人。至2008年，共上网录入吸毒人员381人。

2010年，全县登记在册吸毒人员479人（男372人、女107人），其中：现有吸毒人员235人，戒断巩固三年以上140人，解除社区康复37人，服刑三年及以上释放4人，出国三年以上3人，正在服刑三年以上14人，下落不明6人，累计死亡40人。禁吸戒毒工作坚持“应收尽收”原则，组织开展“大排查”“打零包，大收戒”等专项行动。

（三）禁种与铲毒

1989年4月18日，县公安局印发《关于继续查禁种植罂粟的通知》，要求将查禁种植罂粟工作纳入社会治安综合治理，及时发现及时铲除。对种植罂粟人员，要追查种子的来源；对传播种子人员要依法处理；对开设的烟馆，坚决取缔，严禁吸毒。1991年，县公安局治安科在小寨坝镇石桥村等地铲除农户种植罂粟苗991株。1995年后，县境内种植罂粟逐渐增多，县公安局和各有关部门在禁种毒品工作中，进村入寨向群众宣传禁毒法律、法规，发动群众检举、揭发种植毒品线索，在每年4—6月罂粟开花季节，开展普查铲除罂粟毒苗行动，采取地毯式、经常性检查，落实举报奖励制度等措施，做到发现一株铲除一株，严惩一起，根治一方。至2010年，共铲除罂粟苗19165株，行政拘留2人，刑事拘留2人，查处非法种植罂粟案3起，罚款2000元。

七、易制毒化学品与精神麻醉药品管制

2004年起，县公安局禁毒科针对县境内化工、医药企业逐年增多，生产和使用易制毒化学品单位不断增加的实际情况，采取完善审批手续等措施，加强对生产、销售、使用易制毒化学品单位的管理。要求各有关单位建立销售、购买易制毒化学品台账，做到生产、销售、使用易制毒化学品底数清、情况明。是年，县境内有生产和使用易制毒化学品单位13家，年生产硫酸82万吨、盐酸25万吨，年使用易制毒化学品7920吨。2005年11月1日，国务院《易制毒化学品管理条例》正式施行。是年，县公安局对县境内生产、使用易制毒化学品的厂矿、学校、医院等单位实行登记、建档管理。2006年，县公安局禁毒大队设易制毒化学品管理办公室。

2007年，县公安局禁毒大队与县政府有关职能部门贯彻落实《易制毒化学品管理条例》《麻醉药品和精神药品管理条例》及贵阳市《关于加强我市易制毒化学品和精神麻醉药品管理工作的意见》，联合开展执法检查5次，未发现违规现象。

2008年11月，县公安局禁毒大队在全县范围内开展醋酸酐专项检查行动。经查，县境内有使用醋酸酐企业一家（息烽汉方制药厂，用量较少，检查时该厂醋酸酐库存量为1000毫升），其购买、

运输、使用符合规定。县境内无生产、销售醋酸酐企业。是年，县境内有生产、销售、使用易制毒化学品单位26家。县公安局禁毒大队办理易制毒化学品购买证86份，运输备案证明104份。

第五节 监所管理

一、看守所

（一）设施

1991年，县看守所有监室14间277.44平方米，办公室、厨房607.58平方米。1999年，投资54.2万元，新建办公楼780平方米，安装监室监控系统和在押人员报警装置。2005年11月再次扩建，新增建筑面积1326平方米。2010年，投入资金40万元，安装看守所内AB门，扩建民警谈话室3间。

（二）羁押看管

1991年，调整充实县监所管理委员会成员。1999—2005年，先后制定《外来人员会见 送物服务承诺制度》《关于羁押犯罪嫌疑人 被告人实行换押制度》《干警岗位职责处罚制度》《息烽县看守所在押人员私人财物保管制度》等。其间，1995年5月16日凌晨，5监室8人密谋越狱，正在翻越围墙时，值班武警战士鸣枪、吹哨报警，看守所民警、武警官兵紧急出动，越狱人员蹇某某在慌乱中摔死，其他越狱人员在围墙内被生擒。1999年4月17日，犯罪嫌疑人曾某某被同监室在押人员7人打死，致县公安局3名民警被逮捕（其中1人经法院审理无罪释放），赔偿死者（曾某某）家属人民币24.9万元。此后，采取相应措施，建立《息烽县看守所严管措施》《息烽县看守所关于对“牢头狱霸”防范和打击处理机制》等制度，加强管理，避免事故发生。2010年1月15日起，公安部监管局负责人联系县看守所工作。3月4日，公安部监管局授予县看守所2009年度“一级看守所”称号。同日确定县看守所为对外开放试点所，并选为2010年公安部监管局联系全省的4个看守所之一。

息烽县看守所1991—2010年羁押人员统计表

表7-1-2　　单位：人

项目 年度	押量	其中		项目 年度	押量	其中	
		男	女			男	女
1991	248	236	12	2001	483	438	45
1992	234	225	9	2002	324	293	31
1993	177	166	11	2003	308	278	30
1994	196	186	10	2004	441	417	24
1995	210	194	16	2005	430	412	18
1996	173	165	8	2006	397	372	25
1997	43	39	4	2007	462	433	29
1998	241	212	29	2008	550	521	29
1999	223	204	19	2009	458	440	18
2000	402	378	24	2010	385	353	32

（三）教育改造

1991年，县看守所规定，被羁押人员7～10日内熟背监规，15日内熟知《在押人员行为规范》，监室内《学习园地》每月更新1期，每日学习、生活按常规管理。定期不定期请公安、检察、法院、司法干警到所进行法制宣传教育，鼓励在押人员坦白认罪，检举揭发他人违法犯罪行为，保护自己合法权益，争取从轻、减轻或免除处罚，争取立功受奖。是年，所内广播宣传167次，上法制课31次，监规教育1503人次，个别谈话389人次，在押人员写心得体会353份，为检察机关、公安机关提供违法犯罪线索6条11人。2002年，在押人员提供违法犯罪线索105条，经查证属实破刑事案31件。是年，经市中级人民法院审理，为3名有立功表现的罪犯裁定减刑。2004年，在押人员举报违法犯罪线索12条，破获盗窃案9件。次年10月，县公安局制发《关于进一步规范和加强看守所深挖破案线索工作　促进全局案件侦破的暂行规定》，从搜集情报线索、办案部门与看守所互通信息、加强信息反馈等10个方面作出相应规定。2006—2009年，在押人员提供违法犯罪线索241条，破获刑事案168件。2009年，县看守所被省公安厅监管总队评为二级看守所。

二、行政拘留与收容审查

（一）行政拘留

1991年5月，县投资8万元在大型地看守所旁新建行政拘留所，建筑面积1650.4平方米，设拘留室6间，厨房、厕所各1间，办公楼1栋，安装铁门和自来水。将看守所厨房、浴室、保管室改造为4间拘留室，另修放风场等活动场所240平方米。车辆、电脑、电教设备、洗澡间、图书室、会见室、医务室等与看守所共同使用。2006年7月前，被行政拘留人员生活费用自理。7月，行政拘留所与看守所合设，被行政拘留人员生活费纳入县公安局统一预算，被行政拘留人员用餐由看守所食堂统一配送。1991—2010年，行政拘留所关押被行政拘留人员4429人，其中男性3741人、女性688人。

（二）收容审查

1989年4月，县公安局收容审查所成立，设在县行政拘留所，管理方式与行政拘留所相同。1991—1996年，关押被收容审查人员2057人（男性1896人、女性161人）。1997年1月，因国家取消收容审查制度，收容审查所撤销。

第六节　道路交通管理

一、交通安全宣传

20世纪90年代初，县内采取出专栏、张贴标语等形式开展交通安全宣传。1997年，县交警大队与息烽电视台合作，开辟《息烽交通》栏目，宣传交通法律法规及交通安全常识。

2002年，县交警大队在永靖小学开展“小交警韵律操”活动，组队参加市中小学生“小交警韵律操”比赛获二等奖。开展以“关爱生命、安全出行”为主题的道路交通安全宣传活动，向62所小学发放《小学生交通安全知识读本》5000余册，宣传资料5000余份，交通安全挂图10套。2003年8月，县交警大队组织机动车驾驶员和中小学生8900余人参加贵州省（贵阳赛区）“升华杯”交通知识大奖赛，获“市优秀组织奖”。是年，县交警大队与永靖、阳朗、下阳朗、黑神庙等公路沿线7所中、小学建立校外交通安全辅导联系制度，发放《小学生交通安全知识读本》5000余册。

2005年起，在全县开展道路交通安全“五进”（进农村、进社区、进单位、进学校、进家庭）宣传活动。至2007年，举办交通安全培训班2期，培训村、居干部近200人。为单位上交通安全课70次。组织客运车驾驶员及车主学习9次共计2700人次，出动宣传车135辆次，举办图片展览等宣传活动85次，制作宣传牌40块，印发宣传资料1.1万余份，播放VCD光碟22场，受教育6万余人次。

2008年4月起，县交警大队在中、小学校开展“珍爱生命，拒绝违章”交通安全教育活动，至2010年，发放《交通安全手册》150册，用展板宣传交通安全法规，用案例解答群众咨询。喷绘“喜迎奥运，平安出行”和交通安全宣传栏各30平方米，展板690平方米，印发《致交通参与者的公开信》2万份。组织全县4000多人参加省“迎奥运，文明出行”交通安全知识竞赛。发放宣传资料5.35万份，播放VCD光碟宣传683场次，受教育群众13.3万人。

2010年，县交警大队成立宣传组，在“春运”、6月“安全生产宣传月”和国庆60周年等大型活动期间，集中开展道路交通安全宣传活动，制作事故警示教育展板30块、横幅32条、大型喷绘2幅，印刷宣传资料1.2万份。出动警力402人次、警车105辆次，开展“五进”宣传活动98次，悬挂标语37幅，展出展板980块次，播放VCD光碟430场次，发放宣传资料1.05万份，撰写工作简报102期，受教育群众6.2万余人次。

二、交通治理

1991年，开展无证驾驶、违章载人、客货混装和超载等违章行为常规检查治理。坚持将上级交通警察支队下达的交通安全四项控制数分解到各单位，形成交通安全一级抓一级、一级管一级、层层有责任格局。是年举办驾驶员学习班2期100余人。查扣证照不全、乱停乱放机动车36辆，行政拘留无证驾车人员3人，1998年起，开展规范县城停车秩序活动，在县城北门桥、十字街、文化路、工商局、城建局路段设执勤岗，其他主要街道画出停车标线，每天7时30分—18时30分安排人员执勤。

2001年6月，以县交警大队为主，交通、农机、工商等部门配合，在县境内各条道路上开展大规模整治交通秩序活动，查处各类交通违章165起，违章超员中巴车、小型客车19辆，查扣无牌无证摩托车88辆，强制报废中巴车1辆、吉普车2辆，吊扣驾驶证15人，拘留无证驾车28人。次年，开展无牌无证摩托车专项治理，查扣摩托车185辆，行政拘留5人，督促摩托车上户238辆。

2004年，开展农村农用车、拖拉机、摩托车等违法载人专项治理活动，沿境内210线、养温线、息九线、黑新线等公路进行交通巡逻检查，查处客车超员、货车超载，农用车、拖拉机、摩托车违法载人等交通违法行为42起，扣留违法车辆16台，暂扣驾驶证2个。是年5月，县交警大队启动“道路交通违法信息管理系统”，并与全省道路交通违法信息管理系统联网。2005年5月起，县公安局开展治理公路“三乱”（乱收费、乱罚款、乱摊派）活动，成立“治理公路‘三乱’工作小组”，制定《治理公路“三乱”工作方案》。

2006年3月起，配合全省开展无牌无证和机动车各项违法集中整治行动。在210国道和县城道路重点整治无证驾驶、驾驶无牌无证、挪用号牌、遮挡号牌、悬挂单面号牌、非法定标志机动车的汽车和摩托车的交通违法行为；在县乡道路上重点整治驾驶无牌无证三轮汽车、低速载货汽车、摩托车、报废机动车和无证驾驶机动车的交通违法行为。至6月，查处各类交通违法行为158起，查处无牌无证机动车117辆、摩托车50辆。

2008年凝冻期间，县境内高速公路、国道、县道、乡镇公路交通中断，滞留车辆2000余台和1万余人。县公安局组织警力打击借机哄抬物价，强卖强买等扰乱社会治安行为，实行交通管制，24小时不间断治安巡逻，全天候控制路况，疏通滞留车辆，确保行车安全。是年起，开展农村道路交通安全集中整治活动。至2010年，出动警力1413人次、警车381辆次，设置检查点138个，派出检查组103个次，纠正违法载客151件，检查违章车辆200余辆，违章行为404人次，行政拘留3人。

三、交通事故查处

1991—1999年，县内每年发生交通事故15～25起。2001年起，随着县境内车辆增加，交通事故剧增，是年发生交通事故167起，死亡10人，受伤40余人，经济损失近400万元。2008年，发生交通事故1228起，死亡8人，受伤24人，经济损失136.8万元。查处违章2656起，暂扣机动车472辆，罚款23.73万元，行政拘留10人。2009年，交通事故升至1659起，为历史最高。死亡14人，受伤17人，经济损失136.4万元。查处违章2087起，罚款25.5万元，行政拘留21人，刑事拘留2人。2010年，交通事故1484起，经济损失32.05万元。查处交通违章3734起，罚款36.7万元，行政拘留6人，刑事拘留4人。

四、机动车及驾驶员管理

（一）机动车管理

1994年11月，县内二、三轮摩托车、农用车年检和入户工作归县公安局交警大队管理；大中小型汽车由县交警大队签章后到有资质的年检部门检验。2000年起，农用车年检、入户改由县农机部门管理。是年，县交警大队不再对汽车年检签章，由车主直接到有资质的部门检验。2005年10月起，县内二、三轮摩托车入户由县交警大队办理，年检归扎佐检查站办理。是年，二、三轮摩托车入户1998辆，定期年检1174辆。2006—2007年，二、三轮摩托车入户3999辆。2010年年末，全县有各类机动车1.79万辆。

（二）驾驶员管理

1997年前，县境内机动车驾驶员实行分片区管理。1998年1月，撤销原设的9个机动车和驾驶员管理片区。重建养龙司、九庄等乡镇片区，由协勤人员负责辖区驾驶员的管理和组织学习等。2002年，县交警大队组织521名驾驶员集中培训学习，与287位车主签订安全责任书。2004年，全县驾驶员1.42万人。此后，县内驾驶员逐年增多，至2010年，全县有各类机动车驾驶员1.85万人。

第七节　消　防

一、机构

1991年，中国人民武装警察部队息烽县消防科（现役），受中国人民武装警察部队安顺地区消防支队和息烽县公安局双重领导，担负全县消防工作。1996年1月，因行政区划变更，由安顺地区消防支队转隶贵阳市消防支队管理。1997年10月16日，县消防科和消防中队合并，组建“中国人民武装警察部队息烽县消防大队”（简称县消防大队），受贵阳市消防支队和息烽县公安局双重领导。

二、消防设施

1991年，县消防科、消防中队有“119”火警报警电话2对，话机2台，消防水罐车2辆。1994年1月6日，消防中队营房被烧毁后，重建营房9间，建筑面积286平方米。1996—2001年，先后配备消防空气呼吸器、防化服、隔热服、战斗服等防护装备64件和水罐消防车2辆。2002年11月，县消防大队在永靖镇下阳朗村半边街新建营区，占地5840平方米。建消防大楼1幢，建筑面积1985平方米，有办公室、会议室、官兵宿舍共32间，车库7间，以及篮球场、训练场等。2003年7月竣工投入使用。此后，逐年添置消防器材和办公设备。2010年，县消防大队有通讯专线5对，电话10部，计算机18台（并入“金盾网”），水罐消防车3辆，消防宣传车、抢险救援车、抢险救援指挥车、大型水罐泡沫消防车各1辆，切割机1台、消防机动泵15台、消防栓112个、高位消防水池700口、消防摩托车2辆。

三、消防安全宣传

1991年，县消防科利用元旦、春节、国庆等重大节假日，选派人员到厂矿、企业、重点防火单位上消防课，讲解防火、灭火知识。在集镇设点发放资料、接受群众咨询，出防火专刊、书写张贴防火标语等，多形式广泛开展消防宣传。至2004年，共出动消防宣传车180余辆次，设点宣传90余次，发放各种宣传资料3.78万余份，挂贴宣传标语9230余条，拟写各种宣传稿件208篇，办宣传专栏119期，举办消防培训班42期。

2005年3月，县消防大队在全县中小学开展学生消防安全月活动，消防官兵为学校师生讲授消防知识，表演消防技能，赠送《中小学生消防知识手册》。是年，邀请市消防支队防火监督处法规指导科领导为乡镇派出所所长及派出所消防兼职民警20余人进行消防知识培训。对《中华人民共和国消防法》《贵州省消防条例》《消防监督检查规定》《贵州省公安派出所消防监督检查规定》等进行培训讲解学习。

2007年6月，县消防大队开展“六月安全生产月”消防宣传活动。发放消防宣传资料4000余份，挂出展板7块，播放宣传光碟2张。11月，开展“119”消防宣传活动，在县广播电视台播放一周消防安全知识，组织“119”青年志愿者在县城三角花园设点宣传，接受过往群众咨询150余人次，发放消防宣传资料5000余份。

2008年起，县消防大队依托新闻媒体、网络开展消防宣传，扩大宣传覆盖面和影响力。至2010年，投入资金2万余元，在贵阳电视台、息烽电视台和消防总队消防网、贵阳消防网、息烽公安网等媒体播放宣传视频、刊登宣传稿件700余篇（条）。举办培训班40余次，接受培训800余人，发放宣传资料1.5万余份。

四、执法检查

1991年，消防执法检查坚持突出重点，分类、分级挂牌管理。建立50人消防联络员队伍。检查单位197家次、农村50户以上村寨65个、一般村寨310个次、居民住房501户，整改隐患40起。1996年10月起，以施行《贵州省消防条例》为契机，加大消防执法检查力度，定期不定期适时开展消防执法检查。2005年起，开展火灾隐患“大排查、大整改”活动和人员密集场所消防安全大检查。至2008年，开展专项检查和整治活动20余次，共检查单位（场所）1668家次，发现火灾隐患528处，下发《责令限期整改通知书》35份，下发《消防安全检查意见书》192份，提出整改意见320余条，行政处罚58起，罚款4.96万元。2009年起，组织开展以“公众聚集场所、高层和地下建筑消防安全专项整治”和“公众聚集场所易燃可燃装修材料消防安全专项整治”活动，至2010年，共检查单位1380家次，下发《责令限期改正通知书》83份、《重大火灾隐患责令限期改正通知书》4份，提出整改意见190余条，行政处罚42起。

1991—2010年，全县发生火灾158起，造成直接经济损失132.95万元。

第二章　检　察

1991—2010年，县人民检察院坚持立检为公，执法为民原则，践行“强化法律监督，维护公平正义”工作理念，履行刑事、民事、行政、控告申诉、监所检察和反贪污贿赂、反渎职侵权职责。切实保障公平正义，维护社会稳定，促进社会和谐，为经济建设创造良好的法制环境。20年间，先后7次受到最高人民检察院表彰奖励，2001年、2004年先后被省人民检察院授予“人民满意检察院”“全省先进检察院”称号和命名为“五好检察院”。2008年被省委、省政府表彰为“精神文明建设工作先进单位”。

第一节　机　构

1991年，县人民检察院设刑事检察一科（审查批捕）、刑事检察二科（审查起诉）、反贪污贿赂检察科、法纪检察科、控告申诉检察科、办公室。1992年2月，增设民事行政检察科。是年，先后在县税务局、供销合作联社、信用合作联社、烟草公司设立检察室。1993年，增设小寨坝镇检察室。1994年5月，设反贪污贿赂工作局，撤销反贪污贿赂检察科。1996年7月，设监所检察科，8月，设县看守所检察室。1997年5月，设法警队。是年，县税务局、供销合作联社、信用合作联社、烟草公司等单位检察室撤销。1999年1月设政工科。2001年9月，刑事检察一科更名为侦查监督科，刑事检察二科更名为公诉科，法纪检察科更名为渎职侵权检察科。2002年2月，设纪检组。2005年11月，渎职侵权检察科更名为反渎职侵权局。2010年，设控告申诉科（内设职务犯罪举报中心和刑事赔偿办公室），办公室内设计划财务装备科，政工科内设法警队，反贪污贿赂工作局（内设侦查科、预防科、技术科）；反渎职侵权局内设侦查科。原侦查监督科、公诉科、民事行政监督科、监所检察科、院纪检组职能不变。

第二节　刑事检察

一、侦查监督

1991—2010年，县人民检察院受理县公安机关和本院自侦部门提请批准逮捕各类犯罪案2872件4753人，审查批准（决定）逮捕2565件4215人，不批准逮捕228件439人，退回补充侦查63件117人，追加逮捕98人。审查公安机关应立案侦查而不立案69件，发出《立案通知书》29件、《要求说明不立案理由通知书》67件。对公安机关在侦查活动中超期羁押人犯等违法行为作出《纠正违法通知书》64件。在公安机关侦查活动中，提前介入个案侦查185件。

息烽县人民检察院1991—2010年刑事侦查监督（批捕）统计表

表7-2-1

年度	提请逮捕		批准逮捕		不批准逮捕		退补侦查		追加逮捕	立案监督	
	（件）	（人）	（件）	（人）	（件）	（人）	（件）	（人）	（人）	（件）	（人）
1991	154	281	132	241	14	33	7	17	10	—	—
1992	139	244	120	197	10	33	4	12	2	—	—
1993	123	255	108	192	10	20	5	12	9	—	—
1994	117	201	112	188	5	23	15	24	—	—	—
1995	122	239	102	213	16	38	18	29	—	—	—
1996	117	221	103	190	10	28	14	23	2	—	—
1997	116	178	91	139	24	36	—	—	3	—	—
1998	128	184	106	148	19	33	—	—	8	3	3
1999	126	182	114	163	8	12	—	—	1	—	—
2000	127	209	103	169	12	28	—	—	—	—	—
2001	189	277	151	219	18	38	—	—	3	4	4
2002	163	236	164	137	19	19	—	—	—	—	—
2003	163	235	144	211	4	9	—	—	3	13	19
2004	166	281	142	247	11	22	—	—	4	3	5
2005	121	217	113	205	8	12	—	—	5	2	2
2006	149	235	138	218	12	18	—	—	8	3	3
2007	173	283	160	226	12	16	—	—	2	4	5
2008	155	253	150	246	5	7	—	—	13	13	13
2009	169	310	163	304	5	5	—	—	11	15	16
2010	155	262	149	253	6	9	—	—	14	9	15

二、审查起诉

1991—2010年，县人民检察院受理公安机关和本院自侦部门移送审查起诉各类犯罪案2951件4551人，经审查决定起诉2608件3992人，免予起诉、不起诉176件172人，追加起诉73人。提请抗诉13件15人。其间，2000年起，县人民检察院实行主诉检察官制度，院内设主诉检察官2名。在公诉部门成立以主诉检察官为核心的办案组，由主诉检察官承办重特大、疑难案件，并对办案组成员办理的案件质量进行把关，对办案组成员办理的除重特大、疑难、不批捕、不起诉以外的一般性案件行使审批决定权。2006年，县人民检察院制发《审查起诉部分罪名证据标准》，将刑法规定的八类犯罪及40余个办案活动中常见的罪名细化，使检察人员熟知和掌握常见罪名的证据标准。次年，县检察院与公安机关制定《关于加快办理轻微刑事案件的意见》，建立快速移送审查起诉制度，缩短办案时限，提高诉讼效率。

三、提起公诉

1991年，县人民检察院提起公诉166件239人，免予起诉18件19人。1997年，提起公诉50件76人，不起诉8件16人。2002年，提起公诉161件230人，不起诉19件19人，抗诉2件2人。2003年8月，县检察院获最高人民检察院“第二届全国十佳公诉人暨全国优秀公诉人评选特别奖”。2004年，提起公诉182件291人，不起诉5件5人，追加起诉4人，抗诉6件6人。2008年，提起公诉162件280人，不起诉5件5人，追加起诉19人。1991—2010年，县人民检察院检察员（含助理检察员）出庭支持公诉2608件次。

息烽县人民检察院1991—2010年刑事侦查监督（提起公诉）统计表

表7-2-2

年度	移送起诉		提起公诉		免予起诉		追加起诉	提起抗诉	
	（件）	（人）	（件）	（人）	（件）	（人）	（人）	（件）	（人）
1991	183	280	166	239	18	19	—	—	—
1992	135	196	132	192	3	4	2	—	—
1993	110	173	88	141	12	18	2	—	—
1994	134	210	123	189	38	57	—	—	—
1995	105	188	84	154	20	22	—	—	—
1996	124	201	109	175	18	20	—	—	—
1997	58	86	50	76	8	10	—	—	—
1998	114	163	108	150	2	5	1	—	—
1999	146	199	110	148	8	9	—	—	—
2000	117	174	109	160	8	12	—	—	—
2001	175	239	149	205	8	12	1	—	—
2002	180	249	161	230	19	19	—	2	2
2003	173	246	142	208	4	15	3	4	4
2004	194	315	182	291	5	5	4	6	6
2005	156	248	127	204	5	5	—	—	—
2006	160	247	151	233	4	9	—	—	—
2007	136	217	120	183	6	6	14	—	—
2008	197	317	162	280	5	7	19	—	—
2009	183	314	150	245	1	1	15	—	—
2010	194	325	154	285	1	2	7	1	3

四、刑事审判监督

1991—2010年，县人民检察院审查监督县人民法院刑事判决、裁定245份，对量刑畸轻的13件15人依法提出抗诉。县人民法院依法组成合议庭，按一审程序再审。免予起诉、不起诉196件247人，追加起诉73人。

第三节 民事行政检察

1992—2010年，县人民检察院受理不服人民法院判决、裁定民事、行政申诉案320件，经初查，息诉121件，立案147件，向上级检察院建议提请抗诉（或提请抗诉）47件。上级检察院支持抗诉36件，向县人民法院发出检察建议再审案件15件。市中级人民法院、县人民法院改判15件。办理执行监督案3件，参与县人民法院执行案件现场监督，促成当事人达成和解协议41件，支持起诉5件，督促起诉27件。

第四节 反贪污贿赂检察

一、案件办理

1991—2010年，县人民检察院反贪局立案侦查贪污、贿赂案262件。其中，贪污191件，行贿5件，受贿50件，挪用公款16件。为国家挽回经济损失930.9余万元。其间，2004年4月，立案侦查息烽磷矿发生的贪污、受贿、挪用公款系列窝案，依法查处该矿领导10名，涉嫌职务犯罪提起公诉直接责任人11人，为国家挽回经济损失400余万元。2006年1月，县检察院反贪污贿赂局获省检察院授予集体三等功。

二、预防职务犯罪

1991年，县建立县委领导下的预防职务犯罪工作机制。至2002年，先后与教育、计生、工商、国土、移民、金融、税务、林业等28个单位和部门建立预防职务犯罪协调机制，开展法制教育32次；向发案单位发出检察建议52件次。2003年，在息烽重钙厂挂牌成立全省首家国企重点工程项目预防职务犯罪办公室，制定《息烽县人民检察院预防工作联系制度》《息烽县人民检察院专题调研制度》等15项制度。

2004年，县人民检察院成立职务犯罪预防科。按“教育是基础、法制是保障、监督是关键”工作方针，在全县干部中开展预防职务犯罪活动。2006年，县委成立预防职务犯罪工作领导小组。2007年，预防职务犯罪工作领导小组改称预防职务犯罪工作委员会。是年，预防职务犯罪工作委员会在县农业局、县国税局、县工商局、息烽磷矿、息烽重钙厂等32家单位和部门建立预防职务犯罪联系点。2009年，县检察院在县委党校建立预防职务犯罪警示教育基地，至2010年，全县77家单位2231名干部参加警示教育活动，接受警示教育。县预防职务犯罪工作委员会与县内重点部门、重点工程项目签订预防职务犯罪责任书4份，向自侦部门移送案件线索4份（2件2人立案查处），向被调查单位发出检察建议19份，帮助有关单位完善规章制度80余条，上法制警示教育课67次，听课人数7000余人。

息烽县人民检察院1991—2010年查办贪污、贿赂案件统计表

表7-2-3　　单位：件

项目年份	合计	贪污	行贿	受贿	挪用公款
1991	12	9	—	3	—
1992	13	8	1	2	2
1993	10	7	—	3	—
1994	12	10	—	2	—
1995	14	9	—	4	1
1996	16	11	2	2	1
1997	13	8	—	4	1
1998	12	11	—	1	—
1999	10	7	—	2	1
2000	12	8	—	3	1
2001	13	9	—	2	2
2002	8	8	—	—	—
2003	13	10	—	3	—
2004	23	15	—	5	3
2005	21	13	—	5	3
2006	19	12	2	4	1
2007	9	9	—	—	—
2008	10	8	—	2	—
2009	11	9	—	2	—
2010	11	10	—	1	—

第五节　反渎职侵权检察

1991—2010年，县人民检察院反渎职侵权局立案查处国家机关工作人员滥用职权、徇私舞弊、玩忽职守等犯罪案共129件，其中：非法入侵他人住宅17件，非法拘禁40件，玩忽职守25件，重大责任事故16件，其他31件。其间，2004年起，为确保检察机关正确行使对职务犯罪案的侦查、起诉权，县人民检察院实行人民监督员制度。人民监督员对检察机关查办职务犯罪案件中的“三类案件”（检察机关直接受理的犯罪嫌疑人不服逮捕决定案件、拟撤销案件、拟不起诉案件）、“五种情形”（应当立案而不立案，超期羁押，违法搜查、扣押、冻结，应当给予刑事赔偿而不予以确认或不依法执行赔偿决定，办案人员徇私舞弊、贪赃枉法）实施监督，提出建议意见。2009年12月，县预防职务犯罪工作委员会组织全县副科级以上干部50余人赴贵阳市乌当区反腐倡廉警示教育基地开展警示教育。

第六节 控告申诉检察

1991—2010年，县人民检察院控告申诉检察部门坚持以便民告示牌方式向外公布控告、申诉受理范围，方便群众来访。相继推出“五访”（接访、管访、处访、稳访、结访）模式和“阳光检务车流动检察室”工作平台，共受理申诉案件77件，审查决定立案64件（其中不服逮捕40件、不服起诉15件、不服免诉6件），维持原处理决定58件，改变原处理决定6件。其间，1997年起，坚持检察长接待日制度和检察长接待日登记预约制度。2008、2010年，县人民检察院分别被省人民检察院、最高人民检察院授予全省检察机关“文明接待室”和全国检察机关“文明接待室”称号。

案例一：

2006年7月，县人民检察院控告申诉检察部门受理息烽县康裕来磷肥厂负责人邓某不服县人民检察院不批准逮捕王某的申诉案。邓某认为王某伙同他人潜入息烽县康裕来磷肥厂盗窃电缆线，数额较大，触犯了《中华人民共和国刑法》的有关规定，涉嫌盗窃罪，应予追究刑事责任。县人民检察院对该案进行立案复查，查明王某作案时未满16岁，未达到刑事责任年龄。检察院不批准逮捕的决定正确，对申诉人的申诉理由不予支持，维持原不批准逮捕王某的决定。

案例二：

2007年11月，县人民检察院控告申诉部门受理张某等三人不服息烽县人民检察院对林某某、黄某不捕决定的申诉案。立案复查认定：2006年4月15日中午，张某等三申诉人在贵遵高速公路53千米处的桥面上，因放炮一事与修建扎南路二标段桥二队的工人发生口角、纠纷，张某等三人受伤，但由于当时场面混乱，扎南路二标段桥二队工人众多，无法确认张某等三人的伤是由谁所致。犯罪嫌疑人林某某、黄某犯故意伤害罪的犯罪事实不清，证据不足，县人民检察院以事实不清、证据不足对林某某、黄某作出的不捕决定，适用法律正确，程序合法。申诉人张某等三人提出的申诉理由不能成立，不予支持，维持不捕决定。

第七节 监所检察

1996年7—8月，县人民检察院相继设监所检察科、县看守所监所检察室，规定检察人员每月驻监所时间不少于20天，定期与管理部门召开联席会议，互通监管改造信息。对所内减刑、假释、暂予监外执行，侵犯在押人员合法权利、超期羁押等进行监督。依法对脱逃、重新犯罪等行为加强刑罚执行和监管活动监督。是年，监所检察科配合看守所建立刑事拘留期限档案，制作《羁押人员诉讼期限登记表》，坚持“一案一审查”制度，落实羁押期限届满提示和催办制度。对在押人员的生活保障、劳动安全、羁押期限设检察意见箱，畅通举报投诉渠道，依法纠正违法行为，维护在押人员的合法权利和法律尊严。1996—2010年，监所检察室受理控告申诉7件，对判处暂予监外执行、管制、剥夺政治权利、缓刑、假释等人员考察513人次，在所内上法制课58次，给在押人员谈话2200余人次，提检察建议125条。配合县监管委员会、公安局开展监所安全检查1580次，纠正不安全隐患和违法行为198人次，对99件留所服刑人员减刑、保外就医、暂予监外执行进行专项检查。向县人民法院提出《纠正意见书》1份。

第三章　法　院

1991—2010年，县人民法院在刑事、民事、行政案件审判活动中，坚持以事实为依据，以法律为准绳，坚持公平、公正与合法的审判理念审理各类案件。坚持审判方式改革，与时俱进，在审判活动实践中不断探索、总结，相继推行“巡回法庭”“流动法庭办案车”“夜间法庭”，开通“法律咨询热线”“诉讼直通车”等便民利民举措。作出“当日立案，排期开庭，一月审结，公正裁判”案件审结十六字承诺制。共审理刑事案件2959件、民事案件2.87余万件、经济案件2527件、行政案件399件，有效化解社会矛盾，维护国家、集体和公民的合法权益，多次受到最高人民法院、省高院表彰奖励。其间，2000年、2002年两次被最高人民法院表彰为“人民满意好法院”，2003年，被最高人民法院授予“全国模范法院”称号、省高级人民法院记“集体一等功”1次。

第一节　机　构

一、内设机构

1991年，县人民法院内设办公室、政工科、刑事审判庭、民事审判庭、经济审判庭、行政审判庭、告诉申诉庭、执行庭。1995年4月，设法警队。1997年2月，撤销告诉申诉庭，增设立案庭、审判监督庭和研究室。2000年9月，法警队更名为法警大队。同月24日，增设纪检组。2002年4月，设执行工作局（与执行庭合署办公）、书记员室、监察室。民事审判庭更名为民事审判一庭，经济审判庭更名为民事审判二庭。

二、派出机构

1991年，县人民法院设九庄、养龙、黑神庙、永靖、永阳人民法庭5个派出机构。1992年5月，设立永红人民法庭（厂矿法庭）。1996年5月，撤销永红人民法庭。1997年7月，撤销永靖、永阳人民法庭。1998年7月，设流长巡回法庭。2000年9月，设西洋肥业有限公司巡回法庭。2001年4月，设青山、西山巡回法庭。2008年，撤销流长、西山巡回法庭，设流长人民法庭和西山人民法庭。

第二节　刑事审判

一、案件审理

1991年，县人民法院受理刑事案166件（含经济犯罪37件）242人。审结165件240人，审结率99.4%。判决发生法律效力150件213人，受刑法处罚210人，占98.6%。是年，派出干警87人次、出动车辆23次，与公安、检察、司法配合，开展反盗窃、反暴力性犯罪专项斗争和“打流窜、抓逃犯”统一行动，选择典型案件召开公开宣判大会6次，宣判案件42件68人。受安顺地区中级人民法院委托，宣判并执行死刑7人；审结经济犯罪案件36件，为国家、集体挽回经济损失7万余元。

1992—1996年，审结刑事案660件（含经济犯罪86件）。选择典型案件，在县城、案发地乡

（镇）召开公开宣判大会20余次，宣判案件150件220人。1997年，《中华人民共和国刑法》《中华人民共和国刑事诉讼法》修正及司法解释公布实施。是年，审结刑事案97件142人；上诉24件，二审审结20件，维持18件，部分改判2件。

2001年起，县人民法院推进刑事审判方式改革，扩大简易程序审理案件适用范围，探索普通程序简便审理。是年，审结刑事案119件。2004年起，审理未成年人犯罪案件实行“圆桌审判”方式，坚持“寓教于审，惩教结合”，教育、感化、挽救未成年人。量刑时，对符合缓刑条件的一律适用缓刑，该从轻、减轻的一律从轻、减轻处罚。至2006年，审结未成年被告人59名，适用缓刑、单处罚金、免予刑事处罚34人。2007年7月起，未成年人是主犯或共同犯罪中未成年人占半数以上的案件，移送贵阳市云岩区人民法院审理。2008—2010年，审结各类刑事案508件855人。

1991—2010年，县人民法院审理各类刑事案2959件，被告5335人。其中，侵犯公民人身权利、民主权利883件1369人，占收案数的29.84%；侵犯财产罪1337件2725人，占收案数的45.18%；危害公共安全罪281件333人，占收案数的9.49%；破坏社会主义市场经济秩序罪50件66人，占收案数的1.68%；妨害社会管理秩序罪204件338人，占收案数的6.89%；妨害婚姻家庭罪76件108人，占收案数的2.56%；渎职罪33件42人，占收案数的1.11%；贪污罪95件254人，占收案数的3.21%。

二、案例简介

李某超等9人盗窃耕牛案

罪犯李某超、刘某华、肖某文等9人均系石硐乡农民。1999年12月起，李某超、刘某华、肖某文等9名被告人纠合在一起，或两三人一起，或单独行动，在县境内及毗邻的修文县等地实施盗窃耕牛违法活动。至2002年3月，盗窃耕牛46头，价值8万余元。

县法院审理认为：被告人李某超参与作案28次，盗窃耕牛33头，致19头耕牛无法追回，数额巨大；被告人刘某华参与作案15次，盗窃耕牛17头，致10头耕牛无法追回；被告人肖某文参与作案16次，盗窃耕牛18头，致12头耕牛无法追回，刘某华（1989年因犯抢劫罪被判刑8年）和肖某文（1994年因抢劫罪被判刑5年）系累犯，犯罪情节严重；其余被告人犯罪行为在审理过程中一一查明。县人民法院认定被告人李某超、刘某华、肖某文、刘某全、刘某礼、杨某福、王某元、王某志8人的行为已构成盗窃罪，被告人李某超、李某文的行为构成销售赃物罪，依法对9名被告进行有罪判决：被告人李某超犯盗窃罪和销售赃物罪，分别判处有期徒刑15年和3年，实行数罪并罚，决定执行有期徒刑17年，剥夺政治权利3年，并处罚金人民币4.5万元；被告人刘某华犯盗窃罪，判处有期徒刑12年，并处罚金人民币3万元；被告人肖某文犯盗窃罪，判处有期徒刑11年，并处罚金人民币2万元；被告人刘某全犯盗窃罪，判处有期徒刑10年，并处罚金人民币2万元。被告人李某文犯销售赃物罪，判处有期徒刑2年，并处罚金人民币0.5万元。其余被告人犯盗窃罪分别被判处3～9年不等有期徒刑。

第三节　民事审判

一、案件审理

1991年，县人民法院受理各类民事案件374件，审结369件、结案率98.7%。其中婚姻家庭纠纷205件，占民事案件的55%，审结202件，审结率98.5%，调解、判决离婚的占53.6%，调解和好与判决不准离婚的占46.4%。此后数年，县人民法院受理各类民事案件逐年上升，至1997年，达868件

（含旧存1件）。

1998年1月起，县人民法院在永靖人民法庭设“夜间法庭”，审理民事案件。4月下旬向社会推出“当日立案、排期开庭、一月审结、公正裁判”案件审结十六字承诺制。是年，受理民事案件1272件（含15件旧存）审结1263件，结案率99.3%。2002年9月4日，县人民法院审结县内首例离婚损害赔偿案件，判决因第三者插足而导致夫妻感情破裂的过错方周某赔偿对方精神损失费1万元。10月18日，推出“流动法庭办案车”。

2004年2月8日起，县人民法院开通涉及民工工资案件绿色通道，实行代书诉状、缓交费用、优先立案、优先审理、致力调解和优先执行，加大对民工服务力度。5月起，县人民法院设立“速裁法庭”，当年“速裁法庭”办结民商事案件25件。是年，推行“阳光审判工程”，注重调解，及时化解矛盾，解决纠纷，坚持“能调则调，能判则判，调判结合”原则。充分行使释明权，做好对当事人的诉讼指导和法律宣传，让当事人在自愿基础上化解纠纷，互谅互让达成调解协议，自觉履行权利义务。

2006年9月，县人民法院出台《关于加强诉讼调解工作的若干意见》，对规范和加强诉讼调解工作作出明确要求。是年，受理民事案件1157件（含旧存18件），审结1139件（适用简易程序和普通程序的926件，适用督促程序213件），审结率98.44%。解决诉讼争议标的2329.06万元，平均结案周期23.5天。次年11月起，推出《村级司法联络员制度》，在全县各村聘任司法联络员1名，明确法官联系各村司法联络员。开通“诉讼直通车”，向群众承诺“一旦有纠纷需要诉讼或法律帮助，一个电话，‘诉讼直通车’就会开到你身边，为你提供热情的服务和帮助”。2009年，县法院出台《息烽县人民法院司法便民服务三十三条具体实施意见》，在立案大厅实行“一站式”服务、“一次性”告知、“首问责任制”“同岗替代”“诉讼直通车”“巡回法庭”等便民措施，制作“便民服务卡”3万余份发给群众，向人民群众公开便民措施、联系方式。

2010年，受理民事案件1127件，审结1118件，审结率99.2%，涉诉标的3094万元。是年，为弱势群体司法救助“减、缓、免”诉讼费12.95万元。

1991—2010年，县法院共受理民事案件2.37万件，审结2.34万件，审结率98.64%。

二、案例简介

（一）周某诉杨某双、向某利名誉权损害赔偿纠纷案

2003年3月28日，被告杨某双酒后使用向某利手机向原告周某丈夫发短信称：“你老婆给你戴绿帽子。”原告丈夫收到短信后即与其发生吵闹，导致夫妻感情不和闹离婚。原告于2003年4月23日向县人民法院起诉，要求被告杨某双、向某利赔礼道歉并赔偿精神损失2000元，其他损失300元。后原告因无其他损失300元的证据，当庭放弃该请求。县法院公开审理后认为，被告杨某双在没有事实依据的情况下，酒后发送手机短信损害原告名誉权，且对原告夫妻家庭造成一定不良影响，因而被告杨某双应向原告赔礼道歉，并适当赔偿原告一定的精神损害抚慰金。但本案被告的行为对原告的精神损害并未造成较严重的后果，因此原告的请求不予全部支持。被告向某利不知情，没有串通被告杨某双恶意损害原告名誉权的事实，因而不承担本案民事责任。依法判决被告杨某双向原告赔礼道歉，赔偿原告周某精神损害抚慰金1200元。

（二）刘某川诉县人民医院人身损害赔偿纠纷案

2005年2月16日，原告贵州西洋肥业有限公司搬运工人刘某某驾驶嘉陵50型轻便摩托车进厂上

班途中，被贵州西洋肥业有限公司龚某某驾驶的贵A25037大货车撞击，造成原告右大腿膝关节严重受伤，当日住进县人民医院，经医院诊断：创伤性失血性休克；右小腿毁损伤；右膝软组织挫伤。同日，被告与原告签订手术协议书："由于右小腿系重车碾压毁损伤，无法保留右小腿，为挽救生命，行右下肢截肢术。"在手术过程中，因发现原告小腿上段肌肉挫伤，污染严重，遂对原告做了右大腿截肢手术。2005年3月31日，经贵阳市法医活体检验鉴定中心鉴定，原告的损伤属Ⅴ级（五级）伤残；2005年11月25日，县卫生局委托贵阳市医学会对原告所作手术是否属医疗事故进行鉴定，12月13日，贵阳市医学会作出"贵阳市医鉴（2005）63号"医疗事故技术鉴定书，认为被告对原告诊断为右小腿毁损伤正确，并认为原告膝关节内侧软组织挫伤，右小腿及腘窝部广泛撕脱，且小腿上段肌肉挫伤，污染严重。因此，从右大腿下1/3截肢未违反医疗常规，不构成医疗事故。但被告在行截肢部位上，未履行告知义务，存在明显不足。鉴定结论为：该病例不构成医疗事故。原告认为被告未尽医疗规则，未履行良好的告知义务，存在明显不足，导致原告的损伤加大，应对原告的损伤承担民事责任。为此，原告向县人民法院提起诉讼，要求被告赔偿。县人民法院认为：原告以交通事故受伤后因医疗差错导致损伤加大，要求被告赔偿，被告在对原告治疗过程中，虽对原告伤情诊断正确，手术也未违反医疗常规，不构成医疗事故，但被告在对原告右大腿作截肢手术时，未履行告知义务，存在明显不足，应承担一定责任。为此，依法判决被告县人民医院赔偿原告刘某川医疗损失2万元。

第四节 经济审判

一、案件审理

1991年，县人民法院受理经济纠纷案76件，审结70件，审结率92%，诉讼标的55.2万余元。1994年起，经济审判活动推行"简繁分流，繁简分管"，将适用简易程序审理的经济纠纷案交由人民法庭审理。是年，受理经济纠纷案304件（含法庭206件），结案303件，结案率99.7%。诉讼标的109.19万元。1997年起，鉴于经济纠纷案涉诉被告多住省外，传唤难度大、时间长、当事人诉讼成本高等，审判机关与原告协商，采用原告就被告方式审理案件。至2001年，受理经济纠纷案1572件，诉讼标的2.6亿元。县人民法院选派9批26名审判人员，分赴内蒙古、山东、河南、重庆等省份，为县境内息烽磷矿、息烽铝厂、西洋肥业有限公司审结案件，诉讼标的450余万元。2002年，撤销经济审判庭，经济纠纷案划归民事审判二庭，列入民商事案件管理。

1991—2001年，县法院经济审判庭共收经济案件2520件，结案2513件，审结率99.7%，诉讼标的2.71亿元。

二、案例简介

永靖镇信用社诉县糖业烟酒公司、喻某某借款合同纠纷案

1996年，县人民法院经济审判庭受理永靖镇农村信用社诉县糖业烟酒公司（简称"烟酒公司"）、喻某某借款合同纠纷一案。经审理认定，1995年1月27日，经县烟酒公司担保，被告喻某某向原告信用社借款6万元，定于同年11月30日前归还，按季付息，并由被告烟酒公司用其房屋进行担保。喻某某将借款使用后，未按季偿付利息，也未按合同约定期限归还借款。信用社派员催收后，喻某某仅付至1995年12月20日止的利息，尚欠信用社本金6万元及其算至1996年6月30日止的利息7428

元8角7分。经审理，判决被告借款本金6万元及其算至1996年6月30日止的利息7428元8角7分，由喻某某在12个月内付清，每月付5000元，1996年6月30日后的利息按季付清，息随本清。烟酒公司为喻某某的借款担保期限已过，且信用社与喻某某私下重新达成还款协议，因此视为成立新的法律关系，烟酒公司不再承担本案责任。

第五节　行政审判

一、案件审理

1991年，县人民法院审结行政案2件。至1994年，诉至县人民法院的行政纠纷均在10件以下，多为土地、山林之类。此后，随着法律法规的宣传，行政机关相对管理人运用法律维护自身合法权益的意识增强，行政诉讼案件逐年增多。1995年受理行政案50件（含非诉行政执行43件），至2000年，县人民法院共受理行政案148件（含非诉行政执行43件），年均受理24.67件。

2002年起，行政机关申请执行的非诉行政执行案件，改由行政庭审查，作出是否准予执行裁定。裁定前，实行听证制度。通过听证，使行政管理相对人有机会维护其合法权益。2009—2010年，审结行政诉讼案45件（其中判决维持行政机关具体行政行为25件，经协调当事人撤诉8件，驳回当事人诉讼6件，重新作出具体行政行为6件），非诉行政执行案86件（其中裁定执行73件，不予执行3件，行政管理相对人认识有错或释明自愿履行义务6件，行政机关主动撤回申请4件）。

县人民法院审理行政案件坚持"宽进严出"的立案标准，把协调手段贯穿于行政诉讼始终，只要通过协调能够解决的案件，不论是庭审前、庭审中或是庭审后，都组织双方当事人进行协调。1991—2010年，共审结各类行政诉讼案件399件。其中，维持116件，撤销75件，变更4件，撤诉130件，中止3件，裁定驳回起诉34件，判决履行法定职责7件，判决驳回诉讼请求16件，作其他处理14件。

二、案例简介

贵州省遵义县建筑工程公司诉息烽县人事劳动和社会保障局劳动行政裁决纠纷案

原告贵州省遵义县建筑工程公司承建原息烽银都水泥厂集资楼工程后，原告的直属三处于1999年9月23日将该工程主体以单包工方式承包给李某海完成。此后，李某海聘用民工进行施工。工程完工后，原告与原息烽银都水泥厂进行结算。2000年12月20日，原告的职工宛某平出具证明给李某海，证明欠有李某海单包工工资2.39万元，但在结清余款时应扣除材料损失等。此后，被告向原告发出《劳动监察限期整改指令书》，原告在2005年8月23日的回复中说明李某海不是民工，民工是李某海所雇，民工的工资是李某海所欠，且被告不能适用《中华人民共和国劳动法》的规定。被告于2005年8月31日适用《中华人民共和国劳动法》第五十条和《劳动保障监察条例》第十八条第（二）项规定，作出"息人劳监处决字〔2005〕01号《劳动保障监察行政处理决定书》"，对原告作出"必须在2005年9月7日前支付李某海等52名民工工资2.39万元"的行政处理决定。原告收到被告的处理决定书后，遂向法院提起行政诉讼。

县人民法院审理后认为：被告是县政府的劳动行政部门，按照《中华人民共和国劳动法》规定，依法对用人单位遵守劳动法律、法规的情况进行监督检查，对违反劳动法律、法规的行为有权制止，并责令改正。但原告与李某海之间是民事合同关系，双方的行为应由民事法律进行调整，而被告用《劳动保障监察条例》对原告的民事行为进行处理，适用法律不当，应依法予以撤销。原告起诉的理由充分，予以支持。判决如下：撤销被告息烽县人事劳动和社会保障局在2005年8月31日作出的“息人劳监处决字〔2005〕01号劳动保障监察行政处理决定书”。

第六节　审判监督

1991年4月，县人民法院设告诉申诉庭。是年，接待群众来信来访1531人次，处理简易纠纷21件，告诉立案154件转相关业务庭审理。申诉立案6件（刑事3件、民事2件、经济1件）。1997年起，再审案件由审判监督庭审理。是年，接待来信来访2669件次，其中涉诉2074件，审查立案1514件，申诉立案3件。

2003年起，按最高人民法院关于将无限申诉改为有限申诉规定，县人民法院对当事人提起的申诉实行公开听证，符合立案条件的提交审判委员会讨论、决定再审；不符合立案条件的，当即驳回申诉或动员当事人息诉服判。

2005年，县人民法院在书记员系列管理、人民陪审员制度、审判监督制度三项改革中，扩大审判监督范围，审判监督庭直接参与案件流程管理，把监督向前延伸，推行审前、审中、审后全程监督。是年，县法院提请县人大常务委员会任命人民陪审员5名，人民陪审员参与合议庭审理各类案件47件。

2010年，县人民法院建立案件审理质量评估台账，开展“清理超审限结案”“清理涉诉信访积案”“检查治理国家赔偿案件”“法律文书质量年”等专项治理和为期3年的案件评查活动。清理涉诉信访案3件，通报批评不按时报送法律文书的8个部门，通报批评并处罚对法律文书有错漏现象的13名责任人。开展审判公开，通过县人民法院网、局域网、电子显示屏、触摸屏、公开栏等，向审判人员和人民群众公开审判业务，保障审判人员和人民群众的知情权、监督权和参与权，促进公正高效执法效率。

1991—2010年，县人民法院审结各类申诉案113件（民事97件、刑事14件、行政2件）。经再审，驳回申诉50件，维持原判35件，改判4件，撤诉、调解、中止执行等24件。

第七节　案件执行

1991年，县人民法院收执行案85件，执行70件，执行率82%，执行兑现标的23万元（含物资折款）。1992年，在县税务、运管、粮油总公司等单位设执行室8个，明确执行人员36人；在税务、运管等单位建司法联络室7个；在12个单位设司法联络员56人。分别印发《执行案件规则》《中止执行暂行规定》等制度。是年，收执行案202件，执行182件，执行标的87.19万元，清理旧存执行案139件。1997年，执行室、联络室、联络员相继撤销。

2001年3月起，县人民法院执行工作局划归省高院统一管理、统一协调，开展提级执行和交叉执行行动，处理一批涉及面广、社会影响大、久执未结的系列案、“骨头”案、“钉子”案。是年，开展春季执行会战行动。县人民法院抽派人员组成3个执行小组，分片集中突击执行45天，在乡镇、村及县法院机关召开执行兑现会16次，司法拘留有执行能力而拒不执行的当事人32人，执结执行案

629件，兑现执行标的款物1099.9万元。

2002年8月起，县人民法院实行执行案件立案时不预交执行收费规定。是年，收执行案877件，执结841件，执结率95.9%。2005年，开展夏季执行会战行动。共收执行案762件，执结754件，执结率99%，执行标的1642万元，执行兑现标的款物823.28万元。次年5月，按中央政法委员会《关于切实解决人民法院执行难问题的通知》精神和最高人民法院部署，县人民法院召开集中清理执行积案专项活动动员大会，开展为期40天的集中执行会战行动，清理中止、和解未结积案585件，标的168万元（含物资折款）。是年，收执行案1014件，执结992件，执结率97.83%，执行标的1989.76万元，兑现标的款物1376.58万元。2010年，开展集中清理执行积案活动，对有履行能力拒不履行的被执行人，依法查封财产、强制扣划、拍卖、罚款、司法拘留。是年，收执行案483件，执结468件，执结率96.9%，执行兑现标的款物2477.8万元。其中，强制执行90件，罚款1万元，司法拘留8人。

第四章　司法行政

1991—2010年，全县开展“二五”至“五五”4个五年普法宣传教育规划工作，并顺利通过省、市检查验收。基层司法所办公设施有突破性改变。人民调解组织健全完善，队伍建设不断加强，20年间，调解民间矛盾纠纷2.86万余件，年度调解平均成功率96.39%，为全县文明建设，构建和谐社会作出应有贡献，涌现出小寨坝司法所、小寨坝镇大湾村调解委员会、永靖镇梨安村党支部书记兼村调解委员会主任马发芬等全国先进集体和个人。新形势下的刑释帮教、社区矫正、法律援助、基层法律服务及律师、公证工作得到不断改进和加强。

第一节　机　构

1991年，县司法局内设办公室、人民调解股、法制宣传股、公证处、法律顾问处。4月，人民调解股更名为基层股，法律顾问处更名为县律师事务所，增设养龙区、永阳区、黑神庙区、永靖镇4个法律事务所。1992年，撤区并乡建镇，改设九庄镇、永靖镇、小寨坝镇3个法律服务所。1996年，撤销人民调解股、法制宣传股、公证处、法律顾问处，设基层工作科、宣传教育科。下设事业机构县律师事务所和公证处。是年8月，县律师事务所更名为慰民律师事务所。9月，设县第一法律服务所。1997年9—11月，先后设温泉镇、永靖镇司法所。1998年4月设小寨坝镇司法所。1999年6—9月先后设石硐乡、青山苗族乡、鹿窝乡司法所和法律服务所；九庄镇和养龙司乡司法所。1999年7月8日，设县法律援助中心。县第一法律服务所更名为县中心法律服务所。2000年9月8日，设立流长乡司法所。2001年9月，各乡镇设普法办公室，与乡镇司法所合署办公。

2002年，司法局内设政工科、办公室、法制宣传教育科（依法治理办公室）、律师公证工作管理科、基层工作科、法律援助工作管理科（法律援助中心），各乡镇设司法所。县中心法律服务所更名为贵阳市息烽县中心法律服务所。9月，各乡镇司法所加挂“依法治乡（镇）办公室”牌子。

2010年12月，县司法局内设政工科（警务科）、办公室、计划财务装备科、法规科、基层工作管理科、法制宣传科（县依法治理办公室），律师、公证工作管理科、法律援助工作管理科（县法律援助中心）、社区矫正工作管理科。10乡镇司法所为县司法局派出机构。

第二节　普法宣传教育

一、“二五”普法教育

1991年，县第二个五年普法工作（简称“二五”普法）启动。县委、县政府批转县普法领导小组《关于在全县开展第二个五年普法规划的实施方案》。普法领导小组办公室购买《社会主义法制建设若干问题讲话》和《中华人民共和国宪法》（简称“两本书”）2300套分发给各级干部职工学习。“二五”普法工作首先在县土管局、印刷厂、永靖镇、息烽磷矿4个单位进行试点。是年，在有关单位配合下，通过税法宣传月、社会治安综合治理宣传月、国土教育宣传月、宣传日、“5·19”助残日、“12·30”烟草专卖特别宣传日等活动，开展形式多样、内容丰富的普法宣传教育。出宣传专刊102期，刊登文章126篇、照片59张、图片91张，组装宣传车在乡镇、集镇巡回宣传109次，开展有线广播546次，录音广播198次，编写印发宣传资料4702份，翻印转发宣传资料5048份，组织开展法律宣讲128次，听众7.86万余人，配合宣判大会5次，协助举办法律知识竞赛5次，开展法律咨询1353人次，协助举办培训班16期927人次。1992年6月23日，组织全县2154名干部职工参加全省普及法律知识统一考试，及格率99.7%。9月，组织全县教育系统1477名教职员工参加“两本书”学习考试，平均分89分，及格率100%。1993年，结合乡镇换届，县委抽调人员组成10个工作组深入乡镇开展宪法、选举法、组织法等法律法规宣传。先后出宣传专栏50期，发放宣传资料3400份，有线广播宣传210余次，召开群众大会40余次，有12万人受到教育。征订《农民法律常识读本》1000余本。向私营企业、国有企业、厂矿、乡镇企业发放《中华人民共和国消费者权益保护法》《中华人民共和国反不正当竞争法》合订本5000册。1995年，征订学习书籍和复习资料4700册，考试复习资料2200份，订购普法试卷5400份。7月8日，组织干部职工4810人参加统一考试，参考率92%，及格率99.7%。11月，县“二五”普法教育工作经安顺地区普法领导小组检查验收，综合评分89分，验收合格。

二、“三五”普法教育

1996年9月，县委、县政府印发《关于在全县公民中开展法制宣传教育第三个五年规划》。是年，在县工商局、息烽磷矿、小寨坝镇先行“三五”普法试点，培训村级普法骨干322人。县委、县人大、县政府、县政协、县纪委、县法院、县人民检察院、县人民武装部领导带头学法，连续三次集中听取《中华人民共和国国家赔偿法》《中华人民共和国行政诉讼法》《中华人民共和国行政处罚法》法制讲座。1997年，开展“一书六法两条例”（《社会法制建设基本知识》《中华人民共和国宪法》《中华人民共和国行政处罚法》《中华人民共和国国家赔偿法》《中华人民共和国行政诉讼法》、新修订的《中华人民共和国刑法》《中华人民共和国刑事诉讼法》《行政复议条例》《国家公务员暂行条例》）普法学习，建立以领导干部、执法人员、法律服务工作者和群众骨干为主体的法制宣传员队伍。征订“一书六法两条例”3400余册发给干部职工。11月，组织干部、职工、教师3000余人参加县、市“一书六法两条例”普法学习统一考试，参考率96%，及格率100%。全年举办法制理论骨干培训班23期，受训人员1578人。配合综合治理、禁毒、“6·25”土地日、青少年法制教育、老年人权益保护、保密等专项宣传10余次。建立干部“学法日”制度。出专刊276期，录音广播1760小时，书写固定标语137条（幅）、法律宣传标语162条，发放宣传资料5.87万份。1999年12月，县十三届人大常委会分别听取审议县政府贯彻实施《县人大常委会关于深入开展依法治县工作的决议》和“三五”普法规划工作情况。县司法局为全县171个村（居）委会征订《农村干部法律知识》203册，普法书籍600册，举办法制骨干培训和法制讲座5期。11月2—5日，组织机关、事业单位干部职工参加学法统一考试。2000年2月，县司法局干部为县十三届人民代表大会第三次会议出、列席人员270余人作题为《学习〈行政诉讼法〉 严格依法行政 推进依法治县进程》的法律知识讲座。3月，县司法局、县教育局、县职校联合开办司法中专班，县司法局选派干部任司法中专班专业课兼职教员。8月，市“三五”普法依法治市工作验收组对县实施“三五”普法依法治理工作进行检查验收，实地检查永靖镇南门村、小寨坝镇大湾村、温泉镇幸福村、县水电局、县工商局、县交通局等单位“三五”普法依法治理工作，检查组对各单位“三五”普法工作给予充分肯定，验收合格。

三、“四五”普法教育

2001年8月，县委批转《县委宣传部 县司法局〈关于在全县公民中开展法制宣传教育第四个五年规划〉》，作出《关于在全县公民中开展法制宣传教育第四个五年规划的决定》。9月，县人大常委会作出《关于开展“四五”普法法制宣传教育的决议》，县政府作出《关于开展法制宣传教育第四个五年规划的实施意见》，县委成立普法依法治县工作领导小组，下设办公室在县司法局。11月20日，县召开“三五”普法依法治县总结暨“四五”普法依法治县动员启动大会。是年，征订《公务员依法行政读本》《中华人民共和国婚姻法》等法律书籍1000余册。组织1158名干部职工参加省公务员学法用法考试，参考率98%。

2002—2005年，县依法治县办公室、县司法局相继制定《息烽县领导干部法制讲座制度》《息烽县领导干部学法考试考核制度》《息烽县领导干部法律知识培训制度》《办公会前学法制度》《普法依法治县奖惩制度》《息烽县公务员学法用法制度》《息烽县国家机关公务员（参公 依公执法人员）行政执法活动的公开 公示制度》《息烽县国家行政机关公务员（参公 依公执法人员）定期理论培训制度》《息烽县国家行政机关公务员（参公、依公执法人员）法律知识培训考核制度》等规章制度。征订《教师法制教育读本》《教育法规与政策选编》、中小学生《法制教育》课本3万余册。开展“送法下乡”“法律进社区”“12·4”法制宣传日等法制宣传教育活动，发放宣传资料10万余份，组装宣传车20辆次，制作展板37块，送法律书籍3000余本，上法制课20次，制作横幅40余幅，书写大小标语200多条。2005年6月，县成立4个检查验收组，对各乡（镇）、县直机关及企事业共106个单位“四五”普法依法治县工作进行自查验收。7—10月，“四五”普法依法治县工作分别通过省、市检查组验收合格。

四、“五五”普法教育

2006年，县委制定《息烽县2006—2010年依法治县规划》（以下简称《规划》），全县各级各部门按《规划》要求制定本乡镇本部门“五五”依法治理规划和方案。10月，县委、县政府召开“四五”普法依法治县工作总结表彰暨“五五”依法治县工作动员启动大会，会上表彰“四五”普法依法治县工作先进集体48个、先进个人95名。举办学法培训讲座6期，向农村村民免费发送《安全知识百事通》及其他法律书籍1万余册。

2007年起，开展以“法律六进”（进机关、进乡村、进社区、进学校、进企业、进单位）为重点的法制宣传教育，营造公正高效的法制环境和构建和谐稳定的社会环境。2009年，县委、县政府出台《关于进一步加大“五五”依法治县工作力度，大力开展“法治息烽”创建活动的意见》。围绕建设“生态文明县”“法治息烽”“平安息烽”，结合县城旧城改造、企业改制、土地征用、农民工返乡、环境保护、计划生育等，广泛宣传劳动、就业、社会保障等与人民群众生产生活密切相关及新颁布的法律法规。聘请清华大学法学院教授、博士、研究生等对县内基层法律服务人员进行法律培训。组织参与“治安宣传月”、《消防法》、禁毒、安全生产、“严打‘两抢一盗’，保卫百姓平安”等宣传活动29场次，出动宣传车29台次、宣传人员160人次，办法制宣传栏89期，法律咨询16次，接受咨询1561人次，制作展板52块，作法制讲座15场，培训法制骨干943人次；张贴标语414条，发放宣传资料1.5万余份，拟写信息（简报）19期，创建“法制息烽”普法网页。授予青山苗族乡等12个单位“‘依法治理示范工程’建设示范单位”称号。2010年，“五五”普法、依法治县教育实行目标管理。年初，县政府县长与10个乡镇长及县直企事业（含驻县企业）负责人签订《息烽县2010年依法治县“法治息烽”创建工作目标责任书》，形成一把手负总责，分管领导具体抓，各部门齐抓共管工作格局。是年4月、6月，县“五五”普法依法治县工作通过省、市检查验收。11月，县司法局被全国普法办表彰为全国法治（市、区）创建活动先进单位。2011年，县“五五”普法依法治县工作被中央宣传部、司法部表彰为2006—2010年全国法制宣传教育先进县。

第三节　人民调解

1991年，县内各村（居）、500人以上企业共建人民调解委员会175个，调解员1754人，组织培训433人。调处民间纠纷2514件，调解成功率94%，防止矛盾激化151件198人。次年，县政府下发《关于在各乡镇明确人员管理村级人民调解委员会的通知》，要求各乡镇明确专人管理本乡（镇）村级人民调解委员会工作和帮助调解民事纠纷。1993年，坚持“一年一整顿”制度，采取“补、换、培、稳”方法适时调整充实调解队伍。是年，全县调解委员会173个，调解员812人，组织培训586人。调处纠纷2994件，为历年最多。调处成功率97%，预防矛盾激化13件17人。

1997年9月，开展“创四无活动”（无因民间纠纷激化酿成自杀事件、无刑事案件、无群众械斗和集体上访），排查各类纠纷248件。1999年5月，司法部授予永靖镇犁安村党支部书记兼村调解委员会主任马发芬“全国模范人民调解员”称号，小寨坝镇司法所、小寨坝镇大湾村调解委员会为先进集体。6月30日，《贵州日报》以《八年调解纠纷300件》进行报道。7月1日，《法制生活报》头版头条刊登《为了这片净土的安宁——记全国模范人民调解员马发芬》。2000年，大湾村调委会被评为全省“优秀人民调解委员会”。

2001年3月，县委、县政府成立“息烽县司法调解领导小组”，下设办公室在县司法局。5月，10个乡镇先后成立司法调解中心，建立人民调解员岗位责任、纠纷登记、纠纷排查等制度。2003年5月，按司法部关于人民调解委员会印章的规定，县内乡镇、村（居）、厂矿、企业统一启用“人民调解委员会”印章。9月，对村党支部书记、村（居）委主任就人民调解工作的性质、任务、原则、纪律、纠纷调解范围和程序、纠纷类型、调解协议内容、调解协议效力等方面业务进行培训。

2005年，县委、县政府出台《关于加强人民调解工作的指导意见》，要求加强组织建设，完善人民调解工作的程序和保障机制。县司法局制定建立人民调解员岗位责任、纠纷登记、纠纷排查等各项制度。次年，县司法局下发《关于法律援助与人民解调相结合工作的实施意见》，规范人民调解工作。每个村（居）明确一名专职调解员，每人每月补贴80元。2007年，县司法局开展春季民间纠纷和社会不稳定因素集中排查调处活动，印制《矛盾纠纷排查登记表》《矛盾纠纷排查情况统计表》《矛盾纠纷调解登记表》《人民调解委员会工作情况统计表》等，规范和完善人民调解工作程序和档案。是年，受理各种民间纠纷634件，调处634件，调处率100%，调处成功618件，成功率97.47%；参与处置群体性事件10起；预防矛盾纠纷激化14起；防止群体性上访9起。

2010年，县司法局为人民调解委员会统一制作标牌，设立调解室。是年，全县有乡镇村（居）人民调解委员会183个，调解员911人，其中专职调解员173人。全年调解纠纷973件，调解成功934件，成功率95.99%，防民转刑22件84人，防纠纷自杀2人次，制止群体性事件32件643人。

息烽县1991—2010部分年份民间纠纷调处统计表

表7-4-1

年份	调处民间纠纷（件）	调处成功率（%）	预防民事转刑事件/人	年份	调处民间纠纷（件）	调处成功率（%）	预防民事刑事件/人
1991	2514	94	51/198	2001	1544	98.4	16/82
1993	2994	97	13/17	2002	512	94.4	13/39
1994	2825	92	19/72	2003	1296	98	21/69
1995	2672	98.7	21/85	2005	686	100	22/72
1996	2511	96.7	33/146	2006	751	96	9/45
1997	2481	92	8/37	2007	634	97.47	24/12
1998	1681	96.4	12/49	2008	713	98	7/56
1999	1450	96	16/78	2009	737	97.96	36/157
2000	1642	96	17/68	2010	973	95.99	24/86

第四节　法律服务

1991年，县司法局在四区一镇（永阳区、九庄区、黑神庙区、养龙区、永靖镇）分别设法律事务所。担任区、乡和乡镇企业、个体户法律顾问14家，提供法律帮助69次，帮助追回“三角债”3.8万元，避免经济损失5万余元。代理民事案件25件，代书120份，解答法律咨询509次，开展法制宣传90次，业务收费3212元。次年，撤区并乡建镇后，保留九庄、黑神庙、永靖镇3个法律服务所。1993年，调解民间纠纷124件，代理民事案件16件，非诉讼代理5件，担任法律顾问11家，代书66份，协办公证2件，解答法律咨询870人次，挽回和避免经济损失22.5万元。

1999年4月，县司法局在全省率先开通“148”法律服务热线电话，是年，提供法律咨询服务246件次。《贵州日报》刊登《息烽“148”专用电话成热线》一文，并配发《为法律咨询电话叫好》评论员文章。6月15日，《法制生活报》以《息烽“148”切实为民减讼累》为题，报道息烽“148”法律服务开展情况。2003年，加强基层法律服务工作者执业管理，对无服务执照和上岗证人员一律不准执业。是年3月，组织基层法律服务从业人员参加全省基层法律服务工作者执业培训，聘请专业人员对全县法律服务人员集中培训。

2006年6月，县司法局开通“96188”声讯服务台，为群众提供更方便快捷的法律服务。次年起，乡镇法律服务收费实行“专户统管”，严格收费标准和收支两条线，杜绝打白条收费和收费不开票据等现象。

1991—2010年，基层法律服务代理民事2025件，非诉代理642件，先后担任法律顾问206家，代书法律文书3689份，协办公证127件，接受法律咨询6983人次。

息烽县1991—2010年法律服务统计表

表7-4-2

年份	案件代理（件）	非讼代理（件）	担任顾问（件）	代书法律文书（份）	咨询（人次）	协办（见证公证）
1991	25	69	14	120	509	1
1992	26	2	15	98	145	3
1993	16	5	11	66	870	2
1994	38	12	16	170	851	4
1995	78	34	11	163	912	6
1996	19	8	6	84	947	7
1997	116	83	13	357	1030	5
1998	115	95	22	392	972	31
1999	103	30	13	269	893	16
2000	138	36	7	123	768	18
2001	186	35	5	96	690	20
2002	186	23	9	542	358	21
2003	103	30	13	269	532	16
2004	148	15	7	278	670	17
2005	101	25	10	286	640	8
2006	129	32	7	126	684	15
2007	175	23	7	187	314	10
2008	112	36	9	143	660	16
2009	67	45	16	198	1280	12
2010	146	52	10	98	186	13

第五节　法律援助

一、法律援助案件办理

1994年，国家司法部提出建立法律援助制度。同年，县启动法律援助工作，至1998年，办理法律援助案件11件。1999年7月8日，县法律援助中心正式挂牌执业。是年，办理援助案46件（刑事11件、民事35件），代书73份。2002年，法律援助管理科与法律援助中心合署办公。11月，首家社会团体“息烽县法律援助妇女工作站”成立。至2004年10月，各乡镇法律援助工作站、县残联、未成年人、老年人法律援助工作站相继成立。其间，2003年，法律援助经费列入县财政年度预算。

2005年，县法律援助中心制定服务承诺制度、举报制度、重大疑难案件汇报制度，规范法律援助工作行为。2006年，县司法局对乡镇法律援助工作站、点实行规范化管理，扩大法律援助社会覆盖面。办理援助案393件，处理上访案30余件，接待咨询443人次。2008—2010年，办理法律援助案429件，回访法律援助对象59人。其间，2010年6月24日，司法部法律援助司检查县法律援助工作并给予充分肯定。是年，全县有法律援助中心1个、法律援助工作站15个。

二、案例简介

1997年，张某某因购买的灯泡发生爆炸，致眼睛失明，经多渠道诉讼，难以维护其合法利益。一审败诉后，张某某申请法律援助，县法律援助中心指派专人办理。2001年3月，二审法院撤销原判，发回重审，原审法院重审后，以事实不清，证据不足，驳回原告张某某的诉讼请求，县法律援助中心再次为张某某提供援助，到龙里、遵义、贵阳等地收集证据和进行鉴定，二审法院经过庭审，质证、认证，判被告赔偿张某某人民币2万元。张某某向县法律援助中心送“伸法律援助之手，助残疾人之力”锦旗。贵州省《法制生活报》以《四年索赔无结果，法律援助显生机》为题对案件进行报道。此案被司法部作为当年十大新闻案件进行宣传。

第六节　帮教与社区矫正

一、安置帮教

1999年前，“两劳”刑释解教人员安置帮教工作主要由县公安局管理。是年3月，县委、县政府成立县刑释解教人员安置帮教工作领导小组，下设办公室在县司法局，乡镇司法所设接待站。5月，召开“两劳”刑释人员安置帮教专题会，明确安置帮教工作领导小组成员单位职责，落实司法部、公安部、中央综治委等六部委的要求和部署，对“两劳”刑释人员开展调查。调查统计，1999年前3年，全县有“两劳”人员443人，其中刑释人员389人，解教人员54人（登记365人，签帮教协议240人）。1999—2001年，全县有“两劳”刑释人员694人，其中，重点对象215人，两次以上犯罪16人，无正当职业409人，解除劳教28人。

2004年起，围绕“平安息烽”工程，按照“帮教社会化、就业市场化、管理信息化、工作责任规范化”总体要求，坚持“教育、感化、挽救”原则，从“爱”字出发，“帮”字入手，在“拉”字上下功夫，“改”字上看效果，坚持社会、家庭齐抓共管，做到不脱管、不漏管、底数清、情况明。至2005年，流长乡党政领导组织有关部门帮教乡境内19名刑释解教人员，送去大米250千克、衣物20余件（套）。西山乡司法所、派出所、综治办对“两劳”人员进行家访，送发救济粮750余千克、衣物70余件（套），安置8名刑释人员到驻乡企业就业。九庄镇出资6万元为“两劳”人员改造茅草房15家，发放救济粮5000千克。全镇104名“两劳”人员无一人重新犯罪。2006年，全县有刑释解教人员614人，登记、建档立卡428人，签帮教协议317人，安置就业278人。

2007年，县司法局对2004年至2006年12月刑释解教人员情况进行摸底调查，调查统计，2004—

2006年，全县有刑释解教人员614人，其中：已衔接428名，占刑释解教人员总数的69.7%；未衔接174人，占刑释解教人员总数的28.35%；重新违法犯罪12人，占刑释解教人员总数的1.95%。在已衔接人员中，实际帮教317人，占已衔接人数的74.07%；就业安置的有278人，占已衔接人数的64.95%。

2010年10月，启动安置帮教信息化管理工作。是年，开展培训3期100余人次。收到刑释解教人员通知书145份（刑释116人、解教29人），签帮教协议128份，帮教129人，安置就业131人。

二、社区矫正

2009年起，县司法局开展社区矫正管理工作。是年，开展“五类人员”（判处管制、宣告缓刑、暂予监外执行、裁定假释和剥夺政治权利）摸底排查。排查统计，全县有矫正对象80名，其中，缓刑50名、剥夺政治权利28人、监外执行和假释各1人。2010年，县政府办印发《息烽县开展社区矫正工作的实施意见》，社区矫正工作逐步进入司法行政管理。12月，成立县社区矫正工作委员会，办公室设在司法局。是年，全县有矫正对象91人。

第七节　律师与公证

一、律师工作

（一）律师队伍

1991年，县司法局设法律顾问处，主要接受国家机关、企事业单位、社会团体的聘请，担任法律顾问；接受刑事案件当事人的委托，担任辩护和民事案件诉讼代理人；接受非诉讼事件当事人的委托，提供法律援助或担任代理参加调解、仲裁活动；解答法律询问，代写法律文书；宣传讲解法律等事务工作。是年，法律顾问处有专职律师1人，特邀、兼职律师各2人。1996年，撤销法律顾问处，组建县律师事务所，有特邀律师和招聘法律专业人员各2人。2000年9月起，因特邀律师不再注册登记，律师事务所宣告歇业至2001年6月。2001年7月起，有专职律师1名，法律专业人员2名。2009年，新增专职律师、挂靠兼职律师各1名。2010年底，有执业律师、实习律师各3名。

（二）律师执业

1991年，县司法局法律顾问处为19家行政、企业单位担任法律顾问，提供法律服务131次，参与重大谈判8次，审查修改经济合同29份，追回合法债务22.5万元。承办刑事案件辩护64件，民事代理33件，行政诉讼代理1件，代书法律文书91份，提供法律咨询238件次，接待来信来访506人次。此后，县律师事务所律师为行政、企业单位担任法律顾问、承办刑事案件辩护等业务有所减少。至1998年，先后担任法律顾问65家次，受委托刑事辩护246件，民事代理224件，行政代理15件，代书法律文书765份，非诉代理31件，办理法律援助8件。

1999年，县司法局加强律师执业管理，明确律师办案调查、取证须有2人参加，重大、疑难案件须经集体讨论，当事人监督、单位监督等制度具体落实到案。制发“执法（办案）监督卡”，经检查签字后，随卷宗统一归档，实行错案责任追究制。

2004年，开展律师队伍集中教育整顿活动，经市、县司法局检查，县内律师执业无违规违纪现象。2007年，开展律师执业诚信教育活动，建立完善律师执业接案、建档、收费等规章制度，进一步规范律师执业行为。次年起，对律师执业行为实行当事人监督与单位监督相结合，坚持律师办案监督卡制度。2009年，开展律师执业纪律和职业道德教育，对律师执业实行服务质量评查。

2010年，县司法局在律师中开展以“法律服务和法律援助工作为构建社会主义和谐社会服务”为主题的教育实践活动，保持共产党员先进性、深入实践科学发展观等活动，设立党员律师先锋岗，提高律师诚信为民服务意识。是年，律师事务所律师共受理案件93件，其中：民事案件65件、刑事案件28件。代写法律文书200余份，参与处理涉法上访（信访）案件7件，创收4.46万元。

息烽县1991—2010年部分年份律师执业情况统计表

表7-4-3

年份	担任法律顾问（家）	承办刑事辩护（件）	承办民事代理（件）	承办行政代理（件）	代书法律文书（份）	提供法律咨询（人）
1991	19	64	33	1	91	238
1992	14	48	26	1	93	145
1993	10	24	24	3	49	238
1995	11	35	78	7	163	261
1996	3	31	19	1	136	295
1997	3	18	22	1	107	305
1998	5	26	22	1	126	347
1999	8	14	105	4	198	283
2000	5	10	23	1	124	242
2003	7	6	22	2	158	363
2005	7	7	17	3	194	294
2006	9	10	15	4	178	351
2007	8	3	18	4	133	376
2008	8	12	69	1	171	309
2009	8	9	27	1	186	356
2010	9	28	65	3	200	343

二、公证工作

1991年，县公证处有专职公证员、公证助理和合同制工人各1人。共办理各类公证125件，涉及金额132万元。其中民事公证64件、经济类公证61件。收公证费1700元。次年，共办理公证2139件，为历年最高。其中，民事公证2055件、经济类公证84件，涉及财产金额138.5万元。

1998年，县公证处拓展公证服务领域，首次办理农业种植合同公证。是年，办烤烟种植合同公证223件。1999年，办烤烟种植合同、计划生育合同663件，收公证费2万元。

2001年起，县公证处推行公证接待“首问负责制”。2004年，开展“公正执法树形象”集中教育活动。2006年3月，《中华人民共和国公证法》（以下简称《公证法》）正式颁布施行。县司法局牵头，就《公证法》立法背景、立法精神、实施步骤及公证业务受理范围、公证程序、公证效力等在全县开展《公证法》宣传活动。活动出动宣传车2台，通过县电视台播放《公证法》录音12小时，发放《公证法》宣传资料8000余份，接待群众咨询500余人次。是年，开展公证质量全面检查活动，就公证办证程序、材料审查、出证审批、公证文书规范、诚信执业、职业道德等方面进行检查，共抽查公证卷宗400余件。未发现错证、假证、关系证、人情证以及其他违反职业道德和执业纪律现象，公证文书规范，资料完整。

2010年，县公证处有公证员、公证助理各1名。是年，受理国内公证317件，其中民事类公证314件、经济类公证3件，全部办理完结。

息烽县1991—2010年公证业务统计表

表7-4-4　　　　单位：件

年份	合计	其中		
		民事公证	经济公证	其他公证
1991	125	64	61	—
1992	2139	1298	841	—
1993	564	535	29	—
1994	550	525	25	—
1995	151	48	103	—
1996	299	48	251	—
1997	304	79	62	163
1998	441	117	161	163
1999	1053	835	218	—
2000	809	554	255	—
2001	375	261	114	—
2002	232	28	204	—
2003	355	87	268	—
2004	350	92	258	—
2005	302	149	153	—
2006	806	[illegible]92	14	—
2007	305	[illegible]3	52	—
2008	301	[illegible]	81	—
2009	247	[illegible]5	12	—
2010	301	[illegible]8	3	—

第八篇　社会事务管理

第一章　人事劳动与社会保障

1991—2010年，县人事劳动和社会保障工作部门贯彻落实党和国家深化改革的方针政策，不断推进人事制度改革，推行国家公务员制度，建立完善公务员招考录用、培训、考核、奖惩、任免、调配等制度。大中专毕业生从由政府包揽分配安排工作到由学校、劳动和社会保障部门推荐就业或参加公务员、事业单位招考。劳动用工，对以计划管理和行政审批为特征的劳动招工制度进行改革，落实企业用工自主权，实行“双向选择，市场调节”招工，形成以企业为主体，劳动力市场为依托，法律法规为依据的市场招聘机制。机关、事业单位干部职工工资，经过1993年、2007年两次工资制度改革和历年工资调整，得以大幅度增长，人均月工资由1993年的192.3元调升到2010年初的3204元。社会保障体系逐步建立完善。

第一节　机　构

1991年，县劳动局、人事局单列。劳动局内设办公室、就业办、保险股、仲裁办公室、安全生产监督委员会办公室，1995年设劳动监察股。人事局内设办公室、干部股、工资福利股、代管编制委员会办公室。1996年4月，撤销人事局、劳动局，合并组建县人事劳动局，内设办公室、干部人事股、工资股、职称管理股、劳动股。下设人才交流服务中心、社会保险事业局、劳动就业办公室、劳动安全监察站。2002年3月，县人事劳动局更名为县人事劳动和社会保障局。原承担的安全生产综合管理、职业安全监察和矿山安全监察职能划给县发展计划与经济贸易局，锅炉、压力容器、电梯、防爆电器、起重设备、游乐设施等特种设施安全监察职能划给县质量技术监督局。内设人事劳动争议仲裁办公室，设县劳动监察大队，代替原人事劳动局内设劳动关系与监察科职能。2010年6月，县人事劳动和社会保障局更名为县人力资源和社会保障局，内设办公室、录用调配任免与人才开发科（公务员管理科）、工资福利科、职称管理科、人事劳动争议仲裁办公室、社会保障科。下设县人才交流服务中心、县企业离退休人员托管中心、县社会保险局、县就业局（挂县小额贷款担保中心、县职业技能鉴定办公室牌子）。

第二节　人事管理

一、推行国家公务员制度

1995年，开展机关事业单位“三定”（定机构、定编制、定职能）工作，为推行国家公务员制度作前期准备。全县10个乡镇、45个县直行政机关单位行政定编925人（其中乡镇行政定编319人、县直机关行政定编456人，公安、司法定编150人），共设置职位925个（其中正县级职位4个、副县级17个，正乡、科局级78个，副乡、科局级148个，主任科员和副主任科员113个、科员和办事员565个）。实有行政人员1003人，超编78人，符合过渡公务员条件人员921人，空缺职位4人。对超编人员，采取三种方式处理：男年满58周岁，女年满53周岁作离岗退养，不占单位行政编制；男年满55周岁，女年满50周岁的，本人申请，单位同意，批准退休；安排部分到县属企、事业单位和村任职。

1996年1月起，开展公务员过渡工作。成立县国家公务员制度实施领导小组，下设办公室指导开展公务员过渡工作。印发《息烽县行政机关工作人员过渡为国家公务员　息烽县党群机关工作人员参照试行公务员制度的实施意见》。4月，举办过渡国家公务员上岗知识骨干学习班，后再由各单位组织培训，全县1200余人参加培训。5月25日，组织乡（镇）、县直机关单位640人参加贵阳市公务员全员过渡考试。是年，全县审核批准过渡为国家公务员774人。

2001年起，开展国家公务员培训工作。县组织、人事部门制定《2001—2005年息烽县国家公务员培训规划》，建立《息烽县国家公务员（参公、依公管理人员）考试考核制度》，开展思想道德和行为规范、《保密知识》、十六大精神、《党政领导干部选拔任用工作条例》《WTO知识》《“十五”期间及2010年国民经济形势展望》等学习培训；对晋升科级领导职务的公务员，实行先培训后任职；推进国家公务员学历培训，鼓励公务员通过自学考试及其他成人教育方式提高学历层次，改善公务员队伍知识结构。至2005年，举办培训班4期，培训初任公务员106人，培养在职公务员（含参公管理人员）研究生5名。行政机关公务员大专以上文化程度比例达到85%以上。

2003年起，在编制限额内面向全省公开招考国家公务员。是年，招考录用国家公务员21名。至2010年，累计招考录用国家公务员112名。

2006年，息烽县作为全省开展公务员登记试点县，开展公务员登记工作。参加试点单位51个，行政编制864个，实有943人，登记703人，暂缓登记198人，不予登记1人（被判处有期徒刑缓刑），离岗休养41人，另行登记115人。2008年后，公务员登记作为日常工作按秩序正常开展。

二、大中专毕业生分配

1991年，县成立大中专毕业生分配工作领导小组，下设办公室在县教育局，负责大中专毕业生分配工作事宜。是年对纳入国家统一招生计划、属国家统一分配来县的大中专毕业生，实行按计划为主分配安排工作。对师范院校、卫生医学院校的毕业生，实行“切块”分配给教育和卫生部门安排工作。其他综合院校的毕业生由县大中专毕业生就业工作领导小组直接分配安排工作。对结业肄业生实行自洽单位，县大中专毕业生就业工作领导小组办公室推荐，3个月内无接收单位或虽有接收单位而本人不愿去工作的，取消分配资格。对定向毕业生实行定向分配，10年内不得改变，若在服务期要求调出的，按本科生4000元、专科生3000元、中专生2000元交纳赔偿费。此后，赔偿费标准经过两次调整，至1995年，赔偿费标准调整为本科生8000元、专科生6000元、中专生4000元。

1996年下半年起，县大中专毕业生就业工作领导小组办公室改设在县人事劳动局。2000年，因教育体制改革，普通院校招生实行“并轨”，县停止中等专业学校毕业生由国家统一分配安排工作。2004年起，停止高等院校毕业生由国家统一分配安排工作，大中专毕业生由人事劳动和社会保障部门人才交流服务中心推荐就业或参加相关考试，择优聘用，或自谋职业。

三、专业技术职称评聘

1992年6月前，专业技术职称评聘工作由县科学技术委员会负责，此后由县人事局接管。9月，县职称改革工作领导小组重新组建，下设办公室在县人事局。当月起，开展职称考核工作，至次年2月结束，全县参加考核2147人，考评为优秀312人、称职1770人、基本称职54人、不称职2人。1993年，为188名大中专毕业生初聘专业技术职务。各系列主管部门推荐评审高级职务16人、中级职务119人、初级职务8人。

1997年，县成立工程初级、农业初级、小学高级（代评初级）、中学初级四个系列评委会，评审通过初级专业技术职务96人。

2000年，县成立小学高级评委会和卫生评委会，对78人进行职务晋升资格审查。为157名大、中专毕业生初聘专业技术职务。为全县8个系列1086名初级专业技术人员颁发资格证书。

2004年起，实行专业技术职务结构比例和最高职务档次设置，开展各用人单位专业技术职务结构比例审定，按岗位、结构比例推荐评审专业技术职务。是年，在县委党校、县农业局进行专业技术职务评聘分离试点，建立“个人申报、社会评价、单位聘任、政府调控”的专业技术职务评聘分离管理机制。2005年起，全县推行专业技术职务“评聘分离”制度，专业技术人员职称推荐评审不再受专业技术职务机构比例限制。是年，对147名专业技术人员进行结构比例审查，对在结构比例范围内的138人，同意单位聘任并与工资福利挂钩。

2006年，按照《贵阳市农村实用人才专业技术职称资格评审暂行办法》规定，县制定《息烽县农村实用人才专业技术职称资格评审试点工作实施方案》，在全省率先开展农村实用人才专业技术职称评审。是年，全县有210名农村实用人才取得专业技术职称资格（技师23名、助理技师35名、技术员152名）。至2010年，全县累计评审农村实用人才专业技术职称411人。

第三节　劳动就业与管理

一、就业指导与服务

1991年，县内企业用工有长期固定工、临时工、农民轮换工和合同制工4类。是年，安置就业1074人，办理务工许可证534个624人。1994年，县建立职业介绍所，在永靖、小寨坝两镇分别建立职业介绍站。是年，安置就业997人，组织劳务输出6000余人。1995年，改革固定工制度，在企业实施全员合同化管理，职员实行聘任合同制，工人实行上岗合同制。是年，在省属企业息烽磷矿率先实行劳动合同制，签订劳动合同545人。

1997年，实施再就业工程，县解困与再就业工程领导小组成立。开展县属国有企业摸底调查，确定特困企业7个职工336人。是年，统筹帮困资金8.5万元，划拨帮扶资金8.3万元解决困难员工生活；安置失业人员和下岗职工127人、待业青年1212人，输出农村剩余劳动力2264人。县劳动就业安置和劳动输出工作受到省政府劳动输出领导小组和市劳动局表彰。

2006年12月，在全县范围开展“零就业家庭”调查，对“零就业家庭”人员建立基础台账，按规定进行帮扶，实行动态管理。2007年，县人事劳动和社会保障局、县总工会、县妇联、团县委等联合举办“春风行动”、民营企业招聘周、大中专毕业生服务周等专场招聘会，提供就业岗位7632个，达成就业意向812人。是年，安置“零就业家庭”成员127人就业，消除零就业家庭109户。安置下岗失业人员再就业235人。实现农村劳动力转移就业4950人。

2008年，开展充分就业社区创建工作，完成磷兴园、北门社区2个充分就业社区创建。县委、县政府加强对返乡农民工服务工作的组织领导，在10个乡镇设立返乡农民工接待服务站点，举办帮扶返乡农民工就业创业百日活动和招聘会，组织到场企业38家，提供岗位1000余个，达成用工协议323人，76名返乡农民工实现就业。是年，为返乡农民工3人办理失业保险、31人办理小额贷款担保、126人发放返乡创业扶持资金37.8万元。

2010年，县举办“抗干旱、保民生、促就业”活动、春风行动招聘会、民营企业招聘周、大中专毕业生活动月等招聘活动，累计进场用人单位213家，提供劳动岗位1.75万个，达成就业意向1392人，实现劳务输出1563人。是年，完成城乡统筹就业8611人，扶持自主创业405人，3个社区达到充分就业创建标准。城镇登记失业率控制在3.4%以内。

二、就业培训

1991年，全县完成就业培训716人。此后，根据劳动力市场需求，适时组织各类劳动技能培训。1997年，开展劳动技能培训748人。2001年，县农村剩余劳动力转移与培训工作协调领导小组成立。建成三田劳动就业培训基地，并举办培训班9期，培训817人。是年，实现统筹培训2076人。

2006年1月起，开展职业技能鉴定工作。8月，经省劳动和社会保障厅批准，成立“息烽县人力资源和社会保障局职业技能鉴定站”，负责县内初级工职业技能鉴定。是年，开展农村劳动力职业资格鉴定415人，颁发证书415本。举办县首届非农技能（美发、餐厅服务员、厨师）比武大赛，推荐部分获奖人员参加市农村劳动力比武大赛，分别获厨师二等奖、餐饮服务员三等奖。至2010年，累计开展职业技能鉴定40余期、职业资格鉴定2702人次，颁发证书2019本。

三、劳动监察与仲裁

（一）劳动监察

1991年，县劳动局设安全生产监督委员会办公室，负责全县劳动监察日常工作。1995年，改设劳动监察股。是年，年检锅炉29台，年检率96.67%。检查矿山、煤窑120个次。举办安全培训班2期，参训334人。查处事故15起，结案12起。检查工地14个，发出整改通知书2份。督促补交保险金12.45万元。此后，各项安全检查实现常态化。

1997年，开展矿山（煤窑）安全生产专项监察、检查5次，检查矿山（煤窑）500余个次，查封有安全隐患煤窑24个，炸封、取缔、处理违章开采煤窑98个，下发整改通知书43份，督促整改隐患90余处。劳动监察部门与企业签订安全、环保目标责任书24份。督查审批企业签订集体劳动合同8份，督促补签劳动合同113人。2000年，举办司炉工、水处理工、煤矿特种作业人员和乡镇煤矿安全矿长培训1期，参训222人。

2002年起，开展拖欠农民工工资清查工作。是年，清查建筑施工企业19个（不含水利建设和公路建设部门），涉及民工528人。其中，拖欠民工工资企业2家，拖欠工资20.04万元，涉及民工

73人。

2005年，开展劳动用工、社会保障年度审查，年审用工单位105个，督促补（续）签订劳动合同1200人，鉴证劳动合同1985份，追缴失业保险费31万元，下达整改指导书9份。

2008年，开展打击非法劳动用工专项整治行动，检查用人单位646户次，立案查处违反劳动保障法律法规行为49起，涉及职工829人，下达责令改正决定书51份，罚款3.9万元。开展劳动法律法规宣传活动4次，发放各类宣传资料5000余份，接待劳动者咨询250余人次。

2010年，开展用工信息“网格化”管理。全县配备劳动保障协管员209人，采集录入辖区内用人单位2824户用工1.33万人信息。开展禁止使用童工、劳动合同签订、工资支付及社会保险扩面等专项监察和检查。开展政策法规宣传活动17次，发放宣传资料5000余份，接待咨询1675人次；查处使用童工案件1起，罚款5000元；为民工追讨拖欠工资677.95万元。

（二）劳动仲裁

1994年10月，县劳动争议仲裁委员会受理首起劳动争议案——袁某某诉县粮食局解除劳动合同争议案，经仲裁委员会调处，争议双方达成调解结案。此后，国家法律法规的建立日趋完善，人民群众运用法律手段维护自身合法权益的意识增强，劳动争议诉讼案逐年增多。2009年，受理劳动争议案37件，为历年最高。2010年，受理调处劳动争议案件32件，结案32件；涉案金额361.96万元。

第四节　工资福利

一、机关事业单位工资

1991年，息烽县执行五类地区工资标准。行政事业单位干部职工工资由基本工资、职务工资、工龄工资构成。行政级别工资为基本工资加职务工资，正县级119～165.5元，副县级102～146元，正局、区级86.5～127.5元，副局、区级80～119元，乡、股、科员级68～94.5元，办事员50.5～80元。公安干警工资标准平均高出15%，教职工工资标准平均高出10%。每人每月另加工龄工资（每年0.5元）。5月，调整机关事业单位补助工资（粮油补贴）4806人，月增资2.88万元，人均月增资6元。

1992年1月，调整新参加工作人员工资待遇，参加调整1379人，月增资1.15万元，人均月增资8.33元。2月，调整机关、事业单位在职、离退休人员工龄工资（由每年0.5元调整到1元），参调4555人，月增工龄工资4.32万元，人均月增资9.5元；提高粮食统销价格补贴2326人，月增补贴1.15万元，人均月增5元。4月，调整机关、事业单位离退休人员生活费（调原基本离退休费的10%），53个单位642人，月增离退休生活费9383.8元，人均月增14.6元；调整1952年年底以前参加工作人员工资，原工资在行政11级及其以下调升一级工资的58人，月增资474元，人均月增资8.17元。8月、12月，调整机关和部分事业单位人员奖励工资标准3741人，月增资8.99万元，人均月增资24元。

1993年，县国家机关、事业单位进行第三次工资制度改革，国家机关与事业单位工资实行分类管理，工资标准和工资管理实行“分轨制”，即国家机关实行“职级工资制”，事业单位实行等级工资制。建立正常增资机制，国家机关事业单位工作人员，连续两年考核为称职（合格）以上的，在本职务（岗位）工资标准内晋升一个工资档次；实行职级工资制人员，在任职期内，连续五年考核称职以上或连续三年考核为优秀的，在本职务对应的级别内晋升一个级别；晋升职务（岗位）

的，就近就高靠入新任职务（岗位）的工资档次。全县改革调整国家机关、事业单位4281名正式在职职工工资，人均月增资81.3元，人均月工资由111元上升到192.3元。次年11月，实施集体人员（含民办教师）工资改革，参加改革398人，月增资1.71万元，人均月增资43元。

1995年，首次调整公安、法院、检察院、林业公安等授衔人员警衔津贴，参调130人，月增津贴9996元，人均月增76.89元。1997—2003年，先后4次调整机关、事业单位人员工资标准，人均月增资最高122.93元，最低21.2元。

2004年8月起，推行人事工资信息化管理。

2006年，开展全县国家机关、事业单位工资福利摸底调查，调查统计：全县事业单位在职人员3496人，机关、事业单位离退休（职）人员1697人，民办退养教师42人。机关、事业单位人员死亡后遗属生活困难补助对象330人。次年，实施机关事业单位工资收入分配制度改革，全县102个单位，有在职、离退休人员6663人，套改月增资184.38万元，人均月增资283.67元。完善艰苦边远地区津贴制度，人均月增艰苦边远地区津贴23.97元。

2008年，对县内省属国有企业办全日制普通中小学、职教、幼教教职工79人（贵州开磷社会服务总公司磷化工子校45人、南山煤矿学校34人）按照地方工资进行套改审批。

2010年，县制定出台《息烽县关于公共卫生与基层医疗卫生事业单位绩效工资的实施办法》《息烽县关于其他事业单位绩效工资的实施办法》。开展事业单位岗位设置工作，全县258个事业单位设置岗位4156个（管理岗位677个、专业技术岗位3331个、工勤技能岗位148个）。开展岗位设置工作中，聘用事业岗位3439个（含双肩挑14人），待岗2人、缓聘6人。完成1189名事业单位工作人员岗位设置及新进岗位工资兑现，实现事业单位工资整体入轨。

二、企业工资

1991年，县内企业工人工资除实行技术等级工资外，尚有计时、计件、挂钩浮动、超额超产提成奖励和经营包干等多种形式的工资分配制度。1994年，对县属国有企业进行工资调整，下达调资总额7.96万元。

1995年，推行工资与企业经济效益、承包目标和贡献挂钩，实行多超多奖、欠收扣罚、特殊贡献加奖。是年，对参加工效挂钩的31户企业中的22户（包括供销企业6户）企业进行1994年、1995年挂钩方案核定，对其余9户企业，采取不结算，暂时保留挂钩户头的办法处理。对34户国有、集体企业进行调资升级，参加调资升级职工1616人，人均月增资81.62元。

2007年7月，县企业离退休人员托管中心成立。至2010年，托管中心为原息烽磷肥厂、新兴印刷厂、龙泉磷肥厂、轻工公司、乡企公司等改制企业119名退休人员办理移交托管手续，预留退休人员非统筹项目养老金补助费171万元。除按月发放托管人员养老金和非统筹项目外，每人每月补贴100元，办理医疗保险等。

第五节　社会保险

一、职工养老保险

1991年，县内为国有企业招收劳动合同制工人办理养老保险，保费由单位按企业职工工资总额的15%缴纳、个人按本人标准工资的3%交纳。是年，参保5156人，收养老保险金167.45万元。次年4

月，县政府印发《息烽县城镇集体企业职工养老保险费用社会统筹实施细则》，规定城镇集体企业职工（不含乡镇企业）纳入养老保险，养老保险基金筹集实行“以支定收，略有节余，留有部分积累”原则，按“档次提取，自求平衡，分步到位”的步骤进行。5月，印发《息烽县国营固定职工离退休费社会统筹实施细则》，开始对国有企业固定职工和劳动合同制工人征收养老金。

1998年起，建立企业职工基本养老保险制度，国有、集体、股份制（股份合作制）、联营、私营、外商投资企业和职工，个体经济组织及其从业人员、城镇就业的非城镇户口人员以及其他非工薪收入者均为社会统筹对象。企业职工个人缴纳基本养老保险比例统一按职工本人缴费工资的4%执行，企业职工基本养老金保险个人账户，统一按职工本人缴费工资的11%建立。10月起，企业缴纳基本养老保险费工资基数统一为企业职工个人缴费工资基数之和；职工个人以本人工资收入作为缴费基数，低于上年度社会职工平均工资的，按社会职工平均工资的60%缴纳。

2001年，县设立养老保险查询电话和监督电话。7月起，养老保险基金划入财政专户管理，对符合退休条件的进行公示。2007年7月，小寨坝镇下发《磷化工基地建设被征地农民就业扶助和基本养老保障试点的实施意见》。宣传、动员失地农民参保。2009年，全面启动城镇老年居民养老保险。至2010年，参加养老保险8724人，征收养老保险金3606.14万元。

息烽县1991—2010年基本养老保险统计表

表8-1-1

年份	参保（人）	离退休（人）	基金收入（万元）	基金支出（万元）	累计结余（万元）
1991	4327	1017	167.45	139.06	28.39
1992	4380	841	167.45	122.29	73.55
1993	5059	960	175.11	149.85	98.81
1994	3362	622	146.67	108.52	136.96
1995	3369	650	154.24	80.66	210.54
1996	3406	643	155.14	97.26	268.42
1997	2440	743	186.37	114.43	340.36
1998	2428	951	452.31	317.2	475.47
1999	2619	1480	571.94	458.73	588.68
2000	1865	921	418	406	600.68
2001	2147	965	577	606	571.68
2002	2387	1082	518	720.51	369.17
2003	2541	1144	600	796	173.17
2004	2715	1185	1433.45	905	701.62
2005	3395	1240	1033.03	1044.23	690.42
2006	4604	1288	1323.92	1203.44	810.9
2007	5205	1393	1906.2	1433.45	1283.65

续表

年份	参保（人）	离退休（人）	基金收入（万元）	基金支出（万元）	累计结余（万元）
2008	6967	1432	1643	1771	1155.65
2009	7771	1518	3128.5	1816.51	2467.64
2010	8724	1708	3865	2494.74	3837.9

二、失业保险

1993年5月起，县劳动部门根据《国有企业职工待业保险规定》征收待业保险费，是年征收待业保险费3.15万元。次年，待业保险投保4198人，应收待业保险6.58万元，实收6.53万元，收缴率99%。办理待业保险3件34人，发待业救济金6324元。

1993—1995年，利用“两金”为企业退休人员补发工资31.87万元，慰问离退休职工7.2万元，为停产半停产企业职工解决生活费2.39万元，解决困难职工生活费300人6.67万元。其间，1995年，对被开除和辞退职工进行登记、建档、建卡管理。发放待业救济金7617元。对特困企业职工66人发放救济生活费1.06万元。此后，征收待业保险费逐年增多。1997年，征收待业保险费15.48万元。是年，安置下岗职工19人、城镇失业青年42人。全县结存待业保险基金20.34万元。

1999年1月12日，国务院颁布《失业保险条例》，规定：“城镇企业事业单位按照本单位工资总额的2%缴纳失业保险费。城镇企业事业单位职工按照本人工资的1%缴纳失业保险费。城镇企业事业单位招用的农民合同制工人本人不缴纳失业保险费。”同时《国有企业职工待业保险规定》作废，《失业保险条例》代替《国有企业职工待业保险规定》。

2001年，全县参加失业保险1618人，收失业保险金18万元。2005年1月，失业保险金征收工作由县就业与技能开发中心转县社会保险收付中心收缴。

2007年6月起，失业保险金征收范围扩大到国有企业、城镇集体企业、外商投资企业、港澳台商投资企业、城镇私营企业以及事业单位及其职工。失业保险金征收标准为：职工个人以本人上一年月平均工资收入作为缴费基数。职工本人工资基数超过全市社平工资300%以上部分作为缴费工资基数，低于全市社平工资的60%，按60%作为缴费工资基数。企事业单位按其工资总额的2%缴纳失业保险费；企事业单位职工按本人工资的1%缴纳失业保险费。职工个人应缴纳的失业保险费由所在单位代扣代缴。企事业单位招用的农民合同制工人本人不缴纳失业保险费。收缴的失业保险基金存入在银行开设的“失业保险基金收入账户”，实行收支两条线管理。存入银行和按照国家规定购买国债的失业保险基金，分别按照国家有关城乡居民同期存款利率和国债利息计息。失业保险基金利息并入失业保险基金。失业保险基金专款专用，不得挪作他用和用于平衡财政收支。2007—2010年，共征收失业保险金421万元。

三、医疗保险

2005年7月，根据《贵阳市机关事业单位职工医疗保险实施办法》规定，息烽县启动机关事业单位职工医疗保险，并与贵阳市联网，实行市级统筹。统筹项目分为基本医疗保险、大额医疗补助、个人账户资金注入三个部分。基本医疗保险费由单位和职工共同缴纳，单位按缴费基数的7.5%缴纳，职工个人按缴费基数的2%缴纳；大额医疗补助实行一年一保，按每人每年96元标准补助，由单位和参保人各负担50%；个人账户注入资金标准为：副地级以上干部（含享受待遇）和正教授级人员（含相同职务）每人每月注入600元；正副县级干部（含享受待遇）、副教授级（含相同职务）和工龄满30年（含30年）以上的在职职工，每人每月注入400元；工龄满20年（含20年）以上的在职职工，每人每月注入300元；工龄满10年（含10年）以上的在职职工，每人每月注入200元；工龄10年以下的在职职工，每人每月注入100元。退休人员按其退休时享受的待遇和工龄，比照在职人员标准注入。是年，全县参保单位269家6995人，征缴医疗保险费449万元。此后参保单位、人数逐年增加。至2007年，全县机关事业单位参保增至273户、人数7339人，征缴医疗保险费1001.6万元。

2008年，开征企业职工医疗保险。是年参保1335人，征缴医疗保险费23万元。同年，启动城镇居民医疗保险，当年参保4670人，收缴医疗保险费25.6万元。

2010年，机关事业单位职工医疗保险较2009年扩面1611人，收缴医疗保险费1888.92万元。城镇居民医疗保险较2009年扩面1010人。

四、工伤保险

2005年7月，启动企业职工工伤保险。工伤保险对象为县境内各类企业及有雇工的个体工商户。保费收缴以用人单位上年度职工工资总额为基数，按照确定的缴费费率按月缴纳。征收费率及标准，按照“以支定收，收支平衡”原则，分三个类别进行：风险较小行业控制在用人单位职工工资总额的0.6%以内；风险中等行业控制在用人单位职工工资总额的1.2%以内；风险较大行业控制在用人单位职工工资总额的2.4%以内。平均缴费费率控制在用人单位职工工资总额的1%以内。企业职工工伤保险，实行市级统筹。是年，参加工伤保险企业33个，参保人数1615人，收缴工伤保险费7.5万元。

2006年3月起，对乡镇煤矿、非国有非煤矿山征收工伤保险费，乡镇煤矿企业参加工伤保险当年，缴纳工伤保险标准为每生产1吨煤缴纳2.5元；非国有非煤矿山井工开采（洞采）企业参加工伤保险当年，缴纳工伤保险费标准为每生产1吨矿缴纳1.5元。10月起，县境内建筑企业及在建工程项目纳入工伤保险。建筑企业以工程项目合同价（含追加合同价款）的16%为缴费基数，缴费基准按1.2%为农民工缴纳工伤保险费。同年，启动农民工“平安工程”。收缴工伤保险基金91.91万元。

2007—2010年，累计征缴工伤保险费711.99万元。

五、生育保险

2008年，息烽县根据《贵阳市城镇职工生育实施办法》《贵阳市城镇职工生育保险实施细则》精神，启动生育保险工作。是年参保人数3780人，征缴保险费11.2万元。至2010年，参保人数5946人，累计征缴保险费131.28万元。

六、农村社会养老保险

1991年，国家民政部、省政府确定息烽县为全国农村社会养老保险试点县之一。次年，县成立农村社会养老保险制度改革领导小组，县政府下发《关于认真搞好农村社会养老保险制度改革的通知》，制定《息烽县农村社会养老保险办法》。8月，县民政局在小寨坝镇开展农村社会养老保险制度改革试点。1993年扩大试点面，在全县10个乡镇的18个村进行试点。是年，有4350人参加农村社会养老保险，收取保险费9.76万元（个人缴费6.09万元、集体缴费3.67万元）。此后，农村社会养老保险收缴工作在全县铺开。

1996年，省民政厅、省计生委在息烽县开展“计划生育与扶贫济困相结合”试点工作，要求农村独生子女户、两女结扎户全部统一参加农村社会养老保险。是年，全县农村独生子女户278户、两女结扎户350户参加保险。收取养老保险费23万元。1998年，开展农村社会养老保险清理规范工作，对参保人员进行统一编号建卡管理。并上交省农村社会养老保险事业管理处保费49万余元。1999年，国务院行文明确民政部门不再承担农村社会养老保险业务，2000年起，全县农村社会养老保险业务转由县人事劳动和社会保障局办理。

2008年，县委、县政府印发《息烽县新型农村社会养老保险实施细则（试行）》，6月，县新型农村社会养老保险在鹿窝乡试点，10月，新型农村社会养老保险在全县启动，县新型农村社会养老保险工作领导小组成立，负责组织领导全县新型农村社会养老保险工作。是年，全县参保3005人，收缴养老金385.7万元；领取待遇1516人，发放养老金12.89万元。此后，县委、县政府及有关职能部门通过电视媒介、发放资料、《致全县干部职工的一封信》、组织人员进村入户宣传和上门服务等方式，加大新型农村社会养老保险宣传。要求全县机关干部、教师等带头动员其亲属参保。县民政、残联部门对鳏、寡、孤、独、“五保户”、残疾人、低保对象等特殊困难群体，按照国家相关补助政策，主动帮助其参保。采取实行“一把手负责制”“一周一报制”，层层分解目标任务等措施，推进新型农村社会养老保险的落实，至2010年11月30日，全县参保人数87259人，参保率88.69%，累计征收养老保险费5577万余元。

息烽县2008—2010年城乡居民基本养老保险统计表

表8-1-2

年份	参保（人）	离退休（人）	基金收入（万元）	基金支出（万元）	累计结余（万元）
2008	2448	1727	21.31	819.1	797.79
2009	14660	5699	369.72	1588.74	2016.81
2010	75690	24801	2559.04	6624.4	6082.17

第二章　民　政

1991—2010年，息烽县各项民政事业快速发展。多次成功组织人民群众战胜洪涝、冰雹和干旱等自然灾害，拓宽救灾救助渠道，动员、组织社会各界人士募集款物，帮助灾区迅速恢复生产，灾后人民群众衣、食、住等得到保障。双拥、优抚、安置工作齐头并进，农村义务兵家属优待标准逐年提高。“双拥”活动形成制度，广泛深入开展“双拥”工作，1992年、1995年、1999年、2003年、2007年5次被省委、省政府、省军区命名为“双拥模范县”。基层群众自治组织不断加强，村民自治、民主管理，村务公开逐步实现制度化、法制化、规范化。殡葬改革方面，2005年起，县内尸体火化率100%。农村社会保障体系逐步建立完善，各项社会福利事业有较大发展。

第一节 机 构

1991年，县民政局内设优抚安置组（对外称息烽县退伍安置办公室）、社会民政组、行政财务组。在四区一镇（区级镇）配备民政助理员，24个乡（镇）明确兼职民政干部。1992年，撤区并乡建镇后，各乡镇设民政福利股。1996年4月，内设办公室、社会救济科、优抚安置科、社会行政管理科；下设农村社会养老保险所、烈士陵园管理所。是年，县残疾人联合会与县民政局合署办公。1997年，乡镇民政福利股更名为民政办公室。2001年9月，县老龄委员会与县民政局合署办公。是年，县老龄委员会改称县老龄工作委员会，办公室设在县民政局。组建"息烽县民间组织管理局"（对内称息烽县民政局民间组织管理科），县地名办公室划归民政局领导管理，与区划地名科合署办公。2002年3月，民政局内设办公室、救灾救济科、优抚安置科（含息烽县双拥工作领导小组）、综合科、区划地名科（息烽县地名办公室）。2006年6月，设立县老年活动中心（与县老年大学合署办公，实行一套机构、两个机构名称体制），隶属县民政局管理。2008年7月，地名办公室单独设立，不再与区划地名科合署办公。2010年，民政局内设办公室、救灾救济科、优抚安置科（含县双拥工作领导小组）、综合科、区划地名科、地名办公室。

第二节 优抚安置

一、优抚

1991年，为全县义务兵家属309户发放优待金5.39万元，户均174元；对43户烈属、因公牺牲人员家属、病故军人家属（简称"三属"）和43户伤残军人发放优待金5.71万元，发给8名立功人员立功奖800元，对在乡复员军人720人进行定补。是年，对烈军属、革命伤残、孤老复员军人实行挂牌包户服务，全县建包户服务小组190个，对387户774人实施挂牌服务。

1994年，调整农村军人家属优待金标准：一年兵由200元调到330元，两年兵由210元调到350元，三年兵由230元调到370元。是年，发放农村、城镇军属545户、"三属"38户和在乡伤残军人42人的优待金共14.63万元；为16名军人发放立功奖1600元；发放在乡复员军人定期、定量补助费21.75万元；"三属"和伤残军人抚恤金和保健金6.15万元。县、乡（镇）政府在春节和"八一"期间组织慰问团，慰问优抚对象438户（人），送去慰问金1760元。

1996—2002年，民政部相继提高部分优抚对象抚恤金标准，县民政部门认真抓好落实，及时按新标准发放。2003年1月起，落实贵阳市民政局、财政局《关于实施贵阳市优抚对象抚恤金补助标准自然增长机制》精神，对"三属"、在乡革命伤残军人、老复员军人和回乡退伍军人抚恤金实行自然增长机制——"在上年定补标准基础上，按每年5%递增"。

2004年10月1日起，调整军人死亡一次性抚恤金标准：烈士由原来补助40个月工资提高到80个月，因公牺牲由原来补助20个月工资提高到40个月，病故由原来补助10个月工资提高到20个月。

2005年起，全县农村优抚对象纳入"新型农村合作医疗"范围。农村优抚对象医疗费按合作医疗规定报销后，剩余部分纳入"农村医疗救助"解决。是年，发放211户农村义务兵家属优待金65万元，户均7243元；城镇义务兵家属48户优待金34.7万元，户均3084元。按"优抚对象补助标准自然增长机制”规定，每月补助在乡老复员军人优待金178元，人年均2136元。全年共发放抚恤金156.7万元。

2008年，开展“爱心献忠臣”活动，县民政局划拨14万元帮助27户优抚对象维修住房；为40户无钱治病优抚对象发放临时补助金4万元；为37户生活困难优抚对象发放大米3700千克；慰问农村重点优抚对象、参战人员，每人发给慰问金100元。

2009年9月，县政府印发《息烽县优抚对象医疗保障实施细则》，投入资金18.3万元作优抚对象医疗保障启动经费。是年，下拨资金32.2万元为49户优抚对象修建住房。

2010年，全县有优抚对象7280人，其中：现役军人家属536户1876人，“三属”19户34人、在乡老复员军人505人、军休干部2人、伤残军人120人、带病回乡退伍军人131人、参加对越自卫反击战750人、一般退伍军人3862人。是年，发放各类优抚金554.9万元。为30户优抚对象发放救济粮6000千克；为49户发放城乡低保金8.5万元；为1193名重点优抚对象补助2011年参合参保金3.4万元；为2名优抚对象子女发放“慈善助学”款8000元，助其读大学；为7名优抚对象发放建房款4.2万元；兑现14名在乡老复员军人丧葬补助费4.6万元。

二、安置

1991年，接收退伍军人和志愿兵116人，安排工作22人，94人回农村。是年，县民政局被省政府、省军区、安顺地区行政公署、安顺军分区评为退伍安置工作先进集体，荣获奖励和嘉奖。1992—2002年，接收退伍军人1130人，其中安排工作335人，安排回农村795人。

2003年起，贯彻《贵州省城镇退役士兵安置任务有偿转移和自谋职业试行办法》，对城镇退役士兵实行政府安排和自谋职业相结合，鼓励城镇退役士兵领取一次性经济补助后自谋职业。是年，接收退伍军人、转业士官124人，其中城镇22名，农村102名；安置26人。

2007年，接收退伍军人134人，其中农村109人，城镇23人，转业士官2人。县民政局组织城镇退伍兵参加为期30天的电脑操作技能培训。对20名参加培训考试者，按高分到低分选择岗位，由政府全部安排就业。对3名选择自谋职业者，发给补偿金9.4万元。是年，县召开退伍士兵安置表彰工作会，总结安置工作，表彰安置工作任务完成好的单位和个人。

2010年，接收退伍军人118人。其中，农村103人、城镇13名、三级士官2人。符合安置政策的15人，除1人安置在事业单位工作外，其余14人选择自谋职业，发一次性有偿安置费54万元，每人平均3.86万元。县民政局组织103名农村退伍军人参加人才交流中心培训后，全部推荐到企业就业。

三、“双拥”工作

1991年，元旦、春节、“八一”建军节期间开展拥军优属慰问活动，县、乡（镇）分别成立慰问团或慰问小组慰问驻军部队和县人武部，赠送慰问品113件，慰问金1100元。向前方战士赠送鞋垫540双、锦旗3面，写慰问信273封。全年走访优抚对象653户，帮助优抚对象和退伍军人解决住房困难44户215人。

1993年，县武警中队开展警民共建活动，为10户烟农进行烤烟打顶抹芽。全县各级干部群众为优抚对象办好事实事350余件，向前线军人送鞋垫520双。次年，开展“纪念建军六十七周年系列活动”。举办第八届“八一杯”运动会和老年门球赛、“八一”军民文艺联欢会；县电视台为全县退伍老战士、军烈属、在乡伤残军人、驻县官兵点歌；张贴、悬挂“拥军优属、拥政爱民”标语360余条，出“八一”专刊4期；干部群众为优抚对象办好事实事500余件。全县为380余户军、烈属优抚对象进行烤烟打顶抹芽425亩，收摘烟叶2860千克，抗旱保苗254亩，妇女为部队官兵做鞋垫550双。

1995年，56029部队在县境内执行杭福、贵成光缆施工期间，县城64个单位、30名个人捐款8570元，各中小学捐鸡蛋5105个、手套10双。“五一”劳动节当日，县五大班子领导，县直有关部门，永靖镇、小寨坝镇党委、政府，息烽磷矿党委等到部队慰问，送去肥猪11头、鸡蛋1.2万个、现金0.6万元。

1998年，开展创建拥军优属乡镇、街道、村组和军（警）民共建精神文明活动。全县军（警）民共建单位33个。“八一”期间，县“双拥”领导小组举办“八一杯”篮球运动会和“八一”军民文艺联欢晚会、拥军优属迎春座谈会。春节、元旦期间开展拥军慰问活动，成立慰问团11个，慰问军、烈属，在乡伤残军人、军人、“两队一部”官兵，为优抚对象做好事办实事1300余件，为息烽籍战士寄去鞋垫864双。次年，开展“爱心献功臣行动”，县直机关、各乡镇结对帮扶68对，新增帮扶组织75个，重点扶持全县158户重点优抚对象，捐赠衣被2568件、食品368千克，拨款14.72万元补助67户优抚对象新建和维修住房，补助8户优抚对象医药费2200元，安排战斗英雄陶洪礼（下岗）在息烽集中营从事保安工作，解决再就业问题。

2003年起，开展双拥模范县创建活动，至2006年，投入158.6万元帮助消防大队修建消防大楼、购买办公用品；为县人武部、武警中队安装空调、建图书室、购买笔记本电脑等；团县委在实施“希望工程”工作中，对军、烈属子女给予特殊照顾；县中医院坚持每年为驻县部队官兵免费体检、县人民医院设军人看病优先就诊处；县妇联组织农村妇女为部队战士寄鞋垫2000余双、开展表彰“好军嫂”活动；县广电公司对“三属”、伤残军人实行减半收费；县民政局对全县残疾军人、“三属”、孤老复员军人免费赠阅《科技快报》；县工商局、土管局为退伍军人以及军人家属实行办照优先、地税局对退伍军人自谋职业者实行税收减免优惠；息烽集中营革命历史纪念馆对现役军人实行免费参观和军车免费停放；县内公交车对现役军人一律免费乘坐等。其间，息烽县被表彰为市级“双拥先进县”。县民政局、县人民武装部等7个单位被市评为拥军优属、拥政爱民先进单位。2007年2月，省委、省政府授予息烽县“双拥模范城（县）”称号并表彰。

2008年，配合贵阳市开展争创全国双拥模范城活动，全县成立双拥慰问团11个，慰问小组41个，于春节、雪凝灾害期间开展走访慰问活动。县民政部门筹资32万元为县人武部购买抢险设备，为消防队购买消防器材。县委、县政府协调资金134万元，为武警中队新建、维修营房600平方米。

2010年4月，成都军区某部队前往安顺执行抗旱救灾任务，途经息烽，县里组织慰问活动，送去肥猪4头和矿泉水、鞋垫、慰问信等。是年，县委、县政府下发《关于进一步做好拥军优属工作的意见》，再次提高立功受奖士兵奖金标准。坚持开展拥军优属走访慰问活动，送去慰问金17.47万元、春联1000余副。

四、烈士褒扬

1991年，清明节前后，全县100余家单位干部职工、青年学生及人民群众1万余人在张露萍烈士陵园开展悼念烈士活动——向烈士纪念碑敬献花圈，举行革命传统教育报告会，举行入党、入团、加入少先队宣誓仪式等。1994—2003年，县委、县政府3次投入资金共100余万元，修建通往张露萍烈士陵园公路，完善陵园配套设施。

2003年，投入40万元在息烽宝山公墓区内新建烈士陵园。将县城南八角坟14座烈士墓搬迁到新建烈士陵园。

2005年2月，国家发展和改革委员会将鹿窝红军坟列入全国30条红色旅游精品线。8月，省民政厅拨款4万元，维修九庄镇西门村祖师观红军坟。在九庄小学布置“红军长征过息烽”展览室。是年，县在温泉镇天台村启动修建王涌波等三十二烈士陵园，当年建成后举行竣工揭幕仪式。

2010年，县政府筹资300余万元，对九庄镇西门村祖师观红军烈士陵园纪念点进行改扩建，建28米高纪念碑一座、两组红旗雕塑、毛泽东诗词墙和石雕牌坊等。是年，张露萍七烈士陵园接待重庆、厦门和省内铜仁、黔东南等地区组工干部29批1699人次；清明节前后，县内干部、群众、师生3万余人相继到张露萍七烈士陵园开展悼念活动。

第三节　救　济

一、灾害救济

1991年5月16日，县内永靖镇、石硐乡、九庄镇、西山乡等乡镇遭受冰雹、暴雨袭击，造成房屋损坏327间。7月上旬，县境内遭受暴雨灾害4次，7天降雨量达456毫米，洪灾造成房屋损坏1439户2219间，雷电击死5人，水淹死1人、伤9人等，直接经济损失1620余万元。是年，县政府下拨救济粮313.7万千克，安排解决1.54万户次64103人次生活困难。

1992年，县境内出现倒春寒、风灾、冰雹、干旱、虫害等自然灾害，全县受灾面积45.13万亩，成灾面积32.97亩，因灾造成直接经济损失4071.6万元。县政府先后两次召开救灾紧急会，安排部署救灾工作，调剂烤烟苗230万株，解决杂交玉米种3700千克，组织投入抗旱机具442台等。全年下拨救灾款2.5万元、救济粮97.2万千克，安排救济对象4389户18630人。下拨捐赠粮食5221千克，安排救济灾民105户406人。

1995年6月23日9时许，全县10个乡镇遭暴雨袭击，至次日清晨6时，平均降雨量165毫米，部分地区达200毫米。灾情发生后，国家水利部副部长周文志率国家防汛抗旱指挥工作组到息烽视察灾情。7月10日后，全县持续干旱39天，受灾面积28.5万亩，因灾造成经济损失1.14亿元。县政府组织召开救灾专题紧急会议，安排部署救灾救济工作。是年，先后下拨救济粮59.98万千克、棉衣1000套、棉被300床、衣物350余件等，安排救济4100户1.65万人。

1996年7月1日晚11时至4日上午8时，县境内遭受特大暴雨袭击，全县10个乡镇161个村不同程度受灾，民房、圈舍倒塌721间7000余平方米；校舍垮塌2920余平方米；130家矿山、小煤窑停产，全县农作物累计受灾面积23.18万亩，直接经济损失3650余万元。灾后，县委、县政府下拨国家救灾款物110余万元。补助1020户灾民维修住房，下发救灾粮食93万千克，安排救济9600户4.07万人。

2000年6月24日晚7时，县境内普降大雨，局部降雨量达169.9毫米。全县受灾农户1.13万户4.61万人，死亡4人，受伤1人；农作物受灾3.76万亩，成灾面积1.95万亩，绝收面积6908.49亩，烤烟减产124吨；损坏、倒塌房屋1133间；死亡牲畜62头（只）等。造成经济损失1801万元。灾情发生后，县委、县政府召开紧急会议安排布置抗灾救灾，“四大班子”领导带领有关部门负责人赶赴灾区走访了解灾情，组织干部群众开展抗灾救灾。全县下拨救济粮35.8万千克、棉被290床、棉衣600件、衣物4.7万余件（套），安排救济2840户1.2万人。下拨建房补助款93.18万元，帮助333户灾民、贫困户建房1665间。次年8月，县境内出现持续干旱，受灾农户3.87万户12.94万人，农作物受灾10.1万亩，直接经济损失4279万元。灾情发生后，县委、县政府组织投入人力6.18万人次，机械设备1236台，用电5.9万度，用油20.7吨，浇灌面积2.85万亩，拨款475.5万元抗灾救灾。

2002年6月18—19日，县境内普降大雨，最大降雨量114.8毫米，全县受灾1.37万户5.58万人；农作物受灾3.6万亩；损坏、倒塌房屋1928间；农电、城建、水利、交通等基础设施损坏严重。造成直接经济损失2450万元。灾情发生后，县委、县政府组织民政、供电、公安、交通、水电、卫生、消防等部门负责人召开紧急会议，部署抗灾救灾。紧急转移安置946人，下拨救灾款60万元，救灾粮6.05万千克，发放捐赠衣被2.5万件（床），调运棉被300床，解决受灾群众临时困难。省委常委、市委书记王晓东、贵阳军分区政委何洪江赶赴重灾区阳朗坝现场办公，慰问群众。

2007年7月30日凌晨5时至31日中午12时，县内遭受强降雨袭击，降雨量达112毫米，全县7个乡镇不同程度受灾。县委、县政府迅速启动防汛抗旱紧急预案，主要领导率民政、水电、公安、卫生、农业等单位负责人赶赴阳朗坝现场指导疏散被洪水围困群众，抢救财物。疏散转移群众600余人，抢救物资折款80余万元。市长袁周率市防汛办、水利局、农业局等部门负责人到阳朗坝灾区现场指挥抢险，看望受灾群众。

2008年1月13日，息烽遭受特大凝冻灾害，全县受灾22.6万人，损坏、倒塌房屋206栋9960间；农作物受灾面积7300公顷，绝收面积979.7公顷；因灾死亡大牲畜2409头，直接经济损失2亿元，间接经济损失4亿元。灾害发生后，县委、县政府立即启动应急预案，对铁路、公路滞留旅客3万余人发放价值2万元的食品。救助流浪乞讨人员137人次。发放救灾款87万元，帮助430户灾民及特困户修建房屋；棉被2225床、棉衣1709件、棉鞋477双、救济粮57万千克。是年，县民政局被省民政厅评为抗凝冻工作先进单位。次年3月、4月，流长、鹿窝、养龙司、永靖4个乡（镇）发生冰雹灾害；8月中旬至9月上旬，有6个乡镇遭受干旱灾害，受灾人口11.35人，农作物受灾4043公顷。两次灾害造成直接经济损失1112.56万元。县民政部门下拨救灾款34万元、救济粮50.5万千克、棉被350床，下拨自然灾害救济款174.9万元，补助321户灾民新建住房。

2010年，县内遭受旱灾。全县受灾人口11.6万人，农作物受灾9553公顷，其中成灾面积6967公顷、绝收面积450公顷。造成直接经济损失9191万元。县委、县政府组织群众开展抗旱自救，增加水利投入，新建抗旱应急水源、采取集中供水等，解决人畜饮水困难和抗旱保苗用水，努力将旱灾损失降到最低。

二、社会救济

（一）“五保户”救济

20世纪90年代初，全县对城镇“五保户”每人每月发给生活费10元，月供应口粮15千克，节日进行慰问；农村“五保户”除乡镇统一安排生活外，民政部门给予适当补助。1994年，宣传、贯彻落实国务院《农村“五保”供养工作条例》，县民政部门向乡镇印发《“五保”供养协议书》《“五保”调查审批登记表》各2500份。是年，拨款3.79万元维修永靖镇、养龙司乡敬老院，划拨0.5万元扶持鹿窝乡敬老院办福利商店。1998年，全县有“五保户”498户535人。人均月供养标准75元。其中由敬老院供养52人，人均月供养标准110元，对分散供养“五保户”实行包户服务。次年，全县“五保户”460户611人，人均年供养标准850元。

2006年，贯彻国务院《农村“五保”供养条例》，提高“五保”对象供养标准和服务水平。全年发放“五保”、孤儿供养金52.4余万元（集中供养对象年人均1620元，分散供养对象年人均840

元）。资助“五保”、孤儿481户556人参加合作医疗资金5560元。

2008年，县中心敬老院投入使用，设床位62张，进住农村“五保”老人34名。是年，提高“五保”供养金标准，分散供养“五保”老人从每月70元提高到100元，敬老院集中供养“五保”老人从每月106元提高到120元。全年发放供养金83.49万元、春节慰问金2.87万元、物价补贴3.4万元。凝冻期间为乡镇敬老院80名“五保”老人送去棉被、棉衣、棉鞋各1床（件、双）。次年，按《贵阳市农村“五保”供养暂行办法》要求，规范“五保”供养工作，落实县、乡镇两级财政补助资金。为510户569人发放供养金99.48万元、“两节”慰问金2.77万元、一次性生活补贴5.67万元。投入资金82万元，维修改造养龙司乡、青山苗族乡敬老院，为36户五保户改造住房。2010年，为512户536人五保供养对象发放供养金101万元。

（二）城乡低保

1998年起，息烽县开展城镇居民最低生活保障（简称城低保）工作，成立“最低生活保障工作领导小组”。是年，为196名下岗职工、10名“三无”对象发放生活保障金4.44万元。1999年，息烽县列为贵阳市3个农村居民最低生活保障（简称农低保）试点区（县）之一。4月，启动农低保工作。经调查登记、审查核定，全县有农低保对象（特困户）1091户2077人。县民政部门对农低保对象实行“一户一卡一证”挂牌管理。是年，发放粮食（玉米）9.35万千克、低保金11.97万元。

2004年5月1日起，城镇低保标准从120元/月/人调为135元/月/人。

2009年，开展城乡低保规范化建设年活动，县民政部门派出工作组赴各乡镇培训业务人员5000余人次，发放宣传资料9000余份；制定《息烽县城乡低保规范化建设工作方案》《息烽县城乡低保村（居）级民主评议办法》，全县170个村（居）分别成立评审团，对城乡低保户实行一户一档管理。同年，为全县城低保对象1299户2130人发放低保金370.04万元、两节慰问金17.64万元、一次性生活补贴25.99万元、油价和生活补贴54.47万元；为农村低保对象5544户1.18万人发放农低保金634.58万元、两节慰问金48.6万元、一次性生活补贴112.43万元、油价补贴101.69万元。

2010年，调整提高城乡低保标准：1月起，农低保从70元/月/人提高到110元/月/人；10月起，城低保从200元/月/人提高到240元/月/人。是年，为农村低保对象4423户9283人发放低保金758.6万元，城低保对象1180户1976人发放城低保金405.8万元。县城乡低保工作规范化建设工作得到省、市充分肯定。全市低保工作现场会在息烽召开。

（三）城乡医疗救助

2004年起，县内开展农村特困群众基本医疗保障救助工作。县成立农村贫困医疗救助领导小组，制定《息烽县农村医疗救助实施方案》。县民政局、财政局制定下发《息烽县农村医疗救助基金管理试行办法》。是年，有10户30人享受医疗救助金1.68万元，此后，该项工作形成常态，至2007年，县民政部门资助贫困群众7714户次1.5万余人次参加新型农村合作医疗资金15.3万元；对因患病影响家庭生活的农村贫困群众433户补助医疗救助金74.89万元。

2008年5月，启动城市医疗救助工作，县政府拨款6万元作启动资金。是年，共资助城市低保对象901人参加城镇居民基本医疗保险金7041.4元，救助因病造成家庭生活困难的城市居民8户1.2万元。2009年，为农低保和“五保”对象1.14万人交纳新型农村合作医疗资金22.73万元，为城低保对象1155人交纳城镇医疗保险金1.1万元。对554户农村居民生病住院后实施二次救助，发放救助金115.31万元，户均救助2072元；向39户因病住院城镇居民发放救助金15.46万元，户均救助3964元。

2010年，县政府修订出台农村医疗救助实施办法，降低救助门槛，切实解决群众因病致贫和因病返贫问题。对患大病、重病的城市低保对象56人发放救助金13万元，人均救助2320元；资助农村低保户、“五保”对象和特困户4914户9819人参加“新农合”资金29.5万元；对患病低保户、“五保户”和特困户医疗费用进行二次救助1440人，发放救助金385万元，人均救助2670元。

（四）流浪乞讨人员救助管理

1991年起，县民政部门对流浪乞讨人员的救助主要是发给路费，送回原籍。至2003年，共接待救助流浪乞讨人员近1000人次。2004年起，贯彻执行国务院《城市生活无着的流浪乞讨人员救助管理办法》《城市生活无着的流浪乞讨人员救助管理办法实施细则》，县民政部门增设“息烽县流浪乞讨人员救助管理站”。是年，救助流浪乞讨人员58名、过境麻风病人122名，支付车费、生活费2.5万元。派专人护送有求助需要的外地流浪儿童到贵阳市救助站接受进一步救助。至2010年，共救助流浪乞讨人员1300余人次，支付车费、生活费等2.97万元，其中向市救助站转送流浪儿童8名。

（五）困难群众临时救助

2004年始，县民政部门开展农村特困群众救助工作。是年，县政府制定下发《息烽县特困群众救助管理办法》，全年对510户951人特困群众发放救助金14.91万元。2005年，开展农村特困群众救助向农低保平稳过渡工作，县成立社会救助工作领导小组，开展农村居民最低生活保障对象调查，县财政拨入农村居民最低生活保障金24.73万元，对年人均收入在625元以下的特困群众实行“应保尽保”。是年1—6月，对农村特困群众3797户次7922人次发放救助金130.78万元，月人均补差金额30.87元。

2009年，遵照国家民政部《关于进一步建立健全临时救助制度的通知》和《贵阳市城乡困难群众临时救助暂行规定》文件精神，县政府把“城乡困难群众临时救助”工作列入当年十件实事之一，印发《息烽县城乡困难群众临时救助实施细则》，匹配启动资金10万元。是年，全县救助城乡困难群众35户107人，发放救助金6.35万元。2010年，救助城乡困难群众100户，发放救助金20.58万元。

三、救灾捐赠

1991年，县民政部门组织开展“一方有难，八方支援救灾捐赠活动”，县、区、乡各级成立救灾捐赠领导小组，组织、协调救灾捐赠工作。132个单位6190人参加救灾捐赠，捐款11.2万元、粮票4.9万千克、衣物3000件、水泥50.5吨、化肥21吨等。1994年，县委、县政府向全县发起向贫困山区群众送温暖、献爱心活动，全县4000余人参加，收到捐款1万余元、衣裤5800件。是年，接收安顺地区转交北京市东城区捐赠物资3.2万件。

1995年，县内遭受严重水灾和旱灾，县委、县政府发动机关干部职工、社会各界开展向灾区捐款捐物活动，据不完全统计，参加捐赠活动的有257个单位1.5万余人，捐款42.63万元、衣物353件、浓缩饲料600千克等。是年，接收云岩区捐赠衣物83593件、华侨友谊公司捐款4万元，新华社、省委宣传部等向灾区捐款33.8万元。至2000年，共接收机关干部职工及社会各界人士捐款91.2万元、物资折款7.59万元、衣物14.57万件、化肥142.8万千克、水泥5000千克、书籍560余本等。

2003年，县民政部门在各乡镇社会事务办设立经常性救灾捐赠接收点，明确专人负责，及时公布捐赠情况。县政府于4月、10月组织两次救灾捐赠活动，共接收捐款2.24万元，衣物1157件及文具等。

2008年，县境遭受特大凝冻灾害，灾害期间，县民政部门接收社会各界捐赠款175万元，用于农业基础设施恢复、灾区恢复重建和购置救灾设备等。5月12日，四川汶川地区发生地震，县委、县政府组织机关干部职工、社会各界和企事业单位向地震灾区捐款捐物，截至5月31日，共收到捐款166万余元、物资折价88.6万元，先后3次将捐款汇入贵阳市慈善总会账户，3次组织专人将接收的物资和自购价值60.59万元的救灾物资送往四川汶川地震灾区一线。次年，县境内遭受旱灾，全县干部职工及群众捐款14.5万元，接收省内外抗灾物资折款10万余元。

2010年3月，县民政部门组织开展"抗旱救灾，爱如春雨"捐赠活动，93家单位6826人响应，共收到捐款14.4万元。

第四节　村（居）委换届与村民自治

一、村（居）委换届

1989年，全县169个村（居）委会开展《村民委员会组织法（试行）》颁布实施后的首次换届选举，全县有选民10.51万人，参加投票选举10.38万人，参选率98.7%，选举产生村（居）委主任163名、副主任136名、委员427名。

1993年，全县169个村（居）委会进行第二届换届选举，有选民12.35万人，参加投票选举12.1万人，参选率97.93%，选出村（居）委会主任167名、副主任95人、委员450人。

1995年11月至1996年3月，全县169个村（居）委会进行第三届换届选举。有选民14.62万人，参加投票选举14.24万人，参选率97.4%。选出村（居）委会主任165人、副主任93人、委员496人。

1998年，全县169个村（居）委会进行第四届换届选举。有选民14.02万人，参加投票选举13.48万人，参选率96%。选举产生村（居）委会主任163人、副主任96人、委员554人。

2001年，全县170个村（居）委会进行第五届换届选举。有选民16.21万人，参加投票选举12.97万人，参选率80.44%。选出村（居）委会主任162人、副主任103人、委员525人。

2004年，全县170个村（居）委会进行第六届换届选举。有选民15.12万人，参加投票选举13.29万人，参选率88%。选出村（居）委会主任158人、副主任83人、委员524人。

2007年，全县170个村（居）委会进行第七届换届选举。有选民15.58万人，参加投票选举14.01万人，参选率89.91%。选出村（居）委会主任164人，副主任、委员587人。

2010年，全县174个村（居）委会进行第八届换届选举。有选民14.58万人，参加投票选举11.26万人，参选率77.24%。选出村（居）委会主任172人，副主任、委员575人。

二、村民自治

1991年，全县设四区一镇（区级镇）、24个乡，下辖161个村1642个村民组，8个街道居民委员会。是年，培训村（居）委员会干部337人，改选村委会主任14名，调整村委会委员6名，村民组长97名。建红白理事会139个、互助储金会145个，入会农户2.7万户12人，筹集资金47.4万元。1992年，在流长、温泉、九庄3个乡镇开展民政工作示范乡镇试点，制定完善村（居）委任期目标责任制，村（居）委廉洁、行政生活、财务审批、村民议事等制度。1994年起，开展"村民自治示范活动"，县成立村民自治示范活动领导小组。至1999年，全县8个乡镇147个村达到村民自治示范村考核标准。其间，调整村（居）委成员39名，培训村（居）委干部3460人次、村民组长

2575人次，各村增选科技副主任、配备民政信息（联络）员。九庄镇村民自治工作受到安顺地区表彰。

1999年起，实施“村务公开，民主管理”，县委、县政府下发《关于加强基层民主政治的决定》《关于加强我县农村基层干部队伍建设的实施意见》《关于在全县农村普遍实行村务公开的意见》和《关于进一步加强村民自治示范工作的通知》4个文件。县民政部门组织干部深入村寨调研，帮助村委会统一公开内容：经济发展指标、涉及村民的重要事务、财务收支、计划生育指标、林木和宅基地审批、救灾救济款物发放；统一公开时间和程序；划拨专款统一制作公开栏，设置意见箱“回音壁”，规范村民自治管理行为。是年，《贵州日报》《贵阳民政》报道温泉镇村务公开工作。

2003年，县民政部门派员到乡村指导各村制定完善工作规划、《村民自治章程》及《村规民约》。是年，对阳朗村等50个村民自治模范村通报表彰并授牌。制作专题片《根深叶更茂——息烽县村民自治工作纪实》参加全国村民自治模范县评选。

2004年，开展创建全市示范社区和启动社区信息网络化建设工作。次年，开展村民自治模范县创建工作。9月20日，省民政厅授予息烽县“贵州省村民自治模范县”称号。2006年起，开展“三优精品社区”创建活动。制定下发《息烽县“三优精品社区”示范点建设实施方案》。是年，创建示范社区8个、三优精品社区1个。

2008年，在小寨坝镇红岩村、永靖镇永红村开展农村社区建设试点工作。2009年起，开展村务公开和民主管理“难点村”专项治理工作。制定《息烽县村务公开和民主管理“难点村”治理达标验收评分标准》。是年，县难点村治理工作得到国家民政部、省民政厅、市民政局肯定，被选作贵州省两个典型代表之一参加在江苏南京举行的全国村务公开和民主管理“难点村”治理工作经验交流会。启动社区志愿者服务工作，9个社区注册登记志愿者600余人。

2010年，开展社区整合工作。全县9个社区调整为13个社区。是年，扩大农村社区建设试点，试点村由2个扩大到10个（新增九庄镇杉林村、温泉镇温泉村、西山乡柏香山村、石硐乡前丰村、流长乡水尾村、鹿窝乡杨寨村、养龙司乡堡子村、青山苗族乡冗坝村）。组织培训村（居）委干部300余名。继续对村务公开和民主管理5个“难点村”进行专项治理。

第五节　社团、婚姻登记与殡葬改革

一、社团组织管理

1991年，开展社会团体清理整顿工作。全县清理整顿社会团体13个，其中学术性5个、专业性3个、行业性3个、联合性2个，分别对社会组织进行《社会团体申请登记》和《社会团体法人代表登记》。1993—2001年，全县社团组织有增有减，保持在13～15个之间。2002年5月，组建“息烽县民间组织管理局”管理民间组织。2004年8月，县民政局、农业局联合下发《关于农村专业经济协会培育发展和登记管理的通知》，检查养龙司蔬菜协会、石硐烤烟协会、何家硐煤炭协会、息烽永生私立中学、息烽县非公有制经济协会。2007年，县民政部门开展民间组织清理登记，清理注册登记民间非营业组织32个、社团24个、民办非企业单位8个、县级社团4个、县级民间非企业5个。县民政局联合教育局检查县内教育类民办非企业单位34家，填发处理通知书28份。2010年，全县有注册登记社会组织46家，其中社会团体28家、民办非企业单位18家。是年，年检27家社会团体、13家民办非企业单位。

二、婚姻登记管理

1991年，县民政部门开展婚姻登记“五清、四查、一处理、一兑现”工作。经检查，全县婚姻登记合格率98%。是年，全县登记结婚人数1852对，其中：准予登记1753对、违法婚姻75对、清理后补证59对，其他16对。1992年，清理违法婚姻58对，处罚58对，收罚金1500元。是年，婚姻登记1547对，登记率100%。1993年，全县登记结婚人数2213对，至1999年，登记结婚人数呈下降趋势，其中1996年为1573对，为历年最低。

2003年9月，在各乡镇设立婚姻登记点，负责辖区内婚姻登记工作。县民政局派出工作组到各乡镇村组宣传新《婚姻登记条例》，印发《婚姻登记条例》2万份给村组干部和村民学习。选派县、乡（镇）民政干部及婚姻登记员到贵阳市参加培训。是年11月起，全县婚姻登记实现微机出证。2004年，撤除永靖镇、西山乡、青山苗族乡婚姻登记点，从7月1日起，三乡镇婚姻登记业务由县民政局婚姻登记处承担。2007年7月1日起，所有乡镇婚姻登记点停办婚姻登记业务，统一由县婚姻登记处承办。是年，全县办理婚姻登记2715对，其中结婚2422对、离婚293对，登记合格率100%。

2010年始，开展创建全国规范化婚姻登记文明窗口活动，投入资金4万余元，完成婚姻登记场地设置及制度上墙等工作。是年，办理结婚登记3927对、离婚登记590对，出具婚姻状况证明592份。补领结婚证件758对，补领离婚证件15对。

三、殡葬改革

息烽县推行殡葬改革始于20世纪70年代。1983年12月，县委、县政府出台《关于国家机关工作人员逝世后有关治丧事项的暂行规定》，要求国家机关工作人员死亡后，必须火化。同年，县委组织部转发省委组织部《关于共产党员丧事改革的若干规定》，要求共产党员逝世后，必须火化，丧事从简。1990起，在机关事业单位、厂矿企业及永靖镇街道推行殡葬改革，实行尸体火化。1996年，县殡葬改革领导小组成立，加大殡葬改革力度，利用广播、电视或星期天摆摊设点等方式，宣传有关殡葬改革法律法规，县民政干部深入乡镇、村组宣传移风易俗，推行火葬，厚养薄葬新观念。是年，全县死亡1343人，火化尸体132具，火化率9.8%。其中农业人口死亡1227人，火化尸体16具，火化率2.1%；非农业人口死亡116人，火化尸体48具，火化率41.37%。

2000年9月，县政府办公室印发《关于认真执行〈贵阳市殡葬管理办法〉的意见》，明确各乡镇、驻县厂矿成立殡葬改革领导小组，下设办公室，配备专兼职人员负责处理辖区殡葬管理日常事务；要求县城范围和全县行政、企事业单位及厂矿划为火化区，各乡镇政府所在地的非农业人口死亡后，必须火化；国家机关、企事业单位干部职工死亡后必须火化，否则不予报销丧葬费等。2001年，县政府首次拨款修建农村公益性墓地，为推进殡葬改革提供必要条件。是年，全县死亡825人，火化尸体320具，火化率38.8%。其中非农业人口死亡59人，火化尸体59具，火化率100%；农业人口死亡766人，火化尸体216具，火化率34%。此后，县境内尸体火化率逐年提升。2002年，全县死亡1207人，火化尸体1104具，火化率91.46%。其中非农业人口72人，火化尸体72具，火化率100%；农业人口死亡1135人，火化尸体1032具，火化率90.9%。

2003年，息烽庆云山殡仪馆竣工投入使用。启动息烽宝山公墓及火化车间修建工程。2004年4月，火化车间建成投入使用，至12月，火化尸体910具。是年，建成农村公益性墓地146个，其中建成小寨坝镇中心村片区、永靖镇马当田村、青山苗族乡冗坝村3个示范性农村公益性墓地。

2005年，全县尸体火化率100%。

2007年，县民政局印发《关于进一步规范全县殡葬工作骨灰处置管理的通知》，要求骨灰安葬必须进入经营性公墓或农村公益性墓地，每座墓地占地不超过1平方米等。提倡在公墓区内实行树葬、深埋不留坟头等处理方式。2008年，全县死亡1410人，尸体火化后，骨灰均进入公墓区安葬。是年，全县种长青阔叶树3万余株，绿化坟头6000余个。2008、2009两年，县殡葬改革工作经市目标考核为优秀，受市委、市政府通报表彰。

2010年，县政府出台《关于进一步规范农村公益性墓地建设管理的实施意见》。全县规划建设农村公益性墓地335个，投入资金85万元，用于农村公益性墓地规范化建设。是年，全县死亡1440人，尸体火化率、骨灰入公墓率100%；种植树苗1.2万株，绿化坟头2005座；检查、整顿县境内殡葬石刻用品作坊。

息烽县2001—2010年尸体火化统计表

表8-2-1

年份	死亡数（人）	火化尸体（具）	火化率（%）
2001	825	320	38.8
2002	1207	1104	91.46
2003	1149	1139	99.13
2004	1153	1145	99.3
2005	1312	1312	100
2006	1265	1265	100
2007	1370	1370	100
2008	1410	1410	100
2009	1083	1083	100
2010	1440	1440	100

第六节　社会福利

一、敬老院及老年人活动场地建设

1991年，全县有底寨、养龙司乡干河沟两个敬老院。是年，投入资金13.5万元，在永靖、猫场、九庄、流长、小寨坝5乡镇修建敬老院。至1995年，全县10个乡镇皆建有敬老院。进住五保老人52人。1999年，全县乡镇敬老院有床位100张，进住五保老人66人。

2003年起，实施“星光计划”项目建设。是年，投入60万元，启动建设县城永红、东门老年“星光计划”项目。2006年11月3日，县城东门老年活动中心建成投入使用，占地7919平方米，建筑面积1620平方米，绿化面积3200余平方米。2008年10月22日，县中心敬老院投入使用，设床位62张，当月进住农村五保老人34名。该工程占地1613.7平方米；计划投资120万元，其中市级匹配84万元、县级匹配36万元。

二、福利企业及经济实体

（一）福利企业

20世纪80年代末，县民政部门投资80余万元在县城南郊火车站对面修建县内首个民政福利企业——息烽利民纸箱厂，生产销售纸质包装箱，安排残疾人到厂就业。1993年，为加强企业管理，提高生产效益，对利民纸箱厂实行目标管理。次年，完成生产总值40万元，实现利税4万余元。1995年，利民纸箱厂遭洪水淹没，厂房倾倒，生产设备损坏，生产原材料被水淹坏等，生产受到严重影响，当年仅完成产值14.3万元，实现利税1.1万元。1996—2005年，利民纸箱厂年完成生产总值40万～50万元，年实现利润4万～5.5万元。常年解决6名残疾人就业。2006年，利民纸箱厂实现产值110万元，实现利润12.5万元，产值、利润创历年最高。2007年，因城市建设需要，利民纸箱厂拆除停办。

（二）经济实体

1992年，县民政部门投入资金7万元，创办民政经济实体——回风炉厂1家。此后，县民政部门逐年拨款支持乡镇敬老院创办经济实体，至1996年，有8个乡镇敬老院办起经济实体，年产值（销售）60余万元，实现利税7万余元。1998年，养龙司乡、九庄镇等敬老院的经济实体，所获收入解决敬老院的经费开支后略有结余。1999—2006年，全县乡镇敬老院所办经济实体每年经济收益5.5～6.6万元。

2007年后，根据市民政局“民政部门禁止办经济实体”通知精神，县民政部门的经济实体停办。

三、福利彩票销售

县民政部门销售福利奖券始于20世纪80年代末。1991—1992年，福利奖券销售主要由全县民政系统干部职工利用赶场天边宣传边销售，两年共销售奖券62万元。

1993年起，奖券销售工作推向市场，聘请民政干部以外的人员承担奖券销售工作，按比例提成销售劳务费。是年，销售奖券26万张46万元。1995年7月20日，在县公证处和安顺地区民政局派员现场监督下，清理销毁福利奖券尾券7个品种23615张，面值2.36万元。

1996年起，福利奖券更名为福利彩票。是年12月，县民政部门组织150万张300万元福利彩票销售活动。采取“大规模、大奖组、大宣传、大场面、大队伍、突击销售”方式进行销售，日销售量160万元、筹集福利基金60万元。1998年，销售福利彩票250万元，筹集福利基金52万元。2000年，受电脑型彩票冲击和县境内低温灾害影响，福利彩票销售额仅为64万元，筹集福利基金11.52万元。

2003年起，社会福利彩票销售改由省民政厅统一组织，在息烽设点作常年销售。2009年起，福利彩票销售采取聘请彩票管理专业人员负责销售。是年，彩票销售633.3万元。2010年，全县15个福利彩票销售网点销售即开型福利彩票891万元，创历史最高纪录。

第七节　地名与勘界

一、地名管理

1991年，对县城部分路段进行命名和更名。原沙石坡更名为人民路，百货大楼到北门桥为交通路，北门、蚕桑坡、牛奶场、农机厂一带为蚕桑坡路，县砖厂、川黔公路到落水洞为环城东路，电影院一带命名为文化路等。次年7月，贯彻安顺地区行署《关于全区地名管理下步工作意见》，县政府成立县地名委员会，出台《关于在全县范围内开展地名管理工作安排意见》，11月，举办有29人参加的地名管理业务培训。开展地名实地补查，全县复查，补更地名2193条，补增地名150条，减去地名111条，填写成果表6579份，改写县、乡（镇）概况11份。

1995年，安顺地区地名管理工作在息烽试点。是年，县城和10个乡镇共装订门牌4.53万块，立路牌40块。1996—2001年，完成县境内国道、省道、县道、村及自然村寨标志设置规划和补栽地名标志工作。完成《县乡大辞典》（息烽部分）编写工作。2002年，对县城及城郊部分路段予以命名：县招待所至客运停车场后门桥头命名为河滨路，210国道云环小学至西门湾命名为银杏鹰路，210国道快活岭岔口至永靖镇砖厂命名为太和路，县商业银行岔路至环城路铁路大桥命名为东门路，停车场后门桥头至环城路命名为育才路，210国道下阳朗半边街至张露萍等七烈士陵园命名为汉方路。2007年9月，在涉及有县边界的养龙司、流长两乡进行平安边界宣传活动，出动宣传车10余次，发放《行政区域界线管理条例》等宣传资料5000余份。2008年，完成全县“数字地名”数据库录入工作。在县城育才路、河滨路、东门路开展楼、门牌一条街创建工作，投入经费4.6万元，安装栋牌11块、单位门牌17块、门面牌395块、单位牌85块、住户牌1139块，全县楼、门牌设置安装达到规范性目标要求。

2010年，完成县城19条街道命名、更名、废名工作和9个乡（镇）辖区内55条街道命名工作。

二、勘界工作

1991—1996年，县勘查划界工作处于停止状态。1997年，与修文、金沙两县联合对六广河中心线、周家岩两侧山脊相交处进行边界勘定并签订“界限协议”。与修文联合对边界接壤的九庄、石硐、永靖和修文县的六桶、大石、久长等6乡镇边界进行勘界划定，签订边界协议。在息烽、修文、开阳3县县界交接点埋设双面界桩。2000年，与遵义、金沙两县对本县养龙司乡荆江村与遵义县乌江镇坪塘村、金沙县高田乡港坝村中心线进行勘界划线并签订界桩路线协议。与开阳、修文两县签订本县永靖镇安马村与修文县久长镇卢山村、开阳县双流镇桐心村行政区划界限协议并埋设界桩。2001年，对本县温泉镇、小寨坝镇与开阳县接壤的马场镇、永温乡、金中镇、双流镇等7个乡镇进行勘界并签订协议。对本县温泉镇、养龙司乡、小寨坝镇与遵义县接壤的乌江镇、三合镇、新名镇进行勘界并签订协议、埋设界桩。2010年，分别与遵义、金沙、开阳、修文四县开展联合检查、确认边界工作，制定界线和界点的管理意见、签订界线管理协议。完成《贵阳市地名故事》资料收集上报。

第三章　移民开发

1991年，息烽县乌江渡水电站库区移民办公室（简称县移民办）为正科级常设事业机构，隶属县政府办公室。2002年4月，组建县移民开发办公室（简称移民开发办），为县政府直属正科级事业机构。是年，移民开发办与县国土局、地矿局合并（仍单独办公）。9月27日，县移民开发工作领导小组成立。2010年12月，组建县水利水电工程移民局，为县政府直属事业机构。

第一节　构皮滩水电站库区移民

一、淹没范围

乌江构皮滩水电站位于贵州省余庆县境内，是国家“十五”计划重点工程和贵州省实施“西电东送”战略的标志性工程。构皮滩水电站库区淹没涉及余庆、遵义、瓮安、开阳、息烽5个县的109个乡（镇）1859个村、19066个村民组315.07万人。其中，息烽县境有养龙司乡和温泉镇的6个村29个村民组、64户农户306人。淹没土地1459.9亩，其中耕地604.7亩（田83.3亩、旱地294.8亩、轮歇地226.6亩）、林地658.9亩、牧草地71.8亩，其他地124.5亩。淹没电灌站4座、水轮泵站1座、水电站1座、10千伏输电线路2千米。淹没沟坝500米、坟墓62座。

二、移民搬迁安置

2000年10月起，长江水利委员会设计院和县移民开发办组成联合调查规划组，对乌江构皮滩水电站工程建设区、水库淹没区开展实物指标调查。凡涉及移民个人的实物指标，张榜公布，接受监督，填发个人实物补偿手册。对移民搬迁后获补偿的房屋及附属设施，决定由移民自行撤走或转让。

2002年9月23日，县乌江构皮滩库区移民安置实施规划编制工作领导小组成立，下设实物指标分解落实组、移民安置规划编写组、项目规划设计组、维护稳定工作组，着手县境内库区移民搬迁安置工作。次年8月18日，县委、县政府下发《关于构皮滩水电站息烽库区移民搬迁安置的实施意见》。明确库区移民搬迁安置实行“政府负责、投资包干、业主参与、综合监理”政策。2004年春季，启动移民搬迁安置工作。是年，搬迁安置温泉镇三交村移民22户105人，生产安置109人。调整落实移民安置土地192.97亩，其中耕地155.47亩、林地37.5亩。次年，县构皮滩水电站库区移民工作队组建，下设温泉镇、养龙司乡两个工作组，加大工作力度，推进移民安置工作。至2006年，构皮滩水电站息烽库区移民搬迁安置全部完成，累计搬迁安置移民64户324人（含搬迁后新增人口），生产安置311人。拆迁房屋5480平方米，转让房屋安置耕地467.5亩。移民新建和购房1.16万平方米。

第二节　移民后期扶持

1991—2006年，县内移民后期扶持工作对象为乌江渡水电站库区移民，扶持措施主要是对移民住地的道路修建和硬化、人畜饮水、水利灌溉、土地整治、产业发展和对移民进行技能培训等方面开展工作。其间，1991年，为移民户建水池34个，容积2881.5立方米，微型水池31个，容积210立方米；打水泥田坎2567米，改造望天田52.3亩，土变田15.3亩。至2006年，累计修建水池71个、山塘2口、沟渠12.34千米、提灌站7个、人饮工程17个；造耕地923.2亩，坡改梯620余亩；培训430人次；修机耕道13.6千米；修建鹿窝乡杨寨小学，面积510平方米；修建鹿窝乡卫生院，面积350平方米等。2006年后，后期扶持工作对象增加构皮滩水电站移民。2007年，县发改委、县移民办组织编写《息烽县大中型水库库区和移民安置区基础设施建设和经济发展规划（2006—2026年）》。2008年，实施“雨露计划”，支助34名移民子女到湖南省宁乡县环球职业技术学院学习电子科技、服装设计等技术。学成后，大多到沿海城市工厂就业。是年，硬化通组路13条18.8千米；修建机耕道6条10.1千米；修复灌溉沟渠4.5千米，建公厕2处等。流长乡水尾村获批为全省50个移民示范新村试点之一，投资20万元，改造房屋、美化庭院、建造垃圾处理场等。

2010年，硬化通组路和串户路13条15.15千米，修建机耕道4条1.9千米。帮助群众发展椪柑50亩。投入资金15万元，为温泉中学购置教学设备。是年底，全县有移民人口3323人，移民人均年收入6005元。

第九篇　农业农村

第一章　管理机构

1950年，县设建设科，管理全县农业、交通工作。1954年，始设立农林科，主管全县农业工作。1956年改称农林水科。1957年7月改科为局。随着经济建设的发展，县农业管理机构几经分合变动。至1991年，县农业管理机构有县农业办公室、县农业局、县畜牧局、县林业局、县水利电力局、县农业机械管理局、县乡镇企业管理局。历经4次机构改革，至2010年，县农业管理机构保留县农业局、县林业绿化局、县水利局。

第一节　县农业局

1991年，县农业局内设农业技术推广站、植物保护站、土壤肥料站、农业经济管理站、种子公司、良种场和区农推站。县畜牧局内设品种改良站、兽疫防治站、水产站、牲畜良种繁殖站和区畜牧兽医站。

1995年11月28日，撤销县农业局、县畜牧局独立建制，合并组建县农业局，内设人秘股、业务股、农业技术开发服务中心（简称农业中心）和畜牧水产技术开发服务中心（简称畜牧中心）。农业局承担原农业、畜牧两局的工作。

农业中心：下设农业技术推广站（简称农推站）、植物保护站（简称植保站）、土壤肥料监测站（简称土肥站）、农业经营管理站（简称农经站）、水果蔬菜站（简称果蔬站）、种子管理站、农业中心办公室。

畜牧中心：下设畜禽品种改良站（简称品改站）、兽医防治检疫站（简称兽防站）、水产站畜牧中心办公室。

2002年1月，县农业机械事业局和县农业办公室（以下简称县农办）下辖农业区划办公室划归县农业局管辖。

2010年5月，县撤销县农办和县乡镇企业管理局，将原县农办所辖扶贫开发办、新农村建设办公室和原县乡镇企业管理局所辖项目办划归农业局。是年底，县农业局内设办公室、农业中心、畜牧中心、农业综合科、农业执法大队、农机推广站、农机管理站、农机监理站、农村能源环保办公室、中药材产业办公室和区划办、扶贫开发办、农业农村基层设施建设科、新农村建设办公室。

乡镇农业服务中心：1991年，县内4区1镇设有农业技术推广站和畜牧兽医站。1992年，撤区并乡建镇后，10个乡镇设置农技站、畜牧站；永靖镇、小寨坝镇、九庄镇、温泉镇、流长乡、养龙司乡等6个乡镇设置农机站，1996年石硐乡、青山苗族乡、九庄镇、鹿窝乡成立农机站。乡镇站人员归乡镇管辖，业务上受县业务部门指导。2002年5月，乡镇农技、畜牧、农经、农机四站合并，组建农业服务中心，为乡镇事业单位，业务受县业务部门指导。

第二节　县林业绿化局

1991年，县林业局内设办公室、资源林政管理科、营林科；7月设县森林病虫检疫防治站、县林业科技推广站；林业公安派出所、区林业工作站；下设南山林场、苗圃场、木材公司。

1992年2月，全县设10个乡镇林业工作站，经费实行差额补贴。2000年8月，明确乡镇林业工作站为林业局派出机构，由乡镇和林业局双重领导，以林业局为主，乡镇林业站人、财、物由县林业局统一管理。

1998年，撤销木材公司。

2001年11月，县林业局改称县林业绿化局。2002年3月，设立县森林防火办公室，与林业公安派出所合署办公；11月设立县木材检查站。2003年9月设县林木种苗站，与林业科技推广站合署办公。2004年1月，增设县城镇绿化管理站；9月3日，设立县天然林资源保护工程管理中心。

2010年，县林业绿化局内设办公室、资源林政管理科（法制科）、营林科、森林病虫检疫防治站、林业科技推广站、林业公安派出所、森林防火办公室、林木种苗站、城镇绿化管理站、天然林资源保护工程管理中心，下设苗圃场、乡镇林业工作站、南山林场。

第三节　县水利局

1991年，县水利电力局内设局办公室、水利电力股（勘测设计队）、管理股、水政水资源办公室。下设小桥河水库管理所、下洪马水库管理所、底寨河管理所、养龙司电灌站。4个区水利站；流长变电站（1999年8月划归贵阳市北供电局息烽分局管辖）。1992年撤销4个区水利站，建10乡镇水利站。1993年成立县水利电力开发公司。1998年12月，县自来水公司划归县水电局代管。1999年6月，设立水土保持监督站，与水政水资源办公室合署办公。

2001年9月，县水利电力局更名为县水利局。2002年3月，增设水政监察大队。2010年，县水利局设局办公室、规划建设科、水政水资源办公室、水利工程管理站、水利建设站、水土保持监督站、水政监察大队、抗旱排涝服务队。乡镇水利站为乡镇政府组成机构，业务受县水利局指导。

第二章　综　述

1991—2010年，县内实施以改土、治水和植树造林为中心的农田水利建设和农业生态建设，促进农业农村经济发展。推广农业实用技术，调整产业结构，发展果蔬生产。实施“三良工程”，推行订单农业，发展产业化经营，推进农业综合服务。实施国家天然林资源保护、退耕还林等8大工程，改革集体林业产权制度，森林资源得到有效保护。改革小型水利工程产权制度，建立责、权、利相统一，投资、管理、经营三位一体的农村水利新机制。

第一节　农村经济体制改革

1991年，全县农村实行包干到户的家庭联产承包责任制，且增人不增地，减人不减地。至1997年，人口出生、死亡、出嫁、外迁等原因，造成家庭人口与耕地不平衡现象日显突出，部分农户私下进行土地转包，转包期多为1～3年。少数村出现“两田制”苗头，即村委会对“三户一人”（死亡绝户、农转非户、外迁户和农转非人口）的土地收回进行重新承包，村委会收取管理费。

1998年6月23日，根据中央、省、市的土地二轮承包文件精神，全县开展土地延包工作。填发“农村土地承包经营权证”45994个，承包土地267961亩，承包期50年。同时清理收回“三户一人”土地4979亩。

2001年，青山苗族乡出现农户将自己承包的部分土地出租给别人耕种现象，租地者以土地产出实物的一半作为租金，后降低到当年产量的三分之一。根据土地自然条件不同，土地承包人与经营人的收益分配有“砍扁担”（五五分成）、顺“三七”、顺“四六”或倒“三七”、倒“四六”等方式。其中也有个体与集体产生的流转并改变用途的现象。其他乡镇也有类似情况。

2003年10月，《中共中央关于完善社会主义市场经济体制若干问题的决定》印发后，县内按照土地相关法规进行土地承包经营权流转。是年，全县耕地流转1.23万亩，其中转包7161亩、转让1458亩、互换1226亩、出租1667亩、入股610亩、其他形式169亩。2005年，全县土地流转经营权7933亩，其中农户自发流转7341亩、乡村组织流转592.8亩。

2006年，因土地征用或按法定程序批准（农户分户、移民安置等）调整而导致农户实际承包面积、“四至”与承包经营权证登记内容不一致，或因农户分户、移民等原因需要按照《农村土地承包经营权证管理办法》重新办证、更证、换证2035户13132人。

2007年，全县各乡镇村将土地征用及分配纳入乡镇村政务公开内容。2008年，全县土地流转面积1.88万亩。

2009年9月4日，县制定《息烽县农村土地承包经营权流转实施方案（试行）》。农村土地承包经营权流转按照土地所有权、承包权、经营权分离的原则，在不改变土地集体所有性质和农业用途的前提下进行流转。是年，县成立农村土地流转工作领导小组，办公室设在县农业局，制定《息烽县农村土地承包经营权流转实施方案（试行）》。是年，全县新发生土地流转1397.95亩。

第二节　农业结构调整

一、产业结构调整

1991年前，全县农业生产格局为一粮二烟三油菜，粮食作物以水稻、玉米为主，经济作物以烤烟、油菜为主。1992年，县委、县政府提出“一粮二烟三开发”的经济建设思路。1996年，县政府提出以良种为龙头，稳定粮食种植面积，主攻单产，增加总产，围绕“服务城市、富裕农村，城乡一体、协调发展”的思路，突出农业科技，扩大蔬菜水果面积，发展城郊型农业。至2006年，全县粮食作物内部结构从数量型向优质型转变，饲料玉米及青贮玉米面积逐年增加。由粮食作物和经济作物二元种植结构发展到粮食作物、经济作物、饲料作物三元种植结构，种植比例由62：37：1发展到58：39：3。在耕作制度上，旱地作物由三熟向四熟发展，稻田由两熟向三熟发展。

2009年4月22日，县委、县政府出台《关于2009年促进农业稳定发展农民持续增收的实施意见》，提出加快农业产业结构调整，扩大经果林种植规模，加大生态畜牧业发展，发展无公害、绿色、有机食品，搞好动植物防疫体系建设，支持申请农产品商标。

2010年，全县通过无公害蔬菜产品认证6个、水产品认证4个、果树葡萄1个、生猪1个。实施粮油增产工程25.8万亩，建蔬菜基地6.5万亩、蔬菜大棚330个，建成脱毒马铃薯良种扩繁及商品基地0.2万亩，种植抚育中药材基地1.5万亩，建设菊花、百合名贵花卉基地5.7万平方米；新（扩）建养殖小区15个，新增规模养殖场12户。

二、产业化经营

1996年后，县内蔬菜项目发展很快，逐步形成生产基地。

2002年，县内开始实施奶牛、肉牛项目，提出“六位一体”（畜、草、果、沼气、水、路），资金捆绑使用，养殖相对集中连片。2004年，建成小寨坝镇王家坪、九庄镇和平、西山乡文安3个肉牛基地。

2006年，引进三联乳业、好一多、美满、康庄等市级龙头企业，带动农户发展奶牛、肉牛、肉鸡、肉兔养殖，养殖农户与企业签订产品回收合同。是年，出现订单农业，贵阳苗姑娘、息烽千草等企业与1.5万户农户签订4.5万亩种植辣椒、白菜、大葱、生姜、太子参合同。康庄牧业、天伦公司与950户养殖户签订肉兔回收合同，贵阳三联乳业公司、贵州好一多乳业公司与136户养殖户签订牛奶收购合同，息烽天蓬养殖有限公司与400户农户签订生猪回收合同。

2009年4月，县委出台《关于2009年促进农业稳定发展农民持续增收的实施意见》，要求大力招商引进涉及农业产业化经营的龙头企业，通过政策扶持、项目支持驻县龙头企业。继续推广基地连农户、公司加农户的经营模式，大力发展订单农业，鼓励龙头企业发展农产品品牌。

2010年，全县有蔬菜万亩基地5个、无公害蔬菜基地22个，种植无公害蔬菜4.51万亩。养殖小区发展到47个。认证县级龙头企业9个：贵州太和制药有限公司、贵州腾龙宏升农业科技发展有限公司、息烽县康庄牧业有限公司、息烽天蓬养殖有限公司、奇志养殖场、辉煌牧业有限公司、惠农蛋鸡养殖场、有祥肉牛基地、千草中药材有限公司。

三、农民专业合作经济组织

1998年8月，县内第一家专业技术协会——西山乡蔬菜专业技术协会成立。2002年2月，流长乡营中村养猪协会成立。至2006年，全县有农民专业合作经济组织35个（种植业16个、养殖业17个、渔业1个、沼气池后续服务1个），会员2854人，带动农户5942户。组织销售蔬菜8000吨、干鲜果225吨、肉禽蛋类40吨、奶类1620吨、水产品8吨。2007年8月，按照“民办、民管、民受益”原则，全县农民专业合作经济组织发展到44个。2009年，息烽创新农机专业合作社成立，合作社成员以带机入社为主，入社机具有拖拉机、旋耕机、农用运输车、农机维修设备等。2010年，全县有农民专业合作经济组织60个。

第三节　农业综合开发

一、项目与资金

1993年，息烽县列为贵州省第二期农业综合开发县。至2010年，共实施项目95个，总投资6104万元，其中财政资金3315万元、自筹资金1602万元、专项贷款1187万元。

二、农业综合开发成果

水利建设：完成洪马水库渠道改造配套、老厂灌区扩建配套、小桥河水库渠道配套、底寨河渠道改造防渗、鱼简河渠道改造防渗、九庄河治理工程，改善和恢复农田灌溉4万余亩。

土地治理工程：用生物措施和工程措施改良土壤5.02万亩，改造冷、烂、锈田4.36万亩，修建机耕道41.9千米、田间路10千米，机耕2万余亩。

经济林：造林10万余亩，其中经济林、水果树3.9万亩。

农业技术培训4万余人次。

农业产业化：2007年，在农作物布局与种植结构上，形成粮食28万亩、油菜8万亩、蔬菜4万亩的生产格局。建成南山7000亩秋淡菜基地、养龙司灯塔村万亩无公害蔬菜基地、九庄镇5000亩辣椒基地、以石硐晚熟水果基地为主的近4万亩水果基地；流长乌江库区1700亩网箱养鱼、永靖镇和西山乡为主的2500亩稻田养鱼；以鹿窝乡为主的近千亩草莓基地、流长1000亩优质西瓜基地等。

三、重点项目

（一）坡改梯工程

1991年，县成立以工代赈建设基本农田指挥部，下设办公室，各乡镇成立相应领导小组，负责坡改梯工作。至2004年，国家投入资金2349.48万元，群众集资259万元，共建成坡改梯13.47万亩，配套修建蓄水工程288处5.44万立方米，引水沟渠280条71.7万米，修公路及机耕道216条13.45万米，恢复水毁农田5170亩，治理河道23.5千米。工程覆盖10个乡镇141个村21220户85044人。此后坡改梯纳入基本农田建设。

（二）标准农田建设

1998年，永靖镇雨洒村小坪坝建成600亩标准农田示范工程，省长钱运录到息烽视察工作后，同意由省扶贫办安排扶贫资金45万元，再建500亩高标准农田。该500亩高标准农田建设在老厂村青山点实施，1999年11月动工，2000年4月竣工。建输水主干渠630米，田间支渠3条575.5米，修公路352米、机耕道2条628米、涵洞4处、蓄水池6个990.8立方米；地埂用块石干砌或砼浆砌块石。建成能抵御50年一遇的洪水和30天连续干旱的排灌标准农田。此后，每年都有标准农田建设。2007年改称基本农田建设，至2010年，全县治理农田面积共29154亩。

（三）村寨道路硬化建设

2000年，启动村寨道路硬化项目（又称串户路建设），县成立领导小组，办公室设在县农办。各乡镇成立相应的领导小组，采取国家补助石砂、水泥，群众自筹部分和投工投劳办法，组织农户实施。至2005年，共投入资金1246.65万元，其中市级资金573.3万元、县级资金99.75万元、农户自筹527.1万元，投工投劳16.28万个，共硬化路面703.8千米，受益农户6793户，受益村民4万余人。

2006—2010年，全县共投入资金1630.72万元，其中省级169万元、市级833.6万元，县级自筹494

万元（138.12户农户自筹），硬化路面838千米，受益农户1万余户4万余人。

第四节　农村税费改革

1991年，贯彻省政府《关于切实减轻农民负担的通知》精神，县成立减轻农民负担监督管理领导小组。对全县4个区各抽1个乡和永靖镇1990年农民负担进行摸底调查：户均83.25元、人均18.63元，占当年纯收入的5.73%；其中正常负担人均7.34元，占人均纯收入的2.26%。1993年，各乡镇成立领导小组，查清涉农负担执行项目有57项（中央13项、省37项、地区1项、县4项、乡镇2项），取消16项（中央7项、省2项、地区1项、县4项、乡镇2项），减轻农民负担人均1.15元。次年，发放农民负担监督卡。

1995年，县内“三提五统”（三提是公积金、公益金、管理费，五统是计划生育费、民兵训练费、教育附加费、乡村道路修建费、优抚费）占上年人均纯收入的2.16%，社会负担占1.1%，农民负担占上年人均纯收入的3.31%。次年，“三提五统”占农民负担的2%。

1999年，县委、县政府决定，农业人口“三提”款人均不能超过8元，占上年农民人均纯收入的0.57%；“五统”款人均13.1元，占上年农民人均纯收入的0.94%。农民负担专项检查表明，收费比较混乱的仍是中小学和教育辅导站。是年，清退不合理收费、集资20.5万元。

2000年，县内“三提五统”标准占上年农民人均纯收入的1.3%，全县减轻农民负担60.4万元。是年，全县换发“农民负担监督卡”47960份。

2001年3月28日，县委、县政府召开农村税费改革动员会。根据中共中央农村税费改革试点工作通知精神，全县开展农村计税土地面积、粮食常年产量、农民负担情况调查摸底工作。2002年，全县农村税费改革后，农民上交农业税附加人均5.73元，比上年农民人均负担提留统筹费19.4元少负担13.67元。2004年，全县减轻农民负担212.62万元。

2005年起，全县取消农业税征收。

2006年，全县各乡镇实行涉农收费、价格“公示制”。72所中小学实行义务教育一费制，农村中小学义务教育“两免”（免课本费、杂费）225.94万元。对1万余名困难学生补助生活费123.59万元。161个村实行村务公开和报刊征订“限额制”，84个村实行一事一议制。全年支农、惠农补助621.51万元，其中良种（含种植、养殖）补助98.59万元。

2007年，全县农村中小学实行“两免”金额454.77万元，受益学生3.02万人；补助1826名贫困学生生活费35.1万元。

2009年，涉及农民的良种、农机、农资综合补贴发放到户，惠农政策做到“一公开、三到户、五不准”，即补贴工作公开进行；政策宣传到户，面积申办到户，资金兑现到户；不准调整补贴标准，不准截留、挤占、挪用补贴资金，不准用补贴资金抵扣各种税费、贷款、欠款；不准无故拖延补贴时间；不准在补贴工作中向农民收取任何费用。

第五节　农村合作基金会

1995年11月，按照农业部、中国人民银行有关文件精神，在小寨坝镇、温泉镇开展农村合作基金会试点工作。12月，县内第一家农村合作基金会在小寨坝成立。

1996年7月，根据省委、省政府《关于大力发展农村合作基金会的决定》和农业部、中国人民银行《关于加强农村合作基金会管理的通知》精神，县成立农村合作基金会领导小组，下设办公室在县农业局农经站。11月，全县10个乡镇全部成立农村合作基金会。12月，县农村合作基金会服务中心成立。至1997年10月，全县11个基金会共筹集资金1587万元（4078户），投放借款1474万元（5623户），其中农业614万元（4770户）、乡镇企业435万元（52户）。

1997年，县政府下发《关于清理整顿农村合作基金会工作实施方案》，成立清理整顿农村合作基金会领导小组，于11月撤销县农村合作基金会服务中心和永靖镇农村合作基金会，保留小寨坝等5个基金会，2个基金会并入信用社。

1999年6月1日起，开展清理整顿农村合作基金会工作，至7月30日结束，全县除石硐乡基金会有盈利，不愿意收购和移交外，其余9家基金会决定关闭清盘。

2001年，根据省政府办公厅《关于农村合作基金会清盘关闭工作有关问题的通知》，全县11个基金会关闭清盘，所有债权债务移交给县清偿办公室。

第六节　农业综合服务

一、农业适用技术培训

（一）种植及管理培训

1991—2004年，县内组织农业适用技术培训单位主要有县农业局、县农办、县科技局、县科协和部分乡镇，技术力量以县农业局技术人员为主，并从省农科院、农学院、市蔬办、市农科所等部门请专家传授草莓、西瓜、蔬菜栽培管理技术和硅钙肥改造锈水田技术；县农业局各业务站结合项目进行农作物栽培管理、病虫害防治、施肥；牧草种植、秸秆微贮、科学养羊、防治疾病等技术培训，每年培训1万余人次。2005—2010年，开展送科技下乡活动，利用赶场天设立活动点；结合项目和乡土人才培训，进行蔬菜栽培、畜禽饲养、农业新技术和农机实用技术培训，每年培训1万余人次。其间，2007年10月，县农业局组队参加贵阳市农村农用技术竞赛，获农技推广先锋1名、农技致富带头人2名、农业技术能手1名、农用技术学习型村1个。

（二）农机驾驶员培训

1991—2000年，培训拖拉机驾驶员1000余人。2001年，培训各类农机人员2462人，以后逐年增加。2005年为3395人，此后下降，至2010年，每年培训2000人左右。

二、农业经济信息

1991—2002年，县农经站每年编发《农村经济信息》8～9期，最多一年12期。发放到县有关单位和乡镇。2003年起，在中国农业信息网“一站通”上发布供求信息。2005年，县内建成电话语音系统（以县内农业技术、科技、市场行情为主的电话语音信息服务系统）、电脑网络系统（息烽农业信息网并关联农业部、省及其他相关网站）、电视节目系统，简称“三电合一”；完成农业局局域网建设，发展农经信息员48人。2006年，建立农村信息服务站（点）172个（县级1个、乡级10个、村级161个），有农村信息员209人。通过一站通、息烽农业信息网、电话语音、电视广播、办信息专栏、印发信息资料等方式，发布供求信息2.75万条，促成交易金额4451万元，占农产品总交易额的30%。南山秋淡菜，九庄、鹿窝、流长等乡镇种植的大葱，通过上网发布信息，有广东、广西、重庆、湖南等地客商前来采购，外销蔬菜3.23万吨。2007年，县农经站将“三电合一”语音服务器与电信96188相连，农户可通过电信96188获得农业信息。与县电视台、县远程教育办联合，每周在电视台播放农业节目，并制作VCD光盘500余张，分发到各乡镇、村远程教育点。2009年，开展鲜活农产品网上销售，促销蔬菜1.9万吨、水果1308吨、畜产品2515吨、水产品2855吨。

三、农产品质量安全检测

2006年，县成立食品安全协调委员会，县农业局成立农产品质量与安全管理工作领导小组，下设办公室，由农经站负责日常工作。开始对主要农产品进行检测。是年，申报并通过论证无公害农产品产地6个，其中蔬菜产地2个，大米、肉兔、肉牛、肉鸡产地各1个。无公害农产品2个，即大白菜、小青瓜；无公害农产品产地认定和产品认证一体化5个，即葡萄、肉兔、奶牛、生猪、辣椒。至2008年，无公害农产品一体化认证17个，其中蔬菜10个、畜产品4个、水果2个、稻米1个。已通过论证的无公害农产品产地、产品27个，其中蔬菜22个、畜产品5个。

2010年，对原粮、成品粮、经济作物、生产资料、畜牧产品行情进行监测。将省市级重点龙头企业、农民专业合作社的生产基地和规模养殖场以及茶叶、蔬菜产地、集贸市场全部纳入重点监管和抽检范围，加大对外来农产品的检测力度。

四、“三良工程”

2008年，小寨坝镇实施“三良工程”（良种+良肥+良法）农业生产方式试点获得成功。2009年起，县委、县政府与贵州开磷有限责任公司合作，实施“政企联合，以工哺农”政策，在全县推广“三良工程”，对坡度25度及以下耕地，在水稻、玉米、油菜、马铃薯种植地区（主产区），对推广优良品种和先进种植技术的农户，每亩无偿补助20千克磷酸二铵，所需资金由县财政和开磷共同承担。县成立领导小组，制定实施方案，建立县、乡、村三级示范点，采取“统一品种、统一施肥、统一育苗移栽”方式，抓好良种选择、测土配方、技术指导。至2010年，共实施1180.33万亩，其中水稻133.7万亩、玉米19.4万亩、油菜21.4万亩、马铃薯5.8万亩；水稻增产8246吨，增收1746万元，玉米增产12652吨，增收2602万元，油菜增产5611吨，增收2294万元，马铃薯增产8220吨，共增收9020万元，人均增收586元。

第七节　农村能源建设

1997年起，由县卫生局牵头实施沼气池建设。

2000年，县成立农村能源管理办公室，与县农业局土肥站合署办公。是年，推广100口98A型强回流沼气池，体积8立方米。次年，配套改厕。2002年配套改厕、改圈；2004年，推广贵州省多功能高效强回流B型池，配套改厕、改圈、改灶。2007年，为养殖场和养殖大户修建30立方米的中型沼气池，解决粪便污染问题。2009年，建农村沼气池服务网点18个。至2010年，全县共建沼气池22760口，其中中型沼气池16口。

息烽县2000—2010年沼气池建设及“三改”情况统计表

表9-2-1

年份	建池总数（口）	“三改”情况		
		改圈（个）	改厕（个）	改灶（个）
2000	100	—	100	—
2001	500	—	500	—
2002	4000	4000	4000	—
2003	3240	3240	3240	—
2004	2000	2000	2000	2000
2005	2000	2000	2000	2000
2006	5654	5654	5654	5654
2007	5000	5000	5000	5000
2008	4167	4167	4167	4167
2009	83+中型8	—	—	—
2010	中型8	—	—	—

第八节　新农村建设

1994年2月20日，县委印发《关于我县农村小康建设规划意见》，要求小康建设以村为单元、户为基础，抓好村的建设。1998年3月12日，县委、县政府印发《息烽县小康村建设规划》。至2000年，全县建成小康镇2个、小康村81个。

2003年8月4日，县委印发《关于加大新阶段扶贫开发工作力度　全面推进小康社会建设的决定》。

2005年1月25日，县委、县政府下发《关于进一步提高执政能力　全面推进生态经济县建设的决定》，开展建设生态经济示范村工作。市级点13个村、县级点7个村。实行项目整合，资金捆绑使用，共投入资金861.74万元，其中市级资金514.84万元，县级各部门配套资金346.9万元。是年，西山乡金星村、文安村，青山苗族乡马路岩村，小寨坝镇红岩村4个村进行生态村建设，发展生态养殖。

2006年1月，县委、县政府印发《关于加快建设社会主义新农村的实施意见》，提出从当年起，每年创建10个以上社会主义新农村村寨，用15年时间，使全县161个村基本实现“生产发展、生活宽裕、乡风文明、村容整洁、管理民主”目标。5月26日，全县新农村建设村容村貌整治现场会在流长乡召开。是年，实施省级试点2个（永靖镇立碑村、流长乡水尾村）、县级试点12个。

2007年，实施市级试点3个（永靖镇老厂村田坝、养龙司乡幸福村对门寨、石硐乡前峰村对门坡）、县级试点8个。是年，在小寨坝镇红岩村建市级生态家园富民示范村，治理河道1100米，修建机耕道6千米、串户路10千米、葡萄园硬化公路1.3千米，生态养鱼6亩。安装秸秆气化炉60户、太阳能热水器40个，完成精品户建设30户，示范户建花池750米，改厕、改厨各30间。至2010年，全县共建示范点77个，累计投入资金16811.9万元，其中财政资金10482.41万元、自筹资金6329.5万元。全县电视覆盖率90%。10个乡镇新建精神文明活动中心，部分村建立文化室或阅览室。

全县77个示范点完成村组公路、串户路、机耕道等建设538.6千米，实现村村通公路和村寨串户路硬化。新建“四改一气”16300余套，乡村清洁能源工程93户，改造危房和房屋立面整治3284户；整修山塘64口，治理病险水库，建提灌站、拦河坝、渡槽11座，新建“三小”水池800口、人畜饮水工程28处；建花池、垃圾池890个；完成基本农田建设6.3万余亩，整村推进扶贫开发56个村，硬化村居院坝1.1万平方米，实施烟水配套水池6800立方米。建成西山乡供港澳蔬菜基地1个，建成蔬菜大棚230个，喷灌300亩，建成鹿窝产地蔬菜批发市场2000平方米、阳朗村和小寨坝镇花卉大棚5.7万平方米。

围绕菜、果、烟、花、药、蚕、猪、牛、兔、禽十大产业以及乡村旅游业，形成生态文明新农村产业支撑。粮食结构调整实施粮食增产工程16.4万亩，玉米高产项目1.2万亩，脱毒马铃薯一级良种扩繁基地、商品薯基地2500亩。大葱、牛腿南瓜、辣椒、反季节蔬菜等9.8万亩次，产量8.9万吨，外销6.9万吨。发展果树、中药材各1万余亩。生态养殖出栏肉鸡40万羽。流长乡水尾片区水产品批发市场形成，网箱养鱼达2000余箱；建成养龙司3000亩蔬菜产地批发市场，形成西山柏香山、林丰一线3000余亩县城蔬菜供应基地、小寨坝红岩5000余亩葡萄园、阳朗现代农业示范园区建设格局。永靖镇立碑村实施蔬菜、养殖、交通运输、外出务工增收“四个一百万”工程，实现农户收入从单一向多渠道转向，该村70多户农户存款超过10万元。

围绕退耕还林、石漠化治理、人工造林、封山育林、天然林保护等工程建设，逐步推广山顶种林、山腰种果、山脚种蔬（粮）生产模式，形成“种—养—沼气池”庭园经济系统。养龙司乡幸福村以蔬菜产业为支撑，形成“蔬菜—生猪—沼气池”家庭生态型农业小循环模式。

第三章　种植业

1991年，全县有耕地面积25.6万亩，总产粮食5.6万吨、油菜籽7668吨、花生338吨、蔬菜1.98万吨、水果1219吨。2010年，全县有耕地面积22.8万亩，总产粮食9.2万吨、油菜籽9061吨、花生564吨、蔬菜17.4万吨、水果4590吨。

第一节　生产条件

一、耕地

1991年，全县有耕地面积256159亩（其中田78488亩、土177671亩），人均耕地面积1.3亩。此后，因人口增长和工矿交通以及城镇建设用地的大幅度增加，耕地面积逐年减少。至2010年，全县有农户56913户，农业人口204893人，耕地面积228180亩（其中田72450亩、土155730亩），人均耕地面积1.02亩。

二、劳力

1991年，全县农业户44477户，农业人口196779人，其中劳力96844人，人均耕种2.6亩。改革开放后，农村部分劳力外出务工。2004年，外出务工劳力25493人。2007年，外出务工劳力45734人。2010年，全县有农村人口204893人，其中劳力135955人；全县耕地面积228180亩，在家从事农业劳力67223人，人均耕种3.39亩。

息烽县1991—2010年耕地变化统计表

表9-3-1

年份	农业户（户）	农业人口（人）	劳动力（人）	耕地面积（亩）	其中		人均耕地（亩）
					田（亩）	土（亩）	
1991	44477	196779	96844	256159	78488	177671	1.3
1992	44818	196966	96924	254869	79002	175867	1.29
1993	46246	198667	99720	254527	78766	175761	1.28
1994	46702	198558	100960	253285	77975	175310	1.28
1995	48250	201106	103683	252953	77975	174978	1.26
1996	48997	197266	107791	251945	77624	174321	1.28
1997	49544	199802	108147	251160	77850	173310	1.26
1998	50314	202393	112690	251176	77400	173776	1.24
1999	51424	202452	114323	250920	77820	173100	1.24
2000	51515	214435	115911	249195	77565	171630	1.16
2001	52313	215097	115133	245790	76740	169050	1.14
2002	53128	218708	118535	234225	75210	159015	1.07
2003	54294	216105	118430	231015	74880	156135	1.07
2004	55539	215848	122560	223365	74775	148590	1.03
2005	56502	215824	123830	228645	77490	151155	1.06
2006	58038	213952	135758	228645	77490	151155	1.07
2007	59427	216179	136091	228147	75429	152718	1.06
2008	59427	216179	136091	228093	72381	155712	1.04
2009	60047	222457	143825	228345	72450	155895	1.03
2010	56913	204893	135955	228180	72450	155730	1.02

三、畜力

县内农业生产的主要畜力是役牛。1991年，全县有役牛29491头，每头役牛负担耕地8.7亩。至1995年，役牛年均2.9万头以上，未超过3万头。此后逐年上升，1998年发展到3.67万头，为历史最高，头均负担耕地6.84亩。此后逐年下降，2002年2.56万头，为历史最低，头均负担耕地9.12亩。2003年上升到3.52万头，此后维持在3.4万头左右。2010年，县内役牛存栏3.1万头，头均负担耕地7.34亩。

四、农机具

1991年，县内农机具主要有拖拉机、人力脱粒机等。拖拉机主要用于运输，农忙季节在田坝地区开展机耕。是年，底寨、阳朗、养龙司、小寨坝、九庄、竹花等有田坝的乡建有乡农机站。

1992年引进丰收180型拖拉机、常州产东风704型拖拉机及配套旋耕机、东风250型拖拉机及配套旋耕机，同时开展机耕推广工作。此后，逐年引进、推广微耕机（水田耕整机、多功能微耕机）、小盘拖、插秧机（久保田SPW-48型手扶式插秧机、东洋PF455S型插秧机）、收割机（东杭HL2010型联合收割机、洋马Ce-2型联合收割机、青海产马铃薯收获机）、烘干机以及玉米秸秆揉丝机、铡草机、起垄机等农业机械。

1999年，流长乡、养龙司乡成立农机合作服务队，至2002年，全县成立12支农机合作服务队。

2006年，县开展水稻机械化插秧实验示范120亩，利用洋马Ce-2型自走联合收割机收割水稻1380余亩。2007年，实施水稻机械化插秧示范1500亩，机收面积3600亩。同时组织2台联合收割机到开阳县龙岗镇进行跨区收割水稻300亩。2008年，在小寨坝镇南极及石硐乡进行马铃薯机械化收获示范，在小寨坝镇王家坪村进行玉米机械化收割实验。2010年，全县机插面积5655亩、机收面积13230亩。

息烽县1991—2010年农业机械拥有量统计表

表9-3-2

年份	总动力（千瓦）	拖拉机（台）		农用载重车（台）	农用水泵（台）	机动脱粒机（台）	碾米机（台）
		大中型	小型				
1991	21778	—	—	—	—	—	—
1992	22270	—	—	—	—	—	—
1993	—	—	—	—	—	—	—
1994	22367	173	282	47	334	—	—
1995	23167	—	—	—	—	—	—
1996	34497	57	370	68	464	636	509
1997	34867	57	370	68	473	636	509
1998	—	—	—	—	—	—	—
1999	52935	112	510	113	775	947	400
2000	53787	112	546	122	775	—	—
2001	57423	—	—	—	—	—	—
2002	60892	115	698	619	895	—	—
2003	64600	115	807	661	971	—	—
2004	68870	117	851	715	1036	—	—
2005	77299	154	864	916	1284	—	—
2006	90666	243	1301	1076	1517	—	—
2007	95199	352	1765	1187	1762	326	—
2008	114000	300	1805	—	—	—	—
2009	122210	280	1650	—	—	—	—
2010	129542	274	1726	—	—	—	684

五、肥料

境内有机肥料有厩肥、绿肥（人工种植）、人粪尿、草木灰、饼肥、杂肥等。野生绿肥已少有施用，人工种植绿肥面积多年维持在3万亩以上。

县内施用化学肥料主要有氮肥（尿素）、磷肥（过磷酸钙、钙镁磷肥）、钾肥、复合肥，此外还推广过腐殖酸类肥料。化肥使用量呈逐年增加趋势。

息烽县1991—2010年农用化肥施用情况统计表

表9-3-3　　单位：吨

年份	合计	氮肥	磷肥	钾肥	复合肥
1991	9538	4325	3264	312	1637
1992	10642	4313	3616	370	2343
1997	13093	6262	3363	310	3158
1999	14179	6922	3530	405	3322
2000	14419	7016	3621	520	3262
2001	15463	8119	3171	669	3504
2002	14526	7084	3415	519	3505
2003	16379	7585	3178	578	5038
2004	16791	7647	3238	518	5388
2005	17725	7900	3468	754	5603
2006	18036	8091	3355	949	5641
2007	17651	7584	3174	1427	5466
2008	18586	7730	3516	995	6344
2009	17921	6321	2206	732	8662
2010	18399	5254	2034	306	10805

说明：以上数据按实物量计算。1992年有氨水35吨

第二节　粮食作物

一、种子

（一）水稻

1991—1999年，境内引进汕优系列、冈优系列、威优系列、Ⅱ优系列、金优系列、Ⅰ优、D优、K优、中育87-1、特青198、温优3号等20多个品种。以上品种米质好，亩产400～500千克。

1998年，县农业局从桐梓县引进巴西陆稻，试种9.8亩，获得成功。2001年，在县政协推动下，全县种植巴西陆稻8120亩，因遭受持续33天干旱，成收面积2813亩，平均亩产253.4千克。此后未组织大面积种植。

2000年，种子市场放开后，种子代销个体户销售的品种增多，至2010年，境内种植的杂交水稻

有香优系列、金优系列、Ⅱ优系列、T优系列、中优系列、K优系列、冈优系列、两优系列、特优系列以及丝优、协优、汕优、茂优、D优、B优、绵Ⅱ优、国毫杂优、标优、川优、湘优等70多个品种，亩产500千克以上。

（二）玉米

1990年前，境内种植的品种有郧单1号、黔单4号、中单2号、息单1号等杂交玉米种和群改种墨白94，一般亩产350千克左右。1991年后，引进京杂6号、辽宁1号，此后引进掖单13和贵毕系列。至1999年，境内除墨白、黔单、中单、郧单仍有少数种植外，大部分种植贵毕系列5个杂交组合和息单7号、交三单交、农干3号、干单3号等杂交组合，以白粒居多，亩产273千克左右。

2000年种子市场开放后，品种不断更新，至2006年，境内种植的杂交玉米种有临奥系列、鄂玉系列、登海系列、黔单系列、成单系列、遵玉系列、三北系列、华玉、中单、高油、农大、川单、筑糯、中农、安单、承玉、黔西、毕玉、黔玉、金筑等40多个杂交组合。

2007—2010年，县内玉米主要品种有临奥系列2个、鄂玉系列3个、贵毕系列4个、奥玉系列2个、黔单7个、遵玉系列2个、安单系列2个、成单系列2个以及黔玉、贵单、绿单、三北、承玉、金玉、川单、渝单等150多个组合。

（三）小麦

1991年起，县内先后引进贵农10号、贵麦2号、贵麦3号、贵花1号、川育21526、绵农4号、竹麦1号、黔麦11号、黔麦早2号、节燕3号、中燕1号、黑小燕1号，但大多被淘汰。至2007年，除阿波、百泉565仍有种植外，主要种植绵阳26。其中，贵农10号亩产260千克，贵麦2号和贵麦3号亩产200千克以上。

（四）马铃薯

1991年，县引进米拉马铃薯，亩产800～1000千克。1997年，县扶贫办派员随省扶贫办考察组到（北京）中国农科院蔬菜花卉研究所考察学习后，引进脱毒马铃薯“中薯3号”“费乌瑞它”种薯60吨，在青山苗族乡试种600亩。次年6月组织验收，平均亩产206.6千克。1998年，引进“会-2号”脱毒马铃薯试种40亩，经验收，平均亩产1180.6千克，比本地品种亩产850千克，增产42.1%。脱毒种薯有“坝薯10号”“8009”、费乌瑞它、中薯3号、中薯5号、坝薯10号、鄂薯3号、大西洋、津八9个品种。

二、种子经营与管理

（一）种子经营

1991年，境内种子由县种子公司负责从产地调种，除公司销售外，大部分调拨各区、乡镇农推站代销。种子调进前种子公司进行品种比较试验。1999年起，将种子分装成1千克小包装销售，规定销售种子必须开具发票。

2000年12月1日，《中华人民共和国种子法》颁布实施，主要农作物商品种子的生产和经营实行许可证制度，县内始有个体经营户从事种子经销。个体经营户从2003年的9户发展到2010年的157户，销售品种从48个增加到231个。

2003—2010年，种子管理站共引进水稻、玉米新品种147个进行示范种植，在境内推广的品种有130余个；经省农业厅审查通过的30余个品种中，中优838、金优725、标优2号、奥玉3202、中优63、中优608、科优21、泸香8285、春喜11、正红311、筑黄2号、贵单8号、金玉818等品种在全县种植较普遍。

息烽县1991—2010年种子销售新品种比较实验统计表

表9-3-4

年份	销售种子总量（千克）	其　中				新品种比较试验（个）			
		杂交水稻种	杂交玉米种	杂交油菜种	小麦良种	杂交水稻种	杂交玉米种	杂交油菜	其他
1991	—	—	—	—	—	7	—	4	小麦2
1992	55028	33000	15000	1081	5947	—	—	—	—
1993	76330	41255	32000	3075	—	10	—	10	—
1994	99962	51600	45234	3128	—	—	—	—	—
1995	109556	60235	46102	3219	—	—	—	—	—
1996	149948	66300	79500	3158	990	4	5	3	小麦4
1997	81441	58216	19525	3200	500	5	16	3	小麦7
1998	107105	62469	41536	3100	—	—	—	—	—
1999	145633	62876	82757	3291	—	—	—	—	—
2000	112900	67000	90100	3300	—	17	7	7	—
2001	160515	66800	90315	3400	—	—	6	—	—
2002	159197	65425	89672	4100	—	14	11	—	旱稻11
2003	72750	48000	23000	1750	—	3	5	—	—
2003	91049	58490	30097	2462	—	—	—	—	—
2004	132200	69000	58000	5200	—	—	—	—	—
2005	278735	67479	75149	3889	—	—	—	—	—
2006	443039	69744	90148	4412	—	—	—	—	—
2007	615150	65650	545000	4500	—	2	3	—	—
2008	594700	54000	536000	4700	—	2	1	—	—
2009	559800	68000	485000	6800	—	3	2	—	—
2010	530700	48700	476500	5500	—	4	2	—	—

说明：2000年杂交玉米种中，含外销43900千克

（二）种子管理

1991年，种子管理工作由县种子公司兼管。1997年，对西山乡和流长乡农推站违法调进杂稻种2700千克和杂交油菜种80余千克的行为进行处理。1999年，配合工商部门销毁伪劣种子30千克。2003年5月，成立县种子管理站，加强对种子生产、经营的有效管理。2004—2005年，查办违法经营种子案件8件。2006年，种子行政处罚权交县农业执法大队行使。2007年后，县种子管理站配合执法大队查处违法经营种子案件12起。

三、制种

（一）杂交玉米

1991—1992年，县农业局在九庄镇新田村制杂交玉米种“毕单3号”488亩，因干旱最高亩产61.5千克，平均亩产32千克，总产15616千克。后因缺乏经费停止制种。

1997年，县农业局在九庄镇姜家坡开展杂交玉米制种工作，制杂交玉米种506亩，品种有“贵毕301”“息单7号”“雅玉2号”，共收杂交玉米种子2.67万千克。1998年，制种面积870亩，收种子6.55万千克。1999年增至920亩，品种有“贵毕301、302、402”“干单3号”，收种子7万千克。2000年，制种面积降至377.5亩，品种有“交三单交”“干单3号”，平均亩产50.6千克，由于气候和农民自留种子的影响，共收种子1.2万千克。此后未再制种。

息单7号：20世纪80年代，县农业局农技干部陈昌其利用“墨白94”群体改良种作为选育自交系材料，育成抗旱、较耐瘠、产量高的白粒型、中秆杂交玉米新品种，命名为“息单1号”。1990—1993年，以王家坪为育种基地，在“息单1号”基础上育成白粒杂交种“息单7号”。“息单7号”参加安顺地区品种区域试验，1994年平均亩产461.9千克，居9个参试品种的第二；1995年平均亩产513.6千克，居当年9个参试品种的第一；两年平均亩产417.5千克，比对照种增产8.3%，名列两年汇总第二。1996年1月，经安顺地区品种审定委员会审定通过。“息单7号”的繁育与推广列入1997年贵阳市科技项目。

（二）杂交水稻

1989—1990年，县农业局在养龙司试制杂交水稻种获得成功。1991年，县农业局在王家坪乡瓮沙村试制杂交水稻种50亩，因灾和设置隔离区，实收28.26亩，收杂稻种子3126.5千克，平均亩产110.6千克，最高亩产180千克。1992年，制杂稻种300亩，收种3.45万千克。此后未再制水稻种。

（三）脱毒马铃薯

2000年，县扶贫办在青山苗族乡绿化村办脱毒马铃薯原种繁殖基地，2002年移至小寨坝镇南桥村茅坪。基地有种薯生产土地150亩，建成年产一级种40万千克规模。主要品种有费乌瑞它、中薯3号、中薯5号、米拉、大西洋等。此后，县内脱毒马铃薯种主要由种薯基地供应。2005年，建脱毒微型薯扩繁基地和一级种薯扩繁基地。扩繁7万粒微型种薯120亩；良种扩繁1600亩，收原种7.79万千克，一级种24.5万千克，全县推广脱毒马铃薯6.8万亩。2006年，基地全年生产种薯25万千克。2007年，息烽县成为全省14个脱毒马铃薯基地县之一。至2010年，全县共推广种植脱毒马铃薯30万亩，平均亩产1238千克。

四、种植

（一）水稻种植

水稻是县内主要粮食作物，产量居第一位。以阳朗、下阳朗、底寨、西山小鹿窝、三田、养龙司、九庄、竹花、鹿窝、温泉等平坝地区和水源较好地区为主产区。1991年，水稻种植面积5.8万亩，产量1.98万吨；1992—2001年，种植面积6.7万～7.3万亩，产量2万～3万吨，2000年种植7.3万亩，产量3万吨，为历史最高。此后逐年下降，2010年种植面积5.9万亩，产量2.46万吨。

（二）玉米种植

玉米，境内俗称苞谷，为县内第二位主要粮食作物。以石硐、何家硐、猫场、青山、梨安、小寨坝、王家坪、南极、流长、新场、茅坡、安江等地区种植较多。1991—1997年，玉米种植面积在

9.3万亩左右，由于气候原因，年产量0.75万～1.9万吨，差异很大；玉米品种以墨白为主，玉米粒以白粒居多。随着生活水平提高，玉米由食用型向饲用型转化。1998年西山乡试种高蛋白质玉米450亩。2001年，全县推广优质硬粒型杂交黄玉米7.1万亩。至2002年，小寨坝镇、流长乡、养龙司乡、温泉镇、永靖镇种植高蛋白玉米（中单9409）7600亩，平均亩产311.5千克。2003年，小寨坝镇引进高蛋白玉米黔单11号试种成功，2005年种植面积扩大到4000亩。2006年，实施优质玉米高产示范工程，推广硬粒型黄玉米9万余亩，平均亩产412.5千克，比一般玉米增产22%。是年与贵阳新希望饲料公司签约，以每千克玉米1.45元的价格订单收购，实行统一供种、统一技术、连片种植。2007—2010年，种植面积11万～12万亩，产量3.3万～4.4万吨。

（三）小麦种植

小麦是县内夏收主要粮食作物，产量居粮食第三位。1991—1999年，种植面积8万亩上下，产量1.1万吨左右。随着种植结构调整，2000年小麦种植面积降至5.4万亩，产量7190吨。是年，流长、小寨坝试种面包小麦黔燕1号、中燕1号、节燕3号。2010年种植小麦8970亩，产量1032吨。

（四）大豆种植

大豆，又名黄豆，县内品种有绿、黑、黄三种，多套种于玉米行间。1991年种植面积2.6万亩，此后种植总体趋势下降。1993年产量最高，为1483吨。1994—1999年，产量1000吨左右。2000—2006年，年产量530～690吨。2010年种植面积1.21万亩，产量1150吨。

（五）红薯种植

境内俗称红苕，以5折1计算主粮。种植面积多年在8000～9000亩，产量1100～1600吨。2003—2006年，年种植面积1.3万亩左右，产量3000吨左右。2006—2010年，年种植面积8500～9500亩，亩产150千克左右。

1998年，九庄镇堰塘村村民陈龙志在0.4亩西瓜地里套种红薯，未加追肥，收红薯1500千克（鲜重），折合亩产3750千克。红苕最大个体重6.5千克、一般个体重2.5～3千克。

（六）马铃薯种植

境内俗称洋芋，以5折1计算主粮。主产于梨安、青山、石硐、何家硐、猫场、南极等高寒地区。1991—1995年种植面积4.5万亩左右，产量0.45万～1.1万吨。2001年，推广种植脱毒马铃薯，2005年产量1.6万吨。2007年种植脱毒马铃薯3.76万亩，产量1万吨。2010年马铃薯产量1.5万吨。

（七）杂粮

县内夏收杂粮主要有大麦（又名老麦）、豌豆、胡豆及荞子等，产量波动很大，最高年产1308吨，最低年产373吨。秋收杂粮主要有高粱、小米、麻豆（又名巴山豆）、小豆（又名饭豆）、绿豆、八月豆等，产量随气候变化而增减。最高年产274吨，最低年产67吨。

息烽县1991—2010年粮食作物种植面积、产量统计表

表9-3-5　　单位：亩、千克、吨

年份	1991	1992	1993	1994	1995
播种面积	325712	330253	314140	339694	332153
亩产	173	124	188	177	145
总产量	56458	41013	59103	60010	48079

续表

年份		1991	1992	1993	1994	1995
水稻	播面	58130	72445	63455	70606	72357
	亩产	340	211	327	299	229
	总产	19771	17066	20762	21111	16592
其中：杂交水稻	播面	38172	55352	51405	58646	62681
	亩产	377	231	346	322	251
	总产	14409	13824	17784	18863	15750
玉米	播面	95821	91100	83657	92042	93687
	亩产	203	62	232	166	87
	总产	19490	7497	19386	15263	8150
其中：杂交玉米	播面	53562	30877	56100	54033	49660
	亩产	232	77	240	189	105
	总产	12403	2365	13459	10187	5197
小麦	播面	75090	84443	87967	86342	81898
	亩产	121	113	117	112	136
	总产	9119	9519	10270	9657	11104
大豆	播面	26461	15659	18330	22206	15684
	亩产	45	32	81	64	46
	总产	1185	664	1483	1411	719
红苕	播面	5369	5639	6053	7216	9059
	亩产	214	132	274	273	130
	总产	1151	856	1661	1970	1177
马铃薯	播面	45400	46047	39545	50005	49398
	亩产	105	104	114	197	195
	总产	11899	4768	4521	9871	9615
夏季杂粮	播面	11899	9069	9839	7285	7268
	亩产	59	41	59	78	85
	总产	706	373	581	567	621
秋季杂粮	播面	7542	5851	5294	4000	2802
	亩产	36.3	46.2	83	42	36
	总产	274	270	439	168	101

说明：红苕、马铃薯按5折1计算

表9-3-5续1

年份		1996	1997	1998	1999	2000
播种面积		329888	330645	349935	337680	307935
亩产		209.14	211.38	206.57	225.24	247
总产量		68993	69893	72986	76059	76060
水稻	播面	71933	68685	67472	72750	73065
	亩产	380.69	394.9	390	386.03	418.6
	总产	27384	27124	26339	28084	30585
其中：杂交水稻	播面	58940	64065	63057	67980	67935
	亩产	410.89	400.76	397	392.06	424.41
	总产	24218	25675	25006	26652	28832
玉米	播面	93925	93165	112140	97845	95520
	亩产	180.01	182.27	182	214.76	237.28
	总产	16907	16981	20413	21013	22665
其中：杂交玉米	播面	41580	71805	91529	84285	66135
	亩产	263.11	191.42	189	224.51	240.73
	总产	10940	13745	17326	18923	15921
小麦	播面	86380	87255	85130	83505	54135
	亩产	132.98	136.77	136	143.66	132.82
	总产	11487	11934	11555	11996	7190
大豆	播面	12880	14925	13245	11505	10335
	亩产	80.05	70.62	73	82.05	67.34
	总产	1031	1054	969	944	696
红苕	播面	4968	6060	9918	9555	8205
	亩产	170.69	165.18	143	157.93	204.75
	总产	848	1001	1416	1509	1680
马铃薯	播面	49590	51810	53640	54585	55665
	亩产	213.49	212.14	216	216.69	221.61
	总产	10587	10991	11576	11828	12336
夏季杂粮	播面	6217	6165	6020	5145	9180
	亩产	99.08	101.38	104	110.2	85.62
	总产	616	625	626	567	786
秋季杂粮	播面	3995	2580	2370	2790	1830
	亩产	33.29	70.93	38.82	42.29	66.67
	总产	133	183	92	118	122

表9-3-5续2

年份		2001	2002	2003	2004	2005
播种面积		317130	324465	318525	313320	309375
亩产		178.76	175	215.64	246.37	249.59
总产量		56691	56781	68687	77192	77216
水稻	播面	72300	72465	72060	70770	69765
	亩产	336.03	135.65	315.26	368.7	371.05
	总产	24295	9830	22718	26093	25886
其中：杂交水稻	播面	68775	69210	64650	66495	67080
	亩产	343.02	137.94	327.32	375.8	374.75
	总产	23591	9547	21161	24989	25138
玉米	播面	100665	104505	104640	107880	108720
	亩产	91.89	216.03	187.38	233.27	228.13
	总产	9250	22576	19607	25165	24802
其中：杂交玉米	播面	78090	76425	85800	87225	95025
	亩产	100.77	225.69	195	248.56	236.4
	总产	7869	17248	16748	21681	22464
小麦	播面	47400	46905	39600	35250	30585
	亩产	146.01	148.62	150.71	150.41	150.53
	总产	6921	6971	5968	5302	4604
大豆	播面	12750	13305	12705	11535	11055
	亩产	42.20	46.37	52.11	59.21	61.6
	总产	538	617	662	683	681
红苕	播面	8625	9870	13650	12720	15075
	亩产	178.43	185.82	229.23	246.07	250.41
	总产	1539	1834	3129	3130	3775
马铃薯	播面	57900	61605	62685	61995	62100
	亩产	220.16	221.35	247.65	251.89	261.64
	总产	12747	13636	15524	15616	16248
夏季杂粮	播面	14595	12795	10080	9195	9690
	亩产	89.62	94.72	94.05	107.12	113.21
	总产	1308	1212	948	985	1097
秋季杂粮	播面	2895	3015	3000	3180	2415
	亩产	32.12	34.83	41	57.55	50.93
	总产	93	105	123	183	123

说明：2002年8月9—20日连续12天低温阴雨，影响水稻扬花授粉，减产严重

表9-3-5续3

年份		2006	2007	2008	2009	2010
播种面积		296985	504675	497970	513159	526905
亩产		232.17	171.39	178.45	181.87	173.88
总产量		68952	86498	88864	93329	91620
水稻	播面	64890	66480	62730	62237	59220
	亩产	315.06	391.67	403.51	407.42	416.53
	总产	20444	26038	25312	25356	24667
其中：杂交水稻	播面	57810	66480	62730	62237	59220
	亩产	322.85	391.67	403.51	407.42	416.53
	总产	18664	26038	25312	25356	24667
玉米	播面	111105	112140	110355	113571	119310
	亩产	218.73	300.33	357.53	375.05	377.09
	总产	24302	33679	39455	42598	44991
其中：杂交玉米	播面	84330	112140	110355	113580	119310
	亩产	203.18	300.33	357.53	375.05	377.09
	总产	17134	33679	39455	42598	44991
小麦	播面	33090	31095	20640	20700	8970
	亩产	148.69	150.02	133.24	135.5	115.05
	总产	4920	4665	2750	2809	1032
大豆	播面	11145	11700	9405	10800	12165
	亩产	47.38	89.23	88.35	88.61	94.94
	总产	528	1044	831	957	1155
红苕	播面	14940	9302	9010	8945	8605
	亩产	198.53	155	160	165	162
	总产	2966	1441.81	1441.6	1475.9	1394.01
马铃薯	播面	59805	60375	61620	62235	52260
	亩产	262.94	265.47	280.65	294.17	296.38
	总产	15725	16028	17294	18308	15489
夏季杂粮	播面	2010	11062	10550	9580	10020
	亩产	33.33	95.1	93.2	105.5	108.2
	总产	67	1052	983.3	1010.7	1084.2
秋季杂粮	播面	—	3010	3005	3015	2816
	亩产	—	35.2	38.4	55.1	52.4
	总产	—	106	115.4	166.1	147.6

第三节　经济作物

一、烤烟

（一）品种

20世纪90年代初，县内栽种烤烟品种主要有NC82、K326、红花大金元、斯佩特G-28、斯佩特G-140等。1995年，县烟草局采取全县统一供种，集中育苗办法，推广K326、NC82等优良品种，禁止私人使用劣杂品种。1996年起，推行包衣种子。2001年，烤烟主栽品种有K326、NC82、云烟85。至2004年，统一包衣良种推广率100%，K326为主栽品种，种植面积为全部烤烟面积的80%。2007年，全县烤烟品种实现100%良种化。

（二）育苗与种植

1991年，县内推行“麦、肥、烟”“麦、烟”等分带轮作营养袋（块）育苗，适时移栽，烟叶长至10片时，即开始采摘起烘。1992年，实行合理稀植，每亩种烟1000～1300株；推行重施底肥，早施追肥，及时中耕，防治病虫害，打顶抹芽和去掉脚叶方法，平均亩产烟叶199.4千克。1993年，烤烟种植6.68万亩，收购烟叶14.04万担，创历史最高水平。

1995年，推行地膜覆盖育苗和烟株移栽前施足底层肥，施窝肥，移栽时再施肥的双层施肥技术。1998年，按照国家烤烟生产部署，压缩种植面积和收购量，全县烟草种植面积降为2万亩。2001年，为提高上中等烟比例，烤烟生产向石硐、九庄、青山等地宜种烟区发展。示范点以50亩以上连片种植为重点，实行集中育苗，分户管理，对苗床施用斯美地熏蒸，推行双膜育苗、小苗假植和剪叶技术。2002年，推广漂浮、托盘育苗新技术，育苗307箱。

2003年，漂浮、托盘育苗获得成功，全县漂浮育苗1179箱，托盘育苗231箱。根据省、市《烤烟生产技术方案》，县制定《息烽2003年优质烟生产技术方案》，强化流程管理，推行高厢起垄、拉绳等距移栽等规范移栽种植技术。2005年，引进和使用自动化剪叶器和化学抑芽剂打顶抹芽。2006年，推行标准化“麦套烟”种植，放弃“油菜、烟”套种轮作。

2007年，实行集约化育苗、商品化供苗和提前起垄，直插式移栽；大田管理实行化学抑芽技术。推广“秸秆覆盖”技术。是年种植烤烟1.98万亩，收购烟叶4.5万担，上等烟占49.2%。2010年全县种植烤烟1.87万亩，收购烟叶4.07万担，上中等烟占62.59%。烟农人均收入4183.72元。

（三）烘烤

20世纪90年代初，县内试行机烘技术，烤烟质量有所提高，因投资大，技术性强，推广艰难。烟农仍以河南乔庄式烘房烘烤烟叶为主。1996年，引进远红外涂料涂在加热管上技术，烤烟质量明显提高。是年，上中等烟比例达91%，为历史最好年份。

1999年，推广L-QX立式炉灶——气流下降式烤房和通过调节湿度、温度和烘烤时间，将烟叶烘烤过程分为变黄、定色、干筋三个阶段的“三段式”烘烤技术。当年新建L-QX烤房180余间。至2001年，上中等烟所占比例90.17%。

2003年，县烟草公司在石硐、流长等地召开“立式炉灶气流上升式”和“立式炉灶气流下降式”烤房修建培训会，培训技术人员150余名。2005年，对烟农全面进行“三段式”烘烤技术培训，统一制定“三段式”科学烘烤技术资料，统一按1间烤房配1支干湿球温度计、1张烘烤图表，便于烟农对照操作。是年，县内标准化烤房计2150间，占种烟农户的86%。

2006年8月，公司在石硐乡召开上部烟叶一次性砍烤现场培训会，全面推行上部4～6片烟叶一次性砍烤技术。是年，以集约化烘烤为主，修建小改密（密集型）烤房164间、密集型烤房2间。2007年，通过普通烤房改为密集型烤房改造技术的培训，共完成"普改密"烤房改造347套。2008年，修建"热源外置式"烤房计划251间。2009年，石硐乡、九庄镇、青山苗族乡、养龙司乡、流长乡、鹿窝乡新建烤房群11群共70间。

（四）生产扶持

1999年，全县办烤烟示范点7000亩，按每亩扶持补贴100元（主料烟示范点每亩120元）标准，发给烟农折合人民币205万元。2000年，公司无偿投入农膜1.5吨，集中育苗，并出资上万元从外地调入烟苗200余万株，无偿发给烟农。2001—2007年，公司共无偿投入620万元用于种子、农膜、肥料、农药、培训、烤房建设和用煤补贴。投入资金400万元，用于烟水配套工程。

二、油菜

1991年，境内油菜以油研5号、7号等双低杂交油菜为主，亩产89千克，总产量7668吨。1994年，引进油研系列和秦油2号、杂09、杂61、中油821等品种。此后，应用育苗移栽等配套技术。1999年，亩产突破100千克，总产量9000吨。2005年，境内种植优质油菜2.66万亩，平均亩产136.5千克。2007年，全县种植面积8.39万亩，产量10458吨。2010年，油菜籽产量9061吨。主要品种有油研系列、黔油系列、华油杂系列、中油杂系列、德油系列以及川油、华皖油、广源等26个双低油菜品种。

三、花生

花生主要产于竹花、鹿窝、流长、新场、王家坪等地。种植面积保持在3000亩左右。2007年，全县种植面积4335亩，产量495吨。2010年产量最高，为568.4吨。

息烽县1991—2010年油菜籽、花生种植产量统计表

表9-3-6

年份	油菜籽			花生		
	面积（亩）	亩产（千克）	总产（吨）	面积（亩）	亩产（千克）	总产（吨）
1991	86254	89	7668	3740	90	338
1992	74155	73	5416	2787	48	135
1993	70188	70	5490	2480	160	397
1994	75766	78	6042	2910	140	432
1995	89408	94	8384	3349	117	391
1996	85835	91.4	7846	1400	83.6	134
1997	86165	93.3	8036	1830	100.5	184
1998	83924	97	8140	2950	99	291
1999	84360	108.9	9188	3000	92	276
2000	90375	93.5	8453	3450	87.5	302

续表

年份	油菜籽			花生		
	面积（亩）	亩产（千克）	总产（吨）	面积（亩）	亩产（千克）	总产（吨）
2001	82605	99.2	8196	3900	94.9	370
2002	80595	109.1	8791	4500	85.8	386
2003	77730	106.6	8287	4740	82.3	390
2004	—	—	—	4260	88.7	378
2005	82500	124.1	10236	5160	85.3	440
2006	81525	124.5	10150	4365	74.5	325
2007	83909	124.6	10458	4355	113.6	495
2008	65070	114.46	7448	3624	113.7	412
2009	74403	116.04	8634	2900	124	359.6
2010	91860	98.64	9061	3950	143.9	568.4

四、蔬菜

1991年，县内大宗蔬菜有儿菜（茎用芥菜）、莴笋。是年，底寨、阳朗、三田等地种植儿菜1500亩，平均亩产4000千克，最高亩产6000千克。养龙司乡幸福、堡子、灯塔等村种植莴笋1000亩，亩产1500～2000千克。

1996年，小寨坝镇盘脚营村许明朗父子3人，在海拔1450米的南桥村上新厂试种秋淡蔬菜80亩，在贵阳市蔬菜办技术人员指导下，6月中旬播种，9月收割，亩产大白菜2300千克，产值1840元，收入10万元，获利3万元。

1997年，机关干部和个体户10人携资到小寨坝镇南桥村，种植大白菜、莲花白1597亩。2004年，在海拔1300米以上的永靖镇老厂村、河坎村、硬寨村，小寨坝镇田兴村、南桥村发展夏季反季节冷凉蔬菜9040亩，形成冷凉蔬菜基地，平均亩产3150千克。

2006年，全县蔬菜播种面积4.39万亩，总产量8.86万吨，其中商品蔬菜上市量8.2万吨。初步形成以不同优势蔬菜品种为主的不同区域的4个蔬菜产业带：以永靖镇老厂、河坎、硬寨、联丰，小寨坝镇南桥、田兴，青山苗族乡大林等村为核心的种植夏秋反季节大白菜为主要品种的冷凉蔬菜产业带，规模1.5万亩；贵遵高等级公路一线的永靖镇6个村，西山乡4个村，小寨坝镇4个村，养龙司乡6村，以大头菜、儿菜、牛腿南瓜（密本南瓜）、黄瓜、莴笋、甘蓝、速生菜、香细菜为主的蔬菜产业带，规模2万亩；以县城至九庄、九庄至流长公路沿线的西山乡2个村、青山苗族乡2个村、九庄镇6个村、鹿窝乡6个村、流长乡2个村种植生姜、大葱、香葱、干椒为主的调味品（加工）蔬菜产业带，规模2万亩；乌江河流域的养龙司乡11个村、流长乡5个村、鹿窝乡2个村、九庄镇3个村，利用低热河谷种植以瓜豆、茄、果为主导品种的次早熟蔬菜产业带，规模1万亩。

2010年，全县有蔬菜万亩基地5个、蔬菜大棚350个、无公害蔬菜基地22个。

息烽县1995—2010年蔬菜种植统计表

表9-3-7

年份	播面（亩）	总产量（吨）	其中商品蔬菜		主要品种
			播面	产量	
1995	10260	19800	—	—	萝卜、白菜、四季豆、南瓜、莴笋
1996	12650	24000	1484	2850	萝卜、白菜、四季豆、南瓜、莴笋
1997	15500	31890	1880	3680	萝卜、白菜、四季豆、南瓜、莴笋
1998	16950	37260	2370	4580	萝卜、白菜、四季豆、南瓜、莴笋
1999	17860	36500	3568	6510	萝卜、白菜、四季豆、南瓜、莴笋
2000	18890	38675	6130	11985	甘蓝、萝卜、白菜、四季豆、南瓜、莴笋
2001	19900	41060	9930	19870	甘蓝、萝卜、白菜、四季豆、南瓜、莴笋
2002	21053	41920	14870	32155	儿菜、小青瓜、甘蓝、萝卜、白菜、四季豆、南瓜、莴笋
2003	28793	34390	22390	45695	大葱、牛腿南瓜、儿菜、小青瓜、甘蓝、萝卜、白菜、四季豆、南瓜、莴笋
2004	38743	77486	31252	65860	生姜、辣椒、大葱、牛腿南瓜、儿菜、小青瓜、甘蓝、萝卜、白菜、四季豆、南瓜、莴笋
2005	43618	84700	35260	73300	黄瓜、番茄、生姜、辣椒、大葱、牛腿南瓜、儿菜、小青瓜、甘蓝、萝卜、白菜、四季豆、南瓜、莴笋
2006	51000	76300	—	63100	黄瓜、番茄、生姜、辣椒、大葱、牛腿南瓜、儿菜、小青瓜、甘蓝、萝卜、白菜、四季豆、南瓜、莴笋
2007	53200	97950	—	80100	黄瓜、番茄、生姜、辣椒、大葱、牛腿南瓜、儿菜、小青瓜、甘蓝、萝卜、白菜、四季豆、南瓜、莴笋
2008	109200	191000	—	86000	黄瓜、番茄、生姜、辣椒、大葱、牛腿南瓜、儿菜、小青瓜、甘蓝、萝卜、白菜、四季豆、南瓜、莴笋
2009	122200	203900	—	89000	黄瓜、番茄、生姜、辣椒、大葱、牛腿南瓜、儿菜、小青瓜、甘蓝、萝卜、白菜、四季豆、南瓜、莴笋
2010	140000	174000	—	90000	黄瓜、番茄、生姜、辣椒、大葱、牛腿南瓜、儿菜、小青瓜、甘蓝、萝卜、白菜、四季豆、南瓜、莴笋

五、水果

1991年，县设果品办。1996年，县农业局设立果蔬站，负责果树栽培、管理、防治病虫害培训和指导，引进适合本地生长的优良品种。

1998年，开展果树现状调查工作，查明县内主要种有柑橘、梨、桃、苹果、葡萄、杨梅、李、猕猴桃、柿、樱桃、花红、石榴、枣子、枇杷、杏等果树。总面积2万余亩，投产面积8046亩，总产量5778吨。李、柑橘、桃、梨、猕猴桃5个树种种植面积较大，其中以李分布最广，各乡村皆有。境内以柑橘、李、桃、猕猴桃、梨为主的连片果园61个，其中集体7个、重点农户53家、股份制1个。大部分果园缺乏后续资金、技术和管理经验，果园面积虽有发展，但普遍存在重种轻管，品种、树龄老化，优质品种少、果苗与高秆作物混种、零星分散等问题。

2010年，全县果树生产面积3万亩，产量6000吨，并形成区域化布局。建成以红岩村为主的贵遵公路6000亩水晶葡萄、息九公路西山乡3000亩杨梅，石硐乡、九庄镇、鹿窝乡、流长乡、小寨坝镇、永靖镇等中海拔9000亩梨子、鹿窝乡中低海拔1000亩李枣，流长乡、养龙司乡、温泉镇中低热河谷3000亩柑橘，青山苗族乡、石硐乡等高海拔5000亩核桃等六大产业带。同时，加强果树后续管理工作，经常请省市果树专家来县对果农进行果树修剪、套袋、施肥、病虫害防治等技术培训。

息烽县1991—2010年主要水果产量统计表

表9-3-8

年份	总产（吨）	其中主要水果（吨）									
		柑橘	梨子	葡萄	红枣	柿子	桃子	杨梅	李子	猕猴桃	其他
1991	1219	201	163	50	3	17	224	3	485	—	73
1992	779	107	137	47	2	63	95	4	230	—	91
1993	1174	259	107	59	3	18	152	10	522	—	—
1994	1011	169	172	93	2	38	138	11	330	—	—
1995	1261	282	137	126	4	25	106	5	49	—	77
1996	830	233	57	145	28	30	61	11	—	—	265
1997	1339	351	111	143	7	23	97	12	—	0.4	595
1998	1369	598	195	116	2	24	117	38	—	3	277
1999	—	—	—	—	—	—	—	—	—	—	—
2000	1010	366	178	120	29	27	102	19	—	8	161
2001	1892	792	160	157	30	61	184		—	—	506
2002	1932	683	169	509	36	26	162	34	—	20	294
2003	2111	—	—	—	—	—	—	—	—	—	—
2004	2233	665	324	103	26	14	168	12	—	9	913
2005	2272	824	315	594	11	27	214	12	—	17	301
2006	2518	—	—	—	—	—	—	—	—	—	—
2007	2704	1022	569	667	14	55	286	50	—	38	—
2008	2703	1022	569	667	14	55	286	50	—	38	—
2009	4316	1159	947	1168	13	34	456	29	—	14	—
2010	4590	1036	1069	1511	13	27	491	31	—	8	—

（一）葡萄

1973年，小寨坝镇红岩村车头山村民曾庆彬从遵义引种水晶葡萄，至20世纪90年代，种植农户发展到120户，面积100多亩。红岩村土壤环境和气候条件独特，产出的葡萄甜中带有蜂蜜香味，受到市场欢迎。2001年，全村种植葡萄800多亩，户均收入2000多元。

2004年，小寨坝镇政府在红岩村举办“红壤碧珠”葡萄文化节。2006年，葡萄种植扩展到大寨、关岭、王家坪等4个村12个村民组，种植面积3000亩，挂果面积1000亩。是年，红岩村获“贵阳市十大文明生态村”称号。2007年8月14日，县政府在潮水、红岩村举办主题为“红岩欢歌”的葡萄文化节。此后每年举办葡萄节。2010年，以红岩村为中心的葡萄种植面积9300亩，产量1511吨。

（二）西瓜

1991年，县内西瓜种植面积近千亩。8月，县委、县政府邀请省农科院、省农业厅专家对流长西瓜进行品评鉴定：单瓜重6.75～6.9千克，含糖量9.9%～11.6%，可食率58%～60.8%；含糖量、可食率均超过当年全国西瓜良种鉴评会规定指标；瓜瓤鲜红、质脆皮薄、汁多爽口，上市时间正值邻近的西瓜基地如广西钦州、贵州榕江等地西瓜收获完毕茬口，7月中下旬到8月高温暑热季节，除销往贵阳、遵义、六盘水等县市外，还远销重庆、南充、柳州、南宁、怀化、湛江等地。1998年，种植面积1.45万亩，产量36942吨。是年7月，县成立西瓜营销工作领导小组，并于24日在流长乡营中小学举办息烽县首届“西瓜节”，吸引大批客商，西瓜畅销省内外20个县市，初步形成品牌。2003年后，因受灾或其他原因，县内西瓜生产萎缩，每年种植面积2000～3000亩。

六、花卉

2008年，贵阳市投资360余万元在永靖镇阳朗、猫洞、立碑等村建户种花卉基地，建单体大棚150个（2.7万平方米）及滴灌设施。小寨坝镇开磷集团物业管理公司建连体大棚3万平方米，配套冷库和采后处理车间。是年10月，县农业局组织花农10人到昆明参加40天的花卉栽培技术培训。2009年，建成小寨坝镇开磷集团物业管理公司花卉基地，引进红玫瑰、白玫瑰、百合、马蹄莲等10余个品种进行栽培，上市鲜花2万余枝；永靖镇户种花卉基地种植康乃馨10余个品种81万株。2010年，县投资180余万元，在永靖镇猫洞村建设鲜切菊花项目，改建1万多平方米连体大棚，新增补光、滴灌、喷灌、防虫网及加温等设施，种菊花37.62万株。

七、中药材

1991年，毕节人张创到西山乡西山村种植杜仲、黄檗，套种桔梗、板蓝根、牛膝等1200亩。2003年，县农业局组织人员调查全县中药材，查明县内有药用植物102科298属357种，其中木本65种、竹类4种、菌类4种、木质藤本25种、草本257种。野生中药材资源主要集中在西山、南山高海拔地区。2004年，县农业局设中药产业办公室，开展开发抚育野生药物资源，引种外地药材工作。2007年，县中药材产业办公室在小寨坝镇南中村建息烽县中药材基地。是年，全县采收续断、葛根、五倍子、金银花、南沙参、黄山药等野生商品药材50余吨，销往贵阳、重庆等地。2010年，县内人工栽培的中药材有天麻、喜树、黄檗、板蓝根、桔梗、太子参、杜仲、半夏、苦参、金花石蒜、瓜蒌、五倍子、续断等。

八、蚕桑

2005年底，在九庄镇示范种植桑树184亩。2006年，县政府与平坝县贵州振兴茧丝绸有限公司签订合作协议，由公司对农户实行“五统一”（统一供桑苗、蚕种、蚕药、蚕具；统一小蚕共育；统一技术规程；统一质量标准；统一收购鲜茧）养蚕。是年，从广西调进蚕种29张试养，获得成功。至2008年底，县内桑园扩展至4个乡镇21个村1000余户，面积增加到10791.7亩，其中九庄镇8537.7亩、青山苗族乡704亩、石硐乡1050亩、流长乡500亩，在石硐乡高田坎村、大林村，九庄镇鸡场村、望城村建成4个核心示范园。

2007年11月，息烽县被国家商务部列入“东桑西移”示范县。12月25日，县政府制定《关于进一步加快蚕桑产业发展的实施意见》，要求“基地建设规模化、生产经营产业化、产业管理市场化”，以市场为导向，以增加农民收入、带动农村经济发展为目标，建立蚕业合作经济组织，引进扶持蚕业龙头企业，提出在3～5年时间内将蚕桑产业打造成支柱产业的目标。

息烽县2006—2010年蚕桑生产情况统计表

表9-3-9

年份	养蚕（张）	收鲜茧（千克）	总产值（万元）	平均每张鲜茧（千克）	均价（元）	每张产值（元）
2006	29	870	1.7	30	20	600
2007	188	4139	7.4	22	18	394.2
2008	196	4357	7.9	22.2	18.2	405.3
2009	440	11962	21.9	27.2	18.3	498.4
2010	355	11245	28.5	31.6	25	802.5

第四节　农技农艺

一、农作物病虫草鼠害防治

（一）病虫草鼠害

全县农作物病虫害发生种类多，范围广，常年发生面积3万～5万亩，经过防治后仍损失产量1500～2500吨，遇大发生年损失则更重。重大病虫害有稻瘟病、稻飞虱、稻纵卷叶螟、黏虫、二化螟、玉米螟、大小斑病、油菜蚜虫、霜霉病、小麦锈病、白粉病等。此外，检疫性有害生物在境内发生情况有所增加。1996年发现美洲斑潜蝇，1998年发现南美斑潜蝇，2002年，全县检疫性有害生物普查结果有28种。至2010年，县内农作物主要病虫害有122种，其中病害63种、虫害59种。

（二）防治与检疫

1991年，开展水稻和玉米病虫害综合防治1.9万亩，挽回损失1400吨。1996年起，开展省内调运检疫。是年，市无偿配给123台背负式机动喷雾器，分配到各乡镇组建机械化防治队，平时在本乡镇开展防治工作，出现大面积病虫害时，进行联合防治。1997年起，开展省与省之间调运检疫。综合防治扩大至小麦、油菜。至1998年，综合防治面积17～20万亩，年均挽回损失4900吨。2000年起，开展化学除草、农区灭鼠工作。至2010年，防治面积多年为24万亩。其间，2005—2010年，新增机动喷雾器542台，机械化防治面积4.45万亩次。2007年起，开展县内市场检疫工作。

（三）监测预报

1991年，县植保站是全国农田鼠害监测网点、全省农作物病虫测报网点站。至2010年，先后承担二代黏虫、稻瘟病、稻飞虱、油菜蚜虫的系统测报及农田鼠害监测工作。每年编发《病虫简报》《病虫情交流》《鼠情简报》24期以上，以简报形式向党政领导提供信息，预报病虫鼠情，做好防治工作。其间，2004年前，主要使用糖醋液诱蛾器、黑光灯等诱杀害虫。2005年，引进佳多频振式杀虫灯进行物理诱杀防治，实现虫情监测自动化，提高预测预报准确率。

专记：鼠害防治

20世纪90年代，县内鼠害严重，鼠传染病——流行性出血热、钩体病流行。1988年春，全县开展统一灭鼠工作，根据县植保站鼠种调查和鼠情监测结果，选用慢性抗凝血药杀鼠醚，在老鼠繁殖高峰前，统一投药，灭鼠97.89万只，挽回经济损失286万元，流行性出血热和钩体病发生率比上年同期分别降低59.7%和95.0%。此后，每年由县植保站负责组织全县农区鼠情监测和灭鼠工作。

县植保站潘世昌1986年5月加入贵州省农田鼠害研究协作组，一直从事农区鼠害监测和防治工作，基本摸清县内黑线姬鼠是农田耕作区主要鼠害，褐家鼠、小家鼠为住宅区主要鼠害。2000年起，潘世昌主持全县农田鼠害发生规律及防治（毒饵站灭鼠）技术研究，项目区鼠密度由灭鼠前的平均7.49%下降到0.82%，共计完成农田鼠害综合防治技术推广面积58.8万亩，平均每亩减少粮食损失18.39千克，共计减少粮食损失975.5万千克。2010年，项目研究成果《息烽县主要害鼠发生规律及防治技术研究应用》获贵阳市科技进步二等奖。

1991—2010年，潘世昌在学报及期刊上发表科技论文33篇，其中《黔中地区小家鼠种群数量动态及预测预报模型》（《植物保护学报》2006年）、《小家鼠种群年龄的研究》（《西南农业学报》2003年）、《小家鼠胴体重指标划分种群年龄的研究》（《贵州农业科学》2006年）、《黔中地区小家鼠种群繁殖特征》（《西南农业学报》2007年）连续获贵阳市第八、第九、第十次自然科学优秀论文二等奖。先后获省、市、安顺地区科技进步二、三等奖3项，省农业丰收二、三等奖2项；连续6次获全省农田鼠害监测与治理工作先进个人称号，2次获“贵阳市中青年科技骨干”称号，2次获息烽县专业技术带头人称号。2009年11月获“全省农区鼠害监测与防治突出贡献者”称号。

二、土肥技术

（一）配方施肥

1991年，开展水稻微机施肥，亩产623.9千克，比习惯施肥亩产533.7千克增长16.9%；测土配方施肥亩产646.5千克，比习惯施肥亩产568.1千克增长13.7%。1992年，开展油菜配方施肥，全部育苗移栽，磷肥打底，配方施肥亩产119.6千克，比习惯施肥亩产102.4千克增产12千克。1995年，县统一安排配方施肥任务8万亩，其中水稻5万亩、玉米3万亩，对5个片区9个对照进行验收，配方施肥比未配方施肥，水稻亩增产率50%，玉米亩增产率25%。

1998—1999年，全县推广专用复混肥。玉米8.8万亩、马铃薯3.75万亩、油菜7.1万亩、小麦3万亩。施专用肥的玉米比习惯亩增产率13.6%，马铃薯增产率19%；对上中下不同肥力的3个同田对比点进行验收，油菜每亩增产率分别为15%、19%、24.7%；小麦每亩增产率分别为10.4%、12.9%、19.4%。2006年，配方施肥16万亩。

2010年，推广测土配方施肥面积45.12万亩，其中水稻5.5万亩、玉米12万亩、马铃薯8.55万亩、油菜7.3万亩、蔬菜10.45万亩、果树等1.32万亩。

（二）微肥推广

1991年，全县推广施用微肥（主要为硼肥和锌肥）1.08万亩，其中水稻施锌肥，亩增产率7.5%；喷施磷酸二氢钾亩增产率12%；施增产菌亩增产率5.5%。1992年，实施3000亩油菜施硼肥配套丰产技术，施用硼肥的油菜亩增产率9%。至2009年，施用微肥面积4.2万亩，其中水稻2.78万亩、玉米1.92万亩、蔬菜0.5万亩。

三、耕作制度

（一）旱地分带轮作

1985年起，推广小麦收割后种玉米，再套种红薯，收割后再种小麦（或油菜）。增产效果明显，面积逐年增加。1992年，旱地分带轮作7.1万亩；平均复合亩产536.8千克，比对照增产26.3%。

1995年，推广紧凑型玉米栽培，实施分带轮作多熟制开发和建设“双纲”“吨粮”田土；主要模式有：麦—稻、芋—稻、麦—玉米—苕、芋—玉米—苕、麦—玉米—玉米、草莓—稻、茎用芥菜、短藤瓜—稻、西红柿—玉米—红苕等。

（二）稻田多熟制

1999年，全县推广粮经型稻田多熟制7581亩，其模式为菜（白菜、莴笋、儿菜、大头菜）—（短藤）瓜（青豆、四季豆、茄子、早马铃薯）—杂稻。2001年发展到1.02万亩。2004年，达到2.31万亩，平均亩产值1245.6元。至2006年，旱地多熟制有小麦—玉米—红薯、小麦—烤烟—红薯、马铃薯—玉米—豆（薯）、蔬菜—绿肥—玉米—花生（辣椒或生姜）；稻田多熟制有白菜—早马铃薯—水稻、白菜—短藤瓜—水稻、白菜—早糯玉米—水稻等。

第四章　养殖业

1991年，全县肉类总产4656吨，禽蛋340吨；人均占有量分别为21千克、1.5千克。2010年，肉类总产1.4万吨，禽蛋1716吨；人均占有量分别为54千克、6.6千克。20年间，全县养殖业通过畜种改良，推广猪、牛人工授精、网箱养鱼，推广配合饲料，科学饲养，提高了畜、禽、鱼的出栏率、出肉率和饲料利用率。

第一节　畜禽饲养

一、猪

（一）良种公猪

1991年，全县有种公猪62头，其中良种公猪27头、杂交公猪35头。县畜禽品种改良站（简称县品改站）引进苏白种公猪6头，投放到无良种公猪的边远乡村。此后，县品改站每年引进约克、苏白良种公猪，逐步取代杂交公猪。1992年，小寨坝镇农民许明朗引进杜洛克、长白种猪。1995年，执行国家《种畜禽管理条例》，在养龙司乡试行鉴定公猪，挂牌配种。农民逐渐接受并利用良种公猪与本地母猪进行杂交，农民引进良种公猪的数量逐渐增多。2005年，农户引进杜洛克、大约克等良种公猪31头。此后未再引进。

（二）母猪

1991年，县内母猪多为杂交母猪，品质较差。是年，养龙司乡幸福村村民引进黑母猪4头，至1993年发展到11头。逐步辐射到王家寨、牛头山两村民组，小寨坝镇、青山苗族乡、石硐乡等乡镇。1995年，全县有黑母猪387头。1997年，因粮价上涨，生猪价格低于粮价，仔猪价格由14元/千克降到3.6元/千克，致使母猪存栏下降30%。1999年，市农业局推广二元杂交（简称二杂）母猪。县品改站在小寨坝镇盘脚营村干沟选择41户农户，采用“借猪还猪，滚动发展”办法，投放头均重23千克的二杂母猪50头。2006年，西山乡磨盘，小寨坝镇红岩、南中、石桥，鹿窝乡田坝，青山苗族乡冗坝和养龙司乡蚂蟥等村实行规范化饲养，建规范化母猪圈舍350间，投放二杂母猪500头。

2007年，根据中央、省、市能繁母猪补贴文件精神，全县9483头能繁母猪补贴款47.42万元。是年，开展能繁母猪保险工作，当年投保率84%。2010年，全县有能繁母猪14099头，补贴资金70.5万元，其中市级资金42.29万元、县级匹配资金28.19万元。

（三）人工授精

1990年前，县内生猪繁殖多为本交（自然交配，分为自由交配和人工辅助交配）。县牲畜良种繁殖站采用徒手采精法开展猪人工授精获得成功。1991年，在乡镇建猪人工授精点。1992年，6个猪人工授精点共配种1242头次，受精率87%。1993年，因经费和农户意识等问题，除县牲畜良种繁殖站坚持人工授精外，其余猪人工授精点工作处于停滞状态。1997年，县牲畜良种场猪人工授精配种502头次。1999—2001年，采用民办公助办法建人工授精点6个。小寨坝镇中心村猪人工授精点一年输配母猪880头次，受精率90%，成为省级生猪人工授精示范点。2010年，规范猪人工授精点建设，为全县15个猪人工授精点制订管理制度和操作规程。全年共输配母猪6526头次。

二、牛

（一）品种改良

1991年，石硐乡兽医站采用人工授精配种，产杂交牛7头。次年，因经费缺乏，牛人工授精工作停止。1999年6月，市农业局推进牛品种改良（简称牛改）工作，县内建立5个牛改点。采取“以家为点”办法开展工作。至12月共配318头。采取畜主送1头发情母牛到配种点配种，各补助畜主和输精员5元的办法，以鼓励其积极性；每产1头杂交牛犊，奖励输精员50元。2000年，牛改点增加到15个，配种1820头，受胎率35%，产犊55头。2001年，九庄镇新沙村漆树湾组一村民家的母牛产下一公一母双胞胎；父本为西门塔尔。2002年，牛人工授精配种开始收取服务费，每头30元。2004年，输配发情母牛5087头，受胎率46%，产犊1236头。2006年，牛改配种收费提高到50元/头，产犊奖励降至20元/头。2007年7月，石硐乡红星村半坡组宋天才家的本地黄母牛产下3头牛犊，平均初生重16千克；父本为安格斯。是年，取消产犊奖励，配种服务费提高到100元。2009年产犊3256头，为历年最多。2010年配种6782头，受胎率61%，产犊2930头。

冻精品种：黄牛有西门塔尔、利木赞、红安格斯、黑安格斯；水牛有摩拉、尼里。

（二）肉牛

2000年前，境内无专门肉牛养殖，仅有牛贩将所购得的老残牛经短时饲养后出售。2002年，县内始有肉牛生产基地。是年，出栏肉牛2266头。2005年，县财政划拨专项资金对肉牛养殖户改造牛舍进行补助，每户500元，同时对养殖大户贷款贴息；县农业局对点上农户和养殖大户无偿提供草种、配备人工冻精配种器材、冻精和液氮。是年8月，县畜牧部门购进25头10月龄秦川母牛，投放西山乡胜利村作肉牛养殖基础母牛。小寨坝镇个体户从成都引进西门塔尔种公牛3头。2006年，全县出栏商品牛7668头。至2010年，全县每年出栏肉牛约7000头。

（三）奶牛

1991年，县牲畜良种场有奶牛22头。因缺乏资金，种公牛长期没有更新，母牛品质退化严重，产奶牛头均日产奶不足15千克。至1997年，剩奶牛5头，头均日产奶5千克左右，1999年全部淘汰。

2001年，小寨坝镇余强购进奶牛3头，因缺乏饲养技术，且牛奶销售问题未解决，2005年全部出售。

2002年11月，在市政府支持下，县品改站从四川西昌购进怀孕奶牛100头投放永靖镇雨洒建奶牛基地。2004年3月，再次从西昌购进256头怀孕奶牛。2005年5月，县品改站从陕西乾县购进怀孕奶牛108头投放青山苗族乡大林村建奶牛基地。2006年，全县存栏黑白花奶牛1458头，其中能繁母牛716头、后备奶牛192头、育成牛550头；年产牛奶2918吨。2010年，全县有奶牛620头，产牛奶2010吨。雨洒、大林两奶牛基地所产牛奶由贵阳山花公司收购。

三、马、驴、骡

境内马属西南马，体型小而结实，能拉善驮。主要分布在交通不便的山区，多用于驮煤、粮食或肥料。1991年，全县有马6546匹。随着县内公路建设加快，村村通公路，马匹作用降低，饲养量逐年减少；境内养驴多作种驴用。1991—2001年，饲养量1～5匹。2002年起，已无人饲养；境内养骡多用于驮煤、粮食或肥料，饲养数量减少，2007年尚存28头。2010年，全县有马1487匹，骡1头。

四、羊

1991年，境内饲养主要有麻羊，次为黑山羊及白山羊。是年羊存栏3394只。此后羊存栏量逐年上升，1995年达到1.1万只。其间，1994年，县获小尾寒羊（绵羊）种羊基地建设项目，于1996年2月从镇宁县牲畜良种场引进小尾寒羊16只，其中公羊4只，投放永靖镇坪子上（南山）饲养。因草场刺灌木较多，夏季高温高湿，小尾寒羊难以适应。至10月，死羊6只；产羔羊5只，存活2只。次年将剩余小尾寒羊作肉羊出售。

1996年4月23日，县农业局成立“息烽县隆兴牧业有限责任公司”，各乡镇成立养羊领导小组，县财政借给养羊扶贫贷款30万元发展黑山羊。公司将任务下达给各乡镇畜牧站，采取以物放贷、实行公证办法，从金沙县等地购进种羊1175只，投放给7个乡镇的66户农户饲养。8月，市、县又借给养羊扶贫贷款135万元；公司采取直接借款，派人监督，见羊付款办法，购进种羊3754只，投放127户养殖。至2000年，三年共出栏羊6.5万只。后因周边县养羊兴起，羊价下跌；部分养羊户饲养管理不当，损失较大，加之发展过快，植被破坏严重；公司随之关闭。

2001年，在温泉镇开展用波尔羊冻精改良本地山羊试验。次年产杂交羊108只，后因产羔率太低停止试验。2007年，引进纯种波尔山羊种羊4只，投放给九庄镇新街村养羊大户饲养。2010年，全县存栏山羊1万余只。

五、猫、犬、兔

（一）猫、犬

20世纪90年代初，境内农户养猫为捉老鼠，养犬为看家护院。猫主要以颜色分，麻色猫居多，次为黑猫、花猫、黄猫、白猫。犬亦主要以颜色分，黄色、黑色较多，白色次之；品种有本地狗、下司狗。1991年，全县出售和自宰狗2419只，1992年达2649只。此后因鼠害严重，小商贩所卖鼠药多为毒性强，能引起二次中毒的氟乙酰胺，农民用鼠药毒鼠，继而毒死猫、犬，致使猫、犬数量大减。1994年，出售和自宰狗降至845只，1995年仅164只。在国家研究并推广低毒性新鼠药后，猫、犬数量逐年增多。

1999年，豪杰公司在西山乡建一养狗场，建犬舍260间，养犬最多时有160余只，品种20余个。该场于2001年关闭。此外，县城南门有一人办养狗场，出栏两批，100余只。

（二）兔

2000年，四川人冷定发在养龙司乡王家寨以10余只兔子起家，发展种兔150余只。2003年，县采取“借兔还兔，滚动发展”形式，组织青山苗族乡、小寨坝镇、养龙司乡60余户农户养兔，引进优良肉兔种兔3000只。2007年，市、县投入资金，投放种兔3368只，给养殖小区138户农户饲养。2010年，县内有存栏兔10481只。引进兔种有齐卡肉兔、新西兰兔、加利福尼亚兔、比利时兔、哈白兔。

六、家禽

境内家禽主要有鸡、鸭、鹅。鸡品种较多，除肉鸡、蛋鸡，还饲养过丝毛乌骨鸡、火鸡、斗鸡；鸭主要品种有北京鸭、奥白星肉鸭、火鸭；鹅主要品种有狮头鹅、白鹅。多为引进品种，本地品种极少。其他有野鸡、鸽子、鹌鹑、画眉，亦多为引进品种。全县家禽出栏：1991年14万只，1999年40万只，2005年突破90万只，2010年133万只。

肉鸡：1992年，县畜牧局从惠水县引进贵农黄、罗斯鸡、海赛克斯、衣沙明星和红布洛等肉鸡种蛋进行孵化，提供良种雏鸡1万只。同时试养肉鸡，2个月，平均体重2千克，耗料5千克，料肉比2.5∶1。1994年，推广艾维因、红宝、882、安纳克、罗斯鸡等肉、蛋鸡苗8000只。10月，引进丝毛乌骨鸡100只试养，至年底，成活率70%，体重0.75千克，料肉比4∶1。此后县内养鸡发展较快。2004年，流长乡茶园、大水井、宋家寨、李安寨等8个村发展林下养鸡，与贵阳绿源禽业有限公司签订回收协议，引进铁脚麻鸡、柳州麻花鸡、闽麻鸡，以林下放牧为主，补饲为辅方式，饲养3个月，平均体重2.2千克，料肉比2.75∶1。是年，出栏商品鸡5万只，次年出栏11万只。2008年，推广良种鸡205万只。

蛋鸡：1991年，全县鸡蛋产量319吨。1997年9月，贵阳兰地公司租用县粮食局鸡舍饲养蛋鸡，引进育康8号黄羽蛋鸡雏鸡1万只，次年产蛋134吨。2000年，该公司迁往修文县。2004年3月，石硐乡水头村村民文观仙在外地打工期间学得蛋鸡养殖技术，返乡与其亲戚合伙兴办蛋鸡养殖场，贷款5万元，购进罗曼白蛋鸡1000只试养。至6月，成活率95%，产蛋率90%，试养获得成功。次年，蛋鸡养殖大户发展到7户。2010年，全县鸡蛋产量1583吨。

七、其他动物

（一）蜜蜂

1992年，全县养蜂915箱，产蜜3.9吨。1993年，有蜜蜂1660箱，产蜜7.2吨。2001年、2006年、2010年，分别产蜜1吨、3吨、9.3吨。

（二）野猪

2005年，永靖镇阳朗村柯老五购进4只野猪饲养。2008年，温泉镇尹庵村大槽组龙开峰购进2头野猪（一公一母）进行繁殖，至2010年，野猪增加到100余头，其中种公猪3头、经产母猪30头；出售肥猪5头。

（三）梅花鹿

温泉镇天台村茶园邱代贵在吉林养鹿场打工期间学得梅花鹿养殖技术，于2003年投资8万元引进10只梅花鹿回家饲养，在中国农科院特产研究所技术人员的指导下饲养成功。2007年全部收回成本。2009年，出栏18头，获纯利6万余元。2010年，存栏种鹿1头、母鹿5头、子鹿2头；出售鲜鹿茸2.5千克，兑制鹿血酒5千克。

此外，永靖镇梨安村、青山苗族乡有农民养过菜花蛇。

息烽县1991—2010年畜禽存栏出栏统计表

表9-4-1

年份				1991	1992	1993	1994	1995
畜禽存栏	猪（头）			66135	61063	59346	75362	83697
	其中	能繁母猪		3870	3935	4514	5036	5969
	大牲畜（头、匹）			38490	38701	37654	38488	39965
	其中	牛（头）		31881	32094	31103	31436	32830
		其中	黄牛	12760	12551	12861	12312	12994
			水牛	19099	19516	18223	19106	19828
			奶牛	22	24	19	18	8
		马（匹）		6546	6512	6370	6862	6908
		驴（头）		1	1	6	5	7
		骡（头）		62	94	175	185	220
	羊（只）			3394	4000	5069	8744	11099
	其中	山羊		3394	4000	5069	8744	11099
		绵羊		—	—	—	—	—
	家禽（只）			—	—	184775	—	286523
畜禽出栏	猪出栏（头）			49595	44831	43779	49168	49877
	大牲畜（头、匹）			1054	1452	1673	2904	2099
	其中	牛（头）		824	1002	1119	2517	1788
		其中	黄牛	424	502	615	1486	796
			水牛	400	500	504	1031	992
			奶牛	0	0	0	0	0
		马（匹）		230	450	525	384	311
		骡（头）		0	0	29	3	0
	羊出栏（只）			1530	1343	2016	3161	3625
	禽（只）			142103	179233	134900	153152	156820
	兔（只）			—	199	68	179	237
猪出栏率（%）				75	73.4	73.8	65.2	59.6
牛出栏率（%）				2.6	3.1	3.6	8	5.4
羊出栏率（%）				45.1	33.6	39.8	36.2	32.7

表9-4-1续1

年份				1996	1997	1998	1999	2000
畜禽存栏	猪（头）			88282	95085	98359	105307	110546
	其中	能繁母猪		5108	5208	4640	5977	6713
	大牲畜（头、匹）			43365	46961	47532	48324	47591
	其中	牛（头）		36233	38821	40629	41583	41095
		其中	黄牛	14510	16422	16793	18074	18224
			水牛	21716	22393	23833	23499	22844
			奶牛	7	6	3	10	7
		马（匹）		6907	7894	6664	6484	6238
		驴（头）		1	2	5	11	5
		骡（头）		224	244	234	246	253
	羊（只）			31427	32325	28617	21631	15685
	其中	山羊		31415	32325	28617	21631	15685
		绵羊		12	—	—	—	—
	家禽（只）			282449	269605	425893	470281	449434
畜禽出栏	猪出栏（头）			57928	68426	81509	91130	98809
	大牲畜（头、匹）			1982	2048	2257	2435	2750
	其中	牛（头）		1679	1714	1782	2615	2296
		其中	黄牛	845	807	893	1156	1140
			水牛	834	907	889	1009	1156
			奶牛	—	—	—	—	—
		马（匹）		301	332	456	260	445
		骡（头）		2	2	19	10	9
	羊出栏（只）			13338	16454	17958	17234	14043
	禽（只）			182978	142426	348904	409716	405400
	兔（只）			124	390	412	270	1422
猪出栏率（%）				65.6	72	82.9	86.5	89.4
牛出栏率（%）				4.6	4.4	4.4	6.3	5.6
羊出栏率（%）				42.4	50.9	62.8	79.7	93.1

表9-4-1续2

年份				2001	2002	2003	2004	2005
畜禽存栏	猪（头）			116173	116071	117814	123402	122650
	其中	能繁母猪		6623	6855	9490	9497	10426
	大牲畜（头、匹）			47504	48077	47292	47767	45192
	其中	牛（头）		41863	42382	42870	43559	41427
		其中	黄牛	18179	19055	19908	20689	19307
			水牛	23523	23199	22732	22230	21231
			良种	0	0	120	652	957
			奶牛	161	128	230	640	889
		马（匹）		5422	5396	4231	3494	2780
		驴（头）		5	0	0	0	0
		骡（头）		214	299	71	62	28
	羊（只）			10009	10124	10159	10687	8339
	其中	山羊		10009	10124	10159	10687	8339
	家禽（只）			421368	440713	521066	544722	685887
	其中	鸡		—	—	476950	492971	631472
		鸭		—	—	30099	36740	37767
		鹅		—	—	14017	15011	16648
畜禽出栏	猪出栏（头）			103874	108278	111519	124760	137404
	大牲畜（头、匹）			5293	2493	3923	4708	6147
	其中	牛（头）		3957	2266	2610	4020	5419
		其中	黄牛	1788	1140	1278	1761	2569
			水牛	2169	1126	1332	2158	2783
			奶牛	—	—	—	101	67
		马（匹）		1265	206	1050	688	725
		骡（头）		71	21	263	—	3
	羊出栏（只）			11102	8785	8100	8334	9022
	禽（只）			421368	440713	458294	477164	913018
	兔（只）			1422	—	1726	16194	45901
猪出栏率（%）				89.4	93.3	94.6	101.1	112
牛出栏率（%）				9.5	5.3	6.1	9.2	13
羊出栏率（%）				110.9	86.8	79.7	78	108

表9-4-1续3

年份				2006	2007	2008	2009	2010
畜禽存栏	猪（头）			122592	122683	86287	102300	101100
	其中	能繁母猪		9746	10018	4972	11270	12206
	大牲畜（头、匹）			44343	44164	37159	39210	35591
	其中	牛（头）		40563	41779	33047	37262	34103
		其中	黄牛	18529	19372	14028	34230	31077
			水牛	21443	20600	17481	—	—
			良种	1191	841	910	—	—
			奶牛	591	966	628	687	620
		马（匹）		2591	2357	4084	1944	1487
		驴（头）		0	0	0	0	0
		骡（头）		28	28	28	4	1
	羊（只）			7259	7133	4695	9277	10607
	其中	山羊		7259	7133	4695	9277	10607
	家禽（只）			498819	530851	442501	773073	896761
	其中	鸡		453293	483341	389203	695260	—
		鸭		34734	24455	41041	—	—
		鹅		10792	13055	12257	—	—
	兔（只）			—	—	47474	24391	10481
畜禽出栏	猪出栏（头）			160458	166985	106359	122513	126430
	大牲畜（头、匹）			8113	7836	5311	6083	8041
	其中	牛（头）		8113	7836	4830	5246	7298
		其中	黄牛	3785	3115	2622	—	—
			水牛	3331	4194	2208	—	—
			奶牛	552	46	—	110	—
		马（匹）		465	478	478	837	739
		骡（头）		4	3	3	16	4
	羊出栏（只）			11029	7463	4615	4388	4572
	禽（只）			985516	1051538	708024	1208166	1334904
	兔（只）			66767	74055	74005	44401	40174
猪出栏率（%）				130.9	136.1	123	120	—
牛出栏率（%）				18.9	17.6	15	14	—
羊出栏率（%）				152	105	98	47	—

息烽县1991—2010年肉类、主要畜产品产量统计表

表9-4-2　　　　单位：产量：吨；胴体重：千克/头

年份		1991	1992	1993	1994	1995	1996	1997	1998	1999	2000
肉类总产量（吨）		4656	4529	4254	5030	5080	6564	6791	8932	9969	11020
其中	猪	4281	4051	3811	4422	4555	5786	5968	7821	8823	9946
	牛	96	110	124	236	177	184	173	180	194	238
	羊	28	35	60	74	314	397	390	76	322	200
	马	24	39	42	34	22	21	41	28	20	31
	禽	227	294	217	264	265	221	506	241	606	602
	兔	—	—	—	—	—	—	1	—	1	1
	其他	—	—	—	—	—	—	—	—	3	2
猪胴体重		86	90	87	90	91	100	87	96	89	100
牛胴体重		116	109	111	94	99	109	101	101	90	103
羊胴体重		18	26	30	23	21	24	24	22	19	14
牛奶（吨）		4.2	4.5	3.5	33	28	15	2	2	8	5
蜂蜜（吨）		0.5	0.4	0.7	5	3	6	2	2	3	2
禽蛋（吨）		340	277	318	400	415	493	385	522	681	513
其中	鸡蛋	319	258	271	296	382	304	386	324	—	—
	鸭蛋	17	14	36.6	82	85	66	108	71	—	—
	鹅蛋	3.6	4.5	9.9	22	26	15	28	20	—	—

表9-4-2续1

年份		2001	2002	2003	2004	2005	2006	2007	2008	2009	2010
肉类总产量（吨）		11171	11678	12051	13052	15169	17576	18402	11440	13310	14014
其中	猪	9904	10504	10740	11507	12349	14441	14947	9381	10478	10735
	牛	323	261	398	624	841	1172	1158	630	775	1058
	羊	216	195	141	179	167	213	181	97	93	93
	马	95	11	115	15	61	47	57	0	72	65
	禽	630	683	624	666	1568	1537	1908	1200	1812	1958
	兔	1	—	4	42	134	132	111	54	65	86
	其他	2	24	11	19	49	34	40	78	15	19
猪胴体重		95	97	97	92	90	90	138	88	86	—
牛胴体重		81	115	152	155	155	153	157	130	148	—
羊胴体重		19	22	17	21	19	19	62	21	21	—

续表

年份		2001	2002	2003	2004	2005	2006	2007	2008	2009	2010
牛奶（吨）		—	—	309	1055	1445	2918	3100	3100	2540	2010
蜂蜜（吨）		1	—	2	2	2	3	3	5	7	9.3
禽蛋（吨）		660	—	894	990	1091	1384	1422	950	1623	1716
其中	鸡蛋	—	—	824	895	961	1266	1259	863	1583	—
	鸭蛋	—	—	70	95	130	118	141	79	—	—
	鹅蛋	—	—	—	—	—	—	—	—	—	—

第二节　牧草饲料

一、饲料

青饲料：野生的有各种野菜、野草及树叶。人工栽培的有莲花白、牛皮菜、白菜、莴笋等的下脚叶，红薯藤叶、瓜类藤叶，黑麦草、红三叶、紫花苜蓿等。

粗饲料：多为农副产品，有稻草、谷壳、玉米秆、玉米芯、玉米皮、豆类藤叶等。

精饲料：有玉米、红薯、马铃薯、麦麸、米糠、油粑等，还有酒糟、豆腐渣、豌豆渣、胡豆渣。20世纪90年代中后期，有养殖户从外地购进豆粕、鱼干、鱼粉等。

1991年，县内大部分农户养猪以熟饲料为主，有的在熟饲料中加添加剂；部分农户开始改熟饲为生喂，逐渐使用混合饲料。1992年，部分农户开始用颗粒饲料喂小猪，用浓缩饲料兑熟饲料喂中猪，用熟料喂大猪。至2006年，养猪大户多用生料，一般农户视经济情况，或用熟料，或在熟料中添加浓缩饲料，或阶段性使用生料。

境内养牛，夏秋季节以青草为主，在使役时和严寒天气辅以苞谷。稻草、苞谷秆是牛冬春季节的主要饲草。

为提高秸秆利用率，1993年，推广秸秆氨化技术，1995年，推广秸秆微贮技术和青贮饲料养猪，但农户嫌麻烦，未能继续开展。随着饲养肉牛的兴起，秸秆青贮、氨化技术在养牛大户中得到广泛应用。2010年，县内肉牛、奶牛养殖小区推广秸秆处理技术，利用秸秆3.45万吨。

二、饲料生产销售

1991年6月23日，县畜牧局技术服务部开业，至年底推广鸡混合饲料100多千克，各种添加剂1000多千克；县牲畜良种场产销猪混合饲料40吨。是年，境内有20人推销添加剂、混合饲料。此后猪鸡混合饲料、浓缩饲料、颗粒饲料、添加剂、鱼粉、骨粉在县内销售量逐年增加。1994年，推广仔猪早期断奶补饲技术，使仔猪双月重由不补饲的10千克提高到15～20千克，全年推广仔猪颗粒饲料200吨。

2001年，县内有金鱼浓缩饲料厂产销磷酸氢钙、磷酸二氢钙，流长乡向俊思和巨星饲料厂产销鲤鱼成鱼配合饲料，雨洒奶牛基地办犇鑫浓缩饲料厂和大池饲料厂，产销浓缩饲料。是年，全县推广猪、鸡颗粒饲料825吨、浓缩饲料240吨、饲料添加剂31吨。2003年，犇鑫浓缩饲料厂、大池饲料厂停产，此后其他饲料厂先后关闭。贵阳、遵义、都匀和外省饲料厂生产的饲料大量涌入境内市场，推销人员直接将饲料送到农户家中。至2005年，境内饲料推销人员常年有140余人，销售饲料2000吨，猪鸡饲料、浓缩饲料遍及全县农村。

三、牧草种植

1991年，全县种植牧草64.6亩，主要品种有红三叶、黑麦草、串叶松香草、紫花苜蓿、灰萝卜、燕麦、冬牧。此后虽有种植，但面积增加不多。1998年，引进高蛋白牧草籽粒苋。2002年，推广“紫花苜蓿+玉米+大豆”“多年生黑麦草+经果林”种植模式，试验燕麦与一年生黑麦草混播。是年，全县牧草种植面积增加到2568亩。2004年，引进菊苣、饲用玉米种植。2007年，全县种植牧草1.5万亩，主要分布在奶牛、肉牛、肉兔等26个养殖小区。2010年，县内肉牛、奶牛养殖小区及石漠化治理区域种植牧草1.28万亩。

第三节　养殖小区建设

2001—2002年，养殖小区称项目或基地，2002年开始实施奶牛、肉牛项目，提出“六位一体”（畜、草、果、沼气、水、路），资金捆绑使用，养殖相对集中连片。是年，小寨坝镇王家坪“六位一体”项目，贷款4万元，政府贴息，以物放贷。投放架子牛给农户饲养，育肥后于年底出售。黔西天宝农业发展有限公司与农户签订肉牛养殖合同，饲养84天后，肉牛增重部分，公司按每千克7元回收。全年点上共投放肉牛108头，面上发展肉牛210头。2004年，建成小寨坝镇王家坪、九庄镇和平、西山乡文安3个肉牛基地。

2006年，各级财政共投入建设资金300万元，信贷资金1082万元，贷款贴息资金81万元。对良种、圈舍进行补贴，实行以奖代补制度。农户每购进一头良种奶牛，国家补助1000元，肉兔养殖每户补助一组种兔（10只母兔，2只公兔）。养殖小区新建规范化圈舍4万多平方米，农户传统饲养方式逐步转变成专业化养殖模式。是年，全县有养殖小区37个，其中肉兔22个、二杂母猪7个、野鸡2个、蛋鸡1个、肉牛3个、奶牛2个。引进三联乳业、好一多、美满、康庄等市级龙头企业，带动农户发展奶牛、肉牛、肉鸡、肉兔养殖，培育奇志养殖场、惠农蛋鸡养殖场、合兴兔场等县级龙头企业。养殖农户与企业签订产品回收合同，占养殖小区农户数的55%。至2010年，全县养殖小区发展到47个。

第四节　畜禽疫病防治

一、疫病

2007年4—12月，县兽医防治检疫站（简称兽防站）对全县动物疫病进行普查。县内畜禽有疫病186种及普通病，其中传染病38种、寄生虫病127种（其中多种动物共患病1种）、中毒病21种。传染病中，多种动物共患病3种、猪病14种、牛病4种、羊病3种；禽类共患病1种、鸡病7种、鸭病1种、兔病4种。

人畜共患传染病：炭疽、破伤风、狂犬病、口蹄疫。

猪传染病：猪瘟、猪肺疫、猪丹毒、仔猪副伤寒、仔猪白痢、猪流行性感冒、猪痘、猪流行性腹泻、猪水肿病。经实验室诊断，县内新发猪病有猪蓝耳病、猪细小病毒病、猪圆环病毒病、猪伪狂犬病、猪胸膜肺炎。

牛传染病：牛出败、气肿疽、钩端螺旋体病、结核病。

羊传染病：传染性脓疱口膜炎、角膜结膜炎、胸膜炎。

禽传染病：鸡瘟（鸡新城疫）、鸭瘟、小鹅瘟、禽霍乱、鸡马立克氏病、鸡白痢。

寄生虫病：常见猪蛔虫、牛羊肝片吸虫、前后盘吸虫。

中毒病：常见中毒病，猪11种、牛7种、禽1种。

普通病：常见消化系统疾病。

二、防疫注射

1991年，县内防疫对象主要是“两瘟三病”（猪瘟、鸡新城疫、炭疽病、狂犬病、口蹄疫病），对其他疫病因病设防。实行一年一次（春季）防疫注射。是年，猪瘟防疫注射密度上报为68%。

1993年，猪瘟防疫注射密度降至56%。至8月，境内生猪发病死亡较多，经组织抽查10个乡镇的36个村339个村民组5402户农户，有存栏猪14423头、病猪4668头、死猪2662头，发病率占饲养量的27.3%，死亡率占饲养量的16%。为控制疫情蔓延，全县紧急开展秋季防疫注射。至此，恢复1985年前的一年春秋两季防疫注射。

1994年8月，县政府办公室发出在全县推行畜禽防疫双轨目标管理责任制的通知，明确县、乡镇政府和村民委员会为行政“轨”，负责加强畜禽防疫工作的领导，组织防疫队伍，落实防疫资金，督促收取防疫服务费，兑现奖惩。县、乡镇畜牧业务部门和村防疫员为业务“轨”，负责组织供应防疫药械，检查防疫质量。农户每年交5～6元防疫服务费，村防疫员负责上门为农户所养猪牛进行2次防疫注射。是年秋防，猪瘟防疫密度77.4%，生猪死亡率降至6.7%。

1996年8月，县政府相继印发《息烽县畜禽定点屠宰管理暂行办法》《关于实行畜禽定点屠宰的通告》，通告规定，实行定点屠宰，凡永靖镇城关辖区内单位、个人和屠工、屠商必须到县食品公司定点屠宰场宰杀、加工畜禽。按分散经营原则，凡从事猪肉鲜销的经营单位和个人，应办理“卫生许可证”“兽医卫生合格证”“屠工证”“税务登记证”和“营业执照”，亮证经营。依法进行卫生检疫、检验。

2000年，县农业局制定《息烽县动物疫情报告制度》《息烽县屠宰检疫管理制度》《息烽县动物防疫检疫实验室管理制度》《息烽县动物检疫报告总结制度》《息烽县动物防疫监督证章标志管理制度》。是年，在减轻农民负担工作中，防疫收费被定为农民不合理负担而被取消。至此，由乡镇政府解决部分防疫费用。

2002年4月18日，县农业局印发《息烽县动物及动物产品出入县境检疫换证操作规程（试行）》。6月，县政府办公室转发县农业局《息烽县贯彻执行〈中华人民共和国动物防疫法〉动物产地检疫的实施意见》。2004—2005年，县政府相继出台《息烽县高致病性禽流感控制预案》《息烽县口蹄疫防治应急预案》《息烽县重大动物疫病防控应急预案》《息烽县生猪屠宰市场整治工作方案》。

2005年8月，贵阳乌当区发生禽流感，全市开始禽流感防控工作，至此，禽流感防控工作进入常态化。2007年5月，县政府制定《息烽县高致病性猪蓝耳病防控应急预案》，要求一旦发生疫情，各单位积极行动，各司其职，各负其责，协调配合，齐抓共管，共同抓好重大动物疫病防控工作。

三、疾病治疗

1991年，全县有兽医门诊5个（县级1个，区级4个），由业务技术干部担任，治疗病猪3074头，治愈2794头；治疗牛马376头，治愈351头；治疗犬、猫40只。技术干部使用西兽医诊断技术，中西兽医结合治疗畜病，同时开展剖腹取胎、马的肠吻合、猪的疝气修补等外科手术。至1997年，县乡技术干部因发展工作需要，从事治疗时间逐渐减少，进而不再从事治疗工作，主要负责组织防疫、指导检查、监督管理、实施项目等工作；治疗工作全部由村兽医承担。

四、检疫检验

（一）市场检疫

1991年，全县6个活畜交易市场由县区技术干部和乡兽医共同进行检疫和补打防疫针。规定针头必须煮沸消毒，一户一颗针头。1997年后，技术干部不再参加市场检疫。

（二）肉品检验

1991年，除县食品公司经营的猪肉胴体自检外，县以下食品站肉检工作均由畜牧部门技术干部负责。肉检工作在肉市上进行，经检验合格，在猪肉胴体上加盖圆形合格印章，查出不合格肉胴体，盖高温印章。是年，全县11个肉检点，检出病猪肉胴体131头。

1995年3月，县城肉检点发现一头猪肉尸疑似五号病，追踪至永靖镇个体屠宰场，发现场内16头待宰肥猪中有明显可疑症状，立即采样送省兽防站化验，确诊为五号病后，按规定进行无害化处理，并封闭该屠宰场。此后病猪肉尸上市减少。1996年，县食品公司经营的猪肉由畜牧部门检疫人员驻场进行检疫、检验。1998年5月，启用新的滚筒式肉检验讫印章，可在肉尸背脊皮肤上连续印出检验时间和验讫印章号，更便于消费者识别。

五、兽医卫生监督

定点屠宰：改革开放后，个体屠宰场点增多。1992年，县畜牧局对永靖镇境内的国有、个体生猪菜牛屠宰场点进行调查，11个屠宰场点，除县食品公司屠宰场有20世纪70年代的砖瓦房一间外，个体屠宰场点设施简陋，多为简易工棚，屠宰所需用水不足，无污物处理和排污设施，环境污染严重。政府逐步实行定点屠宰，取缔个体屠宰场点。1996年，根据“集中检疫、统一纳税、分散经营”方针，取缔县城无证经营私人屠坊。畜牧部门检疫人员驻场进行检疫，检验完毕后方准猪肉胴体出场。县内保留县食品公司、黑神庙食品站两家屠宰企业。

卫生监督与监测：卫生监督主要工作有办理屠工兽医卫生证、兽医卫生合格证，检查市场检疫和肉品检验，对市检只检疫收费，不补打防疫针，肉检动刀钩检查少，胴体盖验讫印章数量少或不明显，填写票证不全或不规范等现象提出整改意见。1999年，批评教育违规检疫员，查处违法贩运动物及产品人员26人次，追缴检疫费500余元，责令赔偿货主损失2000元，罚款3040元。处理违法贩运病死猪案一例，焚烧、深埋病死猪7头。2003年，开始奶站监管工作，对奶站生产记录和采样送省检测中心监测。2006年，监测工作进入正常化。主要监测禽流感、鸡新城疫、口蹄疫、结核和布鲁氏杆菌病。2007年5月，配合卫生、工商部门，查处销售未经检疫病死猪肉违法行为6起，强制销毁病猪11头（肉700余斤）。2009—2010年，建立和完善动物疫病可追溯体系。加强屠宰场准入制度，严禁无耳标、无产地检疫证明、证物不符、有病的动物进场屠宰。

第五节　渔　业

一、养殖水域

全县有水域面积3.2万亩，其中可养水面2.52万亩。乌江水库境域内面积2.09万亩。水质良好，适宜渔业养殖。

全县稻田面积7.5万亩，可养殖稻田面积1.5万亩。

水域利用率：1991年2.5%，1996年7.78%，2006年11.7%，2010年22.8%。河流、其他符合渔业养殖的水域均有利用。

二、鱼类养殖

1991年，水产品总产量15吨，鱼类养殖产量5吨，占水产品总产量的31.5%。此后，网箱养鱼发展较快，1999年，水产品总产量1068吨，鱼类养殖产量755吨，占总产量的70.7%，2005年，鱼类养殖产量占水产品总产量的93.2%。2010年，水产品总产量3459吨，鱼类养殖产量3375吨，占水产品总产量的97.5%。

（一）天然养殖

1980年，乌江水库建成蓄水后，主产鱼类有鲤、鲫、鲶、鲂、鳘鲦、马口、草、鲢、鳙等。由于过度捕捞，天然渔业资源逐渐减少。

1997年，流长乡政府与银鱼投资商达成协议，从江苏常州移植1100万枚银鱼卵在库区投放试养成功。1998年1月，投资商与流长、鹿窝两乡签订银鱼养殖和捕捞收购合同。此后又在两乡水域投放银鱼卵。1999年6月下旬开始捕捞，捕捞量31.3万千克。

2003年起，每年2月1日12时至5月31日12时，实施长江禁渔期工作，每年向乌江水库人工投放鱼苗60万尾。

（二）人工养殖

县内淡水鱼养殖主要品种：鲤鱼、草鱼、鲢鱼、鲫鱼、武昌鱼、鳙鱼、云斑鮰、长吻鮠、加州鲈鱼等。特色冷水鱼有大鲵（娃娃鱼）。

主要养殖方式：池塘和山塘水库养殖、网箱养鱼、稻田养鱼、微流水养鱼。

池塘和山塘水库养鱼：主要养殖鲤鱼、草鱼，配养鳙、鲢、鲫等鱼类。以人工种植黑麦草、苏丹草投喂为主，适当投喂米糠、麦麸等饲料。在饮用水源和水质较肥的水库，实行鲤鱼、草鱼配鲢鱼、鳙鱼的养殖模式。1991年，全县山塘水库养殖面积500亩。2010年，养殖面积1625亩，其中池塘466亩、水库830亩。

网箱养鱼：1997年，流长乡党委、政府从四川引进养殖户向俊思，在乌江库区息烽段水域顺江库湾设置网箱64口，计1600平方米，养鱼网箱17口，每平方米产鱼139.9千克。1998—1999年，引进网箱养鱼户12户，带动当地16户农户发展网箱养鱼，新增网箱113口，养鱼网箱达341口。2005年，养鱼网箱增至1022口。2008年，养鱼网箱面积183亩，2010年发展到400多亩。

稻田养鱼：1991年，稻田养鱼1800亩，7月，连日大雨，洪水成灾，几无收获。此后，稻田养鱼面积多年维持在1500亩。2000年，县水产站在西山乡柏香山村进行稻田生态渔业试验示范7户14亩，投放大规格鱼种，饲养5个月，亩产鲜鱼105千克，稻谷512千克。2001年，贵阳市决定在境内建立生态渔业示范区。2002年，全县稻田生态养鱼发展到2957亩。后因投入资金减少和产业结构调整，西山乡生态渔业稻田改种蔬菜。2010年，全县稻田养鱼降至20亩。

特种养殖：县内有人饲养过胡子鲶、罗氏沼虾、克氏螯虾。

2010年，鹿窝乡田坝村村民邓培建在该乡马坉村椅子山利用山洞流水养殖大鲵，从乌当引进大规格大鲵鱼苗70尾饲喂。

（三）种苗生产

1991—1998年，境内无种苗生产。1999年，西山乡小堡村、林丰村分别建鱼苗孵化池孵化鱼苗，是年，自繁鲤鱼苗80万尾。2000年，自繁鱼苗100万尾。此后，小堡村鱼苗孵化池因公路建设被占用，林丰村鱼苗孵化池易遭洪水淹没，停止鱼苗孵化。

第五章　林　业

1991年，全县森林覆盖率24.82%。此后，县内相继实施国家天然林资源保护工程、退耕还林工程、水土保持工程、小流域治理工程、环城林带工程、石漠化治理工程、植被恢复造林工程、薪炭林建设项目等，森林资源得到有效保护，至2010年，森林覆盖率上升到45.83%。

第一节　林业产权制度改革

2008年1月16日，县政府制定《息烽县集体林权制度改革实施方案》，在保持集体林地所有权属于集体的前提下，进一步明确集体林地使用权、林木所有权和经营权，将其落实到户、联户或其他经营主体。通过确权，建立以农村家庭承包经营为主体，多种经营形式并存的林业经营管理体制。对县内尚未落实经营主体的集体商品林、一般公益林、重点公益林及县级以上人民政府规划的集体所有的宜林荒山荒地进行改革。对已明晰使用权和林木所有权、林木使用权的集体林发（换）林权证。是年2月全县开展林权工作，8月完成4.64万宗地、51.48万亩林地勘界确权发证，颁发林权证面积16万亩24986本。全县分山到户率99.48%。为确保林改林权勘界的精度和质量，用GPS采集林权宗地界线数据，Arcpad转绘宗地界线图，ArcpMad绘制宗地矢量图斑，计算宗地面积并打印《林权证》。

第二节　森　林

一、林地面积

1990年，全县有林地面积1.91万公顷，森林覆盖率21.36%。是年，启动长江防护林工程。1995年，全县林业用地面积4.32万公顷，森林覆盖率上升到38.7%。2000年，县内启动天然林资源保护工程。2002年，启动退耕还林工程，林地面积持续增加。2005年，开展森林资源二类调查，查明全县林业用地4.83万公顷，森林覆盖率43.98%。2008年，县内实施石漠化综合治理试点工程。2010年，全县林地面积4.86万公顷，森林覆盖率45.83%。

息烽县1991—2010年森林覆盖率变化情况统计表

表9-5-1

年份	森林覆盖率（%）	年份	森林覆盖率（%）
1991	24.82	2001	41.63
1992	28.26	2002	42.65
1993	31.72	2003	42.95
1994	35.17	2004	43.5
1995	38.7	2005	43.98
1996	39	2006	44.2
1997	39.4	2007	44.7
1998	39.72	2008	45.1
1999	40.03	2009	45.31
2000	40.27	2010	45.83

息烽县2010年林地面积统计表

表9-5-2　单位：公顷

单位	总面积	合计	有林地	灌木林地	未成林地	其他
息烽县	103651	48603.55	36900.26	10502.3	356.77	844.22
永靖镇	15440	6744.44	3636.87	2859.47	7.73	240.37
西山乡	7421	4110.04	3287	805.85	—	17.19
青山苗族乡	5030	2459.22	1878.55	580.67	—	—
石硐乡	11750	4794.37	4419.52	374.85	—	—
九庄镇	11539	4474.56	3557.89	662.33	178.29	76.05
鹿窝乡	9670	4947.24	3921.53	878.43	81.52	65.76
流长乡	10770	4645.63	2728.66	1608.12	74.05	234.8
小寨坝镇	11844	6738.4	6021.44	715.78	—	1.18
养龙司乡	9409	3883.08	3115.18	677.82	15.18	74.9
温泉镇	8740	3883.17	2979.68	849.78	—	53.71
南山林场	2038	1923.4	1353.94	489.2	—	80.26

二、林木蓄积

1991年，全县活立木总蓄积120万立方米，经长江防护林、天然林资源保护、退耕还林等工程建设，至2010年，全县活立木总蓄积241.84万立方米，其中有林地蓄积224.92万立方米、四旁树蓄积16.57万立方米、散生木蓄积3506立方米。

三、重点林区简介

（一）西望山林区

西望山林区位于县城西15千米，地处西山、鹿窝、九庄、小寨坝4个乡镇交界处。林区面积2万余亩，属常绿阔叶混交林，森林覆盖率90%。据查，木本植物种类77科220余种，竹类10余种，珍稀动物10余种，其中被列入国家、省野生植物保护名录的树种有红豆杉、三尖杉、刺楸、鹅掌楸、楠木、山茶花、榉木、杜仲、银鹊树、粗榧、青钱柳等。

（二）天台山林区

天台山林区位于温泉镇境内，面积845亩，是县内植物种群、保护树种和珍稀树种较多的林区，1995年成为贵州林业院校教学基地。林区内有红豆杉、银杏、黄心夜合、榉木、枫香、丝栗等古树群。闽楠、红豆树、白日青、榉木、香果树等被列入国家、省野生植物保护名录。分布有观赏价值较高的樱木石楠、常绿油麻藤、灯台树、枫香、珊瑚朴、乌柿等。

第三节　森林保护

一、林木管护与林政管理

1991年起，县林业部门和各乡镇政府经常组织干部职工及群众学习《中华人民共和国森林法》及《森林法实施条例》等相关法律法规。利用电视、报刊宣传林业法律法规知识，利用赶集天出动宣传车向群众开展宣传活动。举办《中华人民共和国森林法》《森林法实施条例》《防火条例》《退耕还林条例》等培训班；组织县林业行政执法人员参加各级举办的培训班等。县林业部门组织护林人员进行护林，按照省、市下达的森林采伐限额进行操作作业。至1999年，全县共采伐木材86280立方米，占国家下达给息烽县的森林采伐限额13.5万立方米的63.91%。

2000年起，实行聘用常年森林资源护林人员负责林业法律法规宣传、森林病虫害监测防治、森林防火、林木防盗等保护工作。

2003年，县政府出台《息烽县天然林资源保护工程森林管护实施细则》《息烽县预防与扑救森林火灾预案》等文件，明确实施工作办法。

1991—2010年，县内71人先后获得林业行政执法资格。查处乱征滥占林地、乱砍滥伐林木、乱捕滥猎野生动物、乱挖滥采野生植物、森林火灾火警等林业案件1511起，没收盗伐木材1550余立方米，收缴罚没款82.2万元。办理征、占用林地审核审批手续20起，征、占用林地500余亩，收缴森林植被恢复费1400余万元。采伐木材14.33万立方米，占国家下达采伐限额25万立方米的57.32%。

二、森林防火

（一）森林火灾

1991—2010年，县内共发生森林火灾（火警）262起（人为257起，不明原因5起。人为火灾中，生产生活用火82起、上坟烧纸116起、其他59起），过火面积184.92公顷，其中毁林面积72.7公顷，查处256起，处罚77人次，罚款1.36万元。

（二）防范措施

县内采取县政府与乡镇政府，乡镇政府与村支两委，县林业绿化局与乡镇林业站，乡镇林业站与护林员双方签订责任书和管护承包合同、森林防火“包保”责任书的办法，层层落实责任。县政府督查室、县森防办负责督查森林防火工作，在年终目标考核中实行森林防火一票否决制，与政府奖惩挂钩；县林业绿化局制定护林员考核制度，将护林员的报酬与护林效果挂钩。

加强野外火源管理：县林业派出所、森防办、各乡镇林业站工作人员深入林区村寨，协助制订村规民约，规范村民用火行为；每年聘请森林管护人员200人左右，高火险期增加临时护林员300人次，在重点部位严防死守，制止进入林区或在林区边缘用火；各乡镇林业行政执法人员见烟就查，对违规野外用火未引起森林火灾的依法当场处以罚款；重点时段，设立森林防火检查点，全天候派人守护，杜绝火种进山。全县设防火瞭望台4座、防火线500余千米，配备灭火机30台、二号工具3000余把、防火服500套。由县人武部和森防办联合组建森林消防应急分队，扑救森林火灾；重点林区成立由村组干部、护林员组成的森林防火巡查队，负责消除火灾隐患和组织群众扑救火灾。

在防火期内实行全勤上岗，轮流就餐，发挥护林员高山瞭望和地面巡逻作用，对林区进行“全方位、全天候、全时段”监控，及时发现火情，采取应对措施。

三、森林有害生物防治

1991年7月，县森林病虫检疫防治站成立，定编3人。

1992年，九庄镇后陇村50多亩柏木全部出现枯黄干死症状，确诊为云南松毛虫。1999年，温泉天台国有林区一片火烧迹地发生天幕毛虫侵害。2000年，鹿窝乡田坝村马尾松发生松叶蜂虫灾。为防治各类森林病虫害，林业检疫人员定期对全县70余万亩森林进行越冬代调查，并长年监测，有针对性地选择防治方法。

2001年，县内开始对云南松毛虫进行工程防治。

2004年，全县开始对松材线虫病进行工程治理。此后每年春秋两次对全县松林进行全面普查、监测，预测预报，对不明原因枯死松树，取样镜检，在枯死松树发生较多的地块采取喷洒白僵菌、施放肿腿蜂、悬挂天牛诱捕器、设置诱木等措施进行综合防治，清除枯死松，以防止病虫害的发生。

2006年，南山林场坪天坝工区发生松赤枯病和松赤落叶病，县林业检疫部门利用烟剂和人工清除措施综合防治，防治率80%以上。

2009年，永靖镇团元山和南山林场坪天坝工区发生松赤枯病和松赤落叶病，县林业检疫部门利用烟剂和人工清除措施进行综合防治，防治率75%左右。

2010年，西山乡团元山片区、小寨坝镇王家坪村、九庄镇大槽村等部分地块发生银杏大蚕蛾重点危害，用化学药物进行防治，防治率85%以上。

第四节　植树造林

一、采种育苗

县内林木种子大都来自外地，本地自采种数量很少。本地树种主要有马尾松、杉木、柏木、泡桐、香椿、女贞、香樟、玉兰、桂花、白杨、银杏、楸树、柑橘、核桃、桃子、李子、梨子、板栗等。引进树种有柳杉、杂交杨、滇柏、刺槐、喜树、黑松、华山松、水杉、雪松、大枣等。

种苗培育：1991—2000年为计划育苗，县级林业部门根据上级下达的育苗计划，分配到各乡镇林业站、林场或苗圃场，按计划生产，然后由县林业部门统一安排，定价销售。1996年6月，县绿野林业资源开发有限责任公司成立，负责苗木采种、购销。2001年后，苗木生产市场化，县林业部门对采种育苗工作不作具体安排，只提指导性意见，供求情况及价格由市场决定。

2003年9月，县林木种苗站成立，负责林木种苗的生产、管理、技术指导、质量监督、良种选育及开发、推广等工作。是年，县内林业种苗生产经营开始实行《林木种子生产经营许可证》管理，至2010年，登记注册苗木公司12家，大型的有县梨杨富果苗场、县三木雨段苗圃场；育苗面积352.5公顷，育苗数量8500万株；育苗树种主要有核桃、桃、李、梨、柳杉、柏木、华山松、杉木、香樟、紫薇、女贞等。育苗方式主要有播种育苗、容器育苗和扦插育苗。

二、造林模式

（一）工程造林

长江中上游防护林工程：1991—2002年，全县造林面积2.89万公顷，工程总投资944.6万元，其中国家投资382万元，省、市、县配套投资203.7万元，群众投资358.9万元，群众投工投劳140.4万个。

天然林资源保护工程：2000—2010年，人工造林2166.67公顷，累计投资1538.9万元，其中中央投资1862.6万元，地方投资113.3万元。

退耕还林工程：2002年起，对坡度大于25度的坡耕地，动员农民退耕还林，还牧还草。至2007年，共退耕还林人工造林5220公顷（其中荒山造林2466.67公顷）。国家对退耕还林农户进行生活补助：退耕还林后，生态林前8年每年每亩补助原粮300斤，按0.7元/斤折价，每亩补助农民现金210元，每亩困难补助20元；后8年粮食补助减半，每年每亩补助农民折价现金105元，每亩20元困难补助不变。经济林补助标准与生态林相同，仅时间为前5年和后5年。至2010年，项目总投资2.45亿元，其中退耕地粮食补助1.93亿元、种苗费369.43万元、粮食调运费2575.25万元、退耕困难补助2452.62万元、封山育林投资154万元。封山育林始于2007年，至2010年，封山育林933.33公顷。

公益林建设项目：公益林是以提供森林生态和社会服务产品为主要经营目的的重点防护林和特种用途林。2007年，开始实行森林分类经营，将森林面积区划为公益林、商品林两大类。全县公益林面积4.5万公顷，其中国家级公益林2.15万公顷（其中集体2.11万公顷、国有493公顷）、地方公益林2.34万公顷（其中集体2.2万公顷、国有1440公顷）。

国家级公益林由中央财政拨款兑现生态效益补偿基金给林权所有者，每年每亩10元（其中9.75元给林权所有者，0.25元为公共管护支出）；地方公益林由省、市、县三级财政负责补偿基金，比例为省40%，市、县各30%，每年每亩5元。

息烽县2007年公益林面积统计表

表9-5-3　　单位：公顷

单位	合计	国家级公益林	地方公益林
全县	44986.67	21546.67	23440
永靖镇	5808	2348.8	3459.2
西山乡	3057.58	2085.6	971.98
青山苗族乡	2044.34	161.02	1883.32
石硐乡	4709.52	782.19	3927.33

续表

单位	合计	国家级公益林	地方公益林
九庄镇	4981.31	3043.78	1937.53
鹿窝乡	4253.85	2497.97	1755.88
流长乡	4653.3	2846.61	1806.69
小寨坝镇	5581.03	1701.63	3879.4
养龙司乡	4037.4	2425.4	1612
温泉镇	3927.02	3160.35	766.67
南山林场（含国有林）	1933.33	493.33	1440

中德财政合作项目：项目理念为森林可持续经营。德国政府确定450万欧元赠款（折合人民币3843.58万元）；项目总投资1732.07万元，每年由县财政匹配49.6万元上交省项目办，占总资金的17.4%。

2007年6月29日，在贵州省林业厅与德国复兴银行签订的会谈纪要基础上，财政部代表中国政府与德国复兴银行签订财政协议。

项目在县内计划涉及116个村民组，计划实施7000公顷。2008年11月至2009年6月准备；2009年7月至2010年6月试行；2010年7月至2015年12月实施。

石质荒漠化（简称石漠化）综合治理工程：2008年启动，至2010年，建成林草植被3763.67公顷，其中人工造林2166.8公顷（其中经济林1252.87公顷）、封山育林1596.87公顷。工程总投资2729.46万元，其中中央资金2400万元、地方配套资金240万元、地方自筹及群众投工投劳折资89.46万元。

（二）其他工程项目

经济林建设项目：1991—2010年，建成经济林6368.9公顷，主要树种有核桃、梨、李、桃、葡萄、板栗等。其中2005—2010年核桃造林3520公顷。经费为整合农业、水利、林业、扶贫等部门项目资金。

薪炭林建设项目：2001年，实施中央专项投资建设项目，项目期一年。总投资100万元，完成薪炭林人工造林333.33公顷。

植被恢复费造林工程：2005—2010年，全县共恢复森林植被人工造林1025.2公顷、封山育林1166.67公顷。在人工造林中，经济林327.67公顷、防护林（用材林）697.53公顷。工程造林资金来源于征、占用林地收取的植被恢复费，总投资759.2万元。

贵阳市第二环城林带公益林建设工程：2005年，贵阳市第二环城林带公益林建设项目息烽境内面积849.53公顷（其中经济林106.13公顷），苗木补植补造、抚育工作全部结束，实现主要通道沿线快速绿化目的。总投资2200万元，其中县级投资182.4万元。

（三）社会造林

1991年起，县内各单位除参加每年植树节由政府统一发动的义务植树造林活动外，在各单位办公楼及居民区采用栽植大苗的方式植树。县教育系统每年组织学生到指定地点或校园开展义务植树；县水电、交通、城建、环保、林业、人武部、妇联、团委等部门对县城周边、主要公路沿线的荒山荒地，县城公共场所、街道，息烽集中营革命历史纪念馆等进行绿化。至2010年，全县义务植树60万人次，植树460万株。

县农业发展办公室、农业局、水利局、金秋公司、广惠公司、中天公司等部门（单位），先后参与到县林业建设中，形成全社会办林业的局面。以经果林为主，有石榴、猕猴桃、杨梅、金秋梨、板栗、布朗李、核桃、凯特杏、葡萄等10多个品种。至2010年，全县利用农发、水保、扶贫项目等资金造林3200公顷，其中经济林2080公顷。

集体和个体造林先后出现胡学文、雷和毅、王雪金等造林大户和造林专业户，造林866.5公顷，其中经济林52.93公顷。

1991—2010年，全县造林6.33万公顷，以工程造林为主，义务植树为辅，另有少量部门造林、集体造林和个体造林。

第五节　林　场

一、国有林场

南山林场是县内唯一的国有林场，始建于1958年8月。1991年更名为贵州省息烽县南山林场。林场由南向北依次划分为苗圃、场部、二坝田、老安寨、坪天坝、金鸡坪六个工区，总面积2026.07公顷，其中有林地面积827.07公顷、灌木林地面积823.93公顷、疏林地276.53公顷、新造林未成林地96.13公顷，活立木总蓄积量57507立方米。

1986年，经省政府批准，南山林场转为经营性林场。1998年，国家天然林资源保护工程启动后，全县停止木材商品性采伐，林场从采伐木材为主转向以保护森林资源为主。

2010年，林场经营总面积29397亩，其中有林地面积19750亩、灌木林7568亩、疏林地120亩、未成林造林地49亩、宜林地786亩，林地活立木总蓄积83550立方米，其中以人工林为主，森林覆盖率93.3%。

二、集体林场与个体林场

1990年，部分乡村林场实行林业生产承包责任制，将集体林划分到户，由户经营。1991年全县有个体林场6个，经营总面积320公顷。1995年后，林场名存实亡。2010年全县有个体林场5个，经营总面积220公顷。主要树种有杉树、马尾松、柳杉等。

第六节　林产品经营管理

1991年，县林业部门按照《贵州省木材市场管理暂行办法》等法规规定，对县内木材流通方面的非法贩运、非法交易木材进行清理整顿。在工商、公安部门配合下，检查永靖镇、九庄镇、小寨坝镇三个木材市场，坚持查处非法贩运木材行为，堵截木材非法流通，取缔非法营销。至2010年，县内先后引进和新扩建木材经营加工企业37家，每年利用森林采伐木材8000余立方米，加工成农具、家具、办公用品、门窗门合等产品出售；同时引进精细加工企业，对全县小规格材和边角废料进行再加工利用。

第六章　水　利

1991—2010年，县内新建鱼筒河中型水库1座、上沟小（一）型水库1座和3座小（二）型水库。对21座小（二）型水库进行险病处理。新建、整修山塘170处，修建小水池12047口、水窖6291个；配套改造防渗渠道219.44千米。新建、改建电灌站38座。全县有效灌溉面积13.26万亩，比1990年增加117%。修建11个标准水厂、564处农村人畜饮水工程，全县城乡居民生活用水条件有较大改善。

第一节　水利工程

一、蓄水工程

1991年，县内有水库26座，其中险病水库24座；水库总库容1198.5万立方米，兴利库容946.41万立方米。有山塘198口。小水窖总容积7.48万立方米。

息烽县1991年水库统计表

表9-6-1

水库名	库址	库型	坝型	坝高（米）	建竣工时间	总库容（万立方米）	兴利库容（万立方米）	设计灌面（亩）
洪马	永靖镇	小（一）型	砌石拱坝	33	1958—1970年	313	278	8500
小桥河	青山苗族乡	小（一）型	土石坝	46.2	1973—1981年	382	310	7800
麻林	养龙司乡	小（二）型	土坝	7	1955—1958年	14.4	11.7	850
落凼	流长乡	小（二）型	土坝	11	1956—1981年	14.4	9.6	350
长冲沟	小寨坝镇	小（二）型	土坝	6	1956—1957年	10.7	8.7	400
高安所	石硐乡	小（二）型	土坝	15	1957—1959年	48	38.3	1200
何家沟	永靖镇	小（二）型	土坝	11	1957—1967年	13.2	—	500
深冲	青山苗族乡	小（二）型	土坝	13	1957—1958年 1965—1966年	11	10	500
老厂	永靖镇	小（二）型	土坝	4	1957—1958年	10	—	300
烂泥沟	流长乡	小（二）型	土坝	3.3	1957—1976年	10	—	300
盘龙山	九庄镇	小（二）型	土坝	12.9	1958—1960年	47.3	—	1000
钟家山	养龙司乡	小（二）型	土坝	1957年动工，3次续建未竣工，总库容7.2万立方米				
锅圈岩	石硐乡	小（二）型	土坝	14.4	1975—1978年	26.4	20.3	1100
擦耳岩	养龙司乡	小（二）型	拱坝	14.1	1975—1985年	12	—	650
烂田沟	九庄镇	小（二）型	土石坝	27	1976—1978年	90	—	1200

续表

水库名	库址	库型	坝型	坝高（米）	建竣工时间	总库容（万立方米）	兴利库容（万立方米）	设计灌面（亩）
猪嘴田	永靖镇	小（二）型	土坝	12.3	1976年	16.4	11.8	400
犀牛洞	石硐乡	小（二）型	土坝	10	1976—1978年	13	10.8	—
水沟	石硐乡	小（二）型	土坝	14	1977—1982年	13.6	—	450
碾子沟	九庄镇	小（二）型	土坝	18.5	1977—1985年	20.4	16.4	750
马换塘	九庄镇	小（二）型	浆砌块石	11.6	1977—1985年	12.9	—	350
大水井	流长乡	小（二）型	土坝	12	1977—1984年	12	8.9	350
火子冲	石硐乡	小（二）型	土石坝	13	1977—1978年	10	—	250
堰地	鹿窝乡	小（二）型	土坝	12.4	1977—1981年	10	8.4	250
金家厂	永靖镇	小（二）型	土坝	7	1978—1980年	15.3	10.9	—
上寨	石硐乡	小（二）型	土坝	10	1978—1979年	10.9	7.8	300
水头	石硐乡	小（二）型	土坝	10.5	1977—1980年	11.84	—	350

（一）新建水库

鱼简河水库：是县内集排洪、灌溉、供水为一体的中型水库，位于息烽河支流上游，由水库大坝枢纽、渠系灌溉和阳朗排洪工程（排涝面积2000亩）三部分组成。设计洪水标准为50年一遇，校核洪水标准为500年一遇。坝址坐落在西山乡小堡村桐子坝村民组手爬岩处，距县城约14千米。大坝为砼双曲拱坝，最大坝高81米。总库容1050万立方米，兴利库容758万立方米。设计灌溉面积2.64万亩（其中田2.24万亩、水浇地0.4万亩）；向小寨坝磷铵基地和沿途供水365万立方米/年。总投资15619万元。

2002年10月30日，鱼简河水利工程奠基开工。2005年3月27日，大坝砼浇筑完成；4月7日，溢洪道、交通桥贯通。2004年1月，阳朗排洪隧洞工程开工建设。11月，阳朗2号排洪隧洞贯通。年底，1号隧洞打通。2005年8月12日，鱼简河水库主体工程全面完工。

上沟水库：位于小寨坝镇田兴村红岩沟，由大坝枢纽和输水管道工程组成。设计洪水标准为30年一遇，校核洪水标准为200年一遇。大坝为砼拱坝，最大坝高39.2米。水库总库容162万立方米，兴利库容121万立方米，为小（一）型水库，输水管道长10.28千米，年供水能力210万立方米，是向西洋肥业有限公司供水的水源工程。总投资3331.4万元，其中水库2401万元、输水管道930.4万元，资金靠自筹及银行贷款。管道工程自2000年11月5日开工，2001年7月16日完成。大坝于2001年11月23日动工，2004年4月取水口闸门安装完毕，即投入试运行。

马家箐水库：位于石硐乡中坝村马家箐村民组，坝址在九庄河上游马家箐小溪上。为续建工程。20世纪70年代由石硐公社组织农民投工投料兴建，坝基按小（二）型水库规模修建；设计大坝为风化料土石坝，灌溉面积240亩，日供水800立方米。土地下户后停建，大坝建成高度约7米，形成小山塘，库容约2.5万立方米，供马家箐下游40亩农田用水。

2008年1月，贵阳市批复为小（二）型水库，大坝为黏土心墙土石坝型，最大坝高7.5米；总库容

19.2万立方米，兴利库容10.5万立方米。设计洪水20年一遇，校核洪水200年一遇。2009年1月开工，2010年2月完成。马家箐水库供水工程为2007年国家开发银行贷款建设项目，总投资737.87万元。

板厂水库：位于永靖镇联丰村板厂村民组，为小（二）型蓄水灌溉工程，洪水标准按20年一遇设计，200年一遇校核。设计大坝为黏土心墙土坝，最大坝高20.35米（地面以上12.35米）。上游坝面采用干砌块石护坡，下游坝面草皮护坡。背坡中部设一马道，宽1.5米。水库总库容65.23万立方米，其中兴利库容40.63万立方米。设计灌溉田1021亩、旱地600亩，供500多人饮用。一期工程于2001年4月动工，2002年6月完成。二期工程于2002年4月动工，12月因水库淹没赔偿矛盾，受淹农户阻止而停工。只能灌溉下游贵定县——宝莲寺110亩农田。

烂田湾水库：位于温泉镇高潮村烂田湾村民组。大坝坐落在小冲沟上部，为蓄水提灌工程。设计新建土坝1座，坝高10.4米，总库容12.3万立方米，兴利库容10万立方米。新建电灌站1座，扬程80.6米。建渠道3条，长2450米。工程总投资51.25万元，其中以工代赈资金45万元，群众自筹6.25万元（含投工投劳）。灌溉烂田湾等3个村民组470亩农田，其中新增稻田376亩。

2000年8月24日，施工队伍进场，2001年1月13日完工。因工程淹没占地问题未调解清楚，受淹户不准蓄水，故工程未进行竣工验收。提灌站无水可抽，仍只自流灌溉30亩。

（二）险病水库治理

1991—2010年，对小桥河、洪马等2座小（一）型水库和猪嘴田、金家厂、何家沟、深冲、锅圈岩、高安所、犀牛洞、上寨、碾子沟、烂田湾、长冲沟、堰地、落凼、烂泥沟、麻林、钟家山、大水井、水头、火子冲、水沟、盘龙山等21座小（二）型水库进行险病处理。

小桥河水库：1989年，大坝背水坡脚涌出浑水，迎水坡左坝肩出现塌洞。经省、地、县水电部门专家现场鉴定后，定为危险水库。因工程所辖渠道均未防渗，渗漏严重，灌面逐年下降至1010亩。1991年，大坝采用帷幕灌浆防渗，放水隧洞灌浆、水泥砂浆抹面。渠道防渗和电灌站设备更新后，使灌区灌面恢复到2985亩。总投资460万元。1997年，为解决小寨坝镇所在地和磷化工基地2万人的生活用水，增加渠道防渗5.03千米，增建水池，输水管道14.86千米，次年7月正式供水。总投资420万元。

洪马水库：1982年“三查三定”，洪马水库渠系水利用系数仅0.16，水量浪费大，造成水库建成后出现两次干涸、灌区边缘常出现因干旱减产局面。1994年8月，开始渠道防渗改造配套工程，1997年6月完工，经改造防渗干渠，修建隧洞、渡槽，新建梦圆水厂，铺设供水管道后，设计灌溉面积增至8693亩，并成为向县城供水主要水源，日供水5000吨。

1991—2010年，采用水利资金补助和群众集资投劳方式新建山塘9口，总库容8.17万立方米，配套防渗渠道3.01千米，新增灌溉面积324亩；整形改造山塘161口，总库容138.44万立方米，配套防渗渠道62.76千米，恢复灌溉面积5747.7亩。新建、整修山塘170处，总库容135.8万立方米。

（三）整修小水池

县内小水窖建设始于1987年冬，小寨坝镇修建蓄水量约6立方米的圆柱形水窖为试点，建成小水窖32个。1988年，省水电厅将息烽县列入小水窖建设重点县，每个小水窖补助30元。县采取定额补助水泥、砂子，提供模型和技术指导，群众投工投劳和补充材料不足部分。1990年，全县遭遇大旱，小水窖发挥抗旱保苗、牲畜饮水作用，也暴露出蓄水量小、取水不便等弱点。故从当年冬季起以修建水池为主。1991—2010年，全县建成水池12047口、水窖6291个，总容积72.21万立方米，配套改造防渗渠道219.44千米。1998—2000年，市政府每年专项拨款200万元，支持县内水池建设。

二、引水工程

1991年起，县内开始对引水工程进行改造防渗，至2010年，全县改造防渗引水工程122处，新建1处，恢复灌溉面积20121亩，新增灌溉面积814亩。其间，1992年，对大龙滩渠道进行改造防渗，1993年6月完工，新增灌溉面积814亩，改善灌溉面积315亩；解决300人的饮水困难。1996年12月动工修复鹿窝乡老窝寨渠道，加固水毁拦河坝和新建渡槽。1997年3月完工，恢复灌溉面积650亩。2000年，对底寨河渠道进行改造防渗，至2002年，改造干渠36.5千米。恢复灌溉面积4550亩。2005年7月，新修张家沟引水工程，开挖4条隧洞共2980米，安装引水管道1条1262米，铸铁倒虹管1条470米，修建渠道2条共1420米，总投资520万元。年引水量200万立方米，用于补充上沟水库，为温泉镇尹庵片区工业及城镇提供用水。2008年8月完工。

三、提水工程

1991—2010年，全县新建4座小（二）型和3座小（二）型以下电力提灌工程，电机总容量488千瓦，设计新增灌溉面积1885.2亩。同时对38座电灌站进行设备更新和泵房改造，更新电机总容量223千瓦，涉及渠道32.72千米，恢复灌溉面积4231亩。

小南江电灌站：位于乌江水库息烽河左岸流长乡新中村。二级提水，一级为轨道式提水站，扬程100米，配渠道2000米，设计灌溉面积119.2亩。二级站为固定式提水站，扬程78米，修渠道2000米，灌溉152亩，解决485人、186头牲畜饮水。总投资17.85万元。1992年冬至1993年春，建成一级站。2000年1—2月，建成二级站。

街口电灌站：位于鹿窝乡政府所在地的瓮桶河旁，建机房及管理房面积107.3平方米；安装80千伏安变压器1台，水泵配55千瓦电机1套，净扬程88.6米；新建进水池1口，渠道2条0.44千米。总投资18.14万元，灌溉面积230亩。1993年3月动工，当年6月竣工投入使用。

水淹凼电灌站：位于流长乡大水井村中坪村民组，20世纪80年代初，曾用块石、混凝土堵塞最低的两个消水洞，形成蓄水量2万立方米山塘，塘区内无基流，靠拦蓄1.1平方千米集雨面积的洪水。审批总库容3.5万立方米，兴利库容1.6万立方米，灌溉面积386亩。工程总投资27.93万元。1993年11月动工，1994年6月投入使用。提水扬程66.8米。

荆江电灌站：位于乌江水库息烽河右岸养龙司乡荆江村，规模为二级提水，一级站扬程80米、二级站扬程122.5米。灌溉面积857亩，总投资63.5万元。2000年12月动工，2001年4月完工。

息烽县1991—2010年水利设施及灌溉面积统计表

表9-6-2

年份	工程设施（处）	总库容（万立方米）	引水流量（立方米/秒）	装机容量（千瓦）	有效灌溉面积（万亩）	保证灌溉面积（万亩）	建设经费（万元）	累计建设经费（万元）
1991	627	1398	3.51	2528	6.42	4.84	216.27	2105.95
1992	622	1403	3.51	2528	6.28	5.21	50.46	2156.4
1993	623	1406	3.51	2785	6.42	5.28	92.43	2248.84
1994	624	1407.5	3.51	2875	6.55	5.31	187.33	2436.17
1995	624	1407.5	3.51	2875	6.63	5.02	124.5	2560.67

续表

年份	工程设施（处）	总库容（万立方米）	引水流量（立方米/秒）	装机容量（千瓦）	有效灌溉面积（万亩）	保证灌溉面积（万亩）	建设经费（万元）	累计建设经费（万元）
1996	624	1407.5	3.51	2875	6.67	5.29	339.63	2900.3
1997	624	1407.5	3.51	2875	6.79	5.12	714.95	3615.25
1998	624	1407.5	3.51	2875	7.25	5.61	639.5	4254.75
1999	624	1407.5	3.51	2897	7.54	5.94	669.2	4923.95
2000	625	1445.7	3.51	2952	7.83	6.17	704.01	5627.96
2001	627	1518.56	3.51	3119	8.07	6.44	948.72	6576.68
2002	627	1552.24	3.51	3119	8.29	6.63	1840.4	8417.08
2003	627	1547.54	3.51	3174	8.47	6.78	1376.3	9793.38
2004	628	1722.79	3.51	3192.5	8.79	7.07	4868.7	14662.08
2005	628	1741.49	3.51	3192.5	8.93	7.25	1818.37	16480.45
2006	629	1742	3.53	2868	9.14	6.1	580	17060.45
2007	629	1787.67	3.53	2868	10.33	6.39	1420.39	18480.84
2008	630	1686	3.53	2870	11.48	7.62	2779.47	21260.31
2009	643	2754	3.53	2870	12.68	7.74	1234.84	22495.15
2010	644	2779	3.53	2870	13.26	8.24	1555.72	24050.87

说明：本表中总库容包括水池容积

四、饮水工程

（一）水厂

1991—2010年，全县修建标准水厂12个，设计供水能力2.77万吨/日，受益人口18.27万人。总投资3788.24万元。

永靖水厂：位于永靖镇下阳朗村长岭岗，距县城6.5千米。以下洪马水库为水源。2001年5月动工，2002年9月25日完工。水厂生产能力1.5万吨/日，并改造配水管网，新建辅助用房556平方米。清水池出水口高程1143米；钢筋砼结构工艺流程，二氧化氯消毒。改建下洪马水库至龙滩河隧洞进口610米明渠为封闭式箱形渠道，新建塑料输水管道1200米，输水能力1.5万吨/日；清水池至茂安加油站铸铁配水管3300米。工程总投资1239.92万元。

西山水厂：位于西山乡猪场村山背田（小桥河水库管理所院内）。为解决小寨坝镇政府所在地和磷化工基地生活用水，1997年1月，小寨坝镇投资420万元，以小桥河水库为水源，将水库至山背田5.03千米渠道加盖封闭，利用小桥河水管所院内水池调节，从山背田铺设管道14.86千米，利用重力将水输送到小寨坝镇马鞍山高位水池，1998年6月，正式向小寨坝镇政府所在地供水。后因管道经过西山乡底寨、金竹坪工业小区，但不向这两地供水，故而发生群众封堵输水管道纠纷。县水电局拟定山背田建水厂，同时向西山乡3个村和小寨坝镇供水方案。工程于2002年10月开工，2003年3月完工。新建穿孔旋流反应斜管沉淀池2座，重力式无阀滤池2座；改建清水池3口共900立方米；新修管理房39.2平方米，投药消毒间76.6平方米；维修办公楼514.4平方米，库房200平方米；安装投药装置1套，并对厂区进行绿化；铺设配水管网约44千米。水厂日供水5100吨，解决5.5万人饮水。工程总投资290.38万元。

息烽县1991—2010年新建水厂统计表

表9-6-3

水厂名	厂址/水源	动、竣工时间	投资（万元）	性质	供水规模
永靖水厂	永靖镇下阳朗村/长岭岗洪马水库	2001年5月—2002年9月	1239.9	国内银行贷款	1.5万吨/日县城
龙洞水厂	九庄镇桐梓村/泉水	2002年8月—2003年1月	253.3	世行、国行贷款各50%	800吨/日1.25万人
高坎子水厂	养龙司乡堡子村高坎子/地下水	2002年9月—2003年3月	253.8	世行、国行贷款各50%	1100吨/日1.2万人
小寨坝镇饮水工程	西山乡猪场村山背田/小桥河水库	1997年—1998年6月	420	农业开发银行	小寨坝镇、西山乡
西山水厂	（扩建）	2002年10月—2003年3月	290.38	世行、国行贷款各50%	5100吨/日5.5万人
流长水厂	流长乡长涌村马鞍山/泉水	2003年12月—2004年4月	185	世行、国行贷款各50%	400吨/日0.69万人
温泉水厂	温泉镇天台村/上沟水库	2004年5月—2004年10月	298.46	世行、国行贷款各50%	1000吨/日1万人
石硐水厂	石硐乡石硐街/马家箐水库	2004年3月—2004年8月	231.12	世行、国行贷款各50%	500吨/日0.6万人
彭家垭口水厂	永靖镇雨洒村彭家垭口/泉水	2003年12月—2004年4月	427.13	世行、国行贷款各50%	1300吨/日1.8万人
唐家湾水厂	永靖镇硬寨唐家湾后山/泉水	2004年2月—2004年6月	172.35	世行、国行贷款各50%	400吨/日0.39万人
何家硐水厂	石硐乡何家硐	2005年11月—2008年12月	73.8	世行、国行贷款各50%	800吨/日1395人
鹿窝水厂	鹿窝乡政府后面	2005年11月—2008年	43	省水利厅补助	1320人、1033头牲畜

（二）农村人畜饮水工程

县内农村人口居住分散，饮水困难面大，水源和经济条件不尽相同。1991—2010年，县利用国家水利专项资金、移民开发资金、扶贫友好赞助、群众集资投劳等方式筹措资金，以蓄水重力供水、蓄提结合供水等建设方案，建成564处农村人畜饮水工程，解决农村18万余人和11万头牲畜的饮水问题。

第二节　水政·水资源管理

一、管理体制

1997年，息烽县被列为贵州省第四批水土保持监督执法试点县。1998年6月15日，成立县水土保持监督执法领导小组。19日，印发《关于征收水土流失防治费的通知》《息烽县水土保持暂行规定》《关于实行水土保持方案许可制度的通知》《息烽县水土保持方案审批管理办法（试行）》《息烽县水土保持监督员　水土保持管护员管理办法》。

2002年3月6日，设立水政监察大队，利用每年3月22日“世界水日”和3月22—28日“中国水周”，在全县10个乡镇政府所在地和集市，宣传水利法律法规和政策。

二、水费征收

（一）农业灌溉水费

2002年以前，全县水利工程灌溉水费按照《息烽县水利工程管理试行办法》，自流灌溉每亩收大米6.5千克，扬程在50米以下，每亩收大米3.3千克；扬程在50米以上，每亩收大米2.3千克标准，交粮或按市场粮价折合现金随粮计征。

2003年6月，根据《贵州省水利工程供水价格核定及水费计收管理办法》及《实施细则》，县核定下洪马等四个小（一）型水利工程农灌水费价格统一为25元/亩·年。农业灌溉用水亩·年成本：下洪马、小桥河水库45元，底寨河40元，养龙司电灌站35元。三年逐步调整到成本价。受农业产业结构调整影响，国营灌区的农灌面积逐年缩小，农灌用水量逐年减少。至2010年，下洪马水库、小桥河水库、养龙司电灌站分别收到水费7969元、2529元、3849元。

（二）工业水费

县内工业用水多为自备水源供给。小型企业、商业、服务行业用水，靠当地供水单位供给，按方计价。

1992年开始征收水资源费。2006年、2007年、2010年分别征收水资源费10.75万元、20余万元、25.64万元。

（三）生活用水水费

城镇居民生活用水水费由供水单位按照物价部门批准的收费标准收取。农村居民生活用水多由农村人畜饮水工程供给，水费标准未作统一规定，一般只收取管理人员报酬、简单维修费。有的工程未收费。

三、小型水利工程产权制度改革

小型水利工程产权制度改革前，实行分级管理：小（一）型水库由县级管理，小（二）型水库由乡（镇）级管理，山塘由村级管理。

2001年，成立县小型水利工程产权制度改革领导小组。在养龙司乡开展小（二）型以下工程产权制度改革试点，以承包方式发包小（二）型以下工程58处，其中蓄水工程30处、提水工程18处、人畜饮水工程10处。合同规定承包人的权利、责任和义务以及承包人利用所承包工程开展多种经营收入的全部和水费收入的50%归承包人，50%归集体用于工程维修。2002年9月28日，县政府出台《关于对全县小型水利工程进行产权制度改革的实施意见》。

2003年9月5日，全县小型水利工程首次拍卖会在小寨坝镇举行。至2004年，全县小（二）型以下水利工程改制510处，占总处数的90.1%。其中蓄水工程拍卖32处、承包274处、租赁1处、托管1处，共计308处，占蓄水工程总处数的99.4%；引水工程承包153处、托管21处，共计174处，占引水工程228处的76.3%；提水工程拍卖7处、承包20处、托管1处，共计28处，占提水工程28处的100%。拍卖经营的水利工程还有猪嘴田、上寨等2座小（二）型水库。2005年，拍卖长冲沟、水头2处小（二）型水库。此后，小型水利工程未再进行拍卖或承包。

第三节　水土保持

一、水土流失

1991—2010年，全县水土流失面积458.68平方千米，占总面积1036.5平方千米的44.25%，其中轻度流失面积270.13平方千米、中度流失面积142.5平方千米、强烈流失面积22.52平方千米、极强烈流失面积16.2平方千米、剧烈流失面积7.33平方千米。全县每年平均水土流失侵蚀模数1049吨/平方千米。县内造成水土流失的主要因素有自然和人为两种。其间，2005—2010年，征收水土保持补偿费共计47.32万元。

1992年，开始征收水土流失防治费。1998年6月，县政府下发《关于征收水土流失防治费的通知》，对建设和生产活动中造成水土保持设施损坏、水土资源损失的，必须缴纳水土流失防治费。下发《息烽县水土保持暂行规定》，严禁毁林开荒，烧山开荒和在陡坡地铲草皮；严禁乱砍滥伐水土保持林、水源涵养林、防风固沙林等；对水土保持实行监督员制度。

二、水土保持综合治理

1998年11月—2001年，开展永靖镇玄天洞、小寨坝镇王家坪片区小流域水土保持综合治理，治理面积10.69平方千米，遏制水土流失势头。同时，治理阳朗河、头道河、养龙司河、永靖河、九庄河、底寨牛过河、小寨坝磷铵基地厂区排泄沟，小鹿窝河、瓮舍河、水头河坝、管田河、猫场河等部分河段，增大河道行洪能力，避免或减少两岸洪灾损失。

玄天洞小流域综合治理工程：玄天洞小流域内辖永靖镇雨洒村牛洞、上坝、下坝、洒一、洒二5个村民组。该区域土地总面积5813亩（合3.79平方千米），群众陡坡开荒种植，通过扩大种植面积增加总产出。小流域内水土流失面积4112亩，占土地总面积的70.74%，年均侵蚀模数4364吨/平方千米，年流失土壤总量1.2万吨。治理工程从1998年11月至次年春，完成坡改梯治理600亩，营造经果林200亩、水土保持林500亩，封禁治理3303亩，保土耕作1110亩，建渠道465米，修水池10口，铺设人饮供水管3406米，建谷坊5座，立宣传标志碑4块。工程投资120.2万元，其中中央补助25万元、中央借贷50万元、县自筹45.2万元。

王家坪水土保持综合治理工程：涉及小寨坝镇前进、大湾、王家坪3个村，土地总面积9.23平方千米。2000年，工程计划总投资75万元，其中中央财政专项资金50万元、地市配套资金8万元、县级资金17万元。建设规模：坡改梯治理1264亩，营造经果林130亩、水保林5353亩，封禁治理2703亩，封山育草483亩，保土耕作3911亩。修建拦山沟200米、蓄水池8口（容积646立方米）、沉沙凼8口（容积8立方米）、谷坊5座；建立封山育林标志碑6块。工程于2001年1月中旬动工，3月底完成。

第四节　防汛抗旱

1995年以前，县内防汛抗旱工作由每年一届的县防汛抗旱指挥部领导，各有关职能部门具体负责，组织灾区干部、群众实施。

1996年4月，县防汛抗旱指挥部更名为县政府防汛抗旱指挥部，制定《息烽县防汛抗旱预案》，以各小（一）型以上水利工程、各乡镇为单位制定防洪抢险预案。县以武警消防支队、民兵预备役人员组成抢险应急队伍；各乡镇以基干民兵为主组成抢险应急分队。小（二）型以上水库实行行政首长和技术人员包库责任制。并将防汛抗旱工作纳入目标考核；同年7月，在县水利局设置县政府防汛抗旱办公室，负责全县防汛抗旱日常工作。各乡镇成立防汛抗旱领导小组，负责各乡镇防汛抗旱工作。县防汛抗旱办公室组建抗旱服务队，配备队员5人，购置抗旱机具、设备，拥有专用车辆。

第七章　扶贫攻坚

1994年，息烽县被列入国定贫困县后，中央、省、市分别指派单位对息烽从人、财、物各个方面实行对口、定点、结对帮扶，县委、县政府抽调机关工作人员组成扶贫工作队驻村开展扶贫工作。通过各方面的齐心努力，息烽贫困地区的经济和社会各项事业快速发展。1996年，息烽县在国定贫困县中率先越过温饱线，2002年摘掉国定贫困县帽子，2008年进入省建设经济强县行列。

第一节　扶贫攻坚目标

1993年，全县贫困人口14.04万人，占农业人口的70%，其中人均年纯收入200元以下的极贫人口7.4万人，201～300元的3.89万人，301～400元的2.74万人。1994年，《国家八七扶贫攻坚计划》将息烽县列入全国592个贫困县之一。1995年1月，县委、县政府根据《国家八七扶贫攻坚计划》精神，制定《息烽县扶贫攻坚计划》，提出目标：到2000年，全县经济实力明显增强，国民生产总值达3.8亿元，工农业总产值达3.34亿元，财政收入达3000～4000万元。主要工农业产品产量有较大增长，产业结构明显改善，经济布局趋于合理，科学技术和管理水平有较大提高，人民群众生活由温饱向小康迈进，人民群众科学文化素质和道德素质明显提高，社会秩序安定，社会风气更加健康向上。到2002年，全县14.04万贫困人口全部脱贫，年人均收入达到500元以上，生活条件明显改善；人均建成0.5～1亩稳产高产农田；户均建成1亩林、果、药、茶、桑园或其他经济作物；户均向乡镇企业或发达地区转移一个劳动力；户均饲养一个黄牛单位的商品畜；户均有一项家庭支柱产业或其他家庭副业；基本解决人畜饮水困难；实现所有乡镇和90%的村通公路；实现3万亩坡改梯；全县基本普及九年制义务教育；开展农民技术培训和职业技术教育，达到每户至少有一人掌握1～2项农业实用技术；改善医疗条件，建立县、乡、村三级防护网，基本控制地方病；使人口自然增长率控制在11‰以内。

第二节　扶贫攻坚措施

一、各司其职，实行责任制

在县乡两级实行扶贫工作“一把手”负责制，主要领导亲自抓，分管领导具体抓，层层实行目标管理。严格考核奖惩措施。在宣传方面，引导和教育群众树立自立自强思想，依靠自己的双手勤劳致富。

在农业工作中，依靠科技进步，稳定粮食产量，首先解决群众吃饭问题；以治水改土为重点，搞好农田水利基础设施建设，改善农业生产条件，改善农村贫困人口的生产条件和生活环境。推广科学养殖技术，推行畜禽防疫双轨责任制，降低牲畜发病死亡率，提高出栏出肉率。同时培植新的经济支柱，开发西瓜、草莓、折耳根（鱼腥草）、蔬菜等经济作物及水果、药材等经济林木。县制定出台招商引资政策，引进资金、技术、人才，发展乡镇企业。争取资金，兴办扶贫项目。

县内各部门根据自身实际，开展教育扶贫、科技扶贫、文化扶贫、卫生扶贫、交通扶贫、水电扶贫、计生扶贫，拓宽扶贫工作渠道。从1996年起，有计划地开展农业实用技术培训、农民绿色证书培训、农村劳动力非农技能培训，至2008年，全县投入财政资金688万元，培训农村劳动力63.86万人次；至2010年，劳动力就业培训2.62万人，转移劳动力1.97万人；绿色证书培训2万余人次，颁证1万余个。同时，开创“公司+农户”“基地连农户”扶贫新路，探索走“一村一品”产业发展之路。发展养殖小区、蔬菜基地、果树基地等。引导农村剩余劳动力向非农产业转移。

二、落实项目资金

信贷扶贫资金：1994年，到位扶贫信贷资金324.7万元，安排项目7个。此后逐年增加，至2004年，共到位1.37亿元，实施项目255个，累计资金11.84亿元。主要项目有：“温饱工程”、脱毒马铃薯推广、蔬菜；玉米、苕粉加工，经济林、果树、药材种植及加工、鲜花盆景等。猪、羊、禽、鱼养殖及饲料加工。3个医药、2个工业项目。还有广播电视系统改造。

财政扶贫项目资金：1997年，财政无偿扶贫资金开始投入到县内基础设施等项目建设，到2010年，共投入6016.4万元，扶持项目599个，主要投入农村水电路、教育、广播电视；贫困户建房、公路修建、人畜饮水、沟渠改造、地面卫星电视接收站、学校基础设施；基本农田建设、坡改梯工程、卫生室修建、饮水工程、小水池建设、异地扶贫搬迁。蔬菜种植、养牛、村组路；农民适用技术培训、农村党建。

三、实施整村推进扶贫

配套跟进基础设施及文化、通信、教育、卫生等相关事业建设，以保障整村推进开发扶贫的实施。1994年，实现由贵阳到息烽的光缆传输，1996年村村通电；1997年，对极贫村寨实行异地搬迁，国家对困难户补助资金改建新房。1998年乡乡通程控电话，1999年村村通电话和公路；2000年村村通广播电视，两基工作通过省级验收，高标准扫盲验收合格。2003年实现乡乡通油路。2004年全面消除茅草房。

四、社会各界帮扶

在实施“八七”扶贫攻坚计划期间，新华社、省委宣传部，省财政厅派出工作组到息烽定点帮扶。1994年10月，新华社接受帮扶息烽县任务后，先后派出5批10余名干部到息烽挂职。6年中，落实50个扶贫项目，投入资金物资折款360多万元，帮助息烽建“希望小学”2所，修建乡村公路5千米，开发蔬菜基地300亩，建人畜饮水工程13处。是年，全县接收社会各界捐赠物资及现金等折款共2499.6万元。1996年，市委书记亲自联系县内最贫困的青山苗族乡，组织市直机关和国有大型企业37家帮扶县内贫困村；4月25日，县委、县政府召开帮村扶贫动员大会，县长李贵菊与贵阳市37家企事业单位签订帮村扶贫协议书。6月19日，全省“服务万村，创百争万”行动推进会暨青年开发扶贫工作研讨会在息烽召开。1997年4月，贵阳市云岩区与息烽对口协作帮扶，8个驻县工矿企业、38个县直机关、事业单位帮扶71个贫困村和13个经济不发达村。推行“包户限期解决温饱责任制”。投资200余万元在永靖镇河坎村上寨组进行就地改造脱贫试点。7月18日，国务院总理李鹏率国家计委、国家经贸委、铁道部、交通部、农业部、财政部、人民银行、电力部、水利部等部门负责人到永靖镇河坎村上寨村民组视察扶贫工作，叮嘱县、乡、村干部一定要让娃娃上学，要打好扶贫攻坚战，努力改变贫困面貌。强调扶贫工作一定要扎扎实实地做，要落实到村、到户、到人。要重视学习科技文化知识，没有科技知识，即使一时脱贫，一遇天灾人祸就很容易返贫，更谈不上开发性脱贫。

第三节　扶贫成效

1996年，全县贫困村从3年前的131个减少到71个，贫困人口从14.04万人减少到2.94万人。全县农民人均纯收入1200元，人均占有粮食335千克，有7.26万贫困人口基本解决温饱，达到或超过《国家八七扶贫攻坚计划》提出的奋斗目标。被省委、省政府列为全省48个贫困县中率先解决温饱的6个县之一，并授予“率先解决温饱先进县”称号。

1997—1998年，县内对永靖镇河坎村上寨村民组（苗族）、九庄镇新沙村下环山村民组两个极贫村寨实行异地搬迁，国家对困难户补助资金改建新房。

1998年，贫困村减少到20个，按照当年“双600”脱贫标准，最后1.5万名贫困人口越过温饱线，人均纯收入从5年前的391元增加到1436元，人均粮食占有量341千克。提前2年实现《国家八七扶贫攻坚计划》所规定的基本解决温饱目标。2000年，全县农民人均纯收入1567元，建成小康镇2个、小康村81个。

农业人口人均建成0.3亩高产稳产基本农田，户均1亩经济林木，养殖畜禽1.5个黄牛单位。1997年，对极贫村寨实行异地搬迁，国家对困难户补助资金进行房屋改造，改建新房。1998—2003年，共改造贫困户危破房1745户；2001—2004年，共改造农村人居茅草房2627户。至2004年，全县共改善居住条件4672户，投资2963.99万元。

1994—2000年，全县共完成坡改梯5.46万亩，新增耕地2.08万亩，土变田6499亩，人均建成0.3亩稳产高产基本农田；治理病险水库13座；整修山塘109口，水土保持治理面积25.16平方千米，建水池2828口，新增灌溉面积2.08万亩；新建人畜饮水工程38处，解决12.9万人和10.3万头牲畜的饮水困难；新修公路620千米，实现村村通公路目标；133个村完成农村电网改造，实现组组通电计划。同时10个乡镇全部实现通讯数字程控化，122个村通电话。

科技、教育、文化、卫生等社会事业。新建和改造中小学校舍143所，其中新建希望小学18所，教学危房基本消除。10个乡镇新建卫生院，实现村村有卫生室；新建村级计划生育服务站165个。1998年，全县人口自然增长率控制在10.5‰以内。农民每户至少有一名主要劳动力掌握1～2门农业实用技术。全县94个村建立有线电视网络，12315户安装能收视7套以上节目的有线收视设备，41个村安装无线电视接收设备，电视覆盖率90%。10个乡镇均新建精神文明活动中心，部分村建立文化室或阅览室。

乡镇企业发展迅速。1998年末，全县乡镇企业从1993年的162个发展到3711个，总产值从713万元上升到9.19亿元。至2000年，乡镇企业总产值达13.65亿元。

2002年，息烽县摘掉国定贫困县帽子。

第十篇　工　业

第一章　工业布局与结构

20世纪80年代，全县各乡镇大力发展乡镇企业，铸造、加工、采矿等工业企业迅速发展。90年代，县委、政府出台招商引资政策，举全县之力招商引资，一批实力强、管理先进、经济社会效益好的企业来县发展。21世纪，规划建设医药工业园区、工业园区。2009年，全年规模以上工业总产值突破100亿元。2010年，工业园区工业总产值117.4亿元。

第一节　工业布局

1991年，县内工业企业主要分布在小寨坝镇、永靖镇、温泉镇、养龙司乡和川黔公路、原贵遵高等级公路沿线。主要工业企业有贵州息烽磷矿、息烽黄磷厂、息烽重钙厂、南山煤矿。2010年，规模较大工业企业有：贵州息烽磷矿、贵州西洋肥业有限公司、息烽县龙泉磷肥厂、贵阳中化开磷化肥有限公司、南山煤矿、息烽仁都水泥厂、贵州汉方制药有限公司息烽药厂、贵州太和制药有限公司息烽制药厂、息烽拜克汽车配件厂。

第二节　产业结构

1990—2010年，息烽工业产业结构演进的基本轨迹是：依托能源、矿产资源优势的基础工业比例上升，新兴工业比例上升，产业结构由初级层次向高级层次发展演变；围绕磷煤工业、电力、食品加工、医药、建材五大产业，深化改革，加快技术改造，以骨干企业为重点，以优化资本结构为主线，抓大放小，鼓励兼并，规范破产，国有企业活力进一步增强，非公有制工业经济茁壮成长。

1990年，县境有县属工业企业15个（国营12个，集体3个），驻县工业企业6个（除准备搬迁外），工业总产值6034万元。

1995年，乡及乡以上工业企业85个，其中独立核算工业企业71个，非独立核算工业企业14个；按轻重工业分，轻工业企业33个，重工业企业52个。

2008年，有工业企业法人单位82个，从业9098人，其中国有企业12个，股份合作企业1个，其他有限责任公司14个，私营企业55个；采矿业19个，制造业56个，电力、燃气及水的生产和供应业7个。

2010年，纳入统计的规模以上企业、乡及乡以上工业企业16个，均为独立核算工业企业。按轻重工业分，轻工业企业4个，重工业企业12个。

第三节　工业经济

1991年，工业总产值6034万元。50万元以上产值的企业8个。1992年，工业产值7186万元，其中乡以上工业产值4227万元，村及村以下工业产值2958万元，主要工业产品有窖酒、原煤、水泥、磷矿石等。

1993年，乡及乡以上工业总产值（按90不变价）4136.94万元，其中国有工业完成2138.26万元，城镇集体工业完成31.18万元，乡办工业完成1967.5万元。

1996年，乡及乡以上工业产值突破亿元大关，为12892万元。此后，工业产值逐年稳步上升。2001年，以“工业强县”为主攻目标，以“重点项目带动”，县域磷及磷化工支柱产业形成。县域工业总产值跃上10亿元台阶，达到15.71亿元，其中县级工业总产值14.44亿元。2009年，工业总产值突破百亿元，为101.98亿元，其中规模以上工业产值100.03亿元。2010年，工业总产值117.39亿元，其中规模以上工业产值115.31亿元，工业增加值22.72亿元。

息烽县2002—2010年规模以上工业产值统计表

表10-1-1　　　　单位：万元

年份	工业总产值	销售产值	产销率（%）	工业增加值
2002	159115.6	154864.7	97.27	39780
2003	248603	233986	97.12	62150
2004	303314	309426	100.75	75829
2005	430000	316800	96	107500
2006	516000	485237	93.93	155000
2007	678500	—	98.01	—
2008	842979	—	97.52	250578
2009	1000328	—	87.98	298722
2010	1153096	—	90.02	220918

第二章　重工业

县内重工业分为磷化工业、采矿业、电力供应业，其中磷化工为重点行业。1990年，重工业总产值2156.7万元。1993年，重工业总产值3172万元。2000年，重工业总产值40390万元。采矿业以煤矿和磷矿开采为主。其间，电力供应业在输配电建设、配电网管理、变电站建设、电网改造方面有重大发展。

第一节 采矿业

一、煤矿

（一）煤炭资源

县内煤炭资源比较丰富，主要分布在温泉镇、小寨坝镇、养龙司乡、永靖镇、西山乡、青山苗族乡、石硐乡。煤炭储量1758.2万吨，基础储量2197.8万吨，资源总量6014.7万吨，预测资源量2.23亿吨。其中，南山—养龙司一线为无烟煤，其他地方为贫煤及瘦煤，原煤灰份指标A号12.53%～38.85%，挥发份（V2）6.35%～14.2%，全硫（S）1%～4.5%，发热量4000～7500卡/克。

（二）煤炭管理

1991年，有煤窑135个，持证开采12个，多数煤矿属独眼井，以手电、煤油灯照明，木船运输。

次年，有煤矿111个，其中乡镇煤矿29个。

1998年起，实行关井压产，至1999年7月，取缔煤矿1个，关闭28个，煤矿从69个减至40个，产量压缩到15万吨。

2000年4月，实行第二次关井压产，关闭技改后年产量仍达不到3万吨的煤矿20个。保留煤矿20个，设计能力年产78万吨。

2005年，实施煤矿整合兼并重组，形成一批大型煤矿龙头企业，同时鼓励小煤矿做大做强。是年有煤矿21个，其中年产3万吨的15个、6万吨的5个、15万吨的1个。2006年起，对煤矿进行技改扩能，要求技改扩能后的煤矿生产能力不能低于年产9万吨。至2008年，有煤矿企业14家，总设计生产能力年产150万吨，其中4家各年产15万吨，10家各年产9万吨。

2009年4月23日，县政府批准石硐乡星宇煤矿、永靖镇山王煤矿开工建设，年生产能力分别为9万吨。

2010年，有煤矿企业14家，其中，国有煤矿企业1家（林东矿业集团南山煤矿），年生产能力159万吨，乡镇煤矿企业13家，年生产能力129万吨。

（三）技术改造

1991年，南山煤矿使用ABD-21型瓦斯监测系统。1998年和2003年，分别更新安装KJ90系统。

2000年4月起，开展煤矿技改整合，至2005年，每个煤矿实现供两人行走出口，采用矿灯照明，机械通风，轻轨运输，爆破开采，安装瓦斯监测监控系统，实现全县联网。

2006年，县内推广使用WTC瓦斯突出参数仪。是年，在小红寨、马家箐煤矿推行改进支护工艺，率先使用液压金属支护。次年，利发、楠木桥两煤矿使用单体液压金属支护。

2008年起，在县境内煤矿逐步推行煤矿设置专用回风井，推行壁式采煤、支护改革，巷道推广使用锚杆、锚网、锚喷、锚索、砌碹压支架或综采液压支柱，全面淘汰木质支护。次年底，淘汰金属摩擦支柱支护，全面推动通信系统、压风系统、防尘洒水系统等“三条生命线”项目、电法探水预防透水事故项目、井下人员定位系统安装等项目建设。

2010年，投资32万元，将KJ90系统更新为KJ90NB系统。

（四）煤炭生产

1991—2000年，县内煤矿多由乡镇管理。1991年，有乡镇煤矿112个，从业人员1294人，产量

27.83万吨，产值500.73万元。1992年，煤矿增加到200个。1995年，有煤矿119个，从业人员2649人，产量99.1万吨，产值4115万元。1998年后，禁止政府经商办企业，乡镇煤矿停办。县内煤矿转由个体经营。

1998年后，随着国家政策的限制，县内煤矿大都从乡镇管理转化为私营管理，乡镇政府只从安全、税收方面进行管理。1998—2010年，主要有坪土煤矿、利发煤矿、双龙井煤矿、火烧井煤矿。其中规模以上煤矿有鑫悦煤矿。

息烽县1991—2010年煤炭产量统计表

表10-1-2

年份	煤矿个数（个）	年产量（万吨）
1991	112	27.83
1992	94	35.99
1993	137	48.25
1994	116	68.14
1995	102	44
1996	100	50.35
1997	79	47.4
1998	68	36.66
1999	40	15
2000	20	15
2001	18	12
2002	20	51.6
2003	20	91.43
2004	20	69.3
2005	19	56.9
2006	17	39.71
2007	13	31.2
2008	13	34.8
2009	13	84.3
2010	13	31.35

二、磷矿

（一）磷矿资源

息烽磷矿分布在震旦系上部，属高品位磷块岩，主要分布在温泉松林坡、古家沟一带。已探明矿石储量A+B+C+D级1183.14万吨，伴生碘元素储量D级554.2吨，磷矿石保有储量720万吨。属较稳定中型磷矿床。采矿区乔巴山，面积1.2平方千米，最高海拔1018.47米，深部至海拔388米标高以下仍有矿层。

（二）磷矿开采

1990年有矿井7口，从业人员310人，开采磷矿6.17万吨。1994年，温泉采矿场年产磷矿4万吨。

1995年，磷矿价格上涨，有磷矿企业（户）33家，采矿1.9万吨，产值120万元。此后，加大磷矿开采监管力度，严禁无证开采、乱开乱采等。2002年，有采矿企业（户）5家。2008年，有采矿企业2家（贵州息烽磷矿、息烽县惠昌公司），年采矿14万吨，产值1960万元。2009年，贵州息烽磷矿有限责任公司和息烽温泉惠昌磷业有限责任公司共采矿32.23万吨，产值1.21亿元，纳税416.6万元。

2010年，贵州息烽磷矿有限责任公司采矿产值1.76亿元，纳税661.56万元。

第二节　电力供应

一、管理机构

1992年6月，贵阳供电局息烽分局成立，负责息烽、开阳、修文3县及遵义县部分地区的供电。1995年10月，息烽分局划归贵阳市北供电局管理，更名为贵阳市北供电局息烽分局。2007年2月，改称贵阳供电局息烽分局，内设综合管理室、安全监察室、物业办公室、生产技术室、业主项目部、变电检修班、配电检修班、自动化通讯班、变电运行班、配网调度班、营销技术室、用电检查班、电费核算班、抄表班、客服大厅班、集控中心等部门。

二、输配电建设与管理

1999—2006年，县内各变电站35千伏电力线路建设共5条。

35千伏永靖线　2000年2月建成。电压等级35千伏，线路总长21.54千米，10千伏箱式变压器总台数151台，配变总容量27355千伏安，具有10千伏永城Ⅰ回、永城Ⅱ回、永江、永梨、永长、永玄、永阳、永息8条出线。

35千伏九庄线　2000年8月建成。电压等级35千伏，线路总长35.25千米，10千伏箱式变压器总台数132台，配变总容量6510千伏安，具有10千伏九鸡、九何、九镇、九竹4条出线。

35千伏石硐线　2003年5月建成。电压等级35千伏，线路总长26.67千米，10千伏箱式变压器总台数86台，配变总容量3935千伏安，具有10千伏石街、石南、石何、石盘4条出线。

35千伏高坝线　2005年7月建成。电压等级35千伏，线路总长74.7千米，10千伏箱式变压器总台数134台，配变总容量8935千伏安，具有10千伏高荷、高小、高黑、高王4条出线。

35千伏阳朗线　2006年5月建成。电压等级35千伏，线路总长21.98千米，10千伏箱式变压器总台数93台，配变总容量11815千伏安，具有10千伏阳黎、阳长、阳城Ⅰ回、阳城Ⅱ回4条出线。至2009年12月31日，息烽供电分局共管辖110千伏变电站2座、35千伏变电站5座、10千伏开闭所1座。息烽地区配电网共管辖10千伏配电线路49条（含用户专线7条），10千伏线路总长914.7千米（含用户专线总长29.89千米），连同用户专变共有1165台变压器（其中22台为用户专变数），配电变压器总容量99915千伏安（其中用户专变容量11570千伏安）。

三、配电网管理

1990年后，原10千伏息江线为息烽拖电厂用户专线，1993年将该线路移交供电局。10千伏息江线投运后，完成对1千伏息城线线路负荷改接工作，将永靖镇南门村、老厂村、雨洒村、龙爪村、下阳朗村、猫洞村、硬寨村、联峰村、下洪马村、上洪马村、后坝村、河丰村、新萝村、安马村、梨安村等区域负荷改接到10千伏息江线上。

1995年，完成10千伏县城主干线路改造，改造后使用导线型号为95毫米钢芯铝绞线，同时完成10千伏息江线主干线路的改造工作，改造导线型号为75毫米钢芯铝绞线，改造10千伏线路9.5千米。完成35千伏息烽变2号主变3200千伏安增容为7500千伏安的改造，确保县城及周边区域用电需求。

1999年前，下设小寨坝电管站、石硐电管站，代为负责当地配网管理。2000年供电所成立后，由分局和供电所共同承担全县配网管理。主要以35千伏久息线为主供电源。线路采用截面95毫米钢芯铝绞线建设，总长19千米，地线为截面35毫米钢绞线，杆塔基数为75基砼杆。主变容量为两台3200千伏安变压器。县城10千伏主供电源为10千伏息城线，线路型号为截面50毫米的钢芯铝绞线，主供电区域为县城、环城路（老汽车站地段、蚕桑坡地段）、火车站、枧槽沟、老厂、玄天洞、半边街、阳朗、联丰地段。县城区域内用户用电以人民路100千伏安公用变压器及中街100千伏安公用变压器为低压供电，主要供电区域为原县城中街、东风路、交通路、南门；环城路老汽车站及粮食局、三板桥（原供电局）由粮食局100千伏安专用变压器供电；酒厂、北门桥区域由酒厂50千伏安专用变压器供电；蚕桑坡地段由原农具厂100千伏安专用变压器供电。

2000年2月，110千伏永靖变电站建成投运，通过新架和改接，县城区主要由10千伏永梨线、永阳线、永长线、永玄线、永城线、永江线及10千伏息江线、10千伏息城线供电。

2001年12月，从永靖镇110千伏永靖变电站新架1条10千伏永息线至35千伏息烽变，导线使用型号为截面240毫米钢芯铝绞线，线路长3.24千米。同年，35千伏息烽变主变退出运行，建成10千伏息烽开闭所，主供电源为10千伏永息线。10千伏息烽开闭所具有的10千伏出线为：10千伏息烽到小寨坝线、息烽到江土线、息微线、息朝线、息电线、息拖线、息城线、息烽到南山煤矿线。主要供电区域为永靖镇、西山乡、小寨坝镇等乡镇。

2002年，在110千伏永靖变电站未建成前，县城主要由10千伏息城线和10千伏息江线两条线路供电。10千伏息城线全长2.43千米，使用导线为截面95毫米钢芯铝绞线，有公变16台，容量2870千伏安；用户专变19台，总容量2755千伏安。10千伏息江线全长7.3千米，使用导线为截面70毫米钢芯铝绞线，其中专线长29.96千米，有公变8台，总容量980千伏安，用户专变39台，容量4355千伏安。

2005年，完成10千伏息江线1～20号杆主线绝缘化改造，改造导线使用型号为截面150毫米架空绝缘线，线路长度0.95千米。是年，息烽南大街修建工程启动，进行电网改造，使用亮化埋地电缆，4月完成10千伏息城线南大街北段（县永靖砖厂路口至县粮贸大楼路口）公路两侧电缆线路新建工程。10月，500千伏息烽变投运，10千伏息烽开闭所更名为10千伏息城开闭所，同时10千伏息城线更名为10千伏息府线。

2006年9—12月，完成10千伏永城I回线、10千伏永城Ⅱ回线同杆架设双回线工程，使用截面为150毫米架空绝缘线导线进行绝缘化施工改造工作；改造10千伏永城I回线，主线长2.68千米；新建10千伏永城Ⅱ回线，主线长2.68千米；新建10千伏阳城I回线、10千伏阳城Ⅱ回线，同杆架设双回线并使用150毫米架空绝缘线进行绝缘化改造。2007年2月，完成10千伏阳城I回线、Ⅱ回线的投运，10千伏阳城I回线分段174断路器的安装及投运，10千伏阳城Ⅱ回线184断路器的安装及投运。5月，完成10千伏永城I回线、Ⅱ回线的投运，10千伏永城I回线分段171、172、173断路器的安装及投运，10千伏永城Ⅱ回线181、182、183断路器的安装及投运。到2007年5月，县城区10千伏线路网架结构为：

10千伏城网I环，以10千伏永城I回线与10千伏阳城I回线为手拉手的环网供电；10千伏城网Ⅱ环，以10千伏永城Ⅱ回线与10千伏阳城Ⅱ回线为手拉手的环网供电；10千伏城网Ⅲ环，以10千伏永江线与10千伏息江线为手拉手的环网供电。2条准用环网联络：1千伏、10千伏城网I环Ⅱ环联络线路；2千伏、10千伏城网Ⅱ环Ⅲ环联络线路；1条以10千伏息城开闭所为主供电源的10千伏永息线。城区电网形成以1条主供10千伏息城开闭所城区电源为主，以3条环网、2条准用网为主供的县城区负荷网架结构。同时设备情况：10千伏分段断路器11台、10千伏联络断路器7台、10千伏电缆分支箱15台、环网柜2台。至2009年12月底，县城电网结构为：110千伏永靖变、35千伏阳朗变、10千伏息城开闭所，为三角形环形电网供电；110千伏永靖变以110千伏盘靖线和110千伏开永线双回线供电；35千伏阳朗变以35千伏久阳线为单电源供电；10千伏部分以10千伏城网I环、Ⅱ环、10千伏永梨、阳长联络线及10千伏永长、阳长联络线4个电源作准用保障；10千伏息城开闭所以10千伏永息I回线、Ⅱ回线为主供电源，确保三角形、环形电网至少有双电源供电，城区10千伏线路的供电电源可靠性大为提高。

四、变电站建设与管理

新场变电站　新场变电站建成于1965年，时称乌江区温泉乡新场坪输变电站（亦称天台变电站）。1990年，有2条110千伏线路通过变电站输出：其一，由遵义、久长变电站，经由原安江乡入境，至新场坪变电站，出线经由原温泉乡窑上入开阳，经过县内10千米；2007年撤除。其二，从董家坪入境，经养龙司、新场坪变电站、小寨坝、息烽、安马庄出境，经过县内长40千米。共有4条35千伏高压电输出线路，总长41.64千米。其中1条至二七六厂双回线，长5千米；1条经温泉三百块出境入开阳，县段长3千米；1条经养龙司、小寨坝、王家坪等乡至流长变电站，长21.64千米；1条经养龙司、小寨坝至息烽重钙厂，长12千米。10千伏输出线7条99千米：经养龙司、小寨坝20千米；至二七六厂水泵房4千米；经养龙司至安江乡40千米，至县磷肥厂2千米；经温泉街上出境至开阳县段长3.5千米；至温泉乡11.5千米；至赶子18千米。1990—2007年，增加110千伏输出线新烽线（新场坪至息烽磷矿乔巴山）；盘新线（盘脚营火车站至新场坪）、新西线（新场坪至西洋公司）、10千伏新热线（新场坪至热水坪）。该变电站主供变压器压器1990年前为2台15000千伏安变压器，后扩容至2台30000千伏安变压器。2007年，新场变电站属110千伏变电站，有2条110千伏主供电源线，江新I回线、Ⅱ回线，110千伏开高新备用；5条35千伏出线，7条10千伏出线。

流长变电站　1999年8月10日，县政府将流长变电站人、财、物划归贵阳供电局息烽分局所有。2007年，流长变电站属35千伏变电站，有1台3.15兆伏安主供变压器，1条35千伏电源线，6条10千伏出线。

九庄变电站　2000年8月建成，是息烽农网改造第一个建成的农村35千伏变电站。主供变压器容量3.15兆伏安，1条35千伏电源线，4条10千伏出线。

石硐变电站　2005年5月建成投运。主供变压器容量3.15兆伏安。2007年架设1条35千伏电源线，4条10千伏出线。

阳朗变电站　2006年5月建成投运。有1台容量8兆伏安的主供变压器，1条T接35千伏电源线，5条10千伏出线。

永靖变电站　2000年2月建成投运。2007年，建成110千伏永靖变电站后，新架设2台50兆伏安主供变压器，2条110千伏线路供电，其中110千伏开永线为主供电源，110千伏新永线为备用电源。5条35千伏出线，7条10千伏出线。

高家坝变电站　2005年7月7日建成投运。有1台容量5兆伏安的主供变压器，1条T接35千伏电源线，4条10千伏出线。

小寨坝盘脚营变电站 2006年12月建成投运。110千伏盘新线作为新场变的备用电源。

五、电网改造

1999年1月4日，县供电局编制《息烽县农村电网建设改造项目规划可行性报告》和《农电管理体制 农村电网改造工程 城乡用电同网同价总体规划方案》。县委、县政府成立“两改一同价”（农电体制改革、农村电网改造和建设、城乡用电同网同价）工作领导小组及其办公室，制订文件。2001年12月，第一期农村电网改造工程完成161个村4858户，投资4000多万元。2002年3月15日，进行第二期农村电网改造工程，至2004年3月30日完成。经过两期农村电网改造，有161个村65293户进行户改，实现与城镇用电同价；共完成工程投资6748.5万元；新建10千伏线路113.25千米，改造10千伏线路358.73千米；新增10千伏变压器147台，容量13560千伏安；更新10千伏配电变压器73台，容量6415千伏安；新建400伏线路308.45千米，改造440伏线路3141.17千米。

第三节 建材工业

一、建材工业企业

1991年，县内有建材工业企业64家。其中独立核算企业14家，工业产值2154万元。

2004年，有建材工业企业76家，其中规模以上企业有县属仁都水泥厂、县属光辉水泥有限公司2家，共有职工1034人、固定资产2378万元。是年完成产值6097万元。

2005年，有建材工业企业61家，其中砂石厂50家，页岩制砖厂9家，其他2家。

2010年，有建材工业企业29家，其中砂石厂24家，石灰窑3家，页岩制砖厂、玄武岩制砖厂各1家。

二、石灰石、石灰生产

县内石灰石主要用于生产石灰。石灰窑主要分布在210国道沿线。1991年，全县石灰石产量2.67万吨，产值1176万元。随着建筑业发展和高等级公路修建，石灰需求量增大，产量逐年提高，1995年，全县生产建筑用石灰43175吨，产值873万元。2000年以后，逐渐减少。

三、水泥生产

1991年，县内有县水泥厂、大水沟水泥厂和阳朗水泥厂、老鸦河水泥厂4家水泥生产企业，主产普通硅酸盐水泥。是年生产水泥10万吨，完成产值591.39万元，占建材行业工业总产值的26.46%。

1992年12月，老鸦河水泥厂、阳朗水泥厂生产水泥7.82万吨，产值184.7万元。

2000年6月，根据国家五小企业政策，大水沟水泥厂、阳朗水泥厂关闭。老鸦河水泥厂更名为贵阳息烽光辉水泥厂。

四、耐火材料生产

1991年，县内有红砖生产企业6家，生产红砖8573万块，完成工业产值1100万元。

2004年，县内有红砖厂、机砖厂20家，生产红砖1.11亿块，产值1332.7万元。

县建筑材料厂简介：该厂为县属集体企业。1991年有职工154人，固定资产101.3万元，年设计生产能力1200万块。是年生产红砖272万块，产值34.91万元。1992年承包给福建客商，其后承包人几经转换，仍处于亏损状态，承包人无力继续经营，致使承包合同中止。1994年，县建筑材料厂改制，更名为建材有限公司。

第四节　铝加工

县内铝加工工业始于1996年。1997年，息烽铝厂始建。2002年2月，贵州息烽铝厂入驻金星工业园区，投资1500万元，年产铝锭2万吨，年产值3800万元，年纳税250万元。2003年，销售收入15021万元，实现利润244万元，由于电价、原材料价格上涨等原因，2004年3月停产。2006年初，息烽铝厂投入1050万元再次进行技术改造，设计年产铝锭3万吨。10月，48台电解槽全部恢复生产，生产铝锭1800吨，完成工业产值3700万元。因耗能高、污染大，2009年，息烽铝厂停办。

第五节　铸造业

20世纪80年代，县农具厂研制生产回风炉，因美观适用，深受消费者青睐，生产规模逐渐扩大。1991年，县农具厂生产回风炉1366台，增加产值11万余元。1993年，生产回风炉1761台。此后，由于回风炉市场需求大，市场广阔，蕴藏极大商机，县农具厂部分工人辞职回家开办个体回风炉加工作坊，有县城商人转行加入到生产回风炉行业，县城回风炉生产规模短时间内快速扩大，且辐射到西山、养龙司、流长等乡镇。至1995年，县内有50余户生产回风炉，在城北蚕桑坡形成回风炉生产一条街。息烽回风炉远销四川、重庆、湖北各省市和省内各州、市、县，有息烽人外出四川、云南、湖北经营回风炉发家致富。

2000年，全县生产回风炉15.49万台。此后，由于电器普及，燃煤价格上涨，回风炉市场趋于饱和等因素，回风炉生产量逐年下降。2010年，有5家生产回风炉，从业人员15人。

第三章　轻工业

1991—2010年，县内轻工业包括塑料制造业、医药制造业、造纸业、印刷业、鞭炮制造业、服装制造业、白酒酿造业、家具制造业、农副食品加工业、铁锅制造业等行业。

第一节　塑料制品

1991年，县内有个体经营者进行小规模塑料品加工。1993—1997年，县医院生产大输液塑料制品。2002年，贵州开磷宏盛实业有限公司（简称宏盛公司）入驻县城北门福利桥生产编织袋，当年生产编织袋1670万条。2008年，华信塑业有限公司入驻。2010年，生产编织袋4763吨7032万条，总产值8228万元。是年，宏盛公司生产小型塑料编织袋1亿条，集装袋50万条及部分内粘袋、彩印覆膜袋、复合袋、内膜双层袋、集装袋等。

主要企业简介：2002年11月28日，贵州开磷宏盛实业有限公司入驻县城北门福利桥。2005年3

月，贵州开磷宏盛实业有限公司更名为贵州宏盛塑料有限责任公司。2006年10月—2007年，宏盛公司相继取得中华人民共和国危险化学品包装容器生产企业定点证、出口商品包装容器质量许可证资格及危险化学品包装物容器全国工业产品生产许可证。2008—2009年，宏盛公司投资建成4条内粘袋生产线。

第二节　医药制造

1993年10月，县医院生产大输液（生理盐水、葡萄糖生理盐水、葡萄糖注射液）。1994年，生产大输液28.8万瓶，收入56万元；1995年，生产69.1万瓶，收入131万元。1997年，卫生部停止审批生产大输液。2010年，有贵州汉方制药有限公司息烽制药厂和贵州太和制药有限公司息烽制药厂2家制药企业，工业总产值6.21亿元。其中太和制药有限公司息烽制药厂生产药品113.14吨，工业总产值2.29亿元。

第三节　造　纸

境内造纸以刺竹、荆竹和构皮为原料。清代，西望山周边王家坪、大鹿窝、小鹿窝、南望山、黄沙渡等地龚、杨、魏等姓人家分别创办传统手工纸厂，兴盛时期有厂房90间。

1991年，县内有机器造纸厂2家。其中西望山石灰窑魏发凯创办手工作坊生产皮纸，2000年停产。1993年，在酒厂成立造纸分厂，生产瓦楞纸箱、纸板267吨，产值57.7万元，创税0.54万元。1994年，成立贵州省息烽县造纸有限公司，1997年停产。1998年11月，将厂房租赁给花溪恒丰工贸有限公司生产经营，当时有退休职工27人。2000年停产。1999年，息烽黔豫纸厂、宏达纸厂共生产卫生纸1200吨，产值576万元。2005年，息烽黔豫纸厂实施技改，年产卫生纸313吨，产值119万元。2008年，宏达纸厂生产卫生纸120吨，销售产值38.4万元。2009年，根据国家环境保护政策要求，县内纸厂全部关闭。

第四节　印　刷

1991年，县内有县印刷厂和粮食局印刷厂开展印刷业务，主要为机关单位印刷文件、单位宣传资料、账本和书籍、商标、处方笺等。1997年相继停产。是年，县职业技术学校开办印刷厂，后因业务量少，经营不景气，1999年底停办。1999年3月，贵州息烽新兴印刷有限公司成立，从业人员30人，产值50万元。同年年底，英杰印务部开业，至2002年，年产值稳定在10万元左右。2003年，英杰印务部使用电脑排版胶印，从业人员8人。2010年，县境有印刷厂2家，年产值35万元。

第五节　其　他

一、鞭炮制造

县内鞭炮生产主要分布在九庄镇、石硐乡何家硐村、流长乡和县城。采用传统工艺作坊式生产。2000年以后，由于国家安全政策控制，生产作坊逐渐减少。1991年，鞭炮生产业19家，其中乡办1家（九龙烟花爆竹厂）；个体18家，从业人员116人。1998年，九龙烟花爆竹厂承包给河南人陈安众经营，因经营不善，2000年停产。2002年，永靖镇烟花爆竹厂、贵州省息烽县辐光鞭炮厂相继停产。2010年，县内有烟花爆竹生产企业1家。

二、缝纫

20世纪80年代起，因个体经营服装（成衣）户逐渐增多，原县轻工局管辖的县城及各区缝纫社相继停产倒闭，县城及乡镇集镇仅有少量的私人缝纫店从业。1991—2010年，息烽县城有缝纫加工店2～5家不等。乡镇集镇缝纫加工业基本绝迹。

三、制鞋

1991年初，县内有城关制鞋厂1家，从业6人。此后，有农民工外出打工学得制鞋技术后，返乡自主创业，从事制鞋业，多为家庭作坊式，从业3～5人不等，自产自销。

1992年，个体户李枝祥、宋志洪开办皮鞋厂，自产自销。其中李枝祥皮鞋厂年产皮鞋1万双，产值20万元。2003年停产。

1993年，何少云开办息烽春光鞋厂，年产皮鞋5000双，产值2万元；2007年开始生产波鞋。

1999年，蒋兴林在县城交通路开店生产皮鞋。

2000年，田应发开店生产皮鞋，年产1万双。2007年停产。

2004年，董友华在县城中街开店生产皮鞋。

2009年，石硐乡水头村颜加强在浙江打工期间学到制鞋技术，回村生产棉鞋，年产棉鞋3万双；淡季4人从业，旺季20人从业，年产值60万元。

四、白酒酿造

1991年，县内白酒酿造业45家，从业人员152人。酿酒企业主要分布在县城和集镇以及石硐乡，以作坊生产方式为主，采用玉米酿造。酿造规模较大的有县酒厂、县饮食服务公司酒厂和县联营酒厂。县酒厂年产息烽醇和氡泉大曲800吨。是年，县酒厂年产值590.9万元，饮食服务公司酒厂年产100吨。1993年，县酒厂更名为贵州息烽温泉酒厂。是年，安顺民族经济科技发展有限公司承包该厂，生产温泉特曲和福贵醇。1995年，产值14.5万元。因生产不景气，2000年停产。1998年，有白酒小作坊11家。2007年，个体户以原三田乡政府办公楼为厂房，建小南山果酒厂，生产饮料酒，因销路不畅，2010年停产。2010年，共有酿酒小作坊25家，从业人员102人。

五、家具制造

1991年，县内家具生产多属小规模个体生产。2000年以前，家具生产以人工为主，从业人数较多。2000年以后，机器化程度提高，从业人员减少。1999年，家具生产规模较大的有流长邓培俊、刘应中2家。1993年，余万开在县政府大礼堂生产家具，后迁西门环城路。随着外来家具厂冲击，县内家具厂逐渐减少。2010年，共有家具厂6家，其中制门厂3家，其他家具厂3家。

第六节 农副食品加工

菜籽油加工 1991年，菜油加工主要在乡镇集镇进行，是年有菜油加工作坊22家，生产菜油1500吨。县城有粮食局所办油脂化工厂，年产国家标准二级菜油4000吨，从业人员46人，营业收入

199.4万元。2000年以后，县粮食局菜油加工停止，县城出现私营菜油加工作坊。2010年，有菜油加工作坊30家，生产菜油2000吨。

阳朗辣子鸡加工 1992年，黄南武在息烽集中营旧址出口处承包原阳朗公社旧房开辣子鸡餐馆，因味道鲜美，生意兴隆，逐渐形成辣子鸡品牌。以后不断扩大规模，带动阳朗辣子鸡品牌发展，阳朗辣子鸡成为闻名全国的贵州美食。1996年，叶兴林在火车站210国道边加工辣子鸡，生意火爆。2007年，黄南武、叶兴林相继在兰海高速息烽收费站到县城一线建立辣子鸡食府，带动食品工业发展。2009年，叶兴林注册叶老大辣子鸡品牌，建立贵州省息烽县叶老大阳朗辣子鸡食品有限公司。2010年，阳朗辣子鸡加工业30家，工业总产值2.49亿元。

辣椒系列食品加工 1999年，建立玄天商品厂，生产辣椒系列食品。2002年停产。2000年，贵阳苗姑娘食品有限公司入驻。2001年，贵州味美食品工业有限公司和贵州省息烽美满现代农业产业有限公司入驻。是年，年产油辣椒调味品1200万瓶、小米鲊200万件。味美食品工业有限公司年产姜油、葱油、蒜油各2000万瓶。2010年，苗姑娘食品有限公司、味美食品工业有限公司工业总产值分别为1.95亿元、0.47亿元。

大米加工 大米多采用打米机加工，各地建有加工房。1990—1993年，常年有50家加工大米。其中县粮食局打米厂规模最大，1991年产值231.1万元，1993年产值376万元，1995年产值440.3万元。2000年后，县粮食局打米厂停产。全县个体大米加工户常年45家。

第七节 磷矿石加工

1991年，县内磷矿产量23.51万吨，从业199人，外运销售15.64万吨，其中乡办企业温泉磷矿石场产量2.51万吨，产值125.5万元；磷矿石（粉）产销企业有县向阳磷矿粉厂、县燃料公司、国营贵州茂华化肥厂、县永阳磷矿粉厂、县金西矿粉厂、县金阳矿产联营公司、县温泉乡磷矿粉厂、县向阳矿产经营部、县养龙磷矿粉厂、县温泉乡矿产品产销部、县利民矿粉厂、县养龙司矿产品加工厂等12家。1995年，磷矿石（粉）产销企业29家，从业844人，产量11.8万吨，产值521.55万元。1998年，西阳矿粉厂获得出口经营权，产品主要销往日本，年销售15万吨。2010年，有磷矿石经营企业2家，产值4211.55万元；磷矿粉加工企业18家。

第八节 铁锅制造

20世纪80年代，硬寨村村民赵应科在下阳朗开办铁锅厂，生产铁铧和铁锅。1990年，引进锻压机器，由手工作坊生产发展到机器锻压。1991年，下阳朗铁锅厂生产铁锅10万口；从业人员12人。1994年，下阳朗铁锅厂命名为县铁锅厂。1995年，原县铁锅厂职工另建三星铁锅厂和金鑫铁锅厂，当年生产铁锅30万口。金鑫铁锅厂生产半年后停产。三星铁锅厂生产2年后停产。1998年，县铁锅厂生产铁锅50万口，税金12万元。2000年，县铁锅厂更名为贵州息烽长岭岗铁锅厂，产品由生产无柄铁锅转为生产有柄铁锅。2010年，县铁锅厂生产铁锅20万口，产值200万元；从业人员20人。

第四章　化学工业

1991年，县内有化学工业企业7家，1992年增加到8家，2010年减少到6家。主要生产黄磷、磷酸、复合肥、复混肥、磷铵、普钙、硫酸等。

第一节　产　品

县磷化工业主要产品有黄磷、磷酸、复合肥、复混肥、磷铵、普钙、硫酸。1990年，有磷化工企业7家，其中县磷肥厂、县黄磷厂规模较大，当年黄磷厂生产黄磷1120吨。1995年生产黄磷4001.8吨，2007年生产11284吨，2005年生产磷酸49.3万吨、硫酸58.1万吨、黄磷2万吨、农用氮磷钾化学肥料（折合量）71.2万吨；2010年，磷酸产量802693吨、硫酸57.54万吨、黄磷2.3万吨、农用氮磷钾化学肥料（折合量）146.48万吨。2001年，贵州西洋肥业有限公司生产复合肥料10万余吨；2006年，生产复合肥料39.93万吨；2007年，生产复合肥28.8万吨。2009年，西洋复合肥产量由过去四条生产线完成单班日产1600吨上升至日产2400吨；复混肥由过去日产100多吨，突破日产300吨硫酸，一、二期生产线由过去单线生产最高产量日产1200吨上升至1280～1300吨；磷酸单月产五氧化二磷1.7万吨。是年，生产各种肥料累计65万吨，创历史最高水平。2010年，生产硫酸72.2万吨、盐酸6.47万吨、硝酸铵肥86.9万吨、农用氮磷钾化肥39.1万吨。

第二节　产　销

一、贵州开磷磷业有限责任公司

1991年销售黄磷2300吨，收入1928.31万元。2004年2月转由开磷集团营销总公司营销。2007年销售黄磷12708吨，收入14263.99万元。2010年，销售黄磷14873.26吨，销售收入14895.21万元。

贵州开磷磷业有限责任公司1991—2010年黄磷产销统计表

表10-4-1

年份	黄磷产量（吨）	黄磷销售（吨）	销售收入（万元）
1991	2300	2300	1928.31
1992	2227	2227	3242.6
1993	2310	2310	2233.8
1994	2477.4	2477.4	2234.99
1995	4050.2	4050.2	3414.11
1996	3518	3518	2990.3
1997	5078.8	5006	4339.42

续表

年份	黄磷产量（吨）	黄磷销售（吨）	销售收入（万元）
1998	6068	5794.8	4091.86
1999	5663.34	6001.	3966.11
2000	5350.53	5354.2	3338.27
2001	4850.92	5077.41	3245.64
2002	5646.2	5608.2	3584.61
2003	5143.12	5276.37	4082.55
2004	3536.49	3175.04	4143.26
2005	8100.91	6814.73	7183.57
2006	11452.62	11434.6	10607.07
2007	11283.71	12708.14	14263.99
2008	9563.75	10256.43	12563.99
2009	11479.66	12909.48	13562.47
2010	13562.45	14873.26	14895.21

二、贵阳中化开磷化肥有限公司

2004年，生产磷酸一铵10.93万吨，销售11.04万吨；生产磷酸二铵8.54万吨，销售8.28万吨；生产重钙10.13万吨，销售10.57万吨；生产氢钙0.29万吨，销售0.37万吨；生产氟硅酸钠2165.75吨。实现销售收入4.47亿元，利润2200万元。

2005年，产品总量完成45.1万吨，销售收入7.63亿元，实现利润6735.17万元；上缴税费2113.03万元。次年，销售化肥57.34万吨，实现销售收入10.02亿元，利润4100万元，上缴税费2569.16亿元。

2010年，生产五氧化二磷67.95万吨、化肥155.28万吨、氟硅酸钠2.76万吨，实现销售收入34.46亿元，利润3.1亿元。

第三节　科研成果

2000年4月，重钙装置通过技术改造，实现达标达产。同年9月，氢钙装置通过技术改造达到设计生产能力。2005年11月29日申报的“一种磷酸二铵产品的包裹及冷却方法”专利，2006年1月12日申报的“延长硫黄制酸工艺中热副线阀门寿命的方法”专利，被国家知识产权局授予发明专利权。2006年12月，攻克用高镁磷矿石生产磷酸二铵产品外观质量差的难题，生产出颗粒饱满、外观圆润、粒度均匀的精品二铵。是年，合资公司矿浆浓密工作取得成功，满足200万吨矿浆磷酸萃取的需要，保证了矿浆输送工程的全面竣工和成功投用，填补了合资公司自主创新的空白，12月，该项目获得2006年度贵阳市科技创新一等奖。在此基础上，2007年，合资公司开展“开阳磷矿矿浆浓密技术研究”项目，浓密工艺技术重获贵阳市科技进步一等奖、贵阳市优秀技术改造项目一等奖和2007年度贵州省科技进步三等奖。6月11日申报的“一种硫黄喷枪枪体”和“一种硫黄喷枪枪头”两项专利，获国家知识产权局授予的实用新型专利权。2010年，1000吨无水氟化氢试验取得成功，生产出纯度为99.9%的无水氟化氢，达到国家一等品标准。“带结晶过滤器湿法磷酸浓缩装置”获新型专利证书。2010年6月29日申报的“硫酸催化剂筛分器”获实用新型专利证书。

1999年12月24日，重钙厂2000年达标排放年6万吨，成为贵州省首家实现2000年达标排放企业。2001年，重钙厂被国家石油和化学工业局授予“九五期间全国化工环境保护工作先进单位”称号，被贵阳市政府授予“贵阳市文化先进企业”称号，被评为全国“化工环保先进集体”。2003年6月，获得贵阳市政府“贵阳市第三届（1998—2002年）市长环境保护目标优秀奖”。2005年，被贵阳市环境保护局授予“环境友好企业”称号，被贵阳市水利局授予“水资源管理节水工作先进集体”称号。2006年5月，被贵州省环境保护局（厅）授予“贵州省环境友好企业”称号，被贵州省政府授予“全省环境保护先进集体”称号。2008年4月，获得中华全国总工会“全国职工节能减排合理化建议荣誉证书”。2009年4月，获得“2008年度贵阳市节能目标考核先进单位”二等奖。2010年1月，重钙厂荣获国家石化局、中国化工防治污染技术协会“九五”期间全国化工环保工作先进单位奖，被贵阳市精神文明建设指导委员会授予“2009年度贵阳市生态文明创建示范点”称号。

2005年5月，西洋肥业与贵州大学签订“贵州大学与西洋肥业关于开展产学研全面合作协议”。同年8月，西洋肥业省级“贵州大学—西洋肥业技术开发中心”成立，并研发出“硅钙钾肥”等多个新产品，获得国家9项专利权。8月，“贵州西洋集团用贵州大学发明专利——石灰烧结法生产氢氧化铝工业性试验”项目通过省级鉴定。鉴定结论认定本项目达到国内外同类（烧结法）现有生产氢氧化铝生产方法的先进水平。“钾钙肥新工艺新测试方法研究及应用”项目通过省级鉴定，处于国内先进水平。“西洋”牌聚合氯化铝获“贵阳市优秀新产品”三等奖；2006年，“西洋”牌小麦专用肥获“贵阳市优秀新产品”二等奖。镇远农业局20吨硅钾钙肥用于水稻、烤烟等作物进行大面积肥效试验，推广费4万元；贵州省亚热带农作物研究所在贞丰进行500亩甘蔗大面积肥效试验，推广费20万元。2月，硅钙钾肥经过大面积肥效试验，取得由农业主管部门颁发的肥料推广证。11月，“新技术建年产1万吨氢氧化铝”科研项目（总投资2000万元）立项。11月，“不溶性含钾岩石生产硅钙钾肥工业性试验”（总投资500万元）科研项目立项。2008年3月，贵阳市重点技术创新项目“低温连续转化、低温干燥生产高氮肥”项目（总投资1000万元）立项。申请2项国家专利。“一种用磷石膏制硫酸联产水泥的方法”和“一种用磷石膏生产硫化钙的方法”申请专利并获得受理。这两项专利参加在河北廊坊举行的第十七届全国发明展览会展览，获得两项铜奖。2007年8月，主持一次国家专利局在贵州省的专利调研活动。2007—2008年，西洋公司完成合成氨水冷器改造、合成氨余热烘煤技改、合成氨粉尘回收、磷酸闪蒸回浆管道改造、磷酸渣场回水利用改造、磷铵凉水池改造、磷铵蒸汽替代技改、复合肥热风机改造、复合肥转化车间双循环改单循环、硫酸厂送磺管道改造、硫酸厂工业水回收利用、硫酸厂汽机冷却系统改造等项目；实现节电351万千瓦时、节煤900吨、节水58万吨、节油5吨、节省0.7兆帕级蒸汽11887吨、节省液氨3000吨、回收粉尘30吨，为企业带来直接经济效益340.2万元/年。

第四节　地企共建

1997年，重钙厂投资300万元，帮助小寨坝镇修建南极公路约16千米；高家坝至荷包场垭口进村公路约3千米，总投资1200万元。

2000年4月13日，重钙厂向小寨坝镇捐赠“三元复混肥”100吨（价值13万元）。

2005年，西洋公司与县农业局、镇远县农业局、贵州省亚热带农作物研究所合作，进行大面积肥效试验，县农业局将100吨硅钾钙肥用于水稻、土豆、红薯、生姜、大蒜、折耳根（鱼腥草）等作物大面积肥效试验。

2008年，贵州开磷有限责任公司在小寨坝镇开展“良种、良肥、良法”配套工程（简称“三良工程”）试点，为全镇农户无偿提供优质化肥，对种植用地坡度不超过25度的农户，每亩补助肥料20千克，用于油菜、玉米、马铃薯、水稻等主要粮食作物种植。共无偿提供价值1624万元的“开磷牌”磷酸二铵化肥。次年，全县推广“三良工程”（详见本志第九篇第二章第六节第四目）。

第五章　工业园区建设与重要企业

第一节　工业园区建设

1996年，在永靖镇龙爪村、下阳朗村境内建食品医药工业园区，规划面积287.7公顷，总投资8249万元。至2000年，有5家医药企业入驻。至2008年，入驻园区企业11家，固定资产投入3.1亿元，投产企业9家，年产值6.3亿元。2010年，整合到县永靖食品医药工业园。

2010年，县建工业园区，规划面积30.56平方千米，按“一区四园”建设，息烽循环经济磷煤精细化工工业园区（小寨坝镇）；息烽永靖食品医药工业园、息烽温泉尹庵工业园（温泉镇尹庵村）、息烽西山金星工业园（西山乡金星村）、息烽养龙司工业园（养龙司乡养龙司村）。以磷煤化工、食品医药、建材、装备制造产业为主。县成立工业园区建设开发办公室，内设综合协调部、建设开发部、招商引资部负责园区开发事宜。是年底，工业园区有规模以上企业23家，从业8500余人，完成投资36.4亿元，实现工业产值166亿元、工业增加值36.23亿元，税收2.95亿元。

第二节　部分企业简介

一、贵州息烽磷矿

贵州息烽磷矿（简称息烽磷矿），1964年10月成立，位于温泉镇温泉村。1991年，息烽磷矿磷矿石开采为机械化配套作业，年开采20万吨。1994年，相继被化学工业部评为“全国化工思想政治工作优秀企业”，被省经济委员会、企业管理协会、企业家协会授予“贵州省优秀企业”称号。1995年，息烽磷矿有土地18宗，5197.12平方米。1998年，与新西兰五矿公司、贵州汇丰化工有限公司合资成立“贵州汇磷化学有限责任公司”，当年出口磷矿砂6276吨。1999年11月，成立进出口公司，拓展国际市场。2000年，取得天台铁路专线黄磷发运资格；自筹资金兴建年产2500吨6300千伏安黄磷装置及配套设施，建成并投产运行；引进社会车辆参与矿山剥离，扭转原先采剥失调状况。次年，以国家整顿矿山秩序为契机，开展治理矿山周边村民乱采滥挖矿石现象，有效保护国有资源。被省经贸委授予“出口创汇先进企业”称号。2002年，息烽磷矿磷产品被省商检局列为免检产品。2004年，息烽磷矿与职工持股会（职工自然人股东代表组织）、贵州开阳安达磷化工有限责任公司共同出资1351.1万元，组建成立“息烽合力化工有限责任公司”（简称合力公司）。2005年，登记注册成立“全力房地产开发有限公司”。2006年10月，被省国家税务局、地方税务局评为“2004—2005年度A级纳税信用企业”。2009年，投资500余万元对矿山老排土场进行整改治理，采取降坡减载、加固挡土坝及构筑新挡土坝等一系列措施，矿山排土场治理通过安全评审。2010年5月，对职工持股会所持合力股（职工个人持有股份）进行清退。8月，合力公司与彭山县同心水玻璃厂共同投资建设“年产5万吨水玻璃项目”。是年末，企业有职工750人（含离退休职工），其中各类工程技术人员90人（高级3人、中级21人、初级66人）；占地面积46631平方米，房屋建筑面积34101平方米（含职工住宅20501平方米）；拥有挖掘机、装载机、潜孔机、运输车辆等现代化矿山配套机械设备和黄磷生产装置，固定资产原值2590万元；磷矿石保有储量720万吨。被省国家税务局、地方税务局再次评为“A级纳税信用企业”。

二、贵阳中化开磷化肥有限公司

该公司前身为贵州开阳磷矿矿务局息烽重钙厂。地处贵州省贵阳市息烽县小寨坝镇，距离210国道0千米，贵阳到遵义高等级公路1千米，有专用铁路保障运输。1991年3月，成立贵州开阳磷矿矿务局息烽重钙厂（简称重钙厂）。2002年1月2日，“贵州开阳磷矿矿务局息烽重钙厂”更名为“贵州开磷集团息烽重钙厂”。2003年8月5日，贵州开磷有限责任公司、中国化工进出口公司、贵阳市工业投资控股有限公司合资组建贵阳中化开磷化肥有限公司（简称合资公司）。通过新建生产项目和实施技术改造，至2005年5月，合资公司具备年产80万吨硫酸、30万吨磷酸（100%五氧化二磷）、10万吨重钙、36万吨磷酸一铵、24万吨磷酸二铵、1.5万吨氢钙、磨矿100万吨的生产能力。2006年，完成年产30万吨磷酸、80万吨硫磺制酸、60万吨多功能复合肥等项目建设。2007年实施技改，高浓度磷复肥生产能力提高到年产140万吨。

2008年，合资公司引进行业先进生产管理经验，使年产24万吨磷酸二铵生产装置日产量提高到700吨以上，改写该装置投产6年来未能达标达产的历史。同年11月中旬，通过对60万吨磷酸二铵生产装置实施技术改造，取得“单、双管反应器连续运行3天以上不积料”的成效。2009年，完成料浆法重钙和57%磷酸二铵产品的开发并顺利投产，实现浓磷酸分级利用，增加化肥产品种类。完成年产1000吨无水氟化氢中试装置建设。

三、贵州西洋肥业有限公司

2000年3月10日，辽宁海城市西洋耐火材料公司兼并息烽县宏泰化工总厂，成立贵州西洋肥业有限公司（简称西洋肥业公司），注册资本3亿元。是年，启动年产100万吨硫基复合肥工程项目一期工程50万吨项目建设，2001年8月竣工投产。2002年，公司工业总产值80915万元，实现销售收入37278万元，利润8143万元，税金350万元。次年2月，西洋肥业公司与世界“杂交水稻之父”袁隆平合作，袁隆平任“杂交水稻‘良种良肥’技术创新工程”技术顾问。2004年，利用硫基NPK生产工艺，相继研制出水稻专用肥、玉米专用肥、小麦专用肥、大豆专用肥、水果蔬菜专用肥、烟草专用肥等肥种。开发“金光大道”“金色秋天”“加拿芬”“龙腾盛世”等独立品牌。次年，实现销售收入19亿元，利税1.42亿元。2009年，公司建设年产5万吨缓释型高氮复合肥生产线，利用尿醛法工艺喷浆造粒。开发新产品脲甲醛。2010年，生产硫酸72.2万吨、盐酸6.47万吨、硫酸52.47万吨、硝酸铵肥86.9万吨、农用氮、磷、钾化肥39.1万吨，完成工业总产值492020万元。

四、贵州息烽信科环化有限公司

贵州息烽信科环化有限公司（简称信科环化公司）2003年1月成立，位于县温泉镇工业园区，占地面积4万平方米，注册资本3000万元，资产总额5136万元，拥有年产氯化钡1.5万吨、硫脲4000吨的生产能力，时有员工280人。次年1月投入试产，9月实现满负荷生产。2005年，实现工业总产值7838万元，税收655万元，利润258万元。是年被贵阳市委、市政府评为“贵阳市非公有制经济‘十佳’明星企业”“贵阳市非公有制经济安置就业再就业‘十佳’先进企业”“贵阳市十八家循环经济试点企业”。

五、息烽龙泉磷肥厂

1958年，县建息烽磷肥厂，位于温泉镇尹庵村，占地面积44200平方米，建筑面积11043平方米。1990年因亏损停产。1992年，承包给个体经营。1999年10月，租赁给刘必林生产经营，更名为息烽龙泉磷肥厂。租赁后投入资金进行技术改造，建年产普钙3万吨、白肥2万吨两条生产线。2010年，工业总产值10142万元。

六、南山煤矿

位于小寨坝镇盘脚营村大麻窝村民组，1970年10月动工建井。1991年，使用ABD-21型瓦斯监测系统，生产能力30万吨/年，开采单一K5煤层。是年生产原煤21.5万吨。1998—2003年，更新安装KJ90系统，2004年，更名为贵州林东煤业发展有限责任公司南山煤矿。2007年实施改扩建后，设计年产原煤30万吨。2008年10月，建立完成三采区地面永久固定式瓦斯抽放系统。2010年，煤矿占地面积486.37亩，建筑面积71425平方米，有职工1009人，对入井人员实行专人专号、专卡管理。是年生产原煤20万吨。

七、贵州鑫悦煤炭有限公司

2002年11月26日成立，位于养龙司乡蚂蟥村陈家山村民组，下辖息烽利发煤矿和贵州省息烽宏达矿业有限公司，注册资本1500万元。2006年实施技术改造，设计生产能力15万吨。是年实现产值4500万余元、利润580万元。次年全资控股息烽坪土煤矿，公司原煤生产能力增至39万吨/年。2010年12月，公司总资产超过4.2亿元。

八、贵州息烽仁都建材有限公司

公司前身系息烽县水泥厂，位于永靖镇马当田村龙塘湾。1991年，从业人员138人；生产水泥4000吨，工业总产值300万元。1997年11月，贵州仁都工贸有限公司租赁经营息烽县水泥厂，更名为贵阳息烽银都水泥厂，注册商标“银都”牌。次年生产水泥4万吨。1999年，贵阳息烽银都水泥厂被贵阳市评为质量管理先进企业和“重合同、守信用”企业称号，“银都”牌水泥获贵阳市（推荐）产品质量奖。2002年7月，贵州仁都工贸公司购买息烽县水泥厂产权。次年5月更名为贵阳息烽仁都水泥厂，注册商标“仁都”牌，2005年1月26日，经股份制改造，更名为贵州息烽仁都建材有限公司。此后实施技术改造，建成年产10万吨32.5等级普硅水泥生产线，采用微机配料和煅烧工艺，产品连年经省、市质检部门抽检合格，2000年再次被评为“重合同、守信用”企业。2003年通过ISO9001：2000质量体系认证。2007年实现工业总产值1594万元，销售收入1506万元，利税200万元。2008年完成工业总产值1900万元，利税250万元。2010年，生产水泥8.5万吨，工业总产值3000万元。

九、贵州开磷建设公司建材厂

2005年12月，成立贵州开磷磷业公司建材厂，位于小寨坝镇，占地10.67万平方米。当年投资4100万元启动多功能石膏砌块项目建设。2006年4月，成立贵州开磷集团磷业有限责任公司建材厂重庆大学新型建材研发中心，开发资源综合利用循环经济产业。9月，启动1亿块新型耐水石膏标砖项目建设。10月，更名为贵州开磷建设公司建材厂。12月获国家知识产权局颁发“榫条模具”“高强耐水石膏砖及其制备方法”和“砌块模具”发明专利。2007年生产石膏砖631.66万块，工业总产值189.5万元。2008年12月，投资28881万元，启动2×5亿块/年新型磷石膏砖生产线建设。次年3月，投资996.66万元，启动年产10万吨建筑石膏粉项目建设。公司“高强耐水石膏砖”产品荣获贵州省2009年优秀新产品、新技术一等奖。2010年，生产石膏砖3038.35万块，产值911.5万元；生产免税建筑石膏1.28万吨，产值153.48万元。

十、贵阳金元铝业有限公司（贵州息烽铝厂）

1999年投资建设，次年建成投产，主要生产10千克铝锭。2004年停产。2006年公司进行收购重组，投入资金1.2亿余元。2007年实现工业产值3.14亿元。2008年，受凝冻灾害及金融危机影响，生产大幅度下滑，工业产值1.26亿元，安置富余劳动力300多人。2010年停产。

十一、贵州太和制药有限公司

1997年成立，生产基地位于贵阳市高新区息烽医药工业园。公司是以研究、开发云贵高原中草药资源和苗药为主的药品生产企业，主要产品有“平痔胶囊”“骄子”系列产品、“前列倍喜胶囊”等。2001年产值1.5亿元。2002年通过国家食品药品监督管理局GMP（良好生产规范）认证。2003—2007年，先后被贵州省科技厅认定为“民营科技企业”和“高新技术企业”，贵州省银行系统评为“信贷诚信企业”及“AA＋级信誉企业”，获“省级企业技术中心”和信息化建设先进单位称号等，2008年生产药品177.07吨，工业总产值7326万元，工业增加值1685万元，税金175万元。是年获“贵州省名牌产品”、息烽县农业产业化龙头企业称号。2010年，生产药品181.53吨，工业总产值6875万元，工业增加值1443万元，税金258万元。评为贵阳市及贵州省农业产业化龙头企业。

十二、贵州汉方制药有限公司

1992年成立，为汉方集团控股的股份制企业。1996年按GMP标准修建息烽药厂。1998年，销售收入5555.4万元，实现利税687.1万元。2009年2月，公司被贵阳市政府确定为贵州省十大重点制药企业之一。公司与中国医学科学院药物研究所联合开发的国家二类抗癌药“金喜素”（盐酸拓扑替康）获“贵州省1999—2000年度优秀新产品特等奖”，并被国家科技部评为“2001年度国家级星火计划项目”。公司创立的“日舒安”系列产品先后获得“中华医学会百名专家推荐精品”“中国妇女儿童喜爱产品”“中国著名品牌”“中国妇女儿童最喜爱的品牌产品”“中国妇科用药十大影响力品牌”“贵州省二十大重点品牌”等荣誉称号。2008年，公司产值1.6亿元，利税2236万元。2009年，“前列倍喜胶囊”进入《国家基本医疗保险工伤保险和生育保险药品目录（2009年版）》。2010年，实现产值2亿元，利税2500万元。

十三、贵州省息烽县叶老大阳朗辣子鸡食品有限公司

2002—2005年，叶老大阳朗辣子鸡先后在中国国际美食文化艺术节上被评选为“地方名特小吃”，被贵州省贸易厅、贵州烹饪饭店行业协会授予“贵州省名菜”称号，在黔菜美食电视大赛上获得“詹王杯”名火锅称号和“贵州十大名食”“贵州省著名商标”称号等。

2009年11月，成立贵州省息烽县叶老大阳朗辣子鸡食品有限公司（法人代表叶兴林）。在永靖镇柿花坪租用厂房2600余平方米加工生产辣子鸡，总投资600万元。规划年加工辣子鸡240吨，产值1500万元，实现利税600万元。2010年，公司总资产360.6万元，产值428万元。

十四、贵阳苗姑娘食品有限公司

2000年9月成立。2001年投资在息烽食品工业园内建厂，占地50亩，厂房2800平方米，以生产、销售“苗姑娘”系列辣椒调味品、休闲食品为主，产品有三大系列20余个品种。公司在县内青山苗族乡等4个乡镇建立无公害生产基地3000亩。2007年，实现产值580万元，销售544万元，上缴税金18万元，新增固定资产123万元。2008年，工业总产值1000万元，利税883万元。2010年，产值578.58万元，纳税21.87万元。

十五、贵州味美食品工业有限公司

该公司位于永靖镇环城路85号（县食品工业园区），占地面积9934.2平方米，2004年1月投产。至次年底，生产鲜调味油906吨，总产值6730万元，实现利润352万元。其间，公司获得全国工业产品生产许可证（QS），通过ISO9001：2000质量管理体系认证及HACCP食品安全管理体系认证。调味油产品荣获“贵阳市名牌产品”称号等。2006年起，公司全面开拓国内外保健市场，重点推出大蒜精油产品在保健品市场的应用，至2007年，实现总产值12279万元、利润579万元。2008年，投入300余万元进行调味油技术改造，荣获“贵阳市优秀技术改造项目”三等奖。2009—2010年，先后研发出鲜调味油系列18个品种，其中姜油、葱油、调和油获得国家知识产权局的专利保护，循环超声波提取技术的开发与应用项目荣获“贵阳市优秀技术改造项目”三等奖。实现产量3003吨、产值22027万元、利润995.1万元。

十六、贵州省息烽美满现代农业产业有限公司

2003年10月始建，占地165亩，位于永靖镇立碑村，项目总投资3305万元，是以加工优质鸡肉食品、培育优质种鸡和商品鸡苗为主，配套生产无公害饲料和生物有机复合肥为基础的产业。2005年，工业总产值1580.76万元，利税26.68万元，被评为“贵阳市农业产业化重点龙头企业”。2007年，总产值1404.67万元。

第十一篇　交通·邮政·通信

第一章　交　通

1991年，县境内有国道1条54千米，省道1条6千米，县乡道3条89千米。1996—1999年，实施村村通公路工程，改造、新建通村公路549千米。2010年末，县境内有国、省道53.9千米，贵遵高等级公路息烽段37千米，县道25条89.7千米，乡道6条75千米，等外级村公路（未达标验收）361条1180.98千米。每100平方千米内拥有公路149.7千米，每100人拥有公路1.41千米。

第一节　机　构

1991年5月，县交通局内设办公室，管理公路工区、运管所、征稽站、客车站、航管站、港监站、路政队。2003年3月，建立地方海事处，为正科级事业单位，下设顺江海事所、温泉海事所。撤销港监站，设安监科、船检科和处办公室。2007年9月，运输管理所、公路管理所升格为副科级单位，分别行使原县运管所、县公路工区职能。2008年7月，航务管理所并入地方海事处，县征稽站撤销。2010年8月，县交通局更名为县交通运输局，原县建设局城市客运管理办公室划归其管辖，内设办公室、财务审计科和交通规划建设科。

第二节　公路建设

一、高等级公路

（一）贵遵高等级公路息烽段

1995年10月，贵遵高等级公路息烽段动工修建，1997年5月20日通车，道宽12米，息烽段全长28千米。途经4个乡镇24个村，有息烽、小寨坝两个收费站。全段桥梁48座，其中特大桥2座，大桥1座，涵洞169道，隧道2座235米。2007年12月，扎南高等级公路息烽段投入使用后，息烽收费站及匝道停止使用。

（二）扎南高等级公路息烽段

2005年12月开始修建，2007年12月31日竣工通车。息烽段总长38.53千米，其中正线长35.73千米，至县城连线2.8千米。新建息烽收费站和小寨坝收费站。有大桥15座，隧道5个。途经3个乡镇19个村。

二、国道、省道

1991年，国道川黔公路息烽段全长28.3千米（南起K2229+200处，北至K2257+500处）。1992年改称210国道，2009年4月降为县道。

三、县道

1991年，有县城至九庄、黑神庙至新场、高田坎至何家硐3条县道。此后，国家政策支持和地方发展需求，县道建设力度加大。2010年，有县道26条，总长331.86千米，其中二级公路1.19千米、三级公路46.78千米、四级公路283.89千米。

息烽县2010年公路县道统计表

表11-1-1　　　　单位：千米

序号	公路起止		公路等级			
1	起	止	合计	二级	三级	四级
2	小寨坝	梨安	28.3	—	28.3	—
3	洪水营	温泉	5.16	—	—	5.16
4	石碑	南极办事处	12.29	—	—	12.29
5	底寨	马路岩	19.37	—	9.3	10.07
6	方家坪	养龙司	5.99	—	—	5.99
7	桐枝驿	石硐派出所	14.72	—	—	14.72
8	老何线K0+500	鱼简河桥	3.8	—	—	3.8
9	肖家湾	荆江码头	14.7	—	—	14.7
10	农机公司	玄天洞	8.41	—	—	8.41
11	九庄北门桥	黄沙渡口	43.6	1.19	—	42.42
12	张家桥	新民村委会	9.6	—	—	9.6
13	门斗坡	坝子边	26.57	—	—	26.57
14	九庄教场坝	流长	25.36	—	—	25.36
15	黑神庙	顺江码头	31.14	—	—	31.14
16	盘脚营	红岩	7.19	—	—	7.19
17	石硐上场口	梨安	15.44	—	—	15.44
18	养龙司火车站	大岩出行坡	4.28	—	—	4.28
19	关田坝	凤凰池	8.87	—	—	8.87
20	天台	金中小沟	7.23	—	—	7.23
21	龙塘湾	南极	15.47	—	—	15.47
22	刺竹山	长岭岗	9.18	—	9.18	—
23	九庄桥头	多缤洞	5.1	—	—	5.1
24	养龙司	江土村委会	8.04	—	—	8.04
25	茅坡	茅坡村委会	0.87	—	—	0.87
26	养龙司潘家寨	大岩	1.18	—	—	1.18

四、乡道

1991年，全县有乡道3条，总长89千米，多为泥石路面。2000年起，实施乡乡通油路工程，至2002年12月，投资3856万元，多数乡道改造为油路或进行硬化。2010年，全县乡道15条，总长799千米。

五、村组道

1991年，多数村组不通公路。1997年起，国家对村组公路建设实行补助政策，每修1千米公路，国家财政补助7000元，群众投工投劳，将泥巴路改造成泥石路。1998年，实施村村通公路工程。是年，投入资金552.5万元，炸药78吨，修建村公路72条549千米，建成涵洞188座1155米，小桥27座292.72米，1999年实现村村通公路。2006—2007年，升级硬化通村公路564.85千米。2008—2010年，升级改造公路20条。2010年，全县有村组公路361条1180.98千米。

六、专用公路

1993年前，县内有8条专用公路，里程8.2千米。2003年起，投入资金103.5万元，相继修建川黔公路K63+100至银杏鹰药厂、川黔公路K64+100至太和药厂、苗姑娘食品厂公路、养温路K14+200至信科环化氧化钡厂、养温路K12+600至西洋肥业公司公路、川黔公路K70+800至开磷黄磷厂和养温路K73+100至息烽磷矿黄磷厂公路7条专用公路，总长7.38千米。

七、公路及公路桥选介

（一）公路

养温公路：养龙司至温泉公路。1997年进行维修改造。2004年5月，对白石口至养龙站段进行升级改造，达国家四级标准。2005年，完成炒砂铺设。

息九公路：息烽至九庄公路。1993年、2001年、2002年分别进行升级改造，达国家四级标准。全长33千米。

黑新公路：黑神庙至新场公路。2001年至2002年12月，进行升级改造。2004年升级改造，达国家四级标准。2004年7月，因建厂征占，黑新公路改道从中心村黄连沟组到高家坝，2009年再次改道从大干沟到麻柳庄桥边连接黑新公路。

老涟路：老鸦河至涟江公路（原为高田坎至何家硐公路，称高何路）。2008年改为老鸦河至涟江。全长26.57千米。

鹿流公路：鹿窝至流长公路。2000年3月至2002年12月进行升级改造，达国家四级标准。

永青公路：永靖镇立碑村至青山公路。自川黔公路立碑村马场坝组门斗坡起，途经境内河丰至青山苗族乡，全长9千米。

石梨公路：石硐至梨安公路。全长20千米。途经猫场、梨安喜哑。三级公路。

金阳公路：开阳县金钟镇至永靖镇下阳朗村长岭岗组公路。全长20千米，三级公路。

九花公路：九庄镇天鹅桥至修文花朗公路。1993年12月竣工，总投资4.4万元，全长5.5千米。

何大路：石硐乡何家硐至修文大石公路。1994年11月竣工，总投资4.5万元，全长3千米。

金马路：西山乡金竹坪至马路岩公路。1995年12月竣工，总投资298.5万元，全长19.9千米。

玄天路：永靖镇龙爪村至雨洒村玄天洞公路。1995年12月竣工，全长8千米。

龙茅路：永靖镇龙塘湾至老厂村茅坪公路。1998年12月竣工，全长8千米。

竹黄路：九庄镇竹花至黄沙村公路。1999年12月竣工，总投资102万元，全长8.5千米。

鱼简河路：老鸦河至底寨鱼简河公路。2001年8月竣工，总投资130万元，全长7.5千米。

洗后路：洗马塘至后沟公路。2001年10月竣工，总投资60万元，全长2.3千米。

温永路：温泉至开阳永温公路。2002年12月竣工，总投资120万元，全长22千米，四级沥青路面。

关凤路：关田坝至凤池公路。2003年3月竣工，总投资600万元，全长10.3千米。

叶茅路：叶家沟至茅坡公路。2003年3月竣工，总投资380万元，全长7千米，四级沥青路面。

老高路：老鸦河至高田坎公路。2004年12月竣工，总投资330万元，全长15千米，四级沥青路面。

青高路：青山苗族乡青山村至石硐乡高寨村公路。2004年12月竣工，总投资88万元，全长8千米。

盘红路：盘脚营至红岩公路。2004年12月竣工，总投资70万元，全长7.3千米。

小南路：小寨坝至南极公路。2004年5月竣工，全长14千米。

方养路：方家坪至养龙司公路。2005年12月竣工，总投资4.4万元，全长5.5千米。

茅月路：茅坡至月亮湾公路。2005年12月竣工，总投资4.5万元，全长3千米。

养安路：养龙司至安江公路。2005年竣工，总投资120万元，全长8千米，四级沥青路面。

关马路：关田坝至马路岩公路。2007年竣工，总投资16万元，全长15千米。

马鹿路：马路岩至鹿窝公路。2009年竣工，总投资102万元，全长8.5千米。

大小路：大寨至小鹿窝公路。2010年竣工，总投资130万元，全长7.5千米。

（二）公路桥

仙人桥：位于西山乡小鹿窝村尾鲊组。建于清嘉庆八年（1883）；石拱，高11米，长26米，宽5.5米，横跨鹿窝河，通往西望山、潮水等地。

永兴桥：位于潮水村。清道光年间建；单孔石拱桥，高15米，宽5.5米，长28米，通往潮水。

天鹅桥：位于九庄天鹅村。1991年8月被洪水冲毁。政府投资16万元改建平板桥。

洪水营桥：连接开阳县永温与息烽县温泉。1992年，开阳、息烽两县共同投资修建，1993年3月竣工，4月举行通车典礼。

窑上跨河桥：位于温泉村窑上组境内，为钢筋混凝土直桥，1991年建成。

青山桥：位于青山苗族乡青山村。1996年5月修建，2005年6月由贵州省交通厅投资16.5万元重建。

小桥河桥：位于青山苗族乡小桥河。2007年3月由贵州省交通厅投资110万元改建，7月建成通车。

鹿窝桥：位于鹿窝乡。2006年3月由贵州省交通厅投资70万元改建，同年8月完工。

老鸦河桥：位于永靖镇河丰村。2004年4月由贵州省交通厅投资78万元，8月建成通车。

马灌塘桥：位于九庄镇竹花村。2010年5月开始修建，总投资56万元。

底寨文阁桥：位于西山乡柏香山村文阁组，又称文阁大桥。2008年危桥拆除，2010年5月动工重建，12月完工，总投资206万元。

第三节　公路养护

一、国道养护

1991—2010年，国道210线和养温公路由贵州省息烽公路养护段养护。

二、县乡公路养护

1991年，县乡公路养护主要以好路率、差路率、综合值进行考核。是年，县乡公路养护工作获安顺地区第一名。1993年，管养公路119.2千米，其中油路82.3千米，泥路36.9千米。2004年，管养公路116.4千米，其中改建3条23.4千米，乡公路48.2千米。完成水毁工程8处。公路优等路21千米、良等路72.9千米、次等路4.2千米，好路率95.7%，差路率0，养护质量综合值83%。1994年，息烽县被评为省级公路养护先进县。2004年以后，好路率、差路率、综合值不作为考核指标。2006年，每4千米设置一名养护保洁员，定人定线管护，确保路容整洁。是年，公路绿化15千米。2007年，经省公路局年终检查考核，县列养公路好路率100%。2009年，完成永温至温泉公路和息烽至九庄公路大修工程共8.7千米，恢复鹿新公路、黑新线、老何线、九花线、石梨线、金马线、息九线、小南线等挡墙1756.9立方米，清理坍方598立方米。投资99.42万元的老何线、黑新线安保工程通过贵州省公路局验收。2010年，完成金阳公路息烽段、小寨坝至梨安公路大修，息九公路中修，老鸦河至涟江公路、息九公路、九流公路、黑新公路、小南公路等6条公路小修；完成底关公路安保工程。

三、村组公路养护

1991年至2007年5月，村组公路由公路沿线群众负责养护管理，分为日常性养护、季节性养护、临时性养护；实行弹性养护制，忙时干农活，闲时养村道。2007年6月，成立县公路管理所，对村公路养护进行管理。2008—2009年，实行村民自己管理与专门管理相结合。2010年7月9日，将农村公路养护管理纳入目标考核。

第四节　铁　路

川黔铁路息烽段：北起养龙司与遵义乌江董家坪交界处，南至永靖镇梨安村，全长49.33千米，设养龙司、小寨坝、盘脚营、息烽、阳朗、新萝村6个车站，途经养龙司、小寨坝、永靖镇3个乡镇。1991年10月，川黔线电气化改造工程竣工。2006年11月，完成过境公路与铁路平改立工程9座。电气化铁路开通后，铁路部门对列车通行信号、通车信息等进行技术改造，运用微机联网远程监控，由成都铁路局全面实行总控调度。

小寨坝至开阳金钟铁路：1959年县境开阳支线始建，1960年竣工投入使用，途经小寨坝、天台，县境终点在温泉热水坪。

息烽重钙厂货运铁路专线：1991年动工，长1.5千米，总投资1900万元，1995年投入使用，货站年吞吐量45万吨。

第五节　水　路

一、监管水域

1991年，县境通航里程91.7千米，监管水域面积约20平方千米。2010年，乌江库区主航道32.4千米、瓮桶河10千米、雨淋河4千米、息烽河16千米、鱼简河水库3千米、构皮滩水库23千米，共计88.4千米，所辖水域涉及7个乡镇22个村。

二、渡口

1991年，县境有周家岩、花树塘、黄沙、丁家岩、大塘、顺江、荆江，青㭎林、三道拐、大寨、菜子土、对门寨、仲家坪、小南江14个渡口。2005年，改造顺江、大塘、荆江、黄沙、花树塘、周家岩、丁家岩渡口。2008年，构皮滩水库建设完毕，温泉镇三交村大塘口水位上涨，建筑北码头。2010年，改造周家岩、花树塘、黄沙、丁家岩、大塘、顺江、荆江渡口，渡口通行道路硬化成水泥路或梯步。改造青㭎林、三道拐、大寨、菜子土、对门寨、仲家坪、小南江7个自用渡口。

息烽县2010年乌江库区渡口统计表

表11-1-2

名称	地点	改建时间	长度（米）	宽度（米）	水深（米）	年船舶渡运量（万人/次）
顺江渡口	流长乡水尾村	2005年	30	1000	150	2.04
大塘渡口	流长乡前奔村	2005年	20	1200	150	2.92
黄沙渡口	九庄镇黄沙村	2005年	25	1200	120	2.19
花树塘渡口	九庄镇堰坪村	2005年	20	800	120	1.82
周家岩渡口	九庄镇柏茂村	2005年	20	500	110	0.73
丁家岩渡口	鹿窝乡杨寨村	2005年	18	500	110	1.65
荆江渡口	养龙司乡荆江村	2005年	40	1200	150	1.08

第六节　运　输

一、公路运输

（一）运输企业

1991年，粮食局车队从事运输，2000年解体。

2002年3月，息烽瑞达汽车运输有限公司与息烽县社会客运站共同出资，成立息烽县黔通快捷客货运输有限公司。公司地址位于永靖镇花园东路，占地面积6450平方米，建筑面积420平方米，有办公楼1栋，办公室4间，会议室1间；有客运停车场1个，停车位207个；有440平方米货运停车场1个，停车位35个；有中小型普通客车97辆，总座位2301座，经营二、三、四类客运班线37条；有员工100余人。

2004年，息烽瑞达有限责任公司成立，地址位于永靖镇花园东路。2007年，租用公路运输管理所办公室6间、会议室1间办公。有客运停车场1个（3225平方米），内设停车位207个。

2010年3月，县内首家出租车公司——息烽县宏运出租车有限公司成立，有出租车47辆（均安装GPS），在岗驾驶员121人，基本实现经营网络化和信息化。

（二）货运

1991年，县内有解放牌、东风牌、欧曼牌、川路牌、王牌、十通牌、嘉龙牌等大中型货车277辆，有运输服务业6户，从事装卸行业19户。农村运输工具有拖拉机、嘉陵车、马车、板车等。部分村民开始使用摩托车运输。此后，货运车辆增加。1999年村村通公路后，靠马匹运输的情况逐渐减少，乡村摩托车逐渐增加，多用于运输农产品和载客赶集。县城十字街到息烽集中营微型车揽客较多。2000年后，微型车逐渐淘汰，乡镇间使用中巴车载客；摩托车成为遍及城乡的小型运输工具。至2010年，运输车辆1297辆（客车197辆，货车1100辆），其中营业性客运车191辆，客位3660座，客运班线47条；营业性货车863辆。是年，全县有板车18辆，马车13辆。个别边远落后地区仍以人畜运输为主。

（三）客运

1991年，全县有从县城至九庄，县城至流长，县城至养龙司、温泉3条客运线路，有客车29辆；有县城至阳朗、至底寨、至黑神庙3条微型车客运线路，有微型车45辆。

1993年，完成客运量53万人次。

1998年，有农村客运班线8条，客运班车52辆，通达率近40%；有县城至贵阳城市客运班线1条，客运车辆16辆，客运班次16班。是年，县建设局从贵阳公交公司接来下线19座普通型公交车4辆，承包给个体户从事城市客运。

2003年，县内首次投放出租轿车20辆从事客运经营，次年，投放出租车30辆。

2006年，客运车辆基本实现公司化管理。是年，新增19座中巴车5辆。

2008年，全县10个乡镇通客车，村客车通车率92%；农村客运班线29条，客运车辆88辆，日发班（长、短线）435班次；有县城至遵义市、遵义县、贵阳、开阳、修文等跨县（地区）客运班线5条，有客运车51辆，日发班次70班次。

2010年，有城市公交车线路4条（县城至阳朗、十字街至火车站、永靖镇龙爪村至永红村、永靖镇至红旗村），车辆23辆465座；有出租车50辆；有客运班线45条，客运车辆192辆。总运输里程1418千米，其中市际班线3条228千米，车辆7辆；县际班线13条942千米，车辆44辆；县内班线29条248千米，车辆137辆。

息烽县1991—2010年客货运输统计表

表11-1-3

年份	客运量（万人）	旅客周转量（万人千米）	货运量（万吨）	货物周转量（万吨千米）
1991	96	3265	146	2042
1992	162	5462	118	2075
1993	143	4745	120	2101
1994	173	5187	122.5	2205
1995	148	5920	59	1770
1996	175	6647	81	2325
1997	177	6685	84	2520
1998	182	7089	94.57	2833
1999	187	7089	124	3619
2000	206	7132	108.5	3120
2001	225	7828	186.2	9696

续表

年份	客运量（万人）	旅客周转量（万人千米）	货运量（万吨）	货物周转量（万吨千米）
2002	225	7904	185	9800
2003	227	7974	193	9896
2004	244.5	8424	200.9	10264
2005	230	8000	190	9000
2006	280	8500	250	10000
2007	300	9000	260	12000
2008	320	12000	280	13000
2009	320	12000	280	14000
2010	360	14000	300	16000

息烽县2010年客运班线、客车统计表

表11-1-4

序号	起点站	终点站	车辆数	序号	起点站	终点站	车辆数
一、县内班线				28	温　泉	荆　江	4
1	息　烽	江　土	1	29	九流片区		6
2	息　烽	安　龙	1	县　际			
3	息　烽	仲家坪	1	30	息　烽	贵　阳	22
4	息　烽	南　极	2	31	柏　茂	贵　阳	1
5	息　烽	竹　花	1	32	温　泉	贵　阳	2
6	息　烽	红　岩	4	33	新　杨	贵　阳	1
7	息　烽	九　庄	11	34	煤　矿	贵　阳	1
8	息　烽	温　泉	15	35	流　长	贵　阳	1
9	息　烽	流　长	8	36	小寨坝	贵　阳	2
10	息　烽	何家硐	7	37	九　庄	贵　阳	4
11	息　烽	新　杨	1	38	二七六	贵　阳	2
12	息　烽	鹿　窝	3	39	石　硐	久　长	2
13	息　烽	甘　溪	2	40	黑神庙	金　中	2
14	息　烽	青　山	4	41	息　烽	开　阳	2
15	息　烽	荆　江	2	42	息　烽	修　文	2
16	息　烽	小寨坝	12	市（地、州）际			
17	息　烽	久　长	8	43	息　烽	遵　义	3
18	息　烽	猫　场	3	44	磷　矿	遵　义	2

续表

序号	起点站	终点站	车辆数	序号	起点站	终点站	车辆数
19	息　烽	河坎寨	1	45	息　烽	南　白	2
20	息　烽	西　山	6				
21	十字街	火车站	11				
22	息　烽	老　厂	2				
23	息　烽	阳　朗	—				
24	息　烽	底　寨	12				
25	流　长	顺　江	6				
26	温　泉	荆　江	1				
27	息　烽	南山矿	2				

（四）场站建设

1991—2004年，相继建养龙司简易停车场、县城客运站。2005年，投资1100万元，在县城新建16720平方米二级客运站，当年投入使用。2006—2010年，相继建成温泉镇、九庄镇、石硐乡、流长乡、鹿窝乡、青山苗族乡、小寨坝镇客运站。其间，2008年2月动工修建县客运站，2010年3月竣工投入运营。

二、铁路运输

（一）客运

1991年，有重庆至贵阳561次、562次，遵义至贵阳563次、564次列车在息烽站停靠。是年发送旅客210.5万人次。2004年6月，调整为遵义至贵阳7431次、7432次列车在息烽站停靠，是年发送旅客260.85万人次。2007年起，再次调整为重庆至贵阳5613次、5614次和贵阳至北京西站19次列车在息烽站停靠。2010年发送旅客130.66万人次。

（二）货运

县境有新萝村、息烽、盘脚营、小寨坝、养龙司、天台6个火车货运站，其中息烽站为客货两用。

息烽县1991—2010年铁路运输统计表

表11-1-5

年份	发送旅客（万人）	发送货物（万吨）	装车数（车）	卸车数（车）
1991	210.5	433.47	76071	56633
1992	216.38	464.99	80252	60873
1993	244.33	521.36	89233	68682
1994	265.99	544.74	91532	67515
1995	297.19	594.22	100028	88984
1996	319.13	623.77	105754	94422

续表

年份	发送旅客（万人）	发送货物（万吨）	装车数（车）	卸车数（车）
1997	324.62	616.82	103991	90750
1998	337.16	676.04	112957	79222
1999	331.42	677.63	113241	87747
2000	353.73	669.53	113598	89611
2001	304.82	394.01	66922	103380
2002	291.4	818.18	137536	99406
2003	251.71	916.3	152021	112029
2004	260.85	1015.42	168568	122545
2005	274.66	1023.76	168838	121020
2006	128.79	1097.76	178199	135883
2007	129.4	—	—	—
2008	129.71	—	—	—
2009	129.85	—	—	—
2010	130.66	—	—	—

四、水上运输

（一）船舶

1991年，有各类船舶22艘。2006年底，乌江库区及支线航道共有各类船舶38艘。其中客船（矩形钢质船）21艘，总吨位101吨，载客量294人，主机功率9千瓦；货船（矩形钢质船）12艘，总吨位1112吨；非机动船5艘，总吨位122.5吨。2010年，注册登记客船7艘、货船8艘、工程作业船6艘、渡口船14艘、餐饮趸船1艘、渔船435艘、自用船11艘。注册登记船员63人。有渔业船舶建造厂1家。

（二）客货航运

乌江库区形成前，水运依靠传统木船；乌江库区形成后，始有机船运输，主要运送煤炭；木船、汽艇多用于载人。线路由六广河、周家堰至乌江大坝。其中煤炭主要在顺江码头起载。

息烽县1991—2010年货船运输统计表

表11-1-6

年份	货船（艘）	船型	运价（元/吨/千米）	年货运量（万吨/千米）	年货物周转量（万吨/千米）	营业额（万元）
1991	5	矩形钢质	0.2	1	1	0.8
1992	5	矩形钢质	0.25	1	1	1
1993	5	矩形钢质	0.25	1	1	1
1994	5	矩形钢质	0.25	1	1	1

续表

年份	货船（艘）	船型	运价（元/吨/千米）	年货运量（万吨/千米）	年货物周转量（万吨/千米）	营业额（万元）
1995	6	矩形钢质	0.35	1.2	1.2	1.61
1996	6	矩形钢质	0.35	1.2	1.2	1.61
1997	6	矩形钢质	0.65	1.4	1.4	3.25
1998	6	矩形钢质	0.65	1.4	1.4	3.25
1999	6	矩形钢质	0.65	1.4	1.4	3.25
2000	8	矩形钢质	0.8	1.62	1.62	6.48
2001	8	矩形钢质	0.8	1.62	1.62	6.88
2002	10	矩形钢质	放开	4.4	4.4	42.4
2003	12	矩形钢质	放开	4.9	4.9	42.4
2004	12	矩形钢质	放开	5.6	5.6	31
2005	16	矩形钢质	放开	9.6	9.6	79.6
2006	16	矩形钢质	放开	15.6	15.6	96.94
2007	21	—	—	5.1	76.5	—
2008	21	矩形钢质	放开	18	270	—
2009	21	矩形钢质	放开	24	480	—
2010	21	矩形钢质	放开	20	400	—

息烽县1991—2010年渡口客船运输统计表

表11-1-7

年份	渡口船（艘）	船型	运价（元/人/次）	年渡运量（万人/次）	营业额（万元）
1991	12	木质、钢质各6艘	0.5	3.2	1.6
1992	13	木质6艘、钢质7艘	1	3.6	3.6
1993	13	木质6艘、钢质7艘	1	3.6	3.6
1994	13	木质6艘、钢质7艘	1	3.6	3.6
1995	12	木质、钢质各6艘	1	3.4	3.4
1996	12	木质、钢质各6艘	1	3.4	3.4
1997	12	木质、钢质各6艘	1	3.4	3.4
1998	12	木质、钢质各6艘	1.5	3.4	5.1
1999	12	木质、钢质各6艘	1.5	3.4	5.1
2000	12	木质、钢质各6艘	1.5	3.4	5.1
2001	12	木质、钢质各6艘	1.5	3.4	5.1

续表

年份	渡口船（艘）	船型	运价（元/人/次）	年渡运量（万人/次）	营业额（万元）
2002	12	矩形钢质	放开	4.4	6.6
2003	12	矩形钢质	放开	7.2	10.8
2004	12	矩形钢质	放开	7.2	10.8
2005	12	矩形钢质	放开	9.8	14.7
2006	12	矩形钢质	放开	7.2	10.8
2007	12	矩形钢质	放开	9.8	14.7
2008	12	矩形钢质	放开	9.8	14.7
2009	243			89	214.64
2010	12	矩形钢质	放开	9.8	14.7

息烽县1991—2006年客航运统计表

表11-1-8

年份	客船（艘）	船型	运价（元/人/千米）	年客运量（万人）	年旅客周转量（万人/千米）	营业额（万元）
1991	5	矩形钢质	0.15	2.4	6.6	0.99
1992	7	矩形钢质	0.2	2.8	7.2	1.44
1993	7	矩形钢质	0.2	2.8	7.2	1.44
1994	7	矩形钢质	0.2	2.8	7.2	1.44
1995	7	矩形钢质	0.2	2.8	7.2	1.44
1996	7	矩形钢质	0.2	2.8	7.2	1.44
1997	7	矩形钢质	0.3	2.8	8.4	2.52
1998	7	矩形钢质	0.3	2.8	8.4	2.52
1999	7	矩形钢质	0.3	2.8	8.4	2.52
2000	8	矩形钢质	0.45	3.4	9.2	4.14
2001	8	矩形钢质	0.45	3.4	9.2	4.14
2002	9	矩形钢质	放开	5	24	12
2003	9	矩形钢质	放开	4.5	24	12
2004	9	矩形钢质	放开	4.5	24	12
2005	8	矩形钢质	放开	19	210	20
2006	8	矩形钢质	放开	26	210	20

第七节　路政运政管理

1991年，清除路障340处，制止红线内建筑253平方米，拆除违章建筑79平方米。此后，清除路障、制止和查处红线内建筑等，实行常态化管理。1992年5月，在公路沿线7个乡镇19个村巡回宣传公路法规，张贴通告61份，书写宣传标语3条，受教育群众7000余人次。坚持上路检查，制止红线内建筑物17幢179平方米；对息九路、高何路两旁7472株行道树进行石灰刷白。

1994年，县交通部门组织人员上路稽查142天485人次，查扣车辆62台，扣证费94693元，其中罚款6245元。对经营行业实行年度审验，审验率92.8%。发证14个。

1995—2000年，制止红线内建筑197起（户）646平方米；清除路障218处913.5平方米；查处毁坏行道树案件5起，行政拘留2人，罚栽行道树1065棵；查处毁坏桥梁1起；收取公路赔偿费24875元，罚款7020元。

2001年，开展宣传学习贯彻《中华人民共和国公路法》《贵州省公路路政管理等条例》活动。组织干部职工利用赶场天到城关、流长、鹿窝、石硐、九庄等地宣传，散发、张贴路政宣传资料2000余份，接受群众咨询和解答有关路政运政知识。

2002年起，开展超限运输检查专项治理行动，至2007年，查处超限车辆130辆，卸载110吨；处罚恶性超限车辆12辆，收取超限运输费5.47万元、公路赔（补）偿费6.37万元、罚款3300元。

2008年，出动执法人员101人次、车辆79辆次、巡航船艇47艘次，巡航里程1394千米，检查船舶94艘，纠正各类违章12次。2009年，治理超限车辆95辆，收取超限运输费9500元。2010年，印制宣传标语4000余份，利用乡镇赶场天向群众宣传法律法规；处理公路两侧违章堆放物65起452平方米，收取公路赔（补）偿费1.25万元，治理超限车辆195辆，收取超限运输费2.15万元。

第八节　规费征收

1991年，征收汽车养路费192.4万元、汽车管理费19.8万元、拖拉机养路费6.5万元、客运附加费13.5万元、航运管理费721元、船舶折旧费1980元。2008年，征收运输管理费102.5万元、客货运附加费（交通发展基金）146.37万元、汽车养路费1001.87万元、摩托车养路费21.62万元、船舶港务费1400元、船舶检验费5000元。2009年1月1日起，实行"费改税"，停止征收客货运附加费和运输管理费，继续征收船舶检验费、港务费。

第九节　水上交通安全

1991年，安全检查4次，查处船舶37艘次，纠正违章16起。1995年，安全检查32次，渡口检查73次，检查船舶29艘，处理违章22艘次。1996年，成立清理整顿三无船舶领导小组，对22艘乡镇船舶、5艘机动船、8艘渡口船进行登记，取缔私设渡口1处。配合遵义、金沙港监和县渔政部门开展检查工作。2006年，安全检查90余次，出动车辆90余次，人员350人次，重点检查14道渡口、渡船安全和来往船舶。2007年5月4日，县地方海事处在乌江库区顺江码头举办船员安全知识培训班，30名渔船船员参加学习培训。2007年，检查各类船舶80艘，处理违章21起，并对船舶超员超载、无证航行、非客船违章载客、无证驾驶行为实施当场教育警告、违法记分、现场处罚、责令停航等。2008年，检验客船、渡船、货船等29艘。查处和取缔流长街、流长大寨、小寨坝马尔河码头、养龙司荆江4个非法造船点。2010年，现场监督重要渡口和重点航段，发放宣传资料1万余份。

第二章 邮 政

1990年，县邮电局下辖底寨、养龙司、九庄、黑神庙4个邮电支局，6个邮电所、2个邮政代办所。1998年9月1日，邮政、电信分开营业。2005年开始电子商业服务，2007年实施物流服务，2010年，设综合办公室、市场部、金融部、代理业务部、投递部、文化路营业部、中街储蓄所、西山支局、石硐支局、九庄支局、流长支局、黑神庙支局、养龙司支局、西洋支局、温泉支局。开通邮政代收话费、电费、水费、有线电视收视费业务。

第一节 机 构

1990年，县邮电局内设行政办公室、计财供应室、技术业务室，机线、报务、话务、大修、营业发行、分拣投递6个班组和机务站，下辖底寨、养龙司、九庄、黑神庙4个邮电支局，6个邮电所、2个邮政代办所。1998年9月1日，邮政、电信分开营业，11月1日，县邮政局成立，内设综合办公室、经营服务部、会计室、鲜花礼仪部、集邮门市部、投递班。2000年，会计室并入综合办公室，增设储汇室、经警队。2004年，增设市场部、代理业务部。2007年，县邮政速递部独立运营。2008年，增设信贷部。2010年，设综合办公室、市场部、金融部、代理业务部、投递部、文化路营业部、中街储蓄所、西山支局、石硐支局、九庄支局、流长支局、黑神庙支局、养龙司支局、西洋支局、温泉支局。

第二节 邮政业务

一、邮路

1990年，邮电局由县城中街迁入文化路。全县邮路40条。火车邮路：县城至养龙司；委办邮路：县城至九庄（包括底寨、石硐、九庄）；自行车自办邮路：养龙司至三所，养龙司至温泉，大林口至石硐，火车站至县局本埠。1993—2010年，邮路精减为外包邮路2条：息烽—底寨—石硐—九庄；息烽—三所—黑神庙—养龙司—西洋—温泉和四个投递段：上段包括县府路、解放南路、环城东路、文化南路；下段包括解放北路、东风路、筑北大道、东门路、河滨路、环城路、政府路、育才路、柿花坪路；南山段包括虎城中路、半边街、火车站片区、硬寨片区。县局设委代办，乡投递员负责投送。

二、邮政网点

1991年，全县邮政营业网点10个：文化路邮政所、石硐邮政所、九庄邮政所、流长邮政所、养龙司邮政所、温泉邮政所、黑神庙邮政所、青山邮政所、底寨邮政所、中街储蓄所。1992年10月，开办黑神庙储蓄所；1995年4月，开办文化路储蓄所；1996年6月，开办火车站储蓄所。2003年2月，火车站储蓄所搬迁至温泉西洋复合肥有限公司，更名为西洋储蓄所。2010年，县邮政局有县城文化路、石硐、九庄、流长、养龙司、西洋、温泉、黑神庙、底寨等9个支局，南山、鹿窝、阳朗等3个代办点和中街储蓄所。

三、邮政储蓄

1991年，中街邮政储蓄所余额8.81万元，其中定期存款6.35万元、活期存款2.46万元。此后办理邮政储蓄的网点增加，储蓄业务迅速发展。1994年底，邮政储蓄余额732.91万元，是1991年的83.19倍。次年突破千万元，为1238.23万元，其中定期存款883.62万元、活期存款354.61万元。1999年突破两千万元，为2292.14万元，其中定期存款1480.03万元、活期存款812.11万元。2005年突破亿元，为10614.67万元，其中定期存款8123.27万元、活期存款2491.4万元。2010年底，储蓄余额16892万元，其中定期存款8302万元、活期存款8590万元。

息烽县1991—2010年邮政储蓄统计表

表11-2-1　　　　单位：万元

年份	储蓄额	定期	活期
1991	8.81	6.35	2.46
1992	33.65	22.42	11.23
1993	52.21	31.47	20.74
1994	732.91	519.29	213.62
1995	1238.23	883.62	354.61
1996	1634.81	1030.48	604.33
1997	1881.3	1467.85	413.45
1998	1998.61	1468.46	530.15
1999	2292.14	1480.03	812.11
2000	2237.57	1597.01	640.56
2001	2830.69	2256.56	574.13
2002	4185.07	3308.37	876.7
2003	6830.37	5420.62	1409.74
2004	8346.7	6401.18	1945.52
2005	10614.67	8123.27	2491.4
2006	12012.78	8014.13	3998.65
2007	10853.31	6368.13	4485.18
2008	12076	7119	4957
2009	15684	8106	7578
2010	16892	8302	8590

四、函件

1991年，全县收寄函件（含印刷品）0.98万件，计费1.23万元。此后收寄函件逐渐增加：1999年10.33万件，计费10.32万元；2007年20.01万件，计费22.31万元；2009年30.02万件，计费20.65万元；2010年43.64万件，计费20.32万元。

息烽县1991—2010年邮政函件统计表

表11-2-2

年份	件数（万件）	计费（万元）
1991	0.98	1.23
1992	1.98	2.12
1993	2.83	2.34
1994	3.12	3.02
1995	4.32	3.45
1996	5.23	6.02
1997	7.63	7.12
1998	9.86	9.35
1999	10.33	10.32
2000	11.32	11.6
2001	12.98	12.95
2002	13.02	13.01
2003	14.98	13.21
2004	15.23	18.23
2005	16.12	19.12
2006	18	20.01
2007	20.01	22.31
2008	25.08	21.31
2009	30.02	20.65
2010	43.64	20.32

五、包件

1991年，全县邮政包件1.02万件，收费0.18万元。此后，邮政包件直线上升，1997年10.63万件，收费0.76万元。2009年22.73万件，收费9.31万元。2010年，因物流、快递、宅急送等公司兴起，邮政包件数量急剧下滑，是年，邮政包件6.46万件，收费5.31万元。

息烽县1991—2010年邮政包件统计表

表11-2-3

年份	件数（万件）	计费（万元）
1991	1.02	0.18
1992	1.96	0.25
1993	3.21	0.35
1994	4.32	0.48
1995	6.59	0.62
1996	8.12	0.72
1997	10.63	0.76
1998	13.25	0.96
1999	15.21	1.02
2000	16.33	1.31
2001	17.25	1.32
2002	17.35	1.46
2003	17.55	1.57
2004	17.62	1.56
2005	18.68	1.68
2006	18.55	1.32
2007	18.36	10.21
2008	17.41	9.41
2009	22.73	9.31
2010	6.46	5.31

六、汇兑

1991年，兑付汇票2.62万张，收汇1.63万张；1996年，国内汇兑汇票9.15万张；2000年，国内汇兑汇票15.98万；2001年，国内汇票16.31万张，办理特快汇款业务635件。2001年1月起全国联网。2002年，国内汇票4.21万张，兑付汇票13.31万张。2003年起，汇票全部改为电子汇款，国内汇票5.12万张，兑付12.98万张；2005年，国内汇票5.11万张，兑付12.4万张；2006年，国内汇票5.02万张，兑付13.53万张；2008年，国内汇票4.82万张，兑付8.38万张；2010年，国内汇票4.03万张，兑付4.5万张。

息烽县1991—2010年邮政汇兑统计表

表11-2-4

年份	件数（万张）	计费（万元）
1991	4.25	0.21
1992	4.55	0.32
1993	6.35	0.63
1994	6.85	0.83
1995	8.25	0.93
1996	9.15	1.02
1997	9.25	1.12
1998	9.85	1.62
1999	10.1	1.85
2000	15.98	1.95
2001	16.31	1.98
2002	17.52	2.04
2003	18.1	2.08
2004	18.7	2.11
2005	17.51	2
2006	18.55	2.01
2007	15.7	2
2008	13.2	2.01
2009	12.3	2.45
2010	8.53	2.65

七、报刊发行

1991年，报纸发行176.33万份，杂志9.3万份，报刊流转额28.3万元。1995年，订销报纸212.12万份，杂志10.02万份，报刊流转额45.23万元。1996年起，报刊业务与贵州省联网，数据通过计算机传送。1999年，订销报纸202.12万份，杂志9.03万份，报刊流转额65.12万元。2000—2005年，订销报纸720.15万份，杂志37.12万份，报刊流转额489.32万元。2006—2009年，订销报纸912.32万份，杂志46.16万份，报刊流转额456.22万元。2010年，订销报纸385.26万份，各类杂志5.64万份，报刊流转额145万元。订销总量下滑。

息烽县1991—2010年部分年份报刊发行统计表

表11-2-5

年份	报纸（万份）	杂志（万份）	报刊流转额（万元）
1991	176.33	9.3	28.3
1992	187.63	9.65	31.12
1993	198.23	9.86	34.15
1994	208.63	9.98	39.23
1995	212.12	10.02	45.23
1999	202.12	9.03	65.12
2000	101.32	4.04	43.65
2001	122.38	5.25	46.32
2002	123.45	5.35	89.63
2003	124.68	6.85	98.24
2004	123.58	7.51	103.25
2005	124.74	8.12	108.23
2006	108.14	10.78	110.31
2007	206.63	14.12	119.24
2008	285.32	12.63	120.65
2009	312.23	8.63	138.02
2010	385.26	5.64	145

八、机要邮件与集邮

（一）机要邮件

1991—1992年，全县机要邮件3821件，1995年1820件，1998年1321件，2000年3122件，2003年2132件，2005年5414件，2007—2010年,全县机要邮件8388件。

（二）集邮

1991年集邮收入1.23万元，1995年集邮收入1.85万元，1999年集邮收入2.13万元。2006年，集邮门市部由中街迁至文化路营业厅，设集邮展示柜。是年，制作“金色少年”个性化邮票525版，实现集邮收入5.25万元。2009年4月23日，在息烽邮政局一楼大厅客户部为200多名集邮爱好者举办展览，展出邮票藏品20框。

息烽县1991—2010年集邮统计表

表11-2-6　　单位：万元

年份	新邮预订	邮品销售
1991	2.53	1.23
1992	5.63	1.35
1993	7.89	1.46
1994	10.36	1.56
1995	13.56	1.85
1996	16.98	1.88
1997	18.12	1.92
1998	18.24	2.03
1999	18.74	2.13
2000	19.45	10.01
2001	19.58	10.21
2002	20.56	10.58
2003	21.45	11.38
2004	22.14	12.54
2005	23.24	13.56
2006	25.78	14.98
2007	27.58	15.67
2008	29.65	17.2
2009	32.41	19.98
2010	35.25	22.21

九、物流与电子商务

（一）物流

2007年8月1日，贵州省邮政速递物流有限公司息烽营业部成立，负责全县邮政速递业务。2009年，营业部只办理投递邮件，不收寄邮件。2010年，新增邮件收寄业务，实现业务收入11万元。

（二）电子商务（代理业务）

2005年1月起，县邮政局开通代办电信、移动、联通收费业务，当年实现代理收入2.32万元。2006年2月，开通代理保险公司收保费业务，当年实现代理收入3.68万元。2007—2009年，共实现代理收入19.26万元。2010年，与烟草公司合作开通烟草款代扣业务，同年全面开通邮政代收话费、电费、水费、有线电视收视费业务，实现代理收入15.36万元。

息烽县1991—2010年邮政业务收入统计表

表11-2-7

年份	邮政业务收入（万元）	邮政业务量					
		函件		包件		汇票	
		合计（万件）	计费（万元）	合计（万件）	计费（万元）	合计（万件）	计费（万元）
1991	73.25	0.98	1.23	1.02	0.18	4.25	0.21
1992	81.36	1.98	2.12	1.96	0.25	4.55	0.32
1993	90.4	2.83	2.34	3.21	0.35	6.35	0.63
1994	101.22	3.12	3.02	4.32	0.48	6.85	0.83
1995	111.68	4.32	3.45	6.59	0.62	8.25	0.93
1996	124.36	5.23	6.02	8.12	0.72	9.15	1.02
1997	137.87	7.63	7.12	10.63	0.76	9.25	1.12
1998	153.96	9.86	9.35	13.25	0.96	9.85	1.62
1999	170.12	10.33	10.32	15.21	1.02	10.1	1.85
2000	189.22	11.32	11.6	16.33	1.31	15.98	1.95
2001	210.64	12.98	12.95	17.25	1.32	16.31	1.98
2002	234.36	13.02	13.01	17.35	1.46	17.52	2.04
2003	260.45	14.98	13.21	17.55	1.57	18.1	2.08
2004	288.95	15.23	18.23	17.62	1.56	18.7	2.11
2005	321.01	16.12	19.12	18.68	1.68	17.51	2
2006	356.72	18	20.01	18.55	1.32	16.25	2.01
2007	396.36	20.01	22.31	18.36	10.21	15.7	2
2008	440.38	25.08	21.31	17.41	9.41	13.2	2.01
2009	550.48	30.02	20.65	22.73	9.31	12.3	2.45
2010	719.58	43.64	20.32	6.46	5.31	8.53	2.65

第三章　电　信

2002年5月28日，贵州省电信有限公司息烽分公司成立。2004年，县电信局推出IP超市电话，安装有人值守IP公用电话60家（120门）。2008年，贵州省电信有限公司息烽分公司更名为中国电信股份有限公司息烽分公司。是年，长途电话、农村电话、因特网资费普遍降低。2010年，全县通光缆、宽带和有线电话接入网，移动通信全县覆盖率95%；实现村村通电话，其中有线设备开通110个村、无线设备开通51个村。全县共有电信用户5.3万户，其中固定电话3.5万户、宽带用户0.6万户、移动用户1.2万户。有无线基站80个、有人值守公话25家电话60门。

第一节　机　构

1991年，县邮电局内设行政组、经营组和设备维护组。1998年9月，邮政、电信分开经营，成立县电信局和县邮政局。县电信局内设办公室、维护中心、市场经营部、网络维护部、经营服务部。2002年5月28日，贵州省电信有限公司息烽分公司成立，内设综合部、维护安装部、营销部。2006年，在十乡镇设支局营业网点。2008年，贵州省电信有限公司息烽分公司更名为中国电信股份有限公司息烽分公司。

第二节　经营管理

一、对外经营

1994年，邮电管理体制改革，实行政企分开。长途电话、农村电话、因特网资费普遍降低。1996年6月，电信资费结构性调整，取消初装费、附加费和农村电话收费标准，实行低资费标准：网内同价，区间通话前3分钟0.2元，3分钟后每分钟0.1元；区间通话每分钟0.3元，长途电话每分钟0.7元。2006年，公司下设永靖镇、小寨坝镇、养龙司乡、九庄镇、石硐乡等10个乡镇支局网点。至2010年12月31日，全县共有电信用户5.3万户，其中固定电话3.5万户、宽带用户0.6万户、移动用户1.2万户；无线基站80个。当年电信经营收入2773万元。

第三节　电信网络

一、传输电路网

1995年6月30日，国家重点建设工程福州—杭州—贵阳—成都光缆建设息烽段动工，9月完工。10月16日，县邮电局程控电话接入网接入该长途光缆，投入使用。1997年，贵阳市电信局投资404.84万元，实施息烽县城至九庄镇沿线乡镇通信光缆工程，11月5日竣工，全程光缆30芯51千米。1998年，开通息烽至温泉光缆，全程光缆48芯173千米，实现全县通程控、光缆。

二、固定交换网

1992年8月22日，县邮电局正式割接开通从日本引进的二手设备纵横制1000门自动电话交换。1995年6月30日，县城首次开通S-1240型3000门程控电话。10月16日，县邮电局分组交换网。直接进入贵阳市电信局分组交换网，长途电话区号由之前的08638改为0851，结束模拟交换与数字交换并存现状，磁石式交换机退出电信网。1998年，开通可视电话会议系统。2002年，开通ADSL（非对称数字用户线路）宽带业务，逐步实现光纤上网。2010年，全县通光缆、宽带和有线电话接入网，移动通信全县覆盖率95%；实现村村通电话，其中有线设备开通110个村，无线设备开通51个村。

三、无线通信网

1994年，开通县城寻呼通信业务。次年，开通小寨坝、九庄等10乡镇寻呼通信业务。1997年，开通移动电话。1998年，将寻呼通信设备、业务和用户全部划拨联通公司。1999年6月，移动通信业务从电信分离，独立运营。2000年7月，开通ETS-450无线接入系统，建成县城、养龙司两座基站。2002年，开通PHS小灵通无线电话。2008年6月2日，电信收购通联CDMA（码分多址。是指利用码序列相关性实现的多址通信）网络，至2010年，建设移动基站80个，覆盖面80%以上；ETS-450无线接入系统逐步退网。

第四节　电信业务

1991年，县邮电局人工和半自动接续的长途电话业务分代号电话、特种电话、首长电话、紧急调度电话、军政电话、新闻电话、公务电话、业务电话、普通电话9种，总容量500门，实际用户286户。是年，设有航空、天气、特种、水情、军政、公益、新闻、公务、公电、汇款10种电报业务，电报等级、传递顺序为7级。1999年起，改为天气、水情、公益、政务、新闻、公电、汇款、普通8种电报业务，电报传递顺序和时限为4级，电报密码译电为人工译码，电报码编制号译成汉字。2006年后，数字程控电话、传真、联通、移动、PHS（小灵通）、ETS等通信业务取代电报业务。

1992年，县城电话号码为5位数，即：21000～21999。电话号码第一位数“2”代表县编号，第2位数以后的号码代表用户编号。1993年1月9日，县邮电局自动电话进入全国电话自动化网络，长途电话区号为08638。1995年，电话交换网直接进入贵阳本地交换网，同年3月3日，电话号码由5位数升为6位数，即：21000升为721000。1996年7月13日，电话号码由6位数升为7位数，即：721000升为7721000。

1994年，县邮电局建成126台、127台无线寻呼台1座（126台为人工拨号，127台为自动寻呼），容量达到5000门。是年6月，开通传真业务，12月，实现与贵阳地区联网，有寻呼机（俗称BP机）用户350户。至2000年12月，全县均设有传真业务。其后，公用电话和办公自动化迅速发展，传真设备普及到各单位和公用电话业主，电信经营的传真业务逐步取消。

1995年6月30日零时，县城S-1240型3000门程控电话交换机开通（同时停用纵横制自动电话交换机），有用户2460户。10月16日，县邮电局的分组交换设备直接进入贵阳市电信局分组交换网，长途电话区号为0851，采用PAD终端设备，安装分组交换数据网，共有端口48个，用户3家。1998年，建成DDN（数字数据网），有端口48个，用户15家，PDA用户转入到DDN。是年，对3000门数字程控系统实施扩容，数字程控交换机容量扩大至1.2万门，实现各乡（镇）程控电话全面开通，安装电话用户6500户。

1996年，县邮电局建成900兆移动电话基站。5月18日开通移动电话（俗称大哥大）。至1998年，有移动用户815户。1999年6月，电信与移动通信分营，移动电话由移动公司经营。2002年，县电信局建成PHS基站83座。5月1日，开通PHS业务，首期PHS用户5000户。2008年，电信收购联通CDMA移动通信网络，PHS逐步退出历史舞台。至2010年，全县电信移动用户1.2万户。

1997年6月24日，县邮电局可视电话会议开通。

1998年9月，成立国信寻呼公司，有无线寻呼机用户3800户。1999年4月，国信寻呼公司划入中国联通公司。

1999年，建成ISDN（综合业务数字网）设备，有端口48个，开通163账号业务、163上网储值卡业务、96169餐网直通车业务（俗称窄带）。普通拨号上网最高速率56kbit/s（千比特每秒），ISDN

拨号上网提速率128K，用户35户。

2000年，在县城区、车站、学校、人群集中路段先后安装无人值守公用电话亭35个，电话机120部。2004年，IP公用电话和移动通信技术兴起，语音向个人化发展，电话费用降低，至2009年，IP公用电话和IC室外无人值守公用电话淘汰。

2002年，建成ADSL业务，上行速率512kbit/s，下行速率8Mbit/s，用户280户。

2003年，开通乡镇ADSL设备及业务，用户560户。2010年，程控交换机容量扩大至5万门，用户数3.5万户。全县互联网用户8000多户。

2004年，县电信局推出IP超市电话，分别设在学校周边、车站、街道人群密集区域、乡镇等地，安装有人值守IP公用电话60家（120门电话）。2009年，全县有智能公用电话120家（350门电话）。随着通信技术进步和市场繁荣，全县公用电话业务逐步减少，至2010年，有人值守公用电话25家，电话60门。

息烽县2010年电信分公司自办营业厅（网点）统计表

表11-3-1

序号	服务机构名称	所在地址
1	中国电信息烽分公司综合营业厅	永靖镇文化西路19号
2	小寨坝电信支局营业厅	小寨坝镇街上
3	南山煤矿营业厅	南山煤矿
4	养龙司支局营业厅	养龙司乡龙泉大道
5	西洋营业厅	西洋公司
6	温泉营业厅	温泉镇石头田街上
7	流长营业厅	流长乡街上
8	鹿窝营业厅	鹿窝乡街上
9	九庄营业厅	九庄镇新大街
10	石硐营业厅	石硐乡街上
11	青山营业厅	青山乡街上
12	阳朗营业厅	永靖镇阳朗村街上
13	西山营业厅	西山乡底寨街上

第四章　移动通信

1999年8月，息烽移动通信公司成立。2003年，开通动感地带业务。2006年，集团客户部开通大客户经理和大客户业务办理绿色通道。2007年起，双向收费改为单项收费。2010年，有移动通信业务代办点54个。

第一节　机　构

1999年8月，息烽移动通信公司成立，内设办公室、市场部、运维部，设营业厅1个，业务代办点2个。2001年，新增盛达通讯、光辉通讯、现代通讯和中盛通讯4个业务代办点。2004年9月，公司更名为贵州移动通信有限责任公司息烽分公司。2005年，息烽分公司实施“从基础网络运营商向综合信息服务提供商转型”新商业模式。2006年，新增永通通讯、一和通讯2个业务代办点，自办文化西路营业厅、小寨坝营业厅、九庄营业厅、石硐营业厅。2010年，息烽分公司内设综合部、市场部、建维部、集团客户部，有业务代办点54个。

第二节　业　务

一、全球通业务

1999年，在县城开通全球通通信省际自动漫游业务，为跨省漫游用户提供特殊服务。推行标准卡、本地卡、黔中游、彩铃IC卡、轻松卡，月租50元/月，区间通话0.4元/分钟，漫游通话0.6元/分钟（国内、国际长话费另算），不满1分钟按一分钟计费。

2005年，推出全球通商务套餐，实行双向计费。

2008年，推出全球通升级套餐，设88元、138元、188元、288元、388元、488元6个档次，单项收费。

二、神州行业务（含标准卡、本地卡、黔中游、彩铃IC卡、轻松卡）

1999年，推出神州行标准卡：无月租费，市内通话费0.6元/分钟，漫游费0.8元/分钟。

2002年，推出神州行本地卡：无月租费，保底消费19.8元/月的通话费，闲时优惠（22：00—8：00）0.12元/分钟，忙时优惠（8：00—22：00）0.18元/分钟。本地被叫：前1800分钟全网3元包月，超过1800分钟后0.01元/分钟。

2004年，推出神州彩铃IC卡：月租费15元/月（含彩铃功能费5元），市内主叫08：00—00：00为0.16元/分钟，0：00—08：00为0.12元/分钟，被叫1元包月。

2006年，推出神州行黔中游卡：月租费20元/月，市内主叫0.2元/分钟，漫游主被叫0.6元/分钟，省内漫游加收1.5元/天，被叫包月5元/月。

2008年，推出神州行轻松卡：无月租费，每月保底消费19.8元，本地主叫0.22元/分钟，本地被叫5元/月。

三、动感地带（含音乐套餐、G3网聊套餐、随便套餐）

2003年，推出动感地带音乐套餐业务：25元/月，赠送200条短信、彩铃、音乐会员；08：00—22：00，0.18元/分钟，22：00—8：00，0.15元/分钟。

2005年，推出动感地带G3网聊套餐：16元/月，赠送160条短信、30M流量、飞信；07：00—23：00，0.16元/分钟，23：00—07：00，0.09元/分钟。

2006年，集团客户部开通大客户经理和大客户业务办理绿色通道。用户号码段包括135、136、137、138、139，主要经营移动语音、数据、IP电话、多媒体业务及其他增值业务，与206个国家和地区的271个运营公司开通GSM国际及港澳台地区漫游业务。推出动感地带随便套餐，设18元、28元、48元、68元、88元、108元、148元7个档次。

2007年起，双向收费改为单项收费。

2008年，推出飞信、手机阅读、彩铃、彩信、139邮箱、超值短信、个性铃声、图片下载、移动QQ、手机游戏、星座运势、动感资讯业务。

2010年，开展智能手机业务。

第三节　基站网络

1999年，县内首个无线基站在团元山建成。2000年，开通光彩大楼、县政府、蚕桑坡、人民法院、工商局5个GSM移动基站。2002年底，在县城、乡镇驻地、重要工厂区域建移动网络21个，其中县城11个站，九庄、小寨坝、流长、鹿窝、养龙司、石硐、温泉、青山、西山、西洋化肥厂、开磷集团实现网络覆盖。6月，移动通信逐步形成传输。2005年，村网络覆盖基站89个。2008年，建设3G网络，乡镇主要机关、居民区TD网络信号覆盖，县城无缝覆盖。2010年，有基站162个。

息烽县1999—2010年移动业务统计表

表11-4-1

年份	用户数（户）	座机数（个）	基站数（个）	年收入（万元）
1999	3000	—	1	50
2000	8000	—	10	130
2001	12000	—	21	600
2002	16000	1200	35	900
2003	20000	1800	52	1200
2004	24000	2600	70	1500
2005	35000	3000	89	2000
2006	70000	3500	100	4000
2007	80000	3900	116	6000
2008	90000	4200	135	6500
2009	100000	4800	150	7000
2010	120000	5500	162	7500

第五章　联通通信

2004年2月，中国联合通信有限公司息烽分公司（简称息烽联通分公司）成立，设经营部。至2010年，联通息烽分公司建有基站GSM（全球移动通信系统）站点108个、CDMA站点34个，全县161村GSM网络全覆盖，县城及各乡镇政府所在地核心区域3G网络覆盖。实现信息化、智能化、高速化移动手机网络。

第一节　机　构

2005年，息烽联通分公司租赁息烽粮贸饭店办公，设立综合部、市场部、运维部。2007年，新增营业厅和集团客户部，设立小寨坝经营部、九庄经营部。2008年10月1日，联通公司CDMA业务经营主体全部划归中国电信。2009年10月1日，联通3G网络正式启用。

第二节　基站建设

2000年，贵阳联通公司在息烽县建有GSM基站7个。2003年，有GSM基站18个、GSM站点10个。2004年，息烽联通接入端口从零开始，经历7年网通资源整合，累计建宽带接入端口4200个，覆盖县城、黑神庙、西洋肥业等重要区域。2008—2009年，CDMA网络划归中国电信经营。2010年，有息烽联通基站GSM站点108个，CDMA站点34个，全县161个村GSM网络全覆盖，县城及各乡镇政府所在地核心区域3G网络覆盖；新增GSM用户25838户、3G用户1431户，服务用户26640户；实现信息化、智能化、高速化移动手机网络。当年收入969万元。

息烽联通分公司2004—2010年网络通信业务统计表

表11-5-1

年份	GSM新增用户数（户）	CDMA新增用户数（户）	WCDMA新增用户数（户）	全年收入（万元）	服务用户总数（户）	签约社会代理（家）	服务区域覆盖情况
2004	6819	1487	—	121	5178	17	全县半数乡镇
2005	9136	4597	—	342	10780	36	除青山乡外，其余乡镇实现网点客户服务
2006	17786	7478	—	580	17794	47	全县乡镇网点全面覆盖
2007	12289	8431	—	776	25279	54	全县乡镇网点全面覆盖
2008	17786	7416	—	780	25798	36	全县乡镇网点全面覆盖
2009	19172	427	—	1105	24884	46	全县乡镇网点全面覆盖
2010	25838	—	1431	969	26640	41	全县乡镇网点全面覆盖

第十二篇　城乡建设

第一章　管理机构与规划

1984年，县城乡建设环境保护局开始编修《息烽县城总体规划》。1992—1995年，完善县城及各乡镇总体规划。1998年，完成《息烽县1998—2010年总体规划》和全县10个乡镇1998—2010年总体规划。2001—2006年，编制县城和其他9个乡镇的小城镇总体规划、控制性规划及县城河道改造、团元山森林公园等各类专业性规划58个。

第一节　管理机构

1991年，县城乡建设环境保护局内设办公室、质量监督及施工管理站、监理监测站、房地产管理站、村镇建设管理站、规划设计所、排污收费管理站。1995年，撤销县城乡建设环境保护局，设县建设局，建设局内设办公室、房改办公室、建筑规划设计所、安全质量监督与施工管理站、房地产管理站、城管监察中队、村镇建设管理站，县政府人防战备办公室划归县建设局管理。1997年3月，设县城市管理委员会，与县建设局合署办公，实行一个机构、两块牌子的管理体制。2002年，人防战备、城市绿化及城市防洪和城镇规划区地下水资源的管理职能分别划归有关单位。2010年，县建设局更名为县住房和城乡建设局，内设办公室、综合科、安全质量监督与施工管理站、村镇建设管理站、规划管理站、房地产管理站、城建监察大队、市政设施管理站、环境卫生管理站。

第二节　城镇规划

一、息烽县城市总体规划（1997—2010年）

1984年1月，县城乡建设环境保护局开始编修《息烽县城总体规划》。至6月，完成全县25个区、乡镇机关驻地集镇总体规划。

用地规模：建设用地212.6公顷，人均99.8平方米，规划2010年城市建设用地人均指标控制在101.2平方米，城区城市建设用地控制在404.8公顷以内。

城市规划区：永靖镇镇域及水源保护点青山乡、小桥河水库、洪马水库、鱼简河水库。城市规划区面积172.12平方千米。

城区规划范围：东至枧槽沟、大宫山，南至下阳朗火金山，西至柿花坪、团元山，北至蚕山坡、牛角坡，规划面积1042.6公顷。

县域城镇体系规划层次：县城——永靖镇；中心城镇——小寨坝镇；一般城镇——温泉镇、九庄镇、养龙司乡、西山乡、流长乡；集镇——青山、石硐、鹿窝、梨安。

二、息烽县城市总体规划（2010—2020年）

编制《息烽县1998—2010年总体规划》和全县10个乡镇1998—2010年总体规划。

城市规划区：包括永靖、西山和阳朗组团，以及水源涵养地上洪马、下洪马，此次规划将新增的西山乡金星、文安、猪场、柏香山、小堡、林丰、团元山7个行政村和息烽集中营所在的阳朗、猫洞村纳入县城城市规划范围，城市规划区面积113.41平方千米。

城市规划建设用地（中心城）：包括永靖、西山和阳朗3个组团，面积约12.84平方千米。

规划时间：近期2010—2015年，远期2016—2020年。

县域城镇等级规模：县城10万人，小寨坝镇、温泉镇、九庄镇1～5万人，流长镇、养龙司、鹿窝、石硐、青山、新萝1万人。

本次规划城镇等级结构：本次规划调整城镇体系结构为1个中心城区（永靖镇、小寨坝镇、西山乡），2个重点镇（九庄镇、温泉镇），5个一般镇（流长、养龙司、鹿窝、石硐、青山）。

县城包括永靖、西山和阳朗组团，城市人口由规划城市建设区范围内非农业户籍人口、农业户籍人口、暂住半年以上人口三部分构成。预测2015年县城人口9.48万人，2020年县城人口12.57万人。

县城用地规模：县城现状人均建设用地83平方米，本次规划近期2015年采用人均95平方米标准，2020年县城人均约102平方米，2020年城市用地规模达到12.84平方千米。

规划布局：对建设用地功能结构，商业区、新城区和工业园区，文化产业、观光旅游、城市居民休闲区、农业产业用地和生态林地进行布局。

2009年，修编县城总体规划，提出“南移西扩”城建战略，即县城不仅向较为平坦的阳朗片区“南移”，还向具有发展潜力的西山方向“西扩”，以此拓展县城发展空间。修编后的县城总体规划区的建设区域将达到20平方千米，可容纳20万人。

第三节　乡镇规划

一、小寨坝镇总体规划（2003—2020年）

小寨坝镇区建设用地分为五个功能组团片区，即中部中心组团片区，以重钙厂方向为主，形成西部磷化工工业组团片区，在川黔铁路东侧形成东部新组团片区，在小寨坝火车站形成北部组团片区，在重钙厂南侧形成南部新组团片区。确定小寨坝镇的区位定位为交通型、工矿型城镇。

二、小寨坝镇控制性详细规划

规划公共设施用地28.49公顷，人均7.1平方米。将镇区建设用地划分为5个片区，即老镇区中心片区、东部片区、南部片区、西部片区、北部片区。中心片区延续老镇区原有居住、行政、商业功能；东部片区是镇区的新居住小区；南部片区由居住组团和村民住宅组团组成；西部片区是磷化工及仓储用地；北部片区主要功能是交通枢纽。

三、温泉镇建设规划（2000—2010年）

在充分利用现状基础上，沿镇区生活性干道和养温公路形成一环、两中心、三区的带状组团结构环路，行政划分是以通向镇政府道路和自然山体将全镇划分为中心老城区，东部新区和西部发展区。景观轴线：沿新建镇区生活主干道布置公共建筑及新型居住建筑，形成镇区现状风貌景观轴，以镇政府前市民广场及山体自然风貌形成绿化景观轴，养温公路沿线形成传统商业街。

四、九庄镇建设规划（1999年—2015年）

规划用地原则为“相对集中，合理保留，充分利用”。

居住小区，行政办公区和教育文体结合体建筑集中布置。合理保留符合规划发展方向的道路、建筑、公用工程设施、自然绿地。充分利用现状用地中的自然林带山体、农田耕地，以此作为穿插于规划用地中建筑群体的景观主线和各类建筑组团的自然分隔，使全区成为一个高绿化率、生态型城镇。九庄大道中段沿线两侧用地的居住组团、西侧旧区内的部分生产建筑用地。

五、西山乡建设规划（2004—2020年）

规划总用地250.37公顷。将集镇划为2个组团，5个功能区：

中部组团：原底寨街所在地集镇旅游商贸功能组团，是集镇核心所在，可适当发展与旅游有关的商贸、旅馆、餐饮等服务。

北部组团：为行政办公及生活居住区，位于底寨街西北侧，主要设置镇政府新址、公共服务设施、乡域内居民搬迁居住区等，是集镇主要新发展地区。

六、养龙司乡村镇规划（2003—2020年）

确定发展主轴一条，沿养龙司—坝上村—江土村发展；次轴一条，沿养龙司—蚂蟥村—荆江村发展。中心一个，位于养龙司集镇，北部以江土村为重点，发展蔬菜种植、林果业，西部重点发展蚂蟥村，形成一个中心、两个重点的村镇建设布局。

七、流长乡总体规划（2004—2020年）

规划以中心大道及其延伸段，东、西大街，公园路、北环路等主次干道为轴线，把集镇用地分为19个区块，兼顾商住、教育、商业金融、行政管理、集贸和公共绿地等。

八、鹿窝乡村镇规划（2004—2020年）

以集镇—中心村—基层村三级结构体系布局，将集镇新老城区结合部的自然山体规划为集镇休闲绿化小游园，以自然景观和人工景观为主。在贯穿整个集镇的瓮桶河两侧规划分别布置一条2米宽和6米宽滨河绿化带。对集镇10米以上道路进行绿化，并结合集镇景观加强其他绿化建设。对集镇四周山头加强植树造林。

第二章　县城建设

1990年，县城范围面积8.62平方千米，实际建成面积2平方千米。有11条街道和1条环城路，总长10.05千米，街道为南北向；房屋建筑面积58.38万平方米，机关单位办公用房多为砖木结构，民房多为木结构平房。经过旧城改造、新区建设，至2010年，县城城区东至县委党校，南至汉方路，西至团元山，北至蚕桑坡加油站。城区实际建成面积6.1平方千米。新建街道13条，总长8606米，形成4纵2横1环（环城路）街道网络；新建房屋面积249.67万平方米，平房被4～7层砖木或砖混结构楼群取代；建有11层电梯楼房。

第一节 城区建设

一、县城改造

1991年，县城城区包括交通路、解放北路、东风路、解放南路、县府路、人民路和朝晖厂、酒厂、县总工会、饮料厂以及二中等几个房屋建筑比较集中的片区。

1998年，开始县城改造。由贵州宏翔房地产开发公司在原蔬菜公司和饮料厂片区投资动工兴建宏翔花园商住楼房3栋1.5万平方米。

1999年2月，县成立旧城改造领导小组。8月，县政府决定对县城十字街以北地段进行旧城改造和道路拓宽建设（交通路路口、解放北路、东风路路口、东门坝路）。9月，遵义明德房地产开发有限公司在原百货公司仓库地块修建光彩大楼，建商住楼3栋0.7万平方米。

2002年7月，县政府决定对城中城农贸市场地块进行整体改造和开发，拆除农贸市场、县图书馆和涉及交通路地上建筑物，修建集商贸和住宅为一体的建筑群。是年，由遵义市泓塬房地产开发有限公司承建，建筑面积1.03万平方米。

2003年，朝晖厂地块由开磷房地产开发公司动工建设开磷新城，占地6.2万平方米，建8栋8层商住楼，面积4.7万平方米。

2006年，县委、县政府召开县城中街片区旧城改造动员会，举行改造工程奠基仪式。全面改造解放北路、东风路、交通路。至2010年，老客车站地块（正欣城市庄园）、交通路西侧地块（金辉商贸中心）、工会片区地块（深港商贸城）、中街片区（筑北商业大道）、老二中地块（一品城）、中医院办公楼及宿舍地块和县医院18层电梯综合楼主体工程竣工。旧城改造建筑面积47.78万平方米。

息烽县1998—2010年旧城改造项目统计表

表12-2-1

动、竣工时间	开发公司	开发形式	地块名称	性质	楼栋	面积（万平方米）
1998—2001年	贵州宏翔房地产	出让	饮料厂、蔬菜公司	商住	3	1.5
1999—2000年	遵义明德房地产	联建	百货公司仓库	商住	3	0.7
2002—2003年	贵阳恒铭园房地产	出让	城中城农贸市场	商住	2	1.04
2002—2003年	遵义市泓塬房地产	出让	农贸市场	商住	2	1.03
2003—2008年	贵州开磷房地产	出让	原朝晖厂地块	商住	8	4.7
2006—2010年	重庆金穗房地产	出让	中街片区	商住	17	11.52
2007—2009年	息烽伟业房地产	出让	交通路西侧地块	商住	1	1.67

续表

动、竣工时间	开发公司	开发形式	地块名称	性质	楼栋	面积（万平方米）
2007—2010年	遵义正烽房地产	出让	老客车站地块	商住	11	6.82
2008—2010年	息烽伟业房地产	出让	老二中地块	商住	12	13.57
—2010年	贵州万众房地产	出让	工会片区	商住	5	5.23
合计						47.78

二、房屋拆迁

1991年，房屋征收拆迁由县建设局负责。根据国家、省的城市房屋拆迁补偿安置政策，县政府先后颁布《息烽县房屋拆迁补偿安置管理实施细则》和《息烽县房屋拆迁管理暂行办法》，对涉及的房屋户按拆迁面积就地还房或异地重建安置。根据区位实际情况出台拆迁补偿安置临时办法。公益性项目，由政府补助，商品房由开发商负责。按市场物价增长指数调控补偿标准。规定拆除机关、团体、学校、企事业单位的房屋，原则上由建设单位等质量以房换房，交换产权，迁建房屋产权归原单位，拆除营业、居住等民用建筑，采取回迁并按照拆一还一，超出面积补差的原则进行产权调换。对拆迁户在还房期间，发给过渡费予以补偿，过渡期一般1～1.5年。

1997年7月，县政府批准县建设局《关于核定1997年房屋拆迁补偿价格标准的报告》。房屋拆迁补偿价格标准：砖混结构215元/平方米，砖木结构180元/平方米，木结构140元/平方米，其他结构100元/平方米。

1999年5月，成立县房屋拆迁事务所，负责房屋征收，为国有企业性质，隶属县建设局。

2006年，县城中街片区旧城改造项目，东起东风路，西达交通路，南临十字街中心广场，北至花园东路路口。是息烽历史上拆迁量最大的工程，占地面积45904平方米，拆迁户数728户，65945平方米。采取产权调换或货币补偿两种方式进行安置，村民可选择划地迁建。货币补偿：砖混住宅590～620元/平方米，砖木住宅490元/平方米，其他430元/平方米；营业用房：框架6080元/平方米，砖混5570元/平方米，砖木5250元/平方米，其他5150元/平方米；划地迁建：砖混280元/平方米，砖木220元/平方米，其他180元/平方米。

2010年，县教育局宿舍地块项目货币补偿：砖混住宅1700元/平方米，砖木住宅1400元/平方米，其他980元/平方米；划地迁建：砖混住宅630元/平方米，砖木住宅420元/平方米，其他300元/平方米。

息烽县1998—2010房屋拆迁统计表

表12-2-2

年份	项目名称	项目性质	拆迁户数	拆迁房屋面积（平方米）
1998	饮料厂、蔬菜公司	旧城改造	—	—
1999	百货公司仓库	旧城改造	—	—
2000	县东门坝一期	旧城改造	11	928
2002	泉都花园二期（饮食服务公司）	旧城改造	16	922

续表

年份	项目名称	项目性质	拆迁户数	拆迁房屋面积（平方米）
2003	农贸市场（原农贸市场大棚及1号楼）	旧城改造	73	3472
2003	县二中二期（学生宿舍）	旧城改造	5	1360
2004	正兴商业街（东门游泳池地块）	旧城改造	11	2025
2005	东门坝七号地块	旧城改造	17	3438
2005	息烽大道过渡段	道路改造	7	6200
2006	天景嘉园（城关中学及人民路农户）	旧城改造	34	8129
2006	武装部地块	旧城改造	131	10656
2006	筑北商业大道（中街片区）	旧城改造	728	65945
2007	正欣庄园（八角坟老汽车站）	旧城改造	14	1250
2006	金辉商贸中心（交通路西侧1～59户）	旧城改造	27	6801
2007	蓥龙南苑商住楼（文化南路）	旧城改造	4	1485
2007	东风苑（东风路32～50号）	旧城改造	19	1355
2007	龙港商贸城（交警队办公、宿舍楼等，永阳供销社和农资公司仓库）	旧城改造	15	7494
2007	深港商贸城（县总工会地块）	旧城改造	356	47554
2009	水栖怡园（东门6–1地块）	旧城改造	25	3550
2009	龙港馨苑（岸家坡地块）	旧城改造	17	3340
2009	县医院扩建项目	其他	77	13257
2009	王家湾地块土地储备	旧城改造	45	4123
2010	长途客站前沿街地块土地储备（火车站广场）	旧城改造	19	3155
2010	县实验一小	旧城改造	36	7035
2010	县第三中学	旧城改造	21	3094
2010	环城路宾馆（环城路地块）	旧城改造	10	2000
2010	县教育局宿舍地块	旧城改造	99	9000
合计			1817	217568

三、新区建设

东门小区1号、5号、6号地块，东门小区商住楼（教师新村）：项目占地5.65万平方米，建筑面积3.42万平方米。

东门小区6～1号地块（水栖怡园）：占地面积1.7万平方米，建筑面积5.2万平方米。

县消防大队南侧地块：建成房屋面积1.52万平方米。

东门片区7号地块：占地4269平方米，建筑面积1.3万平方米。

晏家坡交警队地块（龙港馨苑）：建设规模8万平方米。

2001年，开始修建县宣传文化中心，2002年竣工，建筑面积4186平方米。

2002年1月9日，县政府与贵州广建房地产开发有限公司签订《息烽县开发建设南大街协议书》。由广建公司出资建设县城南大街（后定名虎城大道）1696米道路，县政府将南大街道路两侧各25米范围内约9.2公顷土地整体出让给广建公司进行房地产开发建设。至2010年，建成商品房面积54万平方米。

2006年6月，新客车站建设动工，建筑面积5158平方米，2007年竣工。

息烽县2001—2010年新建商品房统计表

（不含虎城大道两侧商品房）

表12-2-3

动、竣工时间	开发公司	项目名称	楼栋号	面积（万平方米）	投资（万元）
2001—2003年	贵州中创	教师新村	1、5、6	17	1350
2002—2003年	遵义明德	明星公寓	1	0.47	120
2002—2003年	四川新鋆	金地商住楼	1	0.26	94
2002—2003年	贵州慧恒	慧恒商住楼	1	0.3	103
2002—2003年	贵州汇杰	泉都花园	A、B	1.3	500
2003—2004年	贵州汇杰	泉都饮食城	1	0.68	200
2003—2005年	息烽城市建设	金鑫公寓	1	1.2	900
2004—2005年	息烽伟业	金碧苑商住楼	1	0.54	243
2004—2006年	贵州汇杰	第一商业广场	B	2.0	1300
2005—2006年	贵州宏宇	正兴商业步行街	A、B、C、D	1.62	800
2005—2009年	贵州惠恒	惠恒中心花园	A、B、C、D、E	3.42	2500
2006—2007年	贵州泰维	新贵地带	1	0.29	250
2006—2010年	县城市建设	水栖怡园	A、B、教师公寓1～7	9.2	5489
合计				40.26	14339

息烽县2006—2010年虎城大道两侧商品房建设统计表

表12-2-4

动、竣工时间	开发单位	项目名称	楼栋号	面积（万平方米）	总投资（万元）
2006—2010年	贵州鋆龙房开	广建新苑	22、24、26	4.35	2570
2009—2010年		鋆龙南苑	1、2	1.04	615
2007—2008年	遵义荣天房开	广建新苑	1、8、19、27	5.93	3500
2006—2007年	贵州广建二分公司	广建新苑	12、14、17	6.27	3600

续表

动、竣工时间	开发单位	项目名称	楼栋号	面积（万平方米）	总投资（万元）
2007—2008年	息烽建成房开	佳和苑	3、15、16	3.93	2300
2007—2010年	贵州益荣房开	广建新苑	2、4、6	3.55	2100
2008—2009年	贵州鑫众房开	烽景名苑	18、20、21、23、25	6.36	3750
2008—2009年	息烽新家园	广建新苑	13	1.45	850
2009—2010年	息烽鑫正房开	郦都华府	10	3.05	1800
2007—2008年	贵州广建房开	广建新苑	9	0.95	560
2008—2009年	贵阳经开区东方房开	新城银座	11	2.57	1500
2006—2008年	贵州弘晋房开	龙港新城	1、2、3、4	5.38	3200
2007—2009年		虎成大厦	1	2.81	1800
2008—2009年		龙港商贸城	A1、A2	7.46	4500
2009—2010年		龙港馨园	5、7	1.22	800
合　计				56.33	33445

四、老街改造

1991年，县城有县府路、解放北路、解放南路、东风路、交通路、人民路、蚕桑坡路、铁路新村、文化东路、文化西路、文化北路等11条街道和环城路，总长10.05千米。

1996年，县城街道路面硬化率34.7%。

1998年，改造东风路、蚕桑坡路面，投资39.5万元，建成全长1.04千米混凝土路面。

1999年8月，县政府决定对县城十字街以北地段进行旧城改造和道路拓宽建设，包括交通路路口、解放北路、东风路路口、东门坝道路。

2005年，街道路面全部硬化，县城建成区道路面积增至31.35万平方米。

五、新街建设

1993年，修建花园东路。因缺乏资金，未能竣工。1997年12月，铺装人行道及排水系统，硬化路面后投入使用。

1995年，修建花园南路、花园西路、公园新村路，因资金缺乏未进行硬化。2002年，对路面进行硬化后投入使用。

1998—2001年，先后修建文化南路、镇府路、河滨路、永红路。

2002年2月，贵州广建房地产有限公司投资动工修建虎城大道。最初称为南大街，主干道总长4300米。2005年建成投入使用，定名虎城大道。大道中间为5米宽分隔绿化带，绿化带两边各为11米宽的行车道，行车道两侧各为2米宽绿化带和4.5米宽人行道。是县内第一条有分隔绿化带的道路。

2003年，建育才路，2004年建成投入使用。2006年，将育才路车行道两侧坡度较大的人行道改建为梯级人行道，2007年4月竣工投入使用。

2007年8月，对花园东路、花园西路、花园南路、花园北路和文化东路、文化西路、文化北路及镇府路、河滨路、东门路、公园南路的人行道、排水沟、路灯等进行改造。投资1290万元，至年底，改造道路2万平方米，安装雨、污水管8500米、路灯180盏。

2010年，一品城步行街竣工。

1991—2010年，县城共新建街道13条，总长8606米，除虎城大道为双向6车道城市道路外，其余均为普通城市道路。

息烽县城新建道路统计表

表12-2-5

序号	名称	起止	长/宽（米）	动/竣工年份
1	花园东路	东接交通路北端，西至"城中城"综合市场北出口与文化东路贯通	1200/16	1993/1997
2	花园南路	南起高等级公路管理局息烽管理站职工宿舍，北至县工商局办公大楼房接花园西路，在供电局大楼门口与花园东路支路贯通	200/16	1995/2002/
3	花园西路	东起"城中城"综合市场北出口与花园东路、文化北路连接，西至县职业技术学校旁与息（烽）九（庄）公路搭接	241/16	1995/2002
4	公园新村路	南起高等级公路管理局息烽管理站职工宿舍旁，北至县职业技术学校旁与息（烽）九（庄）公路搭接	204/10	1995/2002
5	文化南路	北接文化东、文化西路，在建设局、教育局办公楼间与文化北路贯通，南接南大街	160/18	1998/
6	镇府路	西起解放北路北端，东至育才路南路口与河滨路贯通	240/18	1999/
7	东门路	西接东风路南路口与十字街连接，东接河滨路南端与永红路贯通	110/20	2000/2002
8	河滨路	南至东门路、永红路路口，北至育才路路口与镇府路贯通	400/20	2000/2002
9	永红路	西接河滨路南端与东门路贯通，东在枧槽沟公路桥头与210国道搭接	184	2001/2006
10	虎城大道	大道北段南在龙港新城与210国道2244千米处搭接，北与文化南路贯通；大道中段北和210国道与北段搭接，南连汉方路	4300/41	2002/2005
11	育才路	西起河滨路北端和镇府路东端，东至息烽二中东侧210国道搭接	485/15	2003/2004
12	体育路	西接滨河路中段，东与210国道2239千米+500米处搭接	260/16	2006/2007
13	一品城步行街	鸿森龙城至县残联段	622/21	2010/2010
		合　计	长8606	

六、标志性建筑

体育场：位于县第二中学对面。2003年，县投资470万元修建，占地33960平方米，建有8条400米标准跑道，阶梯式看台可容5000多观众。

县供电局大楼：位于县城西门。2003年建成，为县内第一栋高11层的电梯大楼（办公楼），建筑面积4500平方米。

虎城大厦：位于贵遵高速息烽匝道出口至息烽大道北侧地块。2007年由贵州弘晋房开公司动工建设，2009年竣工。楼高20层，建筑面积2.81万平方米。为县内第一栋政府综合性办公大楼。

息烽大酒店：位于虎城大道中段，火炬转盘旁。2010年5月动工修建，次年6月竣工。是县内首家三星级酒店。总建筑面积2.2万平方米，楼高20层，有各式客房159间。

第二节　住房建设和管理

一、私人建房

1990年以前，县城私人很少建房。1991年起，私人建房增多，县城私人建房屋多为4层砖混结构。是年，县政府制定《息烽县个人建住房审批的暂行规定》。1993年，县规划修建花园东路，个人建房70余户。1995年，西门片区新增房屋150余幢，建筑面积3万多平方米。至2010年，县城私人建房累计1692户，建筑面积27.58万平方米。是年12月30日，县政府制定《关于加强息烽县城乡个人建房管理的实施意见（试行）》，规定村民改、扩建住宅，新占地面积应当连同原有宅基地面积一并计算。县政府所在地和坝子地区内每户宅基地面积不超过130平方米，其余地区不超过170平方米，建筑面积不超过320平方米。城镇居民申请个人危房改造或者翻建的，应当维持原房屋产权证确定的原址、原面积，并按照规划要求进行改造。

二、单位职工集资建房

20世纪90年代前，事业单位建房多由单位向上级业务部门申请拨款，政府划给宅基地修建职工住房。许多单位将办公楼和职工住房建在一起，或将部分办公用房改作职工宿舍，以缓解职工住房困难。1991年起，县内部分机关事业单位以职工集资，单位出宅基地方式修建职工住房。规定每户面积为：一般干部55平方米，县级75平方米，厅级95平方米（县级和厅级含这一级享受住房待遇的知识分子），离休干部增加10平方米。每套房内设卧室、客厅、厨房和厕所，称为套房。单位建房多为4～6层砖混结构。至1998年底，全县有81个单位1265名职工申请集资建房，共集资1914.83万元，修建住房1265套，面积10.28万平方米。其间，1993年1月6日，县政府决定从是年1月1日起，在行政区域内实施《息烽县城镇住房制度改革实施方案》。按照房改方案，将单位所建住房出售给职工（详见本节第三目《公有住房制度改革》）。

息烽县1991—2000年单位集资建房统计表

表12-2-6

动、竣工时间	集资建房单位	户建筑面积（平方米）	集资户数（户）	集资标准（元/平方米）
1991年—1993年6月	人大办	64.6～75.3	16	120
1991年—1993年6月	永靖法庭	62.9～80.1	4	120
1991年—1993年6月	公安局	64.6～79.7	40	120
1991年—1993年6月	百货公司	63.1～64	8	120
1991年—1993年6月	烟草公司	72.7～96.1	8	120
1991年—1993年6月	广播局	58.3～75.4	23	120

续表

动、竣工时间	集资建房单位	户建筑面积（平方米）	集资户数（户）	集资标准（元/平方米）
1991年—1993年6月	永阳税务局	61.9～82.2	13	120
1991年—1993年6月	县医院	67.03	30	120
1991年—1993年6月	县供销社	61.8～63.6	12	120
1991年—1993年6月	建行	76.8～92.3	5	120
1991年—1993年6月	司法局	60.9～68.8	10	120
1991年—1993年6月	计委	68.2	5	120
1991年—1993年6月	民委	60.9～68.8	6	120
1991年—1993年6月	律师事务所	69.3	2	120
1991年—1993年6月	城建局	65～69.5	20	120
1991年—1993年6月	土管局	61.3～73.4	24	120
1991年—1993年6月	中医院	68.5～80.9	20	120
1991年—1993年6月	工行	51	18	120
1991年—1993年6月	农经委	67.5～81.4	6	120
1991年—1993年6月	农行	66.9～93.8	20	120
1991年—1993年6月	工商局	63.8～72.8	34	120
1991年—1993年6月	燃料公司	86.2～107.5	15	120
1991年—1993年6月	公路工区	70.1	8	120
1991年—1993年6月	交警队	75.7～76.2	8	120
1993年7月—1994年	县委办	59.33～63.6	28	180
1993年7月—1994年	乡企局	75.5～93.3	18	180
1993年7月—1994年	科委	76.3～84.3	10	180
1993年7月—1994年	档案局	79.9～82.5	6	180
1993年7月—1994年	广播事业局	88.18	3	180
1993年7月—1994年	电影公司	53～65	12	180
1993年7月—1994年	教育局	90	8	180
1993年7月—1994年	粮食局	60.17	30	180
1993年7月—1994年	新华书店	68.7～69.8	4	180
1993年7月—1994年	运管所	67.7～106	23	180
1993年7月—1994年	中西药公司	72.1～82.6	6	180
1993年7月—1994年	民政局	86.53	20	180
1993年7月—1994年	工商银行	105.7	4	180

续表

动、竣工时间	集资建房单位	户建筑面积（平方米）	集资户数（户）	集资标准（元/平方米）
1993年7月—1994年	水电局	57.9～67.13	16	180
1993年7月—1994年	永阳供销社	70.1	20	180
1993年7月—1994年	供电局	69.36	23	180
1993年7月—1994年	邮电局	49.35	30	180
1993年7月—1994年	农资公司	81.1～92.1	20	180
1995年—	劳动局	56.5	4	153
1995年—	人武部	98	7	153
1995年—	人行	61	10	131
1997年—	地矿局	147.7	8	135
1997年—	地税局	112.5	8	178
1997年—	乡企局	100	13	200
1997年—	南山林场	91.7	12	273
1998年1月—2000年	公路工区	125	8	280
1998年1月—2000年	公路段	79.4	16	260
1998年1月—2000年	粮食局	93.3	24	280
1998年1月—2000年	中医院	90	30	260
1998年1月—2000年	县法院	47.4	22	260
1998年1月—2000年	食品公司	80	12	250
1998年1月—2000年	农发行	90	20	250
1998年1月—2000年	农办	90	4	260
1998年1月—2000年	新华书店	80	5	250
1998年1月—2000年	国土局	80	5	250
1998年1月—2000年	百货公司	124.4	18	280
1998年1月—2000年	永靖土管所	90	8	260
1998年1月—2000年	永靖卫生院	89	16	260
1998年1月—2000年	永靖派出所	80	20	250
1998年1月—2000年	永靖林业站	80	4	250
1998年1月—2000年	永靖计生站	75.8	24	260
1998年1月—2000年	县医院	109.9	70	250
1998年1月—2000年	温泉疗养院	83.3	24	250
1998年1月—2000年	财保公司	118.2	5	280

续表

动、竣工时间	集资建房单位	户建筑面积（平方米）	集资户数（户）	集资标准（元/平方米）
1998年1月—2000年	供电局	75.8	36	260
1998年1月—2000年	检察院	80.7	22	260
1998年1月—2000年	建行	85.7	21	250
1998年1月—2000年	职校	86.7	30	250
1998年1月—2000年	农业局	82.5	40	260
1998年1月—2000年	国税局	70	18	250
1998年1月—2000年	计生局	99.2	12	250
1998年1月—2000年	县水泥厂	110	16	280
1998年1月—2000年	林业派出所	103	12	260
1998年1月—2000年	南山林场	80	12	260
1998年1月—2000年	高管站	70	10	250
1998年1月—2000年	运管所	87.5	8	250
1998年1月—2000年	永靖教办	90	5	260

三、公有住房制度改革

1992年2月，县成立住房制度改革领导小组，下设住房资金管理委员会、房屋质量等级评估小组、住房制度改革监督小组。6月，建立房地产信贷部（设在县建设银行）。

1993年1月，《息烽县城镇住房制度改革实施方案》实施。3月，住房资金管理委员会与房改办合署办公。县房改办内设资金管理小组、综合业务组、县直机关房改工作小组。10月，出台县职工宿舍评估数据及操作程序实施方案，对单位申请房改售房进行评估。

1994年，按照县城镇住房制度改革实施方案的配套实施办法规定：新建砖混结构单元式套房按标准价180元/平方米出售，旧房按重置价170元/平方米出售，人均年收入5000元以上的职工家庭按成本价257.14元/平方米出售，并按楼层、地段、新旧差异和职工工龄计价售房。是年，县内86个单位参加第一轮房改，办理有限产权，共出售公有住房1801套，售房面积10.76万平方米。个人购买后如果出售，增值部分与单位按照比例分成。

1997年11月，市房改领导小组批复同意实施《息烽县1997年住房制度改革工作安排意见》，规定原已按成本价购买公有住房的职工，按当年成本价补足购房款可以获全产权。至此，全县出售公有住房2080套，均办理“房屋有限产权证”，面积128972.64平方米，收售房款595.55万元。集资建房亦按相关规定陆续出售给职工。

1999年7月1日起，全县停止住房实物分配，全部实行住房分配货币化，同时实行新的公有住房租、售价格标准。

2007年，开展房改房职工补交土地收益和兑现职工增量补贴的测算和方案拟定报批工作。

2008年，按照县政府《关于印发息烽县房改房补交土地收益获取上市权和发放职工住房增量补贴的实施方案的通知》精神，全县启动房改房补交土地收益获取上市权工作，职工持房屋所有权证和市场准入证方可在市场上进行房屋交易。至2010年底，共办理“房地产交易市场准入许可证”1647个，核销职工存量补贴1518.86万元。收缴土地收益金680万元。

四、住房公积金管理

2004年12月，县政府出台《息烽县建立住房公积金制度的实施方案》，施行住房公积金制度。县境内的国家机关、国有企业、社会团体在职职工按规定缴存住房公积金。职工个人缴存的住房公积金和职工所在单位为职工缴存的住房公积金均属职工个人所有。职工住房公积金的月缴存额，以2004年9月职工工资、津贴、补贴、各种奖金和加班工资的月工资总额的5%缴存，单位为职工的月缴存额为职工月平均工资额的5%。

2005年，缴交住房公积金单位122个，职工5352人，缴存金额755.08万元。

2010年12月，缴交住房公积金单位133个，职工6249人，缴存金额964.98万元。

息烽县2006—2010年公积金业务数据统计表

表12-2-7　　　　金额：人、户、万元

年份	归集额	归集人数	提取额	贷款额	贷款户数
2006	868.56	3906	174.74	514	66
2007	1046.2	4803	316.44	2063.3	255
2008	1358.53	6111	465.88	2212.4	254
2009	1591.3	6237	740.6	2366.8	210
2010	1780.22	6249	964.98	2720.4	213

五、商品房

1998年，以建设商住楼1万平方米的宏翔花园为标志，县城房地产开发起步。

2001年，召开县城建设暨东门小区开发推介会，推出项目8个，15家房地产开发商参加推介会。

2002年，县城建设开始加速。启动金地商住楼、慧恒商住楼、泉都花园、“城中城”、东门小区1#、5#、6#楼等项目，建筑面积共计5万平方米。

2003年，县城第一栋电梯商住楼——新城银座（高19层）竣工，建筑面积2.57万平方米。是年，开磷新城开始建设，至2010年建成面积4.7万平方米。

2008年，南大街10号楼动工，2010年竣工。楼高19层，建筑面积2.6万平方米。

2010年，龙港大厦竣工，建筑面积4.3万平方米。

息烽县1998—2010年县城住宅小区统计表

表12-2-8

序号	名　称	规模（平方米）	楼层	建设年份	入住年份	开发公司
1	宏翔花园	11540	7	1998	2000	贵州宏翔房地产开发公司
2	光彩大楼	7800	8	1999	2001	遵义明德房地产开发公司
3	城中城综合市场	10361	—	2001	2003	贵阳恒铭房地产开发公司

续表

序号	名　称	规模（平方米）	楼层	建设年份	入住年份	开发公司
4	东门教师新村	170000	7	2001	2003	贵州中创房地产开发有限公司
5	恒铭园	10440	7	2000	2002	花溪房地产开发公司
6	明星公寓	4765	8	2002	2004	遵义明德房产开发有限公司
7	泉都花园	12554	7	2002	2004	贵州汇杰房地产开发公司
8	慧恒商住楼	30898	7	2004	2008	贵州慧恒房地产开发有限公司
9	金地商住楼	2620	—	2002	2003	四川华莹房地产开发公司
10	金鑫公寓	12000	7	2003	2006	息烽县城建开发公司
11	开磷新城	162000	8	2003	2005	贵州开磷集团房地产开发有限公司
12	南大街广建新苑	610000	—	2003	2005	贵州广建房地产开发有限公司
13	慧恒花园	18000	—	2005	2007	贵州慧恒房地产开发有限公司
14	第一商业广场	20000	7	2004	2006	贵州汇杰房地产开发有限公司
15	正兴商业步行街	16240	5	2005	2007	贵州宏宇房地产开发有限责任公司
16	水栖怡园	92000	—	2006	2008	息烽县城乡建设综合开发公司
17	新贵地带商住楼	2900	7	2006	2007	贵州泰维房地产开发有限责任公司
18	筑北商业大道	115200	7～8	2006	2008	重庆渝万集团金穗房地产开发有限公司
19	金辉商贸中心	10206	7	2006	2008	息烽伟业房地产开发公司
20	正欣庄园（阳光地带）	83000	—	2006	2008	贵州遵义正烽房地产开发有限公司
21	龙港新城	51000	7	2006	2008	贵州弘晋房地产开发有限公司
22	泉都饮食城	16000	—	2006	2008	贵州汇杰房地产开发有限公司
23	烽景名苑	63500	7	2007	2008	贵州鑫众房地产开发有限公司
24	佳和苑	39200	7	2007	2009	息烽建成房地产开发有限公司
25	龙港商贸城	74579	—	2007	2009	贵州弘晋房地产开发有限公司
26	龙港大厦	27800	23	2008	2010	贵州弘晋房地产开发有限公司
27	郦都华府	31000	18	2008	2010	息烽鑫正房地产开发有限责任公司
28	南大街11号（新城银座）	26000	19	2008	2010	贵阳东方房地产开发有限公司
29	一品城A区	137629	—	2008	2010	息烽伟业房地产开发公司
30	深港商贸城	131256	—	2008	2016	贵州万众房地产开发有限公司
31	龙港馨苑	47169	—	2009	2011	贵州弘晋房地产开发有限公司
32	蓥龙南苑	10600	7	2009	2011	贵州蓥龙房地产开发有限公司
	合计	2058257				

第三节　市政建设

一、供水

1990年，县城饮用水主要由大型地水厂供应自来水，日供水量2000立方米。1991年开发玄天洞腹泉，日供水量1000立方米。因水量逐渐减小，日供水量800～400立方米，仅作补充水源。2003年永靖水厂建成投产，日供水1.5万立方米。2010年，县自来水公司日供水能力增至3万立方米。县自来水公司按国家规定标准定期对源水进行净化检测，水质综合检测合格率98%以上。

（一）供水管网

县自来水公司分别于1992年、1998年、2000年、2003年4次改造县城供水管网。供水面积从2.5平方千米增加到8.5平方千米，100毫米以上供水管道从13.8千米增加到65千米；2010年，县城年供水量280万立方米，用水户1.22万户4万人。

息烽县1991—2010年城区供水统计表

表12-2-9

年份	设计供水能力（万立方米/日）	年供水量（万立方米）	用水户（户）
1991	0.2	42	1200
1993	0.3	61	1258
1995	0.3	85	1346
1996	0.35	100	1391
1997	0.35	120	1452
1999	0.35	150	1587
2000	0.35	155	2084
2001	0.35	180	2751
2002	1.8	190	2899
2003	1.8	200	3138
2004	1.8	217	3345
2005	1.8	221	4115
2006	1.8	245	4635
2007	1.8	250	5207
2008	1.8	250	7207
2009	1.8	280	9298
2010	1.8	280	11221

（二）水费收取

1991年，实行总表收费制。是年，县城居民生活用水收费标准0.4元/吨。1992年，执行非生活用水1元/吨、综合用水0.8元/吨标准。1993年，居民生活用水0.6元/吨，收取供水建设费0.3元/吨；生产经营性用水0.8元/吨，收取供水建设费0.4元/吨。2001年9月1日，县城自来水收费执行新的价格标准：生活用水、机关、学校及事业单位用水1.2元/吨、工业用水1.25元/吨、商业用水1.8元/吨、建筑业用水2元/吨、洗浴业用水2元/吨。2003年起，实行“一户一表”制，新增用户供水设施由县自来水公司统一设计安装。2009年，调整水费收费标准：生活用水1.6元/吨、工业用水1.9元/吨、经营服务用水3.2元/吨、行政事业用水2元/吨、市政用水1元/吨。

二、供电

1990年，在县城东南设供电工区，柿花坪置输变电站，变压器容量6400千伏安，进线电压35千伏、出线电压10千伏。城内变压器总容量4360千伏安。随着城区用电量的不断增加，1995年增容为7500千伏安。2000年2月，110千伏永靖变电站（大型地）建成投入运行，2005年和2009年安装2台500千伏变压器，总变电容量增至150万千伏安。架设2条110千伏线路进线（其中1条为备用）；5条35千伏、7条10千伏出线供电。至2010年，在城区6条线路形成3个“手拉手”环网供电的同时，又加装自动化开关，将每条线路分成多段，一旦遭遇供电线路故障，系统将自动判断故障并将其隔离，使相邻非故障段线路迅速恢复供电。

2010年7—8月，县城息九公路路口至三角花园、三角花园至县城十字街地段实施电网入地工程，即供电线路由明线改为入地电缆。其中地基施工和电缆保护管网由住建局负责实施，共计投资339.61万元。

三、路灯

1990年，从城南火车站至城北县人民医院住院部及文化路全长约4千米路段，安装水银路灯194盏；在县府路及十字街、老干局等处安装兰花路灯20盏。

1997年1月，县城路灯由财政局移交建设局管理。是年，投资13万元的县城十字街高杆灯投入使用。高杆灯为圆锥形升降式高杆灯，高25米，安装24颗400瓦灯泡。1998年，安装花园路街心三角花园30米高杆灯和县政府门前6盏兰花灯，并将文化路中央的电线杆移至人行道上，新安装文化南路电灯。2000年，新装镇府路路灯，春节期间临街机关单位及街道居民安装轮廓灯；并投入32万元对县城路灯进行改造。至2001年，县城各沿街主干道共安装路灯183盏。2002年，投入32万元在花园西路增加单臂式路灯60组，县城路灯增加到245盏。2003年，投入22万元在东门小区安装单臂式路灯40组。2004年，新安装南大街高低臂路灯130套、中杆灯6盏、景观灯70套。

2005年，县城开始使用检修车检修路灯，结束人工攀爬人字梯检修路灯的历史。2006年，县城街道共有路灯520盏。2009年，县城东门河道安装夜景灯光，总投资91万元。

四、供气

1996年，县城开始使用罐装液化石油气，气源由贵阳运到县内液化石油气销售点，销售点由贵阳市住建局审批。

1997年，液化石油气开始由县村镇建设管理站管理。每年对液化石油气安全实行严格管理，年审合格的给予换证，不合格者予以停业整顿。是年，取缔经营性燃煤炉灶后，有液化石油气用户4150户，城市气化率31.8%。1999年，全县有液化石油气及灶具经营点共4个。至2001年，县内有液化气供应站、经营部11个。

2005年，重兴液化气公司在养龙司堡子设立储配站并开始对县域供气。储配站储气能力50吨，能满足全县持续供气35天。2007年，储配站从养龙司迁至县城蚕桑坡。

2006年，全县有液化气经营站点18个，用户7100户。

2010年，县内有液化气经营点8个，用户3200户。

五、农贸市场

1992年，在县城建城中城农贸市场，占地面积1.16万平方米。2003年，城中城农贸市场改建为综合市场。建筑面积1.03万平方米，有铺面28个；大棚面积1500平方米，摊位328个。

2010年，在县城建水栖怡园农贸市场，占地面积3200平方米。建筑面积3200平方米，有铺面8个、摊位188个。

六、花园广场

1998年，建三角花园，面积2288平方米，为全封闭花园。2006年进行改造，建成集休闲长廊、桌椅、草坪、花台、假石山为一体的休闲花园。2006年，建北门花园，面积6000平方米，设置假山、草坪、休闲长廊和凉亭。为市民休闲、健身场所。2007年，将原灯光球场改扩建为双拥广场，占地3677平方米，投资280万元；建有长廊、篮球场、观众台、假山、水池等。2008年，建中街广场，占地1808平方米；安装有3匹马塑像和木栏靠椅。是年，建汽车站广场，占地1万平方米。

七、河道治理及污水处理

20世纪90年代末，息烽河、贯城河、下阳朗排洪大沟堵塞严重。2000年前，每逢大暴雨，下阳朗大沟洪水流入白骨洞从石门洞涌出，注入息烽河后在东门田坝泛滥成灾；贯城河河床不畅，由沙石坡汇集而下的洪水殃及“城中城”片区。县委、县政府采取措施，治理河道，防治洪水，处理污水。

息烽河治理：息烽河由东向西流经县城东门至北门桥，县委、县政府于1991、1998、1999年组织机关干部职工，清除石门洞至福利桥700米河段中的垃圾和淤泥2100立方米，加固河堤1730立方米，新砌枧槽沟至东门小区河堤165米。2000年，对息烽河河道进行改道，2002年竣工。河道由实验幼儿园至育才路西路口全部贯通，长395米，深4米，宽8～12米；硬化河床，沿河种植绿化树。2007年，在东门小区息烽河道两侧新安装石围栏，修建拦河橡胶坝。

下阳朗段排洪大沟治理：下阳朗排洪大沟半边街段，2004—2005年修建南大街中段时，修筑排洪大沟，长207米，其中明沟165米、暗沟42米。

贯城河治理：贯城河是源于城西沙石坡的季节河流，由南大街经西门片区流往乡镇企业局办公楼旁注入息烽河。1992—1993年，涉及“城中城”农贸市场地段，筑沟盖板改为暗沟；修筑花园东路时，在其中段修桥1座，并将筑沟盖板改为暗沟至“城中城”农贸市场北端。2004年，改造“城中城”段河道146米。2008年，火车站西段排洪沟整治工程、县城民政路排水工程、城中城农贸市场河道改造工程完工。

县城污水处理厂：2007年，城区建成8600米污水收集管道。2008年8月，动工修建日处理0.7万吨污水处理厂（地址在西山乡林丰村葫芦水村民组息烽河与底寨河交汇处，占地11亩，距县城约4千米）、污水输送管道3790米和相关配套设施。2009年12月试运行，2010年4月，委托贵州绿地环保科技有限公司负责运营。

八、县城垃圾填埋场

1991—2002年，将解放南路与环城路交界处（老客车站）旁的天然大麻窝作为垃圾填埋场，此后垃圾堆放点为西山乡林丰村黄草坝。2008年12月，在小寨坝镇盘脚营村石宝林组王兵槽建县城垃圾填埋场，占地14.5公顷，总库容85.5万立方米，总投资5600万元。2010年12月建成并投入调试运行。有容量66.4万立方米填埋库区，7000立方米调节池1个、渗滤液处理系统和出水水质自动监控系统各1套。日处理生活垃圾90吨，渗滤液处理能力50吨/日（产水率70%）。

第四节　城镇绿化

1995年以前，城镇绿化工作主要为单位的庭院绿化和小范围内的行道树绿化。1996年6月，县绿野林业资源开发有限责任公司成立（简称绿野公司）。是年，在县城部分乡街道种植行道树。2002年，十字街街区、息烽集中营革命历史纪念馆广场、贵遵路出口绿化工程通过设计及立项。是年，绿野公司在东门小区、息烽集中营革命历史纪念馆广场和十字街街区共栽植行道景观树150株，对各街道的死亡树、病死树进行更换补植。2004年1月，县林业局设立城镇绿化管理站，负责全县园林绿化规划编制及实施、建设、更新改造及养护管理、监察、工程验收和相关法律法规宣传等。同时接管绿野公司。是年，对南大街、东门坝河滨路进行绿化，共种植胸径10厘米香樟720余株、柳树120余株，红花檵木、红叶石楠、四季桂、毛叶杜鹃、龟甲冬青7000平方米共60余万株，草坪5000余平方米；“五一”、国庆、春节等节假日期间，利用鲜花、盆景装饰县城十字街等闹市区。此后装饰工作形成常态。2006年，绿化体育路和育才路，种植银杏90株、香樟240株，红叶石楠、金叶女贞等5万余株。

1996—2010年，在北门广场种植香樟树66株；汽车站广场种植银杏、香樟、海棠、紫荆、桂花、天竺桂等100余株，茶花等灌木500余株，草坪300平方米；双拥广场绿化面积4000平方米，种植香樟27株，紫荆、紫薇及各类球形植物200余株，金叶女贞、红花檵木等20余万株。县城所有街道、景点均完成绿化。

二、温泉森林公园建设

1994年8月，省林业厅同意建立“息烽温泉省级森林公园”（包括息烽温泉风景区的温泉和天台山丛林景点）。2004年1月，根据《贵州省息烽县旅游发展总体规划》，在原息烽温泉省级森林公园基础上，将西望山国有林、南山林场坪天坝、场部和苗圃三个工区、玄天洞以及团元山合并建设温泉森林公园，由县林业绿化局负责组织筹建。

2005年，完成《息烽省级森林公园总体规划》，公园包括团元山、西望山、南山、玄天洞、天台山和温泉等六个景区，总面积3554.3公顷。2010年，团元山景区建设竣工。

第三章　城市管理

1991年，县政府制定《息烽县个人建住房审批的暂行规定》。此后出台《息烽县城管监察实施细则》等文件，逐步加强对设计、建房和城市公共设施管理。通过修建农贸市场、停车场等公共设施，加强城市管理，注重环境卫生，县城面貌一新，功能更加完善。

第一节　县城环境卫生

一、机构

1991年，永靖镇政府设环境卫生管理站，负责县城环境卫生。2001年6月，县委决定将永靖镇政府环境卫生管理站更名为县市容环境卫生管理站，划归县城市管理委员会管理。2002年9月，县市容环境卫生管理站更名为县环境卫生管理站（副股级），下设办公室、业务监察科、垃圾清运队。

二、卫生设施

1991年，县城垃圾清运车为3辆川路车，2部小四轮拖拉机；设果皮箱180个。是年，在十字街转新大街位置修建收费公厕1所，收费标准为2角/人/次。

1997年8月，县政府出台《关于加强县城管理工作的意见》。是年，建垃圾房13座、垃圾池8个，设果皮箱120个，县城街道主干道两侧每隔50米设置1个，并开始在背街小巷置果皮箱。1999年，建7所水冲式公厕。2000年，建成封闭式垃圾池6个。2002年，县投资11.5万元配备县城第一辆洒水车。2007年，在蚕桑坡北端新建3000平方米垃圾中转站1座。2008年，新建垃圾转运站3座，配置清运车7辆。

2009年6月1日起，实行公厕免费。

2010年，县环境卫生管理站有垃圾清运车、洒水车和吸污车等16辆。县城有密封式垃圾清洁间43个、垃圾转运站4座；有公厕32所，其中水冲式公厕24所。

三、卫生管理

1991年，县城保洁区域为解放南路、解放北路、县府路、交通路、东风路、人民路、文化路、铁路新村等路段。

1994年1月，县政府决定对县直机关、企事业单位及永靖镇自来水用户收取“城市卫生维护费”，与收自来水费同步进行，按用户用水量每立方0.15元收取。后改为按单位和户收取。

1997年，永靖镇政府成立创建省级卫生城市办公室，对城内机关单位、居民住户实行“门前三包（包卫生、包管理、包绿化），门内达标”制度。县城开始全天保洁，垃圾日产日清。组织机关干部、学校师生8000余人次上街大扫除，清除广告、标语残迹1万余张。9月，取缔县城、阳朗和温泉片区经营性煤火炉灶143户，减少乱堆乱放行为和二氧化硫对空气的污染。至此，县城脏、乱、差现象开始转变。

2002年，县城保洁区域由解放南路路口沿210国道延伸至张露萍等七烈士墓地的旅游线，保洁路段增至14条，每天清扫面积10万平方米，实行凌晨普扫，白天保洁，日清运垃圾量60吨。同时，宣传垃圾袋装化，袋装率60%。是年，县物价局规定永靖镇城关住户的卫生维护费由县自来水公司收取。其他机关、社会团体、企事业单位、学校、各种经营性商业、经营性个体户、服务业、加工店、临时摊点等行业的卫生维护费由县市容环境卫生管理站收取。

2003年，实行保洁人员“清扫一班，保洁一班”路段负责制，每日晨6时前普扫，白天巡回保洁。县城县府路、十字街等主要街道实行夜间保洁。

2004年9月，环境卫生保洁路段实行招标承包制度，将县城环卫作业区域划分为5个作业区、40

名保洁员，面向社会公开竞标承包。11月，县城生活垃圾实行袋装化管理，封闭住房灰道。

2005年，南大街建成投入使用，清扫路段由半边街延伸至云环小学东南侧铁路桥下。2006年，县城清扫路段东至大型地自来水池旁，南至云环小学东南侧铁路桥下，北至响水桥，西至柿花坪屠宰场处，面积20.5万平方米。环卫站临时聘用环卫工人75名。

2009—2010年，实行定岗、定员分片责任制，治理环境卫生、占道经营、查处违章建筑。清除各类“野广告”1.1万余条，清除和覆盖各种制假证等电话号码1100多个，规范沿街门头牌匾1920平方米。清运垃圾3万吨。

第二节　市容管理

一、市容市貌管理

1991—1993年，县城集贸市场均为“马路市场”，每逢赶场天，街道拥挤，垃圾遍地。1994年2月，县政府对县城交通、市场秩序管理作出规定，不得在解放路、东风路、交通路、县府路、文化东路、文化北路和十字街等主要街道摆摊设点，所有摊位统一归行入市。

1996年3月13日，县政府颁发《关于整顿县城容貌的通告》，规定日杂、百货、副食、小吃摊一律进入农贸市场，水果摊、夜市以及赶场天从农村进入的农副产品在划定路段两旁范围内交易。临街建筑实行围栏施工。严禁在街道、公路、院落乱堆乱放物品、乱扔垃圾、乱泼污水。临街、临路不得乱搭凉棚、雨篷和乱建炉灶，已搭建的限期拆除。农贸市场和室内经营摊点由工商部门管理，室外经营摊点由城管部门管理。永靖镇对街道、住房、单位和院落的环境卫生实行“门前三包”，并签订“门前三包”责任书，垃圾做到日产日清。1997年，夜市摊点迁解放北路。星期三文化路集市移至农贸市场内，星期天集市摊点控制在建设局、教育局办公楼门口以北至街心花园一带。1998年4月，夜市迁文化西路。2004年，集中整治文化路、花园路、县府路、十字街、北门桥等重点路段的占道经营，取缔赶场天“马路市场”。西门市场、城中城综合农贸市场建成投入使用。2006年，城管人员每天坚持执法巡逻，对乱搭、乱建、乱放和占道经营等违法违章行为出现一例查处一例。县城完善主要街道标识、标线，文化路十字路口安装红绿灯。2008年，经常组织检查卫生，对卫生死角进行曝光，限时整改。2009—2010年，实行定岗定员分片责任制，设置临时占道经营区域（点）6个，规范占道经营摊点135个。取缔各种占道经营摊点222起，清除店堂延伸占道经营185起、违规早餐点86起、各类“野广告”约3000余条、各类制假证等电话号码约600余个，清洗外墙面895平方米，规范沿街门头牌匾1920平方米，拆除违章建筑27起1万余平方米。

二、县城车辆停放管理

1991年后，随着公用、私人汽车及运营的二、三轮摩托增多，县城各街道、路口处车辆乱停乱放现象突出。

1994年2月5日，县政府作出关于县城交通、市场秩序管理规定，规定所有大客车、中巴车、货车以及九庄、黑神庙方向的微型车只能在社会停车场依次停放候客，阳朗方向的微型车只能在人民路依次停放候客，摩托车只能在国营像馆和理发店之间及百货公司门口依次停放候客，马车、驮马只能在猪市坝停放经营。

1995年前，县内营运车辆的经营管理权由县交通局负责。1996年1月，县城内营运车辆由城管部门管理，县城外营运车辆由交通部门管理。在县城内，车辆行驶由交警部门管理，车容和停放由城管部门管理。3月13日，县政府发出《关于整顿县城容貌的通告》，规定开往贵阳、九庄、小寨坝、石硐的客车停放在社会停车场内，候货的大小汽车、拖拉机、人力车和开往底寨方向的微型车停放花园东路，摩托车停放文化东路、花园东路、环城路的南北两端。所有进城车辆时速必须控制在20千米以内。9月，由贵阳市公交公司调拨的3辆中巴车在县城开通运营，运行路线为蚕桑坡、火车站两条线，价格为0.5元/人。

1997年，取消原文化路停车许可，所有货运车辆和开往底寨的客运车辆一律停放在新大街花园东路，阳朗方向的客运微型车停放在蔬菜公司空坝内，客运的士停放在人民路，人力车分别停放在社会停车场、花园东路、蔬菜公司空坝内，摩托车停放在文化东路、花园路、县医院、汽车站、火车站指定停放点内。

1998年，对人力板车进行整顿，纳入规范管理。是年办证32件。

2002年11月，设立县城市客运管理办公室（2010年10月划归县交通局），统一管理城市小公共汽车、出租车客运行业。

2009—2010年，城管部门查处各类机动车辆占用人行道乱停乱放现象508起。

三、燃气市场管理

1996年，由村镇建设管理站开展燃气管理工作。对全县4家罐装经营点进行安全及销售管理，其中县城2家、小寨坝1家、养龙司1家。

2007年，全县有充气配送站1座，门市经营点18家。

2010年，全县有液化气经营点8家，用户3200户。

第三节　城市管理执法

1990—1996年，县政府先后制定《永靖镇规范管理暂行办法》《息烽县小寨坝镇商业一条街实施暂行办法》《息烽县个人住房审批的暂行规定》《息烽县城管监察实施细则》等地方规章，以保障城市规划、环境保护、房地产管理与县城经济协调发展。

1996、2002年，宣传执行《中华人民共和国房地产管理法》《中华人民共和国城市规划法》和《贵阳市房地管理办法》《贵阳市建设拆迁管理办法》《贵阳市建筑市场管理办法》《贵阳市市容环境卫生管理条例》《贵阳市市容环境卫生监察处罚规定》《贵阳市市政设施管理办法》《贵阳市城镇房屋产权产籍管理办法》《息烽县城管监察实施细则》。

2004年，根据城市管理相关法规，开展集中整治文化路、花园路、县府路、十字街、北门桥等路段的占道经营，全年取缔占道经营及流动摊点2000余起，教育处罚2400余人，查处违反市政设施管理行为21起、违反城市管理34起、占道洗车点3处，拆除违章建筑25起，面积2832.6平方米，规范修车点17处，取缔煤火炉灶60个。

2007年，根据省、市、县“整脏治乱”工作要求，城管大队、环卫站、城市客运管理办公室联合执法，实行定岗、定员分片责任制，开展治理环境卫生、占道经营，查处违章建筑，规范出租车行为等工作，全年取缔占道经营650余起，没收无证占道经营流动摊点130余个，查处各类流动小摊贩450余个、机动车乱停乱放170余起，清除野广告2.5万余张，拆除违章建筑23起，取缔中小学周边流动摊点100余个。

2010年，取缔各类占道经营摊点222起，清除店堂延伸占道经营185起，清退违规设置的早餐点86起，查处机动车占用人行道乱停乱放现象508起，清除城区各类“野广告”约3000余条、各类制假证等电话号码600余个，拆除违章建筑27起，面积10047.6平方米，收缴色情盗版书籍89套、各类非法音像制品40余件，查处进城车辆污染路面行为33起。

第四章　建筑业管理

县城建部门按规定对建筑工程质量进行抽查、抽测和监督，按照有关规定对建筑工程实行招投标管理。对入境开发商进行资质审查，按照《贵阳市商品房销售管理办法》进行商品房销售管理。

第一节　企业资质与招投标管理

一、企业资质

1991年，全县有建筑企业240个。1992年有建筑企业203个，产值803万元（当年价）。1994年有建筑企业63个。1995年有建筑企业130个，产值1487万元。1998年，县建设局对入境的开发商进行资质初审。2001年，建筑企业产值为5175万元。2003年开始，实行建筑工程施工许可制度，未经许可，工程不得开工建设。2004年，县内有建筑企业20个，产值11193万元（当年价）。2008年，全县26个建筑企业，产值21094万元。2010年，建筑企业产值19592万元（当年价）。

二、招投标

2000年1月1日，《中华人民共和国招投标法》施行，在县建设局成立县招投标办公室，由施工管理站负责招投标管理工作。至2005年，共招投标工程65个，面积27.9万平方米，总造价5092万元。

2006年，50万元以上所有市政设施及房屋建筑项目招标均进入贵阳市交易中心进行，全年招投标工程29个，建筑面积42757.2平方米，造价13123.22万元。其中公开招标14个，面积22848.6平方米，造价1981.71万元，邀请招标15个（房开项目），面积29909.6平方米，造价1111.51万元。

2009年，招标工程20个，建筑面积34262.23平方米，总造价1288.24万元。议标工程2个，建筑面积1650平方米，总造价54万元。

第二节　质量安全监督管理

一、质量监督

1991年起，县内建筑工程质量监督管理工作由县建设局施工管理站具体负责，主要对工程质量及施工安全进行监管。

1992—2002年，县建设局施工管理站共监督工程241个；验收工程66个，验收合格率100%，优良率5.6%~10.63%。

2003年起，实行建筑工程竣工验收备案制度，实现从“质量等级核验”向“竣工验收备案”的监督机制和模式的转变。主要由县建设局施工管理站负责具体监管及组织验收工作。至2010年，县建设局共办理建筑施工许可项目152个，建筑面积117.6万平方米。

二、安全监督

1997年，全年组织召开施工企业安全质量管理工作会议2次，参会人员64人次。安全质量监督与施工管理站同各施工企业签订安全目标责任书。由施工管理站对施工企业安全生产实行目标管理、量化考核。此后，县境内的施工管理实行规范化，每年对施工企业责任人或以会代训或专门会议组织培训，对在建工程进行安全质量大检查均在10次以上。

2007年5月31日起，息烽地区建筑工地全部使用扣件式钢管脚架，禁止使用外竹脚架。

2008—2010年，共指导质监工程98个，召开安全质量会议12次，巡回检查20次，召开安全工作会议19次。

第五章　房地产开发

1998年，首家房地产商进入县城。2003年，有11家房地产开发商入驻县城。至2010年，入驻县城房地产企业修建商品房132.79万平方米，其中新区建设125.36万平方米，旧城改造7.43万平方米。乡镇建设也有很大发展。

第一节　房地产业

1991—1997年，单位、个人建房多由县内建筑公司、建筑队或个人承包。

1998年，县计划与经济贸易局引进贵州宏翔开发公司，在原饮料厂地块进行首家房地产开发，以建商住楼1.2万平方米的宏翔花园为标志，县内房地产开发起步。1999年，县工商业联合会引进遵义明德房地产开发公司，在原百货公司仓库地块修建光彩大楼，建筑面积8000平方米。

2001年，县政府进一步完善房地产优惠政策，利用《贵阳日报》等新闻媒体向外宣传息烽开发计划，吸引外资投资息烽建设，并于3月召开县城市建设项目推介会，推出建设项目8个，吸引外资投资建设。是年，入驻县内的房地产投资企业增至5家。

2002年1月9日，县政府与贵州广建房地产开发有限公司签订《息烽县开发建设南大街协议书》。约定由广建公司出资建设县城南大街1696米道路，县政府将南大街道路两侧各25米范围内约9.2公顷土地整体出让给广建公司进行房地产开发建设。

2003年，县内共有11家房地产开发公司入驻。至2005年，全县房屋新开工面积8.64万平方米，竣工面积8.88万平方米，共完成房地产开发投资1.68亿元。

2010年，县内共有20家房地产开发公司入驻。

第二节　房地产管理

一、房地产登记管理

1991年，由县城建局房地产管理站办理房屋建筑、交易及房产登记管理等业务。1996年8月，县政府授权县工商管理局负责房地产登记业务。2001年3月22日，设立县房地产交易中心，负责全县房屋产权、抵押等登记。

息烽县2000—2010年房地产登记管理统计表

表12-5-1

年份	办理房产证		审核房地产抵押登记备案	审查贷款金额	商品房预售登记	
	件	面积（万平方米）	件	（万元）	户、件	面积（万平方米）
2000	420	11.43	338	—	62户	0.56
2001	723	4.2	615	680	80户	0.81
2002	556	1.4	637	1387	80户	0.81
2003	556	45.99	1270	9020	180户	2.02
2004	539	12.73	459	9256	120户	0.78
2005	502	10.88	453	6414	6件	4.23
2006	566	9.75	420	4545	9件	12.04
2007	496	4.35	371	5705	9件	31.01
2008	612	6.63	583	9750	8件	22.19
2009	2604	29.1	1571	77937	6件	10.69
2010	2770	40.65	878	23832	7件	7.3

二、产权产籍及交易管理

1991年，县内只有房地产开发，没有商品房开发。政府、企事业单位造房，主要是用于内部职工福利分配，没有房地产市场。

1995年，县内开始房屋产权登记发证及房地产交易管理，房屋产权证办理执行土地使用证、验收合格证、建设用地规划许可证、建设工程规划许可证的发证制度。

1998年，县建设局按照《贵阳市商品房销售管理办法》进行商品房销售管理。对达到预售条件的，由县建设局审核并颁发预售许可证后预售，预售资金由县建设局监督使用。房屋销售价格由开发商根据其建筑成本结合息烽市场自行定价报县建设局房地产管理站实际核算的面积为准。商品房建筑竣工后，实行综合验收，提供物业管理方案后交付使用。

2000年，根据《贵阳市城镇房屋权属管理办法》，县建设局印发《关于使用商品房〈住宅质量保证书〉〈住宅使用说明书〉的通知》，规定房地产企业在销售商品房住宅时，必须向购房人提供商品房《住宅质量保证书》和《住宅使用说明书》；在订立商品房买卖合同时，必须向购房人明示

《商品房销售管理办法》，预售商品的，必须明示《城市商品房预售管理办法》。至2006年，入驻县内的房地产企业，投资2.7亿元建成光彩大楼、宏翔花园、明星公寓、泉都花园、恒铭园、金鑫公寓、“城中城”、开磷新城、教师新村、慧恒中心花园、龙港新城、正欣商业步行街等商业住宅小区，修建商品房居住面积29.1万平方米。销售两室一厅、三室一厅住房2088套，面积24.65万平方米。

2003年后，受物价等因素影响，商品房价格每年以100元/平方米的价格上涨。至2006年，住房最低销售价580元/平方米，最高销售价880元/平方米。2007年，平均价格950元/平方米。

2010年，县内商品房实行网上签约和网上备案制度。

息烽县1998—2010年商品房预售面积统计表

表12-5-2

年份	审核办理商品房预售许可证（件）	批准预售面积（万平方米）	住房平均价格（元/平方米）
1998	1	1.05	300
2000	1	0.68	311
2001	1	0.46	339
2002	3	2.03	375
2003	2	3.8	415
2004	5	5.02	568
2005	7	5.49	625
2006	10	17.07	705
2007	19	33.12	816
2008	8	22.19	923
2009	9	12.98	1027
2010	8	4.74	1485

三、物业管理

开磷新城、泉都花园、正兴商业步行街3个住宅小区分别由开磷物业管理公司、贵阳新佳丽物业管理公司、息烽庆烽物业管理公司管理，其余小区由业主委员会自主管理。

第六章　农村建设

改革开放后，农民收入逐年增加，农村逐渐走向富裕，农村建设速度加快。

1996年5月11日，县政府印发《关于加快集镇建设的通知》，要求集镇建设必须坚持规划先行，坚持统一规划、统一征地、统一出让、统一开发、统一管理原则。至2005年，各乡镇先后编制集镇规划，并按规划进行集镇建设。至2010年，集镇和农村住房面貌发生巨大变化。

第一节　集镇建设

一、小寨坝镇——黑神庙

1988年，开阳磷矿矿务局在黑神庙兴建黄磷厂、重钙厂，带动境内商业、城建及配套设施建设的发展。1990年，黑神庙集镇面积2.5平方千米，建成面积0.18平方千米。1992年9月，小寨坝镇列入贵州省小城镇建设试点镇。1995年4月，小寨坝镇列为全国500个小城镇建设试点镇之一。1999年，建设部授予小寨坝镇“全国村镇建设先进镇”称号。2010年，黑神庙集镇建成面积2.5平方千米。

（一）街道

1991年，集镇中心街道为川黔公路，长800米，柏油路面。镇内有3条巷道：区供销社至中学，长70米，宽2米，泥石路面，场天为农副产品市场，平时为蔬菜市场；镇中心街道中段急弯处至粮管所，长250米，宽2.5米，水泥路面，场天为蔬菜市场；从黑神庙道班向西南至重钙厂，长250米，宽4米，泥石路面。至1998年，建成新街、文化路、文化东路、贸易路和交通路（即黑神庙路），北端延伸800米，道路平均宽14米，总长2千米；其中4条为混凝土路面，1条为沥青路面。2002—2006年，建成2.3千米南山大道，路宽18米。2008年，建成黑神庙小学至农贸市场东风路，修建南山大道行政中心区道路及排污管网系统。

黑神庙街道统计表

表12-6-1

名称	方位	起止点	长（千米）	宽（米）
竹园路	东西	黑神庙中学至烟叶站家属楼	0.5	10
黑神庙路	南北	杨福群家至黄文才家	1.2	6
磷城大道	南北	南至盘脚营村干沟组李远义家，北至小寨坝村南极路口	4.5	8
复兴路	东西	南大街转盘至开磷集团重钙厂生产区门口（贵遵高速路立交桥）	0.8	12
诚信路	东西	新修客车站路口至上寨村干沟组老高速路	1.2	12
磷城南路	南北	南大街转盘至李云忠家	0.6	12
中心路	南北	竹园路邓培祥家至贸易路聂明武家	1.5	8
富民路	南北	磷城南路毛子祥家路口绕顾景明家至磷城南路陈远杰家路口	0.6	5
民生路	东西南北	诚信路中段路口至磷城南路北段杨昌豪家路口命名（含绕廉租房段路）	1.2	6
新街	南北	路言学家至黄文才家	0.9	8
贸易路	东西	兴园门口至农行	0.6	8
文化路	南北	竹园公园门口至聂明武家	0.5	8
文化东路	东西	黑神庙小学门口至农贸市场	0.4	6

（二）建筑

1990年，黑神庙房屋建筑面积4.86万平方米（未含黄磷厂、重钙厂），其中砖混结构2.03万平方米、砖木结构2.18万平方米、木结构瓦顶3951平方米、土墙瓦顶结构2553平方米。另外，黄磷、重钙厂建筑面积19693平方米，其中工业用房1.09万平方米、办公区及住宅8724平方米。

至1999年，新建镇区54156平方米。长20千米、管径250毫米、日供水4300立方米的供水工程投入使用。新安装200千伏变压器2台，架设低压线路3400米，安装中杆灯1盏、路灯100盏。城镇房屋建筑面积11.25万平方米，其中公共设施面积3.62万平方米、私人建房面积7.63万平方米；厂矿区房屋建筑面积11.27万平方米，其中生产用房6.35万平方米、办公及生活用房4.91万平方米。至2000年，房屋总建筑面积23.87万平方米。

2001—2007年，建成农贸市场、竹文化园、精神文明活动中心、政府职工安居工程住房楼和学生宿舍楼群、镇卫生院住院部门诊楼。

2010年，建成南山大道拆迁安置小区面积20.5万平方米。建成4A级室内农贸市场升级改造和垃圾填埋场，修建阳光党务公开广场、客运站和重钙厂货运停车场。是年底，黑神庙集镇所在地建筑面积47.2万平方米，多为砖混结构。厂矿企业建筑面积21.48万平方米，其中生活用房4.58万平方米。

（三）供水

1991年，镇内使用从干沟抽取的地下水，日供水150立方米。随着厂矿的陆续兴建、人口增多以及小城镇建设的铺开，供水渐成困难。1993年，建立自来水站，实行装表计量收费。1998年7月，小寨坝引水工程建成，自青山小桥河水库起，修建暗渠和铺设管道21.68千米，配套设施有高位蓄水池2个，蓄水量2000立方米，日供水量4300立方米，出水管道总长107.5千米，使供水系统大为改善。2001年7月，在盘脚营干沟钻地下水提水，修建泵房，铺设管道2100米，连接原有供水管网，基本保证镇区内供水需要。2005年3月，改造镇区供水管网。2006年，铺设南山大道管网，改造凤凰山段、小寨坝段主管道以及城区管网，实行一户一表供水。

（四）供电

1991年，镇内供电有2条10千伏线路，安装50千伏变压器2台，用电总负荷450千伏安。2010年，镇内有10千伏线路5条，线路总长506千米，其中10千伏线路150千米、400伏线路56千米、220伏线路300千米，共有配变183台，其中公变140台、专变43台，总容量11375千伏安。

二、温泉镇——石头田

石头田位于县境东北部，距县城39千米，距温泉2千米。集市在养温公路穿越镇区路段。1990年，集镇面积0.27平方千米。至2010年，集镇建成面积0.7平方千米，东至温泉派出所，南至西洋公司水泵房，西至息烽磷矿家属区新楼，北至温泉政府大楼。

（一）建筑

1990年，石头田房屋建筑面积37997平方米。1991年，居民住房主要为砖木和砖混结构，多为一层五间（四列三间），无装修，饮用水、卫生间设在屋外。1995年，温泉镇列入安顺地区22个小城镇建设试点镇之一。1998年，县政府批准实施《温泉镇村镇建设总体规划》。2000年，温泉镇精神文明活动中心大楼、社会停车场、地税所及信用社办公楼和中、小学教学楼相继建成投入使用，建筑面积8538.37平方米。2001年，房屋外面大多数贴瓷砖，屋内刮瓷粉，少数住房安装洗澡设备，室内设卫生间。2004年，建成农贸市场果蔬大棚摊位168个、商品房1号、2号楼，面积2600平方米。2003年，建成农贸市场公厕1座。2005年，修建温泉镇政府办公大楼、计划生育综合楼、王涌波等烈士陵园。至2010年，石头田房屋建筑面积22.7万平方米，多为3～4层砖混或砖木结构房屋，最高6层。大多数住户室内设卫生间，安装洗澡设备。水电、电视普及。

（二）街道

1991年，石头田仅有1条街道，为养龙司至温泉公路的一段，长400米，宽7.5米，水泥路面，赶集日为农副产品市场。2004年，修建长920米、宽20米的永兴路，并植行道树100株。2006年，投资45万元修温泉东路，长400米，宽12米，水泥路面。

（三）供水供电及排污设施

镇内供电有新场坪变电站出线，有10千伏高压线1条，能满足生产生活用电。供水设施有息烽磷矿在白石口安装的提水机，提水入蓄水池经输水管输入各个用户。镇内有阴、阳沟排水。2006年，修温泉东路的同时，修建排水沟400米。

三、九庄镇——九庄

九庄位于县境西部，距县城32.9千米。1991年是九庄区区公所驻地，1992年起为九庄镇政府驻地。

1991年，九庄集镇面积0.36平方千米。2010年，集镇建成面积2.89平方千米，东至乌江复旦学校，南至九庄加油站，西至九庄镇西门村场口组，北至九庄北门桥。中心区域覆盖新街村、西门村、新街社区居委会及天鹅村、望城村部分村民组，主要街道有兴隆路、镇北路、红卫路、九中路、镇新路、红园路、复旦路。

（一）建筑

1991年，九庄总建筑面积3.24万平方米，其中砖混结构1.29万平方米、木瓦房1.18万平方米、草房7669平方米。

1992年，修改完善九庄镇建设规划。

2004年，随商业一条街投入使用，新增建筑面积42万平方米。2008年，九庄镇政府办公及业务用房、乌江复旦学校建成投入使用。2010年，红军烈士陵园主体工程竣工，新大街街道全部硬化，沿街居民住房全部建成，休闲广场、农贸市场、客车站、加油站、公共厕所等市政设施全面竣工并投入使用。九庄建筑面积70.18万平方米，多为3～4层砖混或砖木结构房屋。

（二）街道

1991年，有交通路、镇北路、镇新路、九中路、红卫路、西门路6条街道和青堰路，仅交通路硬化。

1998年，商业一条街动工修建，长1400米，宽20米，2004年竣工，定名兴隆路，共投入资金2000多万元。2008年，乌江复旦学校建成后，青堰路改称复旦路。

九庄镇2010年街道统计表

表12-6-2

街道名称	起点	终点	长度（米）	宽度（米）
兴隆路	天鹅桥	鹿九公路路口	1200	20
镇北路	工商所	北门桥	400	6
红卫路	红军烈士陵园路口	红园路与三合村交叉路口	450	4.5
九中路	原九庄小学	供销社	250	6
镇新路	原百货大楼	红园路口	1000	6
红园路	国土所	三合村路口	1200	8
复旦路	原蔡家桥	乌江复旦学校	300	4

（三）供水供电及排污设施

供排水：20世纪80年代末，九庄建有自来水560立方米蓄水池1个、供水点6个，基本满足全镇用水需要。1992年，安装自来水进家。无专用排水设施，污水从街道两侧排放，仅交通路两侧有排水沟。

供电：1991年，九庄片区有10千伏线路1条、供电线路60千米、配变压器30台，总容量800千伏安。2000年，新建35千伏九庄变电站，有10千伏线路3条、供电线路80千米。2010年，配变压器130台，总容量6650千伏安。

四、养龙司乡——养龙司

养龙司位于县境东北部，距县城30千米，分新街、老街两部分。

1991年以前是养龙司区公所驻地，1992年后为养龙司乡政府所在地。新、老街建成面积0.42平方千米。2010年，养龙司集镇建成面积1.6平方千米，东至川黔铁路，南至灯塔村委会，西至镇政府后面耕地，北至正大饲料厂。

（一）建筑

1991年，养龙司建筑总面积6.02万平方米，其中砖混结构8003平方米、砖木结构14264平方米、木瓦结构3.7万平方米、草房901平方米。2001年，修建小商品市场，2002年竣工。2004年，步行街一期建设工程完工，农贸市场建成投入使用；是年8月，县政府批准实施《息烽县养龙司乡总体规划及建设规划》。至2010年，养龙司有公共建筑楼33栋，私人修建二层以上建筑物729户。建筑总面积17.5万平方米，多为2～3层砖混结构住房，最高4层，大部分住房配有卫生间和洗澡设备。

（二）道路

1991年，新街是养龙司至温泉公路的一段，长约1000米，最宽处宽6米，街中心地段宽仅4米，泥石路面，场天为农贸市场。老街长约500米，路面坑洼。2000年路面硬化。1995年修龙腾路、奋斗路。2003年，龙泉路建成投入使用。2006年建幸福路。2007年建和平路、飞越路。至2010年，养龙司有方养公路、养温公路穿腹而过，新建街道有龙泉路、飞越路、文化路、龙腾路、奋斗路、幸福路6条，总长2820米。

养龙司乡2010年街道统计表

表12-6-3

街道名称	建造时间（年）	起止点	街道长度（米）	街道宽度（米）
龙腾路	1995	三岔路口至卫生院	680	4.5
奋斗路	1995	龙腾路至乡政府办公楼	120	4.5
龙泉路	2003	计生站至烟叶站	690	10
幸福路	2006	烟叶站至方养公路	800	4.5
和平路	2007	派出所至烟叶站路口	310	4.5
飞越路	2007	养龙司电信分局至派出所门口	220	7

奋斗路、龙泉路、文化路、龙腾路4条主要路段安装42盏路灯。

（三）供电供水及排污设施

1991年，由新场变电站供电，有10千伏高压输电线通养龙司，安装10千伏安变压器6台。1999年，改造高压电线600米。

供水设施：有水厂1座、500吨蓄水池1个，位于堡子村高坎子组，建于2003年；抽取地下水，解决养龙司乡堡子、养龙司、幸福、坝上、高坡、灯塔6个村居民用水。

排污设施：仅老街东侧有一排水暗沟，长400米，因无相应配套设施，排水效果不佳，余则任其自流。2003年，修建龙泉路，安装排污管道480米，新建垃圾场1个。有公厕3座，分别坐落在养龙司农贸市场、文化路和奋斗路旁。

五、流长乡——流长

流长位于县境西北，距县城27千米，为县境西北部主要乡村集镇，是该地及金沙县部分地区物资集散地。1992年，流长为乡政府所在地。集镇由一条老街和180县道过境公路形成，集镇面积0.3平方千米。2010年，流长集镇建成面积0.75平方千米，东至供电所，南至客车站，西至茅坡老政府驻地，北至猪市坝。

1996年，完成集镇总体规划修编及集镇道路建设详细规划。1998年，编制顺江码头建设规划。

（一）房屋建筑

1990年，流长集镇房屋建筑面积1.13万平方米，其中砖混与砖木结构4886.56平方米，木瓦房6447平方米。房屋多为平房，少部分为2～3层楼房。随着《小城镇建设总体规划》的实施，先后建成中学教学用房4000平方米、精神文明活动中心400平方米、医院住院部500平方米、交通楼1200平方米、教师宿舍楼3260平方米。至2010年，流长集镇建筑总面积8.8万平方米，多为砖混或砖木结构，3层楼房居多。

（二）街道

1991年，流长只有一条老街和180县道过境公路。

1999年，动工修建商业一条街，2002年建成。主街长265米，宽16米，支路长97米，宽12米。

2010年，流长共有育兴路、育秀路、长征路、和谐路、乌江路、文明路、迎红路7条街道。

（三）供电供水及排污设施

1997年，县在流长建变电站，流长电源由变电站供给，安装10千伏安变压器2台，高压线10千伏安。

1988年，由县城建局、水电局、爱委会共同投资14万元，在长涌村高洞修提水站1个，建蓄水池80立方米、调节池1个，安装管道4千米，次年7月竣工，流长始有自来水。1998年，县乡筹资20万元，群众投工投劳，从长涌村长冲沟高洞处取地下水，经一级泵站提水至长涌村中寨组后面山上蓄水池；日供水150立方米，解决4200人、1200头牲畜的饮水困难。乡成立自来水管理站，供水实行装表计量收费。

污水排放靠街道边沟，顺沟流入稻田。2005年，兴修街道污水沟1800米、排水沟580米，安装供、排水管道2500米。

六、石硐乡——石硐

石硐为乡政府所在地。位于县境西部，距县城23千米，是县境西部主要乡村集镇之一。1992年，规划设计石硐小集镇，规划面积7万平方米。1998年11月3日，县政府批准实施《石硐乡村镇建设总体规划》。

1991年，石硐集镇建成面积0.27平方千米。2010年，集镇面积扩大到2平方千米，东至新大街250米路口，南至石梨公路路口，西至何家硐路口，北至石硐中学。

（一）建筑

1990年，房屋总面积1.24万平方米，其中民房6825平方米。民房中，砖混结构998平方米、砖木结构2028平方米、木瓦结构1915平方米、土瓦结构98平方米。全民、集体房5592平方米，其中砖混结构3406平方米、砖木结构2146平方米、土瓦结构40平方米。

1996年，新建一条街道，长1200米，随即街道两旁新建砖木结构，四五层的平顶房屋。至2005年，累计投入资金约1120万元改造新、老街路面1040平方米，新建计划生育站、烟叶站、农业三站、林业站、供电所、政府办公楼、农产品市场、水厂等。2008年，老街两旁房屋开始改建成两三层楼砖瓦房。至2010年，石硐集镇建筑总面积达到3万平方米，多为砖混或砖木结构。

（二）街道

1991年，集镇中心街道为高何公路的一段，全长600米，宽3.4米，土石路面。街南端为生猪市场，占地200平方米；街北对面小山顶为牛马市场，占地400平方米。2004年硬化路面。1996年新建和谐路，长1200米，宽8.5米，砂石路面。至2010年，石硐有步行街、和谐路、黄金路等3条街道，总长2850米。

（三）供电供水及排污设施

1991年，电源由久长输变电站供给，有10千伏输电线路1条、50千伏安变压器1台。集镇居民用上自来水。污水多流向街面及街后稻田中。至2010年，新老街街道两边修建下水道。

七、青山苗族乡——青山

位于县境西南部，距县城19.5千米，为青山苗族乡所在地。1991年，青山苗族乡没有集镇，政府所在地仅有一条长约40米、宽5米的乡村泥土公路，乡政府机关办公楼、乡卫生院、青山乡民族小学、乡信用社、乡供销社、乡烟叶站等零星分布于公路两边。除乡机关职工及学校老师外，路两旁还有7户人家，其中3家砖瓦房、2家土墙房、2家平房。乡供销社商店是乡里唯一的商店；路边有1家打米、面条加工房和1家粉馆。

1995年，省乡规划设计研究院对青山苗族乡小集镇建设进行规划。2003年，进一步完善《青山苗族乡集镇建设规划》。

2002年，贵阳市帮扶青山苗族乡的10家公司捐助20万元硬化青山苗族乡小集镇第一段街道，捐助17万元修建饮水站。至2010年，建成4条街道，即民族路（东西走向）：东起青山苗族乡客车站，西至山岔麻窝青山苗族乡农业中心办公楼；团结路（南北走向）：南起青苑路西山信用社青山分社办公楼，北至民族路乡卫生院门诊大楼；青苑路（东西走向）：东起团结路西山信用社青山分社办公楼，西至振青路青山苗族乡文化服务中心办公楼；振青路（南北走向）：南起青山苗族乡老卫生院办公楼，北至民族路青山民族中学实验大楼。集镇建成面积约1平方千米，共有房108栋，其中住户房81栋、单位用房27栋，总建筑面积31840平方米。集镇有农贸市场1个；卫生院1所；中、小学、幼儿园各1所；停车场、民族活动场各1个；超市2家；烟酒副食店16家；药店、化肥代销店、饮食店、粮油供应店、理发店、饲料销售店、电话超市各2家；电器销售店、汽修店、缝纫店、中药材收购店、屠宰店、铁铝器销售店、花圈爆竹销售店、娱乐场所共计13家。

青山苗族乡2010年街道统计表

表12-6-4

街道名称	红线宽度（米）	街道长度（米）	街道面积（平方米）
民族路	12	907	10884
文化路	12	139	1668
青山路	12	605	7260
永青路	12	872	10464
团结路	8	121	966
青苑路	8	351	2814
建设路	8	431	3458

供电供水及排污设施：

1991年，电源由永靖镇柿花坪变电站输送，居民生活用水靠井水，无排污设施。1998年，在小桥河水库建水泵站提供生活用水。2004年，安装排污管道。

八、鹿窝乡——鹿窝

位于县境西北部，距县城59千米。鹿窝乡政府所在地。1991年仅有1条街道，长约250米，宽5米，土石路面，街道两旁有30余户人家，其中个体经营户10户，加工业2户。房屋23栋，木架结构为主，其中砖木2层楼房6栋（供销社1栋、粮站2栋、居民3栋。其时乡政府办公室和职工住房为1栋长7间木结构2层楼房，面积400平方米）。

1995年，乡政府在原木结构房地址上新建5层砖混结构政府大楼1栋，1000平方米。1998年11月，县政府批准实施《鹿窝乡村镇建设总体规划》。至2010年，集镇扩大，东至鹿龙村场背后组，南至林口，西至鹿龙村李家窑组，北至马坉村水浇莲组，建成面积0.5平方千米。

居民木结构瓦房多改建成砖木结构房；派出所、烟叶站、农业三站、司法所、信用社、计生站、卫生院先后新建2～3层砖混结构楼房，乡精神文明活动中心面积1270平方米，乡中学教学楼2000平方米。王家仓安置小区房屋建成8000平方米。集镇所在地建筑总面积4.6万平方米，多为砖混或砖木结构。

建设新街长164米、宽7米。安装路灯10盏，改造河道，修建垃圾场、垃圾池。完成街道绿化。清洁卫生由5名保洁员负责。有经商户48户，加工房3户。供电全覆盖。

供电：1991年，电源来自流长供电所，有高压线1条、变压器2台。至2010年，有高压线3条。

供水：1991年，鹿窝乡驻地干部、居民均饮用河水。2005年建鹿窝水厂，日供水量1000立方，供学校、机关、街道居民和附近村组226户2500余人生活用水。

九、西山乡——底寨

位于县境中部，距县城6千米。1991年以前是永阳区公所驻地，1992年起为西山乡政府所在地。底寨有一条长420米、宽4米的老街，土石路面。街道两旁居民住房多为木架瓦顶结构。县城至九庄公路从老街旁边经过并与老街两端相交，公路两侧建房逐渐增多，形成街道。乡政府至息九公路有500米道路相连。

2005年编制规划，以华府路至息九公路一线，征地80亩，平整土地，修通道路，架通水、电线路。作为西望山旅游开发移民安置用地，后改为小集镇建设用地。是年，硬化老街路面。

2010年冬，启动小集镇建设。是年，底寨建筑总面积1.1万平方米，多为4层砖混或砖木结构房屋。集镇东至底寨酱油厂，南至息九公路，西至柏香山国有林，北至河沟，建成面积0.02平方千米。

供水：1991年，西山乡采取由农民找水源和投工投劳，政府提供水管方式解决生活用水问题。2002年2月，国家投资291万元，在猪场村修建水厂，2003年竣工投产。2004—2010年，水厂累计投资200万元，铺设管道180千米，解决猪场、文安、柏香山、林丰、金星、田冲、小堡、小鹿窝8个村1.1万余人的饮水问题。

供电：1985—1999年9月，西山乡由国家电网，经小桥河水管所供电。1999年10月，建底寨供电所，有10千伏安高压线4条，总长81千米。

第二节　农村住房建设

20世纪90年代初期，各乡镇农户房屋以平房、瓦顶居多，木门窗，少有二层楼房。小寨坝镇、温泉镇、养龙司乡农户房屋以砖木结构为主。永靖镇、九庄镇、石硐乡农户房屋大部分为土墙房屋，占60%～70%。西山乡、青山苗族乡农户土墙住房占80%左右。鹿窝乡农户住房以土墙和木架房为主。多无装修，有的以石灰粉刷内墙，室内多为泥土或三合土地面。几无自来水进家，更无洗澡设备。厕所多设在猪圈旁或为猪圈的一部分，共用猪圈粪坑。厕所或无门，或有简易木门，或以旧麻袋或其他旧布遮掩。个别人家尚未专设厕所，直接进入猪圈大小便。

1996年，农户新建房屋多为砖木或砖混结构，二层楼房居多。屋内墙面水泥抹光，部分刷涂料，个别人家刮瓷粉；室内地坪为水泥地面。少数农户房屋进行内外装修。2000年，农业局牵头推广沼气池，次年配套改厕，在沼气池旁修建厕所，三面砖墙，封顶有门，内贴瓷砖，安装陶瓷蹲便池，便池与沼气池用管道连通，配备沼液回流冲厕装置，抽沼液冲洗厕所，既保证厕所的清洁卫生，又将粪便直接冲进沼气池。至2008年，全县农村改厕2.67万个。

2001年，息烽县实施“消灭人居茅草房”工程。是年2月24日，市委书记率市直8家单位到青山苗族乡调研，参与调研单位集资100万元扶持该乡“消灭人居茅草房”。10月30日，共改造茅草房226户，成为贵阳市消灭茅草房第一乡。至2004年，全县共投入资金4200万元，投工17万个，改造农村人居茅草房2627户。至此，全县彻底消灭人居茅草房。

2010年，各乡镇农户新建房屋大多为砖混平顶结构，多为3间2～3层楼房。房屋最高楼层：石硐乡、养龙司乡、西山乡4层，小寨坝镇5层、温泉镇6层。屋外装修多贴瓷砖，室内装修仍以刮瓷粉为主，有贴墙纸者。少数农户室内采用吊顶和打线条方式。部分农户房屋内设卫生间和洗澡设备。

息烽县1991—2010年乡镇农户建房统计表

表12-6-5

乡镇名	部分年度建房户平均建房面积（平方米）					1991—2010年		
	1991年	1996年	2001年	2006年	2010年	总建房户数	占2010年总户数（%）	总建房面积（万平方米）
小寨坝镇	93	75	100	128	236	2834	67	33.48
九庄镇	75	90	121	140	153	7745	81	11.85
温泉镇	—	41	83	117	123	—	—	—
养龙司乡	100	117	168	216	236	5017	79	89.4
石硐乡	84	128	100	113	108	2027	—	19.92
流长乡	95	96	80	100	150	4000	65	33.2
西山乡	86	77	85	136	155	2724	46	21.54
鹿窝乡	—	—	100	107	99	—	—	—
青山苗族乡	—	—	106	141	114	798	56	9.54

第三节　安居工程及危房改造

一、安居工程

1997年，对极贫村寨实行异地搬迁，国家对困难户补助资金改建新房。4月，永靖镇河坎村上寨村民组（苗族）异地搬迁工程动工，由市、县投资200万元，经过7个月施工，建成房屋24幢（可住48户），有自来水、厕所、猪圈与房屋配套，建筑面积4732.8平方米，户均98.6平方米；住宅区内建有宽7米，长306米水泥路1条；改造进村公路7.8千米，建供电线路6千米；由新华社出资修建饮水工程1座，铺设自来水管网680米。

1998年6月28日，九庄镇新沙村下环山村民组异地搬迁工程动工，11月竣工。总投资86.78万元，为长期居住茅草房的46户苗族村民修建新房46幢，总建筑面积3141.98平方米，户均68.3平方米，并配套水、电、路、停车场和篮球场。是年，对154户特困户每户补助3000元，自筹部分资金和投工投劳建房，至11月全部竣工，总建筑面积1.15万平方米，户均74平方米。

2003年，国家投资在小鹿窝村书房田地段修建苗族新村，2005年竣工，修建房屋22幢，原木江山村民组的22户苗族同胞集体迁入新村。

2005年，县委、县政府决定将处于顺向山体滑坡地质灾害点上的青山苗族乡马头山村民组住户整体搬迁。投资186.3万元，在三口洞新建房屋33幢，2835平方米。2007年12月，马头山村民组的33户128人全部迁住新居。

二、危房改造

2007年，根据贵阳市委、市政府《农村危房改造的实施意见》，采取国家补助、农户自筹和投工投劳办法，全县启动农村危房改造工作。2008年，省市县补助资金1678.9万元，其中省级补助资金400万元、市级补助资金681.3万元、县级匹配资金474.2万元、县领导及单位部门筹资68.5万元、乡镇投入24.9万元、其他投入30万元。2009年，实施《贵阳市农村危房改造整区（市、县）推进实施意见》，至2010年，全县共改造农村危房9610户。中央省市县补助资金4628.9万元，其中：中央及省补助资金2359.35万元、市配套1094.5万元、县配套1175.05万元。

三、廉租房

2008年，县启动廉租住房建设工程，由政府筹措资金帮助城镇最低生活保障家庭、住房（无房居住）困难家庭解决住房难问题。工程位于永靖镇解放南路，是年11月开工，次年9月竣工。工程总投资600万元，建筑面积6271.4平方米（100套），其中A栋2～6层，建筑面积4141.4平方米（58套），B栋7层，建筑面积2130平方米（42套）。

2010年，县廉租住房建设工程分别在永靖镇、小寨坝镇、温泉镇进行，总投资6075.11万元，总建筑面积3.65万平方米（588套），其中永靖镇1.1万平方米（220套），位于永靖镇环城路；小寨坝镇2.16万平方米（308套），位于小寨坝镇南大街复兴社区；温泉镇3962平方米（60套），位于温泉镇永兴路。

四、房屋立面整治

2006年，全县对公路、铁路沿线乡镇居民住房进行立面整治，平顶屋面增盖斜顶屋面，墙体进行钢化瓷粉粉刷。2009年，对贵遵高速公路沿线可视范围内房屋进行立面整治，整治1089户，其中永靖镇185户、西山乡386户、小寨坝镇490户、养龙司乡28户，当年完工并交付使用。

第十三篇　商　贸

第一章　国有商业

1997年9月，县国有企业改革改制工作领导小组成立，着手推进商业企业体制改革工作。至2010年，有7家国有商业企业完成改革改制工作。其中，五交化公司、百货公司等4家改为股份制商业企业，蔬菜公司、饮料厂等3家企业改制后注销解散。

第一节　管理机构

1991年，县商业局为县国有商业企业管理机构，内设人秘股、信息股、财会股、统计股。下辖糖业烟酒公司、中西药公司、百货公司、五交化公司、蔬菜水产公司、食品公司、饮食服务公司、民族贸易公司、饮料厂9个商业企业。1997年6月，在县级机构改革中，县商业局并入县计划与经济贸易局。

第二节　体制改革

1991年，县商业局所属各企业以企业行政领导为代表，实行领导班子集体承包，实行利润定额包干，超收全留，欠收自补，工资总额与经济效益挂钩。挂钩基数及比例以劳动部门当年下达的指标为准。其中个人承包、自主经营、定额交利的企业有百货公司、蔬菜公司门市部、饮食服务公司、食品公司和民贸公司276商店；以销定酬承包经营的企业有糖业烟酒公司、五交化公司、民贸公司门市部、百货公司和蔬菜公司多数门市部。1992年，实行企业“经营放开、价格放开、分配放开、用工放开”（简称“四放开”）和全员劳动合同制管理，借以推动企业改革改制。由各单位制定“四放开”改革实施细则，报县经济体制改革委员会（简称县体改委）批转执行。1993年，本着“稳定完善、适当调整、税保国家、利活企业”的指导思想，开展第三轮经营承包。是年下半年，由县体改委、县经济贸易委员会、县商业局组织联合调查组，对商业系统8个公司的人员、收支、承包及存在问题进行调查摸底，重新拟定商业改革试行方案，报县政府审批。1994年，选择百货公司和五交化公司作为试点，组建新兴商业公司和正大商业公司。新兴商业公司和五交化公司一套人马，两块牌子。1996年，全面推行全员劳动合同制管理。是年11月，除饮料厂外，商业系统企业全部实行全员劳动合同制，共有153名职工与企业签订劳动合同。

1997年9月，县国有企业改革改制工作领导小组成立。12月19日，县委、县政府下发《关于放开搞活国有企业的实施方案》，明确国有企业改革改制以产权制度改革为突破口，以盘活资产存量、推动国有资产重组为重点，结合实际，选择产权出售、依法破产、联合、兼并、股份合作制、公司制改造、引资嫁接、托管经营、分离重组、抵押承包等形式进行改革改制。1998年，县政府下发文件，规定由改制企业用资产变现收入，按一定标准缴县社会保险局（简称社保局），社保局承担企业离退休职工、遗属子女的养老金和有关费用发放。1999年，县国有企业改革改制工作领导小组批复百货公司、五交化公司、中西药公司、糖业烟酒公司、饮食服务公司、蔬菜公司、食品饮料厂7家企业进行改革改制。

一、改制企业

（一）蔬菜水产公司（县华泰商业有限公司）

1999年6月，《息烽县蔬菜水产公司产权制度改革实施方案》经公司职代会讨论通过。蔬菜水产公司时有职工21人，有资产总计55.76万元，负债45.34万元，所有者权益10.42万元。可列入改制流动资产和固定资产总计28.83万元，改制成本22.31万元。职工以安置费入股方式组建新企业。可筹集股金19.31万元，购买原批发部的部分资产，国家给予的优惠形成资产1.2万元，职工带资入股形成的资产6.14万元，新企业共有资产26.65万元。公司在改制中，总资产减除各项应予支出成本、负债等，国有资产尚缺0.81万元才能解决企业改制后的职工安置问题。11月，县政府批复：原则同意蔬菜水产公司改革方案，在改制中有关税费的减、免、缓按县文件执行；同意按文件规定将离退休职工结转县社保局；企业改制后剩余国有资产和负债一次性结转县国有资产经营有限责任公司。是年，县华泰商业有限公司成立。2005年，公司注销停业。

（二）食品饮料厂

由于食品饮料厂停产多年，无力支付退休人员养老金，经县政府、县计划经济局决定，将饮料厂出售的土地款作为解决该厂退休人员基本生活费一次性划转县社保局，并与社保局达成协议：食品饮料厂一次性付给社保局13.43万元，其中养老金借款6985元，安置费12.73万元；饮料厂欠交社保局安置费2.13万元，从1999年1月起，由饮料厂从租金和固定资产中偿还；7名退休人员和1名遗属的基本养老金、医疗费、生活困难补助费由县社保局支付；欠发退休人员养老金、医疗费等由饮料厂负责支付。

（三）百货公司（新兴商业公司）

1998年6月底，百货公司共有在册职工37人、离退休人员31人、抚恤对象2人，账面资产总额389万元（其中流动资产163万元，固定资产226万元），负债225万元，负债率57.8%，占有土地9327平方米，评估价321万元。已出售给供电局部分资产收入75万元，交县社保局用于支付离退休职工安置费、遗属抚恤对象安置费以及办理房产、土地转移等各类费用。剩余资产39.86万元向社会公开出售，用于归还银行贷款。百货公司欠各银行贷款205.24万元，其中1986年“两棉赊销”政策性贷款136.44万元，流动资金贷款68.8万元。“两棉赊销”贷款作报损处理，流动资金贷款由新组建的公司承担35万元，其余部分由仍保留法人地位的百货公司承担，并处置剩余资产予以归还。

1999年8月，百货公司进行股份制改造。参加改制职工33人，每人依据工龄按每年454.24元进行安置，改制后成立县新兴百货有限公司。2000年，百货公司存货损失20.48万元。

（四）县五交化公司（正大百货有限公司）

1994年，县五金交电化工原料公司（简称县五交化公司）按照“分离重组”的原则，成立正大商业公司，实施“国有民营”改革。1998年，县五交化公司与正大商业公司合并，进行产权制度改革。

1998年5月底，县五交化公司有在职职工30人、退休职工5人，流动资产74.03万元、固定资产（净值）139.12万元，资产总计213.15万元，负债总计260.92万元（其中欠工行163.84万元、建行40万元）。实际可参加改制的流动资产为4.47万元，房产90.53万元，土地2323.31平方米（价93.4万元），其他固定资产1万元，实际负债为260.92万元。其中，流动负债54.07万元以承担等额负债形式支付，即由新建公司承担61.15万元负债；银行贷款203.84万元，由新建公司承担拨改贷部分贷款40万元，流动资金贷款15万元；其余贷款由五交化公司处置剩余资产后归还。职工安置费部分由职工带资入股23.9万元，应付职工工资、福利由职工带资入股1.58万元，国家给予一次性优惠形成的资产25.57万元，承担负债而形成的资产61.15万元，即新建公司共有资产112.2万元（其中资本金57.2万元，负债55万元）。

是年8月，经县长办公会同意，批复五交化公司改制方案，明确退休职工安置和有关税费减免按文件办理。同意免交土地出让金，继续保留县五交化公司，并由五交化公司处理改制后的剩余国有资产，归还除新建公司承担的55万元银行贷款外的剩余银行贷款。

改制后，新建公司更名为县正大百货有限公司，参加改制职工30人，每个职工依据工龄按每年454.24元工资进行安置。

（五）糖业烟酒公司

1998年11月底，糖业烟酒公司共有在职职工19人、退休职工27人、抚恤人员1人；账面资产64.06万元，负债55.7万元；占有土地3宗，面积2332平方米。1993年实施“国有民营”改制后，实际可列入改制的流动资产25.34万元、固定资产6.27万元，土地1580.46平方米，价款41.41万元，共计73.02万元。产权制度改革将县府路2号房地产（其中土地219.86平方米，房产1.26万元）定向出售给职工，并一次性付款，可变现16.8万元。该款用于支付职工安置费14.13万元，支付应付工资、福利费0.88万元，尚余1.79万元以支付改制必需费用。支付职工安置费后，职工即脱离国有企业职工身份。将灯光球场和东门坝两处房产向社会公开出售，处理流动资产等变现收入78.84万元，用于支付离、退休职工和遗属费用，归还银行贷款、借款以及其他负债。对离、退休职工和遗属，一次性付给县社保局17.28万元后，由县社保局负责离、退休职工养老金及医疗费的发放。糖业烟酒公司在处理完上述各事项后，即办理企业注销手续。

1999年11月，经县长办公会研究批复，同意将离、退休职工结转县社保局；企业改制后剩余的国有资产和负债一次性结转县国有资产经营有限公司；公司改制后，其酒类专卖的行政职能转到县计划与经济贸易局；职工养老保险金由职工自行缴纳，县社保局对其以前已缴纳的部分予以认可。

（六）饮食服务公司（兴源贸易有限公司）

1999年6月底，饮食服务公司有在职职工24人、退休职工30人、抚恤对象4人。账面资产总计169.54万元，其中流动资产18.9万元，固定资产149.98万元（土地以半价入账），所有者权益139.3万元；账面债务30.2万元。可列入改制的流动资产为11.69万元，账面固定资产149.98万元，可供改制的土地及房产为268.68万元；可列入改制的负债为39.79万元，改制成本为99.63万元。改制后，由新成立的股份制企业购买饮食服务公司资产，实际付款额为7.14万元。减除职工安置费（每人按工龄每年

454.24元计算）。尚余柿花坪房地产74.29万元，转交县国资办或国有资产经营有限公司处置。是年11月，饮食服务公司改制方案获得批准。

（七）县中西药公司

1998年6月底，县中西药公司有在职职工32人、退休职工9人、长期养病人员1人、遗属2人；账面固定资产105.34万元、流动资产163.85万元，土地资产评估122.65万元。可列入改制的资产141.24万元，改制所需成本60.38万元。是年，县政府批复县中西药公司《关于请求批准改制方案的报告》，同意成立新的药品经营公司并免交土地出让金，股份制企业“息烽药业有限责任公司”成立，承担职工安置费和改制必须费用，以及原企业负债中的应付工资、福利及工会费等，离、退休人员转至县社保局。

二、未改制企业

（一）县食品公司

1955年9月，县食品公司成立，为生猪、菜牛、菜羊、鲜蛋的购、销、调、存业务机构。1966年6月，接管由各区供销社分出的养龙司、九庄、黑神庙等食品站。1991年，县食品公司购进生猪10640头，购进总额273.77万元，利润5.51万元。是年，县政府支持开发魔芋新品种，生产魔芋片1000多千克，但亏损19万元。1996年，在县食品公司建畜禽定点屠宰场，9月投入使用。同时印制《息烽县人民政府关于实行畜禽定点屠宰的通告》广泛张贴宣传，整顿城关食肉市场，依法取缔无证屠宰场点3个。是年，为平抑肉价，县食品公司调进冻猪肉2500千克，平价销售。落实生猪活储7000头交贵阳肉联厂。

2002年，县食品公司职工（含食品站）31人，其中在岗8人、在职下岗5人、离退休职工18人。公司资产总计36.92万元，其中流动资产21.76万元、固定资产15.01万元、递延资产1.49万元；负债256.58万元。至2010年，账面资产总额117.7万元、账面负债总额287.9万元、账面所有者权益-170.2万元；实物资产：土地九宗共10202.55平方米。年底在册人员45人，其中职工22人、退休职工23人。

（二）民族贸易公司

20世纪70年代初，为解决驻县厂矿生活物资供应问题，先后在贵州朝晖机械厂、贵州汽油机厂、贵州拖拉机电机厂、贵州高强度螺栓厂6个厂矿设立综合商店。1984年，以6个厂矿商店为基础，成立县厂矿贸易公司，次年改称民族贸易公司（简称民贸公司）。1991年开始，驻县厂矿陆续外迁，民贸公司经营状况每况愈下。至2002年，公司在职人员26人、退休13人；公司总资产14.32万元，负债总计41.17万元，企业净资产-22.34万元。2010年1—11月，公司召开职工大会，启动改制工作。大会讨论通过《息烽县民贸公司改革改制方案》和《息烽县民贸公司职工安置方案》。

第二章 供销合作

县供销合作社联合社（简称县供销联社）成立于1952年。因经营需要，先后成立4个区级供销社和农资日杂公司等直属企业。县供销联社原属自收自支单位。1991年，县供销联社内设人秘保卫股、统计股、财务股、审计股、业务股、基层工作股、物价股，下辖土产公司、农资日杂公司和永阳、九庄、黑神庙、养龙司4个区供销社。1993年10月，经县政府批准，设立县供销社总公司，与县供销联社实行两块牌子、一套人马的管理体制。1996年5月，县供销联社将原内设股室改为科室。内设机构调整为办公室、政工科、财会科、审计科、计划统计科、物价业务基层工作科和安全保卫科。2001年9月，县党政机构改革，明确县供销联社是受政府委托行使部分行政管理职能的直属事业单位。2002年，县政府明确县供销联社为财政全额拨款的事业单位。是年5月，县供销联社内设科室改为办公室、市场开发科和业务管理科。2010年5月，在机构改革中，将县供销联社明确为县政府参照公务员管理的其他机构，内设办公室、社有资产管理科、合作经济发展科、计财科。下辖康弘供销有限责任公司、兴盛供销有限责任公司、九庄供销社、永阳供销社以及农资日杂公司、土产公司、县供销社总公司。

第一节　体制改革

1988年，全县各区供销社推行承包经营责任制，企业与分销店、门市部承包人签订完成购、销利润指标合同书，每轮合同期为3年。

1996年5月，县供销联社召开各社、公司法人代表会，安排部署企业实行全员劳动合同制工作。次年，县供销联社在向县政府呈报的《关于推进供销合作社改革与发展的请示》，申明坚持合作制原则，理顺供销合作社组织体制，强化为农业服务功能，加大改革力度。1999年，县政府在《关于对供销社深化改革的批复》中，要求做好基层社和社属企业分块实施，选择公司制、股份合作制、承包租赁、联合、分离重组等多种形式以盘活资产。是年，永阳社、养龙社、九庄社、黑神庙社分别亏损45.97万元、21.42万元、36.47万元、16.6万元。12月，县供销联社成立体制改革领导小组，开展体制改革工作。

2000年，县供销联社所属土产公司、农资日杂公司以及养龙司、九庄、黑神庙供销社101名离、退休人员基本养老金结转县社保局支付。是年，县供销联社报请县委、县政府批复《息烽县供销改革与发展实施意见》，本着“全员身份置换，人员分流；买断资产，重组企业”这一基本形式，开展基层企业体制改革。

2001年5月，县供销联社在养龙司供销社、黑神庙供销社进行体制改革试点。试点工作通过召开职工大会、清理债权债务、委托会计师事务所对社有资产进行全面评估、清收企业内外欠款或由新企业股东出资等多种方式筹集改制成本，安置原企业职工；由新企业职工整体购买原企业资产并承担相应债务，按照《中华人民共和国公司法》规定，重组资本，重建企业。

2002年3月，原养龙司供销社经工商登记注册，组建息烽康弘供销有限责任公司。公司吸收自然人15人、社会法人1人入股，重组资本103.6万元。其中15个自然人现金入股11.3万元，带自身安置费入股12.2万元，承担负债义务所得权利股31.2万元，合计54.7万元，占实收资本的52.8%；社会法人入股（县供销联社并农资日杂公司），由县供销联社代为管理国资公司将缓缴剩余土地出让金15.9万元，以及2001年管理费5万元入股，承担负债义务所得权利股27.9万元，合计48.9万元，占实收资本的47.2%。公司承担原企业负债153.3万元，改制成本56.1万元。

同年9月，原黑神庙供销社经工商登记注册，组建兴盛供销有限责任公司。公司吸收自然人13

人、社会法人1人组成新企业股东，重组资本100.1万元。其中13个自然人现金入股5.1万元，带自身安置费和所得权利股入股36.8万元，合计41.9万元，占实收资本的41.86%；社会法人股（县供销联社并农资日杂公司）由县社代为管理国有剩余资产9.5万元，应收管理费5万元，承担负债所得权利股43.76万元，合计58.26万元，占实收资本的58.2%。公司承担原企业负债218.8万元，改制成本156万元。

2004年1月，县政府批复县土产公司产权制度改革，将资产并入县供销社总公司。2005年12月，县政府批复县农资日杂公司资产并入总公司。是年，县供销联社批复九庄、永阳两供销社改革改制方案。到2010年，全县供销系统的改革改制工作基本完成。

息烽县1991—2010年供销社基层社经营状况统计表

表13-2-1　　单位：万元

年份	永阳社		（康弘）养龙社		九庄社		（兴盛）黑神庙社	
	销售总额	利润	销售总额	利润	销售总额	利润	销售总额	利润
1991	345	5.1	237.71	1.5	360.9	5.08	253.5	1.08
1992	367.78	5.1	309.73	1.54	362.6	5.13	282	1
1993	306.7	0.47	265	–4	398.1	1.4	267	–3.9
1994	263.1	0.22	270	1.19	364.9	0.39	210.37	0.04
1995	222.7	–1.39	251.8	1.15	431	4.04	251.5	0.05
1996	356.4	0.26	284.2	0.03	614.6	5.01	386.7	–2.43
1997	338	273.8	222.8	–9.4	582.9	–1.6	291.4	–3.2
1998	273.8	–27.5	101.7	–1.02	233.2	–4.62	142.2	–1.55
1999	106.8	–45.97	150.4	–21.42	224.6	–36.97	154	–16.6
2000	299.7	–4.8	153.3	–18.3	163.1	–35.1	796.1	–10.8
2001	208.1	0.49	738.1	–9.6	897.5	–4.46	127.7	–9.3
2002	204.3	0.21	268.4	0.72	883.6	–1.02	260.7	0.04
2003	237.5	0.16	210	0.47	511.6	–0.35	510.8	0.09
2004	184.8	1.06	33.89	–1.34	61.13	–0.02	33.67	0.18
2005	273.5	1.05	98.6	0.49	150.12	–0.22	42.8	1
2006	195.4	0.54	22.36	0.02	92.3	1.03	24.57	1.36
2007	270.6	1.03	14.57	0.41	91.02	0	39.26	2.17
2008	351.75	–0.58	64.3	–0.68	111.6	–0.03	13.6	0.2
2009	235.9	1.24	1.79	0.08	102.6	–1.24	12.55	1.37
2010	128.9	3.27	1.67	0.06	28.9	–3.42	15.6	1.46

第二节　农村商业网点建设

一、供销综合服务中心

2003年，遵照贵阳市供销社《关于在全市千人以上行政村设供销社综合服务中心的实施意见》，县供销联社因地制宜，把综合服务中心的设立与企业改革改制工作结合起来，采取分流人员自办、联办，农村能人领办等形式发展服务中心，组织形式有股份制、合作制、承包制、租赁制等。是年7月，启动组建供销综合服务中心工作，选择在青山苗族乡大林村，永靖镇阳朗村、下阳朗村进行试点。

2004年，在力求办一个成功一个，以点带面的工作方针指导下，在永靖镇老厂村、管田村、梨安村，西山乡鹿窝村、柏香山村，青山苗族乡青山村、石硐乡石硐村，九庄乡鸡场村、新街村，鹿窝乡鹿窝村设立10个供销综合服务中心（俗称供销社农家店）。

2006—2009年，县供销联社在各乡镇相继建立农家店135个、超市10个、绿色回收站11个。其中：永靖镇建农家店24个、超市1个、绿色回收站6个；小寨坝镇建农家店19个、超市2个、绿色回收站1个；九庄镇建农家店21个；石硐乡建农家店16个、超市1个；青山苗族乡建农家店5个、绿色回收站1个；养龙司乡建农家店12个、超市3个、绿色回收站1个；鹿窝乡建农家店10个；西山乡建农家店7个、超市1个、绿色回收站1个；流长乡建农家店12个、超市1个；温泉镇建农家店9个、超市1个、绿色回收站1个。

二、农资专业合作社

2004年，县供销联社决定组建石硐乡农资专业合作社。是年9月，按照《农村专业合作社指导办法》，拟定组建工作实施方案，召开石硐乡部门、村组干部会，广泛宣传动员，办理入股社员股金及社员证手续。石硐乡农资专业合作社注册资本30万元。股金由县供销联社及直属企业、基层社和政府部门、村组干部、职工、农民入股构成。其中九庄供销社入股10万元，占总数的33.3%；石硐乡政府部门、村组入股各1万元，各占总数的3.33%；农民、干部、职工入股2万元，占总数的6.67%；县供销社直属企业入股16万元，占总数的53.3%。各社员按股分红，农民社员实行农业生产资料优惠价供应和二次返利。2004年底，石硐乡农资专业合作社正式开业运营。

第三节　农副产品采购

1991年，农副产品购进总值113.19万元，其中非食油脂类2.14万元、土产类2.01万元、干鲜果及干菜调味品类22.73万元、粮油类56.82万元，花生127681千克、葵花712千克。此后，随着市场的开放，农副产品大多流入市场，采购工作日渐萎缩，农副产品购进总值以及物资种类大幅度缩减。1994年，收购总值缩减至21.89万元，其中土产类仅收购0.68万元，干鲜果及干菜调味品类也只有8.52万元，粮油类降至12.66万元。但由于花生价格调高，花生收购量不降反升，为24792千克。1998年，农副产品收购总值再降至6.31万元，其中土产类0.74万元、粮油类0.69万元、中药材0.15万元。此后，随着市场经济的发展，农副产品市场的不断放开，流通渠道出现多极化、多元化，供销社经营日益困难，1999年后，农副产品再无购进。

第四节 农资销售

1991年，供销合作社对化肥、农药、农膜三种农业生产资料实行专营，其他部门、单位和个人一律不准经营。是年，农资销售总额666.06万元。其中销售氮肥5983吨、尿素4882吨、磷肥2165吨、复合肥1409吨、钾肥102吨；销售农药14.91吨、农膜9.83吨、中小型农具9802件。继续实行农户每交售50千克油菜籽，奖售平价化肥5千克的政策。此后多年，由于奖售政策的出台和农业的发展，农资销售总额逐年增加。1993年，对粮食订购实行每交售50千克，奖售平价化肥13千克的政策。1997年，县政府《关于认真抓好1997年全县杂交玉米推广与奖售化肥挂钩供应的通知》规定：农户每种一亩杂交玉米按每包（40千克）72元优惠价供应尿素1包。是年，农资销售总额1573.91万元，其中销售尿素4894吨、磷肥721吨、复合肥1940吨、钾肥500吨、农药2.23吨、农膜5.66吨。

1998年，国务院下发《关于深化化肥流通体制改革的通知》，化肥实行经营放开政策。在市场竞争中，个体经营户迅速抢占市场，并取得化肥生产厂家在县的代理经营权。是年，供销社农资销售总额直线下降，仅749.8万元，不足1997年的二分之一。此后多年，农资销售总额在600～300万元之间。2003年，决定以县供销社总公司为龙头，基层供销社为基础，多渠道组织货源，协调与厂家合作关系，走自主经营的路子。2005年，农资销售总额恢复至1378.76万元。是年，销售氮肥7158吨、磷肥911吨、复合肥1138吨、钾肥10吨、农药1.45吨、农膜19.5吨、中小型农具10500件。2006年，贵州赤天化股份有限公司正式成为县供销社总公司的合同供货单位；县供销社总公司承担县政府委托的重要农业生产资料"淡储旺供"任务，县财政解决其储备费用困难，使得农资销售总额多年维持在1000万元以上。2010年，销售总额降至812万元。其中销售尿素3983吨、磷肥123吨、复合肥33吨、钾肥26吨。

息烽县1991—2010年农用物资销售统计表

表13-2-2

年份	销售总额（万元）	氮肥（吨）	磷肥（吨）	复合肥（吨）	钾肥（吨）	农药（吨）	农膜（吨）	中小型农具（件）
1991	666.06	5983	2165	1409	102	14.91	9.83	9802
1992	782.3	5123	2659	2094	145	5.85	28.32	13682
1993	665.9	4510	2714	2014	1	2.27	25.75	5317
1994	1023.13	6661	1627	2284	—	3.58	39.62	2790
1995	1300.52	4476	1971	2078	—	5.9	57.24	4697
1996	1718.88	4534	2051	2141	—	2.8	33.19	8097
1997	1573.91	5425	721	1940	236	2.2	5.66	—
1998	749.8	5068	766	536	—	5.1	11.88	—
1999	—	4605	410	656	—	10.5	21.25	603
2000	635.9	4055	1366	645	19	2.63	15.35	—
2001	380.5	2488	523	386	5	—	27.88	—

续表

年份	销售总额（万元）	氮肥（吨）	磷肥（吨）	复合肥（吨）	钾肥（吨）	农药（吨）	农膜（吨）	中小型农具（件）
2002	365.38	3402	1181	686	—	7.49	—	—
2003	374.51	3130	270	1034	230	—	—	—
2004	—	4927	475	1028	15	1.8	11.08	—
2005	1378.76	7158	911	1138	10	1.45	19.5	10500
2006	1021.12	4495	1231	1307	—	—	—	—
2007	1142.42	5431	1016	1039	—	—	—	—
2008	1433	8521	266	870	—	—	—	—
2009	1499	6660	199	137	—	—	—	—
2010	812	3983	123	33	26	—	—	—

第三章　粮　油

全县粮油购、销、调、存、加工以及粮油企业的经营管理工作主要由县粮食局负责。1991—2010年，县粮食局进行过数次经营管理体制改革。其间，1992年7月1日，率先在全省范围内取消粮油证，放开经营。1999年5月以后，因经营不善和受市场冲击，粮食局所属企业经营状况每况愈下，难以为继。2010年，县粮食局在机构改革中并入县发展和改革贸易局。

第一节　机　构

1991年，县粮食局下设7个股、4个粮店、5个区（镇）粮管所、8个粮站和4个购销点，负责全县粮油购销、调运、储存等工作。是年11—12月，国有企业搬迁，撤销拖拉机电机厂、拖拉机配件厂和汽油机厂3个厂矿粮店。1992年6月，成立贵州省息烽县粮油食品经营总公司。公司与县粮食局实行两块牌子，一套人马的管理体制。粮食企业开始从计划经济向市场经济转变。局内设股室改为办公室、储运科、财务科、统计科、业务科、政工科、保卫科、基加科、农管科、工青妇办公室。1994年3月，县粮食局在贵阳设立办事处。

1992—1995年，先后对只有投入没有产出的粮油贸易公司酿酒厂、玻璃瓶厂、天台养殖场、植酸厂等亏损大户予以关、停、并、转。1996年8月，粮贸大楼竣工，粮贸饭店开业。局机关由大型地迁入大楼办公。1999年5月，实行政企分开，县粮油食品经营公司不再实行一个机构，两块牌子的管理体制，粮食局列入政府机构序列，为政府管理粮食流通领域的职能部门。局内设办公室、财务统计科、储备调运科、业务科。成立县粮油收储有限责任公司，管辖永靖仓库和底寨、养龙、九庄、黑神庙4所粮管所。2002年，县粮食局内设科室再度改为办公室、财务统计科、市场流通科，直至2010年并入县发展和改革贸易局。

第二节　粮油收购

一、粮食收购

1991年，县内粮食定购继续执行奖售一定数量的化肥、加柴油评议差价、发放预购定金的“三挂钩”政策和超过定购任务83%以上部分加补差价的计价办法。是年，完成定购粮任务：稻谷534吨、大米2489吨、玉米1067吨。在此期间，定购价经过两次调整，每50千克中籼稻由原来的21.6元调为26.1元；每50千克中籼米由原来的33元调为38元；每50千克玉米由原来的18.7元调为21.7元。1993年，定购任务分公粮、余粮两部分，公粮按90元/50千克结算，余粮按大米100元/50千克、玉米66元/50千克价格与农民结算。为确保农业税（公粮）的征收和余粮的完成，规定一律征实，不得折征代金。少数上交大米确有困难的农户，可用0.5千克玉米抵0.5千克大米收购，各计各价；但对以大米上公粮有困难的要以0.8千克玉米，折抵0.5千克大米入库。灾歉减免实行“先征后减”的办法，退钱不退粮。

1994年，取消“三挂钩”政策。从6月1日起，执行全省统一价，即每50千克中籼稻50元，每50千克中籼米72.5元，每50千克玉米46元。从当年起，对全面完成定购粮和农业税任务的前五名乡镇实行奖励，最高奖8000元，最低奖4000元，等级差1000元。1995年，实行定购粮食价外补贴政策，即每50千克大米补贴13元（稻谷9元），每50千克小麦、玉米补贴8元。1996年，为补偿粮食生产成本，定购粮价又进行较大幅度的提高，稻谷提为每50千克72元，大米提为每50千克104.3元，玉米提为每50千克66元。1997年，按国家保护价执行标准收购议价粮，即稻谷每50千克65元，大米每50千克94.2元，玉米每50千克61元；同时规定定购任务实行完成每50千克（贸易粮）供应10千克尿素的奖励政策。

1998年，执行国务院《粮食收购条例》和《粮食购销违法行为处罚办法》，要求农发行和粮食部门加强协调，确保收购资金的需要和严格封闭运行，及时付款和收购不打“白条”。同时，敞开收购，不得限收、拒收、停收，对擅自从事粮食收购活动的，由工商行政管理部门严格查处。是年，共完成粮食定购413.4万千克。1999—2000年，继续按省政府《关于贯彻国务院进一步完善粮食流通体制改革措施的通知》，除认真执行按保护价敞开收购农民余粮，执行优质优价外，还进一步调整定购价，稻谷为每50千克58元（大米按稻谷折算），玉米每50千克48元；保护指导价，稻谷每50千克52元，玉米每50千克50元（白玉米下浮为每50千克40元）。

2001年，玉米退出国家定购任务，只保留稻谷，其收购价执行定购价、保护价两价合一政策，中晚籼稻的定购价按当年农业税计税价格执行，即每50千克52元。由于当年受灾，全县秋粮任务按2355吨分配到各乡镇。是年，实际完成2076吨。2004年，实行对用粮食缴纳农业税的农户进行直补政策，即用实物缴纳的农户，国家按每千克直补0.04元给农户；对各乡镇按征收入库部分，每千克奖励0.02元。是年，计划收购商品粮4000吨，实际完成2232吨。

2005年，县内取消农业税，粮食收购采取价格随行就市、敞开收购政策。是年，收购稻谷1862吨、大米356吨。2006年，收购稻谷4624吨，2010年收购稻谷1579吨。

二、油脂收购

1991年，油菜籽收购按保证任务6750吨，争取任务7600吨，分配给各区（镇）。每50千克中等收购价为74元，并奖售（平价）化肥5千克，返销油饼15千克，返销比例价菜油2.5千克。是年收购油菜籽9092吨，超地区任务6000吨的65.99%。1992年，油菜籽收购由指令性计划改为指导性计划，价格随行就市，定价每50千克60元，并继续实行奖售政策。

1993—1995年，取消“一奖二返”的奖售政策。国家为掌握油源，确保城乡食油供应，县政府明确规定，不准个体户和其他部门到农村收购，粮食部门要与工商、物价、税务、公安等部门密切配合，加强市场管理，制止油菜籽抢购“大战”，以确保完成当年5000吨油菜籽收购任务，收购价格也由每50千克70元调到115元。1996—1997年，油菜籽收购价调为每50千克120元。为完成5000吨收购任务，县政府出台新的奖励办法，即收购价不超过每50千克125元的乡镇，完成任务60%～70%，按每吨10元计奖；完成任务80%～99%，按每吨15元计奖；完成任务100%，按每吨20元计奖；超任务的，按每吨25元计奖。当年完成油菜籽收购6489吨，占任务的130%。1998年，油菜籽收购指导价为每50千克110元，并大力提倡“以粮换籽、以油换籽”业务，各计各价。当年油菜籽收购减至2414吨。

2000年，针对全县无证经营油菜籽个体户增多、偷漏国家税款严重、市场混乱的局面，再次将油菜籽收购价提高到每50千克150元，并要求粮食、工商、物价、税务等部门配合，打击无照经营、欺行霸市、扰乱市场等违法行为。是年，计划收购2700吨，实际收购2711吨。2002年起，油菜籽价格由购销企业根据市场自定，收购量逐年减少。

2003年收购320吨，为30年来收购最低的年份。此后，购销企业实行自主经营，不再统购统销，市场竞争日益激烈，因收购资金严重缺乏，2004年收购油菜籽670吨。此后再无收购。

息烽县1991—2010年粮食、油菜籽收购统计表

表13-3-1　　单位：吨

年份	定购完成实绩			市场收购（含保护收购）			油菜籽收购
	稻谷	大米	玉米	稻谷	大米	玉米	
1991	534	2489	1067	—	179	68	9092
1992	—	—	—	—	169	135	3929
1993	—	—	—	196	2844	855	4528
1994	514	2720	880	92	—	213	2255
1995	70	2091	545	1	134	66	3449
1996	74	1634	932	135	1457	753	6489
1997	2695	1478	976	—	166	710	2838
1998	3272	1651	1336	185	96	486	2414
1999	3400	23	839	2209	22	294	2810
2000	4824	377	1381	26	103	31	2711
2001	2076	—	—	145	392	708	1320

续表

年份	定购完成实绩			市场收购（含保护收购）			油菜籽收购
	稻谷	大米	玉米	稻谷	大米	玉米	
2002	—	—	—	45	1210	516	969
2003	—	—	—	1960	864	1314	320
2004	—	—	—	640	405	1187	670
2005	—	—	—	1862	356	—	—
2006	—	—	—	4624	11	—	—
2007	—	—	—	1507	339	—	—
2008	—	—	—	3097	—	—	—
2009	—	—	—	1292	—	—	—
2010	—	—	—	1579	—	—	—

第三节　粮油销售

一、粮食销售

1991年，提高三种粮食统销价：特二粉由每50千克22元提高到35元；标二米由每50千克13.9元调整为25元；中等玉米由每50千克9.6元调整为16元。但调整后价格仍未理顺购销倒挂，其差额部分由财政给予补贴。5月1日起执行后，对机关、企事业单位在册职工以及离退休人员每人每月补偿6元，民办中小学教师每人每月补助4元。

1992年4月1日起，国家再次提高粮食统销价，达到购销同价。提价后，对计划供应人员，按上年标准同时发放补贴。7月1日起取消粮油证，实行放开经营，价格随行就市。干部职工，离、退休人员按照国家、企业、个人共同负担原则，实行每人每月补贴6元；吃计划供应粮油的民办教师、民政优抚对象和遗属，每人每月补贴3～4元。农村粮食供应保留适当的返销指标，按定购价加合理费用的价格供应。1993年下半年，全国粮价一度上涨，县粮食局积极调运市场调节粮，投放市场优质大米30万千克，在个体户市场大米每千克2元时，粮食部门以每千克1.44元售出，达到平抑粮价、稳定市场的目的。

1995年4月，实行“米袋子”行政首长负责制。1996年9月，为安排灾后城乡居民生活，县粮食局适当下调部分粮价。1998年7月，对粮食批发经营户实行准入制度，凭粮食批发准入证和工商营业执照开展经营活动，不得在农村收购粮食。1999年9月至2001年，粮价放开，粮食销售渠道增多，年销售量锐减，造成陈化粮连年增加，经上级部门同意，共处理陈化粮大米334吨、稻谷3502吨、玉米840吨、面粉78吨。

2002年，国家实行退耕还林政策，每亩退耕地补助粮食150千克，至2004年上半年，共补助粮食6698吨。2004年下半年，改粮食补助为现金补助。2005—2010年，粮食销售总量多在1500吨左右，其中1/3为救济粮。

二、油脂销售

1991年5月1日起，国家调整六种食用油统销价格，其中二级菜籽油由计划供应每千克1.46元调整为4.36元，实现购销同价。1992年，改凭证定量供应为议销，并放开经营。是年，菜油销售量增至769吨，为以后各年最高值。1993年，菜油库存为180余万千克，为减小库存，粮食局动员职工推销菜油，油价降为每千克3.6元。是年，共售出菜油586吨。1994、1995年，县粮食局在贵阳延安中路设立菜油批发窗口，贵阳市多家经销商上门批发，销量一路看好。1999—2003年，由于菜油价格一路上涨，零售价格最高时达每千克8元以上，粮食部门销量大减，最低年仅销售33吨。2004年，价格回落，每千克在7.6～7.8元左右。是年，仅销售60吨。2007年，销售菜油187吨。此后，在市场经济冲击下，再无销售。

息烽县 1991—2010年粮食、油菜籽（油）销售统计表

表13-3-2　　单位：吨

年份	粮食销售合计	其中			菜油销售
		救济粮	因灾缺粮	水库移民	
1991	14348	920	4022	—	120
1992	14192	781	6443	—	769
1993	7217	157	2474	—	586
1994	16465	375	3642	—	475
1995	6665	98	3231	—	168
1996	7180	1607	191	—	197
1997	4061	328	323	—	346
1998	4582	195	105	—	260
1999	7049	202	—	3159	105
2000	2962	695	—	647	136
2001	3200	456	—	—	138
2002	9960	923	—	1003	33
2003	7076	765	—	2571	33
2004	5000	485	—	2124	60
2005	1025	458	—	—	97
2006	844	363	—	—	236
2007	1413	365	—	—	187
2008	1739	573	—	—	—
2009	1864	459	—	—	—
2010	1562	519	—	—	—

第四节　仓储与加工

一、仓储

1991年，全县粮食仓库总容量3945万千克，有各式储油罐17个，总容量475吨。1993—1997年，共投资69.1万元，在永靖镇大型地、鹿窝、九庄竹花，新建、改建拱形仓、简易仓3栋，总库容342万千克。1997年9月，投资32万元（其中省贴息贷款20万元），改建永靖镇大型地苏式仓，增容至300万千克。次年，省财政厅下拨20万元，用于全县粮仓、粮库、地皮及围墙修建。

2003年8月，由于经营成本高、丧失功能以及建设等原因，拆除梨安、猫场、何家硐、新杨、小鹿窝、潮水、安江、阳朗等地粮站，仓房拆除或改作他用。2004年8月，县天安粮油储备库成立；9月，大型地库容18110吨的9栋大仓作为省级储备粮专库投入使用。至2004年，全县共有各种仓型仓库41栋，仓容3660万千克。其中永靖镇仓房11栋，库容2033万千克；西山乡仓房2栋，库容193万千克；青山乡仓房1栋，库容15万千克；温泉镇仓房1栋，库容38万千克；养龙司乡仓房5栋，库容446万千克；九庄镇仓房6栋，库容294万千克；石硐乡仓房4栋，库容115万千克；鹿窝乡仓房2栋，库容160万千克；小寨坝镇仓房6栋，库容292万千克；流长乡仓房3栋，库容74万千克。全县拥有储油罐14个，总容量790吨。各粮所保管、储存菜油的容器以油桶为主。

二、仓储管理

1991—1995年，息烽县连续被安顺地区粮食局评定为无害虫、无霉变、无鼠患、无事故“四无”粮仓达标县。1996年，为落实“一符三专四落实”（保管的实物要与保管账、统计账、会计账相符；专人管理、专仓储存、专账记载；质量落实、数量落实、品种落实、地点落实），根据《贵州省粮油仓库“三报两本　挂牌建卡”实施细则》要求，仓房实行挂牌管理，粮油进出日报制，库存实物每月盘点制，会、统、储每月对账制，做到日清月结。

1998年，投资6万元对大型地天安粮油储备库9栋大仓实行电子计算操作管理。1996—2004年，贵阳市粮食局对所属区市（县）“一符四无”粮仓进行的鉴定验收中，县粮食局均获“一符四无”粮仓达标证书。2010年4月，检查库存粮食，账账及账实皆相符。

三、加工

县内米面加工和油菜籽加工，主要由县粮食局米面厂和油脂化工厂完成。1991年，米面厂加工小麦3716吨，出粉2579吨，出粉率69.4%；加工稻谷17吨，出米12吨，出米率70.59%。此后多年，小麦加工多在1400～2000吨之间；稻谷加工则忽高忽低，高时为1813吨，低时仅31吨。1997年，受市场冲击，米面厂亏损。是年，仅加工小麦545吨，加工稻谷298吨。2000—2003年，稻谷加工仅数百吨。

1991年，县油脂化工厂加工油菜籽2924吨，油脂972吨，出油率33.24%。1995—1997年，因亏损停业。1998年8月，省粮油食品工业公司与县油脂化工厂联营。2000年，加工油菜籽1.1万吨，工业总产值4690万元，利税33.3万元。2002年，省粮油食品工业公司单方撤出协议，生产停止。

息烽县1991—2003年粮油加工统计表

表13-3-3　　单位：吨

年份	小麦加工			稻谷加工			菜籽加工		
	原料	面粉	产出率（%）	原料	大米	产出率（%）	原料	菜油	产出率（%）
1991	3716	2579	69.4	17	12	70.59	2924	972	33.24
1992	1689	1155	68.46	56	38	67.86	2582	923	35.75
1993	2080	1395	67.07	1209	824	68.16	2276	836	36.73
1994	1648	1430	86.77	1813	1206	66.52	1633	549	33.62
1995	2037	1818	89.25	31	20	64.52	889	305	34.31
1996	1418	1263	89.07	34	21	61.76	2348	788	33.56
1997	545	402	73.76	298	205	68.79	2545	901	35.4
1998	83	60	72.28	53	42	81.13	—	—	—
1999	—	—	—	158	109	68.99	—	—	—
2000	—	—	—	208	149	71.63	—	—	—
2001	—	—	—	347	246	65.77	—	—	—
2002	—	—	—	706	485	68.69	—	—	—
2003	—	—	—	705	484	68.65	—	—	—

第五节　调　运

一、粮食调入：息烽县人多地少，属粮食调入县，每年调入的粮食均在700万千克左右。1992年，粮价放开，粮食企业向市场经济转型，计划调入的粮食大幅减少。为确保供应，县粮食局每年组织人员到四川、湖北、湖南、河南、陕西等省采购议价粮补充库存，年均400万千克。1997年以后逐年减少。

二、油脂调出：1991—1994年，县内油菜籽（菜油）主要调往北京。1998年7月，省粮食局下文规定，省内油菜籽一律暂停向省外销售和转运，保证就地加工，增加工业产值。1999年以后，县内油菜籽多调往贵阳、安顺、遵义等地油厂加工。

息烽县1991—2004年粮油调拨统计表

表13-3-4　　单位：吨

年份	粮食调入						油脂调出	
	稻谷	大米	小麦	面粉	玉米	大豆	油菜籽	菜油
1991	664	1039	1020	—	4664	—	560	345
1992	2060	4953	1500	277	1340	240	4435	294
1993	54	1190	1093	—	127	—	7927	11
1994	839	5179	554	1102	1116	315	2161	716

续表

年份	粮食调入						油脂调出	
	稻谷	大米	小麦	面粉	玉米	大豆	油菜籽	菜油
1995	4842	4981	7598	956	2484	237	3214	354
1996	1083	1848	935	42	185	—	6371	633
1997	1145	375	1210	379	123	34	2798	1075
1998	805	77	919	59	—	—	—	33
1999	—	727	—	22	—	—	—	—
2000	1256	374	—	—	144	—	—	61
2001	—	228	—	30	40	—	—	399
2002	42157	—	—	41	—	—	—	—
2003	17173	—	—	39	—	—	—	—
2004	387	—	—	37	1728	—	21	—

说明：2005—2010年无调入发生

第六节 局属企业和单位

20世纪90年代初至21世纪初，县粮食局开展多种经营，先后建设酱油厂、酿酒厂、玻璃瓶厂、养殖场、植酸厂、植物油厂、饲料厂、粮贸饭店等多家企业，设立贵阳办事处、县粮油食品经营总公司。至2004年12月，除部分企业关、停、并、转外，所属县粮食局企业和单位有金穗粮油购销有限责任公司、天安粮油储备库、粮贸饭店、永靖粮店（含军供站）、粮油贸易公司、植物油厂（油脂化工厂）、米面厂、饲料公司、贵阳办事处、汽车队10家。

金穗粮油购销有限责任公司：1992年6月，成立贵州省息烽县粮油食品经营总公司。公司与粮食局实行两块牌子，一套人马的管理体制。1999年，政企分开，撤销总公司，成立县粮油收储有限责任公司，下辖永靖仓库和底寨、养龙、九庄、黑神庙4个粮管所。2003年，粮油收储有限责任公司进行全面改革，更名为金穗粮油购销有限责任公司，4个粮管所改为分公司，永靖仓库和公司抽调人员组成粮油配送中心。

天安粮油储备库：2004年9月，县粮食局争取到1.5万吨省级储备代储任务，购销有限责任公司剥离14人成立县天安粮油储备库。储备库用大型地仓容18110吨的9栋大仓作为省级储备专库。储备库每年置换三分之一陈粮，价差由省储粮总公司解决。稻谷由湖北等省外购进，县粮食局代表政府对储备库使用资产进行监督管理。2008年，储备库有总资产7804.99万元，负债总额6844.21万元，净产值960.78万元。

粮贸饭店：1996年8月，粮贸饭店开业，原有职工64人。2001年12月至2002年12月，有18人解除劳动合同，给予一次性补偿安置。此后，对所属餐厅、歌舞厅、桑拿浴、二楼商场实行承包租赁。由于服务行业竞争激烈，造成粮贸饭店经营困难。到2004年12月，粮贸饭店欠银行贷款521.72万元。

永靖粮店：原有干部职工232人，设4个门市部经营粮油。1998—2003年，4个门市部先后停业。在此期间，先后有17人自愿申请解除劳动合同，按政策给予17人一次性安置。剩余人员开展军粮供应工作。

粮油贸易公司：原有干部职工15人，设2个粮油门市部。2003年，因辞职、调出和正常退休5人外，剩余人员分成两组各自承包门市部，开展以粮油为主的零售经营活动。至2004年12月，共欠银行贷款43.23万元。

植物油厂（油脂化工厂）：植物油厂有3台200型榨机及浸出、精炼等设施，设计年加工油菜籽1.5万吨。1991—1993年，生产的成品油主要调往北京。1995—1997年，因资金缺乏和管理不善，一度停产。1998年8月，省粮食局同意省粮油食品工业公司与该厂联营，生产趋于正常，产量上升。2002年，工业公司因故单方撤出协议，油厂生产停止。2004年5月，通过招商引资，与开阳华兴油脂公司签订20年出租合同。2005年，油厂租赁给贵州省诚信房地产开发公司经营。2006年，该公司终止合同，欠款35万元。

米面厂：米面厂拥有年加工7500吨面粉的磨粉机组一套，年加工大米7500吨的碾米机组一套。1995年，因面粉车间机械陈旧，生产的面粉质量差，县粮食局投资8万元进行技改。1997年，全厂受市场经济影响，造成亏损。1998年初，面粉、面条车间停产关闭，大米车间为购销企业代加工，收取加工费。2004年12月，县粮食局争取到省粮食局对该厂大米车间每年30万元的技改扶持资金，并被省指定为省的粮食“应急”加工点。

饲料公司：1995年，县粮食局投资29万元在北京购买年产5000吨饲料的自动加工机械一套。因饲料生产成本高，售价高于市场粮价，导致销售困难，造成连年亏损。1997年，饲料加工车间和养殖场租赁给贵阳兰地公司经营。2004年，租赁方受市场影响终止合同，饲料公司自此关闭。

2008年，息烽县国有粮食企业改革改制工作领导小组成立，指导国有粮食企业改制重组，进行全面清产核资。县粮食局委托贵阳同信会计师事务所对粮食企业清产核资进行专项审计。是年6—11月，基本完成清产核资；完成国有粮食企业改制重组资产评估和人员调查摸底；完成《息烽县国有粮食企业改制重组工作方案（草案）》和《息烽县国有粮食企业改制职工安置方案（草案）》。

贵阳办事处：1994年，县粮食局在贵阳设立办事处，原有职工19人。2002年辞退或自愿申请解除劳动合同15人，剩余4人除开展正常经营活动外，还担负贵阳固定资产的维护任务。2004年12月，共欠银行贷款528万元。

汽车队：2002年3月，因6辆营运汽车使用年限已到，又无资金更新而停业关闭。欠银行贷款23.38万元。全部职工12人自谋生路。

第四章　专卖专营

县石油公司、盐业公司、烟草公司同属对口上划的国有独资商业企业。1995年，县石油公司划归中国石油化工股份有限公司贵州贵阳石油公司管理，更名为县石油支公司。2000年，县盐业公司划归贵州盐业（集团）有限责任公司下属分公司。2005年，县烟草公司取消法人资格，公司资产无偿划转贵阳市烟草分公司。

第一节　烟　草

一、机构

贵州省息烽县烟草专卖局与贵州省烟草公司息烽县公司为两块牌子，一套人马，受县政府和上级业务主管部门双重领导。1991年，局（公司）内设办公室、专卖办公室、政工股、纪检股、烟叶生产股、卷烟经营股、计划财统股、基础股、审计股、安保股。1992年，划归安顺地区烟草公司，内设11个股室，下辖4个烟叶站、5个独立核算单位。1996年1月，随息烽县划归贵阳市辖，县局（公司）由安顺划归贵阳市烟草专卖局（公司）管理。1997年2月，贵阳市卷烟厂实行改制，成立贵州黄果树烟草（集团）有限责任公司，县公司划归（集团）有限责任公司统一经营。2002年6月，“贵州黄果树集团息烽烟草有限责任公司”更名为“贵州烟草公司息烽县公司”，由贵阳烟草专卖局（分公司）直接领导和管理。2005年8月，取消县烟草公司法人资格，建立县烟叶生产部、县卷烟营销部和县卷烟配送中转站。原县烟草公司资产全部无偿划归贵阳市分公司。2010年，县局（分公司）下设综合办公室、人事劳资科、财务科、安保科、专卖办、稽查大队、卷烟市场营销部、卷烟配送中转站、烟叶生产科（技术推广站）、现代烟草农业办公室，下辖石硐烟草站（基地单元站）、石硐烟草站九庄分站、养龙司分站、流长分站。

二、烤烟收购

1991年，全县收购烤烟8.57万担。1993年，在每个收购站点设立举报箱和样品柜，确保烤烟收购工作公开、公正。是年，收购烤烟14.04万担。1994年，省物价局、省烟草公司为鼓励优质烟生产，对交售优质烟实行奖励：每担上等烟奖50元、中上等烟奖30元。次年4月，提高上中等烟奖励标准：中一、中二、中四烟每担提高30元，中三烟40元、上一烟20元、上二烟25元、上三烟15元、上五烟10元。1996年起，烤烟收购执行40级制分级标准。是年收购烤烟8.37万担，收购总值3372.53万元，其中省奖励1987.75万元，县补贴15.32万元。1997年，收购烤烟9.59万担，其中上等烟0.36万担、中等烟3.53万担、下等烟5.33万担。实现烟叶税收443万元。

1998年7月，国务院下发《关于调整烟叶和卷烟价格及税收政策的紧急通知》，取消各种形式的烟叶收购价格补贴，适当提高烟叶收购价格。是年，按国家烤烟生产部署，压缩烤烟种植面积和收购量，全年收购烤烟3.8万担。2002年，因种植面积剧减，收购量仅0.98万担。是年，针对烤烟收购中的不正之风，建立烤烟收购制度，规范收购行为，查办打击烟叶收购中违规违纪行为，使烤烟收购量回升。次年，收购烤烟3.77万担。2004年，收购烤烟2.88万担，其中上等烟22.55%、中上等烟68%、橘色烟35%。全年实现经营利润315万元。2005年起，烤烟收购量均在4万担以上，优质烟的比例也大幅度提升。2010年，全县收购烤烟4.07万担，其中上等烟占收购量的30.05%、中等烟占收购量的32.54%。

三、卷烟销售

1991年9月，安顺地区行署发文要求强化地产烟销售，规定：凡不承担地产烟销售任务的，由烟草部门吊销其专卖许可证，工商部门变更或注销其营业执照，各县烟草公司在完成地产烟销售任务之前，一律不准经销区外烟。受地产烟销售不畅，以及执行省公司卷烟价格实行双轨制和随行就市的影响，是年仅销售卷烟4928箱。1992年，《中华人民共和国烟草专卖法》开始执行，随着查办力度的加大，销售工作中采取“开拓市场，引导消费，增强效益”的营销策略，使卷烟销售增加到

7656箱。1994年，由于零售商多渠道进货，当年卷烟销售降到多年来最低点，仅销售卷烟4649箱。为维护市场秩序，进一步加强对违法违章的查处力度，以及进一步建立“全面经销、全面配送、专销结合”的销售网点运行机制，至2003年，卷烟销售又回升至7021箱。2004年，销售卷烟7196箱。2005年，销售卷烟7612箱。2006年，销卷烟7815箱，销售金额共计6716万元，单箱产值为8595元。2007年，通过加强零售终端建设，全年销售卷烟8206箱，销售额7968万元。此后，卷烟销量逐年增大，至2010年，销售卷烟10200箱，销售金额突破亿元大关，为14018万元。

息烽县1991—2010年烤烟收购和卷烟销售统计表

表13-4-1

年份	烤烟收购			年份	烤烟收购		
	收购量（万担）	均价（元/担）	卷烟销售（箱）		收购量（万担）	均价（元/担）	卷烟销售（箱）
1991	8.57	109	4928	2001	1	379.05	7000
1992	11.9	114	7656	2002	0.98	399.42	6789
1993	1.4	141	6163	2003	3.77	390	7021
1994	5.9	135.74	4649	2004	2.88	485.86	7196
1995	4.34	187.13	5345	2005	4.75	387.68	7612
1996	8.37	211.34	8423	2006	4.1	341	7815
1997	9.89	229.69	8674	2007	4.5	486	8206
1998	3.8	231	6206	2008	4.29	622.38	8664
1999	4.54	342	—	2009	4	683.5	9597
2000	5.1	335	6600	2010	4.07	575.38	10200

四、烟草专卖

1991年6月，《中华人民共和国烟草专卖法》（以下简称《烟草专卖法》）颁布。是年查处各种案件172起。其中，查处违法生产和销售假冒伪劣卷烟案58起，破获地下卷烟厂2个，收缴卷烟机2台，没收假冒伪劣卷烟2479条，年检卷烟零售户1014户。其中国营、集体132户、个体882户。1992年是执行国家《烟草专卖法》的第一年，烟草系统职工除认真学习和宣传《烟草专卖法》外，在公安、工商、交警等部门配合下，对市场进行巡回检查和设置检查点进行检查等。全年共查处各类违法违章案件287起，没收卷烟382条，假冒卷烟3648条，上缴国库罚款收入23.16万元；年检卷烟零售许可证1280户，占零售户的95%。

1993—1997年，为维护“两烟”市场的正常经营秩序，打击不法烟贩的违法活动，县烟草专卖局与公安、交警、工商、技术监督等部门密切配合，共查处各类违法案件367起，没收假冒伪劣卷烟36257条，查处违法收购烤烟127.5万千克，上缴国库罚没收入379.58万元。1998年，因在执法打私工作中成绩突出，县烟草专卖办公室被国家烟草专卖局评为全国打私工作先进单位。

1999年5月1日至6月30日，在全县范围内开展“百日打假”活动，出动执法人员315人次，检查卷烟经营户815户，没收假冒伪劣卷烟2733条，查处违法渠道进货4955条，吊销烟草专卖零售许可证

1个。是年，共查处各类违法案件45起，上缴国库罚款收入69.4万元。2001年，检查全县卷烟市场250人次，查处违法经营案21起。2003年，查处无证运输案4起，卷烟196件，非渠道进货3起，上缴罚款收入42.05万元。2005年，查处无证贩烟案1起。

2006年，开展市场清理整顿，取缔无证经营户15户。全年办理卷烟零售许可证117户，注销72户。2009年，办理零售许可证253个，注销零售许可证136个。2010年，出动稽查管理人员331人次，检查经营户7326户次，清理市场20个。

第二节　石　油

一、机构

1991年，县石油公司下设办公室，隶属安顺石油公司管辖。1996年，县石油公司划归贵阳石油公司管辖，公司下设办公室、财务股、业务股、油库。1998年，中国石油化工股份有限公司成立，县石油公司划归中国石油化工股份有限公司贵州贵阳石油公司管辖，更名为县石油支公司，内设经理办、财务办、零售管理、综合管理4个业务办公室，下辖黑神庙、城关2个加油站。2001年，收购息烽茂安加油站、天台加油站、养龙站加油站，新建息烽金阳加油站、小寨坝加油站。2006年，因城市规划需要，茂安加油站拆迁至县城西门，2009年建成营业。2010年，县石油支公司下辖金阳、城关、西门、黑神庙、小寨坝、天台和养龙站7个加油站，共有30立方米储油罐16个、15立方米储油罐2个、加油机19台。

二、石油销售

1991年，县石油公司销售轻油1531吨，其中汽油580吨、柴油951吨。此后，随着县内经济发展，道路建设以及机动车和农机具的快速增多，轻油销售量逐年快速增长。2001年，轻油销售5180吨，其中汽油1895吨、柴油3285吨。2006年，轻油销售10125吨，其中汽油3702吨、柴油6423吨。2010年，轻油销售18030吨，其中汽油7780吨、柴油10250吨。

息烽石油支公司1991—2010年轻油销售统计表

表13-4-2　　单位：吨

年份	轻油销售量	其中		年份	轻油销售量	其中	
		汽油	柴油			汽油	柴油
1991	1531	580	951	2001	5180	1895	3285
1992	1670	645	1025	2002	5932	2012	3920
1993	1980	810	1170	2003	6832	2230	4600
1994	2680	955	1735	2004	8180	2630	5550
1995	3105	1122	1993	2005	9400	3215	6185
1996	3200	1200	2000	2006	10125	3702	6423
1997	3725	1370	2355	2007	11700	5015	6685
1998	4017	1532	2485	2008	13100	5972	7128
1999	4352	1650	2702	2009	16300	6995	9305
2000	4708	1770	2938	2010	18030	7780	10250

第三节　盐　类

一、机构

县盐业公司原为县商业局下辖单位，1991年成立贵州省盐务管理局息烽支局后，实行两块牌子，一套人马管理体制，支局下设办公室和财务股。1999年，公司（支局）划归县计划与经济贸易局管辖。2000年11月，公司（支局）划归贵州盐业（集团）有限公司，更名为贵州盐业（集团）有限公司息烽分公司。2002年7月，公司下设财务股、业务统计股和盐政股。

二、盐类营销

1991年、1992年，食盐销售收入136万元，完成利润12.94万元。1993年，全县各乡镇增设零售点20余处，方便群众购盐。1995年，购进食盐1249.5吨，销售1540吨。此后多年，购入量和销售量多维持在1000余吨。1998年建立碘盐加工制度，要求每小包盐误差不得超过2钱，并做到“四不发”：保管员不到现场不发、运输车辆不洁不发、碘盐不合格不发、包装质量不合格不发。2002年3月，与重钙厂签订896吨工业盐购销合同，获利4.5万元；11月，续签300吨购销合同，获利1.5万元。是年，加碘盐、工业盐、多品种盐等购入量增至2098吨，销量增至2186吨。2003年，取消中间流通环节，采取集中配送方式，直接将盐配送到零售点。是年2月，广东发生“非典”（非典型肺炎），不法商贩趁机宣传食盐涨价，导致县内多地出现抢购食盐现象。公司在抓专项宣传的同时，紧急配送食盐59吨，涨价风波迅速平息。2006年，销售各种盐2659.37吨，为历年最高，实现利税38.8万元。是年，深入大型养殖村、养殖场宣传和推进畜牧盐销售工作。当年销售畜牧盐26.56吨。2008年1—2月，县内遭遇罕见强凝冻灾害天气，为支持抗凝冻、保民生工作，动用459.5吨工业盐进行除雪融冰。为防止工业盐流入市场，公司组织人员进行走访回收。是年，销售纸塑料小包碘盐1160.28吨。2009年，购进盐1266.1吨，销售1723.02吨。2010年，购进盐1461.83吨，销售1406.66吨。

息烽县1995—2010年部分年份盐购销统计表

表13-4-3　　单位：吨

年份	购进	销售	年份	购进	销售
1995	1249.5	1540	2004	1914.65	2120.5
1997	1320	1344	2005	2189.1	2364.54
1999	1014	1244	2006	2441.62	2559.37
2000	1256	1201.4	2007	2548	2246
2001	1125	1201.4	2008	2428.23	2409.9
2002	2098.9	2186.21	2009	1266.21	1723.02
2003	1914.65	2120.5	2010	1461.83	1406.66

三、法规宣传与执法检查

（一）法规宣传

1997年5月5日“全国宣传碘缺乏危害日”，公司会同卫生、防疫等部门，在永靖、黑神庙、养龙司、九庄、温泉、流长等地，通过标语、黑板报、设立咨询点及散发资料等办法，向群众宣传碘缺乏的危害，共散发资料5000份，接受群众咨询3000余人次。次年，在县科协、教育、防疫等部门配合下，张贴宣传标语和《盐业管理条例》《食盐专管办法》《贵州省食盐管理条例》等，进行盐业专卖和食用碘盐知识宣传。1999年，《息烽报》专版刊登《盐业管理条例》《食盐专管办法》。此后多年，食盐专卖、科学加碘宣传成常态化工作。

2003年12月，对职工和盐政人员进行《盐业管理条例》《盐业执法办法》等法制宣传、培训。2006年，开展“食用合格碘盐，保证健康安全”主题宣传活动，发放资料4000余份，接受群众咨询3000余人次。次年，制作宣传光碟150张，通过教育部门下发全县各小学，引导学生家庭自觉食用合格碘盐。2008年，在科技“五下乡”“五月综治宣传月”和“5·18”助残日活动中，除发放宣传资料、张贴宣传画、标语以及赠送宣传围裙外，还帮助鹿窝乡建立一个“碘盐示范村”和一个“碘盐示范学校”，宣传普及正确食用碘盐，保证婴幼儿智力和身体健康发育的知识。

2009年，出动车辆和盐政人员深入全县10乡镇进行入户、入校的盐政宣传活动。发放宣传资料2万余份，张贴宣传日主题海报50余张，展出碘缺乏病展板40余块，赠送宣传围裙500余份、购物袋500余个。将鹿窝乡瓮舍村和瓮舍小学定为碘盐示范村、示范学校。执法人员深入示范村、校内开展碘盐健康教育课。

2010年，除以“贵盐集团关爱你的健康”为主题进行营销宣传活动外，5月12—20日，第十七个“防治碘缺乏病日”，出动宣传车7台次、盐政人员21人次，在7个乡镇开展宣传活动，发放宣传资料1万余份，张贴宣传日主题海报40余张，悬挂宣传标语2幅，接受群众咨询5000余人次。

（二）执法检查

1992年，查获江西樟树阁山盐矿和县粮食局酱油厂计划外销售食盐60吨，被安顺盐务分局处以2万元罚款。1995年，发放食盐零售许可证235个，查处案件2起，没收违法盐0.28吨。1997年3月，息烽重钙厂擅自向四川自贡进工业盐300吨。由于查处及时，违法行为得到有效制止。2001年，在温泉查获违法经营户3户，没收违法盐224千克，罚款50元。在猫场查获私盐250千克。通过查有无零售许可证和暗访，对10乡镇256个经营点进行检查、清理，查处违法案件7起，没收私盐500千克，查处无证经营户42户，取缔15户。2004年，查获各类涉盐违法案件4起，查获各类违法盐产品149千克。执法人员深入各农贸市场、学校食堂、饭店、食品加工单位以及季节性的辣椒、香肠、腊肉加工点，集中检查其用盐情况。检查中注销过期经营许可证25户。2005年，依法查处九庄镇纸坊村个体工商户销售散盐行为，封存、扣押其散盐550千克。在对全县经营户的清查中，取缔无证经营户34户，没收违法盐58千克。2007年，取缔无证经营户21户，新办理食盐零售许可证65个。2008年，出动执法车43台次、执法人员145人次，检查经营户921户，查获涉盐案件18起，处罚无证经营户21户。2009年，稽查人员对各乡镇和县城零售商店的食盐价格执行情况进行全面大检查，在抽查的58户零售户中，对违规抬价销售的3户进行处理。2010年，出动执法车68台次、执法人员214人次，查处涉盐案件21起，查获违法盐2.65吨，处罚无证经营零售户19户。

第十四篇　财税·金融

第一章　财　政

县财政多年属于“吃饭”型财政（财政资金只能维持国家机关运转，缺乏用于建设的资金，财政经济建设职能基本丧失）。1991年，本级财政收入1693万元，至2010年，本级财政收入突破3亿元，为30769万元。20年间，本级财政收入增长18倍。1991—2010年，财政支出总额455442万元，其中民生累计支出占财政预算的59.32%。

第一节　机　构

1991年年初，县财政局内设人秘股、监察股、农财股、预算股、企财股和行财股等股室。下辖信用资金管理所和国债服务部。永靖镇、养龙区、黑神庙区、九庄区、永阳区及乡（镇）设财政所。6月，财政局增设国有资产管理办公室。1992年，撤区并乡建镇，建4镇6乡10个财政所。2000年5月，撤销县财政局下辖的信用资金管理所和国债服务部，增设监察科、社会保障财务管理科、基本建设科。2002年，各乡镇成立农业税收管理分局、财务管理办公室。4月，成立县会计核算中心。2003年11月，增设会计事务管理科。2006年8月，增设经济建设科。2007年10月，乡财政所划归县财政局管理。2010年，县财政局内设办公室、综合科、预算科、国库科、经济建设科、农财科、基层财政管理科、行政事业财务科、会计科、国有资产与企业管理办公室和监督检查科。

第二节　财政体制

1991年，中央对地方实行“划分税种，核定收支，分级包干”的财政体制。1992年，县财政实行“分级包干，分灶吃饭”，对乡镇实行“核定基数，收支包干，定额上解，超收分成，一定三年”的县财政管理体制。1994年，实行分税制财政管理体制。1998年，制定《息烽县乡镇级财政体制管理办法（试行）》，实行“划分收支，分级包干，当年平衡，消化赤字，奖快促慢”的财政管理体制。县对乡、镇完成财政收入实行上台阶奖励政策。2005年，县乡财政体制管理原则为“划分收支范围，核定基数，实行激励机制，定额上解，超收分成，基数补助，自求平衡”。

第三节 财政收入和支出

一、财政收入

1991年，县财政总收入2002万元，其中本级财政收入1693万元，上级补助529万元。本级财政收入中，税收收入主要来源于产品税。此后多年，由于税源不稳定，本级财政收入呈不稳定状态。1996年，息烽划归贵阳市辖后，由于招商引资力度加大，上级补助大量增加，财政总收入和本级财政收入增长较快。是年，财政总收入3925万元，其中本级财政收入2445万元，增长34.34%；上级补助增至2447万元，增长近1倍。从1997年起，财政总收入和本级财政收入稳步增长。2004年，地方财政收入突破亿元大关，为10050万元。2005年，本级财政收入11909万元，息烽县跻身于贵州省地方财政收入亿元县行列。2008年，本级财政收入突破2亿元大关，为22221万元。2010年，本级财政收入突破3亿元大关，为30769万元，比1991年的1693万元增长18倍，平均增长率17.24%。

1991—2010年，上级补助收入累计285941万元，占财政总收入（包括财政总收入、上年结余和上级补助）470362万元的60.79%。

息烽县1991—2010年财政收入统计表

表14-1-1　　单位：万元

年份	财政总收入	公共财政预算收入			预算收入同比增长率（%）	政府性基金预算收入	上级补助收入
		小计	税收收入	非税收收入			
1991	2002	1693	1425	268	—	—	529
1992	2090	1768	1612	156	4.43	—	803
1993	2581	2248	2104	144	27.15	—	608
1994	2995	1812	1268	544	-19.4	—	1405
1995	3189	1820	1297	523	0.44	—	1232
1996	3925	2445	1878	567	34.34	—	2447
1997	4535	2920	2139	781	19.43	66	3224
1998	4903	3232	2264	968	10.68	73	3394
1999	5582	3601	2284	1317	11.42	89	4635
2000	6089	3858	2741	1117	7.14	215	5561
2001	6312	4763	2839	1924	23.46	64	8701
2002	9962	6022	4018	2004	26.43	62	10972
2003	12278	7401	5248	2153	22.9	232	11788
2004	16575	8711	6104	2607	17.7	707	12262
2005	22743	11909	8379	3530	36.83	799	17418
2006	27052	14816	10282	4534	24.31	5894	20539
2007	33014	18185	13510	4675	22.74	1245	27770
2008	44535	22221	17390	4831	22.19	507	44828
2009	40906	25588	18886	6702	15.15	617	50176
2010	55175	30769	25652	5117	20.25	17936	57649

息烽县1995—2010年乡镇本级财政收入统计表

表14-1-2　　　　单位：万元

年份	永靖镇	青山苗族乡	西山乡	养龙司乡	温泉镇	九庄镇	石硐乡	鹿窝乡	流长乡	小寨坝镇	合计
1995	282	40	49	73	92	100	82	43	52	130	943
1996	374	53	58	118	134	204	158	77	93	188	1457
1997	459	80	98	110	135	202	173	80	102	220	1659
1998	531	107	122	119	175	165	185	57	62	257	1780
1999	583	118	141	116	193	153	139	57	62	229	1791
2000	656	147	170	132	230	219	146	63	70	278	2111
2001	825	139	150	139	260	96	59	33	55	320	2076
2002	1363	183	226	251	352	265	245	127	118	437	3567
2003	1680	278	302	294	448	297	339	166	176	629	4609
2004	2119	350	407	355	624	353	393	217	220	895	5933
2005	2469	391	482	434	779	405	510	205	222	1207	7104
2006	2441	440	573	495	712	435	625	214	295	1740	7970
2007	2732	526	591	530	960	583	727	382	482	2100	9613
2008	3055	658	679	636	1306	803	713	692	726	2375	11643
2009	3523	626	713	711	1051	910	919	555	531	2541	12080
2010	3802	876	1074	1202	1311	1321	1255	815	733	2898	15287
合计	26894	5012	5835	5715	8762	6511	6668	3783	3999	16444	89623

二、财政支出

1991年，财政支出1992万元，其中，一般公共服务支出359万元、公共安全支出89万元、教育支出445万元、社会保障和就业支出159万元、文化体育与传媒支出36万元、医疗卫生支出163万元、农林水事务支出294万元，其他类支出447万元，上解支出211万元。此后各项支出逐年增长，2001年为12761万元，其中一般公共服务支出、公共安全支出、教育支出分别是1991年的5.2倍、6.6倍、6.5倍，农林水事务支出是1991年的近7倍。2010年，财政预算支出86794万元。

1991—2010年，累计公共财政预算支出455442万元，政府性基金预算支出37308万元。公共财政预算支出年均增长率22.4%。其中一般公共服务支出82237万元、公共安全支出22513万元、教育支出95589万元、社会保障和就业支出36731万元、文化体育与传媒支出10863万元、医疗卫生支出33897万元、农林水事务支出70567万元。教育、卫生、社会保障等民生支出逐年增长。累计民生支出占公共财政预算的比重为59.32%。土地有偿基金累计支出30252万元，占政府性基金预算支出的81.09%。

息烽县1991—2010年财政支出统计表

表14-1-3　　单位：万元

年份	公共财政预算支出									预算支出与上年同比增长率（%）	政府性基金预算支出	上解支出
	合计	一般公共服务支出	公共安全支出	教育支出	社会保障和就业支出	文化体育与传媒支出	医疗卫生支出	农林水事务支出	其他类支出			
1991	1992	359	89	455	159	36	163	294	447		0	211
1992	2621	414	90	519	102	82	152	508	754	34.58	0	155
1993	2714	562	110	737	191	47	231	416	420	3.55	0	140
1994	3133	578	134	830	114	41	306	571	559	15.44	0	96
1995	3756	774	154	987	160	58	337	355	931	19.89	0	87
1996	4642	687	236	991	325	23	385	555	1440	23.59	0	114
1997	5985	969	336	1302	241	38	386	757	1956	28.93	57	75
1998	6501	1001	419	1485	204	264	438	1167	1523	8.62	13	95
1999	7835	1366	369	1983	291	271	473	1212	1870	20.52	87	69
2000	9289	1436	441	2053	438	415	709	1906	1891	18.56	231	157
2001	12761	1878	589	2897	483	500	1101	2042	3271	37.38	110	91
2002	16735	2982	662	3298	1044	692	995	2345	4717	31.14	56	139
2003	18405	3187	869	3900	738	973	1518	2159	5061	9.98	640	268
2004	21184	3964	1204	4185	978	877	1397	2540	6039	15.1	611	172
2005	27760	4961	1523	5514	1888	1217	1744	4429	6484	31.04	2430	640
2006	36167	9349	1761	7692	2982	383	2185	5764	6051	30.28	4418	333
2007	45515	10303	2134	9197	3954	397	3522	7402	8606	25.85	1245	530
2008	65498	12718	2776	14337	6568	936	4592	9513	14058	43.9	2861	1090
2009	76155	13525	4367	15839	6579	1197	5458	14643	14547	16.27	3615	1140
2010	86794	14390	4381	18376	9409	1394	7810	12519	18515	13.97	20258	1040
合计	455442	82237	22513	95589	36731	10863	33897	70567	103045	22.4	37308	6642

息烽县1995—2010年乡镇本级财政支出统计表

表14-1-4　　单位：万元

年份	永靖镇	青山苗族乡	西山乡	养龙司乡	温泉镇	九庄镇	石硐乡	鹿窝乡	流长乡	小寨坝镇	合计	年度增长率（%）
1995	312	46	121	188	97	179	111	69	125	185	1433	
1996	276	40	112	184	102	165	122	63	117	178	1359	–5.16
1997	367	81	149	217	145	237	167	106	169	246	1884	38.63
1998	342	82	140	237	137	205	146	93	160	233	1775	–5.79
1999	433	94	183	264	156	252	187	124	190	274	2157	21.52
2000	571	153	235	328	199	328	247	159	224	361	2805	30.04
2001	259	126	158	174	222	162	110	79	109	234	1633	–41.78
2002	525	159	164	229	194	245	155	105	141	307	2224	36.19
2003	562	264	256	275	327	227	164	173	158	408	2814	26.53
2004	1039	333	336	264	308	237	292	171	187	278	3445	22.42
2005	1076	363	362	332	293	385	316	288	299	581	4295	24.67
2006	1099	410	362	491	398	531	457	243	295	761	5317	23.8
2007	1984	511	500	452	491	651	538	374	358	982	6841	28.66
2008	1717	689	605	734	722	766	610	527	595	1057	8022	17.26
2009	2054	782	665	1010	759	1059	840	540	730	1324	9763	21.7
2010	1926	834	1087	1186	991	1509	1276	813	907	2071	12600	29.06
合计	14542	4967	5705	6565	5541	7138	5738	3927	4764	9480	68367	17.85

第四节 国有资产管理

1992年6月，县成立国有资产管理办公室（简称国资办）。1995年，对29户企业进行清产核资，国有资产总额18277万元，负债总额6895万元，所有者权益总额11807万元。2000年3月，成立县国有资产经营有限责任公司（简称国资公司）。2003年，通过县级行政、事业单位产权登记年检，年检单位138户，资产总额35534万元，负债总额12333万元，净资产总额23201万元。2007年，对全县207户行政事业单位资产进行全面清理核实，认定资产总额63056万元，负债总额20697万元，净资产总额42359万元。2008年非税收入改革中，将县直机关经营性资产划交国资公司经营管理。

国资公司成立后的几年间，盘活国有资产12家，其中房产67676.3平方米、地产238830平方米，总价值17186.64万元。利用闲置资产担保或抵押，向银行及其他金融机构融资，为县城基础设施建设、教育基础设施、磷化工基地建设、铝产品生产、饮用水行业以及下岗职工再就业等融资11593万元。采取直接投资方式，对城建、农业、旅游等12个项目投资1609万元。通过租赁、承包、合作经营、招商引资等方式盘活国有资产，使国有资产得到保值增值，财政税收增加，财政支出压力得以缓解。

2010年年底，县内215家行政事业单位国有资产总量145045万元，其中行政单位59414万元、事业单位85631万元。14家国有企业资本3341万元。

第五节 预算外资金管理

1991年4月，把预算外资金管理与治理“三乱”（乱收费、乱罚款、乱摊派）和“三查”（查乱收费、乱罚款、乱摊派）工作相结合，严格收费立项和票据管理，使管理工作规范化。1995年，沿用“财政代管，专户储存”方式，资金归征收单位支配，逐步推行综合财政预算。1997年，将预算外资金全部纳入财政综合预算平衡，实行预算内外资金统筹管理。1998年，预算外资金实行“收支两条线”管理。2000年，按照“统一政策，分级管理，核定收支，政府调控”原则，对收费单位实行“核定收支计划，收入全额上缴，支出统筹安排，超收比例分成，短收自负，结余留用”的管理办法。2004年，财政部发布《关于加强政府非税收入管理通知》，将行政事业性收费、政府性基金、罚款收入等称为“非税收入”，用以替代使用多年的“预算外收入”概念。2008年11月，非税收入征管改革，实行网络管理，各单位非税收入缴款人直接到银行缴入财政非税收入汇缴专户。

1998—2010年，上缴国库行政性收费16468万元，罚没款6625万元，合计23093万元，占本级财政收入的14.05%。

第六节 农村税费改革

1999年，开始进行农民负担、计税面积、农业人口和农作物产量测算，为农村税费改革作试点前的准备工作。

2002年，开展扩大农村税费改革试点工作。改革前全县农民政策内负担为959.39万元，其中农业税及其附加327.42万元、农业特产税及其附加36.65万元、屠宰税24万元、提留统筹（即村提留、乡统筹，指乡镇或村合作经济组织依法向所属单位包括乡镇、村办企业、联户企业和农民收取的款项）及其他提留统筹437万元，其他134.32万元。改革后农民负担为603.54万元（含农业税及附加，农业特产税及附加），政策内减负355.85万元，减负率37.09%，人均减负17.12元；改革前农民负担总额1672.32万元，改革后减负额1068.78万元，减负率63.91%，人均减负50.7元。政策内常规负担，改革前农民负担总额764.42万元，其中包括农业税及附加、乡统筹、村提留等；改革后农民负担为581.11万元，减负率23.98%，人均减负8.99元。

2004年，农业税税率降低1个百分点，并实行各种补贴。将2002年农村税费改革试点时确定的7%的农业税税率调整为6%。调整后农民农业税及附加总负担率由原来的8.4%降到7.2%。实行对农民用实物缴纳农业税每千克直接补贴0.1元，对农民种植优质水稻每亩直接补贴5元的政策。2005年，取消农业税，提前两年达到国务院决定五年在全国取消农业税的要求。2006年，对种粮农民补贴采用“一折通”形式，将各类补贴直接发放到农民手中。2002—2010年，共补给农民退耕还林、种粮、粮食综合直补等资金10373.33万元。

第七节　车辆、家电下乡补贴

2009年2月1日起，县实施摩托车下乡补贴；3月1日起，实施汽车下乡补贴和家电下乡补贴。至2010年12月31日，县财政共补贴摩托车3235辆，补贴资金171.5万元；补贴汽车1275辆，补贴资金463.42万元（其中微型客车下乡产品723辆，补贴资金261.75万元；轻型载货车下乡产品321辆，补贴资金192.04万元；微型载货汽车下乡产品30辆，补贴资金9.63万元）；补贴家电15250台，补贴资金354.54万元。

第八节　财务管理与监督

一、会计集中核算

2002年4月，县会计核算中心成立，县级财政预算单位会计统一纳入会计核算中心管理，实行统一核算。至2010年，会计核算中心纠正各预算单位不规范报账业务1093笔，累计金额4568.73万元。其中，纠正一般性差错1544.35万元，拒绝报销889.46万元，纠正坐支（单位用自己业务收入的现金直接支付业务支出的行为）26.35万元，纠正手续不完善2108.57万元。由会计核算中心归集上缴财政预算资金5869.97万元，上缴财政专户资金1841.52万元，合计7711.49万元。

二、国库集中收付

2005年9月，开展财政国库管理制度改革工作，增加原会计核算中心国库集中收付职能，建立以国库单一账户体系为基础，资金缴拨以国库集中支付为主要形式的财政国库管理制度。当年国库指标（单位用款计划）结余926.3万元。2006—2010年，各年国库指标结余分别为1966万元、6825万元、12363万元、17024.63万元、14273.26万元；各年代扣代缴建筑安装工程税款分别为53.9万元、309万元、458万元、592万元、753.5万元。

三、财政资金管理

2003年9月，县财政扶贫资金和农业综合开发资金实行县级报账制，首先在会计核算中心试运行。2005年9月，移交财政局农财科。在资金管理方面做到账户统一、核算统一、人员统一、审核统一。至2010年，县级到位资金累计8716.62万元，其中，财政扶贫到位资金5666.4万元，农发行到位资金3050.22万元。

四、财政投资评审

2007年5月，实行财政投资项目评审制度，引进专业人才，开展财政投资评审工作。是年评审项目28个，送审金额0.85亿元，审定金额0.7亿元，审减率16.99%。至2010年，共评审项目639个，送审金额11.17亿元，审定金额8.59亿元，节约资金2.57亿元，综合审减率16.99%。

五、会计事务管理

1995年起，对会计人员实行会计证考试年检制度，经检查无会计证者，须参加培训，合格获证后持证上岗。2003年11月，县财政局增设会计事务管理科，负责会计事务管理工作。建立会计人员信息管理系统，将全县会计人员纳入系统管理。

六、政府采购

2003年1月1日起，实施《政府采购法》，改变社会集团控购管理方式，实行政府采购。至2010年，进行政府采购497（批）次，预算采购资金11792万元，实际采购资金10158万元，节约资金1634万元，资金平均节约率13.86%。其间，2007年，县政府成立采购办，政府采购实行采管分离。

七、财务监督

1991—1999年，每年对行政事业单位进行一次财务、物价大检查。2000年起，改为各司其职，检查工作转为会计信息质量检查和资金使用监管。2001年，清理检查行政事业单位176个，各类银行账户335个，批准保留银行账户303个。2004年11月，清理64家行政事业单位168个银行账户，查出因欠银行贷款不能销户的银行账户5个，不符合开设银行账户的12家单位账户13个。是年，调查处理九庄镇、永靖镇、县供销社公车私挂问题，责令单位按规定办理过户手续，对负有责任的领导人分别进行诫勉谈话。2005年，检查向阳希望小学、县信用联社2004年度会计信息质量状况和疾控中心“收支两条线”执行情况。2007年，出台《息烽县财政性资金审批及拨付程序》文件，规范全县财政性资金拨付手续，修订完善《息烽县行政事业单位会议费管理实施意见》，严格控制会议数量、会期、规模及标准。2010年，开展涉企收费项目检查，取消收费项目13个，涉及金额41.6万元。

第二章　税　务

1991—1994年，县内税务工作由县税务局开展。1994年，县税务局分设为国家税务局和地方税务局。国家税务局负责全县中央税、中央和地方共享税的征收管理。地方税务局负责营业税、个人和企业所得税、固定资产投资方向调节税等13个地方税种的征收管理。

第一节 机 构

1991年，县税务局内设办公室、人事教育股、监察股、计划会计股、税政股、征收管理股、征收股，下派永靖镇、永阳、九庄、小寨坝、养龙司5个税务所。是年9月，税务局增设稽查队。1994年9月14日，县税务局分设为国家税务局和地方税务局。

一、国家税务局

县国家税务局（简称县国税局）内设办公室、人事教育股、监察室、计划财务股、征收管理股、征收股、稽查分局，下派九庄、底寨、石硐、温泉、流长、小寨坝、养龙、永靖8个税务所。1995年5月，撤销征收股，设立征收分局；撤并下派税务所，底寨税务所并入永靖税务所，流长税务所并入小寨坝税务所，石硐税务所并入九庄税务所。1996年6月，县国税局内设机构改股为科。内设机构为办公室、人事教育科、监察室、税政科、征收管理科、征收分局、稽查分局。

1997年11月机构调整后，征收管理科改为管理服务科，税政科改为政策法规科，稽查分局改为稽查局，征收分局改为直属征收管理分局，养龙税务所与温泉税务所合并成立养龙征收管理分局，九庄税务所改为九庄征收管理分局，小寨坝税务所改为小寨坝征收管理分局，撤销永靖税务所，设西山征收管理分局。2001年4月23日，县国税局内设办公室、综合业务科、计划财务科、人事教育监察科，设直属机构为直属征收管理分局、稽查局，设事业单位为信息中心。撤销九庄征收管理分局、西山征收管理分局，保留小寨坝征收管理分局和养龙征收管理分局。7月12日，人事教育监察科分设为人事教育科、监察室，直属征收管理分局改为永靖征收管理分局。2003年6月，贵阳市国家税务局进行机构调整，撤销县国税局计划财务科，内设办公室、综合业务科、财务科、人事教育科、监察室、计划征收科、管理科，直属机构为稽查局，事业机构为信息中心；撤销永靖征收管理分局和养龙征收管理分局，小寨坝征收管理分局改设为小寨坝管理分局。2004年2月，改置小寨坝管理分局为小寨坝税务分局。2005年1月，县国税局内设办公室、综合业务科、征收管理科、人事教育科、监察室、计划征收科、税源管理科。直属机构为稽查局，事业机构为信息中心。稽查局内设办公室、检查科、案件审理科、案件执行科。2007年4月，县国税局内设机构改为办公室、综合业务科、计划财务科、人事教育监察科，设直属机构为直属征收管理分局、稽查局，设事业单位为信息中心。撤销九庄、西山原派出机构，只设养龙征收管理分局、小寨坝征收管理分局。7月，人事教育监察科分设为人事教育科、监察室，直属征收管理分局改为永靖征收管理分局。2009年9月，县国税局内设办公室、政策法规科、收入核算科、人事教育科、监察室、办税服务厅、税源管理科，设1个副科级直属机构（稽查局）、1个正股级事业单位（信息中心）和小寨坝税务分局、养龙税务分局2个副科级派出机构。

二、地方税务局

1994年，县地方税务局（简称县地税局）内设人秘股、征收管理股、征收股、稽查队、会计股、税收股，下辖永靖、西山、青山、石硐、九庄、鹿窝、流长、小寨坝、养龙、温泉10乡镇税务所。1996年4月，县地税局内设办公室、税政科、征收管理科、计划会计科、征收科、税务稽查队。12月，撤销原10乡镇税务所，组建永靖税务所、九庄税务所、小寨坝税务所和温泉税务所。1998年5月，县地税局上划为省政府直属机构。10月，局内设各股改为科，稽查队改为稽查局。1999年2月，增设监察室。2001年12月，实行机构改革，县地税局内设办公室、计划财务科、征收管理科、税政法规科、人事教育科、监察室、征收分局、稽查局，下辖永靖税务所、小寨坝税务所、温泉税务所和九庄税务所。

第二节　税　种

1991年，县税务局征管的税种有产品税、增值税、营业税、城市维护建设税、车船使用税、房产税、城镇土地使用税、屠宰税、牲畜交易税、国有企业奖金税、国有企业工资调节税、印花税、建筑税、个人收入调节税、工商统一税、城乡个体工商户所得税、集体企业所得税、私营企业所得税、中外合资企业所得税、国有企业所得税等20个税种。其中，个人收入调节税、工商统一税、中外合资企业所得税无税收入库。此后多年，税种略有增减。

一、国税税种

县国税局、县地税局分设后，建立分税制财政管理体制。县国税局征管的中央固定收入有关税、海关代征消费税和增值税、中央企业所得税、地方银行和外资银行及非银行金融企业所得税，铁道部门、各银行总行、各保险总公司等集中缴纳的收入（包括营业税、所得税、利润和城市维护建设税）、中央企业上缴利润等。外贸出口退税，除1993年地方已经负担的20%列入地方上缴中央基数外，以后发生的出口退税全部由中央财政负担。

中央与地方共享收入包括增值税、资源税、证券交易税。增值税中央分享75%，地方分享25%。资源税按不同资源品种划分，大部分资源税作为地方收入，海洋石油资源税作为中央收入。证券交易税，中央与地方各分享50%。

1994年，县国税局征收入库税种有消费税、增值税、营业税、城市维护建设税、车船使用税、房产税、城镇土地使用税、屠宰税、印花税、固定资产投资方向调节税、资源税、个人所得税、企业所得税13个税种和教育费附加、国家能源交通重点建设基金、国家预算调节基金3项收费。

1995年，县国税局征收的税种有增值税、消费税、营业税、城市维护建设税、个人所得税以及个体工商户所得税、资源税、印花税、屠宰税、教育费附加、国家能源交通重点建设基金、国家预算调节基金等。

2001年1月1日起，停止征收车辆购置附加费，由国家税务局负责政策管理，交通部门代征税款。

至2010年，国税局在县内征收的主体税种有增值税、消费税、营业税、企业所得税、储蓄存款利息个人所得税5个税种。

二、地方税税种

县地税局自1994年9月成立到2010年，共负责征收营业税、企业所得税、个人所得税、资源税、城镇土地使用税、城市维护建设税、固定资产投资方向调节税、土地增值税、印花税、车船税（车船使用税）、房产税、屠宰税、耕地占用税、契税、烟叶税15个税种和教育费附加、文化事业建设费2项行政收费。其中：

营业税：2009年1月1日起实施，征税范围包括交通运输业、建筑业、金融保险业、邮局通信业、文化体育业、娱乐业、服务业、转让无形资产、销售不动产等。

企业所得税：1994年起征，2008年税率修改，统一为25%。

城镇土地使用税：1995年以前每平方米0.2～2元；1996—2000年，每平方米0.4～2元；2001—2006年，每平方米0.4～2.4元；2007—2010年，每平方米3～12元。

城市维护建设税：征税对象为缴纳增值税、营业税的单位和个人。

固定资产投资方向调节税：1991年起征，2001年1月1日起暂停征收。

土地增值税：1994年1月1日起征，征收对象为有偿转让国有土地使用权、土地上建筑物及其他附属物产权的单位和取得土地增值额的个人。

印花税：对经济活动和经济交往中成立领受的凭证征收。

车船使用税：2007年，该税变更为车船税，实行幅度定额税率。

房产税：1994年实行税制改革，房产税划归地方税务机关征收管理。

屠宰税：1994年，省财政厅、省税务局下发《关于屠宰税征收办法的通知》，由于税务机构分设，屠宰税划归地方税务局征管。是年起，农民自养、自宰、自食的税率，按每头定额征收。从1998年3月1日起，屠宰或收购猪、牛、羊的单位和个人为屠宰税的纳税义务人。但少数民族传统节日自宰、自食的牲畜，农民宰杀伤残的牲畜，军事机关、部队自宰自食的牲畜，教育科研单位因教学、科研需要宰杀牲畜，可免缴屠宰税。2005年5月12日，屠宰税停征。

耕地占用税：执行标准为每平方米20元。

契税：1998年9月10日起征。

烟叶税：2006年4月28日，国务院第464号令，烟叶税取代原烟叶特产农业税，税率20%，由地方税务机构征收。

教育费附加：1994年税制改革后规定“教育费附加分别由国家税务局和地方税务局负责征收”，分别缴入中央金库和地方金库。1996年2月1日，国家税务总局明确“教育费附加”（铁道、银行总行、保险总公司缴纳的除外）由地方税务局负责征收管理。

文化事业建设费：1998年8月1日起征。各营业性娱乐场所，按其营业收入的3%征收；广播电台、电视台、报纸、刊物等广告媒介单位及户外广告经营单位，按其经费收入的3%征收。

第三节　税务征收

1991年，县税务局税收总收入1511.6万元，其中产品税738.5万元、增值税229.6万元、营业税327.2万元、企业所得税167.6万元。1992年，税收总收入1831万元。1993年，税收总收入2032.6万元，其中产品税1069.4万元、增值税278.2万元、营业税421.3万元、企业所得税39.1万元。1994年，县税务局分设为国税局和地税局，税务征收工作按国家规定各司其职。

一、国税局税务征收

1994年，国税局税收总收入1851万元，其中消费税12.8万元、增值税1208.6万元、营业税273.6万元、企业所得税175.8万元。次年，由于营业税、企业所得税剧降，税收总收入仅1481万元。此后，税收总收入逐年增加，至2006年，税收总收入突破亿元，为11380.4万元，其中增值税9442万元、企业所得税1759.3万元。2008年，税收总收入突破2亿元，为20119.4万元。此后两年，总收入略有下降，至2010年，税收总收入19092.2万元。

息烽县国税局1994—2010年税收总收入统计表

表14-2-1 单位：万元

年份	税收总收入	年份	税收总收入	年份	税收总收入
1994	1851	2000	2451.1	2006	11380.4
1995	1481	2001	3218.9	2007	13859.6
1996	1501	2002	3646.2	2008	20119.4
1997	1724.5	2003	4719	2009	10877.7
1998	1833.6	2004	6464.8	2010	19092.2
1999	2100.3	2005	9735.6	—	—

二、地税局税务征收

县地税局建立起税务登记、纳税申报、征管档案管理、发票管理、纳税服务等各项制度。1994年，全县地税征收仅455万元。此后逐年增加，至2001年达2411万元；2006年突破亿元，为10889万元；2009年突破2亿元，为22983万元；2010年突破3亿元，为30514万元。

息烽县地税局1994—2010年税收总收入统计表

表14-2-2 单位：万元

年份	税收收入	年份	税收收入	年份	税收收入
1994	455	2000	1903	2006	10889
1995	604	2001	2411	2007	13628
1996	793	2002	3646	2008	18464
1997	1072	2003	4397	2009	22983
1998	1344	2004	6686	2010	30514
1999	1575	2005	8869	—	—

第四节 税务执法

一、国税稽查

1991年，税务局成立稽查队，开展税收专项检查。稽查对象主要为磷化工行业、房地产、煤炭、医药经销、金融以及个体工商户。1999年，检查户数722户，立案12户，查补税款、罚款等46万元。2000年，推行稽查工作建议委托制，实施一级稽查，狠抓专项检查和要案查处。全年检查244户，立案21户，查补税收、罚款、滞纳金等36万元。2001年，完善一级稽查体制，由县局直属稽查局负责实施稽查工作。全年检查89户，立案24户，查补税款等71万元。2002年，以商业零售发票、免税企业、纳税异常企业为检查重点，共检查56户，查补税收23万元。2003年，推进检查工作由“数量收入型”向“效率执法型”转变，推行稽查选案制和限时办案制度，开展“阳光稽查”和各类专项检查。全年检查22户，立案4户，查补税款1.02万元。2005年，稽查工作性质由监督打击型向执法服务型转变。按照税务总局、省局、市局的专项检查重点，对全县煤炭、免税、免抵退、水泥生产、废旧物资收购等行业进行专项稽查、“阳光稽查”。全年检查52户，立案11户，查补税款、罚款等121万元。2006年，税收专项检查的主要行业为煤炭、房地产、摩托车销售等。是年共检查38户，立案12户，查补税款等162万元。2007年，对食品加工业、房地产、化工原料、医药制造、医药零售等13户税负偏低、申报异常的企业进行重点检查，共检查73户，查补税款、罚款、滞纳金等429万元。2008年，选定煤炭开采、建材生产2个行业7户纳税人为专项稽查对象，选定塑料制品、批发零售、化学原料等7个行业15户税负偏低、申报异常的企业进行检查，共检查14户，立案14户，查补税款47万元。2010年，对房地产、煤炭、医药经销、金融等4行业进行检查。检查15户，立案4户，查补税款、罚款、滞纳金等954万元。

二、地方税稽查

2000年起，县地税局开展执法专项检查。是年，共查补税款3.37万元。2004年，查补税款118.12万元。2006年，查补税款157.55万元。2010年，查补税款119.85万元。11年间，共查补税款（含企业自查补税和滞纳金）588.28万元。

息烽县地税局部分年度税务稽查情况统计表

表14-2-3　　单位：万元

年份	检查行业或对象	查补税款（含自查补税、滞纳金）
2000	固定资产投资方向调节税	3.37
2001	税款货物发票	0.55
2002	加油站	0.43
2003	独、合资企业、建安工程承包人、电力、金融、保险、电信、烟草	26.55
2004	货物运输、医药生产及购销、建筑业、房地产、超市、加油站	118.12
2005	房地产、电力、烟草、电信、银行、保险	18.95
2006	房地产、煤炭	157.55
2007	建安工程、房地产、磷化工	142.91
2010	——	119.85

第三章　金　融

1991—2010年，县金融业取得较大发展。国有商业银行的股份制改造，信用社统一法人的建立，标志着银行逐步走向现代化企业经营管理模式。金融业通过发放商业贷款，在支援工、农业生产、增加群众收入、提高购买力、稳定经济生活等方面发挥支撑作用。2010年，全县有政策性银行1家、商业性银行5家。

第一节　金融机构

一、中国人民银行息烽县支行

1991年，中国人民银行息烽县支行（简称县人行）内设人秘股、会计国库股、货币发行股、计划统计股、稽核金管股、安全保卫股。1994年，增设支行国库股。1996年5月，县人行内设机构调整为营业室、人秘科、金融监管科、保卫科。2001年7月，县人行内设机构调整为办公室、金融机构监管股、会计国库发行股、计划统计股、安全保卫股。原“息烽县纪委驻息烽县金融系统纪检组”更名为“贵州省金融系统纪律检查办公室驻息烽金融系统纪检组”，与监察合署办公。2003年12月，金融监管股从人行划出，建立贵州监管局息烽监管组。2004年，县人行内设机构改设为综合业务股（含办公室）、国库会计股、货币金银股、保卫股。

2005年1月，因业务发展需要，撤销发行库，货币发行业务并入修文县发行支库。人行内设机构调整为办公室、国库会计股、综合业务股。2006年，撤销原3股（室），只设综合管理股和基础业务股。

二、中国工商银行股份有限公司息烽县支行

1991年初，中国工商银行息烽县支行（简称县工行）内设信贷、计划、会计、出纳、储蓄、人事秘书等股室，下辖营业厅、城关储蓄所、城关第一储蓄所、城关第二储蓄所、拖电厂储蓄所、重钙厂分理处、温泉分理处、国营二七六厂第六办事处、南山煤矿代办所9个网点。1992年，撤销拖电厂储蓄所，业务并入城关储蓄所。1994年2月，设立文化路储蓄所。1999年，城关第一储蓄所撤销。11月30日，建设银行息烽县支行划归县工行管理。2001年12月，南山煤矿代办所撤销。2003年1月，撤迁第六办事处，同时将城关第二储蓄所更名为第六分理处，业务并入温泉分理处。2004年5月，温泉分理处撤销，业务划归温泉信用社。2005年10月28日，工行改制，县工行更名为中国工商银行股份有限公司息烽县支行，11月30日挂牌营业。

三、中国农业银行股份有限公司息烽县支行

1991年，中国农业银行息烽县支行（简称县农行）内设人事股、办公室、工商信贷股、计划股、会计股、信合股、稽核监察室、保卫股，下辖营业室、黑神庙营业所、养龙司营业所、永阳营业所、九庄营业所、二七六厂分理处、储蓄专柜城关第一储蓄所、城关第二储蓄所8个营业网点。1993年7月，增设县农贸市场和温泉镇二七六厂两个分理处。1997年1月，农村信用社与农行脱离直属领导关系。2000—2003年，先后撤销城关第一、第二储蓄所、九庄营业所、养龙司营业所。

2004年9月，撤销县农贸市场分理处。年底，县农行内设综合部、业务发展部、计划财务部、保卫部，下辖营业室、永阳营业所、二七六厂分理处、黑神庙营业所4个网点。

2009年1月，县农行更名为中国农业银行股份有限公司息烽县支行。7月正式挂牌营业。

四、中国农业发展银行息烽县支行

1997年3月，中国农业发展银行息烽县支行成立（简称县农发行），内设办公室、信贷计划部、会计出纳部。2008年4月，内设机构改为信贷客户部、会计结算部。

五、贵阳银行股份有限公司息烽支行

2001年5月11日，贵阳银行股份有限公司息烽支行挂牌成立，内设办公室、公司个人金融部、

会计出纳部，下辖1个营业部。11月，成立支行工会组织。2002年2月，增设市场部。5月，成立支行团组织。2003年，设办公室、公司个人金融部、会计出纳部、保卫科、市场部5个部门和1个营业网点。2004年，恢复原4部（室），增设1个营业网点。2006年，内设机构调整为办公室、公司个人金融部、会计出纳部3部（室）。2007年，设办公室、市场营销部、综合结算部（原会计出纳部）3个部（室）和2个营业网点。2008年1月，协助贵阳市住房公积金管理中心成立贵阳市住房公积金管理中心息烽管理部。是年，支行内设机构为办公室、市场营销部、综合结算部，下辖营业部和2个营业网点。2010年9月，更名为贵阳银行息烽支行。

六、邮政储蓄所

县邮政局中街邮政储蓄所建于1990年4月。1992年10月，开办黑神庙储蓄所；1995年4月，县文化路储蓄所开业；1996年6月，火车站储蓄所开业。2003年，火车站储蓄所迁至西洋肥业有限公司，更名为西洋储蓄所。2010年，相继开办石硐储蓄所和九庄储蓄所。

七、息烽县农村信用合作联社

1991年，全县25个乡镇均建有由农民入股、为入股社员服务的信用社，4个区建有区农村信用合作联社。1992年撤区并乡建镇，全县设10乡镇，4个区联社随之撤销，25个信用社合并为永靖镇、小寨坝镇、九庄镇、温泉镇、青山苗族乡、石硐乡、鹿窝乡、流长乡、养龙司乡、西山乡10个信用社。1993年2月，县信用合作联合社正式成立，内设人秘保卫股（履行办公室职责）、社务股、稽核股等机构，下辖10个独立核算的法人社和3个信用分社。1996年底，信用社与农业银行息烽县支行脱离隶属关系后，改由人民银行息烽县支行监管。

2003年12月，贵州省农村信用社联合社成立，息烽联社划归省联社管理。

2005年1月，县农村信用合作联社（简称县联社）挂牌营业。内设综合业务办公室、业务发展部、会计信息部、稽核审计部、监察保卫部、营业部等机构，下辖温泉、养龙司、小寨坝、流长、九庄、石硐、西山7个信用社和阳朗、文化路、永安、东风路、花园路5个信用分社。恢复鹿窝、青山营业网点。2010年，县联社设业务发展部、合规风险部、会计信息部、科技信息部、综合办公室、党委（理事会）办公室（人力资源部）、稽核审计部（事后监督中心）、纪检监察室、安全保卫部，下辖花园路分社、永靖分社、文化路分社、阳朗分社、西山信用社、青山分社、永安分社、石硐信用社、九庄信用社、鹿窝分社、流长信用社、养龙司信用社、温泉信用社、小寨坝信用社、营业部15个网点机构。

第二节　金融管理

一、中国银行业监督管理委员会贵州监管局息烽办事处

2003年12月22日，金融监管股从中国人民银行息烽县支行划出，成立息烽县监管组。2004年3月2日，息烽县监管组更名为中国银行业监督管理委员会贵州监管局息烽办事处（简称银监办）。银监办负责辖区内银行业金融机构的监督工作，重点对农村信用社及其联社、邮政储蓄机构进行现场和非现场检查，收集辖区内有关金融风险信息，以及完成省局交办的其他工作。

二、货币投放与回笼

金融机构发放（支付）现金的渠道有工资、奖金、劳务支出、行政事业费支出；收购工矿、农

副产品支出；发放贷款和支付储蓄存款；支付汇款和有价证券等。回笼（收回）现金的渠道有商品销售收入、服务事业收入、税款收入、储蓄存款收入及收回贷款、汇款、债券等收入。

1991—1995年，全县发行货币10.09亿元，回笼6.29亿元。回笼现金的主要渠道为储蓄存款、商品销售和服务事业收入现金。

1997年，受亚洲金融危机的冲击，国内经济增长速度减慢，投资和消费增长趋缓，市场有效需求不足，呈现出通货紧缩趋势。1998年起，采取扩大内需方针，实行财政政策和货币政策，保持市场物价稳定，促进国民经济持续稳定增长。1996—2000年，全县净投放货币7.57亿元，回笼现金2.36亿元。2001—2004年，全县净投放货币7.19亿元，回笼2.36亿元。

三、现金管理

1994年，人民银行息烽县支行组织县工商银行、农业银行、建设银行、农村信用联社对开户单位进行现金管理检查。检查中采取单位自查和各银行重点抽查相结合的方式，共抽查32个现管单位。发现违反《现金管理暂行条例》的现金坐支户6户，金额为14.6万元；超库限额3户，金额为4.8万元；白条抵库19户中共有117笔，金额为33.6万元。还发现一些单位财会人员业务素质低、财务管理制度不健全、账实不符、假借用途套取现金等情况。

1997年4月4日，中国人民银行总行下发《大额现金支付登记备案规定》的通知，要求凡办理现金收付业务的商业银行、农村信用联社都必须建立大额现金支付登记备案制度。人民银行省分行制定《贵州省大额现金支付登记备案实施办法》，明确大额现金支取只能通过基本存款账户办理，临时性存款账户和专用账户未经批准，不得办理现金支取。对金融机构违反《现金管理暂行条例》和《贵州省大额现金支付登记备案实施办法》，放松现金管理进行不正常竞争的，人民银行要给予限期改正、通报批评、罚款等处罚；对触犯刑法的，移送司法机关处理。

2001年4月，中国人民银行下发《关于进一步加强和改进现金管理有关问题的通知》，要求提高认识，转变现金管理的重点，合理控制现金投放，防止因现金过量投放引起物价上涨。

2005年12月，人民银行息烽县支行对辖区内5家金融机构的现金管理中大额现金支付等情况进行检查。辖区内金融机构对公支付大额现金270笔，金额3460万元；个人支取储蓄大额存款674笔，金额8419万元。其中农村信用联社1笔专用账户支现7万元，未按要求登记，责令其立即整改。

2006年6月，人民银行息烽县支行检查组对农行、信用联社现金管理执行情况进行检查。检查中发现对公支付大额现金130笔，金额1750万元；对个人储蓄存款支付大额现金92笔，金额125万元。这些大额支付未发现开户单位对大额现金提取放松管理的现象。检查中同时发现农行未严格执行大额现金支取台账登记制度，存在漏登个人储蓄大额现金支取10笔，金额160.3万元，漏登对公存款大额现金支取11笔，金额88.1万元，检查组根据《大额现金支付管理办法》有关规定，责令其限期整改。

四、金融市场管理

农村合作基金会的前身为“互助储金会”。1993年，互助储金会资金总额68.6万元，其中村民入股38.6万元，集体资助3.5万元，民政局有偿救灾款26.5万元。1994年5月，全县161个行政村已发展105个互助储金会，入户农户3100户。互助储金会经县民政局批准成立，由各乡（镇）民政股主管业务。1995年后，互助储金会逐步升级为由乡（镇）政府统一管理的农村合作基金会。

1996年，贵阳市农村金融体制改革领导小组下达《对当地农村合作基金会进行调查的通知》。人民银行息烽县支行于下半年对农村合作基金会金融化倾向进行专项调查。调查发现：

（一）股金存款化

股金进出自由，变相高息吸收存款。其中小寨坝镇基金会从1995至1996年7月共吸收股金554.5万元，而7月末股金余额只有222万元。违规吸收财政性存款，以高额利率回报，用“代管资金”名义，吸收乡、镇政府财政、教办、土管所等单位资金，按时间长短计息，月息3‰～12‰，一年定期利率16.8%，均高出金融机构利率2倍左右。

（二）收取高额资金占用费，高息进高息出

所谓资金占用费，实际就是变相放贷。但贷款利率比人民银行的贷款利率高出2.6～3.3倍。有3家基金会从1995年12月至1996年6月共放款60笔，但只有16笔属会员借款，其余皆为非会员借款，严重背离基金会运作原则。

（三）管理行政化

6家基金会、监事会成员或管委会主任大多由乡、镇党政领导兼任并管理行政。1997年，人民银行息烽县支行针对农村合作基金会分流资金潜在风险再次进行调查。调查发现全县所有基金会股金（存款）均多于各家农村信用社存款，基金会为保持收、存款的高息回报而滥放贷款，以致借款人不能如期归还本息，形成潜在风险。1999年，人民银行息烽县支行组织全县农村信用合作社配合当地政府清理整顿农村合作基金会。经清产核资，将符合国务院有关规定的农村合作基金会并入农村信用合作社。至2000年，妥善解决全县农村合作基金会退出市场的问题。

五、代理财政国库

20世纪90年代初，中国人民银行制定《关于提高银行办理国库经收业务管理办法》，规定各级国库经收的国库款项，须当日办理入库和报解；当日不能办理的，最迟于次日上午办理；库款金额不满300元的，月末扫数报解。凡不按规定时间和金额办理解缴，积压、占用国库款项的，每天按应缴金额的万分之三罚款。

1991—1995年，全县各专业银行共经收各级预算收入1.59亿元，其中中央预算收入1264.3万元、地方预算收入1.46亿元。

1996—2000年，经收各级预算收入4.76亿元，其中中央预算收入3140.3万元、地方预算收入4.45亿元。2001—2004年，经收各级预算收入10.2亿元，其中中央预算收入9181.6万元、地方预算收入9.27亿元。

2005年下半年，推进财政国库集中支付制度改革。至2006年，全县有近100家单位正式纳入县财政国库集中支付改革。息烽县率先成为贵阳辖区启动财政国库集中支付制度改革试点县。

2009年11月，人民银行息烽县支行抽调相关股室人员组成检查组，检查工商行、农行、农业发展银行、贵阳商行息烽县支行等金融机构的国库经收工作。检查中发现贵阳商行息烽县支行对企业缴纳税款未通过“待结算财政款项”科目过渡，检查组立即责令其整改。

2010年1月，息烽支库与县财政部门的集中支付业务联网。历时4年的国库集中支付业务手工操作结束。2010年末，人民银行共办理收入业务28717笔，实现预算收入6.54亿元，其中中央级预算收入1.11亿元、省级预算收入5109.17万元、地级预算收入480.85万元、县级预算收入4.87亿元。办理库款支拨业务8596笔，实现预算支出11.19亿元。

六、反洗钱监管

2005年10月，人民银行息烽县支行与县公安局协商制定《中国人民银行　息烽县公安局打击洗钱犯罪工作协调办法》，与县银监办协商制定《中国人民银行　中国银行业监督管理委员会贵州监管局息烽办事处反洗钱工作金融监管协调办法》，明确人民银行、县银监办和县公安局在反洗钱工作中各自应承担的职责。

2008年3月，成立县金融系统反洗钱工作领导小组，办公室设在人民银行。9月，领导小组对辖区内信用联社、工行、贵阳商行、农行、农发行、邮政储汇局6家银行业机构和财保公司、人保公司2家保险业机构反洗钱工作履行职责、反洗钱内控制度落实、客户身份识别、重点可疑交易报送、反洗钱信息保密等情况进行现场和非现场评价。发现以上机构存在缺乏专业培训、对部分大额、可疑交易识别能力不够、业务操作员对系统操作不熟悉等问题，以及反洗钱报表、报告存在迟报、漏报等现象。

2009年9月，人民银行息烽县支行抽调业务骨干和相关人员共4人组成检查组，对贵阳市商业银行息烽县支行反洗钱组织机构、内控制度建设及宣传培训等进行现场检查。发现商行未严格执行“联网核查身份信息核查系统”对个别客户身份进行有效识别，个别账户开户时间与人民币结算管理系统审批时间不符，以及大额交易有漏报现象等，检查组对此向商行息烽县支行提出警告，并在辖区内通报批评。

2010年9月，人民银行息烽县支行对县信用联社的反洗钱工作进行现场检查。检查中查阅单位银行结算账户77户、个人银行结算账户12382户；分析资金交易20笔，交易额1300万元。检查发现信用联社未严格对客户身份进行有效识别，未及时报备大额可疑交易等情况，人民银行息烽县支行对信用联社进行通报批评。

第三节　存、贷款业务

一、工商银行存、贷款业务

（一）存款

1991年，县工行存款余额20253万元。此后多年，存款余额逐步增长，至2001年，存款余额增至30534万元。2007年，存款余额40302万元。2010年，存款余额54906万元。

（二）贷款

1991年，县工行贷款余额7764万元。1993年，继续加大贷款力度，增加国有工业企业流动资金贷款。是年，贷款余额增至10361万元。1998年，县工行对有市场、有效益、有信誉、有还债能力的“四有”企业增加的贷款占新增工业贷款的90%以上。对已建立现代企业制度的息烽重钙厂、中国轻工业贵州化工冶金公司、贵州开磷集团息烽黄磷厂、息烽塑料制品厂、息烽电信局等企业贷款4118万元。是年，县工行贷款余额16055万元。2000—2004年，县工行继续对重钙厂给予贷款支持，5年间累计发放贷款27368万元和技改贷款5500万元。2004年，县工行贷款余额突破2亿元大关，为20764万元。2005—2009年，县工行工业贷款的投向重点是中化开磷化肥有限公司、贵州开磷合成氨有限责任公司、贵州西洋肥业有限公司。2010年，县工行贷款突破6亿元，为63203万元。

息烽县工商银行1991—2010年存、贷款余额统计表

表14-3-1　　单位：万元

年份	存款余额	贷款余额	年份	存款余额	贷款余额
1991	20253	7764	2001	30534	18332
1992	21625	8736	2002	31789	19045
1993	22764	10361	2003	32635	19366
1994	23213	12078	2004	33256	20764
1995	24574	13366	2005	35232	21138
1996	25839	14429	2006	37128	23786
1997	26477	15399	2007	40302	36476
1998	27383	16055	2008	44600	48270
1999	28987	17564	2009	57791	49705
2000	29467	18011	2010	54906	63203

二、农业银行存、贷款业务

（一）存款

1991年，县农行各项存款余额2472万元，其中企业存款418万元、农业存款443万元、集镇储蓄存款1507万元、其他存款204万元。此后，存款余额逐年增加。1998年，存款余额首次突破亿元大关，为10490万元，其中企业存款2699万元、城镇储蓄存款7023万元、农业存款195万元、其他存款573万元。2004年，各项存款余额22286万元，其中企业存款6929万元、机关团体存款3921万元、储蓄存款11002万元、农业存款13万元、其他存款391万元、同业存款（信用社）2146万元。次年，各项存款余额突破3亿元，为30248万元。此后数年，存款增势不减。至2010年，各项存款余额42727万元，其中个人存款22606万元、公司类存款20121万元（事业类存款5029万元、机关类存款10081万元）。

（二）贷款

1991年，县农行各项贷款余额2749万元，其中工业贷款49万元、商业贷款2013万元、个体工商业贷款6万元、乡镇企业贷款154万元、农业贷款491万元、信托贷款15万元、特种贷款21万元。代理人行贷款36万元。此后，贷款余额逐年大幅度增长或偶有减少。1996年，息烽县成为小额扶贫贷款（每户贷款金额2000元）试点县之一。县农行实行“五个不贷”（不是贫困户不贷、没有发展项目不贷、违反计划生育政策不贷、不实行5户联保不贷、不张榜不贷）原则，在鹿窝乡试点以家庭妇女为贷款对象的“孟加拉国模式”贷款失败；在青山苗族乡开展“中国式”贷款获得成功。是年，县农行农业贷款由上年的285万元增至611万元。1999年，县农行第二次发放农村小额扶贫贷款，仍采用“五个不贷”原则，在县内10个乡镇、23个贫困村3524户贫困户投放小额贷款。是年，农行各项贷款余额突破1亿元，为19392万元，其中短期贷款3907万元、中长期贷款6792万元、逾期类贷款8693万元、委托贷款35万元。2003年，各项贷款余额13418万元，其中工业贷款220万元、农业贷款12587万元（扶贫贴息贷款2287万元、扶贫贷款610万元、其他农业贷款9690万元）、私营企业及个体贷款227万元、个人住房贷款261万元。此后，除个别年份有小幅下降外，其余年份均呈增长态势。2010年，县农行各项贷款余额46896万元，其中公司类贷款42290万元、个人贷款4284万元、票据贴现322万元。

息烽县农业银行1991—2010年存、贷款余额统计表

表14-3-2　　单位：万元

年份	存款余额	贷款余额	年份	存款余额	贷款余额
1991	2472	2749	2001	18147	17801
1992	3336	3348	2002	14689	18313
1993	4022	3397	2003	18614	13418
1994	5333	2457	2004	22286	15156
1995	5875	3165	2005	30248	24320
1996	6397	4511	2006	25181	23299
1997	8185	4694	2007	30384	30874
1998	10490	6048	2008	36362	28895
1999	12474	19392	2009	33277	33164
2000	15402	18928	2010	42727	46896

三、中国农业发展银行息烽县支行存、贷款业务

（一）存款

农发行不开办储蓄存款业务，其存款来源主要为粮食风险基金专户存款、粮食补贴和销售回笼款、国资公司经营用划拨的存款等。1997年年底，各项存款金额1063万元。次年，存款余额69万元。此后存款有升有降，至2008年，存款余额升至5216万元。2010年，存款金额2265万元。

（二）贷款

农发行贷款余额主要为涉农项目贷款，其中包括农业产业化龙头企业贷款，政府融资平台涉农项目基础设施贷款等。1997年，贷款余额9055万元。此后多年，贷款余额2000万～3000万元。2006年3月，因贷款余额较小，会计结算业务划转到修文农发行代理。2008年，恢复会计结算业务。是年，贷款余额17567万元。2010年，贷款余额13303万元。

息烽县农发行1997—2010年存、贷款业务统计表

表14-3-3　　单位：万元

年份	存款余额	贷款余额	年份	存款余额	贷款余额
1997	1063	9055	2004	361	1878
1998	69	2833	2005	947	3988
1999	160	2910	2006	—	—
2000	246	2040	2007	—	—
2001	142	1771	2008	5216	17586.5
2002	362	2813	2009	2194.93	13803.5
2003	214	2377	2010	2265.37	13303.5

四、贵阳银行股份有限公司息烽支行存、贷款业务

（一）存款

2001年7月，贵阳银行息烽支行开始为县行政、事业单位办理代发工资业务。年末各项存款余额12326万元，其中储蓄存款余额1381万元。2004年，各项存款余额10242万元。2005年，各项存款余额17238万元。2006年，各项存款余额突破2亿元，为22671万元。其中储蓄存款7458万元，较上年增加41.57%。2008年，各项存款余额37160万元，其中储蓄存款余额14906万元，比上年增长25.2%，比开业初年增长979.36%。2010年，各项存款余额81804万元，比开业初年增长1954.16%。

贵阳银行息烽支行2001—2010年存款余额统计表

表14-3-4　单位：万元

年份	存款余额	同比增加	同比增长率（%）	其中储蓄存款余额	同比增加	同比增长率（%）
2001	12326	—	—	1381	—	—
2002	14826	2500	20.28	1649	268	19.41
2003	18777	3951	26.65	2434	785	47.6
2004	10242	-8535	-45.45	3742	1290	53
2005	17238	6996	68.31	5368	1526	40.78
2006	22671	5433	31.51	7458	2190	41.57
2007	29481	6810	30.04	11904	4446	59.61
2008	37160	7679	20.04	14906	3002	25.22
2009	53583	16423	44.19	23541	8635	57.93
2010	81804	28221	52.67	28368	4827	20.5

（二）贷款

2001年，贵阳银行息烽支行各项贷款余额2189万元，其中公司类贷款2000万元、个人类贷款198万元。2003年，各项贷款余额11758万元，其中向县国有资产投资管理有限公司发放贷款8000万元，向下岗失业人员发放贷款12万元，公司类贷款1684万元，贴现20万元。2008年，各项贷款余额增至22410万元，其中向下岗失业人员发放贷款37笔119万元，住房按揭180笔1287万元，其他个人贷款49万元，向县土地收购储备交易中心发放贷款2000万元，贴现1870万元，公司类贷款4002万元。2010年，各项贷款余额75275万元，其中向国有资产投资管理有限公司发放贷款1600万元，向县土地收购储备交易中心发放贷款2300万元，向下岗失业人员发放贷款244笔1927万元，住房按揭贷款471笔7686万元，新型农村养老保险贷款8145笔2813万元，个人贷款122笔1932万元，公司类贷款16192万元，贴现12560万元。

贵阳银行息烽支行2001—2010年贷款余额和贷款情况统计表

表14-3-5　　　　单位：万元

年份	贷款余额	其中					
		公司类贷款	个人类贷款	向国资公司贷款	向县土储交易中心贷款	向下岗失业人员贷款	住房按揭贷款
2001	2189	2000	198	—	—	—	—
2002	6910	4500	221	—	—	—	—
2003	11758	1684	—	8000	—	12	—
2004	11918	722	—	—	—	6	—
2005	14088	1000	—	—	—	2	18
2006	15676	2939	—	2000	—	—	718
2007	18575	4360	55	—	—	—	416
2008	22410	4002	49	—	2000	119	1287
2009	33070	8650	49	5200	—	708	2948
2010	75275	16192	1932	1600	2300	1927	7686

五、邮政储蓄业务

邮政储蓄分为定期与活期两种，利率以中国人民银行挂牌公布的利率为准，所存款项转存于县人行结算利息。1991年，储蓄余额8.81万元，其中定期6.35万元、活期2.46万元。此后逐年增加。1995年，储蓄余额1235.23万元。2005年突破亿元，为10614.67万元，其中定期8123.27万元、活期2491.4万元。2010年，储蓄余额16892万元，其中定期8302万元、活期8590万元。

息烽县1991—2010年邮政储蓄年末余额统计表

表14-3-6　　　　单位：万元

年份	储蓄额	其中		年份	储蓄额	其中	
		定期	活期			定期	活期
1991	8.81	6.35	2.46	2001	2830.69	2256.56	574.13
1992	33.65	22.42	11.23	2002	4185.07	3308.37	876.7
1993	52.21	31.47	20.74	2003	6830.37	5420.62	1409.75
1994	732.91	519.29	213.62	2004	8346.7	6401.18	1945.52
1995	1238.23	883.62	354.61	2005	10614.67	8123.27	2491.4
1996	1634.81	1030.48	604.33	2006	12012.78	8014.13	3998.65
1997	1881.3	1467.85	413.45	2007	10853.31	6368.13	4485.18
1998	1998.61	1468.46	530.15	2008	12076	7119	4957
1999	2292.14	1480.03	812.11	2009	15684	8106	7578
2000	2237.57	1597.01	640.56	2010	16892	8302	8590

六、农村信用合作联社存、贷款业务

（一）存款

1991年，农村信用合作联社期末存款余额867万元，其中农民储蓄242万元、集体存款49万元、乡镇企业存款27万元、其他存款549万元。1996年，农民储蓄2624万元、乡镇企业存款320万元，分别是1991年的10.8倍和11.85倍。至2003年，信用联社期末存款余额14869万元，其中农民储蓄突破亿元，为10620万元；乡镇企业存款3860万元。2007年，存款余额43843万元，其中农民储蓄33625万元、乡镇企业存款9728万元。2010年，存款余额77296万元，其中农民储蓄62395万元、乡镇企业存款13569万元。

（二）贷款

农村信用合作联社经过管理体制改革，进一步明确贷款以承包户、专业户（重点户）为主，以农业、养殖业为主，以流动资金为主的方针。

1991年，贷款余额1025万元。1998年，贷款余额升至3350万元，其中农户贷款2866万元，占贷款余额的85%；乡镇企业贷款244万元。比1991年增加10倍。由于允许信用联社与银行业务有交叉，允许发放工商贷款，农户贷款余额与其他贷款余额逐年快速增加。2005年，贷款余额21074万元。至2010年，贷款余额61552万元，其中农户贷款49356万元、乡镇企业贷款192万元、其他贷款12004万元。

息烽县农村信用合作联社1991—2010年存、贷款业务统计表

表14-3-7　　单位：万元

年份	存款余额	贷款余额	年份	存款余额	贷款余额
1991	867	1025	2001	8126	8320
1992	1114	1098	2002	10689	11386
1993	1388	1210	2003	14869	12889
1994	1973	1287	2004	21053	17140
1995	2667	1974	2005	31440	21074
1996	3484	2129	2006	36736	24793
1997	4529	2845	2007	43843	26083
1998	5745	3350	2008	49580	34409
1999	5806	4428	2009	61344	50036
2000	5910	5880	2010	77296	61552

第四节　保　险

一、机构

（一）中国财产保险有限公司息烽支公司

1991年，原人保息烽县支公司内设办公室、业务股、计财股。1997年5月，按照《保险法》，人保息烽支公司分设为中保集团财产保险有限公司息烽支公司和中保集团人寿保险有限公司息烽县支公司。1998年10月，撤销中保集团公司，恢复中国人民保险公司息烽县支公司称谓。2003年8月，

中国人民保险公司息烽县支公司更名为中国财产保险股份有限公司息烽县支公司（简称人保财险公司）。公司内设微机室、档案室、会议室、领导办公室、营业室。2004年，内设机构改为业务部、综合部，下辖小寨坝营业部。2010年，公司内设综合部、业务1部、业务2部，下辖小寨坝办公处。

（二）中国人寿保险公司息烽县支公司

1997年5月，中保集团人寿保险公司息烽县支公司由原人保息烽县支公司分设，内设办公室、营销部、服务部。2003年8月，中保集团人寿保险有限公司息烽县支公司更名为中国人寿保险股份公司息烽县支公司（简称寿保公司）。公司内设办公室、营销部、中介部、团险部。2010年，公司内设办公室、个险部、团险部、营保部、客户服务中心。

（三）中国平安保险股份有限公司息烽县支公司

1997年，中国平安保险股份有限公司息烽县支公司成立。公司内设培训部、经理室、办公室。

二、主要险种

（一）机动车辆保险

1991年，按原有规定对车辆保险，并实行第三者责任法定保险。未参加保险的车辆，公安交通监理部门和农村监理部门不予办理年审、过户、办照等手续，车辆不准上路行驶。1996年，《机动车辆保险条款》统一修订为《车辆保险附加保险条款》。1999年重新修订条款，使条款费率市场化。2003年年初，为进一步适应机动车市场需求，人保公司将费率个性化，统一费率分为《营运性机动车条款》《非营运性机动车条款》《家庭自用车条款》和《第三者条款》。2004年11月，对家庭自用车、营运机动车保险条款增加500元以下免赔额。2006年7月1日，开始办理机动车交通事故责任强制保险（简称“交强险”）。

（二）企业财产保险

人保公司息烽县支公司成立后，开办企业财产保险业务，同时增办企业财产保险附加盗窃险。1996年，人保总公司重新修订财产保险条款，将企业财产险分为“财产保险基本险”和“财产保险综合险”两部分，以及盗窃、机器损坏等若干附加险。

（三）货物运输保险

该险种依据人保公司颁发的《国内水路铁路货物运输保险条例》执行，为常年性保险项目。

（四）家庭财产保险

1991年，人保公司息烽县支公司依据《家庭财产保险条款》开展保险业务。2001年，推出《金锁系列家庭财产险》。2002年，推出“金牛家财险”“金锁家财险”“合家欢家财险”等系列险种。

（五）简易人身保险

该险种为人寿保险公司的稳定保险项目。1991年后，推出“福安康”两全保险。

（六）团体意外伤害保险

包括团体人身意外险、子女教育险、学生平安险、煤矿职工人身意外伤害险、锅炉压力容器及第三者责任特约险和游泳池人身意外险等。2007年2月至2008年12月，增加学生幼儿险和短期健康保险。

（七）养老金保险

20世纪90年代，人保公司、寿保公司、平安保险公司相继推出“福寿安康”保险、“养老还本”“鸿寿”养老金、“老来福”终身保险、“老有所养”年金保险等。

（八）农业保险

1991年，为全县烤烟进行统保，办理烤烟保险。1992年，为4万多户农民办理农房长效还本保险。1995年，为农村开办大牲畜保险。2003年，开办林木火灾保险和贷款房屋保险。2009年1月，开办能繁母猪保险，共投保政策性能繁母猪12637头。2010年，政策性能繁母猪保险停办。

（九）其他财产险

1996年实行财产与人寿保险分营后，人保息烽支公司依据《雇主责任保险条款》和《产品保险条款》开办雇主责任和产品险。3月，开办个人抵押房屋保险。1999年7月—2004年12月，相继开办供电责任险、医疗责任险、校园方责任险等。

人寿公司息烽县支公司开办“99鸿福险”“千禧理财”（分红型）、“康宁定期”“康宁终身”“鸿鑫两全”（分红型）、“福馨两全险”“祥和定期”“祥瑞还本”保险，以及人身意外伤害综合险附加住院医疗费保险和附加意外伤害医疗费用保险等。

平安保险公司息烽县支公司开办“养老保险”“子女教育保险”“投资理财保险”“医疗保险”“平安鸿利分红保险”等。

三、保费收入与理赔

（一）人保息烽县支公司

1991—1996年，人保息烽县支公司保费收入932万元，理赔1465件，理赔金额601.2万元。其中机动车险理赔1445件，理赔金额556.3万元。1997年5月，人保息烽支公司分设为中保集团财产保险有限公司息烽支公司和中保集团人寿保险公司息烽支公司，保费业务与理赔业务分开办理。

人保息烽县支公司1991—1996年保费收入和理赔统计表

表14-3-8　　单位：件、万元

年份	保费收入	理赔金额	理赔件数	其中机动车理赔	
				件数	金额
1991	61.9	38.8	154	146	27.1
1992	72.3	91.2	223	219	90.8
1993	72.4	97.2	260	257	92
1994	144.6	65.1	244	243	64.8
1995	290.4	81.7	275	274	81.5
1996	290.4	227.2	309	306	200.1

（二）人保财险息烽支公司

1997年，累计承保405笔，保费收入349万元，理赔377笔，理赔金额126.1万元，其中机动车险理赔124.3万元、企业财产险0.6万元、家庭财产险0.1万元、责任险1.1万元。此后多年，保费收入稳步增加，总赔付在200万元上下浮动。2004年，保费收入1004万元。理赔925笔，赔付金额461.92万元。2006年7月，机动车交通事故责任强制保险正式施行，保费大幅度增加。是年保费收入1192万元，机动车险赔付金额增至518.69万元。2010年，保费收入1142.4万元，总赔付金额473.4万元。

人保财险息烽支公司1997—2010年部分保费收入与理赔统计表

表14-3-9　　　　单位：件、万元

年份	财产保险		责任保险		货运保险		机动车保险	
	保费	赔付额	保费	赔付额	保费	赔付额	保费	赔付额
1997	49	0.6	67	1.1	—	—	230.6	124.3
1998	89	10	7.5	1.9	—	—	350.5	215.1
1999	59.6	0.6	6.4	4.4	86.7	—	263.6	171
2000	149.6	42.8	-2.7	10.9	31.8	—	255.5	171
2001	126.9	39.6	8.2	5.7	52.7	—	318.2	160.3
2002	—	—	—	—	—	—	520	—
2003	128.2	—	10.5	—	146.82	—	593.28	—
2004	128.5	—	—	—	152.2	—	631.8	461.92
2005	213.5	74	—	—	183.8	0.03	546.5	383.4
2006	—	—	—	—	54.39	—	1119.9	518.69
2007	280.1	27.6	2.66	—	180.6	1.2	548.5	411.4
2008	244.6	82.8	43.3	—	136.47	—	623.1	414.1
2009	274.8	34.8	36	5.4	64.62	—	534.3	283.7
2010	212.3	100.9	47.7	1	225.11	—	632.2	314.8

（三）中国人寿息烽支公司

1997年，人寿公司收保费10万元。理赔支付25笔，共5.2万元，此后，保费收入与理赔金额逐年增高。2005年，公司在个险、团体险和银保三个渠道同时开展业务，是年保费收入327.87万元，理赔支付146笔，共140万元。2008年，保费收入1335.87万元。2010年，团体险保费严重缩水，个险较往年有所下滑，保费收入1554.05万元。理赔支付160笔，共170.2万元。

人寿息烽支公司1997—2010年保费收入与理赔统计表

表14-3-10　　　　单位：件、万元

年份	保费收入	理赔		年份	保费收入	理赔	
		件数	金额			件数	金额
1997	10	25	5.2	2004	120	65	42.3
1998	20	—	10	2005	327.87	146	140
1999	40	—	24.9	2006	515.46	150	160.12
2000	58	50	30	2007	912.48	115	120.21
2001	68	58	35.3	2008	1335.87	121	109.08
2002	80	65	42.2	2009	1473.89	124	103.23
2003	100	70	40	2010	1554.05	160	170.2

第十五篇　综合经济管理

第一章　计划（规划）管理

1991—2010年，在统计、工商、安监、质监、物价、国土等经济管理机构的配合下，实现由过去单一的计划管理经济体制向商品经济体制的转换，经济建设取得快速发展。经过“八五”“九五”“十五”“十一五”4个经济建设5年计（规）划的实施，县内国民生产总值从1991年的1.62亿元增加到2010年的55.49亿元，生产总值增加34.25倍；工业总产值从1991年的6340万元增加到2010年的117.4亿元，增加185倍；农业总产值从1991年的1.06亿元增加到2010年的9.74亿元，增加9.2倍；县本级财政收入从1991年的1693万元增加到2010年的3.08亿元，增加18.19倍；农民人均经济收入从1991年的525元增加到2010年的5084元，增加9.68倍。

第一节　机　构

县计划委员会：1991年，县计划委员会（简称县计委）内设办公室、扶贫办公室、农业开发办公室。1995年，在机构改革中与县经济委员会合并。

经济体制改革委员会：1990年8月，经济体制改革办公室成立，1992年5月，经济体制改革办公室更名为县经济体制改革委员会。1995年12月，与县计委、县经委组建县计划与经济贸易局。

县发展改革经济贸易局：1991年，县经济委员会（简称县经委）内设政工科、财贸科、工交科、安全技术科、办公室。1995年，撤销县计划委员会、县经济委员会，合并组建县计划与经济贸易局。是年12月，经济体制委员会并入计划与经济贸易局。局设办公室、政工科、统计科、工业科、商贸科、财会科、体改委办公室。1997年6月，撤销县商业局，并入计划与经济贸易局。

2002年3月，县计划与经济贸易局更名为县发展计划与经济贸易局，局设办公室、发展计划科、经贸合作科、强县办公室（西部开发办公室）、安全监察科（安全生产委员会办公室）。2004年8月，县发展计划与经济贸易局更名为县发展改革局，局设办公室、发展规划科、经贸科（减轻企业负担办公室）、商务科（整顿和规范市场经济秩序办公室）、强县办公室、企业科。

2010年5月，县发展和改革局、县粮食局、物价局、科学技术局、乡镇企业局重新整合组建县发展改革经贸局。局设办公室、体改规划科、项目管理科、投资管理科、商务科、物价监督管理科、粮食流通科、综合执法科（商务执法大队）。

第二节　“五年计划”（规划）与完成情况

一、“八五”计划与完成情况

1991—1995年，是全县经济建设第8个“五年计划”时期。“八五”计划要求到1995年全县国民生产总值达到23465万元，平均年增长8%；工农业总产值达到22018万元，年均增长6.9%。其中工业总产值8626万元，年均增长8%；农业总产值13392万元，年均增长6%；财政收入2500万元；乡镇企业产值8940万元；粮食总产量6350万千克。

1995年，完成国内生产总值3.55亿元（现价），其中第一产业完成1.16亿元，第二产业完成1.37亿元，第三产业完成1.02亿元。是年，境内遭遇雹、水、旱、虫灾，特别是6月下旬，由于特大洪灾和39天伏旱，造成粮、烟减产。粮食总产48079吨，烤烟2808吨。油菜籽未受灾害影响，产量8384吨。农业总产值10291万元，比计划少3392万元。农民人均纯收入855元。乡镇企业总产值2.76亿元，五年间超计划18703万元，年均3740万元。工业总产值1.43亿元，完成计划的105.78%。财政收入1339.6万元，完成计划的100.72%，其中县级财政收入821万元。

二、“九五”计划与完成情况

1996—2000年，是全县经济建设第9个“五年计划”时期。“九五”计划要求2000年国民生产总值达到4.75亿元，年均增长10%，其中第一产业1.31亿元，第二产业13.5亿元，第三产业2.09亿元。工业总产值5.35亿元，年均增长30%；农业总产值1.31亿元，年均增长4%；乡镇企业总产值10.02亿元，年均增长30%；农民年人均纯收入1446元，年均增长10%。

2000年，完成国内生产总值74949万元（五年间超计划增长27449万元，年均增长5489万元）。其中第一产业增加值23179万元，第二产业增加值32340万元，第三产业增加值19430万元。人均国内生产总值3132元。农业总产值36831万元，五年间比计划增长23931万元，年均增长4786.2万元。粮食总产量76060吨，油菜籽总产量8453吨，烤烟总产量3047吨。工业总产值94642万元，五年间比计划增长41142万元，年均增长8228.4万元。乡镇企业总产值138826万元，五年间比计划增长38626万元，年均增长7725.2万元。财政收入9757.6万元，其中地方财政收入4073万元。城镇居民可支配收入4742元，农民人均纯收入1598元。

三、“十五”计划与完成情况

2001—2005年，是全县经济建设第10个“五年计划”时期。“十五”计划要求2005年国民生产总值达到160840万元。其中第一产业增加值31000万元，年均增长6%；第二产业增加值89600万元，年均增长22.6%；第三产业增加值40240万元，年均增长15.7%；人均国内生产总值6180元，年均增长14.5%；农业总产值4956万元；工业总产值293200万元，年均增长28.8%；本级财政收入9500万元；粮食总产量稳定在76000吨左右；农民人均纯收入2300元。

2005年，完成国内生产总值23.7亿元（现价），其中第一产业增加值3.4亿元，第二产业增加值15.1亿元，第三产业增加值5.2亿元。人均生产总值9073元。农业总产值完成5.17亿元，实现农民人均纯收入2372元。粮食总产量77216吨。乡镇企业增加值55545万元。完成工业总产值44.64亿元，其中规模以上工业总产值42.81亿元。完成非公有制经济固定资产投资6.28亿元。财政总收入首次突破2亿元大关，为2.39亿元，其中县级地方财政收入1.27亿元。城镇居民人均可支配收入8253元。

四、“十一五”规划与完成情况

2006—2010年，是全县经济建设第11个“五年规划”时期。“十一五”规划要求到2010年国民生产总值达到54.2亿元（现价），年均增长18%。其中第一产业增加值4.6亿元，年均增长6.5%；第二产业增加值39亿元，年均增长21%；第三产业增加值10.6亿元，年均增长15.3%。人均生产总值20070元，年均增长17.2%；农业总产值7.25亿元，年均增长7%；工业总产值136亿元，年均增长25%，其中规模以上工业总产值130亿元，年均增长25%；地方财政收入2.9亿元，年均增长18%；全社会固定资产投资22亿元；社会商品零售总额7.22亿元；城镇居民人均可支配收入1.21万元，年均增长8%；农民人均纯收入4180元，年均增长12%。

2010年，地方生产总值完成55.49亿元，为规划目标的102.38%，在2005年的基础上翻了一番。其中第一产业增加值完成6.43亿元，为计划目标的139.78%，年均增长13.7%；第二产业增加值完成36.22亿元，年均增长19.1%；第三产业增加值完成12.84亿元，年均增长19.7%。人均生产总值从2005年的9094元增加到23218元，为计划目标的115.68%，年均增长20.6%，达到3572美元。工业总产值完成117.4亿元，为计划目标的85.32%，在2005年的基础上翻一番。其中规模以上工业产值完成115.3亿元，为目标的88.69%。农业总产值完成9.74亿元，为目标的134.34%，年均增长13.5%。财政总收入完成5.5亿元，其中地方财政收入完成3.08亿元，再次突破3亿元。全社会固定资产投资完成50.1亿元，为目标的227.7%，5年累计固定资产投资153.39亿元，是“十五”计划累计投资的2倍多。招商引资到位资金19.18亿元，在2005年的基础上翻一番，年均增长18.3%，5年累计到位资金67.54亿元。社会消费品零售总额完成9.38亿元，为目标的129.92%，年均增长19.1%。农村居民人均纯收入5084元，为目标的121.63%，在2005年的基础上翻一番，年均增长16.3%。城镇居民人均可支配收入14680元，为目标的119.19%，年均增长12.2%。

第二章　统计管理

1992—2010年，息烽县先后组织实施全国第三产业普查、全国第一、二次农业普查、全国第三次工业普查以及全国第一次和第二次基本单位普查等多项重大普查工作。2000年和2010年，分别开展第五次、第六次全国人口普查工作。20年间，随着社会经济的发展和生产关系的变革，统计信息逐步成为社会经济的信息主体，在科学管理和决策中发挥重要作用。

第一节　机　构

1991—1995年，县统计局无内设机构。1996年，内设办公室、业务科和计算站。次年5月，内设机构调整为办公室、社会经济调查科、第三产业统计科、工业统计科、计算站。2002年3月，统计局内设机构改为办公室、综合统计科，同时建立统计执法队。2008年7月，撤销计算站，增设县能源统计站。2010年，县统计局内设科室改为办公室、第一产业统计科、第二产业统计科、第三产业统计科。

第二节　常规统计

一、农业统计

1991—1996年，农业统计延续农村经济、社会、科技和农、林、牧、副、渔生产“一套表”统计，实行以乡为总体的农产品产量抽样调查，用单位和人均产量推算全乡、全县产量。1997年，农业统计以适应新的国民经济核算体系需求的《农村增加值和净产值表》规范农村统计。表种分为两部分，一是乡镇统计表式，年报表共14个，用来统计农村建设、农业机械拥有量、农村电气化、化肥及农业科技推广，农、林、牧、副、渔业生产、收入分配等情况。二是统计计算表式，共11个表，用来统计、计算社会总产值、农业总产值、物质消耗、农村增加值暨收入税净产值及农村商业网点、收入分配等。

1998年，按照贵阳市加强农村统计服务功能的要求，在季报中组织实施农村经济主要指标统计制度，农业总产值中取消副业指标，将副业纳入农业产值中其他农业范畴。1999年，农村统计实行季报、年报制度，报表内容有秋冬播种面积、春耕面积、全年农作物播种面积、夏收作物实际产量、畜牧生产情况，农、林、牧、渔中的消耗和商品产值以及农产品、茶叶水果、林畜业生产情况等。农业总产值的计算采用产品法，即产品产量乘以单价。同年，按照贵阳市统计局要求，在农村统计年报制度中增加乡镇社会经济基本情况卡片，以增强乡镇统计的系统性和完整性。2003年10月，国家统计局下发通知，从2004年起正式实行新的农村发展速度计算方法，采用农产品价格指数缩减法计算农业发展速度，逐步取消不变价格农业总产值统计。2004年起，增加特色农业统计。

二、工业统计

1992年，国家统计局下发《改进工业经济评价考核指标的实施方案》，建立以工业增加值、工业销售产值为龙头的总量指标体系。调整后的工业统计定期报表《工业总产值及主要产品产量》月报中增加工业销售产值。1993年，在工业统计年报中首次增加工业增加值指标。从1998年起，工业统计取消实行多年的按隶属关系划分统计范围的方式，改为按产品销售收入500万元以上（简称规模以上）统计。2000年起，对规模以下工业企业实行每年两次抽样调查。同年，国家统计局决定不再编制2000年不变价格指数，继续1990年不变价格指数体系。2002年3月，省统计局、省经贸委、省计委联合下发《关于认真做好采用价格指数缩减法计算工业发展速度试行工作的通知》，开始用指数缩减法计算工业发展速度。2003年10月，省统计局转发国家统计局通知，正式取消试行多年用不变价来计算工业发展速度的方法。是年，恢复年报中取消多年的工业企业中间插入年调查表的方式，由规模以上工业企业填报，将生产法和分配法结合起来，计算工业企业增加值。对规模以下企业仍采取抽样调查。经过多年改革，工业统计基本形成全调查、抽样调查和必要的科学估算相结合的统计调查方法体系。

三、商业统计

1993年，商业统计（批发和零售业、住宿和餐饮业统计）实行重大改革，取消商品购、消、存数量统计，改为批发零售贸易统计，按零售额区分为小型、大中型批发零售贸易企业。对小型和个体批发零售贸易进行抽样调查。1998年，将“大中型批发零售贸易业”改为“限额以上批发零售贸易业”，“小型批发零售贸易业”改为“限额以下批发零售贸易业”。1999年，国家统计局第二次修订《国民经济行业分类及代码》，增加“食宿和餐饮业”门类，把食宿业、餐饮业分别改为批发零售贸易、餐饮业。2002年，增加非公有制经济社会商品零售总额季报。2005年，将批发零售贸易、餐饮业分别改为批发和零售业、食宿和餐饮业，实行以定期报表代替年报。

四、固定资产投资统计

1991—2010年，固定资产投资统计内容几经调整。

1996年，息烽县划入贵阳市，固定资产投资统计按照贵阳市要求进行，并增加500万元以上项目统计。1998年，将“城镇集体固定资产投资”半年报改为季报，“城镇和工矿区私人固定资产投资”由半年报改为季报。1999年，增加“国债项目投资统计基层标准表”年报。全社会固定资产投资总额包括基本建设、更新改造、房地产开发、城镇和工矿区私人建房、农村非农投资、个体、私营投资、新增固定资产统计等。50万元以下收集资料统计，并对数据进行评估。

2000年，县房地产开发逐渐起步，固定资产投资统计实行月报制，将计划总投资50万元及以上项目纳入固定资产投资统计，房地产开发从固定资产投资统计中分出，单独作为一个专业进行统计。统计的主要内容包括计划总投资和本年完成投资、商品房建设投资及销售情况、土地开发投资、土地开发面积、建筑面积和竣工面积、房地产开发经济效益等。报表分为月报和年报两种，年报增加财务状况表、非工业能源和信息化情况表。2002年，增加非公有制固定资产投资表，按季报送。

息烽县1991—2010年固定资产投资完成情况统计表

表15-2-1　　单位：万元

年份	全社会固定资产投资	增长速度（%）	其中			
			基本建设	更新改造	其他投资	房地产开发投资
1991	1465	—	—	—	—	—
1992	1927	34.54	—	—	—	—
1993	2733	41.83	—	—	—	—
1994	3165	15.81	—	—	—	—
1995	4015	26.86	—	—	—	—
1996	7680	91.28	—	—	—	—
1997	9692	26.2	—	—	—	—
1998	10957	13.05	—	—	—	—
1999	18541	69.22	4041	5040	9133	327
2000	23556	27.05	7353	9221	6672	310
2001	42718	81.35	7629	34440	649	680
2002	51322	20.14	13842	36406	1074	2343
2003	58023	13.06	13887	43194	1122	1824
2004	75088	29.41	33050	41057	981	3050
2005	109218	45.45	36949	54775	943	6535

续表

年份	全社会固定资产投资	增长速度（%）	其中			
			基本建设	更新改造	其他投资	房地产开发投资
2006	156474	43.27	62506	67551	3883	14609
2007	218642	39.73	66829	83172	11390	39988
2008	287184	31.35	42144	145000	16434	41745
2009	378464	31.78	124977	137217	25521	28819
2010	501043	32.39	164421	181048	24991	48869

五、物资统计

1991年，物资统计（包括工业产品销售、原材料供应、物资消耗定额、机电设备供应和物资经济效益指标等情况统计）。年报共10张表，主要由县及县以上全民、集体和其他所有制物资部门、供应机构、销售机构和全部大、中型工业企业填报。定期报表4张。1993年，国家年报制度改革，原材料、能源统计也发生变革，当年年报表减少到3张。1997年第三季度取消物资专业统计，能源消费与库存仅保留在工业和建筑两专业中。

六、劳动工资统计

1992年，年报中《城镇集体所有制单位全部职工数和工资及私营企业 城镇个体劳动者年末人数》改为《城镇集体所有制单位全部职工人数和工资》，免去原私营和个体的数据内容。1993年，年报实行“一套表”制度，劳动工资统计相关指标全部并入“一套表”。1994年，将职工分为合同制职工、正式职工、长期职工和临时职工，工资总额部分也相应发生变化，并在年报中填报《城乡劳动力资源平衡表》。1996年，年报中增设“下岗职工人数”和“下岗职工生活费”指标，并从是年起将劳动工资统计月报改为季报。1997年，年报中增加“享受养老保险职工年末人数”“全年上交养老保险累计金额”“享受失业保险职工年末人数”“全年上交失业保险累计金额”等反映劳动保险方面的指标。1998年，年报不再填报“城乡劳动力资源配置情况”，同时删除年报中关于下岗职工和劳动保险方面的指标，划归劳动部门统计。报表中“职工”划分为“在岗职工”和“离开本单位仍保留劳动关系的职工”两部分，以及其他从业人员。

七、国民经济平衡统计

1993年，正式用国内生产总值取代国民收入指标。1997年，贵阳市建立第三产业统计报表制度，按季报送第三产业统计报表。县统计局开始试算国内生产总值季报，同时在年报中开始计算第三产业总产出，将社会总产值计算改为更全面反映第三产业产出社会总产出指标。2004年，经国家统计局批准，地方国内生产总值改为地方“生产总值”（简称GDP），并对各地区的GDP进行质量评估。

八、其他统计

1992年，综合统计取消国民经济和社会发展基本情况的填写，改用数据库资料替代。重要指标有人口、土地面积、农业、工业、乡镇企业、社会商品零售总额、客运量、邮电业务总量、教育、卫生、财政、金融等12项。1996年3月，在贵阳城调队指导下开始进行物价调查。建立物价调查卡片和台账，计算消费价格总指数和商品零售价格指标等。1997年，在贵阳市统计局统一安排下，息烽县开始执行第三产业统计报表制度。统计范围为辖区内所有第三产业企业、事业、行政单位和社会团体。适时开展财政金融统计（该项统计由财政、银行、税务等部门进行，县统计局按月收集）和社会基本情况统计（主要包括文化、教育、卫生、广播电视、公安、计划生育、气象等。统计数据由业务主管部门按系统制定方案组织实施）。

第三节　专项普查

一、农业普查

（一）第一次全国农业普查

1996年5月5日，县农业普查领导小组成立。6月，从政府办、农业局、乡企局、国土局、水电局、民政局等单位抽调人员组建县农普办，乡、村两级相应成立普查机构。12月31日24时为普查的标准时间，普查内容共38个项目，678个指标。农业普查表分《农村住房调查表》和《乡镇非农企业基本情况卡片》两部分。其中《农村住房调查表》内容包括家庭成员及其从业情况、农业用地、农作物种植、牲畜与家禽、农业科技应用、房屋及建筑物、住房经营类别七部分。《乡镇非农企业基本情况卡片》调整除农业企业以外的各种经济类型的乡（镇）办、村办、村民小组办、联产办和个体等乡镇企业。

贵阳市农普办确定永靖镇的阳朗、老街、立碑、后坝、猫洞、上洪马、下洪马、河丰、南门、龙爪10个村为市级试点单位。县内10乡镇领导和县、乡两级农普办工作人员共104人参加市级普查试点工作。在试点基础上，县农普办将全县4镇6乡划分为164个普查区、1480个普查小区，选聘普查员824人、指导员165人，开展人员培训和宣传动员工作。1997年2月，经过调查摸底和普查登记，各乡镇开始逐级手工汇总数据。1997年10月，普查资料录入、审核、汇总工作结束。

（二）第二次全国农业普查

2005年12月19日，县政府办公室下发《关于开展第二次全县农业普查的通知》，并成立第二次农业普查领导小组。下设农业普查领导小组办公室（简称县农普办）。办公室下设综合业务组、宣传文秘后勤保障组、数据处理组、质量控制与检查组。

2006年1月1日至12月31日为时期指标。住户普查表有19个大项，166个指标；单位普查表有13个大项，211个指标；乡镇普查表有8个大项，97个指标；行政村普查表有10个大项，95个指标。此外，住户普查表中集体户人口情况，共有5套8张表，569个指标。增加的乡镇和行政村普查表中，包括交通、电力、文化、教育、市场、医疗卫生机构、敬老院、农技推广服务，增加社会保障如养老保险、合作医疗、扶贫、救济等项目。

2006年10月20日，县第二次农业普查领导小组组长佘龙与贵阳第二次农业普查领导小组组长罗筑云签署第二次农业普查目标责任书。全县选聘普查指导员161名，普查员904名，并选派县、乡农普办31名人员参加省、市培训。在县、乡两级普查人员培训后，县农普办开展农业普查宣传活动。12月31日24时为全国第二次农业普查标准时点。普查活动中共发放《致农业普查农村住户一封信》1万余份，办宣传专栏322期，张贴宣传画和《全国农业普查条例》1500张。

2007年1月1日，全县第二次农业普查登记工作全面展开。经过清查摸底，全县农业普查涉及农业生产经营4.57万余户，涉农单位39家，10个乡镇161个行政村，1477个村民小组。1月15日，入户登记结束。2007年3月，由县农普办和乡镇农普办共同进行编码，历时一个月，农普编码工作结束。

二、经济普查

（一）第一次全国经济普查

2004年5月31日，县政府发布《关于组织开展第一次经济普查工作的通知》，成立县第一次全国经济普查领导小组，下设办公室在县统计局。10月9日，办公室下设业务组、数据处理组、后勤组。各乡镇分别成立乡镇经济普查工作领导小组和办公室。按第一次全国经济普查领导小组统一部署，2004年12月31日为第一次全国经济普查的标准时点。第一次全国经济普查表式有：法人单位基本情况表、产业活动单位基本情况及附表、规模以上工业6张表、规模以下工业3张表，建筑业、房地产、物业管理、交通运输、电信业分别填报2张表，以及限额上、下批发零售业财务状况、住宿、餐饮业填报企业经营状况、服务业财务状况、行政事业单位财务状况、个体经营户上报经营状况汇总表等。铁路、邮政、银行、保险、证券等行业由铁道部、国家邮政局、人民银行、保监会、证监会上报。10月1日至12月1日，县第一次经济普查领导小组组织开展单位清查。参加清查的基层普查员共147人，县直各单位配合清查的工作人员200余人。清查中共收清查表1000余份，个体经营户清查登记共发放普查表7500份。至12月1日，单位清查工作全面结束，共清查县法人单位644个、产业活动单位291个、个体户6207户。

2005年12月30日，县第一次经济普查领导小组办公室发布第1、2号经济普查主要数据公报，第一次经济普查工作结束。经第一次经济普查统计：2004年年末，全县从事第二、三产业的法人单位616个。其中，企业法人单位162个、机关事业法人单位259个、社会团体法人单位9个、其他法人单位186个；产业活动单位785个，其中从事第二产业97个、从事第三产业688个；个体经营户6779户，其中从事第二产业的733户、从事第三产业的6046户。个体经营户较为集中的5个行业分别是：工业710户，占个体户总数的10.47%；交通运输业1598户，占总数的23.57%；批发、零售业3145户，占总数的46.39%；住宿、餐饮业503户，占总数的7.22%；居民服务和其他服务业428户，占总数的6.31%。第二、三产业就业人员26579人，其中，第二产业就业人员11105人、第三产业就业人员15474人。就业人员中，单位就业人员16879人，占63.5%；个体经营人员9700人，占36.5%。在单位就业人员中，女性5201人，占30.81%。第二、三产业162个企业法人单位实收资本总额1121465万元。总额中由国家投入的资本448106万元，占39.96%；集体投入的资本26141万元，占2.33%；个人投入的资本193682万元，占17.27%；法人资本453536万元，占40.44%。工业企业法人单位92个，就业人员9399人。工业个体经营户710户，就业人员1794人。在工业企业法人单位中，国有企业14个、集体企业5个、私营企业48个、其他企业25个。在工业企业法人单位就业人员中，国有企业1320个、集体企业52个、私营企业2071个、其他企业5956个。建筑业法人企业单位4个，就业人员497人。建筑业个体经营户23户，就业人员212人。建筑业企业法人单位中，国有股份制合作企业1个、集体企业1个、其他有限责任公司2个。建筑业企业法人单位中，房屋和土木工程建筑业占75%，建筑安装业占25%。建筑业企业法人单位建筑总产值2944万元，其中，资质内企业完成2170万元，资质外企业完成774万元。建筑业个体经营户经营收入934.27万元。在建筑业企业法人单位的建筑总产值中，房屋和土木工程建筑业占77.62%，建筑安装业占22.38%。

息烽县2004年工业企业法人单位和就业人员行业分布统计表

表15-2-2

指标名称	企业（个）	平均人数（人）	指标名称	企业（个）	平均人数（人）
合计	92	9399	无机酸制造	1	19
采矿业	28	2159	肥料制造	11	4060
煤炭开采和洗选业	20	1705	磷肥制造	9	1456
非金属矿采选业	8	454	复混肥料制造	2	2604
土砂石开采	5	52	中成药制造	3	810
耐火土石开采	1	11	塑料制品业	2	480
黏土及其他土砂石开采	4	41	非金属矿物制品业	14	502
化学矿采选	2	401	水泥制造	2	228
其他非金属矿采选	1	1	铝冶炼	1	77
制造业	61	6938	水泥制品制造	1	15
农副食品加工业	6	63	砼结构构件制造	1	15
食品制造业	5	248	砖瓦、石材及其他建筑材料制造	10	244
调味品、发酵制品制造	4	247	金属制品业	3	20
酱油、食醋及类似制品制造	1	46	结构性金属制品制造	1	5
其他调味品、发酵品制造	2	69	金属结构制造	1	5
机制纸及纸板制造	5	57	不锈钢及类似日用金属制品制造	2	15
本册印制	1	9	金属制厨用器皿及餐具制造	2	15
化学原料及化学制品制造	18	4658	电力、燃气及水的生产和供应业	3	302
基础化学原料制造	4	445	水生产和供应业	2	57

息烽县2004年主要工业产品产量统计表

表15-2-3

主要产品	计量单位	本年生产量	主要产品	计量单位	本年生产量
原煤	吨	511485.65	磷肥	吨	121967.7
磷矿石（p2o530%）	吨	254794	普通过磷酸钙（p2o5100%）	吨	77128.54
毛油（初榨植物油）	吨	1333.7	重过磷酸钙（p2o5100%）	吨	44839.2
精制食用植物油	吨	397.39	合成复合肥料（实物量）	吨	738381.6
其中：大豆精制油	吨	275.45	磷酸铵肥料（含一铵、二铵）	吨	195364.4
菜籽精制油	吨	121.94	硝酸磷肥	吨	501256.5
机制纸及纸板	吨	1047.95	其他合成复合肥料	吨	41760.7

续表

主要产品	计量单位	本年生产量	主要产品	计量单位	本年生产量
硫酸（折100%）	吨	505349.98	中成药	吨	2937.71
盐酸（含量31%）以上	吨	198246.15	塑料编织袋	吨	2810.63
磷酸（含量85%）	吨	499569.35	水泥	吨	79927
沉淀硫酸钡	吨	1960	原铝（电解铝）	吨	110757
氯化钡	吨	6891	发电量	吨	627.04
黄磷	吨	5834.8	自来水	吨	137
合成氨	吨	45357.57	水泥电杆	吨	3813
氮肥（折含氮100%）	吨	41760.7	水泥预制构件	吨	59467.14
氯化铵（N1100%）	吨	41760.7	砖	吨	3018.45

息烽县2004年工业企业分品种能源消费统计表

表15-2-4

名称	计量单位	消费总量	名称	计量单位	消费总量
原煤	吨	210108.7	汽油	吨	704.86
洗精煤	吨	7154.01	煤油	吨	21.53
型煤	吨	11489.23	柴油	吨	2659.89
焦炭	吨	35	电力	万千瓦时	61652.91

（二）第二次全国经济普查

2008年4月，县政府下发《关于开展第二次全县经济普查的通知》，成立县第二次全县经济普查领导小组，下设办公室在县统计局。是年6月，各乡镇相应建立普查领导小组和办公室。2008年12月31日，为第二次全国经济普查的标准时间点。普查的主要内容包括单位基本属性、从业人员、财务状况、生产经营情况、生产能力、能源消耗、科技活动等。至2009年10月底，完成普查登记及数据处理工作。2010年6月25—28日，县第二次经济普查领导小组办公室对外先后发布第1号、第2号、第3号经济普查主要数据公报，第二次经济普查工作结束。

经第二次经济普查统计：2008年末，全县有从事第二、三产业法人单位686个，其中，企业法人单位173个，机关、事业法人单位299个、社会团体法人单位26个、其他法人单位188个；产业活动单位170个，其中第二产业8个、第三产业162个。在法人单位中，内资企业684个，占全部法人单位的99.7%；外资企业2个，占0.3%。共有个体经营户7159户。永靖镇个体经营户占比重最大，为2553户；其次是小寨坝镇1192户；以下依次为九庄镇734户、温泉镇709户、流长乡502户、养龙司乡477户、石硐乡447户、西山乡270户、鹿窝乡176户、青山苗族乡99户。第二、三产业从业人员26541人，其中第二产业从业人员7852人、第三产业从业人员18689人。从业人员中，单位从业人员15598人，占58.8%；个体经营人员10943人，占41.2%。单位从业人员中，制造业5281人，占33.9%；建筑业272人，占1.7%；公共管理和社会组织3146人，占20.2%；批发和零售业491人，占3.1%；教育2284

人，占14.6%。单位从业人员中，具有研究生以上学历的51人，占0.3%；具有大学本科及大专学历的6009人，占39.5%；具有高、初中学历的9538人，占61.1%；具有高级技术职称的177人，占4.7%；具有中级技术职称的1135人，占30.3%；具有初级职称的2432人，占65%；高级技师35人，占3.4%；技师142人，占13.9%；高级工205人，占20%；中级工2641人，占62.7%。第二、三产业企业法人单位资产总额6691087万元。其中，国有企业440606万元，占6.7%；有限责任公司3295617万元，占50%；股份有限公司14708万元，占0.2%；集体企业25194万元；股份合作企业1062571万元；私营企业1758925万元；其他企业10万元。

个体经营户较为集中的5个行业：批发和零售业3436户、交通运输业1409户、住宿餐饮业711户、居民服务和其他服务业723户、工业479户。

工业企业法人单位82个，年末从业人员9098人。其中，国有企业12个，占14.63%；股份合作企业1个，占1.22%；其他有限责任公司14个，占17.1%；私营企业50个，占60.98%。工业企业法人单位资产合计819710万元，负债合计521448万元，所有者权益298262万元。主营业务收入829310万元，其中采掘业占4.41%，制造业占90.1%，电力、燃气及水的生产和供应业占5.49%。营业利润19107万元，其中，采矿业占14.86%，制造业占84.63%。

建筑业法人企业单位4个，从业人员272人。其中，国有企业2个，其他有限责任公司2个。房屋和土木工程建筑业占50%、建筑安装业占25%、建筑装饰业占25%。建筑总产值5527.5万元。其中，资质内企业2823.3万元、资质外企业2704.2万元。建筑总产值中，房屋和土木工程建筑业占53.3%、建筑安装业占45.9%、建筑装饰业占0.8%。总承包和专业承包建筑业企业房屋建筑竣工面积55060平方米，竣工价值2587.8万元。其中住宅建筑面积4.97万平方米，竣工价值2335.9万元。

交通运输、仓储和邮政业企业法人单位10个，从业人员372人。其中，道路运输业3个，从业人员23人；水上运输业2个，从业人员27人；装卸、搬运和其他运输服务业3个，从业人员303人；仓储业1个，从业人员14人。营业收入3620.7万元。

批发和零售企业法人单位36个，其中批发业24个、零售业12个，从业人员491人。资产总计9141.5万元。其中，批发业资产8042.2万元、零售业资产1099.3万元。主营业务收入31116万元，其中，批发业29659.2万元、零售业1456.8万元。

住宿和餐饮业企业法人单位4个，从业人员66人。其中，住宿业3个，从业人员46人；餐饮业1个，从业人员20人。资产总计686.7万元。其中，住宿业456.7万元、餐饮业230万元。

房地产企业20个，从业人员642人。其中，房地产开发业19个，从业人员345人；物业管理企业1个，从业人员297人。

其他第三产业的法人单位534个，从业人员7301人。其中，企业法人单位21个，从业人员513人；行政事业及其他非企业法人单位513个，从业人员6791人。营业收入3365.6万元，营业利润56.2万元。

其他第三产业中的行政事业单位和其他非企业法人单位固定资产原值3.92亿元，全年收入7.49亿元，全年支出6.7亿元。

息烽县2008年工业企业法人单位和从业人员统计表

表15-2-5

分　类	企业单位数（家）	所占比重（%）	年末从业人员数（人）	所占比重（%）
总计	82	100	9098	100
内资企业	81	98.79	9089	99.9
国有企业	12	14.63	1215	13.35
股份合作企业	1	1.22	523	5.75
有限责任公司	16	19.51	3872	42.56
国有独资公司	2	2.44	406	4.46
其他有限责任公司	14	17.07	3466	38.1
股份有限公司	2	2.44	88	0.97
私营企业	50	60.98	3391	37.27
私营独资企业	35	42.68	836	9.19
私营合作企业	8	9.75	337	3.7
私营有限责任公司	6	7.32	2212	24.31
私营股份有限公司	1	1.22	6	0.07
外资企业	1	1.22	9	0.1

息烽县工业企业法人单位和从业人员行业分布统计表

表15-2-6

分　类	企业单位数（家）	年末从业人员人数（人）	所占比重（%）
总计	82	9098	100
采掘业	19	1725	18.96
煤炭开采和洗选业	13	1393	15.31
有色金属矿采选业	1	1	0.01
非金属矿采选业	4	305	3.35
其他采矿业	1	26	0.29
制造业	56	7224	79.4
农副食品加工业	3	23	0.25
食品制造业	4	183	2.01
饮料制造业	5	29	0.32
木材加工及木、竹、藤、棕、草制品业	1	54	0.59
造纸及纸制品业	3	36	0.4
印刷业和记录媒介的复制	1	6	0.07

续表

分类	企业单位数（家）	年末从业人员人数（人）	所占比重（%）
化学原料及化学制品制造业	12	5245	57.65
医药制造业	4	358	3.93
塑料制品业	3	558	6.13
非金属矿物制品业	12	446	4.9
有色金属冶炼及压延加工业	3	241	2.65
金属制品业	2	17	0.19
通用设备制造业	1	1	0.01
交通运输设备制造业	1	8	0.09
电气机械及器材制造业	1	19	0.21
电力、燃气、水的生产和供应业	7	149	1.64
电力、热力的生产和供应业	2	87	0.96
燃气生产和供应业	1	1	0.01
水的生产和供应业	4	61	0.67

息烽县2008年主要工业产品产量统计表

表15-2-7

产品名称	计量单位	本年生产量
塑料制品	吨	6811.22
磷矿石（折含五氧化二磷30%）	吨	153034
黄磷	吨	22772.79
中成药	吨	4413.96
十种有色金属	吨	6987
原铝（电角铝）	吨	6987
硫酸（折100%）	吨	152635
合成氨（无水氨）	吨	80831
农用氮、磷、钾化学肥料总计（折纯）	吨	850125.33
氮肥（折含N100%）	吨	238072.18
磷肥（折五氧化二磷100%）	吨	612053.15
合成复合肥料（实物量）	吨	399223.13
发电量	万千瓦时	387
精制食用植物油	吨	942
水泥熟料	吨	50978.41
水泥	吨	60700

息烽县2008年工业企业主营收入和营业利润行业分布统计表

表15-2-8　　单位：万元

分　类	主营业务收入	营业利润	收入所占比例（%）	利润所占比例（%）
总计	829310	19107	100	100
采掘业	36566	2840	4.41	14.86
煤炭开采和洗选业	11972	2534	1.44	13.26
非金属矿采选业	24094	286	2.91	1.5
其他采矿业	500	20	0.06	0.1
制造业	747199	16171	90.1	84.63
农副食品加工业	36	3	0	0.02
食品制造业	6352	307	0.77	1.61
饮料制造业	71	3	0.01	0.02
木材加工及木、竹、藤、棕、草制品业	79	57	0.01	0.3
造纸及纸制品业	149	−8	0.02	−0.04
印刷业和记录媒介的复制	16	3	0	0.02
化学原料及化学制品制造业	663796	10725	80.04	56.13
医药制造业	49556	6240	5.98	32.66
塑料制品业	9753	18	1.18	0.09
非金属矿物制品业	3063	588	0.37	3.08
有色金属冶炼及压延加工业	12997	−1809	1.57	−9.47
金属制品业	933	77	0.11	0.4
交通运输设备制造业	398	−34	0.05	−0.18
电力、燃气及水的生产和供应业	45545	97	5.49	0.51
电力、热力的生产和供应业	44974	181	5.42	0.95
水的生产和供应业	571	−85	0.07	−0.44

三、第三产业普查

1993年3月18日，县第三产业普查协调小组及办公室成立。11月6日，全县第三产业普查工作会召开，普查工作启动。1991年和1992年为第三产业普查年份。经过清理单位、调查登记、质量验收、数据处理、资料分析，1995年2月23日，发布《息烽县第三产业规模与水平》《息烽县第三产业经济类型》《息烽县第三产业行业状况》等报告。经过普查，县1992年第三次产业单位761个，从业人员12861人，分别比1991年增加2.28%、7.21%；城乡个体户2846户，比1991年增长19.08%。

四、工业普查

1995年5月9日，县第三次工业普查领导小组及办公室成立。9月28日，召开全县工业普查工作会，第三次工业普查工作正式启动。普查对象为县境内全部工业和附营工业企业生产活动单位，包括村办工业、个体工业、合作经营工业。是年年底，经过普查，有乡及乡以下工业企业85个，其中独立核算工业企业71个（国有企业13个，其中省属1个、县属12个）、非独立核算工业企业14个。工业企业从业人员3030人，其中工程技术人员171人。县乡及乡以上工业企业工业总产值7421.9万元（90价），独立核算单位工业增加值2955.75万元。

五、基本单位普查

（一）全国第一次基本单位普查

1996年8月8日，县政府发出《关于做好全县第一次基本单位普查的通知》，同时成立领导小组及办公室。10月24日，县普查办到开阳县参加普查试点工作。11月，办普查工作人员培训班4期。12月普查工作结束。经过普查，全县法人单位444个，其中乡产业法人单位83个（不包括村民委员会）、产业活动单位522个。

（二）全国第二次基本单位普查

2001年9月30日，为普查标准时间点；2000年10月1日至2001年9月30日，为时期指标。2001年10月29日，县政府办公室下发《关于成立息烽县第二次基本单位普查领导小组的通知》，普查领导小组及办公室成立。2001年10月19日，召开全县基本单位普查培训会，普查工作启动。8月底，普查登记和数据处理工作结束。经过普查，全县共有法人单位579个、产业活动单位343个、有证个体经营户2744户。

六、人口抽样调查

（一）全国1%人口抽样调查

1995年3月，县政府成立全国1%人口调查领导小组办公室，具体组织实施调查工作。调查涉及县内1286户家庭、4个集体户，共5134人。10月1日正式入户登记，10月10日登记结束。12月15日，通过安顺地区1%人口抽样调查办公室评估验收。

2004年，根据贵州省1%人口抽样调查小组办公室抽样实施方案，县内9个乡镇、45个调查小区被抽中，总户数1511户，摸底现有人数4598人，户口在本地的外出人员1488人。调查表分为户记录和人记录，其中户记录调查事项20项、人记录35项。11月1日开始入户登记，10月登记结束。经过复查、编码和手工汇总，12月1日，报表上报市1%人口抽样调查办公室。

（二）人口变动抽样调查

2003年10月9日，市统计局对10个区（市、县）人口变动抽样调查作统一部署。息烽县被抽中31个调查小区，调查户数1754户，人口5969人。11月1—10日为调查登记阶段，16—28日为资料编码阶段，12月28日至2004年1月28日为数据编审、汇总阶段。2003年以后，该项工作每年进行一次。

（三）劳动力抽样调查

2006年，实施劳动力调查制度，2007年起每年进行四次。调查样本由国家在1%人口抽样调查的样本框中抽取。

七、农村住户经济调查

（一）县级农村住户经济调查

1999年，全县有西山乡猪场村、永靖镇新萝村、马当田村、养龙司乡蚂蟥村、九庄镇天鹅村、鹿窝乡马坉村、石硐乡石硐村、流长乡大水井村等8个农村经济调查点。2001年，鹿窝乡马坉村改名为田坝村。

农经住户调查表经过汇总，产生11个汇总表，1450个指标，包括农村住户基本情况、生产情况、产品出售情况、粮食收支情况、总收入、纯收入和可支配收入、总支出情况、现金收支情况、生活消费现金支出结构、购买生产资料情况、消费品总支出情况等11项内容。

（二）乡级农村住户经济调查

1996年，县统计局在已有的8个农经点的基础上延伸30个农经点，平均每个乡镇3个点，每个点10户。调查内容和调查方法与县农经点相同。1997年，因经费原因，农经点减为20个共200户，每个乡镇20户。2003年，县统计局帮助各乡镇安装计算机录入程序，调查数据由各乡镇自行编码、录入。

（三）农村贫困监测

1997年，县利用原8个农经调查点开展农村贫困监测。贫困监测共5个表式：《国家重点扶持贫困县统计监测报表》《社区基本情况调查表》《调查户家庭成员个人情况调查表》《住户基本情况调查表》《住户收支情况调查表》。5个表式共307个指标，每年1月10日送市统计局审核后再报省统计局。

八、人口普查

（一）第五次全国人口普查

第五次全国人口普查标准时间为2000年11月1日0时。普查涉及人口增长、家庭人口、性别构成、年龄构成、民族构成、受教育程度、城乡人口7个方面49个项目。

2000年5月，以行政区划名录清理为基础，将全县分为169个普查区，763个普查小区。经过对普查人员的培训、测试以及试点普查，11月1日，开始进行普查登记工作。是日零时，全县总人口22.15万人，其中男性11.73万人，占总人口的52.96%；女性10.42万人，占总人口的47.04%。11月10日，普查登记结束。11月15—25日，普查领导小组办公室开展人口、出生人口、死亡人口和外出人口4个指标的复查工作。12月20日，完成人口普查数据手工汇总工作。

2001年5月，在《息烽报》发布《息烽县第五次人口普查公报》（第一号）。2002年6月28日，公布《息烽县第五次人口普查公报》（第二号），普查工作结束。

（二）第六次全国人口普查

第六次全国人口普查以2010年11月1日为标准时点。普查涉及人口增长、家庭户人口、性别构成、年龄构成、民族构成、受教育程度、城乡人口、人口的流动性8个方面63个项目。

2009年9月，成立县第六次人口普查领导小组及办公室。办公室设在县统计局。常务副县长担任领导小组组长，统计局局长担任办公室主任，成员由各乡镇、有关单位主要负责人组成。普查中，将全县划分为166个普查区，1005个普查小区，选调普查指导员268人、普查员1164人。2010年9月14—16日，完成全县普查指导员综合业务培训。至10月13日，完成对各乡镇普查员的培训工作。11月1日开始普查登记。

经过普查，全县普查时点的常住人口212897人，与2000年11月1日0时的第五次人口普查221583人相比，10年间共减少8686人，减少率3.93%。2009年11月1日至2010年10月31日，全县平均常住人口21.22万人，年均出生人口2965人，出生率13.97‰。年均死亡人口1369人，死亡率6.45‰。自然增长人口1596人，自然增长率7.52‰。全县常住人口共有家庭7.4万户，家庭人口20.92万人，平均每个家庭人口2.83人。

第四节　统计执法检查

1991年，县统计局首次对县邮电局违反统计法有关规定进行处罚。1994年6月，县人大和县政府牵头成立统计执法领导小组，对全县有关单位进行统计法规执行情况大检查，历时1个月。8月，县统计局执法领导小组对永靖镇、养龙司乡统计违法行为进行通报处理。1997年5月，县统计局对个别单位拒报统计资料进行通报。6月，县政府办公室组织开展统计执法大检查，并制定实施计划。7月8日，县统计执法大检查业务培训会在永靖镇政府会议室召开，各乡镇长、乡企站统计人员和集体企业厂长（经理）、会计、统计人员以及县直有关单位共140余人参加会议。23日，贵阳市统计执法大检查领导小组办公室组织的检查组到县检查。检查发现，永靖镇乡企站、砖厂、阳朗水泥厂等6个单位和厂矿中，两个乡企站第二季度统计台账不完善，两个企业未建统计台账，检查组对四单位签发《统计检查查询书》，责令限期查清统计数据来源，建立健全财务统计台账。是月，对青山苗族乡统计员侵占调查经费一事进行通报处理。1999年11月，县统计局对县自来水公司瞒报统计资料进行处罚。2001—2006年，在相关部门配合下，县统计局相继组织统计执法检查5次。其间，2005年9月，将每年10月定为统计法规执行情况检查月。

第三章　工商行政管理

1991年，县工商局内设办公室、行教科、市场科、企业登记科、个体经济科、行财科、合同商标广告科、经济检查科，下派永靖、永阳、小寨坝、养龙司、九庄等5个基层工商所。1995年12月，工商行政管理局、物价局、质量技术监督局合并，挂县工商局牌子，但各司原职，继续使用各自印鉴。1999年8月，恢复三局机构，县工商局上划贵阳市工商行政管理局管理。2001年，实行精简内设机构，全员竞争上岗，撤销原科室，组建办公室、政策法规科、执行监督科、注册登记科、后勤服务中心。下派机构减为永靖、养龙司、小寨坝和九庄4个工商所。2004年8月，工商局增设纪检监察室。

第一节　市场建设与管理

一、集市场期

1991年，集市有永靖、底寨、养龙司、九庄、黑神庙、阳朗、新场、石头田、石硐、猫场、鹿窝、流长、潮水、梨安和二七六厂15个。场期分别为：每周星期一赶新场；星期二赶鹿窝、底寨；星期三赶永靖、养龙司、九庄；星期四赶流长、猫场；星期五赶黑神庙、石硐；星期六赶九庄、石头田、潮水；星期日赶永靖、养龙司、梨安。俗称“赶转转场”。1992年撤区并乡建镇后，集市逐渐向乡镇政府所在地集中，部分市场已有名无实。1998年，县政府调整集市和场期。调整后的集市基本以乡镇政府所在地为赶场地，市场由当地政府管理。调整后的场期为：每周星期二赶鹿窝；星期三赶永靖、养龙司；星期四赶流长；星期五赶黑神庙、石硐；星期六赶石头田、九庄；星期日赶永靖、养龙司。

二、市场建设

1992年，县委、县政府成立农贸市场建设领导小组，将全县19个集贸市场纳入规划管理，开始修建室内市场和专业市场。5月，由工商局投入部分资金，群众集资一部分，改造鹿窝乡街道市场路面1300平方米。8月，动工修建永靖镇农贸市场。该市场占地面积1.16万平方米，建筑面积1.36万平方米，建水泥摊位396个，另建住宅面积3947平方米，总投资365.1万元。是年，原国营“二七六”厂建室内综合市场1个，占地面积545平方米。次年，青山苗族乡投资，在境内高田坎修建露天牲畜市场1个，占地3000平方米，可容大小牲畜1000余头。市场于当年7月投入使用。

1994年，由县电影院投资3.65万元，建成室内小吃市场162平方米和小商品市场500平方米。工商局投资10万元，改造维修县城综合农贸市场权项1800平方米，总投资8146元，改造维修城中城综合农贸市场进出口路面46.72平方米。1995年，息烽磷矿投资5万元修建温泉石头田露天农贸市场，市场设摊位165个。九庄镇集资10万元，改造街道水泥路面200平方米。2001年12月，工商行政管理局将县城综合农贸市场和五号楼移交国资公司，完成市场建设中的体改工作。

三、市场管理

20世纪90年代初期，工商局遵照《贵州省商贸市场管理办法》规范交易行为和市场秩序。1994年5月，省政府要求工商行政管理机关及时查处市场违法、违章行为，维护市场秩序，保护经营者、消费者合法权益，对“疏忽职守、滥用职权者给予行政处分；构成犯罪的，依法追究其责任”。县工商局组织职工学习文件，利用赶场天向群众宣传。1995年12月，县质监局、物价局与工商局合并后，对市场计量器具和部分强制检定器具实行长期检定证书管理，做到一器一证。

1999年4月，农业部、国家工商行政管理总局下发《关于进一步做好农贸市场管理工作的通知》，要求强化农资市场管理，严厉打击出售假冒伪劣化肥、农药、种子的违法行为；坚决取缔非法经营、无生产证、无照经营的个人或单位；在对农资商品进行的专项治理中，全面落实农资打假辖区责任制，市场巡查制等监管制度，实行“两账一票一书一卡”制度和种子留样备案制，从源头防止假冒伪劣农资商品流入市场。2005年，“红盾护农”活动启动，工商局依法开展农资检查56次，出动执法人员1201人次，查获伪劣化肥378吨，失效敌敌畏、乐果81瓶，失效稻瘟剂、除草剂289包，劣质种子230千克；查处各类伪劣农资商品案14起；没收、销毁各类伪劣农资价值43万元，罚款金额20.4万元。

1992—2007年，打击出售伪劣食品、药品的违法活动和垄断经营、传销和变相传销。此期间出动执法人员深入市场15次，查处经济违章案件469起，处罚金64.34万元。在副食品打假活动中查获假烟17353条，货值81万元，假酒货值6.69万元；查获劣质酱油360千克，劣质月饼460千克以及一批其他变质食品等。2008年，在严厉打击“涉卫星电视广播地面设施违法犯罪”活动中，出动执法人员14人，车辆4次，检查经营户67户，依法扣押天线20米、高频头12个、接收机4台。在文化市场专项检查中，联合县文化局、公安局、城管大队共收缴非法出版物200册，取缔无照出版物销售摊点5户。

第二节　企业登记

1991年年初，全县有工商业121户，企业法人101人，非企业法人20人。随着经济改革开放，政策的扶持，招商引资力度加大，县内工商业得到快速发展。1996年，全县有工商业企业155户，其中私营企业43户。1997—2004年，依法注销企业350户。2006年，新增登记注册企业39户，其中有限责任公司11户、有限责任分公司11户、非企业法人营业单位11户、个人独资企业5户、合伙企业1户。年检中办理企业注销登记12户。2007年，内资企业发展为320户，注册资金2.1亿元；私营企业164户，注册资金0.82亿元。2009年，完成各类主体开业登记1052户，其中个体工商户1007户、有限责任公司21户、个人独资企业7户、合伙企业2个、分支机构15个；办理变更登记972户，其中企业变更登记109户、个体工商户变更登记863户；办理注销登记200户，其中企业注销21户、个体工商户179户。2010年，完成各类主体开业登记1109户，其中个体户新增1036户、私人企业新增52户、内资企业新增9户、农民企业合作社新增12户。年检中吊销企业27户，注销个体工商户60户。

第三节　个体工商户管理

1991年年初，全县有个体工商户2644户，从业人员3400人。随着改革开放，搞活经济的不断深入，个体工商户群体不断发展壮大。2007年，个体工商户4611户，注册资金6600万元，从业人员6157人。

2008年9月1日起，停止征收个体工商户管理费和集贸市场管理费，办理《个体工商户营业执照》人数大幅度增加。当月，县工商局办理个体执照168户，比8月的82户增长105%。是年，个体工商户5494户，注册资金7250万元。

2009年1月，面对金融危机，县工商局走访慰问全县企业和个体工商户。规定各工商行政管理所、局有关科室全年对重点工商个体户和重点企业走访不得少于4次。是年，个体工商户5677户，注册资金1.15亿元，从业人员6856人。

2010年，在“三创一办”活动期间，县工商局对个体工商户坚持准入交易和退市全程监管，加强个体工商户自律制度建设。是年2月起，启动一年一度验收工作。至年底，全县个体工商户6733户，注册资金1.77亿元。应予验照贴花的个体工商户5697户，实际验照贴花3953户，注销60户，验收率70.2%。

第四节　合同、广告、商标管理

一、合同管理

巨额资金和重大安全工程项目合同立案建档。共鉴证合同114份，涉及资金1.2亿元；检查合同

394份；办理动产抵押鉴证15户，金额622万元。2001—2004年，共鉴证合同31份，资金3.5亿元。检查合同31份。

2005年，举办合同法培训班，制定企业信用制度，引导规范当事人签约行为，解决合同示范文件和拟定规程。是年，县工商局共参加招投标合同鉴证会9次。对全县78户企业的主体资格进行审查，确保合同的合法性。2006—2009年，帮助指导签订合同文本430余份，参加招投标会议3次，参加政府采购审查资质13次，对98户企业主体资格进行审查，办理企业动产、不动产抵押登记10户。处置“欺诈合同”4户。2010年，对贵州开磷集团磷业有限公司、贵铁分局遵义工务段息烽盛达工程公司、息烽县城市建设综合开发公司、中国人民保险公司息烽县支公司、贵州息烽磷矿、贵阳中化开磷化肥有限公司、贵州西洋有限公司等6家省级“重合同守信用”企业和市级命名的息烽晨华网络信息中心、贵州西洋有限公司、贵州开磷集团物业管理有限公司、息烽县心连心超市等4家企业进行复核。参加政府采购审核资质19次，办理不动产抵押登记9户。

二、商标管理

1992年6月，县工商局对息烽阳朗水泥厂进行商标注册，经国家工商行政管理局核定，商标标识为“洲洞”，注册号599367。11月，县工商局对已获“黔桂”商标名称的息烽矿泉水厂申请“商誉评估”作出批复，认定商誉评估值为55万元。1993年，县工商局在省、地工商局指导下，扶持全县个体工商户和私营企业发展，开展商标注册工作。1994年4月，县工商局为息烽格来特矿泉水有限责任公司进行商标注册，经国家工商行政管理局商标局核定，使用商品第32类，商标注册证为68604号。次年，重点加强对医疗、药品、食品等与人民生活密切相关的商标监测。共出动执法人员360人次、车辆90台次，查获商标违法案1件，罚款3000元。1998—2002年，工商局为县仁都水泥厂、县康裕来磷肥厂、富源磷业有限公司、“黄南武”辣子鸡、西泽特肥厂、县宏达造纸厂等企业依法办理商标注册手续。2006年，查处商标侵权假冒案3件，罚款11.5万元。查处茅台酒商标标识、彩带、彩合1.2万袋。至2007年，全县有效注册商标22件。2008年10月，“叶老大”辣子鸡获著名商标认定。2009年2月，开展维护“双桥”牌味精商标权益活动，扣押假冒味精86袋，34千克。2010年，成功注册“大青山灰豆腐”“金钯养殖”“黄宇辣子鸡”“雨花瀑布虫茶”“蜂布叮”5个农产品商标。

三、广告管理

1991—1994年，县工商局取消不合法规广告1727件，审查登记发布广告428户次。1994年10月，《中华人民共和国广告法》（以下简称《广告法》）正式颁布，县工商局在全县开展学习、宣传《中华人民共和国广告法》活动，相继制定医疗、药品、糖业、酒类、烟草、食品、饮料等专项广告管理办法，对广告内容、文字、图案、形式等进行服务。至2000年，取消不符合法规广告365件。审查、登记、发布广告139户次。查处医药保健品违法广告3件。2001年起，按照全面结合、重点突出的管理方法，县工商行管理部门加大对户外广告的巡查力度。组织相关人员进行电子政务培训，把经济户口和广告户口数据库逐步理顺、建档；建立以“12315”为基础的工商行政管理综合执法体系，推动社会信用体系建设和广告规范库数据建设。至2009年，出动执法人员136人次、执法车29台次，审查户外广告27件，清除不合法规广告243件，审查、登记、发布589户次，审理广告违法案7件，开业企业户数402户，认领建档42户；开业个体户3869户，认领建档3869户。2010年，广告登记27件，抽查行政许可注册登记类卷宗60件。

第五节　消费者权益保护

1991年，县工商行政管理部门受理调处消费者投诉160件，为消费者挽回经济损失3.9万元。接受消费者咨询1200人次。

1993年，县工商行政管理部门接受投诉256件，挽回经济损失2.61万元。

1994年，县工商行政管理部门开展“消费者信得过企业”评选活动。县乡镇企业公司、养龙司水泥厂、九庄供销社、阳朗水泥厂、格莱特矿泉水厂、县职校加油站等6家企业入选，由县政府颁发荣誉证书和牌匾。是年，受理调处投诉229件。

1996—2003年，县工商行政管理部门累计受理调处投诉911件，接受咨询199人次。

2008年，县工商行政管理部门围绕“抗凝冻保民生”“3·15”宣传活动，现场设立消费者投诉台、“12315”申诉台、企业登记注册咨询台、假冒伪劣商品展示台、工商法律法规宣传咨询台。印发《中华人民共和国消费者权益保护法》《贵州省消费者保护条例》《中华人民共和国产品质量法》《种子管理办法》等相关法律法规1万余份。接待咨询2100人次，宣传群众1.2万人次。

2010年3月，在“3·15”消费者权益活动中，向群众发放《消费者权益保护法》2500册、《中华人民共和国食品安全法》1000份、《工商法律法规汇编》2500册。受理消费者投诉12件，涉及家用电器、机械、百货、房屋装修建材、服务等。其中：属产品质量类投诉6件、计量和其他投诉各3件。

第四章　质量技术监督

1991年，县标准计量管理局专业从事全县计量器具管理工作。1992年12月，县标准计量管理局改称县技术监督局。1995年12月，工商行政管理局、技术监督局、物价局合并组建县工商行政管理局，但各局原印鉴继续使用，人员各司其职。1999年8月，技术监督与工商、物价分开，单独设立县质量技术监督局（简称质监局），实行省以下垂直管理。局下设办公室、业务科、质量技术监督检测所（简称检测所）和特种设备安全监察科。

第一节　计量管理

20世纪90年代初期，加强市场计量规范管理，县标准计量管理部门对商贸计量器具进行定期检定，实行一器一证。对汽车计价器、燃油加油机、售油器、焦度计（屈光度计）、验光镜及固定摊点经销者的各类衡器实行强制管理。1991年，共检定计量器具220台（支）。1992年，检定各类计量器具2244台（支）。是年，县质监局在西洋肥业有限公司、息烽仁都水泥厂等企业设立计量管理站，负责计量管理工作。1993年，检定各类计量器具3863台（支）。其中检定地中衡10台、台案秤334台、杆秤3000支、加油机14台、油表5块；没收违法计量器具7台（支），罚款250元。1994年、

1995年元旦、春节期间，对8个主要农贸市场500多家摊点进行计量检查，检验各种器具1160台，现场处罚违法使用计量器具的商店、摊点65家，依法没收肉贩、水果摊贩使用的“短命秤”26支。1996年，开展县以下乡镇限制使用杆秤的工作。规定公众贸易中心必须使用电子秤、双面度盘秤式案秤，商店、固定摊点必须使用供双方可见的衡器。2008年凝冻期间，在全县开展“关注民生、计量惠民”活动。出动执法人员对县内加油机、地中衡、台案秤、瓦斯计进行严格检定。免费为农贸市场个体工商户检定计量器具100台次；对9家重点耗能企业能源计量器具开展调查摸底，将情况制成电子文档，规范管理；免费检定永靖镇个体工商户案式托盘秤、电子秤、雨洒牛奶场电子计量器具共80余台次。2010年，县技术监督局开展国庆节市场大检查活动，从9月初开始，集中人力，对集贸市场和旅游景点、车站等地商店、摊点的各种计量器具进行逐一检测，严格查处使用不合法计量器具和未按定量包装商品的行为。

第二节 标准化管理和统一代码标识工作

一、标准化管理

1992年4月，国家下发《关于一九九二年进一步开展食品标签通用标准实施检查的通知》，要求各地进一步加强食品标签通用标准的管理工作。县委、县政府协调县工商、卫生、物价等职能部门，深入各农贸市场、商店、摊点、超市及有关企业，对婴幼儿食品、啤酒、乳制品、酱油、饮料、茶叶、面包等食品进行详细检查。经过检查，标签通用标准无假冒伪造，全部合格。

1995年8月，质监局下发《关于企业产品执行标准登记管理的通知》，要求县境内企业、事业单位生产销售的产品所执行的国家标准、行业标准、地方标准和企业标准均要登记备案。2000年，贵阳市政府将息烽县列入工业生产企业消灭无标准生产县。通过抓宣传、培训、核实，确定消灭无标准生产企业133家，产品143个，依法为133家企业办理产品执行标准登记和企业标准备案手续。2002年11月，省、市质监局验收组对消灭无标准生产项目进行验收，县内企业以标准覆盖率97.9%通过验收。质监局对企业产品标准备案进行复审，共有备案企业标准19个，登记标准15个。协助19个企业制定企业标准，并对新办企业产品标准及时进行登记。

2005年起，对全县企业登记备案执行的标准进行清理，将县内9类69种产品标准执行情况输入电子监管网，并完成上报入网赋码方案。2008年，按标准化规定培育创名牌企业6家，名牌产品11个。共办理产品登记标准18个，其中国家标准14个、行业标准3个、备案企业标准1个。2009—2010年，培育名牌产品5个。

二、统一代码标识

1993年7月，县政府下文成立县统一代码标识制度领导小组，下设办公室，县质监局抽人负责全县统一代码标识工作。办公室编写打印统一代码标识宣传提纲1200份，发出办理代码标识通知800份，打印各种表册资料1000份，举办培训班，参训人员200余人。至年底，全县统一代码标识申请单位514家，其中，企业174户、事业单位217户、社团12户、机关110户，申办率95%。

2008年，新办组织机构代码证70个，换证134个，代码机构标识年检310个。次年，继续加强与工商、税务、金融系统联系，完善信息共享网络。组织机构代码新办证90个，换证156个，年检306个。2010年，组织机构新办证165个，换证187个，年检392个。

第三节　产品质量监督

1992年3月，县农资公司从四川购进芬兰进口硫酸钾复合肥180吨，货值24.84万元。经县计量局报送省质检站检测，属劣质复合肥，因处理及时，未造成重大经济损失。1995年1月，检查全县电工产品销售商店，按规定处理查出的197台无安全证的冰箱、电视机、组合音响、电钻等，总价值48万元。是年4月，县质监部门特邀县人大、县政府领导，检查全县18家农资商店，查获劣质“二元复合肥”和普通过磷酸钙33吨、劣质农药3000包、过期失效农药5000包（瓶）。查处非法经营种子11家，查获冒牌杂交水稻种子942千克。2001年2月，出动执法人员36人次，专项检测全县种子、化肥、农药、农膜经销点82家，共检测水稻种4.71万千克、玉米种1.7万千克、西瓜种240箱、菜种200千克、化肥3500吨、农药15批次、农膜5批次，除发现5箱西瓜种过期失效外，其余均符合质量标准。2002年8月，专项检查全县铝合金建筑型材市场，在15个经营户中，查获不合格铝型材6120米，货值5万余元。是年，专项检查建材市场，共检查建筑工地10个、水泥300吨、钢材20吨、预制板1000余米、砖7万块，检测合格率83.3%。2007年，检查种子、农药、化肥100批次，抽检化肥5万余吨。

2008—2009年，县质监局开展专项检查20余次，出动车辆120台次、执法检查人员450人次，共检查企业、小作坊348家次、食品销售店90个次、超市50家次。全面检测县内7个化肥生产企业和化肥销售店、15个建材生产企业、9个建筑工地以及供电部门，查处不合格水泥22吨、不合格铝合金窗架2批次。开展对28大类食品的无证查处和面条等5类食品的专项整顿工作。

第五章　物价管理

1991年，物价局内设办公室，下设物价检查所。1995年12月，县工商局、物价局、技术监督局合并，挂牌县工商行政管理局。1999年8月，恢复县物价局建制。物价局内设办公室、物价科，下设物价检查所。12月，价格事务所成立，与物价科一个机构，两块牌子。2002年3月，内设机构改为办公室、价格管理科（价格认证中心）、收费管理科、价格监督检查科（物价检查所）。2010年5月，县物价局并入县发展和改革局。

第一节　价格管理

1992年3月，县政府印发《息烽县物价局关于深化价格改革　进一步搞活搞好流通工作的报告》的通知，提出进一步放开价格管理权限，让企业有更多的自主权，拓宽价格运行机制，推进价格改革向纵深发展。是年，核定贵州茂华化工厂普钙厂价格，调整非生活用水价格，规定从1993年起，将县管氡泉大曲、息烽醇、息烽大曲、低度息烽窖酒、梦游窖、双喜大曲零售价格放开。1993年，实施息烽油菜籽、菜籽油购销价格放开，粮食销售价格放开，并实行粮价补贴政策。是年，统一中小学校收费标准和统配化肥（尿素）销售价格。1994年5月1日起，化肥不再分计划内外价格，化肥调拨价格和零售价格实行差率或利润率控制。1995年，核定杂交水稻种子、杂交油菜种价格。1998年，调整屠宰生猪收费标准：屠宰、加工、运输各种服务收费标准为18元/头。是年，县物价局、供电分局印发《关于我县农村入户电价实行最高限价的通知》，规定农村入户电价每千瓦时不得超过0.7元，并制定息烽城乡用电同价方案。1999年，核定县杂交玉米、杂交油菜种价格；重新确定各项屠宰服务收费标准。是年，颁发审验行政事业性收费许可证116个，涉及收费项目146项，收费标准323个。收费总额967.35万元。取消和降低收费项目和标准9项。

2001年，调整自来水价格和农村殡葬管理有关收费标准，实施农村供电一户一表安装费用标准，核定下洪马水库水利工程供水价格。成立县物价局价格举报中心和案件审理委员会，在10个乡镇161个村聘请涉农价格和收费义务监督员161名，在4个重点企业聘请涉及价格、收费义务监督员4名，确保“价格、计量信得过”。2004年4月，对化肥价格过快上涨问题启动临时干预措施，实行尿素最高限价管理。对非营利性医疗机构中开展送医服务、药品价格进行检查；对农村新型合作医疗服务收费、药品价格公示情况进行检查；核定县义务教育阶段学生住宿费收费标准等。是年，共审查行政事业性收费许可证169个，其中行政事业性148个、经营服务性21个。2007年5月，以猪肉为重点的副食涨价，物价局组织相关部门召开会议，开展专项调查，为县委、县政府决策提出合理化建议。开展价格服务进校园和景区活动，规范6所重点中小学和息烽集中营革命历史纪念馆等景点景区的收费公示牌，确保明白收费。2008年，县发生雪凝灾害后，按照“抗凝冻、保民生、稳物价”的服务理念，实行临时价格干预措施，对合力超市、农贸市场部分商品价格采取调价备案、提价申报制度和价格提醒告诫干预。安排专人在做好生猪、鸡蛋、仔猪、油料价格定点监测的同时，对粮、油、肉、蛋、禽、菜等价格、重要农业生产资料价格、涉农收费及建材、粮油制成品、副食品价格进行监测。3—4月，对全县行政事业性收费许可证进行年审换证，核发许可证324个，其中正本146个、副本178个，年审验率100%。年审中严把收费项目和标准关，对明文取消的项目一律不上证，对降低收费标准的严格按照文件规定上证。2009年1月，县物价局召开供水价格和污水处理征收标准听证会，参会21人，旁听12人。核定县污水处理、居民生活用水及其他用水收费标准均为0.6元/立方米。调整县城出租汽车收费标准。完成化肥、粮油副食品、成品油等重要商品价格的重点监测，对全县36个非税收入收费单位407项收费项目的重新审核。2010年，对自流供水的西山、九庄、唐家湾、彭家垭口、鹿窝水厂，电力抽水供水的流长、养龙司、石硐、何家硐水厂分别确定水价为2.2元/立方米和2.6元/立方米。明确青山苗族乡参照自流供水水价执行。对低保户用水实行优惠价格。

第二节　收费管理

20世纪90年代初，县物价部门依照《贵州省行政事业性收费管理条例》《贵州省经营性服务价格管理暂行办法》《贵州省〈收费许可证〉管理办法》等法规开展收费管理工作。

1998年起，实施《收费许可证》制度，加强对行政事业单位收费项目、标准的管理和监督，至2004年，共取消不合理收费项目39个，其中涉农项目18项，涉及金额73万元。10个乡镇所在地，161

个村各收费单位悬挂涉农价格和收费公示牌，85所中小学（含教学点）悬挂教育收费公示牌。在各村和工矿企业聘请义务监督员171名，对公示的价格和收费进行监督。

2006年，全县有收费部门37个，收费项目123项，收费总额6314.46万元。其中行政性收费68项，收费总额1445.14万元；事业性收费55项，收费总额4869.33万元。此外，涉企收费17个部门，收费项目46项，收费金额1214.63万元。其他收费部门23个，收费项目77项，收费金额5099.83万元。全县共核发行政事业性收费许可证328个。其中正本145个、副本183个，年审证率100%。2008年，共核发行政事业性收费许可证332个，其中正本146个、副本186个。取消行政事业性收费10项，涉及金额331.2万元。其中涉企收费5项，涉及金额168.7万元；其他收费5项，涉及金额162.5万元。其他取消的收费项目有义务教育杂费（限于城市）、城市房屋拆迁管理费、建设工程质量监督费、公路运输管理费、集贸市场管理费和个体工商户管理费等。

2009年，县物价局会同县财政局清理全县行政事业性收费项目。是年1月1日起，全县取消公路养路费、航道养护费、公路运输管理费、公路客货运附加费、水路运输管理费、水运客货运附加费6项收费，涉及金额120万元。4月，对2008年行政事业性收费许可证进行年审。

2010年，全县有行政事业性收费部门32个，项目64项。其中行政性收费38项，收费总额855.32万元；事业性收费26项，收费总额5709.49万元；涉企收费17个部门，收费项目30个；其他收费部门20个，收费项目34项。收费项目中属于中央制定的收费项目和收费标准21项，中央制定项目、省制定收费标准26项，省级制定收费项目和标准17项。

第三节　价格监督检查

1991年，检查医疗收费项目10个，收费标准505个。制定卫生费收费标准，放开市场调节价格，实行差率管理。物价检查616家，检查824人次，没收非法所得3685元；查处一般价格违法案件10件，没收非法所得3901元，罚款47463元。在物价大检查中，检查单位81户，抽查27户，查处一般违法行为11件，没收非法所得40203元，上缴财政39703元。

1992年4月中旬，进行农业生产资料价格检查。7—8月，重点检查境内铁路各车站客、货运价格，查处金额30.3万元。出动检查人员50人次，参加检查人员320人次，检查国有、集体单位和个体商户517户。查处案件54件，其中重大案件3件，制裁总金额31.98万元，没收非法所得694元，上缴财政1.67万元。

1998—2003年，县物价局印制《中华人民共和国价格法》《关于商品和服务实行明码标价的规定》《明码标价实施细则》《开展明码标价规范日活动的通知》等资料2.5万份，分发各单位和经营户，在全县全面推行明码标价工作。共开展物价监督检查300余次，查出价格违法400余起。受理价格咨询、投诉、举报53起，查出价格违法金额200余万元，其中责令退还消费者43万元、没收和罚款117万元。组织开展教育、民政、计生、工商、国土、建设、农机、乡企、电力、医药、自来水、种子、化肥、道路客货运等专项检查73次，查出价格违法143起，违纪金额217万元，其中责令退还消费者59万元、没收非法所得和罚款108万元。此外，2003年1月，因广东“非典”流行，县内发生抢购板蓝根冲剂现象。2月，县物价局组织力量对县人民医院、中医院、乡镇卫生院、个体诊所及零售药店等医药部门进行检查。至5月，县物价局共出动车辆20台次，出动执法人员75人次，检查医药部门146家次，未发现有价格违法情况。县物价局会同县纠风办、教育局，检查全县110所中小学收费情况。检查中，清退上学期书本费余额8.7万余元。

2004年2—3月，县物价局专项检查全县农业生产资料及涉农收费部门（包括中小学校、民政、计生、屠宰、防疫、检验检疫等部门）的收费执行情况。2005年，对全县73个涉农收费部门进行价格和收费检查。检查中，责令非义务教育学校清退上学期代收的书本费、教辅费、资料费等7.7万元。在秋季教育收费检查中，督促清退代收书本、资料费余额11.5万元。为打击借春运乱涨价、乱宰客的不法行为，在春节期间出动车辆和人员，共检查客运车辆60余辆。2006—2007年，检查春节期间客运情况，检查客运车辆97辆，发现存在价格违法6起，为消费者清退经费2000余元。县物价局会同财政、教育、纠风办等部门，查出县国土局向农民收取土地抵押登记费3.5万元，息烽二中向学生收取补课费13万元，责令清退，无法清退的收缴财政。2008年，物价局会同交警队、运管所等部门，检查车辆30台，发现价格违纪6起，为消费者清退经费1000余元。查出出租车涨价行为13起，罚款2400元上缴财政。

2009—2010年，出动人员和车辆，对客运、成品油、旅游、粮油、种子、化肥、化肥生产用电、医药价格（包括农村合作医疗）、商品明码标价进行监督检查。通过检查，明码标价率超过90%。受理举报投诉案件20余件。

第四节　价格认证

1998—2003年，县物价部门共为公、检、法、司等部门进行价格认证412起，涉及认证金额961万元。针对公安部门办案经费紧张问题，对公安提交的涉案认证基本实行免费评估。2005—2009年，县物价部门共进行价格认证868件，评估金额3300余万元。

第六章　安全生产监督管理

1991年，县设安全生产委员会，统一部署全县安全生产宣传教育及培训工作；设安全监察站，行使国家对矿山、锅炉压力容器及劳动保护的监察职能。2004年，组建县安全生产监督管理局，履行安全生产宣传、培训、监管职责，至2010年，查处安全生产案33件，处以罚金198.18万元。

第一节　宣传教育培训

1991年，县安全生产委员会（简称县安委会）组织各成员单位在“全国安全生产周”活动期间，在县城摆摊设点，通过发放安全生产资料，接受群众法律咨询、悬挂宣传标语等形式，开展以“安全就是效益”和“提高职工安全意识”为主要内容的生产安全宣传。至2002年，相继开展以“遵章守纪，杜绝‘三违’”“不伤害自己，不伤害他人，不被他人伤害”“治理隐患，保障安全”“加强管理，保障安全”为主题的生产安全宣传活动。

2004年组建县安全监管局后，安全生产宣传工作力度进一步加大。开展以“关爱生命、关注安全”为主题的“全国安全生产月”活动，结合《道路交通安全法》的实施，采取法律咨询、安全生产知识演讲和“安全杯”健身展示赛等方式，进行安全生产宣传。共张贴标语2000余条，悬挂宣传画200余幅，播放光碟70余次，发放宣传资料4000余份。接受群众咨询5000余人次。此后，每年开展“全国安全生产月”宣传活动，安全生产宣传工作在县内形成制度化、常态化。2005年9月，邀请省安全培训中心老师到息烽培训乡镇安全监察员31人。县安监局举办安全培训班3期，共培训非煤矿山负责人和安全管理人员200人、危险化学品安全管理人员320人、烟花爆竹经营人员200人、特种作业人员48人。次年，县内组织培训煤矿安全管理人员、企业法人、矿长等140余人次；培训非煤矿山安全管理人员，复审矿长、安全员以及其他生产经营单位安管员、从业人员等1425人。县安监局选派安全生产监管干部32人次参加省、市举办的各类安全生产培训。

2008年6月，县委宣传部、团县委、安监局、文体广电局、司法局、总工会、县依法治理领导小组办公室联合开展“安全生产咨询”“安全生产知识竞赛”“安全生产座谈会”等3项活动，发放各种宣传材料30种约5万份，展出交通事故、危险化学品事故等宣传展板12块，接受群众咨询600余人次，受教育群众约2万人次。组织培训各类从业人员2683人。次年，在党校培训煤矿从业人员和烟花爆竹经营人员937人；组织非煤矿山管理人员和特种作业人员144人到有资质的中介机构培训。

2010年6月，在“全国安全生产月”活动期间，县“全国安全生产月”组委会组织开展安全生产宣传咨询、应急救援演练、安全知识竞赛、企业员工话安全等13项活动，发放各类宣传资料5万份。播放光碟3张，接受教育群众1.5万人。

第二节　监督检查

1984年4月，县成立安全监察站，行使国家对矿山、锅炉压力容器及劳动保护的监察权。1991年，县劳动局内设安全生产监督委员会办公室。2001年，原劳动部门负责管理的锅炉、压力容器、电梯、压力管道、防爆电器、起重机械、特殊危险化学品的行政管理职能统一划归县质监局管理。是年，县质监局下发《关于加强锅容管特监督管理安全监察工作的通知》，要求各有关单位要严格贯彻落实国家关于安全生产的法律、法规，建立和完善锅、容、管、特各种设备管理制度，落实安全生产工作领导责任制，确保县内锅、容、管、特设备安全运行。是年3月起，县质监局对县内使用锅、容、管、特的企业、单位进行全面普查登记，至6月10日止，共普查登记使用锅炉压力容器的单位45家，小烫店、豆腐加工店、浴室37家，登记各种锅炉压力容器110台。检查中，为7个单位办理锅炉压力容器安装报批手续，对违反国家有关规定安装锅炉的中化十六建设公司进行处罚。2004年5月，对县城辖区内危险化学品生产企业进行检查、调查登记工作。检查登记危险化学品生产企业6家。其中，黄磷生产企业2家、氯化钡生产企业1家、硫酸、盐酸生产企业3家。检查中未发现违规现象、不安全操作程序和安全隐患。

2004—2007年，县安监局、质监局或独立，或会同县发展计划与经济贸易局、县国土资源局、县公安局、县建设局等单位，对道（水）路交通安全、煤矿安全、非煤矿山安全、民爆物品安全、人员密集场所、消防、危险化学品安全，建筑、燃气、特种设备安全、烟花爆竹安全等进行专项整治。其中，道（水）路安全专项整治共清理违章占道436起，查扣证照不齐机动车462辆，行政拘留6人，培训考核违章驾驶员380人次；检验摩托车1079辆，办理摩托车驾驶证718个；投资20余万元，完成县城主要街道安全标志、标线设置；查处"三无"（无生产日期、无质量合格证、无生产厂家）船舶1艘，处理违章船舶33艘，分流乘客80人，卸超载货物50余吨。煤矿安全专项整治，培训矿工、群众监督员、瓦斯监控员、矿长和特种作业人员共1675人次，查处各类隐患1916起；炸封或关闭小煤窑91个；非煤矿山安全专项整治，对51家企业进行安全评估，查处无证矿山94个，收缴工具100余件，没收矿产品230吨；查出危害大、稳定性差的地质灾害点139处，下达隐患整改指令书150份；民爆物品安全专项整治，检查涉爆单位、场所1410家次，排除隐患430起；收缴炸药65.7千克、火雷管131枚、电雷管19枚、导火绳70米、自制炸药2千克和烟花爆竹7件等。

开展人员密集场所和消防安全、危险化学品安全专项整治，共检查重点防火单位、学校、网吧近300次，下达整改通知书82份，提出整改意见193条，处罚存在安全隐患的单位5家，罚款3500元。检查危险化学品生产、储存和使用企业80家次，检查剧毒化学品使用单位20家、易制毒化学品生产、使用、经营企业25家，查出隐患65条，下达整改指令书20余份。共安装消防栓79个，修建消防水池836口。建筑、燃气、特种设备安全专项整治，下达整改意见书18份；对3家单位进行立案查处等。此后，每年开展各项安全生产专项整治活动。

其间，县质监部门对锅炉、压力管道、压力容器等特种设备运行状况建立管理台账，实行动态管理。共检查锅炉391台次、压力容器857台次、起重机械167台次、电梯19台次、压力管道11400余米、液化气经营点70户次、液化气充装站12个次、建筑工地18个、浴室8家等。下达监察意见书30份。

2010年，开展煤矿和非煤矿、危险化学品和烟花爆竹、道路交通安全和人员密集场所等安全专项整治活动，共出动执法人员6291人次、车辆1050台次，炸封非法采煤窝点42个；查处非煤矿山安全隐患204条；收缴非法烟花爆竹60余箱、"三无"烟花爆竹产品10箱，取缔无证经营户35家次，吊销非法转让许可证经营户1户，取缔烟花爆竹非法生产窝点1个；检查车辆3750台次，查处交通违法案件1877起，罚款38.02万元，行政拘留10人；查处超员客车32辆次、违章客货车207辆，处理非法营运摩托车647辆、其他非法营运车辆182辆；查处农用车违法行为36起，暂扣无牌无证车辆32台；检查网吧300家次、歌舞娱乐场所56家次、学校270所（次）、医院38家次、商场52家次，查处安全隐患338条等。县质监部门检查锅炉86台次、压力容器347台次、压力管道10000余米、起重机械105台次、电梯45台次、厂内机动车辆65台次；检查液化气经营点15户次、液化气充装站5次，下达安全监察意见书16份，责令整改排除安全隐患22次。是年，帮助和指导特种设备使用单位建立特种设备安全管理制度，与23家特种设备使用单位签订安全"包保"责任书23份，落实特种设备使用单位管理特种设备的主体职责。

息烽县2004—2010年安全生产违法行为行政处罚统计表

表15-6-1

年份	受处罚单位	受处罚原因	处罚金额（万元）
2004	小寨坝镇龙洞煤矿	未执行《整改指令书》；电工无证上岗；安全员、安检员未同时跟班作业	2.5
	光辉水泥厂	采石面无规划；无安全检查和职工教育记录；未采取安全措施，致一人高空坠落死亡	3
2005	小寨坝镇楠木桥煤矿	未建立健全安全生产责任制度；出现重大工伤事故未及时上报；无防尘设施	7.7
	石硐乡小红寨煤矿	特种作业员不足；瓦斯探头损坏；运输巷道帮漏严重；井下作业点未进行粉尘检测	7.6
	鑫悦煤炭有限公司	停产整改期间组织生产	0.8
	永靖镇下阳朗煤矿	停产整改期间组织生产	2.5
	双龙煤矿	未进行粉尘检测和安全检查	2
	马家箐煤矿	未取得“安全生产许可证”组织生产	1.8
	石硐乡石硐煤矿	无双回路电源供电；停业整顿期间组织生产	6
	光辉水泥厂	矿山爆破砸坏村民房屋和过往车辆，砸伤村民	4
2006	永靖镇姜家堰煤矿	下井登记档案作假；拒不执行安全监察指令	3.98
	石硐乡石硐煤矿	在井下瓦斯浓度超限情况下作业	3
	火烧井煤矿	在井下瓦斯浓度超限情况下作业	3
	马家箐煤矿	在井下瓦斯浓度超限情况下作业	3
2007	安黔煤矿	瓦斯窒息事故致一人死亡	0.6
	永靖镇火烧井煤矿	法定代表人超定员组织生产；企业负责人未按规定轮流带班下井	8
	永靖镇狮子山砂厂	安全事故致一人死亡；“安全生产许可证”到期，仍组织生产	10.6
2008	登云预制构件厂	安全事故致一人死亡	10.2
	永靖镇姜家堰煤矿	违章指挥作业	1
	仁都水泥厂	拒不执行安全监察指令	1.1
	鑫悦煤炭有限公司	井下掘进头探放水措施不符合规定	1
	信科环化有限公司	擅自新建、扩建硫脲合成车间、高纯度硫脲车间、盐酸储罐等	5
	石硐乡石硐煤矿	透水事故致一人死亡	5.6
	马家箐煤矿	未按整改指令完成整改工作	2.5
2009	光辉水泥厂	安全事故致一人死亡	13.8
	林东煤业公司	安全事故致一人死亡	0.3
	湘联煤矿	未按安全整改指令完成整改工作	3.8
	坪上煤矿	未按安全整改指令完成整改工作	2

续表

年份	受处罚单位	受处罚原因	处罚金额（万元）
2010	中化开磷化肥有限公司	安全事故致一人死亡	10
	永靖镇火烧井煤矿	掘进头无瓦斯传感器；在技改期间组织生产	65.8
	马家箐煤矿	随意摆放爆破器	2.6
	西洋肥业有限公司	未按安全整改指令完成整改工作	2.9
	安艳烟花爆竹经营店	非法经营、储存烟花爆竹；转让烟花爆竹经营许可证，擅自改变经营许可	0.5

第三节 安全事故查处

2002—2010年，全县共发生各类安全事故376起，死亡190人。其中道路交通事故255起（含铁路交通事故2起），死亡108人；煤矿事故23起，死亡27人；非煤矿山事故6起，死亡6人；工矿企业事故20起，死亡22人；危险化学品生产企业事故1起，死亡2人；危险化学品运输事故1起；化工生产企业事故1起，死亡1人；医药生产企业事故1起，死亡2人；建筑行业事故6起，死亡9人；铁路路外事故12起，死亡12人；房屋火灾事故17起，死亡1人；森林火灾事故33起，过火面积258.1亩，成灾面积13.5亩。

2005年3月24日，贵州西洋肥业有限公司发生中毒窒息事故，致2人死亡，直接经济损失25万元。县安监局根据《使用有毒物品作业场所劳动保护条例》规定，对贵州西洋肥业有限公司处以罚款10万元；对公司有关责任人员给予警告并令其做书面检查等。4月9日，四川大学工程设计院贵阳中化开磷化肥有限公司料浆磷酸一铵装置防腐工程发生重大火灾事故，致5人死亡。贵阳化工机械厂电焊工被吊销资格证书，并被机械厂实施经济处罚；贵阳化工机械厂螺旋机安装作业班长被机械厂实施经济处罚；四川大学工程设计院磷酸项目部施工现场总负责人、河南省孟州市化美防腐保温工程公司负责人、四川大学工程设计院法定代表人、贵阳化工机械厂、河南孟州市华美防腐保温工程公司、四川大学工程设计院、贵州化兴建设监理有限责任公司等个人和单位因对事故负有责任，被贵阳市安监局分别处以0.5万～8万元不等的罚款。6月17日，贵州太和制药有限公司息烽制药厂中药提取罐操作台发生药液喷出事故，致2人死亡。事故主要原因是湖南瑞建节能设备制造有限公司生产的热回流抽提浓缩器设计上存在缺陷。市安监局将调查报告和技术鉴定报告等文函移交湖南永川市安监局处理。县安监局对太和制药有限公司副总经理、太和制药厂厂长、制药厂设备工程部主管分别罚款500元、1000元、500元。7月15日，石硐乡大兴田煤矿发生重大透水事故，致3人死亡，直接经济损失62.8万元。县安监局在查处中首次使用省政府办公厅《关于贯彻落实国务院办公厅进一步加强煤矿安全生产工作紧急通知的意见》，对每个死亡人员家属赔偿20万元。煤矿矿长因重大责任事故罪，被县法院判处有期徒刑三年，缓刑三年；石硐乡乡镇企业管理站技术员被判处有期徒刑一年，缓刑一年；乡镇企业管理站站长被石硐乡政府给予行政记过处分；石硐乡副乡长被县安监局给予行政警告处分。

2006年5月24日，小寨坝镇互通立交桥拆除工程中，因未设置安全提示牌，致使车辆高空坠落，造成2死4伤。贵阳市安监局依据《中华人民共和国安全生产法》对山东省公路工程总公司扎佐至南白高等级公路改扩建工程第九合同段项目部经理罚款4万元；对合同段二工区主任进行警告；施工队长被判处有期徒刑一年，缓刑一年；贵州众品拆除有限公司经理被罚款2万元；监理公司对河北华达公路工程咨询监理有限公司现场监理予以开除处分；驻地高级监理工程师被处罚3万元；山东省公路工程总公司被责令停业整顿；贵州省调整公路开发总公司合同段总监理工程办公室被责成向市安监局作深刻检查。8月21日，永靖镇双龙煤矿发生重大瓦斯爆炸事故，致4人死亡。煤矿法人代表被省煤矿安全监察局、省监察厅移送司法机关追究刑事责任；矿长被吊销“矿长证”并移送司法机关追究刑事责任；驻矿安全督查员、督查小组组长被移送司法机关追究刑事责任；永靖镇企业管理站、安全监察站站长被撤职并移送司法机关追究刑事责任；对永靖镇镇长、县乡镇企业局、煤炭管理局副局长、县安监局局长、副局长、分管安全工作的副县长等人给予记过、警告、书面检查等行政处分；对双龙煤矿超层越界组织生产行为处以100万元罚款。

2008年9月12日，贵州西洋肥业有限公司磷酸分厂散矿仓发生事故，致1人死亡。县安监局对公司处以10万元罚款。公司副总经理、环安部部长分别被处罚2.17万元、1.5万元；磷酸分厂厂长、分厂电工班班长、分厂行车操作工分别被处罚1万元、0.3万元、0.2万元。同月26日，息烽仁都建材有限公司发生事故，造成1人死亡。县安监局对公司处以10万元罚款，对其他相关责任人分别作出罚款处理。

2009年3月5日，贵州鑫悦煤炭有限公司息烽利发煤矿发生顶板事故，致2死1伤。矿长被移送司法机关追究刑事责任；煤矿督查员被县检察院立案调查；当班安全员、跟班矿长、法定代表人被县安监局分别处罚0.2万元、0.5万元、0.2万元。利发煤矿被省煤矿安全监察局林东监察分局处罚19万元。

2010年3月2日，贵阳中化开磷化肥有限公司在对B套浓缩冷凝水收集槽进行焊补作业时发生安全事故，造成1人死亡、1人受伤。该公司因“安全生产主体责任落实不到位，导致事故发生”，被县安监局罚款10万元。

第七章　审　计

1991—2010年，县审计部门坚持以县本级财政预算执行情况及决算和其他财政收支的审计为重点，共完成财政审计64项，查出虚增虚减财政支出、转移财政资金、“与下级往来”核算不实，以及隐瞒预算收入、坐支门面收入、违规超预算购置轿车和个别工作人员非法侵占项目资金等违纪违规资金2598.14万元。兼顾其他，相继开展金融保险、行政事业、农业与环境资源、政府投资项目、领导干部任期经济责任、国有企业、专项资金和外资利用等八个方面的审计业务。

第一节　机　构

1991年1月，县审计局下设财政金融审计股、企业审计股、商粮贸审计股、行政事业审计股等4个专业审计股。1994年4月，县审计局下设办公室、财政金融审计科、企业审计科和行政事业审计科。2002年3月，县审计局下设办公室、审计业务科和经济责任审计科。2010年12月，县审计局下设办公室、政府投资审计监督科、财政金融审计科、行政事业审计科、经济责任审计科。

第二节　审计业务

一、金融、保险审计

1991—2010年，县审计局对中国工商银行息烽县支行、中国农业银行息烽县支行、中国建设银行息烽县支行、中国农业发展银行息烽县支行、贵州省农村信用合作联社息烽县信用联社、中国财产保险公司息烽县支公司、中国人寿保险公司息烽县支公司等金融保险部门的资产、负债、损益情况及财务收支情况进行审计。在审计的19个单位（项目）中，查出收取手续费长期挂账、乱摊成本、虚列费用、多计利息支出、固定资产账实不符以及用假发票虚列支出等违纪违规资金189.5万元。

二、行政事业审计

1991—2010年，县审计局累计完成行政事业单位审计140个，查出超标发给职工福利、劳务奖励、结余资金存入银行支取利息、设置账外账、改变资金投向收取利息以及挪用等违纪违规资金1269.44万元，收缴财政339.4万元。其中：县卫生防疫站违纪资金12.9万元，县移民办结余资金存入银行支取利息，“账外账”以及改变资金投向获取利息等违纪资金326.5万元被收缴。

三、农业与环境资源审计

1991—2010年，县审计局完成对农业、林业、水利等各类专项资金审计项目42个，查出超标资金占用费、资金投入不足、虚列扶贫项目购置轿车、挤占扶贫项目资金、违规发放扶贫补助等违纪违规资金512.8万元。审计局对此处以37.5万元罚款，并将虚列支出购置的桑塔纳轿车一辆没收上缴财政；滞留财政的扶贫资金103.1万元，责成县本级财政将资金拨付到位。

四、政府投资项目审计

2002年，县审计局开始对政府投资项目进行审计。至2010年，共完成审计项目327个，审减资金4174.9万元，占送审金额33255.16万元的12.55%。

五、领导干部任期经济责任审计

2000—2010年，县审计局对县农机厂、县乡镇企业总公司、县自来水公司、县交通局、县粮食局、县林业局、县水利局、县农业办公室以及永靖镇、石硐乡、温泉镇、九庄镇等10乡镇共22个单位主要负责人进行任期经济责任审计。审计查出私设“小金库”、管理不善造成固定资产损失、流动资金损失、挪用专用资金、转移专款、挪用应上缴劳动保护费等违纪违规资金1601.77万元。

六、国有企业审计

1991—1993年，县审计局连续3年对县属国有工商企业实行承包经营审计，查出违纪违规资金137万元，其中收缴财政19.7万元。1994年起，县国有企业不再实行承包经营，烟草、石油、盐业等单位上划集团公司直接管辖，审计监督工作重点随之转到国家财政资金方面。2003—2004年，开展对县国有投资公司和县自来水公司财务收支审计，查出隐瞒应缴国资收益、固定资产账实不符等违纪违规资金183.63万元。

七、专项资金审计

1991—2010年，县审计局开展新型农村合作医疗资金、社会救灾救济资金、义务教育专项经费、煤炭价格调节基金、农村养老保险基金、人口与计生专项经费等27项专项审计和审计调查。查出购置大宗物资未按规定实行政府采购以及虚列支出弥补办公经费，内部结算票据以记做支等违纪违规资金147.11万元。县审计局责令县农业办公室收回违规资金，归还原资金渠道。

八、外资利用审计

1995年起，经上级授权，县审计局审计县卫生局、教育局、水利局等单位负责实施的世界银行贷款项目，截至2007年，累计审计129个单位（项目），提交正式审计报告29份。2008年起，世界银行贷款项目改由省、市审计机关直接审计，县审计工作终止。

息烽县1991—2010年审计局主要审计成果统计表

表15-7-1

年份	审计单位（家）	违纪违规资金（万元）	应上缴财政（万元）	已收缴财政（万元）	审计覆盖率（%）
1991	80	263	6	4	83
1992	44	95	15	6	46
1993	25	60	1	1	26
1994	12	25	—	—	13
1995	9	27	16	16	9
1996	19	640	4	3	20
1997	19	165	8	6	20
1998	20	90	26	26	21
1999	25	374	—	—	26
2000	24	200	49	19	23
2001	27	502	331	318	28
2002	32	492.5	396	356	33
2003	32	419	166	151	33
2004	25	668	7	7	26
2005	32	221	—	—	33
2006	36	945	928	283	36
2007	25	987	124	90	26
2008	18	2360	5.71	5.71	19
2009	19	2690	19	22.22	20
2010	31	1073	3	3	34

第八章 国土管理

1991—2010年，县国土资源管理部门执行国家土地管理法律法规，开展地籍管理、土地规划、土地使用权制度改革、土地开发与保护、土地监察等工作，土地资源得到合理利用和有效保护。

第一节 机 构

一、局机构

1991年，县土地管理局内设办公室，下辖永阳、养龙、九庄、黑神庙和永靖镇5个区（镇）土地管理站。1992年2月，区（镇）撤销土地管理站建置，建10个乡（镇）土地管理所。4月，县设立矿产资源管理办公室，归口县政府办公室。1994年5月，县矿产资源管理办公室对外挂县地质矿产局牌子。

1995年11月，原县土地管理局、地质矿产局、环境保护局、移民办公室合并，成立县国土局，承担环保、地矿、土地、测绘和移民工作。次年4月，县国土局内设机构改为办公室、国土规划建设用地管理科、地籍科、矿产资源管理科。1996年6月，移民办公室由国土局分出，成为独立建制。1997年1月，县国土局增设监察室。5月，内设机构调整为办公室、地籍科（挂县测绘管理办公室牌子）、环境保护科、建设用地管理科、国土法规监督管理科。1999年4月，县编委明确10乡镇土地管理所为县国土局派出机构。6月，县环境保护局由县国土局分出，县国土局环境保护科随之划出。

2001年9月，县国土局更名为县国土资源局。2002年4月，县国土资源局所辖各乡镇土地管理所更名为国土资源所。2003年9月，县国土资源局增设法规监察科。2005年12月，县国土资源局内设机构调整为办公室、人事教育科、法规监察科、用地规划管理科、地矿科，下辖10个乡镇国土资源所。

二、局属事业单位

1991年，县土地管理局下设县城乡建设用地征拨站、土地勘测规划站、地籍管理站、土地法规监察站等4个股所级事业单位。1994年8月，地价评估所成立，地籍管理站加挂县地价评估所牌子。1996年4月，县国土局撤销城乡建设用地征拨站，工作职能划归国土局各有关科室。是月，矿产资源管理站、环保监理站成立，县矿产资源管理站加挂矿产资源管理科牌子。1999年6月，县环保监理站随县环保局从国土局分出。

2003年9月，县土地交易所成立。2005年12月，土地登记所、县国土资源信息管理办公室成立。2008年4月，土地收购储备交易中心成立，撤销土地交易所建制。至2010年，国土资源局所属股所级事业单位有县土地勘测规划站、地籍管理站、土地法规监察站、地质矿产管理站、地价评估所、土地登记所、国土资源信息管理办公室、土地收购储备交易中心8个。

第二节　地籍管理

1991年7月，完成农村宅基地调查确权工作。测绘地籍图、登记38975宗，面积12.26平方千米，发证383宗；城镇地籍调查2331宗，面积2.79平方千米；独立工矿地66宗，面积2.8平方千米。8月，省、地组织验收。此后，开展农村宅基地、国有土地复查补缺工作。至1995年，全县有土地登记发证户49956户、79285宗地，面积1657.07公顷。其中农村集体土地宅基地76298宗，面积1160.73公顷；国有土地2987宗，使用面积496.34公顷。农村宅基地登记发证到户15115户、17429宗，面积256.47公顷。国有土地登记发证1259宗，面积30.41公顷。

1996年，农村集体土地发证21002个、26167宗、22738户，面积279.43公顷。国有土地发证930个、956宗、701户，总面积4404.3公顷。是年8月底，完成流长变电站、九庄自来水供水池、高洞水池、小桥河管理所、小桥河水库、下洪马渠道、长岭岗水池、下洪马黄家大坡水池、下洪马水库管理所、下洪马库区、底寨河管理所、底寨河水管所预留地、底寨河渠道、乌鸦嘴河渠、养龙司电灌站、电灌站水池、电灌渠道等17宗地确权划界工作。办理国有土地使用证17个，总面积3670.88万平方米。

1997年起，开展土地使用权初始登记工作。至1999年，共完成国有土地使用权登记635户、645宗，发证645个；农村集体土地登记1560户、1726宗，发证1660个。

2000年，继续开展国有土地使用权证书年检工作，审核登记发证2350宗，面积101.27公顷。办理土地使用权抵押登记63宗，面积9.8公顷。办理非耕地土地使用权抵押登记4宗，面积0.17公顷。

此后，土地变更登记发证、土地抵押登记、土地使用权登记发证、土地权属变更、证书年检等地籍管理工作形成常态化，常年开展。

2010年，办理国有土地使用权登记发证579个，面积82.16公顷。集体土地登记发证545个，面积6.85公顷。抵押登记87宗，面积38.88公顷，金额668.57万元。

第三节　土地规划

一、第一轮《规划》编制（1990—2000年）

1989年，省土地管理局确定息烽县为编制《土地利用总体规划》试点县。1990年11月，规划编制工作启动。规划以1989年为基期年，2000年为规划目标、任务年。1992年1月完成规划编制。

二、第二轮《规划》编制（1997—2010年）

1996年5月，县土地利用总体规划修编工作启动。规划以1996年为基期年，2000年为近期年，2010为年规划目标年。

1998年10月9日，《息烽县土地利用总体规划（含基本农田保护区规划）》通过省、市专家组评审。2000年3月9日，省政府批准《息烽县土地利用总体规划》。同时，开展10个乡镇的土地利用总体规划编制工作。

三、第三轮《规划》编制（2006—2020年）

2007年，《息烽县土地利用总体规划》编修大纲通过市级专家评审组验收，同意进入第三轮规划修编。2009年，第三轮规划编修（2006—2020年）工作启动。第三轮规划以2005年为基期年，

2010年为近期年，2020年为规划目标年。规划范围为县行政区划范围内的所有土地。县土地总面积103652.62公顷。

息烽县部分年份土地利用规划调控指标统计表

表15-8-1　　单位：公顷

指　标	2005年	2009年	2010年	2020年	指标属性
耕地保有量	31365	33102.59	32670	31653	约束性
基本农田保护面积	25088.17	25785.42	26920	26920	约束性
园地面积	402.99	662.56	670	800	预期性
林地面积	40448.25	46938.73	46500	46000	预期性
牧草地面积	9535.27	—	300	7000	预期性
建设用地总规模	5416.61	4444.59	6110	7332	预期性
城乡建设用地规模	3091.99	3454.25	3470	3777	约束性
城镇工矿用地规模	921.47	838.12	1161	1809	预期性
新增建设用地占用农用地规模	—	—	598	1463	预期性
新增建设用地占用耕地规模	—	—	264	709	约束性
整理复垦开发补充耕地规模	—	—	254	575	约束性
亿元GDP耗地量	228.11公顷/亿元	—	110公顷/亿元	60公顷/亿元	预期性
人均城镇工矿用地	95.2平方米/人	—	100平方米/人	110平方米/人	预期性

第四节　土地使用权制度改革

一、土地使用权出让

1987年，国务院先后颁布《城镇土地定级规程（试行）》《城镇土地估价规程（试行）》等文件。1990年，县内开始土地使用有偿出让工作。至2010年年底，共计出让土地531宗，面积277.18公顷，出让价款38621.2万元。

息烽县1990—2010年土地使用权出让统计表

表15-8-2

年份	出让数（宗）	出让面积（公顷）	出让价款（万元）
1990—2004	415	35.4	2398.41
2005	20	3.46	1595.06
2006	45	61.88	2146.93
2007	13	48.67	2146.93
2008	12	3.57	363.9
2009	8	1.16	69.97
2010	18	123.04	29900

二、非耕地拍卖

1994年，县委、县政府决定在全县开展非耕地公开拍卖工作。同年9月，在西山乡进行试点，拍卖非耕地1宗88公顷，拍卖金7.42万元。此后，非耕地公开拍卖在全县推开，适时组织拍卖，至2000年，全县共拍卖出让非耕地106宗，面积2189.57公顷，收取拍卖金25.38万元。2001年起，停止非耕地拍卖。

息烽县1994—2000年非耕地拍卖统计表

表15-8-3

年份	拍卖数（宗）	拍卖面积（公顷）	开发面积（公顷）
1994	1	88	88
1995	45	1121.09	578.4
1996	28	599.39	843.27
1997	30	316.6	316.6
1998	1	55.87	55.87
1999	0	0	0
2000	1	6.89	6.89

第五节　土地开发与保护

一、土地开发

1991年，全县有可开垦荒草地3600余公顷。1998年，国土管理部门配合农业部门进行荒坡改梯土90公顷，荒坡改梯田6.8公顷。

1999年，组织实施规划管理、保护和土地利用的国土资源大调查。查清全县有15°～25°土地1229.62公顷、25°～35°坡耕地4178.17公顷、大于35°的坡耕地1230.02公顷。开展耕地后备资源调查统计，全县有可成片开发的宜耕地和荒地415.9公顷，其中可开垦的荒草地404.19公顷，可治理的水毁地11.71公顷。开发耕地68公顷。

2000年起，实施耕地占补平衡规划。开发新增耕地图斑14个，增加耕地129.43公顷。至2003年，新增耕地开发图斑立项19个，开发新增耕地144.48公顷。

2004年，国家投资700余万元的九庄片区土地开发项目4个标段全面开工。2005年，完成九庄片区涉及9个行政村的408.27公顷土地开发。修建支渠11610米、斗渠4595米、农梁9532米、田间道路17694米、生产路15586米。建提水泵站1座。2006年实施青山开发项目，开发新增耕地38.57公顷。2007年，实施土地开发项目3个，面积15.26公顷。2009年，石硐乡难冲桥村5个坡土开发项目、石硐村螺蛳垭口土地开发项目完成验收，共新增耕地8.2公顷，并取得新增耕地合格证。

2010年，县国土资源管理部门向省国土资源厅借用1242.05亩新增耕地指标，实现县内“双保行动”和“扩大内需”等建设项目补充耕地异地占补平衡。向市土地开发中心购买516.36亩新增耕地指标，实现小寨坝镇磷煤化工基地2期工业建设项目补充耕地异地占补平衡。

二、土地整理

1991—2006年，国土资源管理部门协助有关农业部门完成以工代赈的坡改梯8733.48公顷，增加有效耕地面积1047.45公顷，治理水土流失158.18平方千米，改造中低产农田2806.67公顷。其间，组织实施荒坡改梯土整理180.67公顷。建成永靖镇老厂村、石硐乡高寨、小寨坝镇南桥村80公顷高标准农田。九庄片区土地整理项目完工验收，新增耕地2.03公顷。

2007—2009年，相继组织实施青山绿化村，九庄镇洞坪子、盘龙山、杨家海，石硐乡高寨村、难冲桥村土地整理项目和永靖镇老厂村高标准农田建设项目，总投资1541.26万元，设计新增耕地面积19.62公顷。

2010年，土地整理项目点共有6个，涉及流长、鹿窝、西山、青山、永靖5个乡镇，总面积849.25公顷。其中，可抵2010年新实施土地整理项目任务722公顷。

三、土地保护

1991年，在编制第一轮土地利用总体规划中，划定基本农田保护区保护面积2.52万公顷。

一等保护区：永靖镇、九庄乡、养龙司乡、小寨坝乡、温泉乡（不含兴隆村）、底寨乡（不含团元山村）、阳朗乡（不含联丰村）、管田村、盘脚营村、马当田村、下阳朗村、硬寨村、鹿窝村、竹花村、新田村、杉林村、潮水村、大寨村、关岭村、大清村、王家坪村、前进村。

二等保护区：鹿窝乡、流长乡、茅坡乡、新场乡、石硐乡、青山乡、梨安乡、安江乡、联合村、胜利村、新寨沟村、红星村、何家硐村、玉龙村、西安村、红岩村、合箭村、龙塘村、甘溪村、瓮沙村、雨洒村、河坎村、老厂村。

三等保护区：南极乡、兴隆村、联丰村、团元山村、上洪马村、大洪村、中坝村。

1997年，在第二轮规划中，全县划定基本农田保护区10个、保护区161个、保护块2.3万个。全县耕地面积32762.64公顷，划定保护面积30141.63公顷，保护耕地占92%。其中一级保护24716.13公顷，占保护面积的82%；二级保护5425.49公顷，占保护面积的18%；规划建设预留地52块，面积983公顷，占保护面积的3%。设立保护标志25块，埋设保护区界桩350个，与农户签订保护责任书52135份。

2000年，开展基本农田保护区调整划定工作，调整县、乡（镇）土地总体规划和基本农田保护区，划定基本农田保护区10个、保护区161个、保护地块12587块，面积27981.1公顷，保护率85.4%。建设预留地227个图斑，287.8公顷。

第六节　土地监察

一、国土资源动态巡查

2002年，县国土资源局先后制定完善《国土资源执法监察巡查制度》《违法行为举报制度》《行政过错追究制度》《错案追究制度》《执法监督制度》《执法监察制度》等一系列制度，并在全县10个乡（镇）161个村建立巡查网络点1476个。是年起，开展国土资源执法监察动态巡查，至2010年，共巡查9275次，发现国土、矿产资源违法案件1564起，现场制止1302起。其中：拆除建筑物20宗，面积3713平方米，没收建筑物面积3577平方米；收缴罚款367.39万元，挽回经济损失436.5万元；取缔无证砂厂、矿山89个、磷矿山4个，封闭磷矿非法采矿点1个；炸封无证煤窑514个次，拆除机械设备30台，收缴皮带49件、工具230件，没收矿产品1735.5吨，查处率100%。立案275起，结案275起，做到立案1起，查处1起。

二、违法占地查处

1991—2010年，共立案查处违法占地2730宗，面积145.6公顷。查处2699宗，结案率98.86%。其中收回土地10.27公顷；拆除建筑物79宗，收回土地2.97公顷，申请法院强制执行131宗，结案131宗，结案率100%。收缴各类违法占地罚款1826.37万元。

息烽县1991—2010年土地违法案件查处统计表

表15-8-4

年份	立案数（件）	结案数（件）	查结率（%）
1991	254	227	92.6
1992	54	54	100
1993	262	262	100
1994	73	73	100
1995	381	381	100
1996	550	550	100
1997	556	556	100
1998	197	197	100
1999	120	120	100
2000	55	53	96.4
2001	32	32	100
2002	0	0	0
2003	69	69	100
2004	—	—	—
2005	19	19	100
2006	16	15	93.7
2007	22	21	95.5
2008	7	7	100
2009	7	7	100
2010	56	56	100

三、土地卫片执法检查

2010年，按照《国土资源部关于开展2009年度土地卫片执法检查工作的通知》精神，县成立土地卫片（卫星图片）执法检查工作领导小组，开展2009年度土地卫片执法检查，完成县境内16个图斑的内外业工作和卫片档案归档及网上在线填报工作。对在卫片执法中发现的3宗卫片土地违法案件进行立案查处，结案率100%。

第九章　招商引资

1998年6月，县成立招商委员会办公室，为县招商委员会日常办事机构。2001年12月29日，组建县一站式服务办公室。2002年3月6日，成立县招商引资局，下设办公室、项目科、招商引资科、投资服务科。

第一节　投资环境建设

1998年5月20日，县政府出台第一部招商引资优惠政策——《息烽县人民政府招商引资优惠政策》（以下简称《政策》）。规定：县外投资者到县兴办乡镇企业，一律由招商办限时代办一切手续。“一站式”服务办公室协调相关部门提供投资政策、项目审批、规划选址、工商登记的咨询和服务工作。

2001—2002年，先后在《参考消息》《大公报》《西部开发报》及新华网等新闻媒体，宣传推介县的投资环境和招商项目，以吸引外商来县考察、投资。县委、县政府领导亲自参加各种大型招商活动，并聘请省、市和企业有关专家组成经济顾问团，为县域经济发展献计献策。

2002年10月，贵阳市投资9000余万元的鱼简河大型水库动工修建，并相继建设上沟、马家箐2个水库和唐家湾、彭家垭口、西山、大坪、养龙司、温泉、九庄、何家硐、石硐、鹿窝10个符合国家饮用水标准的现代化净水厂。在抓好入驻企业围墙外基础设施建设的同时，确保水、电、路、通讯、电视等“六到位”；实现乡乡通油路，村村通公路；电力、通信等设施不断加强，基础设施明显改善，使入驻企业来得了，留得住。是年，全县建立和完善招商引资“一把手工程”制度、项目跟踪落实责任制度、政府与企业双向承包制度、监督检查制度和招商引资奖励制度等“五项安商制度”，确保各项政策措施落到实处。积极进行主动服务、超前服务、跟踪服务、全程服务和免费服务等“五个服务”，及时解决引资入驻项目建设中遇到的各种矛盾和问题。

2007年，修改原招商引资优惠政策，出台《息烽县招商引资政策》。次年，县委、县政府出台《息烽县招商引资奖励政策》。是年4月，成立以县委书记、县长为组长，分管领导为副组长的招商引资工作领导小组，以做好小寨坝磷化工基地、乌江峡、西望山旅游景区开发和县城南大街建设等项目的“产前、产中、产后全程服务”。企业入驻后，及时在价格、税收、基础设施配套上分阶段兑现有关政策和承诺。为加大政策扶持力度，积极支持企业做大做强，本着“扶上马，送一程”原则，针对企业发展资金、流动资金紧缺等困难和问题，及时采用国资抵押担保方式为企业贷款。

2008年，县委、县政府出台《关于开展“整治发展软环境　建设服务型机关”专项工作的实施意见》，从制度和纪律等方面对各级各部门进行强制约束，以保障投资者的合法权益。要求各安商服务单位公开办事政策、办事内容、办事程序、办事人员，承诺服务标准、服务时限。

2009年，县招商局与县新闻中心合作建设县第一个招商网站，利用县政府网站、“息烽欢迎你”“贵州农经网”等网站宣传县招商引资政策。同时，通过青山苗族“四月八”文化节、贵阳避暑季、红岩葡萄节等活动对外宣传息烽。

第二节　引资项目

1998—2010年，县招商引资部门与投资商共签约项目203个，协议总投资307.18亿元，实际到位资金92.06亿元。

息烽县1998—2010年部分年份招商签约项目统计表

表15-9-1

年份	签约单位或个人	签约项目名称
1998	天龙魔芋食品公司	特种蔬菜种植和加工项目；新建贵阳天龙魔芋食品总厂项目
	贵州太和制药有限公司	年产1.2亿粒“单痔胶囊”项目
1999	贵州息烽特种水泥有限责任公司	年产特种水泥12万吨的息烽特种水泥厂建设项目
2000	贵州鸿佳物业发展有限公司	息烽温泉旅游度假区建设项目
2001	贵阳金盛农业发展有限公司	息烽县1000吨气调保鲜库工程建设项目
	贵阳联大绿化食品有限公司	辣椒及蔬菜种植、加工项目
	利尔房地产开发有限公司	房地产开发项目
	贵阳苗姑娘食品有限公司	年产“苗姑娘”系列辣椒50万件项目
	贵州中创房地产开发有限公司	息烽县东门小区开发项目
	贵州厦龙房地产开发有限公司	息烽县城南大街开发建设项目
2002	开磷集团	磷化工加工项目
	西洋肥业公司	年产100万吨硫基复合肥项目
	贵州汉方药业	年产1000万支羟基喜树碱和1000万支盐酸拓扑替康项目
2004	息烽合力化工股份有限公司	黄磷生产项目
	香港大友公司	无患子种植项目
	开磷集团	开磷新城建设项目
2006	陕西澄城铝建公司	息烽铝厂收购项目
	浙江投资商	年产5000万条彩印编织袋厂建设项目
	浙江慈溪娱乐城	液化气管道及分装项目
	贵州华丹完全生物降解塑料有限公司	完全生物降解塑料生产项目
	重庆渝万集团	息烽县城中街旧城改造项目
2007	重庆万盛煤炭有限公司	原煤生产项目
	重庆梁平县邵沟煤炭有限公司	息烽下阳朗煤矿和双龙井煤矿收购项目
	重庆渝万集团	息烽县城中街娱乐城建设项目

续表

年份	签约单位或个人	签约项目名称
2008	江苏投资商朱仁良	筑北港口建设项目
	贵州腾龙宏升农业科技发展有限公司	食用菌种植项目
	贵州开磷有限公司和贵阳公共交通总公司	合成氨尾气综合利用项目
	贵州辉皇畜牧业有限公司	年出栏2000头优质肉牛高效循环农业示范基地扩建项目
	四川特驱家禽养殖有限公司	养鸡、养猪和饲料加工项目
	贵州裕万家林工贸公司	息烽猫场裕万家林场现代林业综合开发产业化经营项目
2009	贵阳成华苗圃场	息烽成华生态园林场建设项目
	湖北投资商	100万吨水泥粉磨站建设项目
	张启云	息烽旅游特色产品研发项目；息烽阳朗河乡村旅游开发项目
	贵州省江西商会	鑫玉龙水会建设项目
	浙江慈溪金星娱乐城	怡乐浴园休闲项目
	东北投资商	金钯养殖基地建设项目
	长虹铸造厂建设项目	四川投资商
2010	贵州海城房地产开发有限公司	四星级宾馆建设项目
	王伦甫	三星级酒店建设项目
	息烽捷浪建材开发有限公司	磷石膏板材生产建设项目
	广州石碣润丰国际蔬菜交易中心	广州石碣润丰国际蔬菜交易中心建设项目
	中国华能赫章风力发电有限公司	华能息烽风力发电厂建设项目
	合肥宁垣工程技术有限公司	科技节能环保备件生产项目
	息烽隆鑫生态园绿化有限公司	息烽县橘橙基地建设项目
	贵州华山水绿化工程有限公司	优质核桃苗圃生产基地建设项目
	息烽红海建材有限公司	磷石膏建材生产线建设项目
	息烽宏鑫沥青浇灌公司	沥青拌合站建设项目
	息烽清涛生态养殖有限公司	生态农业观光肉牛养殖项目
	贵州祥盛益农业养殖有限公司	养殖、种植场及饮料加工厂建设项目
	贵州玖能矿业有限公司	矿产品经营项目
	息烽振兴煤业有限责任公司	煤炭经营项目

第十六篇　教育·科技

第一章　教　育

1991年，全县有幼儿园5所，在园幼儿409人；小学138所，入学率97%；中学17所，初中毛入学率49.9%。1997年，随着“两基”工作的实施，县教育局制定县中小学布局调整规划，逐步整合全县教育资源。至2010年，全县有幼儿园24所，在园幼儿4036人；小学60所，入学率99.5%；中学11所，毛入学率115%。20年间，全县先后实施高标准扫盲，两基（基本普及九年义务教育、基本扫除青壮年文盲）、普实（普及实验教学）和新课程改革，逐步形成由学前教育、义务教育、普通高中教育、中等职业教育、成人教育、特殊教育组成的教育体系。

第一节　教育管理机构

1991年，县教育局内设秘书股、人事股、教育股、计财股、职业教育股、教研室、农教办公室；同时在永阳区、养龙司区、九庄区、黑神庙区设教育办公室，设教办主任和“三教”专干，即普教专干、农教专干、扫盲教育专干。1992年撤区并乡建镇后，在乡镇设教育辅导站。1996年，教育局内设办公室、政工科、招考办、教育科、计财科、教研室6个科室。2000年12月，设办公室、政工科、教育科、计财科、招生考试办公室、教研室、督导室7个科室。2002年，内设机构由7个科室调整为5个，即办公室、督导室、教育科、政工科、计财科；招考办、教研室改为事业单位。2004年，设立县政府教育督导室，改变过去督导室作为教育局内设机构的体制。2010年，县教育局内设办公室、计财科、教育科、政工科4个行政机构和招考办、教研室2个事业单位。

第二节　学前教育

一、幼儿园

1991年，全县有县机关、粮食局、底寨、国营276厂、息烽磷矿幼儿园5所，其中教育部门办3所，企业办2所；班级16个，在园幼儿409人，教师22人。1992年，幼儿入园年龄为：托幼班2～2.5岁，小班2.5～3.3岁，中班3.5～4.5岁，大班城镇为5岁，农村为6岁。1994年，粮食局幼儿园停办。1997年，启动“两基”教育，动员失、辍学儿童复学，小学学生人数增加，校舍紧张，各校附设学前班控制招生数，不再增加学前班，为幼儿园提供发展空间。1999年，全县有幼儿园11所，在园幼儿突破1200人，民办幼儿园从县城向乡镇发展。2002年，取消小学附设学前班，多数学前班教师转入幼儿园任教或自办学前班。至2010年，全县有幼儿园24所，其中公办幼儿园7所、民办幼儿园17所，教职工236人，在园幼儿4036人。

二、学前班

1991年，全县小学附设学前班19个，在班幼儿1250人，教师25人。1992年，县教育局按照《幼儿教育大纲》要求，将学前班年龄定为城镇5岁，农村6岁。1993年，有学前班35个，在班幼儿1680人，教师35人。1996年，国务院、省、市三级妇儿工委联合专家组经过考察论证，将息烽定为贫困地区实施《儿童发展规划纲要》试点县；同年，市教委明确息烽为“贫困地区幼儿教育现状调查与对策研究”课题试点县。探索贫困地区多渠道多形式办班路子和提高幼教质量的途径，推广以乐为主的学前教育模式。1998年3月，县教育局出台《关于进一步办好幼儿园　学前班的意见》。批准学前班130个，在班幼儿2342人，教师131人。2000年，县教育局按照省教育厅关于全省中小学布局结构调整意见，将学前班逐步从小学中剥离出来。2002年，公办小学全部取消附设学前班。2003年，原学前班教师办民办学前班106个，在班幼儿1618人，有教师95人。至2010年，全县有学前班6个，在班幼儿305人。

三、幼教课程·教师

1991年，县内幼儿教师无一具备幼教资格。幼儿教育没有统一教材，由各幼儿园和学前班自行选用教材。1992年，全县统一使用省教委编写的《学前班教材（教师用书）》和《学前班课本（幼儿用书）》。1993年，县教育局在县职校开设幼师班，招收94名初中毕业以上文化的青年和在职幼儿教师进行为期3年的学习，在取得学历合格证后分配到各小学担任幼儿教师。使用贵州人民出版社编印的《语言》《数学》《常识》《美工》《好行为》作为幼儿教育教材。1998年后，县教育局把教师必须具备全日制中等幼儿师范学历作为审批条件之一。2000年，全县153名幼儿教师学历达标121人。2005年，使用教育科学出版社出版的幼儿教育教材。通过说话、计算、游戏、儿歌、手工制作开发智力，促进幼儿能力和个性发展。每周以班级为单位开展评比活动，每学期评选“乖娃娃”或“红花少年”进行表彰。

四、卫生保健与安全

全县幼儿园和学前班保证幼儿每天有2小时以上活动时间，每半年检测身高、体重、视力一次，定期开展幼儿免疫防治；随时排查和消除教室、活动设施设备安全隐患；上学放学由家长接送。学前班不提供就餐，幼儿园提供早中餐，寄宿幼儿活动每天不少于3小时，就餐间隔不少于3.5小时。

息烽县1991—2010年学前教育统计表

表16-1-1

年份	园数（家）	班数（个）	在班人数（人）	学前班数（个）	在班人数（人）	在园班总幼儿数（人）
1991	5	16	409	123	956	1365
1992	5	24	505	125	963	1468
1993	5	24	737	126	1025	1762
1994	4	15	1088	126	1358	2446
1995	7	37	1199	127	1817	3016

续表

年份	园数（家）	班数（个）	在班人数（人）	学前班数（个）	在班人数（人）	在园班总幼儿数（人）
1996	7	42	1337	129	2187	3524
1997	7	58	1697	129	2165	3862
1998	7	74	1899	131	2342	4166
1999	11	88	1784	130	2267	4501
2000	8	143	4026	132	418	4444
2001	7	141	336	128	5712	6048
2002	10	276	235	264	3793	4028
2003	8	136	510	106	3681	4191
2004	10	124	517	99	3052	3569
2005	13	114	897	80	2788	3685
2006	14	122	858	91	2939	3795
2007	13	116	1038	82	2677	3715
2008	25	101	1413	52	1969	3382
2009	20	79	3340	4	132	3472
2010	24	130	3984	18	181	4165

第三节　义务教育

一、学校

1991年，全县有小学138所、教学点48个、初级中学9所、完全中学2所、“戴帽”初中7所、十二年制学校1所、九年制学校1所。青山、安马、江土、茅坡、温泉、竹花、王家坪等小学附设初中。小学教师1202人，初中教师402人。在校小学生31936人，入学率97%、巩固率96.5%、毕业率94%、普及率97.8%；在校初中生7947人，初中阶段毛入学率49.9%、辍学率6.23%。

1993年，全县开始有计划地撤销小学戴帽初中和生源不足的小型村级小学及教学点。1994年，永生私立中学和息烽武术学校创办。1997年，随着“两基”工作的实施，县教育局制定县第一轮中小学布局调整规划，采取“撤并改”办法，将135所小学调整为128所。

1998年，县委、县政府制发《关于实施“国家贫困地区义务教育工程”的意见》，对全县教育资源进行整合，对学校建设重点、办学规模、寄宿制学校分布作出规划和调整。至2002年，全县有小学95所、教学点14个；初中11所、完全中学4所、十二年制学校2所、九年制学校2所。

2003年，再次进行中小学布局调整，将95所小学调整为62所，教学点43个，在全县10个乡镇设置初级中学，初级中学调至11所（不含民办中学）。

2010年，全县有小学60所、教学点22个、初级中学11所、完全中学1所、12年制学校1所。在校小学学生17762人，入学率99.53%，小学教师1136人。有初级中学9所、九年制学校2所、十二年制学校1所、完全中学1所。在校生12152人，入学率115.04%，初中教师581人。

息烽县1991—2010年普通小学统计表

表16-1-2

年份	学校数（所）	教学点（个）	班数（个）	招生数（人）	学生总数（人）	毕业生数（人）	教师数（人）	入学率（%）
1991	138	48	1051	4746	31417	4905	1202	97
1992	136	52	1050	4576	30408	5252	1205	97
1993	137	44	1030	3969	29470	4525	1277	97
1994	138	43	1022	4573	29753	4324	1279	98.5
1995	138	40	1022	4821	29408	4150	1270	98.7
1996	137	36	1032	5040	29482	4396	1280	98.9
1997	139	32	1028	4435	29519	4052	1302	98.9
1998	132	7	951	4220	28825	4301	1369	99.2
1999	121	7	916	3878	28011	4374	1406	99.5
2000	101	12	867	4371	28352	4774	1486	99.2
2001	95	14	827	4699	27430	5007	1398	99.2
2002	95	14	832	4947	27155	4958	1387	99.4
2003	62	43	801	4145	26729	4283	1415	99.4
2004	62	43	775	4267	26452	4140	1413	99.45
2005	62	42	737	3570	25099	4508	1398	99.54
2006	62	39	694	3773	24420	4156	1302	99.8
2007	62	37	657	3093	22518	4375	1252	98.97
2008	60	25	613	2855	20664	4473	1253	99.16
2009	60	25	592	2581	19218	3955	1260	99.31
2010	60	22	561	2620	17762	3853	1136	99.52

息烽县1991—2010年普通中学统计表

表16-1-3

年份	学校数（所）	教学点（个）	班数（个）	招生数（人）	学生总数（人）	毕业生数（人）	教师数（人）	毛入学率（%）
1991	17	20	152	2688	7947	2476	402	68.3
1992	17	20	158	2849	7798	2554	402	69.2
1993	17	20	160	2595	7344	2404	413	70.5
1994	17	21	158	2609	7157	2162	419	72.3
1995	17	21	185	2849	7473	2174	444	79.1
1996	12	—	173	3848	8370	2466	430	88.1

续表

年份	学校数（所）	教学点（个）	班数（个）	招生数（人）	学生总数（人）	毕业生数（人）	教师数（人）	毛入学率（%）
1997	12	—	186	3858	9489	1990	486	93.2
1998	14	—	209	4110	11064	2103	523	108.2
1999	12	—	211	4000	11218	3171	590	106.5
2000	13	17	248	4578	11793	3504	615	107
2001	11	18	228	4372	12412	3279	613	112
2002	11	19	238	4894	13392	3500	624	111.7
2003	11	18	225	3843	12256	4193	612	97.6
2004	13	16	216	3987	11963	3641	599	101.32
2005	14	19	214	4069	11675	3843	560	103.06
2006	15	18	212	4167	11605	3953	570	107.17
2007	16	15	207	4347	11995	3520	567	105.88
2008	11	14	226	4259	12727	3420	578	112.52
2009	11	14	218	4004	12658	3686	589	115.14
2010	11	14	212	3926	12152	4089	581	115.04

二、课程设置与教改

（一）小学课程设置

1991年，执行国家教委《九年义务教育课程计划（试行）》，小学一、二年级设《思想品德》《语文》《数学》《自然》《体育》《音乐》《美术》7科，三年级以上增加《劳动》，四年级以上增加《社会》，同时开设班队活动、体育活动、科技活动；周课时总量一年级29节，二、三年级30节，四、五、六年级31节。2001年，全县片区中心小学从三年级开始开设英语课。2004年秋季，实施新课改后，小学《思想品德》一、二年级改为《品德与生活》，三到六年级改为《品德与社会》，取消四到六年级的《社会》学科。县内实施新一轮课程改革，小学先后选用西南师范、江苏教育、北京师范大学、教育科学出版社等10余家出版社教材。2005年9月，取消小学一到六年级的《自然》，从三年级起设《科学》。同年，一到六年级开设综合实践活动课，将原来的体育课改为体育与健康课。2006年，全县小学统一使用人民教育出版社和江苏教育出版社出版的九年义务教育教材。

2008年，流长小学校长王济金倡导，在该校推行国学经典进课堂，要求学生诵读《弟子规》《三字经》《百家姓》《朱子治家格言》《孝经》《道德经》等。随即推广到流长乡其他中小学。至2010年，流长小学学生“好行为”“好习惯”养成效果明显，国学经典教育产生影响，家长和社会各界人士予以好评。

（二）初中课程设置

1991年，中学开设《政治》《语文》《数学》《英语》《历史》《地理》《生物》《体育》《音乐》《美术》，初二以上开设《物理》，初三开设《化学》。同时，每年安排劳动技术课二周，但多数学校强调文化课，劳动技术课基本未开。1993年，全县使用九年义务教育配套教材，根据需要开设科技活动、健康教育、禁毒教育等课程。2004年实施新课改，将《政治》改成《思想品德》。选用人民教育出版社、北京仁爱出版社、湖南岳麓书社、上海科技出版社、华东师大出版社等出版社出版的教材。在农村普通初中（县及县以下初中）开设“农村实用科技”地方课程，学生学完“农村实用科技”课程考核合格者，发给“绿色证书”。

县内教学推行以教师为主导、学生为主体、训练为主线的教学方法，教育学生学会探索，学会求知，学会生活。

三、学制学籍

（一）学制

9年义务教育，小学实行6年制，初中实行3年制。

1991—1997年，六年级由学校统一命题举行毕业考试，考试合格的发给毕业证书（1996年后发义务教育证书），再由全县统一命题举行升学考试。各中学按照划定的录取分数线录取小学毕业生进入初中学习。息烽中学、城关中学除招收县城小学毕业生外，还面向全县招收优秀学生。初中毕业考试由县统一组织，思想品德、体育考核合格，毕业考试成绩达到毕业规定要求的，准予毕业。高中升学考试由市统一，县教育局组织实施。未升入高中的，或继续复读，或回家务农、务工。

1993年后，实施普及九年义务教育，对应入学的适龄儿童，由乡镇政府下发入学通知，按学校划定的招生片区入学，逐步取消留级制度。1997年3月，取消留级制度；9月，小学升初中实行入学通知书制度，取消小学升学考试，只进行毕业考试，由乡镇政府向小学毕业生发放入学通知，小学毕业生全部进入初中学习。2001年，贵阳市教育局下文要求，从秋季起，全部实行6周岁入学。由于县内条件不具备，只在城关和部分乡镇所在地学校实行。2003年，全县实行6周岁入学，此前为7岁入学。2005年，县教育局转发贵阳市初中毕业与高中招生考试制度改革方案，明确初中毕业考核分为基础性和课程学习评价。基础性评价包括公民道德素养、学习态度与能力、交流与合作、实践与创新、运动与健康、审美与表现；课程学习评价对所学科目进行考核或考试，达到毕业规定标准，准予毕业。

（二）学籍

1989年，息烽在安顺地区率先实行中小学学籍簿卡管理制度。学生入学除登记造册在校学生名册外，还需办理学籍簿和学籍卡。小学学籍由乡镇教辅站管理，学籍簿一式二份，一份学校留存，一份交乡镇教办；初中学籍由县教育局管理，学籍簿一式二份，一份学校留存，一份交教育局。同时办理学籍卡，一人一卡，学生转学要在原学校注销学籍，学籍卡随学生带到所转入的学校，并在转入学校办理学籍登记。学生转学、休学，小学须经教辅站批准，初中须经县教育局批准。

（三）“两免一补”

2003年，国家对西部地区义务教育实行免教科书费、免杂费、补助贫困寄宿生生活费（简称“两免一补”）。是年秋季，县内在九庄镇实施“两免一补”试点。2005年“两免一补”扩大到石硐、鹿窝、流长、养龙司等乡。2006年，对城市低保家庭接受义务教育子女实行“两免”。2007年秋季起，全县所有义务教育阶段学生免交书费和杂费。至2010年，全县共实施“两免一补”4万余人次，补助金额1344.5万元。

息烽县2004—2010年“两免一补”统计表

表16-1-4　　单位：万元

年份	2004	2005	2006	2007	2008	2009	2010	合计
人次	440	1220	6860	7358	8530	9410	9576	43394
金额	4.4	12.2	68.6	109.2	319.8	352.3	478.1	1334.5

第四节　高中教育

一、学校

1991年，全县有息烽中学（2004年更名为县第一中学）、息烽城关中学（1996年更名为县第二中学）、276子校（2000年更名为西洋肥业有限责任公司子弟学校，简称西洋子弟学校）高中部3所高中。有高中教师84人，招收新生368人，在校学生1089人，高三毕业334人。1994年，永生私立完全中学建校。2001年，全县有高中教师121人，招收新生突破1000人。2002年，新世纪学校兴办高中部，梨安中学创办，设高中部。2004年，贵阳星宇中学（独立高中）到息烽办班。2008年，乌江复旦学校办高中部。由于办学条件、师资等因素，县第二中学、西洋子校、梨安中学先后停办高中；新世纪学校和星宇中学停办。2010年，全县有高中3所，其中高级中学1所、完全中学1所、十二年制学校1所。是年有教师202人，在校学生3598人，毕业758人。

20年间，全县高中阶段毛入学率由1991年的11.6%上升到2010年的49.86%；共培养高中学生17343人，毕业9638人；考入大学本科3818人，大专4294人，中专875人。

息烽县普通高中建停情况统计表

表16-1-5

年份	学校名称	学段设置	兴、停办时间
1991	息烽中学（息烽一中）	完全中学（2003年后为高级中学）	2003年停办初中
	城关中学（息烽二中）	完全中学（2003年后为初级中学）	2003年停办高中
	276子校（西洋子弟学校）	十二年制学校（2006年后为九年制学校）	2006年停办高中
1994	永生私立中学建校	完全中学	
2002	梨安中学建校	完全中学	2005年停办高中
2004	新世纪学校	十二年制学校（2002年为九年制学校）	2008年停办
2004	星宇中学建校	高中	2008年停办
2006	乌江复旦学校建校	2008年起为十二年制学校	2008年办高中

息烽县部分年度普通高中设施发展统计表

表16-1-6

年份	学校数（所）	占地面积（平方米）	校舍面积（平方米）	功能室（间）	图书（册）	计算机（台）
1991	3	54175.5	15035	13	26700	
1994	4	55853.5	21665	18	34050	
2002	5	67475.7	33231	26	61177	247
2004	5	59733	35943	24	70020	339
2008	3	102684	36554	16	73050	345
2010	3	112032	45472	23	147688	505

息烽县1991—2010年普通高中教育基本情况统计表

表16-1-7

年份	学校数（所）	班数（个）	招生数（人）	学生总数（人）	毕业生数（人）	教师数（人）
1991	3	22	368	1089	334	84
1992	3	20	333	1005	352	86
1993	3	22	364	945	303	90
1994	4	24	430	1182	288	93
1995	4	24	420	1236	261	105
1996	4	25	382	1111	337	96
1997	4	25	401	1061	346	89
1998	4	24	462	1100	331	87
1999	4	27	541	1294	284	92
2000	4	32	690	1585	323	96
2001	4	41	1265	2369	398	121
2002	5	54	1352	3008	382	176
2003	5	65	1222	3319	611	181
2004	5	64	1306	3088	802	182
2005	5	64	1227	3206	701	197
2006	5	56	1427	3068	693	162
2007	2	53	1184	2992	631	150
2008	4	63	1279	3507	757	161
2009	3	67	1295	3252	746	177
2010	3	69	1395	3598	758	202

二、学制课程与学籍

1991—2010年，县内高中学制均为3年。初中毕业生通过参加升学考试，由市教育局划定最低录取线，录取上线初中毕业生进入高中学习。公办高中按照学生中考成绩择优录取，录取顺序为息烽中学、息烽二中，其他学校实行挂牌招生。

高一、高二开设《政治》《语文》《数学》《英语》《物理》《化学》《历史》《体育》《艺术》《劳动技术》《社会实践》课程。另外，高一开设地理、高二开设生物，高三分为文科和理科，文科不开设《物理》《化学》《生物》，理科不开设《政治》《地理》《历史》。高一学生进校时进行一周军事训练。

学籍簿一式3份，一份学校留存，一份交县教育局，一份交地区（市）教育局。学生在高中学习期间，要参加会考，高三学习结束后，达到毕业标准的，准予毕业，由学校发给经贵阳市教育局验证的普通高中毕业证书。

会考始于1990年，至2005年由省教育厅统一组织，规定《语文》《数学》和《政治》任意一科不合格的，或前述3科合格，其余学科有2科不合格的不予毕业。2006年，省教育厅将会考下放到各地州市组织。贵阳市规定，《语文》和《政治》任意一科不合格的，不予毕业，《语文》《政治》合格，其余学科有3科不合格的不予毕业。

2001年，全县会考合格率68.1%，此后逐年上升，2006年达到81.4%，2009年突破90%，2010年为91.7%。

第五节　中等职业教育

一、息烽县职业技术学校

1986年，在永靖镇下阳朗村长岭岗创办县长岭岗高级农业中学。1988年改称县职业技术学校（简称县职校）。1995年4月，县职校迁县城西门新建，1997年投入使用。1998年7月，县教师进修学校和县电视大学工作站并入，改称县职业教育培训中心。1999年9月，县农业广播学校并入，形成“一套人马、多块牌子、多种功能”的办学格局，担负职业教育、教师培训、电大教育和农村剩余劳动力短期培训等教学任务。2004年，修综合实验大楼，面积1900平方米，设置计算机、电工培训室等。2007年建学生食堂。

学校办学形式有联办、自办和委培3种。学校先后自办农学、化工、幼师、计算机应用、财会电算化、应用电子技术、旅游与饭店管理等专业。与有关部门联合举办畜牧班、林业班、园艺班、财会班、毛纺班、预备役军人班、医士班、汽修专业、数控专业等专业。接受贵阳天长磷化工公司委托，办一年制磷化工专业。专业教师向联办单位和社会各界聘请能胜任专业课的人员担任。学制有二年制和三年制两种。此外面向市场，根据实际需要多形式多渠道开办短期培训班，学员结业时发给结业证书。

1997—2005年，学校开设计算机、幼教、初中、旅游、电子电工、司法等专业，毕业学生2000余人。2006年，和重庆市工业学校联办数控专业。2007—2010年，结合用人市场需求调整专业设置，开设电子技术应用、旅游服务与酒店管理、数控技术，招收新生700余人。

息烽县职业学校1991—2010年所办专业及招生人数统计表

表16-1-8

年份	专业及招生人数	年份	专业及招生人数
1991	财会150人、农学20人	2001	计算机38人、旅游管理22人、电子电工46人、初中241人
1992	畜牧兽医38人、毛纺64人	2002	计算机应用、电子41人、初中130人
1993	预备役102人	2003	计算机应用32人、电子技术应用41人
1994	幼师90人、预备役43人	2004	计算机应用32人、电子技术应用89人
1995	磷化工48人、幼师36人	2005	计算机应用44人、电子技术应用39人
1996	磷化工44人、医士90人、果蔬106人（短期）	2006	数控技术应用120人
1997	医士48人、司法33人、计算机应用51人、果蔬46人（短期）	2007	数控技术54人、电子技术43人、旅游服务37人
1998	计算机应用148人、司法31人	2008	数控48人、电子112人、旅游服务47人
1999	计算机48人、旅游管理35人、初中78人	2009	电子162人、酒店管理47人
2000	计算机42人、旅游管理30人、初中200人	2010	电子技术85人、酒店管理24人

二、农村中学渗透职业教育

1995年，县政府出台《关于推进农村初中阶段教育改革的意见》，明确逐步改革农村初中办学模式，分为普通初中渗透职业教育和职业初中班模式。在长岭岗中学、流长中学进行试点，此后扩展到黑神庙、石硐、养龙司、温泉中学开设农技培训班，逐步实现农村初中各年级渗透职业教育。

2001年，县委出台加快职业教育发展意见。县政府划拨30亩基地给县职校，各乡镇共划拨225亩地给各中学做职业教育基地。2002年，县教育局下发《关于界定在全县乡镇中学实行初二后分流的通知》，强调把职业学校初中试点学校教学班办成教育培训、科技示范推广、农民扶贫开发和农村劳动力转移培训的重要基地，初二学生完成初二学业后在初三年级办理中专入学手续，同时开设专业课，初三毕业后继续留在原学校上一年专业课，经考核，发给贵州省农广校中专毕业证。

2003年，县委下发《贯彻国务院关于基础教育改革与发展的决定的实施意见》，要求继续推行初二后分流和3+1办学模式，实行绿色证书制度。2004年，县职教中心农广校招收2+3专科100人，中专班初二后分流150人。全县乡镇初中学校均建立职教基地，开办初职班，大乡镇初职班学生70人，小乡镇初职班40~50人。2005年，县委、县政府出台《关于加快教育改革和发展的意见》，县教育局下发《关于县职业技术学校2005年度中职招生和农村富余劳动力转移培训的实施意见》，对中职招生和富余劳动力转移培训作出具体安排，并对家庭贫困学生实行职教券政策，每人给予补助500元，推行资源互补联合办学模式，实行暑假工半工半读办学模式，继续实行初二后分流。

第六节 成人教育

县内成人教育以职校和农民文化技术学校为平台，县内各职能部门开展的适用技术培训班为补充，开展职业教育、农民文化技术学习和适用技术培训。职校主要针对初中、高中毕业生和城乡群众就业技能学习培训，教师培训、学历学习。职能部门主要采取短期培训的办法对城乡居民进行适用技术培训。

一、广播电视大学

1991年12月，县电视大学（简称电大）工作站成立。电大先后开设中文、史地、英语、行政管理、财会、法律等专业，学生毕业分配到农村中学任教。1994年，招收成人大专班学生192人，同时开展不脱产业余进修。1998年，电大工作站并入县职业教育培训中心。1999—2010年，县电大教育培训学员2033人。

二、农民文化技术学校

1991年，继续办好农民夜校。1992年，启动高标准扫盲工作，将文盲脱盲任务落实到扫盲教师，扫盲教师深入村组和文盲家中开展送教工作。1994年通过安顺地区验收，全县共扫除文盲1354人。1997年，根据《息烽县“两基”工作总体规划》成立扫盲机构，在乡镇、村开办农民文化技术学校，由小学教师任扫盲教师，乡镇农技人员任农技教师，全县共有专（兼）职教师570人，配置相应教学设施。到1999年，共扫除文盲4596人，举办各种农技培训5810期，培训学员15万余人次。

三、成人自学考试

县成人自学考试始于1984年，是年报考人数159人，以后逐年增加。1991年起，县内报考人员全部报考大专和本科，至1995年，每年400~500人，报考专业14~15个科目。1997年为800人，1998年1634人报考。2004年开考36个专业，1785人报考，计4646科次，为历年最高。2005年1296人报考3310科次。2007年开始实行网上报名。2008年，由于考生减少，区县不再设立考点，考务工作由贵阳市自考办安排，考生在网上报名后直接到市区参加考试。20年间，有1.8万多人次参加自学考试，报考4.2万余科次，合格1.5万余科次，毕业1235人，其中本科52人，专科1183人。

四、成人高考

县内于1986年开始办理成人高考。1991—1998年，全县参加成人高考1520人，录取862人；1999—2001年，年均300人报考；2003—2007年，年均210人报考。此后报考人数逐年减少，2010年164人报考。20年间，参加成人高考共计4652人。

第七节　特殊教育

1994年，县政府出台发展特殊教育意见，成立特殊教育工作领导小组，乡镇设立特殊教育专职干部。1997年，采取在学校办特教班随班就读方式，全县招收一般弱智残儿童200名就读。同年9月，县特殊学校正式开学，借用县体育局的闲置房屋作校舍，利用全县师生员工的捐赠作为启动资金，教职工8人。招收聋哑学生24人，实行吃、住、穿全免费，残疾儿童入学率63.5%，获贵州省特殊教育一等奖。

1999年，教育部拨款10万元，省、市各匹配5万元新建县特殊学校，年底竣工，占地面积7420平方米，建校舍4160平方米，配备教师11人和必要的教学设备。是年秋，开设培智一、聋一、盲三、聋五、聋七5个教学班，在校生33人。2002年学生最多达49人，以后有所减少。2003年，学校始设初中部。此后学校继续增加投入，完善办学设施，购置图书1366册、实验仪器设备388个品种。2010

年，有学生28人。

2006—2010年，共3届学生，毕业37人，其中男19人，女18人。就业5人，创业4人，外出打工14人，在家待业14人。

第八节 民办学校

1989年，浙江人陈江荣创办息烽县永生私立中学，后经贵阳市教育局更名为贵阳市息烽永生中学。1995年在县城西郊（人民路）建校。2010年，有综合教学楼1幢，3200平方米，教室24间；学生宿舍1幢，970平方米；活动场地800多平方米，运动场800多平方米。开办初期，招收初中学生100人，高一学生120余人。2010年，全校有21个班，在校学生1108人，其中初中生92人，高中生1016人。教职工50余人。自创办以来，培养初高中毕业生3800多名，为上级学校输送本科生900余人，专科生800余名。学校每年对贫困学生实行学费减免和对品学兼优的学生进行奖励。1995年，学校被评为息烽县先进学校；2006年，被评为贵阳市先进民办学校；2008、2009年获贵阳市普通高中“入出口”评估二等奖。

1993年，永靖镇个体工商户谭德润在永靖镇南山林场创办武术学校。1997年，开阳县张春茂在息烽永靖镇创办新世纪学校。2002年，贵阳市白云区龙向东到息烽办梨安中学。息烽人李奕、罗昌红、谌智慧、邹元琴、吴学敏、黄明群、张孝云等先后经教育局审批兴办幼儿园。2003年，张孝云在永靖镇举办起航英语培训中心息烽教学点；2005年，万玉梅在永靖镇举办北爱钢琴电子琴培训班。至2010年，全县有20个民办教育机构，其中幼儿园17所、中学1所、培训班2个。

息烽县民办中学、培训班统计表

表16-1-9

学校名称	创办时间、创办人	地点	性质、校舍	停办年份	更名
息烽永生私立中学	1989年陈江荣（浙江）	县城	完中。先租赁后建校舍3200平米		贵阳市息烽永生中学（1997年）
息烽少林武术学校	1993年谭德润（息烽）	梨安	9年制+武术。先租赁，1995买拖电厂子校校舍	2008	
息烽新世纪学校	1997年张春茂（开阳）	县城	12年一贯制	2008	
息烽梨安中学	2002年龙明（白云区）	梨安	投资150万元建校舍	2008	
贵阳星宇中学	2004年与县职校合办高中	县职校	贵阳星宇中学利用县职校校舍	2008	
贵阳市启航英语培训中心息烽教学点	2004年11月张光祥（息烽）	县城	培训。租赁校舍		贵阳市息烽县启航英语培训中心（2005年）
北爱钢琴电子琴培训班	2005年万玉梅（息烽）	县城	培训。租赁房屋		

息烽县民办幼儿园基本情况统计表

表16-1-10

幼儿园名称	创办时间	校址	法人	园长	班数	学生数	教职工数
小花幼儿园	1999年9月	永靖镇花园西路	郭庆群	沈　娅	3	120	6
好孩子幼儿园	1998年5月	永靖镇镇府路	曾凡猛	曾蔷薇	3	60	6
下阳朗幼儿园	1999年9月	永靖镇下阳朗村	向国霞	向国霞	2	78	5
春雷幼儿园	1999年9月	流长乡流长街上	黄明群	黄明群	2	50	2
红光幼儿园	1999年9月	石硐乡石硐街上	邹元琴	邹元琴	2	82	4
坝上幼儿园	1999年9月	养龙司乡坝上村	李由香	李由香	1	28	2
新月幼儿园	1999年9月	小寨坝镇中心村	陆安红	陆安红	3	120	6
阳光幼儿园	2000年3月	永靖镇息九公路旁	李　奕	李　奕	6	182	20
育英幼儿园	2001年11月	养龙司乡养龙司街	谌智慧	谌智慧	5	146	15
晨曦幼儿园	2001年11月	九庄镇街上	吴学敏	罗登菊	2	62	4
小红花幼儿园	2002年10月	温泉镇石头田村	谌志静	熊　敏	2	88	3
柏香山幼儿园	2002年10月	西山乡柏香山村	简玉荣	简玉荣	2	57	3
满天星幼儿园	2004年9月	小寨坝镇中心村	张孝云	宋　丽	5	165	16
福乐幼儿园	2005年11月	永靖镇阳朗村	谭永利	谭永利	2	65	3
希望幼儿园	2010年8月	永靖镇龙爪村	丁宦文	丁宦文	1	13	1
金太阳幼儿园	2010年8月	温泉镇西洋公司	姜增顺	龙开仙	5	125	10
乐乐幼儿园	2010年8月	小寨坝镇重钙厂	杨　进	马　琴	8	280	15

第九节　部分重点学校简介

息烽县实验幼儿园：2002年，县利用招待所办机关幼儿园，县政府投入110余万元，新建教学楼1栋，面积3207平方米；绿化面积460平方米，户外活动场地2160平方米。有多功能活动室、探索发现室、美工室及班级用房。每班呈套房式格局，内设活动室、盥洗室、儿童厕所、睡房。睡房单人单睡，配置幼儿课桌、小床、被褥；中、小型教学玩具、图书、钢琴、电脑、投影仪等。每班还配有空调、电视机、VCD、录音机、电子琴、消毒柜、保温桶。室外有大型多功能滑梯、秋千、跷跷板、平衡桥、金字塔、攀爬等。还配有厨房，厨房设备有和面机、绞肉机、烤箱、冰柜、冰箱、发酵箱、消毒柜、保洁柜、节能灶等。是年，更名为县实验幼儿园。设置托幼班、小班、中班、大班，招收2～6岁儿童入园。县实验幼儿园以“健康、快乐、自信、自主”为办园理念。实行“双向选择制”“分层聘任制”教职工聘任制度。2010年，全园有教职工48名，在园幼儿520人。

息烽县永靖小学：位于永靖镇交通路，为县内最大的完全小学。

清宣统二年（1910），为息烽两级小学堂（校址在今县委、县政府办公楼处）。民国10年（1921）易名为县立第一两级小学。民国26年（1937），军统局息烽特训班占用校址，学校迁往川主庙（现永靖小学校址）与县立第一两级女子学校合并，成为县内第一所男女合校，更名为永靖小学。民国28年（1939）年迁城隍庙内，改名为“息烽县中心国民学校”。民国34年（1945），改为标准中心学校。设1～6年级7班，在校学生300余人。

中华人民共和国成立后，县政府恢复永靖小学，更名为永靖镇完全小学。1967年改称永红小学。1985年再次恢复“永靖小学”校名。1991年初，小学占地面积约5000平方米，建筑面积3670平方米。开设1～6年级33班。2010年，学校占地7680平方米，建筑面积4962平方米。有37个教学班，学生2336人。有专任教师83人。学校拥有图书室、阅览室、仪器室、电教室、音乐教室、体育器材室、医务室、实验室等功能室；有图书6万余册，计算机25台。多年来，学校入学率、巩固率100%。建校以来，学校为社会输送数万名合格小学毕业生。

息烽县云环小学：原名县忠烈保国民学校，位于县城南郊下阳朗，创办于民国30年（1941），后停办。1950年恢复办校，取名为“下阳朗民办小学”，是年有学生200余人，教师6人。1963年转为公办，改名为“下阳朗小学”。1971年，学校附设“戴帽初中班”，学生增加到600多人，教师25人。1980年，停办初中班。1999年，新华社《参考消息》报社捐赠20万元人民币，邵云环烈士的丈夫曹荣飞捐赠10万元人民币，市政府、县政府筹集资金100余万元人民币，在原校址上修建教学楼、邵云环烈士纪念室。为缅怀邵云环烈士，弘扬爱国主义精神，县政府将新建学校命名为“云环小学”。2010年，学校占地7680平方米，建筑面积2250平方米。有11个教学班，466名学生，教职工27人。学校拥有邵云环烈士纪念室、多功能教室、电子阅览室、图书室、科技室、心理咨询室、音乐舞蹈室、乡村学校少年宫、留守儿童之家等功能室。

息烽县第一中学：原名县立初级中学，始创于民国29年（1940），民间称息烽中学，校址在底寨文昌阁，民国31年（1942）暑期，学校迁至县城北门溪流锁。民国35年（1946）冬，迁至县城东门原军统特训班医务所。民国36年（1947），学校又迁往原特训班工字房（今县实验幼儿园处）。至1949年息烽解放时，学校有初中6班，学生280人，教职工19人，毕业初中生222人。1950年4月1日开学复课。1955年，县政府拨款在县城北门（今校址处）新建校舍，次年秋迁入新校舍。1958年增设高中部，更名为贵州省息烽中学。1960年改称息烽县第一中学。1961年更名为息烽中学。1967年改称“新息中”。1990年，学校有教学用房7816平方米。2003年9月，停办初中，办成独立高中。2004年4月16日，再次更名为息烽县第一中学（简称息烽一中）。2007年，学校获“贵阳市区（县、市）普通高中‘入口出口’成绩评估一等奖”。2008—2010年，连续3年获贵阳市区（县、市）普通高中“入口出口”成绩评估二等奖。

2010年，息烽一中占地面积3.47万平方米，有运动场地8800平方米，校舍面积2万多平方米。综合实验大楼为7层框混结构，面积3313平方米，内设理化实验室、多功能教室、阶梯教室、阅览室、音乐室、画室、语音室、微机室、书库等，藏书8万余册。教学大楼为6层框混结构，面积6859平方米，内设教室54间，行政、教研组办公室25间，会议室、洗手间等。学生宿舍楼2栋，为6层框混结构，面积9572平方米，有寝室210间。学生餐厅2个，一次可容纳600人就餐。有在校学生1949人；教师148人。

2001—2010年，息烽一中先后承担国家科研课题《创新写作教学实验与研究》《农村中学贫困生助学问题研究》，市课题《高中英语教学中开放型阅读能力的培养》《促进学生主动学习途径与方法研究》《力的分解演示仪的研究与制作》等，均已结题。全校教师在省级以上报刊发表论文200

余篇。

息烽县乌江复旦学校：原名九庄中学，始建于1958年秋，位于九庄镇青堰村青龙山脚下。最初名为九庄后陇农业中学，校址在九庄镇后陇村。1960年秋，改称息烽县第三中学，1961年秋停办。1965年，县拨款兴办农业中学，第三中学易名九庄农业中学，简称九庄农中，1966年停办。1968年，学校迁址青堰村。1970年，又改名九庄初级中学。1971年升为完全中学。1980年秋，九庄中学高中部停办。

20世纪90年代，由贵州工学院毛建全教授引路，受台湾兹根基金会资助，新修1幢4层楼800平方米的教学楼；此后陆续修建4层楼教师宿舍1幢。学生宿舍楼兼食堂2幢，5层教学楼1幢，内设阶梯教室、办公室等。

2005年，复旦大学百年华诞，复旦之子积极探索高等教育反哺农村基础教育新路子，支持西部地区教育事业，捐资100万元在西部地区建一所复旦实验学校。该项目落户九庄中学，定名为“息烽县乌江复旦学校”。市、县匹配资金，将原老教学楼拆除重建。2008年复办高中部，将九庄小学收并，办成12年一贯制学校。2010年，学校设有阶梯教室、微机室、多媒体教室、物理、化学、生物实验室、通用技术试验室、体育器材室等。初中部设置24个教学班，在校学生1324人；高中部设置18个教学班，在校学生960人。有教师134人，其中复旦大学支教教师4人。

第二章　教　师

1991—1999年，教师主要来源于师范类大中专毕业生分配。2003年，在部分学校试行教师聘用制。2005年，县内教师全部实行聘用制。

第一节　教师队伍

1991年，全县有教师2633人。其中公办和企业教师1739人，分别为幼儿教师20人、小学教师1202人、初中教师402人、高中教师115人。所有教师中，大专以上学历263人、中专学历971人、高中学历125人、初中级以下学历351人；中学高级教师21人、一级教师102人、二级教师182人、三级教师112人；小学高级教师227人、一级教师482人、二级教师270人、未评职称341人，其中民办教师305人、代课教师575人。

至1999年，每年将师范类大、中专毕业生分配到中小学任教，吸收部分非师范类大中专学生从事教师职业，全县共有717名大中专毕业生分配到学校担任教师。同时，通过考核，逐年将民办教师转为公办教师。2001年8月，县政府出台深化大中专毕业生就业制度改革意见，对中专毕业生不再分配，大专、本科毕业生继续分配。是年，对本县户口2000年师范类中专毕业生考试，择优录用45人任小学教师。2003年起，对师范类大专毕业生实行择优录用。大学本科毕业生包分配延续到2004年。2005年，所有毕业生均实行双向选择，竞争上岗、择优录用。进入教师队伍要求具有相应的教师资格证。自2008年起实行面向社会公开招考，至2010年，全县共补充教师1356人。

2010年，全县有教师2176人，其中幼儿教师149人、小学教师1136人、初中教师648人、高中教师202人、特殊教育教师8人、职业教育教师33人。

第二节 教师培训

一、业务培训

1990年，省教委和人民出版社确定息烽为九年义务教育课程、教材试验县，全县连续3年共派出中小学16个学科24名骨干教师和县教研室、学科教研员36人次外出接受人教社举办的一级培训。参加培训人员回来后，连续三年在县内举办中小学和学科以及学校行政人员研讨班，先后培训小学教师788人，初中教师496人，学校行政领导37人。1993—1995年，对小学4～6年级教师进行全员岗前培训。1995年，县教育局制定《息烽县中小学教师继续教育第一阶段实施意见》，开展普通话、三笔字、简笔画学习培训。1997年，派出所有中学副校长和新任校长到贵阳市师专参加校长培训和派出2名副局长到省教育学院学习培训。对全县中小学教师进行计算机初级培训，凡男教师50岁以下，女教师45岁以下分期分批在县职教中心参加培训。1998年，为适应九年义务教育工程需要，县教育局选送校长30人、义务教育教师105人到贵阳师范学校培训。2003年，由县人事劳动局组织对教师进行计算机中级培训。

二、学历培训

20世纪90年代初，县内教师学历偏低，初中教师多数是中专学历，高中教师多数是大专学历。1991年，县教育局制定《关于中学教师离职进修的规定》。1993年，组织学历未达到专科的中学教师参加自考、函授和电大学习，通过考试，取得大专学历。1999年，在小学教师中开展学历拔高培训，凡女教师在40岁以下，男教师在45岁以下，都要进行学历拔高，达到大专以上学历。2001年，教育局制定《教师进修工作意见》，要求1998年12月31日未满40周岁，未获专科学历的小学教师，1999年12月31日未满40周岁，未取得本科学历的中学教师，必须参加学历拔高学习。2004年，教育局下发《关于教师脱产进修的规定》，鼓励教师在职学习，教师脱产进修必须进修本科学历，且专业对口。凡参加学习的教师，每学期补助50～80元。对报考研究生脱产学习或函授学习的学费，70%由教育局承担，学校承担30%，取得学历后，教育局给予一次性奖励6000元。2010年，县内教师小学专科、初中本科学历均为80%。

第三节 教师待遇

1991—2010年，每年“六一”儿童节，各级党委、政府都要到学校慰问师生。教师节开展多种形式的庆祝活动，对先进教师、优秀教育工作者进行表彰。重大节日期间，各级党政负责人看望和慰问退休教师代表和困难教师及生病住院教师。凡任教25年的教师，市政府颁发荣誉证。省政府对任教30年或在乡及村级小学连续任教25年的教师颁发荣誉证，获得省政府荣誉证书的教师退休时享受百分之百的退休金。在此期间，4人次被评为全国教育系统劳动模范，1人被评为全国先进教育工作者，2人被评为全国优秀教师，1人被评为全国优秀德育课教师，10人次受到省部级表彰。

息烽县1991—2007年获得国家、省级奖励教师名录

表16-2-1

姓　名	性别	籍贯	工作单位	荣誉称号	授予单位	获奖时间
李光碧	女	贵州息烽	茅坡小学	全国先进教育工作者	国务院	2005年4月
张永平	男	贵州息烽	温泉小学	全国教育系统劳模	国家教委、人事部	1991年9月
张学智	男	贵州息烽	新沙小学	全国教育系统劳模	国家教委、人事部	1993年9月
罗良恺	男	贵州息烽	县教育局	扫盲先进工作者	国家教委、人事部	1994年10月
张仕凯	男	贵州息烽	石硐高清民校	全国优秀教师	国家教委、人事部	1995年9月
范国炎	男	贵州息烽	县教育局	中华扫盲奖	国家教委	1997年9月
耿全香	女	河南滑县	下小学	全国优秀教师	教育部	1998年9月
舒盛刚	男	贵州息烽	河坎小学	全国模范教师	人事部、教育部	2001年9月
陈永棋	男	贵州息烽	堰坪小学	全国优秀教师	教育部	2004年9月
王忠华	男	贵州息烽	安马小学	全国优秀教师	国家教委、人事部	2007年9月
吕文新	男	贵州息烽	云环小学	全国优秀教师	中国中小学幼儿教师奖励（教育）基金会	2000年9月
陈久琪	男	贵州息烽	息烽一中	全国优秀教师		2001年9月
刘长远	男	贵州息烽	鹿窝小学	省先进工作者	省人民政府	1995年6月
王传喜	男	贵州息烽	梨安小学	省优秀教师	省人民政府	1997年9月
王旭初	男	贵州息烽	城关中学	省优秀教师	省人民政府	1997年9月
方　维	男	贵州息烽	流长小学	省优秀教师	省人民政府	2001年9月
汪政权	男	贵州息烽	息烽二中	省优秀教师	省人民政府	2001年9月
杨明仙	女	贵州息烽	县教研室	省优秀教师	省人民政府	2004年9月
蔡伦忠	男	贵州息烽	督导办公室	“两基攻坚”先进个人	省委省政府	2006年9月

民办教师：1991年，全县有305名民办教师。采取考核办法，逐年予以转正，至1999年，277名民办教师转为公办教师，28名民办教师退养。

一、职称评聘

1993年起，教师职称评审工作实行每年晋级评审，中级以上职称实行空岗补缺评审。至此，教师工资和职称挂钩，教师成为专业技术人员。此前，教师作为国家干部看待，每年填写干部履历表。

2001年，根据省人事厅《贵州省事业单位专业技术职务结构比例实施意见》，小学按乡镇高级5%、中级30%，县城学校高级10%、中级35%的比例实行空岗补缺评聘。中学按乡镇中学高级15%、中级30%，县城学校高级20%、中级35%的比例实行空岗补缺评聘。根据省人事厅《关于2005年度全省专业技术职务评聘工作有关问题的通知》要求，2005年起，事业单位全面实行“评聘分离”制度。2010年，全县有“中学高级”职称教师97人。

二、住房优惠

2002年，开发东门小区，县政府建教师新村1号、5号、6号楼共200余套住房，教师购买教师新

村住房每平方米由县政府补助80元。

三、工资待遇

1993年，对公办教职工工资进行套改，按档次增加工资，中学高级教师最高档次月工资增加228.5元，小学高级教师和中学一级教师最高档次月工资增加175元，小学一级教师和中学二级教师最高档次月工资增加146.5元，小学二级教师和中学三级教师最高档次月工资增加82元。次年，对民办教师按职称增资，小学高级月增45元，一级30元，二级25元，三级20元。1995年，公办教师再次增资，高级职称月增46元，中级职称月增30.5元，初级月增21.5元，员级月增18元，小学三级月增16.5元。1995年10月，教师工资级差金额再次增加。次年，对民办教师进行按教龄增资，20年及以上者月增20元，20年以下者月增10元；1997年，全体民办教师月增资15元，同年10月再次按教龄增资，20年以上者月增15元，以下者月增10元。

1997年7月，对教师工资进行调标，按原职务（技术等级、岗位）工资增加14元后金额进入相应的工资档次。

1999年7月，根据国务院办公厅转发人事部、财政部关于调整机关事业单位工作人员工资标准，对教师工资再次进行调整，实行新的中小学教师专业技术职务等级工资标准。中小学教师工资标准提高10%。

2001年1月，根据国务院办公厅转发人事部、财政部增加调整机关事业单位工作人员工资和增加离退休人员退休费四个实施方案的通知，对全县中小学教师工资进行调整。10月，根据国务院办公厅转发的人事部、财政部关于从2001年10月1日起调整机关事业单位工作人员工资标准和离退休人员离退休费三个实施方案的通知精神，对全县中小学教师的固定工资和浮动工资按国家规定的工资构成比例相应提高。

2003年7月，国务院决定，从2003年7月1日起，调整机关事业单位工作人员工资标准、增加机关事业单位离退休人员离退休费。按照人事部、财政部拟定的《关于调整事业单位工作人员工资标准的实施方案》《关于增加机关事业单位离退休人员离退休费的实施方案》调整全县教师工资。

第四节　教学研究

一、教学研究网络

1991年，息烽为全国义务教育教材试验工作试验县之一，县教育局以此为契机，建立教学研究网络。1992年，在10个乡镇教育辅导站设教研员1人。1995年10月，制定《乡镇教育辅导员教研工作要求》，提出转变教育思想，实现应试教育向素质教育转轨。1996年11月，出台《关于改进和加强全县教研工作的意见》，组建各乡镇中心教研组，片区中心教研组，各中小学组建学科教研组，形成县—乡镇—片区—学校的教研网络。县教研室深入教学一线，组织乡镇和学校开展教学研究，及时纠正教学中出现的问题。1997年，县教研室编制小学《语文》《数学》《思想品德》《自然》四门考试学科的《教学常规（试行意见）》，对备课上课、作业布置与批改、教学辅导与课外活动、检测与评估、教学研究等进行规范。2000年后，全县10个乡镇和乡镇片区中心完小以上学校建立教研工作领导小组，学校建立教导处、思教处、学科教研组等教育科研机构。2004年8月，通过文化考试和试教，择优录用县教育局教研室教研员7名。2006年12月，县教育局印发《关于改进和

加强教学研究工作　建立校本研修制度的意见》，建立校本研修制度，配齐小学、初中所有学科兼职教研员。片区教研组经常到辖区内的学校进行教学调研，给本校教研提供智力支持和专业引领力量。

二、教研活动

1996—2010年，县教育局组织开展《深化全县学校职称改革》《我国贫困农村地区幼儿教育现状调查和对策研究》《快速作文研究》《关于改革薄弱学科研究》，参加“息烽县2000年教育发展规划”调查研讨。县教研室出台《关于进一步加强教育科研的意见》《小学社会　自然学科教研工作意见》、新时期《中小学教学常规管理》等。配合教师继续教育工作、实施素质教育及课堂教学改革，县教研室、各中小学每学期组织开展各科研讨、评荐活动。

县教研室分别到各中小学以公开课和研讨课模式，在不同学科内开展“同课异构”“一课多上多研”教科研活动。通过“不同教师，相同教学内容”“同一教师，相同教学内容，不同班级”进行教学实践的方式，提倡教师从不同教学手段、不同学习方法进行设计和教学。并就一些教学中存在的困惑和共性问题进行讨论，寻找解决问题的措施。帮助各中小学校更新教育教学观念，提高管理水平和学科教学业务能力。

2007年3月，教研室撰写的《点面结合抓培训　促进农村教师队伍整体素质的提高》被教育部课题组评为三等奖。2009年，在全县征集到论文、教学设计680余篇，选出252篇论文、教学设计，编入《园丁寻梦——息烽县教育科研教学论文集》。

20年间，教研室组织开展全县性大型教研活动100余次，参与活动教师近1万人次。涉及中小学各学科，形式有优质课、观摩课、示范课，论文评选、技能才艺展示、教具制作、县际教学交流等。

第三章　学校建设

1996年，全县中小学校存在危房2.5万平方米，占校舍总面积的19.31%。1997年，县成立“希望工程”领导小组，争取世界银行教育贷款投入中小学基础设施建设。1998年，息烽县被列为国家贫困地区义务教育工程县，县委、县政府加大中小学基础设施建设力度，同时争取社会捐资集资和收取教育费附加等，加快学校建设。2000—2010年，全县学校建设有危房改造工程、希望工程、农村中小学寄宿制建设工程、农村薄改工程、校安工程、国开行贷款工程，使全县学校校容校貌焕然一新。

第一节　校舍建设

1991年，学校建设以乡镇为主，进行危房改造。至1995年，全县筹集资金450万元，改造危房1.06万平方米，维修校舍5025平方米。1996—1998年，筹集资金1453.6万元，改造54所中小学和2个乡教育辅导站，消除危房2.21万平方米，新建校舍4.42万平方米。1997—1999年，实施世行贷款和义教工程，改扩建学校35所。2000—2010年，县内学校建设主要依托中学危房改造工程（简称危改工程）、农村中小学寄宿制建设工程（简称寄宿工程）、贫困地区农村薄弱学校校改工程（简称薄改工程）、中小学校舍安全工程（简称校安工程）、国家开发银行贷款工程（简称国开行贷款工程）、希望工程进行。

2001—2005年，县内学校实施危房改造工程项目13个，投资1249万元，其中中央财政专款615.92万元；改造面积2.38万平方米，消除危房1.78万平方米，新建校舍面积2.54万平方米。

2004—2010年，县内农村中小学寄宿制建设工程，对息烽二中、黑神庙、九庄、养龙司、流长中学进行改扩建，新建青山中学。共投入资金1690.9万元，其中中央资金702万元、市级资金317.9万元、县级及以下政府匹配671万元，共建校舍1.5万平方米，其中学生宿舍10560平方米、学生食堂4725平方米，购置床2985张、单人课桌凳1500套。

2006—2010年，共有中央资金“薄改工程”项目11个。改造11所学校校舍面积3.32万平方米，共投资3874万元，其中中央资金1515万元、省级资金726万元、市级资金169万元、县级配套资金1464万元。

2009年，国开行贷款“校安工程”项目3个，其中第一中学新校区5.5万平方米，投资9732万元；第二中学9505平方米，投资1400万元；息烽第一小学9500平方米，投资3850万元。总建筑面积7.4万平方米，投资14982万元，其中省级资金1850万元、县级配套资金6932万元，申请国开行贷款共计6200万元。是年，修建乌江复旦学校小学部，建筑面积6200平方米，投资682万元，全部为中央资金。

希望工程：1996—2010年，全县接受香港和国内单位或个人捐款，援建或改造19所小学，并根据捐款单位或个人意见更名为某某希望小学。具体学校如下：

息烽县部分希望工程援建小学统计表

表16-3-1

年份	捐资单位或个人	捐资金额（万元）	县内投资（万元）	援建或改造	受援学校更名
1996	香港翁业坚	20		核桃坝小学	业坚希望小学
	香港宝莲寺	20		坪上小学	初慧希望小学
	新华社	10		青山小学	新华希望小学
	新华社	20		下阳朗小学	云环小学
1997	贵州通海经济发展有限公司	—		援建林丰小学	林丰希望小学
	中国银行	15	5	杨寨小学	中银杨寨希望小学
	贵阳卷烟厂	20		堡子小学	迅文希望小学
1998	香港九龙庆回归筹委会	30（港币）		向阳小学	向阳希望小学
	香港佛教协会能正法师	10		安马小学	能正希望小学
	贵阳市团委	20		中坝小学	中坝希望小学
	贵阳市地税局	18		三交小学	三交希望小学
	贵阳市电信局	30		茅坡小学	电信希望小学

续表

年份	捐资单位或个人	捐资金额（万元）	县内投资（万元）	援建或改造	受援学校更名
1998	贵阳宇宏公司	20		高峰小学	宏信希望小学
	贵阳市食品公司	10		马路岩小学	马路岩希望小学
2002	云南省红塔集团官房房地产开发有限公司	25		南极小学	官房希望小学
2005	香港苗圃	30	110	新沙小学	新沙希望小学
2005	天津市西青区人民法院	30	90	幺寨小学	幺寨希望小学
2006	香港陈兆洪	35	110		陈兆洪希望小学
2008	省青基会	15	90		联华国际希望小学

除以上项目外，2000—2010年，全县还有其他工程项目70个。建筑面积9.2万平方米，投资8695万元；全部为县政府出资，主要用于新建教学楼、实验楼、学生食堂等。

第二节　教学设施

1991年，全县中小学基本实现有教室、有课桌的标准，建筑多为砖木结构，地面坑洼不平，课桌破损严重。小学只有三角尺、米尺、圆规等教具，中学只有少量物理、化学演示实验器材。是年，县用2.08万元购置教学仪器配发到各中小学。此后，县教育局陆续为各中小学购置教学仪器。1994年，按照“两基”标准配齐息烽中学、城关中学、九庄中学和养龙司中学的教学仪器，全年实验仪器开出率、学生实验，物理达92%，化学90%；演示实验，物理、化学均在95%以上。1996年3月，县教育局在流长乡召开校园建设现场会后，各中小学筹措资金，修建围墙、校门、绿化校园。至年底，60多所学校建有围墙、校门、花池，种植绿化树。1997年启动的世界银行贷款项目中，有115.6万元用于购置教学仪器、图书、课桌；1998年启动的国家义务教育工程项目款中，有72.27万元为教学设施专款，用于购置教学仪器、图书、课桌，配发给全县59所中小学。至2000年，全县新建教师宿舍8550平方米，厕所15个，围墙3万米，操场11.2万平方米，旗台113个，花圃3500平方米，篮球架30副，课桌5800套，图书柜、仪器柜440个。

2002—2004年，为普及实验教学，各级投资600余万元为三类以上中小学新建、改建实验室，配备标准实验桌椅、柜、操作台；购买实验仪器、药品。初中理化生实验仪器品种、数量配备率均95%以上；小学自然仪器品种、数量配备率85%以上。2004年通过普及实验教学验收。2007—2009年，县政府先后投入资金1152.83万元，按《小学数学科学教学仪器配备标准》为小学配置教学仪器，达标率86.21%；按《初中理科教学仪器配备标准》为中学配置理科教学仪器，达标率92.31%。按《贵州省音体美器材配备标准》为中小学配置音、体、美、卫生器材，公办学校达标率100%。通过中国华光科技基金会书海工程外联部分别为息烽二中、石硐中学、永靖小学补充图书9549册、200册、5000册，使小学生均图书达到12.66册，生均图书达标学校占学校总数的90.8%；初中生均图书达到18.94册，图书配备达标率100%。

2010年，县各中学和大型小学均配置计算机网络教室，中小学均按“两基”标准配备课桌、实验仪器，音、体、美教学器材，满足教学需求。

息烽县2010年办学条件统计表

表16-3-2

类别＼办学条件	生均占地（平方米）	生均校舍（平方米）	生均图书（册）	计算机（台）	建立校园网校数（所）
学前教育	5.1	3.69	2.9	—	—
小学教育	28.8	2.5	16.22	754	6
初中教育	23.5	7.1	15.5	669	4
普高教育	24.5	11	33.74	398	2
职业教育	71.1	40	49.1	170	1

第三节 信息化建设

1996年，黑神庙中学购置30多台二手电脑，利用劳技课开设计算机课程，传授计算机的操作知识和技能。2001年，县教育局成立教育信息化领导小组，下设办公室，负责全县教育信息化工作。派出教师参加市级培训并开展二级培训，选派24名女教师到北京参加“明天女教师”信息技术培训，全县有7所学校（息烽一中、息烽二中、黑神庙中学、温泉中学、县职业技术学校、永靖小学、云环小学）开设信息技术课。

2002年10月，教育部、李嘉诚基金会西部中小学现代远程教育扶贫示范工程实施。息烽县被列为项目县，分别在各乡镇中心中小学、息烽一中、息烽二中、南门小学和向阳小学共建24个卫星接收站。2003年4月10日，时任国家副主席曾庆红在省领导陪同下视察黑神庙中学远程教育工作，对该学校开展信息技术教育，利用先进地区优质资源，促进落后地区教育发展，培训基层干部帮助农民掌握技术，了解信息，增收致富的做法予以高度肯定。

2004年，贵州省实施农村中小学现代远程教育模式三项目工程，息烽9个乡镇中学和息烽二中列为项目学校，每校建设30座计算机网络教室、多媒体教室和卫星接收站各1个，配备防盗、防雷设备以及必要教室和桌椅等设施，工程总投资150余万元，至此，全县各初级中学开齐信息技术教育课。

2006年6月13日，县教育局在小寨坝镇召开全县农村中小学现代远程教育经验交流暨表彰会，总结全县2003—2005年农村中小学现代远程教育工作，表彰先进学校11所，先进个人22人。

2007年1月20日，县教育局下发《关于进一步加强农村中小学现代远程教育工作的实施意见》。次年，投入资金140万元，采购电脑300台，在各中心小学组建计算机网络教室，各中心小学至此开齐信息技术课。

2010年7月，县教育局依托贵州教育网建立门户网站，网站包含信息公开、教育资讯、教育党建、校园风采等10个栏目。

第四章　教育管理

1989年，县内学校实行分级办学分级管理。教师资格认定、职称评定，教师聘用、教师业务指导由教育局负责。直属学校教师由教育局直接管理，工资由县财政发放；乡镇学校教师由各乡镇管理，工资由各乡镇的财政发放。2000年起，全县中小学教师收归教育局管理，工资由县财政统一发放。教师乡镇内和乡镇之间调整由各乡镇负责。

第一节　管理与改革

一、体制

1991年4月，县委、县政府下发《关于各级各类学校实行分级办学分级管理的补充意见》规定：中级职称以上公办教师、大学本科毕业的教师、定向分配的教师，在区镇内调整，由各区教办提出意见与教育局协商后，由教育局行文。其余教师在区镇范围内调整，由教办报教育局批准后由乡镇行文。

1992年，撤销区教育办公室，在各乡镇设置教育辅导站。1993年，在小寨坝镇黑神庙中学实施校长负责制试点，实行校长聘班主任，班主任聘科任教师制度。由于这种聘任不利于教师稳定，未推广。1997年，县出台《息烽县校长负责制试行方案》，在南门小学、小寨坝小学等校实施校长负责制、教师聘任制、岗位责任制、结构工资制、目标管理“四制一管理”试点。1998年，首次实施校长竞聘，对九庄、石硐、小寨坝等8所小学校长进行公开选拔，竞聘上岗。1999年9月，县委、县政府下发关于贯彻《中共中央国务院深化教育体制改革　全面推进素质教育的决定》的实施意见，明确基础教育实行县乡两级管理，全县中小学教师的资格认定、工资发放、培养培训、调配交流、考核奖惩等，从2000年起由教育局统一管理。2002年再次对永靖、黑神庙、养龙司等8所小学校长进行公开竞聘。2003年8月，县委、县政府下发关于贯彻《国务院关于基础教育改革与发展的决定》的实施意见，再次明确规定教育局依法履行对全县中小学教师的资格认定、工资发放、培养培训、调配交流、考核奖惩等管理职能，至此，以县为主的管理体制建立，教师的人事管理由教育局负责。

2004年，撤销乡镇教育辅导工作站，有关教育工作由乡镇长直接负责。中学教育教学业务由县级教育部门负责，小学教育教学业务由乡镇中心学校校长负责。同年，在小寨坝镇试行设教育工作领导小组办公室，办公室不设编制，从各校抽人组成，负责辖区内教育行政和业务管理工作。试点工作结束后，在各乡镇成立教育工作领导小组办公室，受乡镇政府和县教育局双重领导。2005年，县政府成立教育督导室，由分管县长任主任，将全县划分为4个责任区，开展督政和督学工作。

二、教学管理

1989年，县教育局转发安顺地区教育局《关于加强学籍管理的意见（试行）修改稿》和《贵州省中学教育常规管理基本要求（纲要）》，全县开始实行学籍簿卡管理制度。1993年，县教育局出台《关于加强初中和小学学籍管理的有关规定》，明确留级比例，小学5%（城）、7%（农），初中5%。1997年，取消留级制度。2002年，县教育局出台《关于加强中小学教学常规管理的意见》，强调健全学校管理制度，完善工作职责，实行乡镇联考，建立教学质量奖惩制度。2004年，开始义务教育课改实验，县成立教材选定委员会，并组织专家组对当年秋季课改实验课程教材进行遴选。2007年，县教育局印发《关于规范普通中小学作息和作息时间的通知》，明确全县各级各类学校的作息时间。2008年，开始高中课改实验。

三、教师管理

1992年，县教育局对教职工事假、病假、婚假、产假、丧假及旷工作出明确界定。1998年，县教育局下发《关于对教师管理工作的补充规定》，要求加强师德教育，提高师德水准和思想素质，言行举止符合道德规范，着装大方，不穿拖鞋、奇装异服，不浓妆艳抹，不带金银首饰进教室，仪表端庄，要求严格劳动纪律并对请假作出规定，一律不准停薪留职，不准参与黄、赌、毒。2001年，转发市教育局《关于进一步加强对禁止教师在8小时工作时间内自行到校外兼职兼课的暂行规定》，8小时以内一律禁止教师自行在外兼课兼职，不得召集学生进行有偿补课。2002年，县教育局下发《关于干部调整　教师调动　支教工作中的纪律规定》，凡是调动的教师必须在三日内到新单位报到上班，凡是组织决定派出支教的教师，必须在接到通知后三日内到支教学校上班。同时，下发《加强支教工作管理意见》，对支教人员的选派对象范围、管理、待遇、时间、考核等作出规定。

2004年10月，根据《贵阳市人民政府关于批转市教育局〈关于实施名校名师工程的意见〉的通知》要求，教育局开展首届县级教育名师评选，汪政权、陈万立、张国生获县级“教育名师”称号。

2006年，教育局出台《对全县教育质量进行奖惩的意见》，明确对校长的奖励办法，在年度考核中，第一名2000元，第二名1500元，第三名1000元，其余800元。2008年，县教育出台《全县教育系统干部职工请假的规定》，对教师请假进行规范，明确各类假的批准权限和请假程序。

四、教师聘用

从2003年开始，逐步实行教师聘任制。是年9月，二中、职业技术学校、永靖小学教师实行聘用制，中学教师81人、小学教师48人签订聘用合同。2004年9月，对县内10所中学、38所小学、县教研室的教师实行聘用制；中学教师434人、小学教师741人、县教研室7人签订聘用合同。2005年9月，对全县2所中学、34所小学、县特殊教育学校、实验幼儿园的教师全部实行聘用制；中学教师191人、小学教师256人签订聘用合同。2008年，实行面向社会公开招考制度。至2010年，全县共补充教师1356人，其中小学教师710人，初中教师506人，高中教师140人。

第二节　招　生

20世纪90年代初，实行大中专招生考试预考制，由县组织预考，预选上线的学生参加国家、省、市（地区）组织的统考。统考时县设置考点组织考试，每年7月7日、8日、9日为全国高等学校统一招生考试日，录取分数线由省统一划定，省招生办负责上线考生的投档和录取工作；中专、高中由地区统考，县设考点组织考试，录取分数线由地区划定，地区招生办负责投档和录取工作，小学升初中招生考试由县统考，乡镇组织考试，按分数高低由息烽中学（县第一中学）、息烽城关中学（县第二中学）和乡镇内中学梯次录取。在高考和中考录取中对少数民族考生、省级以上表彰的三好学生、优秀学生干部实行加5~20分的优惠政策。

2001年，高考增加英语听力考试，实行网上录取。2002年，开始实行高考“3+X”模式，考试科目理科为语文、数学、英语、理科综合（物理、化学、生物）；文科为语文、数学、英语、文科综合（历史、地理、政治）。2003年，全国高考时间改为6月7日、8日，严格考生户籍、民族成分审查，建立考生电子档案。2005年，实行网上填报志愿，网上录取，所有参加高考的学生均填写“诚信承诺书”。

息烽县1991—2010年招生情况统计表

表16-4-1 单位：人

年份	高考参考人数	高考招收人数			中考参考人数	中考招收人数				
		本科	专科	中专		中专	五年制大专	高中	县职校	县外学校
1991	480	36	48	58	3152	134	—	368	38	—
1992	520	42	62	65	3281	147	—	331	168	—
1993	540	45	64	60	2953	153	—	364	26	—
1994	545	48	60	62	2675	165	—	430	251	—
1995	565	19	75	28	2458	179	—	420	114	—
1996	538	38	65	34	2074	245	—	438	130	—
1997	561	69	82	510	2125	274	—	401	104	—
1998	575	55	116	35	2037	428	—	462	33	—
1999	580	132	100	23	2294	713	—	541	50	—
2000	585	128	142	—	2225	667	—	731	43	—
2001	593	195	189	—	2252	302	—	1274	14	—
2002	673	173	189	—	2221	28	9	1464	72	—
2003	911	344	293	—	2005	28	9	1449	276	—
2004	1171	298	386	—	2036	—	—	1359	49	132
2005	1458	373	664	—	1719	—	—	1400	200	180
2006	1284	222	412	—	2100	—	—	1427	418	295
2007	1130	312	276	—	2587	—	5	1184	115	315
2008	1172	395	453	—	2783	—	—	1200	206	384
2009	1201	390	334	—	2351	—	7	1299	82	426
2010	1132	504	284	—	2254	—	—	1359	104	543
合计	16214	3818	4294	875	47582	3463	30	17901	2493	2275

第三节 经费来源

教育经费的来源主要包括县级财政拨款、上级专款、城乡教育费附加、社会捐资集资以及学生缴纳的学杂费等项，县级财政拨款主要用于人员工资，专款、城乡教育费附加和社会捐资集资主要用于学校基础设施建设，学杂费主要用于学校运转。1989年，县教育经费实行分级管理办法。1991年，县委《关于对各级各类学校实行分级办学分级管理的补充意见》，在分级管理基础上就有关事项进一步明确县、乡政府的办学职责。

一、学杂费

1991年，学校杂费标准，小学每个学生每学期3～5元，初中6～7元。1999—2004年，小学县城每个学生40元，农村每个学生25元，初中县城每个学生60元，农村每个学生40元。2004年，实行一费制，小学1～2年级，县城每个学生86元，农村每个学生80元；3～6年级，县城每个学生125元，农村每个学生90元；初中，县城每个学生200元，农村每个学生145元。1991—1999年，普通高中每个学期收学、杂费100元，2000年起，每个学期收380元。

二、农村教育费附加

从1986年起，按不低于上年农民人均收入的1.5%的比例征收，农村教育费附加实行乡征、县管、乡用。由县按各乡镇农业人口总数的90%核定征收人下达各乡镇，乡镇分户造册，开展常年性征收，也可由粮食部门用于秋征时代征，财政所结账。每年11月底上交县“农村教育费附加”专户储存，分乡镇核算，各乡镇定期提取出用款计划，报教育局审批后实施，全部用于校舍建设。同时，县政府根据国家有关规定征收机关、事业单位职工每年按年工资收入总额分段计征的10～50元不等的教育费，用于教育发展。2002年实行农村税费改革后，停止征收教育费附加。

三、上级拨款

1992—1997年，上级拨款161.5万元，城乡教育费附加594.9万元，社会捐资集资151.3万元，其他渠道筹资382.4万元。

1997年，全县启动“两基”工作，按照“两基”标准，县财政拨付教育经费逐年增加。争取到世界银行教育贷款72.5万美元，折合人民币579万元。1998年，息烽列入国家贫困地区义务教育工程项目县，获国家贫困地区义务教育补助款767万元。

息烽县1991—2010年教育经费统计表

表16-4-2

年份	教育经费拨款（万元）	财政总支出（万元）	教育经费占财政总支出（%）
1991	445	1992	22.34
1992	519	2621	19.8
1993	737	2714	27.16
1994	830	3133	26.49
1995	987	3756	26.28
1996	991	4642	21.35
1997	1302	5985	21.75
1998	1485	6501	22.84
1999	1983	7835	25.31
2000	2053	9289	22.1

续表

年份	教育经费拨款（万元）	财政总支出（万元）	教育经费占财政总支出（%）
2001	2897	12761	22.7
2002	3298	16735	19.71
2003	3900	18405	21.19
2004	4185	21184	19.76
2005	5514	27760	19.86
2006	6714	36167	18.56
2007	9197	45515	20.21
2008	14337	65498	21.89
2009	15839	76155	20.8
2010	18376	86794	21.17

专记：“两基”攻坚

全县两基工作分两步走，即先“普六”，再“普九”。经历“普六”验收、“两基”达标验收、两基复查和迎国检三个阶段。“普六”从20世纪80年代初开始实施，1986年通过省政府“普六”验收，1994年通过高标准扫盲验收。“普九”于1996年启动，2000年通过省政府验收，2004年通过省的复查，2009年通过国家复查。

1992年，县内启动高标准扫盲工作，将文盲的脱盲任务落实到扫盲教师，扫盲教师深入村组和文盲家中开展送教工作。1994年通过高标准扫盲验收。

1994年，动员失辍学儿童返校复学，确保在读学生不辍学。1995年，建立流失学生检查报告制度，加大控辍保学力度，对困难学生缓、减、免交书本杂费，将小学学生流失率控制到1.1%。1996年，全县小学入学率98.74%，巩固率99.14%，普及率99.66%，毕业率98.7%。初中入学率72.3%，辍学率7.8%。

1997年，“两基”攻坚开始实施。3月，县政府成立“两基”工作领导小组，各乡镇也成立领导小组，把“两基”工作纳入乡镇和部门的年终考核。县委、县政府组织召开教育工作会，动员和部署全县“两基”工作。7月，开始实施小学教师毕业生整班移交初中，95.3%的小学毕业生升入初中。9月，各乡镇对小学新入学儿童实行入学通知书制度，由乡镇人民法院向适龄儿童发放入学通知书，对不送子女入学的监护人，不批宅基地、不办结婚登记手续、不给予平价化肥、不给贷款。县委、县政府印发《息烽县求助失辍学儿童实施方案》《息烽县消除失辍学儿童实施方案》《息烽县“希望工程”管理细则》，“希望工程”得到社会各界支持，当年受助学生2273人，援建“希望小学”10所。

1998年，争取中央专款279万元、省专款225万元、市专款150万元，自筹113万元，扩建15所中心小学和1所初级中学。加大控辍保学力度，取消小学升初中考试，全面实施小学毕业生整班移交初中。2000年，全县共投入资金2852万元，消除危房2.1万平方米，新增校舍面积52303平方米，生均校舍面积3.8平方米。同时，统一购置图书、教学实验仪器配发到各中小学，小学生均图书6.19册，中学生均图书11.5册。北京师范大学研究生贵州支教团对息烽教育发展进行调研，撰写《修文　开阳息烽三县教育改革与发展的思考》《息烽县教育改革与发展报告》。聘请28名司法干警任各中学法制副校长，上法制课361节，受教育9.63万余人次。“两基”工作通过省级验收。

2002年，县投资55.2万元，为13所小学和11所中学建设成远程信息技术教育实施项目。

2007—2009年，县政府投入1212.83万元，补充中小学电脑、课桌、铁床、图书阅览桌椅，音、体、美器材。投入10多万元建立15个村扫盲图书室，配备图书10余万册；投入60多万元新建6所中小学多媒体教室。2009年，“两基”工作通过“国检”，至此，“两基”工作全面完成。

第五章　科学技术

1991年，全县有科技人员2694人，科技经费3万元。2010年，有科技人员7604人，科技经费499万元。20年间，全县共获科技进步奖国家级二等奖1个、省级2个、地市级14个；县自评科技进步奖71个。工农业科技成果的推广应用，对县内经济增长和农业生产稳定增收起到重要作用。

第一节　机构与队伍

一、行政管理机构

1991年，县设科学技术委员会（简称县科委）。内设办公室、科技情报所。1992年，县成立科技开发中心，与县科委合署办公。12月，成立“息烽县中药材开发公司”，经济上实行独立核算，行政隶属县科委领导。1996年，县科委改称县科学技术局（简称县科技局）。2002年10月17日，成立“息烽县生产力促进中心”，与科技情报所合署办公。2007年，成立“息烽县知识产权局”，与县科技局合署办公，挂知识产权局牌子，无人员编制。2010年7月，撤销县科技局独立建制，合并至县发展改革经济贸易局，保留县科技局牌子及公章。

二、群众学术组织

县科学技术协会，简称县科协。是全县科学技术工作者的群众组织，县科协由县级学会（协）会、乡镇科协和企业、事业单位科协组成。2010年，全县有专业学（协）会6个，老年科技协会（简称老科协）1个，企业科协4个，乡镇科普协会10个，农技协会27个。

三、科技队伍

1991年初，全县有科技人员2694人，其中社科副研究员1人、中等专业学校高级讲师1人、中学高级教师20人、小学中的中学高级教师3人、高级工程师1人、高级农艺师2人、高级兽医师1人、副主任医师6人、副主任药师1人；中级技术职称501人、初级技术职称2157人。

2010年，县域内企事业单位、党政机关、社会团体在职及离退休人员中，有各类专业技术科技人才7604人。其中，获得职称资格证的5240人（高级职称185人、中级2135人、初级2920人），无职称的2364人。

第二节　科技经费实施项目

1991—1998年，最高年科技经费17万元。2001年增加到43万元，此后逐年增加，2008年突破300万元，2010年，全县科技三项费499万元。全县共组织实施省、地（市）、县三级科技项目344个，其中省13个，地（市）39个，县292个。

随着科学技术的发展，科技项目的安排已由原来的农业、工业、卫生、医药等方面延伸到社会科学，如人才管理、社会调查、教学设备、电教、科技培训等方面。

息烽县1991—2010年部分年份科技三项费及实施项目统计表

表16-5-1　　单位：万元

年份	省厅拨款	地市局拨款	县财政拨款	实施省级项目	实施地市级项目	实施县级项目
1991	0	0	3	—	—	玉米群改种选育、水稻特青的高产试验等6个科技项目。
1992	0	3	2	—	玉米群改种的选育	
1993	10.3	5	2	县中药材基地建设	县中药材基地建设	县中药材基地建设
1994	0	10	1	—	县中药材基地建设	县中药材基地建设
1995	0	0	1	—	—	县中药材基地建设
1996	5	5	0	硅钙肥改良锈水田	龙氏养猪法推广、息单7号玉米示范种植	硅钙肥改良锈水田
1997	0	10	1	—	西瓜基地、早秋蔬菜基地、罗氏召虾养殖	县西瓜基地建设
1998	0	0	3	—	—	县西瓜、早秋蔬菜基地
2001	0	10	33.7	—	石硐乡金秋梨基地建设	石硐乡金秋梨基地、温泉镇椪柑基地、养龙司蔬菜基地等6个项目
2002	13	32	44	县花椒基地建设、贵州地道药材GAP试验示范基地	县脱毒马铃薯种薯扩繁与推广、县科技局局域网建设、县科技工作调研	养龙司花椒基地、县脱毒马铃薯种薯扩繁基地、县西瓜基地建设、永靖镇无公害蔬菜基地建设5个
2003	4	6	74.1	养龙司乡万亩蔬菜基地建设	县黄檗GAP试验示范基地、科技扶贫培训	养龙司乡蔬菜新品种试验、鹿窝乡枇杷和无公害两熟糯玉米基地、九庄镇艳红桃示范基地、永靖镇雨洒奶牛基地等12个
2004	5	46	100	县2004年科普宣传活动周	县生产力中心、县椪柑基地、流长生态优质肉鸡推广、科技扶贫培训	县“远程教育”信息库、县脱毒马铃薯基地建设等14个项目
2005	2	62.9	125	县科技“十一五”规划	鹿窝绿宝石梨种植和生态村建设、县三农科技专家服务中心建设、县科技“十一五”规划	流长乡前奔梨低产梨园改造、九庄镇团村肉鸡养殖小区等24个项目

续表

年份	省厅拨款	地市局拨款	县财政拨款	实施省级项目	实施地市级项目	实施县级项目
2006	5	15	130	南极顶牌夏秋反季节大白菜推广	县香葱、生姜无公害种植示范项目、科技扶贫培训	流长乡前奔村经果林种植、小寨坝镇金谷梨种植等24个项目
2007	5	30	178	县2000亩太子参规范化种植基	县政府网站和服务器、贵州皂荚系统开发与产业链、年产1亿块新型耐水石膏砖	县苗圃场果树新品种引种试验示范、中化开磷1000吨无水氟化氢中试等35个项目
2008	9	40	254	养龙司千亩蔬菜园种植技术推广、县灾后重建科技培训	县经果林灾后重建、灾后科技行动计划、养龙司蔬菜基地灾后重建	县政府办公室信息化建设、县禽流感等动物疫病监测等60个项目
2009	5	50	297	县葡萄避雨栽培试验	汉方药厂生产线技术改造、县西山虫茶扩繁技术攻关、优质肉牛高效循环农业示范基地、县杂交玉米超高产攻关	振华蛋鸡养殖、县教育局多媒体教室建设、西山虫茶产业化建设、磷石膏综合利用等68个项目
2010	0	45	454	—	汉方药厂日舒安湿巾生产线扩能、县市政照明高效节能控制系统工程	黄南武辣子鸡标准化保鲜技术试验、西山虫茶规范化管理等33个项目

第三节 科技成果及应用

一、科技成果

1991—2010年，全县获国家级科技进步二等奖1个，省级科技进步二等奖2个；地（市）级奖14个，其中一等奖2个、二等奖2个、三等奖10个；县级奖71个，其中一等奖7个、二等奖10个、三等奖35个、四等奖19个。

息烽县1991—2010年科技进步奖获奖情况统计表

表16-5-2

获奖名称	获奖单位	获奖人	授奖单位等级	授奖年份
磷化工全废料自胶凝充填采矿技术	贵州开磷集团有限责任公司	屈庆麟 杜绍伦 姚金蕊 李文成 蹇明星	国务院二等奖	2009
贵州省农区主要害鼠发生规律防治技术研究及应用	县农业局植保检疫站	简富明 潘世昌等	贵州省政府二等奖	2003
开阳磷矿矿浆浓密技术研究	贵州开磷集团有限责任公司	廖贵芳 罗德忠	贵州省政府二等奖	2007
烟蛀茎生物学特性发生规律及防治研究	县农业局	简富明 狄光华 简定萍	安顺行署一等奖	1991

续表

获奖名称	获奖单位	获奖人	授奖单位等级	授奖年份
良种良法，我县油菜获丰收	县农业局农推站	罗锡忠　狄光华　马书烈　陈孟叔　郑满江	安顺行署二等奖	1991
应用综合农业技术创千亩杂稻高产记录	县农业局	狄光华　罗锡忠　冯世忠　马书烈　皮荣卫	安顺行署三等奖	1991
玉米群体改良种丰产示范	县科委	陈昌其　何国才　吴　建	安顺行署三等奖	1991
息烽县旱地农业的一条新路——玉米地膜覆盖栽培	县农业局	孙润林　文周宇　杨静　郑满江　梅先伦	安顺行署三等奖	1991
黏虫生物学特性及发生规律测报技术研究	县农业局植保站	简富明　宋致书	安顺行署三等奖	1991
息烽县农业害鼠生物学发生规律及防治技术研究	县农业局植保站	潘世昌　简富明　沈成冰　王超悌	安顺行署三等奖	1991
息烽县西瓜基地建设	县科技局	朱品国　曾发贵　杨应华　周　松　王新民	贵阳市政府三等奖	2000
南极顶牌夏秋反季节大白菜推广应用	县农业局蔬菜办	周启康　魏明山　王晓芳　叶春芳　向艳辉	贵阳市政府三等奖	2002
食用橄榄调和油的研究开发	贵州味美食品工业有限公司	王兵等	贵阳市政府三等奖	2004
息烽脱毒马铃薯扩繁与推广	县科技局	文　俊　郑满江　杨应华　张天炽　罗志娟	贵阳市政府三等奖	2004
息烽县牛冷冻精液人工授精技术推广与应用	县农业局品改站	徐忠惠　赵子刚　吴亨进　熊治忠　陈远华	贵阳市政府三等奖	2006
开阳磷矿矿浆浓密技术研究	贵州开磷集团有限责任公司	廖贵芳　罗德忠	贵阳市政府一等奖	2006
息烽县主要害鼠发生规律及防治技术研究应用	县农业局植保站	潘世昌　李　梅　宋致书　马书烈	贵阳市政府二等奖	2010

二、科技推广与应用

（一）农业科技

水稻叶龄模式栽培：1990年，在养龙司试验2.5亩，获得成功。1991年推广5000亩，亩产570.2千克，比对照田516.9千克亩增产53.3千克。1992年推广2.26万亩，在插秧后期长期阴雨，7月中旬后又遇持续干旱的情况下，仍获得最高亩产726.3千克，最低亩产448.7千克，平均亩产507.6千克的产量。1995年推广7万亩，由于6月23日特大暴风雨袭击和连续30多天的干旱，造成水稻大面积灾害损失，使水稻叶龄模式栽培有效面积降到9800余亩，平均亩产470.5千克；高产指挥田57亩，亩产546千克。

水稻抛秧栽培技术：1996年开始试验，采用木盘温室育秧，2000年，抛寄育秧53.8亩，抛寄大田538亩。2003年，在7个乡镇39个村3982户，采用旱地育秧和温室育秧，示范水稻抛秧5612亩，其中大田直抛30亩（有水源保证的冬水田），抛寄二段秧5582亩（前茬为油菜、小麦田）。验收70亩，平均亩产523.8千克，比对照亩产503.2千克增产20.6千克，增产率4.1%；每亩省6个工时。

2006年，在水源较好的永靖镇、西山乡、养龙司、鹿窝乡、温泉镇的30个村4561户农户，采用木盘秧田育秧及配套技术，推广水稻抛秧11250亩，验收19.4亩（代表面积500亩），平均亩产384.5千克，比当年水稻平均亩产323千克增产61.5千克，增产率19%。该技术与手工插秧相比，每亩可节省秧田0.1亩，节省用工2～3个，节约生产成本30%左右，增产5%～10%，劳动强度也大为减轻。

横坡种植：1999年，推广坡耕地横坡聚垄区作2万亩，横坡等高种植0.3万亩，配套选用良种、平衡施肥、防治病虫害等综合措施。其中玉米18910亩，等高种植平均亩产317.7千克，比顺坡亩产301.7千克增产16千克，增产率5.3%。马铃薯套玉米1100亩，5～10度马铃薯产量等高比顺坡减10.8%，10～15度等高比顺坡减1.1%，15～20度等高比顺坡增0.6%。小麦3000亩，等高种植亩产163.5千克，比顺坡亩产157.8千克增产4.8千克，等高比顺坡增产3%。

集多年经验，县土肥站认为，马铃薯在雨水多的年份不宜横坡种植，黏重土壤在雨水多的年份不宜横坡种植。

旱地分带轮作：境内主要推广模式为麦—烟（苕—豆），芋—玉—苕、豆，麦—西瓜—菜等。采用6尺或5尺开厢，秋季种小麦或马铃薯，播幅2尺或3尺，预留行3尺。冬前种植蔬菜或绿肥，次年春季种烤烟或玉米。小麦或马铃薯收获后种苕、豆或菜。经多年测产验收，粮粮型复合亩产平均比常规亩产增加40%，粮经型复合产值比常规亩增加200元以上，增幅25%以上。

旱地宽厢宽带试验：2002—2005年，全县示范种植3470亩，主要种植模式有：绿肥、玉米—白菜、马铃薯—红苕、辣椒、胡萝卜、豆类；菜用豌豆、绿肥—玉米—马铃薯—胡萝卜；绿肥、黑麦草—白菜—玉米—生姜；绿肥、豌豆—芥菜—玉米—反季莴笋；绿肥、紫花苜蓿—白菜—玉米—红苕，共种植4季，平均每亩纯收益1312～1560元。

稻茬油菜免耕栽培：2002—2004年，实施稻茬油菜免耕栽培11145亩，验收185亩，平均亩产138.3千克，最高亩产158.5千克，最低亩产129千克。比常规栽培平均亩产145千克，亩产少6.7千克，降幅4.6%。但稻茬油菜免耕栽培每亩可节约翻犁、整地、中耕除草用工5个，每个工按16元计，可节约资金80元；按油菜每千克2.6元计，相当于油菜籽30.2千克，比常规栽培亩增产23.5千克，亩增产值61.1元。同时有利于改善土壤结构，利用稻茬在油菜生长后期腐烂缓效供肥，减少施用化肥，保护生态环境。

马铃薯稻田免耕、稻草全程覆盖栽培：2002年，在鹿窝乡鹿龙村套作试验4.5亩。亩产折成净作1296.15千克，比常规产量低25.3千克。该技术种植的马铃薯可提前7天上市，省工4个。2006年，推广面积1526亩，验收125亩，平均亩产1445千克，最高1612.8千克，最低1098.5千克。

（二）畜牧科技

科学养猪技术：境内传统养猪为熟饲，饲料单一，营养不全面，饲料利用率低。1991年，用科学养猪技术饲养1头杂交猪，14个月，体重150千克，料肉比4～5：1，屠宰率76%。至2010年，使用科学养猪技术，养1头杂交猪，4～6个月，体重110～120千克，料肉比3.5：1，屠宰率80%。

仔猪早期断奶补饲技术：1995年，鹿窝乡畜牧站试验补饲58头仔猪，投料810千克，总增重677千克，料肉比1.2：1，双月重达21千克，比不补饲仔猪双月重10千克增重11千克。

（三）林业科技

保水剂造林：2004年，在贵阳市第二环城林带工程建设中，全县849.53公顷二环林带造林全部采用保水剂进行造林，提高造林成活率，至2010年，所造林地郁闭成林，长势良好。

营养袋造林：2003年，县内推广营养袋造林技术，提高荒山造林成活率，特别是白云质砂石山造林成活率最高，主要造林树种有柏木、喜树、柳杉、刺槐等。至2010年，全县营养袋造林面积3000公顷。

生物防治：2007年，县林业局在小寨坝南极片区释放肿腿蜂防治松褐天牛135公顷，防治效果80%以上。至2010年，每年5月，在天幕毛虫、银杏大蚕蛾、云南松毛虫等病虫发生区喷洒白僵菌进行防治，面积累计3700公顷，防治效果75%以上。利用引诱剂诱捕害虫，每年4—10月设置诱木、天牛诱捕器等诱捕松褐天牛，防治面积累计1664公顷，防治效果80%以上。

（四）工业科技

石灰烧结法生产氢氧化钠工业性试验：2005年8月15日，贵州省经贸委对“贵州西洋集团用贵州大学发明专利——石灰烧结法生产氢氧化钠工业性试验”项目通过省级鉴定，认定本项目达到国内外同类（烧结法）现有生产方法的先进水平。

利用磷石膏——黄磷炉渣制备新型高强耐水磷石膏砖新工艺：贵州开磷磷业公司研发。2009年获中国石油和化学工业协会颁发的科技进步一等奖。

高强耐水磷石膏砖：2009年获省政府颁发的2009年贵州省优秀新产品、新技术奖。开磷集团旗下企业研制。开发新型建筑材料，实现工业固体废弃物综合利用。

（五）医药卫生

1993年，县医院开展丙型肝炎、脑电图检查、成分输血、光量子血疗及细菌培养等项目获得成功。

苗疆消痛液：是一种治疗关节慢性疼痛的外用酊剂。由县人民医院外科医生邓钧根据县内苗族王氏家族、开阳县苗族马氏家族、贵阳民国时期名医杨老先生遗方，结合临床实践开发而成。经过多年实践，有效性90%以上。2000年，《消痛液局部外用治疗慢性疼痛102例》获县政府科技成果二等奖；2001年经过省卫生厅检验合格，获得生产批文；2005年获得国家专利证书。

第十七篇　卫　生

第一章　机构及人员配置

1991—2010年，县内卫生机构历经合并、撤销、改制、上划、恢复、更名等。至2010年，有县级卫生机构7个、乡（镇）级卫生机构10个、村级卫生机构161个、厂矿企业卫生机构（含疗养院）6个、私营（含私人个体诊所）卫生机构10个、改制卫生机构1个、学校卫生室3个。

第一节　管理机构及人员

一、县卫生局

1991年，县卫生局（挂爱国卫生运动委员会牌子）内设办公室、业务科、县爱国卫生运动委员会办公室。县红十字会设在县卫生局。1996年4月，县卫生局配置行政编制7人、事业编制4人。2000年10月，县卫生局组建卫生综合执法大队，负责全县医疗单位、药店及公共卫生的监督执法，打击市场无证行医、违法经营药品和假冒伪劣药品等工作。

2002年机构改革，调整卫生局职能：药政药检工作职能交由省、市垂直领导的县药品监督管理分局管理；原县人事劳动局负责的职业卫生监察、矿山卫生监察和县财政局负责的公费医疗管理职能划归县卫生局管理；原卫生局管理的卫生质量控制规划、专业技术培训、科研成果推荐评审等工作，交由卫生事业单位承担。撤销业务科，设综合科。县红十字会从卫生局分出，单独建立“息烽县红十字会”。撤销卫生综合执法大队。

2010年，原由省、市垂直管理的县食品药品监督管理分局划归县卫生局管理，组建县卫生食品药品监督管理局，原县食品药品监督管理局更名为县卫生监督局，为县卫生食品药品监督管理局管理的二级局。

二、食品药品监督管理局

2002年，撤销县药品监督检验所，全建制划转给县药品监督管理分局，加挂县药品稽查大队牌子，实行两块牌子、一套人员体制，内设办公室、业务股，为贵阳市药品监督管理局派出机构，正科级建制，主要负责本辖区内药品监督管理工作。同年5月，县药品监督管理分局更名为县药品监督管理局，加挂药品监督管理局稽查队牌子，为独立执法主体。2004年5月，县药品监督管理局更名为县食品药品监督管理局，加挂药品监督管理稽查局牌子，隶属关系不变，内设办公室、食品安全股、药品监督股，工作职能在原药品监督管理基础上增加对辖区内食品、保健品、化妆品的安全监督管理。2010年，县食品药品监督管理局划归县卫生局管理、组建县卫生食品药品监督管理局，原县食品药品监督管理局更名为县卫生监督局，为县卫生食品药品监督管理局管理的二级局。

第二节　医疗机构及队伍

1991年，县内有各级各类医疗卫生机构40个，其中县直医疗机构2个，防疫站、妇幼保健院、疗养院、单采血浆站各1个，区卫生院4个、乡（镇）卫生所24个，厂矿医务室、学校医务室各3个；共有卫生从业人员605人，其中卫生技术人员422人（中医师15人、西医师110人、护师40人、中药师6人、西药师11人、检验师5人、中医士4人、西医士62人、中医士4人、护士71人、助产士5人、西药药剂士8人、中药药剂士2人、检验技士10人、其他中医2人、护理员11人、西药药剂员13人、中药药剂员2人、检验员3人、其他初级卫生技术人员38人）。

2006年，县、乡（镇）医疗卫生单位有职工503人，其中卫生专业技术人员465人，占职工总数的92.45%；县级医疗卫生单位有专业技术人员283人，占专业技术人员总数的60.86%；乡级医疗卫生单位有专业技术人员182人，占专业技术人员总数的39.14%。本科以上学历57人，占职工总数的11.33%；大专学历120人，占职工总数的23.86%；中专学历221人，占职工总数的43.94%；高中及以下105人，占职工总数的20.87%。有高级职称8人，占专业技术人员的1.72%；中级职称51人，占专业技术人员的10.97%；初级职称380人，占专业技术人员的81.72%；无职称26人，占专业技术人员的5.59%。全县医疗机构拥有床位568张，每千人拥有床位2.27张。此外，有村级卫生人员322人。

2010年，全县有各级各类医疗卫生机构166个，其中县级医疗机构2个，县疾控中心、卫生监督所、妇幼保健院、单采血浆站各1个，疗养院1个，乡（镇）卫生院10个、厂矿医务室4个、民营医院2个、个体诊所8个、村卫生室135个；有卫生技术人员782人，其中执业（助理）医师211人、执业护士247人、医技人员99人、乡村医生225人。

一、县直医疗机构

（一）县人民医院

1991年，县人民医院内设科室14个，其中管理科室4个（办公室、总务科、财务科、保卫科）；临床科室6个（内一科、内二科、外科、妇产科、中西医结合科、中医科）；辅助科室4个（医技科、药剂科、防保科、门诊部）。有职工183人，其中卫生技术人员133人（获中级以上技术职称24人）。病床150张，医疗设备60余台。1993年，建“息烽红会血站”，为县人民医院内设独立站，性质为“以副补主”自负盈亏的医院第三产业。1995年，县人民医院内设科室调整：保留办公室、总务科、财务科、保卫科、门诊部、外科、妇产科、中医科、药剂科、防保科。内一科更名为传染科，内二科更名为内儿科。增设护理部、放射科、检验科、政工科、医务科、供应科。撤销医技科、中西医结合科。调整后内设科室共18个，其中管理科室7个、临床科室5个、辅助科室6个。1996年4月，“息烽红会血站”从县人民医院整体（人、财、物）划拨给县卫生局管理。

2005年9月，县人民医院住院部从蚕桑坡（原省职工疗养院）搬出，入住医院新建综合大楼。10月，医院内设科室调整，增设控感科、医保科；保留办公室、总务科、财务科、防保科、护理部、政工科、医务科、门诊部、妇产科、药剂科、放射科、检验科、中医科、供应科。外科分设为外一科和外二科；内儿科分设为内科和儿科；传染科更名为感染科，手术室更名为麻醉科。调整后内设科室共23个，其中管理科室10个（办公室、总务科、财务科、保卫科、护理部、政工科、医务科、防保科、控感科、医保科）；临床科室7个（外一科、外二科、内科、儿科、妇产科、感染科、麻醉科）；辅助科室6个（门诊部、药剂科、放射科、检验科、中医科、供应科）。至2010年，县人民医院有职工334人，其中卫生技术人员286人（获中级以上技术职称73人）。设病床238张，有各种医疗设备200余台，业务用房1万余平方米。

（二）县中医医院

县中医医院（简称县中医院）于1988年10月建院开诊。1991年，内设住院部、门诊部、办公室和财务科。其中，住院部设综合病房；门诊部设中医、西医、骨伤、肛肠、痔瘘、理疗按摩、针灸、中医妇科等诊断室，有医技人员31人，病床26张。2004年，县中医医院内设机构调整为办公室、医务科、控感科、护理部、财务后勤科。2006年6月，再次调整内设机构，保留门诊部、药剂科、内儿科；增设中西医结合外科、骨伤专科、麻醉科、心血管专科、医技科；外妇科更名为妇产科，成立医保合医办公室，财务后勤科分设为财务科和总务科。有医技人员103名。2010年，中医院内设办公室、医务科、控感科、护理部、财务科、医保合医办公室、总务科7个科室；门诊部设中医、西医、外科、骨伤科、肛肠科、针灸科、五官科、发热门诊、肠道门诊等诊断科室；医技科设检验室、X光室、B超室、心电图室、手术室；住院部设中西医结合心脑血管专科、内儿科、中西医结合外科、妇产科、骨伤科、麻醉科、重症抢救观察室、老干病房。有职工197人，其中医技人员171人（副高职称6人、中级职称29人、初级职称136人）。业务用房1.43万平方米，设病床150张。

二、疾控中心

1991年，县设卫生防疫站（加挂县皮肤病防治站牌子），下设防疫组、计划免疫组、食品卫生组、检验组、办公室，时有职工24人。2000年，卫生监督职能划出，由县卫生局卫生综合执法大队负责。2002年，撤销县卫生防疫站和皮肤病防治站，组建县疾病预防控制中心（简称疾控中心），为县卫生局领导的副科级事业单位，内设办公室、流行科、慢性科、监测检验科、财务科、健康教育科6个科室。人员编制27人。

三、县卫生监督所

2002年，撤销县卫生局卫生综合执法大队，组建县卫生监督所，为县卫生局领导的副科级事业单位，内设办公室、业务一科和业务二科，人员编制9人。2003年8月，在各乡（镇）卫生院设立卫生监督办公室，监督员由县卫生局在乡（镇）卫生院医务人员中考核聘任，作为县卫生监督所派驻乡（镇）卫生院的卫生监督员，办公室人员所需经费纳入各乡（镇）财政全额预算管理，共聘任21人。2010年，卫生监督所增编4人。

四、县妇幼保健院

1991年，设县妇幼保健站，为县卫生局领导的副科级事业单位，内设预防保健科、儿科、妇产科、医学影像科、妇女保健科、儿童保健科、医学检验科，人员定编20人。2008年，县妇幼保健站更名为县妇幼保健院。至2010年，有职工22人，其中医技人员19人，其他人员3人。

五、县单采血浆站

1993年，县人民医院筹资建“息烽红会血站”，为县人民医院内设机构。1996年4月，息烽红会血站整体（人、财、物）划给县卫生局，组建“息烽县单采血浆站”，为卫生局管理的副科级自收自支事业单位，事业编制25名。内设办公室、血源科、单采科、检验科、财务科、总务科、保卫科。2006年，单采血浆站改制为企业，次年完成转制，组建“息烽县上升单采血浆有限责任公司”，属上海生物制品研究所下属企业，与县卫生局脱离隶属关系。

六、区、乡镇卫生院、所

（一）区卫生院

1991年，全县有永阳区、养龙区、九庄区、黑神庙区4个全民所有制区卫生院，共有职工95人，病床60张。1992年，撤区并乡建镇后，各区卫生院撤销。

（二）乡镇卫生所、院

1991年，全县有乡镇卫生所24家（集体性质），设置病床36张，有职工115名，其中卫生技术人员83人。1992年撤区并乡建镇后，全县组建为四镇六乡，各乡镇建卫生院，即：永靖镇卫生院、养龙司乡卫生院、小寨坝镇卫生院、九庄镇卫生院、石硐乡卫生院、鹿窝乡卫生院、温泉镇卫生院、西山乡卫生院、流长乡卫生院、青山苗族乡卫生院，隶属乡镇管理。时有医护人员205人，病床69张，业务用房2750平方米。医护人员工资实行差额补助：财政补助80%，医院自筹20%。2002年12月，乡镇卫生院上划县卫生局直接管理，人员经费由差额补助改为财政全额拨款。2010年，乡镇卫生院共有在编职工136人，其中执业医师23人、助理医师29人、护士23人，病床207张。

七、村卫生室

1991年前，未建村级卫生室。1992年，全县建村卫生室113个，卫生人员113人，接生员61人。工资每人每月补助40元，2004年1月起，每人每月补助100元。2007年，村卫生室增至154个。次年1月起，每人每月工资补助调至200元。2010年，村卫生室增至161个，有村医208人。

八、厂矿、企业医院（所、室、疗养院）

（一）林东矿务局南山煤矿医务所

1991年，林东矿务局南山煤矿医务所有干部职工17人，其中医技人员14人；有病床12张。

（二）国营二七六厂职工卫生院

1996年，国营二七六厂职工卫生院有医技人员32人。2001年更名为西洋医院，有医技人员22人。2006年改制为个体医院。

（三）息烽磷矿医务所

1991年，息烽磷矿医务所有干部职工11人，其中医技人员9人。1992年，设病床22张。2010年，有医技人员7人。

（四）开磷集团磷化医务所

1991年，息烽黄磷厂医务室有干部职工15人，其中医技人员14人。1992年设病床4张。1996年更名为息烽重钙厂卫生所，有医技人员26人。2001年更名为重钙厂医务所。2007年更名为开磷集团职工医院磷化医务所。2010年，有医技人员13人。

（五）遵义铁路医院息烽火车站卫生所

1996年，遵义铁路医院息烽火车站卫生所有医技人员14人。2007年减至5人。

（六）贵州省总工会温泉疗养院

1991年，贵州省总工会温泉疗养院（简称温泉疗养院）有干部职工183人，其中医技人员100人；设病床400张。此后，疗养院医技人员逐年减少，至2010年，有医技人员42人。

九、民营医院

（一）协和医院

2008年8月15日注册登记，9月开诊。设内科、外科、妇科、皮肤科、医学检验科、医学影像科、中西医结合科。

（二）阳光医院

2010年6月20日注册登记，12月开诊。设内科、外科、皮肤科、医学检验科、医学影像科、中医科等。

十、个体诊所

20世纪90年代初，县境内有个体诊所数十家，其中公立医院退休医师开办的诊所占相当比重，如县城同德堂中医诊所、王秋云诊所、杨光远牙科（均为县人民医院退休医师开办）。后由于村卫生室的建立、个体诊所人员加入村卫生室、退休医师年龄增大等因素，个体诊所逐渐减少。至2010年，有私人诊所8家，从业人员20余人。

十一、中、小学校卫生室

1991年，息烽中学、城关中学和永红小学各校设卫生室，分别有校医1人。

十二、其他

（一）公医办

1990年，县公费医疗管理委员会成立，下设办公室（简称公医办）在县卫生局，管理全县公费医疗事宜。1995年，公医办改设在县财政局，由财政局管理。2002年，公医办业务划归县卫生局管理。

（二）新型农村合作医疗管理中心

2003年11月10日，设立县新型农村合作医疗办公室，为县卫生局管理的股级事业单位，核定事业编制4名。同时在10个乡镇设新型农村合作医疗办公室，为各乡镇政府领导下的股级事业单位。2006年，县新型农村合作医疗办公室更名为“息烽县新型农村合作医疗管理中心”（简称县合管中心），为县卫生局管理的副科级事业单位，内设办公室、综合业务科。核定事业编制30名。其中县合管中心配备工作人员7名，10个乡镇新型农村合作医疗办公室（简称乡镇合医办）配备23人（暂占县合管中心编制），“乡镇合医办”原机构管理体制不变，实行乡镇与县卫生行政主管部门双重领导。

第二章　医　疗

1991—2010年，县内西医事业快速发展，各种辅助诊断、治疗设备及新技术的引进逐年增多，提高了诊断准确率和治愈率。县内中医有较好基础，1988年建立县中医院后，更推进了传统中医药文化在境内的传承和发扬，2009年，县中医院针灸科成为第一批省级重点专科。全县医技人员加强医学知识的学习和研究，不断总结临床实践，先后发表专著论文论述160余篇，分别刊载于国家、省、市相关权威性刊物，部分论文通过专家学者交流评审，评为优秀专著论文，受到国际医学专家、学者的关注。县人民医院、县中医院突破多项疑难手术，填补县内医疗空白。部分乡镇卫生院相继开展阑尾切除和疝修补等手术。2010年，县级医疗机构门诊20.04万人次，业务收入4907.46万元，较1991年的7.76万人次、142.82万元分别增加157.66%和3336.11%。

第一节 西 医

一、内科

20世纪90年代初，县人民医院西医内科除诊治多发病、常见病外，对出血热、血栓病等重大疾患的诊治进行总结研究，取得良好疗效。1991年，县人民医院成立血栓病防治所，设血栓病床10张，购置血液流变学系列检查仪器微循环显微镜、中风预防仪等设备，引进抗血栓新药“蛇毒清栓酶”，开展对血栓病的防治和科研工作。是年，收治血栓病患者28人。1993年，县人民医院引进“血疗”新技术，开展光量子血液疗法。

2000年起，县人民医院内科开展纤维胃镜及幽门螺杆菌检查、胃镜下黏膜组织检查、胃镜下止血、胆道蛔虫钳取，电子胃十二指肠镜检查、电子结肠镜检查、肠息肉电切除等新技术，均取得较好疗效。

2003年4月，“非典型肺炎”在广东等省、市、自治区流行，根据党中央、国务院和省、市、县各级政府指示，县人民医院成立以院长为组长的“非典”防治领导小组，从各科室抽调业务骨干11人，组成“非典”抢救小组（详见本篇第三章第二节）。

2004年，县中医院开展心源性休克、心肌梗塞等急危重症抢救获得满意效果，开展经食道心脏调搏术获得成功。2007年4月16日，县内小寨坝镇一家化工厂发生“二氧化硫”泄漏事故，中毒群众（包括工人和农民）236人，其中严重患者60余人，经过县人民医院的抢救和一周的治疗，全部康复。

二、外科

1991年，县内西医外科开展各种普外中小手术。次年，县人民医院开展小儿麻痹遗留症矫正术，肾盂、输尿管切开取石术、前列腺切除术、先天性腕关节脱位开放加盖术攻关获得成功。1994年，县人民医院首次开展脊椎骨折减压术、脊髓探查、蝶克氏固定术、肾破裂修补等外科手术取得成功。1995年11月，县中医院开展建院以来首例外科手术——阑尾切除术取得成功。

1998年7月至1999年，九庄镇卫生院在贵阳市第二人民医院专家的指导帮助下，相继开展阑尾切除、疝气修补、鞘膜积液、剖宫产、肠修补、胃修补、剖腹探查等外科手术，结束县内乡镇卫生院不能开展外科手术的历史。

1999—2003年，县人民医院开展子宫肌瘤挖出术、剖宫产妇腹壁美容切口术、髌骨骨折采用AO张力带克氏针——钢丝固定术、脊柱骨折采用鲁氏棒固定、骨盆粉碎性骨臼并骶髂关节分离开放手术复位、弧形钢板固定、颅内胶质瘤摘除、甲状腺次全切除、左肾切除、胸腹联合切口、胃大部切除、颅内血肿清除、开胸探查、腹腔镜胆囊切除、胆肠吻合等手术获得成功。2004年9月，青山苗族乡卫生院首例四肢骨科内固定手术成功。

2005年，县中医院开展首例开颅手术获得成功。次年，开展胰、十二指肠切除术获得成功，开创县内此类手术先例；开展骨盆粉碎性骨折切开复位固定术、肩胛骨粉碎性骨折切开复位固定术，填补县内空白。

2006—2010年，县人民医院相继开展脾脏包膜下血肿清除引流、四肢骨干骨折交锁髓内钉内固定、髋臼骨折切开复位重建钢板内固定、股动静脉断裂吻合、脊椎骨折切开复位并椎弓根内固定、脊椎结核病灶清除、人工全髋关节置换，股骨骨折不愈合、股骨上段截骨定制关节置换，自发性血气胸开胸探查、肺叶切除、张力性气胸、开胸探查救治等手术。开展各种腹腔镜手术200余例。

三、妇产科

1996年，贯彻落实世界卫生组织《世界儿童发展纲要》精神，县人民医院妇产科增设标准无菌产房1间，单人病房4间，建成县内首家“爱婴医院”。2000年，息烽县被指定为“国家降消项目”县。1997年起，以县人民医院妇产科为主，有关科室参与，成立危重孕产妇及儿童抢救小组，为危重孕产妇及儿童急诊提供24小时服务。2007年，开展分娩镇痛、经阴腹联合手术治疗子宫脱垂。至2010年，妇产科除日常为产妇接生外，相继开展经腹膜内子宫下段剖宫产术、宫颈椎形切除术、筋膜内外全子宫切除术、经阴道全子宫切除术、阴道前后壁成形术、子宫肌瘤剔除术、阔韧带肿瘤切除术、外阴及阴道肿瘤切除术、腹腔镜下卵巢肿瘤切除、输卵管卵巢切除、输卵管造口、输卵管伞成形、子宫内膜病灶切除等。

四、五官科

20世纪90年代，县人民医院五官科为30余名白内障患者作白内障囊外摘除术，术后视力恢复为0.5～1.2。2005年，首次利用高频电刀电凝止血技术为鼻腔连续7年出血患者进行手术获得成功。次年，在市一医专家指导下，开展鼻窦炎负压置换治疗，效果显著。2007年，为遵义市桐梓县一名声嘶5年的男性患者做双声带息肉摘除术，术后声嘶症状立即消除。2010年，县人民医院五官科相继开展纤维喉镜检查、局麻下经纤维喉镜行声带息肉及小结摘除术、会厌良性肿瘤摘除术、纤维喉镜下喉异物取出术；鼻内镜检查、鼻内镜微波治疗鼻出血、中下鼻甲成形术、筛前神经切断术、鼻息肉摘除术、前鼻孔成形术、鼻骨骨折复位术、全麻下耳道异物及鼻腔异物取出术、经鼻内镜鼻窦手术及先天性耳前瘘管摘除术等。

1991—2010年，医技人员在临床实践中，不断探索总结，撰写《健康教育对医院感染的影响研究》《婴儿暖箱医院感染控制策略》《腹腔镜胆囊切除术308例临床观察》《奥曲肽治疗急性胰腺炎效果观察》《盐酸纳洛酮治疗脑梗塞疗效观察》《经纤维喉镜摘除声带息肉63例分析》《鼻内镜引导下微波治疗慢性肥厚性鼻炎80例》《腹腔镜下卵巢良性肿瘤剥除缝合术52例体会》等论文近100篇，分别被省级以上刊物刊载，有18篇在全国、省学术会上交流。

第二节　中　医

1991年，县内主要医疗单位县人民医院、县中医院、各区、镇卫生院及县中西药公司设专职中医师坐诊，从事中医诊疗。在县城、乡镇集镇有个体中医诊所，在民间有中草医走村串寨（游医）为患者提供中医诊疗服务，民间中草医以秘方治疗骨伤见长。

1992年撤区并乡建镇后，各乡镇卫生院设专职中医师坐诊。20世纪90年代，县中医院运用中医治疗内、外、妇、儿科等常见病和多发病取得明显疗效。运用耳穴疗法配合“利胆排石汤”治疗急性胆囊炎合并胆石症，最大排石1.5厘米×0.8厘米。以传统中医疗法推拿、按摩、针灸为主治疗腰痛、肩周炎、膝关节炎、面瘫等疾病，辅以中药“补阳还五汤”，治疗中风后遗症半身不遂200余例，多数患者症状、体征不同程度缓解，部分病人疗效明显。采用中医辨证分型办法，以“茵陈蒿汤”为主随症加减，辅以中药制剂田基黄、板蓝根肌注，治疗传染性黄疸型肝炎。一般治疗30余天后，症状、体征消失，肝功检验转为阴性。采用“大承气汤”“金虞匮大黄牡丹皮汤”治疗急慢性阑尾炎急性发作、肠套叠、肠扭转及不完全肠梗阻等急腹症，疗效明显。采用中医整骨“八法”复位，小夹板固定，配合中医分期辨证施治，用“复元活血汤”“接骨丹”“八珍汤”等方剂随症加减，治疗四肢闭合性骨折、锁骨单纯性闭合性骨折，多数患者治疗40天左右康复。1996年起，用活血化瘀法治疗头痛、慢性肝炎；用参苓白术散治疗慢性溃疡性结肠炎以及中药治疗小面积烧伤等，均取得满意疗效。1998年起，县城县府路（水井巷）国文诊所运用小针刀手术治疗骨质增生疗效明显，有不少省内外患者慕名前来就诊。1999年，采用益肾化瘀法治疗哮喘，益肾化瘀除湿汤治疗蛋白尿等。

2002年6月，永靖镇阳朗、老街、猫洞、立碑等村遭受百年罕见洪灾，县中医院组织医技人员深入抗洪救灾一线，诊治各类病人2546人，免费发放价值1万余元药品，煎熬中药普发受灾群众预防传染病流行。次年4月起，购进电脑控制煎药机和包装机，采用中药入煎前冷水浸泡，根据不同药物选择不同火力和煎制时长等，为患者提供煎药服务。2004年，县中医院中医接诊患者1.98万人次。

2005年，县中医院运用针灸理疗、推拿、中药熏蒸、拔火罐等治疗中风偏瘫、脑瘫、偏头痛、月经不调、痛经、小儿遗尿以及各种软组织损伤引起的疼痛。对颈椎综合征、椎间盘突出、网球肘、鼠标手、腰肌劳损等现代职业病的治疗取得满意疗效。是年，县中医院针灸室病床增至12张。

次年起，运用头针、耳针、穴位注射、中药药包热敷、中药穴位敷贴、闪罐、走罐、刮痧等方法为患者治疗。是年，针灸室接待患者2000余人次。

2008年，县中医院开展中药房建设项目建设活动，新购置煎药机、中药封装机、落地式连续投料粉碎机、摇摆式高速粉碎机、空调、除湿机、冷藏柜等设备，进一步提高中药规范管理和加工能力。被省中医药管理局指定为中药新剂型推广单位，新增中药颗粒饮片400余种，满足患者多样化需求。在院内推行配制消肿止痛膏治疗急慢性筋伤、紫草油膏治疗小面积烧伤。县人民医院中医运用针灸治疗面瘫、面肌痉挛、神经性头痛、顽固性呃逆、颈椎病等疗效明显。次年，县中医院配合省卫生厅、省中医药管理局开展“中医中药中国行”活动，现场指导群众鉴别中药真伪，宣传中医药文化、科学理论、独特治疗方法及疗效等科普知识。为息烽第二中学、县实验幼儿园配置预防甲型H1N1流感病和手足口病中药煎剂4000余袋，制作药枕300余个。县中医院针灸科成为省第一批重点专科。是年，引进中药直肠滴入技术。

2010年，运用补肾、凉血解毒、利尿等中医疗法，治疗慢性肾炎、肾病综合征等，疗效明显，有重庆、成都、贵阳等地患者慕名前来就诊。运用中药肚脐外敷治疗婴幼儿肠胃、呼吸系统疾患。是年，县中医院通过“中医管理年”活动检查验收。

1991—2010年，县内中医相继开展针灸、钩活术、拔罐、火针、电针、耳针、推拿、牵引、理疗、中药熏洗、中药热罨包等近30种中医药传统疗法及非药物治疗服务，为中医临床诊疗积累了丰富实践经验。中医药技术人员相继撰写的《黄芩黄连甘草汤治疗心律失常》《清肝托降压汤合硝苯地平控释片治疗高血压头痛75例》《中药复方治疗糖尿病自主神经病变性腹泻56例》《香砂六君子汤治疗慢性胃炎143例》等论文先后在省级以上刊物发表。其中《湿热黄疸诊治》论文1995年4月参加第二届世界传统医学大会暨“超人杯”世界传统医学优秀成果大赛交流，获国际优秀成果奖，作者陈历修被授予“民族医药之星”称号。《中药复方治疗糖尿病自主神经病变性腹泻56例》选送参加“全国内科急危重症学术交流会”“全国中医药研究会临床经验交流会”交流，受到与会专家好评。论文《运用小柴胡诊加减治疗顽固性头痛18例》获中华医学优秀学术奖。

第三节 中西医结合

1991年，县人民医院设中西医结合外科。县人民医院、县中医院分别开展中西医结合治疗出血热。1993年，县人民医院组织医务人员攻关，采取中西医结合方法，诊疗流行性出血热，总结出“平、扩、限、需”补液治疗方案，治愈率由1978年的84%提高到当年的97.5%，死亡率由16%下降到2.5%。1995年起，县中医院医技人员采用中西医结合方法治疗痛风性关节炎、高血压等。2004年起，县中医院医技人员采用中西医结合治疗脑栓塞、脑出血所致偏瘫后遗症、脑外伤及其后遗症、脑萎缩、老年痴呆、小儿脑瘫、高血压、脑动脉硬化、冠心病、肢体麻木、急性脑缺血发作颈椎病、三叉神经痛等心脑血管疾病。2006年起，开展以中药为主、中西医结合治疗小儿肺炎、小儿胃肠道感染、消化不良以及小儿肾炎，取得较好疗效。

1991—2010年，县内医技人员通过对中西医结合理论的研究和实践，撰写《中西医结合治疗流行性出血热肾功能衰竭》《痛风性关节炎的中西医结合治疗》《中西医结合治疗流行性出血热少尿期》《巯甲丙脯酸合丹参治疗高血压》《中西医结合治疗大叶性肺炎23例疗效观察》《浅析中西医结合治疗高血压急症》《中西医结合治疗非溃疡性消化不良观察》等论著，其中《中西医结合治疗流行性出血热肾功能衰竭》获贵州省首届科技成果优秀奖，《浅析中西医结合治疗高血压急症》一文在山东召开的“全国内科急危重症学术交流会”上交流，受到与会专家好评。

第四节 水 疗

水疗亦称浴疗，是利用温泉的特殊水质为患者治病疗疾的独特治疗方法。其机理是通过温泉的放射性氡气蜕变产生α、β、γ射线的电离辐射，经皮肤、呼吸、消化等途径进入体内，对肌体组织产生有益的生物和物理作用而达到缓解或治疗疾病的目的。息烽温泉氡含量11.14马谢/升，富含30多种有益于人体健康的矿物质和微量元素。20世纪50年代末，省总工会息烽温泉职工疗养院运用息烽温泉为患者进行水疗，至今有近60年历史。通过临床观察总结，息烽温泉水疗对心血管系统、运动系统、神经系统、代谢系统，内分泌腺等方面疾病有较好疗效。据该疗养院临床统计，1990—2000年相继收治的8562中长期病例中，疗养1月以上，好转以上（含治愈、近愈）7706例，总有效率90%以上，其中运动系统疾病、皮肤病、呼吸系统疾病、消化系统疾病、神经系统疾病、循环系统疾病有效率分别为96.3%、94.1%、92.1%、91.2%、86.3%、89.6%，其他疾病有效率87.8%。2001—2010年，收治住院20天以上，出院时有疗效评定的13种慢性病病人（西医第一出院诊断）3854例，治愈3545例，总有效率91.98%，其中运动系统疾病、消化系统疾病、神经系统疾病、循环系统疾病、皮肤病有效率分别为93.5%、87.4%、86.6%、91.3%、91.1%，其他疾病有效率

87.9%。收治病例中，疗效排在前四位的依次为运动系统疾病、循环系统疾病、皮肤病及消化系统疾病。

第五节　其　他

一、公费医疗

1990年，县国家机关、人民团体、事业单位等由财政预算开支的在编人员享受公费医疗待遇。1992年6月，县政府出台《息烽县公费医疗管理（试行）办法》，规定：享受公费医疗人员就医门诊费按工龄计发，每月6～9元不等发给个人，实行节约归己，超额自付；住院费根据数额多少，扣减5%～25%和当月门诊费后，在公医办报销；住院费在1万元以上者、离休干部、因公负伤及见义勇为者实报实销。2005年7月1日起，除离休干部、二等乙级以上伤残军人和符合计划生育政策的女职工住院分娩享受公费医疗外，在职职工和退休人员纳入医疗保险，不再享受公费医疗。2006年，全县享受公费医疗87人，其中离休干部54人、二等乙级以上伤残军人33人。2010年，全县享受公费医疗37人，其中离休干部36人、伤残军人1人。

二、新型农村合作医疗

20世纪70年代初，息烽县曾实行生产大队办合作医疗，至20世纪80年代初，合作医疗解体。2003年，息烽县被省委、省政府定为2003年启动省级新型农村合作医疗试点县。11月25日，县政府制定出台《息烽县新型农村合作医疗实施方案》，县、乡镇成立相关组织。2004年始，息烽县实施新型农村合作医疗，资金按个人缴纳和中央、省、市、县财政补贴办法筹集。参保农民看门诊和住院医药费按当年合医实施方案规定标准给予补偿报销。是年，参保农民9.91万人，参保率45.3%。资金筹集标准为参保人员每人每年自筹10元，中央、省、市、县四级财政分别按参保人员每人每年10元、4元、3元、3元补贴，共筹集资金675.12万元；享受补偿15.04万人次，报销金额174.99万元，其中门诊补偿14.9万人次，报销金额86.48万元，住院补偿1469人次，报销金额88.51万元。此后，农民参保人数和参保率逐年上升。2005年起，新型农村合作医疗实行大病统筹，参保人员当年患病住院基本医疗费按补偿比例报销后，个人承担的医疗费用累计在5000元以上部分进入大病统筹管理，分段按比例进行核算报销，报销金额最高2万元封顶。2006年，中央、省、市、县财政补贴标准调整为每人每年20元、6元、4.5元、4.5元。是年，补偿报销金额436.85万元，其中门诊补偿27.8万人次，报销金额157.28万元，住院补偿6005人次，报销金额279.57万元。大病统筹补偿278人次，报销金额97.66万元。2007年，省、市、县财政补贴标准再次调整为每人每年7元、5元、3元。是年农民参保率92.68%；筹集资金1011.08万元。2008年，中央、省、市财政补贴标准作第三次调整，分别为每人每年40元、30元、7元。大病统筹报销金额最高调整为6万元封顶。2008年，参保农民个人自筹资金调整为每人20元。2010年，参保农民19.56万人，参保率96.17%；中央、省、市、县财政补贴标准作第四次调整，分别为每人每年60元、45元、10元、5元，共筹集资金2833.86万元；补偿报销金额2258.96万元，其中门诊补偿53.05万人次，报销金额676.33万元；住院补偿1.63万人次，报销金额1582.63万元；大病统筹补偿707人次，报销金额1317.5万元。

第三章 卫生与疾病防控

1991年，县境内传染病发病率排序前5位依次为痢疾、肝炎、出血热、麻疹、伤寒。1996年，国家将结核病列入乙类传染病防控。随着改革开放深入和市场经济发展，县境内外来人员增多，人群流动频繁等，县境内传染病发病情况发生了新的变化，肺结核、肝炎等病源传播呈现增加趋势。县政府增加投入，开展创建卫生县城、卫生村寨活动，实施改水、改厕工程，改善城乡卫生面貌。县疫病防控部门加大疫病防控知识宣传力度，完成计划免疫接种。深化疫情管理，提高监测能力，对传染病的发生、流行实行定时、定点、系统观察，制定有效防治措施，消除传染病源，遏制疫情发生和蔓延流行。

第一节 爱国卫生运动

一、创建卫生达标活动

20世纪90年代初，县爱国卫生运动委员会（简称爱委会）开展爱国卫生相关法律法规和卫生科学知识宣传教育，组织机关、学校、企事业单位利用节假日开展全民卫生大扫除，清理明沟暗渠和卫生死角，清运污泥、垃圾，参与社会“除害防病”活动。1996年起，开展创建市级卫生达标活动（简称创卫），创卫工作推行目标管理责任制，实施绿化草坪、街道园林绿化，街道、院落清洁，市容市貌整洁工程。1997年，县成立“整顿市容市貌领导小组”，从县城建、工商、公安、交通等部门及永靖镇抽调50人负责治理城镇环境卫生相关工作。至1999年，全县出宣传专栏55期，张贴标语840余条幅，出动宣传车5台，发放宣传资料2.9万余份，在县电视台专题播放25期，接受教育群众近10万人次。清除卫生死角51处；疏通和维修下水道80余条，1.4万余米；清理县城河道700余米；出动运输车辆65台次，清运垃圾1210吨，河道淤泥2100平方米；取缔不规范广告牌和标语86条块；清除、洗刷、覆盖野广告3000余处；拆除街道乱搭建屋棚架78处3360平方米。投入资金430余万元，硬化县城路面1.2万平方米，绿化花园、草坪1850余平方米，补植、种植行道树260余棵；增设果皮箱45个，水泥电杆10棵等。创建市级卫生达标单位23个，其中县政府办、组织部、宣传部、人民银行、保健站、公安局、法院、工行、燃料公司、中医院、农业银行、建设银行、永靖镇政府等13个单位达到全国机关单位卫生达标新标准。

2000年7月，县政府批转县爱委会《创建卫生县城规划》（简称《规划》），拟定“力争2008年达到国家卫生县城标准”。2001年10月，经省市专家验收组检查验收，息烽县城各项创建指标达到“省级卫生县城”标准，验收合格。2002年起，启动创建“市级卫生村寨”工程。

2004年，贯彻《国务院关于加强爱国卫生工作的决定》《中共中央 国务院关于卫生改革与发展的决定》和省、市相关文件精神。4月6日，召开万人创建省级文明县誓师大会，举行万人签名仪式。出动宣传车100余台次，刷写宣传标语400余条（幅），制作宣传标牌84块，出宣传专刊专栏84期，发放宣传资料60万份，利用广播电视等广泛宣传，清除、洗刷、覆盖野广告2000余处，清除卫生死角20余处，清运排污积存垃圾2500余吨，拆除乱搭乱建饮食和水果摊点7个，新修水冲式公厕4座、封闭式垃圾池15座，新置果皮箱300个，种植行道树513株，摆设鲜花2.5万盆，增设、更换、改造部分路段路灯设施。实施县城农贸集市搬迁和规范管理，杜绝占道经营，取缔马路市场。成立以永靖镇治安巡防队为主的灭犬队，灭杀县城区内散养宠物犬及流浪犬200余条。县创卫办协同县委、县政府督查室定期、不定期对“创卫”工作督检督查。在县城十字街、三角花园、东门小区等地段设置“创卫”曝光台，对机关、乡（镇）、企业、学校等单位“创卫”情况公开曝光监督。

2006年，县委、县政府对创卫工作提出“一年重点整治，两年规范管理，三年取得实效，四、五年巩固”要求。至2009年，投入人力5000余人次，清除卫生死角80余处，出动运输车辆40台次，清运垃圾250余吨。投入资金2.31亿元，新建和改造息烽大道、体育路、永红路、育才路等主要街道，新建污水处理厂1个，增设和改造东门小区、息烽大道等路段的路灯设施，新增和维修果皮箱720个，购置垃圾清运、吸污、洒水车22辆，改建垃圾清运站4个、垃圾中转站1个，新增移动公厕10个，改建和维修公厕27座，种植行道树1500棵，新增绿化面积2万平方米。

2010年起，按市委、市政府部署，开展创建“国家卫生城市”“国家环境保护模范城市”“全国文明城市”和协办2011年第九届全国少数民族传统体育运动会（简称“三创一办”）活动，发放创卫宣传资料3万余份，清除卫生死角、野广告5000余处，清理垃圾200余吨。维修或新建垃圾池10个，更换果皮箱215个、垃圾分类桶86个，安装排污管道8000米，新建及维修公厕16个，维修排污沟700米。累计创建“市级卫生村寨”25个。

二、改水改厕

1991年起，县内通过改水工程的实施，加强流行病源体防控，推动农村改水改厕工程。至1996年，改造无害化厕所102口，农村34%以上人口受益。1997年后，加大实施农村改水改厕工程工作力度，从人力、物力、资金上给予倾斜，至2010年，建成能源沼气式厕所2.27万口，改建卫生厕所1.53万座，农村改水受益人口5.83万人。其间，1998—2000年，投入改水资金504.08万元，完成改水工程94处，受益人口3万余人，建成能源式沼气厕所213口，改造卫生厕所3512座。2001—2003年，重点支持西山乡、石硐乡、鹿窝乡等边远山区的改水工程，解决数千人畜饮水问题。投资1240万元新建息烽水厂，日供水量可达1.5万吨，水质达到国家GB5750-85生活饮用水标准，最大限度满足县城人口生活用水和工业生产用水需要，同时解决阳朗、下阳朗、龙爪村等城乡接合部供水问题。建成能源沼气厕所7740口，改建卫生厕所3975座。

三、除害防病

20世纪90年代初，全县开展灭鼠活动，减少鼠害和因鼠带来的各种疫情，降低传染病疫情的发生和流行。1997年，开展秋季灭鼠活动，投放毒饵3吨，鼠密度由投药前的56%下降到投药后的17.9%，其中县城鼠密度由投药前的44.5%下降到投药后的2.24%；发放灭蚊、蝇药奋斗呐35千克，对机关、学校、饮食店、医院等单位喷洒消杀；发灭蟑药物1.5万小包。

1998年起，改秋季灭鼠为春季灭鼠行动，至2000年，共投毒饵34.6吨。2000年监测，鼠密度由投药前的11.9%下降到投药后的2.3%，县城下降到2%。发放灭蚊药60千克，蚊密度由投药前的10.91%下降到投药后0.3%；蝇密度由投药前的40%下降到投药后的2%。发放灭蟑药1912袋，蟑密度由投药前的28%下降到投药后的2.5%。

2001年起，开展创建“灭鼠先进县”活动和春、秋两季灭鼠行动。是年，县城封堵鼠洞600余个，在重点机关、企事业单位安装防鼠门窗、铁网、铁皮156处，设置上、下水道口铁丝网71处，清除藏鼠死角166处。春季鼠密度由投药前的18.1%下降到投药后的2.89%，阳性房间率由8.4%下降到1.54%，环境鼠迹由10处下降到3处。秋季鼠密度由投药前2.7%下降到1.8%，阳性房间率由1.8%下降到1.2%。2002年4月，省、市灭鼠专家组检查验收息烽创建“灭鼠先进县”工作，各项指标均达到国家规定标准，息烽县被省爱委会命名为“省级灭鼠先进县”。2004起，加强除害防病工作，消灭“四害”（老鼠、蚊、蝇、蟑螂）形成常态化，每年坚持开展春、秋两季集中消灭“四害”行动，投放灭鼠、灭蚊、灭蟑药物覆盖率均在90%以上，每年每次投药后监测，“四害”密度均控制在国家规定范围内。至2010年，保持“省级灭鼠先进县”称号。其间，2007年，开展国家级卫生县城创建工作，县成立创建领导小组，制订创建实施方案，在全县组织开展“除四害”活动。县爱卫办结合创建“文明县”和“整脏治乱”工作，采取定期检查与不定期抽查结合，检查验收市级卫生达标机关单位的环境卫生5次。在养龙司乡、西山乡、青山苗族乡开展创建卫生村寨活动。

第二节　疾病防治

一、计划免疫接种

1991年，计划免疫接种卡介苗、脊髓灰质炎疫苗、麻疹疫苗、百白破（简称“四苗”）3.88万人次，“计划免疫”接种运转5次。1992年后，增加乙肝疫苗（合称“五苗”）。1995年起，“计划免疫”接种运转6次。2003年起，按月定点接种，提高预防接种质量。2007年后，增加A群流脑、乙脑疫苗（合称“七苗”）接种。2008年6月后，增加流脑A+C、甲肝疫苗、麻风疫苗、麻腮风疫苗（合称“十一苗”）接种。2010年始，预防接种收归各乡镇卫生院统一管理，各乡镇卫生院设立免疫规划门诊，根据本乡镇实际情况，采取按月、周、日定点接种方式进行接种。

1991—2010年，累计接种（服）脊灰疫苗18.59万人次、百白破18.2万人次、麻疹疫苗5.76万人次、卡介苗5.58万人次、乙肝苗6.71万人次、A群流脑苗11.4万人次、流脑A+C33.29万人次、乙脑苗8.68万人次、甲肝苗9984人次、麻腮苗4914人次。

息烽县1991—2010年计划免疫统计表

表17-3-1　　单位：人次

年份	脊灰苗	百白破	麻疹苗	卡介苗	乙肝苗	A群流脑	乙脑苗
1991	14003	14517	5466	4759	—	13451	3180
1992	12025	12291	4338	4234	160	12838	3822
1993	11850	11214	3955	3804	790	9652	3883
1994	13354	12318	4401	3922	500	—	3812
1995	14400	13395	4732	4321	287	9600	3687
1996	11230	10978	3701	3413	966	11345	2274
1997	11127	10608	3500	3295	3965	9521	3878

续表

年份	脊灰苗	百白破	麻疹苗	卡介苗	乙肝苗	A群流脑	乙脑苗
1998	11208	10760	3527	3363	5323	8673	6529
1999	9310	9149	2991	2927	1719	3717	4884
2000	7926	7893	2663	2532	1485	4760	4035
2001	7267	7359	2573	2304	1412	5900	5422
2002	7000	6944	2419	2202	2772	—	4800
2003	6377	6301	2007	1809	3952	4600	2035
2004	4617	5066	1635	1562	4571	—	5240
2005	5445	5223	1635	1450	4455	—	1000
2006	6098	6052	2043	1788	5450	—	1300
2007	7485	7643	2506	2014	7997	3291	13772
2008	6833	6236	1651	1952	5964	4404	2991
2009	8708	8545	1025	1900	7096	4901	4730
2010	9614	9537	821	2293	8263	7302	5557

二、传染病防控

（一）“非典”防控

2003年4月，非典型性肺炎（SARS，简称“非典”）在广东等省、市、自治区流行。根据党中央、国务院和省、市指示精神，县成立以县长为组长的“非典”防治领导小组，10个乡镇和有关单位成立“非典”防治组织，建立县、乡、村、组、户五级防治网络。有关单位坚持24小时值班，实行“日报告”和“0报告”制度。县人民医院抽调11名医务骨干，组成“非典”抢救小组，建“非典”隔离病房。县政府和医疗单位投入资金100余万元购置防治“非典”药物、器械、物品等，发放宣传资料28万余份，对3500万平方米公共场所，1050辆次过境客车进行药物消毒杀菌。4月20日至8月20日，县人民医院“非典”病房接待门诊病人555人次，其中留病房观察诊治7人，平均每人住院观察一周，均康复出院。对外出返乡的3081人进行防“非典”体检观察，未发现“非典”病例。

（二）霍乱防治

1991—1997年，县内未发生霍乱（2号病）疫情。1998年9月、10月，永靖镇梨安村下坝村民组和邻近的梨安林场发现两例上吐下泻病人，临床检验为“2号病”，经治愈出院，未发生二代传染病源。

2008年8月5日，西山乡鹿窝村尾鲊村民组发生一起每小时上吐下泻数十次的病例，经县人民医院抢救脱险，隔离治疗。采样送检确认为“2号病”。县疾控中心派人深入疫区实施定点封锁，限制人群活动范围，对环境进行消毒杀菌处理，对疫点地区102户346人发放、服用四环素、诺氟沙星、呋喃唑酮等药物；对房屋25栋、厕所5间、圈舍8间、污水沟3条进行消毒杀菌，同时乡政府下令学校停课一周，对全校700余名师生预防服药3天，对学校教室、宿舍、环境进行消毒杀菌。三天后采样37份化验，全为阴性，未出现新病例，解除疫区封锁，恢复正常生产、生活和教学秩序。

（三）麻疹防治

1993年2—3月，九庄镇和平村暴发麻疹疫情，全村总人口827人，发病30例，罹患率分别为：0～4岁组占50%、5～9岁组占30%、15～20岁组占20%。首例发病症状为：发热（最高体温41℃）、咳嗽、眼红，发热6天后头部、面部、全身出现皮疹，持续8天后好转。对患者采取就地隔离治疗，保持室内通风换气和适当温度湿度，辅以药物防治，除死亡1例外，其余病例在发病8天后恢复正常。

1995年7月9日，永靖镇雨洒村小坪坝村民组1名12岁女孩感染麻疹，初期症状不明显，随后传染给姊妹和邻居儿童，共发病20例。患者未痊愈就到雨洒小学上课，致使雨洒、下坝两村民组的15名儿童感染，截至10月6日，共流行发病42例。防疫人员深入现场发放药物，指导防治，由于防治措施得当，感染儿童全部康复。12月，永靖镇马当田村小学一名6岁儿童发病，家长误认为感冒，未隔离治疗，在学校引发麻疹流行，致19个村民组的31名学生感染麻疹。事后，县疾控中心派员深入雨洒、马当田两村开展调查，认为两村发生麻疹流行的主要原因为：医务人员接种工作疏漏；部分家长拒绝给子女接种疫苗；疫苗超过时限致接种成功率下降。防控部门对此采取改进措施。之后，至2010年，未发现麻疹流行。

（四）甲肝防治

1991—2006年，县境内未发生甲肝疫情流行。2007年4月27日，九庄乌江复旦学校发现甲肝疫情流行，经采样、化验，确认81名学生感染甲肝。疫情发生后，市、县、镇各级领导及相关组织，抽调人员组成县疫情控制办公室，成立肠道传染病疫情控制专家组、流调组、信息组分别开展工作。经过防控治疗，81名感染学生全部康复。2008年5月17日，县人民医院收治来自开磷集团子弟学校的3名学生患者，体征为：巩膜黄染、乏力、厌油、尿黄、腹痛、恶心、呕吐等。县疾控中心组织相关人员到该学校现场调查，对学校生活用水采样化验，发现细菌总数、大肠菌群超标。5月20日，市疾控中心派出专家赶赴现场指导开展防控工作。经取样、化验、普查，确认18人为感染甲肝病例（其中学生15例、工人3例）。疫情发生后，县政府成立“开磷学校甲肝疫情防控领导小组”，成立甲肝疫情控制专家组、流行病学调查组、医疗救治组、信息保障组分别开展工作，疫情得到及时控制，未引起扩散蔓延，感染者全部康复。

（五）甲型H1N1流感防治

2009年10月20日，流长中学学生出现多例发热、流涕、鼻塞、咽痛、咳嗽、乏力、呕吐等症状。县疾控中心现场采集病人及密切接触者标本5份送市疾控中心检测。10月21日，检测出其中1份为甲型H1N1流感性标本。县卫生局选派医技人员到流长乡指导救治，对甲流患者采取隔离治疗，对46名密切接触者进行甲型H1N1流感疫苗应急接种。因防控措施得当，未发现第二代病人，避免了疫情蔓延扩散。

2009年10月23日，息烽二中出现多例学生发热、流涕、鼻塞、咽痛、咳嗽、乏力、呕吐等症状。县疾控中心采集病人及其密切接触者标本7份检测，确认其中有2份为甲流感阳性，定性为一起甲型H1N1流感流行。县立即启动甲型H1N1流感应急预案。10月25—26日在该校对2500余名学生和教职员工进行甲型H1N1流感疫苗应急接种，疫情得到有效控制。两名感染甲型H1N1流感的学生经县人民医院隔离治疗，于10月28日康复。观察143名密切接触者，未发现体征异常，完全解除隔离医学观察。

（六）结核病防治

2002年前，结核病防控未列入政府计划。2002年12月，县疾控中心根据政府统一安排，制定《息烽县结核病防治规划（2001—2010）》。2003年，县结核病防控项目启动，县疾控中心为县结核病防控机构，承担全县结核病的诊断、治疗和管理工作。2009年10月，根据《第八轮中国全球基金结核病项目定点医院结核病防治领域项目实施计划》和《定点医院实施结核病防治规划指导意见》要求，通过专家现场评估，确定县人民医院为息烽县“第八轮中国全球基金结核病项目定点医院”。2010年2月1日，结核病防治工作由县疾控中心移交县人民医院。

1991—2010年，全县结核病发病5463例，经过医疗单位治疗，得到有效防控，死亡19例，占发病率的3.4‰，其中县疾控中心2003年3月至2010年12月接诊、治疗485例。

（七）麻风病防治

1954年，县政府在九庄镇蜂子岩建麻风村，集中收治全县麻风病人。1955年，麻风村迁至西山乡西望山凤池寺，更名为麻风医院，时有医师2人、管理人员（院长）1人，开展麻风病防治工作。1994年后，全县新发现麻风病例1起，发病率由1986年的10.8/10万下降到0.4/10万。

1996年起，强化麻风病防治措施，改集中防治为社会（分散）防治模式，建立县、乡、村三级防治网。县皮防站医务人员每月给患者送药一次，坚持“送药到手，首次服药到口，吞下再走”原则，治疗率、覆盖率100%。自1954年麻风村建立到1997年，全县收治麻风病人175人，其中，治愈120人、死亡49人、迁徙6人。

1998年，县麻风病发病率下降为零。次年，完成基本消灭麻风病目标。2000年，对完成多学科综合治疗（MDT）的病人进行清理、复查，未发现复发症状；对麻风病人家属308人进行复查（重点对14岁以下儿童），复查面100%，未发现感染和新生病例。是年2月18日，省卫生厅下发《关于确认息烽县基本消灭麻风病达标》的批复，确认息烽县达到卫生部规定的“基本消灭麻风病县”标准，实现“基本消灭麻风病”总目标。

息烽县1991—2010年主要传染病发病情况统计表

表17-3-2　　单位：人

年份	伤寒	麻疹	出血热	痢疾	甲肝	乙肝	乙脑	梅毒
1991	13	2	45	687	139	81	14	—
1992	7	2	95	292	51	52	7	—
1993	21	45	227	151	50	38	26	—
1994	24	6	408	249	28	18	17	—
1995	30	80	132	323	14	20	25	2
1996	10	35	59	387	35	61	8	3
1997	27	39	43	211	36	37	15	6
1998	9	7	25	317	32	25	23	4
1999	6	1	34	228	90	37	18	—
2000	33	1	20	155	45	47	23	—

续表

年份	伤寒	麻疹	出血热	痢疾	甲肝	乙肝	乙脑	梅毒
2001	49	—	8	92	25	47	10	1
2002	37	5	4	130	33	76	12	—
2003	46	17	4	93	36	161	15	—
2004	43	6	3	34	33	56	7	2
2005	31	—	1	30	18	100	8	7
2006	28	—	5	47	23	108	9	7
2007	54	2	2	28	160	165	—	9
2008	13	12	2	41	50	184	2	11
2009	15	—	5	42	14	144	2	24
2010	13	2	—	42	10	95	—	45

三、地方病防治

（一）碘缺乏病防治

1996年，县卫生防疫站对县城盐库、零售点、居民户开展碘盐监测，采取半定量测定449份，合格50.6%，定量245份，合格52.7%。是年，对159所中小学校3.82万名中小学生强化补碘，服碘油丸2.19万人，服药率57.37%。对息烽中学、县城南门小学、永靖镇马当田小学7～14岁学生1001人甲状腺肿大开展调查，查出甲状腺肿大247人，肿大率24.68%。

1999年，对县盐库采样300份，合格205份，合格率68.33%；零销点采样300份，合格192份，合格率64%；居民食盐采样100份，合格57份，合格率57%。2000年，对全县10个乡镇20个行政村200户居民食盐进行半定量测定全合格，同时接受北京3份质控监测均合格。2001年，对盐库采样172份，合格160份，合格率93.02%；居民食盐采样249户，合格231份，合格率92.77%。2002年，对县盐库碘含量监测90份，合格90份，合格率100%；居民食盐抽查224份，合格205份，合格率91.52%。2005年，开展定点抽查，对9个乡镇36个行政村288户碘盐监测均为合格。

2006年11月起，县疾病预防控制中心用半年时间，开展实现消除碘缺乏病阶段目标评估工作。通过评估显示，居民合格碘盐食用率>90%，8～10岁儿童尿碘中位数>100微克/升，且<50微克/升的比例不超过20%，或<20微克/升的比例不超过10%，儿童甲状腺肿大率<10%。综合指标和技术指标均达到消除碘缺乏病阶段目标标准，实现碘缺乏病阶段目标。

2007起，开展定点抽查加碘监测工作。至2010年，完成定点抽查36个行政村288户居民加碘盐监测采样，经实验室检验，全部合格，未查出非碘盐。

（二）地氟病防治

2000年，县卫生防疫部门按上级有关部门部署，结合息烽实际，选择不同的高氟和低氟区的五所小学学生进行氟斑牙病发病情况调查，共调查小学生2305名，其中，患氟斑牙病393人，患病率17.05%，发病率最高48.7%，最低0.57%。2001年11月，对全县乡镇中心小学8～12岁学生进行氟斑牙调查，共查学生近万名；抽出五所中心学校250名学生作尿氟量查检。2003年，开展按规定年龄段对地氟病氟骨症X光射线拍片150张，其中，轻、中度氟中毒体征各4人，分别占总数的5.3%。初步掌握境内地氟病发病情况。2006年，对青山、西山、石硐乡的6个行政村开展地氟病防治基线调查和健康教育干预督导48/点次的工作；对全县1758名儿童进行氟斑牙调查。

第四章　妇幼保健

1991—2010年，县妇幼保健工作贯彻落实“预防为主，以保健为中心，以基层为重点，面向群体，走保健与临床相结合”方针，拓宽服务面，建立健全县、乡、村三级妇幼保健网络，积极开展孕期保健，提高新法接生及住院分娩率，逐步降低孕产妇死亡率和新生儿破伤风发病率，确保孕产妇安全分娩和新生儿健康成长。孕产期妇女建卡率、产检率分别从1991年的53.89%上升到2010年的99.09%和99.05%。

第一节　妇女保健

一、婚前保健

1991年起，县妇幼保健站在永靖镇开展性病、HIL感染、严重遗传病、精神病、生殖系统疾病等婚前医学检查。至1995年，永靖镇登记结婚男女青年263对，参加婚前医学检查263对，检查率100%，未发现病例。

1998年起，婚前医学检查工作在全县开展。至2003年，全县登记结婚男女青年8682对，参加婚前医学检查2827对，检查率32.56%，检查出患有影响结婚疾病的男性70人，女性84人。根据不同情况，分别提出指导建议意见：建议暂缓结婚男性66人，女性80人；不宜生育男、女各4人。2004年，县妇幼保健站办公楼拆迁修建，婚前医学检查工作暂停。2007年起，婚前医学检查由县计划生育服务指导站负责。

二、孕产期保健

1991年，县妇幼保健站开展对孕产期妇女建卡、产检、产后访视等管理工作。是年，全县有产妇2885人，建卡和产检均为1598人，建卡和产检率53.89%，产后访视1999人，访视率60.29%，住院分娩382人，住院分娩率13.24%；新法接生2711人，新法接生率93.96%。

1995年起，开展高危产妇筛选，对高危孕产妇采取重点监护，科学指导、纠正胎位和特殊处理等。1996年，实施系统管理，开展孕三月早检工作。2010年，全县有产妇3064人，其中活产总数3088人，新法接生3081人，新法接生率99.77%；住院分娩3015人，住院分娩率97.64%；建卡3036人，建卡率99.09%；产前检查3035人次，产前检查率99.05%；产后访视3022人，产后访视率98.62%；孕产妇系统管理2993人，系统管理率97.64%；进行孕三月早检3014人，孕三月早检率98.37%；筛选高危产妇864人，纳入高危产妇管理864人，高危产妇管理率和住院分娩率100%；新法接生3081人次，新法接生率99.77%。

息烽县1991—2010年孕产妇保健统计表

表17-4-1　　　　单位：人

年份	活产数	孕产妇管理						接生情况		高危管理	
		产妇数	建卡数	产检数	早检数	产访数	系管数	住院分娩数	新法接生数	高危产妇数	高危产妇住院分娩数
1991	2884	2885	1958	1958	—	1999	—	382	2711	—	—
1992	2405	2406	2098	2098	—	2085	—	464	2269	—	—
1993	2918	2918	2726	2726	—	2703	—	580	2747	—	—
1994	2909	2909	2705	2705	—	2659	—	584	2727	—	—
1995	3251	3255	3127	3127	—	2998	—	656	2747	46	46
1996	3052	3063	2525	2525	395	2340	1183	689	2572	14	14
1997	2961	2974	2915	2949	1145	2482	1370	463	2492	85	50
1998	2881	2888	2603	2603	1264	2601	1227	589	2603	418	278
1999	2612	2613	2386	2386	1188	2386	1147	661	2368	445	355
2000	2518	2526	2382	2382	1166	2335	1980	672	2427	316	312
2001	2363	2378	2251	2251	1923	2227	1923	845	2300	302	298
2002	2172	2193	2091	2091	1765	2068	1765	925	2114	440	432
2003	2138	2145	2024	2024	1411	1973	1388	1156	2112	395	389
2004	1964	1969	1921	1921	1874	1921	1867	1393	1955	339	332
2005	1855	1865	1826	1826	1816	1825	1805	1495	1849	396	396
2006	2070	2066	2031	2031	2014	2028	1996	1738	2053	432	430
2007	2151	2135	2111	2111	2081	2103	2071	1871	2130	383	381
2008	2369	2343	2324	2324	2291	2331	2281	2143	2346	445	444
2009	2821	2807	2774	2774	2724	2725	2667	2669	2801	640	639
2010	3088	3064	3036	3035	3014	3022	2993	3015	3081	864	864

三、妇科病普查

1991—2007年，先后开展10次妇女妇科病普查工作。共普查3461人次，查出患有妇科病1477例，患病率42.65%。其中患滴虫性阴道炎126例，进行治疗117例；患宫颈糜烂727例，治疗555例；患尿瘘1例，治疗1例；患2度以上子宫脱垂1例，治疗1例；患其他较轻疾病622例。

2010年，全县妇女妇科病普查3.46万人，查出患有妇科病1.02万例，患病率29.5%。其中阴道炎2273例、宫颈炎6122例、宫颈癌23例、乳腺癌1例、卵巢癌44例。通过普查显示，县内妇女患宫颈癌、乳腺癌、卵巢癌疾病呈上升趋势。

第二节 儿童保健

1991年2月16日，国务院颁发《九十年代中国儿童发展规划纲要》（简称NPA），提出到2000年全国儿童生存、保护和发展10个主要目标。其中：婴儿死亡率和5岁以下儿童死亡率分别较1990年降低1/3，孕产妇死亡率和5岁以下儿童中重度营养不良发病率分别较1990年降低1/2。

1996年6月17—26日，国务院妇儿工委专家组到息烽检查NPA实施情况时指出：息烽县为国家级贫困县，经济落后制约了卫生事业的发展，NPA项目实施存在很大差距。提出四项改进措施和奋斗目标：每个乡、镇配备3~5名妇幼保健人员，建立完善县、乡、村三级妇幼保健网；5岁以下儿童呼吸道感染和肠道感染发病率下降10%，患病死亡率下降15%；90%的儿童得到母乳喂养；婴儿死亡率控制在99.8/10万以下，5岁以下儿童死亡率控制在140.7/10万以下，5岁以下儿童重度营养不良发生率控制在36.2%以下。此后，息烽县从人力、物力、资金等方面加大儿童保健工作力度，落实国务院妇儿工委专家组意见。次年4月14—21日，举办177人参加的"国务院妇儿工委办在贫困地区实施NPA试点培训班"，并组织闭卷测试，成绩优秀率90%以上。2000年，3岁以下儿童系统管理率40.55%，5岁以下儿童中重度营养不良率17.73%。2010年，3岁以下儿童系统管理率85.28%，较2000年提高44.73%；5岁以下儿童中、重度营养不良率3.43%，较2000年下降14.3%。

息烽县1991—2010年儿童保健工作统计表

表17-4-2 单位：人

年份	儿童数			7岁以下儿童保健管理			5岁以下儿童营养评价	
	7岁以下	5岁以下	3岁以下	新生儿访视数	保健管理人数	3岁以下儿童系管数	监测数	中重度营养不良数
1991	27455	—	9008	1999	—	108	124	23
1992	36204	—	12489	2098	—	160	160	41
1993	23099	—	7703	2073	—	192	193	62
1994	24391	—	8015	2686	—	135	135	12
1995	29553	—	8509	2999	—	199	199	81
1996	26075	17920	10771	2331	4872	1208	2692	1248
1997	24285	16775	9794	2484	8746	959	7108	1934
1998	23357	16173	9192	2611	9647	1439	2025	3201
1999	22557	15416	8500	2384	10249	1178	8087	2167
2000	22881	15749	8832	2335	18649	3581	14284	2533
2001	21999	14658	7871	2227	11962	4891	14182	1480
2002	20378	13648	7039	2068	12235	3922	6048	1119
2003	18840	12122	6701	1973	11698	4152	9617	1807
2004	17305	10981	6174	1921	12240	4542	7875	530

续表

年份	儿童数			7岁以下儿童保健管理			5岁以下儿童营养评价	
	7岁以下	5岁以下	3岁以下	新生儿访视数	保健管理人数	3岁以下儿童系管数	监测数	中重度营养不良数
2005	15860	10764	6418	1825	11201	4654	7748	467
2006	14622	9916	5775	2028	9473	4330	7134	245
2007	14086	9926	5995	2103	10203	4428	7142	242
2008	14309	10164	6434	2331	10772	4922	8008	174
2009	14978	11071	7474	2725	11469	5839	8461	286
2010	16189	12325	8200	3022	13177	6993	10305	249

第三节　妇幼保健项目实施

一、“降消”项目

2001年起，息烽县贯彻落实《中国妇女发展纲要（2001—2010年）》和《中国儿童发展纲要》，实施降低孕产妇死亡率和消除新生儿破伤风项目（简称“降消”项目）。是年，在县内开通孕产妇“绿色通道”，专设孕产妇信息监测和管理系统，孕产妇住院分娩和紧急转诊接待系统、孕产妇住院和紧急转诊支持系统，在县人民医院成立孕产妇急救中心。2002年，县成立“降消”工作领导小组，县妇儿工委、县卫生局联合成立监督指导小组，各乡镇成立相应组织，抓各项工作的落实。2003年，县卫生局制定《乡村卫生机构管理制度》，规定村妇幼保健人员承担辖区内妇女保健、产后访视，宣传动员孕产妇住院分娩和开展健康教育等工作。2004年，县孕产妇急救中心接待重危产妇35人，抢救成功35人，成功率100%，抢救新生儿15人，抢救成功13人，成功率80%。是年起，县政府配套投入项目资金10.67万元，对妇幼卫生保健人员每年进行一周业务培训，选派乡镇妇幼保健人员到县、市级医院作为期半年至一年的进修学习，10人参加省妇幼大专班学习3年。为县妇幼保健院、各乡、镇卫生院增添医疗设备，为161个村卫生室配备听诊器、血压计、骨盆测量器、高压消毒锅、新生儿访视秤、药品柜、检查床等基础器械。2010年，全县孕产妇死亡率64.77/10万，较2000年的158.35/10万降低93.58/10万。破伤风发病率为零。

息烽县2000—2010年实施降消项目统计表

表17-4-3　　单位：人

年份	产妇数	死亡数	死亡率（1/10万）	活产数	破伤风发病数	发病率（1/10万）	五岁以下儿童数	死亡数	死亡率（‰）
2000	2526	4	158.35	2518	—	—	15749	103	6.54
2001	2378	3	126.15	2363	—	—	14658	82	5.59
2002	2193	1	45.59	2172	—	—	13648	78	5.72
2003	2145	5	233.1	2138	1	46.77	12122	80	6.6
2004	1969	0	—	1964	—	—	10981	68	6.19

续表

年份	产妇数	死亡数	死亡率（1/10万）	活产数	破伤风发病数	发病率（1/10万）	五岁以下儿童数	死亡数	死亡率（‰）
2005	1865	3	—	1855	—	—	10764	42	3.9
2006	2066	0	—	2070	—	—	9916	45	4.54
2007	2135	2	—	2151	—	—	9926	40	4.03
2008	2343	0	—	2369	—	—	10164	53	22.37
2009	2807	0	—	2821	—	—	11071	40	14.18
2010	3064	2	—	3088	—	—	12325	34	11.01

二、“卫IX”项目妇幼子项目

2000年起，息烽县实施“世界银行贷款卫生九项目”（简称“卫IX”项目）妇幼子项目。是年12月，编制《息烽县世界银行贷款卫生IX项目妇幼子项目可行性研究报告》，项目经费概算人民币283.49万元。2001年，开始修建卫生保健场所，创建“爱婴医院”，增添医疗设备，开展宣传培训工作。是年6月，成立县卫生IX项目妇幼子项目特困人群医疗救助领导小组，制定《息烽县特困医疗救助实施方案》，县政府拨专款1万元作特困人群医疗救助配套经费。制定特困人群家庭孕产妇和5岁以下儿童医疗救助标准：孕期保健每例补助40元；新法接生每例补助15元；住院分娩每例补助160元；中度营养不良治疗每例补助15元，重度营养不良治疗每例补助60元；肺炎治疗抢救每例补助160元；腹泻治疗抢救每例补助80元。至2006年，救助特困对象180人次，支付救助金4.9万元。2007年，调高农村特困孕产妇补助标准，全年救助1120人，贫困救助率81.4%，救助金额21.6万元。是年，对照1997年各项指标，孕产妇死亡率下降69.05%，5岁以下儿童死亡率和婴儿死亡率分别下降62.61%和85%，5岁以下儿童营养不良患病率下降86.11%；孕产妇系统管理上升108.13%。孕妇保健率上升58.29%，孕妇住院分娩率由1997年的15.57%上升到86.98%，高危产妇住院分娩率由1997年的58.81%上升到99.48%。是年7—10月，分别接受国家卫生部教育专项评估和卫生部、世行联合督导组检查，确认县卫生IX项目妇幼子项目各项指标已提前完成。

三、公共卫生服务均等化项目

2009年，卫生部、财政部、人口计生委联合下发《关于促进基本公共卫生服务逐步均等化的意见》，卫生部印发《国家基本公共卫生服务规范（2009年版）》，对城乡居民健康档案管理、健康教育、0～36个月儿童健康管理、孕产妇健康管理、老年人健康管理、预防接种、传染病报告和管理、高血压患者健康管理、2型糖尿病患者健康管理、重性精神疾病患者管理等10项基本公共卫生服务项目的考核指标和经费补助作出详细规定。是年，县卫生局制定促进基本公共卫生服务逐步均等化实施方案和细则，明确由县妇幼保健院组织实施。按标准（孕产妇120元/人、3岁以下儿童160元/人、新生儿24元/人）对全县孕产妇2744人、3岁以下儿童5839人、新生儿2695人总共补助133.25万元。2010年，孕产妇补助标准从120元/人提高到160元/人，对3岁以下儿童和新生儿仍执行160元/人和24元/人的补助标准。对上述三种人群实行系统管理。2010年，全县有孕产妇2939人、3岁以下儿童12356人、新生儿2739人，共补助155.06万元。

四、免费增补叶酸预防神经管缺陷项目

2010年11月，根据《2010年度中央转移支付贵州省增补叶酸预防神经管缺陷项目实施方案》和省、市主管部门的要求和部署，在全县实施增补叶酸预防神经管缺陷项目。制定《息烽县实施增补叶酸预防神经管缺陷项目方案》，提出：以神经管缺陷为首要干预目标，对目标人群采取增补叶酸的干预措施，降低神经管缺陷的发生目的。采取利用网络、电视等媒体和发放宣传资料方式，广泛开展增补叶酸预防神经管缺陷相关政策和知识的宣传，扩大增补叶酸项目在县内的社会影响和提高目标人群相关知识知晓率。项目内容是为准备怀孕的农村妇女免费增补叶酸，在孕前3个月至孕早期3个月服用。要求2010年对全县准备怀孕的农村妇女免费增补叶酸，目标人群增补叶酸知识知晓率75%以上，叶酸服用率70%以上，叶酸服用依从率40%。卫生、人口计生部门密切合作、加强沟通，层层分解项目任务，共同做好叶酸发放、管理、随访、信息报送等工作。

第五章　医药与卫生监管

1991—2010年，随着改革开放的不断深化，医药市场进一步开放、活跃，县内游医、药贩使用、销售假药、劣药时有发生。县卫生监管部门贯彻执行《中华人民共和国传染病防治法》《中华人民共和国职业病防治法》《公共场所卫生管理条例》《生活饮用水卫生监督管理法》和《消毒管理办法》等法律法规，坚持每年开展医药监督检查，加大监查打击力度，维护正常医药秩序。加强对辖区内食品、环境、饮用水及劳动卫生的监督管理，维护和保障公民身体健康。

第一节　医药监管

1991年，县医药监管部门适时开展医药检查，全年共检查国营企事业单位54个、集体20个、个体92个，游医药贩65个。检查中药1.31万种、中成药316种、西药2.07万种，查处假药26种、劣药375种，价值8584元；查处无证行医17户；没收罂粟壳1.5千克。采取以帮促管，寓帮于监管之中，协助温泉疗养院等7家单位清理10年以上库存药品333种，价值4905.72元。此后，医药监管检查形成制度，常抓不懈。1996年，成立县医政审评小组，重新审核个体医证、售药证，整顿基本合格的65家个体诊所，发给临时行医许可证。取缔无证行医、售药摊点9家，打击游医药贩41人，没收草药1070包。2001年，审核发放卫生许可证233户，麻醉药品供应卡20人，食品生产经营办证873户，公共场所营业许可证76户。查处无证行医、售药28户。检查医疗用药单位和药品经营单位，查处假劣药品1434种次，价值13.4万元，精神药品和违禁药品88种（其中930片、针剂56支），价值6496元。次年，县内有汉方、太和、银杏鹰三家药品生产企业通过“药品生产质量管理规范”（GMP）认证，37家药品经营户通过“药品经营质量管理规范”（GSP）认证。2004年，加强对医疗机构的消毒检查管理，全年抽检医疗器械291件次，合格264件次，合格率90.72%。2009年，加强精麻药品监督管理，对全县10家使用麻醉药品和精神药品的医疗机构实施网络化管

理，定时维护全县“麻醉药品和精神药品管理系统”，各单位将数据及时汇总上传。定期或不定期组织人员进行精神药品和麻醉药品督导检查，严格按照“五专”进行管理，防止药品经使用环节流入非法渠道。

2010年，出动执法车190辆次，执法人员600余人，检查县级医疗卫生机构20户次、乡镇卫生院40户次、厂矿驻县卫生机构24户次、村卫生室250户次、个体诊所60户次、药店130户次。取缔非法行医3户次，取缔江湖游医32户次；没收销毁非法行医药品器械，价值1.5万余元。开展特殊药品专项检查。检查使用特殊药品原料的药品生产企业1家、经营企业41家，检查覆盖率100%。

息烽县1991—2010年部分年度医药监查统计表

表17-5-1

年份	检查单位（个、次）			查处		
	国有	集体	个体	假劣药（种）	打击非法行医售药（户、次）	罚没（万元）
1991	54	20	92	401	82	0.37
1992	40	91	45	250	34	—
1993	34	—	67	96	86	0.32
1994	32	63	—	62	33	—
1995	33	—	70	220	45	—
1996	24	—	38	126	50	—
1997	—	—	—	453	3	—
1998	—	—	—	411	17	—
1999	—	—	—	237	8	—
2000	—	—	—	146	—	—
2001	—	—	—	58	14	—
2003	—	—	—	—	37	—
2004	—	—	—	—	44	—
2005	—	—	—	—	130	3
2006	—	—	—	—	50	2
2007	—	—	—	—	14	1.03
2008	—	—	—	—	12	0.5
2009	57	680	130	—	24	—
2010	44	290	60	—	35	1.5

第二节　卫生监管

一、食品卫生监管

1991年，县卫生防疫部门在有关单位配合下，利用赶场天开展《食品卫生法》宣传活动，对全县食品生产经营单位、经营户、个体摊点实行分类登记，建档立卡管理；对从业人员坚持预防性健康体检，持证上岗。全年体检615人次，查出患肝炎、痢疾、结核、伤寒、皮肤化脓皮炎（简称“五病”）患者7人，全部督促调离。是年，对县内各主要场镇开展伪劣食品检查6次，检查食品经营户2143户次，罚款20户次，责令停业整改7户，限期改进1户，吊销卫生许可证2户，没收销毁不合格食品5402千克。抽样监测食品204份，合格125份，合格率61%。1992—1993年，培训从业人员500余人次，开展食品卫生检查5次，检查食品经营单位和个体摊点3135户次，罚款13户次，责令停业整改6户次，限期改进14户，没收销毁不合格产品和有毒有害食品912千克。食品监测203份，合格129份，合格率62%。

1994年，县卫生防疫站与县移民办联合成立县内首家餐具消毒公司。是年起，要求永靖镇、小寨坝镇饮食经营户一律使用消毒碗筷，县卫生防疫站定期选派卫生监督员对餐具消毒公司消毒碗筷进行监测。

1996年7月16日，县政府招待所发生食物中毒事件：集体就餐72人，6小时后陆续出现腹泻、恶心呕吐、发热等症状，发病住院治疗51人，无人死亡。经流行病学调查，确诊为细菌性食物中毒。

2001年，抽样监测食品307份，合格248份，合格率80.7%。首次查出县内米面制品含有毒有害物质（吊白块），按规定给予相应处罚。预防性健康体检从业人员1199人，检出“五病”患者20人，检出率1.67%。

2004年，在“禽流感”疫情流行期间，检查禽类屠宰场15户，处罚7户。次年，开展食品卫生专项整治，实施食品卫生分级量化管理，培训卫生监督员72人、餐饮业单位负责人335人；专项整治检查1000余户次，责令整改29户次，罚款5户次；对县城87户推行食品卫生量化分级管理，量化分级管理率70.73%，其中2户（学校食堂）被贵阳市卫生局授予量化分级管理“A级单位”称号。

2007年，加大乡镇食品市场监督管理力度。出动监督人员300余人次，清理整顿集贸市场46次，查处销售伪劣食品、过期食品的食品摊点12户次，没收伪劣、过期食品10余千克。确定青山苗族乡为2007年农村食品安全示范点，出动执法车辆20辆次，执法人员100人次，加强示范点卫生监督工作。次年，开展以学校及学校周边为重点的食品卫生监查整治活动。是年，检查学校食堂28户次，责令整改5户次，检查学校周边经营户187户次，责令整改7户次。

2009年，开展餐饮业及学校食堂量化分级管理工作，评审发放C级信誉度餐饮单位80户次，息烽温泉疗养院食堂经省级评定为A级单位。对九庄复旦中学、温泉中学及长岭岗中学等学校食堂新建项目开展预防性卫生监督审查。对全县各学校食堂的环境卫生状况、卫生许可证及健康证持证情况、加工过程卫生及加工间卫生状况、从业人员个人卫生状况等开展现场监督指导，共检查学校食堂65户次，下达整改意见书15户次。对学校周边饮食店、小吃店及小吃摊点开展重点整治，检查学校周边小吃店、饮食店200余户次，责令停业整改15户次。开展餐饮具卫生管理专项检查300余户次，对不符合要求的5户进行行政处罚等。

2010年，组织县食品安全协调委员会各成员单位在元旦、春节、“五一”、中秋、国庆等节假日和县人代会、政协会期间开展食品安全专项检查，共出动执法检查车辆240台次，执法人员460人次，检查各类餐饮单位954户次，其中大型餐饮单位271户次、小型餐饮店683户次。查处违法经营单位119户次，警告35户次，责令改正75户次，罚款9户5100元。受理投诉举报案件5起，查处5起。培训餐饮单位和学校食堂负责人200余人次，发放食品卫生监督量化分级管理资料200余份。评定C级单位96家（餐饮单位84家、集体食堂11家、幼儿园食堂1家），申报B级单位2家。是年，全县共有餐饮单位403户、学校食堂15户、机关食堂11户、幼儿园食堂14户。

二、公共卫生

1991年，县城有理发店21家、旅社（招待所、宾馆）16家、游泳场馆2个、浴室3个、文化娱乐场所4个、电影院1个、茶室2个、书店及图书馆2个、车站候车室2个。卫生防疫部门坚持对上述场所的卫生进行监管，对从业人员进行健康体检，实行持证上岗。1992年，监查县城和主要场镇公共卫生场所136户，对存在超期使用健康证、理发刀具及毛巾不洁等情况的5家从业单位进行警告并限期改进处理。此后，对公共卫生场所开展监督检查形成制度，常抓不懈。

2003年，“非典”疫情在全国部分省市流行。按市卫生局、文化局有关文件精神，县卫生防疫部门对全县文化娱乐场所和6家单位使用空调的通风条件、环境卫生、食品卫生及消毒措施进行监测检查。是年，培训、体检公共场所从业人员258人，查出HBsAg阳性3例，实施全部调离；对体检合格的255人发给卫生健康证。对151户公用物品进行监测604项次，合格594项次，合格率98.34%。

2004—2007年，县卫生防疫部门对公共场所从业人员进行预防性健康体检473人次，查出HBsAg阳性者3例；抽样公共场所室内空气和用具等物品进行监测1958件次，合格1882件次，合格率96.1%；卫生行政处罚30户次。其中警告27户，责令停业整改1户，罚款2户。

2008年，县卫生防疫部门修订公共场所卫生许可证发放程序和发放标准，制定公共场所卫生许可证办证指南，实行办证公示制。以旅社业为试点开展公共场所卫生监督量化分级管理，按照《贵州省公共场所量化分级管理指南》要求，至2009年，对18家旅社实施公共场所量化分级管理，其中评定级别14户（A级2户、B级3户、C级9户）。

2010年，全县有公共卫生场所218家，其中候车室、图书馆、展览馆各1家、医院候诊室2家、宾馆旅社44家、美容美发室113家、浴室10家、游泳场馆2家、歌舞厅7家、茶室27家、网吧10家。从业人员296人。县卫生防疫部门以创建国家卫生城市工作目标为重点，开展“整脏治乱”，强化卫生监督管理，全年出动执法车辆80台次，执法人员300余人次，检查各类公共场所500余户次，查处无证上岗25人次，下达卫生监督意见书300余份，责令整改12户次；对公共场所卫生质量抽样检测355件次，质量合格347件次，合格率97.7%；卫生培训并颁发合格证288人，核发公共场所许可证173户；对24家公共场所卫生监督进行量化分级管理等级评定：A级3家（旅社）、B级5家（旅社2家、浴室2家、理发室1家）、C级16家（旅社9家、浴室1家、美容美发4家、游泳场馆2家）。

三、饮用水监管

1991年，县卫生防疫部门对县城自来水5个点的末梢水定期进行余氯监测695次，合格520次，合格率74.82%；卫生细菌学检验，合格率64.5%；大肠菌群检验，合格率35.45%。对永阳、九庄、黑神庙、养龙司4个区所在地自来水在丰水期进行卫生细菌学监测，结果均为不合格。

1994年，县卫生防疫部门为县城和各乡镇水厂（站）发放漂白粉640千克，督促做好消毒和加氯工作；对分散式供水点和家庭发放漂白精7700片；对县城5个点末梢水进行余氯测定862次，合格685次，合格率79.54%；细菌总数、大肠杆菌各监测124次，合格116次，合格率90%。1995—2007年，县城自来水监测合格率76.66%～96%，乡镇及20户以上村寨饮用水监测合格率相对较低，主要原因是消毒制度落实不好或未作消毒处理。

2008—2009年，对全县生活饮用水供水单位负责人及其从业人员58人开展相关法律法规及卫生知识培训，发放卫生知识培训合格证58份。开展水源水监测12份，合格5份，合格率41.6%。完成农村生活饮用水监测64份，合格58份，合格率91%。加强水源保护和饮用水消毒。对全县集中供水和农村20户以上饮用水源进行消毒和监测，采取责任分片制，将监测和消毒指导工作任务落实到人。购买漂白粉5500千克、优氯净400千克，并发放到各乡镇。

2010年，培训各类供管水从业人员及水厂负责人46人次。开展检查供水单位90户次，责令整改3户次。抽样监测饮用水115份次，合格113份次，合格率98.3%。

四、学校卫生

1991年，县卫生防疫部门对永靖小学、城关中学1935名学生进行健康体检，查出视力不良258人，占13.3%；沙眼106人，占5.4%；龋齿167人，占8.6%；脊椎弯曲1人，占0.05%；其他392人，占22.4%。对986人进行盐酸左旋咪唑驱虫治疗。1992年，对向阳小学、城关中学60名学生试用五孔镜进行近视矫治，一周后，视力提高0.2～0.5。1993、1994年，对全县178所（次）中小学学生开展肠道蠕虫集体驱虫服药（肠虫清），接受服药4.46万人次，无不良反应。抽样粪检200人，蛔虫阳性22人，感染率11%；鞭虫阳性34人，感染率17%。1995年，县内首次使用阿苯达唑对全县272所（次）中小学学生进行集体驱虫，至1996年，接受服药4.7万人次。服药后询访，无不良反应。对息烽中学、永靖小学2480名学生进行监测，体检1992人，查出视力不良317人，占15.87%；龋齿306人，占15.32%；营养不良192人，占9.6%。2010年3月，对98所中小学学生30054人进行驱虫服药。

五、职业病监管

1991年，县内国有厂矿13家，职工1258人，接触粉尘作业475人，化学因素接触165人，物理因素接触5人。乡镇企业51家，职工1810人，有粉尘、有毒作业点244个，接触粉尘作业1462人。是年，抽查监测作业点37个，合格22个，合格率59.46%（乡镇企业监测4个点，均不合格）。尘肺体检206人，其中复查12人，均未升级。

1994年，对县砖厂、粮食局、农机厂、县酒厂、印刷厂、环管站和阳朗、老鸦河两个水泥厂开展职业病普查，设粉尘监测点9个，监测拍片159人。次年，开展职业危害项目申报，对县内西洋公司、息烽磷矿、重钙厂等17家厂矿企业职业危害因素开展调查，进行职业危害项目申报。

2004年，对19家有害作业单位和存在放射性危害因素的9家医疗机构进行监督管理，持有放射性卫生许可证单位6家，持证率66.67%。开展对西洋肥业有限公司、银都水泥厂、开磷集团、中化肥业、铁锅厂、矽酸盐、页岩砖厂等10家厂矿企业进行粉尘、转化HCl、噪声、放射源、毒物、磷、高温、硫酸雾等监测管理，体检职工2507人，体检率74.99%；监测合格单位8家，合格率80%，建立卫生管理制度9家，占监督总户数的90%；职业危害因素申报8家，占80%，职业危害警示标识设置8家，占80%，对职工防护用品发放10家，发放率100%。2006、2008年，分别对50余家工矿企业开展职业病防护知识宣传教育和培训，发放宣传、培训资料4000余份，培训2100余人次，接受劳动者咨询600人次。

2010年，完成工业企业监测2家，监测有毒有害因素项目58点（次），职业工人体检1632人次，查出职业禁忌症66人。根据《关于职业卫生监管部门职责分工的通知》规定，此后，厂矿企业职业病防治移交质监、人事劳动等部门监管，地方卫生行政部门只负责对医疗单位诊疗放射性危害控制的监督管理。是年，全县有县级医疗卫生单位5家、乡镇卫生院10家、厂矿企业医院5家、村卫生室161家、私人诊所5家。根据《医疗废物管理条例》和《医疗卫生机构医疗废物管理办法》等相关法律法规，依法对全县医疗机构产生的医疗废物进行监管处理。全县各医疗单位产生的医疗废物全部送市特种垃圾处理场集中处理。

第十八篇　文化·旅游·体育

第一章　文　化

息烽文化包括史前文化、龙马文化、古墓葬文化、佛教文化、虫茶文化、温泉文化、民族民间文化、红色文化、当代文学创作等。2005年以后，县境内传统花灯、龙灯、阳戏等民间文化逐渐得到保护、继承和发扬。全县161个村和5个社区全部建起“农家书屋”和实施“文化信息资源共享工程”，科技文化信息资源遍布全县，进入千家万户。

第一节　机　构

一、管理机构

1991年，县文化局下设文物管理所和文化稽查大队。1995年，县文化局与广播电视局合并，组建县文化广播电视局，内设办公室、宣传股、事业股、文物管理所和文化稽查队，下辖广播电视站、有线电视台、文化馆、图书馆、电影公司，代管新华书店。1997年，息烽集中营革命历史纪念馆成立，为文化广播电视局下属副局级单位。2001年，县体育局与县文化广播电视局合并，成立文体广播电视局。2002年6月，县宣传文化活动中心成立，为文体广播电视局下属的股所级事业单位。是年，文体广播电视局内设机构调整为办公室、文化科、体育科、广电科，原文化市场稽查队单列为县旅游文化市场综合执法大队。2010年，县旅游事业局与县文体广播电视局合并，组建县旅游文体广播电视局（县新闻出版局、县版权局）。撤销文化稽查大队，组建旅游文化市场综合执法大队。

二、事业单位

（一）文化馆

1952年初，成立县文化站，1956年改称县文化馆。1991年，县文化馆设排练厅、展览厅、歌舞厅、图书室和办公用房25间。2006年6月，县文化馆从县府路迁至县城东门小区县宣传文化活动中心三楼，内设书画室、琴房、展览室、艺术培训室、舞蹈排练厅。2010年，县文化馆与县宣传文化活动中心合并，对外仍称县文化馆，实行一套机构，两块牌子，隶属县旅游文体广播电视局。

（二）新华书店

1952年，设立新华书店县代销店。1959年，建立新华书店县支店。1991年，新华书店在县城中心十字街有营业厅、书库等设施。1996年，因旧城改造，新华书店迁至文化路。主要经营中小学课本及辅助教材。新华书店业务直属省新华书店管辖。2005年9月，新华书店业务隶属省出版集团公司，行政上由县文体广播电视局代管。2010年，新华书店共有经营房产1992.57平方米，国有资产总值84.34万元，净值为42.04万元。2009—2010年，新华书店向147家农家书屋赠送图书2000余册。

1991—2010年新华书店经营情况统计表

表18-1-1　　单位：万元

年份	销售总额	净利润	纳税总额
1991	114.48	6.34	3.6
1992	116.89	6.12	3.68
1993	121.84	－0.62	4.68
1994	123.91	0.34	8.62
1995	158.17	0.42	7.53
1996	159.21	0.76	3.42
1997	421.53	5.88	13.45
1998	477.35	7.22	17.32
1999	486.32	8.13	14.37
2000	403.57	8.36	19.22
2001	439.81	4.86	7.96
2002	475.61	19.95	15.76
2003	450.37	20.92	18.09
2004	494.87	10.91	16.74
2005	437.05	－2.41	23.45
2006	388.52	6.03	11.36
2007	344.35	0.04	5.06
2008	446.3	6.73	31.38
2009	447.55	－9.72	2.62
2010	460.72	－1.33	2.16

（三）电影公司

1963年，建立县电影管理站。1979年，改称县电影公司。1991年，县电影公司实行目标管理责任制，完成当年指标任务。此后因电视普及，电影放映业迅速衰落，九庄、养龙司两个简易电影院先后关闭。1996年，县电影公司所属电影院在县城改造中拆除，电影公司不复存在。其后，电影工作业务由县广电局直接负责。

（四）图书馆

1979年，县图书馆建立。1990年，县图书馆藏书40656册。1994年，县图书馆被评定为国家标准县三级图书馆。2002年，馆舍因旧城改造拆除，暂借县宣传文化活动中心大楼四楼作馆舍，面积600平方米，设藏书室、借书室、阅览室、会议室、办公室。2005年，县图书馆累计增加藏书5960册，藏书总量为4.66万册。养龙司爱华图书馆藏书6285册，黑神庙育苗图书馆藏书2000册。随着“两基”（基本实现九年义务教育，基本扫除青少年文盲）和普及实验室活动的开展，全县中、小学大多设立图书馆（或图书室）。其中：中学（13所）藏书17.76万册，小学（63所）藏书17.17万册。2009年，迁到虎城大厦三楼，面积2071平方米，内设成人阅览室、儿童阅览室、盲人阅览室、电子阅览室、采编室、借阅室、展览厅、多功能厅、地方文献室、慰民律师图书室等10个服务窗口。其中：阅览室有270多个座席；设有文化共享工程县级支中心，接入10米光缆专线，配置服务器4台，存储容量4TB（百万兆字节）；建成实用、便捷、安全的网络，为读者免费提供查询、下载、复印资料等服务。2010年，县图书馆藏书6.13万册，电子图书24.76万种。全县乡镇有图书室9个、农家书屋161个，共有藏书10.85万册。

1991—2010年，图书借阅50.23万人次，借书量68.59万册次。其中：2005年县图书馆共接待读者5600余人次，借书2600余人次。2006年接待读者6854人次，借阅书籍2114人次，在馆阅读4740人次。图书馆承办“2006年贵阳市公共图书馆馆际协调协作年会”，组织参加市文化局、市图书馆“建设社会主义新农村”主题征文活动，获一等奖1名、二等奖2名、三等奖3名。2007年，图书馆接待读者6418人次。

（五）县文物管理所

1984年4月15日，县文物管理所成立，为县文化局下设事业单位，隶属文化局管辖，同时接受县文物管理委员会领导。1995年机构改革后，县文物管理所为文化广播电视局内设机构。

（六）县广播电视台

1991年，县电视传播电视差转站改为地面卫星接收站，传播3套节目。1993年，县广播电视局网络业务由个人承包，行政上受广播电视局管辖。有线电视站建成后有工作人员6人，用户逾3000户。此后，全县10乡镇分别建立有线电视网，用户逾1.2万户。1996年4月，对县城有线电视网络进行升级改造，开始传输加密节目。年底，实现市、县光缆联网，形成市、县、乡（镇）三级大网络系统，节目增加到31套。1998年，县有线电视站收归广播电视局管理。1999年11月17日，县广播电视台成立，隶属县文体广播电视局。2007年2月14日，县广播电视台实现网台分离，原广播电视台新闻部与《息烽宣传》《“三农”之窗》合并，组建由县委宣传部管理的县新闻中心，成为新闻中心内设新闻二部，仍沿用县广播电视台牌子。原电视网络移交贵阳广电网络公司管理。

（七）息烽集中营革命历史纪念馆

1997年3月18日，息烽集中营革命历史纪念馆成立，为副局级事业单位，隶属县文化广播电视局。其职能是管理保护息烽集中营旧址，负责纪念馆对外开放的接待、宣传、组织，征集、保管息烽集中营历史文物等工作。5月29日，息烽集中营革命历史纪念馆正式挂牌。2004年，纪念馆下设办公室、安全保卫科、宣传教育科、玄天洞管理处。

（八）玄天洞杨虎城将军囚禁处纪念馆

1997年11月，县委、县政府启动玄天洞杨虎城将军囚禁处旧址修复工程。次年10月18日修复竣工，举行开馆仪式，同时成立股所级玄天洞杨虎城将军囚禁处纪念馆。2000年12月，玄天洞杨虎城将军囚禁处旧址划归息烽集中营革命历史纪念馆管理，原玄天洞杨虎城将军囚禁处纪念馆撤销。

（九）宣传文化活动中心

2002年，县宣传文化活动中心成立，大楼竣工，建筑面积4186平方米，内有门厅、多功能厅、电影放映厅、排练厅、展览厅、台球厅、健身房、化妆室、图书室等设施，其中：电影放映厅可容纳700多观众，配置5.1声道放映系统；舞台配置有适应现代歌舞戏剧演出的灯光、音响和多层幕布等设备。中心内设办公室、会议服务部、影视部、宣传文体工作部。2010年，县宣传文化活动中心与县文化馆合并。实行一套机构，两块牌子，隶属县旅游文体广播电视局。

（十）乡镇文化站和村文化室（农家书屋）

1996—2001年，全县10乡镇文化站（宣传文化活动中心）先后建成投入使用。文化站内设阅览室、娱乐室，电影（电视）、录像放映室等。2003年，开始建设农家书屋，当年建成6个，至2007年共建成28个。是年，实施省级农家书屋建设，至2010年，全县161个村建立农家书屋。

第二节　群众文化活动

一、民间传统文化

（一）花灯

县内玩花灯活动多在每年正月初一至十五进行。花灯主要由牌灯、宫灯、鱼灯、宝灯等组成，表演方式主要是由主角“唐二”和“幺妹”出场进行互逗、说唱。1994年，全县花灯出灯30余拨。1995年，县委、县政府拨专款举办“双龙、双灯迎新春”活动，出灯拨数有所回升。1999年、2005年，分别出灯70余拨和90余拨。2009年，流长、九庄花灯列入县非物质文化遗产名录。2010年，全县各乡镇出灯120余拨。

（二）龙灯

县内民间舞龙活动，俗称“玩龙灯”，是春节期间一种群众性传统娱乐活动。龙灯以竹篾扎成骨架，外用桑皮纸或彩缎裱糊，施以彩绘成龙。1992年，全县春节期间出龙灯80余条。1995年，县政府拨专款5000元补助举办当年舞龙活动，有1200余人参加“双龙、双灯迎新春”活动。次年，市委、市政府决定春节前夕在贵阳市区举办大型舞龙活动，县组织养龙司老街灯会的“鹅颈龙”参加。1999年，市举办春节期间舞龙活动，县选派永靖镇代表队参加。2009年，养龙司龙灯列入县级非物质文化遗产名录。

（三）舞狮

县境内舞狮活动多见于乌江沿岸，多在春节期间或喜庆时举行。由2人装扮表演，狮子随锣鼓点表演各种动作。1991—2010年，舞狮活动一直进行。其中以流长乡邓德美的高台舞狮最为有名，每年演出1～2场。

（四）傩戏

县境内傩戏多见于流长乡，有傩戏坛班80余坛，属传统祭祀仪式类戏剧。傩戏因坛班传承不同，演出各异。演出时多戴面具、吹牛角，内涵丰富，唱腔多变，吹、打、跳、唱齐全，并辅以诙谐。主要用于祈福、还愿等。2010年，80坛傩戏队演出100场。

（五）苗族芦笙舞

县境内苗族芦笙舞表演多见于青山苗族乡青山村、冗坝村，永靖镇安马村、河丰村，石硐乡水头村、石硐村等地。芦笙吹奏分喜音和哀音。芦笙舞主要在节日、喜事或丧事中进行。随着芦笙吹奏，表演各种动作，内容有寒鸡步、三半步、勾脚、对脚、转圈等。表演的节目主要有《蒙待央》

《簸箕舞》《够咋》，涉及苗族历史故事和生产生活等内容。

二、群众文化

（一）城镇文化活动

20世纪80年代后期，县内兴起交谊舞热潮，持续到90年代中期。1995年以后，交谊舞的热度逐渐下降。县城开始有人每天晚上到街边空地跳广场舞（有健身舞、健身操、交谊舞等），用VCD（影音光碟）放乐曲伴奏。21世纪初，部分乡镇所在地开始跳广场舞。至2010年，参加跳舞人群以中青年女性居多。

1991年，县开展庆祝中国共产党建党70周年系列活动，6月28日，在县城灯光球场举行“党在我心中”为主题的大型歌舞比赛和文艺演出，1992年“八一”建军节，县文化馆在县城灯光球场组织“双拥”晚会，演出文艺节目26个。1993年的“三八”妇女节、“五一”劳动节、“八一”建军节期间，举办大型文艺演出活动。“十一”国庆节，安顺地区行署慰问团60余人到息烽进行慰问演出，演出文艺节目20余个。1999年，县在灯光球场举办建国50周年庆祝活动，演出文艺节目20余个。县委书记李忠率队参加演出，并担任节目朗诵主角；贵州话剧团笑星、国家一级演员卜小贵在息烽首次登台献艺。2004年5月14、15两日，由贵阳专业艺术团创作，以息烽集中营革命烈士张露萍的遗诗《七月的榴花》为主题的大型歌舞剧在县宣传文化活动中心演出，700余人观看。12月30日，县千人合唱团在“西洋杯”交流音乐会上演出获得成功，省市多家媒体采访报道，美国科本音乐学院教授、指挥家马可·威廉姆斯予以高度评价。2005年8月19日，息烽集中营革命历史纪念馆举行新馆开馆仪式，由贵阳市专业艺术团和县千人合唱团在纪念馆广场联合演出大型文艺节目。歌舞剧表演和千人合唱团合唱《歌唱祖国》《七月的榴花》《保卫黄河》《红星歌》等革命歌曲。2007—2010年元旦、春节期间，举办“龙腾息烽”新春灯谜游艺系列活动。在县文化活动中心演出歌舞、话剧、小品等共264场，放映电影2600余场；文化馆开办音乐、舞蹈、美术、书法、绘画等艺术培训，共培训1600余人；在县城的十字街广场、南大街火炬转盘、火车站广场、老年活动中心等处演出48场。

（二）乡村文化活动

县内农村有玩花灯、玩龙灯、舞狮子、唱阳戏等文化活动。1991年前，多数村寨都有花灯、龙灯演出，1991年后电视普及，玩灯活动减少（详见本节第一目第一、二子目）。

（三）“四月八”与“葡萄节”

2005—2010年，县每年举办青山苗族乡“四月八”活动和小寨坝镇红岩葡萄节活动。“四月八”和“红岩葡萄节”活动成为县乡村文化活动品牌。

（四）文艺下乡活动

2005年，配合省委宣传部主办的“百场戏千场电影进贫困村”慰问演出和贵阳市文化局为期10天的送文化下乡活动，到农村放映电影424场，文艺演出20多场。

（五）民间乐队

县内民间乐队分自娱型和经营型两种。自娱型乐队有挂靠县交通局的交通管乐队，由爱好乐器的机关干部和城镇居民组成。乐器以民族乐器为主，后改为铜管乐。经营型民间乐队出现于20世纪90年代末。因单位搞庆祝活动，从贵阳请来“米兰乐队”助兴，县城民间人士受到启发，陆续自建经营型乐队。经营型乐队有功放机（VCD或DVD）、放音机、落地音箱、电子琴、铜管乐器、电吉它、架子鼓（或大鼓）等设备。2005年，县城有经营型乐队5支，小寨坝2支、阳朗1支。2010年，县城有乐队20支，各乡镇2～3支。

三、文艺竞赛

（一）青少年歌手大赛

1991年春节，县举办第四届青少年歌手大赛，参赛歌手239名，评出美声唱法一等奖1名、二等奖2名、三等奖3名；通俗唱法一等奖1名、二等奖2名、三等奖2名。1992年，县第五届青少年歌咏大赛参赛歌手178名，初赛评出民族唱法、美声唱法一等奖各1名、二等奖2名、三等奖3名；通俗唱法一等奖1名、二等奖2名、三等奖3名。1994年，县第六届青少年歌咏大赛参赛歌手44名，评出一等奖1名、二等奖2名、三等奖3名、优秀奖4名。

（二）诗歌创作比赛

1991年，县举办诗歌创作比赛活动，参赛诗歌188首，评出一等奖1名、二等奖2名、三等奖4名、优秀奖7名。同年，举办建党70周年中学生诗歌创作比赛活动，息烽一中、二中、底寨中学、县职校、温泉小学21名学生参赛，评出一、二、三等奖各1名、优秀奖6名、单位组织奖1名。1992年，县举办诗歌创作比赛活动，有93名作者的作品参赛，评出特优奖、一等奖各1名、二等奖2名、三等奖3名、优秀奖6名。

（三）节假日歌咏大赛

1991年6月27日，县委组织举办庆祝建党70周年歌咏大赛，县内18支代表队878名队员参加，评出一、二、三等奖各1名（队）、优秀奖6名（队）。1996年6月8日，县举行建党75周年大型歌咏比赛，19支代表队参赛，评出一、二、三等奖各1名（队）、优秀奖4名（队）。

第三节　文化市场管理

1991年，县文化稽查大队对县内国营、集体、个体经营的电影、书摊、录像放映室、茶室等进行2次集中检查和4次突击检查，收缴、现场销毁各种非法出版物233本（册）、非法印刷品（日历）4100本（册）、图片189张、年画及挂历1250份。此后，文化市场检查成为常态化工作。1996年，开展文化市场清理整顿活动，全年检查文化娱乐场所156家次，查封麻将机59台，停业整顿文化娱乐经营户4家，查扣录像带205盒，查封违规经营录像放映场2家，责令停业整顿歌舞厅1家，取缔从事色情活动的歌舞厅1家，处理违法人员2人，处理容留未成年人的游戏机室3家，停业整顿无证经营图书1户、无证经营录像制品3户。2002—2003年，县文化稽查大队被评为贵阳市“扫黄打非”先进集体。2005年，组织印刷业和网吧经营户200多人参加市文化局举办的法律法规和安全专项培训。次年，举办两期网吧、电子游戏机经营户培训班，一期业余乐队业务及综合素质培训班。2007年，配合公安、消防、工商、城建等部门，以整治校园周边为重点，对全县文化市场定期检查12次，不定期检查216次，收缴非法音像制品1350余盘、非法盗版书刊1500余本（册）。2009年，开展“迎国庆60周年”专项检查14次，会同公安、消防、工商、安监、城管等部门联合检查19次，文化稽查大队不定期检查306次，夜间巡查216次，共出动检查车辆260台次、执法人员521人次，收缴盗版影碟749盘（其中淫秽光碟40盘）、盗版书刊980余本（册），取缔违法接纳未成年人网吧2家，罚款4000元，取缔无证经营户4家。完成全县网吧视频采集系统平台建设，对进入网吧上网人员实行监控。举办文化市场经营户安全知识、法规培训5次，共培训200余人次。制发宣传资料4000余份。聘请“五老”义务监督员12人、教师行业义务监督员48人，协同监管文化市场。2010年，收缴盗版音像制品3000余张、盗版图书320余本（册）、淫秽光碟15盘、淫秽图书60本，现场砸毁非法经营的小型水果机2台。清理文化行政审批16项、体育行政审批5项、广播电影电视行政审批5项、旅游行政审批8项。12月21日，县文化市场稽查大队被中宣部、文化部、国家广电总局、新闻出版总署联合表彰为基层文化市场管理和执法先进集体。

第四节　宣传刊物与图书出版

一、宣传刊物（含文艺性刊物）

《息烽宣传》：1998年7月，筹备创办县委机关报《息烽报》（详见本志第四篇第一章第八节第三目）。

《“三农”之窗》：2005年4月，《“三农”之窗》创刊，由县政府办公室主办，县农办、农业局、科技局等部门承办，政府办信息科负责编印，内设“惠农政策”“农技天地”“农情简报”“乡镇之窗”“建设新农村”“法律顾问”“市场信息”等栏目。《“三农”之窗》每期发行2万份，向全县10乡镇、涉农部门、村支两委和科技示范户、种植、养殖大户赠阅。2007年9月，《“三农”之窗》改为县委、县政府主办，县文明办、农业局、科技局、科协、农办协办，县新闻中心承办，由新闻中心新闻一部负责编印，发行量不变；内设栏目调整为“领导调研”“政策解读”“聚焦新农村”“农技天地”“以案说法”“农情传递”“健康养生”“生活百科”“息烽民间故事”等。至2010年12月，《“三农”之窗》累计编印68期。

《西望》：2009年10月，《西望》创刊，由县文学艺术界联合会主办，属综合性文艺季刊、内部免费赠阅刊物，以刊载文学、美术、摄影、书法、歌曲等文艺作品为主。设有“文艺理论”“黔中人物”“文化窗口”等栏目。至2010年，编辑印发《西望》文艺四期，分发2000余册。

二、图书出版

《息烽县志》：1985年4月，县地方志办公室成立，着手《息烽县志》编纂工作。经过6年的资料搜集、编写和修改，1992年11月报送贵州省地方志办公室审查验收。1993年5月付印，12月由贵州人民出版社出版发行。该志118万字，通过述、记、志、传、录、图、表、照等8种表述形式，记录上自远古，下至1990年全县山川、地理、建置、政治、经济、文化等方面的变化和发展状况。

《息烽英烈》：1998年，因《烽火不息》进京展览的需要，以贵阳市《烽火不息》展览领导小组，县委、县政府名义，编写出版《息烽英烈》。全书2.8万字。

《筑北灵秀》：1999年5月，由政协贵州省文史资料委员会（简称文史委）、贵州旅游文史丛书编委会编辑的贵州旅游文史丛书《筑北灵秀·息烽卷》由贵州人民出版社出版发行。该书收录县内26位作者的文章87篇，省内著名作家张克、顾汶光的文章3篇。全书25.3万字，多角度描写了县境自然和人文景观，详细介绍了县的旅游资源。

《军统魔窟——息烽集中营》：1999年11月，由政协贵州省文史委、政协贵阳市文史委和政协息烽县文史委共同编辑，由贵州人民出版社出版发行。全书26万字，共收入关于息烽集中营的历史文献和文章39篇。

《息烽50年》：1999年由县委、县政府编辑出版。收入文章35篇，涉及政治、经济、文化、教育、卫生、交通、工农业、信息等方面内容。

《杨虎城将军被囚息烽》：2000年3月，市政协文史委员会和县政协文史委员会重新出版。其中收入杨虎城将军被囚息烽这段历史的研究者和亲历者撰写的史料性文章16篇，收录杨虎城将军诗作15首以及关于张学良被囚大陆的文章1篇。全书7.7万字。

《小寨坝镇志》：2000年4月，小寨坝镇成立镇志编纂委员会，启动镇志编纂工作。2001年5月，镇志初稿经三次审查后，报送市地方志办公室验收。8月，志稿送贵州人民出版社出版发行。该志全面、系统地反映小寨坝镇自然地理、历史文化、政治经济以及民风民俗的变化与发展。全书34.4万字。

《在军统秘密监狱十四年》：2004年3月，由贵州民族出版社出版。该书由息烽集中营革命历史纪念馆编辑，收录韩子栋关于息烽集中营遗文7篇，附录韩子栋女儿韩秀融《深切怀念我的爸爸韩子栋》一文。全书11万字。

《英烈传》：2005年2月，息烽集中营系列丛书《英烈传》的撰写工作启动。7月完成。8月由贵州民族出版社出版。该书分别为罗世文、杨虎城、张露萍（女）、黄显声等30位烈士立传。全书22万字。

《息烽遗事》：由县老科技工作者协会、县文体广播电视局、县旅游局共同编辑。2009年6月，由贵州科技出版社出版发行。《息烽遗事》收集文章88篇，记载息烽集中营旧事、西望山佛教故事、乌江峡传奇故事等。全书19.5万字。

《息烽民间故事选》：由县老科技工作者协会编辑。2009年10月，由贵州科技出版社出版发行。收集文章132篇，内容包含婚姻爱情、人物传奇、神话传说等。全书21.5万字。

《息烽县人民医院院志》：1994年开始编纂，2009年出版。全书约40万字，详细记载县医院近70年（1939—2008年）的历史。

《鹿窝村志》：2008年启动，2012年出版。全书11万余字。详细记述鹿窝村自然环境、民族人口、政党、群团、农林、水利、教育、文化、卫生、经济、社会等情况。是县内迄今为止唯一一部村志。

第五节　文学艺术

一、小说

《利剑斩毒魔》：系县公安局干警杜兰甫于1998年创作的长篇小说，由贵州民族出版社出版。全书27万字，描写公安干警在“缉毒”战线上的斗争和贡献；同时也用一定篇幅揭示毒品对社会的严重危害。

二、散文

2003年6月，息烽中学教师陈久琪的散文集《真情无畏》由银河出版社出版。2008年，县文学协会会员的《卖鸡蛋的妇女》《风雨过后是彩虹》《中国没有过不去的坎》等散文发表于《贵阳日报》《茉莉文学》等刊物。2009—2010年，《西望》共刊载散文120余篇。

三、诗歌

1988—1990年，朱登麟的诗作先后获贵州省首届大学生诗歌大奖赛二等奖、“丁玲杯”诗歌校园作品大奖赛优胜奖、全国“玫瑰杯”爱情诗大奖赛三等奖、贵阳晚报社“长城杯”诗歌大奖赛二等奖。其诗歌《篱笆》与卿山义的诗歌《红帆船》同时入编《当代青年新诗一千家》。1991—2010年，朱登麟、罗孝华各自创作诗歌千余首。此外，龙振祥、郑传明、杨晓红、陈久琪、徐春等人也大量创作并发表诗歌。陈久琪、徐春、罗孝华先后分别出版个人诗歌专集《故乡永是春》《大地露珠》《白狐》。2009—2010年，《西望》共刊载诗歌136首。

四、书法、国画

1991年，县文化馆将原每年一度的书画展改为每年为一个区举办一次书画展。春节期间，“迎春书画展”在黑神庙区举办，共展出书法作品73件，参观者逾4000人次。1994年，县文化馆为养龙司乡青年农民书画家郑维江举办个人作品展。1998—2004年，郑维江先后获韩国东洋书画文化交流协会书画展赛铜奖、世纪名家书画展创作奖、中国牡丹书画院、牡丹之乡书画名人邀请展金奖、当代著名书画家精品年展一等奖、当代著名书画家精品赴欧洲巡展特优奖等奖项。其作品被国内外多家单位收藏。

五、油画

县内油画创作者甚少。20世纪80—90年代中期，息烽中学美术教师向明国的油画创作较为有名，其代表作有《农家小院》《野叟》《暴风雨》《哺》《苗家竹楼》《森林之歌》等。2000—2010年，县文化馆职工柳红梅的油画创作较有特色，其代表作有《阳光》《最美的风景》《相依》等。

六、民间工艺

剪纸画：俗称“剪纸”，又名“窗花”。1991年，息烽磷矿宣传科干部盛家风创作的剪纸画在省民间艺术展览中获三等奖。1992年，盛家风以乌江水电站为题材的剪纸画《高峡出平湖》入展文化部民间艺术研究会举办的全国民间艺术作品展，《苗岭之春》参加1995年县内举办的迎春书法、美术、摄影、民间工艺作品展，获一等奖。

烙画：又称木烙画、烫画。20世纪80年代初，拖配厂宣传科干部刘时祥在县内最先进行木烙画创作。1993年，县五金公司职工毛德昌在县城创办首家经营性烙画制作室。是年8月，息烽中学教师张思亮的烙画《清明上河图》在安顺黄果树参展，受到国家领导人钱其琛的高度评价。1999年，息烽烙画参加在昆明举办的世界博览会，受到好评。2010年，刘子辉创作大量烙画，代表作有《鹏程万里》《咏梅图》等。

七、摄影

1991—1995年，县内有艺术摄影爱好者30余人。1999年，骆凡邦的《民族欢歌——石硐乡民族歌舞表演》《青山玉带——青山公路奇景》《西山风光》《忠魂不朽——七烈士陵园纪念碑》等15幅作品入选大型画册《当代贵州》。同年，骆凡邦的《深山古刹——玄天洞》《山城新景》等5幅作品入选贵阳市出版的大型画册《热土》。2005年，贵阳市文明办和贵阳市文学艺术界联合会、贵阳市摄影家协会联合举办的《争创文明城市　共建美好家园》摄影作品展及出版的画册中，县内骆凡邦、徐天国、李景华、刘静等人的15幅作品入选。其中，骆凡邦的《述说》获三等奖，刘静的《息烽新貌》获优秀奖。2008年，在“中国·贵阳避暑季息烽2008红岩葡萄节”系列活动中，县摄影家协会会员和部分摄影爱好者组成“息烽之夏·息烽美景”摄影组，到西山、小寨坝、永靖镇、流长、鹿窝等地开展摄影采风活动，共拍摄图片2000余张，其中50余张入展贵州图片库“2008中国贵阳避暑季网络摄影展”。2009年，在贵阳市举办的“贵阳市改革开放三十年成就摄影联展”“争创文明城市，共建美好家园摄影展”“纪念红军长征胜利70周年摄影展”“整脏治乱，构建和谐贵阳摄影展”等展览中，县摄影家协会会员的数十幅作品入展。2010年，贵阳市文明办主办贵阳市“三创一办”成果摄影联展，县摄影家协会会员的20余幅作品入展。是年，县有关单位配合协助影视拍摄制作单位完成《烽火不息》《杨虎城将军的最后岁月》等一批电影、电视剧制作。

八、歌曲

1991年，县委、县政府在安排布置建党70周年系列庆祝活动中，重点抓歌曲创作。活动收到14名作者创作的16首歌词。黄及翔、黎昌念、周元章、盛年、周建生等人创作的《党啊　伟大的旗手》《没有党　哪有黄河儿女这一天》《共产伟业贯千秋》《吹进山里的风》《颂歌献给党》《党的阳光暖心窝》《振兴中华全靠党》《你似青松》《党的生日颂党恩》《怀念王涌波》等10首歌词入选。经省民族学院音乐系讲师唐德松谱曲后，在庆祝“七一”歌咏合唱比赛中受到安顺地区专家的好评。1992年，《安顺文艺》第二期将10首歌曲作为专辑，题名《榴花集》发表。2009年，音乐协会会员李景华创作《乌江　你是一条多彩的龙》《息烽美景看不够》等近10首歌曲在省、市级刊物上发表。2010年，县音乐协会配合“三创一办”活动，组织会员创作出《神奇的息烽温泉》《息烽玄天洞》《息烽我的家》等歌曲。

九、舞蹈

2000年10月，贵阳市民宗局举办少数民族文艺汇演，县参赛的《刷把舞》获三等奖。2001年，县文化馆从舞蹈培训班挑选12名学员，在省群众艺术馆专业舞蹈老师指导下，编排舞蹈《苗岭的早晨》，参加贵阳市举办的以歌颂民族团结为主题的大型文艺演出，获得成功。2003年，贵阳市举办民族民间文艺演出，县排练的舞蹈《苗山欢歌》获演出组织奖。是年12月，县文联成立舞蹈协会。2004年5月，贵阳市民宗局主办，市文化局、体育局、教育局协办的“四月八”活动中，县参赛的舞蹈《西望山之春》获优秀集体表演奖。2007年，县创作的原生态舞蹈《簸簸芦笙舞》和民族民间舞《苗家节拍》在贵阳赛区决赛中分别获二等奖和优秀奖。2009年，开展舞蹈大赛息烽分赛区海选，全县十三个海选点拍摄图片2000多张。在参加贵阳市“多彩贵州”舞蹈大赛电视新人选拔赛活动中，总分排列全市第四名；原生态舞蹈《蒙朵革》获贵阳市“多彩贵州”舞蹈大赛决赛第五名。首次电视舞蹈新人选拔赛中，选手刘亮取得全省16强好成绩。2010年8月，青山苗族乡的芦笙舞《蒙待央》在贵州省第七届少数民族传统体育运动会上获表演项目金奖。2011年10月，获全国第九届少数民族传统体育运动会金奖。

十、戏剧小品

1991年6月，黎昌念编剧并导演的方言话剧小品《解围》参加安顺地区税务系统文艺会演比赛，获三等奖。1994年，县文化馆编创的方言话剧小品《除夕夜》入选参加全省电力系统举办的文艺会演。2004年10月，县国税局创作编排的话剧小品《郎舅之间》参加贵阳市税务系统文艺会演，获三等奖。2010年，县文联配合开展“多彩贵州”小品大赛息烽分赛区海选工作，组织专业教师深入机关、乡镇、企业和学校指导编排参赛小品。7月，县建设局和九庄镇选送的小品《等人》《合作医疗好》拔得头筹，并代表县参加贵阳市“多彩贵州”小品大赛海选赛。

第六节　文化产业

2006年，县文化体制改革工作和文化产业发展领导小组成立。2007年，县委、县政府下发《关于深化文化体制改革　加快文化产业发展的实施意见》，县委宣传部下设文化体制改革工作和文化产业发展办公室。2009年，县内有贵州省广电网络公司息烽分公司、3家标牌广告制作公司、8家网吧、4家歌舞厅、4家印刷厂、16家复印打印店、6家图书经销店、7家音像制品经营店等文化产业经营单位。2010年，刘子辉在县委、县政府协调和支持下建成息烽子辉烫画工艺品厂。

第七节　非物质文化遗产

一、非物质文化遗产普查及保护

2006年，县启动非物质文化遗产普查工作，成立非物质文化遗产普查领导小组，下设办公室，从县文化广播电视局文化科、文管所、文化馆抽调人员到办公室工作，组建30人的普查队伍。县政府划拨10万元为普查办公室购置电脑、照相机、摄像机、录音笔等设备。普查工作在10个乡镇全面展开。至2009年，收到10个乡镇非物质文化遗产普查登记表300余份，经两次审查筛选，确定20个项目为重点调查项目。其中：民间文学2项、传统音乐7项、传统舞蹈1项、传统戏剧2项、传统技艺5项、时岁节令1项、民间习俗1项、民间武术1项。进行重点调查，走访传承人20人，形成调查报告20份（约20万字），拍摄照片60幅，拍摄制作音像制品20盒，搜集实物10件，形成文字资料80份，电子资料50G。2009年，制定《息烽县非物质文化遗产2009—2014年保护规划》和《息烽县非物质文化遗产保护规定》，完成县非物质文化遗产项目库建设和申报省级非物质文化遗产名录，对15个重点项目确立保护措施，落实保护经费。

二、非物质文化遗产书籍

1990年6月，县文化局成立县民间文学“《三套集成》编纂办公室”，在全县征集到民歌1961首、谚语5730条、故事800多个（篇），经过分类、整理、筛选，完成县《三套集成》送审稿编纂，送审稿获省文化厅认可，部分作品编入《贵州省民间文学三套集成》。其中民间谚语1960条、民间歌谣341首、民间故事128个（篇）。

2009年，文体广播电视局黄登贵编著约15万字的《息烽记忆》，于2010年内资出版发行。

第二章　体育事业

1991年，县体育运动委员会（简称县体委），下设县业余体校。1996年，县体委更名为县体育事业局。2001年，县体育事业局、文化广播电视局合并，组建县文化体育广播电视局，内设体育科。

第一节　体育设施建设

1991年，投入资金100余万元，在县城北门修建县首个人工游泳池。是年，由县政府拨款10万元，县老体协贷款4万元，征地2.68亩，在县城修建门球场2个、简易网球场1个，为老年人提供平时锻炼和两项运动的比赛场地。

1999年，县实施省第二批全民健身工程，投入资金16.7万元对县城灯光球场（俗称大操场）进行改造，平整混凝土场地，更换铁架篮板，维修四周堡坎及观众席位、器材房和控电房，配置碘钨灯场地照明系统，添置比赛用扩音器材等。次年，投入资金12余万元，对县城人工游泳池进行功能性改造：将室内游泳池改建为旱冰场，游泳教室改为乒乓球运动室，会议室改建成健身房，购置健身器材等。2004年，县国有资产投资管理有限公司对游泳池整体置换，将游泳池撤迁重建。重建后的游泳池（海域游泳馆）用于青少年业余训练和比赛。

2003年，投资470万元，在县城北面修建田径运动场。田径运动场占地3.4万平方米，按国家标准设计建400米标准跑道8条，4周阶梯式看台可容观众5000余名。场内设主席台、裁判席、运动员休息室、活动室、管理人员办公室、贵宾接待室等。次年，开展全国第二次体育场地普查工作。普查统计，全县有各类体育运动场地182个，其中学校161个、体育系统6个、其他15个。

2005年起，实施农民体育健身工程。是年，投入资金700余万元建体育场，体育场占地7.03万平方米，按国家标准设计建400米跑道8条和足球场，可以承接田径、足球、篮球等体育项目比赛。东西看台设5000座观众台，内设主席台、运动员休息室、活动室、场管办公室、贵宾接待室等。至2010年，投入资金5.6万元购置健身器材，在县宣传文化活动中心设健身房，周边空地安装健身设施和器材，为县城居民提供日常休闲健身场地；争取上级资金350余万元，新建村级农民体育健身工程篮球场45个、乡镇农民体育健身工程篮球场6个、健身路径工程5条，在县城东门建老年活动中心网球场1个。

第二节　培训与训练

1991—1999年，全县体育培训、训练、辅导工作由县业余体校负责，常年开展乒乓球、田径、游泳、篮球等体育项目的培训和训练，承担对选派到省、地（市）参赛代表队的训练任务。2001年，县体育局、县文化广播电视局合并后，县业余体校解散。体育培训、训练工作主要依托息烽中学、城关中学、小寨坝中学等有条件的学校进行，县文化体育广播电视局体育科派员参与组织和指导，根据各学校师资、场地等条件，分别择重田径、体操、篮球等运动项目培训和训练，对象主要是中学生。2002年起，增加拳击、举重、摔跤等竞技类体育项目的培训训练。2003年底，市体育局、市体校在县城关中学设立“拳击布局点”，选派教练员从事拳击体育项目训练。2005年，成立县体育项目培训中心。市体育局、市体校为县举重、拳击布局点挂牌，息烽县正式成为贵阳市举重、拳击体育培训基地之一。2010年，全县有三级以上社会体育指导员995名，其中：国家级1名、一级5名、二级30名、三级959名。分别在息烽中学、城关二中、永靖中学、黑神庙中学、永靖小学布局田径、篮球、足球、棋类、拳击、举重等奥运项目业余训练网点。

第三节 体育运动

一、群众性体育运动

1991年，分别举办县首届“独生子女健美比赛”、县第五届储蓄杯、“五一”税务杯篮球运动比赛。举办纪念五四运动、县第五届“八一”杯运动会，设篮球、门球、乒乓球等运动项目的比赛。1993年，举办各类群众体育运动32次，8650余人参加。1995年，九庄镇被评为“全国农村体育先进单位”。1996年，成立县全民健身委员会和“农民体育协会”。1999年，各乡镇成立“全民健身指导委员会”。县政府目标办行文，将知识分子体质达标测试列入年终目标考核，推动全民健身、农民体育活动的普及。是年，在全县开展体质达标测试，举办副局级以上领导干部“三人制”篮球赛。2004年，组织开展体育三下乡（送技术下乡、送指导下乡、送培训下乡）活动，纪念全民健身周十周年。次年，举办“西洋肥业”杯全民健身展示会，各乡镇晨练点、老年大学、老体协等12支参赛队350余人参加展示活动。2006年，举办贵阳市第三十五届（息烽赛区）全民健身跑活动，县四大班子领导、机关干部、厂矿企业职工、学生等3500余人参加。2010年，开展元旦健身跑、大型广播体操暨千人拔河展示、“百村农民篮球赛”乡、县预选赛、“天翼迎春杯”羽毛球比赛、“健强杯”拔河比赛、登山比赛等活动。开展全国第三次国民体质监测工作。

1991—2010年，县体育主管部门贯彻“发展体育运动，增强人民体质”精神，每年利用元旦、春节、“三八”“五四”“八一”、国庆等节日，组织开展体操、健美、篮球、门球、乒乓球、环城跑、游演、拔河、登山、舞龙舞狮、象棋等群众性体育活动。连续10余年组织机关干部职工开展元旦环城跑活动，参加活动4万余人次。

二、老年人体育运动

（一）老年人体育协会

1984年，县老年人体育协会成立（简称老体协）。1991年，县老体协下设县医院老体协、商业局老体协、永靖镇老体协、农行老体协、粮食局老体协、县机关老体协6个分会，有会员437人。2003年，10个乡镇老体协挂牌成立。2010年，全县有中老年晨、晚练健身站点33个、健身气功站点9个，培训中老年社会体育指导员200余名。

（二）老年人体育活动

1991年，县承办两场有省、地及兄弟县市300多名老年队员参加的大型老年人运动会，开展门球、象棋、麻将、钓鱼、吊瓶、老年健身舞等比赛项目。是年，县老体协组队到遵义参加全省老年门球比赛、开磷集团老年门球邀请赛。县粮食局老体协代表队到贵阳参加省老年迪斯科选拔赛等。

1992年，“国际老年节”期间，县老体协组队分别参加国营二七六厂和开磷集团老年人门球友谊赛。选派20余名门球队员到贵阳参观省举办的老年人体育运动比赛。至1994年，相继组织老年人开展体育比赛活动10余次（其中，组队外出参加老年人体育活动友谊赛、邀请赛3次）。

1995年6月，县承办安顺地区东五县（平坝、修文、开阳、清镇、息烽）第十届老年门球协作赛，县代表队取得团体第一名。1997年10月，贵阳市三县一市（修文、开阳、息烽、清镇市）等老年门球邀请赛在息烽举办。2000年，贵阳市老年乒乓球赛在息烽举办，息烽老年代表队获团体第七名。2010年，每逢元旦、春节、中秋、“三八”节、国庆节等节假日，县老体协适时组织老年人开展体育运动比赛，组队参加省、地（市）及邻县老年人体育运动比赛和邀请来县开展比赛。县内老年人体育运动项目主要有门球、台球、棋类、扑克、麻将、川牌、太极拳、太极剑、吊瓶、爬山、跑步、老年健身操、老年健身舞等。老年人根据自身爱好和身体状况选择参加。平时活动多为自发性组织。其间，2007年，举办县首届老年人运动会；设置棋类、柔力球、太极拳、健身操、太极扇等8个比赛项目。

三、校园体育

1991年起，在全县中小学贯彻实施《中小学生体育合格标准》《国家教委初中升学考试体育工作方案》。1995年，对全县237名初中毕业生进行体育考试。县城中学生达标率80%以上、厂矿子校学生达标率65%、乡镇中学学生达标率28%。次年，举办全县首届“园丁杯”篮球运动比赛，息烽中学和永靖小学分别获得第一、二名，并代表县参加贵阳市“园丁杯”篮球赛。1997年5月，举办县第九届中学生运动会。次年，石硐小学被市授予“百日冬季锻炼先进集体”称号。县体育局、教育局联合举办县第六届小学生运动会和第三届“园丁杯”篮球赛。2003年底，贵阳市体育局、市体校在县城关中学设立“拳击布局点”，开展拳击体育项目训练，推进学校体育运动的开展。次年起，全县中小学按体育课占总课时10%～11%的比例安排体育与健康课。2005年，在县内推广“全国中小学生第八套广播体操”（小学《雏鹰起飞》、中学《舞动青春》）。参加贵阳市中小学广播体操录像比赛，永靖小学获小学组一等奖，黑神庙中学获初中组一等奖。次年11月，黑神庙中学体育教师姚启珍的初中体育录像课参加第二届全国中小学体育教学观摩展示活动获二等奖。2008年，县中小学生代表队在“贵阳市中小学生运动会田径比赛暨贵阳市青少年田径锦标赛”区、市、县组中，获团体总分第三名，3人获新单项第一名，4人获单项第二名。

四、体育竞赛活动

1991—2010年，县体育主管部门按上级体育部门的安排和要求，组织和选拔县内体育运动员参加全国、省、市（地）各级举办的体育竞赛活动，并取得较好成绩。息烽籍运动员陈双获全国青年拳击锦标赛60千克级第五、第九名各1次，两次获得全省拳击锦标赛60千克级第一名、冠军赛第二名。邢志平获省残疾人运动会乒乓球单打冠军。县老年门球代表队两次获贵阳市“国际老年节”门球赛（丙级）团体第一名、贵阳市第九届运动会老年健身舞团体第一名。少数民族代表队获贵州省第四届少数民族运动会“抱鹅蛋”团体二等奖、斗牛团体三等奖等。

息烽县1994—2005年部分年份省以上体育比赛获奖统计表

表18-2-1

级别	年份	赛事名称	比赛项目	运动员	名次
竞技类	1994	第三届全国农民运动会	拳术	谭　宋	第9名
	1999	全国青年拳击锦标赛	拳击60千克级	陈　双	第8名
	2000	全国青年拳击锦标赛	拳击63.5千克级	陈　双	第5名
竞技类	1998	省拳击冠军赛	60千克级	陈　双	第2名
			51千克级	吴德海	第1名
	1998	省剑击锦标赛	—	张天毓	第2名

续表

级别	年份	赛事名称	比赛项目	运动员	名次
竞技类	1999	省剑击锦标赛	—	张天毓	第2名
				张天毓	第1名
竞技类	2000	省拳击锦标赛	60千克级	陈　双	第1名
			63.5千克级	陈　双	第1名
竞技类	2001	省拳击锦标赛	63.5千克级	陈　双	第1名
竞技类	2004	省青少拳击锦标赛	60千克级	何　智	第1名
			57千克级	皮世友	第1名
			45千克级	熊　维	第3名
			42千克级	何　飞	第3名
			51千克级	张学成	第3名
			54千克级	侯　军	第3名
			60千克级	贺　文	第5名
			54千克级	涂孝乾	第5名
			45千克级	姚小平	第5名
		省青少摔跤锦标赛	45千克级	欢　欢	第1名
竞技类	2004	省“世纪茶楼杯”青少年摔跤锦标赛	男69千克级	黄正雄	第2名
			女45千克级	杨　婷	第2名
			女45千克级	蔡顺英	第2名
			男42千克级	罗　虎	第4名
			男45千克级	王　云	第1名
			男69千克级	欢　欢	第1名
			男42千克级	陆　强	第2名
			男63千克级	冯文斌	第3名
			男52千克级	何子众	第3名
竞技类	2005	省青少年拳击锦标赛	54千克级	张学成	第1名
			64千克级	何　智	第1名
			42千克级	张永亮	第1名
			42千克级	吕衡阳	第2名
			48千克级	付　乐	第2名
			45千克级	熊　雄	第2名
			42千克级	何　飞	第3名
			51千克级	黄广顺	第3名
		省青少摔跤锦标赛	45千克级	欢　欢	第2名

续表

级别	年份	赛事名称	比赛项目	运动员	名次
民族体育类	1998	省青少年“抱鹅蛋”锦标赛	63.5千克级	陈　双	第1名
	1999	省第四届少数民族运动会	抱鹅蛋	团　体	第2名
			斗　牛	团　体	第3名
残疾人类	1999	省残疾人运动会	乒乓球单打	邢志平	第1名
群众类	1999	省第八届白云风筝节	风筝（板子类）	刘燕青	前3名

第三章　广播·影视·网络

1991年，县广播电视局内设办公室、宣传股、音像股，管理全县有线广播和无线电视转播。其后，县广播事业经历从有线广播到调频无线广播的转变。1993年5月，县有线电视站成立，与广播电视局组成“一套人马，两块牌子”机构。1995年，县内精简机构，广播电视局与文化局合并，成立县文化广播电视局。1999年，成立县农村公益电影放映队，每年放映农村公益电影1000多场。2008年，全县完成电视数字化整体转换。

第一节　广　播

1978年年底，全县建成农村有线广播网。1986年7月，县调频广播实验台建成开播，开始采用调频技术传输息烽广播节目。1991年，使用重庆无线电厂生产的10瓦高频发射机1台、上海无线电厂生产的100瓦调频发射机1台、方形发射天线1幅，以县城团元山为中心，半径15千米范围内可直接用调频收录机接收信号。通往各乡镇广播站原有线路改为调频无线传输，改善播音效果。调频台每天播音4次，除转播中央、省电台节目和《息烽新闻》外，在春节、国庆、“五一”“八一”等重要节日期间，播出县里举办庆祝活动节目实况。

1998年，农村有线广播停止使用。2005年，贵阳广播电台在县开通4套调频广播，频率分别为88.9兆赫、90.9兆赫、102.7兆赫、104兆赫，发射功率4×1000瓦，覆盖永靖镇、小寨坝镇、西山乡、青山苗族乡4个乡镇和石硐乡、九庄镇、养龙司乡、流长乡、温泉镇、鹿窝乡6个乡镇部分地区，覆盖半径为25千米，直接播放贵阳广播电台广播节目。

第二节　电　视

一、电视设施

（一）电视差转

1991年，县城团元山安装有6.2米抛物面天线1座、分米波电视发射机2台，发射频道为35频道、

41频道，功率100瓦，转播中央电视台1套、2套节目；安装7频道电视信号发射机2台，接收云雾山贵州电视台信号。是年，建成石硐乡、猫场乡地面卫星电视差转台。至1994年，流长乡、温泉镇、西山乡、青山苗族乡相继建成电视发射差转台，均发射1套节目。1996年，电视差转改为接收亚太、A卫星，但仍转播贵州电视台上星信号。2000年，接收亚太卫星转播贵州台的设备严重损坏，县广播电视台投入资金维修团元山发射台铁塔、县城至团元山上山道路和高压线路。

（二）有线电视

1993年5月，县政府投入资金50万元，建成县城有线电视网络。网络前端设备有卫星接收机、调制器、混合器，网络宽带为300兆赫，同时传输8套卫星电视节目，覆盖用户2800户，每天播出18小时。是年，相继建起九庄镇、小寨坝镇、石硐乡有线电视网络，分别传输8套节目。1995年，建成温泉镇有线电视网络，用户120户。1996年12月，向贵阳市有线电视责任有限公司租用电信光缆，县有线电视网络与贵阳市有线电视网络联网，实现市、县、乡光缆联网，传输32套节目，24小时向用户转播。2003—2008年，县广播电视台筹措资金，将石硐乡、养龙司乡、流长乡网络改造为HFC（混合光纤同轴电缆网）网络。2009年，县广电网络分公司向省公司争取经费137万余元，完成阳朗片区有线电视网络改造和县城商住小区的新建工程。网络新增数字电视用户2798户，处理各类故障3800起，抢修光缆26次，更换光接收机5台。2010年，乡（镇）、厂矿、企业有线电视整体转换，实现电视网络数字化传输，用户逾1.95万户，传输电视节目70余套。

二、广播电视村村通

1998年起，实施“村村通广播电视”工程，投入资金15.33万元，建成地面卫星接收站15座，入户780余户。至2002年，累计投入资金123.58万元，建成地面卫星接收站116座，入户4740余户。

2003年起，改用数字信号接收，每个天线以5～8个用户为一个接收单元，每户使用一台数字接收机，可看20套节目。是年，投入39.82万元，建地面卫星接收天线30座，入户120户。至2007年，累计投入资金749.61万元，建成地面卫星接收天线9681座，入户30422户。

2008—2010年，采取“一户一锅一机”接收中星9号卫星，接收47套电视节目。用户信息录入100%，实现有线电视数字化转播2000户。其间，2010年，启动小寨坝镇有线电视数字化整体转换工程。

三、有线电视台自办节目

1990年元旦，县广播电视局第一组自办电视新闻节目《息烽新闻》正式开播。1993年，县有线电视站县城线路安装完成，《息烽新闻》节目由县有线电视站播出，覆盖县城2800余户。1998年，县有线电视台收归县文体广播电视局，《息烽新闻》覆盖面增至3000余户。次年，对县城有线电视网络传输系统进行升级更新。2005年，《息烽新闻》由原来每周一组增至每周两组，周二、周五播出，周一、周三、周四、周六重播。在自办节目中增加节目预告、科技、文艺类节目和天气预报，机房全天24小时传输中央、省卫星电视节目和贵阳电视台有线电视节目。2005年，在县新闻中心开设《保持共产党员先进性》《来自南大街的报道》《关注“三农”》等栏目；独立制作完成《乌江南岸拥军潮》《正视贫困与落后》《重拳出击》《大尖山三年迈出三大步》《依靠科技谋发展》《希望永红村“三无两有”纪实》《息烽风光》《息烽“两基”》等20余部电视专题片。2010年12月，《贵阳新闻》荟萃平台开通，《息烽新闻》由每周两组改为每周五组。

第三节　电影放映

1991年，县电影公司实行目标管理责任制，坚持城乡兼顾，重点放在农村的原则，当年放映电影2804场，占任务指标3675场的76%，观众149.33万人次，占任务指标165.35万人次的90%；放映收入154.11万元，占任务指标124.95万元的123.4%；发行电影收入56.7万元，占任务指标50.2万元的112.9%。次年，各项指标任务的完成比例较1991年严重下滑。

1993年后，因电视机基本普及城镇家庭，电影业迅速衰落。县电影院改用16毫米小放映机在小放映厅放映。1996年，县电影院和九庄、养龙司两个简易电影院停业关闭。县电影院在旧城改造中拆除，电影公司实行改制，将放映剧场、营业门厅、职工宿舍等一次性分配给在职和退休职工后，宣布解体。此后电影管理工作由县广电局负责。

1999年，县农村公益电影放映总队成立，下设9个放映小队，投入放映设备10套，当年放映农村公益电影1932场，观众10万人次。2002年，县文化活动中心影剧院继承电影放映事业。举办“第四届农民电影节”，下乡放映50场，县文化中心剧场放映14场，观众2900余人次，票房利润7000元。2004年，文化中心剧场放映20场，观众7000人次，票房利润9000元。2005年，举办“第六届农民电影节”，下乡放映30场，县文化中心剧场放映56场，观众1.4万人次，票房利润1.2万元。2009年，制定《息烽县农村公益电影实施方案》，将1932场放映任务分解到10乡镇，当年放映1959场。其中科教片46场。2010年，放映1932场，其中科教片129场；社区广场放映50场，宣传片136场；县文化活动中心商业演出20余场，放映100余场，观众10余万人次。

第四节　网　络

一、政府信息网络

2005年10月，创建县政府网主页（网址：WWW.gzxf.gov.cn），并建政府大楼局域网。上网范围为县四大班子、县纪委、县法院、检察院、县委组织部、宣传部、息烽报社，以及县政府重要经济和社会发展工作部门。2007年3月，县新闻中心承办县政府网，网络部负责维护更新和管理县政府网及新华网息烽网页、林城贵阳网站息烽县网页。2009年5月，对县政府网进行全新改版，将网站建设纳入政府部门目标考核。9月，对县政府网站再次进行改版，强化“在线办事”“公众服务”和“交流互动”，将网页划分为政务公开、对外宣传、网上办事、公众参与等功能区。新闻中心与永靖镇、县科技局、司法局、温泉疗养院、息烽集中营革命历史纪念馆等单位合作，相继建立“群众心声之家”“依法治县网”“科技信息网”“息烽温泉”等二级网站。至2010年，县政府网站共有一级栏目8个、二级栏目69个，年更新量8000余条，月均访问量11.97万人次。

二、广播电视网络

2006年11月，县广播电视台实现网台分离。2007年2月，组建县广电网络分公司，隶贵阳市广电网络公司。5月，贵阳广电网络公司息烽分公司正式成立。县广电网络公司更新设备，增加光节点，更换光机、扩大器11台，分支、分配器等转输器件上万个，光缆、电缆线40余千米，新建数字电视机房28平方米，实现县电视台自办节目在全县范围内数字化、模拟网络频道同步传送。10乡（镇）

所在地实施数字电视整体转换，县城区城内有广电国干线路1条46千米，贵阳地区环线1条80千米，县至乡（镇）长途干线光缆198千米，确保县、乡区域数字电视的备份传输。

2008年3月，贵州省广播电视信息网络股份有限公司挂牌成立，贵阳市广电网络公司息烽分公司更名为贵州省广播电视信息网络股份有限公司息烽分公司。县广电网络公司共有有线电视直管用户8410户（其中数字电视7967户、模拟电视443户）。2010年，县召开各乡（镇）主要领导参加的有线电视网络整合动员大会。县广电网络公司相继与小寨坝镇、流长乡、南山煤矿等单位签订整合整转协议。至是年10月底，广电网络公司共有有线电视直管用户1.15万户（其中数字用户1.03万户、模拟用户1200户）。

第四章　文　物

县内文物分为史前文物、古墓葬、古建筑、摩崖石刻、碑碣、红色革命遗址和馆藏文物等几个部分。

第一节　不同历史时期文物

一、史前文物与遗址

恐龙化石：1998年，永靖镇后坝村鸦米寨村民在团元山南麓的山梁上发现恐龙化石。6—7月，经省博物馆等单位考古专家现场挖掘，发掘出恐龙化石2具。现存于县文管所。

大风洞遗址：位于石硐乡难冲桥村大土组东部一山顶。遗址洞穴相对高程80米，洞口高15米，宽12米，洞向东发育40米，深部发育有天窗与外界相通。洞口砌有石墙，石墙中部开有石门，门高1.9米，宽1.5米。调查发现石制品10件、残磨石器1件，以及牛、鹿牙齿和动物碎骨、蚌壳等物。石洞为新石器时代古人类住地。

打油洞遗址：位于石硐乡石硐村桃子坪组一半山腰间。洞口朝向东北（33度），高约10米、宽20米、深70米，洞口砌有石墙，洞内靠西侧有人工石砌平台两级，为古人类活动遗址。经调查，采集陶片数件、铜手镯1件、烧骨3件、碎骨数件以及牛牙、鹿牙和小石化人牙等物。

下洞遗址：位于石硐乡何家硐村何家硐组，洞口高4米，宽10米，深100余米，洞口残存石墙厚约1米。调查中采集到石器、陶片、烧骨、碎骨及鹿牙等物。

多缤洞西洞遗址：位于九庄镇桐枝驿村下寨组一半山腰上，洞高7米、宽26米、深50米。调查中在洞内地表采集到少量石制品和动物化石。

石门洞遗址：位于永靖镇马当田村坪上组，洞口高约12米、宽20.5米，洞内地表由洞口向洞内斜下，其间砌有四级堡坎，成三级平台。洞内采集到少量石制品及丰富的动物碎骨、钉螺、宝塔螺、鱼、鼠、竹鼠、豪猪、猕猴、鹿、牛等动物化石。

王家坪洞顶遗址：位于小寨坝镇王家坪村王家坪组。洞口高约3米、宽7米，洞深20米后折向90

度发育30米。洞口砌有石墙，墙高3米、长7米、厚1米。调查中采集石制品2件。

石斧、石锛：1956年，在底寨车田河发现石斧、石锛各1件。石斧顶部稍宽，厚5.5厘米，刃口略呈弧形，宽4.5厘米；石锛顶部较窄，厚6.3厘米，一面开刃，刃宽4.6厘米。经鉴定，为新石器时代晚期制品。

二、古墓葬

新杨汉墓：位于新杨杨寨村民组村民责任地中。墓为2座封土包，南北排列，间距15米，坟墓直径3.5米，南坟高2米，北坟高1.7米。另有封土包1座，直径10米，高1.5米，人称“万人坟”。1984年列为县级文物保护单位。

新杨花坟：位于新杨新民村石关口村民组。为3座圆形石墓，坐北朝南，东西排列，均高1.5米，直径3米，墓前均有石碑，墓主分别是王曾氏、王启忠、王赐元。墓前3米处，建有高0.28米青石回栏，墓前段立有3门4柱5楼式石牌坊。1984年列为县级文物保护单位。

李孟明墓：位于石硐乡猫场村王大山村民组，为圆形石墓，高2米，直径3米。墓前竖有3门4柱5楼牌坊形石碑，碑刻“皇明特敕授定远将军李祖孟明公之墓”；落款为“咸丰九年十二月谷旦阖族修建”。墓两侧各配衣冠冢1座。1984年列为县级文物保护单位。

蔡兴隆墓：位于养龙司乡坝上村关山堡。为典型石室墓，封土高2米，直径约10米。墓前石碑刻“护国将军蔡祖兴隆之墓”，左刻“咸丰七年丁巳九月二十五日建立”。1984年列为县级文物保护单位。

蔡普化墓：位于养龙司乡坝上村关山堡，坐东北向西南，高1.5米，直径约5米，前有拜台，原有残碑一块，后蔡氏族人将其埋入墓中，碑刻“蔡公普化之墓”，碑额有二龙戏珠浮雕图案。蔡普化为明代养龙长官司首任长官，世袭“征蛮将军右军都督同知”之职。1984年列为县级文物保护单位。

蔡朝元墓：位于养龙司乡幸福村钟家山村民组。墓冢坐北向南，高2.4米，直径5.9米，墓前有碑、围墙、石板天井等，墓主系蔡朝元及妻冯氏、女儿蔡汝贞。石碑高1.67米，宽0.57米，中刻“皇清侍赠文林郎蔡公讳朝元字滋乾府君寿域”。

牟海奇墓：位于县城东门田坝高阜处。为椭圆形石墓，高1.5米，长7米，宽5米，有长方石柱碑体，中刻“前明都统将军始祖考牟公海奇府君墓”。此墓原在阳朗上坝河，清道光二十六年（1846）迁葬于此，人称“将军坟”。1984年列为县级文物保护单位。

三、古建筑古遗址

凤池寺：位于西望山凤凰池畔。清顺治十年（1653），由僧人语嵩兴建，雍正十年（1732），僧洪亮重修。后毁于战乱，光绪年间重建。原有上、下两殿及西侧厢房，共4栋22间，均为木架结构，现仅存上殿1栋。民国22年（1933），冯玉祥将军慕名游览，在佛龛左侧上书“圣贤气节，民族精神”8字，并落名款“冯玉祥”3字，寺僧请工匠刻石，至今尚清晰可辨。1984年列为县级文物保护单位。

瞿昙寺遗址：位于西山村苦草坪村民组。清顺治十六年（1659），僧瞿昙始建。雍正六年（1728），僧妙空补修。此后多次改修、重修。庙宇以上、下殿、玉皇殿为中轴线，左右配殿形成对称格局。后毁于战乱。清光绪年间，寺僧重建玉皇殿及两侧配殿。殿前有高0.9米、长10米石栏杆，裙板上饰有浮雕图案。1984年列为县级文物保护单位。

毗卢寺遗址：位于鹿窝乡三友村麻窝田村民组。建于明洪武年间，万历六年（1578），水西宣慰使安国亨重建，清嘉庆十一年（1806）和光绪年间两次重建。1958年，上殿拆修鹿窝乡政府；1963年，拆除中下殿，修建九庄区医院。现仅存三殿基址和三重台阶。1978年，在中殿地基上建三友民校。

报恩寺遗址：位于鹿窝乡老窝村老窝村民组。明万历年间，水西宣慰使安国亨之母奢氏托僧人佛照主持修建；清顺治年间，僧嵩眉重建，嘉庆十一年（1806）和光绪年间重修和补修。庙宇由上、中、下三殿组成。1963年拆除，在其基址上修建鹿窝小学。

水头寺遗址：位于西山山脉车头山脚下。清初所建，除山门外，殿分上、中、下三殿。上殿尚存部分神龛，中殿仅存两个防火用水池，下殿天井成为周家院坝。

华严寺遗址：位于鹿窝乡大石头村填筑坪村民组。明代僧人寂受建，清雍正、光绪年间重建。文革“破四旧”运动中，上、中、下三殿被毁，仅存西厢房。

底寨华氏四合院：位于西山乡柏香山村新寨组寨子中。是晚清贵州实业家华之鸿在底寨修建的院落，占地400余平方米，为穿斗式悬山小青瓦顶木结构建筑，由前厅、后堂和两侧厢房组成。2002年修缮，前厅通面阔19.4米，进深6.4米；后堂通面阔17米，进深3米；两厢房阔7米，深3米；天井平面呈长方形，长9.2米，宽7.7米。2003年列为县级文物保护单位。

四、碑碣

盟誓碑：位于鹿窝乡三友村三友民校前左侧70米。碑高1.4米，宽0.86米，碑额左右分别刻“日”“月”二字，中刻“万古从林”4字，左刻“永乐五年正月盟誓”。1984年列为县级文物保护单位。

语嵩塔：位于西山乡西山村凤池寺村民组，为语嵩骨灰存葬处。塔侧有高2.4米、宽1.27米石碑，额题“望松碑”3字，碑文部分风化，字迹尚依稀可辨。

五、摩崖石刻

县境内摩崖石刻以西望山为最多，共有“西望山”“伏狮”“鹿溪”“雨花瀑”“佛香湾”“天柱峰”“龙脊”“天风岭”“翠微巅”“天门石”“万杉岭”“凤凰池”“万壑呼嵩”“崛起南天”“龙首峰”“石楼关”“万卷书”等30余处。此外，九庄蜂岩寺、青山苗族乡绿化村后寨寺顶坡、南望山玄天洞景区、息烽温泉景区、温泉三交村三妹岩等地也有少量摩崖石刻。

六、革命历史文物

县内革命历史文物主要有息烽集中营旧址、张露萍等七烈士墓、玄天洞杨虎城将军囚禁处、钱壮飞殉难处、板桥烈士墓等。

七、馆藏文物

县内馆藏文物主要有息烽集中营革命历史纪念馆收藏的张露萍、张蔚林、赵力耕、冯传庆、王锡珍、陈国柱、杨虎城、黄显声、许晓轩、车耀先、阎继明等烈士的遗物和黄彤光、韩子栋、周科征、朱承永等幸存者生前捐赠或死后由其子女捐赠的衣物、皮箱、书信、印章等。

第二节　文物普查和保护

2007年4月起，县开展第三次文物普查，成立第三次文物普查领导小组，下设办公室在文体广播电视局。至2009年，对全县10乡镇170个村（居）委会进行走访调查；对150余处拟普查对象进行实地查访。调查登记不可移动文物88处，其中：原有文物记载资料28处、新发现文物60处；史前遗址13处、古墓葬16处、古建筑9处、石窟、寺庙及摩崖石刻9处、近代重要史迹代表性建筑39处、其他2处。普查中采集GPS（全球定位系统）数据100余条，绘制平面草图90余幅、普查点位置示意图200余幅，拍摄照片500余张，采集系统中收录图纸101幅、照片202张。

息烽县2010年文物保护单位统计表

表18-4-1

保护单位名称	保护级别	地　点
息烽集中营旧址（含玄天洞）	全国重点保护单位	永靖镇猫洞村
张露萍等七烈士墓	县级文物保护单位	永靖镇下阳朗村快活岭
西山凤池寺	市级文物保护单位	西山西山村凤池组
西山瞿昙寺	县级文物保护单位	西山西山村苦草坪组
九庄红军坟	县级文物保护单位	九庄镇西门村共和组祖师观山顶
鹿窝红军坟	县级文物保护单位	鹿窝乡老窝村沟头组报恩寺
鹿窝毗卢寺盟碑	县级文物保护单位	鹿窝乡三友村麻窝村民组
新杨花坟	县级文物保护单位	鹿窝乡瓮舍村下河坝组
新杨汉墓	县级文物保护单位	鹿窝乡杨寨村下寨组
底寨蔡兴隆墓	县级文物保护单位	西山小堡村水头组
底寨华氏四合院	县级文物保护单位	西山柏香山村新寨组
猫场将军坟	县级文物保护单位	石硐猫场村王大山组下大坡
将军儿子墓	县级文物保护单位	石硐高寨村毛栗组大坟坡
永靖镇牟海奇墓	县级文物保护单位	永靖镇永红村东一组
养龙司蔡普化墓	县级文物保护单位	养龙司坝上村出口组官山堡

说明：红军南渡乌江遗址、没量坑红军烈士殉难处、板桥烈士墓、西望山摩崖石刻群、华严寺、川黔古驿道息烽段等系2010年以后公布的文物保护单位，故未录入此表

第五章　旅　游

1996年10月，县旅游事业局成立。1998年，明确县旅游事业局为县政府直属事业单位，行使部分行政管理职能，主管全县旅游业。2002年，县旅游事业局内设办公室、旅游管理科、旅游开发科。2009年9月，县旅游事业局更名为县旅游局。2010年，县旅游局和县文体广播电视局合并，组建县旅游文体广播电视局（县新闻出版局、县版权局）。

第一节 红色旅游资源

一、息烽集中营旧址

息烽集中营旧址包括集中营本部、玄天洞杨虎城将军囚禁处和快活岭张露萍等七烈士墓三个部分。集中营本部位于县城南6千米的阳朗坝猫洞村，1938年设立，1946年撤销，先后关押过杨虎城、马寅初、黄显声、罗世文、车耀先、张露萍、许晓轩等共产党人、爱国将领和爱国民主人士1200余人，其中600多人被秘密杀害或折磨致死，400多人下落不明，幸存者不足100人。

玄天洞杨虎城将军囚禁处位于永靖镇雨洒村上坝组，距离集中营本部8千米。玄天洞是南望山山脉中的一个古洞。明朝末年，四川道人半月于此修道，在洞中供奉玄武大帝，故名玄天洞。1938年10月至1946年7月15日，杨虎城将军及其夫人谢葆贞、幼子杨拯中被国民党军统关押于此。

张露萍等七烈士陵园位于县城南3千米处的快活岭。1945年7月14日，张露萍、张蔚林、冯传庆、赵力耕、王锡珍、陈国柱、杨洸7人被国民党军统特务杀害于此。烈士陵园占地面积500平方米，设有陈列室、接待室、展厅、办公室，烈士墓2座、纪念碑1个、七角亭2座。

二、红军长征南渡乌江战斗遗址

1935年3月28日—4月1日，中央红军第一方面军所属第一、三、五军团和毛泽东、周恩来、朱德率领的中央军委，军委第一、二纵队3万余人，在乌江北岸向南岸渡江。红军在乌江沿岸梯子岩、大塘、泡木井渡口以及沿江的九庄、流长等乡镇同国民党反动武装和地方军阀展开大小近十次战斗，歼敌1000余人，近200名红军牺牲。中央主力红军于4月1日全部过江。

（一）江口渡口遗址

位于县鹿窝乡杨寨村罗家山和金沙县后山乡岩脚寨一带。江口渡口是南北两岸渡口的总称，南岸地势多为绝壁，只有大沙心上的大岩有一条路，在半山腰分为两条路通向罗家山。大岩地势险要。国民党为守住渡口，在大沙心修筑一座碉堡，并派一个班的兵力在大岩旁的天然溶洞和大岩上面的罗家山寨子雷洪奎家驻防。守敌共约一连人。

1935年3月29日，红一、三军团在乌江北岸江口岩脚寨一带攻破南岸江口渡口，打垮守敌后，乘胜而上，追向罗家山，国民党地方武装仓皇逃跑。红军攻下江口渡口后，架好浮桥，主力部队陆续过江。

（二）梯子岩渡口遗址

位于大塘渡口与顺江渡口之间。1935年3月29日，红五军团伪装成国民党王家烈部队，从乌江北岸金沙县后山乡抵达乌江边实施偷渡，被南岸守敌发现并进行阻击。傍晚，红军75名勇士，各携长、短枪1支，组成渡江突击队，在炮火掩护下，乘筏强攻梯子岩渡口成功。接着架通竹木浮桥，顺利过江，直插乌江上游大塘渡口，守敌逃往流长。红军于次日中午攻克流长。

（三）大塘渡口遗址

位于梯子岩渡口与江口渡口之间，是敌人防守最严的一个渡口。渡口南岸在今县流长乡前奔村境内。南岸壁立千仞，由北向南望，左边一条小道由手扒岩通向水落洞，右边一条小道由观音岩通向水落洞，两条小道在水落洞汇合后，直通流长集镇。除两条小道之外，这一带皆为悬崖峭壁，无路可走。敌人凭据有利地势，在水落洞一带修3座碉堡，其中观音岩岩口1座、手扒岩岩口1座、水落洞后面的沙岗1座，3座碉堡呈犄角之势，一连守敌凭据碉堡防守。红军采用佯攻战术，并派熟悉水性者泅渡南岸，与包抄攻打大塘渡口的红军接应。突破江口的红军过江后，从水落洞的后山麻坪一带突然攻打沙岗的碉堡内守敌，敌人弃碉堡而逃，大塘渡口被攻下。1935年3月29日，红军先遣部队攻下乌江三大渡口之后，控制乌江南岸至4月1日，红军大部队相继过江，在流长集结，后分三路向南挺进，佯攻贵阳，实现调滇军入黔的战略意图。

三、其他战斗遗址

（一）潮水战斗遗址

位于县小寨坝镇潮水村。1935年3月31日，红军一、三军团及中央军委纵队经王家坪至潮水。敌军在盘脚营、营盘坡、潮水河东岸一带，以潮水河为天然屏障，构筑工事，据守山头和潮水河东岸的马渡河等地，阻击红军行进。红军在潮水河西岸小桥、潮水寺后山和蔡家寨等地与敌军激战，敌军死伤多人，红军一路攻占盘脚营、三合土，至三田一带佯攻县城。

（二）底寨战斗遗址

位于县西山乡柏香山村。红军长征过息烽期间，由于黑神庙、盘脚营和县城有国民党重兵防守，红军除派部分兵力佯攻黑神庙、盘脚营和县城守敌外，中央军委纵队和其他军团从潮水过小鹿窝至底寨向青山、阳朗等地挺进。1935年4月2日，国民党为堵击红军，派十六军李抱冰部一个团从县城出发，以底寨河为天然屏障，盘踞团元山、龙洞坡一线，居高临下构建2座碉堡和工事进行据守。红军采用佯攻策略，在底寨、沙帽河一带与敌人战斗6小时，红军大部队通过底寨，向南挺进。

（三）黑神庙战斗遗址

位于县小寨坝镇潮水村马鞍山。黑神庙是川黔公路上县境内重要集镇。1935年3月31日，红军一、三军团，中央军委纵队经王家坪，到达潮水、底寨等地。为配合佯攻县城，面对国民党军队的严密防守，红军以潮水河为界，分三路佯攻黑神庙守敌。第一路从王家坪过沙子溪，经三步跳上高家坝；第二路从瓮沙过花滩河到黑神庙的青㭎林、黄连沟至桶井坝一带；第三路从单山坡到何家坝，在潮水河西岸与敌军战斗。三路红军佯攻黑神庙，牵制守敌，为主力部队通过息烽赢得时间。

（四）青㭎林战斗遗址

位于县流长乡长涌村。1935年3月30日上午，红一、三军团突破江口渡口后，从罗家山下三坪、小岩口，东渡瓮桶河，一部分从东北周家坡、麻坪等地包抄攻打大塘，另一部分直插流长集镇。红军刚翻过瓮桶河东岸的丁家岩，与国民党军59师黄道南团一个营在青㭎林一带遭遇，双方在小冬坳、扇子水井和高坡交火。敌军凭借有利地形堵截红军，红军分别在扇子水井和高坡山顶上构筑工事，英勇还击，终于击败敌军。红军连长杨启和两名战士在战斗中牺牲。

（五）蚕桑坡战斗遗址

位于县永靖镇红旗村蚕桑坡。1935年3月30日上午，驻守流长的国民党军354团一个营被红军击溃，沿江各区区长纷纷向国民党息烽代理县长毛钺告急。此时，毛钺和国民党354团训练员江涛在县城对居民进行反共宣传，并强迫居民拆房砍树，沿街设置障碍和构筑临时工事，准备抵抗。31日，红1师3团向蚕桑坡守敌发起围攻，摧毁敌军4座小碉堡，打死敌人连长、副连长各1名及士兵10余名。敌军倚仗有利地形，死守蚕桑坡主堡，并以机枪居高临下封锁前沿阵地，红军两次进攻皆失利，牺牲营长、连长各1名，负伤10余人，战斗4小时后，红军撤往潮水、底寨一带。下午3时，敌军唐云山93师由遵义赶到息烽，在城内构筑防御工事，大街小巷均设置障碍物。4月1日，红一军团根据朱德总司令"佯攻息烽县城"的指示，集中2个师的主力包围县城，敌人见势收缩于蚕桑坡、牛角坡等14处大小碉堡内，不敢出击。当晚，敌军李抱冰部进至县城以北，2个团集结黑神庙，3个团集结养龙站。4月2日拂晓，敌军93师进入县城后，分头向底寨、阳朗坝出击，均遭围城红军痛击，被迫龟缩城内。当晚8时，朱德总司令在息烽青山中寨向各军团下达"通过息烽，向东南前进"的紧急电令。红军各军团大部队及军委纵队随即从猫场、老鸦河、底寨、中寨等地先后出发，继续长征。

（六）阳朗战斗遗址

位于永靖镇阳朗村。1935年4月2日晚，红1师3团从底寨进入阳朗，与敌镇南乡常备队遭遇，战斗两小时，俘虏常备队队长吴志均等20余人。4月3日晨，红一军团第1师1、2团在阳朗一线构筑工事，封锁敌93师、53师南进，顽强抗敌6小时，掩护主力跨越川黔公路向开阳、修文挺进。待主力全部通过公路后，边打边向下洪马方向前进。是日晚，红1师3个团翻越狼鸡岭，入开阳境。至此，中央红军全部离开县境。

第二节　自然人文

一、温泉

（一）息烽温泉

息烽温泉地处县东北角，离县城41.2千米，有公路直达。息烽温泉名列中国八大名泉和世界三大氡泉。常年水温53℃～56℃。天然矿泉水分别从4个泉眼涌流而出，日流量为1300多吨。经中国科学院地球化学研究所等有关科研单位取样化验，鉴定为"含偏硅酸和锶的重碳酸钙型'氡泉'"。"氡"对风湿病、慢性消化道疾病、慢性肝胆疾病、心血管病、高血压、糖尿病和痛风等均有疗效。除"氡"外，息烽温泉矿泉水尚含其他30余种微量元素。

史载：清同治年间，当地人就在此"挖坑为池、露天沐浴、疗疾治病"。民国35年（1946），贵州省主席杨森拨专款开发。次年7月14日，杨森率全省军政名流、文人学士和80多个县的县长前来参加落成典礼，并勒"白石涌泉"四字于白石口的悬崖绝壁上。蒋介石、冯玉祥、何应钦等要员曾到此沐浴。1956年，贵州省总工会投资建息烽温泉疗养院，1958年建成投入使用。1995年，息烽温泉景区被省政府命名为省级风景名胜区，景区总体规划面积20.77平方千米。

息烽温泉除疗养院外，还有八大自然、人文景观。

天台丛林：为温泉八大景观之首，位于养温公路12千米处的天台村天台山，面积约700余亩。丛林内莽莽苍苍、古树参天、遮天蔽日。丛林外群山环抱，溪水淙淙。明嘉靖年间，僧人自玉于此建天台寺，现仅存废墟。废墟周围是保护较好的原始森林，多古木大树。其中最大的一棵榉树，树干直径2米多，主干挺直，在20米以上才有分枝，树上藤萝缠绕、苔藓满布。天台丛林有穿山甲、林麝、蟒蛇、山羊、狐狸、果子狸等珍稀动物和猫头鹰、锦鸡、雉鸡、箐鸡等珍贵飞禽。

白石涌泉：位于温泉景区入口前1千米处的公路右侧，一堵白色悬崖耸立其间。岩壁中部为"白石涌泉"石刻。悬崖与对面的乔巴山隔路相望，养温公路蜿蜒于两山间，峰回路转，岩壁下一股清泉涌出，奔流不息，似一幅天然高山流水图。该泉水经鉴定为优质矿泉水。

豸角凌云："豸角凌云"是一棵高30米的石笋，耸立山巅，凌突争雄。传说中有神兽名"獬豸"，能识人之善恶，并以其角攻击恶人。"豸角"即"獬豸"之角。远观豸角，一笋独立，直刺天穹；又似一支巨笔，笔尖朝上，傲然挺立，倒写天上文章。

奇石观瀑：位于温泉疗养院三疗区西面约500米处。大小岩石，千态万状，分布于瀑布两侧，水石相搏，琤琮有声。仰看两峰夹峙处，一线飞瀑似银河落自九天。瀑布落差30余米。

清流鸣琴：沿温泉疗养院清水河曲折向上约500米处，可见一条绿荫掩映的山谷，进入谷底，仰观天际，但见双峰对峙，峭不可攀。悬崖上苍松翠柏，藤蔓缠绕；崖底一泉汩汩涌出，积成一汪10余平方米的水潭，水质清澈，味道甘甜。泉水由右向左，盘旋蜿蜒，缓缓流下多级平台，形成10余级高低不一的瀑布，发出不同频率的响声。1945年被游览的文人命以此名。

慈云生佛：温泉疗养院东面，有一面高逾100米、长约1000米的悬崖绝壁。悬崖中段有一条裂隙，仿佛鬼斧神工将绝壁一分为二。绝壁上岩浆水不断滴落，经亿万年沉积，凝成一尊天然观音像，形神兼备，惟妙惟肖。

高桥天生：自温泉向南，盘山公路曲折蜿蜒，约2千米处，可见一座天然石灰岩拱桥。桥身南北走向，桥长30余米，高20余米，宽约5米，桥面平整可行汽车。桥孔前壁陡峭如削，桥拱中间高，两侧低，呈椭圆形，跨度约8米，上宽7～8米，下宽10米，高约17米。前壁右上方刻有“高桥天生”4个大字。

洪水古营：位于温泉村洪水河畔。洪水河是息烽、开阳两县界河，两岸岩壁陡峭，在温泉村一侧的山崖上有一座人工建造的营盘。清咸丰九年（1859）5月，何德胜领导的农民起义军攻陷瓮安，旋即向开阳、息烽（当时属修文管辖）进军。为抗击何德胜的起义军，息烽地方武装在此修建能容纳上千人的屯兵营盘。营盘地势险要，四面悬崖绝壁，西面山崖上有一条人工小路直达山顶，岩石上刻有“洪水古营”4个大字。至今有近200年历史。

（二）新萝温泉

位于永靖镇新萝村梨安林场边沿，属县城建设规划区，出水点紧靠贵遵高速公路和210国道，县城有二级公路直达景区。井口水温为46℃，日出量1500吨，水质无色无味，富含30余种微量元素，其中除锶、硒、铜、锌、钡、锰、铬、矾等14种人体必需的矿物元素外，还有硫、氡、碳酸钠等。锶含量达到矿泉水界限值，且小于界限指标，具有矿泉饮用水开发价值。氡含量达到国家医疗矿泉标准，具有医疗泉浴开发价值。

二、西望山

西望山地质构造为中生代侏罗系红色砂页岩，地貌奇特，奇峰怪石，重峦叠嶂，异峰突起，山间幽壑深谷，古树参天，清泉飞瀑，林海茫茫，有“一峰一世界，数步一重天”之境界。有仙人峰、凤凰池、盘陀石、玉乳泉、狮子峰、动胆石、天门石、万卷书等八大景观。

仙人峰：位于凤凰池左侧之轿顶山下，系一独立天表的巨大石笋，高30余米，胸部直径4米，体型如人，面南屹立，顶戴头盔，身披铠甲，双目凝视远方，似正在观察时局、指挥三军的一员武将，当地人称石将军。仙人峰下段的石壁上凿有“崛起南天”4字。

凤凰池：在仙人峰右侧的天风岭下，四周为茂密的箭竹林覆盖，池直径宽处百余米，面积300余平方米，水深4～5米。池水清澈甘甜。池边石壁上刻有“凤凰池”3字。

盘陀石：位于仙人峰前的大沟岭岗上，为两块鼓状圆形巨石相叠而成，直径20余米，高约15米。当地人称“朝阳鼓”。两块巨石由七块不足一米见方的卵石支撑在一陡峭的岭岗悬崖之上，状若垒卵，形势艰险，堪称奇观。

玉乳泉：位于语嵩塔右侧，为六棱形石井，边距1.43米，井深1.5米，井底有一块半球形石，呈乳房状。乳嘴为一直径3厘米的小孔，泉水自其中汩汩渗出，清洌晶莹，饮之清心爽目。为西望山“三宝”（虫茶、禅贡米、玉乳泉）之一。

狮子峰：位于轿顶山与莲花山之间，一堵砂石页岩拔地而起，高80余米，形若狮首。其后为下凹的狮腰和凸起的臀部，狮身总长300余米，侧卧峰顶，面向东南，雄踞山巅，下临大壑，其状威武慑人。狮首下的一块岩石上凿有“伏狮”2字。

动胆石：位于天门石右侧约100米处，系不规则梯形状叠石，高20余米，底宽12米，下大上小，顶宽约6米。站立其上，胆战心惊。顶端有“动胆石”摩崖石刻，每字80厘米见方。

万卷书：位于天门石对面，直线距离百米左右，一堵巨型页岩突立于山间岩壁上，高约25米，宽8米，形似若干书卷重叠而成，故名“万卷书”。此景与“天门石”遥遥相对，站在“天门石”上，可饱览“万卷书”风采，故有“打开双扇门，熟读万卷书”佳句。北侧悬崖上刻有“万卷书”3字。

天门石：位于凤池寺南约200米处，在流水淙淙的雨花谷上，四堵擎天巨石拔地而起，南北对峙成门，故曰“双扇门”。外两巨石为外门，高百丈有余，突兀屹立于丛林山水间。特别是南面一扇门石，高度居四门之冠，一石柱拔地而起，状甚雄奇。石柱腰间刻有“天柱峰”3字，为民国年间省内著名学者任可澄手笔。两扇内门虽小，其高度仍在100米之上，当地人称“幺门”，右边“幺门”石壁上凿有“天门石”3字。

三、南望山

南望山是县境内两大山脉之一，与西望山遥遥相望，海拔1300～1700米，夏季气候凉爽宜人。最高峰南极顶，海拔1749.6米，为县境内第一高峰。南望山有奇特的石林景观。南部有3万多亩面积的南山林场，场内有宾馆、饭店、休闲娱乐设施，已对外开放。南望山中有板厂、老厂、下洪马、何家沟、金家厂、上沟、猪嘴田7个水库，建有高山水库垂钓场。上沟水库奇特，水源一日三潮，俗称“三潮水”；下沟有三个洞穴日夜不停向外吹风，更为奇特的是夏天吹凉风，冬天吹暖风。各水库区有良好的生态环境和自然村寨，建有环湖酒店度假村、农家乐；旅游线上植被良好，森林繁茂，古树参天。尤为罕见的是一株“冠盖如云”的“摇钱树”，秋收季节，枝头果实如串串铜钱，别有意趣。

四、团元山

团元山公园位于县城西郊，面积2平方千米，平均海拔1250米，属省级森林公园。1988年，在园区内的最高峰龙奔山发掘出10余米长、生长于1.7亿年前的肉食类巨型恐龙化石。2001年，发现团元山陨石坑，经卫星图片确认，坑内直径3千米，外环直径约20千米，专家鉴定为7000万年前由天体陨石撞击形成。红岩林甘泉位于团元山中部。团元山属丹霞地貌，地质构造为侏罗纪石英砂质岩，团元山泉水为砂岩地层渗水，清澈甘甜，达到国际Ⅰ类水体标准。

五、溶洞

多缤洞：原名“躲兵洞”，位于九庄镇桐枝驿村。1984年，省科学院专家考察此洞，见洞景千姿百态，五彩缤纷，遂改其名为“多缤洞”。该洞长21.4千米，有“地下长廊”之称。洞中水陆并存，由六支水洞和七支干洞组成，多洞一体，多洞互通，曲径通幽，五层洞道层叠交织，洞中有水，水上有滩，滩下有瀑。洞厅大小皆备，厅厅有景，各不相同。为喀斯特洞穴艺术宝库和地下岩溶地貌博物馆，号称“天下奇观”。

银子洞：位于西山乡林丰村水岭沟组。距贵（阳）遵（义）老高速公路50米，距水岭沟组乡村旅游广场2千米。从银子洞垂直下去，即分左道和右道。左道风景优于右道，经过50米有一个“大厅”，“厅”内钟乳石千姿百态。左道的岔道较多，1.5千米的地方叫熬硝硐，有一个大石堆，石堆下面有暗河、钟乳石、瀑布、奇石等。

龙滩洞：位于九庄镇杉林村、柏茂村、新沙村、黄沙村境内。该洞为水洞，全长约3500米，呈S形布局。洞中分为“两段三峡”。龙滩洞的进口在上峡，位于距新沙村下环山村民组450米的龙洞沟底。上峡峡谷宽5～20米不等，崖壁多处直如刀切，洞腔逐渐空阔，五条石坝自然形成五个高低不一、宽窄不同、长短有别的水滩。中峡共有七个滩，总长约1.7千米，洞顶高100余米，水面宽50米以上。下峡长约1.5千米，入口狭小，500米以内多为峡廊壁道，宽3～5米。水流湍急，四个积水滩分布在中、下部，最大滩长110米，水面宽约50米，连接洞内瀑布，从剑壁峡汇入乌江库区。

六、乌江峡

乌江峡由鹰嘴峡、赤壁峡、玉龙峡、猴愁峡、叠翠峡、碧绿峡、玉泉峡和手扒岩等景点组成，素有“小三峡”之称。峡谷内有1978年修建的乌江水电站筑坝形成的人工湖（乌江库区），人工湖在县境内全长84千米，湖面百舸争流，两岸峰峦叠翠，景色十分壮丽。

鹰嘴峡：全长1.18千米，是乌江库区较为险峻的峡谷。南岸岩壁上矗立着一堵200多米高的岩石，状如巨鹰展翅欲飞，甚是雄伟壮观。

赤壁峡：全长7.3千米，整个峡区景色壮观。峡内有一巨大岩石屹立山巅，状似骆驼，因名骆驼峰。南岸岩壁上一峰矗立，前人呼之为石笋，今人称为导弹峰。

玉龙峡：峡内主要景点为玉龙山和乌江水库大坝。因玉龙山与乌江水库大坝相连，故玉龙峡又称大坝峡。玉龙山山势陡峭，半山石壁上刻有“铁索横江”4个大字。

猴愁峡：全长5.85千米，峡内有一对巨型岩石矗立于库区江岸，青葱秀美，如两位少女并肩而立，故名姊妹峰。为峡内著名景点。

叠翠峡：全长1.8千米，连接息烽、金沙两县的水上交通要道黄沙渡口即在此处。峡内自然景观奇特，江面平静，渡船往来穿梭，饶有诗情画意。渡口旁边有两座小石山凸出江面，形似两颗将要咬合的虎牙，人称“二虎山”，左山岩壁上刻一“忍”字，右山岩壁上刻一“让”字，传说为明代官吏徐驹所题。

碧绿峡：位于乌江库区上游。又名剑壁峡。自乌江乘舟溯流而上，在进入黄沙古渡1000余米的江面上，即可听到水从高处轰然坠落的声音；遥见南岸岩壁间，一帘瀑布飞泻而下，飘逸迷人。为峡内主要景点。

玉泉峡：全长0.5千米，泉水自悬崖绝壁的溶洞中流出。峡谷岩壁上有一个形似月亮的溶洞，名“月亮洞”。玉泉峡是乌江峡中最短的一峡。

手扒岩：又名梯子岩，为峡谷南岸最高峰，海拔1172米，悬崖峭壁，高不可攀，前人在梯子岩的半山腰开凿出一条狭窄栈道，行人须用手扒住栈道边的绝壁才能到达山顶，故得此名。

七、青山湖

青山湖，又名小桥河水库，位于青山苗族乡绿化村与冗坝村交界处，距县城14千米，距210国道出口8千米。处于川黔铁路、贵遵高等级公路、210国道线之间，交通方便。湖面面积314亩，风景秀美。青山湖旁边的冗坝村乡村旅游点已发展乡村旅社10家，有床位80个。

八、中国·堡子半边天文化发祥地

“半边天”文化发源于建国初期的县养龙司乡堡子村农业生产合作社。在党对农业的社会主义改造和农业合作化运动高潮中，养龙司乡堡子村农业合作社妇女社员破除“妇女下田，天干三年”的封建思想，带头参加农业生产，实现男女同工同酬。提出“会开机器会种田，妇女能顶半边天”口号，1955年10月，省妇联第99期简报转发堡子的先进事迹，12月，该简报被《中国农村社会主义高潮》一书收录，毛泽东主席亲笔题写编者按：“这一篇文章不长，容易看，建议各乡各社普遍照办。”在毛主席的重视和推荐下，堡子经验成为农村社会主义建设的一个样版。中央人民广播电台等多家权威主流媒体多次报道，全国各地都有人到堡子参观学习。1969年，堡子村党支部书记易华先（女）被贵州省选为特邀代表，参加中国共产党第九次全国代表大会。堡子村成为全国推行男女同工同酬第一村和“半边天”文化发祥地，全国妇联、省妇联领导亲临堡子村考查“半边天”文化。2009年12月，全国妇联主席陈至立代表全国妇联授予堡子村“全国妇女教育基地”称号。2010年，投资建设“中国·堡子半边天文化陈列馆”。

第三节 风景区规划

1993年6月，《息烽风景名胜区总体规划》通过专家论证。9月，县政府批准实施《息烽风景名胜区总体规划》。规划设计面积173.12平方千米，包括温泉、乌江峡、西望山、多缤洞4大景区和玄天洞、息烽集中营旧址、张露萍等七烈士墓3个独立景点。1995年3月，省政府将息烽风景名胜区列为省级风景名胜区。2000—2001年，由贵州省城乡规划设计研究院编制的《息烽风景名胜西望山景区规划》通过省级专家论证。2003年，由贵阳市城市规划设计研究院编制的《息烽集中营保护规划》通过省级专家论证。2004年，编制团元山森林规划、息烽集中营革命历史纪念馆保护规划及环境治理规划和贵州千山旅游发展有限公司开发乌江旅游景区规划的初步设计，规划面积20平方千米。2010年，由贵州省城乡规划设计研究院编制《息烽风景名胜区温泉景区控制性规划》《息烽温泉景区疗养院片区修建性详细规划》，由贵州省城乡规划设计院编制《息烽风景名胜区西望山景区控制性详细规划》。

一、温泉景区

温泉景区除有著名的温泉八景（天台丛林、白石涌泉、奇石观瀑、慈云生佛、清流鸣琴、豸角凌云、天生高桥、洪水古营）外，还有清水河上端幽深宁静的峡谷和下游洋水河的山水风光。以温泉浴和观景游览为主要内容，将其10个景物景观组成天台山、温泉、洋水河3个景点。

在疗养院东边建旅游村，并利用温泉水建鱼池、鱼缸，开展观光养殖业旅游。

开发温泉四周景点和新的旅游项目，如洋水河垂钓、涉水探险。利用西洋公司、息烽磷矿开展企业旅游，利用景区支线铁路，组织体验火车驾驶、火车超市等项目。在天生高桥等处开展民族体育活动。

规划在温泉镇建旅游镇。在天台山、温泉镇、温泉洋水河建停车场，其余各景点之间以步行线相连。

二、乌江景区

景区以峡谷风光为主，19个景物景观组成7个景点，称为“七峡”，即鹰嘴峡、玉龙峡、赤壁峡、猴愁峡、碧绿峡、叠翠峡、玉泉峡。

乌江景区以乘船游乌江观赏峡谷风光为主要游览内容。规划在县内乌江支流瓮桶河、雨淋河、漩塘等开展网箱养鱼，游人垂钓捕鱼等。在碧绿峡一带开展露营、野炊。在红军南渡乌江第一渡口“梯子岩”建陈列室，收集红军南渡乌江资料、实物等用于宣传教育。在村寨周围开展观光农业及果园旅游，建农庄、旅游村、旅游点、码头和停车场。

三、西望山景区

西望山有景物景观31个，将其组成12个景点。以森林旅游、观奇峰异石和访古探秘为主。利用山上良好植被、水源及农家开展避暑休闲活动。

西望山景区在县中部，便于与其他景区联系，规划上山公路与到各乡镇村公路衔接，停车场置于各出入口间，在景区中部瞿坛寺附近建旅游村，解决景区游客食宿。

四、团元山景区

团元山有侏罗纪公园和鱼简河2个景点。以科普教育、休闲旅游为主。在风景区内桦槁坪村和鸦米寨建旅游点。

侏罗纪公园除参观侏罗纪恐龙化石遗址外，保护好发掘地，竖碑立牌。建恐龙化石陈列馆（收集贵州恐龙化石及照片资料）；建演播厅，开展讲学、播放科教电影等活动；建模拟恐龙的生活环境1处，吸引游客游玩，同时作为拍摄电影、电视的基地，建娱乐点。

五、多缤洞景点

洞外环境保护，洞内步道行道修建，灯光照明，供游人考察探秘、观景。在洞内不影响观景的宽阔处设置3～4个服务点，在同心村建服务部和停车场。

第四节　旅游开发

西望山景区开发：1992年，县政府同意张创开发西望山，种植杜仲、黄檗等中药材，后因水土流失、和尚墓遭破坏和被盗等而停止。2002年，县委书记陈长发到西山调研，明确环境保护、群众异地搬迁和保护政策。2003年，贵州千山旅游发展公司开发西望山，但不久停止。2007年，成都昭觉寺演法大和尚考察西望山后，筹集资金300万元，在凤池寺旁建寮房1座。

温泉景区开发：1992年5月，副省长刘玉林到温泉视察工作，指示搞好温泉旅游。7月，省规划院派人到现场进行实地勘测。2002年3月，成立息烽温泉风景名胜区开发协调领导小组。2006年12月，省委副书记王富玉主持召开省委专题办公会，研究息烽旅游资源开发事宜，确定将温泉景区列入省重点建设项目，获取政策、资金等保证，进一步促进县旅游资源开发。2009年5月，县长张定超、县委常委、分管旅游的副县长、县旅游局、招商引资局代表到省总工会与工会相关领导再次就温泉开发建设事宜进行协商，但未能达成一致意见。

乌江峡景区开发：2002年，省公路工程总公司建成荆江旅游区并对外开园，后因景区有关手续不全和公司领导人经济问题，景区开园后不久停业。2003年6月，贵州千山旅游发展有限公司进驻息烽，着手开发西望山和乌江峡的前期准备工作。2005年8月，县政府与贵州千山旅游发展有限公司签约：由贵州千山旅游发展有限公司投资7.5亿元开发乌江峡景区。公司首先在瓮桶河上游老窝村一带启动开发建设。至2007年，乌江峡红色旅游景区建设工程投资1.1亿元。2010年，景区开发工作停止。

第五节　旅游管理

1996—2007年，县旅游管理部门每年分别与全县各旅游景区（点）签订安全生产“三包”责任书，安全落实到人。2007年，“五一”和“十一”前分别对贵阳市海外等3家旅行社在县内设立的门市部进行检查，发现一家证照不全，责令其及时补充完善。2008年4月，息烽集中营革命历史纪念馆免费对外开放后，全国各地前来参观的游客剧增。为规范旅游市场秩序，县旅游局到现场对外来旅游团队进行检查，对未持导游证的导游和黑导游进行批评并登记备案。是年，对全县旅游企业进行质量监督检查40余次，对发现的问题提出整改意见，杜绝旅游市场无证、无照、超范围经营和非法转让许可证等“三黑”违法活动。2009年，县旅游市场实现“安全、质量、秩序、效益”四统一目标。对全县旅游景区（点）、宾馆、饭店、旅游涉外定点单位检查5次，检查面100%。2月起，县旅游局与县人力资源和社会保障局联合举办餐厅服务员培训班，提高服务水平。5月，组织全县各乡镇分管旅游工作的领导、县直机关有关部门代表、各旅游景区（点）、旅游涉外定点接待单位、部分乡村农家乐、乡村旅社从业人员共178人，在翠竹园宾馆参加县首届旅游基础知识讲座，听取县委常委、分管旅游工作的副县长曹垒发、贵阳市旅游学校教师李悦对《息烽县旅游资源状况及旅游发展现状及方向》《导游基础知识》等专题进行系统讲解。是年，继续在全县旅游系统开展“满意在息烽”主题活动，检查全县13家乡村旅社，检查面100%。

1996—2010年旅游人次、旅游收入统计表

表18-5-1

年份	接待人次（万人次）	旅游收入（万元）
1996	20	200
1997	25	250
1998	30	350
1999	42	550
2000	19	720
2001	23	860
2002	27	1050
2003	45	2405
2004	46.34	4016
2005	137.21	4277.9
2006	91.07	4233.3
2007	81.2	4300
2008	111.2	7800
2009	180.14	45600
2010	195.79	63000
合计	1073.95	139412.2

第六节　旅游特产

一、阳朗辣子鸡

阳朗辣子鸡最早是永靖镇阳朗村村民黄南武（女）在经营餐馆的过程中选用当地饲养的土公鸡和优质干辣椒、大蒜头、花椒等原材料，用独特的方法烹制而成，以其香、辣、鲜、糯为特色，在黔味食品中独树一帜。因其原产地在息烽集中营革命历史纪念馆所在地阳朗坝（村），故名阳朗辣子鸡。现已成为贵州名特小吃品牌，产品畅销省内外。以黄南武、叶兴林（叶老大）为代表的100多家辣子鸡经营户，分布在息烽火车站至息烽集中营革命历史纪念馆阳朗坝一带，被称为“阳朗辣子鸡一条街”。

二、苗族刺绣

苗族刺绣是县苗族服饰（衣、裙、绑腿带）文化的主要表现形式。县苗族有大花苗、小花苗、青苗、川苗等不同支系，各个支系都有各自的刺绣特色，其中青苗刺绣以青色为主，大花苗、小花苗刺绣以红黑色为主，川苗刺绣以白青色为主。青苗的花飘带、背扇、环衣最有特色。花飘带是苗族刺绣中的一个重要组成部分，也是苗族青年男女定情的信物。苗族刺绣题材广泛，山川、河流、草、木、虫、鱼、神话人物等，无不毕肖于针下。其构图高度图案化，讲究对称之美。苗家妇女在刺绣过程中广泛运用飞针、跳针、梭花、堆花、背针、蜡染、数纱织花、插花等技法和工艺，使绣品画面层次分明，形象逼真。刺绣内容丰富，其中女性服饰较男性服饰更为多姿多彩。最有特色的青苗和大花苗服饰分老式和新式，老式以青布为主料，花纹图案较少，新式花纹图案较多。大花苗服饰上衣配合花团锦簇的百褶裙，花样图案大，色泽艳红。县苗族刺绣一直保持传统风格，纯手工制作，具有较高艺术品位，产品远销省内外和港澳地区，被多家博物馆收藏。2008年，青山苗族乡举办苗族刺绣培训班，邀请苗族老艺人授课。

三、西望山虫茶

西望山虫茶的母体为西山望白茶。白茶树生长于西望山原始丛林，属常绿乔木，其干、根、叶皆可熬茶饮用。据《本草纲目》记载：虫茶有清热、祛暑、解毒、健胃、助消化等功能。2009年，经贵州师范大学分析测试中心鉴定，西望山虫茶含有人体必需的铜、锌、铁、锰、钙、镁、磷等多种微量元素。人体所需的8种氯基酸中，虫茶就含有7种。其组合比例接近国际FAO（联合国粮食及农业组织）模式，氖氨酸和氮氨酸总含量分别是传统茶叶的66.5倍和81.1倍，多数指标超过冬虫夏草的含量。用虫茶泡出的茶水色泽暗红，味道醇厚，被誉为灵山瑰宝，茶中“茅台”。

西望山虫茶制作：每年3月采摘白茶树嫩叶后，有一种叫夜香螟蛾的小虫就会爬到白茶树上，吃下部分没有被采摘的老白茶树叶，然后在白茶树上拉出一堆堆小米大小的颗粒状虫屎，人将虫屎取回晾干或用火烘干，用筛子筛去杂物，剩下的虫屎颗粒就是天然虫茶；每年3月，采摘白茶树嫩芽，经过炒、揉、晒或烘等工序，制成白茶，再拌以少许西望山禅贡米，装入篾制茶笼或布袋，密闭并悬挂于通风处，待其长出夜香螟蛾，将笼中（袋中）白茶吃尽，拉下虫屎，然后用筛子除去杂物，剩下的虫屎即为人工虫茶。人工虫茶制作时间一般在一年以上或两年左右。

第六章　息烽集中营革命历史纪念馆

1996年，贵阳市委、市政府决定对息烽集中营旧址进行修复。1997年，贵州省委、省政府公布息烽集中营革命历史纪念馆为贵州省爱国主义教育基地。2001年，中宣部公布息烽集中营革命历史纪念馆为全国爱国主义教育示范基地。息烽集中营旧址经过两期修复开放，至2010年，共接待党和国家领导人17位，到此参观并接受爱国主义教育者逾300万人次。

第一节　修复工程

一、一期修复工程

1996年年底，贵阳市委、市政府决定对息烽集中营旧址进行局部修复。市领导多次到现场考察、办公，召集息烽县委、县政府及市文化局共同研究，制定修复方案，组建“息烽集中营旧址修复领导小组”，下设办公室处理修复工程日常事务。是年，市政府拨专款400万元作为修复经费，具体工程由县委、县政府组织实施。县成立拆迁征地组、修复工程组、资料组，从城建、国土、交通、文化、永靖镇等单位抽出人员到各组工作。修复工程征地76亩，国有土地转让11.1亩，共计87.1亩。按原样原址修复周养浩办公室、总机室、信斋、平斋、义斋、明心亭、明心湖桥及碉堡、司号亭各1座。维修仁斋、爱斋、军统人员办公室、收发室、岗亭、猫洞刑讯处、绿化草坪及其他附属设施等。新建展厅、影视厅、接待室、大型群像石雕《忠魂曲》及安装供电、供水、消防设施等。工程于1997年5月20日竣工，29日对外开放。

此后，1999年贵阳市商业银行捐资40万元，在原址按原样修复大礼堂；2002年，集中营集资重建中山室；同年，省委组织部以全省共产党员名义捐资55万元党费，修复忠、孝两斋房；大连市政府捐资在原址按原样修复和斋和诚静堂。

二、二期修复工程

2003年4月10日，中共中央政治局常委、国家副主席曾庆红到息烽集中营革命历史纪念馆参观，作出要“把息烽集中营旧址保护好，把纪念馆配套设施建设好，把全国爱国主义教育示范基地作用发挥好”的指示。5月13日，贵阳市委召开常委会议，成立息烽集中营革命历史纪念馆二期修复工程领导小组；提出“保持原貌、征集史料、挖掘内涵、加强建设、依法修建、规划先行、专家论证、精心组织”的工程建设意见。县委、县政府成立建设办公室，下设规划设计建设、征地拆迁安置、文物征集整理布展三个工作小组分别开展工作。市财政划拨1000万元作建设启动资金。

二期修复工程征地3.25公顷，新建新馆3800平方米，扩建纪念活动广场、停车场、展厅前场地1.6万平方米，修专用公路238米，安装自动消防系统1套及其他附属工程。总投资1603.4万元。2005年8月工程竣工，同月19日举行新馆开馆仪式。

三、玄天洞修复工程

1997年11月26日，县成立玄天洞修复工程领导小组，着手杨虎城将军囚禁处玄天洞的修复工作。修复工程包括：在原址按原样修复塔脚寺（三清宫，原宪兵队驻地）、老洞左厢房（原宪兵中队队部）、玄天洞山门、地母洞前地母庙（原军统特务队驻地）、碉堡4座及其他附属设施。修县城至玄天洞公路8000米。1998年10月，修复工程竣工，同月18日对外开放。

2003年7月，对县城至玄天洞公路进行扩宽改造，总投资549万元。

第二节　开　馆

1997年5月，息烽集中营旧址一期工程完成，5月29日，举行息烽集中营革命历史纪念馆开放揭幕仪式。省委常委、贵阳市委书记主持开馆仪式，贵阳市市长宣布该馆作为贵阳市爱国主义教育基地的决定，省委副书记王思齐发表讲话，省、市领导王思齐、胡克惠、胡圣生，幸存者刘谦、杨虎城将军女儿杨拯英等为“忠魂曲”群雕揭幕。揭幕仪式后，省、市领导和来宾集体参观纪念馆陈列室和修复后的集中营旧址。在贵阳视察工作的全国政协副主席杨汝岱也前来参观。首次开馆的陈列室面积约100平方米，展线长50米，展出图片100余幅。

2005年8月，息烽集中营旧址二期修复工程完成和新馆落成，19日举行新馆开放仪式。新馆共有4个展厅，面积1164平方米，展线长500米；展出图片350余幅；展出历史文物（含部分复制件）160余件。新展厅采用现代科技手段复原刑讯室、小萝卜头囚室等，同时设置5个多媒体，滚动播放幸存者亲口讲述息烽集中营内幕的视频，让参观者产生更为深切的感受。

第三节　宣传接待

一、宣传

1997年10月，省委、省政府决定在次年3月全国“两会”期间，在北京举办“遵义会议”和“息烽英烈”（后定名《烽火不息》）大型展览。1998年3月13日上午10时，《烽火不息》展在中国革命历史博物馆开展，设序、地狱、抗争、忠魂、幸存者、结束语等6个部分，展出图片220余幅、历史文物70余件、猫洞刑讯室模型1座，展线总长180余米。省委副书记、省长吴亦侠主持展览开幕仪式，中共中央政治局委员、国务委员李铁映为开幕式剪彩，全国人大常委会副委员长曹志、全国人大民族事务委员会主任王朝文、团中央书记处书记胡舟华等领导出席开幕式。

展出期间，中共中央政治局委员、中宣部部长丁关根，国务院副秘书长刘奇葆等领导，杨虎城将军长子杨拯民，息烽集中营幸存者的子女周鸿、韩秀融、徐陵、宋振镛及张露萍烈士生前战友甘惜芬等参观展览。《烽火不息》展在京展出17天，接待观众10余万人次，向参观人群发放折页、简介、画册、图片等宣传品5000余件。除国内观众外，有来自俄罗斯、美国、德国、日本、意大利、瑞典等国家的游客参观展览。有30多家主流媒体近100余名记者到现场采访，中央电视台《东方时空》专栏10次播出对展览的专访。《人民日报》《新华社每日电讯》《中国青年报》《中国少年报》《北京晚报》《贵州日报》《贵阳晚报》等报刊共发表通讯、消息、专访等60余篇（条）。

2007年7月，县选派人员参加在遵义举行的重庆、贵阳、遵义、广安四地区红色旅游发展第四次联席会议，建立四地区红色旅游联线。2008年8月，以“红色经典，秀美息烽”为题的息烽集中营历史图片展览在上海、江西上饶、贵阳等地巡回展出。利用“5·18”国际博物馆日开展宣传活动，向游客发放宣传资料，在《东方之旅》《贵州旅游指南》《山水襟怀——贵阳红色旅游》《假日自助游》《中国文博单位要览》等刊物上撰文宣传息烽集中营革命历史纪念馆。2009年6月28日，参加贵阳市避暑节活动在息烽举办的“青春红歌会”，以唱红歌文艺演出形式宣传红色旅游资源。是年11月，邀请中央电视台《大风车》栏目组拍摄息烽集中营革命历史纪念馆宣传片。2010年，协助中央电视台《探索·发现》和《鉴证发展之旅》栏目组拍摄以张露萍烈士为题材的专题片《魔窟女杰》。

二、接待

1997年，息烽集中营革命历史纪念馆接待游客9.7万人次，门票收入46.85万元；1998年，接待游客10万人次，门票收入66.58万元；1999年，接待游客9万人次，门票收入37.36万元；2000年，接待游客9.3万人次，门票收入50.72万元；2001年，接待游客12.64万人次，门票收入73.34万元；2002年，接待游客10.43万人次，门票收入60.51万元；2003年，接待游客10.33万人次，门票收入59.91万元；2004年，接待游客14.43万人次，门票收入83.68万元；2005年，接待游客32万人次，门票收入195.71万元；2006年，接待游客16万人次，门票收入213.42万元；2007年，接待游客4.47万人次，门票收入66.93万元。

2008年4月20日，纪念馆免费对外开放，当年接待游客47.88万人次，门票收入22.82万元；2009年和2010年，分别接待游客71.23万人次和72.17万人次。

息烽集中营革命历史纪念馆重大接待统计表

表18-6-1

接待对象	身　份	时　间
杨汝岱	全国政协副主席	1997年5月29日
罗　干	中共中央政治局委员	1997年7月9日
李　鹏	中共中央政治局常委、国务院总理	1997年7月18日
王忍之	中国社会科学院党组成员	1997年11月30日
李铁映	中共中央政治局委员	1998年3月13日
曹　志	全国人大常委会副委员长（北京参观《烽火不息》展览）	1998年3月13日
丁关根	中共中央政治局委员、中宣部部长	1997年3月14日
布　赫	全国人大常委会副委员长	1997年10月20日
阿兰·布罗迪	联合国基金会高级官员	1998年4月7日
越南人民共和国文化部代表团	越南人民共和国文化部代表团	1998年8月13日
《北京周报》采访团	《北京周报》采访团（其中外国友人3人）	1998年5月23日
孙家正	文化部部长	1998年9月7日
肖　扬	最高人民法院院长	1999年1月19日
习近平	福建省委副书记、代省长	1999年4月10日
彭丽媛	中国著名歌唱家	1999年4月10日

续表

接待对象	身 份	时 间
周光召	全国人大常委会副委员长	1999年7月30日
曹 志	全国人大常委会副委员长	1999年11月17日
吴邦国	中央政治局委员、国务院副总理	1999年11月17日
顾秀莲	全国妇联副主席	2000年10月8日
刘云山	中宣部副部长	2000年10月8日
万国权	全国政协副主席	2001年7月21日
张克辉	全国政协副主席	2001年9月25日
姜春云	全国人大常委会副委员长	2001年11月13日
迟浩田	中共中央政治局委员、中央军委副主席，国防部部长	2001年12月19日
任建新	全国政协副主席	2002年4月2日
铁木尔·达瓦买提	全国人大常委会副委员长	2002年5月15日
曾庆红	中共中央政治局常委、国家副主席	2003年4月10日
韩启德	全国人大常委会副委员长	2003年4月14日
回良玉	中央政治局委员、国务院副总理	2003年5月17日
单霁翔	国家文物局局长	2003年8月3日
吴官正	中共中央政治局常委、中纪委书记	2004年5月3日
李兆焯	全国政协副主席	2005年8月15日
赵 维	文化部副部长	2005年9月8日
裴怀亮、赵刚	中国国防大学副校长	2005年9月8日
秦绍德	复旦大学党委书记	2005年9月8日
郭 欣	国家海事局副局长	2005年9月10日
叶辛等	著名作家，上海作家采风团	2005年9月14日
梁 衡	《人民日报》副总编、作家	2005年9月15日
乌云其木（女）	全国人大常委会副委员长	2005年9月25日
隋明太	国务委员、武警总队政委	2005年11月18日
李长春	中共中央政治局常委	2005年12月13日
王文荣	国防大学副校长	2006年4月17日
白立忱	全国政协副主席、全国供销总社主任	2006年4月20日
张全景	原中央候补委员、中组部部长	2006年4月30日
刘峰岩	中纪委副书记	2006年5月6日
梁光烈	中央委员，中央军委委员，国务委员兼国防部部长、国务院党组成员	2009年4月13日

第十九篇　社会生活

第一章　人民生活

20世纪90年代初，境内取消商品凭票供应。90年代后期，城乡居民的消费观念和生活方式发生改变，在饮食、居住、服饰上，传统性逐渐淡化，转变为追求时尚。城镇住宅楼房配套设施齐全，一些农民建起二、三层的砖混结构楼房，逐步用上自来水，农村改厕工作逐渐铺开。城乡公路交通设施日趋完善，人们出行逐渐以车代步。

第一节　居民就业状况

一、单位就业人数

1991年，全县单位从业人员7448人。

1995年，全县单位从业人员8073人，其中女性2530人，城镇集体单位从业人员584人。

2001年，全县单位从业人员9575人，其中女性3263人，城镇集体单位从业人员408人。

2010年，全县单位从业人员1.94万人，其中女性5914人，城镇集体单位从业人员298人。

二、劳动就业

1991年5月，县成立劳动力管理领导小组，制定《息烽县劳动力管理暂行规定》。是年安置就业1074人。1993—1995年，劳务输出累计1.16万人。1994年，建立县职业介绍所，在永靖镇、小寨坝镇建立职业介绍站。1997年，县成立解困与再就业工程领导小组和办公室，对下岗职工进行分流安置。至2000年，安置下岗再就业342人。2001年，县成立农村剩余劳动力转移与培训工作协调领导小组和办公室，制定农村剩余劳动力转移与培训实施意见，举办非农技能培训（计算机操作员、沼气池修建及灶具维修、井下采掘车驾驶员、中式烹调等），统筹培训2076人；组织参加贵阳市劳务交流会，转移农村剩余劳动力3703人。下岗职工再就业117人。2007年，安置“零就业家庭”109户127人；城乡统筹就业9544人，其中下岗失业人员220人、农村富余劳动力7894人、城镇失业人员1430人。2009年，推行培训、创业、就业三位一体的工作模式，转移农村劳动力6592人。2010年，开展创业、计算机操作员、美发、焊工、计算机维修培训，城乡统筹就业8611人，其中城镇新增就业人员2398人、农村劳动力转移6213人。新增创业405户，带动就业1875人；全县城镇登记失业率控制在3.4%以内。

第二节　居民收入

一、城镇居民收入

1991年，全县对国家机关、企事业单位干部职工进行工资调整，当年人均工资1477元。1992年，年人均工资2088元。此后，按照调整、晋升职务、职称、技术等级、学历变动、奖励、津贴、岗位补贴等方式晋升工资。1995年，城镇居民人均可支配收入3747元。1999年，调整机关事业单位工作人员工资标准，人均月增加工资115元。2001年，增加离退休人员生活费。增发当年12月份的基本工资或基本离退休费。是年，城镇居民人均可支配收入5000元。随着企业改革改制和引进民营企业，企业职工经济收入增加。2006年，国家调整职工工资。2007年，城镇居民人均可支配收入突破1万元，2010年为1.47万元。

二、农村居民收入

1991年，县内农民年人均纯收入525元，随着改革不断发展和深入，农民收入逐年增加。1996年，农民人均纯收入1200元。1998年，农村实行第二轮土地承包后，部分农民的生产观念发生变化，开始从传统农业生产方式向现代农业转变，调整种植和养殖业结构，种养科技含量提高，增产增收；乡镇企业快速发展，农民增收；部分农民外出打工、经商。2004年，农民人均纯收入2000元，此后，农民人均收入增长幅度较大，2007年为3187元，2010年突破5000元。

第三节　居民消费

1991—1999年，随着经济发展，县内城乡居民消费水平逐步提高。2000年，城镇居民年人均消费支出3498元，此后逐年上升，2010年为7591元。恩格尔系数由39.5%上升到40%。

从消费结构上看，2000年食品消费支出占39.5%，衣着消费13%，家庭设备用品及服务8%，医疗保健6.3%，交通和通讯6.8%，教育文化娱乐服务8.9%，居住7.2%。2010年，食品消费支出占40%，衣着消费17%，家庭设备用品及服务10%，医疗保健6%，交通和通信9%，教育文化娱乐服务9%，居住10%。城镇居民食物消费基本满足，消费重心向家庭设备、居住、交通和通信方面转移，尤以衣着变化较大。

息烽县2000—2010年城镇居民生活消费情况统计表

表19-1-1　　单位：元/年/人

年份	2000	2001	2002	2003	2004	2005	2006	2007	2008	2009	2010
消费支出	3498	3487	4382	5485	5294	6072	6099	6633	7282	7829	7592
其中：服务性支出	—	—	1144	1392	1527	1668	1781	1739	1773	1806	1694
食品消费	1382	1479	1606	1714	1890	1968	2131	2510	2790	2999	3037
衣着	453	498	557	501	621	839	864	995	999	1054	1327
家庭设备	281	274	216	575	304	436	343	400	551	814	754
医疗保健	221	257	369	350	270	355	368	366	394	317	460

续表

年份	2000	2001	2002	2003	2004	2005	2006	2007	2008	2009	2010
交通和通信	237	284	456	515	574	694	737	839	775	788	676
文教娱乐	311	314	498	666	874	928	734	787	869	619	704
居住	252	497	549	996	392	449	740	558	745	980	740
杂项商品和服务	117	131	131	168	218	183	184	180	159	257	255
恩格尔系数（%）	39.5	42.4	36.6	31.3	35.7	32.4	34.9	37.8	38.3	38.3	40

2002年，农村居民年人均消费支出1607元，2010年为3391元，增长1倍。恩格尔系数由48.52%降至37.69%。农民收入增加，食物需求基本满足，消费重心开始向穿、用等方面转移，居住和家庭设备用品比例较大。农村居民消费水平虽与城镇居民差距较大，但随着经济发展，也逐步由温饱型向小康型发展，城乡差别、区域差别逐步缩小。

息烽县2002—2010年农村居民生活消费情况统计表

表19-1-2　　单位：元/年/人

年份	2002	2003	2004	2005	2006	2007	2008	2009	2010
消费支出	1607	1391	1582	1864	1964	2517	2818	2873	3391
其中；食品消费	780	772	853	907	898	1250	1204	1213	1278
衣着	47	49	65	72	83	131	146	179	—
家庭设备及服务	63	69	64	84	69	108	142	301	—
医疗保健	182	38	44	92	114	192	64	184	—
交通和通信	68	73	103	135	132	174	218	217	—
文教娱乐服务	128	167	148	252	150	139	105	107	—
居住	229	191	259	284	490	446	870	604	—
杂项商品和服务	402	31	46	21	28	56	68	67	—
恩格尔系数（%）	48.52	55.47	53.89	48.64	45.71	49.68	42.73	42.23	37.69

第四节　衣食住行

一、服饰

（一）服装

20世纪90年代初，县内居民自购布料到裁缝铺做服装比较普遍，服装多以蓝、灰、黑色为主，讲究大方、结实耐穿，服装款式以中山服、春秋装为主。青年男士夏天喜穿短裤，女士多穿长裙或长裤。90年代中后期，追求美观时髦，西装、夹克、羊毛衫、运动衫、太空服、连衣裙、健美裤、七分裤相继出现，花色品种不断翻新。男青年有穿大红大绿衣服者。中老年人尤其是农村老年人多保持传统服装习惯。

进入21世纪，服装来源逐渐由自制服装向成衣转化。城镇部分居民着礼服、休闲服等。年轻女士多穿短上衣、高腰衣、短裙、超短裙、短裤、超短裤，寒冬和早春亦然。保暖内衣、羽绒服、皮衣皮裤、各种档次的大衣，已不再是人们过冬的稀罕衣物。市场上儿童服装款式新颖，各种档次服装应有尽有。农村人劳作时着装简朴，但进城时着装已较为讲究，与城镇居民差别不大。城镇居民人均衣着消费，2000年为453元，2010年为1327元。

（二）鞋帽首饰

20世纪90年代，城镇居民多穿各式皮鞋，女士喜穿高跟鞋。农村人多穿解放鞋（胶鞋）。女士戴首饰，使用化妆品增多。进入21世纪，城镇居民穿鞋向多样化发展，除皮鞋外，还选择休闲鞋、旅游鞋等，既要款式新颖，又要质量上乘，少数人讲究穿戴名牌。女士鞋类甚多，除高跟鞋外，有休闲鞋、旅游鞋、筒靴鞋、雪地鞋。农村居民穿皮鞋的增多。首饰、挎包、手提包逐渐成为青年男女的时尚饰品。首饰多为金、银、玉制品，男士主要有公文包、领带夹，女士主要有耳坠、项链、手提包。使用化妆品的人增多，男性主要用发胶、摩丝和护肤品，女性常用润肤霜、增白霜、防晒霜和香水，部分女性还用摩丝、口红、描眉、眼影和面膜。

帽子：部分老年人冬季戴雷锋帽、鸭舌帽，春夏戴防晒帽；婴儿常戴六瓣帽、毛线帽等。进入21世纪，男女青年戴帽子、配墨镜逐步成为时尚。

发型：20世纪80年代，县内女性发型流行双小辫或大麻花辫。90年代，“马尾”发型为多数女孩喜爱。部分女性将头发烫成卷发，“爆炸头”加紧身裤成为年轻女孩的另类时尚。步入21世纪，“理发师”升格为“发型设计师”，各种欧、美、日、韩时尚发型进入境内。染发、烫发、拉直、复古等应有尽有，马尾发型和披肩发型比较流行。爱美女性多在发廊做自己喜欢的发式和染发。“做头”成为城镇女性的生活时尚。

二、饮食

县内小吃有各种粉、面、包子、馒头、油条、发糕、泡粑、糍粑、甜酒粑、苞谷粑、烧饼、汤圆、凉粉、米皮、油果子、麻花饺、蒸饺、水饺、抄手、丝娃娃、油炸马铃薯、烧苞谷、烤红薯、汉堡包以及各种肉类蔬菜烧烤串等。县城水井巷陈家烧饼受多数消费者喜爱。

饮食习惯：城镇一般一日三餐，早餐多面条、米粉、包子、馒头、油条、豆浆或牛奶；年轻人喜在餐馆吃羊肉粉、牛肉粉、蹄花粉、辣鸡粉（面）、脆臊面（粉）、大排面、肠旺面等。农村农闲时两餐，一般劳作时三餐，农忙时有四餐者。

20世纪90年代，县内城镇居民已能在市场上自由选购粮食和各种肉食。主食以大米为主，面食为辅，偶食玉米、薯类。有的餐馆主食除大米饭外，还备有苞谷饭，供食客选用。年轻女子和小孩喜在街头吃马铃薯做成的小吃，有麻辣马铃薯、大锅马铃薯等；肉食以猪肉、鸡肉为主，辅以牛肉、羊肉、鸭肉或鹅肉。进入21世纪，城镇居民购买猪肉已不挑肥拣瘦，而是挑瘦嫌肥。鱼虾也逐渐成为普通人家的常菜。

城镇宴席多在饭店操办，农村仍以自办为主。方桌逐步改为圆桌，每桌人数由8人演变为10人；而且由男女分桌逐步变为男女同桌。宴席一般在中午12时至下午6时，随到随开，俗称流水席。

城镇酒席，20世纪90年代，每桌13～15个菜肴，120～150元；进入21世纪，每桌15～17个菜肴，300元左右，另配上烟、酒、饮料、餐巾纸。县城饭店多由四方桌、长条凳改为圆桌、独凳或靠椅，圆桌上置一圆形玻璃转盘，菜肴搁转盘上旋转，便于就餐者夹菜。有的饭店除大堂外，还设有单间，单间除饭桌外，还置有自动麻将机，供客人饭前饭后娱乐。

农村宴席，在20世纪90年代，每桌12～13个菜肴，80～100元；进入21世纪，每桌12～13个菜肴，150～200元，另配上烟、酒、饮料、餐巾纸。2005年后，农村有组织一条龙餐饮服务队，农户自己备料，服务队带厨师、厨具、餐桌及凳子，每桌收取40元左右加工服务费。

2008—2010年，县工商联、工商局、卫生局、旅游局、新闻中心联合，在小寨坝红岩葡萄节先后举办“十大美食”评选活动、“息烽县首届地方风味小吃电视演艺大赛”“息烽十大名菜”电视演艺大赛。按照比赛规则及评分标准，评选出十大美食，地方风味小吃、大众喜爱小吃和十大名菜。

十大美食：阳朗辣子鸡、小米鲊、排骨炖萝卜、菌香鸡、吉祥玉子虾、柴灰豆腐、啤酒鸭、潮水鱼火锅、鲜果爆嫩兔、小锅米粉。

地方风味小吃：砂锅粉、红烧肉粉、凉粉、麻花、牛肉粉、黄粑、糯米饭、青豆腐、春卷、羊肉粉。

大众喜爱小吃：馋嘴米皮、烤鱼、豆腐脑、臭豆腐、羊肉串、烤鸡、香酥豆腐、二槌砸鱼、爆炒螺蛳、怪噜豆腐。

十大名菜：金丝豆腐（永靖镇好百合餐馆）、葡萄鱼丸（小寨坝镇渝黔食府）、香辣掌中宝（永靖镇黄南武辣子鸡总店）、贵烽泡菜鱼（永靖镇贵烽酒楼）、苗王豆腐（永靖镇明香餐馆）、郑氏桂花鸡（永靖镇滋味食府）、青山风味山羊肉及牛肉（青山苗族乡王发祥餐馆）、一品香酥丸（流长乡晨龙山庄）、独秀葫芦鸭（永靖镇叶老大辣子鸡酒楼）、御牛红汤（永靖镇蜗牛居餐馆）。

饮酒：饮酒多为男性。有酒瘾的老年人一日三餐饮少量酒，以舒筋活血。多在节假日、红事、白事、喜庆或晚餐时饮酒。农村多饮散装苞谷酒；城镇多饮瓶装窖酒、曲酒、啤酒。20世纪90年代，县内饮酒风盛行，有迟入席者罚酒三杯，结束时喝团圆杯风气。喜欢劝酒敬酒，猜拳行令，并以各种理由劝客多饮。进入21世纪，虽劝酒但不勉强，多不猜拳行令或劝酒。宴席多同时摆酒、饮料、香烟，女子、儿童不饮酒则喝饮料。

饮茶：境内历来有饮茶习惯。城镇人多饮青茶、毛尖茶。城镇一般现沏茶敬客，农村夏天喜用苦丁茶，客人到家，多从茶壶或茶缸中倒茶水相待。敬茶多半杯，递茶时，双手递给客人以示恭敬。红、白喜庆有1～2名女子敬客人茶水习俗。进入21世纪用饮水机、矿泉水、一次性水杯，敬客人一杯后，由客人自便。农村家庭主人站待客人饮完茶，接过茶杯后方才坐下的习俗已不多见。

三、居住

1991年前，境内房屋多为木架房、土墙房、小青砖房、小红砖盖小青瓦房或小平房，房屋内外几无装修，还有少量茅草房和危房。城乡居民住房内多无卫生间，也无洗浴设备，需到住房外如厕，洗澡用一大盆盛水或到公共浴室。

20世纪90年代，居住条件逐步改善，凡新修住房，均砖混结构平顶，城镇四五层楼房，农村三间二、三层楼房居多。城乡民居卧室、客厅、饭厅、厨房、卫生间配套。卫生间安装蹲便器或坐便器，洗浴设备由热水包换成电热水器、太阳能热水器。人们开始注重房屋装修，安装防盗门。进入21世纪，房屋外墙贴瓷砖，内墙刮瓷粉、刷乳胶漆，安装铝合金门窗、防盗门，地面贴瓷砖或铺木地板。2006年，全县对公路、铁路沿线乡镇居民住房进行立面整治，平顶屋面增盖斜顶屋面，墙体进行钢化瓷粉粉刷。至2010年，全县消灭茅草房和危房；县内商住楼第一栋高19层的电梯大楼——南大街“新城银座”竣工。

住房面积与设施：1992年，农村人均住房面积15.79平方米，1996年，城镇居民人均住房面积20.75平方米。2010年，农村人均住房面积44平方米。城镇居民人均住房面积39.2平方米。从房屋产权看，房改私房占43.33%，商品房占33.33%。从建筑式样看，单栋住宅占6.67%，四居室占3.33%，二居室和三居室各占36.67%，其他占10.66%。从房屋设施看，电力线、电视线、宽带线（网线）、自来水进家，有厕所、浴室的人家占63.33%。

家具：20世纪90年代初中期，家具均采用木材请木工制造，用油漆或土漆漆面，后逐渐以宝丽板代之。境内一般人家室内仅有老式木床、柜子、条凳和方桌等。90年代后期，成品家具进入县内市场，自制家具逐步减少。进入21世纪，成品家具逐渐占领家具市场，各式衣柜、装饰柜、电视柜、桌椅、沙发、席梦思床、组合式家具进入城乡家庭。部分家庭用长方桌和独凳、靠椅取代传统的四方桌和长条凳。

家用电器：20世纪90年代初，城镇居民大部分家庭拥有黑白电视机，少数经济条件好的家庭购买彩电。90年代中后期，城镇家庭逐步换上彩电并配置音响设备，取代黑白电视机、收音机、电唱机。电冰箱、洗衣机、电饭煲、电磁炉、饮水机、微波炉、电烤箱等陆续进入城镇家庭。21世纪初，全县实现村村通广播电视、电话。城镇居民家用电器更新升级，洗衣机由单缸至双缸到全自动；电视机由黑白到彩电到液晶彩电或超薄大屏幕彩电；电冰箱由单门到双门；城镇居民普遍使用电饭煲、电高压锅、电炒锅、电热水器，取暖多用电暖炉取代回风炉（烧煤）。部分单位和少数人家安装空调。照相机、摄像机逐渐进入城镇家庭。农村居民使用电器及更新时间较城镇稍晚。冬春季节，农村用回风炉烧煤取暖较为普遍；全县农村电网改造后，农村居民多用电饭锅煮饭、电磁炉炒菜，用电能取暖约占10%。

燃料：20世纪90年代初，境内以煤作主要燃料，有本县自产煤、金沙煤、六广煤和黔西煤等。夏秋季节用土灶煮饭，冬春用回风炉煮饭、取暖。为减少环境污染，1996年，要求县城饭店、小吃店使用液化石油气（简称液化气），部分居民亦开始使用液化气。2006年，全县有液化气用户7100户。后因成本较高，除饭店、小吃店继续使用液化气外，居民用户减少。2010年，居民液化气用户3200户；电能用户城镇约占50%，乡村约占10%左右。

电话：20世纪90年代初，电话还只是办公设备，并经历从手摇电话到数字电话、程控电话的转变。传呼机、“大哥大”（移动电话）一度是有钱人和社会地位的象征。1996年，县政府给机关科级以上干部安装家庭电话（座机）、配传呼机，此后电话、传呼机逐步进入家庭。2000年后，开始使用移动电话。至2010年，手机逐渐进入寻常百姓家。

四、出行

20世纪90年代初，道路多土石路面，交通工具少，居民出行，乘车困难，多为步行。随着经济发展，公路建设加快，实现乡乡通油路，村村通硬化路。客运车辆逐渐增多，私人有轿车，农村50%的农户拥有摩托车。至2010年，居民出行，多乘客车或自己驾车。

客车：1991年，县内有息烽至贵阳客运班线1条、区乡客运班线4条，日发班车12班，居民出行主要靠步行。1996年9月，县城开始有公交车营运。1999年，全县村村通公路，农村客运线路增至8条。农村摩托车逐年增加，成为农户短途出行的重要交通工具。2003年，县城有出租轿车营运。2008年，县内有息烽至贵阳、开阳、修文、遵义市、遵义县客运班线5条，日发车70班次。10个乡镇全部通客车，有农村客运班线29条，日发车435班次。2010年，全县有客运班线43条，其中市际客运班线3条、县际16条、县内24条；县城有公交车线路4条，出租车50辆。

火车：1991—1999年，火车在川黔铁路县境段年发送旅客200多万人次，2000年最高，达350万人次。川黔铁路电气化改造工程竣工后，列车经多次提速，川黔铁路县境段仅停靠息烽站，短途旅客改乘公路客车，县境段铁路旅客发送量减少，2010年，发送旅客130万人次。

客船：乌江库区蓄水后，县域干流、支流航道总长62千米。境内有客船营运，年客运量由1991年的6.6万人次增至2010年的24万人次。

居民出门办事、探亲访友，陆路乘客车、火车、骑摩托车，水路坐客船都十分方便。农户赶集往返，多乘坐客车或摩托车，少数农民赶集后乘出租车回家。

五、其他

办公设备：20世纪80年代末，县城首家（郑舟成开办）复印部开业。1990年，县政府办公室开始使用电脑。20世纪90年代中期，县组织培训机关事业单位50岁以下干部职工学习电脑操作技术，各单位开始配备电脑。90年代末，电脑开始进入县城居民家庭。进入21世纪，机关事业单位拥有电脑数量由每单位1台到一科室1台甚至多台，配上打印机、复印机、传真机，办公方便快捷。随着电脑、打印机、复印机的使用，中文打字机和油印机退出历史舞台。

宠物：20世纪90年代中后期，猫、犬作为宠物进入城镇居民家中。猫的品种不多，犬的品种较多，大型的有狼狗、牧羊犬、沙皮犬、松狮犬、昆明犬、虎头犬及藏獒；小型的有北京狮子狗、腊肠犬、博美、吉娃娃、蝴蝶犬、金巴狗等。境内宠物犬野交乱配居多，故出现许多叫不出品种名称的小型犬。农村亦有农户饲养宠物犬。

纸巾：20世纪90年代初，县内居民多用手帕做面部卫生用具，书报废纸、草纸作卫生纸。90年代中期，城镇开始使用纸巾。县内居民使用纸巾主要有卫生纸和餐巾纸。至2010年，卫生纸取代书报废纸和草纸，纸巾取代手帕，成为人们生活中必不可少的卫生用品。

此外，农村杀年猪，有请邻居吃“刨汤”习俗。农村个别60岁以上老年人仍有吸土烟（旱烟）习惯。

第二章　民　俗

随着社会进步，县内民族习俗发生改变。除苗族还保留部分独特习俗外，其他少数民族习俗逐渐趋同汉族。县委、县政府把精神文明建设与物质文明建设提到同等地位，境内社会风尚朝着健康、文明方向发展。

第一节　传统节日

一、除夕·春节

又称“过年”，以每年农历腊月末日至次年正月初三为节。进入腊月，农村各户要打糍粑、二块粑，煮甜酒、办过年货。腊月二十三日，每家要烧香烛纸钱敬灶，送灶神菩萨上天；供糍粑寓意塞灶神菩萨之口，免其上天后在玉皇大帝那里说主家坏话。腊月二十四日，每家要在屋内外打扫卫生，叫“打扬尘”，作好过年准备。多数农户杀年猪，杀年猪时要在猪圈门口烧香、点烛、烧纸钱，杀猪后拿几张纸钱蘸点猪血，将纸钱烧在主家大门前，表示敬天地，来年养猪顺利。贴春联，贴门神，有的大门前、阁楼处挂红灯笼。吃年晚饭，摆好丰盛酒菜，家庭主要成员在神龛（香火）上点香点烛，龛下烧纸，献酒献饭，放鞭炮，祭祖后，全家人入席，吃团年饭。饭后，由长辈向小孩发压岁钱。20世纪90年代初，每小孩发压岁钱5～10元，家庭经济条件好的发10～20元；90年代后期发12～120元；此期间，农户挂彩灯、放烟花、鞭炮数量较少，大部分人家一般购买10～50元的鞭炮，菜肴以猪肉为主。进入21世纪，每小孩发压岁钱50～100元，经济条件好的发200～1000元，甚至有更多者。菜肴渐臻丰富，肉食、各种饮料、水果、糖果普及。挂彩灯的人家较多。烟花、鞭炮消费数量较大，除禁放鞭炮区域外，多数人家少则上百元，多则上千元。20世纪90年代前，有出嫁的姑娘不能回娘家过年习俗，意为亏舅子，只有过年后才回娘家拜年。20世纪90年代后，城里人逐步打破此习俗，同城居住的子女都可回家过年。

年前，县里要召开年终总结会、表彰会和各种座谈会，向各界人士和全县人民拜年。机关单位从初一到初七放假，初八上班。为享受“黄金周”，有的选择外出旅游，有的选择到宾馆饭店订餐，过一个轻松愉快的春节。

除夕，境内人家有上“子时香”习惯，每家要在神龛上烧香、点烛、放鞭炮。直到凌晨一点，除旧迎新。

20世纪90年代，境内农村有腊月三十夜“守田坎”习惯，一般由男人蹲守，多数串户喝酒，打扑克玩通宵。还有送财神和未普及自来水的偏远村寨仍存在挑金银水习俗。进入21世纪，随着生活节奏加快，养龙司、茅坡、新场、流长一带男子睡懒觉（俗称睡老荒瓜）习惯逐渐消失。退耕还林还草、土地流转数量增多，三十夜“守田坎”逐年减少。自来水的普及，农村人家凌晨“挑金银水”习俗不复存在。除新场、流长地区还有送财神习惯外，其余地区少见。

正月初一，又称大年初一、岁首，是农历开始的第一天，农村特别重视这一天“求吉利”。早起扫地不能从家里往外面扫，只能从外面往家里扫，意为新年里不能把金银财宝扫走，应把金银财宝扫回家。清早吃汤圆，随后全家老幼备带香、烛、纸、鞭炮去祖坟山拜祖坟。正月初三，开始走亲访友，互请春酒，每家一天轮流请到正月十五。人们在春节期间喜打长牌、翻三花、打三五反、推十点半等。此后，喜打麻将、长牌、翻五张、斗地主等。

春节从初一到十五，各地玩花灯（有的叫神灯）、龙灯（花夹龙），农户接灯、开财门，有的捆猪（即杀猪）还灯愿。花灯由民间灯会自发组织，初一出灯，十五收灯。20世纪90年代前，晚上到居民家中玩灯，90年代起，从初八上班起到机关单位玩灯。初十由县里组织玩龙灯，各家龙灯齐聚县城共贺新春。正月初二，县文化馆组织猜灯谜、对对子活动。

二、元宵节

民间称“过大年”。境内居民多以正月十四日为元宵节、少数以正月十三日为元宵节，条件较好人家一般在当日晚上燃放烟花爆竹，增加喜庆气氛。20世纪90年代后期，县里每年正月十五晚九时在体育场燃放烟花，气氛仅次于春节。境内有俗语：“三十夜的火，十四夜的灯。”正月十四、十五日晚，农村家家户户到亲人坟前，焚烧冥钞，燃亮香烛，谓之“亮灯”。进入21世纪，随着电视、网络的普及，玩灯闹“元宵”习俗逐渐减少。县未再组织燃放烟花。

三、清明节

清明是传统祭祀节日，分公祭、私祭。公祭：每年清明节前或当天，县里组织机关单位职工、各界人士和中小学生扫墓，祭奠革命先烈，进行革命传统教育。进入21世纪，在烈士墓前举行入党、入团或加入少先队仪式。私祭：男女老幼到坟山为先祖扫墓、挂青（以白纸制作冥钱，挂在亲人的坟上，意为挂念亲人，表示坟主后继有人）、清扫坟地、为坟培土。若是姑娘挂青，青上系红带，孙辈挂青系黄带。扫墓挂青时间有清明前十天、后十天之说。少数居民采摘清明草打清明粑。清明节期间，农村常聚集同姓家族，修家谱、订族规、同吃清明酒，称“清明会”。20世纪90年代，偶有家族沿袭此俗。2008年起，政府将清明节定为法定节假日。各地家族集中办清明会逐年增多。在祖坟前举行扫墓仪式，护坟垒坟。清明会上，由族长及家族中德高望重的长辈或族人讲话，教育族人遵纪守法，善待父母、子女，尊师重教，和睦相处，清白传家；重视文化和科学，教育子女好好读书，努力工作；廉洁自律，勤劳致富，自觉拒毒拒赌，抵制不良行为。

四、端午节

农历五月初五日，俗称端阳，相传此日百草皆是药。家家户户在房屋门窗上挂菖蒲、艾叶，并取艾叶戴在衣扣间，以此辟邪。有将菖蒲、艾叶扎成狗状，称艾狗，挂在大门口或房前墙上。或将艾枝扎成“天虎”悬挂于大门前上端，大门两侧挂菖蒲为剑，并用红纸书写“端阳五月五，天师骑天虎；手提菖蒲剑，扫邪归地府”。早上吃粽子，中午用雄黄磨酒饮用，搽皮肤以防蚊虫蚂蚁叮咬；有的将雄黄酒或大蒜水洒房前屋后，避免蛇虫接近。傍晚，部分人结伴散步，称“游百病”，意将病患游掉。过了五月初五，还过五月十五，称“大端阳”。民间有“有心过端午，六月不嫌迟”之说。进入21世纪，此种习俗逐渐减少。20世纪90年代前，汉族有接已出嫁女儿和女婿回家过端午节习俗，此后逐渐淡化，但仍沿袭未婚女婿到女方家送节习俗。

五、中元节

又称“月半”，亦称“鬼节”。境内居民农历七月十三日为节（少数居民以农历七月十四日为节），民间有晚辈接逝世长辈过月半习俗。重在祭祀，意在记住逝去的亲人，安慰在世老人。节前备办冥钱，用白纸裱糊为包袱，称为“袱纸”。袱纸正面书写已逝亲人的称谓、姓名及敬奉者姓名，背面写“封号”二字。节日晚，以菜肴饭食置于神龛前的方桌上，将备好的袱纸按家袱、客袱分长晚辈依次堆放在桌前的地上焚化，意为寄钱给已故亲人，让他们在阴间“有钱花”。有的地区有小孩玩香瓜习俗，用瓜或茄子插上香，成群结队地串寨。进入21世纪，焚烧袱纸人家仍然普遍。有的还烧冥币和纸做的“电视机”“电冰箱”“小汽车”等，让逝去的亲人成为“有钱人”，享受“现代化”。烧纸的地点，农村在堂屋或院内，城镇因为是楼房和单元房，居民只得到街道两旁和小区内进行。

六、中秋节

以农历八月十五日为节，有吃月饼、全家团聚赏月吃团圆饭的习俗。青山苗族地区多数苗族人家于此日杀鸡做菜肴，接女儿、女婿过节。

七、其他节日

重阳节：20世纪90年代初，县内农村尚保留重阳节打糍粑习俗，有“重阳不打粑，豺狗咬你妈”之说。90年代中后期，此习俗逐渐淡化以至消失。2008年，重阳节成为国定老年节。此后，县委、政府每年于此日组织慰问老干部和老年人。

跳花厂：又称跳花场，俗称跳厂。青山苗族乡花厂位于青山村核桃坝。中华人民共和国成立后，县内未再跳花厂。20世纪90年代，周边县、区举办花厂节，有“二月二”“二月八”“三月三”。青山、安马等地苗族青年多去乌当区落湾、石头寨，修文县洒坪等地参加。2007年，青山苗族乡举办“四月八”活动。至此，在原址恢复跳花厂。

二月二：县内民间有二月二“龙抬头”说法，有给小孩剃头的习俗。

三月三：农村叫“蚕子会”，又称嚼蚕子，有农民炒苞谷花吃，有的将苞谷花拿到土里，烧香、点烛、烧纸，边吃苞谷花边说“嚼死土蚕子”。进入21世纪，此种习俗减少。

四月八：苗族祖先祭日。1995年，青山苗族乡首次举办“四月八”活动，有芦笙舞、苗族舞、唱苗歌、斗画眉等内容，3000余人观看。后中断数年，其间青山、西山、梨安等地苗族青年男女，背上自己绣制的服饰去贵阳、乌当、花溪、开阳、修文等地参加“四月八”活动。2007—2010年，县、乡政府主持，民间协办，每年在青山苗族乡举办“四月八”活动。节日期间，有苗族舞、芦笙舞、斗鸡、斗画眉、牛王争霸赛、跳花场等。周边贵阳市区、乌当、花溪、修文、开阳、清镇、黔西苗族舞技人员参加，每年有3000~5000人共度“四月八”。

六月六：境内有六月六晒衣服习俗，将存放已久的衣物、被褥搬到屋外晾晒。

牛王节：农历十月初一牛王节，20世纪90年代前，农家有打糍粑犒劳耕牛习俗，将糍粑捏在两只牛角上，有的还在牛头上插上花，然后牵牛去吃水。据说牛看见水中的倒影，会开心地发笑。之后将糍粑喂牛，以奖赏其一年的辛劳。此俗今已不存。

20世纪末，城镇有少数年轻人学西方过情人节、圣诞节、母亲节和父亲节。

第二节　婚丧习俗

一、汉族婚姻习俗

自息烽建县，境内讲究同姓不开亲（联姻），注重门当户对，遵循父母之命、媒妁之言，形成“三回九转”婚姻俗定形式。三回即头道茶（问亲）、二道茶素茶（提亲）、三道茶烧香（订婚）（又有一说是开庚）；九转即提亲、相亲、回话、提茶、烧香（订婚）、开庚、送期、过礼、结婚。进入21世纪，城乡青年男女利用进厂打工、社会交往、走亲访友，自由恋爱。婚姻习俗有所简化。老年男女丧偶或离婚者，也可再婚，受到社会理解和法律保护。

（一）汉族婚姻

20世纪90年代前，农村婚姻还带有父母之命、媒妁之言，但男女自由恋爱开始增多。男方看中女方或双方自愿，都要由男方请媒人备上礼品到女方家提亲，俗称“头道茶”，也称“口信茶”。第二次向女方家提亲称“二道茶”，也称“素茶”，定亲。三道茶烧香（订婚）。提亲时衣服鞋袜、糖食果品等礼品须是双数，且逐次增多。三道茶后，男方家根据女方家提供的女方生辰八字，选择结婚吉日，列成期单送到女方家，称“送期”。之后，双方筹备婚事，“制嫁妆”。婚前二日，男方家送猪肉到女方家，以备筵席。婚前一日，女方家操办筵席，亲朋好友馈赠礼品或礼金祝贺，“准新娘”以布帕遮面哭嫁；男方家带彩礼、花轿，雇请吹鼓手一行数人到女方家接亲，亦称“过礼”。结婚日，“准新娘”离家前在神龛前哭别亲人，也叫“辞祖”。亲人以言或以礼金祝福。“准新娘”迈出堂屋大门哭毕，不能回头，由女方家送亲客送行，随男方家接亲人前往男方家。男方家张贴对联、燃放爆竹迎接新娘。“进亲”时，新郎为新娘戴花、行礼，带至堂屋，分男左女右，在神龛前举行结婚仪式，称“拜堂”。由一个威望高、能说会道的人，主持行口令，举行拜堂仪式，称“进亲拜堂”，礼毕后，新郎新娘双双进入洞房。入洞房前，先由一对儿女双全的老龄夫妇为其铺床，新郎新娘进入洞房后为“结纳”并喝“交杯酒”。晚上同辈的亲朋好友聚在洞房，为新娘出难题，说调皮话，让新娘出窘，称为“闹新房”。婚后三日晨，新媳妇用压箱米煮饭并亲自下厨，饭后，新婚夫妇带礼品回女方家拜望岳父岳母，称作“回门”。

随着改革开放，社会经济不断发展，婚姻习俗发生较大变化。

相亲：20世纪90年代，男方请媒到女方家提亲，女方家人没有意见，由媒人约定时间双方相亲，叫“取同意”，由男方打发女方现金，又叫“见面礼”，少则1200元，多则2000元，随后订婚（烧香）、开庚、送期等。进入21世纪，相亲程序基本没少，打发女方的钱数目增多，一般不搞三回九转，烧香、送期、完婚一起完成。出嫁女子不再哭嫁。压箱米改用葵花、花生、糖果。辞祖、送亲、进亲、交亲、谢厨、回门习俗仍然保留。80后、90后青年男女虽自由恋爱，婚前仍然要找一亲朋或同事当媒人，以便保全女方面子，商谈婚礼条件，协调双方事务和彩礼见证。

彩礼：20世纪90年代初，订婚、烧香由男方家为女方家送去衣料4～8套，4～6色水礼（糖、水果、酒、点心等）。90年代中后期，多将订婚、烧香衣料折算为钱，叫礼金，从几千元增加到上万元。进入21世纪，彩礼一般几万元，多的高达十几万元。礼金多由女方家用于买家具，结婚时送去男方家作嫁妆。过礼仍照旧，由男方家在女方家办酒前一天送猪肉半边到女方家。

20世纪90年代末至21世纪初，小寨坝、王家坪、潮水等地彩礼1.8万～2.8万元之间，流长、新场等地1.2万～2万元之间。2010年，小寨坝、王家坪、潮水等地彩礼升至3.8万～4.8万元，流长、新场等地升至3万～4万元，最高8万～10万元。

嫁妆：20世纪90年代初，大部分由女方家制嫁妆，多为床、桌凳、碗柜、三开柜、写字台，由女方家请木工加工。20世纪90年代中后期，男女双方约定，如男方买家具，女方买家用电器、床上用品、炊事用具等。进入21世纪，嫁妆由过去的木制品向现代家用电器转变，电视机、洗衣机、电风扇、息烽回风炉等相继进入嫁妆行列。富裕家庭还有摩托车、小汽车。多为女方买，男方家多送几万元彩礼。

接亲：20世纪90年代初，接亲多为步行。随着交通条件改善，开始包客车或借面包车、吉普车接亲，货车拉家具。进入21世纪，用小轿车接亲。2005年后，小轿车接亲成为风尚，从2辆增加到20多辆，均要双数。新娘子坐的小车要用花进行装饰，称“花车”。2008年，在县城和城乡接合部，出现新郎拉板车、铁斗车接新娘，新郎脱光衣服，全身画花，戴上草帽，胸前挂旧皮鞋，用板车拉着新娘游街，或将新郎脸涂花，往新郎身上砸鸡蛋，把新郎裤子撕烂，并在新郎胸前挂脏牌取乐等恶俗现象。

结婚：20世纪90年代，男女双方婚配，多数要择属相相配。结婚时要用男女双方“八字”择期，如用节日结婚也要看节日期是否吉利。多数结婚由男方家请一名押礼先生领队，用唢呐锣鼓，吹吹打打，将新娘从女方家接到男方家。城镇青年人结婚出现婚纱照、摄影。进入21世纪，城乡有买鲜花，请大型乐队、腰鼓队进行婚庆的现象。结婚时拜堂，请当地夫妻健在、儿女双全、福好命好的老人“牵亲”（拜堂前将新郎新娘牵入堂屋和拜堂后将新郎新娘牵入洞房），司仪喊礼，新郎、新娘在堂中拜天地、祖宗、父母，新郎父母要备红包打发新娘改口叫爸爸妈妈。请福好命好的女人铺新床，床上放枣、花生、桂圆、桐子各数枚（寓意早生贵子）。新郎新娘入洞房要喝交杯酒。城乡青年男女婚前多拍摄婚纱照，结婚时请摄影师进行婚礼全程摄制，制成光碟，以作永久纪念。若男女双方婚前同居或女方怀有小孩，就不拜堂（俗称“四眼人”不能拜堂，否则不吉利），由新郎引新娘进新房即可。闹新房习俗逐渐减少，至2010年基本不闹新房。婚事大操大办之风盛行，互相攀比，宴席价格由百余元一桌升至三四百元，规模由10桌增加到20桌乃至更多。

婚姻观念：20世纪90年代，部分年轻人实行晚婚晚育，大龄男女增多。到21世纪，大部分年轻人实行晚婚晚育，未婚同居、未婚先孕、未婚生育现象增多。城镇离婚率增高，农村离婚率较低。再婚自由，社会舆论减少。老年人再婚不再受社会舆论指责，城镇儿女支持父或母再婚的较多，少数子女主动为自己父或母找老伴。农村反对的较多。

（二）汉族丧葬习俗

20世纪90年代，人临终时，穿上老衣，将其抬至堂屋神龛前，守候人候其死去，称“送终”。人死后，烧三斤六两纸钱，谓之“落气钱”，并鸣放爆竹报丧。装棺入殓时，死者所穿衣服套数必须是奇数；若父母在世，死者穿孝衣入殓。入殓完毕，灵柩按男左女右规矩停放堂屋（温泉地区停放左边）。脚下点一盏菜油灯，叫“过桥灯”（在医院死亡、非正常死亡或小孩死亡，忌讳停放堂屋）。随后以白皮纸打成冥钱（按死者一岁一束，每十岁加一束制作），悬挂于长竹竿一端，插在房前或院子边，称为“望山钱”。在农村，孝子披麻戴孝，请一人（知客司）带领，到寨邻各家门前（孝子不能进门）逐一磕头请人帮忙，被请人家必到，未请到的人家则可不去。远亲则派人或电话通知。21世纪初，已有少数地区改变这一习俗。

请道士设灵堂做道场，做5～7天道场居多，也有做3天、9天甚至11天的。晚上通宵守灵，道士为死者超度亡魂。下葬前一天，亡者女家和亲友下祭，亡者女家做灵房、金童玉女、祭马，有的下猪羊祭，有唢呐锣鼓吹打前来祭祀，亲友用6尺白布或床单、被面等来祭祀（祭幛）。

出殡时棺木上面放一只公鸡“踩丧”。罩上丧罩，八人抬丧，一人撒纸钱（称买路钱）。孝子行前，送葬队伍随后。边走边放炮仗。抬丧的边走边高喊“起”，表示孝家“起”得快，发得快。抬丧过沟、过桥时孝子要卧在地上，让抬丧的抬棺木跨过，表示背老人过沟过河。

下葬前，孝家请“阴阳”择好地，在葬地先烧香、烛、纸钱，动土挖井（葬坑），井内撒上朱砂、硫黄、白酒，用“踩丧”鸡放在井里，称“雄鸡跳井”。鸡要鸣叫，表示孝家吉利，鸡若不鸣叫，道士要设法使其鸣叫，然后将鸡捉起后下葬。接着帮忙的寨邻砌好坟。孝子回家时，要从来路回家，不能走近路，孝子女性每人要捡一把树枝回家，称“抱柴（财）归家”。送火烟包（用稻草扎成的长条状物，按死者每一岁扎一圈制作）：下葬当晚，孝子送火烟包，一头点燃，放坟上，第二天晚上送至半路，第三天晚上送至寨前。第七日，为死者烧冥钱，连续七次，称“化七”或“烧七”。招山：即给死者“买地”，要烧香、纸钱、烛，在坟东、南、西、北、中挖坑，用鸡蛋、石灰划界。

进入21世纪，葬期多为三天，称急葬，请道士开路，绕棺过“殿”。2001年6月1日起，全县推行遗体火化，县城设殡仪馆，统一到殡仪馆祭奠，骨灰入公墓，占地不得超过1平方米。2004年4月，设在永靖镇管田村宝山的庆云山殡仪馆火化车间投入使用，县内遗体不再运往久长或贵阳火化。2007年6月，全县各乡镇以村为单位，每村建一座公益性墓地，取消大棺材和垒大坟，下葬占地不超过1平方米。对不入公墓的强制进入公墓地。至2010年，火化率、骨灰入公墓率100%。尸体火化后，装入骨灰盒或小棺木入土安葬。下葬习俗基本未变，用毛石或成形石垒砌坟茔，家庭条件好的镶以墓碑。祭祀多将祭幛改为花圈下祭。

二、少数民族婚丧习俗

2010年，全县除汉族外，少数民族有28个，16006人，占全县总人口的5.3%。其中苗族11367人，占全县少数民族人口的71%；布依族3568人，占少数民族人口的22.3%；彝族939人，占少数民族人口的5.1%；其他少数民族132人，占少数民族人口的0.8%。

苗族、布依族、彝族是较早的世居少数民族，呈大散居、小聚居分布；其他25个少数民族是1949年后，或因部队转业、工作分配，学校毕业分配、婚姻，或随“三线”建设而到息烽，且多分布在机关、厂矿、企事业等单位。

布依族、彝族大多数已不会讲本民族语言，婚丧习俗基本与汉族相同；布依族仍保留亡人入殓后在棺后放一碗米饭（称“倒头饭”）习俗。其他少数民族人数较少，且多分布在机关、厂矿、企事业单位，其婚丧习俗基本与汉族相同。

苗族还保留较多婚丧习俗。县境苗族，按语音分类法，分为川黔滇方言一土语苗族（大花族）、二土语苗族（小花族）、三土语苗族（川苗族）、贵阳次方言苗族（青苗族）和落伯河次方言苗族5个族群。青苗族人数占苗族总人数2/3以上。各个族群的婚丧习俗大同小异。

（一）苗族婚姻习俗

提亲：男女双方通过跳厂，玩“四月八”等社交活动，男方看中女方，由男方家请一媒人带一壶酒，两升大米或苞谷、黄豆（称“一壶两升”），去女方家提亲。女方家长一般不作答复，由女方家伯叔陪媒人吃饭喝酒答复。媒人得同意口信后，去神龛下磕头感谢，表示提亲成功。

玩月亮：取得同意后，男方家择吉日，请一男青年作陪郎，请两位芦笙师带领新郎和陪郎，吹着芦笙去女方家，在天黑后到达。进屋后，主人接过芦笙放好，由芦笙师用苗话指导新郎、陪郎在神龛前磕头，再给女方祖父母、父母磕头。主人安排客人吃宵夜后休息。

劝亲：次日，芦笙师请女方伯、叔劝亲，说：“亲戚们，某家托我带某某来认爹、认娘。”女方伯、叔说：“我家一斗米只赶一场，没有哪样说的。”芦笙师指导新郎、陪郎给岳父母、伯、叔磕头，早饭后告辞，主人发还芦笙送出大门。

踩门：又叫送期，男方家请媒人背“一壶两升”去女方家送期，女方家接期后，各自准备办酒结婚。

过礼：女方家办酒头一天，男方家请人背“猪把腿”（带猪尾后脚半截猪肉）约50斤去女方家过礼。

接亲：女方家办正酒的日子，男方家请人挑“一壶两升”，原吹芦笙人员和新郎、陪郎一道，天黑去新娘家。进门后，新郎、陪郎在神龛下，向祖宗、岳父母、舅父母、姑父母、姨父母、伯、叔父母磕头完毕，由知客师安排宵夜后休息。

次日早饭后发亲，新郎、陪郎在神龛下磕头后，主持人向芦笙师敬酒，发还芦笙。芦笙师怀抱芦笙，行45度鞠躬礼，吹芦笙出门上路，新郎随后，新娘、陪娘来到堂屋中央，由新娘弟弟撑开红油纸伞递给新娘和陪娘，出阁上路。舅、姑、姨父母带头走前（称三步客、主送亲）。随后送亲人依次形成送亲队伍，少则50～60人，多则100多人。陪郎背新娘服饰走在送亲队伍后面。

穿礼服：快到男方家时，送亲队伍停下，由新娘伯、叔母给新娘穿绣制的新衣裙、金银头饰，陪娘打扮和新娘一样。

挂红：趁新娘穿衣打扮之机，新郎回家接受亲友们挂红，每挂一段红，新郎要叩头答谢、敬酒。

进亲：新郎披红去新娘穿衣处，并带一段红亲手拴在新娘右臂上，接新娘进家。来到新郎家大门口，两位未婚女青年接过新娘、陪娘进入新房，随后送亲男、女各进客房。

进亲后，新娘、陪娘随送亲女客同宿，不与新郎同宿，送亲队伍在新郎家住1～3天。新郎家办完回门酒，新娘、陪娘随送亲队伍返回娘家。有的新娘在娘家居住一年才去新郎家坐家；有的三天后由新郎接回住几天又回娘家，新郎再接，两家常来常往，新娘怀上小孩才坐家。

20世纪90代初，苗族还有较多人家沿袭上述习俗。90年代中后期，改变婚姻习俗人家逐渐增多。至2010年，除少数人家仍保留上述习俗外，大多数苗族人家与汉族一样，婚姻自主，相识请媒，纳彩结婚，婚后坐家。

境内花苗族办喜事必须请舅爷、姑爷、姨爹；青苗族红白喜事必须先请“三步客”，即舅公、姑公、姨公。

各语系苗族婚姻习俗简介：

一土语苗族：说媒—送期—结婚（接亲—送亲—吃晌午—穿衣打扮回—车马—迎风接驾—认亲）

二土语、三土语苗族：提亲—吃定桩酒—结婚（交彩礼—迎风—发亲—送

亲—吃晌午—进亲—交亲—改老名）—回门—坐家。

贵阳次方言苗族：提亲—吹芦笙（玩月亮）—劝亲—踩门—结婚（过礼—接亲—穿衣—挂红—进亲）—回门—坐家。

落伯河次方言苗族；提亲—烧香—结婚（交彩礼—发亲有哭嫁情节—拍灰—穿衣—回车马—踩堂—扫地担水—认亲）—回门—坐家。

（二）苗族丧葬习俗

苗族老人死后入棺，棺木横放堂屋中央，男人头向东方，女人头向西方。由苗族鬼师用苗语超度亡人。所有亡者不论老辈小辈依次超度，用亡者老名（苗名）祭祀。一、二、三土语苗族在堂屋中央吊一大鼓，由鬼师用苗语唱祀，边打鼓，边吹芦笙，围鼓转圈。青山一带苗族从20世纪80年代开始开孝。苗族丧葬中有用纸做“望山钱”者，有不用“望山钱”者，最特别的是将鸡皮拴在竹竿上做“望山钱”。下葬头天，亲友下祭，又叫献亡。祭礼有猪羊鸡，不论大小，一、二、三土语苗族用绳拴一只脚，绳拉至棺木上，由鬼师用苗语念经做法术交给死人。次日出殡下葬。丧葬后续祭祀活动有“对场十三”“对月”“百期”“周年”等。20世纪末，为减少亲友往返，有人家将后续活动在下葬后一次做完；至2010年，只有少数人家后续活动仍分开举行。另外，有的人家请鬼师祭祀后又请道士做道场。有的宗族如小寨坝落伯河次方言苗族和汉族一样，请道士做道场。

境内花苗族丧事必请“四步客”，即舅爷姑爹、寨老、小叔、掌坛师；若死者是已婚男性，请姑爹坐首位，若是女性，请舅爷坐首位。

苗族丧葬祭祀活动由鬼师主持，一个宗族有一位鬼师（掌坛师）和2～3名助手，鬼师要熟悉本宗族的丧葬规矩和本宗族的人际范围。青山苗族乡王姓家族鬼师由族人推选有能力的人进行

培养；其他宗族多由爱好者提“一壶两升”拜师学艺，由鬼师口口相传。苗族鬼师无偿为族人办丧事。至2010年，因30岁左右的年轻人多不会本民族语言，加之做鬼师无报酬，其传承已后继乏人。

第三节 家庭与礼尚往来

一、家庭

1991—2010年，境内家庭一般以男人为一家之主，沿袭“男主外，女主内”习俗。少有三代同堂、四代同堂家庭。多子女家庭，儿子成家后便陆续分家另居，父母独居或跟其中一家同住，一般跟幼子。在外工作的子女，即使不分家也是另居。家庭小型化（3～4人）已成趋势。祖辈带孙子成为普遍现象。

二、生养习俗

20世纪90年代，农村多子女家庭较多。父母给儿子完婚后，将自己部分房产分给儿子、儿媳居住，待生小孩、办满月酒后才分家的较多。计划生育政策实施后，若育龄夫妇第一胎是男孩，多数家庭不再多生；若连续两胎都是女孩，部分育龄夫妇为生男孩，外出躲藏生子，有的连续生三四个女孩，少数人直到生男孩后方才停止生育。城镇有工作的，为保工作，大多数育龄夫妇都只生一个小孩，也有极少数人超生和隐瞒偷生现象。城乡孕妇均自然顺产，剖宫产比例20%左右。产后男方家拿12个红蛋和1只鸡去女方娘家报喜，生男孩送公鸡，生女孩送母鸡。约定“打三朝”（男方家办“月米酒”）时间。一般是小孩出生后十天半月由女方娘家邀约青老年妇女到女婿家坐玩三天。接喜讯后，女方娘家要向亲友发红蛋，请吃月米酒。并备大米、鸡蛋、婴儿大小衣物、背扇等到产妇家；亲友们多数送钱，进行庆贺。女方亲友返回时，男方给每人用手巾或毛巾包上葵花、花生、糖果和两个红鸡蛋，以示感谢。婴儿满月后外出，均用背扇将婴儿背在背上。

进入21世纪，结婚后即行分家趋势上升，夫妻二人外出打工增多，孩子留家由祖辈代养。部分青年夫妻将孩子接到打工地就读，只留父母在家，这两种现象较为普遍。农村青年人超生现象逐渐减少，部分育龄夫妇连生两个女孩后自愿不再多生，城镇有工作的育龄夫妇超生和隐藏偷生现象得到控制。孕妇难产、怕痛、择期要求剖腹产现象增多，剖宫产比例曾高达60%，经县卫生部门加强管理，降至40%左右。孩子出生后，男方仍沿旧习去女方娘家报喜，发红蛋，约定办满月酒时间。女方娘家仍要送小孩衣物和钱，但不再送大米和鸡蛋。女方亲友吃酒后当天回家，不再住玩三天。城乡普遍大办满月酒。婴儿满月后外出，受外地人的影响，部分人将婴儿背在胸前。

坐月子：妇女产后静居卧床调养，时间通常为一个月，俗称“坐月子”。产妇要吃甜酒鸡蛋，喝鸡汤，以激发奶水和补充营养。传统习俗产妇禁忌颇多，不能吃生冷食物，菜肴盐味要很淡，不能吃花椒、葱蒜：不能摸冷水，不能洗头洗澡等；天气再热，头上都要包帕子或戴帽，卧房门窗关闭，不能扇扇子或吹风，不能哭泣。在此期间，严禁孕妇、戴孝者及其他人进入产妇卧房。进入21世纪，随着社会发展和科学知识普及，产妇禁忌逐渐减少。

三、生日寿庆

县内居民生日多以农历为准。通常年长者除寿庆、幼儿除周岁外，其他年岁的生日纪念都比较平淡，俗称“过生日”。婴幼儿做生，除满周岁要请客送礼外，平时做生（叫“长尾巴”）。给小孩宴请做生日的少见，大多为家庭宴，备办一个生日蛋糕，家人庆祝。年轻人过生日亦较普遍，特别是初、高中学生，三五成群进餐馆过生日。

给老年人过生日，叫“做生”，境内一般年纪上60岁者才做生。此后，每逢进“十”岁之年，子孙即要为其祝寿庆贺。

20世纪90年代，给60岁以上老人祝寿，邀请亲友乡邻前来祝贺，大摆宴席，收受贺礼或现金。小辈为老人上寿，写祝辞、写寿联、办酒席。小孩、年轻人过生日极少。进入21世纪，城乡普遍给老人祝寿，大办酒席。一般要备办“寿碗”，凡前来祝寿的亲友乡邻，均发给“寿碗”一个，意为赶寿。为百岁老人做寿时，场面更为隆重。

四、乔迁、升学、当兵

（一）乔迁

20世纪90年代初，搬家须择良辰吉日，时间一般定在天亮之前，寓意越搬越亮。城乡搬家主要以帮忙打火炮（放鞭炮）冲喜为主，不宴请，不收礼金。后多数人家建房或买新房都要择期乔迁，搬家前要进“水火”，由主人做一甑大米饭背着进新居，意为迁居后反正都有吃。带香、烛、纸钱、水、火夜间进新房，随后搬入家具。进完水火，多数人家办酒席，称“烧锅底”，亲友们在新房前用上等花布或床单、被套挂彩，贴对联，请唢呐锣鼓吹打庆贺。有的地区女主人娘家礼物较多，锅、瓢、碗、碟等炊具全套送齐，有的用一器皿盛上米或汤圆12个，在上面放12枚硬币，意为一年四季招财进宝。客人们或送锅瓢碗筷等炊具，或送礼金。进入21世纪，乔迁除上述习俗外，有的亲友请乐队，花灯、龙灯来开财门等，表示庆贺。办酒席少则十几桌，多则几十桌。

（二）升学

20世纪90年代，学子考上大中专学校，亲友们适当送点钱给考生，支持其上学就读。进入21世纪，城乡大家小户，无论子女考上任何学校，皆大肆操办酒席，收取礼金礼品，一时间形成不良风气。

（三）当兵

20世纪90年代，青年当兵服兵役，送兵头一天晚上，乡村干部和亲友们陪当兵青年过夜，其间亲友给当兵青年适当送纪念品，第二天一早，由全村村民吹唢呐，打起锣鼓，给应征青年戴上大红花，少则几十人，多则100多人将应征青年送往乡镇，由乡镇集中送县。进入21世纪，凡服兵役当兵都办酒席，由当兵家属办酒席请客，摆桌收礼。

涉及礼尚往来的有婚礼、葬礼、乔迁、寿诞、月米、升学、当兵；二婚、三婚，新建住房或房屋加层、钉门（安装大门）甚至粉刷旧房，三朝、满月、百日，考上大学或没有考上自费就读，甚至虚拟宴请。少则十几桌，多则几十桌，收礼金上万元或几万元。受请赴宴之人必不可空手，而且礼金也逐年增多。2009年，县纪委明文规定除红白喜事外，禁止乱办酒席，此风在一定程度上得以遏制。

第四节　其他习俗

一、农耕

种植：20世纪90年代初，农耕仍是牛耕锄种，铲灰积肥，打秧青，割青草垫猪，牛圈积肥。

农作物需除草2～3道（称薅苞谷、薅秧子）。由于农业科技不断普及，农耕讲究科学选种，并根据土壤结构和特性合理种植、密植、精耕细作。农业种植观念从以粮为主转变为以粮食、经济作物并重，粮食种植面积减少，蔬菜、果树种植面积增加。进入21世纪，农业机耕不断发展，使用拖拉机犁土、打田，使用插秧机、稻谷脱粒机的农户逐渐增多，小型耕整地机械进入部分农户。部分农户购置打米机、粉碎机、脱粒机、压面机、榨油机、打浆机等。至2010年，全县有小型耕整地机械2800余台，农产品加工机械3200余台。水稻、玉米、烤烟普遍使用良种，水稻实施两段育秧，玉米、烤烟种植育苗移栽。部分蔬菜、农作物用大棚种植，按配方施肥。使用除草剂除草等。科学种植已成习惯。

养殖：20世纪90年代，由于普及科学养畜，农村生饲料养猪已逐步替代传统熟饲料养猪，养越年大肥猪的农户逐渐减少，养猪大户增多。农村除饲养必要的耕牛外，饲养的肉牛增多；养禽种类增多，有肉鸡、蛋鸡、野鸡等；网箱养鱼已成规模。科学养殖渐成趋势。

二、商贸

集市贸易：集市是农村进行贸易的主要场所。届时，人们不约而同从四面八方赶来，俗称“赶场”。农民赶场主要是交易农副产品，玩耍购物者为少数。集市上人来人往，吆喝叫卖，人头攒动，热闹非凡。各类商品交易都有专门地段，如菜市、肉市、粮食、服装、五金、杂货等，牲口市多在另一地点，各就各位，约定成俗。集市上交易农副产品，计量仍以木杆秤为主，个别小商贩用电子秤；部分商品以个、碗、块、堆论价。

店铺贸易：20世纪90年代初中期，县城商铺甚少门头（店牌）。进入21世纪，几乎每个商铺都设置门头。门头由早期的灯箱布（喷绘门头），逐步发展为铝塑板、彩钢扣板，PVC雕刻门头，以及发光字门头。门头多用汉字，少数用外国品牌译音汉字，个别直接用英语、拼音做招牌，有的加注汉字。店铺都进行装修，多亮丽堂皇。许多中小成衣店铺设置橱窗，陈列服装模特。至2010年，乡镇集市街道两旁商铺亦多设置门头。

大铺小店开业时，一般都要鸣放鞭炮，此后县城因禁放鞭炮，改为张灯结彩，举行仪式，请乐队吹奏乐曲，腰鼓队打着横标沿主要街道游行，以吸引过客。此后，店铺开业沿袭此习俗。部分店铺还供奉“财神”，电子红烛长亮不灭；有的摆上一尊招财猫，以示招财进宝。商店雇用店员，付酬方式一般为底薪加销售业绩提成。店铺每天开张时，比较注重第一位顾客是否成交，认为这是当天生意好坏的预兆。进入21世纪，县城销售家具、建材（主要是装修材料）的商店多在南大街，城内多送货上门；饲料销售店铺多在花园西路一带，饲料赊销和送货上门的增多。

服务行业：20世纪90年代，城乡先后有复印店、洗衣店、歌舞厅、足疗保健、盲人按摩、农机修理、家电维修、摩托车修理、汽车修理、鲜花店、礼仪乐队等。

礼仪乐队以西洋乐器为主，为民间红白喜事、商店开业等各种庆典开展歌舞演出服务，乐队自备乐器音响，节目主要有唱歌、小品等。2009年11月，“欢天喜地婚庆礼仪策划中心”在县工商局注册登记。地址在县城东门田坝教师新村一号楼。主要业务是婚庆礼仪策划、婚礼服务；婚庆、轿子接亲、扎花车、出租婚庆设备、会议用花、寿庆、开业典礼和服务。至2010年，县内有礼仪乐队10余支，每支乐队6人左右。腰鼓队一般10～20人。

屠宰行业：1995年，县城出现畜禽宰杀小作坊，为顾客宰杀鸡、鸭、鹅、兔等，用拔毛机拔毛，液化气烧毷（rǒng）毛，取出内脏，清洗干净，并根据顾客需要砍成块状。此后增加烧洗猪皮、猪头、腊肉服务。杀猪卖肉者皆为男子。1998年，县城始有一女屠工与其丈夫共同卖肉。此后，女屠工逐渐增多，有中年妇女和年轻女子。多为夫妻屠工搭档，或为父女屠工联手。进入21世纪，乡镇也出现女屠工。男人主要负责买猪杀猪，女人负责在市场上守摊卖肉，其砍肉技术不亚于男屠工。2010年，县城农贸市场有杀鸡坊7个，猪肉市场有女屠工40余人，小寨坝集镇有女屠工20余人，流长街上有女屠工3人。

20世纪90年代初期，县内卖鱼均不破杀。此后鱼贩卖鱼，多应顾客所需为其刮鳞破杀，取出内脏，清洗干净。90年代中期，县城有人购买切肉机在农贸市场代客切肉，可切肉片、肉丝、打肉末，一般按顾客自报猪肉重量收费，每斤1角钱。进入21世纪，屠工自备切肉机，为其顾客免费切肉或打肉末。

三、建房

农村修建房屋都要选择宅基地，以主人“八字”选择坐向，修建时要选择吉日动工，要烧香、烛、纸钱敬土地菩萨和鲁班神。房子落成后要钉门。农村宅基地统称阳宅，选择视野广阔而前有向山，后有靠山之地（名曰：前看朱雀、后看玄武，左看青龙、右看白虎）。还要看靠山的来龙去脉，如靠山一层高过一层（叠起）为吉宅，预示子孙人才辈出。20世纪90年代，农村大部分修建房屋都以砖混为主，用红砖、蒸汽砖、水泥砖作墙体，外墙多无粉饰，内墙刮瓷粉，地面铺瓷砖。屋面多为平顶。进入21世纪，农村新建房屋外墙多贴瓷砖或用水泥砂浆粉糊，并安装铝合金门窗。2006年起，县内对公路铁路沿线村居民宅全面整治，将平顶屋面增盖斜顶屋面，墙体进行钢化瓷粉粉刷。

四、称谓

20世纪90年代初，境内人的称谓，一般称同志、大哥、大姐，年长者称大爷、大伯、大叔，夫妻之间叫名字，店主叫服务员，手工业者叫匠人。此后基本不称同志，多称师傅、老师；工商企业流行称老总、某工、老板；年高者称老人家，夫妻间互叫老公老婆；木匠、石匠、泥水匠称木工、石工、泥水工，剃头匠称理发师或美发师，杀猪匠称屠工，或统称师傅。机关工作人员之间多称职务，如为副职，均把“副”字去掉；带“长”字的职务，称呼时多去掉“长”字，如“某局长”，只称“某局”。

五、阳戏

流长乡（新场四坪村）保留有300多年历史的“阳戏”，因其文化底蕴深厚，古朴神秘，唱腔多变，九板十三腔尽显民间艺术神韵，堪称戏剧的“活化石”。当地部分人家每逢许愿祷告，都要请唱阳戏。2009年被省政府命名为非物质文化遗产。

六、迷信

1991—2010年，县内迷信习俗有还愿、算命、吉凶预兆、观花、信风水、画符，母畜生产后挂栏（吊淘米水瓶）等较为常见。求神治病、打醮、丢钱、挂镜、滚蛋、端水碗等少见。

许愿还愿；农村多数有许愿习俗，特别是家有不祥，如久病、没有男孩等，许下为逝去的先人垒坟、立碑，向龙灯会进宝等诺言，如果得偿所愿，必须一一兑现，否则神会降灾。特别是进龙宝生儿子，取名“龙宝”，并杀肥猪，请龙灯会到家玩龙灯还愿。

滚鸡蛋：有的地区滚鸡蛋叫魂，针对小孩或生病的人，连滚三次后与包袱或散纸同烧后看吉凶。

祈雨：境内有“敬龙井”习俗，或称“打龙滩”。逢久旱不雨，村民自发捐钱，在龙洞出水处杀肥猪祭祀，办酒席、敬龙王爷，请道士念经求雨。

算命：城乡司此业者多系中老年男性，间亦有妇女。其算命方式以看面相、手相、拆字为主，亦有于地上摆放签筒，让顾客抽签以卜吉凶祸福者。

吉凶预兆：城乡较多的是眼跳，称“左眼跳财，右眼跳灾”，用一小点红纸贴在眼皮上，表示不祥消除。

挂镜：农村边远地区，少数人家在大门头上挂一镜子，称“照妖镜”，认为能使各种妖怪原形毕露，无处可逃；个别人家用木刻一怪象挂在大门头上，叫吞口，据说能吞去各种妖怪。

养畜产仔：农村将胎盘挂在能产果实的树枝上（叫挂衣胞）。母猪产仔用一瓶淘米水挂在猪圈门上，叫挂拦，防母猪奶水被带走，仔猪缺奶。

葬坟：有信风水习俗，叫阴阳坐向，按死者生辰“八字”决定。

城乡人与人发生纠纷时，部分以“赌咒”来表白自己的真伪。

七、陋习

酗酒：20世纪90年代，酗酒者多为青壮年人，三五成群划拳打码赛赌酒量。酒后丧失理智，寻衅闹事；因酒后致伤、致残、致死事件时有发生。进入21世纪，外出打工者增多，酗酒者逐渐减少，但仍不乏少数嗜酒者。

赌博：20世纪90年代初，城乡盛行纸牌推三花、铺金花、斗地主、斗鸡、麻将，农村还盛行“摇苞谷子”等方式。90年代末21世纪初，城镇有人开设“精武馆”“茶室”“娱乐室”，有人开设电器赌场（老虎机、水果机、恐龙机）招揽人员进行赌博。此后麻将遍及城镇农村，街道、饭店、家庭甚至殡仪馆，随处可见麻将机和打麻将人员。中老年人常以一元二元作赌注以增加刺激性。打麻将人员由男多女少发展到男女几乎各占一半。也有少数沉迷于麻将，嗜赌如命之人。

八、禁忌

（一）语言禁忌

在苗族同胞面前，忌说“苗”“苗子”“好苗哦”“苗得很”等歧视性语言。在布依族同胞面前，除前志说到的“重”“三百斤”，忌说“仲家子”“四个七十五”等歧视性语言。在与彝族同胞交往中忌说“蛮子”。

逢喜事、喜庆日、特殊时间，忌说不吉利语言，名曰“讨口风”。如修房造屋不能说与“垮”字有关的语言；外出不能说“死”，坐车船不能说“翻”，开车的人吃鱼不能“翻”转盘里的鱼。

（二）行动禁忌

忌脚：忌出门，忌会外人，于天未亮时，用竹竿拴谷草插于门外，闭门躲灾。外人见此“忌脚”标志，即主动离去。后来，“忌脚”成为少有走动的亲友的诙谐见面语。

忌越：凡刚落成的新居大门，在门未做好、未“开财门”前，忌人跨越。为防不懂礼节的人犯忌，事先用物件遮挡。凡扁担之类易折之物，禁人跨越，尤忌女人，喻易折。封建礼教忌女人跨越男人头顶，喻会带来霉运。忌从客人面前过，忌女人从男性老人面前过。忌公公进入儿媳房间、大伯子（兄长）进入弟媳房间，忌公公与儿媳或大伯子与弟媳同坐一条板凳，忌公公与儿媳或大伯子与弟媳单独同行或开玩笑。

忌无礼：有老人在场，晚辈忌翘“二郎腿”。老人说话忌抢话、插话。与客人或老人进餐时，忌抢上座、正座；装烟倒茶、添饭敬酒，须恭敬，不能太满，双手呈上，左手前实递，右手后虚递，态度须恭敬；路遇老人，须停步让路，忌抢行。

（三）正月初一忌讳：

忌说不吉利的话，如死、破、鬼、杀、输、倒等。

忌讳打破东西，若不慎打破，要说“打发了”。

忌讳吵架、骂人（意初一吵架全年不安）。

忌讳抬死人和遇殡葬。

忌讳剃头。

忌讳杀鸡，传说此日为鸡生日。

（四）平时忌讳

有产妇忌讳生人进屋，少数人忌讳进产妇房。

孝子不能披麻戴孝进民房。

猪、牛不能进民房（民间有“猪来穷，狗来富”之说），若有误入，要给房主挂红，放鞭炮“冲喜”。

少数人忌讳进灵堂。

青山苗族乡格老冲、大洼、水淹槽王姓苗族忌讳吃狗肉。

青山苗族乡一、二、三土语杨姓苗族忌讳吃猪心。

若某日犯红沙，忌讳出门。忌讳修造、结婚等。

孕妇不进其他人家有牲畜生产的畜圈门（意为怕把母畜的奶带走）。男人不进“龌龊房”（产妇房）。

生辰八字与亡人下葬日相冲的不能送葬或参与下葬。有伤病者不能进灵堂，“防遇龌龊”（感染）等。俗语有“正月不看‘鹰打鸟’，二月不看‘虎咬山’，三月不看‘蛇扭丝’，四月不看‘人重双’”之说，主防不吉、遭灾等。

第三章　谚语·歇后语·方言

谚语，是人民群众集体创造并口口相传，反映人民智慧和生活生产实践的言简意赅、富有哲理的较为定型的艺术短语。歇后语，境内又叫“展言子”。是由前后两部分组成的固定语句，前一部分像谜语，后一部分像谜底，通常说出前半截，“歇”去后半截，让人去领会或猜想出它的寓意。少数谚语、歇后语逐渐被淘汰，大部分仍流行于民间，同时又有一些新的谚语、歇后语产生。在农村，对时令、气象、生产谚语用得较多。从年龄角度讲，老年人用得较多，年轻人用得较少。

第一节　谚　语

一、生活事理

一儿一女一枝花，多儿多女累爹妈。

一行服一行，螺蛳服米汤。
一个钉子一个眼，一个萝卜一个坑。
一勤跟三懒，不懒也要懒。
一懒跟三勤，不勤也要勤。
人怕闹，火怕撬。
人要忠心，火要空心。
人怕三对面，树怕一墨线。
人争一口气，佛争一炷香。
人活一张脸，树活一张皮。
人多力量大，柴多火焰高。
人多好种田，人少好过年。
人比人，气死人。
人是桩桩，全靠衣裳。
人靠衣裳马靠鞍。
大马过得江，小马过得河。
不经一事，不长一智。
不是那家人，不上那家门。
儿多母苦，肥多苗壮。
儿不嫌母丑，狗不嫌家贫。
当面亲家母，背面老虔婆。
上回当，讨回乖。
上梁不正下梁歪，中梁不正倒下来。
吃得亏，打得堆。
吃人三餐，还人一席。
吃人口软，拿人手短。
吃不穷穿不穷，不会打算一世穷。
死要面子活受罪。
当家才知盐米贵，养子方知父母恩。
金窝银窝，不如自己的狗窝。
好事不出门，坏事传千里。
老鸦笑猪黑，自己不觉得。
闲时不烧香，急时抱佛脚。
留得青山在，不怕没柴烧。
做事做到头，杀鸡杀断喉。
输钱就为赢钱起，吃烟就为吃喝皮。
万恶都从私字起，千好都从公字来。
有时省一口，缺时当一斗。

有志不在年高，无志空长百岁。

有理走遍天下，无理寸步难行。

有了一顿怂（“怂”意为使劲吃），没得吃谷种。

良药治病，忠言利人。

众口难调，孤掌难鸣。

羊肉没得吃，惹得一身骚。

听人劝，得一半。

言多必失，线长必断。

饭后一杆烟，害处大无边。

饭后百步走，要活九十九。

远水不解近渴，远亲不如近邻。

村看村，户看户，群众看干部。

孝死不如孝生。

单纱不成线，独木不成林。

油灯不拨不亮，道理不辩不明。

泥人经不住雨打，假话经不住调查。

药苦能治病，甜言能误人。

看着别人吃豆腐牙齿快。

看自己，一朵花；看别人，豆腐渣。

鸭子死了嘴壳壳硬。

真药治不了假病，酒醉解不了真愁。

船载千斤，掌舵一人。

常在河边走，哪有不湿鞋。

猫猫不在家，耗子打翻叉。

猫儿有猫儿路，耗子有耗子路。

娘生十子不嫌多，十子养娘嫌啰嗦。

越耍越懒，越吃越馋。

湿柴怕猛火，猛火要柴多。

跟好人学好人，跟巫婆扛假神。

斑鸠四两鸽半斤，麻雀二两不用称。

躲得过初一，躲不过十五。

强中还有强中手，能人背后有能人。

慢工出细活，三天出个牛打脚。

懒人办事借口多，女人成堆闲话多。

为人不学艺，挑断箢篼系。

身正不怕影子斜，人正不怕影子歪。

师傅领进门，修行在各人。

知识在于积累，才干在于学习。
伸手不打孤身汉，开口莫骂老年人。
活到老，学到老，越学越觉知识少。
晴带雨伞，饱带干粮。
说归说，笑归笑，动手动脚无家教。
独柴难烧，独儿难教。
有借有还，再借不难。
话不好说说在前头，背篼不好背在后头。

二、农事物候

人勤地不懒，三分种来七分管。
人误地一时，地误人一春。
白露不勾头（指水稻），割来喂老牛。
正月种豆二月瓜，三月菜籽开黄花。
七葱八蒜九栽姜，过了重阳火进房。
八月豌，九月胡，十月冷得娃娃哭。
头伏芝麻二伏荞，三伏四伏压红苕。
母猪好，好一窝；公猪好，好一坡。
苞谷薅得嫩，当上一道粪。
冬季清除田边草，来年田肥害虫少。
芒种忙忙栽，夏至谷怀胎。
芒种打田不坐水，夏至宰羊少一腿。
庄稼一枝花，全靠粪当家。
庄稼无牛空起早，生意无本枉自跑。
好土出好苗，好树结好桃。
实现水利化，旱涝都不怕。
种地不掏沟，犹如强盗偷。
种地不用巧，施肥除尽草。
种子年年选，产量季季增。
误了一年春，十年扯不撑。
清明前后，栽瓜种豆。
前人栽树，后人歇凉。
一棵松树一把伞，一棵柳树一口泉。
山上多栽树，等于修水库，雨时能蓄水，旱时能吐出。
治河之本在治山，治山之本在兴林。
春到人间，植树当先。
春栽杨柳夏栽桑，正月植树好时光。
植树造林，莫过清明。

要栽松和柏，不叫春晓得。

种竹怕春知，栽杉怕雨淋。

阳坡松树阴坡杉，半阴半阳栽油茶。

造林不整地，等于做游戏。

山多是个宝，无林富不了。

荒山变成林，如同聚宝盆。

林中常栖鸟，树木虫害少。

灰喜鹊，灰喜鹊，一生专把害虫捉。

啄木鸟，嘟嘟嘟，树干害虫它能除。

山上不栽树，水土保不住。

吃水不忘挖井人，歇荫不忘栽树人。

一九二九，怀中插手；三九四九，冻死猪狗；五九六九，隔河看柳；七九六十三，路上行人把衣单；九九八十一，庄稼老二田中犁。

一杠（彩虹）杠东，一天三冲；一杠杠西，干断河溪。

一点一个泡，大雨还未到。（预示小雨变大雨）

二月初二晴，山中树木发两层。（预示有倒春寒出现）

二月二打雷，来年稻如锤。（预示当年水稻籽粒饱满）

七月秋风雨，八月秋风凉。

三天太阳两天雨，农家户户有余米。

小满不满，干断田坎；立夏不下，犁耙高挂。

大寒不寒，人马不安。

久晴必有久雨，久雨必有久晴。

太阳反照，明天晒得鬼叫。

日落西山胭脂红，不是雨来便是风。

天黄有雨地黄晴，石壁回潮雨来临。

中秋月不明，雨洒上坟灯。（即农历正月十四、十五）

云朝贵阳城，大雨淋死人；云朝遵义府，晒破牛屁股。

云朝贵阳城，大雨淹到门；云朝遵义府，晒破大田土。

云朝东，车马通；云朝南，水涟涟。

云朝西，雨凄凄；云朝北，好晒麦。

云朝六广，大雨长淌；云朝九庄，晒破卤缸。

云朝东，雨无踪；云朝西，披蓑衣。

立秋晒得苦，二十四个“秋老虎”。

不怕重阳十三雨，只怕立冬一天晴。

立冬无雨一冬晴，立冬有雨一冬淋。

冬月打雷谷堆堆，腊月打雷坟堆堆。

白露过一天，蚊子死一千。

有雨天边亮，无雨顶上光。
有雨山戴帽，无雨云缠腰。
先打雷后下雨，抵不上一泼大露水。
两春夹一冬，冷到谷雨中。
鸣雷立秋，干断河沟。
庄稼老二不要夸，三月还要冻桐花。
重阳无雨望十三，十三无雨一冬干。
夏至有雨十八泼，夏至无雨干断河。
夏至有雨十八河，大寒无雨是干冬。
寒露油菜霜降麦。
朝出红霞雨涟涟，晚出红霞火烧天。
晚上下雨白天晴，一人做来养十人。
燕子高飞晴天告，燕子低飞雨天报。
清明不明烂旱种，谷雨无雨撒迟秧。
凌夹雪，半个月。

第二节 歇后语

十五只吊桶打水——七上八下。
八仙过海——各显神通。
马屁股上钉掌——离蹄（题）太远。
大姑娘坐花轿——头一回。
大路边打草鞋——有的说长有的说短。
百货大楼卖西装——一套一套的。
百岁老人过生日——难得有一回。
百米赛跑——争分夺秒。
半夜做买卖——暗中交易。
半夜吃黄瓜——叫（嚼）得响。
半夜吃桃子——专拣耙（pā）的捏（意为专拣弱的欺）。
半斤换八两——谁也不吃亏。
半路上出家——从头学起。
半天云中挂口袋——装疯（风）。
电筒里装马列主义——只照别人不照自己。
自行车下坡——不踩（睬）。
老者唱戏——过说。
竹筒倒豆子——干脆利落。
坟旮旯卖布——鬼扯。

闭起眼睛跳舞——盲目乐观。
闭起眼睛训话——瞎说。
闭起眼睛下围棋——黑白不分。
闭起眼睛哼小调——心里有谱。
肚子里撑船——内航（行）。
芝麻开花——节节高。
坐飞机搽雪花膏——香飘万里。
和尚打架——抓不到辫子。
豆腐盘成肉价钱——划不来。
板凳倒立——四脚朝天。
板凳上玩麻将——抓打不开。
泥菩萨过河——自身难保。
狗咬乌龟——找不到头。
狗吃牛屎——图多（贪多之意）。
狗拿耗子——多管闲事。
刷子脱毛——有板有眼。
拔河比赛——两头扯。
油炸花生米——干脆。
星星跟到月亮走——沾光。
茶壶煮汤圆——有货倒不出。
哑巴吃汤圆——心中有数。
背心穿在衬衫外——乱套。
按方抓药——照办。
扁担挑缸钵——两头都滑脱。
鸡蛋炒鸭蛋——混蛋。
鸡蛋里头挑骨头——无中生有。
耗子钻风箱——两头受气。
病好打医生——恩将仇报。
铁路警察——各管一段。
猫儿不吃死耗子——假慈悲。
圆桌会议——不分上下。
黄鼠狼给鸡拜年——没安好心。
猪八戒照镜子——里外不是人。
猪尿包打人——气胀人。
菜刀切豆腐——两面讨光生。
裁缝扯布——排（纱）杉（县内地名）
裁缝不带尺——存心不良（量）

裁缝的尺子——量人不量己。

船上磕头——跪舟（贵州）。

斑马的脑袋——头头是道。

锭子舂海椒——有点辣手（锭子，即土语“拳头”）。

满口金牙齿——尽说黄话。

超载的火车——任重道远。

矮子过河——安心（“淹”的谐音，谓决心已下）。

搬石头打天——不自量力。

懒婆娘的裹脚——又臭又长。

磨子做枕头——想转了（想通了之意）。

擀面杖吹火——一窍不通。

癞疙宝（即蟾蜍）吃豇豆——悬吊吊的（不踏实）。

癞疙宝打哈欠——好大的口气。

第三节　方　言

息烽话语音，大致可分为3个音区。九庄音区：包含九庄、竹花、鹿窝、石硐、何家硐一带；息烽音区：含黑神庙、永靖、阳朗、底寨一带；养龙司音区：含新场、茅坡、安江、养龙司、温泉一带。境内汉族语音、词汇和少数民族语言，在《息烽县志》（1993年12月第1版）已有叙述，详见该志第三十篇第五章。随着交通、文化的发展和普通话的推广，语音除地区差异外，出现年龄和城乡差异，老年人和农村村民受外来影响较小，语音变化较慢，多守方音，青年人及城镇居民语音变化较快。20世纪60年代后出生的居民多会讲普通话，出门到外省或在境内遇外省人讲话听不懂时，多改用普通话对话。

息烽话中，地方词汇比较丰富。1991—2010年，青少年中很少使用老的地方词汇，而流行一些新的地方词汇。

一、方言词汇

摆平：把事情处理好；平息事态。

好大一匹酸菜：小事一桩。

小菜一碟：小问题，容易解决的事。

小儿科：不值一提的事。

弯酸：不耿直，矫情。

弹起：挺直腰杆、拿出本事；有本事、了不起。

杀飞车：坐火车不买票，逃票。

傻（hǎ）儿：傻包、傻兮兮：不聪明、不懂世故、不明事理。

憨包：同傻包。

刷马子：指男青年找对象、谈恋爱。

翘脚：指人死了。同翘辫子。

耙（pā）耳朵：软弱，缺乏男子汉气概。指害怕老婆的人。

喷（pēn）到：巴结、依靠、傍。

来电：来劲；有了特别的感觉，有激情，有希望。

扯得很：说假话、编故事；滑头、不诚实。

老辫婆：传说中的女鬼、女妖；对疯癫、恶煞、邋遢女人的贬称。哄孩子时常说：“乖乖嘞，老辫婆来了！”

老背背：偷娃娃、拐卖人口的人。

老鬼：平辈老年人之间的昵称，小辈对老辈不敬的称呼；对资深男人的戏称。

搅屎棍：形容把水搅浑，把问题搞复杂，唯恐天下不乱的人；不理解意图乱发议论的人；喜欢找茬的人。

尖梭梭：物件堆得很高很满；某种工具或武器尖细锋利。

支坨子：出卖。与人办事自己先溜，明知有风险或会得罪人，会招惹是非，让别人上前，自己往后缩。得利公沾，失利自保。

精怪：小聪明、自私；有阅历、经验丰富；捉摸不透。

搞笑：制作笑料，幽默；言行惹人发笑；事情做得不好。

搞定：把事情办好；完成了某项任务；解决了某个问题。

赶会：趁机沾光；入伙。又叫搭便车、搭顺风车。

搭便车：坐不用花钱的交通工具，搭熟人的车顺便去。

搭顺风车：方向一致的情况下搭车前往。

放羊：缺乏管理，纪律松弛，放任自流。

放水：不按规定管理，纵容作弊。

放血：杀人。用黑帮的方式寻仇。

出血：为某件事付出代价。主要指经济上。

冲（chòng）棒：说话做事冒失，不稳重，不知天高地厚。又叫冲宝、二冲棒、二冲宝。

冒皮皮：同冲棒。

背时：是没有抓住机遇，运气不好，不顺利。

倒坎：受挫、垮台、失败。

玩假差：虚晃一枪，并不付诸行动。

保长：借指做人做事不尽人意或不开窍，倒二不着三。

倒二：做事抓不住主次，不着调；不服人尊敬。

二、方言成语

叽喊辣叫：吵闹或为一件小事说个不停。又说叽啦舞叫。

正一作二：表态度的口气，意为认真的。

晃打服希：糊里糊涂。

鬼头刀把：形容不正经。

冷火秋烟：很冷清。

憨迷憨眼：傻气。

皮皮翻翻：形容事理纷乱；或物件毛糙；或形容多嘴多舌的性格状态。

马干吃尽：形容某人爱占便宜，强势。

青格郎当：形容人颓唐或狼狈相。
妖二合三：形容喜欢穿着打扮（贬义），或和一些不三不四的人在一起。
吆二喝三；吼吼闹闹，成群结队，不安分。
呼三喝四：同前义，并有召集之意。
假巴一二：假惺惺、装模作样、虚情假意。
和二和三：顺风倒，没主见。
活摇活甩：没有定论、没有定夺、没有决断。
哭稀烂流：形容小儿爱哭或大人很没有出息的样子。
瘦壳朗精：形容很瘦。
厚皮石脸：脸皮厚。
悬皮奁脸：调皮，不正经。例如：“讨嫌死刻，悬皮奁脸嘞。”
邀不到台：形容了不起（贬义）。
吆喝吼道：咋呼，吵闹，风风火火。
麻打火勾：含糊不清、蒙混过关。形容假装粗心，乘机占便宜。
舔口咧嘴：很馋的样子。
焉巴屁臭：形容人或物没精神，无精打采。
抓拿骗吃：到处骗吃骗喝，引申为骗子。
啰哩八嗦：话多、絮叨、烦人。
搞倒事喽：发财、走运、得到好处。有时也作反语用，如：“考试作弊被抓到，搞倒事喽！”
滴滴个儿、滴滴点、点点个：喻东西少。
哈迷日眼：很傻的意思。
日迷胎眼：做事不稳慎，吊儿郎当、稀里糊涂。
怪眉日眼：行为古怪、乖张，说话办事让人不舒服、不愉快。又说怪眉怪眼。
憨吃哑胀：形容吃得多，吃东西无节制。
花迷撂眼：脸很脏。引申为不讲究。
瞌睡眯晞：没睡醒，疲倦的样子。
二昏二昏：头昏致做事找不到头脑、方向；酒醉的样子。
二假二假：形容装模作样，洋洋得意，高傲自大。
干扯湿扯：不诚实、虚伪；耍滑头，能办的不办。
打擦边球：借势、赶趟，在政策规定的范围边缘做事。
背时倒坎：时运不济，倒霉，失败。
打不到山势：辨不清方向，找不到路径。
倒二不着三：做事不着调，颠三倒四，该做的不做，不该做的反倒很认真。
倒尖不兔：假聪明。既聪明又犯傻。

人　物

一、人物传（以人物生年先后为序）

宋仕岭（1924—2008），男，汉族，河南省南乐县人。初中文化。中共党员。

1949年到息烽县工作，历任公安助理员、区委副书记、书记、县宣传部副部长、县人民检察院检察长、革委会副主任、湘黔修路团政委、县委副书记。多次被县委评为先进工作者。1974年11月任县委书记。

任县委书记期间，积极开展视察调研活动。常常深入边远乡镇进行调研，到山区贫困群众的家里访贫问计，了解生产生活情况，形成许多高质量的调研报告，为县委、县政府的决策提供了可靠的依据。为把老百姓关注的事情办好，他经常召集有关部门共同协商，并会同有关部门领导积极与上级部门沟通，寻求支持，协调争取项目，多方筹集资金，切实加强农村基础设施建设。在任期间，他几乎走遍了息烽的山山水水，访问了上百户农村困难群众，成为全县各族人民称赞的知民意、办民事、得民心的好书记。1980年4月，任县人大主任。1983年离休。

陈历修（1926—1996），男，汉族，息烽县九庄镇人。大专学历，中医副主任医师。1953年9月参加工作，曾任县医院中医师、中医教师。

陈历修年轻时跟伯父学习中医8年。1953—1958年，在息烽县九庄区联合诊所从事医师工作。1958年8月至1959年8月，先后在贵阳中医进修学校、成都中医学院师资班学习。此后在贵阳中医研究所任助教。1962年9月回县人民医院中医科工作，其间，自己动手设立中药加工房和中药库房，使中药管理逐步规范。1964年受县卫生局委托，负责举办全县“中医药质量管理提高班”，自编教材，选择130种药材，运用切、炒、晒、蒸、煮等传统方法进行加工示范，将全县中药加工管理提高到一个新的水平。1986年，县医院中医科正式列编，陈历修任中医科首任科主任。

1987—1988年，参加息烽县中药资源普查，对境内1124种中药材进行归档整理，获安顺地区药源资源普查一等奖，并获贵州省中药资源普查“先进个人”称号。

1988年9月退休后，在县城交通路开办“同德堂”诊所。1995年撰写的《湿热黄疸症治温热黄疸》一文获第二届世界传统医学大会优秀成果大奖赛优秀成果奖，其本人同时获“民族医药之星”称号。入选《中国名医列传·当代卷》。

李国良（1933—2010），男，汉族，四川省云阳县人。中共党员。1951年2月参加中国人民志愿军抗美援朝战斗，1956年转业到遵义地区医院工作。1962年调到息烽县人民医院，先后在外科、妇产科及放射科从事诊疗工作，任综合病房医生组组长、外妇科主任、外科主任。

1962年，经李国良努力，县人民医院中断多年的外科手术得以恢复，并在极其简陋的设备条件下，请遵义专区医院派人支援，成功抢救了一位难产孕妇的生命。1963年，县医院购置万能手术床、无影灯、外科手术器械等设备，建起初具规模的手术室，同时在病房内布置一个产房，结束了产妇在病床上生小孩的历史。1963年后，李国良相继开展肠修补术、肠吻合术、膀胱切开取石术、疝修补术、慢性骨髓炎病灶清除术、会阴侧切胎头吸引术、产钳术、剖腹产等手术。1965年以后，先后开展胃大部分切除胃室肠吻合术、尿道修补术、卵巢囊肿切除术、子宫全切除术、外伤性肝破裂肝修补术。1985年开展甲状腺瘤摘除术、甲状腺部分切除术、直肠癌根治术。1986年，李国良的论文《外伤性肝破裂六例治疗体会》获县科技成果二等奖、安顺地区科技成果三等奖；其本人被县委、县政府授予县科技拔尖人才称号。此外，李国良还先后被评为县科教系统先进工作者、卫生系统先进个人、职业道德标兵、计划生育先进个人、优秀共产党员、全区先进卫生工作者。

黄及翔（1934—2009），男，汉族，息烽县底寨文安村人。中共党员。青少年时代在息烽中学读书。1950年9月参军，曾任部队文书、教员、文艺宣传干事。转业后曾任息烽电厂出纳员，省人民广播电台、艺术干校学员。1959年7月被错误处理，1979年2月恢复工作。1983年2月至1984年6月，在息烽县党史办工作。1984年7月至1985年2月，任政协息烽县委员会秘书长、政协办公室副主任、政协文史委员会委员。1985年3月至1987年4月，任息烽县文化局副局长兼息烽县文化馆馆长。1990年至1993年4月，任政协息烽县委员会第三届副主席；1993年5月至1998年2月，任政协息烽县委员会第四届副主席。在此期间，组织编写《息烽文史资料》一、三、四辑；深入10个乡镇，认真了解社情民意后，提出议案30余条。

黄及翔对地方文史研究有较浓厚的兴趣，并取得一定的成绩。1978年，他参与征集红军长征过息烽的文史资料，不辞辛苦，深入流长、瓮沙、青山等地，采访红军长征目击证人，撰写了《中央红军在息烽》《徐保长打错了算盘》等10余篇文章，为挖掘、宣传息烽的红色文化做出了贡献。

黄及翔工作之余，爱好诗歌、书法和音乐，有诗歌和音乐作品发表于报刊杂志和录入1993年出版的《息烽县志》。

刘厚生（1936—1999），男，汉族，四川省岳池县人。中共党员。中专文化。西南水利学校毕业。1954年7月分配到贵州省水利局农水总队实习。此后先后在贵定县专属水利队、息烽县农水局水利组工作，担任过技术员、工程师、息烽县水利局（后更名为水利电力局）副局长、局长等。

刘厚生在息烽水利局工作期间，参与和主持息烽县多项水利工程设计。1984年12月，获全国水利电力系统劳动模范荣誉称号，并到北京出席表彰大会，受到李鹏总理等党和国定领导人的接见。

1985年，为解决息烽水资源严重不足问题，主持设计建设小水窖，将雨水集中储存于小水窖，缺水时取出使用，有效解决人畜饮水困难。在66个行政村修建3100多个小水窖。1989年12月8日，国务院副总理田纪云、省长王朝文等领导到息烽县永靖镇马当田村坪上村民组参观小水窖建设工程，给予了高度评价。刘厚生先后获安顺地区科协先进工作者、安顺地区水利电力局先进工作者、省水利电力厅先进生产工作者称号和水利电力部颁发的“献身水利水保事业32年荣誉证书”。

1990年4月，刘厚生当选县十一届人大常委会副主任。1993年调县政府工作，主持设计修建息烽枧槽沟饮水工程。1995年退休。

邱德林（1937—1997），男，汉族，息烽县养龙司乡荆江村人。中共党员。1982年在北京语言文学自修大学学习，1985年获大专学历证书。

1958年6月参加工作。1970—1985年，历任小寨坝公社党委书记、黑神庙区委常委、县教育局副局长、县委政策研究室副主任、县文化局局长。

1985年10月，调任县志办公室主任。在县志办工作期间，组织整理、校点和重印民国《息烽县志》。1986年3月，主持编写《息烽县志》，组织各单位收集资料，撰写专志。至1989年3月，基本完成资料收集和专志编写任务。全县共收集资料2770余万字，并整理立卷归档共400余卷；撰写专志45部，出版专志8部。1989年3月24日，成立由12人组成的总纂班子，布置分纂任务，邱德林除负责全书总纂外，还分纂凡例、概述、人物。至1991年11月，总纂送审稿打印装订完毕，经审稿、修改，送安顺地区行署、省方志办验收。1993年12月，《息烽县志》出版发行。1998年2月19日，《息烽县志》在省政府举行的贵州优秀志书颁奖大会上获优秀志书三等奖。

邱德林先后在《贵州方志》《贵州地方通讯录》《贵州文史丛刊》《贵州文物》《史志林》《安顺文艺》等刊物上发表文章14篇，发表专业论著《浅谈新方志主题的提炼》《略谈人物传的文体文风》《读民国息烽县志序》等文章，其中《浅谈新方志主题的提炼》一文分别收入贵州人民出版社1991年10月出版的《贵州方志文萃》和黄山出版社出版的《中国地方志综览》。

1988年7月获编辑职称。先后获省“先进工作者”、县“优秀知识分子”称号。曾任贵州省群众文化学会安顺分会会员、贵州省文史研究会会员、贵州省地方志协会会员。

张其沾（1940—2008），男，广东省大浦县漳溪镇（现西河镇）人。中共党员。大专文化。农艺师职称。1961年8月由遵义农校毕业，分配到息烽县农林水利局工作。1963年调九庄区农业技术推广站工作。1981—1987年，历任九庄区公所副区长、永阳区公所副区长、永阳区委副书记（多分管农业工作），县农村工作部副部长、农业局局长。1990年7月调任县委统战部部长。1991年3月至1998年3月，历任县政协第三届、第四届、第五届委员会副主席、秘书长，县委统战部部长、党组副书记。同时任中国共产党息烽县第五、六、七、八次党代会代表、第七届县委委员，第八届、十一届息烽县人民代表大会代表。

在农业部门工作期间，1982年，获息烽县人民政府1981年油菜高产二等奖、水稻高产奖，《黔油九号在我区的推广及栽培技术》一文发表在《息烽科技》上。1982年获农艺师职称。1987年，《加强领导，依靠政策和科技，促进县水稻生产发展》一文在《安顺地区水稻研讨会专辑》上发表。1989年10月，获农业部颁发的全国农业系统成人教育先进工作者荣誉称号。主持农业局工作期间，县农业局多次被地区行署评为二等、三等先进单位。

在统战部工作期间，他钻研业务，创新方法，积极搞好港澳台胞工作。因其工作出色，县委统战部多次被安顺地区评为先进集体，其本人也被安顺地委评为统战工作先进工作者。1994年，其撰写的调研报告《抓住机遇，加快产业机构调整发展，发挥优势，加快农村经济发展》得到省政协安顺地区工委专题研讨会肯定和县委的高度重视。1997年9月，获政协贵州省委员会颁发的“全省政协工作先进个人”荣誉称号。2003年6月退休。

简富明（1954—1997），男，汉族，息烽县永靖镇红旗村人。中共党员。大学文化。1982年毕业于贵州农学院植物保护系，分配到息烽县农业局植保站工作。1995年获高级农艺师职称。一生致力于农作物病虫害研究，先后获得省劳动模范、市先进工作者、县优秀共产党员称号，享受省政府特殊津贴。

简富明主持或参与实施多项省、地科研项目，并获得多项科技成果奖。其中主持实施的《二代黏虫发生规律及测报技术研究应用》项目，1994年获安顺地区科技进步2等奖。根据其研究成果，省内建立了黏虫预报因子分级标准和多因子数学预报模型，使黏虫测报工作科学化和标准化，提高了测报质量及预报准确率，并在全省植保系统推广应用。简富明在国家及省内学术刊物上发表科研文章20余篇，其中《印度谷螟生物学特性研究》（《西南农业学报》1993年载）叙述印度谷螟生物生态特性、发生规律及防治技术，填补了国内该虫生态研究方面的空白，引起学术界高度重视，文章被多次转载、引用，并获中国植物保护学会优秀论文奖。《葡萄透翅蛾研究初报》（《昆虫知识》1982年载）和《烟蛀茎蛾生物学特性及发生规律研究》（《植物保护学报》）填补了贵州省在这方面的研究空白。

谭洪玉（1956—1997），男，汉族，息烽县流长乡人。中共党员。中师文化。1974年7月高中毕业回乡务农和当代课教师。1977年7月考入息烽师范学校，毕业后任教于新场小学初中班和流长中学。1986年8月加入中国共产党。1990年8月调任中共黑神庙区委员会纪检员。1993年任小寨坝镇党委副书记。是年10月，在谭洪玉牵头和组织下，首次安装黑神庙新老街闭路电视396户。其分管乡镇企业工作期间，对乡镇企业的立项、建设严把质量关，并为近百名农村富余劳动力提供就业机会。1997年2月，为解决小寨坝人畜饮水困难，“小寨坝镇供水工程指挥部”成立，谭洪玉担任副指挥长统管供水工程工作。4月27日，谭洪玉携指挥部成员去遵义购置工程急需的器材。返回途中，停车在乌江老君观青㭎坡路边拆换轮胎时遭遇车祸，谭洪玉与另外2名指挥部成员遇难。29日，小寨坝镇党委、人大、政府、镇属各单位及驻镇单位、厂矿主要负责人、黑神庙群众等约1万余人为谭洪玉等3人举行追悼大会，并立“饮水思源”一碑，以为纪念。

二、已故副县级以上领导人简介

姓　名	生平简介
李国栋	（1925.12—2003.04），男，汉族，河南省项城县南屯区狮子李营村人。中共党员。1948年12月，在解放军二野十八军五十二师一五五团一营机枪连当战士。立营功1次、连功4次。历任班长、副排长、排长、副连长、连长。1958年5月，转业到息烽县工业科工作。1961年后，历任县纸厂厂长、支书，农机厂支书、革委会主任、农机局副局长、县经委副主任。1980年5月，任息烽县人民政府副县长。1984年5月，任息烽县人大常务会副主任。1985年退休。

续表

姓　名	生平简介
司云高	（1929.05—2008.04），男，汉族，河南省长垣县人。高小文化。中共党员。1946年10月，在长垣县常五镇当兵。1949年，在渡江战斗和进军西南途中立三等功1次。1950年2月，转地方公安部门工作，历任侦查员、股长、副局长。1957年10月任息烽县公安局局长、教导员。1974年4月，任息烽县轻工业局局长。1981年1月，任息烽县人大常委会副主任。
黄生谷	（1941.04—2008.04），男，息烽县人。高中文化。中共党员。1961年1月参加工作。1969年起任养龙区安江公社革委会副主任、团委书记；安江公社革委会主任、党委书记；养龙区副书记兼安江公社书记、区长；养龙区人大工委主任。1992年3月后任县人大财经委主任、县委统战部部长；县政协五届副主席兼秘书长、党组成员。2003年5月退休。
任国元	（1945.12—2010.05），男，汉族，息烽县人。中共党员。1964年8月当兵。在部队历任排长、指导员。1974—1979年获团嘉奖4次。1979年10月转息烽九庄工作，历任区委宣传委员、公社党委书记、区公所副区长兼武装部部长、区委副书记、区长、区委书记、镇党委书记，县委常委、政法委书记，县人大常委会副主任、党组副书记。
童德权	（1948.12—2002.11），男，汉族，贵州开阳县人。大专文化。中共党员。1968年2月应征入伍。同年4月参加援越抗美战斗，先后任班长、排长、副连长。在部队立个人三等功2次。1979年11月，转业到开阳县人民检察院工作，历任检察员、科长、副检察长。1993年3月，调任息烽县人民检察院副检察长、代理检察长、检察长、党组书记。1997年12月，任息烽县人民政府助理研究员。1998年3月，任息烽县人大常委会副主任。

三、人物简介（以人物生年先后为序）

易华先（1933—　　），女，汉族，息烽县养龙司乡堡子村人。中共党员。1955—1986年先后任堡子合作社、麻林大队妇女主任，1965—1971年任麻林大队副支书。

1953年，中央颁布《关于发展农业生产合作社的决议》，全国迅速掀起了农业大生产热潮。由于当时包工定额不合理，严重影响妇女生产积极性。以堡子合作社的易华先、赵玉华等为代表的妇女，针对生产中“男的做一天活得7分，女的只能得2.5分”的不平等现象，率先提出“新中国提倡男女平等，男女应该同工同酬，评一样多的工分”“同出一天工，男女要记同样工分”的权益要求，但未获批准。

当年冬季，由于大部分男社员撵马车出去运米，田地无人耕种，造成当年油菜籽收成减少近半。社管组委员会分析原因，认为是女社员的劳动积极性没有调动起来。为证明女人的劳动能力并不低于男人，争取同工同酬待遇，妇女们与男人开展劳动竞赛。妇女赵玉华和男社员吴柄柱撒菜籽比赛，结果赵玉华撒的菜籽又匀又多，但记分时仍只得2.5分。妇女们都很气愤，以易华先、赵玉华等为首的妇女再次向合作社提出抗议。

围绕男女同工同酬的问题，堡子合作社引起了一场大争论。经过社党支部、合作社反复研究，最终同意了易华先等人的意见，明确规定：不论男女，都根据生产质量的好坏和生产数量的多少来评定工分。此举大大调动了妇女们的生产积极性。堡子合作社的23名妇女，除一个年纪较大的在家带小孩外，其余都参加了集体生产，原来要十天才能完成的生产任务，只要五六天就可以完成，堡子合作社的粮食产量大幅度提高。堡子村成为全国“男女同工同酬”第一村。

堡子村的典型事迹被时任养龙区妇联主任肖贵荣写成简报，传到当时的贵定专区妇联等有关部门，得到广泛宣传。1955年10月，贵州民主妇女联合会《通报》第99期刊载了报道堡子村典型事迹的《在合作社内实行男女同工同酬》一文。12月，毛泽东主席在主持编写《中国的农村社会主义高潮》一书时收录了此文，并亲笔题写编者按：“这一篇文章不长，容易看，建议各乡各社普遍照办！”堡子经验作为推进农村社会主义建设和落实男女平等政策的样板，在全国广泛推广。

1958年5月25日，毛泽东主席指出：贵州堡子的妇女提出男女同工同酬，现在时代不同了，男女都一样，妇女能顶半边天了！从此，“妇女能顶半边天”的口号响遍大江南北，堡子村妇女同胞以一种自信、自立、自尊、自强的主人翁姿态走上历史舞台。易华先作为农民代表，出席党的第十一次全国代表大会，受到时任中共中央主席华国锋的亲切接见，并合影留念。

冯世忠（1937.07—　　），男，汉族，贵州贵阳人。中共党员。大学本科学历。高级农艺师。1961年7月毕业于贵州农学院，8月分配到息烽县农业局工作。曾任养龙司区农推站站长、县农业局农推站站长。

冯世忠一直在息烽县从事水稻、玉米、油菜、马铃薯等农作物高产栽培和新品种新技术的引进试验示范推广工作，先后实施20万亩优质油菜高产、水稻旱育浅植配套增产、10万亩两杂高产、K优3号引种、小麦综合丰产、5000亩杂稻高产和玉米群改种优势运用等农作物栽培管理项目。分别荣获贵州省农业丰收二等奖2项、三等奖6项，安顺地区科技进步二等奖1项、三等奖3项、四等奖1项，贵州省农业技术推广成果二等奖1项。1985年3月，被贵州省科学技术协会评为省农村科普活动先进个人。1987年4月，获贵州省科技扶贫服务团先进个人称号；12月，被评为安顺地区科技先进工作者和安顺地区农业局先进个人。1980年3月，获省政府授予的农业劳动模范称号。1993年5月，获省政府颁发的长期从事农业科学技术推广成绩工作奖。2001年1月退休。

陈昌其（1943.11.19—　　），男，汉族，福建晋江县人。中共党员。北京农业大学农学遗传选种专业毕业。1970年8月到息烽九庄区农推站工作，1974年11月调县农业局，1980年4月调县科委（后更名为科技局），长期从事农业科学技术推广和杂交玉米制种工作。1987年1月—1990年8月，抽调到县烤烟办。曾任县科委副主任、县科技局副局长、县猕猴桃开发办副主任、县科技局主任科员。

陈昌其在九庄农推站工作期间，大搞引种试验及“五四〇六”“九二〇”腐殖酸类肥料等新技术的推广。在海拔1000米以下地区试种双季稻，获得成功。开展旱地育秧、小麦带土移栽、工厂化育秧、旱播水管新式育秧。在九庄望城开展一年三熟（麦—包—苕）制试验，亩产750千克以上。调县农业局工作后，他坚持引种试验，从河南新乡地区农科所引进的小麦百泉“565”，经过试种成功后在全县大面积推广，还为兄弟县市提供种子。

陈昌其从1978年开始杂交玉米育种工作，为尽快育成杂交玉米种，曾三次去海南岛进行繁殖。经过多年努力，利用“墨白94”群体改良种作为选育自交系材料，育成抗旱、较耐瘠、产量高的白粒型、中秆杂交玉米新品种“息单1号”。在“息单1号”的基础上又经过多年努力，育成白粒杂交种“息单7号”。1996年，经安顺地区品种审定委员会审定通过。“息单7号”的繁育与推广列入1997年贵阳市科技项目。

陈昌其参与编写的《息烽县烤烟优质适产技术》被评为国家“八五”期间优秀科技成果。曾获省级科技成果奖1项，安顺地区科技成果奖4项，县级科技成果奖6项和国家科委、香港学者协会等单位的“振华科技扶贫奖励基金”服务奖。获省科技先进工作者称号1次、安顺地区行署先进科技工作者称号2次、县优秀知识分子称号2次、县优秀共产党员称号4次，被安顺地区行署和县委、县政府授予首批地级和县级专业技术拔尖人才称号。2003年10月退休。

黄南武（1946.04—　　），女，汉族，息烽阳朗人，阳朗辣子鸡创始人。1979年，黄南武在息烽集中营革命历史纪念馆附近的210国道边开了一家辣子鸡小吃店。经过长期实践，摸索出一种制作辣子鸡的技术，炒出的辣子鸡又辣又糯，味香色美，成为独特的地方风味小吃，不仅每年为国家创利税，还起到促进就业、带动农村种植业、养殖业发展的作用。阳朗辣子鸡成为与息烽集中营旧址、息烽温泉齐名的三大品牌。2009年9月，黄南武获全国“三八红旗手”称号。

阳维龙（1958.09.17—　　），男，汉族，息烽县人。中共党员。大学学历。高级工程师。全国低压电器专业委员会委员，全国低压电器标准化技术委员会委员，中国电工技术学会高级会员，享受国务院特殊津贴专家。2002年，获贵州省产学研联合先进个人称号。2007—2010年，先后获慈溪市高层次引进人才奖、慈溪市创新博士称号、慈溪市科技创新推动奖、慈溪市劳动模范称号。

阳维龙一直从事低压电器产品研发设计及制造工作。1982—2003年，在遵义长征电器九厂工作期间，先后担任设计员、科长、副总工程师；2003年至2004年4月，任长征电器股份有限公司技术中心副主任；2004年4月至2006年3月，任长征电器股份有限公司低压事业部总工程师。2006年4月至2010年，任宁波奇乐电气集团有限公司总工程师兼技术中心主任。

阳维龙主管研发的电器产品多次获得省市奖励。1991年，“DW15、DWX15断路器节银攻关”获第二届中国青年科技博览会新星奖。1994年，“DW40型智能万能式断路器”获贵州省新产品奖，1998年“智能型框架式断路器”获贵州省科技进步一等奖。2001年，“大容量、高分断、无飞弧、智能化、万能式断路器”获中国机械工业联合会科技进步二等奖。2007年，“TP1-可通信自动转换开关电器”获慈溪市科技进步一等奖。2010年，“大容量万能式断路器”获实用新型专利。

发表论文《DW40万能式断路器智能脱扣器的设计》《提高断路器可靠性浅谈》《万能式断路器智能控制器的应用及发展趋势》《舰船用三位置自动转换开关的研制开发》《大容量整体结构6300万能式断路器的研制开发》等。

聂朝俊（1958.10—　　），男，汉族，息烽县小寨坝镇桶井坝人。中共党员。1977年在息烽县水电局工作。1978年考入贵州农学院林学系林学专业学习。1982年分配到贵州省林业勘察设计院（以下简称省林勘院）森调一队工作，历任干部、副队长。1988—1990年，任省林勘院总体规划设计队队长、生产计划财务科科长、行政支部书记。1993年，任省林勘院副院长。2000年，任院长、党委副书记。2004年2月，获国家注册咨询工程师。2005年3月，被评为工程技术应用研究员。2006

年，任省林业厅党组成员、省林业调查规划院院长、党委副书记。

陈久琪（1959.01— ），男，汉族，息烽县流长乡人，中共党员，研究生学历，中学高级教师。1985年毕业于贵州师范大学，分配到息烽县第一中学任语文教师。1998年，参加创办息烽县教研刊物《息烽教坛》，并兼任主编。此后兼任过息烽电大《中国古代文学》和《写作》课程主讲教师、《贵阳教育》报刊社执行编辑、贵阳市中师函授学校教师和市教科所教研员。2010年，被贵州师范大学求是学院特聘为写作主讲教师。多次担任贵阳市教育系统举办的中小学教师以及学生征文大赛评委。

1991—2010年，先后被评为息烽县优秀教师、语文学科带头人、县专业技术带头人、县首届杰出青年、贵阳市优秀教师、市十大杰出青年、市优秀青年志愿者、贵州省级骨干教师。获贵州省希望工程贡献奖、共青团中央和中国志愿者协会“中国青年志愿服务奖”奖章，被中国中小学幼儿园教师基金会授予“全国优秀教师”称号。出版诗集《故乡永是春》和散文集《真情无畏》。

吴玉平（1960.07.01— ），男，汉族，贵州贵阳人。1987年12月加入中国共产党，贵州工学院地质系地勘专业毕业。1982年1月到贵州息烽磷矿工作，曾先后担任息烽磷矿技术员、工程师、采矿车间主任、治安科副科长、矿长助理。1989年11月考入贵州省化工厅，任计划处主任科员、助理调研员等职。1999年11月任息烽磷矿副矿长，2001年11月任矿长，2013年11月任党委书记、董事长。

吴玉平任息烽磷矿副矿长时，该磷矿经40多年露天开采，磷矿资源已近枯竭，企业处于亏损状态。他立足企业实际，带领企业干部职工，组织企业生产经营工作，使企业连续多年实现盈利，先后荣获贵州省“五一劳动奖状”、省“厂务公开民主管理示范单位”、省“双百佳企业”、国家二级企业、省“出口创汇先进企业”、省“劳动关系和谐企业”、省国资委“优秀基层党组织”、省“纳税免检企业”、县“十佳纳税企业”等称号。吴玉平也因此获得贵州省“五一劳动奖章”、省化工事业发展“突出贡献奖”，贵阳市“先进劳动者”、市工业经济提速增效先进个人等奖项和称号。

马书烈（1962.05— ），男，汉族，息烽县温泉镇尹庵村人。中共党员，大专文化，高级农艺师。1983年7月毕业于安顺农校农学专业，1997年6月在职就读，毕业于贵州农业学院农学专业。曾任息烽县农业技术开发服务中心办公室主任。

马书烈从事过杂交水稻、玉米、油菜、马铃薯等农作物高产栽培和新品种新技术的引进试验示范推广工作，先后参加农业部、贵州日报社等单位组织实施的基层农业技术推广体系建设、网络传媒知识、科技进步、西部开发、农民教育等项目建设。独立撰写的《息烽县发展蚕桑业的优势和发展对策》《领导联部门、帮企业、哺个人——全力建设息烽新农村》《息烽创新农业产业结构调整工作机制》等文章分别在《中国蚕业》《建设社会主义新农村理论与实践》《科技促进发展》等国家级刊物刊载。参加或主持编制了息烽县国民经济和社会发展“十一五”规划纲要、息烽农业科技园总体规划和息烽县新型农民科技教育培训教材。先后荣获农业部、贵州省农业厅、中共贵阳市委、贵阳市人民政府、息烽县人民政府等单位的农业丰收计划一、二、三等奖，科技进步一、二、三、四等奖，优秀共产党员和先进个人称号共30余项次。

杨　波（1962.06—　　），男，苗族，息烽县石硐乡水头村人。高中学历。自幼酷爱苗族传统文化。高中毕业后，正式向父亲学习芦笙吹奏。常在苗家丧葬祭祀仪式中进行芦笙表演。1997年4月，在家乡组建第一支芦笙队伍，被推举为队长。1997—2008年，杨波多次参加“多彩贵州”及其他文艺展演，展示出较高的才艺。2008年5月，杨波应聘为青山苗族乡“民族文化进校园”专职教师。同年，杨波编排的芦笙舞蹈获“多彩贵州”舞蹈大赛三等奖。2009年9月，杨波编排的芦笙舞蹈《蒙待央》获贵阳市第八届民族运动会金奖；2010年10月，获贵州省第七届民族运动会金奖；2011年，获中华人民共和国第九届少数民族运动会金奖。《蒙待央》成为息烽苗族芦笙舞蹈的代表作品。杨波编排的芦笙舞蹈成为青山苗族乡“四月八”活动的必选节目，深受当地群众喜爱。

高爱琴（1966.05—　　），女，山西省太原市人。1988年毕业于沈阳药学院化学制药专业。国家首批执业药师。曾多次承担大型制药企业的设计与施工工作。贵州太和制药有限公司总经理。

1997年贵州太和制药有限公司组建后，高爱琴兼管药品开发工作。相继研发“前列倍喜胶囊”“心脑联通胶囊”“参术胶囊”“的确凉退热贴”“降压一贴宁”等系列产品，并制定猪鬃草、刺猬皮、灯盏细辛、柿叶、蝼蛄等药材的质量标准（收载于2003年出版的《贵州省中药材、民族药材质量标准》一书）。其中，前列倍喜胶囊获2003年贵州省名牌产品及贵阳市名牌产品称号，平痔胶囊2003年获“贵阳市优秀新产品二等奖”。“亲水性生物黏附凝胶”项目获贵州省科技成果鉴定证书，并获国家《专利申请初审合格通知书》。

在高爱琴的带领下，太和制药公司从一家注册资金400万元的作坊式企业，发展到拥有三条现代化专业生产线，总资产1.4亿元的花园式现代化企业。公司于2002年通过国家食品药品监督管理局GMP认证，2003年被贵州省科技厅认定为“民营科技企业”和“高新技术企业”，同年被贵州省银行系统评为“信贷诚信企业”及“AA+级信誉企业”，2004年获“省级企业技术中心”称号，2007年被评为信息化建设先进单位，同年被纳入“贵阳市知识产权试点单位”，2008年被评为息烽县农业产业化龙头企业，2010年被评为贵阳市及贵州省农业产业化龙头企业。

潘世昌（1966.11—　　），男，汉族，贵州遵义县人。中共党员，本科学历，高级农艺师。1985年7月参加工作。历任息烽县植保站副站长、站长。

潘世昌一直从事农作物病虫鼠害监测预报及防治工作。1986年5月，加入贵州省农田鼠害研究协作组，对农区主要鼠害、农作物主要病虫害发生规律及防治技术进行调查研究。先后参与国家、省、市科技合作专项资金项目5项；参加编写《贵州农区鼠害监测与防治技术标准》1部，参与制订贵州省地方、行业鼠害标准5项。根据研究成果进行灭鼠，大面积防治效果达到75%～90%，鼠密度降至3%以下。

潘世昌在学报及期刊上发表科技论文33篇，其中《黔中地区小家鼠种群数量动态及预测预报模型》刊登在2006年《植物保护学报》上，《小家鼠种群年龄的研究》载于2003年《西南农业学报》，《小家鼠胴体重指标划分种群年龄的研究》载于2006年《贵州农业科学》，《黔中地区小家鼠种群繁殖特征》载于2007年《西南农业学报》。连续获贵阳市第八次、第九次、第十次自然科学优秀论文二等奖。另有5篇论文分别获贵州省首届青年科学技术大会四等奖、贵州省农学会优秀论文奖、贵阳市农学会优秀论文奖。

潘世昌先后获贵州省、贵阳市、安顺地区科技进步二、三等奖3项，贵州省农业丰收二、三等奖2项，连续6次获全省农田鼠害监测与治理工作先进个人称号，2次获“贵阳市中青年科技骨干”称号，2次获“息烽县专业技术带头人”称号。2008年12月，获贵阳市政府特殊津贴。2009年11月，获“全省农区鼠害监测与防治突出贡献者”称号。

陈运凯（1967.07— ），男，农民，小寨坝镇排杉村祝家沟人。曾就读于排杉小学、小寨坝中学、息烽城关中学。1986年10月入伍，1987年10月至1989年9月，参加云南老山对越防御作战。先后4次荣立三等功，3次被总部表彰为先进个人。1993年7月，毕业于昆明陆军学院后勤干部训练大队，曾参加彝良、庐山抗震救灾，并任副指挥长。历任战士、班长、学员、司务长、助理员、参谋、股长、科长、处长、13集团军后勤部副部长等。

肖立书（1967.09— ），男，息烽县石硐人。中共党员，毕业于贵州大学物理系半导体物理与器件专业，高级工程师。1989年参加工作。历任振华集团永光电工厂三车间技术员、振华集团永光电工厂后部工段工段长、振华集团永光电工厂电镀车间副主任、主任，振华集团永光电工厂生产部部长、振华集团永光电工厂厂长助理兼生产部部长、振华集团永光电工厂副厂长、振华集团永光电工厂副厂长兼中国振华（集团）科技股份有限公司思美特分公司副总经理、中国振华（集团）科技股份有限公司片式器件分公司常务副总经理、贵州振华云科电子有限公司总经理、振华集团永光电子有限公司总经理、中国振华集团董事长。

周启康（1968.01— ），男，汉族，息烽县人。中共党员，研究生学历，高级农艺师。1991年8月参加工作。曾任县农业局果树蔬菜办公室主任和土壤肥料监测站工作负责人。

从事过土肥、农推、果蔬工作。先后参与实施农业部测土配方施肥项目、农业部土壤肥力监测项目、贵州省无籽西瓜示范推广项目、贵州省反季节蔬菜推广项目、贵阳市经果林建设项目等；在《农业与技术》《自然科学》《中国西瓜甜瓜》《贵州农业科学》《耕作与栽培》等期刊上发表科技论文21篇。主编《息烽县耕地地力评价》1部44万字。参与制定息烽县水稻、玉米、油菜、马铃薯、葡萄五大作物土壤肥料科学配方。曾获科技成果奖励7项，其中农业部丰收二等奖1项、省农业丰收一等奖1项、市科技进步二等奖1项、市科技进步三等奖1项、安顺地区科技进步三等奖1项、县科技进步一等奖1项、市蔬菜科技二等奖1项。2007年2月和6月，分别获贵阳市优秀科技工作者提名奖和县“专业技术带头人”称号。

蒲　剑（1968.06— ），男，汉族，息烽县养龙司人。1986—1990年，在武汉大学政治系行政管理专业、法律系经济法专业学习，获法学学士学位。1990—1993年，任湖北省邮电工程局秘书。1993—1996年，在北京电影学院导演系电影导演创作硕士学位研究生班学习，获文学（电影）硕士学位。

1998—2006年，多次在北京电视台、中央电视台6频道、南京电影制片厂、中国传媒大学的电视、电影制作中担任编剧、导演或制片主任。其间，2001年，由其编剧并导演的电影《生生长流》获第三届中国少数民族题材影视创作优秀电视电影奖。

发表《世界著名电影导演研究》之《基耶斯洛夫斯基的电影世界》《中国优秀电影电视剧赏析》之《生活是一团麻——电视连续剧〈一地鸡毛〉评析》《思考电视电影》《电视电影，真的来了》《〈大沙暴〉：中国电影的证明》《拿什么奉献给你中国电影的百年寿辰？》《电视电影的艺术扫描》《两个人的战争——电视剧〈中国式离婚〉导演分析》《影视语言》《2006中国电视剧发展报告》（创作综述部分）等多篇论文。多次参加国内外学术交流。

郑维江（1971.12—　　），男，汉族，息烽县养龙司乡陇上村人。中国柳倩艺术研究学院名誉教授。2001年荣获中国文联颁发的“中国历代书画名家——当代名家金奖艺术家”证书。

1995年，县文化馆为其举办个人书画展。1998年出版《当代著名书画家丛书——郑维江书画作品集》。2007年与吴冠中、程十发、蔡国强、刘大为、陈丹青、陆镜清、李玉兰、白庚延、张晓刚9人被前中国书法家协会秘书长刘正成发专文列为“2007年中国画坛十大影响人物”，同时被书法界大众提名“2007年中国书坛十大影响人物”候选人，并被《中国青年书法》《墨林快事》等报刊作为2007年中国书坛十大影响热议人物刊登。作品及简历录入《中国历代书画名家大辞典》《百年经典中国美术全集》《中国历代书画名家宝典》《中国当代著名书画家珍品选》《中国硬笔书法史》等近百部书籍。

曾受邀参加“中国近现代书画展”“当代著名书画家精品年展”“中国水墨画日本展”等国内外数十次大型书画展览。有作品被中国历史博物馆以及国内外众多美术馆、纪念馆、碑林等单位和其他个人收藏。

四、人物名录

息烽籍在县外担任过副师、副厅、副地级以上实职的领导干部名录

姓　名	性别	出生年月	籍贯	文化程度	工作单位	主要职务	任职起始时间
鲁红卫	男	1961年10月	息烽	大学本科	省水利厅	副厅长	2006年11月
陈训通	男	1949年12月	息烽	大学本科	安顺市人大	副主任	2003年4月
黄生忠	男	1943年12月	息烽	大专	安顺市人大	副主任	2000年12月
李彦西	男	—	息烽	研究生	安顺学院	党委书记	2008年
魏明禄	男	1962年3月	息烽	研究生	贵阳学院	党委副书记	2008年9月
蔡启明	男	1963年7月	息烽	—	劳动和社会保障部办公厅、 国家公务员局综合司	副主任 司　长	2006年3月 2008年4月
冯贵富	男	1966年8月	息烽	研究生	中国边防部队云南总队	副指导员	1993年

获省部级及以上先进人物名录

姓　名	性别	出生年月	籍贯	工作单位或地点	获奖时间	荣誉称号（奖项、福利）	授予单位
简富明	男	1954年5月	贵州息烽	县农业局	1994年12月	劳动模范	省人民政府
况力夫	男	1947年5月	四川巴县	县农业局	1995年2月	全国农业科技推广先进工作者	农业部、国家科委、人事部
冯世忠	男	1937年7月	贵州贵阳	县农业局	1993年5月	农业科学技术推广奖	省人民政府
冯世忠	男	1937年7月	贵州贵阳	县农业局	1993年10月	政府特殊津贴	国务院
冯曙建	男	1958年8月	贵州息烽	息烽广播电视台	2002年2月	全国广播电影电视系统先进工作者	人事部 国家广电总局
马书烈	男	1962年5月	贵州息烽	县农业局	1996年4月	农业丰收计划二等奖	农业部
张朝仙	女	1964年7月	贵州遵义	县农业局	1999年3月	先进调查员	农业部
吴　昊	男	1975年10月	贵州息烽	县农业局	2002年9月	农业丰收计划二等奖	农业部
潘世昌	男	1966年2月	贵州遵义	县农业局	2003年12月	科技进步二等奖	省人民政府
廖德平	男	1970年4月	贵州息烽	县农业局	2005年3月	先进调查员	农业部市场与经济信息司
邓学平	男	1957年9月	贵州息烽	县农业局	2005年1月	先进个人	中国渔政渔港监督管理局、渔政指挥中心
魏明山	男	1963年8月	贵州息烽	县农业局	2006年9月	农业丰收计划三等奖	农业部
徐忠惠	女	1968年7月	贵州息烽	县农业局	2006年9月	农业丰收计划二等奖	农业部
郑满江	男	1964年12月	贵州息烽	县农业局	2010年12月	先进工作者	农业部
曾发金	男	1948年9月	贵州息烽	县公安局	1991年10月	先进工作者	公安部
蔡汝达	男	1994年5月	贵州息烽	养龙司灯塔村	1995年4月	贵州省劳动模范	省委、省政府
李光碧	女	1953年3月	贵州息烽	茅坡小学	2000年6月	贵州省先进工作者	省委、省政府
李光碧	女	1954年3月	贵州息烽	茅坡小学	2005年4月	全国先进工作者	国务院
韩思权	男	1978年3月	贵州息烽	养龙司乡农业中心	2006年9月5日	农牧业渔业丰收奖第三名。第18完成人	农业部
李正常	男	1963年9月	贵州息烽	养龙司乡人民政府	2008年4月	第二次全国农业普查先进个人	国务院第二次全国农业普查领导小组办公室 国家统计局
黄全秀	女	1936年12月	贵州修文	县计生委	1991年2月	计划生育优秀工作者	省委省政府
张可人	男	1962年12月	贵州息烽	县人口计生局	2003年9月	全国人口计生科技工作先进个人	国家计生委
吴文源	男	1951年2月	贵州息烽	县计生药具站	2005年2月	全省人口计生30年先进工作者	省委、省政府
蒋月华	女	1962年9月	贵州印江	县计生指导站	2008年2月	全国计划生育流动服务车项目先进个人	国家计生委

续表

姓　名	性别	出生年月	籍贯	工作单位或地点	获奖时间	荣誉称号（奖项、福利）	授予单位
樊高荣	女	1947年9月	贵州息烽		1983年9月	全国“三八”红旗手	全国妇联
赵贤英	女	1964年2月	贵州息烽	息烽县残联	2007年9月	全国妇联系统信访工作先进工作者	全国妇联、国家信访局
文关仙	女	1956年12月	贵州息烽	石硐乡水头村	2008年1月	全国农村妇女“双学双比”活动女能手	全国农村妇女“双学双比”活动领导小组
黄南武	女	1946年4月	贵州息烽	永靖乡阳朗村	2009年9月	全国“三八”红旗手	全国妇联
朱代琴	女	1955年12月	贵州息烽	石硐乡难冲桥村	2010年3月	全国城乡妇女岗位建功标兵	全国妇联

获国家、省级奖励教师名录

姓　名	性别	籍贯	工作单位	荣誉称号	授予单位	获奖时间
罗良恺	男	贵州息烽	教育局	扫盲先进工作者	国家教委、人事部	1994年10月
范国炎	男	贵州息烽	教育局	中华扫盲奖	国家教委	1997年9月
张永平	男	贵州息烽	温泉小学	全国教育系统劳模	国家教委、人事部	1991年9月
张学智	男	贵州息烽	新沙小学	全国教育系统劳模	国家教委、人事部	1993年9月
张仕凯	男	贵州息烽	石硐高清民校	全国优秀教师	国家教委、人事部	1995年9月
耿全香	女	河南滑县	下洪马小学	全国优秀教师	教育部	1998年9月
舒盛刚	男	贵州息烽	河坎小学	全国模范教师	人事部、教育部	2001年9月
陈永棋	男	贵州息烽	堰坪小学	全国优秀教师	教育部	2004年9月
李光碧	女	贵州息烽	茅坡小学	全国先进教育工作者	国务院	2005年4月
王忠华	男	贵州息烽	安马小学	全国优秀教师	国家教委、人事部	2007年9月
吕文新	男	贵州息烽	云环小学	全国优秀教师	中国中小学幼儿园教师基金会	2000年9月
陈久琪	男	贵州息烽	息烽一中	全国优秀教师		2001年9月
刘长远	男	贵州息烽	鹿窝小学	省先进工作者	省人民政府	1995年6月
王传喜	男	贵州息烽	梨安小学	省优秀教师	省人民政府	1997年9月
王旭初	男	贵州息烽	城关中学	省优秀教师	省人民政府	1997年9月
方　维	男	贵州息烽	流长小学	省优秀教师	省人民政府	2001年9月
汪政权	男	贵州息烽	息烽二中	省优秀教师	省人民政府	2001年9月
杨明仙	女	贵州息烽	县教研室	省优秀教师	省人民政府	2004年9月
蔡伦忠	男	贵州息烽	督导办公室	两基攻坚先进个人	省委省政府	2006年9月

副高级职称以上科技人员名录
教育系统专业技术人员名录

姓　名	性别	出生年月	籍贯	工作单位	文化程度	专业技术职务	评定时间
陈万立	男	1963年9月	贵州息烽	息烽一中	本科	中学高级	1996年12月
王旭初	男	1957年11月	贵州息烽	息烽一中	本科	中学高级	1996年5月
皮世福	男	1958年8月	贵州息烽	息烽一中	本科	中学高级	1995年9月
龙兴无	男	1958年7月	贵州息烽	息烽一中	本科	中学高级	1996年12月
汪政全	男	1955年8月	贵州息烽	息烽一中	大专	中学高级	1996年12月
刘勋杰	男	1963年9月	四川仁寿	息烽一中	本科	中学高级	2005年8月
王先泽	男	1955年11月	贵州息烽	息烽一中	本科	中学高级	1996年12月
李庆国	男	1960年11月	山东	息烽一中	本科	中学高级	1996年12月
陈洪玉	女	1959年7月	贵州息烽	息烽一中	本科	中学高级	1996年12月
李福宏	女	1960年8月	贵州息烽	息烽一中	大专	中学高级	1996年12月
吕世春	男	1965年3月	贵州息烽	息烽一中	本科	中学高级	1996年12月
李志忠	男	1965年10月	贵州息烽	息烽一中	本科	中学高级	1996年12月
黄开诚	男	1965年5月	贵州息烽	息烽一中	本科	中学高级	1996年12月
杨秀杰	男	1962年12月	贵州息烽	息烽一中	本科	中学高级	1996年12月
吴应康	男	1962年10月	贵州息烽	息烽一中	本科	中学高级	2005年8月
李克勇	男	1963年3月	贵州息烽	息烽一中	本科	中学高级	1996年12月
王乾刚	男	1963年10月	贵州安顺	息烽一中	大专	中学高级	1996年12月
贺家军	男	1964年6月	贵州息烽	息烽一中	本科	中学高级	1996年12月
叶长勇	男	1961年7月	贵州息烽	息烽一中	本科	中学高级	1996年12月
陈　华	男	1962年6月	贵州息烽	息烽一中	本科	中学高级	2005年8月
黄开菊	女	1965年10月	贵州息烽	息烽一中	本科	中学高级	1996年12月
宋　玲	女	1963年10月	贵州息烽	息烽一中	本科	中学高级	1996年12月
付　群	女	1966年3月	贵州息烽	息烽一中	本科	中学高级	1996年12月
黄文兵	男	1968年10月	湖南衡阳	息烽一中	本科	中学高级	2005年8月
方富俊	男	1962年10月	贵州息烽	息烽一中	本科	中学高级	1996年12月
蒋德玉	男	1963年6月	贵州息烽	息烽一中	本科	中学高级	2003年10月
李玉珍	女	1967年5月	贵州开阳	息烽一中	本科	中学高级	1996年12月
李显荣	女	1964年10月	贵州息烽	息烽一中	本科	中学高级	2003年10月
刘　红	女	1968年8月	贵州息烽	息烽一中	本科	中学高级	2004年8月
甘红梅	女	1967年12月	贵州息烽	息烽一中	本科	中学高级	2004年8月

续表

姓　名	性别	出生年月	籍贯	工作单位	文化程度	专业技术职务	评定时间
罗朝勇	男	1967年3月	贵州息烽	息烽一中	本科	中学高级	2004年8月
王玉琼	女	1969年5月	贵州息烽	息烽一中	本科	中学高级	1996年12月
徐　瑶	女	1974年10月	贵州息烽	息烽一中	本科	中学高级	2000年12月
陈久琪	男	1961年11月	贵州息烽	息烽一中	本科	中学高级	2009年1月
罗文敏	男	1929年11月	贵州务川	息烽一中	大专	中学高级	1988年6月
高仁厚	男	1929年11月	贵州金沙	息烽一中	本科	中学高级	1988年6月
李子员	男	1931年9月	湖南	息烽一中	大专	中学高级	1993年10月
张永明	男	1933年6月	河北	息烽一中	大专	中学高级	1993年10月
郭人清	男	1934年5月	湖南郴州	息烽一中	本科	中学高级	1993年10月
黄有余	男	1940年1月	贵州金沙	息烽一中	大专	中学高级	1993年10月
朱应长	男	1943年11月	贵州息烽	息烽一中	本科	中学高级	1993年10月
朱杰生	男	1942年7月	湖南桂东	息烽一中	本科	中学高级	1993年10月
凌宗问	男	1949年7月	重庆永川	息烽一中	大专	中学高级	1994年6月
孙明权	男	1954年12月	贵州息烽	息烽一中	本科	中学高级	2005年12月
曾兴富	男	1949年10月	贵州息烽	息烽一中	本科	中学高级	1994年6月
张思亮	男	1948年11月	贵州息烽	息烽一中	大专	中学高级	1994年6月
童金华	男	1953年9月	贵州息烽	息烽一中	大专	中学高级	1994年6月
邱　群	男	1957年8月	贵州息烽	息烽一中	本科	中学高级	1993年10月
任莉萍	女	1958年5月	河南禹县	息烽一中	大专	中学高级	1993年10月
曾庆仁	男	1938年4月	不详	息烽一中	不详	中学高级	1988年6月
袁光富	男	1938年4月	不详	息烽一中	中专	中学高级	1988年6月
向明国	男	1937年9月	贵州贵阳	息烽一中	本科	中学高级	1988年6月
王筑英	女	1945年8月	江苏武进	息烽一中	本科	中学高级	1988年6月
戴传声	男	1941年10月	贵州印江	息烽一中	本科	中学高级	1988年6月
丁颖脱	男	1929年3月	安徽怀宁	息烽一中	本科	中学高级	1988年6月
魏明凯	男	1956年9月	贵州息烽	息烽二中	大专	中学高级	1995年9月
胡应能	男	1958年8月	贵州息烽	息烽二中	大专	中学高级	2001年5月
张兴无	男	1962年11月	贵州息烽	息烽二中	大专	中学高级	2002年12月
何卫东	男	1962年11月	贵州息烽	息烽二中	大专	中学高级	2003年5月
边德志	男	1962年9月	贵州息烽	息烽二中	本科	中学高级	2005年12月
金世荣	女	1963年4月	贵州息烽	息烽二中	大专	中学高级	2003年12月
钟兴闻	女	1963年11月	贵州息烽	息烽二中	本科	中学高级	2002年12月

续表

姓　名	性别	出生年月	籍贯	工作单位	文化程度	专业技术职务	评定时间
李成凤	女	1964年6月	贵州息烽	息烽二中	本科	中学高级	2005年12月
王　庆	男	1965年2月	贵州息烽	息烽二中	本科	中学高级	2003年12月
骆艳红	女	1965年5月	贵州息烽	息烽二中	本科	中学高级	2005年4月
金爱莲	女	1965年6月	辽宁葫芦岛	息烽二中	本科	中学高级	2005年12月
陈仕富	男	1966年8月	贵州安顺	息烽二中	大专	中学高级	2005年12月
陈立新	女	1966年7月	内蒙古	息烽二中	本科	中学高级	2005年12月
冉彩霞	女	1970年8月	贵州息烽	息烽二中	本科	中学高级	2006年6月
卢　明	男	1958年4月	贵州息烽	息烽二中	大专	中学高级	2006年12月
赖胜钢	男	1956年10月	贵州息烽	息烽二中	本科	中学高级	2006年12月
杜忠强	男	1956年5月	贵州息烽	息烽二中	大专	中学高级	2006年12月
杨少荣	男	1958年6月	贵州息烽	息烽二中	大专	中学高级	2009年12月
李奎华	男	1963年10月	贵州息烽	息烽二中	大专	中学高级	2010年12月
唐金龙	男	1962年12月	四川乐至	息烽二中	大专	中学高级	2009年12月
杨朝均	男	1964年2月	贵州息烽	息烽二中	大专	中学高级	2009年12月
杨佳贵	男	1965年11月	贵州息烽	息烽二中	本科	中学高级	2009年12月
王梅霞	女	1965年11月	贵州息烽	息烽二中	大专	中学高级	2009年12月
聂培群	女	1966年9月	贵州息烽	息烽二中	大专	中学高级	2009年12月
朱定华	女	1967年11月	贵州息烽	息烽二中	本科	中学高级	2009年12月
江东竹	女	1969年11月	贵州息烽	息烽二中	本科	中学高级	2006年12月
刘祖芳	男	1939年10月	贵州息烽	息烽二中	本科	中学高级	1988年12月
黄少平	男	1948年10月	贵州息烽	息烽二中	大专	中学高级	2002年12月
刘仕华	男	1953年10月	贵州息烽	息烽二中	大专	中学高级	2002年12月
陶寿兰	女	1950年5月	贵州息烽	息烽二中	大专	中学高级	1996年10月
胡嘉仁	男	1950年9月	贵州息烽	县职校	本科	中学高级	1997年9月
胡　翃	女	1968年9月	贵州息烽	县职校	本科	中学高级	2005年12月
王槐霞	女	1964年9月	贵州息烽	县职校	本科	中学高级	2004年12月
刘录勋	男	1961年1月	贵州息烽	县职校	本科	中学高级	2001年12月
张世均	男	1941年9月	河南	县职校	本科	中学高级	1993年12月
晏　奎	男	1970年10月	贵州息烽	县职校	本科	中学高级	2009年12月
刘光湘	男	1949年5月	湖南衡阳	县职校	本科	中学高级	1993年12月
李良峰	男	1974年5月5日	贵州息烽	永靖中学	本科	中学高级	2011年12月
谌贻云	男	1968年8月	贵省息烽	永靖中学	本科	中学高级	2008年12月

续表

姓　名	性别	出生年月	籍贯	工作单位	文化程度	专业技术职务	评定时间
宋云英	女	1960年3月	贵州息烽	永靖中学	大专	中学高级	2004年12月
雷　波	男	1971年6月	贵州息烽	永靖中学	本科	中学高级	2009年12月
王　毅	男	1964年10月	贵州息烽	乌江复旦学校	专科	中学高级	2006年12月
王曙光	男	1960年11月	山东平原	乌江复旦学校	专科	中学高级	1997年9月
冯永伦	男	1961年12月	贵州息烽	乌江复旦学校	专科	中学高级	2010年12月
雷安明	男	1973年3月	贵州黄平	乌江复旦学校	本科	中学高级	2008年12月
陈春叶	男	1975年3月	湖南邵阳	乌江复旦学校	本科	中学高级	2009年12月
杨光庆	男	1967年10月	贵州余庆	乌江复旦学校	本科	中学高级	2006年12月
谢光荣	男	1964年4月	贵州余庆	乌江复旦学校	专科	中学高级	2008年12月
杨晓明	男	1962年9月	贵州道真	乌江复旦学校	本科	中学高级	2002年12月
杨　华	男	1966年4月	贵州务川	乌江复旦学校	本科	中学高级	2006年12月
练红会	女	1970年7月	广东兴中	乌江复旦学校	本科	中学高级	2008年12月
徐德仁	男	1968年4月	山东诸城	乌江复旦学校	本科	中学高级	2007年7月
刘梦桃	女	1972年2月	湖南新邵	乌江复旦学校	硕士	中学高级	2010年12月
庹大成	男	1958年5月	贵州息烽	流长中学	本科	中学高级	—
刘大强	男	1967年2月	贵州息烽	流长中学	本科	中学高级	—
杨秀松	男	1958年9月	贵州息烽	流长中学	专科	中学高级	—
李先菊	女	1964年	贵州息烽	流长中学	专科	中学高级	—
王　毅	男	1966年12月	贵州息烽	青山中学	本科	中学高级	2010年10月
尹文书	男	1958年8月	贵州息烽	黑神庙中学	专科	中学高级	2001年12月
邓学恒	男	1959年4月	贵州息烽	黑神庙中学	专科	中学高级	2003年12月
袁绍林	男	1964年5月	贵州息烽	黑神庙中学	专科	中学高级	2003年12月
曾显德	男	1964年4月	贵州息烽	黑神庙中学	专科	中学高级	2002年12月
徐志凤	女	1964年11月	贵州息烽	黑神庙中学	专科	中学高级	2004年12月
王方贵	男	1965年9月	贵州息烽	黑神庙中学	专科	中学高级	2000年11月
周　勇	男	1967年1月	贵州息烽	黑神庙中学	专科	中学高级	2006年12月
李德贵	男	1966年11月	贵州息烽	黑神庙中学	专科	中学高级	2005年12月
杨　刚	男	1966年10月	贵州息烽	黑神庙中学	专科	中学高级	2005年12月
明　凤	女	1956年11月	贵州息烽	黑神庙中学	专科	中学高级	2001年12月
刘德馨	男	1937年11月	贵州息烽	黑神庙中学	中专	中学高级	1988年6月
方忠海	男	1966年9月	贵州息烽	黑神庙中学	专科	中学高级	2010年12月
聂培莲	女	1969年8月	贵州息烽	黑神庙中学	专科	中学高级	2010年12月
袁兴宇	男	1966年9月	贵州石阡	黑神庙中学	本科	中学高级	2004年11月

续表

姓　名	性别	出生年月	籍贯	工作单位	文化程度	专业技术职务	评定时间
张永智	女	1962年4月	贵州息烽	温泉中学	大专	中学高级	2002年12月
龙开学	男	1955年8月	贵州息烽	养龙司中学	本科	中学高级	2000年11月
周素芳	女	不详	贵州息烽	永靖小学	大专	小中高	1988年12月
汪大光	男	1933年12月	贵州息烽	永靖小学	中师	小中高	1988年12月
周志武	男	1947年1月	贵州息烽	教研室	大专	中学高级	1996年12月
杨时政	女	1938年4月	贵州息烽	教研室	高中	特级教师	1988年9月
姚廷华	男	1930年9月	贵州息烽	教育局	高中	中学高级	1988年9月
张国生	男	1962年8月	贵州安顺	教研室	研究生	中学高级	2001年12月
张明学	男	1954年8月	贵州息烽	中铁二院工程集团	大学	高级工程师	1996年

卫生系统副高级职称以上技术人员名录

姓　名	性别	出生年月	籍贯	工作单位	文化程度	专业技术职务	评定时间
钟厚之	男	1934年1月	贵州遵义	县人民医院	专科	副主任医师	1988年3月
卓贤华	女	1936年8月	四川	县人民医院	大学	副主任医师	1988年3月
陈历修	男	1926年4月	贵州息烽	县人民医院	专科	副主任医师	1988年3月
许忠和	男	1938年1月	贵州息烽	县人民医院	大学	主任医师	1993年1月
魏家屿	男	1942年2月	江苏	县人民医院	大学	副主任医师	1993年9月
余文才	男	1953年6月	贵州威宁	县人民医院	大普	副主任医师	1996年9月
刘长英	女	1953年9月	贵州息烽	县人民医院	大普	副主任医师	1998年12月
蔡显斌	男	1964年10月	贵州息烽	县人民医院	本科	副主任医师	2000年12月
钱中华	男	1962年10月	贵州息烽	县人民医院	专科	副主任医师	2004年12月
范　波	男	1966年8月	贵州息烽	县人民医院	本科	副主任医师	2005年12月
陈绍兰	女	1963年5月	贵州湄潭	县人民医院	专科	副主任护师	2006年12月
梅兰瑱	女	1962年12月	四川	县人民医院	专科	副主任检验技师	2006年12月
张军荣	男	1964年2月	贵州息烽	县人民医院	专科	副主任检验技师	2006年12月
杨维凤	女	1964年7月	四川	县人民医院	专科	副主任护师	2007年12月
张　捷	男	1971年2月	贵州息烽	县人民医院	专科	副主任医师	2009年12月
边丽虹	女	1966年4月	贵州息烽	县人民医院	本科	副主任医师	2010年12月
苏庆承	男	1930年6月	云南昆明	县中医院	大学	副主任医师	1988年3月
文昌碧	女	1940年7月	重庆	县中医院	大学	副主任医师	1988年3月
卢　碧	女	1955年10月	贵州息烽	县中医院	大学	副主任医师	1996年6月

续表

姓　名	性别	出生年月	籍贯	工作单位	文化程度	专业技术职务	评定时间
邬昌纯	男	1950年10月	重庆璧山	县中医院	大学	副主任医师	1997年12月
周宗秀	女	1973年11月	贵州息烽	县中医院	大学	副主任医师	2010年12月
杨发文	男	1969年8月	贵州息烽	县中医院	大学	副主任医师	2008年12月
陈久芸	女	1964年12月	贵州	县中医院	大学	副主任医师	2005年6月
宋永春	男	不详	贵州息烽	县中医院	大学	副主任医师	—

农业系统副高级职称以上技术人员名录

姓　名	性别	出生年月	籍贯	工作单位	文化程度	专业技术职务	评定时间
冯世忠	男	1937年7月	贵州贵阳	县农业局	大学	高级农艺师	1987年12月
祝伯龙	男	1925年10月	贵州开阳	县农业局	专科	高级兽医师	1988年4月
简富明	男	1954年5月	贵州息烽	县农业局	大学	高级农艺师	1995年10月
潘世昌	男	1966年2月	贵州遵义	县农业局	大学	高级农艺师	2004年10月
周启康	男	1968年2月	息烽流长	县农业局	大学	高级农艺师	2005年10月
马书烈	男	1962年5月	息烽温泉	县农业局	大专	高级农艺师	2010年10月
陈岳安	男	不详	湖南	县水利局	—	高级工程师	—

附　录

文献资料（一）

息烽县扶贫攻坚计划

消灭贫穷，实现共同富裕，是社会主义的本质要求和社会主义优越性的体现，是改革和发展的要求，也是维护社会稳定的重要条件。扶持贫困地区尽快改变贫穷落后的面貌，是党中央、国务院的一贯方针，不仅大幅度增加了扶贫投入，制定了一系列扶持政策，而且对扶贫工作进行了根本性的改变与调整，实现了从救济式扶贫向开发式扶贫的转变。为了解决我县14万贫困人口的脱贫问题，到2000年实现脱贫致富奔小康的目标，根据国家《“八七”扶贫攻坚计划》的精神，结合我县扶贫工作的实际，特制定本攻坚计划，作为指导我县今后六年扶贫开发工作的纲领性文件。

一、基本情况

（一）息烽县是列入国家“八七”扶贫攻坚的县。全县总面积1037.45平方千米，有耕地面积25.5万亩（习惯亩），其中田7.8万亩，土17.7万亩；现有人口224655人，其中农业入口199627人，农业劳动力10.1万多个。

近几年，虽然我县扶贫工作取得了一定的成绩，但扶贫开发的任务仍十分艰巨。据1994年8月贫困户调查统计，全县贫困人口14万人，占农业人口的70%，其中人均纯收入在200元以下的人口7.4万人，占农业人口的37%。201元至300元的人口3.9万人，占19.5%，301元至400元的2.7万人，占13.5%。这些贫困人口主要分布在深山区、石山区和少数民族聚居区，共同的特点是：交通不便，经济发展缓慢，文化教育落后，人畜饮水困难，生活生产条件恶劣。要解决这些地区群众的温饱问题，难度大，必须打一场攻坚仗。

二、奋斗目标和总体蓝图

（二）解决广大贫困人口的温饱问题，并帮助和引导他们脱贫致富奔小康，是摆在全县各级党政干部、职工和人民群众面前的一个重要的任务。建立社会主义市场经济体制，以及国家对贫困地区的扶持，给我县带来了发展的机遇和更加广阔的前景。面临机遇和挑战，抓紧扶贫开发，尽快改变我县经济、文化、社会的落后状态，消灭贫困，是关系到我县社会安定、民族团结、共同富裕的功垂千秋万代的伟大事业。因此，我们必须遵循邓小平同志建设有中国特色社会主义的理论和党的基本路线，坚持效率优先、兼顾公平的原则，进一步加强扶贫开发工作，切实贯彻党在农村的和各项方针、政策，稳定以家庭联产承包为主的责任制，解放思想，振奋精神，把握机遇，真抓实干，齐心合力打好扶贫攻坚战。

（三）在大力提高经济效益和发展生产力的基础上，到21世纪末使我县14万贫困人口全部脱贫，贫困户年人均纯收入达到500元以上，生活条件有明显的改善。

（四）扶持贫困户创造稳定解决温饱的基础条件：人均建成半亩到一亩稳产高产基本农田；户均建成一亩林、果、药、茶、桑园或其他经济作物；

户均向乡镇企业或发达地区转移一个劳动力；

户均饲养一头黄牛单位的商品畜；

户均有一项家庭支柱产业或其他家庭副业。

（五）加强基础设施建设

——基本解决人畜饮水困难。到2000年，解决4万人、6万头牲畜的饮水困难。

——实现所有乡镇和90%的村遥公路，新惨县乡公路7条，102千米。

——实现所有乡镇和有条件的村通电话。解决3个乡镇微波或光缆通话，部分乡镇安装程控电话。

——实现3万亩坡改梯。每年完成5000亩以上坡改梯。

（六）改变教育、文化、卫生落后状况

——全县基本普及九年制义务教育，通过开展农民技术培训和职业技术教育，达到每户有1个掌握1～2项农业适用技术的劳动力。

——改善医疗卫生条件，建立县、乡、村三级防保网，基本控制地方病。

（七）实行计划生育，使人口自然增长率控制在11‰以内，生育高峰期控制在12‰以内。

（八）按照以上要求，到2000年，实现全县经济实力显著增强，国民生产总值达38000万元（90价，下同），工农业总产值达33360万元，财政收入3000～4000万元，主要工农业产品产量有较大增长；产业结构明显改善，经济布局趋于合理；科学技术和管理水平有较大提高；人民群众生活由温饱逐步向小康迈进；人民群众科学文化素质和思想道德素质明显提高；社会秩序安定，社会风气更加健康向上。

三、指导思想和工作方法

（九）扶贫攻坚的指导思想是：以邓小平同志建设有中国特色社会主义理论和党的基本路线为指针，以市场为导向，以发展经济、发展生产力、解决群众物质文化生活为目的，坚持开发式扶贫，鼓励广大干部、群众发扬自力更生、艰苦奋斗的精神，在国家的扶持下，依靠科技进步；发挥当地资源优势，发展商品生产，逐步实现脱贫致富奔小康的发展目标。

（十）采取以下方式搞好扶贫开发工作：

——发挥我县区位优势、资源优势、交通优势，按照市场需求，开发有竞争力的名特稀优产品和拳头产品，重点发展投资少、见效快、覆盖广、效益高、不破坏生态环境或对生态环境影响甚小的项目。

——统一规划、连片发展有助于直接解决群众温饱问题，帮助他们脱贫致富的种植业、养殖业，逐步形成一定规模的商品生产基地或区域性的支柱产业。2000年建成3万亩优质烤烟基地，1万亩蚕桑基地，2万亩果品基地，3万亩药材基地和蔬菜基地等，使之成为我县的支柱产业。大力发展以猪、牛、羊和家禽为主的养殖业，使畜牧业产值在农业总产值中的比例在35%以上。

——坚持贸工农一体化、产加销“一条龙”的原则。积极发展既能充分利用当地资源，又能大量安排贫困户劳动力就业的资源开发型和劳动密集型的乡镇企业，外联市场内联农户，带动群众儆贫致富。在永靖镇、小寨坝、温泉3个镇建立乡镇企业工业小区，发展磷化工、煤加工企业，使之成为我县的支柱产业。

扶贫企业的普通工人中，应有70%是贫困户劳动力；企业投产后，每年从纯剩润中提取15%作为扶贫开发基金，由县扶贫办收取，按预算外资金管理，在农业银行专户专存，专项用于扶贫开发。

——围绕提高产品质量，开发新品种、降低物耗、提高劳动生产率、改善劳动条件等方面抓好投入少、效益高、见效快的科技成果的推广利用，推动企业技术改造，促进产品结构的调整和技术水平的提高。

——通过拍卖非耕地使用权，土地有偿租用、承包、转让、馈赠使用权等方式，加快荒地、荒山、荒坡、荒水的开发利用。力争2000年前，把所有能拍卖的荒山拍卖，开发利用，大种经济林木，使之成为全县财政的后续财源之一。

——积极培育劳动力市场，有计划、有组织地发展劳务输出。提供信息，介绍职业，实地培训，开拓输出领域，扩大输出空间，提高输出效益。

积极引导、鼓励贫困户劳动力合理、有序地向非农产业转移。

——坚持以公有制为主体，多种经济成分共同发展。鼓励个体、私营经济发展。放心、放胆、放手地抓好个体、私营经济的发展。到2000年，个体、私营经济在全县国民经济中的比例在三分之一以上。

四、资金投入与使用

（十一）用足用好国家和省用于扶持贫困地区发展经济的财政扶贫、信贷扶贫和以工代赈资金。扶贫信贷资金主要用于建设各种支柱产业、龙头产品商品基地，兴办乡镇企业；支援不发达地区发展资金、扶贫开发基金和以工代赈资金，主要用于贫困地区的基础设施建设。

县财政每年从支援不发达地区发展资金中拿出5%，用于扶贫项目的前期准备。

（十二）扶贫资金的投放要与使用效益和贷款的回收直接挂钩，建立综合的考核指标，实行严格的贷款使用责任制；严格扶贫资金的审计制度，严禁挤占、挪用，违者必纠。

（十三）县扶贫开发办公室要建立好项目库，并同计委、财政、乡企、林业、区划、经委、城建、农业、农行等部门共同规划、设计、论证、筛选项目。坚持扶贫项目由相应的经济实体承包开发，承贷承还扶贫资金；坚持扶贫项目必须覆盖贫困户，把效益落实到贫困户。

（十四）在安排和申报扶贫项目时，要向资源条件好、群众生活较为贫困的乡（镇）、村倾斜。

五、广泛动员、协同作战

（十五）扶贫开发工作是一项关系全民事业的宏伟工程，各行各业各部门以及有条件的企事业单位、人民团体，要根据各自的实际，把扶贫开发工作纳入本单位、本部门工作的重要议事日程，充分发挥各自的优势，一如既往地支持、参与扶贫工作，各尽所能，各尽其力，在资金、物资、技术等方面向贫困乡（镇）、村、组倾斜，积极、真诚地帮助他们脱贫致富奔小康。

（十六）计划部门：要结合县的“九五”计划，制定有利于贫困地区经济和社会发展的宏观规划，管好和用好以工代赈资金，做好涉及扶贫开发的宏观协调工作，组织和推动贫困乡（镇）、村与经济发展较快的乡（镇）、村的经济合作。

（十七）工商、商业、供销部门：要搞好服务工作，积极帮助经济落后、条件较差的乡镇建立农产品商品基地，若建商业设施，开拓市场，搞活流通。引导贫困户依托市场，走向市场。

（十八）农林牧水部门：农业部门要深化农村改革，加强农业技术推广体系建设，农民技术培训，实用技术推广，培训一批稳定的农业技术骨干，加快农业现代化步伐。加强农业综合开发，改造中低产田土，大力推广效益显著的农业科技成果，发展“高产、优质、高效”农业；林业部门要以保护和发展森林资源为目标，以加快造林、绿化步伐为重点，以长防林工程为龙头，积极支持贫困山区发展速生丰产用材林、名特优经济林以及各种林副产品，形成以林果种植为主的区域性支柱产业，防止水土流失，改善生态环境；水利部门要加快贫困山区基本农田建设和小流域综合治理，巩固和改善现有水利设施，配套完成小水窖，采用多形式解决人畜饮水困难，增加农田灌溉面积，提高防汛抗旱能力；畜牧部门要加强“双轨”制的实施工作，大力推广科学养畜，加强畜禽疫病防治工作，努力提高畜牧业在我县国民经济中的比重。

（十九）科技部门：要制定科技扶贫战略规划；把发展国民经济、加快扶贫开发作为科学技术开发的主战场，指导和推动扶贫开发工作转到依靠科学技术和提高农民素质的轨道上来，加快科技成果向现实生产力的转化，动员各方面的力量开展多形式的科技开发和科技服务，认真抓好扶贫开发的，科学研究和科技示范。

（二十）教育部门：要继续贯彻“教育必须为社会主义现代化服务，必须同生产劳动相结合，培养德、智、体全面发展的建设者和接班人”的方针，积极搞好教育扶贫工作；进一步深化教育改革，优化教育结构，提高教育质量和办学效益；积极普及九年制义务教育，做好农村青壮年的扫盲工作，加强成人教育和职业教育。

（二十一）交通部门：要配合实施以工代赈计划，增强交通扶贫观念，做到思想重视，投入倾斜，工作抓紧，开拓奋进，改善贫困山区交通条件，为经济发展和扩大对外开放提供交通运输保障。

（二十二）劳动部门：要通过积极培育劳动力市场，为贫困户劳动力开拓外出就业的门路，做好就业服务和技术培训工作，努力扩大合理有序的劳务输出规模。

（二十三）民政部门：要通过建立健全社会保障体系，加强贫困山区的救灾和救济工作，努力提高贫困山区抗灾救灾实力。

（二十四）民族工作部门：要把解决少数民族贫困地区温饱问题，引导少数民族同胞发展经济，脱贫致富奔小康作为工作重点，协调和配合有关部门对少数民族地区进行智力支边、人才培训、科技咨询，发展少数民族贫困地区教育文化卫生和科技事业。

（二十五）广播电视、文化部门：要与乡镇政府配合，每个乡镇建立地面卫星接收站或差转台，有线电视站，扩大电视收视率和有线广播覆盖范围，建立乡镇文化站、图书销售点等，采取灵活多样的形式改善群众文化生活。

（二十六）卫生部门要坚持“防、保、治”的原则，稳定贫困乡村医疗队伍，完善医疗预防保健网，提高乡村医生业务水平和服务质量，消灭和控制法定的传染病和地方病。

（二十七）计划生育部门：要把计划生育工作与扶贫开发工作结合起来，加强计划生育工作，优生优育，降低人口自然增长率。

（二十八）充分发挥工会、共青团、妇联、科协、工商联、残联等组织的作用。工会要组织好企业管理技术人员和能工巧匠对贫困山区开展传授技术、培训人才、攻克技术难点，救治亏损乡镇企业，开展经济协作；共青团组织要调动广大团员青年的积极性，鼓励贫困山区的团员青年带头学技术，学科技，学文化，扩大希望工程的范围和规模，提高贫困山区适龄儿童的入学率和巩固率；妇联要进一步动员贫困乡村妇女积极参与“双学双比”竞赛活动，兴办家庭副业，发展庭院经济，兴办一些适合妇女特点的扶贫项目；科协要继续发挥科普网络的优势，把科学技术引向广大农村，推广适用技术，提供科技信息，让科学技术广泛适用于贫困山区的生产实践；工商联要进一步发挥自身优势，帮助贫困地区培训人才，推广技术，沟通信患，搞活流通，发展经济技术合作；残联要继续做好贫困残疾人的康复扶贫工作。

（二十九）各级司法机关，执法执纪人员，要履行好为实施本计划保驾护航的任务。

六、组织领导和监督机制

（三十）各级党委、政府要加强对扶贫开发工作的领导，把扶贫开发工作列入重要议事日程，心中时刻装着贫困山区、贫困群众。要经常深入贫困乡村、少数民族村寨，搞调查研究，同群众谈心，亲自帮助他们解决实际问题。要善于动员和组织各方面的力量，开创扶贫开发工作的新局面。要把改变贫困乡、贫困村落后面貌的作为考核领导干部政绩的一个重要方面。对贫困山区的农民群众要动感情，绝不能漠不关心，麻木不仁；对开展扶贫工作要动脑筋，绝不能因循守旧，无所作为；对抓好扶贫工作要动真格，不能只说不干，摆花架子。

（三十一）各乡镇要根据本计划制定具体的实施计划，乡镇长要亲自抓，负总责，及时解决扶贫开发工作中的重要问题，集中使用财力、物力，定期检查工作，保证按期完成本计划所规定的任务。

（三十二）扶贫开发工作要纳入法制化管理的轨道，虚心接受人民代表大会及其常务委员会的法律监督和工作监督。

（三十三）充分发扬民主，广泛团结和调动各方面的人士，搞好扶贫开发工作。对扶贫开发工作的有关重要事项，重大决策、人民群众普遍关心的“热点”问题，要事前提交政协协商，广泛征求意见，建议和批评。

（三十四）本计划自一九九五年一月一日起施行。

中共息烽县委　息烽县人民政府
关于人才强县战略的实施意见

为深入贯彻《中共中央、国务院关于进一步加强人才工作的决定》《中共贵州省委、贵州省人民政府关于实施人才强省战略的决定》和《中共贵阳市委、贵阳市人民政府关于实施人才强市战略的若干意见》，进一步加大我县人才工作力度，结合我县实际，就实施人才强县战略提出如下实施意见。

一、实施人才强县战略是我县面临的一项重大而紧迫的任务

（1）充分认识实施人才强县战略的重要性和紧迫性。人才资源是第一资源，人才是经济社会发展中最重要的决定因素。随着经济全球化进程的不断加快，人才争夺日趋激烈，已成为国家、地区竞争的焦点。综合国力的竞争，更加倚重于人才队伍的整体素质。改革开放以来，我县人才队伍建设取得一些成效，人才总量有所增加，结构和分布有所改善，培养造就了一大批党政人才、专业技术人才和农村实用人才，为推动息烽经济社会发展发挥了重要作用。但是，随着经济社会发展日益加快，我县人才工作已不能适应当前形势发展的需要，人才工作存在一些亟待解决的问题。要全面实现建设小康社会和建设经济强县的目标，人才是关键。全县各级党委和政府必须全面贯彻落实“三个代表”重要思想，从战略和全局的高度，深刻认识人才在经济社会发展中的基础性、战略性、决定性作用，进一步增强人才队伍建设的责任感、紧迫感，把人才工作纳入我县经济社会发展的总体布局，把具有一定知识和技能、能够进行创造性劳动的各类人才集聚到息烽经济社会发展的各项事业上来，走人才强县之路。

（2）实施人才强县战略的总体思路。以邓小平理论和“三个代表”重要思想为指导，全面落实党的十六大精神和全国、全省、全市人才工作会议精神，进一步强化“人才资源”的意识，确立人力资本是最重要的资本，人才队伍建设是最重要的建设的观念，坚持党管人才原则，坚持科学的人才观，坚持以人为本，紧紧抓住培养、吸引、用好人才三个关键环节，加强党政人才、专业技术管理人才队伍建设，加快集聚能够提高全县科技水平、带动产业升级、实现经济增长方式由粗放型向集约型转变的科技型人才；加快集聚能够按照国际惯例，运用先进的手段，提高机关、事业单位的现代化管理水平、提高工作效率的管理型人才；加快集聚能够优化社会环境、维护社会秩序、促进社会稳定的服务型人才。正确处理好引进人才和稳定现有人才的关系，通过观念创新、机制创新、制度创新，努力开创人才工作新局面。

（3）实施人才强县战略的总体目标。按照统筹人才工作力量、统筹人才资源开发与经济社会发展、统筹重点产业需求与人才队伍整体建设、统筹当前需求与长远发展的要求，充分开发县内县外两种人才资源，努力建设一支忠诚实践“三个代表”重要思想的党政领导人才队伍，一支推动科学进步和技术创新的专业技术人才队伍，一支掌握熟练劳动技能的中高级人才队伍，一支活跃在农村生产第一线的农村实用人才队伍，为息烽的经济建设和社会发展提供坚强的人才保证和智力支持。

二、以能力建设为核心，以高层人才队伍建设为重点，推进人才资源整体开发

（4）加快构建现代国民教育体系。人才培养，教育为先。要切实把教育作为人才队伍建设的基础性工作摆在优先发展的战略地位，大力发展教育产业，扩大教育资源总量。深化教育改革，优化教育结构，合理配置教育资源。坚持教育创新，全面推进素质教育，提高教育质量。统筹城乡教育，提高义务教育水平，在农村继续巩固“两基”成果，高水平、高质量普及九年义务教育，扩大优质教育资源，逐步普及高中教育，大力发展学前教育，延长人均受教育年限。加强职业高中教育，增加职业技能课程，调整学科和专业设置，大量培养各类高技能人才和实用人才。完善和规范以政府投入为主，多渠道筹措经费的教育投入机制。调动社会资金和外资投资发展民办教育、职业教育和技能培训，形成公办学校和民办学校共同发展的格局。

（5）突出重点，促进各类人才协调发展。

一是实施“高层次人才培养工程”，建设一支高素质党政人才队伍。以加强思想政治建设和执政能力建设为核心，以知识更新为重点，有计划地培养高层次党政人才，选拔综合素质好、有发展潜力的年轻后备干部，有针对性地开展个性化、差别化的培训，通过理论学习和到发达地区或艰苦环境挂职锻炼等方法，培养一批高素质、复合型的党政领导干部。按照《息烽县2003—2007年干部教育培训规划》，有计划地开展干部培训工作，改革和创新培训内容和培训方式，办好县委党校乡（局）级干部培训班和中青年干部培训班。有计划地选送一批干部到省委、市委党校和各类院校学习深造。每年选派一定数量的乡（局）级干部和后备干部到发达地区挂职学习锻炼。通过多种形式的培养锻炼，提高党政人才科学判断形势的能力、驾驭市场经济的能力、应对复杂局面的能力、依法执政的能力和总揽全局的能力。同时，重视抓好党外干部、妇女干部和少数民族干部的培训培养工作。

二是以盘活现有专业技术人才为基础，以稳定、培养和引进急需的优秀人才为重点，努力培养造就一支规模适当、素质优良、结构合理、富有创新能力的专业技术人才队伍。认真组织实施《贵州省2001—2010年专业技术人才队伍建设规划纲要》，确立“人才是第一资源和最重要资本”的观念，牢固树立开放和竞争的观念，树立符合市场经济的引人用人观念，树立以业绩来评价人才的观念；建立与社会主义市场经济相适应的专业技术人才队伍管理体制；建立有利于优秀人才脱颖而出的运行机制；加强聚集优秀人才的载体建设。立足我县经济结构战略性调整的需要，选拔培养一批具有自主创新能力、勇于创新创业的专业技术带头人和优秀中青年科技骨干。逐步建立和形成基础教育、高等教育、职业教育和在职教育相互衔接、互为补充的教育培养体系，以满足经济社会发展对人才的需求。

三是实施高技能人才培养工程。启动我县技能人才振兴行动计划，结合经济结构调整和市场需求，围绕建立一支以中级技工为主体，高级技工、技师为骨干，适应我县经济发展和技术进步需要的各类复合型技能人才队伍。加强职业技术教育，采取岗位培训、个人自学提高等方式，加快高技能人才的培养。深化职业技能培训制度的改革，全面推行和完善职业资格证书制度和技师考核评价制度。努力创造高技能人才成长的良好机制和环境，进一步改善我县技能人才的结构比例，发展壮大技能人才队伍。

四是实施农村实用人才培养工程。整合培训资源，创新培训形式，完善农村现代远程教育网络，拓展信息传送渠道，发挥职业学校，培训中心的作用，把农业科技示范场、科技园区作为农村

实用人才的实践基地。继续抓好县委党校每年两期村干部培训班，并有计划地选送村干部到外地参观学习培训，使每年村干部的培训率都在90%以上。继续做好“绿色证书”的培训、农民科技知识的培训和农村富余劳动力转移就业培训工作，每年培训1000名以上农村乡土人才。扶持农村乡土科技带头人优先参与由政府资金支持的农业项目。进一步加强农民技术人员、乡镇企业专业技术人员职称评定工作，参照国家和省专业技术职务评审标准，对农村实用人才制定县内认同的技术等级。

（6）重视各类经济组织和社会组织的人才工作。把新的社会阶层中的各类人才纳入党和政府的工作范围，在政治上对各类经济组织和社会组织人才一视同仁，在政府奖励、职称考评、成果评奖、创业投资等人才政策上统一安排，在面向社会的资助、基金、培训项目、人才信息库等公共资源运用上平等开放，在改善创业环境和工作生活条件上积极提供服务。进一步完善和规范市场体系，整合城乡劳动力市场和人才市场，完善服务功能，积极为各类经济组织引进人才提供人才评估和推介服务。拓宽视野，注重从我县各类新经济组织和社会组织中选拔部分优秀人才到党政机关任职。

（7）加快构建终身教育体系，把人才培训和继续教育作为提高人才素质的重要途径。鼓励单位和个人开展继续教育，对取得硕士以上学位的学习费用，按有关政策由人才工作协调小组协调合理分担。建立和完善带薪学习、在职进修、出国（出境）培训等多途径多形式的学习培训制度。积极开展创建“学习型组织”“学习型社区”活动。构建各级各类干部的知识培训体系，探索系统性、个性化的培训新模式，提高教育培训的针对性。充分利用我县远程教育网络平台，逐步建立“息烽县干部在线学习园地”，建立优势互补，覆盖全县的教育培训网络，形成终身化、网络化、开放化、自主化的终身教育体系。

三、以引进紧缺急需人才为重点，创造人才汇集的吸引环境，以较大的竞争力引进人才

（8）畅通人才引进“绿色通道”，放开引进紧缺人才。开辟我县急需的城建、农业、教育、卫生、水利等方面的专门人才及高层次人才“绿色通道”。进一步完善人才流动和引进的政策，改革户籍、人事关系、身份对人才引进的刚性制约，取消人才引进审批制，实行人才准入制、备案制。政府人事部门牵头设立“一站式”人才引进服务窗口，实行人才引进限时办理制度。建立“工作居住证制度”。在人事管理、领办创办企业、成果转化、社会保险、子女入学、入托等方面，与所在地居民同等对待，确保我县急需的高层次人才引得进、留得住、用得好。鼓励省内外、市内外高级人才通过短期培训、项目合作、兼职及技术承包、技术入股、成果转让、考察讲学、担任业务技术顾问等柔性方式来我县工作。根据全县经济社会发展和重大建设项目需要，加强对紧缺人才的预测和规划，提高紧缺人才引入的针对性和有效性。对我县支柱产业发展、重大工程建设和社会事业发展等方面急需的中高级专业技术人才和管理人才，要采取一人一策、一事一策，不拘一格、千方百计加以引进。

（9）积极实施项目引才工程，突出以事业引人。要把人才载体建设作为重要的抓手，做大、做活、做强人才载体，使之成为吸引人才的“磁场”，培养人才的“摇篮”，各类人才施展才干的“舞台”。要依托我县的支柱产业、优势产业和重大项目建设，大力集聚省内外、市内外优秀人才到我县创业。加大招商引资力度，大力引进多种形式的非公有制企业，鼓励人才到非公有制企业献智创业，使之成为未来人才重要的吸纳者和开发者。在制定和完善招商引资各项政策的过程中，不断补充和完善招才引智的各项政策，给各类人才应有的地位、应有的舞台和应有的回报，让人才

的价值得到充分的体现。此外，还要为他们提供良好的工作和生活环境，帮助他们解决各种后顾之忧，促进人才的健康发展。

四、坚持改革创新，建立人才辈出、人尽其才的激励机制，激发人才的积极性和创造性

（10）建立和完善人才评价机制。坚持党政人才的评价重在群众认可、专业技术人才的评价重在社会和业内认可的原则，组织人事部门要加快改革各类人才评价方式，积极探索主体明确、各具特色的评价方法。加强分类分级考评，建立和完善以绩效为核心、定性与定量相结合的综合考评体系。牢固树立本地人才和引进人才同等重要的观念。在人才评价和使用上一视同仁。改革人才评价方式，完善人才评价手段，积极应用现代人才测评技术，努力提高人才评价的科学水平。推行职称评审制度，实行评聘分离，打破专业技术职务终身制。加强专业技术人员能力建设和业绩考核，对业绩特别突出的专业技术人员，其职称评审不受学历、资历、职务结构比例限制。建立专业技术职务任职资格注册管理制度，推进专业技术人才评价的社会化。

（11）建立有利于优秀人才脱颖而出的选人用人机制。认真贯彻《党政领导干部选拔任用工作条例》，加大领导干部公开选拔和竞争上岗的力度，建立完善党政领导人才实绩考核和评估机制，把实绩突出、群众公认的优秀人才选拔到领导岗位。按照公开、平等、竞争、择优的原则，不拘一格选用人才，积极营造优秀年轻人才脱颖而出的良好环境。推行机关中层干部竞争上岗，完善党政机关干部年度考核制度。坚持并改进考试录用制度，完善选调制度，注重选拔年轻干部、高学历干部及有基层工作经验的干部充实党政机关。全面推行事业单位人员聘任制。完善退休制度，事业单位可根据工作需要和本人自愿及身体健康状况，按管理权限批准，适当延长退休年龄：具有副高专业技术职称的可延长1～5年；具有正高级专业技术职称资格或关键岗位上的在岗高级技师，可适当延长退休年龄1～10年。

（12）建立和完善人才分配激励机制。建立资金技术、专利等知识产权入股制度和技术创新人员持股制度。鼓励事业单位结合自身特点，争取灵活多样的分配形式，激活内部分配，实现实际收入与档案工资的分离。逐步探索和实行市场工资机制，做到工资与经济效益和工作业绩挂钩。研究制定按生产要素分配的有关政策，对专业技术人员实行专利、技术或科技成果入股等政策。对特殊人才可采取协议工资、项目年薪等特殊的分配方式。引进急需的高层次人才，工资待遇完全放开。鼓励高层次人才以专利、发明、技术、管理等要素参与分配，分配比例由受益单位和本人协商确定。高层次人才将本人有自主知识产权的科技成果转让到本县各类企事业单位的，可选择一次性买断、分期支付、利益提成、作价入股等收益分配方式。制定允许企事业单位人才兼职兼薪的管理办法；让拥有知识、技术、资本等要素的各类人才通过创新创业致富。

（13）建立规范有效的人才奖励制度。坚持精神奖励和物质奖励相结合的原则，建立以政府奖励为导向、用人单位奖励为主体、社会力量为补充的人才奖励体系，发挥经济利益和社会价值双重激励作用。规范和完善各类人才奖项评选标准和办法，实现有效奖励和有序奖励。坚持和完善“息烽科学技术奖”，设立“息烽县杰出人才奖”，对在全县经济建设和社会发展中做出突出贡献的专业技术人员给予重奖。对获得国家级、省级、市级奖励的各类人才，按照同等标准给予奖励。

（14）建立健全人才保障制度。根据各类人才的特点和需要，建立健全机关、企事业单位人才流动中的社会保险衔接办法，加快机关和事业单位社会保障制度改革，完善企业社会保障体系。建立健全人才补充养老、人身、意外、医疗、家庭财产等保险制度和重要人才政府投保制度。完善高层次人才补贴制度，对县级专业技术带头人每年每人补助学习资料费600元，中青年科技骨干每年每人补助300元；适当提高我县知识分子补贴标准；对农村乡土科技带头人除给予优惠政策外，还要给予适当奖励。

五、坚持党管人才原则，切实加强对人才工作的领导

（15）加强党对人才工作的领导。党管人才主要是管宏观、管政策、管协调、管服务。县委对人才工作统筹规划，把握人才工作的重大方针政策，将人才资源状况纳入经济社会发展统计指标体系之中，通过动态的人才工作指标加强对人才工作的有效监测，切实做好人才队伍建设的宏观指导、组织协调和督促检查工作。

成立县人才工作协调小组，负责全县人才工作和人才队伍建设战略规划、政策研究、宏观管理和协调落实，形成县委统一领导，组织部门牵头抓总，有关部门各司其职，密切配合的人才工作新格局。人才工作协调小组下设办公室，负责处理日常工作。建立人才工作目标责任制，加大督促检查力度，把人才工作纳入年度目标考核内容，作为考核各级党政领导干部尤其是党政一把手政绩的重要依据。

（16）加大对人才开发工作的投入。健全政府、社会、用人单位和个人多元投入机制。县财政2004年预算安排20万元的专款，作为人才资源开发资金，并随着经济的增长每年有所增加。资金由县人才工作协调小组统筹，并制定管理办法，专项用于人才资源开发的各项工作。加强对资金使用的监督管理，提高人才投入效益。

（17）营造尊重劳动、尊重知识、尊重人才、尊重创造的良好氛围。各级党委和政府要充分认识人才工作的极端重要性，与时俱进，开拓创新，准确把握新形势下人才工作的特点和规律，以搞好服务、营造良好环境为工作重点，以充分发挥各类人才的积极性、创造性为出发点和落脚点，积极探索人才工作的新思路，努力开创人才工作的新局面。要充分利用新闻媒体，加强人才资源开发舆论宣传，全力营造尊重劳动、尊重知识、尊重人才、尊重创造的良好社会氛围，形成鼓励人才干事业、激发人才干事业、支持人才干成事业的社会环境。充分发挥工会、共青团、妇联等群团组织在人才工作中的重要作用。完善领导干部联系制度，积极主动、满腔热情地为他们排忧解难，营造良好的服务环境。要实行依法管理，加快推进人才工作法治化建设，增强人才工作的规范和有效性，营造良好的法治环境。

中共息烽县委　息烽县人民政府
关于进一步提高执政能力全力推进生态经济县建设的意　见

中共贵阳市委七届十三次全会对加快生态经济市建设、加强执政能力建设进行了全面动员和部署。为切实贯彻落实市委七届十三次全会精神，推动我县经济社会持续快速健康发展，结合实际提出如下意见。

一、深刻认识进一步加强执政能力建设，全力推进生态经济县建设的重要意义

加强执政能力建设，是党的十六届四中全会站在时代和战略的高度，全面分析当前形势和任务提出的新要求，是各级党组织正确应对严峻挑战、顺利完成历史使命和不断提高执政能力和领导水平的迫切需要。市委七届十三次全会提出了加强执政能力建设的若干措施，为进一步加强全市党组织建设作出了指导。

强化执政理念，提高执政能力是新时期党建工作的核心。新形势下强化执政理念，就是要在新时期的发展中始终贯穿科学的发展观这条主线，更好地体现"立党为公、执政为民"。加强执政能力建设，就是要坚持把理想信念教育放在首位，真正从理论上提高执政修养，增强为民执政、"执好政"的主动性和紧迫性。加强执政能力建设，就是要不断提高发展先进生产力、发展先进文化的能力，在实现最广大人民的根本利益中更好地践行"三个代表"重要思想。加强执政能力建设，就是要坚持发展这一执政兴县第一要务，始终把维护稳定作为首要职责，把依法办事作为核心原则，把会抓发展作为基本能力，将党的方针政策和上级指示精神与县情结合起来，积极推进思路创新和工作方法创新，卓有成效地领导和加快县域经济发展，不断改善人民生活质量，提高人民生活水平。

建设生态经济县是全县融入"大贵阳"框架全面建设小康社会的必然选择。市委七届十一次全会对今后一段时期贵阳市的经济和社会发展进行了总体部署，提出了实施建设"大贵阳"战略。息烽县作为贵阳市的组成部分之一，审时度势，结合县情提出了贯彻落实建设"大贵阳"的意见，强调必须举全县之力，在建设"大贵阳"中实现提速发展，强县升位。市委七届十三次全会作出了加快建设生态经济市的决定，进一步明确了当前和今后一个时期全市经济、政治、文化等领域的发展方向和战略目标。面对全市新的发展形势和发展任务，息烽作为贵阳市经济发展相对滞后的县，工作的任务重、发展的压力大。必须牢固树立和落实科学的发展观，切实加强执政能力建设，不断提高统筹发展的能力和领导发展的水平，按照全面建设小康社会"四步走"发展战略，将自身发展积极融入"大贵阳"框架，将全力推进生态经济县建设作为实施可持续发展的有效载体和工作主线，不断促进强县升位和跨越式发展，确保与全市同步实现"两个率先"目标。

有效推进生态经济县建设是检验我县执政能力建设的一个标准。市委七届十三次全会提出建设生态经济市，对全县的发展提出了更高的要求。能否有效推进生态经济县建设，是检验全县各级执政能力建设的一个标准；能否构建一个物质文明、政治文明、精神文明协调发展的和谐社会，是对

全县各级执政能力的严峻考验。一方面，全县生态经济的发展和和谐社会的构建，有赖于全县各级党组织执政能力的不断提高；另一方面，生态经济的发展和和谐社会的构建将不断推动全县的执政能力建设。为此，全县各级党组织要不断加强自身建设，提高自身素质，在强力推进生态经济发展中，不断提高战略思维能力和领导发展的能力，联系群众和依靠群众工作的能力，科学执政、民主执政和依法执政的能力，驾驭社会主义市场经济和构建社会主义和谐社会的能力，建设社会主义先进文化和拒腐防变、抵御风险的能力。

二、总体思路和奋斗目标

总体思路：以邓小平理论和“三个代表”重要思想为指导，牢固树立和落实科学的发展观，坚持发展这个执政兴县第一要务，不断加强执政能力建设，把建设“大贵阳”和实现“两个率先”作为第一目标，紧扣全面建设小康社会“四步走”战略，依托“生态经济市”定位，按照“谋发展、抓重点、调结构、进强县”的发展思路，全力推进工业强县、科教兴县、环境立县战略，谋求更加科学、更加合理、更加协调的发展；重点抓好城乡基础设施建设、农业综合生产能力建设、重点产业项目建设、人才队伍建设和发展环境建设；全力“提升一产、主攻二产、加快发展三产”，力争在支柱产业发展上实现重点突破，努力构建循环经济持续发展，旅游开发扎实推进，农业综合效益明显提高，人居环境不断改善，城乡一体化进程加快，可持续发展能力增强，物质文明、政治文明、精神文明协调发展的和谐社会。

奋斗目标：第一步，2005—2010年，全面启动生态经济县建设，实现进入“建设贵州经济强县”目标。力争到2010年，部分乡镇初步达到生态经济乡（镇）建设要求，建成一批生态经济示范村和绿色社区。生态经济产值占全县生产总值80%以上，对财政的贡献率达80%以上，对农民增收的贡献率达到80%以上。森林覆盖率达45%，城镇绿地率达43%以上。规模以上企业50%通过ISO14000环境管理体系认证，大气环境质量、水环境质量达到或优于国家标准。第二步：2011—2020年，生态经济县建设全面推进，实现全面建设小康社会目标。力争到2020年，各乡镇基本达到生态经济乡（镇）建设要求，工业企业基本实现清洁生产，规模以上企业100%通过ISO14000环境管理体系认证，生态经济产值占全县生产总值85%以上，对财政的贡献率达85%以上，对农民增收的贡献率达到90%以上。第三步：2021—2050年，循环经济全面实施，基本实现现代化。全县生态经济效益明显，布局合理，基础设施完善，城乡社会和谐，人居环境优美，人民生活安康，可持续发展能力明显增强，物质文明、政治文明、精神文明和谐统一。

三、围绕“三大战略”，抓好“五大建设”，全力推进生态经济县建设

以科学的发展观为统领，以经济建设为中心，以转变经济增长方式为主线，以发展生态产业为基础，以创造良好生态人居环境为根本出发点，围绕工业强县、科教兴县和环境立县“三大战略”，抓好城乡基础设施、农业综合生产能力、重点产业项目、人才队伍和发展环境“五大建设”，着力形成一、二、三产业互动，城乡经济互流的格局，全面加快构建和谐社会进程。

（一）着力增强综合服务能力，全力抓好城乡基础设施建设

坚持建设和管理并重，着力提高综合服务能力，建立较为完备的城乡公共基础设施服务体系。

突出加强水利基础设施建设。深入推进农业综合开发和高标准农田建设，加大水土保持力度，大力实施土地整治。坚持大中小并举，蓄、引、提、排、灌结合，逐步建成较为完备的供水保障网络。完善鱼简河水库配套工程，规划建设一批骨干水利工程和配套水利设施，加快病险水库和小流

域综合治理，初步形成空中水、地表水、地下水互为补充的农灌网络；大力实施“三小”工程、“解困工程”“渴望工程”和“母亲水窖工程”，提高城乡供水能力，加快农村人畜饮用净化自来水工程建设，初步解决工程性缺水问题。

切实加快经济路和旅游路为重点的交通网络建设。加快小寨坝铁路编组站扩容建设。完善客运停车场为主的交通配套设施，强力推进乡村公路提级硬化，力争2010年基本实现村村通等级公路、组组通公路和村寨串户路硬化。加强配套水运设施建设，扩大乌江水路运输量。初步形成川黔铁路、210国道、贵遵高等级公路及其复线和乌江库区、构皮滩库区为中枢的交通网络。

大力推进农村服务设施建设。加强和巩固农村电网改造，完善配变电设施，确保城镇、农村和企业生产生活用电质量。加强城乡传输网络、电话网络、数字网络和移动通信网络建设，逐步推进语音、数据、图像“三网合一”光缆进村入寨，实现互联网、电话网、广播电视网综合传输。到2010年，全面实现自然村寨通广播电视电话，力争80%以上的村建立农经信息网接收点，宽带网络入村率达80%，村通广播电视和通信网络的质量得到有效提高。继续做好防灾减灾体系建设，完善气象灾害预警系统、地质灾害预警系统和人工增雨防雹指挥作业系统。

不断加快城镇功能性基础设施建设。完善城镇供水、供电管网设施，加快城镇道路、供电、通信、消防、绿化、给排水和排污等基础设施建设，大幅度提高城镇供气普及率和垃圾处理率。围绕综合型、工矿型、工矿旅游型、商贸型、民族特色型等定位，以人为本，建设功能齐全、布局合理、经济繁荣、生态协调、环境优美的城镇体系，建设与生态环境和谐、节约耕地的生态型村寨。不断完善以大宗农产品批发市场为中心、产地市场为骨架、集贸市场为基础的农村多元化市场服务体系。

（二）着力提高综合效益，全力抓好农业综合生产能力建设

强化农业基础地位，全面推进“三农”工作。坚持以增加农民收入为核心，注重农业产业的规模和效益，不断提高农业的投入和产出比率。依托全市“农业经济板块”建设，科学统筹区位、交通、气候、市场等资源，不断优化全县农业区划和产业结构布局，大力发展生态农业和绿色农业。围绕服务城市、富裕农村，重点抓好蔬菜瓜果等城郊高效农业、茶果药材和现代畜牧等山区生态农业板块的规划。按照高产、优质、高效、生态、安全的要求，加快无公害农产品生产基地规模化建设，形成一批具有地方特色和市场竞争力的鲜活畜禽水产品、蔬菜等以无公害农产品为主的特色农业基地，并通过基地辐射带动提高全县农业的规模化水平。加快生态农业科技示范园的开发与建设，按照农产品质量认证体系标准，建立健全农村社会化服务体系，严格农业投入品管理，实施无害化生产，提高农产品品质。大力推进农业科技创新，继续抓好农业综合开发，积极发展以畜牧业为核心，草、畜、沼、果、水、路“六位一体”生态农业，大力推广农业废弃物沼化循环利用的生态模式，不断提高农业的综合效益。重点扶持与生产基地配套的生态龙头企业，加快发展农副产品精深加工、储藏、保鲜、运输业，扶持一批辐射面大、带动面广、规模较大、生态效益明显的农产品加工龙头企业，以农业商品化促进农业产业化，以农业产业化加快农业生态化，以农业生态化推动农业现代化。

（三）加快发展新型工业和生态旅游，全力抓好重点产业项目建设

大力实施“工业强县”战略。以发展循环经济为突破口，加快工业结构调整，加快发展科技含量高、经济效益好、资源消耗低、环境污染少、人力资源优势得到充分发挥的新型工业，主攻

二产，加速推进“工业强县”战略进程。坚持以项目为载体，每年都争取让一些项目进入全市循环经济实施计划，真正把发展循环经济落实到项目上。充分发挥企业主体作用，抓好循环经济试点工作，不断将试点成果向企业延伸。根据环境容量，按照循环经济理念进一步优化工业布局结构，不断加快企业生态转型和环保生产进程，强力推进小寨坝新型工业区、尹庵磷化工业区、阳朗食品医药工业基地综合生态化建设。力争到2010年，基本形成具有较强竞争力的生态支柱产业和县域特色经济框架。

大力培育工业支柱产业。充分发挥磷化工企业相对集中的优势，重点抓好贵阳循环经济息烽磷复肥基地建设。以贵阳中化开磷和西洋肥业为龙头，依靠科技进步，整合产业要素，延长产业链，综合利用废气废渣废水。大力推进磷矿资源保护性开发、做好优势磷化工产品扩张性开发。力争到2010年，全县磷化工产品实物总量达380万吨以上，磷化工产业产值达58亿元。扶优扶强绿色食品加工和现代制药业。大力发展带动型产业和龙头型企业，积极发展姜、葱、蒜等种植，重点扶持味美、美满等具有一定规模的农产品深加工龙头企业发展壮大。依托汉方、太和、银杏鹰等药业企业，在建立和巩固GMP药业生产基地的基础上，大力发展GAP中药材规范种植，扶持其不断研制和开发新产品，提高制药市场占有份额，做大做强制药业，力争2010年全县药业产值达到10亿元以上。

积极发展以生态旅游为龙头的服务业。充分发挥自然生态资源与人文生态资源相对集中的优势，积极培育特色旅游产业，以此带动三产加速发展。坚持保护与开发并重，将旅游开发与生态环境建设、历史文化遗产保护同步规划、同步实施，高起点、高水平编制旅游发展规划和重点景区建设规划。坚持以“重温革命史、休闲观光游”为主题，不断改善旅游基础设施建设，打造以息烽集中营旧址为重点的革命历史教育游、以乌江峡为重点的红色旅游、以西望山为重点的休闲观光游、以温泉为重点的度假疗养旅游路线，力争到2010年全面建成集革命传统教育、红色旅游、自然山水风光、人文景观于一体的筑北旅游精品线。不断完善行、游、住、食、购、娱等要素功能，延长服务链，倡导绿色营销。努力发掘文化特色产品，开发旅游商品，加强旅游促销。改造提升交通运输、商贸物流、餐饮等传统服务业，全力推动信息、金融、保险等现代服务业，加快发展城镇房地产、社区服务、法律服务等需求潜力大的服务业。通过对社会服务体系的改组改造并与其他体系嫁接，提高服务体系在科技、信息、供给等方面的综合服务能力。

（四）着力构建智力支撑体系，全力抓好人才队伍建设

坚持“科教兴县”战略，按照《人才强县战略实施意见》（息党发〔2004〕16号），全面实施人才强县、“专家治县”，积极围绕生态经济发展培养和配备人才。结合生态经济建设作好人才预测和教育培训规划，结合全县经济和社会发展“十一五”规划编制好人才规划。紧紧抓住培养、吸引、用好人才三个环节，不断加强以党政人才、企业经营管理人才和专业技术人才为主体的人才队伍建设。实施人才资源整体性开发，用好现有人才，培养后备人才、引进急需人才，为建设生态经济县提供根本依托。

积极营造聚才环境。全面放开人才市场，积极营造尊重知识、鼓励创新的环境，加大科技投入，鼓励支持以企业为主体的技术创新，加快科技成果向现实生产力的转化，加速高新技术产业的发展；加强农村新品种、新技术的引进和推广运用。制定切实可行的激励机制，综合利用产业聚才、项目引才等手段，集聚一批高素质党政人才、企业经营管理人才和专业技术人才；同时采取特殊政策，建立外来人才的绿色通道，在生态经济领域和重点产业项目上引进一批专业人才，并建立

领导干部联系专家制度和人才流动机制，吸引高层次人才为生态经济县建设服务。

重视资质人才的教育培养。强化示范特点，发挥辐射效应，注重实验功能，扎实抓好科技园区建设；巩固和发展“普实”教育成果，深入推进现代远程教育网络和职业技术教育学校、农技培训机构、劳动就业培训基地等城乡基础教育载体建设；切实加强公共卫生和基层文体设施建设，不断为全县科技、教育、文化、卫生、管理等实用人才队伍建设提供一个大容量、综合性、立体化的育才平台。在充分利用全县基础教育载体加快人才培育的同时，积极通过岗位轮换、借地育才、对外交流等方式，不断加强对企业法人和经营者的循环经济理念培训；不断加大对生态经济建设高层次人才的培养；着眼于农村劳动力资源的综合开发，扎实推进农村劳动力的技能型培训转移工作，并不断通过县乡村实用人才培训和农民教育工程加大对农村生态经济建设人才的培育，切实为建设生态经济县提供坚强有力的智力支撑。

不断创新用才机制。深化人事制度改革，建立健全以公开、平等、竞争、择优为导向，有利于优秀人才脱颖而出、充分施展才能的选人用人机制，并在公开、公正原则基础上做到个人激励与群众激励并重，充分激发人才队伍活力。进一步放活人才使用的所有制和地域界限，广泛开展对外合作交流，充分利用和发挥非政府组织、学术团体和机构、私营公司或企业、民间基金组织等的技术优势，共同开展生态保护与建设。

（五）着力加快城乡一体化进程，全力抓好发展环境建设

抓好生态环境建设和保护，推进可持续发展。依托“生态经济市”定位，坚持发展与环境综合决策，强力推进县域经济社会的可持续发展。加强资源保护，禁止毁林开荒和乱挖乱采野生植物；坚持工业污染防治与城镇环境保护、农村环境保护与城镇综合整治、生态建设与生态保护“三结合”；大力实施节能、节水和资源综合利用工程。搞好“封、造、防”为主的生态环境建设，突出实施好“三环三线一景区”（环城、环镇、环库；河流、铁路、公路沿线；旅游景区）为重点的林带建设，形成以西望山、乌江库区、城镇乡村、通道沿线为核心的林带交错的生态屏障。加强退耕还林工程管理，巩固退耕还林成果，扩大牧草、林竹、林茶、林药、林果等种植规模。鼓励种植生态林和经济林兼用树种，大力发展有经济效益的生态林，提高人工造林质量，加快以速生丰产用材、工业原料、中药材原料为重点的商品林基地建设，力争全县森林覆盖率2010年达到45%。大力推进城镇园林化、河岸森林化、道路林荫化、农村庭院花园化。继续加强山、水、林、田、路综合治理，扎实推进生态文明村建设，积极开发清洁能源，配套改圈、改厕、改灶、改厨和改造串户道路，力争2010年全县农村“五改一气”农户覆盖率达60%。

加快政府职能转变，抓好政务环境建设。按照“经济调节、市场监管、社会管理和公共服务”目标，突出抓好政府职能转变，深化行政体制改革和企事业单位改革，真正实现政企分开和政事分开，努力提高行政服务质量和效率。完善在利用产业导向和优惠政策引资开发高新技术、污染防治、节能降耗和资源综合利用项目，引进先进技术、人才、设备和管理经验等方面全方位对外交流与合作所需配套的资金、信贷、土地、税收等优惠政策，积极为外来投资者提供良好的投资环境。

深入推进“文明县”建设，努力构建和谐社会。坚持以“卫生与秩序”为突破口，不断推进“文明县”建设。全面加强农村思想政治和社会哲学工作，突出加强未成年人思想道德教育。积极通过机关、学校、企业、家庭、社会等平台加强公众的生态知识、生态文明宣传教育，不断增强全

县人民的环境意识、生态理念和法制观念，鼓励公众参与生态环境的保护和建设。不断深化城乡生态文明建设，大力推进绿色社区创建，促进文明社区和文明家庭建设；切实推进优美乡镇创建，塑造特色生态城镇；扎实推进生态示范村创建，综合整治农村环境；积极实施生态家园富民计划，创建“全面小康示范村”。切实加强文化基础设施建设，积极保护和合理开发民间艺术、民俗文化，丰富生态文化内涵，大力培育具有地方特色的生态文化产业。深入推进可持续发展战略和计划生育基本国策，逐步建立人口与资源、环境承载力相适应的人口生态体系。大力发展科技、教育、卫生和社会保障等事业，不断提高全县人民的科技文化综合素质。不断调整、优化人与人之间、人与自然之间的关系，增强社会诚信意识，促进人与自然和谐相处，加快建设和谐社会进程。

（六）以机制创新为保障，不断推进生态经济县建设

加强生态经济发展规划和管理。全面贯彻《贵阳市建设循环经济生态城市条例》，在全面调查全县生态产业、生态环境、生态文化资源的基础上，结合城镇总体规划和生态功能区划，尽快制定《息烽县生态经济县建设规划》、各生态乡（镇）建设规划以及生态经济示范点建设规划。加强法律监督、民主监督、群众监督和舆论监督，进一步完善县、乡（镇）政府内部的监察制度，加强对全县各级领导干部执行生态、环境、资源等方面法律规章情况的监督，确保生态经济县建设规划顺利实施。

建立多元化投入机制。全面放开生态建设投入限制，建立生态经济县建设的多元化投入机制。完善财政管理体系，优化财政支出结构，加大对生态经济建设的投入。县财政每年安排一定的工作经费，用于生态经济县建设规划、考核、奖励，并逐年递增。生态经济县建设重大工程和重点项目，优先纳入国民经济和社会发展计划，统筹安排，认真组织实施。各乡镇和县各有关部门进一步完善环境设施使用和服务收费制度，依法征收城镇污水、垃圾、废物等收集和处置费，实行统一收集、付费处置。按照“政府引导、社会参与、市场运作”的要求，鼓励不同经济成分和各类投资主体，以独资、合资、承包、租赁、拍卖、股份制、股份合作制和BOT等不同形式参与生态经济县建设。完善自然资源与环境有偿使用机制，按照“谁受益、谁补偿、谁破坏、谁恢复”的原则，对资源受益者依法征收资源开发和生态环境补偿费。积极争取国债资金及上级部门资金，广泛吸引外资、民资及其他社会资本。进一步增强开放意识，加强生态经济建设的对外交流与合作，积极争取国内外各类投资。

四、加强执政能力建设，提高领导发展的水平

为全力推进生态经济县建设提供坚实保证实施生态经济县建设是一项需要全县人民长期不懈奋斗的事业，是一项跨部门、跨行业的综合系统工程。要实现生态经济县建设提出的各项战略任务目标，必须树立和落实科学发展观，切实加强党的执政能力建设，不断提高全县各级党组织和领导班子的执政能力和领导水平。

（一）加强理论武装，突出思想政治建设，不断提高用“三个代表”重要思想指导实践的能力

坚持用“三个代表”重要思想武装党员和领导干部。继续完善学习制度，加强对“三个代表”重要思想的学习，坚持用“三个代表”重要思想武装头脑，不断提高运用“三个代表”重要思想的立场、观点、原则和方法分析问题、解决问题的能力。增强学习的自觉性，广泛学习市场经济、科技、法律、金融、文化、历史等方面的知识，不断拓宽知识面，掌握新情况，解决新问题。坚持理论联系实际，善于运用理论指导实践，牢固树立和认真落实科学发展观，不断提高全县各级领导

干部科学判断形势、驾驭市场经济、应对复杂局面、依法执政和总揽全局的能力。加强理想信念教育，大力弘扬以爱国主义为核心的民族精神和以改革创新为核心的时代精神，着力培育和塑造“团结一心、知难而进、奋力拼搏、敢为人先”的息烽精神，使全县人民始终保持昂扬向上的精神状态。加强思想政治宣传，认真总结各个阶段推进生态经济县建设的工作经验和先进典型，加大宣传力度，营造全县上下共同推进执政能力建设和生态经济发展的良好氛围。

坚持抓好领导班子思想政治建设。推进生态经济县建设，实现强县升位和跨越式发展，关键在各级领导班子。全县各级各部门要紧扣抢抓机遇、加快发展这个根本主题，以建立创新型、团结型、实干型领导班子为目标，不断提高领导班子创造力、凝聚力和战斗力。大力推进领导班子思想政治建设经常化和制度化，一级抓一级、一级带一级、层层抓落实，努力促进全县各级党政机关、企事业单位领导班子思想政治建设整体推进和共同提高。

坚持开展好党员先进性教育活动。以开展“做合格党员”活动为载体，认真落实中央、省、市关于开展保持共产党员先进性教育活动的一系列安排部署，高质量、高标准开展好保持共产党员先进性教育活动。坚持把学习实践“三个代表”重要思想作为主线贯穿教育活动始终，进一步增强广大党员学习实践“三个代表”重要思想的自觉性和坚定性。坚持把加快息烽发展作为开展先进性教育的出发点和落脚点，以科学发展观统领经济社会发展全局。通过教育活动，力争使全县党员队伍在思想境界、综合素质等方面有较大提高，党员队伍的先锋模范作用得以有效发挥，实现提高党员素质、加强基层组织、服务人民群众和促进各项工作的目的。

（二）牢固树立和落实科学的发展观，突出科学发展，不断提高驾驭市场经济的能力

一是科学制定中长期发展规划。正确审时度势，认真结合县情，立足当前，着眼长远，在遵循生态经济县建设规划前提下，科学制定县域经济和社会发展、产业发展、区域开发、城镇总体建设等中长期规划，因地制宜确定一系列符合息烽发展的新的战略、思路、目标和任务，推进可持续发展战略的实施。二是坚定不移地推进主导产业发展。按照“谋发展、抓重点、调结构、进强县”的发展思路，全力推进工业强县、科教兴县和环境立县战略，重点抓好城乡基础设施建设、农业综合生产能力建设、重点产业项目建设、人才队伍建设和发展环境建设，全力“提升一产、主攻二产、加快发展三产”，力争在主导产业发展上实现重点突破。三是努力转变经济增长方式。以“提高质量、优化效益”为中心，注重经济增长结构、质量和效益的有机调整，充分发挥比较优势，加快生态经济县建设。对特色农业的发展，要推行专业化、标准化生产，实行规模化、产业化经营。对工业的发展，要大力倡导无污染、低能耗的项目进入，以节约资源、保护环境为目标，形成有利于低投入、高产出、少排污、可循环的政策环境和发展机制，全面建设集约型社会。对旅游业的发展，要加强统筹规划，保护旅游资源，开发特色项目，改善交通条件，开拓客源市场。四是进一步解放思想，深化改革。坚持把解放思想置于万事之先，引导干部群众走出认识误区，与时俱进，开拓创新，脚踏实地，艰苦创业。认真研究解决关系全县发展的重大问题，坚决摒弃一切制约发展的观念和体制机制弊端，积极推进县属国有企业改革、农村经济体制改革和干部人事制度改革，解放和发展生产力，全力推进生态经济县建设。五是切实提高领导经济工作的能力。进一步建立健全县委常委会经济形势分析会制度，健全经济工作报告制度、通报制度以及重大经济决策、重大项目沟通协调制度，不断完善领导经济工作的体制机制和方式，从总体上提高县委科学把握发展机遇、正确应对挑战的能力。

（三）健全和完善党的领导制度和领导方式，突出制度建设，不断提高党组织总揽全局协调各方的能力

一是建立健全联系通报制度。建立和完善党内情况通报制度、情况反映制度和重大决策征求意见制度，逐步推进党务公开。认真贯彻《中国共产党党员权利保障条例》，切实保障党员的民主权利。认真贯彻《中国共产党党内监督条例（试行）》和《中国共产党纪律处分条例》，建立健全党员有效监督所属党组织和上级党组织工作的机制。二是健全县委领导制度和规则。认真执行县委议事规则，健全常委会向全委会负责、报告工作和接受监督制度，健全重大决定由全委会表决通过制度，实行干部任职票决制。全委会召开会议时，可根据议题事先征求同级党代会代表意见或邀请部分代表列席会议。三是完善领导体制和工作机制。按照总揽全局、协调各方的原则，进一步完善领导体制和工作机制，加强对县人大、政府、政协等组织的领导，发挥这些组织中党组的领导核心作用，实现县委对各级组织、各个领域和各项事业的有效领导。积极支持各级各部门依照法律和章程独立负责、协调一致地开展工作。

（四）全面推进法制社会建设，突出依法治县，不断提高发展社会主义民主政治的能力

一是不断完善政治制度。进一步坚持和完善人民代表大会、政治协商制度，充分发挥统一战线的优势和作用，全面贯彻党的民族、宗教、侨务方针政策，切实做好党外知识分子、非公有制经济人士和其他社会阶层人士工作。二是大力推进依法治县。督促、支持和保证国家机关依法履行职责，在法治轨道上开展各项工作，保障公民和法人的合法权益。支持县法院和县检察院依法独立公正地行使审判权和检察权，加强对司法活动的监督和保障，保证司法公正，维护司法权威。三是推进决策科学化、民主化。大力推进民主决策制度和工作运行机制建设，完善重大决策的规划和程序，建立和完善专家咨询、部门联合会诊、公众参与的决策机制，通过多种渠道和形式广泛集中民智，增强决策的透明度，使重大决策的确立、重要工作的确定、重点项目的安排、主导产业的发展建立在科学、协商、民主的基础上。建立决策失误追究制度，健全纠错改正机制。对生态经济建设决策实行公众听证制度，提高公众参与程度，科学有效地推进生态经济县建设。四是扩大基层民主。进一步完善基层政权、基层群众性自治组织、企事业单位的民主管理制度，保证基层群众依法行使选举权、知情权、监督权等民主权利，保证人民依法享有广泛的权利和自由。

（五）全面推进“平安息烽”建设，突出社会稳定，不断提高构建社会主义和谐社会的能力

一是关心群众生产生活。继续推进就业再就业工作，建立比较完善的城镇、农村社会保障体系，完善覆盖城乡的最低生活保障制度，切实保障被征地农民、农民工的合法权益，妥善处理好失地农民的生产生活问题；加快构建覆盖城乡的新型社会救助体系，积极发展社会福利和慈善事业，努力做到少年有所学、青年有所为、老年有所养、病者有所医、弱者有所助、困者有所济。二是加强信访和矛盾纠纷排查调处工作。进一步落实信访工作责任制，完善领导干部下访约访、越级上访劝返等制度。依法开展信访工作，引导群众以理性、合法的形式表达利益要求、解决利益矛盾。健全预防化解矛盾纠纷机制，综合运用政策、法律、经济、行政等手段和教育、协商、调解等方法，依法及时合理地处理群众反映的问题。三是深入开展平安创建活动。努力形成集打击、防范、控制于一体的治安防控体系，健全快速有效处置群体性事件和突发事件的工作机制，形成统一指挥、功能齐全、反应灵敏、运转高效的应急机制，完善贯彻“严打”方针的经常性工作机制。不断完善考核标准和考核办法，大力推进“平安息烽”建设。四是切实维护社会公共安全。落实安全生产责任

制，强化安全生产监督管理，加强劳动保护。加快构建各类自然灾害的预测预警和综合防御体系。完善各类公共突发事件应急预案。

（六）切实加强干部队伍建设和基层组织建设，突出选好配强领导班子，不断提高自身素质和团结带领广大群众干事创业的能力

认真抓好各级领导班子和干部队伍建设。一是增强领导班子解决自身问题的能力。坚持民主集中制原则，健全党内组织生活制度，认真开展批评与自我批评，切实加强班子成员之间的联系与沟通，增进领导班子的团结。二是严格按照《干部任用条例》选拔任用干部。坚持用好的作风选人，选作风好的人，真正把德才兼备、肯干事、能干事的优秀干部选拔进各级领导班子。严格控制选任制领导干部任期内的职务变动，各乡镇党委、政府领导班子正职在一个地方原则上应工作满一届。三是切实抓好优秀年轻干部的培养选拔工作。配齐乡镇党政领导班子中30岁左右的年轻干部，同时在县直机关、部门领导班子中配备一定数量的30岁左右的年轻干部。调配干部时优先充实年轻干部。让更多的年轻干部到基层锻炼。大胆破格提拔特别优秀的年轻干部。四是加大干部交流力度。按照《息烽县乡（科）级党政领导干部交流制度》的规定，有计划地对县直机关、乡镇领导班子成员进行交流。五是加强后备干部队伍建设。对乡（科）级后备干部实行动态管理，采取培训、挂职轮岗锻炼等措施，加强后备干部的培养锻炼。加快培养选拔少数民族干部、妇女干部和非中共党员干部的步伐，使少数民族干部、妇女干部和非中共党员干部的数量符合有关规定并在现有基础上有所增加。

切实加强农村基层组织建设。按照中央、省、市提出深入开展新一轮农村基层组织建设“三级联创”活动的要求，以强力推进“双带致富”“远程教育”和“双千工程”为载体，以创建“农村基层组织建设先进县”“五好乡镇”和“五好村”为目标，不断加强农村基层组织建设。积极推进“两推一选”等制度，注意从农村知识青年、退伍军人、致富能人、外出务工回村优秀党员中选拔村党支部书记。大力抓好村党支部书记、村（居）委会主任的学历培训和实用技术培训工作，使全县161个村的党支部书记、村（居）委会主任基本达到中专以上文化程度，掌握1～2门致富技能，进一步提高农村基层组织带领群众致富发展的能力。

进一步深化干部人事制度改革。坚持和完善民主推荐、民主测评、考察预告、差额考察、考察情况反馈制、任前公示、任职试用期制、考察工作责任制、干部任免票决、公开选拔、竞争上岗等制度。扩大党员和群众对干部选拔任用的知情权、参与权、选择权和监督权。积极探索加强干部考察、防止和减少用人失察失误的办法和措施。加大调整不称职、不胜任现职领导干部的工作力度。按照树立正确的政绩观的要求，研究探索领导班子和领导干部实绩考核评价指标体系。推进建立干部能上能下、能进能出机制的进程。加强干部监督管理工作，建立“便利、安全、高效”的举报机制，加大对群众反映干部问题的查核力度，着力整治用人上的不正之风和腐败现象。

拓宽干部教育培训方式，狠抓大规模党员干部培训。建立和落实干部学习考核制度和激励机制，促进干部学习的深入。按干部管理分级负责原则，开展分层次、分类型、多渠道、多形式、重实效的培训。继续办好每年的乡（科）级和中青年干部培训班，同时采取理论培训、到发达地区挂职学习或到艰苦环境锻炼相结合的方式，抽调一定数量的年轻干部到省、市机关和省内外经济发达地区挂职锻炼，选派一定数量的乡（科）级领导干部和专业技术人员到省内外有关院校学习。

继续抓好机关、学校、社区、企业和新经济组织党建工作。机关党组织要严格组织生活，加强对党员特别是单位领导的教育和监督，促进机关工作的正常开展。学校党组织要把加强和改进学校党建工作与贯彻党的教育方针政策紧密结合起来，分析、研究在新形势下如何抓好素质教育、提高教学质量、巩固义务教育成果等问题。社区党建工作应按照建设“三优社区”的目标，抓好社区党建工作的示范带动，逐步扩大社区党建工作的覆盖面，充分发挥社区党员的先锋模范作用和社区党组织的战斗堡垒作用。加快解决国有企业在改制、改组过程中党组织变更、设置和发挥作用问题，同时做好停产、关闭、破产国有企业党建工作。积极探索新经济组织党组织组建形式、活动内容和活动方式，努力扩大新经济组织党组织覆盖面，力争在符合条件的新经济组织中党组织组建率达80%以上。

进一步加强党员的发展和教育管理工作。按照发展党员“十六字”方针，以坚持标准、保证质量为核心，重点做好在生产、工作一线和知识分子群体中发展党员工作。农村党员发展工作要把35岁以下、高中以上文化程度、具有“双带致富”能力的农村青年致富能人作为重点培养对象。同时做好在其他社会阶层先进分子中发展党员工作。按照从严治党的方针，严肃查处不合格党员，保持党员队伍的先进性和纯洁性。积极探索党员教育管理的新机制、新方法，加强流动党员、下岗职工党员和离退休党员的教育和管理，以帮助解决再就业问题和生活实际困难为重点，搞好改制企业和下岗职工党员的管理和服务。

（七）密切党同人民群众的血肉联系，突出作风建设，不断提高拒腐防变和抵御风险的能力

一是深入开展“争做廉洁从政表率”活动。加强对各级领导班子和领导干部“两个务必”和“为民、务实、清廉”教育，不断提高各级领导班子和领导干部组织群众、宣传群众、教育群众、服务群众的能力。二是坚持开展机关效能建设，切实改进工作作风。以提高服务质量和办事效率为核心，完善制度，强化考核，严禁有令不行、办事拖拉、吃拿卡要、态度刁蛮，积极探索建立行为规范、运转协调、公正透明、廉洁高效的长效机制。坚持下基层调查研究制度，县级领导每年至少有3个月时间下基层调查研究，坚持轻车简从，多深入困难多、矛盾多、问题多的地方，切实为人民群众排忧解难。切实精简会议、文件，改进会风文风。坚持厉行节约，反对铺张浪费，简化公务接待。严格规范和控制各种检查、评比、达标活动。三是强化对领导班子特别是对主要领导干部的监督。建立健全巡视制度和领导干部个人重大事项报告制度、述职述廉制度、民主评议制度、谈话诫勉制度、经济责任审计制度，依法实行质询制、问责制、罢免制。四是严格落实党风廉政建设责任制。坚持“党委统一领导、党政齐抓共管、纪委组织协调、部门各负其责、依靠群众的支持和参与”的体制和机制，按照中央和市委的部署，着重抓好党风廉政建设和反腐败各项任务的落实，重点抓好领导干部廉洁自律工作，筑牢思想道德和党纪国法两道防线。坚持标本兼治、综合治理，惩防并举、注重预防，加强廉政教育和制度建设，严肃查处违纪违法案件，不断提高领导干部拒腐防变的能力。

县委号召：全县经济和社会发展正步入一个非常重要的关键时期，既面临良好的发展机遇，也面临严峻挑战，各级各部门党组织要进一步准确把握全县的发展定位，进一步强化发展责任，紧紧抓住历史机遇，勇敢地迎接挑战，以时不我待的紧迫感和责任感，振奋精神，集中精力，转变作风，扭住发展不动摇，锁定发展新目标，拿出工作新举措，干出强县新业绩。全县上下务必坚持求真务实、真抓实干的作风，少说空话，多干实事，少说闲话，多干正事，真正把执政能力建设和生态经济县建设的各项任务落到实处并取得实实在在的成果，为实现强县升位和跨越式发展目标做出更大的贡献。

中共息烽县委　息烽县人民政府关于加快建设社会主义新农村的实施意见

为深入贯彻党的十六届五中全会、省委九届八次全会和市委七届十五次全会精神，县委、县政府决定用5—15年的时间，举全县之力，扎实开展社会主义新农村建设工作，加快我县全面建设小康社会步伐。结合县情，提出如下实施意见。

一、正确认识建设社会主义新农村的重大历史意义

（一）建设社会主义新农村是全面建设小康社会，构建社会主义和谐社会的客观要求

建设社会主义新农村是重大而长期的历史任务，也是加强“三农”工作的重大战略举措，事关全面建设小康社会和社会主义现代化建设的全局。近年来，县委、县政府以邓小平理论和“三个代表”重要思想为指导，采取综合措施，大力提升一产，主攻二产，加速发展三产，全县经济社会发展成效明显，物质文明、政治文明、精神文明建设取得长足进步，农村面貌发生较大改变。初步具备了以城带乡，以工促农，建设社会主义新农村的条件。

但我县农村各项事业发展同全面建设小康社会目标相比还存在较大差距，主要表现在：农业产业化进程不快，劳动生产率低，农村经济发展的物质基础还不够厚实；农民科技、文化素质不高，持续增收路子不宽；村寨规划滞后，建设杂乱无章，脏、乱、差现象不同程度存在；基础设施较为薄弱，农业抵御自然灾害的能力弱；农村社会事业发展滞后。这些困难和问题决定了我县建设社会主义新农村这一历史任务的长期性、艰巨性。

（二）建设社会主义新农村是抓好“三农”工作的有力举措，是今后工作的重中之重

解决“三农”问题是一项长期的历史任务，是全党工作的重中之重。当前，农民求发展、谋发展、抓发展的热情高涨，要求提高自身生活水平，改变农村落后面貌的愿望十分强烈。建设社会主义新农村顺应了农村的发展要求和经济社会的发展趋势，是做好“三农”工作的有力举措。因此，要把建设社会主义新农村放在经济社会发展的突出位置，用建设社会主义新农村统揽“三农”工作全局。全县上下要充分认识建设社会主义新农村的重大历史意义，深化对县情的再认识，按照“生产发展、生活宽裕、乡风文明、村容整洁、管理民主”的总要求，扎实抓好社会主义新农村建设工作。

二、建设社会主义新农村的指导思想、基本原则和目标任务

（一）指导思想

以邓小平理论、“三个代表”重要思想为指导，深入贯彻党的十六大和十六届五中全会精神，坚持党在农村的基本路线、方针、政策，坚持科学的发展观和“多予少取放活”的方针。实事求是，紧紧依靠群众，加大投入，提高农业综合生产能力，发展农村经济，富裕农民，美化村寨，改善农村人居环境，提高农民基本素质，加强农村基层党组织建设、民主法治建设，把农村物质文明、政治文明、精神文明建设同建设社会主义和谐社会有机结合起来，全面建设富裕、文明、民主的社会主义新农村。

（二）建设社会主义新农村的基本原则

一是实事求是、因地制宜、区别对待、量力而行的原则。依托产业布局及发展，实事求是地制定建设规划，对乡镇和村区别对待，不硬性统一标准、模式，不强行硬推，坚持依托产业建新村，搞好规划建新村，整理改造变新村，量力而行，逐步建设，做到以人为本，不拘一格。

二是典型示范、突出重点的原则。在2005年创建的生态经济示范村基础上选择11个基础条件好，群众积极性高的村作为试点，各乡镇要选择1～2个村寨作试点。

三是政府引导，群众自力更生的原则。尊重群众意愿，充分发挥农民主体作用，引导扶持，不包不揽。深入宣传发动，引导群众摒弃“等、靠、要”思想，积极投身社会主义新农村建设，实行整体申报审批制度，不申请不创建，不竞争不选点；坚持村民自治，不增加农民负担。

四是循序渐进、逐步推开、确保成效的原则。因势利导，逐步推开，不急功近利，不搞形式主义，切忌不切实际地全面铺开。先在基础条件好、群众积极性高的村寨进行示范建设；条件不具备的村寨暂不全面铺开，可按要求逐步实施，条件较差的贫困村重点抓好扶贫开发工作，注重巩固建设成果。

五是“三个文明”协调发展的原则。在发展农村经济，增加农民收入，抓好农村物质文明建设的同时，大力推进农村政治文明、精神文明建设，做到乡风文明、管理民主。

（三）目标任务

从2006年起，每年创建10个以上的社会主义新农村村寨，用15年的时间，使全县161个村基本实现“生产发展、生活宽裕、乡风文明、村容整洁、管理民主”的目标。

在生态经济村建设的基础上，经过5～15年的努力，全面实施“六个工程”，即“四改一气”工程、危房改造工程、“三小”工程、农村安全饮水工程、“四旁”绿化工程、进村公路硬化和串户路硬化工程；建成社会主义新农村的每个村有一个支撑发展的产业、一个作用明显的民间组织、一套民主实用的管理制度、一个规范的宣传栏、一幢设施齐全的综合楼、一个公共文体娱乐场所、一条水泥串寨路、一个优美的环境；每户农户有一条致富门路、一门以上的实用技术、一幢合格美观的住房、一个优美的庭园、一条水泥串户路、一口沼气池、一种良好的生活习惯、一间清洁的厕所。做到“四个提高”，即提高农民素质、提高农业综合生产能力、提高党的基层组织战斗力、提高农村文明程度和民主管理水平。

三、实现“四个突破”，强力推进社会主义新农村建设

（一）发展新产业，组建新组织，在农村经济发展的产业支撑上有新突破

把提高农业综合生产能力，发展农村经济，促进农民持续增收放在显著位置。

1. 加快农业产业结构调整步伐，提高农业产业化水平，增加农民收入。把农业产业结构调整和产业化建设作为农民增收的助推器，大力发展特色农业和品牌农业，不断提高农产产业化建设的规模以及组织程度，帮助农民规避、降低发展种、养业的市场风险，千方百计促进农民持续增收，重点是在“十一五”期间，定位于城郊型、市场型农业，结合区位、气候等优势，抓好蔬菜、调味品等种植、养殖主导产业发展。一是以生态养殖小区建设为契机，大力发展畜禽养殖业，建成畜禽养殖小区70个，辐射农户3500户；二是紧跟市场动向，建设订单外销蔬菜基地，建成无公害蔬菜基地8.5万亩；三是依托龙头企业，扩大调味品原料基地规模，建成调味品原料基地5万亩；四是实施粮食增产工程15万亩；五是巩固、发展烤烟生产，建成优质烤烟生产基地3万亩；六是建成优质果树基地

1万亩、中药材种植基地7.5万亩；做到每个乡镇有一个主导产业、一批专业村，使产业结构调整真正成为农民增收的重要支撑。统筹布局重大产业项目，避免重复建设。

2．组建农村新经济组织。培育壮大农村各类经济组织，围绕农业产业化，推广行之有效的经济组织组建和运作模式，建设好连接市场、企业、农户的纽带；做到乡镇、村主导产业均有协会等专业组织牵头发展，各类经济组织覆盖农户达70%以上，提高农民和农业产业化的组织程度。

（二）在农村基础设施建设上有新突破

"十一五"期间，一是加强交通设施建设，提级改造县乡公路100千米，硬化通村公路1100千米，新建县城、九庄等14个汽车客运站和黄沙等5个码头以及丁家岩等14个渡口；二是加强水利基础设施建设，建成两岔河中型水库，建成迷洗、高硐等5座小一型水库和水落洞等4座小（二）型水库；新建、改造山塘62处，新建小水池6000个、提灌站7个，完成76千米渠道防渗，建成农村安全饮水工程224处，解决农村3.5万人饮水困难，农田保灌面积达11.2万亩；三是改善农业生产条件，建设高标准农田1.5万亩，实施沃土工程7.5万亩，大力实施坡改梯、土地整治等农业综合开发工程3万亩，建成机耕道350千米；四是完成农村危房改造3476户，全县农村基本消除危房；五是完成全县村寨的串户路建设；六是建成2万口沼气池，使农村70%以上的农户户均1口沼气池；七是实施退耕还林5万亩，全县森林覆盖率达45%；八是夯实生态建设基础，实施石漠化治理22万亩；九是进一步加强农村通讯、广播电视等基础设施建设，完成全县村村通广播电视工程；十是建成20个农产品规范化、专业化市场。

到2010年，第一产业增加值达4.5亿元，年均增长7%，农民人均纯收入达4230元，年均增长12%；2015年，第一产业增加值达6.15亿元，年均增长6.5%，农民人均纯收入达6500元，年均增长9%；到2020年，全县农业经济质量明显提高，农业基础设施更加完善，生态环境明显改善，农民生活更加富裕。

（三）创造新环境，在规划建设新村寨和整治村容村貌上有新突破

1．规划先行，建设新村寨。统筹考虑村经济发展、社会事业发展、集镇建设规划，实行公共设施统一布局、综合配套、相互联通、分步建设，把制定规划同村寨统筹发展、易地扶贫搬迁等结合起来。重点做好村寨建设规划，全县村寨按照规划建设。编制规划要征求村民意见，按程序严格审批，坚持先规划后建房，不规划不批建的原则，确保规划的权威性、统一性、导向性，改变村寨自发建设，盲目发展状态，防止村寨建设千篇一律。注重保护耕地，保护传统民居、民族建筑。有计划的引导散居户逐步向规划建设区集中。2010年，全县40%的村实现"乡村风情浓郁、村镇结构合理、功能配套完善、交通便捷畅达、生产生活便利"目标；2015年，全县80%的村达到这一目标；2020年全县所有村达到这一目标。

2．创造新环境。2010年实现95%以上的农户饮用卫生安全的自来水，2008年全面完成农村"四改一气"工程。实施"四旁绿化"工程，美化环境。以"四改一气"和"四旁绿化"为纽带，发展庭园经济，形成"养殖＋沼气＋经济作物"的生态发展模式；加强农村环境污染防治，落实卫生保洁制度，实现30户以上村寨垃圾集中处理，生活污水通过排水沟排放，杜绝临棚乱搭、墙面乱画、庭院乱挂、柴草乱垛、粪土乱堆、垃圾乱倒、污水乱泼、禽畜乱跑现象，实现村寨路面硬化、村寨绿化、庭院净化、环境净化、村巷亮化。抓好林业生态建设，2015年全县森林覆盖率达48%，2020年全县森林覆盖率达50%以上。

（四）塑造新风尚，培育新农民，在提高农村文明程度上有新的突破

1．塑造新风尚，提高农村文明程度。着力提高农民的思想道德素质，引导群众革除陈规陋习。提高农民的科学文化水平和致富本领。加强农村文化阵地和文化队伍建设。开展健康向上、具有地方特色的文体活动，用先进文化占领农村文化阵地。开展“富在农家、学在农家、乐在农家、美在农家”活动。加强生态环保教育，增强基层干部和农民的可持续发展意识。转变农民生育观念，提高人口素质，全面推行优质服务，人口与计生工作实现村民自治。进一步推进殡改工作，实现村村有公益性墓地。认真抓好“普法”工作，增强农民的法制观念和诚信意识。坚持在村党支部的领导下，以不断健全基层民主选举制度，规范基层民主决策程序，完善基层民主管理机制，强化基层民主监督力度为核心，切实加强农村民主法治建设。

2．培育新农民，提高农民综合素质。以实地讲课，农村远程教育等为载体，大力开展农业适用新技术和非农技能培训，完成84个贫困村10000人科技扶贫培训。确保农村新增劳动力人均受教育年限2010年达到10年，2015年达到11年，2020年达到12年。到2010年，通过各种形式的教育培训，使18岁以上，45岁以下的农村劳动力基本掌握1～2门实用技术，增强农民的竞争能力和自我发展能力，促使广大农民成为具有一定专业技能、文明守法、诚信经营、自我发展能力较强的新型农民。

四、抓好“四个统筹”，促使社会主义新农村建设深入开展

（一）统筹城乡协调发展

以旧城改造和乡镇扩容为着力点，完善城镇功能，推进小城镇建设，发展城镇经济。着力抓好招商引资，加快乡镇企业发展，引导乡镇企业按产业布局向小城镇集中，把发展乡镇企业同转移农村富余劳动力结合起来，发展各种服务行业和交易市场，培育新的经济增长点，不断提高城镇化水平。加强流动人口管理。逐步建立城乡统一的劳动就业、义务教育等制度，形成有利于城乡相互促进，共同发展的局面。重点广开农村富余劳动力就业渠道，促进农村富余劳动力更多更好的转移，不断增加农民非农收入，2010年，有序转移农村富余劳动力3.5万人。依托旅游景区资源开发和保护，发展好“农家乐”等乡村旅游，评定乡村旅舍100家，促进农村富余劳动力就地转移。

（二）统筹农村社会事业发展

一是改善农村医疗卫生条件，加强乡镇卫生院和村卫生室建设，“十一五”期间，建成100个村（居）卫生室，完善新型农村合作医疗和农村贫困家庭医疗救助制度，使农民合作医疗参合率达到80%以上，努力做到小病不出村，常见病不出乡，大病不出县，实现人人享有初级卫生保健。二是实行农村最低生活保障制度，根据农村经济发展状况，逐步提高农村低保水平；落实好“五保”供养政策和“五老”精神，提高“五保”供养水平，到2010年“五保”供养水平人均达1200元，扎实抓好农村敬老院建设。三是抓好农村教育事业，大力加强和改进未成年人思想道德建设，继续实施“科教兴县”战略，大力发展职业教育，建成并办好1个职业教育中心，财政新增教育经费主要用于农村教育，促进农村教育均衡发展；积极推进农村中小学“三小”工程（小伙房建设、小厕所改造、小基地创业）建设；2010年乡镇中学办成寄宿制初中，新建10个乡镇幼儿园；2007年，义务教育阶段家庭经济困难学生均享受“两免一补”政策，使学生不因家庭经济困难而辍学；2010年，全县农村全部实现免费义务教育，全县农村义务教育阶段中小学基本实现标准化办学。四是加强农村文化体育运动场所等文化体育基础设施建设，建成10个乡镇体育场和123个村（居）宣传活动室，加强农村优秀民族、民间文化资源的开发、整理和保护，推进文化产业的健康发展。五是严格执行耕

地占补平衡制度和基本农田保护“五不准”，节约使用土地，确保全县旱涝保收田土面积达到人均0.5亩。六是全面完成84个贫困村整村推进扶贫工作，力争到2010年全县农村贫困人口全面脱贫。

（三）统筹涉农资金使用，加大建设投入

把有限的资金用在农民最需要的地方，提高公共财政对农村的覆盖范围。

一是调整财政支出结构，建立稳定增长的财政支农机制和年度统筹资金、项目的工作机制，确保财政对农业的投入逐年增长。二是认真贯彻落实国家给予农民良种补贴、购置农机具补贴等支农惠农政策。三是每年从新增加的教育、卫生、文化经费中安排70%的资金用于农村，科技专项资金向农村倾斜，农村税费改革上级转移支付的50%用于农村义务教育。四是将每年留县级的土地出让金，按不低于30%的比例，专项用于土地整理和复垦、宜农未利用地的开发和基本农田建设以及改善农业生产条件。五是每年从各部门、各单位纳入财政专户管理的预算外收入中统筹安排10%的资金用于支持新农村建设。六是任何单位和个人不得减免育林基金、水资源费、水土保持补偿费、森林植被恢复费、水利建设基金等，确保此类基金全部征收并用于农、林、水利等建设。七是千方百计、全力以赴争取市级在价格调节基金、小城镇建设等资金中专门安排的用于新农村建设和村寨规划建设的资金以及市财政专项安排用于农村合作医疗的资金，并将争取的资金专项用于新农村基础设施、合作医疗等各项建设事业。八是积极争取金融企业对社会主义新农村建设的大力支持。

抓好项目库建设，努力争取上级资金支持。实施项目组装配套，资金捆绑使用，各部门资金、项目要向新农村建设倾斜，发动群众投工投劳，提高资金使用效率，实行项目建设资金财政、审计全程监督，确保资金安全。

（四）统筹各方力量，建设新农村

建设社会主义新农村需要各方面的力量团结协作，狠抓落实。驻县企、事业单位要结合自身实际，积极参与社会主义新农村建设。实行县级领导联系建设社会主义新农村制度，县四大班子领导要做示范，每个县级领导、县直有关部门领导确定一个联系点，做到县直机关帮扶自然村寨，党员干部驻村帮户。对农村沟渠、道路等基础设施建设和种植、养殖等项目安排要坚持统筹考虑、实施。县领导的联系点和县直机关帮扶的自然村寨每年要整合投入一定资金，由乡镇以水泥等实物帮扶示范点。各乡镇明确专人协调联系，蹲点指导。县抓乡镇，乡镇抓村，层层示范落实，推进社会主义新农村建设。

五、落实“三项创建”，为社会主义新农村建设夯实基础

（一）创建生态经济示范村

抓好生态经济村创建工作，按照“完善、充实、巩固、提高”的思路，加强基础设施建设，改善农村人居环境，增加农民收入，走生产发展、生活富裕、生态良好的发展道路，促进农村经济社会与生态环境的协调发展。发展循环经济，保护生态环境，大力宣传生态文化，切实增强农民的生态环保意识、可持续发展意识，加快建设资源节约型、环境友好型社会。

（二）加强农村基层党组织建设，创建党建示范村

以创建党建示范村为载体，进一步加强村级班子建设，配强选好村党支部领导班子，抓好农村党员干部培训和农村党员的发展、教育和管理工作，重点抓好农村流动党员教育、管理及在农村外出务工青年中发展党员工作；以开展保持共产党员先进性教育为契机，探索、落实干部经常受教育，农民长期得实惠的有效方法。开展农村无职党员设岗定责活动。继续抓好“双千工程”“双带

致富”工程、“支部加协会”和农村远程教育，深入开展“三级联创”活动，创建“五个好”村党支部，不断提高农村党组织的战斗力、创造力、凝聚力。加强基层民主政治建设，抓好村务公开、涉农收费公开和民主决策、民主管理、民主监督制度建设，保障农民群众的选举权、知情权、决策权、参与权和监督权。逐步推行村民代表大会和村民监事会制度，不断提高自治水平。

（三）加强农村文化建设，创建文明示范村

加强农村文化建设，以文明示范村为依托，全面提升农村文明程度。加大综治、禁毒工作力度，通过村民“一事一议”，将农村反对黄赌毒、抵制“法轮功”等邪教、反对封建迷信和宗派宗族势力形成村规民约，并健全完善，到2008年全县80%以上的村寨达到“平安村寨”标准。宣传倡导《公民道德建设实施纲要》，加强理论教育和农村思想政治工作，实施好“文明新风进万家”工程，继续开展“文明村”“星级文明户”“文明家庭”等评选活动，在农村营造文明、科学、健康的生活风尚；丰富农民精神文化生活，满足农民多层次精神文化需求；引导农民树立正确的婚育观。2010年全县60%以上的村达到文明村标准；2015年全县80%以上的村达到文明村标准；2020年全县所有村达到文明村标准。

六、加强领导，强化措施，为建设社会主义新农村提供坚强保障

（一）加强领导，形成强大工作合力

成立息烽县建设社会主义新农村工作领导小组以及相关工作机构，各乡镇、各有关部门相应成立领导机构和办事机构，对建设社会主义新农村工作进行统一指挥、协调。各乡镇和有关部门要结合各自的工作实际，认真制定长期工作计划，细化年度工作方案，分解落实工作任务，拿出具体工作措施，做到目标明确、专人负责、权责清晰、奖惩挂钩。工作中要主动对接、积极协调、相互配合、搞好服务，形成强大的工作合力。

（二）深化农村改革，为新农村建设提供强大动力

坚定不移地坚持统分结合双层经营体制为核心的农村基本经济制度。巩固农村税费改革成果，防止农民负担反弹，基本完成乡镇机构改革、农村义务教育和县乡财政体制改革任务。依法做好征地安置补偿工作，确保被征地农民生活水平不低于征地前生活水平，解决好失地农民的长远生计问题。鼓励非公有制经济长入农村，加快农村经济发展。鼓励、支持金融企业对农户和农村中小企业发展生产给予支持。

（三）转变行政模式，充分发挥村级组织和群众的主体作用

1. 紧紧依靠群众，调动农民的积极性、主动性和创造性，充分认识农民是建设社会主义新农村的主体，尊重群众意愿。在30户以上的自然村寨建立村民理事会，以村民理事会为组织形式，通过一事一议，进而把阶段性集中建设同日常管理有机结合起来，做到群众自我组织、自我管理、自我教育、自我服务、自我监督，长效管理，促使社会主义新农村建设逐步规范化、制度化。具体工作中，须经80%以上的农户书面签字同意，才能以村的名义申报建设社会主义新农村。

2. 切实转变行政理念，依法行政，从以行政推动为主的工作模式转变到以引导服务为主的工作模式上来。乡镇要切实把工作重点从直接抓生产经营、催种催收等具体事务转到对农户和各类经济主体提供政策服务和营造发展环境上来，正确定位工作职责，不越位，不缺位，不包揽，努力提高公共管理和社会服务水平；宣传好、落实好党和国家的法律、政策，保障农民合法权益，维护农村社会稳定，巩固党在农村的执政基础。

（四）维护农村社会稳定，为新农村建设创造良好环境

坚持群防群治，推进社会治安防控体系建设，充实群防群治队伍，完善“专职联防”和“十户联防”制度，加强农村社会治安综合治理，农村治安、刑事案件发案率逐年下降，破案率逐年上升，群众安全感达95%以上。坚决打击敌对势力、敌对分子和“法轮功”等邪教组织。正确处理人民内部矛盾，把矛盾和纠纷化解在基层和萌芽状态；建立健全矛盾纠纷处理机制，完善社会稳定预警机制，积极预防和处置群体性事件。抓好安全生产警示教育，普及安全生产知识，完善安全生产责任制，加强监管队伍建设，有效遏制安全生产事故发生。

（五）深入广泛宣传，促使建设社会主义新农村深入人心

建设社会主义新农村涉及面广、任务重，时间长，需要全社会的积极参与和广泛支持。各乡镇、有关部门要层层发动，采取群众喜闻乐见、效果良好的宣传途径和形式，深入广泛宣传，关键是引导和教育群众摒弃“等、靠、要”思想，积极参与社会主义新农村建设工作。宣传媒体要大力宣传在建设工作中涌现出来的先进个人和集体、所取得的经验和成就，对工作不力、成效不明显的，予以曝光。

（六）建立科学合理的考核机制和定期督查制度

县委督查室、县政府督查室将此项工作列入县委、县政府综合目标管理、考核，制定专门的奖惩措施，重点对项目建设的进展情况、资金和领导力量的到位情况等定期督查，对工作成效明显的单位通报表彰，对工作落实不力，成效不明显的给予通报批评。组织部门要将此项工作的开展情况列为干部考核任用的依据。各领导小组每季度召开一次工作协调会，通报情况、总结经验、解决问题，每年召开一次现场会，推广典型，推进社会主义新农村建设。

中共息烽县委　息烽县人民政府
关于印发《息烽县关于进一步加快实施“旅游活县”战略的意见》的通知

为深入学习实践科学发展观，认真贯彻落实县委十一届六次全会精神，充分发挥旅游资源优势，进一步培育和壮大旅游产业，推进“旅游活县”战略，增强县域经济活力，加快生态文明县建设，实现“建强升位”目标，特提出如下实施意见。

一、理清思路，明确目标

1．进一步提高对“旅游活县”战略的认识。旅游业作为现代先导型的朝阳产业，具有综合性强、关联度高、拉动力大、产业链长和可持续发展的特性。息烽县旅游资源丰富，比较优势明显，旅游产业发展空间十分广阔。为此，县委审时度势，在十一届四次全会上提出了“旅游活县”战略目标，明确了旅游业在全县经济社会发展中的重要地位。加快培育和发展旅游业，是扩大消费、带动产业发展、拉动经济增长的需要，是转变经济发展方式、优化产业结构的需要，是提升地区影响力、扩大对外开放的需要。“旅游活县”战略的提出，是深入贯彻落实科学发展观的必然要求，也是经济社会和谐发展的客观需要。因此，全县上下要进一步提高对实施“旅游活县”战略重要性、必要性和紧迫性的认识，充分审视到全县旅游产业发展的优势和有利条件，坚定发展信心和决心，抢抓机遇，围绕建设生态文明县和“建强升位”这一目标，加快旅游产业发展。

2．实施“旅游活县”战略的指导思想。以邓小平理论和“三个代表”重要思想为指导，深入贯彻落实科学发展观，按照“政府引导、企业主打、行业主管、社会联动”的发展思路，充分挖掘利用我县红色文化、绿色文化、温泉文化、民族民间文化、“半边天”文化、佛教文化、溶洞奇观和地貌特征等旅游资源，以旅游景区开发为重点，切实加强旅游基础设施建设、加快发展乡村旅游，大力开发旅游产品，构建宣传、文化（艺）、旅游、体育、教育“五位一体”的旅游发展新格局，加快旅游市场化、产业化、社会化进程，努力把旅游业培育成增强县域经济活力的朝阳产业，成为第三产业发展的龙头，推进全县经济社会又好又快发展。

3．“旅游活县”战略的发展目标。（1）到2010年，力争接待省内外游客突破180万人次，实现旅游总产出达5亿元以上；到2012年，力争来息游客突破260万人次，旅游总产出达7.2亿元以上。（2）到2010年，基本完善息烽集中营景区功能性配套设施建设；启动新温泉的开发并初具开发条件；启动西望山景区道路、步道等基础设施建设，加大对外招商引资力度，推进温泉景区、西望山景区、多滨洞、团元山、乌江峡红色旅游区建设开发，到2012年全面进行实质性的开发建设。（3）到2012年，乡村旅游发展工作取得初步成效，力争创建1个省级乡村旅游特色乡（镇），2个市级乡村旅游点，10个乡村旅游示范点，200家乡村旅舍和100家乡村旅游示范户，实现乡村旅游接待人数以每年30%左右的速度递增。

二、突出重点，强化措施

4．夯基础，造环境。一是加快旅游交通网络建设。抓好息烽至开阳公路、息烽县城至玄天洞、九庄至黄沙、竹花至新杨公路、关田坝至凤凰池、小寨坝至荆江公路和息烽至金沙乌江大桥建设。2009年完成龙塘湾至茅坪、九庄至石硐公路改扩建30千米，硬化村公路30千米，完成永温至温泉、息烽至九庄公路大修8.7千米。启动息烽县城至玄天洞、小寨坝至流长配套公路、沙帽河至鹿窝、小寨坝至温泉旅游公路建设。建成息烽社会客运站和8个乡镇客运站。加快推进小寨坝铁路编组站、息烽火车站扩容增量，2009年建成火车站广场。全力配合贵阳至重庆息烽段快速铁路建设。力争新建贵阳港息烽港区及配套公路，改扩建顺江等3个码头和仲家坪等7个渡口。要把县、乡公路改造建设优先安排在重点旅游景区（点）、乡村旅游示范点。二是完善城市旅游功能。建成息烽游客接待服务中心，提升息烽旅游接待服务的能力和水平。要加快建设一批星级宾馆，提高旅游接待规模、接待水平和接待能力。规范建成息烽旅游风味小吃一条街、旅游商品一条街、文化娱乐一条街。进一步完善城市园林绿化景观建设，美化市容市貌。加快息烽温泉省级森林公园、团元山景区、县城广场、河道景观建设。在城区主要街道、重要公共场所、主要旅游景点及旅游公路沿途改造和新建高标准的公共厕所。三是推进旅游信息化进程。大力发展旅游电子商务，健全旅游统计体系、旅游信息调查体系和假日旅游预订体系，并通过政府网站和旅游网站对外发布。在重点窗口部门、交通客运站、星级酒店建立电子显示咨询服务平台，及时把握旅游者的需求动态，提供优质的旅游市场信息服务。

5．细规划，谋长远。要高标准完善旅游发展规划，合理布局旅游资源。按照县委建设生态文明县和“建强升位”的总体要求，及时修编《息烽旅游业发展总体规划》，科学规划红色旅游、休闲旅游、探险旅游、观光旅游、文化旅游、民俗旅游等为一体的筑北旅游精品景区，形成特色鲜明、点线相连的旅游网络。要科学规划和发展乡村旅游，组织编制全县乡村旅游发展总体规划和乡村旅游示范点的修建性详规，建成一批具有一定规模和层次的乡村旅游示范点。规划要一步到位，分步实施。规划一经审批，必须按规划进行招商和建设，确保旅游业持续健康发展。

6．树品牌，突重点。一是继续树立“红色旅游”品牌。充分利用好息烽集中营革命历史纪念馆和息烽乌江景区被十三部委确定为红色旅游经典景区暨精品线路的比较优势，突出红色旅游的主导地位。拓展收入渠道，增创发展新优势，建设集中营游客综合服务功能区，为游客消费创造良好条件和环境。二是突出抓好重点旅游景区开发。完善配套设施建设，加大旅游招商引资力度，做好旅游宣传促销，扎实推进集中营景区、乌江峡、西望山、温泉、多滨洞、团元山等景区（点）开发建设，并取得实质性进展。三是大力发展乡村旅游。鼓励干部职工、工商业主、经营能人和民营企业家投资修建乡村旅舍，带头参与乡村旅游发展。加大对乡村旅游的规划建设和指导，围绕息烽阳朗片区，小寨坝潮水红岩片区，养龙司乡幸福、堡子片区，西山林丰、柏香山片区，流长水尾、新中片区生态文明新农村示范点五大板块和流长前奔、青山苗族乡冗坝村、西山新寨沟等示范点建设，大力发展以休闲、度假、观光、探险和体验游为主的乡村旅游业，加强乡村旅游示范点、示范户建设，形成产业集聚，提升示范效应。四是加快旅游商品开发。依托息烽独特丰富的旅游商品资源，按照统筹规划、合理布局的原则，在保护好现有特色产品的前提下，积极引资开发独具息烽特色的农产品、风味小吃、手工艺品、民族刺绣等旅游商品，对西望山虫茶、核桃干果、中药材、烙画、刺绣、阳朗辣子鸡、氡泉产品、乌江鱼、牛肉为主的畜牧产品、各类鲜果等独具特色的旅游商品和其他农副土特产品进行高层次开发，最大限度提高附加值。要重点扶持苗姑娘、味美等具有自主品牌的农产品深加工企业，提高市场上市率，争创中国名牌和驰名商标，丰富和提高我县旅游商品的种类和质量。

7. 重投入，促发展。加大县财政旅游扶持导向性投入，确保县旅游发展专项基金随财政收入的增长逐年递增。主要用于旅游整体形象的宣传促销、重点项目开发、人才培训、旅游商品开发研制、兑现奖励扶持政策等。（1）加大旅游招商引资力度。一是鼓励招商引资开发旅游资源，借助外力加快发展，认真落实招商引资优惠政策，竭尽全力为企业搞好服务。对重点景区乌江峡、西望山、息烽温泉等开发项目，只要是有利于息烽发展的，可采取一企一策的办法。对引入开发旅游资源项目并成功投入营运的，按招商引资有关奖励办法予以奖励。二是加大对旅游项目用地的政策扶持力度。对符合土地利用总体规划的重点旅游建设项目，政府给予大力支持，依照程序优先办理土地手续。鼓励农户以土地转包、出租、互换、转让、入股等方式向有技术专长、资金实力、经营能力的专业大户合理流转，促进乡村旅游规模集约发展。支持投资者或农户在荒山、荒坡、荒滩进行乡村旅游开发，鼓励农户利用自己承包的林地、果园或者宅基地发展乡村旅游。（2）加大政策奖励扶持力度。一是鼓励企业开发旅游商品。在县域内开发影响力大和具有自主知识产权的旅游商品的企业一次性给予5万元奖励。对在当年政府或行业协会主办的旅游商品设计评比中，获国家级金、银、铜奖的单位或个人，分别奖励5万元、3万元、1万元；获省级金、银、铜奖的单位或个人，分别奖励3万元、2万元、1万元；获市级金、银、铜奖的单位或个人，分别奖励2万元、1万元、0.5万元。对县域内旅游商品生产企业，对新开发生产本县旅游特色商品项目贷款在10万元以上的，给予3年贴息扶持。凡经销息烽县旅游特色商品年销售额50万元及以上，按年销售总额的1%给予奖励；50万元（不含50万元）以下10万元以上的按年销售总额的0.5%给予奖励。二是鼓励创建星级酒店和旅行社。对新建三星级以上星级宾馆并投入营运的企业，按照招商引资有关奖励办法给予奖励；对旅行社每年组团来息烽县人次前三位分别给予1万元、0.5万元、0.3万元的奖励，对县内组建旅行社的企业给予鼓励并根据运行情况予以奖励。三是鼓励和支持企业实施品牌战略。大力扶持旅游企业、景区（点）上等级、上规模。被国家旅游局评定机构或授权组织评定为国家AAA、AAAA、AAAAA级的旅游景区，分别一次性给予10万元、20万元、30万元的奖励，被评定升级为国家AAAA、AAAAA级的旅游景区，分别一次性给予20万元、30万元的奖励；被批准为省级旅游度假区、国家级旅游度假区的，分别一次性给予10万元、30万元的奖励。四是鼓励企业主动参与营销。旅游企业凡参加省、市统一组织的活动，推介息烽县旅游资源、旅游景点、旅游线路或旅游产品的，对展位费和布展费分别给予20%～30%补助。经审核批准，对在主要交通干道上设置广告专题宣传我县旅游整体形象、旅游线路和旅游景点的，按照实际财务投入的情况予以奖励（最高不超过4万元）。（3）加大乡村旅游发展扶持。要把乡村旅游发展与生态文明新农村建设有机结合起来，整合资源、项目、资金加快发展。对每个乡村旅游点建设给予5万元扶持；对全县经有关部门评定达到不同级别的乡村旅舍每户分别给予0.5万元、0.3万元、0.2万元、0.1万元的扶持，对达到市级标准的乡村旅游示范户给予0.3万元的扶持；达到县级标准的乡村旅游示范户给予0.1万元的扶持。同时，要积极争取更多的县内乡村旅游发展项目列入省旅游发展资金支持的计划。对一次性贷款投资200万元以上的乡村旅游项目，县财政按贷款利息的50%给予3年期的贴息扶持。

8. 抓整合，聚合力。一是要加强县内县外旅游整合。推进旅游合作，建立区域旅游无障碍通道。探索建立互利互惠、合作共赢模式，加快形成优势互补、资源互享、客源互送、线路互推、信息互通的旅游发展新格局。推进跨区域旅游资源和精品线路的联合开发，强化旅游品牌的联合宣传促销和旅游市场的整顿规范，加强区域间旅游产品的联合开发。特别是集中营、乌江流域、多缤洞、息烽温泉景区的开发，要与周边地区旅游开发紧密结合，加强合作。二要形成合力。要整合宣传、旅游、文化（艺）、体育、教育资源，形成“五位一体”，构建旅游发展新格局，齐心协力共同建设旅游精品，共同开发旅游线路，共同开拓旅游市场，共同促进旅游对外宣传促销，形成全县一盘棋、上下一条心，积极主动推进旅游业的大发展。各部门各乡镇在对外接待中，要把推介息烽一日游、二日游、三日游等纳入接待目录。

9．善管理，上水平。一要加强旅游市场监管。建立旅游市场综合治理联合执法制度，健全旅游行政执法体系和质量监督网络，健全投诉机制，加大部门联合执法力度，切实保障旅游消费者和旅游经营单位的合法权益。建立县旅游行业协会组织，发挥其在旅游业发展中的媒介、自律、服务和监督作用，规范旅游企业经营行为，营造良好的旅游经营环境。二要提高旅游服务质量。要加强旅行社规范化管理，强化服务意识，提高旅游接待水平。强化旅游标准化管理，加快星级宾馆、星级饭店、乡村旅游接待点和乡村旅舍的建设和评定工作，加强旅游行业质量信誉等级管理，不断提高服务质量。三要加强旅游队伍建设。激活现有人才，充分发挥不再担任乡科级领导职务人员的人力、智力、组织等优势，进一步充实旅游干部人才队伍。加快旅游人才的培养和引进，大力推进岗位培训，实行旅游从业人员资格认证和考试制度，加强旅游从业人员思想道德、业务素质和诚信建设，增强服务意识，不断提高旅游从业人员的整体素质和管理水平。要强化县域内旅游行业和从业人员的息烽意识，营造“人人了解息烽，人人宣传息烽，人人为息烽旅游发展做贡献”的良好氛围。四要强化旅游安全管理。按照“谁主管、谁负责”的原则，进一步加强对全县旅游行业的监管，切实加强旅游安全防范体系建设，加强旅游安全监管和执法队伍建设，建立完善旅游安全防范预案，层层落实安全生产责任制，确保旅游业健康发展。

三、加强领导，提供保障

10．加强领导。充分发挥县旅游发展领导小组作用，健全旅游工作协调机制，负责对全县旅游业发展统一规划、统一管理、统一协调，研究和解决旅游业发展中的重大问题，负责全县旅游业发政策措施的制定和落实。领导小组成员单位要从旅游业发展的全局出发，强化旅游发展意识，按照各自的职能分工共同培育息烽旅游业。每年召开全县旅游发展大会，表彰对息烽旅游发展做出突出贡献的单位、企业和个人，安排部署旅游业发展工作。

11．明确责任。对招商引资开发重点旅游景区的企业，要建立县级领导联系帮扶制度，帮助企业解决前期手续、建设开发、营运开发中遇到的困难和问题，县直各单位部门、各乡镇要按照各自的职能分工，落实帮助重点企业的责任，在工作中要从全县旅游业发展的大局出发，善于运用政策打“擦边球”、勇于不计个人利益顾全大局，以真心、真诚帮助旅游企业发展。此外，还要建立县领导和部门帮助发展乡村旅游示范点制度，帮助示范点理清思路，制定目标，落实措施，解决问题，搞好服务，形成齐抓共管的强大合力。各乡镇要明确责任，把各项政策措施真正落到实处。

12．营造声势。在旅游的对外宣传上，要坚持“红色经典·灵秀息烽”的形象主题，坚持有效性、持续性、统一性。要开设专栏、专题，采取走出去，请进来的办法，采取搞活动，造声势的措施，加大旅游宣传力度。建立息烽旅游网站，强化网上宣传，增加网站服务的内容，确保及时更新。要本着政府引导、景区和企业为主，多渠道增加宣传投入，保证旅游市场促销需要。各旅游景区（点）每年投入一定的经费用于对外宣传促销。要营造良好的旅游氛围，在贵遵高速公路、210国道等交通干线、县城中心广场、主干道和游客集散地设置旅游公益广告牌、指示牌。要精心组织开展“林城贵阳——避暑季”息烽系列子项目活动，“苗族四月八”“县树”“县花”、旅游形象大使、旅游服务之星评选，旅游景点摄影大赛，美食大赛，红色旅游文化节等节庆活动，认真策划组织开展旅游论坛等旅游主题宣传活动，营造良好的旅游氛围，树立息烽旅游形象。

13．强化督查。县委督查室和县政府目标办要将全县旅游发展工作纳入对各乡镇及相关部门的年度目标考核，严格奖惩。县委组织部要将旅游发展工作实绩纳入干部政绩考核内容，作为干部提拔任用的重要依据，对发展县内旅游业成效显著的干部要大胆提拔任用，对长期没有起色，履行职责不力的干部予以调整。县委督查室、县政府目标办要搞好督促检查，促进工作落实。各有关部门要根据本意见的精神和自身的实际，制定具体的工作方案和措施，确保各项目标任务落实到位。

中共息烽县委办公室 息烽县人民政府办公室关于做好养龙司乡、石硐乡、西山乡撤乡设镇相关工作的通知

息委办字〔2013〕114号

各乡（镇）党委、政府，新华社区，县委各部委，县直国家机关各部门，人武部，各人民团体，省属、市属驻县企事业单位：

根据《省人民政府关于同意息烽县养龙司乡石硐乡西山乡撤乡设镇的批复》（黔府函〔2013〕152号）精神，将我县养龙司乡建制设置为养龙司镇、石硐乡建制设置为石硐镇、西山乡建制设置为西山镇，实行镇管村体制，原所辖行政区域和政府驻地不变。为确保养龙司、石硐、西山尽快完成撤乡设镇相关工作，现将有关事宜通知如下：

一、所涉及的相关单位和县直有关部门要积极配合做好养龙司、石硐、西山撤乡设镇的相关工作。

二、养龙司、石硐、西山三个镇所辖部门原公章由所在镇政府负责收集后统一上缴县档案局，并及时做好公章、印信、证件、门牌更换及交通指示牌调整的申报工作。

三、公安部门要积极配合养龙司、石硐、西山3个镇做好群众相关证件的更换工作。

四、原养龙司、石硐、西山三个乡所有机构要与县直相关部门对接并做好撤乡设镇更名后相关工作。

五、养龙司、石硐、西山三个镇要在行文、公务活动中使用规范名称。

中共息烽县委办公室

息烽县人民政府办公室

2013年8月22日

中共息烽县委　息烽县人民政府关于促进农民增加收入的实施意见

息党发〔2004〕18号

（2004年5月12日）

为认真贯彻落实中央，省、市农业农村工作会议精神，切实做好全县促进农民增收工作，根据县的实际，提出如下实施意见：

一、增强做好促进农民增收工作的责任感和紧迫感

近年来，全县在以增加农民收入为核心、切实推进解决“三农”问题做了大量工作，有效地促进了农村经济的繁荣，农业结构调整步伐加快，农村改革稳步推进，农民收入增加，农村社会稳定。同时必须清醒地看到，当前全县农业农村发展还面临突出问题，农民增收困难，农民人均收入增长缓慢，城乡二元结构仍然相当明显。如不尽快扭转这种局面，不仅影响农民生活水平的提高，而且不利于全县建设小康社会目标的实现。因此，在新形势下促进农民增收，既是当前紧迫的任务，又是长期的工作；不仅是重大的经济问题，也是重大的政治问题。

促进农民增收的总体思路是：全面贯彻中央和省、市农业农村工作会议精神，按照“谋发展、抓重点、调结构、进强县”的工作思路，以增加农民收入为核心，抢抓建设“大贵阳”机遇，统筹城乡经济协调发展，走“多予、少取、放活”的路子，采取综合措施，大力推进农业产业化和城乡一体化，发展壮大农村二、三产业，加大农村剩余劳动力向非农产业有序转移的力度，进一步加速农业农村基础设施建设，不断创新助农增收机制，力争全县农民人均纯收入在贵阳市各区、县（市）间排名前移，为“两个率先”目标的实现做出贡献。

二、夯实农业基础，为农民增收创造条件

县、乡两级财政要千方百计加大对农业和农村基础设施建设投入，确保财政每年对农业总投入的增长幅度高于财政收入的增长幅度。坚持建设与管理并重，按照“用途不变、范围不变、对象不变”的原则，采取承包、租赁、拍卖、股份等形式，切实建立起农业和农村基础设施配套管理的有效机制，充分发挥农业和农村基础设施最大的综合效益。针对全县农业发展“瓶颈”，应着力抓好以下工程建设：

水利农田工程　从2004年起，用2年时间新建和改造人饮工程120处，解决农村12000人、畜饮水困难。建成小水池4000口，完成渠道新建防渗60千米，电灌站更新140千瓦，新建改造山塘40口。建成3座小（二）型水库，完成鱼简河水库和阳朗排洪工程建设。继续实施好九庄镇农业综合开发土地治理项目，切实抓好2004年2000亩基本农田建设。

交通工程　不断加大县、乡（镇）、村等级公路建设改造力度。2004年，完成100千米县乡公路硬化、250千米贫困村村级公路硬化。2010年全面基本实现全县村通等级公路。

茅草房和危房改造工程　在2004年全面消除农村人居茅草房的基础上，从2005年起，启动农村

贫困农户危房改造工程，力争用3～5年时间完成1500户特困农户的危房改造。

林业生态工程　继续实施好退耕还林、天然林资源保护工程。2004年示范种植中药材白术、板蓝根、桔梗0.27万亩、黄檗0.1万亩、水果林带0.5万亩，实施贵阳市第二环城林带工程造林1.3万亩。积极探索生态文明村建设。

生态能源工程　从2004年起每年投入1400万元（含贷款与农民自筹），新建沼气池4000口，配套改圈、改厕、改灶、改厨、改造串户道路，力争到2010年实现全县农村“五改一气”工程覆盖农户面达60%。2004年建成沼气池2000口，配套改厕2000间、改圈2000间。

通信工程　大力加强农村通信、农业信息化建设，力争到2010年，80%以上的行政村建立农经信息网接收点，努力提高农村综合经济信息服务能力和水平。鼓励通讯企业进入农村市场，力争用3～5年时间使全县农村自然村寨通电话率达90%以上。从2004年起，每年计划投资120万元，完成30个自然村通广播电视工程，到2009年，全县50户以上的自然村寨基本通广播电视。

教育工程　加大对农民科学技术培训和实用技术培训力度，提高农民的科技素质。每年完成“绿证”培训1500人和新一轮农民技术培训4万人次。在2004年完成新一轮技术培训5.6万人次、“绿证”培训1550人，非农技能培训5600人。进一步提高农村义务教育的质量，加快农村后备劳动力的文化基础教育、职业技能培训，广泛推广“3+1”农村普及教育与职教有机结合的模式，探索建立农村特困学生助学金制度，全力提高劳动者素质。2004年在30个边远贫困村修建远程教育接收点，建成134个村级小学卫星接收站，完成10个乡镇中学多媒体教室的建设。

医疗卫生工程　从2004年起，每年增加的卫生事业经费主要用于发展乡村卫生事业，再用2年时间完成2个县级医院的新建和改造，用3年时间完成10个乡镇卫生院的改造。逐步建立新型农村合作医疗制度，努力解决好农民因病致贫、返贫问题。

“双带致富”工程　从资金、项目、金融等方面逐年加大对农村党员干部培训和“远程教育”的投入，力争用2～3年时间把全县村党支部书记轮训一遍，使其真正掌握1～2门致富技能。从2004年起，逐步启动1330名农村党员干部及村级后备干部的培训工作。

三、立足实际，创新思维，不断探索促进农民增收的途径

着眼于统筹城乡发展，打破城乡二元结构，以基地为载体，以项目为龙头，千方百计形成和壮大地方特色产业，逐步形成一批符合农产品质量标准的具有地方特色和市场竞争力的农产品基地，通过基地的辐射带动提高全县农业的规模化水平。力争到2007年建成10万亩特色农产品基地。

（一）努力提高粮食综合生产能力

进一步加强耕地特别是基本农田的保护力度，坚决防止和切实治理乱占滥用耕地现象，严格实行基本农田保护和耕地占补平衡制度，开展经常性的基本农田保护执法检查，切实抓好农田水利基础设施建设，稳定粮食播面，加强粮食生产。落实好粮食收购补贴政策，大力推广农业实用技术，引进和推广适宜全县种植的新品种，不断提高科学种植水平。

（二）切实加大传统种植业的结构调整

围绕服务城市、富裕农村，充分发挥乡镇区域比较优势，调整农业生产布局，调整农产品结构，加快对传统种植业的改造。按照农产品质量认证体系加快五大种植基地的规模化建设。一是以南山山脉为主的淡季蔬菜生产基地；二是以养龙司为主的无公害蔬菜生产基地；三是以永靖、西山为主的稻田养鱼基地；四是以九庄为主的龙头企业产品生产基地；五是以石硐、九庄为主的优质烤

烟生产基地。力争2004年完成蔬菜总产量8万吨（其中上市蔬菜3.6万吨）。完成2.2万亩烤烟种植任务，并从2005年起每年安排上年烤烟农特税的10%用于烤房改造、技术培训及生产补贴等。

（三）做好做大做强畜牧业

认真贯彻落实省、市关于加快畜牧业发展的各项政策措施，抓住品种改良、饲草饲料、疫病防治、优质畜产品基地和畜产品加工等关键环节，逐步建立财政、个体、集体、外来资金等多元化投入机制。从2004年起，县财政在已确定每年预算安排畜牧专项补助资金100万元的基础上，随财力的增长而增加投入，扶持畜牧业发展。通过小额贷款重点扶持奶牛基地、优质商品肉牛基地、优质生态商品肉禽基地上规模、上档次。2004年，建成3个“六位一体”养殖基地，种植牧草5000亩，出栏商品牛1000头；商品肉鸡150万羽；肉兔2万只；依托乳业龙头企业发展农户饲养奶牛600头，进一步做大仔猪养殖基地。提高畜禽水产养殖在农民人均纯收入和全县农村经济发展中的比重，力争2010年实现畜牧业产值占农业总产值的50%。

（四）加大农业招商引资力度，扶持发展农村二、三产业

一是加大对龙头企业的扶持。加快生态农业科技示范园的开发与建设，重点扶持与生产基地配套的龙头企业，力争2004年实现农产品加工业产值超过1200万元，2007年、2013年分别达到1.5亿元和5亿元。财政部门逐年增加支持农业产业化发展的专项资金，安排一定资金用于辐射面广、带动力强、科技含量高、市场竞争力强的龙头企业的技改贷款贴息。力争通过3～5年的努力使全县农业主导产业形成“龙头企业+生产农户+生产基地”的产业化经营格局。二是进一步加强农业与药业、食业的衔接互动。以利益为纽带，对药业、乳业和食品加工业类龙头企业给予政策扶持。积极鼓励农户通过土地使用权、资金或农产品入股等方式与龙头企业形成利益共同体，以合同、订单等方式促进企业与农户联合，并在技术、信息上给予支持，确定企业、农户、政府及部门的权利和义务，促进厂地优势联合，使种植业、养殖业成为企业的原料基地，实现企业增效与农民增收的双赢。龙头企业不论所有制形式和经营形式，只要能带动农户增收，财政、金融和税收方面都要一视同仁地给予支持。同时，积极探索建立农业综合开发、扶贫开发和农业产业化经营项目风险化解机制，对向贫困乡镇和贫困农户预付农产品收购定金的龙头企业，可使用扶贫信贷资金帮助解决原料收购资金紧缺的问题。三是引导企业、农民积极发展农村二、三产业。引导企业重点发展农产品加工业的储藏、保鲜、运销业，因地制宜积极发展信息产业、物流配送、咨询服务、旅游、餐饮住宿、娱乐休闲、交通运输等行业和各类专业市场、集贸市场、批发零售市场。因地制宜地引导农民创办一些投资少、见效快的农副产品加工企业，结合结构调整、自然风光、民族特色及农业科技园区建设，发展商贸流通，推进农产品销售及相关服务业的发展。

（五）有序开发和转移农村劳动力

继续调整农村劳动力就业结构，促进农村劳动力向技能型劳动力转变，加快务工型劳动力向创业型劳动力的转变。一是加强对农民的教育培训。以市场需求为导向，以提高就业能力和就业率为目标，以转移就业前的引导性培训和职业技能培训为重点，按照不同行业、不同工种对从业人员技能的基本要求，安排培训内容，采取提前介入用工单位、签订劳动力输出“订单”、发布用工信息等多种办法，提高劳动力转移的组织化程度。组织开展针对性强、层次较高的培训活动，鼓励各类教育培训机构、用人单位开展对农民的职业技能培训。县乡财政安排农民职业技能培训专项资金，从2004年起，探索培训经费直接补助给参加培训转移的农民的办法。二是切实维护农民工利益。进

一步清理和取消农民进城就业的不合理收费，简化农民跨地区就业和进城务工的各种手续，防止变换手法向进城就业的农民及用工单位乱收费，严禁企业违法拖欠和克扣农民工工资。本地农民进城务工，劳动部门免费办理外出务工证，公安部门只办理流动人口暂住登记、免收暂住人口管理的相关费用。计生部门免收流动人口婚育证办证费和流动人口计划生育管理服务费，免收节育手续保证金。卫生部门对通过培训进城务工的农民，免费安排一次体检，免费发放“健康证”“体检合格证”。三是大力推进小城镇户籍制度改革。凡在城镇有相对固定住所、稳定职业和生活来源以及在农林牧场从事种植、养殖、农林产品加工的农业户口，均可申报登记城镇居民常住户口；其共同居住的父母、配偶、子女，可随迁办理城镇常住户口。教育行政主管部门建立完善保障进城务工就业农民子女接受义务教育的工作制度和机制，做到收费与当地学生一视同仁。

（六）强力推进小城镇建设

按照“小城镇、大战略”思路，把小城镇建设作为全面振兴全县农村经济的重要增长点和突破口，同壮大县乡经济、发展乡镇企业、推进农业产业化经营、移民搬迁等结合起来，增强小城镇吸纳农村人口、带动农村发展的能力。到2010年，力争使县城人口达到10万人。同时把小寨坝镇建成县城级磷化工城；把九庄镇、石硐乡、流长乡、养龙司乡建成以农副产品交易为主的商贸型城镇；把温泉镇、西山乡和鹿窝乡建成以旅游服务业为主的旅游型城镇；把青山苗族乡建成民族特色型城镇。逐步完善城镇功能，结合农业结构调整规划建设和完善一批有规模、具特色的农产品集贸市场和专业批发市场，对自产自销农副产品的农民免收城乡集贸市场管理费。通过直销、配送等多种形式，形成上下连通、内外结合的市场营销网络，不断提高农产品的商品率。

（七）加强农民减负工作，切实维护农民利益

一是深化农村税费改革。认真执行中央关于降低农业税税率和取消烤烟外的农业特产税等有关政策，严格按照减税比例调减到户，真正让农民得到实惠；认真执行农民销售自产农产品不缴纳增值税的政策规定，对农民进入各类市场销售自产农产品所得暂不征收个人所得税；对专营种植业、养殖业的个体工商户或个人，凡其经营项目属于农业税、牧业税范围且已征收农业税、牧业税的，对其所得不再征收个人所得税。二是加强涉农价格管理和监督。物价部门加强涉农价格管理和监督检查，重点监督化肥、农药、种子、柴油、农膜、农村电价、水价、农村中小学教育收费、民政、计划生育、防疫检验、婚姻登记等收费。进一步完善涉农价格和收费公示制度，形成整治涉农价格和收费秩序的长效机制。依法打击一切坑农、伤农、害农行为，充分发挥农村价格网络的作用，密切监控农资价格动态，及时解决带倾向性、苗头性的农资涨价问题。切实稳定农产品价格。三是推进土地使用权流转。按照“自愿、有偿、依法、规范”的原则，引导农民推进土地流转和发展适度规模经营。提倡和鼓励土地向种田能手和种粮大户集中的流转形式，县有关部门和乡镇帮助农民建立土地流转库，完善土地流转手续，规范土地流转行为。严禁强制收回农民土地承包权（不含“三户一人”土地）重新进行发包。

（八）健全和完善支农帮农机制

一是多渠道增加对农业农村的投入。继续深化农村信用社改革，加大信贷支农力度，认真落实《贵阳市深化农村小额扶贫贷款工作意见》，充分发挥小额扶贫贷款资金的使用效益。二是建立和完善相配套的农村社会化服务体系。按照农产品质量认证标准，以农业商品化促进农业产业化，以农业产业化带动农村现代化。大力培育和开发名特新优产品，力争通过几年的努力，使我县的特

色优势农产品在省内外市场有一定的知名度和竞争力。积极发展农村专业合作经济组织。按照“民办、民管、民受益”的原则，扶持和发展壮大以多种形式组建农民参与的各种专业合作经济组织、协会，充分发挥其在信息传递、技术服务、市场营销和维护农民合法利益等方面的积极作用。同时建立配套的有效约束监督机制。依托现有的政府网站、农经网等信息网络，建设集采集、分析、发布、交易于一体的县、乡（镇）、村信息平台，引导农村经纪人利用现代科技手段增强服务功能，促进品牌农业、商品农业发展。三是努力提高农产品质量安全水平。认真实施贵阳市食用农产品安全监督管理规定，加快我县农产品检验检测、安全监测及质量认证体系建设，强化农业投入品管理。逐步实施农产品市场准入制，2004年申报完成4个省级无公害蔬菜基地，建立1个质量监测站。四是逐步建立失地农民促进就业和社会保障制度。随着全县各类工程建设项目的推进，被征地农民失地后的生活保障问题日益突出。要切实落实最严格的耕地保护制度，完善土地征用程序和补偿机制，妥善安置失地农民，促进农村社会稳定。五是完善扶贫开发机制。认真执行省、市、县关于加强新阶段扶贫开发力度全面建设小康社会的决定，坚持以增加贫困人口收入为目标，以改善贫困乡、村生产生活条件为重点，以提高贫困人口素质为根本，实施基础设施工程、增收减负工程、科教扶贫工程、社会救助工程、双带致富工程。建立和完善农村医疗保险、最低生活保障制度，抑制因灾、因病返贫，努力实现贫困乡、村物质文明、政治文明、精神文明协调发展。

四、加强对农业农村工作的领导，确保各项工作落到实处

全县各级各部门要树立科学的发展观和正确的政绩观，把促进农民增收作为解决好“三农”问题重中之重的工作放在更加突出的位置。要以求真务实的工作作风，建立党政“一把手”亲自抓的负责制，切实把促进农民增收的成效作为衡量工作重要指标，完善监督考核机制，改进服务方式方法，真正把中央，省、市、县帮助农民群众增加收入的各项措施落到实处，让农民群众真正得到实惠。实施人才兴农战略，大力开发农村人才资源，培养、引进农业经营管理、农业科技、党政管理等方面的人才，为农业农村经济发展提供人才保证和智力支持。加强农村基层组织建设，选好配强村党支部书记，并切实抓好村党支部书记的培训，不断增强其带头致富、带领群众致富的能力；全面深化“三级联创”活动，进一步巩固和发展“学教”活动成果，不断完善“让干部经常受教育，使农民长期得实惠”的长效机制。

做好新阶段、新形势下的农业农村工作，促进农民增加收入，推动农村经济社会全面进步意义深远，责任重大。只有从实现好、维护好、发展好农民群众根本利益的高度出发，结合实际，狠抓落实，才能不断开创全县农业农村工作的新局面。

文献资料补充息烽县人大常委会关于流长乡、鹿窝乡撤乡设镇有关问题的决定（二）

息烽县人大常委会
关于流长乡、鹿窝乡撤乡设镇
有关问题的决定

息人常〔2016〕14号

（2016年8月30日县第十六届人大常委会第四十四次会议通过）

经贵州省人民政府黔府函〔2016〕121号文件批准，撤销流长乡、鹿窝乡，设立流长镇、鹿窝镇，根据有关法律法规规定，息烽县第十六届人大常委会第四十四次会议决定：

一、撤销流长乡、鹿窝乡设立流长镇、鹿窝镇。

二、流长乡、鹿窝乡第七届人民代表大会更名为流长镇、鹿窝镇人民代表大会。换届后的流长镇、鹿窝镇第一次人民代表大会为流长镇、鹿窝镇第一届人民代表大会第一次会议。

三、流长乡、鹿窝乡第七届人民代表大会代表更名为流长镇、鹿窝镇人民代表大会代表，任期至届满。

四、流长乡、鹿窝乡第七届人民代表大会选举产生的流长乡、鹿窝乡第七届人民代表大会主席团、主席，人民政府乡长、副乡长，分别更名为流长镇、鹿窝镇人民代表大会主席团、主席，人民政府镇长，副镇长。

息烽县人民代表大会常务委员会

2016年8月30日

前志补遗（三）

佚文四篇

《毗陵六逸诗抄》序

王嗣衍

毗陵六逸，予曩客燕邸，即耳其名，而言者不详。岁丙申，移守兹郡，辄与绅士大夫接。庄编修荪服、徐主事辛斋为予道之甚悉，且出其遗稿以相示，虽皆出于感发悲愤，然或以情胜，或以气胜，或以渊博胜，要自有不可磨灭者。惜其所遇独奇，未获少展其抱负，而各赍志以没。昔人谓孟东野穷而后工于诗，六逸其殆工于诗，而益穷其遇者欤！前此宋大中丞欲汇成帙，付剞劂不果，孙子一士来宰是邑，毅然独任之，不数月告成。夫表章幽隐，正吾辈事，六逸有知，其亦可无憾也夫！康熙五十六年夏六月，贵阳王嗣衍序。

王嗣衍，字芷园，息烽县城人，生卒年月不详。康熙二十六年举人，康熙三十六年进士，授知府衔，出任陕西白河县知事。

游西望山记

刘泽滋

吾黔西望山，乃苗岭之秀峰也。久欲览胜登临，奈学业羁身，无暇及此，殊为恨恨。今岁试验期毕，校中放假，师友约集游览，一以避暑，一以骋怀，同行者共三十余人，余亦与焉。

山之麓距校二十里许，至则日将午，借农家少憩，至是而升，则重岩深邃，曲折通幽，山中竹木郁郁森森，日光为之掩蔽，只闻百鸟喧鸣，水声潺潺。约行两句钟，忽然开展，乃莲花山也。横行约数里，谷口一亭，浑疑路断，亭中少憩，见一联云：“层层望去层层高，山上探山山更迴；步步行来步步险，路间觅路路几无。”亭左一石峭立如狮，其后有路可通。曲折而上，不数十武，数孤峰岿峙目前。古木苍翠，烟云缭绕，隐隐有寺，名曰华严，刹址坍塌，亭阁毁坏，今虽重建，然工程不过十之二。于大殿见铜佛三尊，约高七尺；小铜佛四尊，形象均不完备。相传为开山祖师雨松（语嵩）自滇省铸来者。转而之西，至客院，院壁石刊一联，书法遒劲，不识何人手笔，联云：“尘浣胸中，绿竹高低千径绕；云飞足底，青蓬远近万峰朝。”辗转游览，见断碣残碑，不禁起今昔之感。未几，暮色苍苍，归鸦哑哑，投宿寺中，僧炊黍进。

次日，金鸡三唱，甜梦初回，信笛一声，促起，整队前游。山径幽曲，穿林陟岩，搴裳始过。复自南折里许，至山之一端，旁有尖峰二，高冲云汉。适晴天一色，白雾横山，四顾茫茫，一碧无际。且行且览，尤胜于平日之所闻者。惜路途险窄，高悬万仞，进步维艰。折而北，至夹谷中攀缘上，突然接于眼帘者，瞿昙寺也。庙貌倾颓。破垣碎瓦，满目荒烟，惟古木参天，浅草龙茸。刹址之宏，罕有伦比。询其由，则毁于苗乱。为之嘅然。乃饭于寺，饭罢谋登峰。虽赤日中天，而凉风拂面，寒气侵骨，始知高地之温度减少，诚不虚也。逾一岭，遥望数峰，高插九霄。询于师，知为苗岭之秀峰。徐徐前进，唯见空谷闲云，自来自去，幽壑中水若断若续。至峰麓，古路曲折，两旁碑碣残断无余，惟古松古柏，满目皆是。道旁一小岩，怪幻不可状。一亭依岩建，有联云："正途一直可通行，请将眼孔抬高，何必待人来引路；捷径千条休错走，好把脚跟站稳，不妨随我去凌霄。"小憩亭内，遥望丛岩中，泉涓涓缘之以下，如滴露，如垂珠，一片幽情雅趣，令人乐而不忍去。然志在高山，无暇顾及，起而行，路险多曲。凡历石百有余级，仰见石刊三大字曰：凤池寺。四围树木阴翳，淡烟笼罩，佛殿僧舍，隐隐参差在上。甫登寺，俨若置身于浮云空青之间。历四旧刹。小憩客院，僧煮茗进。茶罢，寺僧导引出客院，折而南，绕林木，过小桥，见一池。僧曰：此即凤凰池也。相传有凤凰游其间。池面积约七百余方丈。有亭翼然临于池上者，壮观亭也。亭新建。吾师立成一联云："举袂快风飘，恍如一片清虚，搜归眼底；凭栏惊日映，俨似千层浩渺，吞贮胸中。"徘徊观望，风景绝佳。池周枯木垂藤，峻峰峭石，倒映池中，俨若图画，且水鸟三四游泳其间，洵可乐也。池畔一高峰，与寺斜对。少焉，由亭之左，缓步而升。至峰间一古亭，内有联云："好高的定要争高，到此间骨软筋疲，偏又想高高走去；踏稳了方能靠稳，莫以后心慌脚乱，宜更加稳稳行来。"亭左一峻石屹立，高数丈，宛如人形，朝拱其寺。仙人峰因此得名也。山数峰，惟此峰高可上。亭中少坐，复前行，至峰顶，四顾无边。晴天无雾，看东枕紫江，西窥黔邑（黔西城之东山，晴天可睹），南屏龙场，北视播州，乌江之水环绕西北，迢遥千里。所谓登东山而小鲁，不诚然哉？

览毕，历观寺左右各景，凡动胆石、万卷书、天门石、玉笋峰、盘陀石等，皆奇妙玲珑。继至玉乳泉，一石乳大可合抱，中通小孔，水涓涓而出。乳四周勷以池。池畔有亭，倾颓已久。游览毕，返寺，遂宿焉。是夜，僧与师叙谈，此山之庙，在昔共十有八，盛于明；历数百年，贵州兵燹，悉毁于苗乱。今不得其人，空负名山，致成此现象。予侍师侧，悉闻所言，吁人杰地灵，诚不虚也。

翌晨起，梳洗毕，绕殿巡行，见正殿楹联云："看仙翁手拍云端（仙人峰在寺前），浑疑桂院高凌，约汝三清游上界；待老子头昂霄外，漫道竹疆远隶，让他五岳镇中州。"系刘韫良撰。转而之北，至东廊，即客院，昨宿处之前面也。院前亦刊一联云："福地少人知，绝好修真来此地；仙乡容我住，其如归隐待何年。"亦刘撰。吾师等亦志两联于客院。其一云："苔边笔扫云皆润，松下琴眠日更长。"其二："振袂手探红日近，披襟肩裹绿云深。"饭后，师以山中寒重，不可久停，遂整队由山后归。

途中景况，与来时无异。且行且憩，至第二日午后始至校。身虽已在校中，而魂魄精神，犹依稀放浪乎山巅空谷焉。握笔为之记。时民国七年八月二日事也。

刘泽滋，民国息烽县第二高小学生。

息烽温泉序

王廷华

地之为名，或取之于山水，或称之于人物，或得意之于事，命其名者也。如吾息南山之麓有热水在焉，水之热度达到百分之九十六七，故历代相传皆以“热水”呼之。至民国三十四年（1945），王君天梯奉令建筑池宇，布置一切，引旁溪流水渗入其中，供人游泳。浴罢歌曰：强邻逼处兮耻莫忘，长期抗战兮足以当。不战自退兮明礼让，得陇望蜀兮逞豪强。元首断断兮盟邦倾向，元旦轰轰兮帝国请降。民族复兴兮快畅，收回失地兮奔忙。温泉游泳兮无他望，欲得澡身寿而康。寿而康兮心莫放，养我浩然乐无疆。又曰：道路平平，泉水温温。洗心涤虑，四海澄清。且开工之日值倭奴寇我黔疆，退兵之时，人谓温泉一开，烽烟永息。得意若此，人民莫不欢欣。即呈请省主席子惠杨公题其名曰：“息烽温泉。”意在温泉可以息烽，非息烽之温泉也。其义广矣。于情于理于景，名实相符，较之“热水”有天渊之别。吾人敢不志之？

王廷华，字质彬，号养气山人，息烽九庄桐枝驿人。曾任民国修文县参事会参事、息烽县县议会副议长等职。著有《莲蓬集》传世。

论语嵩语录及塔铭书

陈　垣

塔铭为钱邦芑撰并书，篇中“并书”二字，似当补入。碑凡十三行，行七十字。今《语录》所附塔铭，阙字之外，尚有漏字。谨将敝箧所藏，另抄呈校：《锦江禅灯》十一，《黔南会灯录》二，皆载语嵩为破山弟子雪臂峦法嗣。今碑中所谓长破杲者，即雪臂峦庚子以前旧号。《黔诗纪略》作长破果，传写误也。语嵩先参之破雪，亦破山弟子；与语嵩同日得法之书云，即《黔诗纪略》所称为天峰和尚者也。语嵩大弟子佛宗号嵩目，佛海号嵩眉，皆见《黔南会灯录》四。佛智号醒闲，又作省贤，见《五灯全书》一〇五。远庵则木陈弟子，见《五灯全书》七十三。湘潭孝廉郭金台，隆武丙戌举人，见《小腆纪传》五十八。吴门刘居士，见《山晖语录》十一《与钱中丞书》。《五灯全书》八十七载远庵为语嵩揭龛偈，有“三千里外扶筇至，万指丛中拨手归”之语，与塔铭所载远庵举火偈不同。《锦江禅灯》十一载语嵩病中示偈，有“吾年五十七，无补法门益，拜扫上天童，老病相摧逼”之语，亦与塔铭所载不合，当是后人缘饰，且生于辛亥，卒于丙午，亦非五十七也。

语嵩与钱邦芑、方于宣关系最深，其住牟尼山，即二人所邀请，今《语录》与二人书问亦特多。于宣晚节披猖，《语录》卷十《答神生偈》，有“休恋途中风景好”之句，曾于《黔诗纪略》见之；今观《语录》卷七《与神生法语》，又有“无端妒杀人，几个知休歇！不休歇，惹得子规啼夜月”之语；卷十二《与神生偈》，又有“佛恩国恩何如报，孝莫亲兮忠莫君，今日夜郎珍重汝，金汤法化度迷津”之句，语嵩之于于宣，可谓尽忠告之道。虽其所示句语，孰先孰后不可知，然大意总是劝其不宜出，出则必须忠于君国，惜于宣不能听，卒至身败名裂而后已。当语嵩卒时，于宣恐已先卒，塔铭通篇不及于宣一字，殊可注意。《贵州通志》卷二云语嵩化后，钱邦芑为作塔铭，方于宣序其语录行世，《滇黔佛教考》据此以为于宣当卒在语嵩后，大误。今观《语录》于宣序，乃永历八年撰，其刊行当在语嵩生前。其所记皆永历时事，其中人事，钱、方面外，如相国文居士安之、东川吕居士大器、金一程居士源，皆《小腆纪传》有传，莫子偲以为足备掌故，最称卓识。往考顺治宫廷事，亦曾利用憨璞、茚溪等语录，以补公私记载所不及，偲翁实先得我心也。《嘉兴藏》尚有《燕居语录》，为今本《嘉兴藏目录》所未载，今本《目录》止于又续藏之四十三函，其末数种为黔南语录，《佛教考》藏经篇曾论之。其第四十四函之第一种即为《云山燕居申语录》八卷，倘能物色得此，必于黔中掌故，更有裨益。燕居与山晖争席事，为吾人所不取，然《黔南会灯录》称黔南宗风，兴自燕居、语嵩、云腹三人，则《燕居语录》似不可不一考也，未识黔中有传本否？今因语嵩连类及之，处地北而语天南，必又有笑其陋者。匆匆不具。乙酉七月四日。

右碑连题目十三行，行七十字。《黔乘》所载有缺漏。民国二十四年（1935）江苏省立国学图书馆第八年（此处文字疑有误——编者注）刊有拓本影片，仅得碑上半截。兹特据初拓片补足，一字不漏。

陈垣跋

注：此文为陈垣回复贵州籍政治家、实业家、学者朱启钤的一封书信。

陈垣，生于1880年，卒于1976年。广东新会人，历史学家、宗教学家。

文艺作品选录（四）

文学作品

一、诗　歌

篱　笆（外一首）

朱登麟

把那些青涩的许诺
密匝匝编进我长长的期待
你给我圈定的日子
便开始了梅雨季节

我滴滴答答的哀求
都把你檐前的青石板敲出坑了
常青藤把隐秘的心思
发疯似的四处宣讲
那条羞羞答答想伸进你卧室的句子
被乱草涂改得结结巴巴的
风囫囵吞枣
不肯揿响五月的门铃

深夜，我站得酸疼的脚
关节炎没天没地撒娇
额角沁出星星点点惨白的花苞

亲爱的，某个黎明
太阳掀开你酣睡了一个雨季的窗帘
你肯定很惊讶——
我披挂满身的瓜瓜豆豆
为何都气鼓鼓的
瞪你

石菩萨

挣脱凶险的峭壁
大模大样往山腰一站
立地成佛
俯瞰一片高原
几十个寨子提心吊胆

五步蛇钻进钻出
七窍内繁殖血污和恐怖
从阴森森的瞳孔
鸦群扑簌簌窜出
腐臭的身下长出无数条山路
恶狠狠抓紧一群山峦
纠结月黑夜的焚风
叩打每扇失血的柴扉
索取香火
诅咒和祈祷战战兢兢
踩痛土地的胸脯

传说在每个石棱上簇生
方丈之内庄稼不敢生长

报春花无数次衔落流血的影子
寒号鸟的眼泪弥漫山塬
阳光站在半壁叹气
一条公路轰轰开到面前

只探头睁怀疑的眼光一闪
吓得打开峭壁匆匆逃遁

高原 仍在一段阴湿的山谷下
战栗

朱登麟，男，生于1966年。20世纪80年代起从事文学创作，现为贵州省作家协会会员。诗歌《篱笆》曾获贵阳晚报社“长城杯”诗歌大奖赛二等奖，并入选《当代青年新诗一千家》；《石菩萨》曾获贵州省首届大学生诗歌大奖赛二等奖。

攀沿阳光（外一首）

罗孝华

一

阳光陡泻如岩
踩着耀眼的台阶
文字积成的青苔上
阳光洒落密密的标点
一排排歌刺破苍穹
桅杆在风中挣脱翅膀
慵倦的鸟
你的痛苦打湿华丽的乐章
幻美的秃顶山系
可曾刻下铭心的愿望
可曾在爱的蚌壳
剥出一片忧伤

二

攀住一些历史的藤蔓
凭吊古人遗弃的秋千
寂寞点点
阳光的意义
挺立在石头多皱的掌心

三

岁月伸长胳膊
将体毛的珠贝撷取
那水体的流动
被人类的玻璃体容纳

四

为了爱
一只猿坠入阴森的地狱
火舌窜动着诗意
猛扑踏青的女子
古钟被拉响
一个帝王浅淡的意象
被托向神秘的远古

五

阳光陡泻如岩
金辉的城堡
抑扬豪迈的厮杀
云在凄凉的铠甲后面
流着悲壮的鲜血

六

银镯铜器
闪动的冷辉咄咄逼人
当天使痛失乐园
魔鬼离开地狱
谁用一轮遮羞的明月
挂在时间的墙壁

七

龟裂的大地
怒雨淋湿号角
战旗追缴宁静

八

阳光陡泻如岩
峭壁上读不尽的尸骨
照亮了热血和光芒
一片圣洁的云
走在富丽的大地上
整个宇宙
弥漫着她的体香

三　月

哗响的三月
唤醒焦渴的田园
虚幻的果
晃出叶的迷阵
晨光清凉的句子无人解读
田边地角的杂草已经除尽
逼向天心的叩问
将飞燕的影子击落
叮当的农具
吻过一大片处女地
心的寂寞被腾空
将绿色搬进门
生命的储仓需要填进
一些不卑不亢的句子
希望之门悬吊的深锁
等待三月
锻打成一把闪光的钥匙
佩挂在时间的银链上

罗孝华，男，生于1970年，乡村医生。1999年出版诗集《白狐》。作品入选《中国二十世纪微型文学作品选集》《新世纪诗选》《21世纪贵州诗歌档案》《中国好诗歌》等。

迎来“九七”

——写在香港回归的日子

陈久琪

百年前那滴血的黄昏
历史在暗室里
显影出一串清晰的数据
一九九七
母亲悲壮的呼唤
铸成儿子眼角的冰凌
伴着强盗庆功宴的乐声
屈辱流淌成
一段艰辛难忘的岁月
黑暗宣扬了沉默的预言
磅礴而起的狂飙
盘旋着意志的火焰
还我中华还我香港
镰刀与铁锤的铿锵
强壮了血性民族的筋骨
炎黄子孙的呐喊
搅动了整个宇宙
雄啸而成的主题
催报黎明
香港回归，祖国统一
米字旗将一瞬坠地
义勇军进行曲
定会把中华的辉煌升起

陈久琪，男，笔名仲石。高中语文教师。已出版诗集《故乡永是春》、散文集《真情无畏》等。

红帆船

卿山毅

发过一千次誓了
心是一片茫茫的海
要逐你于无际的边沿
你不再属于我的海域

你美丽的帆使人嫉妒
每一个岛都欢迎你着陆
你既然不属于我的海域
为什么总在心里漂游

潮涨潮落，黄昏的我
已经奄奄一息
苍穹的边沿，一块红霞
是你回来了吗

你不再回来了
我不再是你的梦
而夜深之时，你不安的马达
与我的心脏一起跳动

我不能逐走你
你常常入我的梦
我逐不走你
尽管我发过一千次誓

卿山毅，男，息烽西山人，曾为教师，后辞职下海。诗歌《红帆船》曾入选《当代青年新诗一千家》。

二、散　文

红色流长（外一篇）

朱登麟

流长是红色的。山山水水的流长，就象抽象派画家笔下的一面旗，展开在历史的记忆和现实的想象之中，红得炫目。

地处边关的流长，三面环水，沟谷深切，是地图里一块孤傲的高地。桀骜不驯的乌江在她的脚下咆哮奔腾千年不息。她高高在上、卓尔不群，起伏的山峦构成道道雄关，成为它命中注定的伤痛和骄傲。千百年高昂的头颅，渴望一次震颤人心的旷世冲动。

于是就有了那一次惊心动魄的摆渡。

民国《息烽县志·建置志·关梁篇》载：息烽地形最为险要者，莫如乌江，缘乌江为川黔必由之道。古人有诗、赋赞曰：“冥冥巫峡气，滔滔洞庭波。蹈常忽善变，极力翻臼窠。”“断壁千寻而削列，迅湍一线以长穿……骇浪惊翻，激流奔下；迅淏雷訇而电激，层花卷石而谽閜。”相传明逃亡皇帝朱允炆被永乐帝朱棣驱赶，率3000死士至此，遭遇狙击，血染乌江，最后不得不解散队伍，与当地人结盟（至今在西望山上还留有盟誓碑），建文帝无奈削发为僧，归隐山林。史载：明军征播（播州，即今遵义以北一带）时，童元镇兵刃于此，溺尸至江水不流。又载：明王节愍公祥，与白文选大战乌江败死葬此地。节愍时有“小霸王”之称，山因以名“霸王坡”。

滔滔乌江，成为多少人帝王将相迷梦中的一种宿命。

而名震寰宇的红军，注定要成为打破宿命创造奇迹的先行者。

71年前，那个遍野油菜花飘香的季节，和煦的阳光驱散了大地上的阴霾。

3月28日，红军主力一军团、三军团、四军团、五军团、九军团集结北岸，准备南渡乌江。而此时，国民党军孙渡部正从赤水河至黔西间的340千米战线上收缩队伍往南追击；周浑元、吴奇伟部正从金沙泮水一带“兼程猛进”迫近；而南岸各渡口均有重兵把守，层层设防，碉堡林立。军情如火，容不得片刻的迟疑。

当夜，红军先头部队神不知鬼不觉来到江对岸金沙县后山乡的悬崖丛林中。星光灿烂，脚下汹涌的乌江水，激荡着一股企盼已久的莫名的兴奋。

当时的乌江，河流深切，两岸悬崖峭壁，怪石对峙，丛林幽深，江水从嶙峋怪石丛中奔流而下，迅猛湍急，恶浪滔天，折桨断楫，吞舟嚼船，山势险恶，易守难攻。江口、大塘、梯子岩三个渡口，或水面较宽，水势较缓，易于行船；或地势陷落，水面较狭，易架浮桥，成为红军抢渡乌江的首选。

严格地说，这只是一场局部的闪电战，或者说只是一次速战速决的战斗，是毛泽东“只要把滇军调出云南来就是胜利”的大战略中的一个环节。但它的战略意义是巨大的，它既是一次借机摆脱敌人围追堵截的战略终点，又是一次开辟新战场走向更大的胜利的战略起点。红军用急行军摆脱了追击，用声东击西的佯攻牵制了敌人的主力，设疑军迷惑了敌人的排兵布阵，用包抄战术有效打击了守军的有生力量，最后顺利地用最小的牺牲换来了突围的胜利，达到了“把滇军调出云南”的战略目标。战略选择和战术运用上的睿智，确非古时那些只知强攻死打的帝王将相所不及。

从3月28日夜至4月1日，红军主力用不到4天的时间完成了这一次惊心动魄的摆渡。红色的浪潮淹没了流长，把这块迷茫的土地染成了红色——那些千百年来落寞地散落在乌江岸边的山崖、村庄、田园、码头、渡口被染成了红色；那些世世代代渴望翻身做主人的干涩的额头被染成了红色；那些徒步重走长征路探寻人类社会历史进程的脚步被染成了红色；那些带着几分兴奋、几分迷茫、几分虔诚前往红军烈士陵园祭奠的稚嫩的眼睛被染成了红色……

71年的风云变幻，71年的沧桑巨变。当又一波红色的浪潮带着追忆和感恩的热浪铺天盖地汹涌而至时，71年前用战火铸造辉煌的流长，又恢复了它旗帜般原生态的红色。

水上流长

流长是飘浮在水上的一座岛。乌江及其两条支流87千米的水域像一条华丽缎带，柔软地缠绕着它，遮盖着它半身的伤痕。流长的一切都跟水有关，水孕育了它，也带给它干渴，使它成为周遭地区旱象最重的一片旱塬。流长是山与水的畸形派对，是干涸与枯竭之间对立统一的结合。

透过矛盾看流长，我们更愿意把它解读成一个水乡——因为我们亲眼看到一车车的水产品从这里运往远方，因为一条乌江养活着沿岸世世代代的乡人。

但让流长真正成为水乡的是乌江大坝的修筑。传统的流长更像一个激流险滩中披头跣足的舞者，为了生存，不断搏击着来自自然界和自己内心的重重恶浪。“峡束湍已豪，水落势益壮。飞鸟不敢前，潜鱼哪能傍！”这条沿岸峭壁耸峙的河流，切割出一道深深的鸿沟，用豪放不羁的奔流，亿万年与流长人的命运纠缠不休。

“水光潋滟晴方好，山色空蒙雨亦奇”。一座大坝，构建起一个高峡平湖、风光旖旎的乌江峡，也构建了流长水乡的梦幻风骨。使流长的春夏秋冬、阴晴圆缺，有了别样的风情。波光荡漾的乌江，网箱连串成排，渔船划破清波。晨昏白鹭蹁跹，夜晚渔火闪烁。生活在水上的流长人，用闲适的桨声和激情的渔歌，激活了浩浩乌江，打捞起一江春色。

站在岸上看乌江，扑面而来的是浩如烟海的柔之美；站在水上看流长，刺破青天的是岩崖凸突的刚之壮。乌江为流长而生，流长为乌江而活。是流长塑造了乌江？还是乌江养育了流长？出于水养于水殁于水的流长人，用阳刚与阴柔的完美结合，构建起水上流长鲜明的性格。

流长是一座岛，一座形式和内容、物质和精神各个层面上的岛。

“五百门”散记

郑传明

它是一个特定时代的传奇；它是一段飘渺的记忆；它是一嗓大乌江上的船工号子；它是二万五千里长征路上一曲红色的革命壮歌！

——题记

“五百门”是乌江河上的一个古渡口。这个名字听起来似乎很生涩，可它却真真实实地存在过和存在着。或许是前世承载过太多的喧嚣与热闹，今生的五百门累了倦了，它以“惯看秋月春风”的豁达沉沉地睡去，全然没有在意人们对它的种种揣度与翻检。

“五百门”具体的位置在息烽县九庄镇的黄沙村，现在人们习惯叫它黄沙渡。其实真正的古渡口因为乌江大坝的修建，早已淹没在水下，我们只能凭借至今尚能辨识的、标注着“嘉庆十五年”“贵阳府黄沙渡盐关岭南河邑信士”落款字样的“阿弥陀佛”碑和大河两岸的峭崖上巨大的摩崖石刻“忍”“让”二字，来确定渡口的大概位置。而这些宝贵的历史遗迹也鲜明地向我们传达出一个信息：五百门曾经是“川盐入黔”的重要渡口。

史料记载，“川盐入黔”的主要有四个口岸，即仁怀的仁岸、綦江的綦岸、叙永的叙岸和涪陵的涪岸。除涪岸外，其余三个口岸的盐巴都要通过息烽。从叙岸入黔的盐道一条经水西九驿渡乌江，从六广河进入今天的贵阳市境内，另一条则由金沙过乌江黄沙河，经“五百门”、九庄、猫场、梨安、久长、扎佐进入贵阳。

“五百门”这个名字的来历已无可考证。当下我们只能从当地老人们不甚清晰的言谈中获知，这地方原来是川盐集散地，渡口两侧峭崖壁立，只有中间一段狭窄的豁口可以上下互通，因而被人们辟为码头。而码头以上陡峭蜿蜒的古盐道两边，曾经排列着五百家盐号，专事经营盐巴。而每家盐号门前必定有一个专供过往商贩烧水做饭的火塘。于是人们就综合这两个方面的因素，冠之以“五百门”之名。可以想象，在大山横亘、沟谷纵横的黔地，在没有现代运输机械的肩挑背扛时代，“背盐工”们在经过长时间负重跋涉之后，有一盆热水泡泡脚、有一个温馨的旅店打打尖，那是何等的惬意！

岁月的沧桑淡化了人们对于辛酸往事的回忆，可我们无法摒弃对于历史真实的探究心理。踏着光洁的青石板垒砌而成的古盐道，脑海里浮现出来的是“盐巴老二”手拄“拐脚木”，将前胸尽量贴近地面，一步步从渡口向上攀爬的情景，耳边回响的是乌江船工铿锵有力的纤夫号子：嘿哟咗嘿，不松气喇嘛嘿哟咗嘿，加把劲呀嘛嘿哟咗嘿，五百门喇嘛在前头哟，滚开水呀嘛嘿哟咗嘿，热炕头呀嘛嘿哟咗嘿……

盐运的繁荣为九庄这个边鄙小镇带来了空前的繁荣，并由此衍生出了许多盐商巨富。九庄望城坡的党氏一族，就是因为先祖党鲲南经营盐巴而成为一方巨富。即便是在今天，九庄人仍然被视为“生意精”，深谙商场经营之道。

“五百门”向世人展示的除了建立在多数“盐巴老二”汗水和辛酸基础上的商贸繁荣外，还以其雄浑的气势书写着中国工农红军转战黔中大地的精彩篇章。遵义会议后，中国工农红军四渡赤水，为世界军事指挥史添上了最具魅力的一笔，将蒋介石数十万部队扔在了赤水河以北地区。1935年3月31日，红军进抵乌江北岸的金沙后山一线，趁着暴雨突破乌江天险，集结于息烽九庄、流长、鹿窝一线，做出要攻打贵阳的姿态，让坐镇指挥的蒋介石仓皇逃离。南渡乌江之后，数万红军才算真正跳出了国民党军的重重包围圈，开启了北上抗日的新征程。史料记载，南渡乌江战役中，担任突击任务的红三军团及中央后勤机关大部分人马就是从“五百门”登岸的。不幸的是，惨遭失败的国民党反动派丧心病狂地向集结在九庄的红军实施报复性轰炸，为了掩护群众转移，150多名红军指战员英勇牺牲在九庄镇。

千里乌江依旧奔流不息，历史已然成为尘封的记忆。然而这并不能改变这里曾发生过和正在发生着的一切。冥思苦想之际，江风过耳，那呜咽之声，不就是这山崖、这水岸对于“五百门”前世今生的倾心叙述吗？

郑传明，男，教师，后从政。

大爱无言

蔺中原

每当看到星空中有飞机从头顶悄然飞过，我就会不自觉地想起那一次远行来。

飞机起飞之前，我帮父母系好了安全带。可能是看到了父母的苍苍白发，美丽的空姐微笑着走过来亲自检查了他们的安全带。我们这一趟是飞往海南，主要是去看海。

母亲这一辈子最远到过清镇，还是修红枫湖的时候。听说我要带她和父亲去海南看海，她急忙摇头，连说了几个“不”字。母亲一向节俭，她怕花钱。父亲则说“海有啥看法？如果能去海南，去拜拜南海观音还可以。”近年来父亲信佛，经文里常提到南海观音菩萨，却未曾亲眼见过。我说：“去吧，不仅看海，还看南海观音。”母亲拿眼白了一下父亲。父亲说：“白我做啥子？都这个年龄了，还有几年好活？”

飞机开始起动，在航道上缓缓行驶。正月的天气还很寒冷，刚上飞机时天空还飘着微雪。我说：“飞机进入云层后会出现颠簸，严重时感觉就像坐三轮车在石子铺就的路上跑一样。”我这样说，是让父母心里有个准备，万一出现了颠簸不至于害怕。去年7月，我与妻子和女儿跟团去九寨沟旅游，飞机刚起飞进入云层，我们就遇上了强对流。一次约3秒钟的失重，机上多数人都发出了尖叫。下了飞机，心才落地。父亲说：“你怎么能拿飞机与三轮车相比呢？”一脸的不信任，那眼神仿佛我在吹牛。

飞机开始远离地面，坐在窗边的母亲努力地望向地面。父亲坐在母亲的旁边，也把头够过去贴着玻璃窗向下看。母亲一会儿说“你看那个”，一会儿说“你看这个”，边说边用手指。父亲则应着：“哪个？哪个？”边说边向母亲指的方向看去。窗外一片漆黑，地面的灯火离我们越来越远。父亲和母亲却仍然脸贴着玻璃向着斜下方那遥远而暗淡的灯火眺望。我一下子莫名其妙地被感动得一塌糊涂。

从我记事起，几十年来我从未看到父亲和母亲这么近距离地说过话，更别说牵手、拥抱和更为亲密的举动。在我的想象之中，他们的婚姻同《故事会》上描写的他们那个年代的婚姻故事一样，父母之命，媒妁之言。我很难把爱情这两个字放到他们的婚姻和生活之中。父亲十三岁学会赌博，三十岁学会酗酒。在那个出工不出力的年代，大家都在拿工分度日的时候，他却撵马车、修水库，在外面搞副业，走南闯北，想干一番事业。可是辛苦赚来的钱或票在兜里还没放热就输到了别人的兜里。有时母亲会劝他别赌了，血汗钱输了不值，父亲便会对母亲吼道：“你们女人，就是头发长见识短！我还不是想多赢一些，那样全家都不遭罪。”冬日的晚上，母亲带着我们兄妹四人围在火炉边，有时会莫名地流出泪来，伤心地说，要不是你几个小龟儿，老子死了还好过些。

四年前一个秋天的午后，父亲醉酒后把右脚的髌骨摔成了三块。在青山医院做完接骨手术后，母亲在院里悉心照料了父亲一个多星期。我敢说，这是父亲与母亲结婚几十年来单独在一起最长的一段时间，也是唯一没有吵嘴的一段时间。出院后，父亲像变了个人似的。母亲告诉我们说，父亲在医院里跟为他换药的医师聊，说自己很讨嫌，原以为这次摔伤了没有人会理他，没想到……

机身抖动了一下，我知道飞机进入了云层。喇叭里传来空姐甜美的声音，说后面可能会遇上强对流，飞机会出现一定的颠簸，请大家再次检查安全带是否系好。父亲看了看自己的，又用手去拉了拉母亲的。而就在这时，我们明显地感觉到飞机开始倾斜，有一股无形的力量由下而上使飞机在迅速飞升，紧接着便是几秒钟的失重，并伴有剧烈的颠簸。机上没有人说话，不知什么时候母亲已把头转了过来，父亲和母亲都表情严肃，正注视着前方，我分明看到父亲的左手牢牢地抓住母亲放在扶手上的右手，手背上青筋突起。我突然鼻子一酸，眼睛一热，就觉得有泪水在眼眶里转。

终于，飞机穿破云层，开始平稳地飞行了。我对父母说，现在可以看到星星了。父亲有些不信，而母亲却说已经看到了。我把父亲的安全带解开，父亲就轻易地把头够了过去。看着白发苍苍的父母脸贴着玻璃看星星，我突然觉得他们就像两个数星星的孩子。我趁假意整理眼镜之机擦掉了眼角的泪水。我终于明白了，父母之间有大爱，正所谓大爱无言。

早该带父母出门走走了。

蔺中原，息烽县九庄镇乌江复旦学校数学教师。

梦里水乡（外一篇）

胡友国

老家其实也只隔那么十来千米，似乎邻近而又遥远。记忆里，它曾经美丽而又贫穷。

这是镶嵌在中国大地上的一小块马血泥地，泛着暗红。它有好几个阳坡和阴坡，然后又逶迤往南拐，在右侧甩下一条深沟，就如传说中玉帝作好的地图被水打湿揉皱了的一般。近万块大大小小的梯田一弯弯地分布在这些阳坡和阴坡上。那些木架的瓦屋就零散地坐落在这些梯田中间的空地里。田埂上偶有一株两株不是很高大的枫树，在深秋里泛着红黄的颜色。

这里是水的世界。冬田犁了或春田耙了的时候，有月亮的夜晚，满坝满坡都是月光，满坝满坡的镜子。月亮就在水里，你走到哪它就跟到哪。要是春天，那蛙声咕咕咕，咯咯咯，会让你的酣梦生出许多怪诞有趣的情节。

我曾到过广东的茂名，那里热带夏天的秧苗极单瘦，像个没发育的瘦小女孩，哪像我们的秧苗总是蓬蓬勃勃满坝满坡的青绿。轻风翻动秧苗的叶子，泛点白的绿浪一波波赶潮似的，到了面前便倏地不见了，留下一阵稻秧的微香。那时我喜欢站在大田的田坎上看大人们薅秧，他们男男女女站成弯弯的一排，弓着身子，用手在秧苗间抓那些水案板和剪刀菜，然后站起身来用脚将那一团团草踏进田泥里去。一个男人用浑厚悠长的声音起头唱道："薅秧哦呵喂——吆哦——"其余的男人就接口齐声和道："呀喂——吆哦喂——"那声音就随了绿浪荡送到满坡的田坝。

我第一次下田薅秧是在一个星期天，就在我家门口的大田里。那时稻秧也开始抽穗扬花，很小很小的白，有一股馨香。肥田的稻秧比我还高。那天我一直跟在新娶的大嫂身边，大嫂好看，牙白，两束头发晃悠悠的，稻花就洒在她头上和新的青布衣服上，于是田里就有了很好闻的三种味：大嫂的香、稻花的香，还有脚拱起的咕咕冒着气泡的黑泥香。大嫂问我："薅秧可好玩？"我点头说："好玩。"

大嫂是去年冬天嫁过来的，本是干山坡上的人。她是前年跟她叔娘来相亲的。一见我家水井就在后檐沟边冒着清水，就说："啧啧啧，水桶都不要哇！"并说她们地方挑一担水要一早的工夫。我精明的母亲就从她们的眼神里看出些端倪来，笑着说："我们这里的人家从来不用水桶的哦。"母亲临时决定将早饭改成打糍粑，因为糍粑可以说是我们的特产。大嫂那时我还只能叫姐，她有些怕羞，只是不怕我，敢跟我说话。她见井里有鱼，就说："好多漂亮的鱼哟！"我卖弄说："这不算，前天涨水，单在一个牛脚印窝里，我就捡了一大盆。"她便张大了那好看的嘴，作吃惊状："哇——！"

我学得了一身游泳的好本事，能把水当床，睡在水上半天也不会下沉。其实水田里还是最初的教练场。头次游泳是在自家门口的小田里。那田太肥，秧栽得稀，秧行里能过我们的身子。那时人太傻，脚把水花踢得老高，最后被牛娃的爷爷闻声逮个正着。我们被光着身子押到大人们干活的现场，牛娃被他爸用竹条狠抽，母亲也愤怒地拿了竹条过来，到了我面前却莫名其妙地愣住了，并没有抽我。我一直想不通那天母亲为何变恶为慈，后来从外人嘴里听出了秘密，说那天母亲见我一身的黑泥，只两个眼珠骨碌碌打转，让她没舍得下手。

以后的游泳场就在栽过冬小麦的水稻田里，那里泥底子硬实，起不了浑水，后面的土坎上到处都咕嘟咕嘟吐清泉呢。我们学乖了，拴了牛，也不扑腾，像一条条水鳗在秧行间静游，回来身上干净，没一个瞒不住大人眼睛的。再后来就敢下丈余深的堰塘了，那田里洗澡的事就被我们看成了小儿科。

我们的麻谷是出了名的好，饭舀在碗里白亮亮地泛着点油性。初中要走读，我每天吃饭早，那饭我从来不等菜，只泡米汤再放点盐，那时我们都这样说：米汤放盐赛过年。

我是第一个走出田坝的人，离家那时满坡的谷子金黄，枫叶也正红得灿烂。许多乡亲来送我，吃饭，喝水酒，送我一块八角的零票和一大堆足以让家生光的祝福。我走上大路，回了一下头，乡亲们的笑脸和那如画的风景就一下定格在我记忆里了。

碾　米

故乡的歌是一支清远的笛，总在有月亮的晚上响起。

——席慕蓉

长到12岁的时候，父母就不让我吃闲饭了，得劳动。要吃饭，就得背谷子下河去碾米。

十三口人要吃饭，碾米可不是件简单事。从家门口往下，走过自己生产队的地盘，再走过二队和三队的水田埂，一直下到那个老远就听到河水咆哮，听见“黑窜鸟”飞鸣，还在岩畔上就仿佛有水飞沫溅到脸上的深沟里才是碾坊。我背的是“裹底背”，背篼又大又厚实，谷子却不多，但很沉。第一次背谷子下河，路滑，险些栽倒在水田里。

碾米房只是两间低矮的土坯草房，矮得大人们一伸手就可以触到屋檐上的草。碾米的人不少，碾坊周围拴满了驮马。一些人来，一些马去。一些在夜晚碾完了米的人点起火把背米上岩畔，一些人又打着灯笼赶着驮了谷子的马从岩畔上下来。那些驮马多在脖颈上挂了串铃铛，无论是上岩畔还是下岩畔，都嗅当嗅当响。那路也就一直有火把灯笼在上在下，一直有人在吆喝，一直有驮马的铃铛响。

100斤谷子碾下米来大概要半个钟头。碾坊外面硕大的水车的水斗在懒洋洋地翻倒着水：哗——哗——哗——。屋内石槽里的大石磙叽咕——叽咕地顺那圆石槽滚动，一圈，两圈……。

碾米要依个先来后到，大人们很有耐性地坐着听那叽咕叽咕的石磙响，男人抽旱烟，女人纳鞋底，没事就说些家常闲话，猪呀牛呀的，一直到等米碾好；小孩就不行，呆坐在一个地方会感到无聊。于是我就趴在那大石磙的横轴上，顺着那石槽转圈，作免费的“旅游”。这项玩腻了，就到河上面的地方去“观光”。我想探寻河的源头，可却无法办到：林子很深，葛藤很粗又很长，带刺的荆棘又多又密，走了不到250米，就再没去路，于是只好沿路返回。

碾坊近处的河道上是很好玩的，沙石都奇大，又光又浑圆，爬上去可以睡觉；下来掰开那些小的圆石头，偶尔可逮着个螃蟹。那河水奇清，是真真的纯净，不含一星半点杂质，用脚想搅浑它都难，不论你怎样搅它，只一松开脚，那浑水立即就没了，仍是纯纯的清亮。

挨到晚上就有些恼火，外面不能去，茅屋内一盏孤灯伴着那大石磙叽咕叽咕的声响。没吃饭的人就陆续地借主人家的灶火弄点简单的饭吃。第一天碾米，很不习惯这样的生活。弄饭也要依个先来后到，我家做饭要在两家人之后了。碾坊主人是对60多岁的老夫妻，与我同姓，我们叫幺伯和幺伯娘。我一饿就表现出饿相来，靠在娘的身上。幺伯娘看了我几眼，说：“幺儿，来。”就牵了我的手，进到里间屋里，把那盖着大碗的小碗拿开，是一碗热的面糊糊，她拿了筷子给我说：“幺儿，吃饱了再说。大人们经饿，不管他们。”我一边吃，她一边用那温热的手掌给我擦糊在嘴边的面糊糊。

吃过了饭，幺伯的青㭎柴火就旺了起来，烧得嚓嚓跳火花。那一圈人在听幺伯摆龙门阵，摆的是乾隆马再兴，至今还记得那故事中的精彩部分，记得说那男子的妻子实在是漂亮无比，他每耕作时都把妻子的画像插在犁沟的两头，犁铧走到那一头，就看一眼那画像，犁到这一头，又看一眼，忽然一阵风将那画像刮到京城里，有那好事的捡得了后把它交给了皇上……

那晚上我一点没睡意，尽听故事，尽幻想这故事。

天亮上路，背着米上那岩畔可费呆力了。那米虽不多，却像背砣石头般重。走不到岩畔的一半，就累得汗水滴答，脚如灌铅，胸腔打鼓。没多会，后面来了匹白额的黄母马，铃铛随头的摇动哩当哩当响。我正靠一边让它过去，那赶马的中年人就立在我面前，没说二话，就从我肩上接过背篼，玩儿似的就挂在了他的一只肩上，一直挂着。我满心欢喜地空着两手跟他走，一路听着那悦耳的马铃声，听着他口里的小曲儿，一直走到我家门口，他才笑着把背篼给我……

平生就碾过一回米，却忘不了这碾米的记忆。

胡友国，男，息烽县乌江复旦学校语文教师。

寂寞如茶（外一篇）

李　星

独自待在书屋里，沏一壶热茶，陶然于古筝名曲之中，心无所羁，怡然自乐……我喜欢享受这样的寂寞，古乐相伴，随心所至，为茶所思。

一曲“平湖秋月”缓缓舒展开来，宛如撒在地板上的缕缕阳光，灿烂而含蓄；又像雾霭迷离的幻境中，无数小溪掠过山涧汇合成为一条宽阔的河流，潺潺湲湲，在一望无垠的平原流淌，最后融入波澜不惊的湖中，清冷的月光下，烟波飘渺的湖面让人平和而淡定。

沁人心脾的清香弥漫了整间小屋，提壶倒茶、端杯观色、闻香慢呷，所有的压抑和浮躁都在这袅袅茗香中消失得无影无踪。没有了语言，没有了文字，也没有了自己，有的只是一种淡然、宁静、闲适的心境。

记得禅宗有这样一个故事：一个屡屡失意的年轻人找一位高僧寻求解脱。和尚无言，用温水给年轻人泡了杯茶，问：“这茶可香？”年轻人摇了摇头。和尚说：“不会吧，这可是上等的铁观音。”年轻人仔细品了品，依旧摇了摇头。和尚微笑，又拿了一个杯子放了茶，取一壶滚沸的水高高冲下，随着茶叶的翻滚，清香袅袅，氤氲而出，转眼间沁满了禅房。年轻人由此顿悟。

散文家林清玄说：“一片茶叶如果不能被丢进壶中泡制，就失去了释放芳香的机会，也就失去了一片茶叶的生命本质。”细碎、纤弱的茶叶，一旦投入滚烫的水中，便会释放出原本看不到的一切内涵，毫无保留地贡献出生命积蓄的精华，变成一壶浓郁甘醇的茶水，从而完成自己价值的升华。那些不曾经历风雨之人，就像温水沏的茶叶，只在生活表面漂浮，浸泡不出生命的芳香；那些栉风沐雨的人，如被沸水冲沏的酽茶，在沧桑岁月里几度沉浮，散发出沁人的清香。

我不懂什么茶道、茶经与茶艺，只是想起古人喝茶的境界：“楚云散尽，燕山雪飞；江湖归梦，从此忘机。”于是，快乐而单纯地陶醉于这样一种宁静祥和之中。昔有陶潜先生独爱菊，是因为菊清高，孤傲；而濂溪先生爱莲之出淤泥而不染，是若有所失才心有旁骛，换言之，有心而寄情于物。既然古人高士尚且如此，自幼喜好附庸风雅的我，泡一壶清茶而困于午后那自以为脱俗的“雅室”内，戚戚之意亦在情理之中。

人都有物质与精神的追求和需要，无论是对事业、权利、地位、财富，还是对爱情、荣誉、健康等。在追求的过程中，一些人背着沉重的包袱去面对生活，带着厌世的镣铐去表演人生，人生之剧可能表演得精彩绝伦吗？

我们都是平凡之人，如果真想做到不妄自尊大，也不妄自菲薄；不处处强人一头，也不甘事事矮人半肩；恬淡睿智，心平气和，与人为善，的确是很不容易。做人如茶，尽敛苦涩，散发清香，以宽容、谦和的心态对人对事，快乐的源泉就在心中。

茶添书香

读书不仅需要时间，更需要心境。我喜欢在夜里，找一本心仪的书，静静地坐在柔和的灯光下，让思绪伴着书中文字飘远。

我不吸烟，自然不喜欢在云山雾海里手持书卷。倒一杯热水放在桌上，拈几片茶叶丢进杯里，把思绪泡成一杯浓淡适中的绿茶，让缕缕清香弥漫整个书房。

不知道还有多少人与我一样远离红尘，超然于城市的疲惫与喧嚣，陶醉于一个又一个夜里。我喜欢夜的安静。夜，带给我绵长、平和的思索与感悟……台灯就这样一直亮着，快接近午夜了，楼层里已没有任何声音，整个世界显得空旷而幽远。探头朝窗外望去，几盏如同哨兵的路灯孤独地守望着繁华而清冷的街道，窗户是一面暗色的镜子，照出我平静的容颜。

心绪渐入书，思绪渐入情，一些震撼心灵的文字沉淀着特别的感怀。流连中，走进忧郁或孤寂的心境，想象作者经历了怎样一番情感折磨或一段心声，几许感伤，话不尽的心殇，就在目光停留的瞬间，已留下我几多叹息，无声而悠长。“每一本书都是一个用黑字印在白纸上的灵魂。”人生就是一部无字之书。没有阅读的人生是残缺的。学会读书，就学会了阅读人生。“路漫漫其修远兮，吾将上下而求索”。我们无时无刻不在撰写人生之书的每一个章节。与书为伍，仿佛与圣贤相对而坐，聆听教诲，感到心灵充实丰盈，思想豁然开朗。掩卷遐思，古今多少人，古今多少书，多少情与思，多少哲与理，尽在不言中。呷一口热茶，想起茶庄姑娘告诉过我，绿茶叶嫩，宜用紫砂壶，水温只需80℃左右即可，不然会焐坏了叶子。其实，透明的杯也极好，可以看得更真实，那是一场死与生的演绎。原本干瘪的叶片，袅袅浮起，如出水芙蓉，俏嫩可人。枯萎的生命，瞬间焕发生机，一杯绿翠，清香四溢。或许人生也如茶吧。我们不能做一片永远皱缩着的叶子，总要融入被腾腾热气包围的沸水中。做人应该是这样的，慢慢去适应社会，慢慢被社会容纳，就像茶叶入水的过程，这个过程里，谁也无法摆脱磨难与困惑，也许这就是成长所付出的代价吧？成长的历程总会浸透淡淡的苦涩，当生命像茶叶一样慢慢舒展开来，清水就有了绿意，人生就有了希望。

这个世界越来越忙碌，现代生活越来越丰富多彩，满眼的物欲充斥着我们的视野，只有带着品茶时的那份淡泊和宁静，那份超脱和弃舍，人生才会有苦后回甘的欣慰和怡然。此时再也不是当初那片干涩的茶叶，我们已经能够勇敢而坦然地面对一切。当用心去品味，我们才幡然明了，原来有很多事情只有经历了才能够真正懂得。

就这样，在随心所至的感悟中拥一室清幽，求其心境，静中养气。一盏清灯下的灵魂，见心见性；一本好书里的文字，放纵心灵；一杯绿茶里的变幻，品味人生。

李星，男，小学教师。

三、散文诗

触摸西望山

陈久琪

我在西望山下行走。晨光把千仞险岩从雾障中剥出：涧泉如珠，飞瀑似练。小鸟鼓噪起名山胜境的激情，血液温润着肌肤。岁月在沧桑的记忆上镌刻成一方古朴，“永乐盟誓”的壮景便涉过五百年历史的深渊，闪烁在眸底。

我在西望山中行走。阳光被参天横柯挥洒成细碎的银片。足迹融进茵茵草坂的幽静，方方扁扁的修竹，摇荡起那晶莹欲滴的梦。满山的摩崖碑刻展露出万古丛林迷人的情韵。当温馨挤入思维的缝隙，时间便倾倒在纷繁芜杂的僧侣世界。任那镏金染彩的庙宇饱含了粗犷豪放的呼唤，也掀不动秋蝉的孤独寂寞。

我在西望山上行走。异石奇峰，呈现如诗如画般的境界。天风岭裸露出它的遒劲刚健，夕阳切割成了叠嶂层峦的纵横沟壑，大笔写意绘出浩渺千里的云海峰波。灵魂的倩影仿佛震颤于杜康的醇度，感觉便搁浅在那深奥神圣的诗海岸边，再无力寻回那丝鸢飞戾天的尘迹。

说明：此作曾被用作贵州省电视台拍摄制作的息烽风光片解说词。

四、小说

茶　蛊

朱登麟

九叔和泥土滚打了一辈子，拿手的活儿是种烤烟。那心里除了喜欢那有着醉人芬香的土地外，再喜欢的就是喝茶了。他喝茶不仅是他有了茶瘾，而更多的还是那喝茶里似乎有着他做一个老人的身价、派头和一份神仙味儿。所以，他从不乱喝生冷水，唯恐丢了自己的那一份做人的东西。

立夏过后，下了几场透雨，满坡的烟苗儿就像突然发现了什么惊喜事儿似的，可劲儿长了起来……九叔拿了一把刃口很宽很亮的锄头给烟苗锄草和培土，一边弯下腰去摘那些已经蔫巴发黄了的脚叶，一边就把它丢在烟杆脚下，掏泥盖上。九叔是“老烤烟”了，这个活儿他做得很熟。

正午的太阳特凶，烤烟的茎秆上全渗出细密的油珠子，宽厚的烟叶也全耷拉下去，提不起早晨那股兴致勃勃的冲劲儿来。九叔就把根部的泥土堆得很厚，隆起一个个小土包。这样做有利于减少水分散失。时而有蚯蚓被他白亮的锄刃一下子斩成两段，九叔看着那两截悸动不已的活活的肉，心里总会有一阵子怪怪的发抖。于是就不得不把活儿做得更细，遇到蚯蚓就把它扒出来，垒到烤烟根部的湿泥中去。九叔这个人就是这样，啥事儿都认真得过分，像跟谁较着劲儿似的，以至于寨子里大人细娃都怕他。

九叔一埋头就是几个时辰，认真去照料他的烟苗儿，等发觉有什么东西在腹里一阵一阵滚过的时候，太阳已略微偏向西天了。九叔抬起头来，发觉嗓子眼里燥得厉害，那一股慌慌劲儿更翻腾得来劲。再活动活动腰杆，竟发觉浑身四处硬是使不出劲儿来。九叔吓了一跳，暗想今天是着了鬼了，怕是很多年以前那老病儿又来了。便赶紧停了锄头，回头去看身后薅过的烟苗，每棵根部都罩着个浑圆的坟丘，像是一个个强力的城堡护卫，使人和烟苗都很放心。垒过土和没有垒过土的就是不同，那烟苗儿的精气神儿就不一样。九叔一边眯了眼前前后后地作比较，一边合着两只粗厚手掌使劲搓，掌缝中漏下一条条黑黑的油垢来，那是打烟脚叶时手上沾的烟油。

搓够了，等手上有了一种轻松感，九叔又埋着头去拿锄头。可心里那一阵慌慌劲儿又上来了。九叔骤然想起什么来，暗笑自己怎么这样老糊涂了，连那个好东西都竟然想不起来。就撒手丢了锄头，快步奔到石坎子上去，坎子上放着个黑虎墩墩的砂罐，罐儿上盖着个带把盖儿，盖儿下就盛着九叔那口心爱之物：一罐子酽茶。九叔走到石坎上，不慌不忙先在裤腿上蹭了蹭手上的泥土和烤烟油垢，才慢慢蹲下去，抬起砂罐，口对着罐嘴儿，仰了脖子喝。有一滴清凉的液体顺着喉管滴溜溜滑进肠胃，顿觉全身透过一阵爽劲。再喝，整个茶罐都调翻转了，只听到茶叶渣子“噗——噗”地掉在盖儿上，就是没有一滴茶水再滴下来。九叔就觉着怪：明明每天带这一砂罐浓茶，都要喝到傍黑收工时候。今儿个这茶让谁喝了去？莫不是老伴儿不留心熬少了？怎么半晌午不到就没了呢？还是有过路人趁人不注意给喝了呢？

九叔抬起头来张望，见东邻的土里许大菩萨把腰弯成一张弓，正撅了屁股“吭哧吭哧”地握着锄头在刨。西邻是后生子何猪儿的地，也种着烟；可那烟苗儿蔫不拉叽像些痨病鬼。土板得像块铁，狗尾草比烟苗还高。九叔一见心里就来气。想起何猪儿平时在县城走东街串西巷，四处油舌滑嘴的作为，便有些忿忿的。九叔承包的这几块地就是何猪儿家的。九叔从农推站做烤烟辅导员退休回来，就琢磨着趁手脚还活动，好好的做两茬烤烟。这些年在农推站搞实验地，下乡蹲点搞辅导，积累了一肚子种烟经验，九叔还不想丢掉这技术。而且又闲不惯，看何猪儿庄稼做得跟鸡刨似的，一大坡肥油油的地就这样一季季给耽误着，九叔就觉得心里隐隐发疼。一个庄稼人如此作践土地，这不知作的哪辈子孽？想当年给地主家做活，也没敢这样粗疏过！九叔想，但没有说出来。九叔晓得这个话在这些年有多大个分量，觉得说了也无非是让人笑话“老古董”。九叔直接去找何猪儿，何猪儿当时正摆弄着一台从县水泥厂贱价买来的破打砂机，请了四五个师傅给他修理，又是点烟又是陪笑，像别人儿子似的。九叔就看不惯，又忍不住那坡地的诱惑，就说了。没想何猪儿倒那么爽快，什么条件也没要，就答应把瘦骨嶙嶙的坡土转包给九叔，却不肯把东边这最大最肥最平整的一块地给九叔。九叔气得鼻子吹灰，心想：你娃儿是想让我老头子出丑啊。凭你做庄稼那点能力，老子做石旮旯也比你做坪子土强。这样一想又犯上了“犟”劲，跟何猪儿也跟那块肥地较上了劲。因此九叔对这一坡土，又亲自拿锄头把稍大块的坷垃拍散，然后垫上厚厚一层用细筛筛出来的煤灰和岩泥做底肥。整土、育苗、移栽、施肥、除草，除了叫在乡中学教书的小儿子给背过几回岩泥和煤灰外，没一样工序九叔让别人插手帮衬过，都是自己亲手亲脚干。因此九叔的烟苗一栽上就出手不凡，长势压过了这一坡所有的人家。而何猪儿那一块肥地，自打栽上烟秧子就没见他来地头转悠过一次。看着那些稀稀拉拉蔫头奄脑的烟苗，九叔心里一阵痛快一阵难受的。有几次他锄草锄到地界上，总想把锄头移过去几株，甚或整个儿什么报酬也不要，替何猪儿把那块地一并料理了。可想来想去他还是忍住了。妈的，你等着吧，看看是哪个丢丑！九叔暗暗下狠劲儿想，却又觉得这想法很有些不对劲。

这样想着的时候，九叔实际上已经三步并做两步，颠颠地跑到了西邻的许大菩萨面前。许大菩萨和九叔家是住隔壁，一层木板隔着两家人，平时吃饭喝水都要相互打一声招呼的。许大菩萨比九叔小六岁，是个有名的天垮下来有房子顶着不关自己事儿的角色。也是遇什么事都没多大主见的人。那几年肥料特紧缺，九叔每年都要从农推站想法子给他弄几包回来。而且每年烘烟时节，九叔都要亲自回来给他掌火，致使他的烤烟每年都能在全寨子里卖出好价钱，因此他对九叔特别肥贴。“大菩萨”这个诨号，还是九叔给他起的呢。

许大菩萨见九叔走过来，毛手毛脚的，就不知是什么事，停了锄，抬头给他打招呼：“九叔——”

九叔不搭理他，气呼呼的走过去，瞪起眼吼道：“是不是你喝了我的茶？”

许大菩萨便明白过来，嘻嘻地陪着笑说：“我还说你是发的哪样瘟火？是那个，我不喝那个东西——你晓得的嘛。”

九叔便拍拍脑壳，他是真的老糊涂了：许大菩萨是从不喝茶的。渴了，便抱着大木瓢咕咚咕咚灌半瓢凉水下去。即使在坡上干活，也最多不过是牛饮水那样翘起屁股把头伸到水沟里去胡乱喝一气。九叔对许大菩萨什么都对劲，就不喝茶这一项上，十分的看不起他。半世年纪的人了，有事没事弓起腚子趴沟坎上喝水，或抱了大木瓢咕咚咕咚，真不是个劲。而且儿大女成人了，至少该提个茶壶显显神儿，老资格嘛，阅世深有派头嘛。若是能像他九叔那样不是涩得叫别人咋舌的茶不饮，要把茶叶放砂罐里炒得略带烟香味儿，掺上开水熬得翻天冒鼓的再喝，那才有个老庄稼人的粗犷而又不失深沉老到的滋味。因此九叔几次熬茶，硬叫许大菩萨喝，见他蹙了额头、吃药似的闭了眼猛喝一口，但难过得直冲他苦笑。九叔对许大菩萨摇摇头，叹息一声，就不再说什么话，垂头丧气的又踅回自家土里来。想来想去总觉不对头，是不是那老婆娘做了什么鬼呢？九叔想起每次他把茶罐里还可以泡出一壶黄水来的茶叶渣子倒掉，说淡了，“没得吃才淡了！”老伴总要叨咕上半天，说九叔作孽，要是前些年，连比这个淡的渣儿都得嚼吞掉呢。但又不像，老伴念归念，可每年还是细细的给他摘、炒、揉、晒茶叶。这几年老伴做茶叶的手艺确实提高了不少，这不是为他九叔又是为谁？

九叔就这么胡思乱想着，锄头再不像先前那样乖巧听使唤，垒的土也不似先前那样匀整有韵味。回头看后来垒的这几棵苗，蔫不拉叽像在生九叔的气似的。九叔便不想再干下去，收了锄头和剩的肥料，在把砂罐和一些杂物一起装进背篓里的时候，才发现那放砂罐的地方一片湿，砂罐底还滴着水珠儿。一看是砂罐漏了，便恨恨地骂了一句，也不知是骂砂罐还是骂人，却也没有舍得把那漏了底的砂罐丢掉，口干茶瘾发作便想回家去。一抬头见半山腰的水沟边，一个人正撅了屁股跪在沟坎上，头深深的伸进沟里喝水。九叔以为是许大菩萨，又想取笑他两句。细看又不像，便转过头看，许大菩萨仍躬了腰在下劲儿使锄头。等他回过头来时，那人已经喝好水站了起来：虎虎的一个年轻汉子，是何猪儿。九叔想把头调开，不想何猪儿先笑起来，脸上的肌肉扯做一堆，先跟他打起招呼来：“九叔，收活儿哇！”

“收啦！”九叔没好气地说，正眼也不看他。

何猪儿“咚咚”从坡上跑下来，看看自己的地，又看看九叔的，最后又看九叔的脸，说：“九叔，真有您老的，您那地比我的就是不同。”

九叔气呼呼地说：“你小子，一季里没跟烟苗儿照个面，它还舔你肥屁股怎的！”

何猪儿说：“九叔，也不是的，您看这水渠到处都漏了，赶明年那几坝田还吃大米不？今冬村里要修水渠，我得赶着去买水泥什么的。砂子我们这山上石头多。去远处买不合算。估摸着不如去买台砂机来自己打，一方面自己赚几个，另一方面队里也可以省几个。你说我哪还抽得出时间管它？她娘儿几个连田里还照看不过来哩，赶明年村里要建加工房，我承包得成的话，这块地搞不好全部包给你哩。”

九叔心里那个气儿还没消：庄稼人，可不能没个稳劲，四乡里野，能野出个啥明堂？便软不软硬不硬的丢了一句：“你小子有能力，好福分，不似我们这些泥巴子命！”说过之后，又觉有些不对劲。真不知今天是着了哪路魔了，怎么说什么干什么都不顺气？还是那罐茶他娘的闹的。便不再说话，搭眼认真看何猪儿，发觉这后生子也不像原来见的那样年轻了，额头眼角都挤了几条很深的皱纹，脑门子上一圈子青晕，像被太阳终日晒起的。而且敞着个胸，挺着个健壮的胸板儿，眼神儿也不是自己印象中那种吊儿郎当没分量的样子。便背了背篓扛了锄头往坡下走。突然又像想起什么似的，回过头来冲坡上喊：

“大菩萨也——收活儿喽——”

晚饭后，一天的炎热终于渐渐淡去。

月亮从山垭口的几茎茅草尖上升起来，水一样凉爽，洒满一院子。饭后的九叔，又另用一个新砂罐熬了一壶酽酽的茶，一个人坐在月地里喝。不知怎的，总喝不出个滋味，又想扬了嗓子喊许大菩萨，猛想起许大菩萨不喝茶，便又觉得十分扫兴。想着是新砂罐不如那旧砂罐的原因，心里忿忿的，就端了茶罐回屋里，翻箱倒柜找出一只白瓷缸子：缸面洁白，但缸壁留了些细细的擦痕，缸底还留有一圈洗不去的烧过黑迹。

九叔端详这只缸子，心里有一种莫名其妙的烦躁。这是他前些年熬茶用的，那时缸壁上糊了厚厚一层茶垢，加瓢清水也能熬出一缸酽茶来。有一天九叔上山砍犁弓，被他在县城医院当护士的幺儿媳妇回来看见，想着孝敬公爹就用煤灰渣加草酸给他洗得一干二净。九叔回来以后发觉他这么多年来不知熬了几百斤茶叶才熬成这个样子的茶缸不见了，对老伴和儿子大发雷霆，用这洗干净的白瓷缸子熬茶，怎样也觉品不出该有的茶味。就一气之下跑到城里坛罐厂买了一只茶罐，就不再用那口白瓷缸子了。九叔当时的心思是：你嫌老子不卫生，老子干脆用砂罐熬，黑对黑，要和幺儿媳妇较劲。为这事，寨上的一些年轻人给九叔的茶罐编了许多的话头，如“九叔的茶缸——越黑越有味”“九叔的茶缸——讨幺儿媳妇的嫌”。如此等等，被后生小子们滥用，越传越广。如今，九叔面对这只洗过的茶缸，想起幺儿媳妇曾为此委屈得伤心哭了一场，竟觉得有些内疚。而且看这只洗过的白瓷缸，确实比以前黑不溜秋的样子是好看得多。

晚上，九叔在床上辗转反侧，总不能睡着，合上眼就仿佛看见幺儿媳妇泪涟涟的样子和何猪儿越显黑瘦的脸。这两件毫不相干的事情不知怎么着了魔似的硬往他脑壳里钻。便系了鞋走出屋来，敲墙壁想叫醒许大菩萨，想了想又没叫，独个儿在院子里走了一回，见月亮已升到中天，四下里到处是如潮的蛙鸣。月光很明，照得地上如同白昼。九叔回屋，换上白天做活穿的解放鞋，院墙下扛了锄头，一个人做贼似的蹑手蹑脚跑到坡上，就着月光在何猪儿家的那块好地上刨起来。

刨到地尽头的时候，月儿已经停在西边山尖上的几棵芭茅草尖上了。九叔回过头去看，那些半人高的毛狗草全倒下了，露出一棵棵油碧的烟苗来，微风吹过，那一片片肥厚的叶片巴掌般哗哗地在月下拍响，像是过节一样兴奋。九叔突然感觉嗓子眼里燥得厉害，肚腹里滚过一阵又一阵那种慌慌的感觉，火燎似的难耐，知道又是那茶瘾儿上来了。他一抬头看到了半山腰下的水渠，一沟的清水映着月光，金子般一闪一闪地翻动着。九叔看看四下没人，便如飞地跑上沟坎，撅起屁股跪下去，把头深深地伸进水沟里去——

怪事，这沟里的凉水竟是这般甘甜！

书画作品（含油画）

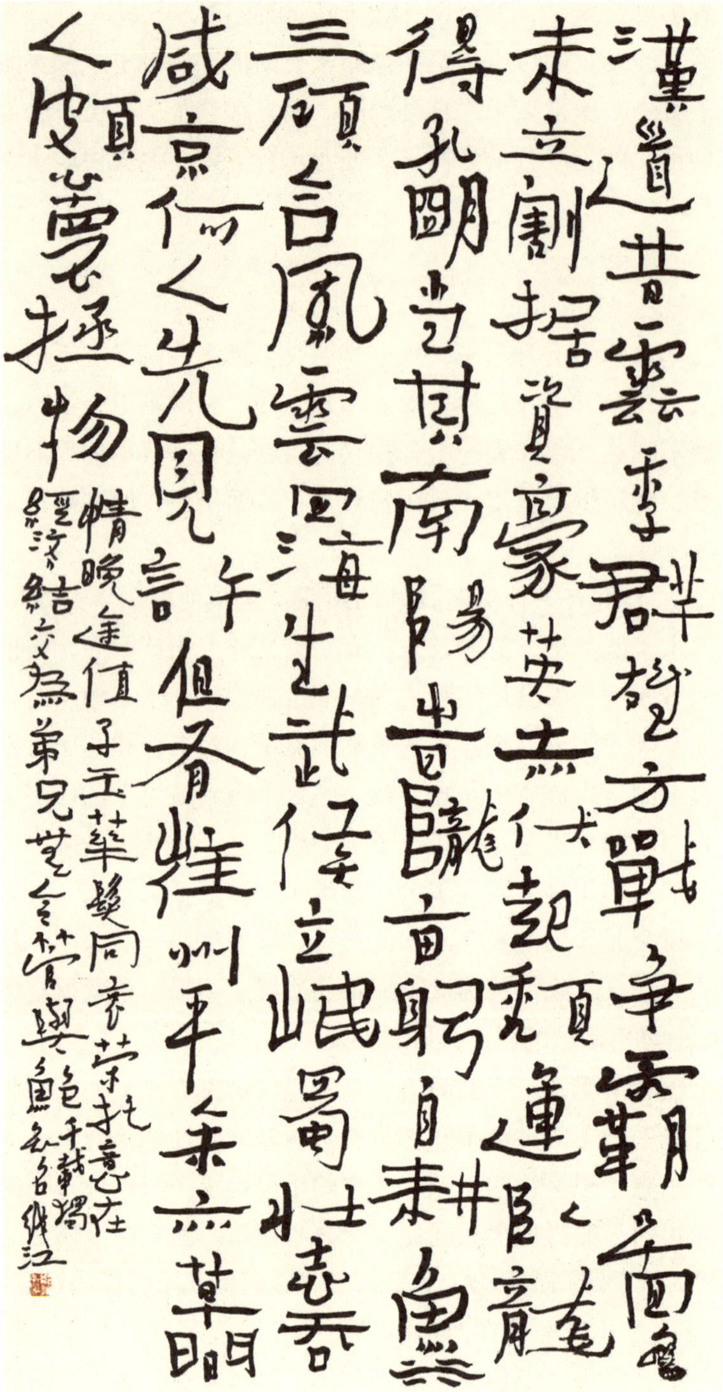

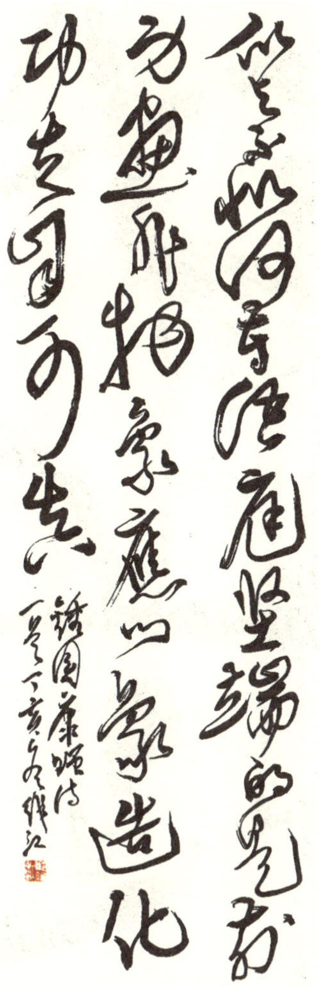

秋风

水墨交响

雨后江山

荷意

无题

郑维江，男，生于1971年。书画家。1998年出版《郑维江书画作品集》。作品获众多奖项并入编近百部大型辞书和作品集。

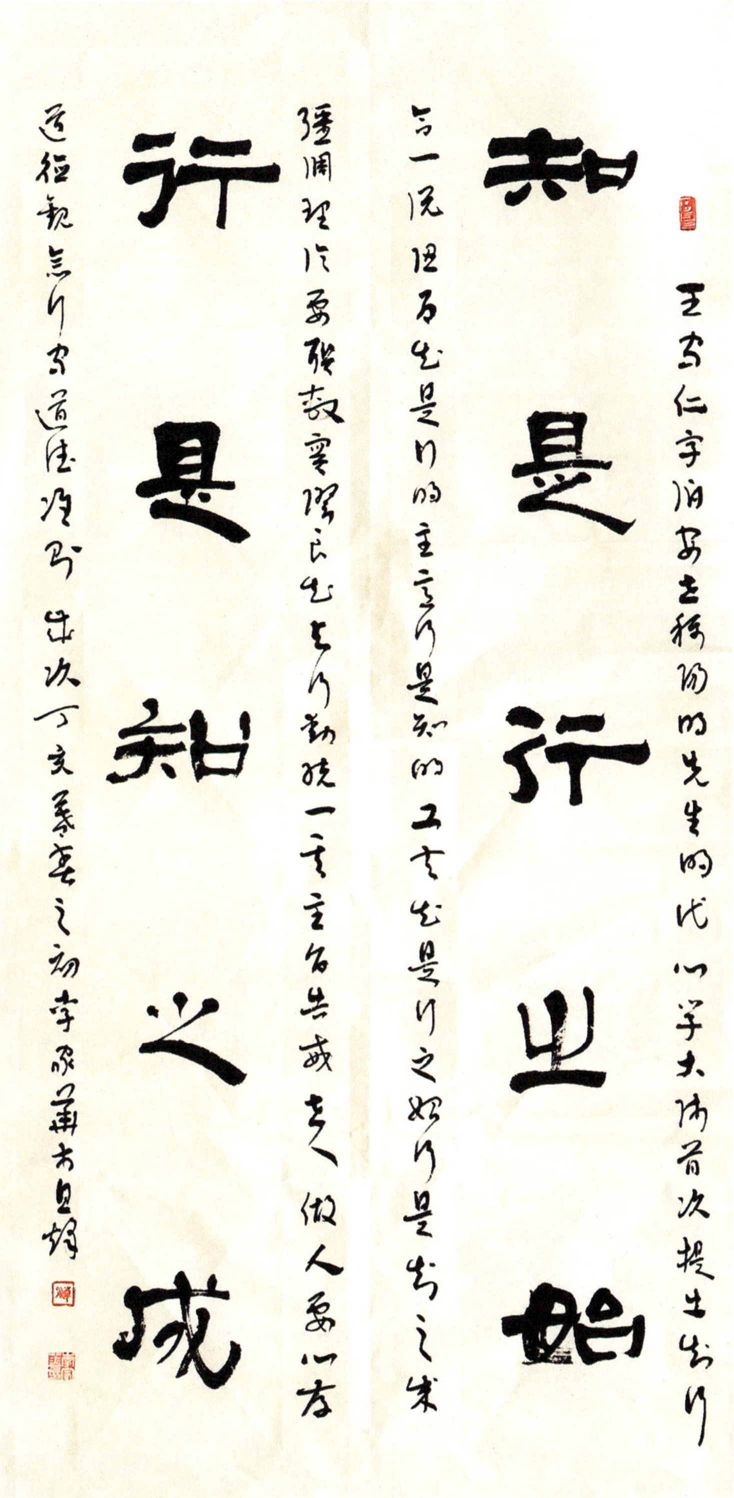

李家华，男，教师。

阳光

柳红梅，女，生于1976年。毕业于贵州大学艺术学院油画专业。县文化馆职工。

烙画、版画

清明上河图局部

清江晨雾

刘子辉，男，民间工艺品制作者。

父亲和他的兄弟

徐强，男，37岁。毕业于贵州大学艺术学院美术系。县文化馆职工。

音乐作品

息烽玄天洞

1=F $\frac{4}{4}$
♩=76

方富俊
李世俊 词
王霁晴 曲

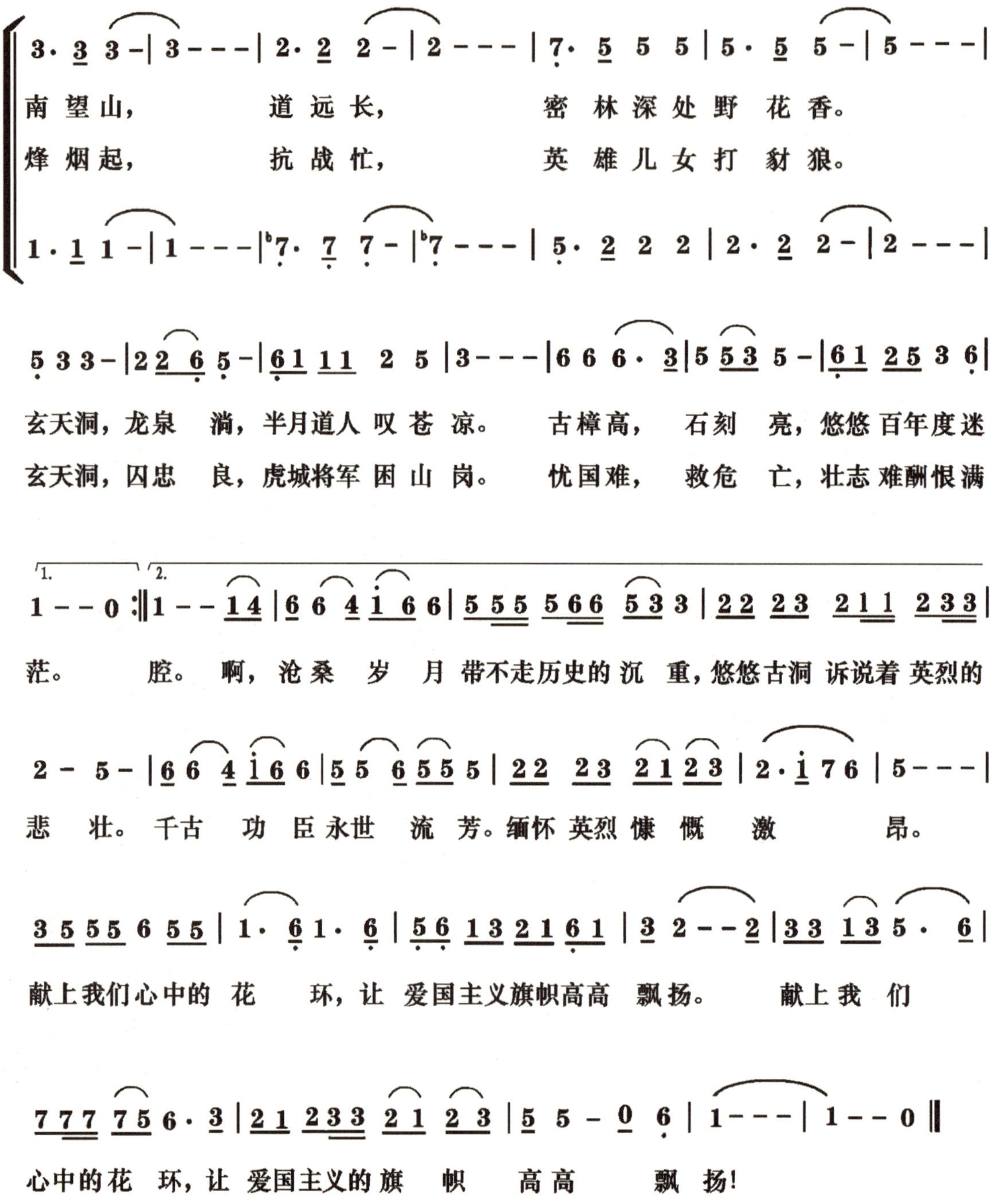

壮歌起息烽

（男中音与混声合唱）

朱登麟 词
邓承群 曲

1=C $\frac{4}{4}$

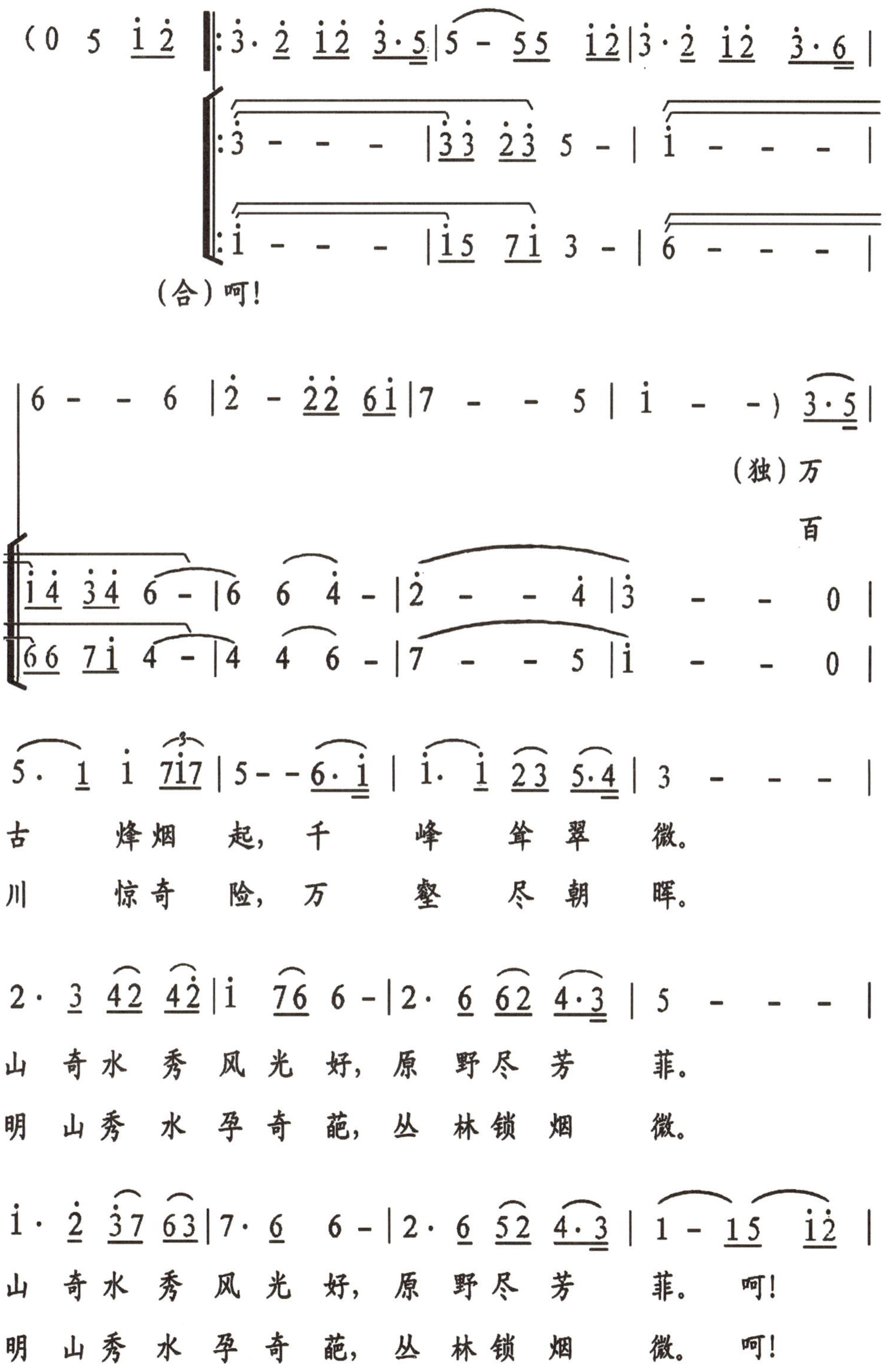

温泉水暖，苗寨歌飞。
江山秀美，人文荟萃。
呵！温泉水暖，苗寨歌
呵！江山秀美，人文荟
西望山麓蜂蝶舞，乌江峡畔渔歌醉。呵！
息烽英烈名千古，龙马精神放光辉。呵！
呵！
飞。呵！
萃。呵！
锦绣江山美如画，山川多妩媚。
壮歌一曲冲霄汉，山河更壮
美。
山河更壮美。

请到青山苗乡来

男女二重唱

1＝G $\frac{4}{4}$

♩＝86

朱登麟　词

蒋仁春　曲

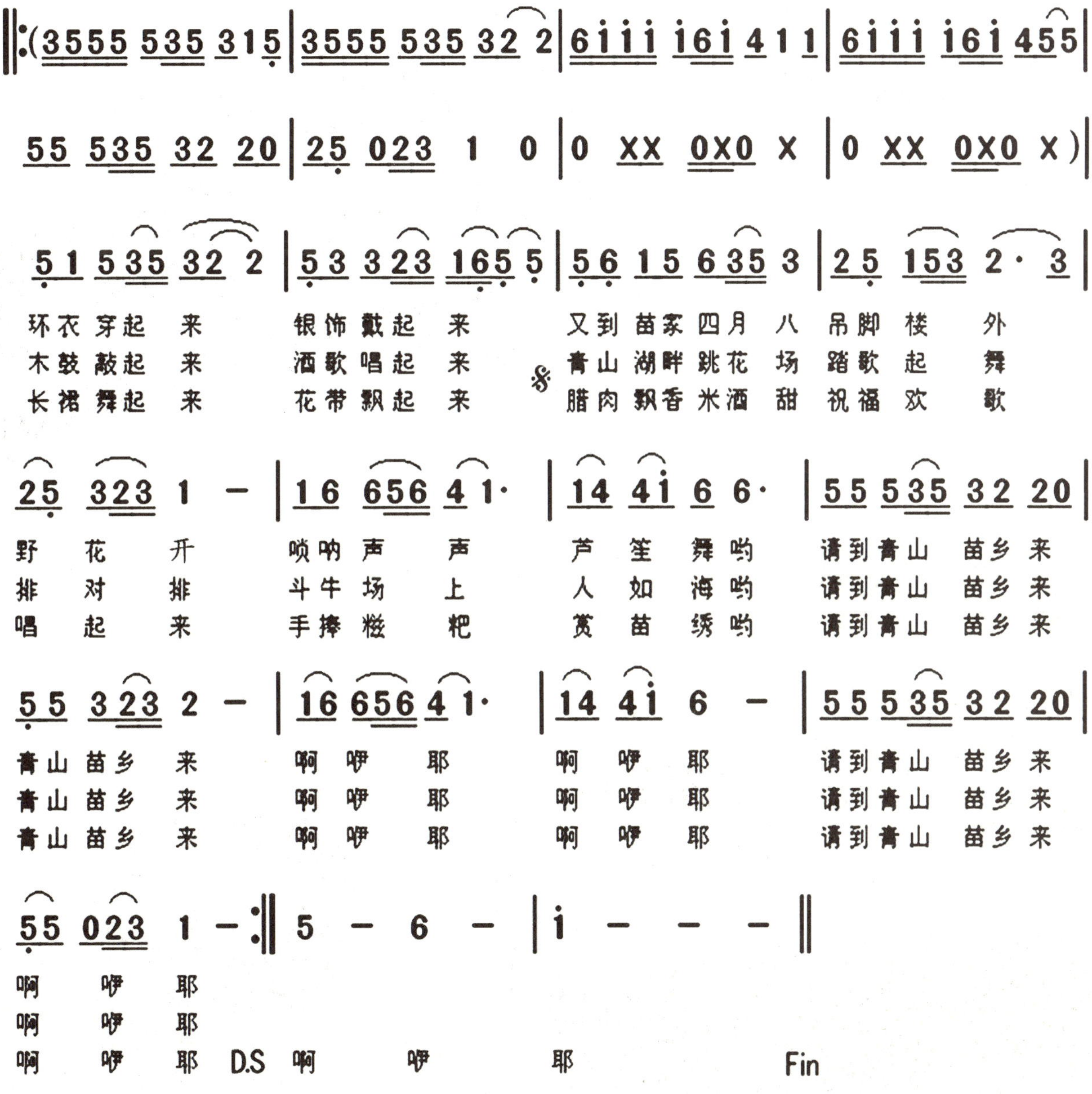

注：第二段不用间奏

摄影作品

暗香（曾兴富　摄）

捕（陈继康　摄）

团元山云海（颜　阳　摄）

希望的田野（赵立祥　摄）

牧归（罗 旭 摄）

无限风光（何 超 摄）

岁月如歌（冯曙建　摄）

索　引

说　明

一、本索引采用主题分析方法编制。

二、本索引按主题词首字汉语拼音音序（同义词按音调）排列，若首字拼音相同时按第二字音序排列，以此类推，首字为阿拉伯数字或英文字母者，作“非音序”集中排列在本索引末。

A

B

C

D

E

F

G

H

J

K

L

M

N

P

Q

R

S

T

W

X

Y

Z

非音序